READINGS
IN
KNOWLEDGE
REPRESENTATION

WITHDRAWN

READINGS
IN
KNOWLEDGE
REPRESENTATION

edited by

Ronald J. Brachman
Schlumberger Palo Alto Research
Currently at
AT&T Bell Laboratories

and

Hector J. Levesque
University of Toronto
and
The Canadian Institute for Advanced Research

MORGAN KAUFMANN PUBLISHERS, INC.
SAN MATEO, CALIFORNIA

389109

Tennessee Tech. Library
Cookeville, Tenn.

To our families

Library of Congress Cataloging-in-Publication Data
Main entry under title:
Readings in knowledge representation.
Bibliography: p.
Includes index.
1. Artificial intelligence.   2. Linguistics—Data
processing.   I. Brachman, Ronald J., 1949–
II. Levesque, Hector J., 1951–
Q335.R43   1985   006.3   85-16400
ISBN 0-934613-01-X (pbk.)

Morgan Kaufmann Publishers, Inc.
2929 Campus Drive, San Mateo, California 94403
© 1985 by Morgan Kaufmann Publishers, Inc.
All rights reserved.
Printed in the United States of America

No part of this publication may be reproduced, stored in
a retrieval system, or transmitted in any form or by any
means—electronic, mechanical, photocopying, recording,
or otherwise—without the prior written permission of the
publisher.

90 89   5 4

CONTENTS

ACKNOWLEDGMENTS

What seemed at first to be a simple and straightforward job of collecting together some good papers has turned into a complex and elaborate task. We would never have gotten this far without the help of a number of people. First we owe our thanks to Robin Wallace and Amy Atkinson for help in composing, producing, and following up on the incredible number of permission letters needed for this project. We must also thank our employers, Fairchild Camera and Instrument Corporation, and subsequently Schlumberger Computer Aided Systems, for their support and facilities. Peter Patel-Schneider helped immensely, both by reading drafts of our original material and by cajoling our printer into appropriate behavior. And we are grateful to Victoria Gilbert for her help with the index. Our publisher, Mike Morgan, has been the keystone in this project, and despite starting a new company in midstream, has managed to hold everything together from start to finish. We would also like to thank Nils Nilsson for helping us get the project initiated. His encouragement and wise counsel were among the most important ingredients needed to produce this volume.

The editors are also pleased to thank the following authors and publishers for permission to include copyrighted material in this volume:

Patrick J. Hayes, "Some Problems and Non-Problems in Representation Theory," *Proc. AISB Summer Conference*, University of Sussex, 1974, 63–79. Copyright © 1974 Society for the Study of Artificial Intelligence and Simulation of Behavior. All rights reserved. Reprinted by permission of the AISB and the author

John McCarthy, "Epistemological Problems in Artificial Intelligence," *Proc. IJCAI-77*, Cambridge, MA, 1977, 1038–1044. Copyright © 1977 by International Joint Conferences on Artificial Intelligence. All rights reserved. Used by permission of the International Joint Conferences on Artificial Intelligence, Inc., and the author; copies of the Proceedings are available from Morgan Kaufmann Publishers, Inc., 95 First Street, Los Altos, CA 94022, USA.

Brian C. Smith, Prologue to "Reflection and Semantics in a Procedural Language," Ph.D. thesis and Tech. Report MIT/LCS/TR-272, M.I.T., Cambridge, MA, 1982. Copyright © 1982 by Massachusetts Institute of Technology. All rights reserved. Reprinted by permission of the Massachusetts Institute of Technology and the author.

Hector J. Levesque and Ronald J. Brachman, "A Fundamental Tradeoff in Knowledge Representation and Reasoning (Revised Version)." Original version appeared as "A Fundamental Tradeoff in Knowledge Representation and Reasoning" (by Hector J. Levesque), *Proc. CSCSI-84*, London, Ontario, 1984, 141–152. Copyright © 1984 by the Canadian Society for Computational Studies of Intelligence. All rights reserved. Reprinted by permission of the CSCSI.

Hubert L. Dreyfus, "From Micro-Worlds to Knowledge Representation: AI at an Impasse," in *Mind Design*, 161–204, edited by J. Haugeland, Cambridge, MA: The MIT Press, 1981. This version is excerpted (with minor revisions) from the Introduction to the second edition of his *What Computers Can't Do* (New York: Harper & Row, 1979). Copyright © 1979 by Hubert L. Dreyfus. All rights reserved. Reprinted by permission of Harper & Row, Publishers, The MIT Press, and the author.

M. Ross Quillian, "Word Concepts: A Theory and Simulation of Some Basic Semantic Capabilities,"

Behavioral Science **12,** 1967, 410–430. Copyright © 1967 by James Grier Miller, M.D., Editor. All rights reserved. Reprinted by permission of Dr. Miller and the author.

Roger C. Schank and Charles J. Rieger III, "Inference and the Computer Understanding of Natural Language," *Artificial Intelligence* 5(4), 1974, 373–412. Copyright © 1974 by North-Holland Publishing Company. All rights reserved. Reprinted by permission of the publisher and the authors.

Patrick H. Winston, "Learning Structural Descriptions from Examples," in *The Psychology of Computer Vision*, 157–209, edited by P. H. Winston, New York: McGraw-Hill Book Company, 1975. Copyright © 1975 by McGraw-Hill, Inc. All rights reserved. Reprinted by permission of the publisher and the author.

Anthony S. Maida and Stuart C. Shapiro, "Intensional Concepts in Propositional Semantic Networks," *Cognitive Science* 6(4), 1982, 291–330. Copyright © 1982 by Ablex Publishing Corporation. All rights reserved. Reprinted by permission of the publisher and the authors.

Ronald J. Brachman, "On the Epistemological Status of Semantic Networks," in *Associative Networks: Representation and Use of Knowledge by Computers*, 3–50, edited by N. V. Findler, New York: Academic Press, 1979. Copyright © 1979 by Academic Press, Inc. All rights reserved. Reprinted by permission of the publisher.

William A. Woods, "What's in a Link: Foundations for Semantic Networks," in *Representation and Understanding: Studies in Cognitive Science*, 35–82, edited by D. G. Bobrow and A. M. Collins, New York: Academic Press, 1975. Copyright © 1975 by Academic Press, Inc. All rights reserved. Reprinted by permission of the publisher and the author.

Marvin Minsky, "A Framework for Representing Knowledge," in *Mind Design*, 95–128, edited by J. Haugeland, Cambridge, MA: The MIT Press, 1981. Originally published as Memo 306 of the Artificial Intelligence Laboratory of the Massachusetts Institute of Technology. Excerpts were reprinted in *The Psychology of Computer Vision*, edited by Patrick H. Winston (New York: McGraw-Hill, 1975). Copyright © 1981 by Bradford Books, Publishers. All rights reserved. Reprinted by permission of The MIT Press and the author.

Daniel G. Bobrow and Terry Winograd, "An Overview of KRL, a Knowledge Representation Language," *Cognitive Science* 1(1), 1977, 3–46. Copyright © 1977

by Ablex Publishing Corporation. All rights reserved. Reprinted by permission of the publisher and the authors.

Patrick J. Hayes, "The Logic of Frames," in *Frame Conceptions and Text Understanding*, 46–61, edited by D. Metzing, Berlin: Walter de Gruyter and Co., 1979. Copyright © 1979 by Patrick J. Hayes. All rights reserved. Reprinted by permission of the author.

John McCarthy, "Programs with Common Sense," in *Semantic Information Processing*, 403–418, edited by M. Minsky, Cambridge, MA: The MIT Press, 1968. Copyright © 1968 by The MIT Press. Parts taken from "Programs with Common Sense," in *Proc. Symposium on Mechanisation of Thought Processes*, Vol. 1, 77–84, London, 1959. Copyright © 1959 Her Majesty's Stationery Office. Parts taken from "Situations, Actions, and Causal Laws," Stanford Artificial Intelligence Project Memo No. 2, Stanford University, July, 1963 (work supported by ARPA, under contract SD-183). All rights reserved. Reprinted by permission of The MIT Press, the National Physical Laboratory (Teddington, Middlesex, England), and the author.

Richard W. Weyhrauch, "Prolegomena to a Theory of Mechanized Formal Reasoning," *Artificial Intelligence* **13**(1,2), 1980, 133–170. Copyright © 1980 by North-Holland Publishing Company. All rights reserved. Reprinted by permission of the publisher and the author.

David W. Etherington and Raymond Reiter, "On Inheritance Hierarchies with Exceptions," *Proc. AAAI-83*, Washington, D.C., 1983, 104–108. Copyright © 1983 by The American Association for Artificial Intelligence. All rights reserved. Reprinted by permission of the AAAI and the authors.

Robert C. Moore, "The Role of Logic in Knowledge Representation and Commonsense Reasoning," *Proc. AAAI-82*, Pittsburgh, PA, 1982, 428–433. Copyright © 1982 by The American Association for Artificial Intelligence. All rights reserved. Reprinted by permission of the AAAI and the author.

Johan de Kleer, Jon Doyle, Guy L. Steele, Jr., and Gerald Jay Sussman, "AMORD: Explicit Control of Reasoning," *Proc. Symposium on Artificial Intelligence and Programming Languages*, SIGPLAN Notices 12(8), and *SIGART Newsletter*, No. 64, August, 1977, 116–125. Copyright © 1977, Association for Computing Machinery, Inc., reprinted by permission of the ACM and the authors. All rights reserved.

Terry Winograd, "Frame Representations and the Declarative/Procedural Controversy," in *Representation and Understanding: Studies in Cognitive Science*,

185–210, edited by D. G. Bobrow, and A. M. Collins, New York: Academic Press, 1975. Copyright © 1975 by Academic Press, Inc. All rights reserved. Reprinted by permission of the publisher and the author.

Randall Davis, Bruce Buchanan, and Edward Shortliffe, "Production Rules as a Representation for a Knowledge-Based Consultation Program," *Artificial Intelligence* **8**(1), 1977, 15–45. Copyright © 1977 by North-Holland Publishing Company. All rights reserved. Reprinted by permission of the publisher and the authors.

Randall Davis and Bruce G. Buchanan, "Meta-Level Knowledge: Overview and Applications," *Proc. IJCAI-77,* Cambridge, MA, August, 1977, 920–927. Copyright © 1977 by International Joint Conference on Artificial Intelligence. All rights reserved. Used by permission of the International Joint Conferences on Artificial Intelligence, Inc., and the authors; copies of the Proceedings are available from Morgan Kaufmann Publishers, Inc., 95 First Street, Los Altos, CA 94022, USA.

Raymond Reiter, "On Reasoning by Default," *Proc. TINLAP-2, Theoretical Issues in Natural Language Processing-2,* University of Illinois at Urbana-Champaign, 1978, 210–218. Copyright © 1978 by the Association for Computational Linguistics. All rights reserved. Reprinted by permission of the ACL and the author.

Ronald J. Brachman, Richard E. Fikes, and Hector J. Levesque, "KRYPTON: A Functional Approach to Knowledge Representation," FLAIR Technical Report No. 16, Fairchild Laboratory for Artificial Intelligence Research, Palo Alto, CA, May, 1983. This is a revised version of an article published under the same name in *IEEE Computer,* **16**(10), 1983, 67–73. Copyright © 1983 IEEE. Reprinted, with permission, from *Computer,* Vol. 16, No. 10, pp. 67–73, October 1983. All rights reserved.

Aaron Sloman, "Afterthoughts on Analogical Representation," *Proc. Theoretical Issues in Natural Language Processing,* Cambridge, MA, 1975, 164–168. Copyright © 1975 by Aaron Sloman. All rights reserved. Reprinted by permission of the author.

Brian V. Funt, "Problem-Solving with Diagrammatic Representations," *Artificial Intelligence* **13**(3), 1980, 201–230. Copyright © 1980 by North-Holland Publishing Company. All rights reserved. Reprinted by permission of the publisher and the author.

Thomas D. Garvey, John D. Lowrance, and Martin A. Fischler, "An Inference Technique for Integrating Knowledge from Disparate Sources," *Proc. IJCAI-81,* Vancouver, B. C., August, 1981, 319–325. Copyright © 1981 by International Joint Conferences on Artificial Intelligence. All rights reserved. Used by permission of the International Joint Conferences on Artificial Intelligence, Inc., and the authors; copies of the Proceedings are available from Morgan Kaufmann Publishers, Inc., 95 First Street, Los Altos, CA 94022, USA.

Patrick J. Hayes, "The Second Naive Physics Manifesto," in *Formal Theories of the Commonsense World,* 1–36, edited by J. R. Hobbs and R. C. Moore, Norwood, NJ: Ablex Publishing Corp., 1985. Copyright © 1985 by Ablex Publishing Corporation. All rights reserved. Reprinted by permission of the publisher and the author.

Chuck Rieger, "An Organization of Knowledge for Problem-Solving and Language Comprehension," *Artificial Intelligence* **7**(2), 1976, 89–127. Copyright © 1976 by North-Holland Publishing Company. All rights reserved. Reprinted by permission of the publisher and the author.

James F. Allen, "Maintaining Knowledge about Temporal Intervals," *Communications of the ACM* **26**(11), 1983, 832–843. Copyright © 1983, Association for Computing Machinery, Inc., reprinted by permission of the ACM and the author. All rights reserved.

John McCarthy, "First Order Theories of Individual Concepts and Propositions," in *Machine Intelligence 9,* 129–147, edited by J. E. Hayes, D. Michie, and L. I. Mikulich, Chichester, England: Ellis Horwood, Ltd., 1979. Copyright © 1979 by Ellis Horwood, Ltd. All rights reserved. Reprinted by permission of the publisher and the author.

INTRODUCTION

The notion of the *representation of knowledge* is at heart an easy one to understand. It simply has to do with writing down, in some language or communicative medium, descriptions or pictures that correspond in some salient way to the world or a state of the world. In Artificial Intelligence (AI), we are concerned with writing down descriptions of the world in such a way that an intelligent machine can come to new conclusions about its environment by formally manipulating these descriptions.

Despite this apparent simplicity in general goal, the research area of Knowledge Representation has a long, complex, and as yet non-convergent history. Despite the fact that just about every current AI program has what is called a "knowledge base" containing symbolic descriptions represented in some "representation scheme," there is still a vast amount to be understood before, for example, the knowledge in one system can be shared with another. There are tremendous subtleties in the notions of "representation," "knowledge," and their combination in AI.

The papers in this volume have been collected to allow the reader with a general technical background in AI to begin to explore these subtleties. None of the papers here is tutorial, or is explicitly addressed to the AI beginner. Rather, these are the original articles by prominent researchers that have dictated the research directions in the field for the last quarter-century. They cover the gamut from proposals for formal representation regimes to representations of particular domain fragments to critiques of the entire Knowledge Representation enterprise. We have concerned ourselves here primarily with producing a complete Knowledge Representation sourcebook for those who would be ready to take a graduate-level course in the subject.

As hinted above (and as detailed somewhat below), Knowledge Representation is a deceptively simple field to enter. Almost every novice AI student will be asked to invent languages suitable for capturing the regularities of some domain. Further, a number of surveys exist that introduce the four or five leading representational methodologies sufficiently to get the interested beginner off the ground (see, for example, [Barr and Davidson 81], [Mylopoulos and Levesque 83], and [Nilsson 80]). But fundamental difficulties exist in representing and reasoning at the level of real-world complexity, and no surveys or textbooks exist that can guide us through those problems. Since such a textbook is probably an impossibility at this point in time, a collection of the papers that have delved the deepest into these problems seems the best resource to provide for the field now. Thus we have attempted to collect the most important ideas in Knowledge Representation, in their original presentations, and accompany them with a certain amount of introductory material that will supply, we hope, a modicum of coherence to a generally fragmented and variegated area.

At this point in the history of Knowledge Representation research (relatively short, if we restrict ourselves to work done in an AI context[1]), it has been possible to comb virtually the entire literature in our search for the crucial papers to include in this volume. While we have no doubt omitted some that are on a par with those collected here, we have brought together a critical mass of writings that

---

[1]McCarthy and Hayes [1969] date the beginning of serious work in AI to papers by Turing and Shannon in 1950, although most agree that the initial impetus for concentrated work in the field was the Dartmouth conference in 1956.

touch on virtually all of the important research issues in the history of the field. Each of the papers was selected because it introduced something new and important, and in a graduate course specializing in Knowledge Representation, no doubt all of these papers would be required reading. Our only regret is that there are papers that we would have loved to have included that simply were never written.

As always with collections of this sort, this book is a reflection of the perceptions of the field by its editors, and certainly others would have produced different volumes. We have concentrated on articles that we feel have substantially influenced the course of work in the field, and have highlighted authors who have written thoughtfully on the field as a whole. There are relatively few articles included that simply present new formalisms, or that address themselves mainly to implementation concerns. And, of course, there are many different points of view represented here, not all of which we particularly agree with (indeed, it would not be possible to agree simultaneously with all of the views represented). However, it was important to us to include as much of the seminal thinking on the subject as could fit in a reasonable volume.

In the rest of this Introduction, we try to put some perspective on the book by giving a brief, impressionistic view of Knowledge Representation, and by surveying the topics of current major interest in the field. Where possible, we indicate which papers in our collection are most relevant to the topic at hand.

The Knowledge Representation Hypothesis

Much has been written of the discord and disagreement in the field of Knowledge Representation (KR). In a 1979-80 survey of the field, Brachman and Smith [1980] found "wide-ranging diversity within the Knowledge Representation community." This survey was also cited in [Newell 82] as evidence for "a veritable jungle of opinions. There is no consensus on any question of substance." However, in the subsequent five years, perhaps partially influenced by those very writings, the field has found some important common themes emerging. Perhaps the agreement is tacit, but there do seem to be some substantial common bonds among researchers currently working in Knowledge Representation.

First, there is growing awareness of a longer, richer heritage for KR than just the last thirty years or so of AI research. Although traces of formal logic can be found as long ago as Aristotle, the idea of using a calculus to represent and manipulate ideas seems to have originated squarely with Leibniz [1646–1716]:

> There is little doubt, however, that Leibniz' ideas, which far outstripped in detail and understanding any earlier hints, were his own spontaneous creation. "While I was yet a boy with a knowledge only of common logic, and without instruction in mathematics, the thought came to me, I know not by what instinct, that an analysis of ideas could be devised, whence in some combinatory way, truths could arise and be estimated as though by numbers" (*Elementa Rationis*). He was thereafter constantly occupied with such notions and attempted to contrive an alphabet of thought, or *characteristica universalis*, which would represent ideas in a logical way, not things in a pictorial way, and would be mechanical in operation, unambiguous, and nonquantitative. (*The Encyclopedia of Philosophy*, Vol. 4, p. 538)

This agrees remarkably well with most current views of KR. The trend is for knowledge to be represented as explicitly as possible, and (relatively) declaratively, in some formal language. The term "knowledge-based system" is currently a popular one in Artificial Intelligence. What makes AI systems knowledge-based is not that it somehow takes knowledge to write them, nor just that they behave as if they had knowledge, but rather that their architectures include *explicit knowledge bases*—more or less direct symbolic encodings in the knowledge in the system. This is certainly true of expert systems, for example, currently the most visible and common type of AI system.

Brian Smith has captured this underlying methodological assumption in what he calls the *Knowledge Representation Hypothesis*:

> Any mechanically embodied intelligent process will be comprised of structural ingredients that a) we as external observers naturally take to represent a propositional account of the knowledge that the overall process exhibits, and b) independent of such external semantical attribution, play a formal but causal and essential role in engendering the behaviour that manifests that knowledge. [Smith 82, p. 2]

In some sense, it is only with respect to this hypothesis that AI representation research can be distinguished from any number of other areas involving symbolic structures, such as database management, programming languages, and data structures.

In order to have an explicit knowledge base, a system must rely on some well-specified language for encoding its beliefs. That role is played by a *knowledge representation language*. Beyond that, in just about all imaginable cases of interest, a system will be concerned with more than just the literal set of sentences (or frames, or production rules, or whatever) representing what it knows. A representation system must also provide access to facts *implicit* in the knowledge base. In other words, a representation component must perform *automatic inferences* for its user.

Work on representation languages and general inference schemes is an important part of KR research. In addition, most in the field would probably assent to one of the current clichés of AI that says that it is in the knowledge itself that the power lies. In other words, the ability of an intelligent system to diagnose real diseases, to troubleshoot real circuits, etc., resides in the detailed explicit knowledge base that represents the system's understanding of its domain.

Simultaneously producing good candidates for each of the three ingredients—the representation language, the inference regime, and the particular domain knowledge—is essentially the central problem of Artificial Intelligence. In a slightly different way, David Israel characterized the crux of "the representation problem":

All parties to the debate agree that a central goal of research is that computers must somehow come to "know" a good deal of what every human being knows about the world and about the organisms, natural or artificial, that inhabit it. This body of knowledge—indefinite, no doubt, in its boundaries—goes by the name "common sense." The problem we face is how to impart such knowledge to a robot. That is, how do we design a robot with a reasoning capacity sufficiently powerful and fruitful that when provided with some subbody of this knowledge, the robot will be able to generate enough of the rest to intelligently adapt to and exploit its environment? [Israel 83b, p. 37]

If the three ingredients to the representation problem were as simple as they might appear, the papers collected in this volume would never have existed. Unfortunately, while most of us agree on the general problem to be solved, we have hardly begun to understand what to do in any of the three cases. In fact, the whole underlying Knowledge Representation Hypothesis is not so much an explanation of rational cognitive behavior, as it is a working hypothesis about a reasonable way to build intelligent systems. The only thing we know for sure about this hypothesis is that it is the only one we currently have.

Still, our research proceeds and has its successes. Leaving aside the haziness surrounding our basic enterprise, what exactly are the problems we currently face as a field, and where do we stand after some thirty years of AI research on the subject? Let us take a very brief look at some of the issues that have prompted the important contributions that we include in this book.

Knowledge Representation and Logic

The role of formal logic in Knowledge Representation has been hotly contested from the beginning and many of the papers included here make at least some reference to logic. Part of the problem has to do with the history and goals of KR and their differences from those of symbolic logic. After Leibniz, the next big push in formal logic was the work of Frege at the turn of the century who, along with Russell, Peano, and others, gave logic much of the flavor it has today. The goal of this early work was to put mathematics and mathematical reasoning on a sound theoretical footing. Indeed, until recently, the major application of symbolic logic and one of the great successes of twentieth century mathematics, has been the analysis of formal theories of sets and numbers.

The goals of Knowledge Representation, however, even at the very beginning, were quite different, and perhaps much more in line with Leibniz' original dream. KR schemes were used to represent the semantic content of natural language concepts, as well as to represent psychologically plausible memory models. In neither case was there a clear relationship to formal *languages* of any kind (as Woods among others points out [Chapter 11]). Gradually, however, KR schemes began to be used as a very flexible and modular way to represent the facts that a system needed to know to behave intelligently in a complex environment.

This view of Knowledge Representation, involving propositional representations of the beliefs of a system, along the lines of the Knowledge Representation Hypothesis, has slowly come to dominate the field. With it has come an emerging consensus about at least some of the issues relating KR and logic. For example, the need for *semantics* for representation languages is pretty much agreed upon. Without some concrete specification of the meaning of a notational convention, what is implied by an expression in that language is unclear, and comparisons to other notational systems are impossible. This is not to say that representation languages require formal semantics *à la* Tarski, say, but they do need more than just a statement of what some program does with them. Without such, there is no independent means of knowing whether the conclusions drawn by an AI program are correct or complete. Nor is it the case, just because we understand a representation language propositionally, that we must understand it as a notational variant of the language of standard first-order logic. Indeed, the emerging view is more that representation languages are perhaps non-standard logical languages—non-standard in their syntax, semantics, and use. So while it has become important to relate representation languages to classical first-order logic, the actual role to be played by *that* language, its semantics, and full theorem-proving remains controversial.

It is somewhat misleading, however, to think of KR only in terms of the representation language involved. Because the role of a representation system is to manage *beliefs* expressed in the language, it is much more than just the implementation of any logical calculus. In particular, again following the Knowledge Representation Hypothesis, the symbolic structures in a knowledge base cause the system to behave one way or another. As such, there is a temporal extent to KR structures that is certainly not a property of purely formal languages.

There are a number of issues raised by this belief management aspect of Knowledge Representation. Foremost perhaps, is that *reasoning* will be necessary to determine what is implicit in the explicit beliefs a system has. As discussed by Levesque and Brachman [Chapter 4], the degree of incompleteness of these beliefs will determine to a large extent how difficult it will be to ferret out their implications. Moreover, depending on the extent of this incompleteness, it will often be necessary for a system to make assumptions or use defaults to fill in gaps in its beliefs and then revise these conclusions in a non-monotonic way as new information about the world is acquired. Arguably, a logic by itself cannot and should not attempt to provide specifications of how this type of rational belief revision should take place. What it *should* provide for KR, however, is a clear statement (based on the semantics of the KR language) of what the logical consequences of reasoning one way or another would be.

So in the end, the relation between KR and logic is still a subtle and difficult one. Although violent disagreement has been replaced somewhat by a sense of calm and commonality, this remains perhaps the central question of the entire Knowledge Representation enterprise.

Issues in the Representation of Knowledge

When presenting a number of papers in a volume such as this, their order of appearance is always a problem, since the papers can usually be classified in more than one way. Although we have grouped the papers in terms of seven categories, to be described below, important issues in Knowledge Representation link papers across many of these categories. Here, we provide a quick overview of some of the issues dealt with by the papers included in this collection. For each issue, we indicate which papers most directly address the point.

A first group of issues focuses on the overall adequacy of a knowledge representation system:

- *Expressive Adequacy* [Brachman, Chapter 10], [Woods, Chapter 11], [Moore, Chapter 18]. What are the standards for measuring the expressive adequacy of a representation language? Should every language be a notational variant of the language of full first-order logic? At the very least, a knowledge representation language should be very clear about precisely what knowledge it is representing, something that has not always been true in the past.

- *Reasoning Efficiency* [Levesque and Brachman, Chapter 4], [de Kleer *et al.*, Chapter 19], [Brachman *et al.*, Chapter 24]. It is one thing to come up with a representation of knowledge that is sufficient to logically imply any fact of interest, but quite another matter to actually calculate these implications, especially when the representation language is expressive enough. How can we balance the need to provide correct, rational inferences with the need to produce them in a timely fashion?

Another cluster of issues that arise repeatedly involves what might be called the basic epistemology of a Knowledge Representation system:

- *Primitives* [Schank and Rieger, Chapter 7], [Brachman, Chapter 10], [Bobrow and Winograd, Chapter 13]. One of the ongoing discussions in KR research involves the role of primitive knowledge structures. The important questions to be considered are what primitives are appropriate to build into a representation (if any) and at what level?

- *Meta-Representation* [Smith, Chapter 3], [Weyhrauch, Chapter 16], [Davis and Buchanan, Chapter 22]. Another recurring theme in representation research involves the use of structures that represent knowledge about other structures in the system. The nature of these and how they can be exploited is still an active area of research.

- *Incompleteness* [Levesque and Brachman, Chapter 4], [Moore, Chapter 18], [Brachman *et al.*, Chapter 24]. Exactly what a Knowledge Representation language allows one to leave unsaid about a domain determines how incomplete the system's knowledge can be. This, in turn, determines to a large extent how sophisticated a reasoner is required to perform inferences over expressions in that language.

Given the important role played by logic in the field, several papers focus on aspects of Knowledge Representation not covered by standard logic:

- *Definitions vs. Facts* [Woods, Chapter 11], [Brachman *et al.*, Chapter 24]. A given connection between two structures in a Knowledge Representation system could mean that the meaning of one structure depends on the meaning of the other, or simply that there is a contingent relationship between the entities that the two structures represent. This distinction, between defining terms on the one hand and simply recording facts of the domain on the other, is not possible in standard logic. A related issue here is the contrast between an object-oriented view and a sentence-oriented view of representation. The former advocates clustering all facts about an object in one place, while the latter emphasizes more complex statements involving individuals or groups of individuals whose identities need not be known.

- *Universals vs. Defaults* [Hayes, Chapter 14], [Etherington and Reiter, Chapter 17], [Reiter, Chapter 23]. Among the most commonly employed representation techniques is a generalization/specialization relation, giving rise to a so-called IS-A hierarchy. But do these links represent universal set inclusions (*e.g.*, as in "all elephants are mammals"), or stereotypical cases ("birds fly")? Both kinds of statement are important, but research is needed to determine how they can amicably co-exist in the same system. Further, the exact import of the stereotypical version needs to be determined.

- *Non-Deductive Reasoning* [Quillian, Chapter 6], [Schank and Rieger, Chapter 7], [Winston, Chapter 8]. Many AI programs use reasoning techniques (such as inductive generalization and concept intersection) that are far removed from anything resembling standard logical inference. How exactly to make sense of this kind of reasoning behavior without simply saying that it means whatever the program does remains a difficult open problem.

- *Non-Monotonic Reasoning* [McCarthy, Chapter 2], [Etherington and Reiter, Chapter 17], [Reiter, Chapter 23]. Given the importance of default knowledge and the fact that our understanding of the world changes over time, it is clear that computational representation systems will need to reason non-monotonically, discarding previous conclusions in the presence of new information. What is not so clear is whether they should take the more or less direct tack that has dominated research in the area so far and reflect this non-monotonicity in the logic itself.

Several papers are concerned with representing knowledge in ways that are quite different from simple yes-no sentences:

- *Procedural* [Dreyfus, Chapter 5], [de Kleer *et al.*, Chapter 19], [Winograd, Chapter 20]. Is there a difference of any consequence between representing something as a procedure or as a declarative statement? We tend to distinguish between "knowing that" and "knowing how" but to what extent should this distinction bear on formal representation of commonsense knowledge? Is it somehow possible to integrate skills with our more traditional logical forms of representation?

- *Analogical* [Hayes, Chapter 1], [Sloman, Chapter 25], [Funt, Chapter 26]. A lot of our reasoning seems to be based on direct visualizations of scenes and situations, rather than on theories of any kind. Properties of such representations, such as granularity, appear to make them quite different from propositional representations and moreover, seem to offer distinct computational advantages.

- *Probabilistic* [Davis *et al.*, Chapter 21], [Garvey *et al.*, Chapter 27]. There has been a recent burst of interest in reasoning methods that avoid the exactitude of standard logical deduction. Perhaps spurred on mostly by work in expert systems, which typically rely on non-integral levels of confidence, more and more representation work includes a fuzzy or subjective aspect to it. What techniques are appropriate for less exact reasoning, and how it integrates with more determinate deduction remain to be determined.

Finally, papers can be grouped in terms of what the knowledge being represented is actually about:

- *Substances* [Hayes, Chapter 1], [Hayes, Chapter 28]. A thorny problem for representation systems that carve up the world roughly the way logic does is dealing with material substances. Something like a pound of butter or a quart of milk only has some of the properties of objecthood in that, for example, it readily merges with other "objects" of the same type.

- *Causality and Time* [McCarthy, Chapter 15], [Rieger, Chapter 29], [Allen, Chapter 30]. How to represent an event as something changing in time (rather than by stating what is true before and after the event) remains an open problem for standard (static) representation languages, and one that crops up repeatedly when representing knowledge about the physical world.

- *Knowledge* [Maida and Shapiro, Chapter 9], [McCarthy, Chapter 31]. To represent knowledge about other agents it is often necessary to deal with propositional attitudes such as their beliefs, desires, and intentions, which take propositions as arguments. The problem here is to allow a language to refer to propositions without running into paradoxes that accompany self-referential propositions.

Of course there are many other connections among the papers, and some of these will be mentioned in the introductions to the individual papers.

Organization of the Book

The body of the book is divided into seven sections, generally grouping together sets of papers that approach representation in a related way. Each paper is introduced by a brief description of its contents and import; we have tried to give the reader a bit of historical perspective on the papers, as well as some sense of how they all fit together. Our introductions are not intended to be abstracts of the articles, but rather stage-setting comments to give the reader an idea of why the paper was included in the collection and what to expect from it.

The opening section, *The Knowledge Representation Enterprise*, comprises papers that discuss general issues in Knowledge Representation. They present different views of, among other things, what Knowledge Representation is really all about, and taken together, offer a perspective for understanding all of the work that goes on in the field.

The next five sections represent the technical development that has happened over the last thirty years. The first two of these cover the typical home-grown AI representation languages (*i.e.*, not based directly on predicate logic) that have dominated most of the work in the field. Our section on *Associational Representations* highlights *semantic networks*, arguably the most popular of all techniques employed to represent knowledge in AI programs. The section also gives some evidence of the very roots of network representations ([Quillian, Chapter 6]), as well as a survey of their development and metamorphoses over the years ([Brachman, Chapter 10]). This group of papers is topped off in Chapter 11 with Woods' retrospective analysis of problems with naive uses of network representation.

At this point in our history, work on semantic networks has essentially merged with work on *Structured Object Representations*, exemplified by *frame* representations. The next section of our book highlights this recent work, starting off in Chapter 12 with Minsky's seminal paper that changed the focus of work from associations to larger chunks of knowledge representing stereotypical situations. This section is short, mainly because a number of papers in the volume that relate to structured object representations appear in other sections (*viz.* [Levesque and Brachman, Chapter 4], [Maida and Shapiro, Chapter 9], [Brachman, Chapter 10], [Etherington and Reiter, Chapter 17], [Winograd, Chapter 20], [Brachman *et al.*, Chapter 24]).

As mentioned earlier, first-order logic has always played a central role in Knowledge Representation research, and our next section, *Formal Logic-Based Representations*, includes papers that advocate and investigate this approach to representation and inference. Among these is McCarthy's early paper [Chapter 15] on representing and using common-sense information. Also included in Chapter 18 is Moore's explicit characterization of the role of logic in this enterprise.

Another important trend in representation research is covered in our next section, *Procedural Representations and Production Systems*. The value of using procedures to represent knowledge provided for some heated argument in the early to mid-1970's that is discussed by Winograd in Chapter 20. Production rules are a procedural style of representation that has dominated work in expert systems since the time of the two papers included here. The four papers together provide a sample of ways to represent knowledge procedurally, and the advantages to be gained by so doing.

The last section on representation schemes, *Other Approaches*, contains papers that are not easily categorized, or that represent new and emerging trends in the field. These include a paper on default reasoning, one on a hybrid approach to representation (integrating two different representation schemes), two on more pictorial, less linguistic representations, and one on inexact, evidential reasoning. As detailed above, these represent among the most important issues being pursued in the field at this time.

The final section of our volume concerns itself with *Representations of Commonsense Knowledge*. Here we change direction completely, and look at representations of particular parts of the world that are relevant across a wide range of applications. The section starts out with an attempt by Hayes in Chapter 28 to shift the field's attention away from formalism *per se*, and onto actually representing everyday knowledge of the physical world. The other papers in this section concern themselves similarly with formalizations of other important aspects of experience, such as causality, time, and knowledge itself.

The volume is completed with a partially annotated bibliography. We have collected together over 300 references to papers and books in Knowledge Representation research, and have provided brief comments on a number of the more important ones. While not intended to be complete, our bibliography is a helpful way to survey the bulk of the relevant literature, and to find references not included in the volume itself.

I / The Knowledge Representation Enterprise

1 / Patrick J. Hayes
Some Problems and Non-Problems in Representation Theory

At the time this paper was written, there was a good deal of research in logical, network, and procedural representation systems, but very little basis for communication among the advocates of the different approaches. Part of the problem was that inventors of representation schemes were (and continue to be) fairly vague about what the expressions in their schemes were supposed to mean. This paper was one of the first to attempt to clarify this issue. Hayes points out that without a semantic theory of some sort, it is not only impossible to compare or evaluate different representation schemes, but the schemes should not even be considered to be representational. He shows, for example, how arguments about representation differences between semantic networks and logic only make sense given *interpretations* of the schemes. Similarly, it is impossible to contrast analog and propositional schemes without some clear notion of what they are supposed to represent (in this context, Hayes spends considerable time discussing the predecessor to the Sloman paper [Chapter 25]). The situation is even more complex for procedural representation schemes, since normally these can be *implemented* in each other. It is only by looking at meaning that representational differences in these schemes can be observed. Hayes goes on to examine some of the representational problems involved with schemes that have roughly Tarskian semantics: the frame and qualification problems (also discussed in [Reiter, Chapter 23] and [McCarthy, Chapter 2]), the control of reasoning (addressed in [de Kleer *et al.*, Chapter 19] and [Davis and Buchanan, Chapter 22]), and the representation of substances (taken up again in his later "Naive Physics" paper [Chapter 28]). He concludes by dismissing what he sees to be non-issues, such as the declarative/procedural controversy (see [Winograd, Chapter 20] for a different viewpoint) and fuzzy logics. Although this paper is one in the earliest in the area, the observations it makes are still quite relevant a decade later.

Appeared in *Proc. AISB Summer Conference,* University of Sussex, 1974, 63–79.

Some Problems and Non-Problems in Representation Theory

Patrick J. Hayes

0.   Introduction

The purpose of this paper is to give a brief survey of some general issues and problems in representing knowledge in AI programs. This general area I will call representation theory, following John McCarthy. Its boundaries are, like those of all interesting subjects, not crisply defined. It merges in one direction with programming language design, in another with philosophical logic, in another with epistemology, in another with robotics. Nevertheless, it is an increasingly important aspect of AI work. Since my main concern here is to draw attention to problems which seem to me to be difficult, and issues which seem to be important, this paper should be read as an appeal for help rather than a statement of achievements (and comments, criticisms and suggestions are welcome).

Inevitably, to believe that some issues are important, and some problems difficult, is to believe that others aren't. At the end of the paper I draw attention to some specific points of disagreement with other authors. It may be helpful, however, to point out immediately that my goals here are not philosophical, but technical. Some commentators on an earlier draft seemed to take it as an essay in philosophical analysis in the modern Oxford style. My aim rather is to substitute, for informal and apparently endless philosophical discussion, the precision of mathematics. (This aim is not achieved in this paper, I hasten to add, but is I hope brought nearer.) To emphasise this, I will, when introducing a technical word intended (ultimately) to have a precise meaning, underline it.

1.   Semantics

There are many ways known of systematically representing knowledge in a sufficiently precise notation that it can be used in, or by, a computer program. I will refer generally to such a systematic representational method as a scheme. It is not a very good word, but one cannot say 'language' as that begs an important question (see section 2). Examples of schemes include logical calculi, some programming languages, the systematic use of data structures to depict a world (e.g. as in the early Shakey's use of an array as a room-map), musical notation, map making conventions, circuit diagrams, 'JCM Schemas', 'Conceptual Dependency' notation, 'Semantic Templates' (all in [21]), etc. A configuration is a particular expression in a scheme: an assertion, a program, a data structure, a score, a map, etc. Thus one might, formally, define a scheme to be a set of configurations.

All of these examples are formal in the sense that the question, whether a particular arrangement of marks is a well-formed configuration, always has a definite answer: there is a definite notion of well-formedness. Many ways which humans have of conveying meaning will not be allowed as schemes, for they fail this criterion: drawings, photographs, poems, conversational English, musical performances, TV pictures, etc. In brief, I wish to draw a distinction between (formal) schemes, in which knowledge can be stored and used by a program, and on the other hand, (informal) scenes or perceptual situations _requiring_ the deployment of knowledge for their successful interpretation.

I am aware of several philosophical problems in analysing this distinction further. As a rough-and-ready guide, schemes can be recognised by the fact that one can construct _ill-formed_ 'configurations'. There is no such thing as an ill-formed photograph. Natural language is a borderline case, as are accurate line drawings of polyhedra.

Schemes are usually intended as vehicles for conveying meanings about some 'world' or environment. In order to be clear about this important topic, a scheme must have an associated _semantic theory_. A semantic theory is an account of the way or ways in which particular configurations of the scheme correspond to (i.e. have as their meanings), particular arrangements in the external world, i.e. the subject matter about which the scheme is intended to represent knowledge. Some of the schemes referred to above have very precise semantic theories, others have none (and seem to rejoice in this lack: see section 7 below), others (music, maps, circuit diagrams) have informal semantic theories which can be made precise by the approach outlined in section 2 below.

It is not at all fashionable in AI at present to give semantics for new representational schemes, and this is, I believe, a regrettable source of confusion and misunderstanding. Now, one cannot _prove_ such an opinion, of course. One _can_ point to other fields where syntactic confusion and proliferation of ad-hoc formalisms has been or is being replaced by the development of semantic insights: notably, philosophical logic and the design of programming languages. One _can_ point to the way in which, in AI itself, elementary semantic ideas have _been_ re-invented by various authors over the years (especially the Frege/Tarski notion of individuals and relations between them, which crops up with remarkable regularity [25, 26]). And one _can_ point to several important questions which simply cannot be answered _without_ a semantic theory. Of these, the most urgent concern the equivalence or otherwise of different formalisms. Is there a difference in meaning between a conjunction of atomic predicate-calculus assertions and the corresponding semantic network? Is there anything which can be expressed in the notation of Merlin [16] which cannot be expressed in a logical notation? The answer to both these questions is _yes_, in fact: but without a semantic theory the questions cannot even be precisely formulated. Finally, discussion in the AI literature, on, for example, the different roles of deductive, inductive and analogical reasoning and the relative merits or demerits (either technical or philosophical) of various formalisms, is often ill-informed or at best vague due to a lack of a clear model theory for the systems under discussion.

Nothing so far has been an argument for any particular _sort_ of semantic theory: for example, some kinds of 'intensional', 'operational', 'meaning-intentional' or 'procedural' semantics, may eventually enable the meanings of configurations in a scheme to be rigorously defined. However, as a matter of fact, the only mathematically precise account which I have seen of how a scheme can talk of entities outside of the computer, is the Tarskian model theory for first-order logic (but see section 2 below). I believe there are important reasons for going beyond this semantics, but many of the arguments in the AI literature against the use of predicate logic as a scheme are based on misunderstandings of one kind or another, especially the assumption that the use of predicate calculus necessarily involves the use of a general-purpose theorem-proving program. (See section 7 for more discussion.) To defend first-order logic is unfashionable: however, I do want to emphasise that it is the semantics of predicate logic which I wish to preserve. I have no brief for the usual syntax: networks, for example, can be used as a syntactic device for expressing predicate calculus facts. Some other authors advocate rather the use of predicate calculus syntax either without semantics [19], or with an alien semantics imported from computational theory [6]. This is throwing out the baby and keeping the bathwater.

To insist on a semantic theory is not, of course, to insist that the expressions comprising a program's beliefs are accurate, i.e. that what they express about the world is in fact the case. (This common misunderstanding may be caused by the phrase "truth-recursion", which leads people to think that metamathematics guarantees infallibility.) Without a semantics, one cannot even say precisely what is being claimed about the world: that is the point.

It is important to emphasise that to regard a formalism 'simply' as a programming language: that is, a way of getting the machine to do what one wants, is to adopt a rather different point of view towards it. (Unless, that is, the semantics of the scheme are concerned with machines and what they do.) For example, many people argue that PLANNER is to be regarded 'simply' as a programming language which provides useful facilities for the sorts of programming one finds oneself involved in when writing AI programs. Much of the force of the criticism in [23] for example, is from this position. While this is a perfectly respectable point of view, it is different from the one which regards PLANNER as a scheme which refers to external worlds of, say, blocks. It is even different from the idea that PLANNER is a scheme which refers to problem-solving processes or the like. For the 'programming language' view encourages the user (for example), if he needs a new semantically primitive notion, like negation, to encode it - that is, to implement it - in PLANNER in some way. In terms of schemes this is a change of scheme, since the semantics have been enriched.

To put it extremely: the only difference, in this view, between (say) CONNIVER and (say) FORTRAN, is user convenience: for one could implement the one in the other. (I have heard precisely this view forcibly maintained by professional systems programmers). Hewitt characterises the essence of PLANNER in terms of schemas [13]. While this syntactic approach works up to a point, the relationships between programming languages are, I feel, greatly clarified by giving them natural semantics. The trivial universality which FORTRAN possesses can then be eliminated by the requirement that in embedding one language in another there is a corresponding embedding of the meanings of programs. "Implemented in", as a relation between languages, then ceases to be an embedding since the meaning of (say) THCONSE does not correspond to the meaning of the rather large piece of (say) FORTRAN which would be in the implementation (actually, several pieces scattered about the program but related by context.) The former has to do, presumably, with goals and facts and such things: the latter, probably, with arithmetic relationships between numbers which represent list structures in some way.

In saying all this, one must admit that there is much force in the position that it is too early in AI to settle on particular schemes with fixed semantics. According to this view, AI programs should be implemented using all possible programming skill and ingenuity and we should leave to the future the (perhaps rather arid) task of tidying-up. Much very good AI work has been done from this standpoint, and will probably continue to be done. I do not wish to give the impression of arguing against pragmatic expediency in writing advanced programs. But I do feel that it is not too early to investigate schemes with organised semantics, both on general grounds of scholarliness and because I believe that such schemes are ultimately _easier_ to use in programming.

2.   Linguistic and direct representations

Several authors have drawn attention to a distinction between representations consisting of a description in some language and representations which are in some sense more direct models or pictures of the things represented. I first met this distinction in [1], and it has been more recently emphasised by Sloman [22]. It seems to be clearly important but I have met with surprising difficulty in trying to make the distinction precise.

One problem is to suitably define what is meant by a descriptive language, for we must not beg the question by being too restrictive in our definitions of language.   Thus Sloman's emphasis on what he calls _analogical_ representations is really a plea for the consideration of a wider class of languages than those in which the only semantic primitive is the application of a function to arguments (Sloman's term is 'Fregean' languages, like predicate calculus and PLANNER. Some authors seem to have interpreted Sloman as arguing _against_ the use of descriptive representations [3], but this is a misunderstanding.)

Another problem is that a representation which appears to be a direct model at one level of analysis, may, upon enquiring further, be itself represented in a descriptive fashion, so that it becomes impossible to describe the overall representation as purely either one or the other. For example, a room may be directly represented by a 2-dimensional array of values which denote the occupants of various positions in the room: but this array may itself be implemented by the programming system as a list of triplets <i,j,a[i,j]>, i.e. by a sort of description. It seems essential, therefore, to use a notion of _level_ of representation in attempting to make the distinction precise.

Third, _any_ representation must also be a direct representation of something. For, the pattern of marks which is a configuration of the scheme, can convey meaning only by virtue of the fact that its parts are physically arranged in some definite way. This physical arrangement has to be a _direct_ representation of (at least) the way in which meanings of some configurations are compounded into meanings of larger configurations.

Fourthly, the notion of direct representation seems to depend upon some _similarity_ between the _medium_ in which the representation is embedded, and the thing represented. Thus a map of a room is a direct representation of the spatial relationships (in the horizontal place) in the room, by virtue of the similarity between the 2-dimensional plane of the paper and the 2-dimensional plane of the floor of the room. The paper is a direct homomorph of the room: they are the same sort of structure (2-D Euclidean space), admitting the same sorts of operations (sliding, rotation, measurement), but the map is a simplification of the reality, in the sense that certain properties present in reality (colour, exact shapes, etc.) and certain relations (the third dimension, comparisons of value) are missing in the map. Another example is an ordered vector of items in a core store: here the medium is the address structure of the store, which is similar to the integers in respect of its ordering relationships, but not (for example) in respect of its cardinality (stores are finite).

Putting all this together, one arrives at the following general position. There are things called media in which one can construct certain configurations of marks or symbols: that is, arrangements of marks in which relations exhibited directly in the medium hold between the marks. A language is defined (syntactically) by a set of 'primitive' symbols and a set of grammatical rules which define new configurations in terms of old ones. One gets the usual ideas of parsing. (It could be mathematically interesting to see how much of formal language theory can be generalised to this setting from the conventional 'string' case of 1-dimensional media. One can certainly define context-free, and context-sensitive grammars, but I am not so sure about finite-state, for example.) A model for such a language is provided by a set of entities acting as meanings of the primitive symbols; and, for each grammatical rule, a semantic rule which defines the meaning of the configuration in terms of the meanings of its parts. (One needs variables and variable-binding expressions also, so this account needs elaboration and qualification, but space does not permit a full discussion.) This, so far, is the usual Tarskian idea of a truth-recursion, generalised to this more general notion of language. But now, we also insist that each medium-defined relation used in constructing configurations corresponds to a similar relation in the meanings, and that the representation is a structural homomorph of the reality with respect to these relations. That is, the meanings of configurations must exist in a space which is similar to the representing medium, and the syntactic relations which are displayed directly by the symbol-configurations of the language, must mirror semantic relations of the corresponding kind. The directness of a direct representation lies in the nature of the relationship between the configurations and the reality they represent (it is a relation of homomorphism rather than denotation). A scheme is not direct because of any syntactic features (such as being 2-dimensional) of its schemes, or because of any special qualities (such as being continuous) of the worlds it describes.

It is possible to give formal grammars for simple maps, to emphasise how this account fits the facts, along the lines of Rosenfeld's isotonic grammars [18]. To emphasise again: map-making conventions are, in this view, a language, of which the maps are expressions. The relationship of these expressions to reality is that the primitive symbols denote features of a terrain in a way defined by the map key, and the positional relationships between symbols directly display corresponding relationships between the denoted features.

In electrical circuit diagrams, lines joining symbols denoting components directly denote, in their topological structure this time, the electrical connectivities in the actual circuit. Another example is provided by the simple narrative convention. In "He got up. He got dressed. He went out. He walked to the shop ...", we understand a time-sequence which is directly denoted by the ordering of the (timeless) separate propositions. This convention is also used in programming languages and cartoon strips, with the same sort of semantics. A final example is provided by networks. A network is a configuration which is a relational structure. Web grammars are the appropriate parsing device. The most obvious way of giving this a semantics is by declaring that a model is any relational structure into which the network can be homomorphically embedded. According to this semantics, a network has the same meaning as the conjunction of predicate calculus atoms corresponding to the arcs of the network. (It is a straightforward exercise in system programming to convert a list of such atomic assertions into a network, represented in the core-store medium by using 'addresses' as the direct analog of 'is connected to', for efficient retrieval.) As we will see, however, one can give a rather different semantics to networks, which makes them more expressive in an important way.

A more complete and rigorous account of this will be published elsewhere. The major problem is to find a general precise characterisation of what is meant by "medium" and "similar". I am currently working on an algebraic account (in which a medium is a category), but it is not yet altogether satisfactory. (Suggestions are welcome.)

The importance of all this, apart from the intrinsic interest of the subject, seems to me to lie in three points. (1) It shows that direct representations are not incompatible with linguistic representations, and can be given a precise model theory along Tarskian lines (which supports Sloman's view in [22]). (2) It suggests ways in which efficient deductive systems may be generalised from work in computational logic. (3) The notion of 'medium' captures the idea of levels of representation mentioned earlier. For a medium may not be physically directly present, but may itself be represented by configurations in some quite other medium, as in the array example. Or again, consider a simulation language like SIMULA.

This provides a medium consisting of processes and events and certain relations between them. This medium, taken in its own terms, gives a direct representation of time which is often extremely useful. But if one goes deeper, time is represented in a quite indirect way involving numerical descriptions and long chains of inference. This 'looking-deeper' means not treating SIMULA as a medium to be used to represent, but rather as a reality which is itself represented in some medium (say, FORTRAN or assembly language). The choice of primitive relationships defines both the medium and the level at which analysis will cease.

This shows, incidentally, that Sloman's arguments for the utility of analogical representations, based on the idea that they are somehow more efficient in use than Fregean representations, are fallacious. For an analogical representation may be embedded in a medium which is itself represented in a Fregean way in some other medium. Any discussion of efficiency must take into account the computational properties of the medium.

3.   Exhaustiveness and plasticity

An important fact about schemes with Tarskian semantics is that a configuration in such a scheme is, in general, a partial description of the environment. It constrains the form of a satisfying world, but does not (in general) uniquely determine one. And even if it does uniquely determine a world (is categorical, in the technical term), this fact can only be determined by metamathematical analysis: there is no sense in which one can say in the scheme itself, "this is a complete description."

Now this means that one has the opportunity of adding information ad lib, further specifying the world. (Hence the idea of conjunction arises very naturally). The process of adding information can be arrested only by the whole configuration becoming inconsistent, i.e. making an assertion about the world which is so strong that no such world exists. Different schemes will have different particular notions of consistency, but this general outline follows from the abstract properties of the satisfaction relationship between configurations and worlds. This ability to accept new pieces of information and to gradually accumulate knowledge piecemeal is one of the most valuable aspects of Tarskian schemes. Thus, the idea of a 'knowledge base' of separate pieces of information, to which new pieces can be added freely without a need, in particular, to pay attention to control flow or other organizational matters, is very familiar and important.

This possibility of adding information is one aspect of a schemes's plasticity, i.e. the ease with which changes can be made to configurations in the scheme. Plasticity is essential for nontrivial learning, and for any system working on limited information in an uncertain world.

However, there are times when one does want to be able to make a claim of exhastiveness in a representation. For example, we might want to represent that all the relations of a certain kind, between the entities represented in the configuration, are also represented in the configuration; or, that all the facts about some entity, which are in some sense relevant to some problem or task, are present in the configuration.

One important example of the need for this sort of assumption is the well-known frame problem. Consider a traditional description of the monkey-bananas problem, in natural English. How do you know there isn't a rope from the box, over two pulleys, and down to the bananas (so that as you move the box, the bananas ascend out of reach)?* Well, we assume that the simple description has given us all the relevant information to do with causal chains in the situation: we assume it is an exhaustive account of the machinery of the room. Much of the difficulty of the frame problem lies in the impossibility of expressing this assumption in the predicate calculus. (Using the causal-connection theory developed in[9], we could say there was no causal connection between the box and the bananas; but that is not strictly true: the monkey can throw one at the other, for example. In any case it is unsatisfactory as a general solution.)

---

*This example due to Alan Newell

(Parenthetically, I would like to take this opportunity of suggesting that we should stop talking about the frame problem. There are, it is now clear, several independent difficulties bound up in the normal formulation. One was just noted; another is the lack of a good representation of the way in which causal chains follow trajectories determined by mechanisms in the environment; another is the heuristic problem of organising inferences involving causality. The presence of state-variables in the language is not part of the problem, as some authors seem to have believed.)

Another, rather different, example of a claim of exhaustiveness is provided by the sort of analogy reasoning epitomised by Evan's well-known program, and formalised in the Merlin system [16]. This is normally regarded as essentially non-deductive reasoning, but it can be regarded as deductive reasoning from some rather strong hypotheses. Thus, suppose we decide that a certain collection of properties of an individual, taken together, constitutes an exhaustive description of it, from a certain 'point of view'. For example, we might say that a man was a mammal with a nose and feet. What could this mean? Well, it might mean that certain facts about men can be established by the use of these properties only: that is, an essentially proof-theoretic assertion. Now, with this meaning, if we replace the properties in the description with others (of the same 'type', in some sense: e.g. with corresponding sort structures in a multi-sorted logic), then corresponding facts can be established relative to the alternative properties. Thus, in the example of [16], if a pig is a mammal with a snout and trotters, then we can regard a pig as a man with a snout for a nose and trotters for feet. The existance of the 'analogy' follows from the (presumed) sufficiency of the list of properties. It follows deductively from the claims expressed in the putatively exhaustive descriptions of men and pigs.

This account of analogy (which is related to Kling's ideas) suggests natural explanation of (for example) the breakdown of an analogy (the claim of exhaustiveness fails: e.g. some property of men needs other hypotheses than those of noses and feet), and naturally relates 'analogical' and 'deductive' reasoning.

Now, there is a way in which a direct representation can be considered to be exhaustive, by a slight alteration to the semantic rules. We may insist that the medium-defined relations of a configuration completely mirror the corresponding relations in the reality: that is, that a medium-defined relation holds between subconfigurations if and only if the corresponding relation holds in the world between the entities denoted by the subconfigurations. Let us call such a representation, strongly direct.

For example, a map is strongly direct in this sense: all the 2-dimensional spatial relationships which hold between towns, rivers, etc. also hold in the map between the symbols denoting them. (They are also, often, exhaustive in a stronger sense; that all the entities (towns, rivers) present in the reality are denoted by symbols in the map. Thus we say, of a map with a river missing, that it is wrong, not just incomplete. It misleads us because we assume that if a river isn't marked, it isn't there.)

An example of a direct representation which isn't strongly direct is provided by networks: a relation may well not be displayed in the graph. However, we can also use networks as a strongly direct representation, if we consider the medium to be the algebra of relational structures with a given signature. Thus we would insist that either all or none of the instances of a certain relation are displayed in the network. A family tree is a strongly direct representation in this sense, relative to the relationships 'child of' and 'married'. With this semantics, (which can be specified algebraically) a network is no longer equivalent in meaning to the simple conjunction of the atomic facts represented in it. (If we call this conjunction C, it is equivalent to C with the added rule: if $C \not\vdash \emptyset$ then $\neg\emptyset$, for any atom $\emptyset$ in the appropriate vocabulary.) Winston's use of networks to describe concepts [26] seems to be closer to this latter semantics than to the former one, for example.

In unpublished work at Stanford, Arthur Thomas is developing a different approach to combining exhaustiveness with a Tarskian semantics, based on Hintikka's 'model sets'.

Strongly direct representations are less plastic than direct/Tarskian representations, in that information cannot be accumulated piecemeal in them. To add information to a strongly direct representation is to alter the information expressed by it. Alterations, as opposed to mere additions, raise problems of their own.

The trouble with alterations is that the information being altered may have been used earlier as a premis in a deduction of some kind. Thus, other pieces of information which obtain their support in some sense, from the altered information, are now endangered, and should probably be re-examined. This seems to require the system to keep an explicit record of how it formed its beliefs: a history of its own thinking. And this seems prohibitively expensive (of either space or time: one could recompute rather than store), due to exponential factors in the amount of information required.

Under some circumstances, it may be possible to re-evaluate a belief on criteria independent from its original derivation, as for example in adjusting the fit of lines to a gray-level picture (this observation due to Aaron Sloman), but in general I do not think one can avoid the problem.

This dilemma seems insoluble. There must be a clever series of compromises which steer us between its horns, but I don't know of any work in this direction.

More far-reaching alterations to a representation which one can envisage include changes to the basic ontology, to the sorts of entity to which it refers. The introduction of substances into a scheme oriented towards describing individuals is such a change, for example (see section 6). Minsky and Papert [15] give another rather simpler example: the change from a two-place relation of support between objects to a support relation between an object and a collection of objects, needed to describe e.g. an archway or a table. As they remark, this alteration seems to require a complete rebuilding of all knowledge about support, for the actual logical grammar of the assertions has changed. However, in this and similar cases one can see the general outlines of how it might be done. The fundamental step is to introduce the new notion of support as a new primitive idea (this is the really 'creative' act), and then define the old notion in terms of the new one, i.e regard the old concept henceforth as an abbreviation for its definition in terms of the new one. In the example, support (a,b) would be defined as support (a, {b}). This preserves the old theory of support as a special case of a new, more general, theory (which is yet to be defined). There is, however, a strong constraint on the new theory, viz. that it 'explains' the old theory. Thus, statements of the new theory which translate statements of the old theory must be derivable (in the new theory).

This corresponds to the idea that the alteration is somehow a refinement of, or an improvement upon, the former representation. A similar change, but in which the new concept completely replaced the older concept, which was rejected as wrong or unusable, could not be handled this way.

This whole issue of plasticity in representation is important not only for learning, but also for everyday program development reasons, and for debugging. For we must be able to modify and improve the representations of knowledge in the programs we write, and this is often far from easy.

4.   Evidential Reasoning

There is a continual need, especially in perception, to represent information concerned with one belief being evidence for another. It seems clear that one needs to make reasonings concerning such matters explicit so that they can be properly related to other reasonings, and can be adjusted in the light of experience (see section 3). The problem is how to adequately express the notion of one knowledge-fragment (or collection of fragments) being 'good evidence' for another.

There seem to be several notions of good evidence, but all can be put into a common framework: A is good evidence for B (under assumption Th, say) if the conjunction (A & not B) is somehow unlikely or implausible (or: if this follows from Th). Thus, for example, if A entails B then A is very good evidence for B, for then (A & not B) is impossible. In Guzman's work [8] back-to-back 'T's are good evidence for occlusion of one body by another, since the former without the latter is an unlikely coincidence. In a world where lines of bricks were common, back-to-back 'T's would be weaker evidence since the conjunction of such an observation with the hypothesis of a single occluded body would be less implausible: the possibility of a line of bricks being occluded would be an alternative explanation of the evidence.

This sort of observation suggests an account of 'plausible' as follows: (A & not B) is implausible if B entails A (occluded body entails back-to-back 'T's) and no other B of the suitable sort (e.g. no other hypothesis about physical arrangements of bodies) entails A. If there are several such explanations of A then A is evidence that one of them holds, but it doesn't distinguish which one. This decision has to be made on some other basis, for example by the use of Baye theorem in a probabilistic scheme, or by choosing the simplest hypothesis or the one most compatible with other entrenched beliefs.

An important problem is how to discover the collection of possible or likely explanations. (This point was emphasised to me by Aaron Sloman). How many ways can back-to-back 'T's arise? I can think of three, and am pretty convinced there aren't any more; but I have no idea where that conviction comes from, or how I would prove it. The 'theory' of lighting and perspective which is welded into Waltz's program has this nice exhaustive character, expressed in effect as a collection of explicit disjunctions. This works up to a point, but how could a program derive these lists from a description of, for example, the lighting conditions and geometry of the scene?

Involving the background theory of lighting, etc., in this way is not just of academic interest. A vision system which could make hypotheses about the lighting conditions, the sorts of reflectivity in the scene, etc. would find it necessary to be explicit about the role of such assumptions in interpreting pictorial phenomena. Thus we might have: if there is strong unidirectional lighting then shadows have sharp edges and are dark; so if this is the corner of a shadow then it will have a dark interior: $Th \supset (\overline{B} \supset \overline{A})$; from which we may use corners with sharp edges and dark interiors as evidence for shadows. Reasonings like this will be essential in any system with the ability to perceive a range of scenes. (Similar remarks apply to other perceptual situations, e.g. understanding speech, handwriting, children's stories.)

5. Control

A system which makes inferences to generate new facts must control its inference-making capabilities in some way. This control itself requires the storing and using, by the system, of information about the deductive process. That is: the system must represent and use knowledge about its own deductive behaviour.

In conventional programming languages this information is sometimes represented implicitly in, for example, the ordering of statements in the body of a program (which is a strongly direct representation of the time-order of control flow, provided jumps are forbidden) and sometimes explicitly in, for example, the correspondence in names which relates procedure calls to their corresponding procedure bodies. In PLANNER-like languages, the latter representation breaks down since 'procedures' are called not by name but by pattern matching, and is replaced by the more flexible device of advice lists. The ordering information is still represented implicitly, however.

Now, this metadeductive information needs to be made explicit and separated from the factual information represented in the scheme, for reasons of semantic clarity, plasticity and deductive power. For example, the residue of PLANNER upon separating out control information is a logic which resembles intuitionist predicate calculus. Results like this are important: they give us an inkling of how a semantic theory might be put together. (Unfortunately, intuitionist logic itself has a rather murky semantics.) The control information which can be represented in PLANNER is rather limited, as the CONNIVER authors emphasise [23]. Their solution, to give the user access to the implementation primitives of PLANNER, is however, something of a retrograde step (what are CONNIVER's semantics?), although pragmatically useful and important in the short term. A better solution is to give the user access to a meaningful set of primitive control abilities in an explicit representational scheme concerned with deductive control. This is the basic idea of the GOLUX project now underway at Essex [11].

The problem is to find a good set of control primitives. What is control? One answer to this is to pick on a fixed mechanism (the interpreter) associated with the language, and to relate control to this mechanism in, more or less, the way an order code relates to an actual computer. But this tends to be inflexible and arbitrary. The GOLUX answer is that control is a description of the behaviour of the interpreter. The exact nature of the interpreter is not defined, only that it constructs proofs according to some predefined structural rules. The descriptions in control assertions constrain its behaviour more or less tightly. It is, I believe, important that control information be represented in a scheme compatible with the scheme used for 'factual' information, so that control can be involved in inferences, added to, and changed.

Control primitives in GOLUX include predicates on, and relations between, partly constructed proofs in the search space; descriptions of collections of assertions; and primitives which describe temporal relations between events such as the achievement of a goal (e.g. the construction of a proof). The major source of difficulty is the tension between the expressive power of these primitives and their implementability: it is important that they be sufficiently simple that their truth can be rapidly tested against the actual state.

GOLUX is based on recent ideas in computational logic [10, 12]. Other authors have also recently emphasised that computational logic provides a powerful theoretical framework for problem-solving and computational processes [14, 28, 19], although we are not in complete agreement as to which is the best framework.

A common area of difficulty both here and in evidential reasoning is to get a good notion of a 'theory': an organised body of knowledge about some subject-area.

6.   Substances, Parts and Assemblies

Every representational scheme known to me is based ultimately, like predicate calculus, on the idea of separate individual entities and relations between them.

But our introspective world-picture also has quite different 'stuff', viz. substances: water, clay, snow, steel, wood. Linguistically, these are meanings of mass terms. Substances are fundamentally very different from individuals, and I know of no scheme which seems capable of satisfactorily handling them. I became aware of this problem from reading Davidson [5].

We often speak as though substances were individuals having properties and relations one to another and to more conventional individuals: steel is dense, blood is thicker than water, his head is made of wood. The relation "made of" seems particularly important. But appearances are deceptive.

Does 'water is wet' mean the same as 'all samples of water are wet'? I think it does: we certainly want to be able to infer from 'water is wet', that 'this sample of water is wet'. This suggests at first sight that we should treat pieces of stuff as individuals, which seems fairly acceptable.

But these individuals are also rather strange, especially for fluids. If you put together two pieces of water you get one piece, not two: we have to speak of quantity (of stuff) before we can use arithmetic. (It is significant that, as Piaget has shown, children properly understand the concept of quantity only at quite a late stage of development.) Moreover, we should distinguish properties which a piece of stuff has by virtue of its being a piece (size, shape), from those which it has by virtue of its being made of stuff (density, hardness, rigidity): for the former, but not the latter, can be easily altered by physical manipulations. It really seems that we cannot get away from substances no matter how hard we try.

Let me emphasise that this problem is not a by-product of a nominalist philosophical position. I have no objections to platonic, abstract, non-physical individuals. That's not the difficulty. The difficulty is 'individuals' which appear and disappear, or merge one with another, at the slightest provocation: for they play havoc with the model theory.

This seems to me to be one of the most difficult problems in representation theory at present. The only way I can imagine handling substances is by regarding each substance as a (special sort of) individual, to which such properties as hardness, density, etc. are attributed. These individuals can be regarded as platonic ideals, or alternatively as the physical totality of all samples of the substance: you can take your nominalism or leave it. We have the naive axiom

$$\text{Stuff}(x) \ \& \ \text{madeof}(y,x) \ \& \ z(x). \ \supset z(y)$$

(e.g.: a lump of hard stuff is hard).

which transmits properties from substances to pieces of them. (Care is needed: steel ships float, for example; a fact which often amazes young children.) Notice this axiom is first-order (in a sugared syntax). Quantity is now a function from (pieces)x(stuff) to some scale of measurement, so we can express conservation of quantity through some physical alteration Q by:

$$\text{quantity}(\text{piece},\text{stuff}) = \text{quantity}(Q(\text{piece}),\text{stuff}).$$

And so on. This works up to a point, but seems to me to be essentially unsatisfactory.

There is a close analogy between being made of a substance, and being made up of a number of parts. And a corresponding analogy between quantity (of stuff) and number (of parts). Sand and piles of small pebbles are intermediate cases: and we often treat an assembly of individuals as a fluid, e.g. as in "traffic flow". The major difference seems to be that different scales of measurement are used in common-sense reasoning (but not in physics, where quantity is number of atoms), as the "paradox of the heap" shows. This runs as follows: a heap with one stone in it is small. If you add just one stone to a small heap, it's still a small heap. Hence by mathematical induction all heaps are small. The 'paradox' comes by switching from the informal quantity scale of 'small-large' to the precise number scale. Induction is not valid in the former, which (for example) exhibits hysteresis.

Things are often made up of parts joined or related in some way. Obvious examples are physical objects made of pieces glued or assembled together: cups, cars, steam engines, animals. But there are others: processes made up of subprocesses; time-intervals made up of times. The idea of organised collections of entities being regarded themselves as entities permeates our thinking.

Now this fact strikes at the root of an 'individual-based' ontology in the same sort of way that substances do. They only way of handling collections is to count both the collection and its parts as individuals, related by some sort of made of or has-as-part relation. But then these assembled individuals behave in odd ways: they sometimes merge (two heaps make one heap) like pieces of stuff: sometimes they can be disassembled, cease to exist for a time and then perhaps be reassembled: is it the same individual? (Our intuition says: yes, in most cases).

Modal logicians now have very elegant semantic theories which can accommodate such odd behaviour in individuals. But these allow any pattern of vanishing, reappearing and changing properties. The point is to find a way of representing the fact that composite individuals have this special way of vanishing (being taken apart), and to distinguish, for example, those composites which cannot be reassembled (animals, cups) from those that can (cars, steam engines): and to do all this in a framework which assumes that things, by and large, don't just vanish and reappear spontaneously. Composites are thus a different sort of individual, in a very deep sense.

A related issue is how to state criteria upon which we reify a collection into a composite individual. Physical compactness is sometimes sufficient (a heap), but not always necessary (the wiring system of a house), for example. Of course, one does not expect a single general answer, but I do not know of any reasonable answers at all, even for special cases.

I have already remarked on the similarities between being made of (stuff) and being made up of (parts). Is this anything more than a facile analogy? Is there some common framework in which the fundamental ontological notion, rather than existence, is space-occupancy? It might be useful to strive for a representation which allowed the simultaneous expression in different schemes of both 'existence' and 'space-occupancy'. (The schemes would, I believe, have to be essentially different.) Indeed, in a crude way one can see how it might be done directly by "arrays of facts": the array subscripts give one access via spatial relationships to the local presence of objects, which also partake of relationships (represented by a network, say) between themselves and other, non-space-filling, individuals (such as colours). Decomposability is indicated in the array also by 'break lines' which separate the space into regions: different sorts of connection could be fairly easily handled (glued, detachable ...). But this is very crude and has several crucial drawbacks (notably plasticity: imagine moving an object through the space, preserving its shape.)

7.   Some non-issues

7.1   Irrelevant classifications

Much heat is generated by disputes based on classifications which do not correspond with the facts, or which at least have outlived their usefulness. Two such are the "generality vs. expertise" debate and the more recent "procedures vs. assertions" debate. Both of these arise from a revulsion against a particular early naive idea about how to organize intelligent programs, which one could (perhaps unfairly) call the general problem-solver fallacy. (Seymour Papert calls it, the blinding white light theory.)

This was the early insistence that problem-solving methods had to be wrapped up in black boxes called problem-solvers, whose (only) input was a problem and whose (only) output a solution. Problem-solvers were supposed to be as powerful and as general as possible. One had not to "cheat" by "giving" the problem-solver the solution in any sense, e.g. by reprogramming it or cleverly coding the problem in some way (this is made explicit in [7]). Unfortunately, of course, this collection of rules means that there is no way of getting subject-matter-dependent knowledge into the black box; for it cannot be there a priori (violates generality), and it cannot be put into the problem (cheating), and there aren't any other inputs. This is a caricature, but not much of a caricature. Much work in automatic theorem-proving was done with the implicit idea that the theorem-provers were to be regarded as problem-solvers in this sense (c.f. the widely felt 'need' for adequate criteria of relative efficiency of theorem-provers: "my problem-solver is more powerful than yours". (See [2,10] for a fuller discussion).

The MIT school have now succeeded admirably in destroying this idea, but unfortunately have gotten it confused with some others. Surely we need both generality and expertise: the fallacy is not the emphasis on generality, but the insistence upon the black box and the "no cheating" rules. The general mechanisms of means-end analysis, heuristic search and computational logic should not be rejected, but rather incorporated into more flexible systems, rather than wrapped up in closed 'problem-solving subroutines' or 'methods' or whatever. Thus, to reject conventional uniform theorem-proving systems because they work with assertional rather than 'procedural' languages, is to miss the point. (Whether a language is considered to be a programming language or not, is largely a matter of taste, in any case. LISP can be regarded as (an incomplete) higher-order predicate calculus, or as a first-order applied predicate calculus: predicate calculus can be regarded as a programming language, although by itself not a very good one.) The force of the MIT criticism of computational logic is directed against the 'problem-solver' view and its consequences, especially the lack of any accessible and manipulable (programmable) control structure in conventional theorem-proving systems. The GOLUX system referred to earlier is an attempt to fill this lack directly with an especially devised control language.

A more recent attack on conventional theorem-proving [17] is that it is too concerned with "machine oriented" logic, and not enough with "human oriented" logic. I confess to being quite unable to understand what this could possibly mean.

7.2   Semantics

Some authors, usually concerned with comprehension of natural language, use 'semantic' as a vague term roughly synonymous with 'to do with meanings', where this means the same as 'not to do with grammars'. This follows a long and honourable tradition in linguistics (c.f. the use of such terms as "semantic markers" and the idea that linguistic deep structure is semantics).

I wish to emphasise however that this is not the same usage as that adopted here and in formal logic. And it is, I believe, very misleading. It militates against an understanding of the fundamental point that the meanings of linguistic expressions are ultimately to be found in extra-linguistic entities: chairs, people, emotions, fluids.....

As a recent example, Wilks' "semantic units" [24] are syntactic objects in a scheme: nowhere does he tackle the difficult and vital problem of describing exactly what sorts of extra-linguistic entities his "semantic units" refer to. It is easy to say: we must have substances and things and ...; but what are these? There does seem to be the beginnings of some sort of sketchy semantic theory behind Wilks' formulae (actions have agents which are animate, etc.), but it is not articulated: and if it were, all the problems I have discussed would promptly appear. Similar remarks apply to Schank's work [20], and others.

I am not arguing that natural language should be given an extensional semantics. I distinguish sharply between a natural language, which is an informal and probably not even completely defined means of communication in the real world (is "Eh?" a sentence? Eh?), and a formal deductive scheme for representing knowledge. (It has been suggested to me that the distinction may be related to Sassure's distinction between Langue and Parole, but I have not investigated this.) I suspect that those who deny the usefulness of extensional semantics would also deny the validity of this distinction. That is probably a perfectly respectable philosophical position: but I submit that it is bad engineering.

7.3   Fuzziness and Wooliness

Several authors have recently suggested that more exotic logics, especially 'fuzzy logic', are necessary in order to capture the essentially imprecise nature of human deduction. While agreeing that we have to look beyond first-order logic, I find the usual arguments advanced for the use of fuzzy logic most unconvincing.

Introspection does not suggest to me that intuitive reasonings are essentially imprecise; still less that they are precise in terms of a real-valued truth-value in the unit interval (which is what fuzzy logic would have us accept). Even ignoring introspection, fuzzy logic does not seem very useful, for where do all those numbers come from? (This is McCarthy's point.)

The typical example brought forward to illustrate the need for fuzzy logic concerns the everyday use of such words as 'large', 'small', 'old', 'expensive'. Now it seems to me that, when I say a heap is small, I mean just that. If asked, "Is what you say true?", I will correctly answer "yes", and become impatient with the protagonist. These are <u>precise</u> words but they refer to <u>vague</u> measuring scales. As remarked earlier, for example, the scale 'small-large' exhibits a different topology from the integers or from real intervals: it is more like a tolerance space [27] and it may have hysteresis (an intermediate heap will be considered small if it began as small and grew, and considered large if it began as large and shrank), and it may have gaps in it. The point however is, that we should keep the vagueness of the scale localised into <u>it</u>, rather than letting it infect the whole inferential system. This enables different 'fuzzy' measuring scales to coexist, which is important. We should investigate what sorts of measurement scales are useful for various purposes.

The most drastic alteration to the actual logic which seems to be needed to handle words like this is to move from a 2-valued to a 3-valued logic, and it is not absolutely clear that even this small step is really necessary.

The view expressed here is different from the one I held some years ago. I have become more respectful, since then, of the unexplored possibilities of predicate logic.

Acknowledgements

Many people have helped me with conversations, suggestions and criticisms. I would like especially to thank John Laski (section 1); Aaron Sloman (sections 2 and 4); Harry Barrow (section 3); Jim Doran (section 4); Bruce Anderson, Carl Hewitt, Johns Rulifson (section 5); Seymour Papert, Gerald Sussman, Bruce Anderson (section 7.1). More generally, I owe much to many conversations with Richard Bornat, Mike Brady, Jim Doran and Bob Kowalski. Alan Bundy, Aaron Sloman and Yorick Wilks made many useful criticisms on an earlier draft.

References

(1) S. Amarel. More on Representations of the Monkey Problem. <u>Internal Report</u>, Carnegie-Mellon University (1966)

(2) D. B. Anderson & P. J. Hayes. The Logician's Folly. DCL Memo 54, Edinburgh University (1972)

(3) R. Balzer. A global View of Automatic Programming. <u>3rd IJCAI proc.</u> Stanford (1973) (<u>see</u> "Problem Acquisition", paragraphs 3 & 4)

(4) E. Charniak. Jack & Janet in Search of a Theory of Knowledge. <u>3rd IJCAI proc.</u>, Stanford University (1973)

(5) D. Davidson. Truth and Meaning. <u>Synthese 17</u> (1967)

(6) M. van Emden & R. Kowalski. The Semantics of Predicate Logic as a Programming Language.

(7) G. Ernst & A. Newell. Some Issues of Representation in a General Problem-Solver. <u>Proc. Spring Joint Comp. Conf.</u> (1967)

(8) A. Guzman. Computer Recognition of Three-Dimensional Objects in a
       Visual Scene. Report MAC-TR-59, MIT (1968)

(9) P. J. Hayes. A Logic of Actions. Machine Intelligence 6, Edinburgh
       University Press (1971)

(10) P. J. Hayes. Semantic Trees. Ph.D. thesis, Edinburgh University,
       (1973)

(11) P. J. Hayes. Computation & Deduction. Proc. MFCS Symposium, Czech.
       Academy of Sciences, (1973)

(12) P. J. Hayes. Simple and Structural Redundancy in Nondeterministic
       Computation. Research memorandum, Essex University (1974)

(13) C. Hewitt. PLANNER. MIT AI Memo 258 (1972)

(14) D. Loveland. A Hole in Goal Trees. Proc. 3rd IJCAI, Stanford (1973)

(15) M. Minsky & S. Papert. Progress Report. AI Memo 252, MIT. (1972)

(16) J. Moore & A. Newell. How can Merlin understand? Internal memo,
       Carnegie-Mellon University (1973)

(17) A. Nevins. A Human Oriented Logic for Automatic Theorem Proving.
       MIT AI Lab. Memo 268 (1972)

(18) A. Rosenfeld. Isotonic Grammars. Machine Intelligence 6, Edinburgh
       University Press (1971)

(19) E. Sandewall. Representing Natural Language Information in Predicate
       Calculus. Machine Intelligence 6, Edinburgh (1971)

(20) R. Schank. The Fourteen Primitive Actions and their Inferences.
       Stanford AIM-183, Stanford University (1973)

(21) Schank & Colby (eds). Computer Models of thought and language.
       Freeman (1974)

(22) A. Sloman. Interactions between Philosophy and Artificial Intelligence
       Artificial Intelligence 2, (1971)

(23) G. Sussman & D. McDermott. Why Conniving is Better than Planning.
       MIT AI memo 255A, 1972

(24) Y. Wilks. Understanding Without Proofs. Proc. 3rd IJCAI, Stanford
       (1973)

(25) T. Winograd. Understanding Natural Language. Edinburgh University
       Press (1971)

(26) P. Winston. Learning Structural Descriptions from Examples. Ph.D.
       Thesis, Report MAC-TR-76, MIT (1970)

(27) C. Zeeman. Homology of Tolerance Spaces. Warwick University, 1967

(28) R. Kowalski. Predicate Calculus as a Programming Language. DCL Memo 70, Edinburgh University (1973)

(29) E. Sandewall. The conversion of Predicate-Calculus Axioms, Viewed as Non-Deterministic Programs, to Corresponding Deterministic Programs. Proc. 3rd IJCAI, Stanford (1973)

2 / John McCarthy
Epistemological Problems of Artificial Intelligence

In an earlier paper [McCarthy and Hayes 69], a distinction was made between the epistemological and heuristic aspects of Artificial Intelligence. Roughly, the former deals with what information can be formally represented, while the latter focuses on how that information can be made available to a finite computational device. In the current paper, with the benefit of a decade or so of experience, McCarthy reviews what he considers to be the major outstanding epistemological problems. Indeed, as he points out, even if we had arbitrarily fast computers, we would still be a long way from true intelligent behavior. There are just too many areas of knowledge that we still do not know how to formally represent in any satisfactory way. Among those mentioned by McCarthy are propositional attitudes, concurrency, properties of space and time, causes and abilities, properties of materials, and the relationship between reality and appearances. Some of these have been dealt with to a certain extent since the paper was written, for example, in [Hayes, Chapter 28] and [Allen, Chapter 30]. McCarthy himself sketches an approach to the first of these problems in terms of a formalization of concepts, a topic he expands on in [McCarthy, Chapter 31]. A more fundamental epistemological problem is also raised, namely the *frame problem,* and a closely related one, called the *qualification problem.* Basically, the problem is to come up with a formalization that allows but does not require the seemingly endless qualifications and hedges present on any true general statement (see [Reiter, Chapter 23] for more on this; also, this is one of the key points of Dreyfus' skepticism about the possibility of ever capturing commonsense knowledge [Dreyfus, Chapter 5]). The mechanism McCarthy introduces for dealing with the problem is called *circumscription,* a new form of reasoning that he has gone on to develop in considerable detail in [McCarthy 80] and [McCarthy 84].

Appeared in *Proc. IJCAI-77,* Cambridge, MA, 1977, 1038–1044.

EPISTEMOLOGICAL PROBLEMS OF ARTIFICIAL INTELLIGENCE

John McCarthy
Computer Science Department
Stanford University
Stanford, California 94305

Introduction

In (McCarthy and Hayes 1969), we proposed dividing the artificial intelligence problem into two parts - an epistemological part and a heuristic part. This lecture further explains this division, explains some of the epistemological problems, and presents some new results and approaches.

The epistemological part of AI studies what kinds of facts about the world are available to an observer with given opportunities to observe, how these facts can be represented in the memory of a computer, and what rules permit legitimate conclusions to be drawn from these facts. It leaves aside the heuristic problems of how to search spaces of possibilities and how to match patterns.

Considering epistemological problems separately has the following advantages:

1. The same problems of what information is available to an observer and what conclusions can be drawn from information arise in connection with a variety of problem solving tasks.

2. A single solution of the epistemological problems can support a wide variety of heuristic approaches to a problem.

3. AI is a very difficult scientific problem, so there are great advantages in finding parts of the problem that can be separated out and separately attacked.

4. As the reader will see from the examples in the next section, it is quite difficult to formalize the facts of common knowledge. Existing programs that manipulate facts in some of the domains are confined to special cases and don't face the difficulties that must be overcome to achieve very intelligent behavior.

We have found first order logic to provide suitable languages for expressing facts about the world for epistemological research. Recently we have found that introducing concepts as individuals makes possible a first order logic expression of facts usually expressed in modal logic but with important advantages over modal logic - and so far no disadvantages.

In AI literature, the term *predicate calculus* is usually extended to cover the whole of first order logic. While predicate calculus includes just formulas built up from variables using predicate symbols, logical connectives, and quantifiers, first order logic also allows the use of function symbols to form terms and in its semantics interprets the equality symbol as standing for identity. Our first order systems further use conditional expressions (non-recursive) to form terms and λ-expressions with individuaal variables to form new function symbols. All these extensions are logically inessential, because every formula that includes them can be replaced by a formula of pure predicate calculus whose validity is equivalent to it. The extensions are heuristically non-trivial, because the equivalent predicate calculus may be much longer and is usually much more difficult to understand - for man or machine.

The use of first order logic in epistemological research is a separate issue from whether first order sentences are appropriate data structures for representing information within a program. As to the latter, sentences in logic are at one end of a spectrum of representations; they are easy to communicate, have logical consequences and can be logical consequences, and they can be meaningful in a wide context. Taking action on the basis of information stored as sentences, is slow and they are not the most compact representation of information. The opposite extreme is to build the information into hardware, next comes building it into machine language program, then a language like LISP, and then a language like MICROPLANNER, and then perhaps productions. Compiling or hardware building or "automatic programming" or just planning takes information from a more context independent form to a faster but more context dependent form. A clear expression of this is the transition from first order logic to MICROPLANNER, where much information is represented similarly but with a specification of how the information is to be used. A large AI system should represent some information as first order logic sentences and other information should be compiled. In fact, it will often be necessary to represent the same information in several ways. Thus a ball player habit of keeping his eye on the ball is built into his "program", but it is also explicitly represented as a sentence so that the advice can be communicated.

Whether first order logic makes a good programming language is yet another issue. So far it seems to have the qualities Samuel Johnson ascribed to a woman preaching or a dog walking on its hind legs - one is sufficiently impressed by seeing it done at all that one doesn't demand it be done well.

Suppose we have a theory of a certain class of phenomena axiomatized in (say) first order logic. We regard the theory as adequate for describing the epistemological aspects of a goal seeking process involving these phenomena provided the following criterion is satisfied:

Imagine a robot such that its inputs become sentences of the theory stored in the robot's data-base, and such that whenever a sentence of the form "*I should emit output X now*" appears in its data base, the robot emits output X. Suppose that new sentences appear in its data base only as logical consequences of sentences already in the data base. The deduction of these sentences also use general sentences stored in the data base at the beginning constituting the theory being tested. Usually a data-base of sentences permits many different deductions to be made so that a deduction program would have to choose which deduction to make. If there was no program that could achieve the goal by making deductions allowed by the theory no matter how fast the program ran, we would have to say that the theory was epistemologically inadequate. A theory that was epistemologically adequate would be considered heuristically inadequate if no program running at a reasonable speed with any representation of the facts expressed by the data could do the job. We believe that most present AI formalisms are epistemologically inadequate for general intelligence; i.e. they wouldn't achieve enough goals requiring general intelligence no matter how fast they were allowed to run. This is because the epistemological problems discussed in the following sections haven't even been attacked yet.

The word "epistemology" is used in this paper substantially as many philosophers use it, but the problems considered have a different emphasis. Philosophers emphasize what is potentially knowable with maximal opportunities to observe and compute, whereas AI must take into account what is knowable with available observational and computational facilities. Even so, many of the same formalizations have both philosophical and AI interest.

The subsequent sections of this paper list some epistemological problems, discuss some first order formalizations, introduce concepts as objects and use them to express facts about knowledge, describe a new mode of reasoning called circumscription, and place the AI problem in a philosphical setting.

Epistemological problems

We will discuss what facts a person or robot must take into account in order to achieve a goal by some strategy of action. We will ignore the question of how these facts are represented, e.g., whether they are represented by sentences from which deductions are made or whether they are built into the program. We start with great generality, so there many difficulties. We obtain successively easier problems by assuming that the difficulties we have recognized don't occur until we get to a class of problems we think we can solve.

1. We begin by asking whether solving the problem requires the co-operation of other people or overcoming their opposition. If either is true, there are two subcases. In the first subcase, the other people's desires and goals must be taken into account, and the actions they will take in given circumstances predicted on the hypothesis that they will try to achieve their goals, which may have to be discovered. The problem is even more difficult if bargaining is involved, because then the problems and indeterminacies of game theory are relevant. Even if bargaining is not involved, the robot still must "put himself in the place of the other people with whom he interacts". Facts like a person wanting a thing or a person disliking another must be described.

The second subcase makes the assumption that the other people can be regarded as machines with known input-output behavior. This is often a good assumption, e.g., one assumes that a clerk in a store will sell the goods in exchange for their price and that a professor will assign a grade in accordance with the quality of the work done. Neither the goals of the clerk or the professor need be taken into account; either might well regard an attempt to use them to optimize the interaction as an invasion of privacy. In such circumstances, man usually prefers to be regarded as a machine.

Let us now suppose that either other people are not involved in the problem or that the information available about their actions takes the form of input-output relations and does not involve understanding their goals.

2. The second question is whether the strategy involves the acquisition of knowledge. Even if we can treat other people as machines, we still may have to reason about what they know. Thus an airline clerk knows what airplanes fly from here to there and when, although he will tell you when asked without your having to motivate him. One must also consider information in books and in tables. The latter information is described by other information.

The second subcase of knowledge is according to whether the information obtained can be simply plugged into a program or whether it enters in a more complex way. Thus if the robot must telephone someone, its program can simply dial the number obtained, but it might have to ask a question, "*How can I get in touch with Mike?*" and reason about how to use the resulting information in conjunction with other information. The general distinction may be according to whether new sentences are generated or whether values are just assigned to variables.

An example worth considering is that a sophisticated air traveler rarely asks how he will get from the arriving flight to the departing flight at an airport where he must change planes. He is confident that the information will be available in a form he can understand at the time he will need it.

If the strategy is embodied in a program that branches on an environmental condition or reads a numerical parameter from the environment, we can regard it as obtaining knowledge, but this is obviously an easier case than those we have discussed.

3. A problem is more difficult if it involves concurrent events and actions. To me this seems to be the most difficult unsolved epistemological problem for AI – how to express rules that give the effects of actions and events when they occur concurrently. We may contrast this with the sequential case treated in (McCarthy and Hayes 1969). In the sequential case we can write

1) $s' = result(e, s)$

where s' is the situation that results when event e occurs in situation s. The effects of e can be described by sentences relating s', e and s. One can attempt a similar formalism giving a *partial situation* that results from an event in another partial situation, but it is difficult to see how to apply this to cases in which other events may affect with the occurrence.

When events are concurrent, it is usually necessary to regard time as continuous. We have events like *raining until the reservoir overflows* and questions like *Where was his train when we wanted to call him?*.

Computer science has recently begun to formalize parallel processes so that it is sometimes possible to prove that a system of parallel processes will meet its specifications. However, the knowledge available to a robot of the other processes going on in the world will rarely take the form of a Petri net or any of the other formalisms used in engineering or computer science. In fact, anyone who wishes to prove correct an airline reservation system or an air traffic control system must use information about the behavior of the external world that is less specific than a program. Nevertheless, the formalisms for expressing facts about parallel and indeterminate programs provide a start for axiomatizing concurrent action.

4. A robot must be able to express knowledge about space, and the locations, shapes and layouts of objects in space. Present

programs treat only very special cases. Usually locations are discrete – block A may be on block B but the formalisms do not allow anything to be said about where on block B it is, and what shape space is left on block B for placing other blocks or whether block A could be moved to project out a bit in order to place another block. A few are more sophisticated, but the objects must have simple geometric shapes. A formalism capable of representing the geometric information people get from seeing and handling objects has not, to my knowledge, been approached.

The difficulty in expressing such facts is indicated by the limitations of English in expressing human visual knowledge. We can describe regular geometric shapes precisely in English (fortified by mathematics), but the information we use for recognizing another person's face cannot ordinarily be transmitted in words. We can answer many more questions in the presence of a scene than we can from memory.

5. The relation between three dimensional objects and their two dimensional retinal or camera images is mostly untreated. Contrary to some philosophical positions, the three dimensional object is treated by our minds as distinct from its appearances. People blind from birth can still communicate in the same language as sighted people about three dimensional objects. We need a formalism that treats three dimensional objects as instances of patterns and their two dimensional appearances as projections of these patterns modified by lighting and occlusion.

6. Objects can be made by shaping materials and by combining other objects. They can also be taken apart, cut apart or destroyed in various ways. What people know about the relations between materials and objects remains to be described.

7. Modal concepts like *event e1 caused event e2* and *person e can do action a* are needed. (McCarthy and Hayes 1969) regards ability as a function of a person's position in a causal system and not at all as a function of his internal structure. This still seems correct, but that treatment is only metaphysically adequate, because it doesn't provide for expressing the information about ability that people actually have.

8. Suppose now that the problem can be formalized in terms of a single state that is changed by events. In interesting cases, the set of components of the state depends on the problem, but common general knowledge is usually expressed in terms of the effect of an action on one or a few components of the state. However, it cannot always be assumed that the other components are unchanged, especially because the state can be described in a variety of co-ordinate systems and the meaning of changing a single co-ordinate depends on the co-ordinate system. The problem of expressing information about what remains unchanged by an event was called *the frame problem* in (McCarthy and Hayes 1969). Minsky subsequently confused matters by using the word "frame" for patterns into which situations may fit. (His hypothesis seems to have been that almost all situations encountered in human problem solving fit into a small number of previously known patterns of situation and goal. I regard this as unlikely in difficult problems).

9. The *frame problem* may be a subcase of what we call the *qualification problem*, and a good solution of the qualification problem may solve the frame problem also. In the *missionaries and cannibals* problem, a boat holding two people is stated to be available. In the statement of the problem, nothing is said about how boats are used to cross rivers, so obviously this information must come from common knowledge, and a computer program

capable of solving the problem from an English description or from a translation of this description into logic must have the requisite common knowledge. The simplest statement about the use of boats says something like, "*If a boat is at one point on the shore of a body of water, and a set of things enter the boat, and the boat is propelled to the another point on the shore, and the things exit the boat, then they will be at the second point on the shore*". However, this statement is too rigid to be true, because anyone will admit that if the boat is a rowboat and has a leak or no oars, the action may not achieve its intended result. One might try amending the common knowledge statement about boats, but this encounters difficulties when a critic demands a qualification that the vertical exhaust stack of a diesel boat must not be struck square by a cow turd dropped by a passing hawk or some other event that no-one has previously thought of. We need to be able to say that the boat can be used as a vehicle for crossing a body of water unless something prevents it. However, since we are not willing to delimit in advance possible circumstances that may prevent the use of the boat, there is still a problem of proving or at least conjecturing that nothing prevents the use of the boat. A method of reasoning called *circumscription*, described in a subsequent section of this paper, is a candidate for solving the qualification problem. The reduction of the frame problem to the qualification problem has not been fully carried out, however.

Circumscription - a way of jumping to conclusions

There is an intuition that not all human reasoning can be translated into deduction in some formal system of mathematical logic, and therefore mathematical logic should be rejected as a formalism for expressing what a robot should know about the world. The intuition in itself doesn't carry a convincing idea of what is lacking and how it might be supplied.

We can confirm part of the intuition by describing a previously unformalized mode of reasoning called *circumscription*, which we can show does not correspond to deduction in a mathematical system. The conclusions it yields are just conjectures and sometimes even introduce inconsistency. We will argue that humans often use circumscription, and robots must too. The second part of the intuition - the rejection of mathematical logic - is not confirmed; the new mode of reasoning is best understood and used within a mathematical logical framework and co-ordinates well with mathematical logical deduction. We think *circumscription* accounts for some of the successes and some of the errors of human reasoning.

The intuitive idea of *circumscription* is as follows: We know some objects in a given class and we have some ways of generating more. We jump to the conclusion that this gives all the objects in the class. Thus we *circumscribe* the class to the objects we know how to generate.

For example, suppose that objects a, b and c satisfy the predicate P and that the functions $f(x)$ and $g(x, y)$ take arguments satisfying P into values also satisfying P. The first order logic expression of these facts is

2) $P(a) \land P(b) \land P(c) \land (\forall x)(P(x) \supset P(f(x))) \land (\forall x\, y)(P(x) \land P(y) \supset P(g(x, y)))$.

The conjecture that everything satisfying P is generated from a, b and c by repeated application of the functions f and g is expressed by the sentence schema

3) $\quad\quad \Phi(a) \wedge \Phi(b) \wedge \Phi(c) \wedge (\forall x)(\Phi(x) \supset \Phi(f(x))) \wedge (\forall x\, y)(\Phi(x) \wedge \Phi(y) \supset \Phi(g(x, y))) \supset (\forall x)(\Phi(x) \supset P(x))$,

where Φ is a free predicate variable for which any predicate may be substituted.

It is only a conjecture, because there might be an object d such that $P(d)$ which is not generated in this way. (3) is one way of writing *the circumscription* of (2). The heuristics of circumscription – when one can plausibly conjecture that the objects generated in known ways are all there are – are completely unstudied.

Circumscription is not deduction in disguise, because every form of deduction has two properties that circumscription lacks – transitivity and what we may call *monotonicity*. Transitivity says that if $p \vdash r$ and $r \vdash s$, then $p \vdash s$. Monotonicity says that if $A \vdash p$ (where A is a set of sentences) and $A \subset B$, then $B \vdash p$ for deduction. Intuitively, circumscription should not be monotonic, since it is the conjecture that the ways we know of generating P's are all there are. An enlarged set B of sentences may contain a new way of generating P's.

If we use second order logic or the language of set theory, then circumscription can be expressed as a sentence rather than as a schema. In set theory it becomes.

3') $\quad (\forall \Phi)(a \in \Phi \wedge b \in \Phi \wedge c \in \Phi \wedge (\forall x)(x \in \Phi \supset f(x) \in \Phi) \wedge (\forall x\, y)(x \in \Phi \wedge y \in \Phi \supset g(x, y) \in \Phi)) \supset P \subset \Phi)$,

but then we will still use the comprehension schema to form the set to be substituted for the set variable Φ.

The axiom schema of induction in arithmetic is the result of applying circumscription to the constant 0 and the successor operation.

There is a way of applying circumscription to an arbitrary sentence of predicate calculus. Let p be such a sentence and let Φ be a predicate symbol. The *relativization* of p with respect to Φ (written p^{Φ}) is defined (as in some logic texts) as the sentence that results from replacing every quantification $(\forall x)E$ that occurs in p by $(\forall x)(\Phi(x) \supset E)$ and every quantification $(\exists x)E$ that occurs in p by $(\exists x)(\Phi(x) \wedge E)$. The circumscription of p is then the sentence

4) $\quad\quad p^{\Phi} \supset (\forall x)(P(x) \supset \Phi(x))$.

This form is correct only if neither constants nor function symbols occur in p. If they do, it is necessary to conjoin $\Phi(c)$ for each constant c and $(\forall x)(\Phi(x) \supset \Phi(f(x)))$ for each single argument function symbol f to the premiss of (4). Corresponding sentences must be conjoined if there are function symbols of two or more arguments. The intuitive meaning of (4) is that the only objects satisfying P that exist are those that the sentence p forces to exist.

Applying the circumscription schema requires inventing a suitable predicate to substitute for the symbol Φ (inventing a suitable set in the set-theoretic formulation). In this it resembles mathematical induction; in order to get the conclusion, we must invent a predicate for which the premiss is true.

There is also a semantic way of looking at applying circumscription. Namely, a sentence that can be proved from a sentence p by circumscription is true in all minimal models of p, where a deduction from p is true in all models of p. Minimality is defined with respect to a containment relation $\leq$. We write that $M1 \leq M2$ if every element of the domain of $M1$ is a member of the domain of $M2$ and on the common members all predicates have the same truth value. It is not always true that a sentence true in all minimal models can be proved by circumscription. Indeed the minimal model of Peano's axioms is the standard model of arithmetic, and Gödel's theorem is the assertion that not all true sentences are theorems. Minimal models don't always exist, and when they exist, they aren't always unique.

(McCarthy 1977a) treats circumscription in more detail.

Concepts as objects

We shall begin by discussing how to express such facts as "*Pat knows the combination of the safe*", although the idea of treating a concept as an object has application beyond the discussion of knowledge.

We shall use the symbol *safe1* for the safe, and *combination(s)* is our notation for the combination of an arbitrary safe s. We aren't much interested in the domain of combinations, and we shall take them to be strings of digits with dashes in the right place, and, since a combination is a string, we will write it in quotes. Thus we can write

5) $\quad\quad combination(safe1) = $ "45–25–17"

as a formalization of the English "*The combination of the safe is 45–25–17*". Let us suppose that the combination of *safe2* is, co-incidentally, also 45–25–17, so we can also write

6) $\quad\quad combination(safe2) = $ "45–25–17".

Now we want to translate "*Pat knows the combination of the safe*". If we were to express it as

7) $\quad\quad *knows(pat, combination(safe1))$,

the inference rule that allows replacing a term by an equal term in first order logic would let us conclude

8) $\quad\quad *knows(pat, combination(safe2))$,

which mightn't be true.

This problem was already recognized in 1879 by Frege, the founder of modern predicate logic, who distinguished between direct and indirect occurrences of expressions and would consider the occurrence of *combination(safe1)* in (7) to be indirect and not subject to replacement of equals by equals. The modern way of stating the problem is to call *Pat knows* a referentially opaque operator.

The way out of this difficulty currently most popular is to treat *Pat knows* as a *modal operator*. This involves changing the logic so that replacement of an expression by an equal expression is not allowed in opaque contexts. Knowledge is not the only operator that admits modal treatment. There is also belief, wanting, and logical or physical necessity. For AI purposes, we would need all the above modal operators and many more in the same system. This would make the semantic discussion of the resulting modal logic extremely complex. For this reason, and because we want functions from material objects to concepts of them, we have followed a different path - introducing concepts as individual objects. This has not been popular in philosophy, although I suppose no-one would doubt that it could be done.

Our approach is to introduce the symbol *Safe*1 as a name for the concept of safe1 and the function *Combination* which takes a concept of a safe into a concept of its combination. The second operand of the function *knows* is now required to be a concept, and we can write

9) $knows(pat, Combination(Safe1))$

to assert that Pat knows the combination of safe1. The previous trouble is avoided so long as we can assert

10) $Combination(Safe1) \neq Combination(Safe2),$

which is quite reasonable, since we do not consider the concept of the combination of *safe*1 to be the same as the concept of the combination of *safe*2, even if the combinations themselves are the same.

We write

11) $denotes(Safe1, safe1)$

and say that *safe*1 is the denotation of *Safe*1. We can say that Pegasus doesn't exist by writing

12) $\neg(\exists x)(denotes(Pegasus, x))$

still admitting *Pegasus* as a perfectly good concept. If we only admit concepts with denotations (or admit partial functions into our system), we can regard denotation as a function from concepts to objects - including other concepts. We can then write

13) $safe1 = den(Safe1).$

The functions *combination* and *Combination* are related in a way that we may call extensional, namely

14) $(\forall S)(combination(den(S)) = den(Combination(S)),$

and we can also write this relation in terms of *Combination* alone as

15) $(\forall S1\ S2)(den(S1) = den(S2) \supset den(Combination(S1)) = den(Combination(S2))),$

or, in terms of the denotation predicate,

16) $(\forall S1\ S2\ s\ c)(denotes(S1,s) \wedge denotes(S2,s) \wedge denotes(Combination(S1), c) \supset denotes(Combination(S2), c)).$

It is precisely this property of extensionality that the above-mentioned *knows* predicate lacks in its second argument; it is extensional in its first argument.

Suppose we now want to say "*Pat knows that Mike knows the combination of safe*1". We cannot use $knows(mike, Combination(Safe1))$ as an operand of another *knows* function for two reasons. First, the value of $knows(person, Concept)$ is a truth value, and there are only two truth values, so we would either have Pat knowing all true statements or none. Second, English treats knowledge of propositions differently from the way it treats knowledge of the

value of a term. To know a proposition is to know that it is true, whereas the analog of knowing a combination would be knowing whether the proposition is true.

We solve the first problem by introducing a new knowledge function $Knows(Personconcept, Concept)$. $Knows(Mike, Combination(Safe1))$ is not a truth value but a *proposition*, and there can be distinct true propositions. We now need a predicate $true(proposition)$, so we can assert

17) $true(Knows(Mike, Combination(Safe1))$

which is equivalent to our old-style assertion

18) $knows(mike, Combination(Safe1)).$

We now write

19) $true(Knows(Pat, Knows(Mike, Combination(Safe1))))$

to assert that Pat knows *whether* Mike knows the combination of safe1. We define

20) $(\forall\ Person, Proposition)(K(Person, Proposition) = true(Proposition)\ and\ Knows(Person, Proposition)),$

which forms the proposition *that* a person knows a proposition from the truth of the proposition and that he knows whether the proposition holds. Note that it is necessary to have new connectives to combine propositions and that an equality sign rather than an equivalence sign is used. As far as our first order logic is concerned, (20) is an assertion of the equality of two terms. These matters are discussed thoroughly in (McCarthy 1977b).

While a concept denotes at most one object, the same object can be denoted by many concepts. Nevertheless, there are often useful functions from objects to concepts that denote them. Numbers may conveniently be regarded has having *standard concepts*, and an object may have a distinguished concept relative to a particular person. (McCarthy 1977b) illustrates the use of functions from objects to concepts in formalizing such chestnuts as Russell's, "*I thought your yacht was longer than it is*".

The most immediate AI problem that requires concepts for its successful formalism may be the relation between knowledge and ability. We would like to connect Mike's ability to open safe1 with his knowledge of the combination. The proper formalization of the notion of *can* that involves knowledge rather than just physical possibility hasn't been done yet. Moore (1977) discusses the relation between knowledge and action from a similar point of view, and the final version of (McCarthy 1977b) will contain some ideas about this.

There are obviously some esthetic disadvantages to a theory that has both *mike* and *Mike*. Moreover, natural language doesn't make such distinctions in its vocabulary, but in rather roundabout ways when necessary. Perhaps we could manage with just *Mike* (the concept), since the *denotation* function will be available for referring to *mike* (the person himself). It makes some sentences longer, and we have to use and equivalence relation which we may call *eqdenot* and say "*Mike eqdenot Brother(Mary)*" rather than write "*mike = brother(mary)*", reserving the equality sign for equal concepts. Since many AI programs don't make much use of replacement of equals by equals, their notation may admit either interpretation, i.e., the formulas may stand for either objects or concepts. The biggest objection is that the semantics of reasoning about objects is more complicated if one refers to them only via concepts.

I believe that circumscription will turn out to be the key to inferring non-knowledge. Unfortunately, an adequate formalism has not yet been developed, so we can only give some ideas of why establishing non-knowledge is important for AI and how circumscription can contribute to it.

If the robot can reason that it cannot open safe1 because it doesn't know the combination, it can decide that its next task is to find the combination. However, if it has merely failed to determine the combination by reasoning, more thinking might solve the problem. If it can safely conclude that the combination cannot be determined by reasoning, it can look for the information externally.

As another example, suppose someone asks you whether the President is standing, sitting or lying down at the moment you read the paper. Normally you will answer that you don't know and will not respond to a suggestion that you think harder. You conclude that no matter how hard you think, the information isn't to be found. If you really want to know, you must look for an external source of information. How do you know you can't solve the problem? The intuitive answer is that any answer is consistent with your other knowledge. However, you certainly don't construct a model of all your beliefs to establish this. Since you undoubtedly have some contradictory beliefs somewhere, you can't construct the required models anyway.

The process has two steps. The first is deciding what knowledge is relevant. This is a conjectural process, so its outcome is not guaranteed to be correct. It might be carried out by some kind of keyword retrieval from property lists, but there should be a less arbitrary method.

The second process uses the set of "relevant" sentences found by the first process and constructs models or circumscription predicates that allow for both outcomes if what is to be shown unknown is a proposition. If what is to be shown unknown has many possible values like a safe combination, then something more sophisticated is necessary. A parameter called the value of the combination is introduced, and a "model" or circumscription predicate is found in which this parameter occurs free. We used quotes, because a one parameter family of models is found rather than a single model.

We conclude with just one example of a circumscription schema dealing with knowledge. It is formalization of the assertion that all Mike knows is a consequence of propositions P and Q.

21) $\Phi(P0) \wedge \Phi(Q0) \wedge (\forall P \; Q)(\Phi(P) \wedge \Phi(P \text{ implies } Q) \supset \Phi(Q))$
$\supset (\forall P)(knows(Mike, P) \supset \Phi(P))$.

Philosophical Notes

Philosophy has a more direct relation to artificial intelligence than it has to other sciences. Both subjects require the formalization of common sense knowledge and repair of its deficiencies. Since a robot with general intelligence requires some general view of the world, deficiencies in the programmers' introspection of their own world-views can result in operational weaknesses in the program. Thus many programs, including Winograd's SHRDLU, regard the history of their world as a sequence of situations each of which is produced by an event occuring in a previous situation of the sequence. To handle concurrent events, such programs must be rebuilt and not just provided with more facts.

This section is organized as a collection of disconnected remarks some of which have a direct technical character, while others concern the general structure of knowledge of the world. Some of them simply give sophisticated justifications for some things that programmers are inclined to do anyway, so some people may regard them as superfluous.

1. Building a view of the world into the structure of a program does not in itself give the program the ability to state the view explicitly. Thus, none of the programs that presuppose history as a sequence of situations can make the assertion "*History is a sequence of situations*". Indeed, for a human to make his presuppositions explicit is often beyond his individual capabilities, and the sciences of psychology and philosophy still have unsolved problems in doing so.

2. Common sense requires scientific formulation. Both AI and philosophy require it, and philosophy might even be regarded as an attempt to make common sense into a science.

3. AI and philosophy both suffer from the following dilemma. Both need precise formalizations, but the fundamental structure of the world has not yet been discovered, so imprecise and even inconsistent formulations need to be used. If the imprecision merely concerned the values to be given to numerical constants, there wouldn't be great difficulty, but there is a need to use theories which are grossly wrong in general within domains where they are valid. The above-mentioned *history-as-a-sequence-of-situations* is such a theory. The sense in which this theory is an approximation to a more sophisticated theory hasn't been examined.

4. (McCarthy 1977c) discusses the need to use concepts that are meaningful only in an approximate theory. Relative to a Cartesian product co-ordinatization of situations, counterfactual sentences of the form "*If co-ordinate x had the value c and the other co-ordinates retained their values, then p would be true*" can be meaningful. Thus, within a suitable theory, the assertion "*The skier wouldn't have fallen if he had put his weight on his downhill ski*" is meaningful and perhaps true, but it is hard to give it meaning as a statement about the world of atoms and wave functions, because it is not clear what different wave functions are specified by "*if he had put his weight on his downhill ski*". We need an AI formalism that can use such statements but can go beyond them to the next level of approximation when possible and necessary. I now think that circumscription is a tool that will allow drawing conclusions from a given approximate theory for use in given circumstances without a total commitment to the theory.

5. One can imagine constructing programs either as empiricists or as realists. An empiricist program would build only theories connecting its sense data with its actions. A realist program would try to find facts about a world that existed independently of the program and would not suppose that the only reality is what might somehow interact with the program.

I favor building realist programs with the following example in mind. It has been shown that the Life two dimensional cellular automaton is universal as a computer and as a constructor. Therefore, there could be configurations of Life cells acting as self-reproducing computers with sensory and motor capabilities with respect to the rest of the Life plane. The program in such a computer could study the physics of its world by making theories and experiments to test them and might eventually come up with the theory that its fundamental physics is that of the Life cellular automaton.

We can test our theories of epistemology and common sense reasoning by asking if they would permit the Life-world computer to conclude, on the basis of experiments, that its physics was that of Life. If our epistemology isn't adequate for such a simple universe, it surely isn't good enough for our much more complicated universe. This example is one of the reasons for preferring to build realist rather than empiricist programs. The empiricist program, if it was smart enough, would only end up with a statement that "*my experiences are best organized as if there were a Life cellular automaton and events isomorphic to my thoughts occurred in a certain subconfiguration of it*". Thus it would get a result equivalent to that of the realist program but more complicated and with less certainty.

More generally, we can imagine a *metaphilosophy* that has the same relation to philosophy that metamathematics has to mathematics. Metaphilosophy would study mathematical systems consisting of an "epistemologist" seeking knowledge in accordance with the epistemology to be tested and interacting with a "world". It would study what information about the world a given philosophy would obtain. This would depend also on the structure of the world and the "epistemologist"'s opportunities to interact.

AI could benefit from building some very simple systems of this kind, and so might philosophy.

References

McCarthy, J. and Hayes, P.J. (1969) Some Philosophical Problems from the Standpoint of Artificial Intelligence. *Machine Intelligence* 4, pp. 463–502 (eds Meltzer, B. and Michie, D.). Edinburgh: Edinburgh University Press.

McCarthy, J. (1977a) Minimal Inference – A New Way of Jumping to Conclusions (to be published).

McCarthy, J. (1977b) First Order Theories of Individual Concepts (to be published).

McCarthy, J. (1977c) Ascribing Mental Qualities to Machines (to be published).

Moore, Robert C. (1977) Reasoning about Knowledge and Action, 1977 *IJCAI Proceedings*.

3 / Brian C. Smith
Prologue to "Reflection and Semantics in a Procedural Language"

This paper is drawn from a curious source: it is the Prologue to a 500-page doctoral thesis by Brian Smith on a dialect of LISP. Even more curious, perhaps, is the approach and tone, having more in common with cognitive science and philosophy of mind than computer science. Nonetheless, what it says about Knowledge Representation is very relevant, and provides an illuminating perspective on the entire field. The main observation is that almost all of our research is based on what Smith calls the *Knowledge Representation Hypothesis* which, in a nutshell, says that a critical component of an intelligent system is a set of data structures that we can interpret as sentences representing what the system knows. The fact that these data structures could be arrays, records, graphs, or even a single bit (under the right interpretation) means that the hypothesis covers a very wide range of representational approaches (Levesque and Brachman in Chapter 4 use this observation as the basis for comparing what would otherwise be syntactically very dissimilar representation schemes). In fact, at first glance, it is hard to imagine the hypothesis being false, and it is certainly assumed in the contributions to this volume, with the exception of [Dreyfus, Chapter 5] (and it is largely irrelevant in [Sloman, Chapter 25] and [Funt, Chapter 26]). Smith sees the historical development of this representational focus as a solution to the problem of providing a system with generality, flexibility, and modularity. Moreover, to achieve similar properties in its reasoning abilities, it appears that a system needs to explicitly represent its own operations and structures. This is the *Reflection Hypothesis*, present as far back as McCarthy's original work [McCarthy, Chapter 15], and an important assumption behind the meta-representation frameworks such as presented in [Weyhrauch, Chapter 16] and [Davis and Buchanan, Chapter 22]. It is this second hypothesis that Smith goes on to explore in his dissertation in the context of the procedural language LISP.

Appeared in Ph.D. dissertation and Tech. Report MIT/LCS/TR-272, M.I.T., Cambridge, MA, 1982.

Prologue

Brian Cantwell Smith

It is a striking fact about human cognition that we can think not only about the world around us, but also about our ideas, our actions, our feelings, our past experience. This ability to *reflect* lies behind much of the subtlety and flexibility with which we deal with the world; it is an essential part of mastering new skills, of reacting to unexpected circumstances, of short-range and long-range planning, of recovering from mistakes, of extrapolating from past experience, and so on and so forth. Reflective thinking characterises mundane practical matters and delicate theoretical distinctions. We have all paused to review past circumstances, such as conversations with guests or strangers, to consider the appropriateness of our behaviour. We can remember times when we stopped and consciously decided to consider a set of options, say when confronted with a fire or other emergency. We understand when someone tells us to believe everything a friend tells us, unless we know otherwise. In the course of philosophical discussion we can agree to distinguish views we believe to be true from those we have no reason to believe are false. In all these cases the subject matter of our contemplation at the moment of reflection includes our remembered experience, our private thoughts, and our reasoning patterns.

The power and universality of reflective thinking has caught the attention of the cognitive science community — indeed, once alerted to this aspect of human behaviour, theorists find evidence of it almost everywhere. Though no one can yet say just what it comes to, crucial ingredients would seem to be the ability to recall memories of a world experienced in the past and of one's own participation in that world, the ability to think about a phenomenal world, hypothetical or actual, that is not currently being experienced (an ability presumably mediated by our knowledge and belief), and a certain kind of true self-reference: the ability to consider both one's actions and the workings of one's own mind. This last aspect — the self-referential aspect of reflective thought — has sparked particular interest for cognitive theorists, both in psychology (under the label *meta-cognition*), and in artificial intelligence (in the design of computational systems possessing inchoate reflective powers, particularly as evidenced in a collection of ideas loosely allied in their use of the term "meta": meta-level rules, meta-descriptions, and so forth).

In artificial intelligence, the focus on computational forms of self-referential reflective reasoning has become particularly central. Although the task of endowing computational systems with subtlety and flexibility has proved difficult, we have had some success in developing systems with a moderate grasp of certain domains: electronics, bacteremia, simple mechanical systems, etc. One of the most recalcitrant problems, however, has been that of developing flexibility and modularity (in some cases even simple effectiveness) in the reasoning processes that use this world knowledge. Though it has been possible to construct programs that perform a specific kind of reasoning task (say, checking an circuit or parsing a subset of natural language syntax), there has been less success in simulating "common sense", or in developing programs able to figure out what to do, and how to do it, in either general or novel situations. If the course of reasoning — if the problem solving strategies and the hypothesis formation behaviour — could *itself* be treated as a valid subject domain in its own right, then (at least so the idea goes) it might be possible to construct systems that manifested the same modularity about their own thought processes that they manifest about their primary subject domains. A simple example might be an electronics "expert" able to choose an appropriate method of tackling a particular circuit, depending on a variety of questions about the relationship between its own capacities and the problem at hand: whether the task was primarily one of design or analysis or repair, what strategies and skills it knew it had in such areas, how confident it was in the relevance of specific approaches based on, say, the complexity of the circuit, or on how similar it looked compared with circuits its already knew. Expert human problem-solvers clearly demonstrate such reflective abilities, and it appears more and more certain that powerful computational problem solvers will have to possess them as well.

No one would expect potent skills to arise automatically in a reflective system; the mere *ability* to reason about the reasoning process will not magically yield systems able to reflect in powerful and flexible ways. On the other hand, the demonstration of such an ability is clearly a pre-requisite to its effective utilisation. Furthermore, many reasons are advanced in support of reflection, as well as the primary one (the hope of building a system able to decide how to structure the pattern of its own reasoning). It has been argued, for example, that it would be easier to construct powerful systems in the first place (it would seem you could almost *tell them* how to think), to interact with them when they fail, to trust them if they could report on how they arrive at their decisions, to give them "advice" about how to improve or discriminate, as well as to provide them with their own strategies for reacting to their history and experience.

There is even, as part of the general excitement, a tentative suggestion on how such a self-referential reflective process might be constructed. This suggestion — nowhere argued but clearly in evidence in several recent proposals — is a particular instance of a general hypothesis, adopted by most A.I. researchers, that we will call the ***knowledge representation hypothesis***. It is widely held in computational circles that any process capable of reasoning intelligently about the world must consist in part of a field of structures, of a roughly linguistic sort, which in some fashion *represent* whatever knowledge and beliefs the process may be said to possess. For example, according to this view, since I know that the sun sets each evening, my "mind" must contain (among other things) a language-like or symbolic structure that represents this fact, inscribed in some kind of internal code. There are various assumptions that go along with this view: there is for one thing presumed to be an internal process that "runs over" or "computes with" these representational structures, in such a way that the intelligent behaviour of the whole results from the interaction of parts. In addition, this ingredient process is required to react only to the "form" or "shape" of these mental representations, without regard to what they mean or represent — this is the substance of the claim that computation involves *formal* symbol manipulation. Thus my thought that, for example, the sun will soon set, would be taken to emerge from an interaction in my mind between an ingredient process and the shape or "spelling" of various internal structures representing my knowledge that the sun does regularly set each evening, that it is currently tea time, and so forth.

The knowledge representation hypothesis may be summarised as follows:

> *Any mechanically embodied intelligent process will be comprised of structural ingredients that a) we as external observers naturally take to represent a propositional account of the knowledge that the overall process exhibits, and b) independent of such external semantical attribution, play a formal but causal and essential role in engendering the behaviour that manifests that knowledge.*

Thus for example if we felt disposed to say that some process knew that dinosaurs were warm-blooded, then we would find (according, presumably, to the best explanation of how that process worked) that a certain computational ingredient in that process was understood as *representing* the (propositional) fact that dinosaurs were warm-blooded, and furthermore that this very ingredient played a role, independent of our understanding of it as representational, in leading the process to behave in whatever way inspired us to say that it knew that fact. Presumably we would convinced by the manner in which the process answered certain questions about their likely habitat, by assumptions it made about other aspects of their existence, by postures it adopted on suggestions as to why they may have become extinct, etc.

A careful analysis will show that, to the extent that we can make sense of it, this view that *knowing is representational* is far less evident — and perhaps, therefore, far more interesting — than is commonly believed. To do it justice requires considerable care: accounts in cognitive psychology and the philosophy of mind tend to founder on simplistic models of computation, and artificial intelligence treatments often lack the theoretical rigour necessary to bring the essence of the idea into plain view. Nonetheless, conclusion or hypothesis, it permeates current theories of mind, and has in particular led researchers in artificial intelligence to propose a spate of computational languages and calculi designed to underwrite such representation. The common goal is of course not so much to speculate on what is actually represented in any particular situation as to uncover the general and categorical form of such representation. Thus no one would suggest how anyone actually represents facts about tea and sunsets: rather, they might posit the general form in which such beliefs would be "written" (along with other beliefs, such as that Lasa is in Tibet, and that π is an irrational number). Constraining all plausible suggestions, however, is the requirement that they must be able to demonstrate how a particular thought could emerge from such representations — this is a crucial meta-theoretic characteristic of artificial intelligence research. It is traditionally considered insufficient merely to propose true theories that do not enable some causally effective mechanical embodiment. The standard against which such theories must ultimately judged, in other words, is whether they will serve to underwrite the construction of demonstrable, behaving artefacts. Under this general rubric knowledge representation efforts differ markedly in scope, in approach, and in detail; they differ on such crucial questions as whether or not the mental structure are modality specific (one for visual memory, another for verbal, for example). In spite of such differences, however, they manifest the shared hope that an attainable first step towards a full theory of mind will be the discovery of something like the structure of the "mechanical mentalese" in which our beliefs are inscribed.

It is natural to ask whether the knowledge representation hypothesis deserves our endorsement, but this is not the place to pursue that difficult question. Before it can fairly be asked, we would have to distinguish a strong version claiming that knowing is *necessarily* representational from a weaker version claiming merely that it is *possible* to build a representational knower. We would run straight into all the much-discussed but virtually intractable questions about what would be required to convince us that an artificially constructed process exhibited intelligent behaviour. We would certainly need a definition of the word "represent", about which we will subsequently have a good deal to say. Given the current (minimal) state of our understanding, I myself see no reason to subscribe to the strong view, and remain skeptical of the weak version as well. But one of the most difficult questions is merely to ascertain what the hypothesis is actually saying — thus my interest in representation is more a concern to make it clear than to defend or deny it. The entire present investigation, therefore, will be pursued under this hypothesis, not because we grant it our allegiance, but merely because it deserves our attention.

Given the represention hypothesis, the suggestion as to how to build self-reflective systems — a suggestion we will call the *reflection hypothesis* — can be summarised as follows:

> *In as much as a computational process can be constructed to reason about an external world in virtue of comprising an ingredient process (interpreter) formally manipulating representations of that world, so too a computational process could be made to reason about itself in virtue of comprising an ingredient process (interpreter) formally manipulating representations of its own operations and structures.*

Thus the task of building a computationally reflective system is thought to reduce to, or at any rate to include, the task of providing a system with formal representations of its own constitution and behaviour. Hence a system able to imagine a world where unicorns have wings would have to construct formal representations of that fact; a system considering the adoption of a hypothesis-and-test style of investigation would have to construct formal structures representing such a inference regime.

Whatever its merit, there is ample evidence that researchers are taken with this view. Systems such as Weyrauch's FOL, Doyle's TMS, McCarthy's ADVICE-TAKER, Hayes' GOLUM, and Davis' TERESIUS are particularly explicit exemplars of just such an approach.[2] In Weyhrauch's system, for example, sentences in first-order logic are constructed that axiomatize the behaviour of the LISP procedures use in the course of the computation (FOL is a prime example of the dual-calculus approach mentioned earlier). In Doyle's systems, explicit representations of the dependencies between beliefs, and of the "reasons" the system accepts a conclusion, play a causal role in the inferential process. Similar remarks hold for the other projects mentioned, as well as for a variety of other current research. In addition, it turns out on scrutiny that a great deal of current computational practice can be seen as dealing, in one way or another, with reflective abilities, particularly as exemplified by computational structures representing other computational structures. We constantly encounter examples: the wide-spread use of macros in LISP, the use of meta-level structures in representation languages, the use of explicit non-monotonic inference rules, the popularity of meta-level rules in planning systems.[3] Such a list can be extended indefinitely; in a recent symposium Brachman reported that the love affair with "*meta-level reasoning*" was the most important theme of knowledge representation research in the last decade.[4]

The Relationship Between Reflection and Representation

The manner in which this discussion has been presented so far would seem to imply that the interest in *reflection* and the adoption of a *representational* stance are theoretically independent positions. I have argued in this way for a reason: to make clear that the two subjects are not the same. There is no *a priori* reason to believe that even a fully representational system should in any way be reflective or able to make anything approximating a reference to itself; similarly, there is no *proof* that a powerfully self-referential system need be constructed of representations. However — and this is the crux of the matter — the reason to raise both issues together is that they are surely, in some sense, related. If nothing else, the word "representation" comes from "re" plus "present", and the ability to *re-present* a world to itself is undeniably a crucial, if not *the* crucial, ingredient in reflective thought. If I reflect on my childhood, I re-present to myself my school and the rooms of my house; if I reflect on what I will do tomorrow, I bring into the view of my mind's eye the self I imagine that tomorrow I will be. If we take "representation" to describe an *activity*, rather than a *structure*, reflection surely involves representation (although — and this should be kept clearly in mind — the "representation" of the knowledge representation hypothesis refers to ingredient structures, not to an activity).

It is helpful to look at the historical association between these ideas, as well to search for commonalities in content. In the early days of artificial intelligence, a search for the general patterns of intelligent reasoning led to the development of such general systems as Newell and Simon's GPS, predicate logic theorem provers, and so forth.[5] The descriptions of the subject domains were minimal but were nonetheless primarily declarative, particularly in the case of the systems based on logic. However it proved difficult to make such general systems effective in particular cases: so much of the "expertise" involved in problem solving seems domain and task specific. In reaction against such generality, therefore, a *procedural* approach emerged in which the primary focus was on the manipulation and reasoning about specific problems in simple worlds.[6] Though the procedural approach in many ways solved the problem of undirected inferential meandering, it too had problems: it proved difficult to endow systems with much generality or modularity when they were simply constituted of procedures designed to manifest certain particular skills. In reaction to such brittle and parochial behaviour, researchers turned instead to the development of processes designed to work over general representations of the objects and categories of the world in which the process was designed to be embedded. Thus the *representation hypothesis* emerged in the attempt to endow systems with generality, modularity, flexibility, and so forth with respect to the embedding world, but to retain a procedural effectiveness in the control component.[7] In other words, in terms of our main discussion, representation as a method emerged as a solution to the problem of providing general and flexible ways of reflecting (not self-referentially) about the world.

Systems based on the representational approach — and it is fair to say that most of the current "expert systems" are in this tradition — have been relatively successful in certain respects, but a major lingering problem has been a narrowness and inflexibility regarding the style of reasoning these systems employ in using these representational structures. This inflexibility in *reasoning* is strikingly parallel to the inflexibility in *knowledge* that led to the first round of representational systems; researchers have therefore suggested that we need reflective systems able to deal with their own constitutions as well as with the worlds they inhabit. In other words, since the *style* of the problem is so parallel to that just sketched, it has seemed that another application of the same medicine might be appropriate. If we could inscribe general knowledge about how to reason in a variety of circumstances in the "mentalese" of these systems, it might be possible to design a relatively simpler inferential regime over this "meta-knowledge about reasoning", thereby engendering a flexibility and modularity regarding reasoning, just as the first representational work engendered a flexibility and modularity about the process's embedding world.

There are problems, however, in too quick an association between the two ideas, not the least of which is the question of to *whom* these various forms of re-presentation are being directed. In the normal case — that is to say, in the typical computational process built under the aegis of the knowledge representation hypothesis — a process is constituted from symbols that we as external theorists take to be representational structures; they are visible *only to the ingredient interpretive process of the whole*, and they are visible to that constituent process *only formally* (this is the basic claim of computation). Thus the interpreter can see them, though it is blind to the fact of their being representations. (In fact it is almost a great joke that the blindly formal ingredient process should be called an *interpreter*: when the LISP interpreter evalutes the expression (+ 2 3) and returns the result 5, the last thing it knows is that the numeral 2 denotes the number two.)

Whatever is the case with the ingredient process, there is no reason to suppose that the representational structures are visible to the whole constituted process *at all*, formally or informally. That process is made out of them; there is no more *a priori* reason to suppose that they are accessible to its inspection than to suppose that a camera could take a picture of its own shutter — no more reason to suppose it is even a coherent possibility than to say that France is near Marseilles. Current practice should overwhelmingly convince us of this point: what is as tacit — what is as thoroughly lacking in self-knowledge — as the typical modern computer system?

The point of the argument here is not to prove that one *cannot* make such structures accessible — that one *cannot* make a representational reflective system — but to make clear that two ideas are involved. Furthermore, they are different in kind: one (representation) is a possibly powerful *method* for the construction of systems; the other (reflection) is a kind of behaviour we are asking our systems to exhibit. It remains a question whether the representational method will prove useful in the pursuit of the goal of reflective behaviour. That, in a nutshell, is our overall project.

The Theoretical Backdrop

It takes only a moment's consideration of such questions as the relationship between representation and reflection to recognise that the current state of our understanding of such subjects is terribly inadequate. In spite of the general excitement about reflection, self-reference, and computational representation, no one has presented an underlying theory of any of these issues. The reason is simple: we are so lacking in adequate theories of the surrounding territory that, without considerable preliminary work, cogent definitions cannot even be attempted. Consider for example the case regarding self-referential reflection, where just a few examples will make this clear. First, from the fact that a reflective system A is implemented in system B, it does not follow that system B is thereby rendered reflective (for example, in this dissertation I will present a partially-reflective dialect of LISP that I have implemented on a PDP-10, but the PDP-10 is not itself reflective). Hence even a *definition* of reflection will have to be backed by theoretical apparatus capable of distinguishing between one abstract machine and another in which the first is implemented — something we are not yet able to do. Second, the notion seems to require of a computational process, and (if we subscribe to the representational hypothesis) of its interpreter, that in reflecting it "back off" one level of reference, and we lack theories both of interpreters in general, and of computational reference in particular. Theories of computational interpretation will be required to clarify the confusion mentioned above regarding the relationship between reflection and representation: for a system to reflect it must re-present *for itself* its mental states; it is not sufficient for it to comprise a set of formal representations inspected *by its interpreter*. This is a distinction we encounter again and again; a failure to make it is the most common error in discussions of the plausibility of artificial intelligence from those outside the computational community, derailing the arguments of such thinkers as Searle and Fodor.[8] Theories of reference will be required in order to make sense of the question of what a computational process is "thinking" about at all, whether reflective or not (for example, it may be easy to claim that when a program is manipulating data structures representing women's vote that the process as a whole is "thinking about suffrage", but what is the process thinking about when the interpreter is expanding a macro definition?). Finally, if the search for reflection is taken up too enthusiastically, one is in danger of interpreting everything as evidence of reflective thinking, since what may not be reflective *explicitly* can usually be treated as *implicitly* reflective (especially given a little imagination on the part of the theorist). However we lack general guidelines on how to distinguish explicit from implicit aspects of computational structures.

Nor is our grasp of the representational question any clearer; a serious difficulty, especially since the representational endeavour has received much more attention than has reflection. Evidence of this lack can be seen in the fact that, in spite of an approximate consensus regarding the general form of the task, and substantial effort on its behalf, no representation scheme yet proposed has won substantial acceptance in the field. Again, this is due at least in part to the simple absence of adequate theoretical foundations in terms of which to formulate either enterprise or solution. We do not have theories of either representation or computation in terms of which to define the terms of art currently employed in their pursuit (*representation*, *implementation*, *interpretation*, *control structure*, *data structure*, *inheritance*, and so forth), and are consequently without any well-specified account of what it would be to succeed, let alone of what to investigate, or of how to proceed. Numerous related theories have been developed (model theories for logic, theories of semantics for programming languages, and so forth), but they don't address the issues of knowledge representation directly, and it is surprisingly difficult to weave their various insights into a single coherent whole.

The representational consensus alluded to above, in other words, is widespread but vague; disagreements emerge on every conceivable technical point, as was demonstrated in a recent survey of the field.[9] To begin with, the central notion of "representation" remains notoriously unspecified: in spite of the intuitions mentioned above, there is remarkably little agreement on whether a representation must "re-present" in any constrained way (like an image or copy), or whether the word is synonymous with such general terms as "sign" or "symbol". A further confusion is shown by an inconsistency in usage as to what representation is a relationship between. The sub-discipline is known as the *representation of knowledge*, but in the survey just mentioned by far the majority of the respondents (to the surprise of this author) claimed to use the word, albeit in a wide variety of ways, as between formal symbols *and the world about which the process is designed to reason*. Thus a KLONE structure might be said to *represent Don Quixote tilting at a windmill*; it would not taken as representing *the fact or proposition of this activity*. In other words the majority opinion is not that we are *representing knowledge* at all, but rather, as we put it above, that *knowing is representational*.[10]

In addition, we have only a dim understanding of the relationship that holds between the purported representational structures and the ingredient process that interprets them. This relates to the crucial distinction between that interpreting process and the whole process of which it is an ingredient (whereas it is *I* who thinks of sunsets, it is at best a *constituent of my mind* that inspects a mental representation). Furthermore, there are terminological confusions: the word "semantics" is applied to a variety of concerns, ranging from how natural language is translated into the representational structures, to what those structures represent, to how they impinge on the rational policies of the "mind" of which they are a part, to what functions are computed by the interpreting process, etc. The term "interpretation" (to take another example) has two relatively well-specified but quite independent meanings, one of computational origin, the other more philosophical; how the two relate remains so far unexplicated, although, as was just mentioned, they are strikingly distinct.

Unfortunately, such general terminological problems are just the tip of an iceberg. When we consider our specific representational proposals, we are faced with a plethora of apparently incomparable technical words and phrases. *Node, frame, unit, concept, schema, script, pattern, class,* and *plan*, for example, are all popular terms with similar connotations and ill-defined meaning.[11] The theoretical situation (this may not be so harmful in terms of more practical goals) is further hindered by the tendency for representational research to be reported in a rather demonstrative fashion: researchers typically exhibit particular formal systems that (often quite impressively) embody their insights, but that are defined using formal terms peculiar to the system at hand. We are left on our own to induce the relevant generalities and to locate them in our evolving conception of the representation enterprise as a whole. Furthermore, such practice makes comparison and discussion of technical details always problematic and often impossible, defeating attempts to build on previous work.

This lack of grounding and focus has not passed unnoticed: in various quarters one hears the suggestion that, unless severely constrained, the entire representation enterprise may be ill-conceived — that we should turn instead to considerations of particular epistemological issues (such as how we reason about, say, liquids or actions), and should use as our technical base the traditional formal systems (logic, LISP, and so forth) that representation schemes were originally designed to replace.[12] In defense of this view two kinds of argument are often advanced. The first is that questions about the *central* cognitive faculty are at the very least premature, and more seriously may for principled reasons never succomb to the kind of rigourous scientific analysis that characterizes recent studies of the *peripheral* aspects of mind: vision, audition, grammar, manipulation, and so forth.[13] The other argument is that logic as developed by the logicians is in itself sufficient; that all we need is a set of ideas about what axioms and inference protocols are best to adopt.[14] But such doubts cannot be said to have deterred the whole of the community: the survey just mentioned lists more than thirty new representation systems under active development.

The strength of this persistence is worth noting, especially in connection with the theoretical difficulties just sketched. There can be no doubt that there are scores of difficult problems: we have just barely touched on some of the most striking. But it would be a mistake to conclude in discouragement that the *enterprise* is doomed, or to retreat to the meta-theoretic stability of adjacent fields (like proof theory, model theory, programming language semantics, and so forth). The moral is at once more difficult and yet more hopeful. What is demanded is that we stay true to these undeniably powerful ideas, and attempt to develop adequate theoretical structures on this home ground. It is true that any satisfactory theory of computational reflection must ultimately rest, more or less explicitly, on theories of computation, of intensionality, of objectification, of semantics and reference, of implicitness, of formality, of computation interpretation, of representation, and so forth. On the other hand as a community we have a great deal of practice that often embodies intuitions that we are unable to formulate coherently. The wealth of programs and systems we have built often betray — sometimes in surprising ways — patterns and insights that eluded our conscious thoughts in the course of their development. What is mandated is a *rational reconstruction* of those intuitions and of that practice.

In the case of designing reflective systems, such a reconstruction is curiously urgent. In fact this long introductory story ends with an odd twist — one that "ups the ante" in the search for a carefully formulated theory, and suggests that practical progress will be impeded until we take up the theoretical task. In general, it is of course possible (some would even advocate this approach) to build an instance of a class of artefact before formulating a theory of it. The era of sail boats, it has often been pointed out, was already drawing to a close just as the theory of airfoils and lift was being formulated — the theory that, at least at the present time, best explains how those sailboats worked. However there are a number of reasons why such an approach may be ruled out in the present case. For one thing, in constructing a reflective calculus one must support arbitrary levels of meta-knowledge and self-modelling, and it is self-evident that confusion and complexity will multiply unchecked when one adds such facilities to an only partially understood formalism. It is simply likely to be unmanageably complicated to attempt to build a self-referential system unaided by the clarifying structure of a prior theory. The complexities surrounding the use of APPLY in LISP (and the caution with which it has consequently come to be treated) bear witness to this fact. However there is a more serious problem. If one subscribes to the knowledge representation hypothesis, it becomes an integral part of developing self-descriptive systems to provide, encoded within the representational medium, an account of (roughly) the syntax, semantics, and reasoning behaviour of that formalism. In other words, if we are to build a process that "knows" about itself, and *if we subscribe to the view that knowing is representational*, then we are committed to providing that system with a *representation* of the self-knowledge that we aim to endow it with. That is, we must have an adequate theories of computational representation and reflection *explicitly formulated*, since *an encoding of that theory is mandated to play a causal role as an actual ingredient in the reflective device*.

Knowledge of any sort — and self-knowledge is no exception — is always theory relative. The representation hypothesis implies that our theories of reasoning and reflection must be explicit. We have argued that this is a substantial, if widely accepted, hypothesis. One reason to find it plausible comes from viewing the entire enterprise as an attempt to communicate our thought patterns and cognitive styles — including our reflective abilities — to these emergent machines. It may at some point be possible for understanding to be tacitly communicated between humans and system they have constructed. In the meantime, however, while we humans might make do with a rich but unarticulated understanding of computation, representation, and reflection, we must not forget that computers do not share with us our tacit understanding of what they are.

Notes

1. Bobrow and Winograd (1977), and Bobrow and Winograd, et al. (1977).
2. Weyhrauch (1978), Doyle (1979), McCarthy (1968), Hayes (1979), and Davis (1980), respectively.
3. Metalevel rules in representation were discussed in Brachman and Smith (1980); for a collection of papers on non-monotonic reasoning Bobow (1980); macros are discussed in Pitman (1980).
4. Brachman (1980).
5. Newell and Simon (1963); Newell and Simon (1956).
6. The proceduralist view was represented particularly by a spate of dissertations emerging from MIT at the beginning of the 1970s; see for example Winograd (1972), Hewitt (1972), Sussman et al. (1971), etc.
7. See Minsky (1975), Winograd (1975), and all of the systems reported in Brachman and Smith (1980).
8. Searle (1980), Fodor (1978 and 1980).
9. Brachman and Smith (1980).
10. See the introduction to Brachman and Smith (1980).

11. References on *node, frame, unit, concept, schema, script, patter, class,* and *plans* can be found in the various references provided in Brachman and Smith (1980).
12. See in particular Hayes (1978).
13. The distinction between central and peripheral aspects of mind is articulated in Nilsson (1981); on the impossibility of central AI (Nilsson himself feels that the central faculty will quite definitely succumb to AI's techniques) see Dreyfus (1972) and Fodor (1980 and 1983).
14. Nilsson (1981).

References

For references noted above but not included in this list, see the bibliography at the end of this volume.

Bobrow D. G., (ed.) *Artificial Intelligence,* **13**:1,2 (Special Issue on Non-Monotonic Reasoning), (1980).

Brachman, R., "Recent Advances in Representation Languages," invited presentation at the First Annual National Conference on Artificial Intelligence, Stanford, California, (August 1980), sponsored by the American Association for Artificial Intelligence.

Davis, R., "Applications of Meta Level Knowledge to the Construction, Maintenance, and Use of Large Knowledge Bases," Ph.D. thesis, Stanford University, Stanford, California; also in Davis, R., and Lenat, D., (eds.), *Knowledge-Based Systems in Artificial Intelligence,* New York: McGraw-Hill (1980).

Doyle, J., "A Truth-Maintenance System," *Artificial Intelligence* 12:231–272 (1979).

Dreyfus, H., *What Computers Can't Do,* New York: Harper and Row (1972).

Fodor, J., "Tom Swift and his Procedural Grandmother," *Cognition* 6 (1978); reprinted in Fodor, Jerry, *Representations,* Cambridge: Bradford, 1981.

——, "Methodological Solipsism Considered as a Research Strategy in Cognitive Psychology," *The Behavioral and Brain Science,* **3**:1 (1980) pp. 63–73; reprinted in Haugeland (ed.), *Mind Design,* Cambridge: Bradford, 1981, and in Fodor, J., *Representations,* Cambridge: Bradford 1981.

——, *The Modularity of Mind,* Cambridge: M.I.T. Press (1983).

Hayes, P. J., "The Naive Physics Manifesto," unpublished manuscript (May 1978).

——, Personal conversations on the GOLUM deduction system (1979).

Hewitt, C., "Description and Theoretical Analysis (using Schemata) of PLANNER: A Language for Proving Theorems and Manipulating Models in a Robot," M.I.T. Artificial Intelligence Laboratory TR-258 (1972).

Minsky, M., "A Framework for the Representation of Knowledge," in P. Winston (ed.), *The Psychology of Computer Vision,* New York: McGraw-Hill (1975) pp. 211–277.

Newell, A., and Simon, H., "The Logic Theory Machine: A Complex Information Processing System," *IRE Transactions on Information Theory,* Vol. IT-2 No. 3, (1956) pp. 61–79.

——, "GPS, a Program that Simulates Human Thought," in E.A. Feigenbaum and J. Feldman (eds.), *Computers and Thought,* New York: McGraw-Hill (1963).

Nilsson, N. "Artificial Intelligence: Engineering, Science, or Slogan?" *AI Magazine,* **3**:1 (Winter 1981–1982), pp. 2–8.

Pitman, K., "Special Forms in LISP," *Conference Record of the 1980 LISP Conference,* Stanford University (August 1980), pp. 179–187.

Searle, J. R., "Minds, Brains, and Programs," *The Behavioral and Brain Sciences* **3**:3 (1980) pp. 417–457; reprinted in Haugeland (ed.), *Mind Design,* Cambridge: Bradford, 1981, pp. 282–306.

Sussman, G., et al., "Micro-PLANNER Reference Manual," M.I.T. Artificial Intelligence Laboratory Memo AIM-203a (1971).

Weyhrauch, R. W., "Prolegomena to a Theory of Mechanized Formal Reasoning," Stanford University Artificial Intelligence Laboratory, Memo AIM-315 (1978).

4 / Hector J. Levesque and Ronald J. Brachman
A Fundamental Tradeoff in Knowledge Representation and Reasoning (Revised Version)

If we assume Brian Smith's Knowledge Representation Hypothesis [Smith, Chapter 3], we can interpret the data structures in a Knowledge Representation system as if they were declarative sentences. In this paper, Levesque and Brachman argue that the proper role of such a system is to perform a class of inferences determined by the truth conditions of these sentences. Among other things, the system should be able to determine when the truth of one sentence is implicit in another. However, depending on the range of sentences that have to be dealt with, this task can be relatively trivial or completely unsolvable. Thus, as the title suggests, there is a tradeoff between the expressiveness and the tractability of a Knowledge Representation scheme. The paper illustrates this point by looking at a variety of formalisms (simple databases, logic programs, semantic networks, and frame systems) in terms of the range of first-order logic sentences they can express and the kind of reasoning that they require. One observation is that expressiveness often amounts to the ability to leave certain things unsaid, with full first-order logic at one extreme and databases (and "analogues") at the other. The main conclusion of the survey, however, is that neither expressiveness nor tractability by itself determine the value of a representation language (Allen's time representation [Chapter 30] is given as an example of a formalism that has quite consciously and very effectively traded expressive power for computational advantage). There is no single *best* language, it is argued, only more or less interesting positions on the tradeoff. The paper encourages the design of Knowledge Representation languages with this dimension in mind, contrary perhaps to the views in [Hayes, Chapter 28] and [Moore, Chapter 18] regarding the suitability of full first-order logic as *the* representation framework. It also presents some surprising results about the complexity of computing a kind of inference in simple frame representations.

Original version appeared as "A Fundamental Tradeoff in Knowledge Representation and Reasoning" (by Hector J. Levesque), *Proc. CSCSI-84*, London, Ontario, 1984, 141–152.

41

A Fundamental Tradeoff in
Knowledge Representation and Reasoning
(Revised Version[1])

Hector J. Levesque

Ronald J. Brachman

May, 1985

Abstract

A fundamental computational limit on automated reasoning and its effect on Knowledge Representation is examined. Basically, the problem is that it can be more difficult to reason correctly with one representational language than with another and, moreover, that this difficulty increases dramatically as the expressive power of the language increases. This leads to a tradeoff between the expressiveness of a representational language and its computational tractability. Here we show that this tradeoff can be seen to underlie the differences among a number of existing representational formalisms, in addition to motivating many of the current research issues in Knowledge Representation.

1 Introduction

This paper examines from a general point of view a basic computational limit on automated reasoning, and the effect that it has on Knowledge Representation (KR). The problem is essentially that it can be more difficult to reason correctly with one representational language than with another and, moreover, that this difficulty increases as the expressive power of the language increases. There is a tradeoff between the expressiveness of a representational language and its computational tractability. What we attempt to

---

[1]This is a revised version of "A Fundamental Tradeoff in Knowledge Representation and Reasoning," by Hector J. Levesque, which appeared in the *Proceedings of the CSCSI/SCEIO Conference 1984*, London Ontario, May, 1984. It includes substantial portions of two other conference papers: "The Tractability of Subsumption in Frame-Based Description Languages," by Ronald J. Brachman and Hector J. Levesque, which appeared in *Proceedings of AAAI-84*, Austin, Texas, August, 1984; and "What Makes a Knowledge Base Knowledgeable? A View of Databases from the Knowledge Level," by the same authors, which appeared in *Proceedings of the First International Workshop on Expert Database Systems*, Kiawah Island, South Carolina, October, 1984.

show is that this tradeoff underlies the differences among a number of representational formalisms (such as first-order logic, databases, semantic networks, frames) and motivates many current research issues in KR (such as the role of analogues, syntactic encodings, and defaults, as well as the systems of limited inference and hybrid reasoning).

To deal with a such a broad range of representational phenomena, we must, of necessity, take a considerably simplified and incomplete view of KR. In particular, we focus on its computational and logical aspects, more or less ignoring its history and relevance in the areas of psychology, linguistics, and philosophy. The area of KR is still very disconnected today and the role of logic remains quite controversial, despite what this paper may suggest. We do believe, however, that the tradeoff discussed here is fundamental. As long as we are dealing with computational systems that reason automatically (without any special intervention or advice) and correctly (once we define what *that* means), we will be able to locate where they stand on the tradeoff: they will either be limited in what knowledge they can represent or unlimited in the reasoning effort they might require.

Our computational focus will not lead us to investigate specific algorithms and data structures for KR and reasoning, however. What we discuss is something much stronger, namely whether or not algorithms of a certain kind can exist at all. So the analysis here is at the *Knowledge Level* [21] where we look at the content of what is represented (in terms of what it says about the world) and not the symbolic structures used to represent that knowledge. Indeed, we examine specific representation schemes in terms of what knowledge they can represent, rather than in terms of how they might actually represent it.

In the first section below, we discuss what a KR system is for and what it could mean to reason correctly. Next, we investigate how a KR service might be realized using theorem proving in first-order logic and the problem this raises. Following this, we present various representational formalisms and examine the special kinds of reasoning they suggest. We concentrate in particular on frame-based description languages, examining in some detail a simple language and a variant. In the case of this pair of languages, the kind of tradeoff we are talking about is made concrete, with a dramatic result. Finally, we draw some tentative general conclusions from this analysis.

2   The Role of Knowledge Representation

While it is generally agreed that KR plays an important role in (what have come to be called) knowledge-based systems, the exact nature of that role is often hard to define. In some cases, the KR subsystem does no more than manage a collection of data structures, providing, for example, suitable search facilities; in others, the KR subsystem is not really distinguished from the rest of the system at all and does just about everything: make decisions, prove theorems, solve problems, and so on. In this section, we discuss in very general terms the role of a KR subsystem within a knowledge-based system.

2.1   The Knowledge Representation Hypothesis

A good place to begin a discussion of KR as a whole is with what Brian Smith has called in [28] the *Knowledge Representation Hypothesis*:

> *Any mechanically embodied intelligent process will be comprised of structural ingredients that (a) we as external observers naturally take to represent a propositional account of the knowledge that the overall process exhibits, and (b) independent of such external semantical attribution, play a formal but causal and essential role in engendering the behaviour that manifests that knowledge.*

This hypothesis seems to underly much of the research in KR. In fact, we might think of *knowledge-based systems* as those that satisfy the hypothesis by design. Also, in some sense, it is only with respect to this hypothesis that KR research can be distinguished from any number of other areas involving symbolic structures such as database management, programming languages and data structures.

Granting this hypothesis, there are two major properties that the structures in a knowledge-based system have to satisfy. First of all, it must be possible to interpret them as *propositions* representing the overall knowledge of the system. Otherwise, the representation would not necessarily be of *knowledge* at all, but of something quite different, like numbers or circuits. Implicit in this constraint is that the structures have to be expressions in a language that has a *truth theory*. We should be able to point to one of them and say what the world would have to be like for it to be true. The structures themselves need not *look* like sentences—there are no syntactic requirements on them at all, other than perhaps finiteness—but we have to be able to understand them that way.

A second requirement of the hypothesis is perhaps more obvious. The symbolic structures within a knowledge-based system must play a *causal role* in the behaviour of that system, as opposed to, say, comments in a programming language. Moreover, the influence they have on the behaviour of the system should agree with our understanding of them as propositions representing knowledge. Not that the system has to be aware in any mysterious way of the interpretation of its structures and their connection to the world;[2] but for us to call it knowledge-based, *we* have to be able to understand its behaviour as if it believed these propositions, just as we understand the behaviour of a numerical program as if it appreciated the connection between bit patterns and abstract numerical quantities.

2.2 Knowledge Bases

To make the above discussion a bit less abstract, we can consider a very simple task and consider what a system facing this task would have to be like for us to call it knowledge-based. The amount of knowledge the system will be dealing with will, of course, be very small.

Suppose we want a system in PROLOG that is able to print the colours of various items. One way to implement that system would be as follows:

```
printColour(snow) :- !, write("It's white.").
printColour(grass) :- !, write("It's green.").
printColour(sky) :- !, write("It's yellow.").
printColour(X) :- write("Beats me.").
```

A slightly different organization that leads to the same overall behaviour is

```
printColour(X) :-
    colour(X,Y), !, write("It's "), write(Y), write(".").
printColour(X) :- write("Beats me.").

colour(snow,white).
colour(grass,green).
colour(sky,yellow).
```

The second program is characterized by explicit structures representing the (minimal) knowledge[3] the system has about colours and is the kind of system that we are calling knowledge-based. In the first program, the association between the object (we understand as) referring to grass and the one referring to its colour is implicit in the structure of the

---

[2]Indeed, part of what philosophers have called the *formality condition* is that computation at some level has to be uninterpreted symbol manipulation.

[3]Notice that typical of how the term "knowledge" is used in AI, there is no requirement of *truth*. A system may be mistaken about the colour of the sky but still be knowledge-based. "Belief" would perhaps be a more appropriate term, although we follow the standard AI usage in this paper.

program. In the second, we have an explicit *knowledge base* (or KB) that we can understand as propositions relating the items to their colours. Moreover, this interpretation is justified in that these structures determine what the system does when asked to print the colour of a particular item.

One thing to notice about the example is that it is not the use of a certain programming language or data-structuring facility that makes a system knowledge-based. The fact that PROLOG happens to be understandable as a subset of first-order logic is largely irrelevant. We could probably read the first program "declaratively" and get sentences representing some kind of knowledge out of it; but these would be very strange ones dealing with writing strings and printing colours, not with the colours of objects.

2.3   The Knowledge Representation Subsystem

In terms of its overall goals, a knowledge-based system is not directly interested in what specific structures might exist in its KB. Rather, it is concerned about what the application domain is like, for example, what the colour of grass is. How that knowledge is represented and made available to the overall system is a secondary concern and one that we take to be the reponsibility of the KR subsystem. The role of a KR subsystem, then, is to manage a KB for a knowledge-based system and present a picture of the world based on what it has represented in the KB.

If, for simplicity, we restrict our attention to the yes-no questions about the world that a system might be interested in, what is involved here is being able to determine what the KB says regarding the truth of certain sentences. It is not whether the sentence itself is present in the KB that counts, but whether its truth is *implicit* in the KB. Stated differently, what a KR system has to be able to determine, given a sentence α, is the answer to the following question:

Assuming the world is such that what is believed is true, is α also true?

We will let the notation KB $\models \alpha$ mean that α is implied (in this sense) by what is in the KB.

One thing to notice about this view of a KR system is that the service it provides to a knowledge-based system depends only on the truth theory of the language of representation. Depending on the particular truth theory, determining if KB $\models \alpha$ might require not just simple retrieval capabilities, but also *inference* of some sort. This is not to say that the *only* service to be performed by a KR subsystem is question-answering. If we imagine the overall system existing over a period of time, then we will also want it to be able to augment the KB as it acquires new information about the world.[4] In other words, the responsibility of the KR system is to select appropriate *symbolic structures* to represent knowledge, and to select appropriate *reasoning mechanisms* both to answer questions and to assimilate new information, in accordance with the truth theory of the underlying representation language.

So our view of KR makes it depend only on the semantics of the representation language, unlike other possible accounts that might have it defined in terms of a set of formal symbol manipulation routines (e.g., a proof theory). This is in keeping with what we have called elsewhere a *functional* view of KR (see [15] and [5]), where the service performed by a KR system is defined separately from the techniques a system might use to realize that service.

3   The Logical Approach

To make a lot of the above more concrete, it is useful to look at an example of the kinds of knowledge that might be available in a given domain and how it might be represented in a KB. The language that will be used to represent knowledge is that of a standard first-order logic (FOL).

3.1   Using First-Order Logic

The first and most prevalent type of knowledge to consider representing is what might be called simple *facts* about the world, such as

- Joe is married to Sue.

- Bill has a brother with no children.

- Henry's friends are Bill's cousins.

These might be complicated in any number of ways, for example, by including time parameters and certainty factors.

Simple observations such as these do not exhaust what might be known about the domain, however. We may also have knowledge about the *terminology* used in these observations, such as

---

[4]It is this management of a KB over time that makes a KR subsystem much more than just the implementation of a static deductive calculus.

- *Ancestor* is the transitive closure of *parent*.

- *Brother* is *sibling* restricted to males.

- *Favourite-cousin* is a special type of *cousin*.

These could be called definitions except for the fact that necessary and sufficient conditions might not always be available (as in the last example above). In this sense, they are much more like standard dictionary entries.

The above two example sets concentrate on what might be called *declarative* knowledge about the world. We might also have to deal with *procedural* knowledge that focuses not on the individuals and their interrelationships, but on *advice* for reasoning about these. For example, we might know that

- To find the father of someone, it is better to search for a parent and then check if he is male, than to check each male to see if he is a parent.

- To see if x is an ancestor of y, it is better to search up from y than down from x.

One way to think of this last type of knowledge is not necessarily as advice to a reasoner, but as declarative knowledge that deals implicitly with the combinatorics of the domain as a whole.

This is how the above knowledge might be represented in FOL:

1. The first thing to do is to "translate" the simple facts into sentences of FOL. This would lead to sentences like

   $$\forall x\, \text{Friend}(\text{henry}, x) \equiv \text{Cousin}(\text{bill}, x).$$

2. To deal with terminology in FOL, the easiest way is to "extensionalize" it, that is, to pretend that it is a simple observation about the domain. For example, the *brother* statement above would become[5]

   $$\forall x \forall y\, \text{Brother}(x, y) \equiv (\text{Sibling}(x, y) \land \text{Male}(y)).$$

3. Typically, the procedural advice would not be represented explicitly at all in an FOL KB, but would show up in the *form* of (1) and (2) above. Another alternative would be to use extra-logical annotations like the kind used in PROLOG or those described in [19].

---

[5]This is a little misleading since it will make the *brother* sentence appear to be no different in kind from the one about Henry's friends, though we surely do not want to say that Henry's friends are *defined* to be Bill's cousins.

The end result of this process would be a first-order KB: a collection of sentences in FOL representing what was known about the domain. A major advantage of FOL is that given a yes-no question also expressed in this language, we can give a very precise definition of $KB \models \alpha$ (and thus, under what conditions the question should be answered *yes*, *no*, or *unknown*):

> $KB \models \alpha$ iff every interpretation satisfying all of the sentences in the KB also satisfies α.[6]

There is, moreover, another property of FOL which helps solidify the role of KR. If we assume that the KB is a finite set of sentences and let *KB* stand for their conjunction, it can be shown that

> $KB \models \alpha$ iff $\vdash (KB \supset \alpha)$.

In other words, the question as to whether or not the truth of α is implicit in the KB reduces to whether or not a certain sentence is a *theorem* of FOL. Thus, the question-answering operation becomes one of *theorem proving* in FOL.

3.2   The Problem

The good news in reducing the KR service to theorem proving is that we now have a very clear, very specific notion of what the KR system should do; the bad news is that it is also clear that *this service cannot be provided*. The sad fact of the matter is that deciding whether or not a sentence of FOL is a theorem (i.e., the decision problem) is unsolvable. Moreover, even if we restrict the language practically to the point of triviality by eliminating the quantifiers, the decision problem, though now solvable, does not appear to be solvable in anywhere near reasonable time.[7] It is important to realize that this is not a property of particular algorithms that people have looked at but of the *problem* itself: there *cannot* be an algorithm that does the theorem proving correctly in a reasonable amount of time. This bodes poorly, to say the least, for a service that is supposed to be only a part of a larger knowledge-based system.

One aspect of these intractability results that should be mentioned, however, is that they deal with the *worst case* behaviour of algorithms. In practice, a given theorem proving

---

[6]The assumption here is that the semantics of FOL specify in the usual way what an interpretation is and under what conditions it will satisfy a sentence.

[7]Technically, the problem is now co-NP-complete, meaning that it is strongly believed to be computationally intractable.

algorithm may work quite well. In other words, it might be the case that for a wide range of questions, the program behaves properly, even though it can be shown that there will always be short questions whose answers will not be returned for a very long time, if at all.

How serious is the problem, then? To a large extent this depends on the kind of question you would like to ask of a KR subsystem. The worst case prospect might be perfectly tolerable if you are interested in a mathematical application and the kind of question you ask is an open problem in mathematics. Provided progress is being made, you might be quite willing to stop and redirect the theorem prover after a few months if it seems to be thrashing. Never mind worst case behaviour; this might be the *only* case you are interested in.

But imagine, on the other hand, a robot that needs to know about its external world (such as whether or not it is raining outside or where its umbrella is) before it can act. If this robot has to call a KR system utility as a subroutine, the worst case prospect is much more serious. Bogging down on a logically difficult but low-level subgoal and being unable to continue without human intervention is clearly an unreasonable form of behaviour for something aspiring to intelligence.

Not that "on the average" the robot might not do alright. The trouble is that nobody seems to be able to characterize what an "average" case might be like.[8] As responsible computer scientists, we should not be providing a general inferential service if all that we can say about it is that by and large it will probably work satisfactorily. If the KR service is going to be used as a utility and is not available for introspection or control, then it had better be *dependable* both in terms of its correctness and the resources it consumes. Unfortunately, this seems to rule out a service based on theorem proving (in full first-order logic).

3.3 Two Pseudo-solutions

There are at least two fairly obvious ways to minimize the intractability problem. The first is to push the computational barrier as far back as possible. Research in Automatic Theorem Proving has concentrated on techniques for avoiding redundancies and speeding up certain operations in theorem provers. Significant progress has been achieved here, allowing open questions in mathematics to be answered [30,31]. Along similar lines, VLSI

---

[8] This seems to account more than anything for the fact that there are so few average case results regarding decidability.

and parallel architectural support stands to improve the performance of theorem provers at least as much as it would any search program.

The second way to make theorem provers more usable is to relax our notion of correctness. A very simple way of doing this is to make a theorem proving program always return an answer after a certain amount of time.[9] If it has been unable to prove either that a sentence or its negation is implicit in the KB, it could assume that it was independent of the KB and answer *unknown* (or maybe reassess the importance of the question and try again). This form of error (i.e., one introduced by an incomplete theorem prover), is not nearly as serious as returning a *yes* for a *no*, and is obviously preferrable to an answer that never arrives. This is of course especially true if the program uses its resources wisely, in conjunction with the first suggestion above.

However, from the point of view of KR, both of these are only pseudo-solutions. Clearly, the first one alone does not help us guarantee anything about an inferential service. The second one, on the other hand, might allow us to guarantee an answer within certain time bounds, but would make it very hard for us to specify what that answer would be. If we think of the KR sevice as reasoning according to a certain logic, then the logic being followed is immensely complicated (compared to that of FOL) when resource limitations are present. Indeed, the whole notion of the KR system calculating what is implicit in the KB (which was our original goal) would have to be replaced by some other notion that went beyond the truth theory of the representation language to include the inferential power of a particular theorem proving program. In a nutshell, we can guarantee getting an answer, but not the one we wanted.

One final observation about this intractability is that it is *not* a problem that is due to the formalization of knowledge in FOL. If we assume that the goal of our KR sevice is to calculate what is implicit in the KB, then as long as the truth theory of our representation language is upward-compatible with that of FOL, we will run into the same problem. In particular, using English (or any other natural or artificial language) as our representation language does not avoid the problem as long as we can express in it at least what FOL allows us to express.

---

[9]The resource limitation here should obviously be a function of how important overall it might be to answer the question.

4 Expressiveness and Tractability

It appears that we have run into a serious difficulty in trying to develop a KR service that calculates what is implicit in a KB and yet does so in a reasonable amount of time. One option we have not yet considered, however, is to *limit* what can be in the KB so that its implications are more manageable computationally. Indeed, as we will demonstrate in this section, much of the research in KR can be construed as trading off expressiveness in a representation language for a more tractable form of inference. Moreover, unlike the restricted dialects of FOL analyzed in the logic and computer science literatures (e.g., in terms of nestings of quantifiers), the languages considered here have at least proven themselves quite useful in practice, however contrived they may appear on the surface.

4.1 Incomplete Knowledge

To see where this tradeoff between expressiveness and tractability originates, we have to look at the use of the expressive power of FOL in KR and how it differs from its use in mathematics.

In the study of mathematical foundations, the main use of FOL is in the formalization of infinite collections of entities. So, for example, we have first-order number and set theories that use quantifiers to range over these classes, and conditionals to state what properties these entities have. This is exactly how Frege intended his formalism to be used.

In KR, on the other hand, the domains being characterized are usually finite. The power of FOL is used not so much to deal with infinities, but to deal with *incomplete knowledge* [19,13]. Consider the kind of facts[10] that might be represented using FOL:

1. ¬Student(john).

   This sentence says that John is not a student without saying what he is.

2. Parent(sue,bill) ∨ Parent(sue,george).

   This sentence says that either Bill or George is a parent of Sue, but does not specify which.

3. $\exists x$ Cousin(bill,x) ∧ Male(x).

   This sentence says that Bill has at least one male cousin but does not say who that cousin is.

---

[10]The use of FOL to capture *terminology* or laws is somewhat different. See [4] for details.

4. $\forall x\, \text{Friend}(\text{george},x) \supset \exists y\, \text{Child}(x,y)$.

> This sentence says that all of George's friends have children without saying who those friends or their children are or even if there are any.

The main feature of these examples is that FOL is not used to capture complex details about the domain, but to avoid having to represent details that may not be known. *The expressive power of FOL determines not so much what can be said, but what can be left unsaid.*

For a system that has to be able to acquire knowledge in a piecemeal fashion, there may be no alternative to using all of FOL. But if we can restrict the kind of the incompleteness that has to be dealt with, we can also avoid having to use the full expressiveness of FOL. This, in turn, might lead to a more manageable inference procedure.

The last pseudo-solution to the tractability problem, then, is to restrict the logical form of the KB by controlling the incompleteness of the knowledge represented. This is still a pseudo-solution, of course. Indeed, provably, there cannot be a *real* solution to the problem. But this one has the distinct advantage of allowing us to calculate exactly the picture of the world implied by the KB, precisely what a KR service was supposed to do. In what follows, we will show how restricting the logical form of a KB can lead to very specialized, tractable forms of inference.

4.2   Database Form

The most obvious type of restriction to the form of a KB is what might be called *database form*. The idea is to restrict a KB so that it can only contain the kinds of information that can be represented in a standard database. Consider, for example, a very simple database that talks about university courses. It might contain a relation (or record type or whatever) like

COURSE

ID	NAME	DEPT	ENROLLMENT	INSTRUCTOR
csc248	ProgrammingLanguages	ComputerScience	42	S.J.Hurtubise
mat100	HistoryOfMathematics	Mathematics	137	R.Cumberbatch
csc373	ArtificialIntelligence	ComputerScience	853	T.Slothrop

· · ·

If we had to charaterize in FOL the information that this relation contained, we could use a collection of function-free atomic sentences like[11]

Course(csc248)   Dept(csc248,ComputerScience)   Enrollment(csc248,42)   . . .
Course(mat100)   Dept(mat100,Mathematics)   . . .
     . . .

In other words, the tabular database format characterizes exactly the positive instances of the various predicates. But more to the point, since our list of FOL sentences never ends up with ones like

Dept(mat100,mathematics) ∨ Dept(mat100,history),

the range of uncertainty that we are dealing with is quite limited.

There is, however, additional information contained in the database not captured in the simple FOL translation. To see this, consider, for instance, how we might try to determine the answer to the question,

How many courses are offered by the Computer Science Department?

The knowledge expressed by the above collection of FOL sentences is insufficient to answer this question: nothing about our set of atomic sentences implies that Computer Science has at least two courses (since csc373 and csc248 could be names of the same individual), and nothing implies that it has at most two courses (since there could be courses other than those mentioned in the list of sentences). On the other hand, from a database point of view, we could apparently successfully answer our question using our miniature database by phrasing it something like

Count c in COURSE where c.Dept = ComputerScience;

this yields the definitive answer, "2". The crucial difference here, between failing to answer the question at all and answering it definitively, is that we have actually asked *two different questions*. The formal query addressed to the database must be understood as

---

[11]This is not the only way to characterize this information. For example, we could treat the field names as function symbols or use *Id* as an additional relation or function symbol. Also, for the sake of simplicity, we are ignoring here integrity constraints (saying, for example, that each course has a unique enrollment), which may contain quantificational and other logical operations, but typically are only used to verify the consistency of the database, not to infer new facts. None of these decisions affect the conclusions we will draw below.

How many tuples in the COURSE relation have ComputerScience in their Dept field?

This is a question *not* about the world being modelled at all, but about the *data* itself. In other words, the database retrieval version of the question asks about the structures in the database itself, and not about what these structures represent.[12]

To be able to reinterpret the database query as the intuitive question originally posed about courses and departments (rather than as one about tuples and fields), we must account for additional information taking us beyond the stored data itself. In particular, we need FOL sentences of the form

$$c_i \neq c_j, \qquad \text{for distinct constants } c_i \text{ and } c_j,$$

stating that each constant represents a unique individual. In addition, for each predicate, we need a sentence similar in form to

$$\forall x[\text{Course}(x) \supset x = \text{csc248} \lor \cdots \lor x = \text{mat100}],$$

saying that the only instances of the predicate are the ones named explicitly.[13] If we now consider a KB consisting of all of the sentences in FOL we have listed so far, a KR system could, in fact, conclude that there were exactly two Computer Science courses, just like its Database Management counterpart. We have included in the imagined KB all of the information, both explicit and implicit, contained in the database.

One important property of a KB in this final form is that it is much easier to use than a general first-order KB. In particular, since the first part of the KB (the atomic sentences) does not use negation, disjunction, or existential quantification, we know the exact instances of every predicate of interest in the language. There is no incompleteness in our knowledge at all. Because of this, *inference reduces to calculation.* To find out how many courses there are, all we have to do is count how many appropriate tuples appear in the *COURSE* relation. We do not, for instance, have to reason by cases or by contradiction, as we would have to in the more general case. For example, if we also knew that either *csc148* or *csc149* or both were Computer Science courses but that no Computer Science course other than *csc373* had an odd identification number, we could still determine that

---

[12] The hallmark, it would appear, of conventional Database Management is that its practitioners take their role to be providing users access to the data, rather than using the data to answer questions about the world. The difference between the two points of view is especially evident when the data is very incomplete [14].

[13] This is one form of what has been called the *closed world assumption* [25].

there were three courses, but not by simply counting. But a KB in database form does not allow us to express this kind of uncertainty and, because of this expressive limitation, the KR service is much more tractable. Specifically, we can represent what is known about the world using just these sets of tuples, exactly like a standard database system. From this perspective, a database is a knowledge base whose limited form permits a very special form of inference.

This limitation on the logical form of a KB has other interesting features. Essentially, what it amounts to is making sure that there is very close structural correspondence between the (explicit) KB and the domain of interest: for each entity in the domain, there is a unique representational object that stands for it; for each relationship that it participates in, there is a tuple in the KB that corresponds to it. In a very real sense, the KB is an *analogue* of the domain of interest, not so different from other analogues such as maps or physical models. The main advantange of having such an analogue is that it can be used directly to answer questions about the domain. That is, the calculations on the model itself can play the role of more general reasoning techniques much the way arithmetic can replace reasoning with Peano's axioms. The disadvantage of an analogue, however, should also be clear: within a certain descriptive language, it does not allow anything to be left unsaid about the domain.[14] In this sense, an analogue representation can be viewed as a special case of a propositional one where the information it contains is relatively complete.

4.3 Logic Program Form

The second restriction on the form of a KB we will consider is a generalization of the previous one that is found in programs written in PROLOG, PLANNER, and related languages. A KB in logic program form also has an explicit and an implicit part. The explicit KB in a PROLOG program is a collection of first-order sentences (called Horn sentences) of the form

$$\forall x_1 \cdots x_n[P_1 \land \cdots \land P_m \supset P_{m+1}] \quad \text{where} \quad m \geq 0 \text{ and each } P_i \text{ is atomic.}$$

In the case where $m = 0$ and the arguments to the predicates are all constants, the logic

---

[14]The same is true for the standard analogues. One of the things a map does not allow you to say, for example, is that a river passes through one of two widely separated towns, without specifying which. Similarly, a plastic model of a ship cannot tell us that the ship it represents does not have two smokestacks, without also telling us how many it does have. This is not to say that there is no *uncertainty* associated with an analogue, but that this uncertainty is due to the coarseness of the analogue (*e.g.* how carefully the map is drawn) rather than to its content.

program form coincides with the database form. Otherwise, because of the possible nesting of functions, the set of relevant terms (whose technical name is the *Herbrand universe*) is much larger and may be infinite.

As in the database case, if we were only interested in the universe of terms, the explicit KB would be sufficient. However, to understand the KB as being about the world, but in a way that is compatible with the answers provided by a PROLOG processor, we again have to include additional facts in an implicit KB. In this case, the implicit KB is normally infinite since it must contain a set of sentences of the form $(s \neq t)$, for any two distinct terms in the Herbrand universe. As in the database case, it must also contain a version of the closed world assumption which is now a set containing the negation of every ground atomic sentence not implied by the Horn sentences in the explicit KB.

The net result of these restrictions is a KB that once again has complete knowledge of the world (within a given language), but this time, may require inference to answer questions.[15] The reasoning in this case, is the *execution* of the logic program. For example, given an explicit PROLOG KB consisting of

```
parent(bill,mary).
parent(bill,sam).
mother(X,Y) :- parent(X,Y), female(Y).
female(mary).
```

we know exactly who the mother of Bill is, but only after having executed the program.

In one sense, the logic program form does not provide any computational advantage to a reasoning system since determining what is in the implicit KB is, in general, undecidable.[16] On the other hand, the form is much more manageable than in the general case since the necessary inference can be split very nicely into two components: a *retrieval* component that extracts (atomic) facts from a database by pattern-matching and a *search* component that tries to use the non-atomic Horn sentences to complete the inference. In actual systems like PROLOG and PLANNER, moreover, the search component is partially under user control, giving him the ability to incorporate some of the kinds of procedural knowledge (or combinatoric advice) referred to earlier. The only purely automatic inference is the retrieval component.

---

[15] Notice that it is impossible to state in a KB of this form that $(p \lor q)$ is true without stating which, or that $\exists x P(x)$ is true without saying what that x is. However, see the comments below regarding the use of encodings.

[16] In other words, determining if a ground atomic sentence is implied by a collection of Horn sentences (containing function symbols) is undecidable.

This suggests a different way of looking at the inferential service provided by a KR system (without even taking into account the logical form of the KB). Instead of automatically performing the full deduction necessary to answer questions, a KR system could manage a *limited form of inference* and leave to the rest of the knowledge-based system (or to the user) the responsibility of intelligently completing the inference. As suggested in [10], the idea is to take the "muscle" out of the automatic component and leave the difficult part of reasoning as a problem that the overall system can (meta-)reason about and plan to solve [11].

While this is certainly a promising approach, especially for a KB of a fully general logical form, it does have its problems. First of all, it is far from clear what primitives should be available to a program to extend the reasoning performed by the KR subsystem. It is not as if it were a simple matter to generalize the meager PROLOG control facilities to handle a general theorem prover, for example.[17] The search space in this case seems to be much more complex.

Moreover, it is not clear what the KR service itself should be. If all a KR utility does is perform explicit retrieval over sentences in a KB, it would not be much help. For example, if asked about $(p \lor q)$, it would fail if it only had $(q \lor p)$ in the KB. What we really need is an automatic inferential service that lies somewhere between simple retrieval and full logical inference. But finding such a service that can be motivated *semantically* (the way logical deduction is) and defined independently of how any program actually operates is a non-trivial matter, though one we have taken some steps towards this in [16] (and see [22]).

4.4   Semantic Network Form

Turning now to semantic networks, a first observation about a KB in this form is that it only contains unary and binary predicates. For example, instead of representing the fact that John's grade in cs100 was 85 by

Grade(john, cs100, 85),

we would postulate the existence of objects called "grade-assignments" and represent the fact about John in terms of a particular grade-assignment *g-a1* as

Grade-assignment(g-a1) ∧ Student(g-a1,john) ∧
        Course(g-a1,cs100) ∧ Mark(g-a1,85).

---

[17]Though see [29] for some ideas in this direction.

This part of a KB in semantic net form is also in database form: a collection of function-free ground atoms, sentences stating the uniqueness of constants and the closed world assumption.

The main feature of a semantic net (and of the frame form below), however, is not how individuals are handled, but the treatment of the unary predicates (which we will call *types*) and binary ones (which we will call *attributes*). First of all, the types are organized into a taxonomy, which, for our purposes, can be represented by a set of sentences of the form[18]

$$\forall x[B(x) \supset A(x)].$$

The second kind of sentence in the generic KB places a constraint on an attribute as it applies to instances of a type:

$$\forall x[B(x) \supset \exists y(R(x,y) \land V(y))] \quad \text{or} \quad \forall x[B(x) \supset R(x,c)].[19]$$

This completes the semantic net form.

One property of a KB in this form is that it can be represented by a labelled directed graph (and displayed in the usual way). The nodes are either constants or types, and the edges are either labelled with an attribute or with the special label *is-a*.[20] The significance of this graphical representation is that it allows certain kinds of inference to be performed by simple graph-searching techniques. For example, to find out if a particular individual has a certain attribute, it is sufficient to search from the constant representing that individual, up *is-a* links, for a node having an edge labelled with the attribute. By placing the attribute as high as possible in the taxonomy, all individuals below it can *inherit* the property. Computationally, any mechanism that speeds up this type of graph-searching can be used directly to improve the performance of inference in a KB of this form.

In addition, the graph representation suggests different kinds of inference that are based more directly on the structure of the KB than on its logical content. For example, we can ask how two nodes are related and answer by finding a path in the graph between them. Given for instance, Clyde the elephant and Jimmy Carter, we could end up with an

---

[18] See [2] for a discussion of some of the subtleties involved here.

[19] There are other forms possible for this constraint. For example, we might want to say that *every R* rather than *some R* is a *V*. See also [12]. For the variant we have here, however, note that the KB is no longer in logic program form.

[20] Note that the interpretation of an edge depends on whether its source and target are constants or types. For example, from a constant *c* to a type *B*, *is-a* says $B(c)$, but from a type *B* to a type *A*, it is a taxonomic sentence (again, see [2]).

answer saying that Clyde is an elephant and that the favourite food of elephants is peanuts which is also the major product of the farm owned by Jimmy Carter. A typical method of producing this answer would be to perform a "spreading activation" search beginning at the nodes for Clyde and Jimmy. Obviously, this form of question would be very difficult to answer for a KB that was not in semantic net form.[21]

For better or worse, the appeal of the graphical nature of semantic nets has lead to forms of reasoning (such as default reasoning [24]) that do not fall into standard logical categories and are not yet very well understood [9].[22] This is a case of a representational notation taking on a life of its own and motivating a completely different style of use not necessarily grounded in a truth theory. It is unfortunately much easier to develop algorithms that appear to reason over structures of a certain kind than to *justify* its reasoning by explaining what the structures are saying about the world.

This is not to say that defaults are not a crucial part of our knowledge about the world. Indeed, the ability to abandon a troublesome or unsuccessful line of reasoning in favour of a default answer seems intuitively to be a fundamental way of coping with incomplete knowledge in the presence of resource limitations. The problem is to make this intuition precise. Paradoxically, the best formal accounts we have of defaults (such as [26]) would claim that reasoning with them is even *more difficult* than reasoning without them, so research remains to be done.

One final observation concerns the elimination of higher arity predicates in semantic networks. It seems to be fairly commonplace to try to sidestep a certain generality of logical form by introducing special representational objects into the domain. In the example above, a special "grade-assignment" object took the place of a 3-place predicate. Another example is the use of encodings of sentences as a way of providing (what appears to be) a completely extensional version of modal logic [18].[23] Not that exactly the same expressiveness is preserved in these cases; but what *is* preserved is still fairly mysterious and deserves serious investigation, especially given its potential impact on the tractability of inference.

---

[21] Quillian [23] proposed a "semantic intersection" approach to answering questions in his original work on semantic nets. See also [7] for followup work on the same topic.

[22] A simple example of a default would be to make *elephant* have the colour *grey* but to allow anything below *elephant* (such as *albino-elephant*) to be linked to a different colour value. To determine the colour of an individual would involve searching up for a value and stopping when the first one is found, allowing it to preempt any higher ones. See also [3].

[23] Indeed, some modern semantic network formalisms (such as [27]) actually include all of FOL by encoding sentences as terms.

4.5 Frame Description Form

The final form we will consider, the frame description form, is mainly an elaboration of the semantic network one. The emphasis, in this case, is on the structure of types themselves (usually called *frames*), particularly in terms of their attributes (called *slots*). Typically, the kind of detail involved with the specification of attributes includes

1. *values*, stating exactly what the attribute of an instance should be. Alternatively, the value may be just a *default*, in which case an individual inherits the value provided he does not override it.

2. *restrictions*, stating what constraints must be satisfied by attribute values. These can be *value* restrictions, specified by a type that attribute values should be instances of, or *number* restrictions, specified in terms of a minimum and a maximum number of attribute values.

3. *attached procedures*, providing procedural advice on how the attribute should be used. An *if-needed* procedure says how to calculate attribute values if none have been specified; an *if-added* procedure says what should be done when a new value is discovered.

Like semantic networks, frame languages tend to take liberties with logical form and the developers of these languages have been notoriously lax in characterizing their truth theories [12,3]. What *we* can do, however, is restrict ourselves to a non-controversial subset of a frame language that supports descriptions of the following form:

> (Student
>   **with a** dept **is** computer-science **and**
>   **with** $\geq$ 3 enrolled-course **is a**
>   (Graduate-Course
>   **with a** dept **is a** Engineering-Department))

This is intended to be a structured type that describes Computer Science students taking at least three graduate courses in departments within Engineering. If this type had a name (say A), we could express the type in FOL by a "meaning postulate" of the form

$$\forall x \, A(x) \equiv [\text{Student}(x) \wedge \text{dept}(x, \text{computer-science}) \wedge$$
$$\exists y_1 y_2 y_3 \, (y_1 \neq y_2 \wedge y_1 \neq y_3 \wedge y_2 \neq y_3 \wedge$$
$$\text{enrolled-course}(x, y_1) \wedge \text{Graduate-Course}(y_1) \wedge$$
$$\exists z(\text{dept}(y_1, z) \wedge \text{Engineering-Department}(z)) \quad \wedge$$
$$\text{enrolled-course}(x, y_2) \wedge \text{Graduate-Course}(y_2) \wedge$$
$$\exists z(\text{dept}(y_2, z) \wedge \text{Engineering-Department}(z)) \quad \wedge$$
$$\text{enrolled-course}(x, y_3) \wedge \text{Graduate-Course}(y_3) \wedge$$
$$\exists z(\text{dept}(y_3, z) \wedge \text{Engineering-Department}(z)))].$$

Similarly, it should be clear how to state equally clumsily[24] in FOL that an individual is an instance of this type.

One interesting property of these structured types is that we do not have to state explicitly when one of them is below another in the taxonomy. The descriptions themselves implicitly define a taxonomy of *subsumption*, where type A subsumes type B if, by virtue of the form of A and B, every instance of B must be an instance of A. For example, without any world knowledge, we can determine that the type *Person* subsumes

> (Person **with every** male friend **is a** Doctor)

which in turn subsumes

> (Person **with every** friend **is a**
>   (Doctor **with a** specialty **is** surgery)).

Similarly,

> (Person **with** $\geq$ 2 children)   subsumes
> (Person **with** $\geq$ 3 male children).

Also, we might say that two types are *disjoint* if no instance of one can be an instance of the other. An example of disjoint types is

> (Person **with** $\geq$ 3 young children)   and
> (Person **with** $\leq$ 2 children).

Analytic relationships like subsumption and disjointness are properties of structured types that are not available in a semantic net where all of the types are atomic.

There are very good reasons to be interested in these analytic relationships [4]. In KRYPTON [5,6], a full first-order KB is used to represent facts about the world, but subsumption and disjointness information is also available without having to add to the KB a collection of meaning postulates representing the structure of the types. The reason this is significant is that while subsumption and disjointness can be defined in terms of logical implication,[25] there are good special-purpose algorithms for calculating these relationships in some frame description languages. Again, because the logical form is sufficiently constrained, the required inference can be much more tractable.

---

[24] What makes these sentences especially awkward in FOL is the number restrictions. For example, the sentence *"There are a hundred billion stars in the Milky Way Galaxy"* would be translated into an FOL sentence with on the order of 10^{22} conjuncts.

[25] Specifically, type A subsumes type B iff the meaning postulates for A and B logically imply $\forall x[B(x) \supset A(x)]$.

4.6   An Example of the Tradeoff

As it turns out, frame description languages and the subsumption inference provide a rich domain for studying the tradeoff between expressiveness and tractability. To see this, we will look in some detail at a simple frame description language called $\mathcal{FL}$ whose types and attributes are defined by the following grammar:

$$
\begin{aligned}
\langle type \rangle ::= {} & \langle atom \rangle \\
& | \ (\text{AND } \langle type_1 \rangle \ldots \langle type_n \rangle) \\
& | \ (\text{ALL } \langle attribute \rangle \ \langle type \rangle) \\
& | \ (\text{SOME } \langle attribute \rangle)
\end{aligned}
$$

$$
\begin{aligned}
\langle attribute \rangle ::= {} & \langle atom \rangle \\
& | \ (\text{RESTR } \langle attribute \rangle \ \langle type \rangle)
\end{aligned}
$$

The $\mathcal{FL}$ language is intended as a simplified (though less readable) version of the frame-based language used in the previous section. So, for example, where we would previously have written a description like

(person **with every** male friend **is a** (doctor **with a** specialty)),

the equivalent $\mathcal{FL}$ type is now written as

(AND person (ALL (RESTR friend male) (AND doctor (SOME specialty)))).

To state exactly what these constructs mean, we now briefly define a straightforward extensional semantics for $\mathcal{FL}$ (which also provides us with a precise definition of subsumption). This will be done as follows: imagine that associated with each description is the set of individuals (individuals for types, pairs of individuals for attributes) that it describes. Call that set the *extension* of the description. Notice that by virtue of the structure of descriptions, their extensions are not independent (for example, the extension of (AND t_1 t_2) should be the intersection of those of t_1 and t_2). In general, the structures of two descriptions can imply that the extension of one is always a superset of the extension of the other. In that case, we will say that the first *subsumes* the second (so, in the case just mentioned, t_1 would be said to subsume (AND t_1 t_2)).

More formally, let $\mathcal{D}$ be any set and $\mathcal{E}$ be any function from types to subsets of $\mathcal{D}$ and attributes to subsets of the Cartesian product, $\mathcal{D} \times \mathcal{D}$. So

$$\mathcal{E}[t] \subseteq \mathcal{D} \quad \text{for any type } t, \text{ and}$$

$$\mathcal{E}[a] \subseteq \mathcal{D} \times \mathcal{D} \quad \text{for any attribute } a.$$

We will say that $\mathcal{E}$ is an *extension function* over $\mathcal{D}$ if and only if

1. $\mathcal{E}[(\text{AND } t_1 \ldots t_n)] = \bigcap_i \mathcal{E}[t_i]$

2. $\mathcal{E}[(\text{ALL } a \ t)] = \left\{ x \in D \mid \text{if} \quad \langle x, y \rangle \in \mathcal{E}[a] \quad \text{then} \quad y \in \mathcal{E}[t] \right\}$

3. $\mathcal{E}[(\text{SOME } a)] = \left\{ x \in D \mid \exists y \left[\langle x, y \rangle \in \mathcal{E}[a] \right] \right\}$

4. $\mathcal{E}[(\text{RESTR } a \ t)] = \left\{ \langle x, y \rangle \in D \times D \mid \langle x, y \rangle \in \mathcal{E}[a] \text{ and } y \in \mathcal{E}[t] \right\}$.

Finally, for any two types t_1 and t_2, we can say that t_1 *is subsumed by* t_2 if and only if for any set D and any extension function $\mathcal{E}$ over D, $\mathcal{E}[t_1] \subseteq \mathcal{E}[t_2]$. That is, one type is subsumed by a second type when all instances of the first—in all extensions—are also instances of the second. From a semantic point of view, subsumption dictates a kind of necessary set inclusion.

Given a precise definition of subsumption, we can now consider algorithms for calculating subsumption between descriptions. Intuitively, this seems to present no real problems. To determine if s subsumes t, what we have to do is make sure that each component of s is "implied" by some component (or components) of t. Moreover, the type of "implication" we need should be fairly simple since $\mathcal{FL}$ has neither a negation nor a disjunction operator.

Unfortunately, such intuitions can be nastily out of line. In particular, let us consider a slight variant of $\mathcal{FL}$—call it $\mathcal{FL}^-$. $\mathcal{FL}^-$ includes all of $\mathcal{FL}$ except for the RESTR operator. On the surface, the difference between $\mathcal{FL}^-$ and $\mathcal{FL}$ seems expressively minor. But it turns out that it is computationally very significant. In particular, there is an $O(n^2)$ algorithm for determining subsumption in $\mathcal{FL}^-$, but the same problem for $\mathcal{FL}$ is intractable. In the rest of this section, we sketch the form of our algorithm for $\mathcal{FL}^-$ and the proof that subsumption for $\mathcal{FL}$ is as hard as testing for propositional tautologies, and therefore most likely unsolvable in polynomial time.[26]

We here simply present, without comment, an algorithm for computing subsumption for $\mathcal{FL}^-$:

Subsumption Algorithm for $\mathcal{FL}^-$:   SUBS?$[s,t]$

1. Flatten both s and t by removing all nested AND operators. So, for example,

    (AND x (AND y z) w)   becomes   (AND x y z w).

2. Collect all arguments to an ALL for a given attribute. For example,

---

[26] Details of all proofs can be found in [17].

$$(\text{AND } (\text{ALL } a \ (\text{AND } u \ v \ w)) \ x \ (\text{ALL } a \ (\text{AND } y \ z))) \quad \text{becomes}$$
$$(\text{AND } x \ (\text{ALL } a \ (\text{AND } u \ v \ w \ y \ z))).$$

3. Assuming s is now $(\text{AND } s_1 \ \ldots \ s_n)$ and t is $(\text{AND } t_1 \ \ldots \ t_m)$, then return **true** iff for each s_i,

   (a) if s_i is an atom or a SOME, then one of the t_j is s_i.

   (b) if s_i is $(\text{ALL } a \ x)$, then one of the t_j is $(\text{ALL } a \ y)$, where SUBS?$[x,y]$.

This algorithm can be shown to compute subsumption correctly. For the purposes of this paper, the main property of SUBS? that we are interested in is that it can be shown to calculate subsumption for $\mathcal{FL}^-$ in $O(n^2)$ time.

We now turn our attention to the subsumption problem for full $\mathcal{FL}$. The proof that subsumption of descriptions in $\mathcal{FL}$ is intractable is based on a correspondence between this problem and the problem of deciding whether a sentence of propositional logic is implied by another. Specifically, we define a mapping π from propositional sentences in conjunctive normal form to descriptions in $\mathcal{FL}$ that has the property that for any two sentences α and β, α logically implies β iff $\pi[\alpha]$ is subsumed by $\pi[\beta]$.

Suppose p_1, p_2, ..., p_m are propositional letters distinct from A, B, R, and S.

$$\pi[p_1 \vee p_2 \vee \ldots \vee p_n \vee \neg p_{n+1} \vee \neg p_{n+2} \vee \ldots \vee \neg p_m] =$$
$$(\text{AND } (\text{ALL } (\text{RESTR } R \ p_1) \ A)$$
$$\ldots$$
$$(\text{ALL } (\text{RESTR } R \ p_n) \ A)$$
$$(\text{SOME } (\text{RESTR } R \ p_{n+1}))$$
$$\ldots$$
$$(\text{SOME } (\text{RESTR } R \ p_m)))$$

Assume that α_1, α_2, ..., α_k are disjunctions of literals not using A, B, R, and S.

$$\pi[\alpha_1 \wedge \alpha_2 \wedge \ldots \wedge \alpha_k] =$$
$$(\text{AND } (\text{ALL } (\text{RESTR } S \ (\text{SOME } (\text{RESTR } R \ A))) \ B)$$
$$(\text{ALL } (\text{RESTR } S \ \pi[\alpha_1]) \ B)$$
$$\ldots$$
$$(\text{ALL } (\text{RESTR } S \ \pi[\alpha_k]) \ B))$$

What this mapping provides is a way of answering questions of implication by first mapping the two sentences into descriptions in $\mathcal{FL}$ and then seeing if one is subsumed by the other. Moreover, because π can be calculated efficiently, any *good* algorithm for subsumption becomes a good one for implication.

The key observation here, however, is that there can be no good algorithm for implication. To see this, note that a sentence implies $(p \wedge \neg p)$ just in case it is not satisfiable. But determining the satisfiablity of a sentence in this form is NP-complete [8]. Therefore, a special case of the implication problem (where the second argument is $(p \wedge \neg p)$) is the complement of an NP-complete one. The correspondence between implication and subsumption, then, leads to the observation that subsumption for $\mathcal{FL}$ is co-NP hard. In other words, since a good algorithm for subsumption would lead to a good one for implication, subsumption over descriptions in $\mathcal{FL}$ is intractable.[27]

5   Conclusions and Morals

In this final section, we step back from the details of the specific representational formalisms we have examined and attempt to draw a few conclusions.

An important observation about these formalisms is that we cannot really say that one is *better* than any other; they simply take different positions on the tradeoff between expressiveness and tractability. For example, full FOL is both more expressive and less appealing computationally than a language in semantic net form. Nor is it reasonable to say that expressiveness is the primary issue and that the other is "merely" one of efficiency. In fact, we are not really talking about efficiency here at all; that, presumably, is an issue of algorithm and data structure, concerns of the Symbol Level [21]. The tractability concern we have here is much deeper and involves whether or not it makes sense to even think of the language as computationally based.

From the point of view of those doing research in KR, this has a very important consequence: we should continue to design and examine representation languages, *even when these languages can be viewed as special cases of FOL*. What really counts is that these special cases be interesting both from the point of view of what they can represent, and from the point of view of the reasoning strategies they permit. All of the formalisms we have examined above satisfy these two requirements. To dismiss a language as *just* a

---

[27] As mentioned in section 3.2, the co-NP-complete problems are strongly believed to be unsolvable in polynomial time.

subset of FOL is probably as misleading as dismissing the notion of a context-free grammar as just a special case of a context-sensitive one.

What truth in advertising does require, however, is that these special cases of FOL be identified as such. Apart from allowing a systematic comparison of representation languages (as positions on the tradeoff), this might also encourage us to consider systems that use more than one sublanguage and reasoning mechanism (as suggested for equality in [20]). The KRYPTON language [5,6], for example, includes all of FOL *and* a frame description language. To do the necessary reasoning, the system contains both a theorem prover and a description subsumption mechanism, even though the former could do the job of the latter (but much less efficiently). The trick with these *hybrid systems* is to factor the reasoning task so that the specialists are able to cooperate and apply their optimized algorithms without interfering with each other.

These considerations for designers of representation languages apply in a similar way to those interested in populating a KB with a theory of some sort. A good first step might be to write down a set of first-order sentences characterizing the domain, but it is somewhat naive to stop there and claim that the account could be made computational after the fact by the inclusion of a theorem prover and a few well chosen heuristics. What is really needed is the (much more difficult) analysis of the logical form of the theory, keeping the tradeoff clearly in mind. An excellent example of this is the representation of *time* described in [1]. Allen is very careful to point out what kind of information about time cannot be represented in his system, as well as the computational advantage he gains from this limitation.

For the future, we still have a lot to learn about the tradeoff. It would be very helpful to accumulate a wide variety of data points involving tractable and intractable languages. Especially significant are crossover points where small changes in a language change its computational character completely (an instance of which was illustrated in section 4.6). Moreover, we need to know more about what *people* find easy or hard to handle. There is no doubt that people can reason when necessary with radically incomplete knowledge (such as that expressible in full FOL) but apparently only by going into a special problem-solving or logic puzzle mode. In normal common sense situations, when reading a geography book, for instance, the ability to handle disjunctions (say) seems to be quite limited. The question is what forms of incomplete knowledge *can* be handled readily, given that the geography book is not likely to contain any procedural advice on how to reason.

In summary, we feel that there are many interesting issues to pursue involving the tradeoff between expressiveness and tractability. Although there has always been a temptation in KR to set the sights either too low (and provide only a data structuring facility with little or no inference) or too high (and provide a full theorem proving facility), this paper argues for the rich world of representation that lies between these two extremes.

Acknowledgements

Many of the ideas presented here originally arose in the context of the KRYPTON project. We are deeply indebted to the Fairchild AI Lab (now the AI Lab of Schlumberger Computer Aided Systems Research) for making this research possible and to Richard Fikes, Peter Patel-Schneider, and Victoria Gilbert. We would especially like to thank Peter, and also Jim des Rivières for providing very helpful comments on a earlier draft of this paper, and S. J. Hurtubise for not.

Bibliography

[1] Allen, J., "Maintaining Knowledge about Temporal Intervals," *Communications of the ACM*, Vol. 26, No. 11, November, 1983, 832–843.

[2] Brachman, R. J., "What IS-A Is and Isn't: An Analysis of Taxonomic Links in Semantic Networks," *IEEE Computer*, Vol. 16, No. 10, October, 1983, 30–36.

[3] Brachman, R. J., " 'I Lied about the Trees,' " *AI Magazine*, Vol. 6, No. 3, Fall, 1985.

[4] Brachman, R. J., and Levesque, H. J., "Competence in Knowledge Representation," *Proc. AAAI-82*, Pittsburgh, PA, 1982, 189–192.

[5] Brachman, R. J., Fikes, R. E., and Levesque, H. J., "Krypton: A Functional Approach to Knowledge Representation," *IEEE Computer*, Vol. 16, No. 10, October, 1983, 67–73.

[6] Brachman, R. J., Gilbert, V. P., and Levesque, H. J., "An Essential Hybrid Reasoning System: Knowledge and Symbol Level Accounts of KRYPTON," *Proc. IJCAI-85*, Los Angeles, CA, August, 1985.

[7] Collins, A. M., and Loftus, E. F., "A Spreading-activation Theory of Semantic Processing," *Psychological Review*, Vol. 82, No. 6, 1975, 407–428.

[8] Cook, S. A., "The Complexity of Theorem-Proving Procedures," *Proc. 3rd Ann. ACM Symposium on Theory of Computing*. New York: Association for Computing Machinery, 1971, pp. 151–158.

[9] Etherington, D., and Reiter, R., "On Inheritance Hierarchies with Exceptions," *Proc. AAAI-83*, Washington, DC, August, 1983, 104–108.

[10] Frisch, A., and Allen, J., *Knowledge Representation and Retrieval for Natural Language Processing*, TR 104, Computer Science Dept., Univ. of Rochester, 1982.

[11] Genesereth, M. R., "An Overview of Meta-Level Architecture," *Proc. AAAI-83*, Washington, DC, August, 1983, 119–123.

[12] Hayes, P. J., "The Logic of Frames," in *Frame Conceptions and Text Understanding*, D. Metzing (ed.). Berlin: Walter de Gruyter and Co., 1979, 46–61.

[13] Levesque, H. J., *A Formal Treatment of Incomplete Knowledge Bases*, Technical Report No. 3, Fairchild Laboratory for Artificial Intelligence Research, Palo Alto, CA, 1982.

[14] Levesque, H. J., "The Logic of Incomplete Knowledge Bases," in *On Conceptual Modelling: Perspectives from Artificial Intelligence, Databases, and Programming Languages*, M. L. Brodie, J. Mylopoulos, and J. Schmidt (eds.). New York: Springer-Verlag, 1984, 165–186.

[15] Levesque, H. J., "Foundations of a Functional Approach to Knowledge Representation," *Artificial Intelligence*, Vol. 23, No. 2, July, 1984, 155–212.

[16] Levesque, H. J., "A Logic of Implicit and Explicit Belief," *Proc. AAAI-84*, Austin, TX, August, 1984, 198–202.

[17] Levesque, H. J., and Brachman, R. J., "Some Results on the Complexity of Subsumption in Frame-Based Description Languages," in preparation.

[18] Moore, R. C., *Reasoning about Knowledge and Action*, Technical Note 191, SRI International, Menlo Park, CA, 1980.

[19] Moore, R. C., "The Role of Logic in Knowledge Representation and Commonsense Reasoning," *Proc. AAAI-82*, Pittsburgh, PA, August, 1982, 428–433.

[20] Nelson, G., and Oppen, D. C., "Simplification by Cooperating Decision Procedures," *ACM Transactions on Programming Languages and Systems*, Vol. 1, No. 2, 1979, 245–257.

[21] Newell, A., "The Knowledge Level," *The AI Magazine*, Vol. 2, No. 2, Summer, 1981, 1–20.

[22] Patel-Schneider, P. F., "A Decidable First-Order Logic for Knowledge Representation," *Proc. IJCAI-85*, Los Angeles, CA, August, 1985.

[23] Quillian, M. R., "Semantic Memory," in *Semantic Information Processing*, M. Minsky (ed.). Cambridge, MA: MIT Press, 1968, 227–270.

[24] Reiter, R., "On Reasoning by Default," *Proc. TINLAP-2*, University of Illinois at Urbana-Champaign, 1978, 210–218.

[25] Reiter, R., "On Closed World Data Bases," in *Logic and Data Bases*, H. Gallaire and J. Minker (eds.). New York: Plenum Press, 1978, 55–76.

[26] Reiter, R., "A Logic for Default Reasoning," *Artificial Intelligence*, Vol. 13, Nos. 1,2, April, 1980, 81–132.

[27] Shapiro, S. C., "The SNePS Semantic Network Processing System," in *Associative Networks: Representation and Use of Knowledge by Computers*, N. V. Findler (ed.). New York: Academic Press, 1979, 179–203.

[28] Smith, B. C., *Reflection and Semantics in a Procedural Language*, Ph.D. Thesis and Tech. Report MIT/LCS/TR-272, MIT, Cambridge, MA, 1982.

[29] Stickel, M. E., "A Prolog Technology Theorem Prover," *Proc. of the 1984 Symposium on Logical Programming*, Atlantic City, 1984, 211–217.

[30] Winker, S., "Generation and Verification of Finite Models and Counterexamples using an Automated Theorem Prover Answering Two Open Questions," *Journal of the ACM*, Vol. 29, No. 2, April, 1982, 273–284.

[31] Wos, L., Winker, S., Smith, B., Veroff, R., and Henschen, L., "A New Use of an Automated Reasoning Assistant: Open Questions in Equivalential Calculus and the Study of Infinite Domains," *Artificial Intelligence*, Vol. 22, No. 3, April, 1984, 303–356.

5 / Hubert L. Dreyfus
From Micro-Worlds to Knowledge Representation: AI at an Impasse

Hubert Dreyfus is a longstanding critic of Artificial Intelligence and this recently revised paper presents a very clear exposition of his doubts about the success of the field as a whole and, in particular, the limitations of Knowledge Representation. A major theme of the paper is that intelligence depends crucially on a collection of skills (such as the ability to recognize certain kinds of situations) that are acquired by practice and experience but that are not represented symbolically. Moreover, claims Dreyfus, the difficulties and limitations encountered by Artificial Intelligence researchers are due at least in part to their attempt at treating the entire world as an explicitly representable object. To illustrate this point, Dreyfus looks at the work of Winston on learning [Winston, Chapter 8], Minsky on frames [Minsky, Chapter 12], Schank on scripts (see [Schank and Abelson 77] for background), and Bobrow and Winograd on KRL [Bobrow and Winograd, Chapter 13]. The analysis is quite detailed, and represents a point of view remarkably like the one Winograd currently holds (see [Winograd and Flores 85]) about his own past work and the entire field (down even to the use of compound words like "always-already-in-a-situation"). The main drawback of his anti-formalist anti-mechanist position is precisely that it is so "anti." There is unfortunately very little that Dreyfus can offer as a constructive counter-proposal that is not somewhat vague and hand-waving (one critic has even accused him of thinking of the brain as "wonder-tissue"). However, Dreyfus' critique is sound enough to be sobering, and this point of view simply cannot be ignored by KR practitioners.

Appeared in *Mind Design*, 161–204, edited by J. Haugeland, Cambridge, MA: The MIT Press, 1981.

From Micro-Worlds to Knowledge Representation:
AI at an Impasse

HUBERT L. DREYFUS

SINCE THE COMPLETION, nearly a decade ago, of the first edition of *What Computers Can't Do* (Dreyfus, 1972), there has been considerable change and development in artificial intelligence research. None of this more recent work leads me to relax my overall skepticism, but it does call for new and detailed discussion. In this article I review and examine a representative sample of AI as it has developed in the seventies. The work discussed falls into two categories, which can be assigned to the first and second halves of the decade, respectively.

The Early Seventies: Micro-Worlds

Inasmuch as it was the most impressive new achievement at the time, we begin with Winograd's (1972) natural language understanding program: SHRDLU. SHRDLU simulates a robot arm which can move a set of variously shaped blocks, and allows a person to engage in a dialogue with the computer—asking questions, making statements, and issuing commands about this simple world of movable blocks. The program is an integrated system which makes use of syntax, semantics, and facts about blocks. It is thus, as Winograd cautiously claims, "a computer program which 'understands' language in a limited domain, by including a model of the subject being talked about and a context of discourse" (1973). Furthermore, this program explores the new idea of representing this knowledge in the form of procedures. The resulting dialogue is strikingly natural. Here is a sample. (The sentences in capital letters are computer print-out. The parentheses contain Winograd's comments.)

1. pick up a big red block.

OK.

(The system answers "OK" when it carries out a command. In order to pick up the red block, it had to clear it off by finding a space for the green one and moving the green one away.)

2. grasp the pyramid.

I DON'T UNDERSTAND WHICH PYRAMID YOU MEAN.

(There are three pyramids in the scene, so the program does nothing.)

3. find a block which is taller than the one you are holding and put it into the box.

(The system has to figure out what is meant by "one" and "it", as well as using deduction to decide which block it is holding.)

BY "IT", I ASSUME YOU MEAN THE BLOCK WHICH IS TALLER THAN THE ONE I AM HOLDING.

(Printed out to keep us informed.)

OK.

(The hand has to set down the red block to pick up the taller blue one.)

4. what does the box contain?

THE BLUE PYRAMID AND THE BLUE BLOCK.

5. what is the pyramid supported by?

(Earlier the system responded to "the pyramid" by saying, "I don't understand which pyramid you mean". Now, it assumes that we mean the one just mentioned.)

THE BOX.

. . . .

9. can the table pick up blocks?

NO.

(The semantic rules make this a nonsensical question which therefore must be false.)

10. can a pyramid be supported by a block?
YES.
(The deductive system finds an actual example, so it knows this is possible.)

11. can a pyramid support a pyramid?
I DON'T KNOW.
(The question makes sense, but there is no example in the scene, so there is no easy way to tell without being able to examine the robot's programs.)

12. stack up two pyramids.
I CAN'T.
(The robot tries and fails.)

13. the blue pyramid is mine.
I UNDERSTAND.
(This datum is added to the data base.)

14. I own blocks which are not red, but I don't own anything which supports a pyramid.
I UNDERSTAND.
(Two new theorems are created for proving things about "owning".)

15. do I own the box?
NO.

(Winograd, 1972; pp. 8–11)

If being a major advance means being more general than its predecessors, then SHRDLU, since it no longer depends for its analysis of language on external constraints of the sort essential to Bobrow's STUDENT, is a major achievement. Winograd himself points out the superiority of his program over earlier language understanding programs.

A program may succeed by carefully choosing the problem it will attack, so that some simple special-purpose solution will work. ELIZA (Weizenbaum, 1964) and STUDENT (Bobrow, 1967) are examples of programs which give impressive

performances owing to a severe and careful restriction of the kind of understanding they try to achieve. If a model is to be of broader significance, it must be designed to cover a large range of the things we mean when we talk of understanding. The principles should derive from an attempt to deal with the basic cognitive structures. (1973; p. 167)

If, however, "a major advance" means that a step has been made in dealing with the basic cognitive structures needed to cover everyday understanding—that, thanks to SHRDLU, there is now reason to be optimistic about the possibility of AI—then no progress at all can be claimed. To justify this negative judgment we must first find out how the optimists of the early seventies were able to convince themselves that with SHRDLU AI was at last on the right track. Workers in AI were certainly not trying to cover up the fact that it was SHRDLU's restricted domain which made apparent understanding possible. They even had a name for Winograd's method of restricting the domain of discourse. He was dealing with a *micro-world*. And in a 1970 internal memo at M.I.T., Minsky and Papert frankly note:

Each model—or "micro-world" as we shall call it—is very schematic; it talks about a fairyland in which things are so simplified that almost every statement about them would be literally false if asserted about the real world. (p. 39)

But they immediately add:

Nevertheless, we feel that they [the micro-worlds] are so important that we are assigning a large portion of our effort toward developing a collection of these micro-worlds and finding how to use the suggestive and predictive powers of the models without being overcome by their incompatibility with literal truth.

Given the admittedly artificial and arbitrary character of micro-worlds, why do Papert and Minsky think they provide a promising line of research?

To find an answer we must follow Minsky and Papert's perceptive remarks on narrative, and their less than perceptive conclusions:

In a familiar fable, the wily Fox tricks the vain Crow into

dropping the meat by asking it to sing. The usual test of understanding is the ability of the child to answer questions like: "Did the Fox think the Crow had a lovely voice?" The topic is sometimes classified as "natural language manipulation" or as "deductive logic", etc. These descriptions are badly chosen. For the real problem is not to understand English; it is to *understand* at all. To see this more clearly, observe that nothing is gained by presenting the story in simplified syntax: CROW ON TREE. CROW HAS MEAT. FOX SAYS "YOU HAVE A LOVELY VOICE. PLEASE SING." FOX GOBBLES MEAT. The difficulty in getting a machine to give the right answer does not at all depend on "disambiguating" the words (at least, not in the usual primitive sense of selecting one "meaning" out of a discrete set of "meanings"). And neither does the difficulty lie in the need for unusually powerful logical apparatus. The main problem is that no one has constructed the elements of a body of knowledge about such matters that is adequate for understanding the story. Let us see what is involved.

To begin with, there is never a unique solution to such problems, so we do not ask what the Understander *must* know. But he will surely gain by having the concept of FLATTERY. To provide this knowledge, we imagine a "micro-theory" of flattery—an extendible collection of facts or procedures that describe conditions under which one might expect to find flattery, what forms it takes, what its consequences are, and so on. How complex this theory is depends on what is presupposed. Thus it would be very difficult to describe flattery to our Understander if he (or it) does not already know that statements can be made for purposes other than to convey literally correct, factual information. It would be almost impossibly difficult if he does not even have some concept like PURPOSE or INTENTION.

(1970; pp. 42-44)

What characterizes the period of the early seventies, and makes SHRDLU seem an advance toward general intelligence, is the very concept of a micro-world—a domain which can be analyzed in isolation. This concept implies that although each area of discourse seems to open out into the rest of human activities, its endless ramifications are only apparent and will soon converge on a self-contained set of facts and relations. For example, in discussing the micro-world of bargaining, Papert and Minsky consider what a child needs to know to understand the following fragment of conversation:

Janet: "That isn't a very good ball you have. Give it to me and I'll give you my lollipop.

(p. 48)

And remark:

We conjecture that, eventually, the required micro-theories can be made reasonably compact and easily stated (or, by the same token, *learned*) once we have found an adequate set of structural primitives for them. When one begins to catalogue what one needs for just a little of Janet's story, it seems at first to be endless:

| Time | Things | Words |
| Space | People | Thoughts |

Talking: Explaining. Asking. Ordering. Persuading. Pretending
Social relations: Giving. Buying. Bargaining. Begging. Asking. Presents. Stealing . . .
Playing: Real and Unreal. Pretending
Owning: Part of. Belong to. Master of. Captor of
Eating: How does one compare the values of foods with the values of toys?
Liking: good. bad. useful. pretty. conformity
Living: Girl. Awake. Eats. Plays
Intention: Want. Plan. Plot. Goal. Cause. Result. Prevent
Emotions: Moods. Dispositions. Conventional expressions
States: asleep. angry. at home
Properties: grown-up. red-haired. called "Janet"
Story: Narrator. Plot. Principal actors
People: Children. Bystanders
Places: Houses. Outside

The surprising move here is the conclusion that there could be a circumscribed "micro-theory" of flattery—somehow intelligible apart from the rest of human life—while at the same time the account shows an understanding of flattery opening out into the rest of our everyday world, with its understanding of purposes and intentions.

was clearly also Winograd's hope at the time he developed SHRDLU:

The justification for our particular use of concepts in this system is that it is thereby enabled to engage in dialogs that simulate in many ways the behavior of a human language user. For a wider field of discourse, the conceptual structure would have to be expanded in its details, and perhaps in some aspects of its overall organization. (Winograd, 1972; p. 26)

Thus, for example, it might seem that one could "expand" SHRDLU's concept of owning, since in the above sample conversation SHRDLU seems to have a very simple "micro-theory" of owning blocks. But as Simon points out in an excellent analysis of SHRDLU's limitations, the program does not understand owning at all, because it cannot deal with meanings. It has merely been given a set of primitives and their possible relationships. As Simon puts it:

The SHRDLU system deals with problems in a single blocks world, with a fixed representation. When it is instructed to "pick up a big red block", it needs only to associate the term "pick up" with a procedure for carrying out that process; identify, by applying appropriate tests associated with "big", "red", and "block", the argument for the procedure and use its problem-solving capabilities to carry out the procedure. In saying "it needs only", it is not my intention to demean the capabilities of SHRDLU. It is precisely because the program possesses stored programs expressing the intensions of the terms used in inquiries and instructions that its interpretation of those inquiries and instructions is relatively straightforward.
(Simon, 1977; p. 1062)

In understanding, on the other hand,

the problem-understanding sub-system will have a more complicated task than just mapping the input language onto the intentions stored in a lexicon. It will also have to create a representation for the information it receives, and create meanings for the terms that are consistent with the representation." (p. 1063).

So, for example, in the conversation concerning owning:

although SHRDLU's answer to the question is quite correct,

Angry: State

  caused by: Insult
         deprivation
         assault
         disobedience
         frustration
         spontaneous

Results: not cooperative
      lower threshold
      aggression
      loud voice
      irrational
      revenge

Etc.

(pp. 50–52)

They conclude:

But [the list] is not endless. It is only large, and one needs a large set of concepts to organize it. After a while one will find it getting harder to add new concepts, and the new ones will begin to seem less indispensable. (p. 52)

This totally unjustified belief that the seemingly endless reference to other human practices will converge so that simple micro-worlds can be studied in relative isolation reflects a naive transfer to AI of methods that have succeeded in the natural sciences. Winograd characteristically describes his work in terms borrowed from physical science:

We are concerned with developing a formalism, or "representation," with which to describe . . . knowledge. We seek the "atoms" and "particles" of which it is built, and the "forces" that act on it. (Winograd, 1976; p. 9)

It is true that physical theories about the universe can be built up by studying relatively simple and isolated systems and then making the model gradually more complex and integrating it with other domains of phenomena. This is possible because all the phenomena are presumably the result of the lawlike relations of a set of basic elements, what Papert and Minsky call "structural primitives." This belief in local success and gradual generalization

> the system cannot be said to understand the meaning of "own" in any but a sophistic sense. SHRDLU's test of whether something is owned is simply whether it is tagged "owned". There is no intensional test of ownership, hence SHRDLU knows what it owns, but doesn't understand what it is to own something. SHRDLU would understand what it meant to own a box if it could, say, test its ownership by recalling how it had gained possession of the box, or by checking its possession of a receipt in payment for it; could respond differently to requests to move a box it owned from requests to move one it didn't own; and, in general, could perform those tests and actions that are generally associated with the determination and exercise of ownership in our law and culture. (p. 1064)

Moreover, even if it satisfied all these conditions, it still wouldn't understand, unless it also understood that it (SHRDLU) couldn't own anything, since it isn't a part of the community in which owning makes sense. Given our cultural practices which constitute owning, a computer cannot own something any more than a table can.

This discussion of owning suggests that, just as it is misleading to call a program UNDERSTAND when the problem is to find out what understanding is (cf. McDermott, 1976, p. 4; this volume, p. 144), it is likewise misleading to call a micro-*world* when what is really at stake is the understanding of what a world is. A set of interrelated facts may constitute a *universe*, a domain, a group, etc., but it does not constitute a *world*, for a world is an organized body of objects, purposes, skills, and practices in terms of which human activities have meaning or make sense. It follows that although there is a children's world in which, among other things, there are blocks, there is no such thing as a blocks world. Or, to put this as a critique of Winograd, one cannot equate, as he does, a program which deals with "a tiny bit of the world," with a program which deals with a "mini-world" (Winograd, 1974; p. 20).

In our everyday life we are, indeed, involved in such various "sub-worlds," as the world of the theater, of business, or of mathematics, but each of these is a "mode" of our shared everyday world.[1]

That is, sub-worlds are not related like isolable physical systems to larger systems they *compose*; rather they are local elaborations of a whole which they *presuppose*. If micro-worlds *were* sub-worlds, one would not have to extend and combine them to reach the everyday world, because the everyday world would have to be included already. Since, however, micro-worlds are *not* worlds, there is no way they can be combined and extended to the world of everyday life. As a result of failing to ask what a world is, five years of stagnation in AI was mistaken for progress.

A second major application of the micro-world technique was in computer vision. Already in 1968, Adolfo Guzman's SEE program could analyze two-dimensional projections of complicated three-dimensional "scenes," consisting of piles of polyhedra. Even this early program correctly analyzed certain classes of scenes which people find difficult to figure out; but it had serious limitations. In 1972, David Waltz generalized Guzman's methods, and produced a much more powerful vision system. Together, these programs provide a case study not only in how much can be achieved with the micro-worlds approach, but also in the kind of generalization that is possible within that approach—and, by implication, the kind that isn't.

Guzman's program analyzes scenes involving cubes and other such rectilinear solids by merging regions into bodies using evidence from the vertices. Each vertex suggests that two or more of the regions around it belong together, depending on whether the vertex is shaped like an L, an arrow, a T, a K, an X, a fork, a peak, or an upside-down peak. With these eight primitives and commonsense rules for their use, Guzman's program did quite well. But it had certain weaknesses. According to Winston, "The program could not handle shadows, and it did poorly if there were holes in objects or missing lines in the drawing" (1975; p. 8). Waltz then generalized Guzman's work and showed that by introducing three more such primitives, a computer can be programmed to decide if a particular line in a drawing is a shadow, a crack, an obscuring edge, or an internal seam in a way analogous to the solution of sets of algebraic equations. As Winston later sums up the change:

> Previously it was believed that only a program with a complicated

---

1. This view is worked out further in Heidegger (1972); see especially p. 93 and all of section 18.

are under some external constraint (in this case the laws of geometry and optics). What one would not expect is that the special-purpose heuristics which depend on corners for segregating rectilinear objects could in any way be generalized so as to make possible the recognition of other sorts of objects. And, indeed, none of Guzman's or Waltz's techniques, since they rely on the intersection of straight lines, have any use in analyzing a scene involving curved objects. What one gains in narrowing a domain, one loses in breadth of significance. Winston's evaluation covers up this lesson.

It is wrong to think of Waltz's work as only a statement of the epistemology of line drawings of polyhedra. Instead I think it is an elegant case study of a paradigm we can expect to see again and again, and as such, it is a strong metaphoric tool for guiding our thinking, not only in vision but also in the study of other systems involving intelligence.
(1975; p. 8)

But in a later grant proposal he acknowledges that:

To understand the real world, we must have a different set of primitives from the relatively simple line trackers suitable and sufficient for the blocks world.
(1976; p. 39)

Waltz's work is a paradigm of the kind of generalization one can strive for *within* a micro-world all right, but for that very reason it provides no way of thinking about general intelligent systems.

The nongeneralizable character of the programs so far discussed makes them engineering feats, not steps toward generally intelligent systems, and they are, therefore, not at all promising as contributions to psychology. Yet Winston includes Waltz's work in his claim that "making machines see is an important way to understand how we animals see" (1975; p. 2), and Winograd makes similar claims for the psychological relevance of his work:

The gain from developing AI is not primarily in the usefulness of the programs we create, but in the set of concepts we develop, and the ways in which we can apply them to understanding human intelligence.
(1976; p. 3)

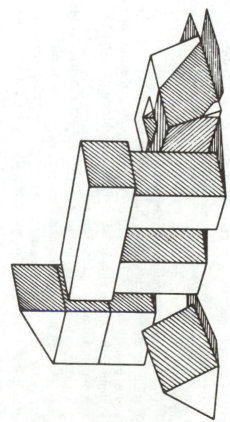

Figure 1.

control structure and lots of explicit reasoning power could hope to analyze scenes like that in figure [1]. Now we know that understanding the constraints the real world imposes on how boundaries, concave and convex interiors, shadows, and cracks can come together at junctions is enough to make things much simpler. A table which contains a list of the few thousand physically possible ways that line types can come together accompanied by a simple matching program are all that is required. Scene analysis is translated into a problem resembling a jigsaw puzzle or a set of linear equations. No deep problem solving effort is required; it is just a matter of executing a very simple constraint-dependent, iterative process that successively throws away incompatible line arrangment combinations.
(1976; pp. 77–78)

This is just the kind of mathematical generalization within a domain that one might expect in micro-worlds where the rule-governed relation of the primitives (in this case the set of vertices)

These comments suggest that in the early seventies an interesting change was taking place at M.I.T. In previous papers Minsky and his co-workers sharply distinguished themselves from workers in Cognitive Simulation, such as Simon, who presented their programs as psychological theories, insisting that the M.I.T. programs were "an attempt to build intelligent machines without any prejudice toward making the system . . . humanoid" (Minsky, 1969; p. 7). Now in their book *Artificial Intelligence*, a summary of work done at M.I.T. during the period 1967-72, Minsky and Papert (1973) present the M.I.T. research as a contribution to psychology. They first introduce the notion of a symbolic description:

What do we mean by "description"? We do not mean to suggest that our descriptions must be made of strings of ordinary language words (although they might be). The simplest kind of description is a structure in which some features of a situation are represented by single ("primitive") symbols, and relations between those features are represented by other symbols—or by other features of the way the description is put together. (p. 11)

They then defend the role of symbolic descriptions in a psychological account of intelligent behavior by a constant polemic against behaviorism and gestalt theory which have opposed the use of formal models of the mind.

One can detect, underlying this change, the effect of the proliferation of micro-worlds, with their reliance on symbolic descriptions, and the disturbing failure to produce even the hint of a system with the flexibility of a six-month-old child. Instead of concluding from this frustrating situation that the special-purpose techniques which work in context-free, gamelike, micro-worlds may in no way resemble general-purpose human and animal intelligence, the AI workers seem to have taken the less embarrassing if less plausible tack of suggesting that even if they could not succeed in building intelligent systems, the *ad hoc* symbolic descriptions successful in micro-world analysis could be justified as a valuable contribution to psychology.

Such a line, however, since it involves a stronger claim than the old slogan that as long as the machine was intelligent it did not matter at all whether it performed in a humanoid way, runs the obvious risk of refutation by empirical evidence. An information-processing model must be a formal symbolic structure, however, so Minsky and Papert, making a virtue of necessity, revive the implausible intellectualist position according to which concrete perception is assimilated to the rule-governed symbolic descriptions used in abstract thought:

The Gestaltists look for simple and fundamental principles about how perception is organized, and then attempt to show how symbolic reasoning can be seen as following the same principles, while we construct a complex theory of how knowledge is applied to solve intellectual problems and then attempt to show how the symbolic description that is what one "sees" is constructed according to similar processes.   (1973; p. 34)

Some recent work in psychology, however, points exactly in the opposite direction. Rather than showing that perception can be analyzed in terms of formal features, Erich Goldmeier's (1972) extension of early Gestalt work on the perception of similarity of simple perceptual figures—arising in part in response to "the frustrating efforts to teach pattern recognition to [computers]" (p. 1)—has revealed sophisticated distinctions between figure and ground, matter and form, essential and accidental aspects, norms and distortions, etc., which he shows cannot be accounted for in terms of any known formal features of the phenomenal figures. They can, however, according to Goldmeier, perhaps be explained on the neurological level, where the importance of Prägnanz— i.e., singularly salient shapes and orientations—suggests underlying physical phenomena such as "regions of resonance" (p. 128) in the brain.

Of course, it is still possible that the Gestaltists went too far in trying to assimilate thought to the same sort of concrete, holistic, processes they found necessary to account for perception. Thus, even though the exponents of symbolic descriptions have no account of perceptual processes, they might be right that the mechanism of everyday thinking and learning consists in constructing a formal description of the world and transforming this representation in a rule-governed way. Such a formal model of everyday learning and categorization is proposed by Winston in his 1970 thesis, "Learning Structural Descriptions from Examples," (see Winston, 1975). Given a set of positive and negative instances, Winston's self-proclaimed "classic" program can, for example, use a descriptive repertoire to construct a formal description of the class of arches. Since Winston's program (along with those of Winograd and Guzman) is often mentioned as a major success of the micro-worlds technique, we must examine it in detail.

This program, too, illustrates the possibilities and essential limitations of micro-worlds. Is it the basis of a plausible general approach to learning? Winston thinks so:

Although this may seem like a very special kind of learning, I think the implications are far ranging, because I believe that learning by examples, learning by being told, learning by imitation, learning by reinforcement and other forms are much like one another. In the literature on learning there is frequently an unstated assumption that these various forms are fundamentally different. But I think the classical boundaries between the various kinds of learning will disappear once superficially different kinds of learning are understood in terms of processes that construct and manipulate descriptions.   (1975; p. 185)

Yet Winston's program works only if the "student" is saved the trouble of what Charles Sanders Peirce called abduction, by being "told" a set of context-free features and relations—in this case a list of possible spatial relationships of blocks such as "left-of," "standing," "above," and "supported by,"—from which to build up a description of an arch. Minsky and Papert presuppose this preselection when they say that "to eliminate objects which seem atypical . . . the program lists all relationships exhibited by more than half of the candidates in the set" (1973; p. 56). Lurking behind this claim is the supposition that there are only a finite number of relevant features; but without preselected features all objects share an indefinitely large number of relationships. The work of discriminating, selecting, and weighting a limited number of relevant features is the result of repeated experience and is the first stage of learning. But since in Winston's work the programmer selects and preweights the primitives, his program gives us no idea how a computer could make this selection and assign

these weights. Thus the Winston program, like every micro-world program, works only because it has excluded from its task domain the very ability it is supposed to explain.

If not a theory of learning, is Winston's program at least a plausible theory of categorization? Consider again the arch example. Once it has been given what Winston disarmingly calls a "good description" (p. 158) and carefully chosen examples, the program does conclude that an arch is a structure in which a prismatic body is supported by two upright blocks that do not touch each other. But, since arches function in various ways in our everyday activity, there is no reason to suppose that these are the necessary and sufficient conditions for being an arch, or that there are any such defining features. Some prominent characteristics shared by most everyday arches are "helping to support something while leaving an important open space under it," or "being the sort of thing one can walk under and through at the same time." How does Winston propose to capture such contextual characteristics in terms of the context-free features required by his formal representation?

Winston admits that having two supports and a flat top does not begin to capture even the geometrical structure of arches. So he proposes "generalizing the machine's descriptive ability to acts and properties required by those acts" (p. 194) by adding a functional predicate, "something to walk through" (p. 193). But it is not at all clear how a functional predicate which refers to implicit knowledge of the bodily skill of walking through is to be formalized. Indeed, Winston himself provides a *reductio ad absurdum* of this facile appeal to formal functional predicates:

To a human, an arch may be something to walk through, as well as an appropriate alignment of bricks. And certainly, a flat rock serves as a table to a hungry person, although far removed from the image the word table usually calls to mind. But the machine does not yet know anything of walking or eating, so the programs discussed here handle only some of the physical aspects of these human notions. There is no inherent obstacle forbidding the machine to enjoy functional understanding. It is a matter of generalizing the machine's descriptive ability to acts and properties required by those acts. Then chains of pointers can link TABLE to FOOD as well as to the physical image

criteria necessary and sufficient for category membership but, rather, in terms of a prototype of a typical category member. The most cognitively economical code for a category is, in fact, a *concrete image* of an average category member. (1977; p. 30)

One paradigm, it seems, is worth a thousand rules. As we shall soon see, one of the characteristics of the next phase of work in AI is to try to take account of the implications of Rosch's research.

Meanwhile, what can we conclude concerning AI's contribution to the science of psychology? No one can deny Minsky and Papert's claim that "Computer Science has brought a flood of . . . ideas, well defined and experimentally implemented, for thinking about thinking" (1973; p. 25). But all of these ideas can be boiled down to ways of constructing and manipulating symbolic descriptions, and, as we have seen, the notion that human cognition can be explained in terms of formal representations does not seem at all obvious in the face of actual research on perception, and everyday concept formation. Even Minsky and Papert show a commendable new modesty. They as much as admit that AI is still at the stage of astrology, and that the much heralded breakthrough still lies in the future:

Just as astronomy succeeded astrology, following Kepler's discovery of planetary regularities, the discoveries of these many principles in empirical explorations on intellectual processes in machines should lead to a science, eventually. (1973; p. 25)

Happily, "should" has replaced "will" in their predictions. Indeed, this period's contribution to psychology suggests an even more modest hope: As more psychologists like Goldmeier are frustrated by the limitations of formal computer models, and others turn to investigating the function of images as opposed to symbolic representations, the strikingly limited success of AI may come to be seen as an important disconfirmation of the information processing approach.

Before concluding our discussion of this research phase, it should be noted that some problem domains are (nearly enough) micro-worlds already; so they lend themselves to AI techniques without the need for artificial restrictions, and, by the same token,

of a table, and the machine will be perfectly happy to draw up its chair to a flat rock with the human given that there is something on that table which it wishes to eat. (pp. 193–194)

Progress on recognition of arches, tables, etc., must, it seems, either wait until we have captured in an abstract symbolic description much of what human beings implicitly know about walking and eating simply by having a body, or else until computers no longer have to be told what it is to walk and eat, because they have human bodies and appetites themselves!

Despite these seemingly insurmountable obstacles Winston boasts that "there will be no contentment with [concept learning] machines that only do as well as humans" (p. 160). But it is not surprising that Winston's work is nine years old and there has been little progress in machine learning, induction, or concept formation. In their account Minsky and Papert (1973) admit that "we are still far from knowing how to design a powerful yet subtle and sensitive inductive learning program" (p. 56). What is surprising is that they add: "but the schemata developed in Winston's work should take us a substantial part of the way." The lack of progress since Winston's work was published, plus the use of predigested weighted primitives from which to produce its rigid, restricted, and largely irrelevant descriptions, makes it hard to understand in what way the program is a substantial step.

Moreover, if Winston claims to "shed some light on [the question:] How do we recognize examples of various concepts?" (1975; p. 157), his theory of concepts as definitions must, like any psychological theory, be subject to empirical test. It so happens that contrary to Winston's claims, recent evidence collected and analyzed by Eleanor Rosch on just this subject shows that human beings are not aware of classifying objects as instances of abstract rules but rather group objects as more or less distant from an imagined paradigm. This does not exclude the possibility of unconscious processing, but it does highlight the fact that there is no empirical evidence at all for Winston's formal model. As Rosch puts it:

Many experiments have shown that categories appear to be coded in the mind neither by means of lists of each individual member of the category, nor by means of a list of formal

nongeneralizability is not the same kind of Waterloo. Game playing, particularly chess, is the most conspicuous example. Though some extravagant early predictions were not fulfilled, large computers now play fairly high caliber chess, and small machines that play creditable amateur games are being marketed as toys. But game players are not the only examples; excellent programs have been written for analyzing certain kinds of mass spectroscopy data (Feigenbaum, 1977), and for assisting in the diagnosis and treatment of some diseases (Shortliffe, 1976). Such work is both impressive and important; but it shouldn't give the *wrong* impression. In each case, it succeeds because (and to the extent that) the relevant domain is well circumscribed in advance, with all the significant facts, questions, and/or options already laid out, and related by a comparatively small set of explicit rules—in short, because it's a micro-world. This is not to belittle either the difficulty or the value of spelling out such domains, or designing programs which perform well in them. But we should not see them as any closer to the achievement of genuine artificial intelligence than we do the "blocks-world" programs. In principle, interpreting mass spectrograms or batteries of specific symptoms has as little to do with the general intelligence of physicists and physicians, as disentangling vertices in projections of polyhedra does with vision. The real, theoretical problems for AI lie elsewhere.

The Later Seventies: Knowledge Representation

In roughly the latter half of the decade, the problem of how to structure and retrieve information, in situations where *anything* might be relevant, has come to the fore as the "knowledge representation problem." Of course, the representation of knowledge was always a central problem for work in AI, but earlier periods were characterized by an attempt to repress it by seeing how much could be done with as little knowledge as possible. Now, the difficulties are being faced. As Roger Schank of Yale recently remarked:

Researchers are starting to understand that tour-de-forces in programming are interesting but non-extendable . . . the AI people recognize that how people use and represent knowledge is the key issue in the field. (1977; pp. 1007-1008)

Papert and Goldstein explain the problem:

It is worthwhile to observe here that the goals of a knowledge-based approach to AI are closely akin to those which motivated Piaget to call . . . himself an "epistemologist" rather than a psychologist. The common theme is the view that the process of intelligence is determined by the knowledge held by the subject. The deep and primary questions are to understand the operations and data structures involved. (1975; p. 7)

Another memorandum illustrates how ignoring the background knowledge can come back to haunt one of AI's greatest tricks in the form of nongeneralizability:

Many problems arise in experiments on machine intelligence because things obvious to any person are not represented in any program. One can pull with a string, but one cannot push with one. One cannot push with a thin wire, either. A taut inextensible cord will break under a very small lateral force. Pushing something affects first its speed, only indirectly its position! Simple facts like these caused serious problems when Charniak attempted to extend Bobrow's "Student" program to more realistic applications, and they have not been faced up to until now. (Papert and Minsky, 1973; p. 77)

The most interesting current research is directed toward the underlying problem of developing new, flexible, complex data types which will allow the representation of background knowledge in large, more structured units.

In 1972, drawing on Husserl's phenomenological analysis, I pointed out that it was a major weakness of AI that no programs made use of expectations (see pp. 241f and 250, in the 1979 edition). Instead of modeling intelligence as a passive receiving of context-free facts into a structure of already stored data, Husserl thinks of intelligence as a context-determined, goal-directed activity—as a *search* for anticipated facts. For him the noema, or mental representation of any type of object, provides a context or "inner horizon" of expectations or "predelineations" for structuring the incoming data: a "rule governing *possible* other consciousness of [the object] as identical—possible, as exemplifying essentially predelineated types" (Husserl, 1960; p. 53). As I explained in chapter 7:

We perceive a house, for example, as more than a façade—as having some sort of back—some inner horizon. We respond to this whole object first and then, as we get to know the object better, fill in the details as to inside and back. (1979; p. 241)

The noema is thus a symbolic description of all the features which can be expected with certainty in exploring a certain type of object—features which remain "inviolably the same: as long as the objectivity remains intended as *this* one and of this kind" (p. 51) —plus "predelineations" of those properties which are possible but not necessary features of this type of object.

Then, in 1974, Minsky proposed a new data structure remarkably similar to Husserl's for representing everyday knowledge:

A frame is a data-structure for representing a stereotyped situation, like being in a certain kind of living room, or going to a child's birthday party....

We can think of a frame as a network of nodes and relations. The "top levels" of a frame are fixed, and represent things that are always true about the supposed situation. The lower levels have many *terminals*—"slots" that must be filled by specific instances or data. Each terminal can specify conditions its assignments must meet....

Much of the phenomenological power of the theory hinges on the inclusion of expectations and other kinds of presumptions. A frame's terminals are normally already filled with "default" assignments. (pp. 1–2/ 96)[2]

In Minsky's model of a frame, the "top level" is a developed version of what in Husserl's terminology "remains inviolably the same" in the representation, and Husserl's predelineations have been made precise as "default assignments"—additional features that can normally be expected. The result is a step forward in AI techniques from a passive model of information processing to one which tries to take account of the context of the interactions between a knower and his world. Husserl thought of his method of transcendental-phenomenological constitution, i.e., "explicating" the noema for all types of objects, as the beginning of progress

toward philosophy as a rigorous science, and Patrick Winston has hailed Minsky's proposal as "the ancestor of a wave of progress in AI" (1975; p. 16). But Husserl's project ran into serious trouble and there are signs that Minsky's may too.

During twenty years of trying to spell out the components of the noema of everyday objects, Husserl found that he had to include more and more of what he called the "outer horizon," a subject's total knowledge of the world:

To be sure, even the tasks that present themselves when we take single types of objects as restricted clues prove to be extremely complicated and always lead to extensive disciplines when we penetrate more deeply. That is the case, for example, with a transcendental theory of the constitution of a spatial object (to say nothing of a Nature) as such, of psycho-physical being and humanity as such, cultures as such.   (1960; pp. 54–55)

He sadly concluded at the age of seventy-five that he was "a perpetual beginner" and that phenomenology was an "infinite task,"—and even that may be too optimistic. His successor, Heidegger, pointed out that since the outer horizon or background of cultural practices was the condition of the possibility of determining relevant facts and features and thus prerequisite for structuring the inner horizon, as long as the cultural context had not been clarified the proposed analysis of the inner horizon of the *noema* could not even claim progress.

There are hints in the frame paper that Minsky has embarked on the same misguided "infinite task" that eventually overwhelmed Husserl:

Just constructing a knowledge base is a major intellectual research problem. . . We still know far too little about the contents and structure of common-sense knowledge. A "minimal" common-sense system must "know" something about cause-effect, time, purpose, locality, process, and types of knowledge. . . . We need a serious epistemological research effort in this area.   (p. 74/124)

Minsky's naïveté and faith are astonishing. Philosophers from Plato to Husserl, who uncovered all these problems and more, have carried on serious epistemological research in this area for two

2. *Editor's note:* numbers after the slash refer to pages in this volume.

thousand years without notable success. Moreover, the list Minsky includes in this passage deals only with natural objects, and their positions and interactions. As Husserl saw, intelligent behavior also presupposes a background of cultural practices and institutions. Observations in the frame paper such as: "Trading normally occurs in a social context of law, trust, and convention. Unless we also represent these other facts, most trade transactions will be almost meaningless" (p. 34/102) show that Minsky has understood this too. But Minsky seems oblivious to the hand-waving optimism of his proposal that programmers rush in where philosophers such as Heidegger fear to tread, and simply make explicit the totality of human practices which pervade our lives as water encompasses the life of a fish.

To make this essential point clear, it helps to take an example used by Minsky and look at what is involved in understanding a piece of everyday equipment as simple as a chair. No piece of everyday equipment makes sense by itself. The physical object which is a chair can be defined in isolation as a collection of atoms, or of wood or metal components, but such a description will not enable us to pick out chairs. What makes an object a *chair* is its function, and what makes possible its role as equipment for sitting is its place in a total practical context. This presupposes certain facts about human beings (fatigue, the ways the body bends), and a network of other culturally determined equipment (tables, floors, lamps) and skills (eating, writing, going to conferences, giving lectures, etc.). Chairs would not be equipment for sitting if our knees bent backwards like those of flamingos, or if we had no tables, as in traditional Japan or the Australian bush.

Anyone in our culture understands such things as how to sit on kitchen chairs, swivel chairs, folding chairs; and in arm chairs, rocking chairs, deck chairs, barber's chairs, sedan chairs, dentist's chairs, basket chairs, reclining chairs, wheel chairs, sling chairs, and beanbag chairs—as well as how to get out of them again. This ability presupposes a repertoire of bodily skills which may well be indefinitely large, since there seems to be an indefinitely large variety of chairs and of successful (graceful, comfortable, secure, poised, etc.) ways to sit in them. Moreover, understanding chairs also includes social skills such as being able to sit appropriately (sedately, demurely, naturally, casually, sloppily, provocatively, etc.) at dinners, interviews, desk jobs, lectures, auditions, concerts (intimate enough for there to be chairs rather than seats), and in waiting rooms, living rooms, bedrooms, courts, libraries, and bars (of the sort sporting chairs, not stools).

In the light of this amazing capacity, Minsky's remarks on chairs in his frame paper seem more like a review of the difficulties than even a hint of how AI could begin to deal with our common sense understanding in this area:

> There are many forms of chairs, for example, and one should choose carefully the chair-description frames that are to be the major capitals of chair-land. These are used for rapid matching and assigning priorities to the various differences. The lower priority *features* of the *cluster* center then serve . . . as properties of the chair *types* . . .   (p. 52/117; emphasis added)

There is no argument why we should expect to find elementary context-free *features* characterizing a chair *type*, nor any suggestion as to what these features might be. They certainly cannot be legs, back, seat, etc., since these are not context-free characteristics defined apart from chairs which then "cluster" in a chair representation, but, rather, legs, back, etc. come in all shapes and variety and can only be recognized as *aspects* of already recognized chairs. Minsky continues:

> Difference pointers could be "functional" as well as geometric. Thus, after rejecting a first try at "chair" one might try the functional idea of "something one can sit on" to explain an unconventional form.   (p. 52/117)

But, as we already saw in our discussion of Winston's concept-learning program, a function so defined is not abstractable from human embodied know-how and cultural practices. A functional description such as "something one can sit on" treated merely as an additional context-free descriptor cannot even distinguish conventional chairs from saddles, thrones, and toilets. Minsky concludes:

> Of course, that analysis would fail to capture toy chairs, or chairs of such ornamental delicacy that their actual use would be unthinkable. These would be better handled by the method

of excuses, in which one would bypass the usual geometrical or functional explanation in favor of responding to *contexts* involving *art* or *play*. (p. 52/ 117; emphasis added)

This is what is required all right, but by what elementary features are *these* contexts to be recognized? There is no reason at all to suppose that one can avoid the difficulty of formally representing our knowledge of chairs by abstractly representing even more holistic, concrete, culturally determined, and loosely organized human practices such as art and play.

Minsky in his frame article claims that: "the frame idea . . . is in the tradition of . . . the 'paradigms' of Kuhn" (p. 3/ 97), so it is appropriate to ask whether a theory of formal representation such as Minsky's, even if it can't account for everyday objects like chairs, can do justice to Thomas Kuhn's analysis of the role of paradigms in the practice of science. Such a comparison might seem more promising than testing the ability of frames to account for our everyday understanding, since science is a theoretical enterprise which deals with context-free data whose lawlike relations can in principle be grasped by any sufficiently powerful "pure-intellect," whether human, Martian, digital, or divine. As Kuhn notes: "In the absence of a paradigm or some candidate for paradigm, all the facts that could possibly pertain to the development of a given science are likely to seem equally relevant" (Kuhn, 1970; p. 15). Minsky interprets as follows:

According to Kuhn's model of scientific evolution 'normal' science proceeds by using established *descriptive schemes*. Major changes result from new 'paradigms', new ways of describing things. . . Whenever our customary viewpoints do not work well, whenever we fail to find effective frame systems in memory, we must construct new ones that bring out the right *features*. (p. 58/ 121; emphasis added)

But what Minsky leaves out is precisely Kuhn's claim that a paradigm or exemplar is *not an abstract explicit descriptive scheme* utilizing formal *features*, but rather a shared *concrete* case, which dispenses with features altogether:

The practice of normal science depends on the ability, acquired from exemplars, to group objects and situations into similarity sets which are primitive in the sense that the grouping is done without an answer to the question, "Similar with respect to what?" (Kuhn, 1970; p. 200)

Thus, although it is the job of scientists to find abstractable, exact, symbolic descriptions, and *the subject matter of science* consists of such formal accounts, the *thinking* of scientists themselves does not seem to be amenable to this sort of analysis. Kuhn explicitly repudiates any formal reconstruction which claims that the scientists must be using symbolic descriptions.

I have in mind a manner of knowing which is misconstrued if reconstructed in terms of rules that are first abstracted from exemplars and thereafter function in their stead. (p. 192)

Indeed, Kuhn sees his book as raising just those questions which Minsky refuses to face:

Why is the *concrete* scientific achievement, as a locus of professional commitment, prior to the various concepts, laws, theories, and points of view that may be *abstracted* from it? In what sense is the shared paradigm a fundamental unit for the student of scientific development, a unit that *cannot* be fully reduced to logically *atomic components* which might function in its stead? (p. 11; emphasis added)

Although research based on frames cannot deal with this question and so cannot account for commonsense or scientific knowledge, the frame idea did bring the problem of how to represent our everyday knowledge into the open in AI. Moreover, it provided a model so vague and suggestive that it could be developed in several different directions. Two alternatives immediately presented themselves: either to use frames as part of a special-purpose micro-world analysis dealing with commonsense knowledge as if everyday activity took place in preanalyzed specific domains, or else to try to use frame structures in "a no-tricks basic study" of the open-ended character of everyday know-how. Of the two most influential current schools in AI, Roger Schank and his students at Yale have tried the first approach. Winograd, Bobrow, and their research group at Stanford and Xerox, the second.

Schank's version of frames are called "scripts," Scripts encode the essential steps involved in stereotypical social activities. Schank uses them to enable a computer to "understand" simple stories. Like the micro-world builders, Schank believes he can start with isolated stereotypical situations described in terms of primitive actions and gradually work up from there to all of human life.

To carry out this project, Schank invented an event description language consisting of eleven primitive acts such as: ATRANS—the transfer of an abstract relationship such as possession, ownership, or control; PTRANS—the transfer of physical location of an object; INGEST—the taking of an object by an animal into the inner workings of that animal, etc. (Schank, 1975a; p. 39); and from these primitives he builds gamelike scenarios which enable his program to fill in gaps and pronoun reference in stories.

Such primitive acts, of course, make sense only when the context is already interpreted in a specific piece of discourse. Their artificiality can easily be seen if we compare one of Schank's context-free primitive acts to real-life actions. Take PTRANS, the transfer of physical location of an object. At first it seems an interpretation-free fact if ever there was one. After all, either an object moves or it doesn't. But in real life things are not so simple; even what counts as physical motion depends on our purposes. If someone is standing still in a moving elevator on a moving ocean liner, is his going from A to B deck a PTRANS? What about when he is just sitting on B deck? Are we all PTRANSing around the sun? Clearly the answer depends on the situation in which the question is asked.

Such primitives can be used, however, to describe fixed situations or scripts once the relevant purposes have already been agreed upon. Schank's definition of a script emphasizes its predetermined, bounded, gamelike character:

We define a script as a *predetermined* causal chain of conceptualizations that describe the *normal sequence of things* in a familiar situation. Thus there is a restaurant script, a birthday-party script, a football game script, a classroom script, and so on. Each script has in it a *minimum number of players and* objects that assume certain roles within the script . . . [E]ach *primitive* action given stands for the most important *element* in a *standard set of actions*. (1975b; p. 131; emphasis added)

His illustration of the restaurant script spells out in terms of primitive actions the rules of the restaurant game:

Script: restaurant
Roles: customer; waitress; chef; cashier
Reason: to get food so as to go down in hunger and up in pleasure
Scene 1 entering
PTRANS—go into restaurant
MBUILD—find table
PTRANS—go to table
MOVE—sit down
Scene 2 ordering
ATRANS—receive menu
ATTEND—look at it
MBUILD—decide on order
MTRANS—tell order to waitress
Scene 3 eating
ATRANS—receive food
INGEST—eat food
Scene 4 exiting
MTRANS—ask for check
ATRANS—give tip to waitress
PTRANS—go to cashier
ATRANS—give money to cashier
PTRANS—go out of restaurant

(1975b; p. 131)

No doubt many of our social activities are stereotyped, and there is nothing in principle misguided in trying to work out primitives and rules for a restaurant game, the way the rules of Monopoly are meant to capture a simplified version of the typical moves in the real estate business. But Schank claims that he can use this approach to understand stories about *actual* restaurant-going—that in effect he can treat the sub-world of restaurant going as if it were an isolated micro-world. To do this, however, he must artificially limit the possibilities: for, as one might suspect, no matter how stereotyped, going to the restaurant is not a self-contained game but a highly variable set of behaviors which open out into the rest of human activity. What "normally" happens when one goes to a restaurant can be preselected and formalized by the programmer as default assignments, but the background has been left out so that a program using such a script cannot be said to understand going to a restaurant at all. This can easily be seen by imagining a situation that deviates from the norm. What if when one tries to order he finds that the item in question is not available, or before paying he finds that the bill is added up wrongly? Of course, Schank would answer that he could build these normal ways restaurant-going breaks down into his script. But there are always *abnormal* ways everyday activities can break down: the juke box might be too noisy, there might be too many flies on the counter, or as in the film *Annie Hall*, in a New York delicatessen one's girl friend might order a pastrami sandwich on white bread with mayonnaise. When we understand going to a restaurant we understand how to cope with even these abnormal possibilities because going to a restaurant is part of our everyday activities of going into buildings, getting things we want, interacting with people, etc.

To deal with this sort of objection Schank has added some general rules for coping with unexpected disruptions. The general idea is that in a story "it is usual for non-standard occurrences to be explicitly mentioned" (Schank and Abelson, 1977; p. 51); so the program can spot the abnormal events and understand the subsequent events as ways of coping with them. But here we can see that dealing with stories allows Schank to bypass the basic problem, since it is the *author's* understanding of the situation which enables him to decide which events are disruptive enough to mention.

This *ad hoc* way of dealing with the abnormal can always be revealed by asking further questions, for the program has not understood a restaurant story the way people in our culture do, until it can answer such simple questions as: When the waitress came to the table, did she wear clothes? Did she walk forward or backward? Did the customer eat his food with his mouth or his ear? If the program answers, "I don't know," we feel that all of its right answers were tricks or lucky guesses and that it has not understood anything of our everyday restaurant

behavior.[3] The point here, and throughout, is not that there are subtle things human beings can do and recognize which are beyond the low-level understanding of present programs, but that in any area there are simple taken-for-granted responses central to human understanding, lacking which a computer program cannot be said to have any understanding at all. Schank's claim, then, that "the paths of a script are the possibilities that are extant in a situation" (1975b; p. 132) is insidiously misleading. Either it means that the script accounts for the possibilities in the restaurant game defined by Schank, in which case it is true but uninteresting; or he is claiming that he can account for the possibilities in an everyday restaurant situation which is impressive but, by Schank's own admission, false.

Real short stories pose a further problem for Schank's approach. In a script what the primitive actions and facts are is determined beforehand, but in a short story *what counts as the relevant facts depends on the story itself.* For example, a story that describes a bus trip contains in its script that the passenger thanks the driver (a Schank example). But the fact that the passenger thanked the driver would not be important in a story in which the passenger simply took the bus as a part of a longer journey, while it might be crucially important if the story concerned a misanthrope who had never thanked anyone before, or a very law-abiding young man who had courageously broken the prohibition against speaking to drivers in order to speak to the attractive woman driving the bus. Overlooking this point, Schank claimed at a recent meeting that his program, which can

3. This is John Searle's way of formulating this important point. In a talk at the University of California at Berkeley (October 19, 1977), Schank agreed with Searle that to understand a visit to a restaurant, the computer needs more than a script; it needs to know everything that people know. He added that as it stands his program cannot distinguish "degrees of weirdness." Indeed, for the program it is equally "weird" for the restaurant to be out of food as it is for the customer to respond by devouring the chef. Thus Schank seems to agree that without some understanding of degree of deviation from the norm, the program does not understand a story even when in that story events follow a completely normal stereotyped script. It follows that although scripts capture a necessary condition of everyday understanding, they do not provide a sufficient condition.

extract death statistics from newspaper accident reports, had answered my challenge that a computer would count as intelligent only if it could summarize a short story.[4] But Schank's newspaper program cannot provide a clue concerning judgments of what to include in a story summary because it works only where relevance and significance have been predetermined, and thereby avoids dealing with the world built up in a story in terms of which judgments of relevance and importance are made.

Nothing could ever call into question Schank's basic assumption that all human practice and know-how is represented in the mind as a system of beliefs constructed from context-free primitive actions and facts, but there are signs of trouble. Schank does admit that an individual's "belief system" cannot be fully elicited from him; although he never doubts that it exists and that it could in principle be represented in his formalism. He is therefore led to the desperate idea of a program which could learn about everything from restaurants to life themes the way people do. In one of his papers he concludes:

> We hope to be able to build a program that can learn, as a child does, how to do what we have described in this paper instead of being spoon-fed the tremendous information necessary.
>
> (1972; pp. 553-554)

In any case, Schank's appeal to learning is at best another evasion. Developmental psychology has shown that children's learning does not consist merely in acquiring more and more information about specific routine situations by adding new primitives and combining old ones as Schank's view would lead one to expect. Rather, learning of specific details takes place on a background of shared practices which seem to be picked up in everyday interactions not as facts and beliefs but as bodily skills for coping with the world. Any learning presupposes this background of implicit know-how which gives significance to details. Since Schank admits that he cannot see how this background can be made explicit so as to be given to a computer, and since the background is presupposed for the kind of script learning Schank has in mind, it seems that his project of using preanalyzed primitives to capture common sense understanding is doomed.

A more plausible, even if in the last analysis perhaps no more promising, approach would be to use the new theoretical power of frames or stereotypes to dispense with the need to preanalyze everyday situations in terms of a set of primitive features whose *relevance is independent of context*. This approach starts with the recognition that in everyday communication "'Meaning' is multi-dimensional, formalizable only in terms of the entire complex of goals and knowledge [of the world] being applied by both the producer and understander" (Winograd, 1976b; p. 262). This knowledge, of course, is assumed to be "A body of specific beliefs (expressed as symbol structures . . .) making up the person's 'model of the world'" (p. 268). Given these assumptions, Terry Winograd and his co-workers are developing a new knowledge representation language (KRL), which they hope will enable programmers to capture these beliefs in symbolic descriptions of multidimensional prototypical objects whose *relevant aspects are a function of their context*.

Prototypes would be structured so that any sort of description from proper names to procedures for recognizing an example could be used to fill in any one of the nodes or slots that are attached to a prototype. This allows representations to be defined in terms of each other, and results in what the authors call "a *wholistic* as opposed to *reductionistic* view of representation" (Bobrow and Winograd, 1977; p. 7). For example, since any description could be part of any other, chairs could be described as having aspects such as seats and backs, and seats and backs in turn could be described in terms of their function in chairs. Furthermore, each prototypical object or situation could be described from many different perspectives. Thus nothing need be defined in terms of its necessary and sufficient features in the way Winston and traditional philosophers have proposed, but rather, following Rosch's research on prototypes, objects would be classified as more or less resembling certain prototypical descriptions.

Winograd illustrates this idea by using the traditional philosophers' favorite example:

4. At the Society for Interdisciplinary Study of the Mind, Symposium for Philosophy and Computer Technology, State University College, New Paltz, N.Y., March 1977.

The word "bachelor" has been used in many discussions of semantics, since (save for obscure meanings involving aquatic mammals and medieval chivalry) it seems to have a formally tractable meaning which can be paraphrased "an adult human male who has never been married". ... In the realistic use of the word, there are many problems which are not as simply stated and formalized. Consider the following exchange:

Host: I'm having a big party next weekend. Do you know any nice bachelors I could invite?

Friend: Yes, I know this fellow X.

The problem is to decide, given the facts below, for which values of X the response would be a reasonable answer in light of the normal meaning of the word "bachelor". A simple test is to ask for which ones the host might fairly complain "You lied. You said X was a bachelor.":

A: Arthur has been living happily with Alice for the last five years. They have a two year old daughter and have never officially married.

B: Bruce was going to be drafted, so he arranged with his friend Barbara to have a justice of the peace marry them so he would be exempt. They have never lived together. He dates a number of women, and plans to have the marriage annulled as soon as he finds someone he wants to marry.

C: Charlie is 17 years old. He lives at home with his parents and is in high school.

D: David is 17 years old. He left home at 13, started a small business, and is now a successful young entrepreneur leading a playboy's life style in his penthouse apartment.

E: Eli and Edgar are homosexual lovers who have been living together for many years.

F: Faisal is allowed by the law of his native Abu Dhabi to have three wives. He currently has two and is interested in meeting another potential fiancee.

G: Father Gregory is the bishop of the Catholic cathedral at Groton upon Thames.

[This] cast of characters could be extended indefinitely, and in each case there are problems in deciding whether the word "bachelor" could appropriately be applied. In normal use, a word does not convey a clearly definable combination of primitive propositions, but evokes an *exemplar* which possesses a number of properties. This exemplar is not a specific individual in the experience of the language user, but is more abstract, representing a conflation of typical properties. A prototypical bachelor can be described as:

1. a person
2. a male
3. an adult
4. not currently officially married
5. not in a marriage-like living situation
6. potentially marriageable
7. leading a bachelor-like life style
8. not having been married previously
9. having an intention, at least temporarily, not to marry
10. ...

Each of the men described above fits some but not all of these characterizations. Except for narrow legalistic contexts, there is no significant sense in which a subset of the characteristics can be singled out as the "central meaning" of the word. In fact, among native English speakers there is little agreement about whether someone who has been previously married can properly be called a "bachelor" and fairly good agreement that it should not apply to someone who is not potentially marriageable (e.g. has taken a vow of celibacy).

Not only is this list [of properties] open-ended, but the individual terms are themselves not definable in terms of primitive notions. In reducing the meaning of 'bachelor' to a formula involving 'adult' or 'potentially marriageable', one is led into describing these in terms of exemplars as well. 'Adult' cannot be defined in terms of years of age for any but technical legal purposes and in fact even in this restricted sense, it is defined differently for different aspects of the law. Phrases such as 'marriage-like living situation' and 'bachelor-like life style' reflect directly in their syntactic form the intention to convey stereotyped exemplars rather than formal definitions.

(Winograd, 1976b; pp. 276-278)

Obviously if KRL succeeds in enabling AI researchers to use such prototypes to write flexible programs, such a language will be a major breakthrough and will avoid the *ad hoc* character of the "solutions" typical of micro-world programs. Indeed, the future of AI depends on some such work as that begun with the development of KRL. But there are problems with this approach. Winograd's analysis has the important consequence that in comparing two prototypes, what counts as a match and thus what counts as the relevant aspects which justify the match will be a result of the program's understanding of the current context.

The result of a matching process is not a simple true/false answer. It can be stated in its most general form as: "Given the set of alternatives which I am currently considering . . . and looking in order at those stored structures which are most accessible in the *current context*, here is the best match, here is the degree to which it seems to hold, and here are the specific detailed places where match was not found. . . ."

The selection of the order in which sub-structures of the description will be compared is a function of their current accessibility, which depends both on the form in which they are stored and the *current context*.

(1976b; p. 281–282; emphasis added)

This raises four increasingly grave difficulties. First, for there to be "a class of cognitive 'matching' processes which operate on the descriptions (symbol structures) available for two entities, looking for correspondences and differences" (p. 280), there must be a finite set of prototypes to be matched. To take Winograd's example:

A single object or event can be described with respect to several prototypes, with further specifications from the perspective of each. The fact that last week *Rusty flew to San Francisco* would be expressed by describing the event as a typical instance of *Travel* with the mode specified as *Airplane*, destination *San Francisco*, etc. It might also be described as a *Visit* with the actor being *Rusty*, the friends a particular group of people, the interaction warm, etc. (Bobrow and Winograd, 1977; p. 8)

But *etc.* covers what might, without predigestion for a specific purpose, be a hopeless proliferation. The same flight might also be a test flight, a check of crew performance, a stopover, a mistake,

a golden opportunity, not to mention a visit to brother, sister, thesis adviser, guru, etc., etc. Before the program can function at all the total set of possible alternatives must be pre-selected by the programmer.

Second, the matching makes sense only *after* the current candidates for comparison have been found. In chess, for example, positions can be compared only after the chess master calls to mind past positions the current board positions might plausibly resemble. And (as in the chess case) the discovery of the relevant candidates which make the matching of aspects possible requires experience and intuitive association.

The only way a KRL-based program (which must use symbolic descriptions) could proceed, in chess or anywhere else, would be to guess some frame on the basis of what was already "understood" by the program, and then see if that frame's features could be matched to some current description. If not, the program would have to backtrack and try another prototype until it found one into whose slots or default terminals the incoming data could be fitted. This seems an altogether implausible and inefficient model of how we perform, and only rarely occurs in our conscious life. Of course, cognitive scientists could answer the above objection by maintaining, in spite of the implausibility, that we try out the various prototypes very quickly and are simply not aware of the frantic shuffling of hypotheses going on in our unconscious. But, in fact, most would still agree with Winograd's (1974) assessment that the frame selection problem remains unsolved:

The problem of choosing the frames to try is another very open area. There is a selection problem, since we cannot take all of our possible frames for different kinds of events and match them against what is going on. (p. 80)

There is, moreover, a third and more basic question which may pose an in-principle problem for any formal holistic account in which the significance of any fact, indeed what counts as a fact, always depends on context. Winograd stresses the critical importance of context:

The results of human reasoning are *context dependent*, the

structure of memory includes not only the long-term storage organization (what do I know?) but also *a current context* (what is in focus at the moment?). We believe that this is an important feature of human thought, not an inconvenient limitation.

(Bobrow and Winograd, 1977; p. 32)

He further notes that "the problem is to find a formal way of talking about .. current attention focus and goals" (1976b; p. 283). Yet he gives no formal account of how a computer program written in KRL could determine the current context. Winograd's work does contain suggestive claims, such as his remark that "the procedural approach formalizes notions like 'current context' .. and 'attention focus' in terms of the processes by which cognitive state changes as a person comprehends or produces utterances" (pp. 287–288). There are also occasional parenthetical references to "current goals, focus of attention, set of words recently heard, etc." (p. 282). But reference to the current context is vague and perhaps even question-begging. If a human being's current goal is, say, to find a chair to sit on, his current focus might be on recognizing whether he is in a living room or a warehouse. He will also have short-range goals like finding the walls, longer-range goals like finding the light switch, middle-range goals like wanting to write or rest; and what counts as satisfying these goals will in turn depend on his ultimate goals and interpretation of himself as, say, a writer, or merely as easily exhausted and deserving comfort. So Winograd's appeal to "current goals and focus" covers too much to be useful in determining what specific situation the program is in.

To be consistent, Winograd would have to treat each type of situation the computer could be in as an object with *its* prototypical description; then in recognizing a specific situation, the situation or context in which *that* situation was encountered would determine which foci, goals, etc. were relevant. But where would such a regress stop? Human beings, of course, don't have this problem. They are, as Heidegger puts it, already in a situation, which they constantly revise. If we look at it genetically, this is no mystery. We can see that human beings are gradually trained into their cultural situation on the basis of their embodied precultural situation, in a way no programmer using KRL is trying to capture. But for this very reason a program in KRL is not always-already-in-a-situation. Even if it represents all human knowledge in its stereotypes, including all possible types of human situations, it represents them from the outside like a Martian or a god. It isn't situated in any one of them, and it may be impossible to program it to behave as if it were.

This leads to my fourth and final question. Is the know-how that enables human beings constantly to sense what specific situation they are in the sort of know-how that can be represented as a kind of knowledge in *any* knowledge representation language no matter how ingenious and complex? It seems that our sense of our situation is determined by our changing moods, by our current concerns and projects, by our long-range self-interpretation and probably also by our sensory-motor skills for coping with objects and people—skills we develop by practice without ever having to represent to ourselves our body as an object, our culture as a set of beliefs, and our propensities as situation—action rules. All these uniquely human capacities provide a "richness" or a "thickness" to our way of being-in-the-world and thus seem to play an essential role in situatedness, which in turn underlies all intelligent behavior.

There is no reason to suppose that moods, mattering, and embodied skills can be captured in any formal web of belief, and except for Kenneth Colby, whose view is not accepted by the rest of the AI community, no current work assumes that they can. Rather, all AI workers and cognitive psychologists are committed, more or less lucidly, to the view that such noncognitive aspects of the mind can simply be ignored. This belief that a significant part of what counts as intelligent behavior can be captured in purely cognitive structures defines cognitive science and is a version of what I call the psychological assumption (Dreyfus, 1979; ch. 4). Winograd makes it explicit:

> AI is the general study of those aspects of cognition which are common to all physical symbol systems, including humans and computers.
>
> (see Schank et al., 1977; p. 1008)[5]

5. He means "physical symbol system" in Newell and Simon's sense; see this volume, Chapter 1.

But this definition merely delimits the field; it in no way shows there is anything to study, let alone guarantees the project's success.

Seen in this light, Winograd's grounds for optimism contradict his own basic assumptions. On the one hand, he sees that a lot of what goes on in human minds cannot be programmed, so he only hopes to program a significant part:

[C]ognitive science . . . does not rest on an assumption that the analysis of mind as a physical symbol system provides a *complete* understanding of human thought. . . . For the paradigm to be of value, it is only necessary that there be *some significant aspects* of thought and language which can be profitably understood through analogy with other symbol systems we know how to construct. (1976b; p. 264)

On the other hand, he sees that human intelligence is "holistic" and that meaning depends on "the entire complex of goals and knowledge." What our discussion suggests is that all aspects of human thought, including nonformal aspects like moods, sensory-motor skills, and long-range self-interpretations, are so interrelated that one cannot substitute an abstractable web of explicit beliefs for the whole cloth of our concrete everyday practices.

What lends plausibility to the cognitivist position is the conviction that such a web of beliefs must finally fold back on itself and be complete, since we can know only a finite number of facts and procedures describable in a finite number of sentences. But since facts are discriminated and language is used only in a context, the argument that the web of belief must in principle be completely formalizable does not show that such a belief system can account for intelligent behavior. This would be true only if the context could also be captured in the web of facts and procedures. But if the context is determined by moods, concerns, and skills, then the fact that our beliefs can in principle be completely represented does not show that representations are sufficient to account for cognition. Indeed, if nonrepresentable capacities play an essential role in situatedness, and the situation is presupposed by all intelligent behavior, then the "aspects of cognition which are common to all physical symbol systems" will not be able to account for any cognitive *performance* at all.

In the end the very idea of a holistic information processing model in which the relevance of the facts depends on the context may involve a contradiction. To recognize any context one must have already selected from the indefinite number of possibly discriminable features the possibly relevant ones, but such a selection can be made only after the context has already been recognized as similar to an already analyzed one. The holist thus faces a vicious circle: relevance presupposes similarity and similarity presupposes relevance. The only way to avoid this loop is to be always-already-in-a-situation without representing it so that the problem of the priority of context and features does not arise, or else to return to the reductionist project of preanalyzing all situations in terms of a fixed set of possibly relevant primitives—a project which has its own practical problems, as our analysis of Schank's work has shown, and, as we shall see in the conclusion, may have its own internal contradiction as well.

Whether this is, indeed, an in-principle obstacle to Winograd's approach only further research will tell. Winograd himself is admirably cautious in his claims:

If the procedural approach is successful, it will eventually be possible to describe the mechanisms at such a level of detail that there will be a verifiable fit with many aspects of detailed human performance . . . but we are nowhere near having explanations which cover language processing as a whole, including meaning. (1976b; p. 297)

If problems do arise because of the necessity in any formalism of isolating beliefs from the rest of human activity, Winograd will no doubt have the courage to analyze and profit from the discovery. In the meantime everyone interested in the philosophical project of cognitive science will be watching to see if Winograd and company can produce a moodless, disembodied, concernless, already adult surrogate for our slowly acquired situated understanding.

Conclusion

Given the fundamental supposition of the information processing approach that all that is relevant to intelligent behavior can be formalized in a structured description, all problems must appear to be merely problems of complexity. Bobrow and Winograd put this final faith very clearly at the end of their description of KRL:

> The system is complex, and will continue to get more so in the near future. . . . [W]e do not expect that it will ever be reduced to a very small set of mechanisms. Human thought, we believe, is the product of the interaction of a fairly large set of inter-dependent processes. Any representation language which is to be used in modeling thought or achieving "intelligent" performance will have to have an extensive and varied repertoire of mechanisms.
>
> (Bobrow and Winograd, 1977; p. 43)

Underlying this mechanistic assumption is an even deeper assumption which has gradually become clear during the past ten years of research. During this period AI researchers have consistently run up against the problem of representing everyday context. Work during the first five years (1967–1972) demonstrated the futility of trying to evade the importance of everyday context by creating artificial gamelike contexts preanalyzed in terms of a list of fixed-relevance features. More recent work has thus been forced to deal directly with the background of commonsense know-how which guides our changing sense of what counts as the relevant facts. Faced with this necessity researchers have implicitly tried to treat the broadest context or background as an object with its own set of preselected descriptive features. This assumption, that the background can be treated as just another object to be represented in the same sort of structured description in which everyday objects are represented, is essential to our whole philosophical tradition. Following Heidegger, who is the first to have identified and criticized this assumption, I will call it the metaphysical assumption.

The obvious question to ask in conclusion is: Is there any evidence besides the persistent difficulties and history of unfulfilled promises in AI for believing that the metaphysical assumption is unjustified? It may be that no argument can be given against it, since facts put forth to show that the background of practices is unrepresentable are in that very act shown to be the sort of facts which *can* be represented. Still, I will attempt to lay out the argument which underlies my antiformalist, and, therefore, antimechanist convictions.

My thesis, which owes a lot to Wittgenstein (1953), is that whenever human behavior is analyzed in terms of rules, these rules must always contain a *ceteris paribus* condition, i.e., they apply "everything else being equal," and what "everything else" and "equal" mean in any specific situation can never be fully spelled out without a regress. Moreover, this *ceteris paribus* condition is not merely an annoyance which shows that the analysis is not yet complete and might be what Husserl called an "infinite task." Rather the *ceteris paribus* condition points to a background of practices which are the condition of the possibility of all rulelike activity. In explaining our actions we must always sooner or later fall back on our everyday practices and simply say "this is what we do" or "that's what it is to be a human being." Thus in the last analysis all intelligibility and all intelligent behavior must be traced back to our sense of what we *are*, which is, according to this argument, necessarily, on pain of regress, something we can never explicitly *know*.

Still, to this dilemma the AI researchers might plausibly respond: "Whatever the background of shared interests, feelings, and practices necessary for understanding specific situations, that knowledge *must* somehow be represented in the human beings who have that understanding. And how else could such knowledge be represented but in some explicit data structure?" Indeed, the kind of computer programming accepted by all workers in AI would require such a data structure, and so would philosophers who hold that all knowledge must be explicitly represented in our minds, but there are two alternatives which would avoid the contradictions inherent in the information-processing model by avoiding the idea that everything we know must be in the form of some explicit symbolic representation.

One response, shared by existential phenomenologists such as Merleau-Ponty and ordinary language philosophers such as Wittgenstein, is to say that such "knowledge" of human interests and practices need not be represented at all. Just as it seems plausible that I can learn to swim by practicing until I develop the necessary patterns of responses, without representing my body and muscular movements in some data structure, so too what I "know" about the cultural practices which enables me to recognize and act in specific situations has been gradually acquired through training in which no one ever did or could, again on pain of regress, make explicit what was being learned.

Another possible account would allow a place for representations, at least in special cases where I have to stop and reflect, but such a position would stress that these are usually nonformal representations, more like images, by means of which I explore what I *am*, not what I *know*. We thus appeal to *concrete* representations (images or memories) based on our own experience without having to make explicit the strict rules and their spelled out *ceteris paribus* conditions required by *abstract* symbolic representations.

The idea that feelings, memories, and images *must* be the conscious tip of an unconscious framelike data structure runs up against both *prima facie* evidence and the problem of explicating the *ceteris paribus* conditions. Moreover, the formalist assumption is not supported by one shred of scientific evidence from neurophysiology or psychology, or from the past successes of AI, whose repeated failures required appeal to the metaphysical assumption in the first place.

AI's current difficulties, moreover, become intelligible in the light of this alternative view. The proposed formal representation of the background of practices in symbolic descriptions, whether in terms of situation-free primitives or more sophisticated data structures whose building blocks can be descriptions of situations, would, indeed, look more and more complex and intractable if minds were not physical symbol systems. If belief structures are the result of abstraction from the concrete practical context rather than the true building blocks of our world, it is no wonder the formalist finds himself stuck with the view that they are endlessly explicable. On my view the organization of world knowledge provides the largest stumbling block to AI precisely because the programmer is forced to treat the world as an object, and our know-how as knowledge.

Looking back over the past ten years of AI research we might say that the basic point which has emerged is that *since intelligence must be situated it cannot be separated from the rest of human life.* The persistent denial of this seemingly obvious point cannot, however, be laid at the door of AI. It starts with Plato's separation of the intellect or rational soul from the body with

its skills, emotions, and appetites. Aristotle continued this unlikely dichotomy when he separated the theoretical from the practical, and defined man as a rational animal—as if one could separate man's rationality from his animal needs and desires. If one thinks of the importance of the sensory-motor skills in the development of our ability to recognize and cope with objects, or of the role of needs and desires in structuring all social situations, or finally of the whole cultural background of human self-interpretation involved in our simply knowing how to pick out and use chairs, the idea that we can simply ignore this know-how while formalizing our intellectual understanding as a complex system of facts and rules is highly implausible.

Great artists have always sensed the truth, stubbornly denied by both philosophers and technologists, that the basis of human intelligence cannot be isolated and explicitly understood. In *Moby-Dick* Melville writes of the tattooed savage, Queequeg, that he had "written out on his body a complete theory of the heavens and the earth, and a mystical treatise on the art of attaining truth; so that Queequeg in his own proper person was a riddle to unfold, a wondrous work in one volume; but whose mysteries not even he himself could read" (1952; p. 477). Yeats puts it even more succinctly: "I have found what I wanted—to put it in a phrase, I say, 'Man can embody the truth, but he cannot know it'".

Acknowledgement: I am grateful to John Haugeland for editorial suggestions on transforming this from a book introduction into an independent article.

References

For references noted in the preceding article, but not shown below, see the bibliography at the end of this volume.

Dreyfus, H. L. (1972; 2nd ed., 1979). *What Computers Can't Do*, New York: Harper and Row.

Goldmeier, E. (1972). *Similarity in Visually Perceived Forms*, New York: International Universities Press.

Husserl, E. (1960). *Cartesian Meditations*, The Hague: Martinus Nijhoff.

Kuhn, T. (1970). *The Structure of Scientific Revolutions*, 2nd, ed., Chicago: University of Chicago Press.

Melville, H. (1952). *Moby Dick*, New York: Modern Library College Editions.

Minsky, M. (1974). A Framework for Representing Knowledge. Cambridge, Mass.: MIT AI Lab Memo 306.

Minsky, M., and Papert, S. (1970). Draft of a proposal to ARPA for research on artificial intelligence at MIT, 1970–71.

———— (1973). *Artificial Intelligence*, Condon Lectures, Oregon State System of Higher Education, Eugene, Oregon.

Rosch, E. (1977). "Human Categorization." In *Advances in Cross-Cultural Psychology*, Vol. 1, N. Warren, ed. London: Academic Press, 1977.

Schank, R. C. (1975a). "The Primitive Acts of Conceptual Dependency." In *TINLAP-75*.

———— (1975b). "Using Knowledge to Understand." In *TINLAP-75*.

Schank, R. C., et al. (1977). "Panel on Natural Language Processing." In *IJCAI-77*, pp 1007–1013.

Simon, H. A. (1977). "Artificial Intelligence Systems That Understand." In *IJCAI-77*, pp 1059–1073.

Weizenbaum, J. (1965). "ELIZA—A Computer Program for the Study of Natural Language Communication between Man and Machine," *Communications of the Association for Computing Machinery*, 9 (1965), 36–45.

Winograd, S. (1976). "Computing the Discrete Fourier Transform," *Proceedings of the National Academy of Science*, 73 (1976), 1005–1006.

Winograd, T. (1973). "A Procedural Model of Language Understanding." In *Computer Models of Thought and Language*, R. Schank and K. Colby, eds. San Francisco: W. H. Freeman, 1973.

———— (1974). Five Lectures on Artificial Intelligence. Stanford, Cal.: Stanford AI Lab Memo 246.

———— (1976a). "Artificial Intelligence and Language Comprehension." In *Artificial Intelligence and Language Comprehension*, Washington, D.C.: National Institute of Education.

———— (1976b). "Towards a Procedural Understanding of Semantics," *Revue Internationale de Philosophie*, Nos. 117–118 (1976), 260–303, Foundation Universitaire de Belgique.

Winston, P. H., and the Staff of the MIT AI Laboratory (May, 1976). Proposal to ARPA, Cambridge, Mass.: MIT AI Lab Memo 366.

Wittgenstein, L. (1953). *Philosophical Investigations*, Oxford: Basil Blackwell.

II / Associational Representations

6 / M. Ross Quillian
Word Concepts: A Theory and Simulation of Some Basic Semantic Capabilities

M. Ross Quillian's pioneering work on semantic memory models in the mid to late 1960's has greatly influenced almost all subsequent work in Knowledge Representation. Quillian is generally acknowledged to have originated the idea of a *semantic network*, in which dictionary-like definitions are encoded with nodes interconnected with associative links. This relatively difficult-to-find paper is a nice summary of Quillian's 1966 Ph.D. dissertation, in which he produced a simulation program intended to be able to "compare and contrast the meanings of arbitrary pairs of English words." Although the work described in this paper is somewhat simplistic compared to what has since appeared (*e.g.*, compare Quillian's networks to the complexity of KRL [Bobrow and Winograd, Chapter 13]), and was designed primarily as a psychological model of human language behavior, Quillian's memory model was responsible for a large number of concepts that have become fundamental to work in the field, including the type/token distinction and spreading activation search for inference. This work and its influence on representation history is treated in [Brachman, Chapter 10].

Appeared in *Behavioral Science* **12**, 1967, 410–430.

COMPUTERS IN BEHAVIORAL SCIENCE

WORD CONCEPTS: A THEORY AND SIMULATION OF SOME BASIC SEMANTIC CAPABILITIES[1]

by M. Ross Quillian

Bolt, Beranek, and Newman, Cambridge, Massachusetts

In order to discover design principles for a large memory that can enable it to serve as the base of knowledge underlying human-like language behavior, experiments with a model memory are being performed. This model is built up within a computer by "recoding" a body of information from an ordinary dictionary into a complex network of elements and associations interconnecting them. Then, the ability of a program to use the resulting model memory effectively for simulating human performance provides a test of its design. One simulation program, now running, is given the model memory and is required to compare and contrast the meanings of arbitrary pairs of English words. For each pair, the program locates any relevant semantic information within the model memory, draws inferences on the basis of this, and thereby discovers various relationships between the meanings of the two words. Finally, it creates English text to express its conclusions. The design principles embodied in the memory model, together with some of the methods used by the program, constitute a theory of how human memory for semantic and other conceptual material may be formatted, organized, and used.

A Memory Model

THE purpose of the research reported here is both to develop a theory of the structure of human long-term memory, and to embody this theory in a computer model such that the machine can utilize it to perform complex, memory-dependent tasks. The concepts of primary concern for storage in the model memory are those generally called the "meaning" of commonplace words, such as "machine," "family," "chair," and so on, it being assumed that such word meaning concepts are held in memory in a manner not fundamentally different from long-term concepts in general. The model employs much of the machinery traditionally used in psychology for representing concepts—conjunctive, disjunctive, and relational sets of attributes, criteriality, and so on, (see for example, Bruner, Goodnow, and Austin, 1956). It also utilizes other representational devices, some of which bear a close resemblance to those used by "transformational" linguistics for representing the "deep structure" of sentences (see Chomsky, 1965). However, the model's general organization is quite distinct from either of these representational systems.

Although the model is proposed as part of a theory of human memory organization, it is not at present intended to handle all the kinds of information that people presumably store in their heads. It is designed to hold only denotative, factual information, and not a person's plans for doing things (see the "schemata" of Piaget, 1950), a person's feelings about words (Osgood, Suci, and

[1] Research contributing to this report was done partly at Carnegie Institute of Technology, partly at the System Development Corporation, and was supported in part by NIH Grant, MH 07722.

A much more extended treatment of the same and related research is given in Quillian (1966). The work is being continued at Bolt, Beranek, and Newman Inc., Cambridge, Mass. This manuscript, at one stage or another, has benefited from critical readings by George W. Baylor, Daryl J. Bem, Walter R. Reitman, and Robert F. Simmons. To all of these the author expresses grateful thanks, as well as to Mrs. Jean Long and Miss Barbara Zimmerman, who have encoded much of the data. Along with almost anyone who attempts to test a psychological model by computer simulation, the author is also deeply indebted to Herbert A. Simon and Allen Newell.

Tannenbaum, 1957) nor his knowledge of the conditional probabilities of word sequences. The theory also deals only with the structure and use of well-developed memory, having little to say as yet about the *acquisition* of stored information. At present the problem of how humans acquire long-term concepts is simply finessed by taking the information to be encoded into the memory model from two already developed sources. These are, first, an ordinary English dictionary and, second, the fund of common knowledge that anyone who encodes this dictionary information into the model must have, that is, his own semantic memory.

The model memory consists, basically, of a mass of nodes, interconnected by different kinds of associative links. Each node may for the moment be thought of as named by an English word, but by far the most important feature of the model is that a node may be related to the meaning of its name word in one of two different ways. The first is directly; that is, its associative links may lead directly into a configuration of other nodes that represents the meaning of its name word. A node that does this is called a type node. In contrast, the second kind of node in the memory refers indirectly to a word concept, by having one special kind of associative link that points to that concept's type node. Such a node is referred to as a token node, or simply token, although this usage implies more than is generally meant by a "token," since, within the model memory, a token is a permanent node. For any one word meaning there can be exactly one and only one type node in the memory, but there will in general be many token nodes scattered throughout the memory, each with a pointer to the single unique type node for the concept. To see the reason for postulating both type and token nodes within the memory, it will be useful to reflect briefly on the way words are defined in an ordinary dictionary.

For defining one word, the dictionary builder always utilizes tokens of other words. However, it is not sufficient for the reader of such a dictionary to consider the meaning of the defined word to be simply an unordered aggregation of the other word concepts used in its definition. The particular configuration of these word concepts is crucial; it both modifies the meanings of the individual word concepts that make up its parts, and, with them, creates a new gestalt which represents the meaning of the word being defined. In our memory model, the configurational meaning of a concept is captured by building up, for each definition, what is best thought of as one plane of token nodes. Each and every token node lies in such a plane, and has both its special associative link pointing "out of the plane" to its type node and other associative links pointing on within the plane to other token nodes comprising the configuration. In short, token nodes make it possible for a word's meaning both to be built up from other word meanings as ingredients, and at the same time to modify and recombine these ingredients into a new configuration. Although the detailed structure of a plane will not be described until later in this paper it will be useful for understanding the model's overall organization to look at Figure 1 at this point.

Figure 1a illustrates the planes of three word concepts, corresponding to three meanings of "plant." The three circled words "plant," "plant 2," and "plant 3," placed at the heads (upper left-hand corners) of the three planes, represent type nodes; every other word shown in the figure's planes represents a token node. The nonterminated arrows from tokens indicate that each has its special pointer leading out of its plane to its type definition, that is, to a type node standing at the head of its own plane somewhere else in the memory. Each of these planes, in turn, is itself entirely made up of tokens, except for the type word which heads it. Figure 1b illustrates one of these planes. Therefore, the overall structure of the complete memory forms an enormous aggregation of planes, each consisting entirely of token nodes except for its "head" node which is always a type node.

Now, what is the full content of a word concept in such a memory? Let us define a full word concept, as distinguished from its plane or "immediate definition," so as to include all the type and token nodes one can get to by starting at the initial type node, or "patriarch," and moving first within its immediate definition plane to all the token

Key to Figure 1

Associative Link (type-to-token, and token-to-token, used within a plane)

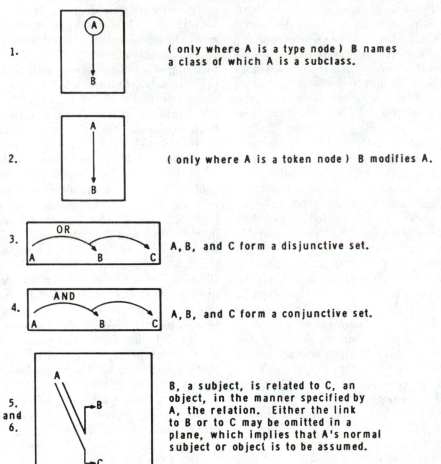

1. (only where A is a type node) B names a class of which A is a subclass.

2. (only where A is a token node) B modifies A.

3. A, B, and C form a disjunctive set.

4. A, B, and C form a conjunctive set.

5. and 6. B, a subject, is related to C, an object, in the manner specified by A, the relation. Either the link to B or to C may be omitted in a plane, which implies that A's normal subject or object is to be assumed.

Associative Link (token-to-type, used only between planes)

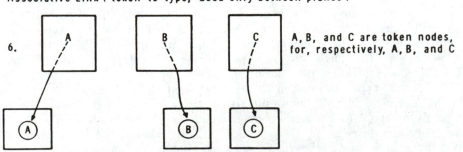

6. A, B, and C are token nodes, for, respectively, A, B, and C

Fig. 1. Sample Planes from the Memory.

nodes found there, then on "through" to the type nodes named by each of these nodes, then on to all the token nodes in each of their immediate definition planes, and so on, until every token and type node that can be reached by this process has been traced through at least once.

Thus one may think of a full concept

analogically as consisting of all the information one would have if he looked up what will be called the "patriarch" word in a dictionary, then looked up every word in each of its definitions, then looked up every word found in each of these, and so on, continually branching outward until every word he could reach by this process had been looked up once. However, since a word meaning includes structure as well as ingredients, one must think of the person doing the looking up as also keeping account of all the relationships in which each word he encountered had been placed by all earlier definitions.

To summarize, *a word's full concept is defined in the model memory to be all the nodes that can be reached by an exhaustive tracing process, originating at its initial, partriarchical type node, together with the total sum of relationships among these nodes specified by within-plane, token-to-token links.*

We now assert that such a memory organization is useful in performing semantic tasks, and constitutes a reasonable description of the general organization of human memory for such material.

To take the latter point immediately, suppose, for example, that a subject were asked to state everything he knows about the concept "machine." Each statement he makes in answer is recorded, and when he decides he is finished, he is asked to elaborate further on each thing he has said. As he does so, these statements in turn are recorded, and upon his "completion" he is asked if he cannot elaborate further on each of these. In this way the subject can clearly be kept talking for several days, if not months, producing a voluminous body of information. This information will start off with the more "compelling" facts about machines, such as that they are usually man-made, involve moving parts, and so on, and will proceed "down" to less and less inclusive facts, such as that typewriters are machines, and then eventually will get to much more remote information about machines, such as the fact that a typewriter has a stop which prevents its carriage from flying off each time it is returned. We are suggesting that this information can all be usefully viewed as part of the subject's concept of "machine." The order in which such a concept tends to be brought forth, from general, inclusive facts to obscure or less and less closely related ones, suggests that the information comprising a word concept in the subject's head is differentially accessible, forming something that may be viewed as a hierarchy beneath the patriarch word. Our memory model's general organization is designed to make a full concept exactly this sort of hierarchically ordered, extensive body of information.

Clearly, a subject could produce hierarchical outputs similar to his output for "machine" for any one of innumerable other word concepts: "war," "family," "government," and so on, so that the overall amount of information he could pull out of his memory in this way seems almost unlimited. The sheer amount of information involved in such concepts argues strongly that both the human subject's memory, and our model of it, contain as little redundancy as possible. In this regard we note that the information a subject can generate as the meaning of "machine" will include all the information he can generate for "typewriter," among other things, and there is no need to restate the information constituting his concept of "typewriter" each time it occurs as part of the concept named by some other word such as "machine," "office," and so on. In short, a word concept like "machine" seems to be made up, in large part, of a particular ordered arrangement of other word concepts such as "typewriter," "drill press," and so forth.

Again, a large memory structured as we have outlined above capitalizes on this redundancy, by running the pointer from every token node for a word meaning to the same type node. Note that in such a memory any given type node will have many token nodes, located in various other planes, all pointing to it, and its full concept may well contain token nodes pointing back to the type node that heads one of these planes. In other words, there is no restriction to prevent reentries or loops within a full concept, so that all routines that search through or process concepts in the memory must take account of these possibilities. Viewed most abstractly, the model memory forms

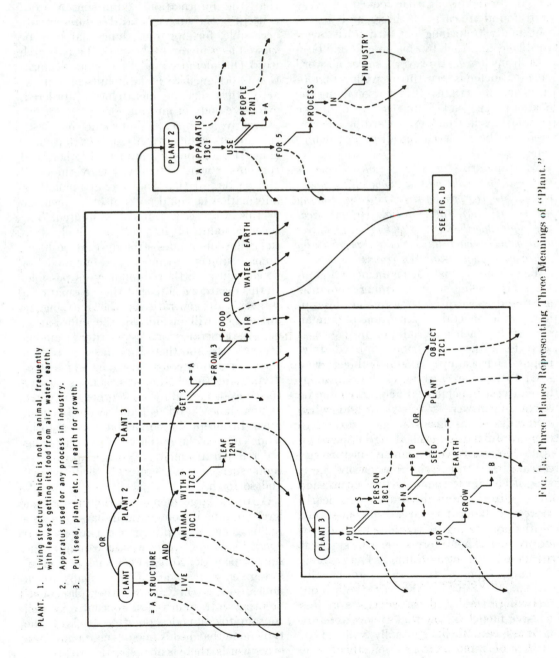

PLANT. 1. Living structure which is not an animal, frequently with leaves, getting its food from air, water, earth.
2. Apparatus used for any process in industry.
3. Put (seed, plant, etc.) in earth for growth.

FIG. 1a. Three Planes Representing Three Meanings of "Plant."

FOOD: 1. That which living being has to take in to keep it living and for growth.
Things forming meals, especially other than drink

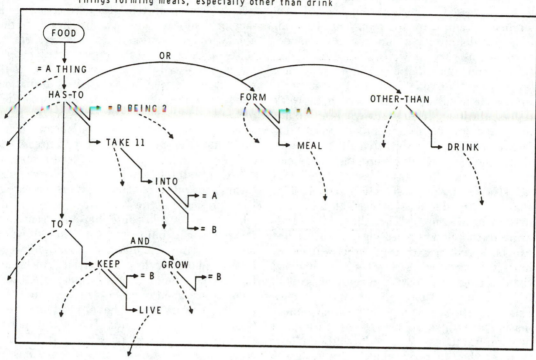

FIG. 1b. The Plane Representing "Food."

simply a large, very complex network of nodes and one-way associations between them. Most importantly, in such a model of semantic memory there is no predetermined hierarchy of superclasses and subclasses; every word is the patriarch of its own separate hierarchy when some search process starts with it. Similarly, every word lies at various places down, within the hierarchies of a great many other word concepts. Moreover, there are no word concepts as such that are "primitive." Everything is simply defined in terms of some ordered configuration of other things in the memory.

Two Constraints on the Memory

Having established the general structure of the model memory as consisting of "planes" each made up of one type and a number of token nodes, it is further necessary to determine the format of the nodes themselves, and the specific varieties of associative links between nodes to be used within a plane.

As to the nature of the nodes themselves, we assume that the relevant units of human conceptual stores are not in fact words, nor are they sentences, nor are they visual pictures; instead they are closer to what we ordinarily call "properties." This assumption is now common in work on concepts (see, for example, Hunt, 1962, or Kelly, 1955), since properties provide a more elemental and, hence, more flexible medium than visual pictures or words, and since either a mental picture or a language concept may be thought of as some bundle of properties (attribute values) and labeled associations among them.

Thus, the nodes of the memory model actually correspond more to properties than to words, although, as will be shown below, this actually need be little different from considering them to be words.

A much more important constraint arises from our assumption that, in order to continue to parallel the properties of human semantic memory, the model must be able to link nodes together into configurations that are at least as varied and rich as the ideas expressed in natural language. Hence, simply attempting to represent natural-language definitions accurately in the model becomes a very powerful constraint dictating the model's structural properties. Over a considerable period of attempting to encode English text into such network representations, it has always been found necessary to have available several different *kinds* of associative links, rather than the simple undifferentiated associations assumed in most classical psychological studies of word association. At the same time, the model must represent all information in a form that is sufficiently standardized to allow processing by rules that can be specified explicitly, or it will be no more manageable as a theory of memory than is English itself. (See Simmons, 1963, for the most thorough attempt to use English itself as a computer's store of information on which to base the performance of complex tasks.) The representation now used in the memory model therefore lies at a level somewhere between the freedom of English itself and the standardization of, say, symbolic logic. In the memory model, complex configurations of differentiated associations must be built up to adequately represent the meaning inherent in dictionary definitions. These are the structures we have called planes. (It will be seen below that the kinds of links utilized in the model to represent configurational meaning correspond roughly to the "syntactic" interrelations between words of text: verb-to-subject, pronoun-to-referent, word-to-modifiers, phrase-to-other-phrase via some conjunction, and so on.)

While the attempt to get the meaning of English definitions accurately represented as planes of nodes within the memory model constitutes one major constraint on its structure, a second is provided by the attempt to write programs that can do something interesting by using this memory. To some degree these two constraints on the model balance one another: the first urges elaboration and complexity to represent the meaning of definitions accurately, while the second urges that the model be

as simple and standardized as possible to make processing feasible.

In selecting a task to perform with a memory model, one thinks first of the ability to understand unfamiliar sentences. It seems reasonable to suppose that people must necessarily understand new sentences by retrieving stored information about the meaning of isolated words and phrases, and then combining and perhaps altering these retrieved word meanings to build up the meanings of sentences. Accordingly, one should be able to take a model of stored semantic knowledge and formulate rules of combination (such as the "projection rules" of Katz and Postal, 1964) that would describe how sentence meanings get built up from stored word meanings. A good many reasonable speculations about such combination rules can in fact be made. (For example, see Cliff, 1959. For a good over-view of these and the empirical work they have produced, see Osgood, 1963.) The bulk of an earlier paper (Quillian, 1963) and of Katz and Postal's recent work consists of such speculations.

It further seems likely that if one could manage to get a small set of basic word meanings adequately encoded and stored in a computer memory, and a workable set of combination rules formalized as a computer program, he could then bootstrap his store of encoded word meanings by having the computer itself "understand" sentences that he had written to constitute the definitions of other single words (Quillian, 1962b). That is, whenever a new, as yet uncoded, word could be defined by a sentence using only words whose meanings had already been encoded, then the representation of this sentence's meaning—which the machine could build by using its previous knowledge together with its combination rules—would be the appropriate representation to add to its memory as the meaning of the new word. Unfortunately, two years of work on this problem led to the conclusion that the task is much too difficult to execute at our present stage of knowledge. The processing that goes on in a person's head when he "understands" a sentence is very large indeed, practically all of it being done without his conscious knowledge.

As one example, consider the sentence, "After the strike, the president sent him away." One understands this sentence easily, probably without realizing that he has had to look into his stored knowledge of "president" to resolve a multiple meaning of the word "strike." (Consider, for example, the same sentence with the word "umpire" substituted for "president.") Just what subconscious processing is involved in unearthing and using the fact that presidents more typically have something to do with labor strikes than with strikes of the baseball variety is by no means obvious, and a good part of this paper is devoted to stating one way that this can be accomplished, given that it has been decided that "president" is the correct word to attend to. Since sentence understanding involves a great number of such, at present, poorly understood processes, the two language functions that the present program performs are considerably humbler than sentence understanding.

The first of these functions is to compare and contrast two word concepts: given any two words whose meanings are encoded in the model memory, the program must find the more compelling conceptual similarities and contrasts between their meanings. Since, in the usual case, each of the two words to be compared will have several possible meanings, the program is also to specify, for each semantic similarity or contrast it finds, just which meaning of each word is involved. This is one step toward the resolution of semantic ambiguity in text. The second major task of the program is to express all the similarities and contrasts found between the two compared words in terms of understandable, though not necessarily grammatically perfect, sentences.

Although the above tasks are only a part of what apparently is involved in sentence understanding, their performance in a fashion comparable to human performance still calls for a basic degree of semantic horse-sense in which, heretofore, computers have been conspicuously lacking and which, apparently, must be based on an extensive and expressively rich store of conceptual knowledge. Thus, being able to get a computer to perform these tasks indicates to some degree the plausibility of the semantic memory model used.

In briefest form, the program that is presently running is used as follows:[2]

1. The experimenter selects a group of words whose definitions are to provide the total store of information in the memory model during a given series of tests.

2. He looks up each of these words in some ordinary dictionary.

3. He encodes each of the definitions given for each word into a specified "semantic" format, and loads them into the machine with a program that combines them into a single network of token and type nodes and associative links, the machine's model of a human memory.

4. The experimenter is then free to select arbitrarily any pair of words in the store and to ask the program to compare and contrast the meanings of those two words (requiring that its answers be expressed in sentences).

5. He may give some fluent speaker the same pair of words, asking him also to compare and contrast them.

6. He can compare the sentences the program generates to those the human has produced or, more simply, he can just judge for himself whether or not the machine's output is one that might reasonably have been produced by a subject.

If the above procedure reveals any changes the experimenter would like to see in the program's performance, he must then revise either some part of the program,

[2] The major effort at representation of a human-like memory structure in a computer so far has probably been the construction of list processors (see, for example, Newell, 1963). These provide counterparts to "associative links" and to "labeled associative links," plus processes for manipulating data stored in such form. By writing the present model and program in one of these, namely, IPL, it has been possible to begin upon the substantial foundation of design and development existing in that language, and to use "associations" and "labeled associations" freely as building blocks for the model memory.

or some part of the memory structure or content, or all of these, and further test new examples to see if the program now operates in a manner closer to what he desires. Repetitions of this kind of test-correct-retest cycle constitute the essence of the research method; however, it is important to realize that for the purposes of developing a theory of memory, the result of this development process should *not* be thought of as the computer outputs the program will now produce, but rather as what now may or may not have become clear about the characteristics of workable concept-like memories. The more general of these characteristics have been outlined above; unfortunately, the rest amount to more or less fine details of the theoretical memory and of how its provisions should be used to build up configurations corresponding to particular meanings of English text. Therefore, the next section explains these technicalities in some detail; after that, we return to a more general level to describe the actual program's performance.

Details of the Model Memory

As stated above, the relational complexity built up in an English definition is always represented in the memory by a configuration of token nodes linked together to form one "plane." Each token in a plane is linked to its type node (which lies out of the plane) by a kind of association that we show in Figure 1 as a dotted line, while it is related to other token nodes (in the plane) by one or more of the six distinct kinds of associative link listed in the key to Figure 1. In encoding dictionary definitions, these intraplane links are used, respectively, as follows:[3]

1. Dictionary definitions require the use of the subclass-to-superclass pointer whenever they define a word by stating the name of some larger class of which it is a subclass. For example, in the dictionary definition of "plant" shown in Figure 1a, the word's third meaning is said to be a subclass of the class of "putting."

2. Any word or phrase used adjectively or adverbially dictates use of the modification pointer.

3. The multiple meanings of a word, and any phrase such as "air, earth, or water," require the formation of a disjunctive set.

4. Any phrase like "old, red house" or "old house with a red porch" requires that the modifiers of "house" be formed into a conjunctive set.

5-6. Together these two links form the open-ended category, by means of which all the remaining kinds of relationships are encoded. This is necessary because in natural language text almost anything can be considered as a relation, so that there is no way to specify in advance what relationships are to be needed (see Raphael, 1964). This means that a memory model must provide a way to take any two tokens and relate them by any third token, which by virtue of this use becomes a relationship.

It will be recalled that we feel that the nodes of conceptual memory are most usefully considered to represent properties rather than words as such. Representing a

---

[3] Stated this way, it appears that the semantic model amounts in structure to a kind of parsing system, and that encoding dictionary definitions into it is in part, at least, similar to parsing these definitions.

This is true, and in fact what appears on one plane of the memory model has many points of correspondence with what Chomsky (1965) calls a "deep structure." In particular, the ternary relationships formed by our subject-object links are a lot like what used to be called the structure of "kernel" sentences. However, our use of terms such as "subject," "object" and "modifier" does not always correspond to that of linguistics; and, also, a plane encodes the meaning of a number of sentences, whereas a deep structure is explicitly limited to the representation of what can be represented in a single sentence (Ibid., p. 138ff). Also notice that the correspondence, in as far as it exists, is between one of our planes and one of Chomsky's deep structures, not between a plane and a generative grammar. A generative grammar is an attempt to state explicitly when and how structural information can be related to sentence, whereas the job of a person encoding dictionary definitions into our memory model is simply to get a representation of their structures, that is, to go ahead and use his language-processing abilities, rather than to describe these. Hence our coder does transformations, rather than describing them.

property requires the name of something that is variable, an attribute, plus some value or range of values of that attribute. This feature is achieved in the memory model by the fact that every token is considered to have appended to it a specification of its appropriate amount or intensity in the particular concept being defined. Omitting this specification from a token, which is generally what is done, means that no restriction is placed on the total range of variation in amount of intensity open to the attribute. On the other hand, whenever such specification does appear overtly with a token node, it consists principally of numerical values, stating how the node's total possible range of amount of intensity is restricted. These values allow encoding restrictions to a fineness of nine gradations, that is, they permit nine degrees of "absolute discrimination" to be represented (see Miller, 1956). The exact use and rationale for this kind of specification "tag" has been described elsewhere (Quillian, 1962b, 1963), along with that of the two other tags (representing the "number" and the "criteriality" of a token; see Bruner et al., 1956) that are available in the model. Here it will only be noted that in encoding dictionary definitions all grammatical inflections, along with all words such as "a," "six," "much," "very," "probably," "not," "perhaps," and others of similar meaning vanish, that is do not become nodes themselves but instead dictate that various range-restricting tags be appended to the token nodes of certain other words. Removing all inflections during encoding permits all nodes in the memory model to represent canonical forms of words, which is of importance both in reducing the model's overall size, and in locating conceptual similarities within it (see the following section).

Certain other words besides those mentioned above are also dropped during the encoding process, such as "and," "or," "is," "which," "there," and "that," these being interpreted either directly as relationships that are basic structural aspects of the model or else as directions to the coder about how he is to form the plane structure —as specifications for how the configurations of tokens on a plane are to be structured. Punctuation similarly shows up only in the associative structure of the model.

All pronouns, as well as all words used to refer again to something mentioned previously in the definition, are replaced in the model by explicit references to the earlier nodes. (In Figure 1 such referencing is being done by =A and =B, where some higher token node in the plane has been designated temporarily to be A or B by giving it a prefix of =A or =B. A more recent version of the loading program also allows referring to any token node in any plane, by a sort of "indirect addressing" feature.) This ability to, in essence, reuse tokens repeatedly in a plane, perhaps modifying them slightly each time, is extremely important in making the model correspond to human-like memory. In the course of coding a great many words into the current and earlier network representations, I have come to believe that the greatest difference between dictionary entries and the corresponding semantic concepts that people have in their heads is that, while dictionary makers try hard to specify all the distinctions between separate meanings of a word, they make only a very haphazard effort to indicate what these various meanings have in common conceptually. Although they may not be aware of it, there is a very good reason for this seeming oversight: the best the dictionary maker has available for showing common elements of meaning is an outline-like format, in which meanings with something in common are brought together under the same heading. However, as anyone who has ever reorganized a paper several times will realize, an outline organization is only adequate for one hierarchical grouping, while in fact the common elements existing between various meanings of a word call for a complex cross-classification. That is, the common elements within and between various meanings of a word are many, and any one outline designed to get some of these together under common headings must at the same time necessarily separate other common elements, equally valid from some other point of view. By making the present memory network a general graph, rather than a tree (the network equivalent of an outline), and by setting up tokens as distinct nodes, it becomes possible to loop as many points as necessary back into any single node, and hence in effect to show any and every common element within and between the meanings of a word. The =A notation causes the network-building program to create such a link.

In all this, it is clear that not only dictionary definitions but also much of the everyday knowledge of the person doing the coding are being tapped and represented in the memory model being built up. For instance, the reader will already have noticed that a numeral is suffixed to the end of some words (a "1" is to be assumed whenever no such numeral appears). This is simply because it is convenient to have each sense of a word named distinctly within the memory, in order to be able to use these in building other configurations. This means that a person building such configurations for input to the model must always decide which possible sense is intended for every token, and use the appropriate suffix.

In attempting to encode dictionary definitions it was found that the memory must provide a mechanism for stating that certain nodes in the immediate definition plane of a type node are variable parameters. A value for one of these parameters will be provided only when the word in whose concept the parameter symbol appears is used in text. Other words within that surrounding text will then form certain parts of the current word's concept; the parameter symbols tell how. To accomplish this, parameter symbols are of three kinds, corresponding to certain ways that other words in text may be related to the word to which the parameter symbols belong. S is the parameter symbol whose value is to be any word related to the present word as its subject; D is the parameter symbol whose value is to be any word related to the present word as its direct object; and M is the parameter symbol whose value is to be any word that the present word directly modifies.

Therefore, to include a parameter symbol in a word's definition plane is to state where within that concept related subjects, objects, and modificands are to be placed, if one or more of these is provided by the text in which the present word is used. For example, when the verb "to comb" is defined by the phrase, "to put a comb through (hair), to get in order," this definition is saying that, when used in text, the verb "to comb" is likely to have an object, which is then to be integrated into its meaning in a certain place, namely, as the object of the node "through." In coding the above definition of "to comb," the object parameter symbol, D, would be used as a sort of "slot" to hold a place for this object until "comb" is actually used in text. It is important not to confuse the sense in which D refers to some object of "comb" and the sense in which there are object links within a plane. D always refers to an object of the word in whose defining plane it appears, while its placement in that plane—indicated by the kind of link from some other token node to it—is another matter. For example, notice in Figure 1a, in the plane for "plant 3," the symbol D (which happens also to have been labeled by = B). This D symbol has been placed as the subject of "in 9," but it is still a D, because it refers to any direct object of the verb "to plant." The symbol D specifies that any such object of "plant" is to be integrated into the meaning of "plant 3" at the place where the D is placed.

A dictionary definition, in addition to stating where within a concept particular sorts of parameter value information are to be "placed," may offer one or more clue words about what such information is likely to be. Thus, in the definition of "to comb" quoted above we are told that its direct object is likely to be "hair."

Clue words play several roles in the memory model, one of which corresponds approximately to the role that transformational linguists ascribe to "selectional restrictions." In other words, the material comprising a full word concept in the memory model can be viewed as consisting of two sorts of information. On the one hand, there is information about the content of the concept itself; on the other there is information about what that concept is likely to combine with when the word is used in text. This latter information is represented by the clue words associated with its parameter symbols. It is significant that this same distinction has been identified in verbal association studies, the associations subjects give to words being divided into paradigmatic (content information) and syntagmatic (parameter clue information) (see, for example, Deese, 1962). Ervin (1961) has shown that the number of content associations, relative to syntagmatic associations, given by young children steadily increases with age.

In the versions of the memory model used in the programs to be described in this paper, clue words have been sought and coded only reluctantly, both they and the parameter symbols having initially been included only because the sort of information comprising them was embarrassingly present in some dictionary definitions. However, it turns out that parameter symbols of some kind play a very crucial role in any such memory, because they make it possible to recognize that two different ways of stating the same thing are in fact synonymous. (See Quillian, 1966.)

As a final point, we note that the model's range readings on tags, together with its ability to form disjunctive sets of attributes, provide it with a ready facility for representing information having a great deal of vagueness. This is essential. It is the very vagueness of the meaning of most language terms that makes them useful—indeed, speech as we know it would be completely impossible if, for instance, one had to specify exactly which machines he made reference to every time he said "machine," and similarly, for every other term whose meaning contains some ambiguity.

To summarize, the memory model, together with the process by which dictionary information is encoded into it, are such that what begins as the English definition of a word seems better viewed after encoding as a complexly structured bundle of attribute values—a full concept, as defined above—whose total content typically extends to an enormous size and complexity throughout the memory. Over all, the memory is a complex network of attribute-value nodes and labeled associations between them. These associations create both within-plane and between-plane ties, with several links emanating from the typical token node, and many links coming into almost every type node.

Performance of the Search Program

It will be recalled that the present program is designed to compare and contrast the meaning of any two word-concepts in the memory store, and then to generate English text to express each of its findings. Notice that this is not the same task as merely using the two words in sentences, a vastly simpler job, for which one need not even consider the semantic concepts associated with the words (Yngve, 1960).

The actual processing system is made up of three separate programs. The first of these transforms input data (definitions which have been encoded as described in the last section) into IPL form and interlaces these to form the total memory model. This program will not be considered further here. The second program compares and contrasts the two given word concepts. It puts out anything found, but in a form expressed in the model memory's own internal language of nodes and links. The third program takes these findings one at a time, and for each generates English text sufficient to express its meaning. Thus, this third program states (in a sort of "me Tarzan, you Jane" style of English) each similarity or contrast of meaning that the second program has found between the two given words.

It is in the operation of the second program, the comparing and contrasting of two concepts, that the interlocking, token-type structure of the overall memory begins to pay off. For, in order to do this job, it is no longer necessary in such a memory to line up some representation of each of the two concepts side by side and try to compare them. Instead, the entire investigation is simply a matter of searching for points in the memory at which the two full concepts intersect (recall how a full concept was defined in the first section above). To see how this is accomplished, recall that the entire memory is a network of nodes and connecting links. Beginning with the two nodes that the program is given to compare (the two patriarch words), this program works alternately on one full word concept and then the other, moving out node by node along the various tokens and types within each. While it will be convenient to visualize this as creating two slowly expanding spheres of activated nodes around each patriarch, actually there is no geometric significance to the expansion of a concept; the nodes in one concept may be located anywhere in the memory model.

The program simulates the gradual activation of each concept outward through the vast proliferation of associations originating from each patriarch, by moving out along these links, tagging each node encountered with a special two-part tag, the "activation tag." Part of this tag always names the patriarch from which the search began, that is, the name of the concept within which the current node has been reached. Now, the program detects any intersection of meaning between the two concepts simply by asking, every time a node is reached, whether or not it already contains an activation tag naming the other patriarch, that is, showing that this node has previously been reached in the tracing out of the other concept. If there is no such tag, the program next checks to see if there is already an activation tag naming the current patriarch, that is, indicating that this node has been reached previously in tracing out this same concept. If so, the program must take account of this, to inhibit retracing out from the node again and hence repeating its effort, perhaps getting into a loop. Only if neither such tag is found is the node tagged, and further search leading to the nodes it points to considered legitimate.

The second part of each activation tag is the name of the "immediate parent" of the current node,—the node at which the associative link leading directly to it originated. Thus, the "activated" areas of the memory are turned from a one-way network into a two-way network, and, whenever a tag from the opposite patriarch is found, these "immediate parent" parts of activation tags permit the program to trace back "up" from the intersection node to the two patriarchs. This produces two paths, except when the intersection node is one of the

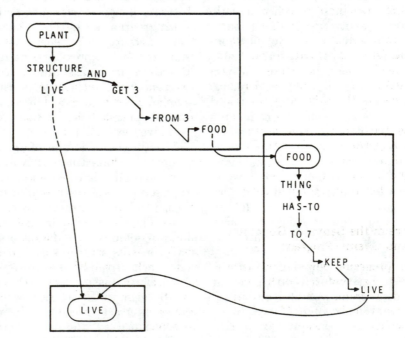

FIG. 2a. Two Paths Direct from Plant to Live.

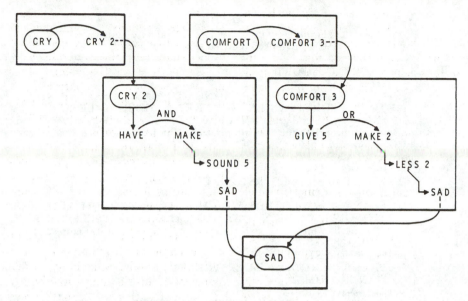

FIG. 2b. A Path from "Cry" and a Path from "Comfort" Which Reach the Same (that is, an intersection) Node.

patriarchs, in which case only a single path is needed, leading from one patriarch directly to the other. Examples of such paths and pairs of paths occur in Figures 2a and 2b, respectively. The paths from a patriarch to an intersection node produced by the second program should not be confused with the "activation" it makes from each patriarch. While this activation is equivalent to an expanding "sphere," a path is only one particular "line" from the center of the sphere to some point within it, one at which it intersects the other full concept's "sphere."

Expanding the two concepts alternately is extremely important; in effect this makes both concepts into searchers for each other, and gives both the maximal number of targets to look for at any given stage of the search.

Performance of the Sentence Generator and Overall Program

The third program, which generates a piece of text to express each path given it by the second program, produces output of the sort illustrated in Table 1. (In this table the paths which the third program has been given to work on are omitted, although the paths for examples 1 and 2 are those of Figure 2.)

The most important point about the sentence producer is that there would seem to be considerable justification for considering it, when taken in conjunction with the first two programs, as an inference maker rather than just a retriever of information. From a relatively small amount of input data, the overall program will indeed derive a very large number of implicit assertions (see calculations below), and make each such assertion explicit in the form of English text. As an example of its most interesting type of "inferential" behavior to date, the reader's attention is directed to the output shown in Table 1 as example 2B. The path that this output expresses is the longer of those shown in Figure 2a. As can be seen from a study of Figure 2a, this kind of performance is made possible by the fact that the memory model closely interconnects related information which has been fed in from a great many different definitions, so that, in order to answer some particular question, the search program can trace out a "plane-hopping" path. While a path lying completely within one plane (except for its

TABLE 1

EXAMPLE OF OUTPUT FROM THE CURRENT PROGRAM

(Paths have been omitted, but see Figure 2)

Example 1. Compare: CRY, COMFORT
    A. Intersect: SAD
      (1) CRY2 IS AMONG OTHER THINGS TO MAKE A SAD SOUND.[4]
      (2) TO COMFORT3 CAN BE TO MAKE2 SOMETHING LESS2 SAD.
        (Note that the program has selected particular meanings of "cry" and "comfort" as appropriate for this intersection. The path on which this output is based is shown in Figure 2b.)

Example 2. Compare: PLANT, LIVE
    A. 1st Intersect: LIVE
      (1) PLANT IS A LIVE STRUCTURE.
    B. 2nd Intersect: LIVE
      (1) PLANT IS STRUCTURE WHICH GET3 FOOD FROM AIR. THIS FOOD IS THING WHICH BEING2 HAS-TO TAKE INTO ITSELF TO7 KEEP LIVE.
        (The paths which these two replies express are shown in Figure 2a.)

Example 3. Compare: PLANT, MAN
    A. 1st Intersect: ANIMAL
      (1) PLANT IS NOT A ANIMAL STRUCTURE.
      (2) MAN IS ANIMAL.
    B. 2nd Intersect: PERSON
      (1) TO PLANT3 IS FOR A PERSON SOMEONE TO PUT SOMETHING INTO EARTH.
      (2) MAN3 IS PERSON.
        (Here the program is treating "person" as an adjective modifier of "someone.")

Example 4. Compare: PLANT, INDUSTRY
    A. 1st Intersect: INDUSTRY
      (1) PLANT2 IS APPARATUS WHICH PERSON USE FOR5 PROCESS IN INDUSTRY.

Example 5. Compare: EARTH, LIVE
    A. 1st Intersect: ANIMAL
      (1) EARTH IS PLANET OF7 ANIMAL.
      (2) TO LIVE IS TO HAVE EXISTENCE AS7 ANIMAL.

Example 6. Compare: FRIEND, COMFORT
    A. 1st Intersect: PERSON
      (1) FRIEND IS PERSON.
      (2) COMFORT CAN BE WORD TO4 PERSON.

Example 7. Compare: FIRE, BURN
    A. 1st Intersect: BURN
      (1) FIRE IS CONDITION WHICH BURN.
    B. 2nd Intersect: FIRE
      (1) TO BURN2 CAN BE TO DESTROY2 SOMETHING BY4 FIRE.
    C. 3rd Intersect: BURN
      (1) FIRE IS A FLAME CONDITION. THIS FLAME CAN BE A GAS TONGUE4. THIS GAS IS GAS WHICH BURN.
        (The sentence producer starts a new sentence whenever it needs to say something more about something it has used adjectively.)

---

[4] "AMONG OTHER THINGS" and "CAN BE" are canned phrases which the program inserts when the next thing it is going to mention is one out of a set of things recorded in its memory. At one point, the program was programmed to insert "AMONG OTHER THINGS" whenever it was about to assert one fact out of such a set. We expected this to make its output have a proper, scientifically cautious ring. However, where it had been saying, (rather clodishly, we felt) "TO CRY IS TO MAKE A SAD SOUND," it now said: "TO CRY, AMONG OTHER THINGS, IS, AMONG OTHER THINGS, TO MAKE, AMONG OTHER THINGS, A, AMONG OTHER THINGS, SAD SOUND." (!) In short, it turns out that if the program is really made to hedge whenever it knows more than it is going to say, one sits around the console all day waiting for it to get around to saying anything. This may not be such a bad simulation of certain individuals, but wasn't what we had had in mind. Thus, the program is now severely restricted as to just when it can hedge. Science marches on.

TABLE 1—*Continued*

Example 8.   Compare: BUSINESS, COMFORT
    A. 1st Intersect: PERSON
       (1) BUSINESS5 IS ACT3 WHICH PERSON DO.
       (2) COMFORT2 IS CONDITION3 WHICH PERSON HAVE NEED4.
         (The code contains information indicating that "person" should be plural here,
           but the sentence producer does not yet make use of this information.)
    B. 2nd Intersect: PERSON
       (1) BUSINESS5 IS ACT3 WHICH PERSON DO.
       (2) COMFORT CAN BE WORD TO4 PERSON.
Example 9.   Compare: MAN, BUSINESS
    A. 1st Intersect: PERSON
       (1) MAN3 IS PERSON.
       (2) BUSINESS CAN BE ACTIVITY WHICH PERSON MUST DO WORK2.
         (Something wrong here. I believe a miscoding in the input data.)
    B. 2nd Intersect: GROUP
       (1) MAN2 IS MAN AS9 GROUP.
       (2) BUSINESS2 IS QUESTION3 FOR ATTENTION OF GROUP.
Example 10. Compare: MAN, LIVE
    A. 1st Intersect: ANIMAL
       (1) MAN IS ANIMAL.
       (2) TO LIVE IS TO HAVE EXISTENCE AS7 ANIMAL.
    B. 2nd Intersect: LIVE
       (1) MAN IS A LIVE BEING2.

terminal points) amounts only to a representation of some piece of the information put into the memory, a "plane-hopping" path represents an idea that was implied by, but by no means directly expressed in, the data that was input. By analogy, suppose we fed a machine "A is greater than B," and "B is greater than C." If then, in answer to the question "what is A greater than?" the machine responded "B," we would not want to call this an inference, but only a "recall." However, if it went on to say, "A is also greater than C," then we would say that it had made a simple inference. The kind of path that we have been calling "plane-hopping" is exactly the representation of such an inference, since it connects information fed in in one definition with that fed in in another. But the fact that our planes are not simple propositions but rather sizeable configurations, every node of which provides the possibility of branching off to another plane, means that the number of "inferential" paths becomes very large as paths of any appreciable length are considered. Moreover, the possibility that a path may contain fragments from several planes, would seem to indicate clearly that the inferences need not be at all simple, although we do not as yet have actual computer output with which to demonstrate this very conclusively.

Assuming a "complete" semantic memory —one in which every word used in any definition also has a definition encoded—a concept fans out very rapidly from its patriarch. It appears that in such a full model memory the average node would branch to at least three other nodes, considering both its ties to tokens and to its type, if it is itself a token. This means that the average number of paths of, say, up to ten nodes in length emanating from any type of node would be over 88,000, each of which would require at least one unique sentence to express. This is to be compared to 2,046 paths emanating from such a type node if no token-to-type links are available. Another way to look at the potential of a memory store such as the theory specifies is to compute what the present programs could generate if one could get, say, definitions of 850 words encoded and stored in a model memory. There would then be 360,000 word pairs to ask it about. Since at a conservative estimate a memory model this size would provide ten nontrivial semantic connections, and hence sentences or sentence sets, between the average word pair, the present programs would have the capability to generate well over three-and-one-half million short batches of text to express this total conceptual knowledge, ignoring all that information present only in longer paths. Definitions of 850 words comprise considerably more information than one could model in the core of today's computers, but calculations such as these seem relevant in evaluating the potential of the model as a general theory of long-term conceptual memory.

While a path represents an idea, it is up to the sentence-producing program to get that idea expressed in English. Thus this program must check a path for restriction tags and other features which make it necessary to insert words such as "not" or "among other things" into the sentence generated to express its meaning.

In attempting to express the meaning of a path, this program also deletes, rearranges, and adds words to those given in the path. It works not only with nodes mentioned in the path itself but sometimes looks *around* these nodes in the memory model to retrieve additional information and to check on things it considers saying.

In expressing a complex path such as that of Figure 2a, this text-producing program realizes when the capability of its sentence grammar is being exceeded and starts a new sentence. (See for example, 7.c.1 of Table 1.) Unfortunately, it does this rather often, and a more powerful grammar would clearly be one which, instead of the two sentences shown in Table 1 as example 3.A.1 and 3.A.2, would produce the single sentence: "A plant is not an animal but a man is." Some of the minor improvements of this sentence over the two which the program now produces would not be difficult to program, but the unification of the two paths into one is a bit more complicated. Clearly, this involves something very close to what Chomsky calls transformations.

In summary, although we have not described the operation of the sentence producer in detail, it should be clear that it has little in common with other sentence generation programs, and, in fact, its whole philosophy is contradictory to a good part of the spirit of modern linguistics, inasmuch as this attempts to treat syntactic facts in isolation from semantic ones. Thus other sentence generation programs pro-

duce sentences that, in syntax, are grammatical, but which are in meaning either completely random (Yngve, 1960), or random permutations of the "dependency" constraints imposed by an input text (Klein and Simmons, 1963). The program is also designed in complete contradiction to the subordinate place for semantic information that the formulation of Katz and Postal (1964) would seem to imply for a performance model.[5] As a theory, the program implies first that a person has something to say, expressed somehow in his own conceptual terms (which is what a "path" is to the program), and that all his decisions about the syntactic form that a generated sentence is to take are then made in the service of this intention. The sentence producer works entirely in this fashion, figuring out grammatical properties of sentences only as these are needed to solve the problem of expressing a path given to it by the search program.

Thus far, the programs have only been tested on very small model memories, built from no more than 50 or 60 definitions (about 5,000 IPL cells), and on only a few such memories (see Table 2). A small total memory means that most branches of the proliferating search of a concept are always getting cut short by reaching a type node for which no definition has yet been encoded. One of the most surprising findings from running the program has been that even with this relative paucity of overall information, the program almost always succeeds in finding some intersections of meaning. Actually, Table 1 lists only a selected sample of the program's output for each compared pair of words; there are usually five or six pairs of sentences generated for each problem pair given to it, although most of these are only trivial variations of a couple of basic sentences such as those we have selected for Table 1. The larger the model memory, the greater

[5] While on the one hand the transformationalists explicitly deny that their work is a model of performance, at the same time they often seem willing to draw psychological conclusions from their models. (See, for example, Katz and Postal, 1964, pp. 1–2; Chomsky, 1965, pp. 139–141).

TABLE 2

WORDS WITH DEFINITIONS ENCODED FOR USE IN MODEL MEMORIES[6]

instrument	cause	live
insurance	attack	level
invent	argue	lift
interest	business	letter
iron	burn	learn
ice	build	leather
idea	bread	land
friend	behave	kiss
develop	cry	know
event	country	laugh
earth	desire	light
exist	sex	language
drink	plant	law
fire	family	lead
flame	meal	jelly
experience	animal	journey
fact	food	jump
comfort	man	judge
cloth		

NOTE: Space limitations have so far required that definitions of no more than twenty of these words be used to constitute a model memory during a given series of word comparisons. Since this paper was written, almost all of the 850 words of basic English have been encoded, but not yet run in the program.

the number of search branches that remain active, so that the search program becomes able to unearth a great many more semantic connections at a relatively shallow depth beneath any two patriarchs. Ultimately this can only improve the program's performance, although it may also require that more concern be given to directing searches than is so far the case. At present, but for one exception, a search just "progressively proliferates" along all possible branches from the two patriarchs (until

---

[6] It is hoped that the program can be tested on somewhat larger memory models in the not too distant future, although it would also be interesting to attempt to improve the dictionary entries from which data are taken. So far definitions given in Ogden (1942) have been used. This was selected in order to make sure that definitions loop back into one another as often as possible, and because its definitions are short. It now seems there is no worry at all about having enough intersections, and several other dictionaries have been investigated as possible sources of input data. *Funk and Wagnalls* (1959), although not consistent on this point, makes much the most thorough effort to arrange the various meanings of a word into some sort of outline, hence indicating which meanings have something in common.

it has covered a given number of nodes, such as 400).

The one exception to this blind, "breadth first," search occurs whenever two concepts are found to intersect on a word used prepositionally, such as "for 5" in the concept "plant 2." Instead of treating this as a substantive semantic intersection, the search program merely concentrates an immediate burst of search activity out from the two tokens of the preposition. The reasoning here is simply that, while a match on such a word is not in itself sufficient to be treated as a significant conceptual similarity, it is a good bet to examine immediately the subjects, objects, and modifiers of such prepositions, rather than continue the usual search schedule which normally would not get to these nodes for some time. Unfortunately there is not yet enough evidence available to assess the value of this search heuristic, since its effectiveness, if any, will not show up until the memory model is relatively large.

Discussion

In the current programs, all activation tags are erased after comparison of two-word concepts is completed, but in order to illustrate the generality of the memory model their relevance to two other phenomena will be mentioned. The first of these is the state a person gets into by reading part of a text; namely he gets "in context." In this state he will, for example, be able to decide which of several possible meanings of a new word that he encounters in the text fits the context. To explain this, let us suppose that the person's memory is indeed organized and utilized as is our model memory. Suppose, for example, that the text is about baseball. As the subject has been reading, he has been firing activation "spheres" from the patriarch nodes corresponding to many of the words in the text. The activation tags applied in this manner are not immediately erased, so that they accumulate throughout much of the memory, on nodes such as "batter," "ball," "pitcher," and so on. Now, upon encountering, say, the word "strike," the reader fires one activation sphere from the type node heading its baseball meaning, another from the one heading its labor union meaning. Clearly, intersections will pile up very quickly beneath one of these meanings, and much more slowly beneath the other. The ambiguity is resolved almost instantaneously; if the reader is a human, he would say that one meaning is "in context," the other not. (An experiment demonstrating the use of the model for such automatic meaning resolution is described in Quillian, 1966.)

The considerable effort that has been invested in building automatic parsing programs (see Bobrow, 1963), all assumes that natural language can be dealt with without using any such semantic contextual information, or at least without using it until after all parsing has been accomplished by purely syntactic information. This may be so, but it seems to me more likely that to attack the problem in this way is to pose the wrong, and probably an insoluble, problem. I suspect that successful mechanical language processors must stay much closer to the way humans process language, in which syntax and semantics are surely interwoven at every stage.

Katz and Foder (1963) and Katz and Postal (1964) propose to describe the "structure of a semantic theory," with almost exactly the same machinery Chomsky has used to advantage for describing syntactic structure. However, aside from also assuming that stored semantic information is always to be placed beneath the syntactic information associated with a word, Katz and his coworkers seem to offer us little more about how this information is to be represented than to assert that it can always be arranged into a single tree structure of "markers" and "distinguishers." We have already described (above) why such a single outline type of organization will not suffice to capture the information which people know and use in dealing with words.

As a theory of semantics our memory model has greater flexibility and expressiveness, and correspondingly greater complexity and cumbersomeness to process, than that of formats generally considered, such as set theoretic or symbolic logic frameworks. However, various attempts to translate English into such terminologies have as yet not met with any general success, and in some cases it is clear that there are formidable difficulties in the way (Darlington, 1964). Others have proposed isolating a set of semantic "elements," either by linguistic methods (Lamb, 1964) or psychologically, by analyzing word meanings into Titchnerian sensory units (Quillian, 1961, 1962a). Even if some such reduction is possible, however, its relation to the way people really encode semantic information, and even its usefulness to any sort of empirical semantic investigation, seem unclear. The problem of semantics, it seems to me, lies more in how to represent and arrange information than in how to discover more of it, a problem to which dictionary and encyclopedia compilers have applied themselves with some diligence.

In any case, the model of memory proposed here is both purely semantic and very elaborate, and one may speculate about what changes will be required if it is to serve as a basis for the explanation and simulation of other functions that people perform with the aid of long-term memory. Programming such new tasks is crucial to establish the generality of the memory model. Doing so would further test the current features of the model, and get at some of its properties that are hardly tested at all by the current programs, such as the parameters S, D, and M. As the model is tested by programming such tasks, changes in its details are inevitable. The pertinent question is whether or not a model essentially similar to this one is likely to prove useful for supporting the simulation of other memory-dependent functions, and, of course, for guiding other research on memory functions.

In summary, four key assumptions about word concepts stored in memory have been made: that the information in them is large, differentially accessible, exceedingly rich in expressive power, and yet composed of units that represent properties. The realization of these features in an explicit model has required a complicated network of associative links, plus a number of other devices. The resulting model has been tested for its ability to allow the meaning of English text to be encoded accurately and, once a model memory has been built up in this way, for its ability to support simulation of two behaviors: the recognition of semantic similarities and contrasts, and the expression of these in sentences. It has been asserted that the memory model and the programs processing it constitute a theory of the general structure and corresponding uses of human memory, although we are aware that a behavioral theory couched in computer terms is sufficiently unfamiliar to make some psychologists feel uneasy.

For those who, like this author, are disposed to consider this model a psychological theory, a great many new problems open up. In addition to exploring the sufficiency of the memory model for other types of behavior, there is the task of discovering how variations in such a structure affect performance, and subsequently of correlating specific features of the model with individual variations of subjects' behavior. Some computer-framed theories have, at least for specific problem-solving behaviors, reached this level of development (see, for example, Newell, Shaw, and Simon, 1962; Simon and Feigenbaum, 1964; or Simon and Kotovsky, 1963). At that point the "information-processing" methodology merges with the main stream of psychological research. For those whose interest is primarily in artificial intelligence per se, let me conclude by suggesting that further advances in reproducing human performance with a computer critically depend on giving such programs memories which can effectively provide them with a "knowledge of the world."

References

Banerji, R. B. A language for the description of concepts. Unpublished dittoed paper, Systems Research Center, Case Institute of Technology, 1964.

Bartlett, F. C. *Remembering, a study in experimental and social psychology*. Cambridge: Cambridge University Press, 1932.

Bobrow, D. G. Syntactic analysis of language by computer—a survey. *Proc. Fall Joint Computer Conference*, 1963, 24, 365–387.

Bruner, J. S., Goodnow, J. J., & Austin, C. A. *A study of thinking*. New York: John Wiley, 1956.

Chomsky, N. *Aspects of the theory of syntax*. Cambridge: M.I.T. Press, 1965.

Cliff, N. Adverbs as multipliers. *Psychol. Rev.*, 1959, 66, 27–44.

Darlington, J. Translating ordinary language into symbolic logic. Memorandum MAC-M-149, Project MAC, Massachusetts Institute of Technology, 1964.

Deese, J. On the structure of associative meaning. *Psychol. Rev.*, 1962, 69, 161–175.

Ervin, S. M. Changes with age in the verbal determinants of word association. *Amer. J. Psychol.*, 1961, 74, 361–372.

Funk and Wagnalls new "standard" dictionary of the English language. New York: Funk and Wagnalls, 1959.

Hunt, E. B. *Concept learning: An information processing problem*. New York: John Wiley, 1962.

Katz, J. J., & Foder, J. A. The structure of a semantic theory. *Language*, 1963, 39, 170–210.

Katz, J. J., & Postal, P. M. An integrated theory of linguistic descriptions. Cambridge: The M.I.T. Press, 1964.

Kelly, G. *The psychology of personal constructs: Volume I*. New York: W. W. Norton, 1955.

Klein, S. Automatic paraphrasing in essay format. SP-1602/001/00, System Development Corporation, Santa Monica, 1964.

Klein, S., & Simmons, R. F. Syntactic dependence and the computer generation of coherent discourse. *Mechanical Translation*, 1963, 7, 50–61.

Kuno, S., & Oettinger, A. Lecture notes for course in language data processing. Harvard Summer School, Harvard University, 1964.

Lamb, S. The sememic approach to structural semantics. In K. A. Romney & R. D'Andrede (Eds.) Transcultural studies in cognition. *Amer. Anthropol.*, 1964, 66, Part 2, 1–74.

Miller, G. A. The magical number seven, plus or minus two: Some limits on our capacity for processing information. *Psychol. Rev.*, 1956, 63, 81–96.

Newell, A. (Ed.) IPL-V programmer's reference manual. Memorandum RM-3739-RC, RAND Corporation, Santa Monica, California, 1963.

Newell, A., Shaw, J. C., & Simon, H. A. The processes of creative thinking. In H. E. Gruber, G. Terrell, & M. Wertheimer (Eds.) *Contemporary approaches to creative thinking*. New York: Atherton Press, 1962, Pp. 63–119.

Ogden, C. K. *The general basic English dictionary*. New York: W. W. Norton, 1942.

Osgood, C. E. On understanding and creating sentences. *Amer. Psychol.*, 1963, 18, 735–751.

Osgood, C. E., Suci, G. J., & Tannenbaum, P. H. *The measurement of meaning.* Urbana: University of Illinois Press, 1957.

Piaget, J. *The psychology of intelligence.* (Tr. M. Cook, & D. E. Berlyne) London: Routledge & Kegan Paul, 1950.

Quillian, R. A design for an understanding machine. Paper presented at a colloquium: Semantic problems in natural language. King's College, Cambridge University, September, 1961.

Quillian, R. A revised design for an understanding machine. *Mechanical Translation*, 1962, 7, 17-29. (a)

Quillian, R. A semantic coding technique for mechanical English paraphrasing. Internal Memorandum of the Mechanical Translation Group, Research Laboratory of Electronics, Massachusetts Institute of Technology, August 1962. (b)

Quillian, R. A notation for representing conceptual information: An application to semantics and mechanical English paraphrasing. SP-1395, System Development Corporation, Santa Monica, 1963.

Quillian, R. *Semantic Memory.* Unpublished doctoral dissertation, Carnegie Institute of Technology, 1966. Also Report AFCRL-66-189, Bolt, Beranek, and Newman, Cambridge, Massachusetts, October, 1966.

Quillian, R., Wortman, P., & Baylor, G. W. The programmable Piaget: Behavior from the standpoint of a radical computerist. Unpublished dittoed paper, Carnegie Institute of Technology, 1965.

Raphael, B. A computer program which "understands." *Proc. AFIPS*, Fall Joint Computer Conference, 1964, 577–589.

Reitman, W. R. *Cognition and thought: An information processing approach.* New York: John Wiley, 1966

Simmons, R. F. Synthetic language behavior. *Data Processing Management*, 1963, 5 (12), 11–18.

Simon, H. A., & Feigenbaum, E. A. An information-processing theory of some effects of similarity, familiarization, and meaningfulness in verbal learning. *J. verb. Learn. verb. Behav.*, 1964, 3, 385–397.

Simon, H. A., & Kotovsky, J. Human acquisition of concepts for sequential patterns. *Psychol. Rev.*, 1963, 70, 534–546.

Yngve, V. H. A model and an hypothesis for language structure. *Proc. Amer. Phil. Soc.*, 1960, 104, 444–466.

(Manuscript received November 28, 1966)

❧

Pictorial form is the possibility that things are related to one another in the same way as the elements of the picture.

LUDWIG WITTGENSTEIN

7 / Roger C. Schank and Charles J. Rieger III
Inference and the Computer Understanding of Natural Language

This paper concerns itself with the crucial problem of specifying language-free inferences in a natural language understanding context. While Schank's earlier work on Conceptual Dependency—a representation based on structures built out of a small number of primitive actions—was clearly influential, it gains some of its most important force from the work Rieger did on determining how inferences can be generated from it. As detailed in this article, inferences can be spontaneously generated from a Conceptual Dependency structure by considering only easily specified patterns of primitive relations, thus avoiding any language-dependency. Schank and Rieger illustrate this point with a set of twelve kinds of inferences that help add to a parsed sentence information that is likely to be correct. They also spend considerable time discussing the implementation of their ideas in the MARGIE program. Among the more interesting aspects of this work is the length to which they go to position themselves opposite work on formal deduction (*à la* [Moore, Chapter 18], say). The work has perhaps more of a formal flavor to it than the authors would like to admit, but their protest against deduction is well taken and is similar to others' (*e.g.*, see [Minsky, Chapter 12] and [Garvey *et al.*, Chapter 27]). On the other hand, their problem probably has more to do with the need for default reasoning [Reiter, Chapter 23] and the inexactness of normal thought processes than with the narrow view of deduction taken here.

Appeared in *Artificial Intelligence* **5**(4), 1974, 373–412.

Inference and the Computer Understanding of Natural Language[1]

Roger C. Schank[2] and Charles J. Rieger III[3]

Computer Science Department, Stanford University, Stanford, Calif. 94305, U.S.A.

Recommended by E. Sandewall

ABSTRACT

The notion of computer understanding of natural language is examined relative to inference mechanisms designed to function in a language-free deep conceptual base (Conceptual Dependency). The conceptual analysis of a natural language sentence into this conceptual base, and the nature of the memory which stores and operates upon these conceptual structures are described from both theoretical and practical standpoints. The various types of inferences which can be made during and after the conceptual analysis of a sentence are defined, and a functioning program which performs these inference tasks is described. Actual computer output is included.

CONTENTS

1. Introduction

The question of what belongs to the domain of parsing and what is part of the domain of inference inevitably comes up when attempting to put together a system in order to do natural language understanding. This paper is intended to explain the difference within the context of Conceptual Dependency

[1] This research was supported by the Advanced Research Projects Agency of the Department of Defense under Contract SD-183.

The views and conclusions contained in this document are those of the authors and should not be interpreted as necessarily representing the official policies, either expressed or implied, of the Advanced Research Projects Agency or the U.S. Government.

[2] Present address: Computer Science Department, Yale University, New Haven, Connecticut 06520, U.S.A.

[3] Present address: Computer Science Department, University of Maryland, College Park, Maryland 20740, U.S.A.

Artificial Intelligence 5 (1974), 373–412

Copyright © 1974 by North-Holland Publishing Company

Theory [6, 7, 8], categorize the kinds of inferences that are necessary within such an understanding system, and outline the basic elements and processes that make up the program at Stanford that currently handles these inference tasks.

We shall assume in this paper that it is the desire of those researchers who work on the problems of computational linguistics to have a system that is capable of responding intelligently, on the basis of its own model of the world, in reaction to a given input sentence. Thus, we assume here that a system responds as follows (for example) is both an interesting and useful system if it accomplishes these things:

(1) INPUT: I am going to buy some aspirin for my cold.
    OUTPUT: Why don't you try some chicken soup instead?

(2) INPUT: John asked Mary for a book.
    OUTPUT: A book about what?

(3) INPUT: Do you want a piece of chocolate.
    OUTPUT: No, I don't want to spoil my appetite for dinner.

(4) INPUT: John went to the store.
    OUTPUT: What did he want to buy?

Before getting into the descriptions of the various kinds of inferences to which a conceptual memory should be sensitive, the notion of inference and how it differs from logical deductions (for instance in a theorem-prover or question-answerer) should be made clear.

In its broadest sense, we consider an inference to be a new piece of information which is generated from other pieces of information, and which may or may not be true. The intent of inference-making is to "fill out" a situation which is alluded to by an utterance (or story line) in hopes of tying pieces of information together to determine such things as feasibility, causality and intent of the utterance at that point. There are several features of all inferences which should make clear how an inference differs in substance and intent from a formal deduction:

(1) Inference generation is a "reflex response" in a conceptual memory. That is, one of the definitions of "processing conceptual input" is the generation of inferences from it. This means that there is always an implicit motivation to generate new information from old. In a theorem-prover or question-answerer, deductions are performed only upon demand from some external process.

(2) An inference is not necessarily a logically valid deduction. This means that the new information represented by the inference might not bear any formal logical relationship to those pieces of information from which it is generated. A good example of this is called "affirmation of the consequent", a technique fruitfully utilized by Sherlock Holmes, and certainly utilized by people in everyday situations. Briefly, this refers to the "syllogism" $A \supset B$, B;

therefore A. In this sense (and there are other examples), conceptual memory is strikingly different from a formal deductive system.

(3) An obvious consequence of (2) is that an inference is not necessarily true. For this reason, it is useful for memory to retain and propagate measures of the degree to which a piece of information is likely to be true. Memory must also be designed with the idea that *no* information is inviolably true, but rather must always be willing and able to respond to contradictions.

(4) The motivations for inference generation and formal deduction are entirely different. Formal deductions are highly directed in the sense that a well-defined goal has been established, and a path from some starting conditions (axioms and theorems) to this goal is desired. Inferences on the other hand are not nearly so directed. Inferences are generally made to "see what they can see". The "goal" of inferencing is rather amorphous: make an inference, then test to see whether it looks similar to, is identical to, or contradicts some other piece of information in the system. When one of these situations occurs, memory takes special action in the form of discontinuing a line of inferencing, asking a question, revising old information, creating causal relationships or invoking a belief pattern.

(5) A memory which uses the types of inference we will describe needs some means of recourse for altering the credibility of a piece of information when the credibility of some piece of information which was used in its generation changes. In other words, memory needs to remember *why* a piece of information exists. In contrast, a formal deductive system in general doesn't "care" (or need to know) where a fact came from, only that it exists and is true.

Having made these distinctions between conceptual inference and other types of logical deductions, we will describe some distinct types of inference.

2. Inference and Parsing

We take as one of our operating assumptions, that the desired output for a conceptual analyzer is a meaning representation. Since it is possible to go directly from an input sentence into a meaning representation (see [4, 6, 11] for descriptions of computer programs that do this), we shall disregard any discussion of syntactic parsing output.

What then should be present in a meaning representation? We claim that it is necessary for a meaning representation to contain each and every concept and conceptual relation that is explicitly or implicitly referred to by the sentence being considered.

By explicit reference we mean the concepts that underlie a given word. Thus we have the concept of John for "John" and the concept of a book for "book" in sentence (5):

(5) John bought a book.

However, we claim in addition that an adequate meaning representation must make explicit what is implicit but nonetheless definitely referenced in a given sentence. Thus, in (5) we have the word "bought" which implicitly references two actions of transfer, one whose object is the book and the other whose object is some valuable entity. We assume that hearers of (5), unless specifically told otherwise, will assume that this object is "money".

It is here then that we shall make our first distinction between the province of parsing (or the extraction of explicit and implicit information) and that of inference (the adding-on of probably correct information). The word "buy" has a number of senses in English, but the surrounding information disambiguates "buy" so that in (5) it can only mean that two actions of transfer occurred and that each action caused the other's existence. Furthermore, it is always true that whenever one of these transfer actions is present (hence called ATRANS for abstract transfer) it is also true that an actor did the other of these transfer actions, and there was a recipient and a donor of this object.

We now state our first inference type which we call LINGUISTIC-INFERENCE:

1. An instance of LINGUISTIC-INFERENCE exists when, in the absence of specific information to the contrary, a given word or syntactic construction can be taken to mean that a specific but unmentioned object is present in a predicted case for a given ACT with a likelihood of near certainty.

In the above example, the ACT is ATRANS, its predicted cases are OBJECT, RECIPIENT (includes receiver and donor) and INSTRUMENT. The word "buy," by definition references its cases. However, in addition "buy" has as a linguistic inference the object "money," as the object of the ATRANS whose actor is the subject of the sentence in which "buy" appears.

We assign to the conceptual analyzer the problem of handling explicit reference, implicit reference, and linguistic inference within a meaning representation because these are consequences of words. Using Conceptual Dependency notation (where ⇔ denotes the relation between actor and action; ⟵O denotes the relation between action and object; ⟸ denotes causality dependence; and

the meaning of this sentence is in fact quite beyond what the sentence explicitly says. Sentence (7) does not explicitly state what John did. Rather we must call upon some other information to decide if John threw something at Mary or if he swung his hand at her (and whether his hand was holding some object). Notice that the same ambiguity exists if we had sentence (8), but that one meaning is preferred over the other in (9):

(8) John hit Mary with a stick.
(9) John hit Mary with a slingshot.

We shall claim that for (7) when no other information is explicit, the most likely reading is identical with the reading for (10):

(10) John hit Mary with his hand.

Thus, (7) is another example of linguistic inference and it is the responsibility of the conceptual analyzer to assume "hand" as the thing that hit Mary on the basis of having seen "hit" occurring with no syntactic instrument. (Note that syntactic instrument is quite different from the conceptual INSTRUMENTAL case mentioned earlier.) Before we get into inferences that are not linguistic it will be necessary to explain further the elements of the meaning representation that we use as the input to our inference making procedures.

We would like to point out at this point that we assign the problem of extracting conceptual structures and making linguistic inferences to the domain of the conceptual analyzer. This is because the information that is used for making the decisions involved in those processes is contained in the particular language under analysis. From this point on in this paper we shall be discussing inferences that come from world knowledge rather than from a particular language. It is those interlingual processes that we assign to the domain of a memory and inference program such as we shall describe in Section 6.

3. The Twelve Primitive Actions

Conceptual Dependency theory is intended to be an interlingual meaning representation. Because it is intended to be language free, it is necessary in our representations to break down sentences into the elements that make them up. In order to do this it is necessary to establish a syntax of possible conceptual relationships and a set of conceptual categories that these relate. Furthermore it is necessary that requirements be established for how a given word is mapped into a conceptual construction.

There are six conceptual categories in Conceptual Dependency:

PP   Real world objects,
ACT   Real world actions,
PA   Attributes of objects,

---

denotes the relation between action, object, recipient and donor), the conceptual analyzer (described in [4]) outputs the following for (5):

```
          p
JOHN <========> *ATRANS* <——O—— MONEY
                    R——> *ONE*
                          \——> JOHN
          p
*ONE* <========> *ATRANS* <——O—— BOOK
                    R——> JOHN
                          \——> *ONE*
```

Two more common examples of linguistic inference can be seen with reference to sentences (6) and (7):

(6) Does John drink?
(7) John hit Mary.

In (6), it is reasonable to assume that the referenced object is "alcoholic beverages" although it is unstated. It is a property of the word "drink" that when it appears without a sentential object "alcoholic beverage" is understood. (In fact, this a property of quite a few languages, but from this it should not be thought that this is a property of the concept underlying "drink". Rather it is an artifact of the languages that most of them share in common cultural associations.) Thus, given that this is a linguistic inference, and that our conceptual analyzer is responsible for making linguistic inferences, our analyzer puts out the following conceptual structure for it:

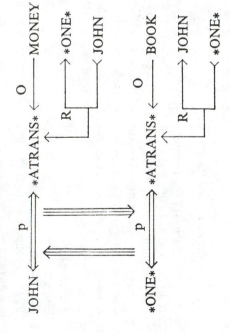

```
         ?
JOHN <========> *INGEST* <——O—— LIQUOR
                    D——> *INSIDE* <—— JOHN
                          \——> *MOUTH* <—— JOHN
```

The ACT INGEST is used here. We shall explain the notion of a primitive ACT in the next section.

In (7), we again have the problem that what hearers usually assume to be

The most important category for our purposes here is the ACT. A word maps into an ACT when it specifically refers to a given possible action in the world. Often verbs only reference unstated actions and make specific reference to states or relationships between these unspecified actions. As an example we have sentence (11):

(11) John hurt Mary.

Here, the real world action that John did is unstated. Only the effect of this action is known: namely that it caused Mary to enter a "hurt" state. Similarly, in (12) the word "prevent" is not a specific real world action but rather refers to the fact that some unstated action caused that some other action (that may or may not be specified later on in the sentence) did not occur.

(12) John prevented Mary from giving a book to Bill.

The analyses of these sentences (11) and (12) are as follows:

```
            p
  JOHN <===> *DO*
         ||
         ||
            p
  MARY <===  *HEALTH* = (X - 2)       (indicates HEALTH has gone
         <=  *HEALTH* = (X)            down 2 points on a 10 point
                                       scale)
```

and

```
            p
  JOHN <===> *DO*
         ||
         || c/
            p                 O
  MARY <===> *ATRANS* <------ BOOK
                        R
                        |--> BILL
                        |--< MARY
```

Since many verbs are decomposed into constructions that involve only unstated actions (denoted by DO) and/or attributes of objects (PA's) and since we require that any two sentences that have the same meaning be

---

AA   Attributes of actions,
T   Times,
LOC Locations.

These categories can relate in certain specified ways which are considered to be the syntactic rules of conceptualizations. There are sixteen of these conceptual syntax rules, but we shall list here only the ones that will be used in this paper:

PP ⇔ ACT
indicates that an actor acts.

PP ⇐ PA
indicates that an object has a certain attribute.

            O
ACT ← PP
indicates the object of an action.

          R→PP
ACT ←
          ‹PP
indicates the recipient and the donor of an object within an action.

          D→PP
ACT ←
          ‹PP
indicates the direction of an object within an action.

          I
ACT ← ⇔
indicates the instrumental conceptualization for an action.

X
⇑
Y
indicates that conceptualization X caused conceptualization Y. When written with a "c" this form denotes that X COULD cause Y.

          →PA2
PP ⇛
          ‹PA1
indicates a state change of an object.

PP1 ← PP2
indicates that PP2 is either PART OF or the POSSESSOR OF PP1.

In Conceptual Dependency, tenses are considered to be modifications of the main link between actor and action (⇔), or the link between an object and its state (⇐). The main link modifiers we shall use here are:

p   past.
f   future.
(null)   present.
ts = x   begin a relation at time x.
tf = x   end a relation at time x.
c   conditional,
/   negation,
?   question.

represented in one and only one way, the set of primitive ACTs that are used is important.

We have found that a set of only twelve primitive actions is necessary to account for the action part of a large class of natural language sentences.

This does not mean that these primitives are merely category names for types of actions. Rather, any given verb is mapped into a conceptual construction that may use one or more of the primitive ACTs in certain specified relationships plus other object and state information. That is, it is very important that no information be lost with the use of these primitives. It is the task of the primitives to conjoin similar information so that inference rules need not be written for every individual surface verb, but rather inference rules can be written for the ACTs. This of course turns out to be extremely economical from the point of view of memory functioning.

The twelve ACTs are:

ATRANS   The transfer of an abstract relationship such as possession, ownership, or control.
PTRANS   The transfer of physical location of an object.
PROPEL   The application of a physical force to an object.
MOVE   The movement of a bodypart of an animal.
GRASP   The grasping of an object by an actor.
INGEST   The taking in of an object by an animal.
EXPEL   The expulsion from the body of an animal into the world.
MTRANS   The transfer of mental information between animals or within an animal. We partition memory into CP (conscious processor), LTM (long-term memory), and sense organs. MTRANSing takes place between these mental locations.
CONC   The conceptualizing or thinking about an idea by an animal.
MBUILD   The construction by an animal of new information from old information.
ATTEND   The action of directing a sense organ towards an object.
SPEAK   The action of producing sounds from the mouth.

The following important rules are used within Conceptual Dependency:

(1) There are four conceptual cases: OBJECTIVE, RECIPIENT, DIRECTIVE, INSTRUMENTAL.

(2) Each ACT takes from two to three of these cases obligatorally and none optionally.

(3) INSTRUMENTAL case is itself a complete conceptualization involving an ACT and its cases.

(4) Only animate objects may serve as actors except for PROPEL.

We are now ready to return to the problem of inference.

4. Language-Free Inferences

The next class of inference we shall discuss includes those that come from objects and relate to the normal function of those objects. As examples we have sentences (13) and (14):

(13) John told Mary that he wants a book.
(14) John likes chocolate.

These sentences have in common that they refer to an action without specifically stating it. In these examples, this missing act concerns the probable use of some object. In (13) that ACT is probably MTRANS (i.e., people usually want books because they want to MTRANS information from them) and in (14) that ACT is probably INGEST (i.e., people normally "like" chocolate because they like to INGEST it). While it is certainly possible that these were not the intended ACTs (John could like burning books and painting with chocolate) it is highly likely that without contrary information most speakers will assume that those ACTs were referenced. In fact, psychological tests have shown (see [5], [10], for example) that in many cases most hearers will not actually remember whether the ACTs were specifically mentioned or not. Notice in the first example that the missing MTRANS (of information from the book) is an inference which occurs AFTER the meaning representation of the sentence has been established (i.e., this sentence is analyzed as "if someone were to ATRANS a book to me it would cause me pleasure"). On the other hand, the missing INGEST in the second example is inferred during the analysis because the REPRESENTATION itself depends upon the analyzer knowing what it means to "like" a food. Therefore, the determination of an object's probable relation to an actor is never strictly a part of just the analyzer or just the memory, but rather a task of conceptual analysis in general.

It is important to mention that, regardless of the ultimate correctness of the chosen ACT, Conceptual Dependency predicts that an ACT is missing because verbs like "want" and "like" are represented as states. In the parsing of each of these sentences it is found that an actor and an object are present with no ACT to link them. This causes a search to be made for the correct ACT to fill that spot.
We thus have our second and third inference-types:

2. An instance of ACT-INFERENCE is present when an actor and an object occur in a conceptualization without an ACT to connect them, and the object in question has a normal function in the world. In this case the normal function is assumed to be the implicitly referenced ACT.
and

3. A TRANS-ENABLE-INFERENCE occurs with conceptualizations

involving one of the TRANS ACTs. It is inferred that the TRANS conceptualization enables another conceptualization involving the same actor and object to take place. The specific act for this inferred conceptualization then comes about via ACT-INFERENCE. Inferences of this type are frequently useful for inferring the intended use of a physical or mental object.

The finished analyses for (13) and (14) after ACT-INFERENCE and TRANS-ENABLE-INFERENCE take place are then:

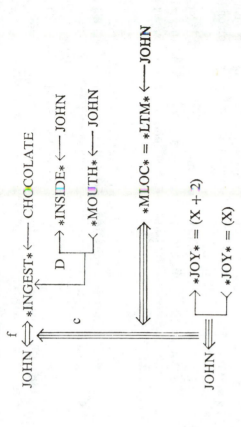

(which eventually leads to:)

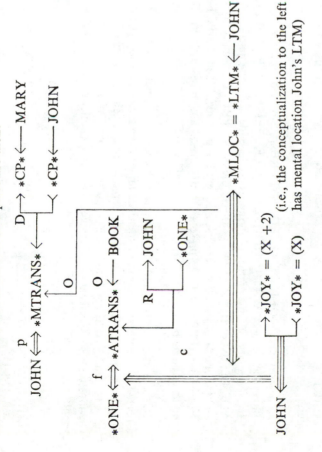

i.e., John wants to read the book, and

The next kind of inference that we shall discuss has to do with the results of a given ACT. Consider sentences (15), (16) and (17):

(15) John went to South Dakota.
(16) John told Mary that Bill was a doctor.
(17) John gave Mary a book.

Each of these sentences refers to an ACT that has a predictable result. Here again, when no information is given that contradicts this prediction, it is reasonable to assume that the normal result of the action was achieved. (Here, as in most of the examples given in this paper, it is necessary in English to use the conjunction "but" to indicate that the inferred result did not take place. Thus, unless we add "but he didn't get there' to (15), the hearer will assume he did.)
We thus have our fourth example of inference:

4. RESULT-INFERENCE can be made whenever a TRANS ACT is present and no information exists that would contradict the inferred result.

Thus, whenever PTRANS is present, we can infer that the location of the object is now the directive case of PTRANS. Whenever ATRANS is present we can infer that there is a new possessor of the object, namely the recipient, and lastly, whenever an MTRANS occurs we can assume that the information that was transferred to the conscious processor (CP) of the brain became present there. Thus for (16), Mary can be assumed to "know" the information that was told to her since "know" is represented as "exist in the long

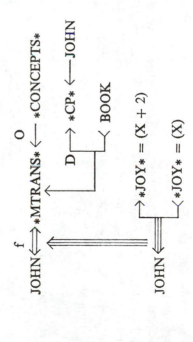

term memory (LTM)" and "tell" involves MTRANSing to the conscious processor which leads to LTM. A program that deals with this problem will be discussed later on in this paper.

The fifth kind of inference that we shall discuss is called OBJECT-AFFECT-INFERENCE. This kind of inference also concerns the result of an ACT but here we mean result to refer to some new physical state of the object involved. Sentences (18) and (19) illustrate this problem:

(18) John hit Mary with a rock.
(19) John ate the egg.

Both (18) and (19) make an implicit statement about a new physical state of the item that is in the objective case. In (18) we can guess that Mary's state of physical health might have been diminished by this ACT (i.e., she was hurt). In (19) we know that the egg, no matter what state it was in before this ACT, is now in a state of not existing at all anymore. Thus we have inference-type 5:

5. An instance of OBJECT-AFFECT-INFERENCE may be present with any of the physical ACTs (INGEST, EXPEL, PROPEL, GRASP, MOVE). The certainty of any of these inferences is dependent on the particular ACT, i.e., INGEST almost always affects the object, PROPEL usually does and the effects of the others are less frequent but possible. When OBJECT-AFFECT-INFERENCE is present, a new resultant physical state is understood as having been caused by the given ACT.

The analyses for (18) and (19) are given below. Note that if "rock" is replaced by "feather" in (18) the inference under discussion is invalid. Thus, in order to accomplish this inference correctly on a machine, the specifications for under what conditions it is valid for a given ACT must be given. Obviously these specifications involve mass and acceleration as well as fragility in the case of PROPEL.

$$
\begin{array}{l}
\text{JOHN} \Longleftrightarrow \overset{p}{} *\text{PROPEL}* \overset{O}{\longrightarrow} \text{ROCK} \\
\qquad\qquad\quad D \longrightarrow \text{MARY} \\
\qquad\qquad\qquad\quad \longleftarrow \text{JOHN} \\
\text{ROCK} \Longleftrightarrow *\text{PHYSCONT}* \\
\overset{\wedge}{\text{MARY}}
\end{array}
$$

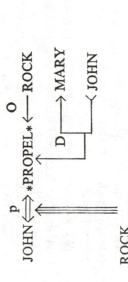

(*PHYSCONT* represents the state of physical contact; many such states are used)

and

$$
\begin{array}{l}
\text{JOHN} \Longleftrightarrow \overset{p}{} *\text{INGEST}* \overset{O}{\longleftarrow} \text{EGG} \\
\qquad D \longrightarrow *\text{INSIDE}* \longleftarrow \text{JOHN} \\
\qquad\qquad\qquad \longleftarrow *\text{MOUTH}* \longleftarrow \text{JOHN}
\end{array}
$$

The next kind of inference we shall discuss concerns the reasons for a given action. Until now, we have only considered the effects of a given conceptualization. However, in order to conduct an intelligent conversation it is often necessary to infer the reason behind a given event. Consider sentences (20), (21) and (22):

(20) John hit Mary.
(21) John took an aspirin.
(22) John flattered Mary.

We would like a computer to have the ability to respond to these sentences as follows:

(20a) What did Mary do to make John angry?
(21a) What was wrong with John?
(22a) What does John want Mary to do for him?

In order to accomplish this, we need to use some of the inference-types discussed above first. Thus, in (20), we must first establish that Mary might be hurt before we can invoke an appropriate belief pattern. By belief pattern we mean a sequence of causally-related ACTs and states that are shared by many speakers within a culture. Such a sequence usually deals with what is appropriate or expected behavior and is often a prescription for action on the part of the hearer.

The belief pattern called by (20) is commonly described as VENGEANCE. It states that people do things to hurt people because they feel that they have been hurt by that person. This belief pattern supplies a reason for the action by the actor. Thus we come to the sixth kind of inference:

(6) An instance of BELIEF-PATTERN-INFERENCE exists if the given event plus its inferred results fit a belief pattern that has in it the reason for that kind of action under ordinary circumstances.

In example (21) we have an instance of the WANT belief pattern which refers to the fact that people seek to obtain objects for what they can use them for (this is intimately related to inference-type 2 discussed above). Sentence (22) refers to the RECIPROCITY belief pattern (which deals with "good" things (i.e., those that cause positive changes on the JOY scale), VENGEANCE taking care of the "bad" ones). RECIPROCITY comes in two types. The one being used here is anticipatory. That is, the action is being done with the hope that the nice results achieved for one person will enable that person to do something which will yield nice results for the original actor.

We will further discuss (20) later on in this paper when we outline the procedure by which our computer program produces (20a) in response to it.

The next kind of inference we shall discuss is called INSTRUMENTAL-INFERENCE. It is the nature of the primitive ACTs discussed earlier that they can take only a small set of ACTs as instrument. Thus, for example, whenever INGEST occurs, PTRANS must be its instrumental ACT because by definition PTRANS is the only possible instrument for INGEST. The reason for this is that in order for someone to eat something it is necessary to move it to him or him to it. Thus, whenever INGEST is present we can make the legitimate inference that the object of INGEST was PTRANSed to the mouth (nose, etc.) of the actor. If this inference is incorrect, it is only because the direction of motion was mouth to object instead. Also, whenever PTRANS appears, the instrument must have been either MOVE or PROPEL. That is, in order to change the location of something it is necessary to move a bodypart or else apply a force to that object (which in turn requires moving a bodypart). Thus we have the seventh inference type:

7. INSTRUMENTAL-INFERENCE can always be made, although the degree of accuracy differs depending on the particular ACT. Whenever an ACT has been referenced, its probable instrument can be inferred.

The list of instrumental ACTs for the primitive ACTs follows:

INGEST	instrument is PTRANS.
PROPEL	instrument is MOVE or GRASP (ending) or PROPEL.
PTRANS	instrument is MOVE or PROPEL.
ATRANS	instrument is PTRANS or MTRANS or MOVE.
CONC	instrument is MTRANS.
MTRANS	instrument is MBUILD or SPEAK or ATTEND or MOVE.
MBUILD	instrument is MTRANS.
EXPEL	instrument is MOVE or PROPEL.
GRASP	instrument is MOVE.
SPEAK	instrument is MOVE.
ATTEND	no instrument is needed, although MOVE often applies.

Using this table it is possible, for example, to make the following inferences from these sentences:

(23) John is aware that Fred hit Mary.
(24) John received the ball.

Since (23) refers to CONC and CONC requires MTRANS as instrument, we can infer (from the possible instruments of MTRANS) where John got his information. He could have MBUILDed it (not likely here because Fred hit Mary is an external event); he could have perceived it from his senses by ATTEND eye to it himself; or by ATTEND ear to someone else which MTRANSed it to him. Since (24) refers to PTRANS, we have two possible instruments MOVE or PROPEL. From this we can infer that the ball was handed to him (move someone else's bodypart) or else it was rolled or thrown (or underwent some other manner of applying a force to a ball).
The next type of inference is PROPERTY-INFERENCE:

8. Whenever an object is introduced in a sentence, certain subpropositions are being made. The most common instance of this is the predication that the object being referenced exists. The inference of these subpropositions we call PROPERTY-INFERENCE.

In some instances, PROPERTY-INFERENCE is dependent on other inference types. Thus, in the sentence "John hit Mary", not only is it necessary to make the PROPERTY-INFERENCE that both John and Mary exist, but it is also necessary to realize that John must have arms in order to do this. This inference is thus dependent on the LINGUISTIC-INFERENCE that, unless otherwise specified, "hit" refers to "hands" as the object of the PROPELing.

PROPERTY-INFERENCE is necessary in a computer understanding system in order to enable us to respond either with surprise or a question as to manner if we know that John does not have arms. Furthermore, in answering questions, it often happens that the checking of subpropositions associated with PROPERTY-INFERENCE will allow us to find an answer with less work. Thus for sentence (25):

(25) Did Nixon run for President in 1863?

Two separate subpropositions that can be proved false allow the question to be answered most efficiently. Establishing that "Nixon was alive in 1863" is false or that "there was a presidential election in 1863" is false is probably the best way of answering the question.

We have not discussed to this point the standard notions of logical inference for two reasons: (a) the problems involving logical inference are already fairly well understood, and (b) we do not view logical inference as playing a CENTRAL role in the problem of computer understanding of natural language. However, there exists a related problem that bears discussion.

Consider the problem of two sentences that occur in sequence. Often such sentences have additional inferences together which they would not have separately. For example, consider:

(26a) All redheads are obnoxious.
(26b) Queen Elizabeth I had red hair.
(27a) John wants to join the army.
(27b) John is a pacifist.

In (26), (26b) has its obvious surface meaning, but also can mean either one of two additional things. Either we have the inference that Queen Elizabeth I was obnoxious according to the speaker, or if (26b) were spoken by a different speaker from (26a), there exists the possibility that (26b) is intended as a refutation of (26a).

For (27), a sophisticated language analyzer must discover that (b) is essentially a contradiction of (a) and hence the inference that the speaker of (b) believes that the speaker of (a) is in error is probably correct. We thus introduce inference-type 9:

9. An instance of SEQUENTIAL-INFERENCE is potentially present when one sentence follows another and they share a subject or a proposition. When subpropositions or inferences of subpropositions can be detected as common to both conceptualizations, and satisfy certain set inclusion or contradiction rules, SEQUENTIAL-INFERENCE may apply.

The next kind of inference is quite straightforward:

10. An instance of CAUSALITY-INFERENCE is present if two sentences are connected by an "and" or by their appearing in sequence. Then if one could have caused the other, it can be inferred that this is what happened.

Consider sentences (28) and (29a) and (29b):

(28) John hit Mary and she died.
(29a) John hit Mary.
(29b) John died.

In these sentences it is usually correct to assume causality. For (28) we infer that the hitting caused Mary's death. For (29) we infer that (a) caused (b). It is our knowledge of the world, however, that would cause us to wonder about the connection in (29) but not in (28). A good program would discover this to be a different kind of causality from the straight result present in (28). Kinds of causality are discussed in [7]. Another important inference type BACKWARD-INFERENCE. This

type of inference can be made whenever an action has occurred that required another action to precede. The possible actions that can be inferred for a given ACT as BACKWARD-INFERENCE are often quite similar to those which can be inferred as instruments for a given ACT. We use this kind of inference whenever an object is acted upon. Thus if we have:

(30) John ate a banana.

we can infer that the banana must have been PTRANSed to him at some time. Likewise, whenever a mental item is operated upon its previous MTRANSing can also be inferred. If we have:

(31) John knows where Mary is.

then we can infer that this information must have been MTRANSed to John at some point (either from his eyes or from someone else MTRANSing this information to him). Thus we have inference type 11:

11. All conceptualizations are potentially subject to BACKWARD-INFERENCE. Depending on the nature of the object, one of the TRANS ACTs can be inferred as having enabled the current conceptualization's occurrence.

The last kind of inference we shall discuss concerns the intention of the actor. Consider the following sentences.

(32) John hit Mary.
(33) John told Bill that he wants to go to New York.

We assume that a person does something because he wants to do it and that he wants to do it because of the results that he expects to achieve. Thus a valid inference here is that it is the intention of the actor that the things inferred with OBJECT-AFFECT-INFERENCE or RESULT-INFERENCE will occur, and that these things are desired by the actor.

Thus from (32) using inference-type 6 we get that "Mary is hurt pleases John". From (33), using inference-type 5, we get that "being located in New York will please John" and "Bill knowing this pleases John". Thus we have inference-type 12:

12. INTENTION-INFERENCE is assumed whenever an actor acts unless information to the contrary exists.

5. Observations

Using the inference types discussed above we can see that an effective analysis of a sentence is often quite a bit more than one might superficially imagine. If we start with the sentence "John hit Mary," for example, our conceptual analyzer would perform the following conceptual analysis:

6. The Program

There currently exists at the Stanford Artificial Intelligence Laboratory a functioning program which works in conjunction with the analysis program written by Riesbeck [4] and the generation program written by Goldman [2]. This program is capable of making some but not all of the inferences described here and of generating responses which demonstrate the kind of understanding to which we have been referring in this paper.

We will now describe the theory of the operation of this program and trace in detail one of the examples we have discussed. Please bear in mind that it is the intent of both the program and this paper to be as theoretically correct as possible. Therefore on occasion we have sacrificed efficiency for theory. It was not the intent of this program to do a dazzling job on a few isolated examples. Rather we have tried to produce a program that is easily extendable that will further the cause of computer understanding.

After conceptual analysis of "John hit Mary" is complete, MEMORY gains processing control (MEMORY having been called upon for knowledge of objects and people, and asked to supply the missing linguistic and object-affect information).

Before examining the flow of an example, a brief explanation of MEMORY's data structures and goals is in order. All propositional information is stored in list positional notation, with the predicate first and the conceptual case slots following. The internally-stored form of a proposition is called a *bond*, and is stored as a single entity under a LISP generated atom (*superatom*). In this way propositions are easily embedded, and, except for their bond, look like *simple concepts*. Simple concepts have only an *occurrence set* to define them (superatoms have occurrence sets too). The occurrence set is a set of pointers to superatoms which contain instances of the simple concept. MEMORY is therefore fully two-way linked. The totality of knowledge about a simple concept are those propositions pointed to by the occurrence set.

In addition to bonds and occurrence sets, superatoms have other characteristics. Most important among these are STRENGTH, MODE, TRUTH, REASONS and OFFSPRING. STRENGTH is a measure of how much credibility a proposition has, and usually represents a composite credibility from those propositions from which it arose. MODE modifies the proposition truth-wise (negations are stored as MODE = FALSE). TRUTH is a flag which is TRUE if this proposition is true in the world at the present time. (This one is for convenience, since this information could be determined from the time modifications or nesting of the proposition.) REASONS is the set of superatoms which participated in the generation of this proposition in the system (i.e., what facts were used to infer this proposition), and OFFSPRING

(34)

```
              p         O
   JOHN <===> *PROPEL* <---- *PHYSOBJ*
        <===       |
                   D ---> MARY
                     <--- JOHN

   *PHYSOBJ*
        ^
        <===> *PHYSCONT*
   MARY
```

During and after the language analysis the consultation of the above inference processes would yield the following results:

LINGUISTIC
OBJECT AFFECT
BELIEF PATTERN — add "hand" as object of PROPEL.
add causal "recipient (Mary) be hurt".
add potential cause of the entire event as Mary DO cause John be hurt cause John be angry.

INSTRUMENTAL PROPERTY — add instrument of MOVE "hand".

add predication that John and Mary exist and that John has hands and that they were in the same place at the same time.

INTENTION — add that John knew that it would cause him pleasure if Mary was hurt and that is why he did it.

The graph after analyzer-initiated inferences have filled out the meaning representation, but before MEMORY gains direct processing control is:

(35)

```
              p        O          part
   JOHN <===> *MOVE* <---- HAND <---- JOHN
        <===        I

              p        O          part
   JOHN <===> *PROPEL* <---- HAND <---- JOHN
        <===        |
                    D ---> MARY
                      <--- JOHN

          part
   JOHN ----> HAND
                 ^
                 <===> *PHYSCONT*
            MARY
```

is its inverse (i.e., what other propositions has this one played a part in inferring). These last two are very important because they give MEMORY recourse to retrace its paths and modify STRENGTHs, or to discuss its reasoning. There is one last feature of the system clock which is stored each time the superatom or concept is accessed. It is chiefly used for reference establishment.

Inferencing is done breadth-first to a heuristically controllable depth. Inferences have the same data structure as described above, namely, each new inference becomes a superatom, complete with its occurrence set and the other properties mentioned. Inferences are organized as lambda functions under predicates, and are invoked directly by conceptualizations. Pattern matching is done within these lambda functions in the form of program tests and branches. Times are processed along with each proposition, and the system emphasizes an awareness of time relationships, since out-of-date propositions are never discarded, but rather modified by new time relations. A forgetting function is viewed as peripheral to the types of tasks we are currently performing. Briefly, these tasks are the following:

(1) To establish referents of all concepts appearing in a conceptual graph. This requires full access to the inference mechanism, and is not compartmentalized as a well-defined preprocessor.

(2) To serve as a passive data bank and access mechanism for the analysis and generation phases. This includes answering simple queries during the analysis such as "is there a concept which is a human and has name John" as well as performing arbitrarily involved proofs. Typical of proof requests are time relation proofs required by the conceptual generator.

(3) To store the analyzed contents of each sentence. This involves (1) as a subtask, and in general involves the storage of a number of subpropositions. Old information is detected as such, so that unless MEMORY has insufficient information to identify an event or state, its existence in MEMORY is discovered. This, of course, applies to the maintenance of simple concepts as well: MEMORY tries to identify all concepts and tokens of concepts and tokens of concepts with existing ones, and notes which it was unable to identify.

(4) To perform appropriateness checking on all peripheral implications of an input. This primarily involves such tasks as making sure that actors are alive and well and in the right places for their actions, and that the actions are reasonable.

(5) To generate unsolicited inferences of the types described earlier and elevate some of them to the status predictions of three basic classes in response to every new input. (A prediction is simply an inference the system has chosen to focus on as being noteworthy at some point.) These three

classes of predictions are (a) completatory predictions, (b) causal predictions, and (c) result predictions. Completatory predictions augment conceptualizations by supplying a most likely candidate for some missing information. Causal predictions try to relate the input to belief patterns in the computer memory which could explain the reasons behind the input. Result predictions establish possible outcomes caused by the input, and also access belief patterns.

(6) To maintain a record of inferencing and prediction activity, and be able to answer questions about and discuss reasons for inferred information. This capability includes the ability to modify STRENGTHs and MODEs when assumptions which lead to them change at some future time.

(7) To answer "who", "whether", "when" and "why" type questions concerning the conceptualizations it has been given, together with their inferences.

We now return to the example "John hit Mary". The conceptualization has form (36). This is the positional form of the analyzed version (34) shown at the end of Section 5. Notice that, although the words "JOHN", "HAND", etc. were used in that diagram, what the analyzer actually passes to memory are *descriptive sets*: sets of conceptual propositions which MEMORY can use to identify the actual referents of the concepts described. The notation

$$Cn: \{(P1)...(Pk)\}$$

is used to denote some concept having descriptive propositions P1, ..., Pk, which has not yet been identified as a concept with which MEMORY is familiar (the referent has not been determined). For the examples, #⟨word⟩ will stand for the unique concept which "⟨word⟩" references (and will be unambiguous in these examples).

(36)

```
((CAUSE ((PROPEL C1:{(ISA—#PERSON)(NAME)—"JOHN")}
                 C2:{(ISA—#HAND)(PART—C1)}
                 C1
                 C3:{(ISA—#PERSON)(NAME—"MARY")}
            ))
       ((PHYSCONT C2 C3))
     )
     (TIME—C4:{(ISA—#TIME)(BEFORE—#NOW)})
)
```

MEMORY's first task is to establish the referents of as many of the simple concepts (C1,...,Ck) as possible. [3] discusses this procedure and its problems in some detail, and a short example is included as Appendix B. We will assume here that all referents have been correctly identified. After this phase, the conceptualization has form (37).

(37)
```
((CAUSE ((PROPEL #JOHN #C0001 #JOHN #MARY))
        ((PHYSCONT #C0001 #MARY))
  (TIME—#C0002))
```

where C0001 is the concept in MEMORY for John's hand, C0002 is the concept in MEMORY for the time of the causal event.

Next, MEMORY fragments the conceptualization into subpropositions, each of which will be submitted to the inferencer. The average English sentence contains many conceptual subpropositions. A subproposition is any unit of information which is conveyed directly (without non-analyzer-initiated inference) by a conceptualization. Subpropositions can be classified into three categories: (1) explicit-focussed, (2) explicit-peripheral, and (3) implicit. Explicit subpropositions are always complete conceptualizations, whereas implicit subpropositions are generally communicated through single, isolated dependencies.

To illustrate these categories, consider the sentence:

"The engine of Beverly's new car broke down while she was driving on the freeway late last night."

The explicit-focussed proposition is: "a car engine broke down". This is the "main reason" for the conceptualization's existence. It is not necessarily always the most interesting subproposition for MEMORY to pursue, however.

Some of the explicit-peripheral propositions are:
1. the car is new,
2. the car is owned by Beverly,
3. the time of the incident was late last night,
4. the location of the incident was on the freeway,
5. Beverly was driving a car.

These are additional facts the speaker thought essential to the hearer's understanding of the conceptualization. They are "peripheral" (dependent) in the conceptual dependency sense, and for the purposes of parsing. However, they frequently convey the most interesting information in the conceptualization.

Some of the implicit propositions are:
1. cars have engines as parts,
2. people own things,
3. Beverly performed an action,
4. cars can be *PTRANS*ed (i.e., they are moveable),
5. the car, engine and Beverly were on the freeway (i.e., the actors and objects involved in an event have the event's location).

Briefly, these are very low-level propositions which affirm conceptual case restrictions, and which must strictly adhere to MEMORY's knowledge of normality in the world. These typically lie on the borderline between what was said and what the hearer nearly always infers without further thought.

In the example "John hit Mary", the fragmentation process yields the following subpropositions from the input conceptualization:

1. JOHN PROPELLED SOMETHING
2. A HAND WAS PROPELLED
3. JOHN MOVED SOMETHING
4. A HAND WAS MOVED
5. A HAND IS PART OF JOHN
6. SOMETHING WAS PROPELLED FROM JOHN TO MARY
7. A HAND AND MARY WERE IN PHYSICAL CONTACT
8. JOHN PROPELLED HIS HAND
9. 8 CAUSED 7
10. IT WAS BEFORE "NOW" THAT 1-9 OCCURRED

We do not pursue all of these in the following description, but bear in mind that MEMORY subjects each of the above 10 subpropositions (some of which are redundant in the information they convey) to inferencing.

Having been "perceived" externally, the causal relation (9 above) is stored as a superatom, assigned strength 1.0, given TRUTH T, MODE T and REASONS T (there are no reasons, it is just true). In addition, its superatom is entered on the inference queue, which now has this single entry. Inferences organized under CAUSE are then called. Two nominal inferences with strength propagation factor 1.0 are that the two parts of the causal relation are themselves true: the PROPEL and PHYSCONT propositions are thus inferred with propagated strength still 1.0, TRUTH T, MODE T and REASONS a list of one item: the superatom for the causal proposition. In addition, TIME propositions are created for these two new superatoms using #C0002. These receive STRENGTH 1.0, TRUTH T, MODE T, having as REASONS a list of one item which is the superatom for the causal time proposition. These two new time propositions are not, however, added to the inference list. The PROPEL proposition, when subjected to inferencing will, among other things, look to see if an instrumental is present, and, seeing that one isn't, will add the most likely one: (MOVE #JOHN #C0001 #JOHN #MARY). This will in turn be added to the inference queue. When its inferences are generated, among them will be the inference that #JOHN has at least one movable hand. Were MEMORY to find a contradiction at this point, it would have access to the MOVE completatory inference which produced the contradiction, and would alter its strength of belief and note that a contradiction had occurred. Later, a response concerning this problem might be generated.

Among the other inferences organized under CAUSE, one has an invocation pattern which is matched by this (CAUSE(PROPEL...)(PHYSCONT...)) pattern. This is the inference that recognizes that someone's PROPELling an object has caused the contact of that object with an animal. The inference is that the animal is likely to have been hurt:

(38) (NEGCHANGE #MARY #PSTATE)

Notice the reason for organizing this inference under CAUSE rather than PROPEL or PHYSCONT: PROPEL alone says nothing about actual contact, only that an actor has propelled an object in a direction. PHYSCONT alone is not enough, because it also appears in sentences like "John is touching the wall," where there are no such violent dynamics. This pattern also knows that the outcome of a propelling which causes physical contact can lead to different kinds of inferences based on the features of the propelled object and the target object. For example, it knows that to hit a bodypart of an animal is the same as hitting the animal, and that a measure of the amount of injury done is a function of the hardness, heavyness, sharpness, etc. of the propelled object, and of the particular bodypart hit.

The NEGCHANGE inference is thus stored as a superatom and added to the inference queue. Its REASONS are the original CAUSE and the facts that (ISA #MARY #PERSON) and (ISA #PERSON #ANIMAL). Notice that the actual inference rule is not recorded as a reason, since a semblance of it can always be reconstructed from its parts.

This same CAUSE pattern also asserts the actor's volition since it detects no information to the contrary: John wanted this causal relation to exist. This is a general operating assumption of MEMORY: that it is essential at every point in inferencing to keep track of the intentionality of actions. Actions which stand by themselves are always assumed to be volitional. Likewise, causal relationships such as this one (where an action causes a state), are assumed to be the result of the actor's volition. (Deciding an actor's intent in most cases is a difficult problem. [3] discusses problems of this nature in some detail.)

At this point, (39) is stored and entered on the inference queue. Its REASON is simply the original superatom. Notice that MEMORY has now made an important distinction between the physical and intentional components of the event. They will proceed in parallel.

(39)

((MLOC ((CANCAUSE ((NEGCHANGE #MARY #PSTATE))
                   ((POSCHANGE #JOHN #JOY))))

#C0003
(TIME—#C0002))

(#C0003 is John's LTM)

We return now to (38). (NEGCHANGE #MARY #HEALTH) accesses inferences organized under NEGCHANGE. MEMORY first checks to determine what caused this situation and finds the REASONS which were generated along with the NEGCHANGE. Had MEMORY not found any REASONS, it would have attempted to apply world knowledge to make a prediction. This knowledge is stored using the predicates CAUSE and CANCAUSE, and is accessed by the MEMORY query: find all probable causes of (NEGCHANGE #PERSON #HEALTH), i.e., find all X such that (CANCAUSE X (NEGCHANGE #PERSON #HEALTH)), and similarly for CAUSE. This situation would occur in the following type of story: "Mary was hurt." "John had hit her with a rock." where one member of the predicted set is borne out by the next line of the story. Such a process is called "knitting" (see [3]), and is the chief measure of "understanding" in several-line stories.

In addition to this determination of causality which was trivially satisfied in this case, MEMORY detects applicability of the following belief pattern: when a person undergoes a NEGCHANGE (on any scale, since all scales are positive), he will want to undergo a POSCHANGE on that scale. MEMORY thus infers (40):

(40)

((MLOC((CANCAUSE((POSCHANGE #MARY #HEALTH))
                 ((POSCHANGE #MARY #JOY))))

#C0004

(TIME—#C0005))

#C0004 is Mary's LTM,
#C0005 is (AFTER C0002)

This subsequently will be detected by the belief pattern (organized under MLOC) that when a person wants a future event, he will perform some action to try to achieve that event or state. Once again, CAUSE and CANCAUSE information is called into play to predict Mary's likely actions. An example of this type of information is:

((CANCAUSE((INGEST #PERSON #MEDICINE))
          ((POSCHANGE #PERSON #HEALTH))))

Using information collected in this manner, a prediction of Mary's future actions is made. This prediction has the form of a bond, and indicates that any or all of the actions listed are possible. Notice that only actions are being predicted. If some causes of the state the actor desires are not actions but rather states or statechanges themselves, further CANCAUSE and CAUSE chains are considered until an action is found. For instance, suppose Mary wants a NEGCHANGE on her own health scale. One cause of a NEGCHANGE on the health might be to have one's heart in PHYSCONT with a knife. Since this is not an action, memory must be searched for things which could cause the required PHYSCONT. Among them would be the action of PROPELling the knife to that location. This PROPEL might then be a valid action prediction for Mary at that point.

At this point, (41) is generated, and inferencing on this line is stopped.

(41)
((PREDICTIONSET #MARY
((INGEST #MARY #MEDICINE #UNSPEC #C0006)
((PTRANS #MARY #MARY #UNSPEC #C0007))))

where C0006 is Mary's INSIDES,
C0007 is a token of a #HOSPITAL

We now return to (39). This inference accesses the belief pattern organized under MLOC which we have labelled VENGEANCE: if a NEGCHANGE (on any scale) of a person, P1, would cause a POSCHANGE on the joy scale for someone else, P2, then P2 must be angry at P1. MEMORY therefore infers (42):

(42) ((MFEEL #JOHN #ANGER #MARY)(TIME—C0002))

Stored under MFEEL is the belief pattern that the reason people are in a state of directed anger toward another person is probably that the second person did something which caused a NEGCHANGE on some scale of the first person. MEMORY first looks to see if Mary is known to have done something which caused a NEGCHANGE in John. In this example it finds none. Had one been found from a previous sentence, MEMORY would have again "knitted" one piece of knowledge with an existing one. In this example, having found no actions on the part of Mary, MEMORY generates a prediction about Mary's PAST actions, once again utilizing CAUSE and CANCAUSE knowledge of the world. After making prediction (43), MEMORY also poses a question of the form "What did Mary do?", stores the question, and notes its potential answer as being of interest to the prediction just made.

(43)
((PREDICTIONSET #MARY
((CAUSE ((PROPEL #MARY #PHYSOBJ #UNSPEC #JOHN))
((PHYSCONT #PHYSOBJ #JOHN)))
((ATRANS#MARY #PHYSOBJ #JOHN #MARY))))

i.e., Mary either hit John first, or took something from him. (It should be clear that we are not intending to specify an exhaustive prediction list. Rather we seek to demonstrate the PROCESSES which occur in MEMORY.) At this point MEMORY stops inferencing and poses the question "What did Mary do to John?"

(44)
((CAUSE (DO #MARY *?*))((NEGCHANGE #JOHN #UN-SPECIFIED)))
(TIME—C0010))

where C0010 is BEFORE C0002.

To summarize, MEMORY has taken the conceptual analysis underlying an English sentence and generated new probabilistic information from it in an attempt to relate it to knowledge MEMORY may already have stored. The new information took three basic forms: (a) predictions about the causes of the input, (b) predictions about the possible results of the input, and (c) predictions about future and past actions of people. The effects of inferencing are seen at the end either in the form of a question or a comment which indicates that the sentence indeed interacted with some of MEMORY's knowledge and belief patterns.

Appendix A. Computer Examples

What follows is output from the MARGIE system currently operating at Stanford. MARGIE is a combination of three programs each of whose output is shown here. The analysis program produces conceptual structures from a given input sentence. The memory program stores this output in a special format and makes inferences about it based on its knowledge of the world. It then recodes these inferences into Conceptual Dependency structures. These structures are then read by a generating program that codes them into semantic structures that are English based (after Fillmore [1]). A modified version of a program written by Simmons [9], then encodes these structures into English.

The examples presented here are intended only to show the flavor of the inference-making program. The entire system is quite a bit more powerful than these examples demonstrate. That is MARGIE can answer questions about what it has been told, ask questions about what it would like to know, as well as parse sentences more complex than those shown here. Here we merely want to indicate the inference capability.

In the interest of space, we have manually edited out some of the less interesting (generally repetitive from example to example) inferences. This explains the apparent discrepancy between the number of "INFERENCES" and "THINGS TO SAY" in the following examples.

TYPE INPUT
*(JOHN TOLD MARY THAT BILL WANTS A BOOK)

OUTPUT FROM PARSER:
TIM00: ((VAL *T*))
TIM01: ((BEFORE TIM00 X))

TIM02: ((AFTER TIM00 X))
TIM03: ((AFTER TIM00 X))
TIM04: ((AFTER TIM00 X))
((ACTOR (JOHN1) ⇔ (*MTRANS* TO (*CP* PART (MARY1) REF-
(*THE*) FROM (*CP* PART (JOHN1) REF (*THE*)) MOBJECT -
((CON ((ACTOR (*ONE1*) ⇔ (*ATRANS*) OBJECT (BOOK1 -
REF (*A*)) TO (BILL1) FROM (*ONE1*)) TIME (TIM04)) ⇐C ((ACTOR
(BILL1) ⇔ T (*JOY*) ⇔ F (*JOY*)) INC (2 TIME (TIM03)))) ⇔ (*MLO-
C* VAL (*LTM* PART (BILL1) REF (*THE*)))) MODE (NIL) FOCUS
(⇔ VAL PART)) TIME (TIM00)) TIME (TIM01))

PARTIALLY INTEGRATED RESULT:
((*MTRANS* #JOHN1) (*MLOC* (CANCAUSE ((*ATRANS* (#SO-
MEONE) (G0012) (#SOMEONE) (#BILL1)) (TIME—G0014))) (STATE-
CHANGE (#BILL1) (#JOY) #UNSPECIFIED #UNSPECIFIED (TI-
ME—(G0017)) (INC—(#TWO)))) (G0019)) (TIME—(G0015))) (G0022)) (G-
0025)) (TIME—(G0028)))
INTEGRATION RESULT: G0038
INFERENCES:
(G0040 G0036 G0047 G0057 G0056 G0055 G0063 G0062 G0065 G0070)
THINGS TO SAY:
((ACTOR (BOOK REF (*A*)) ⇔ (*XABT* VAL (*?*))))

(A BOOK ABOUT WHAT)

((CON ((CON ((ACTOR (MARY) ⇔ (*ATRANS*) OBJECT (BOOK REF
(*A*)) FROM (MARY) TO (BILL)) TIME (G0014) FOCUS (ACTOR))
⇐C ((ACTOR (JOHN) ⇔ F (*JOY*) ⇔ T (*JOY*) TIME (G0017) INC (2)))
⇔ (*MLOC* VAL (*LTM* REF (*A*) PART (JOHN))) CERTAINTY -
(0.8) TIME (G0015))

JOHN POSSIBLY WANTS MARY TO GIVE BILL A BOOK)

((CON ((CON ((ACTOR (*ONE1*) ⇔ (*ATRANS*) OBJECT (BO-
OK REF (*A*)) FROM (*ONE1*) TO (BILL) TIME (G0014) FOCUS ((A-
CTOR))) ⇐C ((ACTOR (BILL) ⇔ F (*JOY*) ⇔ T (*JOY*) TIME (G0017) -
INC (2)))) ⇔ (*MLOC* VAL (*LTM* REF (*A*) PART (BILL))) TIME -
(G0015)) ⇔ (*MLOC* VAL (*CP* REF (*A*) PART (MARY))) TS (G002-
8))

(MARY EXPECTED BILL TO WANT A BOOK)

((CON ((CON ((ACTOR (*ONE1*) ⇔ (*ATRANS*) OBJECT (BOOK RE-
F (*A*)) FROM (*ONE1*) TO (BILL) TIME (G0014) FOCUS (ACTOR))-
) ⇐C ((ACTOR (BILL) ⇔ F (*JOY*) ⇔ T (*JOY*) TIME (G0017) INC (2)))-
⇔ (*MLOC* VAL (*LTM* REF (*A*) PART (BILL))) TIME (G0015))
(BILL WANTS A BOOK)

((CON ((CON ((ACTOR (*ONE1*) ⇔ (*ATRANS*) OBJECT (BO-
OK REF (*A*)) FROM (*ONE1*) TO (BILL) TIME (G0014) FOCUS ((A-
CTOR)) ⇐C ((ACTOR (BILL) ⇔F (*JOY*) ⇔T (*JOY*)) TIME (G0017)
INC (2))) ⇔ (*MLOC* VAL (*LTM* REF (*A*) PART (BILL)))) TIME (-
G0015)) ⇔ (*MLOC* VAL (*LTM* REF (*A*) PART (MARY))))

(MARY KNOWS BILL WANTS A BOOK)

((ACTOR (MARY) ⇔ (*ATRANS*) OBJECT (BOOK REF (*A*)) FROM-
(MARY) TO (BILL) TIME (G0017) CERTAINTY (0.8))

(MARY MIGHT GIVE BILL A BOOK)

((CON ((CON ((ACTOR (BOOK REF (*A*)) ⇔ (*POSS* VAL (BILL))) TS-
(G0014) TIME (G0066)) ⇐C ((ACTOR (BILL) ⇔F (*JOY*) ⇔T (*JOY*)) -
INC (2 TIME (G0067)))) ⇔ (*MLOC* VAL (*LTM* PART (BILL) REF (-
THE))))

(BILL THINKS HE WOULD LIKE TO COME TO HAVE A BOOK)

((CON ((CON ((ACTOR (BOOK REF (*A*)) ⇔ (*POSS* VAL (*ONE1*)))-
TF (G0014) TIME (G0070)) ⇐C ((ACTOR (BILL) ⇔F (*JOY*) ⇔T (*JOY-
*)) INC (2 TIME (G0071)))) ⇔ (*MLOC* VAL (*LTM* PART (BILL) RE-
F (*THE*)))))

(BILL THINKS HE WOULD LIKE SOMEONE TO CEASE TO HAVE A -
BOOK)

((CON ((CON ((ACTOR (*ONE1*) ⇔ (*PTRANS*) OBJECT (BOOK REF-
(*A*)) FROM (*ONE1*) TO (BILL)) FOCUS ((ACTOR)) TIME (G0074))-
⇐C ((ACTOR (BILL) ⇔F(*JOY*) ⇔T (*JOY*)) INC (2 TIME (G0075)))) -
⇔ (*MLOC* VAL (*LTM* PART (BILL) REF (*THE*)))))

(BILL WANTS TO GET A BOOK FROM SOMEONE)

((CON ((CON ((ACTOR (BOOK REF (*A*)) ⇔ (*LOC* VAL (BILL)) TS -
(G0014) TIME (G0078)) ⇐C ((ACTOR (BILL) ⇔F (*JOY*) ⇔T (*JOY*)) I-
NC (2 TIME (G0079)))) ⇔ (*MLOC* VAL (*LTM* PART (BILL) REF (*-
THE*)))))

(BILL THINKS HE WOULD LIKE A BOOK TO COME TO BE NEAR
HIM))

((CON ((CON ((ACTOR (BOOK REF (*A*)) ⇔ (*LOC* VAL (*ONE1*)) -
TF (G0014) TIME (G0082)) ⇐C ((ACTOR (BILL) ⇔F (*JOY*) ⇔T (*JOY-
*)) INC (2) TIME (G0083)))) ⇔ (*MLOC* VAL (*LTM* PART (BILL) RE-
F (*THE*)))))

(BILL THINKS HE WOULD LIKE A BOOK TO CEASE TO BE NEAR
SOMEONE)

((CON ((CON ((ACTOR (*ONE1*) ⇔ (*ATRANS*) OBJECT (BO-
OK REF (*A*)) FROM (*ONE1*) TO (BILL)) TIME (G0014) FOCUS ((A-
CTOR)) ⇐C ((ACTOR (BILL) ⇔F (*JOY*) ⇔T (*JOY*)) TIME (G0017)
INC (2))) ⇔ (*MLOC* VAL (*LTM* REF (*A*) PART (BILL)))) TIME (-
G0015)) ⇔ (*MLOC* VAL (*LTM* REF (*A*) PART (MARY))))

(MARY KNOWS BILL WANTS A BOOK)

((CON ((CON ((ACTOR (BILL) ⇔ (*MTRANS*) MOBJECT (*CONCEP-TS*) FROM (BOOK REF (*A*)) TO (*CP* PART (BILL)) INST ((ACTOR-(BILL) ⇔ (*LOOK—AT*) OBJECT (BOOK REF (*A*)))) FOCUS ((ACT-OR)) TIME (G0086)) ⇐C ((ACTOR (BILL) ⇔F (*JOY*) ⇔T (*JOY*)) IN-C (2) TIME (G0087)))) ⇔ (*MLOC* VAL (*LTM* PART (BILL) REF (*T-HE*)))))

(BILL WANTS TO READ A BOOK)

TYPE INPUT
*(JOHN HIT MARY)

OUTPUT FROM PARSER:
TIM00: ((VAL *T*))
TIM01: ((BEFORE TIM00 X))
((CON ((ACTOR (JOHN1) ⇔ (*PROPEL*) OBJECT (*HAND* PART (J-OHN1) FROM (JOHN1) TO (MARY1) INST ((ACTOR (JOHN1) ⇔ (*M-OVE*) OBJECT (*HAND* PART (JOHN1)))) TIME (TIM01)))) TIME (NI-L) ⇐ ((ACTOR (*HAND* PART (JOHN1)) ⇔ (*PHYSCONT* VAL (M-ARY1)) TIME (TIM01) MODE (NIL) FOCUS (CON ACTOR))))

PARTIALLY INTEGRATED RESULT:
((CAUSE ((*PROPEL* (#JOHN1) (G0009) (#JOHN1) (#MARY1)) (TI-ME—(G0012)) (INST—(*MOVE* (#JOHN1) (G0009) (#UNSPECIFIE-D) (#UNSPECIFIED)))) ((*PHYSCONT* (G0009)) (#MARY1)) (TIME-—(G0012))))

INTEGRATION RESULT: G0021
INFERENCES:
(G0023 G0022 G0016 G0019 G0024 G0026 G0027)
THINGS TO SAY:
((CON ((CON ((ACTOR (MARY) ⇔F (*PSTATE*) ⇔T (*PSTATE*)) IN-C (−2) CERTAINTY (1.0) TIME (G0031)) ⇐C ((ACTOR (JOHN) ⇔F (*J-OY*) ⇔T (*JOY*)) INC (2) TIME (G0032)))) ⇔ (*MLOC* VAL (*LTM* -PART (JOHN) REF (*THE*)))) CERTAINTY (1.0) TIME (G0012))
JOHN WANTED MARY TO BECOME HURT)
((ACTOR (MARY) ⇔F (*PSTATE*) ⇔T (*PSTATE*)) INC (−2) CERT-AINTY (1.0) TIME (G0012))

(MARY BECAME HURT)

((ACTOR (JOHN) ⇔ (*PROPEL*) OBJECT (*HAND* REF (*A*) PART -(JOHN)) FROM (JOHN) TO (MARY) INST ((ACTOR (JOHN) ⇔ (*MOV-E*) OBJECT (*HAND* REF (*A*) PART (JOHN)) FROM (*ONE*) TO (-*ONE*)) FOCUS ((ACTOR)) TIME (G0012) FOCUS ((ACTOR)) CERT-AINTY (1.0))

(JOHN SWUNG HIS HAND TOWARD MARY)

((ACTOR (*HAND* REF (*A*) PART (JOHN)) ⇔ *PHYSCONT* VAL (-MARY))) TIME (G0012) CERTAINTY (1.0))

(JOHNS HAND TOUCHED MARY)

((ACTOR (JOHN) ⇔*i(*MFEEL*) MOBJECT (*ANGER*) TO (MARY)) -FOCUS ((ACTOR)) CERTAINTY (1.0) TIME (G0012))

(JOHN WAS ANGRY AT MARY)

((CON ((CON ((ACTOR (MARY) ⇔F (*PSTATE*) ⇔T (*PSTATE*)) IN-C (2) TIME (G0035)) ⇐C ((ACTOR (MARY) ⇔F (*JOY*) ⇔T (*JOY*)) I-NC (2) TIME (G0036)))) ⇔ (*MLOC* VAL (*LTM* PART (MARY) REF -(*THE*)))) CERTAINTY (1.0))

(MARY WANTS TO FEEL BETTER)

((CON ((ACTOR (MARY) ⇔ (*?*) TIME (G0028) FOCUS ((ACTOR)) C-ERTAINTY (1.0)) ⇐ ((ACTOR (JOHN) ⇔T (*ONE*) ⇔F (*ONE*) INC-(−2) TIME (G0028) FOCUS (ACTOR)))

(WHAT DID MARY DO TO JOHN)

TYPE INPUT
*(JOHN ADVISED MARY TO SELL BILL A BANANA)

OUTPUT FROM PARSER:
TIM00: ((VAL *T*))
TIM01: ((BEFORE TIM00 X))
TIM02: ((AFTER TIM01 X))
TIM 03: ((AFTER TIM01 X))

((ACTOR (JOHN1) ⇔ (*MTRANS*) TO (*CP* PART (MARY)) REF (*-THE*)) FROM (*CP* PART (JOHN1) REF (*THE*)) MOBJECT ((CON -(CON ((ACTOR (MARY1) ⇔ (*ATRANS* OBJECT (BANANA) REF (*-A*)) TO (BILL1) FROM (MARY1) TIME (TIM03)) ⇐⇔ ((ACTOR (BILL1) ⇔ (*ATRANS*) OBJECT (*MONEY* REF (*A*)) TO (MARY1) FROM (-BILL1) FOCUS ((CON ACTOR)) TIME (TIM03))) ⇐C ((ACTOR (MAR-Y1) ⇔T (*JOY*) ⇔F (*JOY*)) INC (2) TIME (TIM02) MODE (NIL)))) F-OCUS ((ACTOR)) MODE (NIL) TIME (TIM01))

PARTIALLY INTEGRATED RESULT:
((*MTRANS* (#JOHN1) ((CANCAUSE ((DUALCAUSE ((*ATRANS* (-#MARY1) (G0004) (#MARY1) (#BILL1) (TIME—(G0006)) ((*ATRA-NS* (#BILL1) (G0013) (#BILL1) (#MARY1) (TIME—(G0006)))) ((ST-ATECHANGE (#MARY1) (#JOY) #UNSPECIFIED #UNSPECIFIE-D) (TIME—(G0015)) (INC—(#TWO)))) (G0017) (G0020) (TIME—(G00-07))))

INTEGRATION RESULT: G0032
INFERENCES:
(G0049 G0045 G0040 G0031 G0066 G0023 G0086 G0083 G0084 G0099 G01-00)

THINGS TO SAY:

((CON ((CON ((CON ((ACTOR (MARY) ⇔ (*ATRANS*) OBJECT (BAN-ANA REF (*A*) FROM (MARY) TO (BILL)) TIME (G0006) FOCUS ((A-CTOR))CERTAINTY (1.0))⇐⇒((ACTOR(BILL)⇔(*ATRANS*)OBJEC-T (*MONEY* REF (*A*) FROM (BILL) TO (MARY)) TIME (G0006) F-OCUS (ACTOR))))⇐C ((ACTOR (MARY) ⇔F (*ONE*) ⇔T (*ONE*)))-TIME (G0015) INC (2)) CERTAINTY (1.0) ⇔ (*MLOC* VAL (*LTM* R-EF (*A*) PART (JOHN)))) TIME (G0007) CERTAINTY (1.0))

(JOHN BELIEVES THAT MARY WOULD BENEFIT BY MARY SELLS BILL A BANANA)

((CON ((CON ((CON ((ACTOR (MARY) ⇔ (*ATRANS*) OBJECT (BAN-ANA REF (*A*) FROM (MARY) TO (BILL)) TIME (G0006) FOCUS ((A-CTOR))CERTAINTY(1.0))⇐⇒((ACTOR(BILL) ⇔(*ATRANS*)OBJEC-T (*MONEY* REF (*A*) FROM (BILL) TO (MARY)) TIME (G0006) F-OCUS (ACTOR))))⇐C ((ACTOR (MARY) ⇔F (*ONE*) ⇔T (*ONE*)))-TIME (G0015) INC (2)) CERTAINTY (1.0) ⇔ (*MLOC* VAL (*CP* REF-(*A*) PART (MARY)))) TS (G0007) CERTAINTY (1.0))

(MARY BEGAN THINKING ABOUT MARY SELLS BILL A BANANA BENEFITS MARY)

((CON ((CON ((ACTOR (MARY) ⇔ (*ATRANS*) OBJECT (BANANA-REF (*A*) FROM (MARY) TO (BILL)) TIME (G0006) FOCUS ((ACTO-R))CERTAINTY (1.0))⇐⇒((ACTOR (BILL) ⇔(*ATRANS*)OBJECT (*-MONEY* REF (*A*) FROM (BILL) TO (MARY)) TIME (G0006) FOCU-S ((ACTOR))))⇐C ((ACTOR (MARY) ⇔F (*ONE*) ⇔T (*ONE*)) TIM-E (G0015) INC (2)) CERTAINTY (1.0))

(MARY CAN BENEFIT FROM MARY SELL BILL A BANANA)

((ACTOR (MARY) ⇔ (*MBUILD*) FROM ((ACTOR (MARY) ⇔ (AT-RANS*) OBJECT (BANANA REF (*A*) FROM (MARY) TO (BILL)) TI-ME (G0006) FOCUS ((ACTOR)) CERTAINTY (1.0)) TO ((ONE*)) CERT-AINTY (1.0))

(MARY CONSIDERED GIVING BILL A BANANA)

((ACTOR (MARY) ⇔ (*ATRANS*) OBJECT (BANANA REF (*A*)) FR-OM (MARY) TO (BILL)) TIME (G0033) FOCUS ((ACTOR)) CERTAINT-Y (0.60))

(MARY POSSIBLY WILL GIVE BILL A BANANA)

((CON ((CON ((ACTOR (BILL) ⇔ (*ATRANS*) OBJECT (MONEY REF-(*A*) FROM (BILL) TO (MARY)) TIME G0033)) ⇐ ((ACTOR (MARY))-⇔F (*ONE*) ⇔ T (*ONE*)) TIME (G0033) INC (2))) ⇔ (*MLOC* VAL-(*LTM* REF (*A*) PART (JOHN))) TIME (G0006) CERTAINTY (0.50))

(JOHN POSSIBLY BELIEVES THAT MARY WOULD BENEFIT FROM BILL GIVE MARY MONEY)

((CON ((CON ((ACTOR (MARY) ⇔ (*ATRANS*) OBJECT (BANANA-REF (*A*) FROM (MARY) TO (BILL)) TIME (G0033))⇐⇒C ((ACTOR (-BILL) ⇔F (*ONE*) ⇔T (*ONE*)) TIME (G0033) INC (2))) ⇔ (*MLOC*-VAL (*LTM* REF (*A*) PART (JOHN))) TIME (G0006) CERTAINTY (-0.50))

(JOHN POSSIBLY BELIEVES THAT BILL WOULD BENEFIT FROM MARY GIVE BILL A BANANA)

((CON ((CON ((ACTOR (BILL)) ⇔ (*INGEST*) OBJECT (BANANA REF-(*A*)) TIME (G0034))⇐C ((ACTOR (BILL) ⇔F (*JOY*) ⇔T (*JOY*)) T-IME (G0034) INC (2))) ⇔ (*MLOC* VAL (*LTM* REF (*A*) PART (BIL-L))) TIME (G0006) MODE ((*?*)))

(DOES BILL WANT TO EAT A BANANA)

TYPE INPUT
*(JOHN PREVENTED MARY FROM HITTING BILL BY CHOKING-MARY)

OUTPUT FROM PARSER:
TIM00: ((VAL *T*))
TIM01: ((BEFORE TIM00 X))
TIM02: ((BEFORE TIM01 X))
((CON ((CON ((ACTOR (JOHN1) ⇔ (*GRASP*) OBJECT (*NECK* PAR-T (MARY1)) TIME (TIM02) ⇐ ((ACTOR (MARY1) ⇔ (*INGEST*) OB-JECT (*AIR* REF (*A*) FROM (*MOUTH* PART (MARY1)) TO (*IN-SIDE* PART (MARY1)) TIME (TIM02) MODE ((*CANNOT*))) FOCU-S (CON ACTOR)) ∧ ((CON ((ACTOR (MARY1) ⇔ (*INGEST*) OBJEC-T (*AIR* REF (*A*) FROM (*MOUTH* PART (MARY1)) TO (*INSID-E* PART (MARY1)) TIME (TIM02) MODE ((*CANNOT*))) ⇐ ((CON ((-ACTOR (MARY1) ⇔ (*PROPEL*) OBJECT (*HAND* PART (MARY1))-TO (BILL1) FROM (MARY1) INST (ACTOR (MARY1) ⇔ (*MOVE*) O-BJECT (*HAND* PART (MARY1))) TIME (TIM01) MODE ((*CANNO-T*)) ⇐ ((ACTOR (*HAND* PART (MARY1)) ⇔ (*PHYSCONT* VAL (-BILL1))) TIME (TIM01) MODE ((*CANNOT*)) FOCUS (CON ACTOR))-) MODE ((*NEG*)))) FOCUS ((CON ACTOR))))
PARTIALLY INTEGRATED RESULT:

(MARY BECAME HURT)

((CON ((ACTOR (MARY) ⇔ (*PROPEL*) OBJECT (*HAND* REF (*A*) PART (MARY)) FROM (MARY) TO (BILL) INST ((ACTOR (MARY) ⇔ (*MOVE*) OBJECT (*HAND* REF (*A*) PART (MARY) FROM (*-*ONE*) TO (*ONE*) FOCUS ((ACTOR))) TIME (G0006) FOCUS ((ACTOR)) MODE ((*CANNOT*)) ⇐ ((ACTOR (*HAND* REF (*A*) PART (MARY)) ⇔ (*PHYSCONT* VAL (BILL)) TIME (G0006) MODE ((*CANNOT*)))) MODE ((*NEG*) CERTAINTY (1.0))

(MARY NOT HIT BILL)

((CON ((CON ((CON ((ACTOR (MARY) ⇔ (*PROPEL*) OBJECT (*HAND* REF (*A*) PART (MARY)) FROM (MARY) TO (BILL)) TIME (G0005)) ⇐ ((ACTOR (*HAND* REF (*A*) PART (MARY)) ⇔ (*PHYSCONT* VAL (MARY)) INC (2))) ⇔ (*PHYSCONT* VAL (BILL)) TIME (G0005)))) ⇐ C ((ACTOR (MARY) ⇔ F (*JOY*) ⇔ T (*JOY*)) INC (2)) ⇔ (*MLOC* VAL (*LTM* PART (MARY) REF (*-THE*)))) CERTAINTY (1.0) TIME (G0005))

(MARY WANTED TO HIT BILL)

((CON ((CON ((ACTOR (BILL) ⇔ F (*PSTATE*) ⇔ T (*PSTATE*)) INC (--2) CERTAINTY (1.0) TIME (G0006)) ⇐ C ((ACTOR (MARY) ⇔ F (*JO-Y*) ⇔ T (*JOY*)) INC (2) TIME G(0006))) ⇔ (*MLOC* VAL (*LTM* PA-RT (MARY) REF (*THE*))) CERTAINTY (1.0) TIME (G0005))

(MARY WANTED BILL TO BECOME HURT)

((ACTOR (MARY) ⇔ (*MFEEL*) MOBJECT (*ANGER*) TO (BILL)) F-OCUS ((ACTOR)) CERTAINTY (1.0) TIME (G0005))

(MARY WAS ANGRY AT BILL)

((CON ((ACTOR (BILL) ⇔ (*?*) TIME (G0028) FOCUS ((ACTOR)) CE-RTAINTY (1.0)) ⇐ ((ACTOR (MARY) ⇔ T(*ONE*) ⇔ F (*ONE*)) INC (--2) TIME (G0028) FOCUS (ACTOR))

(WHAT DID BILL DO TO MARY)

((ACTOR (JOHN) ⇔ (*MFEEL*) MOBJECT (*ANGER*) TO (MARY)) F-OCUS ((ACTOR)) CERTAINTY (0.8) TS (G0005))

(JOHN POSSIBLY BECAME ANGRY AT MARY)

Appendix B. Inference and Reference Establishment

We include this appendix to illustrate briefly how inferences are useful in establishing references to tokens of real world concepts. A scheme has been devised which permits MEMORY to proceed with other aspects of "understanding" even though all referents may not have been established before

---

((ANDX ((CAUSE ((*GRASP* (#JOHN1) (G00002)) (TIME—(G0005))) ((-CANNOT ((*INGEST* (#MARY1) (G0012) (G0016) (G0021)) (TIME—(-G0005))))) ((CAUSE (CANNOT ((*INGEST* (#MARY1) (G0012) (G00-16) (G0021)) (TIME— (G0005))))) (NOT (CAUSE (CANNOT ((*PROPE-L* (#MARY1) (G0024) (#MARY1) (#BILL1)) (TIME—(G0006)) (INST-—(*MOVE* (#MARY1) (G0024) (#UNSPECIFIED) (#UNSPECIFIE-D)))))) (CANNOT ((*PHYSCONT* (G0024) (#BILL1)) (TIME—G0006))-))))))))

INTEGRATION RESULT: G0047

INFERENCES:

(G0032 G0046 G0027 G0031 G0035 G0045 G0053 G0058 G0066 G0079 G00-70 G0074 G0079)

THINGS TO SAY:

((CON ((ACTOR (JOHN) ⇔ (*GRASP*) OBJECT (*NECK* REF (*A*) P-ART (MARY))) TIME (G0005) FOCUS ((ACTOR)) CERTAINTY (1.0)) -⇐ ((ACTOR (MARY) ⇔ (*INGEST* OBJECT (*AIR* REF (*A*)) FRO-M (*MOUTH* REF (*A*)) TO (*INSIDE* REF (*A*)) TIME (G0005) F-OCUS ((ACTOR)) MODE ((CANNOT*)) CERTAINTY (1.0)) CERTAI-NTY (1.0))

(JOHN CHOKED MARY)

((CON ((ACTOR (MARY) ⇔ (*INGEST*) OBJECT (*AIR* REF (*A*)) F-ROM (*MOUTH* REF (*A*)) TO (*INSIDE* REF (*A*)) TIME (G0005)-FOCUS ((ACTOR)) MODE ((*CANNOT*)) CERTAINTY (1.0)) ⇐ ((CON-((ACTOR (MARY) ⇔ (*PROPEL*) OBJECT (*HAND* REF (*A*) PART-(MARY)) FROM (MARY) TO (BILL) INST ((ACTOR (MARY) ⇔ (*MO-VE*) OBJECT (*HAND* REF (*A*) PART (MARY)) FROM (*ONE*) T-O (*ONE*) FOCUS ((ACTOR))) TIME (G0006) FOCUS ((ACTOR)) MO-DE ((*CANNOT*))) ⇐ ((ACTOR (*HAND* REF (*A*) PART (MARY)) -⇔ (*PHYSCONT* VAL (BILL)) TIME (G0006)) MODE ((*CANNOT*)))) -MODE ((*NEG*) CERTAINTY (1.0)) CERTAINTY (1.0)))

(MARY NOT HIT BILL BECAUSE MARY WAS UNABLE TO BREATH-E)

((ACTOR (JOHN) ⇔ (*GRASP*) OBJECT (*NECK* REF (*A*) PART (-MARY)) TIME (G0005) FOCUS ((ACTOR)) CERTAINTY (1.0))

(JOHN GRABBED MARYS NECK)

((ACTOR (MARY) ⇔ (*INGEST*) OBJECT (*AIR* REF (*A*)) FROM (-*MOUTH* REF (*A*)) TO (*INSIDE* REF (*A*))) TIME (G0005) FOCU-S ((ACTOR)) MODE ((CANNOT*)) CERTAINTY (1.0))

(MARY WAS UNABLE TO BREATHE)

((ACTOR (MARY) ⇔F (*PSTATE*) ⇔T (*PSTATE*)) INC (--2) TIME (-G0005) CERTAINTY (1.0))

understanding begins. This scheme also provides for the eventual establishment of these referents as another goal of the inference process. It is not hard to see that, in general, the solution of the reference problem for some concept can involve arbitrarily intimate and detailed interaction with the deductive processes of MEMORY, and that these processes must be designed to function with concepts whose features are not completely known.

Consider the sentence

"Andy's diaper is wet."

Assume a very simple situation for the sake of example: that MEMORY knows of exactly two concepts, MC1, MC2 such that $X \in \{MC1, MC2\}$:

(D1) (ISA X #PERSON)
(D2) (NAME X "ANDY")

(i.e., MEMORY knows two people by the name Andy). However, possibly in addition to much other information, MEMORY also knows

(AGE MC1 #12 MONTHS) and (AGE MC2 #25 YEARS).

This is a typical reference dilemma: no human hearer would hesitate in the correct identification of "Andy" in this sentence using these pieces of knowledge (in no particular context). Yet the natural order of "establish references first, then infer" simply does not work in this case. In order to begin inferencing, the referent of "Andy" is required (i.e., access to the features of C1 in memory), but in order to establish the referent of "Andy" some level of deduction must take place. This is something of a paradox on the surface.

Actually, the fault lies in the assumption that reference establishment and inferencing are distinct and sequential processes. The incorrectness of this assumption is but another example of the recurring theme that NO aspect of natural language processing (from phonology to story comprehension) can be completely compartmentalized. In reality, reference establishment and inferencing are in general so intimately interrelated so as to be functionally almost indistinguishable. Nevertheless, there is an interesting sequence of processing which will solve this class of reference problem.

(We point out that there are many other interesting inferences to be made from this sentence. A glaring one is, of course, "what kind of fluid?" The inference which supplies this information is an example of LINGUISTIC-INFERENCE, and is quite similar to the case in which "hand" is inferred as the missing object implied by "hit". One difference is that, while "hand" is predicted from an ACT, "urine" is predicted from a PP, namely "diaper". Another difference is that "hand" is supplied in response to MISSING information, while "urine" is supplied to make a general concept more specific. We will ignore this and all other inferences not needed in the following description.)

At the point the reference problem is undertaken, the state of this conceptualization is the following:

(*LOC* C1: {(ISA C1 #FLUID)}
C2: {(ISA C2 #DIAPER)
(*POSS* C2 C3: {(ISA C3 #PERSON)
(NAME C3 "ANDY")}})

i.e., there is some fluid located at the diaper which is possessed by a person whose name is Andy. Once the correct "#ANDY" has been identified, the referent of "diaper" can be established, using the principle that explicit subpropositions of a certain class (*POSS* among these) should appease the reference-finding mechanism. That is, "The diaper", occurring out of context with no conceptual modification, is referentially ambiguous, while "The diaper possessed by X" is a signal to MEMORY that the speaker has included what he feels is sufficient information either to identify or create the token of a diaper being referenced. However, this diaper processing must wait for the *POSS* proposition to be stored in MEMORY and this in turn involves the determination of reference to the possessor (the problem at hand). The reference to #FLUID is simply solved: the concept #FLUID is invoked as part of the definition of what it is to be wet, and MEMORY simply creates a token of this mass-noun concept. MEMORY realizes that references to mass nouns frequently occur with no explicit conceptual modification, and does not bother to identify them further unless contradictory inferences result from them later on. This token of #FLUID stands for the fluid which is currently in "Andy"'s diaper. Now only the person referent remains to be solved.

Using its standard intersection search, MEMORY uses the two descriptive propositions to locate MC1 and MC2 as possible candidates for the referent of P. Since no more can be done at this point, MEMORY creates a concept. MC3 (which will turn out in this case to be temporary) whose occurrence set (see beginning of Section 6) consists of the two propositions D1 and D2. In addition, MEMORY notes that this concept has been created as the result of ambiguous reference (specifically, it adds MC3 to the list !REFUN-ESTABLISHED). This done, a token of a diaper which is possessed by MC3 can now be created. This token too, by virtue of its referencing another possibly incorrectly identified concept in MEMORY, will be subject to reference reevaluation, pending identification of MC3. At this point, MEMORY has an internal form of the conceptualization, albeit incomplete, so inferencing begins.

Of interest to this example is the subproposition "MC3 possesses a diaper". Subpropositions are briefly discussed in Section 6. [3] describes in more detail the methods by which all subpropositions are extracted for examination by the inference mechanism. In this example we have a clear-cut example of where an explicit-peripheral subproposition plays a major part in the understanding of the entire conceptualization: one inference memory can make from

(*POSS* X: {(ISA X #PERSON)} Y: {(ISA Y #DIAPER)})

with a high degree of certainty is that the possessor is an infant; namely:

(AGE X #ORDERMONTHS)

(#ORDERMONTHS is a "fuzzy" concept which will match any duration concept within its "fuzzy" limits). The proposition (AGE MC3 #ORDER-MONTHS) is therefore added to MC3's occurrence set, and other inferencing proceeds. Eventually, all inferencing will die out or be stopped by depth controls. At that point, MC3 is detected as still having been unestablished, so reference establishment is again undertaken. This time, however, new information is available which resolves the conflict: the AGE predicate is recognized as matching the AGE proposition stored on the occurrence set of MC1. MC1 MC3 has thus been identified. Its occurrence set, which has probably been augmented by other inferences, is then merged with that of MC1 to preserve any additional information communicated by the input or its inferences and MC3 is purged. Finally, all subpropositions of the original input are resubmitted to the inferencer in hopes of generating new information by making use of MC1's now-accessible occurrence set. Duplicated information is immediately rejected on this and subsequent passes. This procedure is repeated until no new information turns up. At that point, any unidentified references are communicated externally in the form "X who?" or "what X?"

REFERENCES

1. Fillmore, C. The case for case. *Universals in Linguistic Theory*, E. Bach and R. Harms (eds.), Holt, Rinehart and Winston, New York (1968).
2. Goldman, N. The generation of English sentences from a deep conceptual base. Ph.D. Thesis, Computer Science Dept., Stanford University, Stanford, Calif. (1974).
3. Rieger, C. Conceptual memory. Ph.D. Thesis, Computer Science Dept., Stanford University, Stanford, Calif. (1974).
4. Riesbeck, C. Computer analysis of natural language in context. Ph.D. Thesis, Computer Science Dept., Stanford University, Stanford, Calif. (1974).
5. Sachs, J. Recognition memory for syntactic and semantic aspects of connected discourse. *Perception and Psychophysics* **2** (1967).
6. Schank, R. Conceptual dependency: A Theory of natural language understanding. *Cognitive Psychology* **3** (October 1972).
7. Schank, R. Semantics in conceptual analysis. *Lingua* **30** (1972), 101–140.
8. Schank, R. The fourteen primitive actions and their inferences. Stanford A.I. Memo 183, Computer Science Dept., Stanford University, Stanford, Calif. (1973).
9. Simmons, R. and Slocum, J. Generating English discourse from semantic networks. *Commun. ACM* **15** (October 1972).
10. Wettler, M. Zur Speicherung syntaktischer Merkmale in Langzeitgedächtnis. *Proc. of 28th Congress*, Eckensberger, L. (ed.), DGFP-Hogrefe, Göttingen (in press).
11. Wilks, Y. An artificial intelligence approach to machine translation. *Computer Models of Thought and Language*, R. Schank and K. Colby (eds), Freeman, San Francisco (1973).

Received May 1973; revised September 1973; accepted April 1974

8 / Patrick H. Winston
Learning Structural Descriptions from Examples

This paper describes a form of learning involving an associative network formalism. The idea is to present a system with a sequence of descriptions representing examples and non-examples of a concept, and have the system induce the properties of the concept itself. Essential to this approach is the notion of a *near-miss*, that is, something that is almost an instance of the concept. While examples allow the system to construct a general description based on the commonalities it discovers, it has no way of determining what features represent accidental properties of these instances or essential properties of the concept being learned. On the other hand, a discrepancy between a near-miss and its current model allows the system to mark the feature in question as an essential component of the concept. Obviously, a system built along these lines will be very sensitive to the order in which examples and near-misses are presented, but perhaps this is not so unlike a student relying on the careful guidance of an instructor. Moreover, the learning is very dependent on the language used to describe instances, non-instances, and concepts. In particular, the system operates by matching its current model to the current input (a description matching operation not unlike that of KRL [Bobrow and Winograd, Chapter 13]), noting the differences, and updating the model appropriately based on whether the input was an example or a near-miss. The sensitivity of this operation to the exact syntactic form of the current model and input means that this reasoning is quite unlike logical inference over the "obvious" translations of the networks into logic (as described in [Hayes, Chapter 14], for example). Apparently, one would have to axiomatize both the form and the content of Winston's networks to understand the information they contain, yet another complication making the true role of logic in Knowledge Representation such a slippery affair.

Appeared in *The Psychology of Computer Vision*, 157–209, edited by P. H. Winston, New York: McGraw-Hill Book Company, 1975.

LEARNING STRUCTURAL DESCRIPTIONS FROM EXAMPLES

Patrick Henry Winston

5.1 KEY IDEAS

How do we recognize examples of various concepts?

How do we learn to make such recognitions?

How can machines do these things?

How important is careful teaching?

In this paper I describe a set of working computer programs that sheds some light on these questions by demonstrating how a machine can be taught to see and learn new visual concepts. The programs work in the domain of three-dimensional structures made of bricks, wedges, and other simple objects.

Centrally important is the notion of the near miss. By near miss I mean a sample in a training sequence quite like the concept to be learned but which differs from that concept in only a small number of significant points. These near misses prove to convey the essentials much more directly than repetitive exposure to ordinary examples.

Good descriptions are equally important. I believe learning from examples, learning by imitation, and learning by being told uniformly depend on good descriptions. My system therefore necessarily has good methods for scene description and description comparison.

I also argue the importance of good training sequences prepared by good teachers. I think it is reasonable to believe that neither machines nor children can be expected to learn much without them.

Fig. 5.1

5.1.1 Scene Description and Comparison

Much of the system to be described focuses on the problem of analyzing toy block scenes. There are two very simple examples of such scenes in Fig. 5.1. From such visual images, the system builds a very coarse description as in Fig. 5.2. Then analysis proceeds, inserting more detail as shown in Fig. 5.3. And finally there is the very fine detail about the surfaces, lines, vertexes, and their relationships.

Such descriptions permit one to match, compare, and contrast scenes through programs that compare and contrast descriptions. After two scenes are described and corresponding parts related by the matching program, differences in the descriptions can be found, categorized, and themselves described. Of course, one hopes that the descriptions will be similar or dissimilar to the same degree that the scenes they represent seem similar or dissimilar to human intuition.

The program that does this must be able to examine the descriptions of Fig. 5.3 with the help of a matching program and deduce that there is a supported-by relation in one case, while there is an in-front-of relation in the other. Of course the matcher must be much more powerful than this simple example indicates in order to face more complex pairs of scenes exhibiting the entire spectrum between the nearly identical and the completely different.

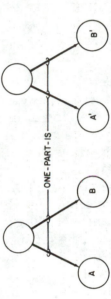

Fig. 5.2

from Fig. 5.4(c). And then from Fig. 5.4(d) it learns the fact that for one object to be supported by the others is a definite requirement, not just a coincidence applying to all of the samples.

Such new concepts can in turn help in making other, more complex abstractions. Thus the machine uses previous learning as an aid toward further learning and further analysis of the environment.

Identification requires additional programs that use the results of comparison programs. There are many problems and many alternative methods involved because identification can be done in a variety of ways. In one simple form of identification, the machine compares the description of some scene to be identified with a repertoire of models, or stored concepts. Then there is a method of evaluating the comparisons between the unknown and the models so that some match can be defined as best. But many sophistications lie beyond this skeletal scheme. For one thing, the identification can be either sensitive to context or prejudiced toward locating a particular type of object. Elementary algorithms for both of these kinds of identifications are discussed later.

5.1.2 Learning and Identification

To build a machine that can analyze line drawings and build descriptions relevant to some comparison procedure is interesting in itself. But this is just a step toward the more ambitious goal of creating a running program that can learn to recognize structures. I will describe a program that can use samples of simple concepts to generate models.

Figure 5.4 and the next few following it show a sequence of samples that enables the machine to learn what an arch is. First it gets the general idea by studying the first sample in Fig. 5.4(a). Then it learns refinements to its original conception by comparing its current impression of what an arch is with successive samples. It learns that the supports of an arch cannot touch from Fig. 5.4(b). It learns that it does not matter much what the top object is

5.1.3 Psychological Modeling

Simulation of human intelligence is not a primary goal of this work. Yet for the most part I have designed programs that see the world in terms conforming to human usage and taste. These programs produce descriptions that use notions such as left-of, on-top-of, behind, big, and part-of.

There are several reasons for this. One is that if a machine is to learn from a human teacher, then it is reasonable that the machine should understand and use the same relations that the human does. Otherwise there would be the sort of difference in point of view that prevents inexperienced adult teachers from interacting smoothly with small children.

Moreover, if the machine is to understand its environment for any reason, then understanding it in the same terms humans do helps us to understand and improve the machine's operation. Little is known about how human intelligence works, but it would be foolish to ignore conjectures about human methods and abilities if those things can help machines. Much has already been learned from programs that use what seem like human methods. There are already programs that prove mathematical theorems, play good chess, work analogy problems, understand restricted forms of English, and more. Yet in contrast, little knowledge about intelligence has come from perceptron work and other approaches to intelligence that do not exploit the planning and hierarchical organization that seems characteristic of human thought.

Another reason for designing programs that describe scenes in human terms is that human judgment then serves as a standard. There will be no contentment with machines that only do as well as humans. But until machines become better than humans at seeing, doing as well is a reasonable goal, and comparing the performance of the machine with that of the human is a convenient way to measure success.

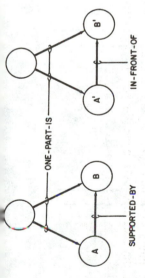

IN-FRONT-OF

ONE-PART-IS

SUPPORTED-BY

Fig. 5.3

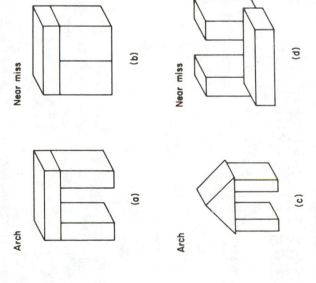

Arch

Near miss

(a)

(b)

Arch

Near miss

(c)

(d)

Fig. 5.4

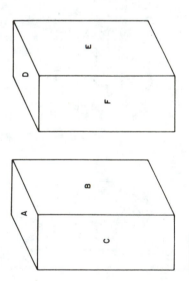

Fig. 5.5

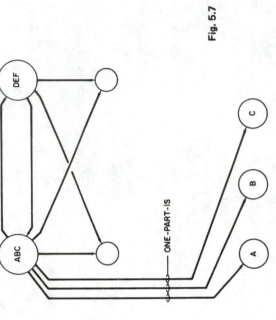

Fig. 5.7

5.2 BUILDING DESCRIPTIONS

The network seems to have the appropriate blend of flexibility and simplicity needed to deal straightforwardly with scenes. It is the natural format. Like words in a dictionary, each object is naturally thought of in terms of relationships to other objects and to descriptive concepts. In Fig. 5.5, for example, one has concepts such as OBJECT-ABC and OBJECT-DEF. These are represented diagrammatically as circles in Fig. 5.6. Labelled arrows or pointers define the relationships between the concepts. Other pointers indicate membership in general classes or specify particular properties. And pointers to circles representing the sides extend the depth of the description and allow more detail as shown in Fig. 5.7.

Now notice that notions like SUPPORTED-BY, ABOVE, LEFT-OF, BENEATH, and A-KIND-OF may be used not only as relations, but also as concepts. Consider SUPPORTED-BY. The statement, "The WEDGE is

SUPPORTED-BY the BLOCK," uses SUPPORTED-BY as a relation. But the statement, "SUPPORTED-BY is the opposite of NOT-SUPPORTED-BY," uses SUPPORTED-BY as a concept undergoing explication. Consequently, SUPPORTED-BY is a node in the network as well as a pointer label, and SUPPORTED-BY itself is defined in terms of relations to other nodes. Figure 5.8 shows some of the surrounding nodes of SUPPORTED-BY. I will generally call such related nodes satellites.

Thus, descriptions of relationships can be stored in a homogeneous network along with the descriptions of scenes that use those relationships.

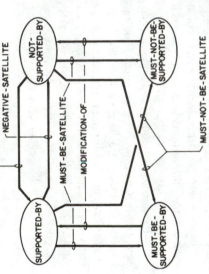

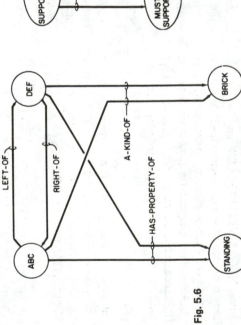

Fig. 5.6

This permits big steps toward program generality. A program to find negatives need only know about the relation NEGATIVE-SATELLITE and have access to the general memory net. There is no need for the program itself to contain a distended table. This way programs can operate in many environments, both anticipated and not anticipated. Algorithms designed to manipulate networks at the level of scene description can work as easily with descriptions of objects, sides, or even of functions of objects, given the appropriate network.

5.2.1 Preliminary Scene Analysis

Consider now the generation of a scene description. The starting point is a line drawing, with or without perspective distortion, and the result is to be a network relating and describing the various objects with pointers such as IN-FRONT-OF, ABOVE, SUPPORTED-BY, A-KIND-OF, and HAS-PROPERTY-OF.

My system's first step in processing a scene is the application of a program written by H. N. Mahabala[1] which classifies and labels the vertexes of a scene according to the number of converging lines and the angles between them. Figure 5.9 displays the available categories. Notice that Mahabala's program finds pairs of Ts where the crossbars lie between collinear uprights.

These are called matched Ts. Such pairs occur frequently when one object partially occludes another.

Mahabala's program creates names for all of the regions in the scene. Various properties are calculated and stored for these regions. Among these are a list of the vertexes surrounding each region and a list of the neighboring regions.

These results are then supplied to descendants of a program developed by Adolfo Guzman.[2] This program conjectures about which regions belong to the same objects. Surprisingly it contains no explicit models for the objects it expects to see. It simply examines the vertexes and uses the vertex classifications to determine which of the neighboring regions are likely to be part of the same object. Arrows, for example, strongly suggest that the two regions bordering the shaft belong to the same body. This sort of evidence, together with a moderately sophisticated executive, can sort out the regions in most simple scenes.

5.2.2 Selected Relation and Property Algorithms

These programs by Guzman and Mahabala provide information required by my own description-building programs now to be described. There are programs which look for relations between objects and programs which look for properties of objects. Generally these programs produce descriptions that are in remarkable harmony with those of human observers. Sometimes, however, they make conjectures that most humans disagree with. On these occasions one should remember that there is no intention to precisely mimic psychological phenomena. The goal is simply to produce reasonable descriptions that are easy to work with. Right now it is important to design and experiment with a capable set of programs and postpone the question of how the programs might be refined to be more completely lifelike, if desired.

Above and Support

T joints are strong clues that one object partly obscures another, but then one may ask if the obscuring occurs because one object is above the other or because one is in front of the other. Even in the simple two brick case there seems to be an enormous number of configurations. Figure 5.10 shows just a few possibilities.

But in spite of this variety, there is a simple procedure that often seems to correctly decide the ABOVE versus IN-FRONT-OF question. Consider the lines that form the bottom border of the obscuring objects in Fig. 5.10. Finding these lines is the first job of the program. Next the program finds other objects whose regions share these lines. In general these other objects are below the original, obscuring object.

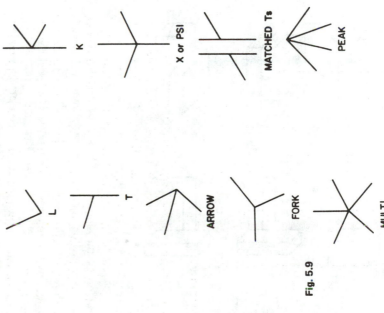

Fig. 5.9

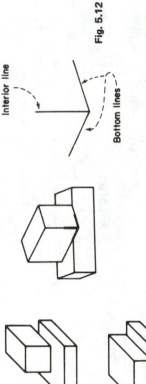

Interior line

Bottom lines

Fig. 5.12

I call these interior lines. Next the program examines the lower of each interior line's vertexes. This is ignored unless it is an arrow, psi, or a K. Then information about bottom lines is gleaned from each of the arrows, psis, and Ks in the following way:

1. If the vertex is an arrow, then the two lines forming the largest angle (the barbs) are bottom line candidates. (See Fig. 5.12.)
2. If the vertex is a psi, then the two non-collinear lines are bottom line candidates. (See Fig. 5.13.)
3. If the vertex is a K, then the two adjacent lines, those forming the smallest clockwise and the smallest counter-clockwise angles with the interior line are bottom line candidates. (See Fig. 5.14.)

This is really a rule and two corollaries, rather than three separate rules. Psis and Ks result primarily when arrows appear incognito, camouflaged by an alignment of objects as illustrated by Figs. 5.13 and 14. Consequently, the corresponding rules amount to locating the arrow-forming parts of the vertex and then acting on that basic arrow.

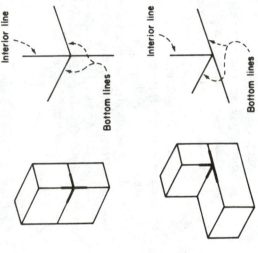

Interior line

Bottom lines

Fig. 5.13

Interior line

Bottom lines

Fig. 5.14

Fig. 5.10

This algorithm works on all the simple two-block situations depicted in Fig. 5.10. It even works correctly on the much more complicated, many-object scene in Fig. 5.11, shown with the bottom lines highlighted.

The difficult part is to find the so-called bottom lines, which correspond roughly to one's intuitive notion of bottom border. The process proceeds by first noting those lines that lie between two regions of the object in question.

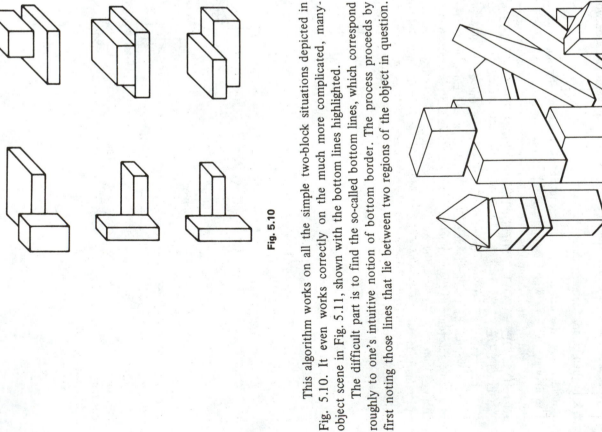

Fig. 5.11

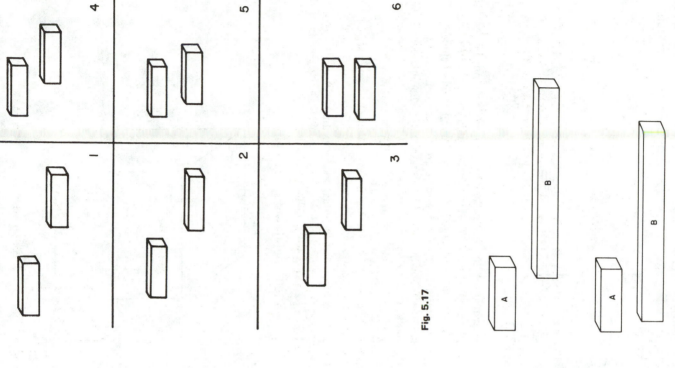

Fig. 5.16

Fig. 5.17

Fig. 5.18

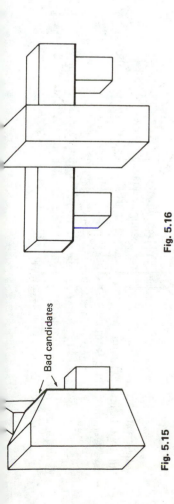

Bad candidates

Fig. 5.15

One further step is necessary before a line can become an approved bottom line. As shown by Fig. 5.15, some of the lines which qualify so far must be eliminated. They fail because they are too vertical, or more precisely, because they are too vertical with respect to the arrow's shaft. The effective way to weed out bad lines is to eliminate any bottom-line candidate which is more vertical than the shaft of the arrow suggesting that candidate.

Of course the program extends rudimentary bottom lines through certain vertexes. Figure 5.16 shows the obvious situations in which the bottom line property is extended through the crossbar of a T or the shafts of a pair of matched Ts.

Left and Right

Consider the spectrum of situations in Fig. 5.17. For the first pair of objects, the relations LEFT-OF and RIGHT-OF are clearly appropriate. For the last, they are clearly not appropriate. To me, the crossover point seems to be between the situations expressed by pairs 4 and 5.

Now notice that the center of area of one object is to the left of the left-most point of the other object in those cases where LEFT-OF seems to hold. It is not so positioned if LEFT-OF does not hold. Such a criterion seems in reasonable agreement with intuitive pronouncements for many of the cases I have studied. It also yields reasonable answers in Fig. 5.18 where in one case A is to the left of B and in the other case it is not. Notice that the relation is not symmetric, however, as the center of area of the much longer brick, brick B, indicates B is to the right of A in both cases.

Extra consideration is needed if one object extends beyond the other in both directions. No matter what the center of mass relationships, humans are reluctant to use either LEFT-OF or RIGHT-OF in such a situation. One must additionally specify a rule against this, leaving the following for LEFT-OF:
Say A is left of B $\Longleftarrow \Rightarrow$

1. The center of area of A is left of the leftmost point of B.
2. The rightmost point of A is left of the rightmost point of B.

The rule for RIGHT-OF is of course parallel in form.

Deciding if one object is to the left of another stimulates far more argument than do questions involving relations like IN-FRONT-OF and SUPPORTED-BY. People have difficulty verbalizing how they perceive LEFT-OF and tend to waver in their methods, but implications are that criteria change depending on whether the objects involved are also related by IN-FRONT-OF, ON-TOP-OF, BIGGER-THAN, and so on. The orientations of objects involved are also a strong influence, and my procedure could probably do better by asking basically the same questions as before, but about lines through the left-most, right-most, and center-of-area points in the direction of orientation instead of what amounts to vertical projection of the points to the x axis.

Marries

The abuts and aligned-with relations arise frequently, perhaps because of human predilection to order. As intuitively used, however, neither of these words corresponds to the notion I want the machine to deal with. To avoid confusion, I therefore prefer to use the term marry, which I define as follows:

An object marries another if those objects have faces that touch each other and have at least one common edge.

Thus the objects in Fig. 5.19 are said to marry one another. Those in Fig. 5.20 do not because they have no common edge. Similarly those in Fig. 5.21 do not because they have no touching faces. The MARRIES relation is sensed by methods resembling those previously described.

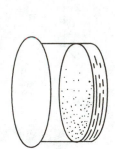

Fig. 5.19

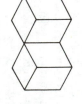

Fig. 5.20

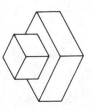

Fig. 5.21

Size

Piaget has shown that at a certain age children generally associate physical size with greatest dimension. They will, for example, adamantly maintain that a tall thin beaker has more water in it than a short fat one even though they have seen them filled from other beakers of equal size.

Adults do not develop as far beyond this as might be expected. I do not think we really use the notion of volume naturally. Apparent area seems much more closely related to adult size judgment. Notice that beaker A in Fig. 5.22 appears to have about the same amount of water in it as does beaker B, even though it must contain twice as much. Unless a subject consciously exercises a formula for volume, he is likely to report that object B in Fig. 5.23 is approximately ten times larger than object A, even if told both objects are cubes. The true factor of 27 times seems large when the trouble is taken to calculate it.

Fig. 5.22

Consequently, the size-generating program does not use volume. Instead it calculates the area of each shape produced by the shape detecting algorithm. Next it adds together the areas of all shapes belonging to an object to get its total area. Then using these areas it can compare two objects in size or consult the following table for a reasonably believable discrete partitioning of the area scale:

0.0% to	0.5% of the visual area →	tiny
0.5 to	1.5 of the visual area →	small
1.5 to	15 of the visual area →	medium
15 to	35 of the visual area →	large
35 to	100 of the visual area →	huge

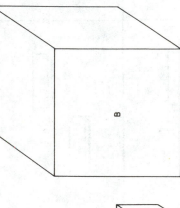

Fig. 5.23

5.3 DISCOVERING GROUPS OF OBJECTS

When a scene has more than a few objects, it is usually useful to deepen the hierarchy of the description by dividing the objects into smaller groups which can be described and thought of as individual concepts. Figure 5.24 seems to divide naturally into two groups of objects, one being three objects tied together by SUPPORTED-BY pointers, and one being three objects on top of a fourth.

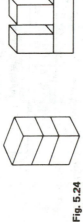

Fig. 5.24

Recognition of such groups seems to be a two part process of conjecture followed by criticism and revision. Conjectures follow from searches for objects linked by pointer chains or for objects bearing the same relation to some grouping object that binds the potential group members together. Criticism and revision is then needed to exclude from membership those objects that are weak compared with the average for the group.

5.3.1 Sequences

A simple kind of group consists of chains of **SUPPORTED-BY** or **IN-FRONT-OF** pointers. The first act of the grouping program is to find sets of objects that are chained together in this way. All such sets with three or more elements qualify as groups.

Using chains to define groups requires a rule for handling the situation illustrated by the scenes in Fig. 5.25. On the left a chain of **SUPPORTED-BY** pointers splits into two branches at the point where object C is supported by two objects, D and E. On the right two chains of **SUPPORTED-BY** pointers join at M which supports both I and L. The current version of the grouping program terminates chains at junction points without further fuss. This seems reasonable for it is natural to think of the scenes in Fig. 5.25 as a set of groups consisting of A-B-C, G-H-I, and J-K-L.

Another problem arises when objects tied together by a simple chain of relations should not constitute a group because of other factors. Here a need for the criticism part of the grouping process becomes clear. Figure 5.26 shows one kind of situation that can occur. In this scene the machine first conjectures a single object conglomerate, grouped together by virtue of an unbroken chain of SUPPORTED-BY pointers. But most humans see a short tower on top of a board on top of another tower. This must be partly

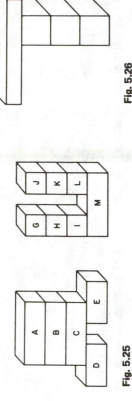

Fig. 5.26

Fig. 5.25

because of the size differences and partly because of the fact that the top group is not directly over the other objects. My system uses either of these radical changes as grounds for breaking the chain.

5.3.2 Common Relations and Properties

For this kind of grouping, the basic idea is again to make a generous hypothesis as to what objects may be in a group and then to eliminate objects which seem atypical until a fairly homogeneous set remains. When several objects relate to some other object in the same way, they are immediately solid candidates for a group. The legs on the table in Fig. 5.27 are typical. They form a convincing group partly because they have the same relation to the table top and partly because all are bricks and all are standing.

All candidates for group membership must be related to one or more particular objects in the same way. For the table, all four objects are related to the board by SUPPORTED-BY. This restriction is a useful heuristic because uniform relationship to a single object seems to have strong binding power. The bricks in Fig. 5.28 naturally constitute two groups, not one.

Now it is necessary to criticize the group with a view toward finishing with a group whose members all have about the same right to group membership. Said another way, established groups where the members are very much alike should have high standards for entry while weaker groups should be more penetrable. The somewhat involved criticism algorithm now

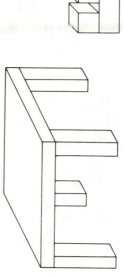

Fig. 5.28

Fig. 5.27

presented helps insure this characteristic in a group by iteratively casting out the clear losers from those proposed.

The flow chart in Fig. 5.29 and the example in Fig. 5.30 help explain. The program first forms a common-relationships-lists, a list of all relationships exhibited by more than half of the candidates in the set. Objects A through F are immediately perceived to be a possible group because they all have a SUPPORTED-BY relationship with a single object G. The relationships exhibited by the candidates are:

A, B, and C:

1 SUPPORTED-BY pointer to G
2 MARRIES pointer to G
3 A-KIND-OF pointer to BRICK
4 HAS-PROPERTY-OF pointer to MEDIUM-SIZE

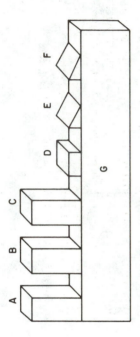

Fig. 5.30

D:

1 SUPPORTED-BY pointer to G
2 MARRIES pointer to G
3 A-KIND-OF pointer to BRICK
4 HAS-PROPERTY-OF pointer to SMALL

E and F:

1 SUPPORTED-BY pointer to G
2 MARRIES pointer to G
3 A-KIND-OF pointer to WEDGE
4 HAS-PROPERTY-OF pointer to SMALL

Three relations appear in the common-relationships-list because they are found in more than half of the candidates' relationships lists:

Common-relationships-list:

1 SUPPORTED-BY pointer to G
2 MARRIES pointer to G
3 A-KIND-OF pointer to BRICK

After this common-relationships-list is formed, all candidates are next compared with it to see how typical each is. The measure is simply the shared fraction of the total number of properties in the candidate list and the common-relationships-list. Said in a more formal way, the measure is

$$\frac{\text{Number of properties in intersection}}{\text{Number of properties in union}}$$

where the union and intersection are of the candidate's relationships list and the common-relationships-list.

Using this similarity formula to compare the various objects of the Fig. 5.30 example with the common-relationships-list, one has:

A vs. the common-relationships-list → 3/4 = .75

B vs. the common-relationships-list → 3/4 = .75

C vs. the common-relationships-list → 3/4 = .75

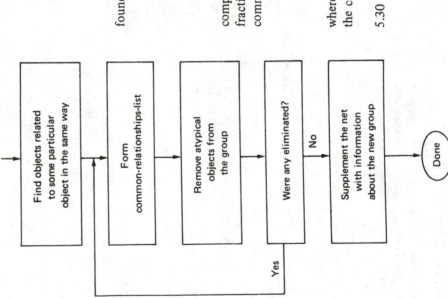

Fig. 5.29

Find objects related to some particular object in the same way

Form common-relationships-list

Remove atypical objects from the group

Were any eliminated?

Yes

No

Supplement the net with information about the new group

Done

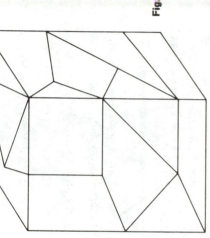

Fig. 5.31

D vs. the common-relationships-list → 3/4 = .75

E vs. the common-relationships-list → 2/5 = .20

F vs. the common-relationships-list → 2/5 = .20

A, B, C, and D do not have scores of 1 only because the common-relationships-list does not yet have a property indicating size. The reason is that there is no size common to more than half of the currently possible group members, A, B, C, D, E, and F.

The much lower scores of E and F reflect the additional fact that as wedges they are different from the standard type. They are immediately eliminated according to the following general rule:

Eliminate all candidate objects whose similarity scores are less than 80 percent of the best score any object attains. This insures that the group will have members all with a nearly equal right to belong.

Next the process is repeated because those properties common to the remaining candidates may differ from those properties common to the original group enough that one or more changes should be made to the common-relationships-list. This repetition continues until the elimination process fails to oust a candidate or until fewer than three candidates remain.

After the first elimination of objects leaves A, B, C, and D, there is a new common-relationships-list:

Common-relationships-list:
1 SUPPORTED-BY pointer to G
2 MARRIES pointer to G
3 A-KIND-OF pointer to BRICK
4 HAS-PROPERTY-OF pointer to MEDIUM-SIZE

Notice that there is now a size property since three of the four remaining objects have a pointer to medium size. The new comparison scores are:

A vs. the common-relationships-list → 4/4 = 1

B vs. the common-relationships-list → 4/4 = 1

C vs. the common-relationships-list → 4/4 = 1

D vs. the common-relationships-list → 3/5 = .6

This time D is rejected because its uncommon size causes a low score, leaving a stable group in which the objects are all quite alike.

5.3.3 Other Kinds of Grouping

There obviously cannot be a single universal grouping procedure because attention must be paid not only to the scene involved, but also to the needs of the various programs that may request the grouping activity. I have discussed two grouping modes that programs can now do in response to various demands. There remain many others to be explored.

One of these involves looking for things that fit together. Children frequently do this at play without prompting, and adults do it extensively in solving jigsaw puzzles.

Another kind of grouping, one particularly sensitive to the goals of the request, is grouping on the basis of some specified property. The idea is to pick out all things satisfying some criteria, such as all the big standing bricks. The result could be a focusing of attention.

Still another way to group involves overall properties that are not obvious from purely local observations. Techniques in this area are again largely unexplored, but it seems that overall shape can sometimes impose unity on a complete hodge-podge. Figure 5.31 illustrates this point. All of the objects fit together to form a brick-shaped group. This is clearly not inherited from any consistency in how the parts are shaped or how they interact with their immediate neighbors.

5.3.4 Describing a Group Using the Typical Member

The machine needs some means of describing groups. The method it uses seems to work, but there is room for improvement.

First, the parts of the group are gathered together under a node created specifically to represent the group as a conceptual unit. Figure 5.32 illustrates this step for a group of three objects, A, B, and C, all arranged in a tower.

Next comes a concise statement of what membership in the group means. This is done through the use of a typical-member node. Properties and relations that the group members share contribute to this node's description. For our A B C case, the typical member is described as a kind of brick, as lying, and as on top of another member of the group. Notice also the FORM pointer to SEQUENCE which indicates the kind of group formed.

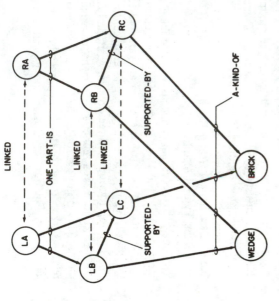

Fig. 5.32

5.4 NETWORK SIMILARITIES AND DIFFERENCES

Powerful scene description programs are essential to scene comparison and identification. Matching is equally important since the machine must know which parts of two descriptions correspond before it can compute similarities and differences. Figure 5.33 briefly illustrates. A process explores the two descriptive networks and decides which nodes of the two best correspond in the sense that they have the same function in their respective networks. The nodes in a pair that so correspond are said to be linked to each other. The job of the matching program is simply to find the linked pairs. Node LC and node RC in Fig. 5.33 both have only A-KIND-OF pointers to BRICK. Since no other nodes have similar descriptions, it is clear that LC and RC should be a linked pair. Similarly, LB and RB should be a linked pair since both have SUPPORTED-BY pointers to WEDGE and both have A-KIND-OF pointers to WEDGE and both have SUPPORTED-BY pointers to parts of a pair of nodes already known to be linked.

Of course the job of the matching program is not so easy when the two scenes and the resulting two networks are not identical. In this case the process forms linked pairs involving nodes that may not have identical descriptions, but seem similar nevertheless.

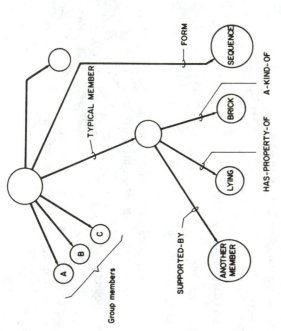

Fig. 5.33

5.4.1 The Skeleton and Comparison Notes

Once the matching process has examined two networks and has established the linked pairs of nodes, then description of network similarities proceeds. The result is simply a new chunk of network that describes those parts of the compared networks that correspond. This chunk is called the skeleton because it is a framework for the rest of the comparison description. As Fig. 5.34 suggests, each linked pair contributes a node to the skeleton. Certain pointers connect the new nodes together. These occur precisely where the compared networks both have the same pointer from one member of some linked pair to a member of some other linked pair. Notice that the skeleton is basically a copy of the structure that the compared networks duplicate.

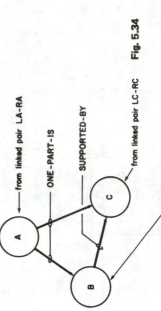

Fig. 5.34

5.4.2 Evans' Analogy Program

Embodying difference descriptions in the same network format permits operation on those descriptions with the same network programs. Thus two difference descriptions can be compared as handily as any other pair of descriptions. Those familiar with Tom Evans' vanguard program, ANALOGY,[3] can understand why this is a powerful feature, rather than simply a contribution toward memory homogeneity. Evans' program worked on two-dimensional geometric figures rather than drawings of three dimensional configurations. Nevertheless his ideas generalize easily and fit nicely into the vocabulary used here.

Figure 5.37 suggests the standard sort of intelligence test problem involved. The machine must select the scene X which best completes the statement: A is to B as C is to X. In human terms one must discover how B relates to A and find an X that relates to C in the same way.

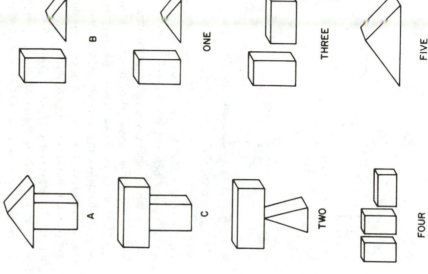

Fig. 5.37

Complete comparison descriptions consist of the skeleton together with a second group of nodes attached to the skeleton like grapes on a grape cluster. Each of the nodes in this second category is called a comparison note or C–NOTE for short. The most common type of comparison note is the intersection comparison note which describes the situation in which both members of a linked pair point to the same concept with the same pointer. Suppose, for example, that a pair of corresponding objects from two scenes are both wedges. Then both concepts exhibit an A–KIND–OF pointer to the concept WEDGE as shown by Fig. 5.35. In English one can say:

1. There is something to be said about a certain linked pair.
2. There is an intersection involved.
3. The associated pointer is A–KIND–OF.
4. The intersection occurs at the concept WEDGE.

Figure 5.36 shows how each of these simple facts translates to a network entry. First, a pointer named C–NOTE extends from the skeleton concept corresponding to the linked pair to a new concept that anchors the intersection description. The A–KIND–OF pointer identifies this concept as a kind of intersection. Finally other pointers identify the pointer, A–KIND–OF, and the concept, WEDGE, associated with the intersection.

All of the comparison notes look like this intersection paradigm.

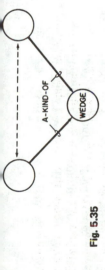

Fig. 5.35

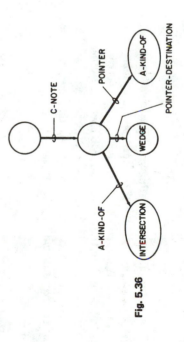

Fig. 5.36

Using the terminology of nets and descriptions, one solution process can be formalized in the following way: First compare A with B and denote the resulting comparison-describing network by

$$d\{A:B\}$$

Similarly compare C with the answer generating descriptions of the form $d\{C:X\}$. The result is a complete set of comparisons describing the transformations that carry one figure into another. Next one should compare the description of the transformation from A to B, $d\{A:B\}$, with the others to see which is most like it. The best match is associated with the best answer to the problem. If M is a metric on comparison networks that measures the difference between the compared networks, one can say

choose X such that

$$M(d\{d\{A:B\}:d\{C:X\}\})$$

is minimum

The metric I use is not fancy. It is the one discussed later that serves to identify some scene with some member of a group of models. It works because the identification problem entirely parallels the problem of identifying a given A to B transformation description with some member of the group of answer connected C to X transformations. The identification program, together with a short executive routine, handles the problem of Fig. 5.37 easily, correctly reporting scene three as the best answer. Reasonably enough, the machine thinks scene one is the second best answer.

Of course if the machine's answers are to be those of the problem's formulator, then the machine's describing, comparing, and comparison measuring processes should all give results that resemble his. Moreover, a really good analogy program should have available alternatives to these basic describing, comparing, and comparison measuring processes. Then in the event no single answer is much better than the others, the program can try some of its alternatives as one or more of its basic functions must not be operating according to what the problem maker intended. Evans' program is superior to mine in this respect because it can often compare two drawings in more than one way. It can visualize some changes as either reflections or any of several rotations.

Given my formulation of the analogy problem, it is easy to see how certain interesting generalizations can be made. After all, once an X is selected, the network symbolized by $d\{d\{A:B\}:d\{C:X\}\}$ describes the problem, and as a descripiton, it can be compared with the descriptions of other problems. By thus applying the comparison programs for the third time, one can deal with the question: Analogy problem alpha is most like which other analogy problem? Alternatively, one can apply the analogy solving program to problem descriptions instead of scenes and answer the question: Analogy

problem alpha is to analogy problem beta as analogy problem gamma is to which other analogy problem? This involves four levels of comparison. But of course there is no limit, and with time and memory machines could happily think about extended analogy problems involving an arbitrary number of comparison levels.

Scene L   Scene R

Fig. 5.38

5.4.3 A Catalog of Comparison-Note Types
The Supplementary-Pointer and the Exit

Consider the scenes in Fig. 5.38 and their descriptions in Fig. 5.39. Scene L has the pointer SUPPORTED-BY between LA and LB, but scene R does not have a pointer between the objects linked to LA and LB. The note describing this situation is called a supplementary-pointer comparison note and has the form shown in Fig. 5.40.

Suppose now we consider a standing brick and compare it with a cube. Here the linked concepts would differ only in that the brick has an additional pointer identifying it as standing. This differs from the supplementary-pointer case in that STANDING is a node outside the scene description. A pointer to the concept EXIT signals this situation. Exits involve concepts generated by the scene description program as well as concepts like STANDING that reside in the net permanently. If one scene contains more objects than another, the concepts left over and not matched end up in exit packages.

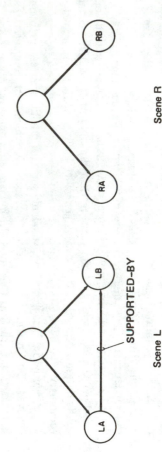

Scene L   SUPPORTED-BY   Scene R

Fig. 5.39

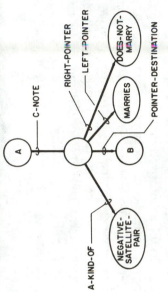

Fig. 5.40

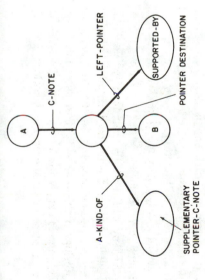

Fig. 5.41

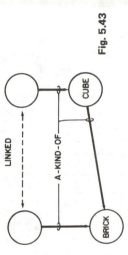

Fig. 5.42

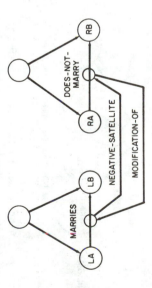

Fig. 5.43

Pointer Modifications

Suppose the left and right networks in Fig. 5.41 are compared. Notice the MARRIES pointer between LA and LB and the DOES-NOT-MARRY pointer between RA and RB. These could be handled individually as unrelated supplementary-pointer comparison notes, but this would ignore the close relationship between MARRIES and DOES-NOT-MARRY. Consequently a different type of comparison note is used that recognizes the relationship. It is the negative-satellite-pair comparison note. With it, the comparison looks as shown in Fig. 5.42. To find such negative-satellite-pair comparison notes, the comparison programs peruse the descriptions of unmatched pointers between linked pairs for evidence of relationship. For example, MARRIES is described in part by a NEGATIVE-SATELLITE pointer to DOES-NOT-MARRY. Now of course there are other pointers that are also just one step removed from a basic relation. All such pointers that are modifications of the basic relation are called satellites because they cluster around the basic relation to which they are attached by the pointer MODIFICATION-OF. Uncertainty, for example, is expressed by PROBABLY satellites or MAYBE satellites. The MUST satellites and the MUST-NOT satellites are others of particular importance in model construction. These inform the model matching programs that the presence or absence of some pointer is vital if some unidentified network is to be associated with a particular model network containing such a pointer.

Each type of satellite is associated with a type of comparison note forming an open-ended family. Thus in addition to negative-satellite-pair comparison notes, there are probably-satellite-pair comparison notes, maybe-satellite-pair comparison notes, must-satellite-pair comparison notes, must-not-satellite-pair comparison notes, and so on.

Concept Modifications

Frequently the members of a linked pair both have pointers to closely related concepts. For example, if a brick in one scene is linked to a cube in another, the situation is as shown in Fig. 5.43. This is very much like the pointer-satellite idea with A-KIND-OF replacing MODIFICATION-OF. In any case, the description generator recognizes this and similar situations and again generates a group of comparison note types. The first of these is the A-KIND-OF chain illustrated by the above situation. This causes the comparison note of Fig. 5.44.

The a-kind-of-chain comparison note also includes situations in which one concept is related to another not directly, but rather through two or three A-KIND-OF relations. Suppose, for example, a cube is linked with an

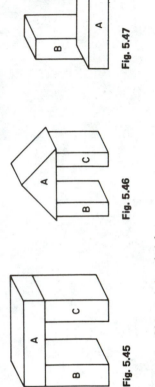

Fig. 5.45

Fig. 5.46

Fig. 5.47

1. Object A is a brick.
2. Object A is supported by B and C.

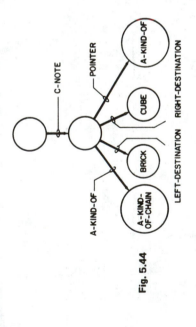

Fig. 5.44

LEFT-DESTINATION   RIGHT-DESTINATION

object for which no identification can be made. There is still an a-kind-of-chain comparison note because CUBE is linked to the general concept OBJECT by a sequence of A-KIND-OF relations.

Another kind of popular concept modification is the a-kind-of-merge comparison note. These a-kind-of-merge comparison notes occur if there is no A-KIND-OF chain as described above, but each concept has a chain of A-KIND-OF pointers to some third concept. For example, WEDGE and BRICK are both connected to the concept OBJECT by A-KIND-OF.

5.5 LEARNING AND THE NEAR MISS

I can now discuss the problem of learning to recognize simple block configurations. Although this may seem like a very special kind of learning, I think the implications are far ranging, because I believe that learning by examples, learning by being told, learning by imitation, learning by reinforcement and other forms are much like one another.

In the literature of learning there is frequently an unstated assumption that these various forms are fundamentally different. But I think the classical boundaries between the various kinds of learning will disappear once superficially different kinds of learning are understood in terms of processes that construct and manipulate descriptions. No kind of learning need be desperately complicated once the descriptive machinery is available, but all constitute opaque, intractable processes without it.

To begin with I want to make clear a distinction between a description of a particular scene and a model of a concept. A model is like an ordinary description in that it carries information about the various parts of a configuration, but a model is more in that it exhibits and indicates those relations and properties that must and must not be in evidence in any example of the concept involved.

Suppose, for example, the description generating programs report the following facts in connection with the arch in Fig. 5.45.

Now suppose the description containing these facts are compared with the scene in Fig. 5.46, where object A is a wedge, and with the scene in Fig. 5.47, where object A lies on the table. In both cases comparison could be made and differences appropriately noted, but the identification of one or the other of these new scenes as arches would be equally likely if the machine knows only what one arch looks like without knowing what in that description is important!

Humans, however, have no trouble identifying the scene in Fig. 5.46 as an arch because they know that the exact shape of the top object in an arch is unimportant. On the other hand, no one fails to reject the scene in Fig. 5.47 because the support relations of the arch are crucial. Consequently, it seems that a description must indicate which relations are mandatory and which are inconsequential before that description qualifies as a model. One need not require any descriptive apparatus not already on hand. One need only substitute emphatic forms like MUST-BE-SUPPORTED-BY for basic pointers like SUPPORTED-BY or, in some cases, add new pointers.

In the learning of such models, near misses are the really important learning samples. In conveying the idea of an arch, an arch certainly should be shown first. But then there should be some samples that are not arches, but do not miss being arches by much. Small differences permit the machine to localize some part of its current opinion about a concept for improvement. If one wants the machine to learn that the uprights of an arch cannot marry, one should show it a scene that fails to be an arch only in this respect. Such carefully selected near misses can suggest to the machine the important qualities of a concept, can indicate what properties are never found, and permit the teacher to convey particular ideas quite directly.

It is curious how little there is in the literature of machine learning about mechanisms that depend on good training sequences. This may be partly because previous schemes have been too inadequate to bear or even invite extensive exploration of this centrally important topic. Perhaps there is also a feeling that creating a training sequence is too much like direct programming of the machine to involve real learning. This is probably an

is better described by theories using the notions of programming and self-programming, rather than by theories advocating the idea of self-organization. It is doubtful, for example, that a child could develop much intelligence without the programming implicit in his instruction, guidance, closely supervised activity, and general interaction with other humans.

5.5.1 Elementary Model Building Operations

The machine's model building program starts with a description of some example of the concept to be learned. This description is itself the first model of the concept. Subsequent samples are either examples of the concept or near misses. One has a sequence of more and more sophisticated models.

Frequently, several responses may appropriately address the comparison between the current model and a new sample. When this happens, branches occur in the model development sequence and it is convenient to talk about a tree of models. Later I discuss in more detail how the alternative branches occur in the model development sequence. This section considers the case in which the matching program finds only one difference between the current model and a new example or near miss. The tables at the end of this section summarize the results.

The A-Kind-of-Merge: Example Case

Suppose the initial model consists of a plain brick while the example is a wedge. Figure 5.48 shows the resulting comparison description. Only one difference is found: the object of the model is related to BRICK while the object of the example is related to WEDGE. But since both BRICK and WEDGE relate by A-KIND-OF to OBJECT, the a-kind-of-merge comparison note occurs. Several explanations and companion responses are possible. One is that the source of the comparison note may in general point to either of the things pointed to by the A-KIND-OF pointer in the two scenes. Thus the object could be either a WEDGE or a BRICK. Another possibility is that the A-KIND-OF pointers from the object do not matter at all and can be dropped from the model. Still another option and the one preferred by the program is that the object may be any member of some class in which both WEDGE and BRICK are represented. In the example two such classes are simply the concepts OBJECT and RIGHT-PRISM. These are both located as the intersection of A-KIND-OF paths. The program responds by replacing the pointer in the comparison network that points to the a-kind-of-merge comparison note by an A-KIND-OF pointer to one of the intersection or merge concepts. In this case an A-KIND-OF pointer is installed between the comparison note origin and the concept OBJECT. Here the altered comparison network is the new model shown in Fig. 5.49. Note that this primary response I have selected for the machine represents a moderate stand with respect to a rather serious induction problem. I have avoided the extremes of pointing to

THING or the OR of brick and wedge, but just where in the spectrum to settle on is a difficult question. Another reasonable position would be to choose RIGHT-PRISM, for example.

The Supplementary-Pointer: Near Miss Case

Now suppose Scene 1 in Fig. 5.50 represents the current model while Scene 2 contributes as a near miss. The matching routine soon discovers that Scene 1 produces a SUPPORTED-BY relation between the two objects whereas Scene 2 does not. A supplementary-pointer comparison note results. Of course the implication is that the concept studied requires the two objects to stand together under the support relation. Consequently, when such a supple-

mentary-pointer comparison note turns up, it transforms to the emphatic MUST version of the pointer involved. Thus the new model is the one in Fig. 5.51.

Of course the supplementary pointer can turn up in the near miss as well as in the current model. Suppose Scene 1 in Fig. 5.50 is the near miss

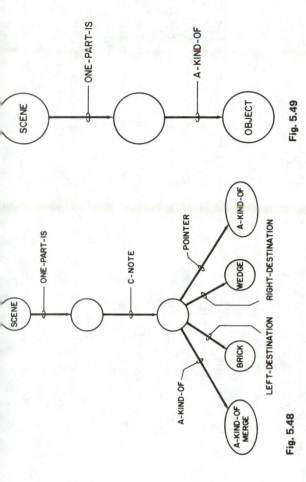

Fig. 5.49

Fig. 5.48

Scene 1

Scene 2

Fig. 5.50

TABLE 5.1 Action of concept generator: Example case

Comparison note type	Pointer involved	Response
A-kind-of-chain	—	Point to intersection with model's pointer
A-kind-of-merge	—	Point to intersection with model's pointer
Negative-satellite pair	—	Drop model's pointer
Must-be-satellite pair	—	Retain model's pointer
Must-not-be-satellite pair	—	Contradiction
Supplementary-pointer or exit	Negative-satellite or fundamental pointer in the model	Drop model's pointer
	Negative-satellite or fundamental pointer in the example	Ignore
	Must-be-satellite	Contradiction
	Must-not-be-satellite	Retain model's pointer

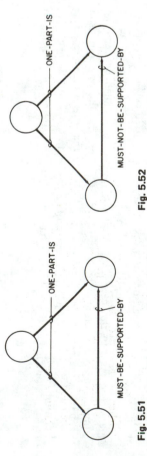

Fig. 5.51

Fig. 5.52

instead of the current model. One concludes A cannot be on B. The supplementary-pointer comparison note now indicates a relation that apparently cannot hold. Appropriately, the MUST-NOT version of the supplementary pointer is substituted in and the new net appears as in Fig. 5.52.

The Must-Satellite-Pair

Frequently comparison between the current model and a new sample displays comparison notes that do not reveal any new feature, but rather result from previous refinements in the model. Suppose, for example, that the current model has a MUST-MARRY pointer in a given location, while the sample has a MARRIES pointer. Now clearly the MARRIES pointer is appropriate in the description and the must-satellite-pair comparison note consequent to matching it with MUST-MARRY should be replaced again by MUST-MARRY. Thus the emphatic form in a must-satellite-pair situation is retained and not interfered with by refinement operations attempted subsequent to its formation.

The A-Kind-of-Merge: Near Miss Case

Sometimes a comparison note offers two or more nearly equal explanations. Consider the very simple current model and near miss in Fig. 5.53. The comparison note is an a-kind-of-merge announcing that the current model points with HAS-PROPERTY-OF to STANDING, the near miss to LYING, and both LYING and STANDING have A-KIND-OF paths to ORIENTATIONS. Now the near miss may fail either because it is lying or because it is

not standing. Responding to these explanations, the model builder might replace the a-kind-of-merge comparison note by a MUST-NOT-HAVE-PROPERTY-OF pointer to LYING or by a MUST-HAVE-PROPERTY-OF pointer to STANDING. Since most concepts humans discuss are defined in terms of properties rather than antiproperties, the MUST version is considered more likely. (Tables 5.1 and 5.2 summarize the points made in this section.)

5.5.2 Coping with Multiple Differences

Comparisons yielding single comparison notes are rare. More often, the model builder must make sense out of a whole group of comparison notes. If the comparison involves a near miss, any one of the comparison notes might be the key to proper model refinement. Moreover, many of the comparison notes have alternative interpretations that make further demands on executive expertise.

The model builder must therefore consider all the comparison notes and all the possible interpretations of each. Then it must produce the set of hypotheses that form the model tree's branches. These in turn must be ranked so that the best hypothesis may be pursued first.

The case of refinement through an example is simpler than through near misses. Since none of the observed differences are sufficient to remove the example from the class, it is assumed that all of the differences found act in concert to loosen the definition embodied in the model. Consequently each

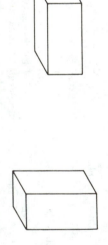

Current model   Near miss

Fig. 5.53

The most obvious way to search for key differences is by level. This assumes only that the differences nearer the origin of the comparison description are the more important. This certainly is a reasonable heuristic since a missing group of blocks generally impresses a human as being more important than a shape change, which in turn dwarfs a minor blemish. Consequently, the program determines the depth of the comparison notes which are nearest to the origin of the comparison description. All those candidates found at greater depth are considered secondary.

The highest level differences allow quick formation of little hypotheses about why the near miss misses and what to do as a consequence. A complete hypothesis specifies one comparison note as the sole cause of the miss and it further specifies which interpretation of that comparison note is assumed. Consequently there is a hypothesis for each interpretation of each potentially central comparison note.

The comparison note specified as crucial by a hypothesis is transformed as if it were the only comparison note. The other comparison notes are assumed by the hypothesis to be insufficient cause for the near miss. Consequently as a new model is formulated according to the hypothesis, all of the comparison notes but one are treated exactly as if the near miss were not a miss at all!

So far a single comparison note is assumed to be the exclusive cause of the miss. Were all possible combinations considered as well, not only would the branching increase enormously, but the ranking of those branches would be difficult. I have therefore decided that only one special combination of two comparison notes is ever permitted to form a hypothesis.

Hypotheses based on two contributing comparison notes are added to the hypothesis list only when two comparison notes with nearly identical descriptions occur.

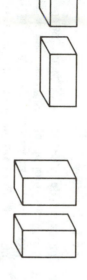

Current model   Near miss

Fig. 5.54.

TABLE 5.2 Action of concept generator: Near miss case

Comparison note type	Pointer involved	Response
A-kind-of-chain	—	If model's node is at the end of the chain add must-not-be satellite to near miss' node
		If near miss' node is at the end of the chain, use must-be satellite to model's node
A-kind-of-merge	—	Replace model's pointer by its must-be satellite
		Replace model's pointer by must-not-be satellite of near miss' pointer
Negative-satellite pair	—	Replace model's pointer by its must-be satellite
Must-not-be-satellite pair	—	Retain model's pointer
Supplementary-pointer or exit	Fundamental pointer in the model	Replace pointer with its must-be satellite
	Fundamental pointer in the near miss	Insert pointer into the model using must-not-be satellite
	Negative-satellite in the model	Replace pointer with its must-not-be satellite
	Negative-satellite in the near miss	Insert pointer into model using must-be satellite

comparison note can be transformed independently and a new model generated by their combined action. There is no problem of deciding if one difference is more important than another.

Consequently, if all the comparison notes had but one interpretation, only one new branch would be generated. The a-kind-of-merge comparison note has two possible interpretations, however, and if one such comparison note occurs, it is only reasonable to create two branches instead of one. The action on the other comparison notes is the same for both branches.

Near misses cause more severe problems. If two differences are found, either of them may be sufficient to cause the sample to be a near miss, while the other difference may be equally sufficient or merely irrelevant. If the differences have multiple interpretations or more than two differences occur, the number of possibilities explodes and the machine cannot work by simply generating an alternative for each possibility. The model builder clearly must decide which interpretation of which differences are most likely to cause the near miss.

Consider Fig. 5.54. Since exactly the same thing characterizes both blocks in the near miss, there is no particular reason to suppose that one difference should be singled out. Consequently a third hypothesis is formed, namely that both differences act cooperatively. This additional hypothesis takes precedence over the two hypotheses that consider the differences separately. It seems heuristically sound that coincidences are significant. The machine creates new models with such hypotheses by transforming both of the specified comparison notes in the miss-explanation mode.

5.5.3 Contradictions and Backing Up

By now one may wonder why the program should deal with alternatives to the main line of model development at all. To be sure, maximum likelihood assumptions may be wrong, but then how could the machine ever know when such a decision is an error? The answer is that the main line assumptions may lead to contradiction crises which in turn cause the model building program to retreat up the tree and attempt model development along other branches.

Consider the very simple situation already presented back in Fig. 5.53. Think again of the left side as the current model and the right side as the near miss. The current model and the near miss combination generate an a-kind-of-merge comparison note for which the priority interpretation is that examples of the concept must be standing. The alternative that examples must not be lying causes a side branch in the model development tree. But suppose one really wants the concept to exclude lying but not insist on standing. Showing the machine a tilted brick does the job. A tilted brick certainly is not standing and its description has no HAS-PROPERTY-OF pointer to STANDING. Yet the current model has a MUST-HAVE-PROPERTY-OF pointer to STANDING. This is a contradictory situation.

When contradictory situations occur, the program assumes it has made an incorrect choice somewhere, closes the branch to further exploration, and backs up to select another alternative.

In the case at hand, an alternative is found and the must-not-be-lying interpretation of the comparison between the scenes leads to a new intermediate model. This in turn is refined by the tilted brick scene which originally caused the contradiction on the former main line. No contradiction occurs on the new path because the MUST-NOT-HAVE-PROPERTY-OF/LYING combination of the intermediate model has nothing to clash with in the example. Indeed the new example lends no new information to model development along this path, the model being the same before and after comparison. The new example served solely to terminate development of an improper path in the model development.

5.6 SOME GENERATED CONCEPTS

In this section I explore some of the properties of the model generator through a series of examples. In the course of this discussion, words like house, arch, and tent occur frequently as they are convenient names for the ideas the machine assimilates. Be cautioned, however, to avoid thinking of these entities in terms of functional definitions. To a human, an arch may be something to walk through, as well as an appropriate alignment of bricks. And

certainly, a flat rock serves as a table to a hungry person, although far removed from the image the word *table* usually calls to mind.

But the machine does not yet know anything of walking or eating, so the programs discussed here handle only some of the physical aspects of these human notions. There is no inherent obstacle forbidding the machine to enjoy functional understanding. It is a matter of generalizing the machine's descriptive ability to acts and properties required by those acts. Then chains of pointers can link TABLE to FOOD as well as to the physical image of a table, and the machine will be perfectly happy to draw up its chair to a flat rock with the human, given that there is something on that table which it wishes to eat.

5.6.1 The House

Figure 5.55(a) illustrates what house means here. Basically the scene is just one wedge on top of one brick. But lacking human experience, this one picture is insufficient to convey much of the notion to the machine. The model builder must be used, and it must be permitted to observe other samples.

Suppose the model builder starts with the scene in Fig. 5.55(a). Then its description generation apparatus contributes the network which serves as the first unrefined, unembellished model of Fig. 5.56. Now suppose the scene in Fig. 5.55(b), a near miss, is the next sample. Its net is that shown in Fig. 5.57. The only difference is the supplementary pointer SUPPORTED-BY. Glancing at Table 5.2, it is clear that the overall result is conversion of the

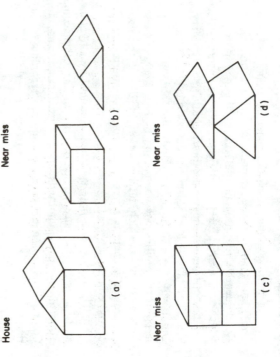

House

Near miss

(a) (b)

Near miss

Near miss

(c) (d)

Fig. 5.55

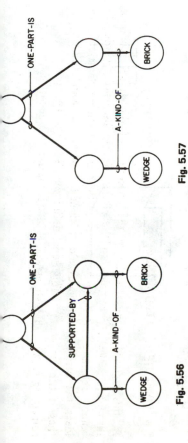

Fig. 5.56

Fig. 5.57

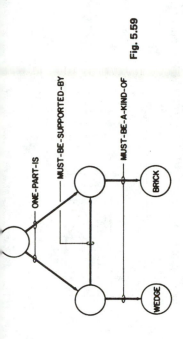

Fig. 5.59

SUPPORTED-BY pointer in the old model to MUST-BE-SUPPORTED-BY in the new model. Thus the new model is that of Fig. 5.58.

Much is yet to be learned. For one thing, the top object certainly must be a wedge. Showing the machine the near miss of Fig. 5.55(c) conveys this point immediately. Similarly the near miss of Fig. 5.55(d) makes the brick property of the bottom object mandatory. But notice that both of these steps cause bifurcation of the model tree. The reason is that the machine cannot be completely sure the miss occurs because the old property is lost or because the new property is added. The program prefers the old-property-is-lost theory and moves down the corresponding branch unless contradicted. In both of these situations, the preferred theory is correct resulting in the final model shown in Fig. 5.59.

5.6.2 The Tent

Think of the tent as two wedges marrying each other. As such it illustrates the handling of two similar differences simultaneously.

The base model is the description of the scene in Fig. 5.60(a) and the first sample is the near miss in Fig. 5.60(b). Two a-kind-of-merge comparison

notes result, one from each of the two objects because they are bricks, not wedges. Since they differ only in source, the hypothesis that both act together has priority. Now this result is complemented by the near miss in Fig. 5.60(c) which informs the machine of the importance of the MARRIES relation. Again dual comparison notes announce the loss of a pair of MARRIES pointers, and twin MUST-MARRY pointers are installed.

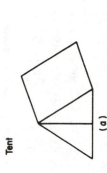

Tent

(a)

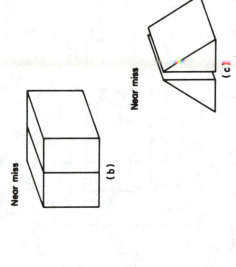

Near miss

(b)

Near miss

(c)

Fig. 5.60

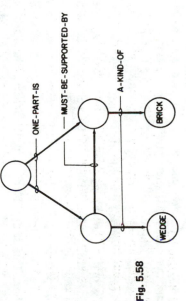

Fig. 5.58

5.6.3 The Arch

The arch involves a mixture of the elements seen in the previous examples. Because of the wider variety of differences encountered, it produces a bushy model tree and a challenge to routines that select priority hypotheses.

An arch with sides neatly aligned with the lintel forms the first model. Combining this with the scene in Fig. 5.61(a) the machine deduces that the MARRIES relations between the top and the supports are not crucial.

Next the near miss of Fig. 5.61(b) indicates that the support relations are crucial. Again, both new MUST-BE-SUPPORTED-BY pointers are handled jointly, and are installed at once.

The machine learns perhaps the most important fact from the near miss in Fig. 5.61(c). Here the two supports touch, supplying two MARRIES pointers to the description. This cannot be allowed. Responding, the machine inserts MUST-NOT-MARRY pointers between the two supports in the model. Some may think that in asserting the MUST-NOT-MARRY relations, the machine overlooks what they consider to be the real principle, that of a hole or passage. But for a child building with blocks, to have a hole and to have two non-touching supports are very nearly the same idea. Consequently the machine's opinion seems adequate for the moment.

Finally, the top object is not necessarily a brick. The sample in Fig. 5.61(d) teaches the machine that anything in the class OBJECT will do, since OBJECT lies but one step removed by an A-KIND-OF pointer from both WEDGE and BRICK.

Fig. 5.62

Figure 5.62 shows the resulting model. I give it in somewhat more detail than usual to convey a feeling for the complexity the programs actually deal with.

5.6.4 The Table

When a concept involves groups of objects, the model generation problem really is no more difficult. It becomes a matter of concentrating on relationships of the typical members of the groups studied.

Study the table in Fig. 5.63 and the description in Fig. 5.64. The essential features of the table are introduced by the following sequence of steps:

First the table should have bricks for legs. This idea is easily conveyed by the near miss non-table of Fig. 5.65(a). Moreover, this conception of table excludes structures such as that in Fig. 5.65(b), a fact which is handily incorporated through a MUST-NOT-MARRY pointer. Next, since the non-

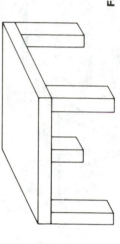

Fig. 5.63

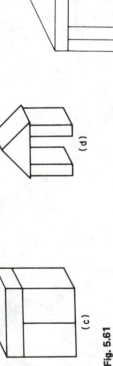

Fig. 5.61

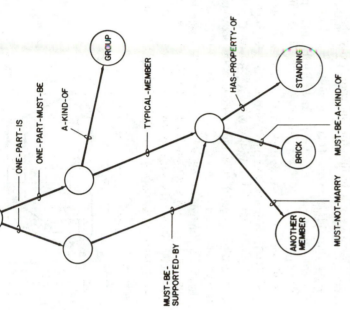

Fig. 5.64

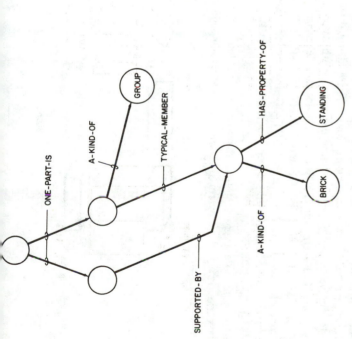

Fig. 5.66

table in Fig. 5.65(c) has only two supports, no grouping occurs, which leads to insistence on a group in the next model refinement. Finally, the scene in Fig. 5.65(d) leads to replacement of the SUPPORTED-BY pointer by MUST-BE-SUPPORTED-BY. Figure 5.66 shows the last model in this development.

5.7 IDENTIFICATION

Once there are programs that describe scenes, compare description networks, and build models, one may go on to using these programs as elements in a variety of other goal-oriented programs. The problem-solving programs described in this section have the following kind of responsibilities:

1. To see if two scenes are identical.
2. To compare some scene with a list of models and report the most acceptable match. This is the identification problem in its simplest form.
3. To identify some particular object in a scene. This is not the same as identifying an entire scene because important properties may be

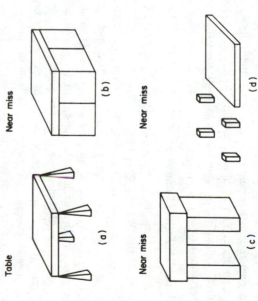

Fig. 5.65

hidden and because context may make some identifications more probable than others.

4. To find instances of some particular model in a scene. It is frequently the case that the presence of some configuration can be confirmed even though it would not be found in the ordinary course of scene description. This requires the ability to discern groups with the required properties in spite of a shroud of irrelevant and distracting information.

5.7.1 Exact Match and Discovering Symmetry

If two scenes are identical, then the networks describing those scenes must be isomorphic. The nodes of the two networks must relate with each other in the same ways, and the nodes must relate to general concepts such as BRICK and STANDING in the same ways. Consequently, comparing two such networks produces a simple kind of comparison description. There is a skeleton, which indicates how the parts of the scenes interrelate, and there is a group of intersection comparison notes that describe how the parts of the scene are anchored to the general store of concepts. None of the other types of comparison notes appear because identical scenes cannot produce two networks with the necessary aberrations of form.

Conversely, if comparison of two networks results in intersection comparison notes only, then the parent scenes must be identical in the sense that the description generating mechanisms employed produce exactly matching networks. There can be variation, but nothing so great as to vary the action of the description generator. The scenes in Fig. 5.67 are identical with respect to the descriptive power of my programs because in both cases the relations observed are LEFT-OF and RIGHT-OF. More capable programs might complain that FAR-TO-THE-LEFT-OF and FAR-TO-THE-RIGHT-OF hold in one scene, while only LEFT-OF and RIGHT-OF hold in the other. The scenes are clearly not identical with respect to a program with such a capability.

It is interesting to note in passing that the exact match detector is a major part of a curiously simple program that checks for a certain kind of left-right symmetry. The method is as follows:

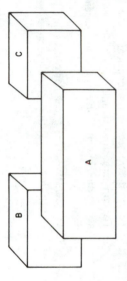

Fig. 5.68

1. Copy the description of the scene exactly.
2. Convert all LEFT-OF pointers in the copy to RIGHT-OF, and all RIGHT-OF pointers to LEFT-OF.
3. Compare the original description against the modified copy. If the match is exact, the scene is symmetric.

This is, of course, an abstraction of the familiar condition for y-axis symmetry in the mathematical sense, whereby symmetry is confirmed if and only if for every point in the scene, (x, y), the point $(-x, y)$ is also in the scene. Switching LEFT-OF and RIGHT-OF pointers is the analog of x-coordinate negation and network matching corresponds to a check for invariance.

To see how this works, consider the scene in Fig. 5.68. The center object A is flanked by B on the left and by C on the right. Figure 5.69 shows the resulting description. There are nodes corresponding to objects A, B, and C, and there are LEFT-OF and RIGHT-OF pointers indicating their relationships.

Figure 5.70 shows the copy of the network with the LEFT-OF and RIGHT-OF pointers switched. Notice that the original network and the copy are identical. Node A matches with A', B with C', and C with B'. Since there are no differences, the machine concludes the scene is in fact symmetric.

The machine knows LEFT-OF and RIGHT-OF are opposites because they are linked together by OPPOSITE pointers. Consequently, it is

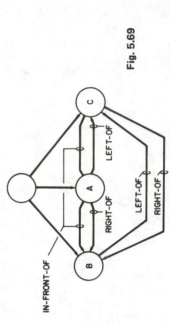

Fig. 5.69

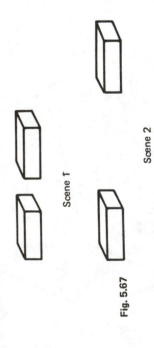

Scene 1

Scene 2

Fig. 5.67

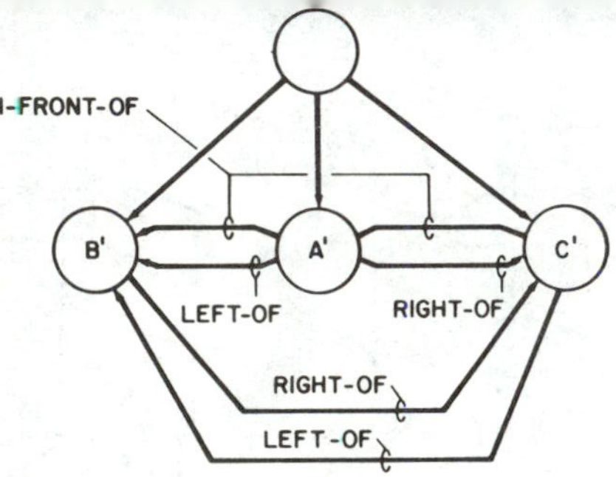

unnecessary to tell the program explicitly to substitute RIGHT-OF for LEFT-OF and vice versa. One need only ask the symmetry program if there is symmetry with respect to either the pointer LEFT-OF or RIGHT-OF. The machine itself can conjure up the appropriate substitutions by working through the OPPOSITE pointer from whichever relation is supplied, be it LEFT-OF or RIGHT-OF. Similarly, if one asks for symmetry with respect to LEFT-OF or RIGHT-OF, the program realizes that the proper substitutions are BELOW for ABOVE and ABOVE for BELOW.

An interesting combination is a simultaneous LEFT-RIGHT and an IN-FRONT-OF–BEHIND SWITCH. This one gives the machine a chance of realizing that two scenes are simply front and back views of the same configuration as are the scenes in Fig. 5.71.

Eventually I think the machine can come upon the symmetry notion in the same way it now learns about arches and houses. But at this point I do not think there is enough comparison describing capability. The needed step is the introduction of a program that generates global comparison notes from the local ones already at hand, thereby introducing the kind of hierarchy into the comparison descriptions that is already the standard in scene descriptions. One obvious ability of such a program would be that of noticing a preponderance of similar comparison notes. This and some of the double comparison ideas proven useful in doing analogy problems are the things the machine needs to learn about symmetry.

Fig. 5.70

5.7.2 Best Match for Isolated Structures

Suppose a scene is to be identified, if possible, as a HOUSE, PEDESTAL, TENT, or ARCH. The obvious procedure is to match its description against those for each of the models and then somehow determine which of the four resulting difference descriptions implies the best match.

Recall that models generally contain must-be satellites and must-not-be satellites while ordinary descriptions do not. Consequently, comparing an ordinary description against a model leads to a variety of comparison notes not found when ordinary descriptions are compared. Among these are must-be-satellite pairs, must-not-be-satellite pairs, and various flavors of exits and supplementary-pointers. Such comparison notes are decisive in the identification process.

Consider the case where some pointer in a scene's description corresponds to its must-not-be satellite in the model. This clearly means a relation is present that the model specifically forbids. The resulting must-not-be-satellite-pair comparison note in the difference network is such a serious association impediment that identification of the unknown with the model is rejected outright, without further consideration. This means that the near-arch in Fig. 5.72 cannot be identified as an arch because the network describing the near-arch has MARRIES pointers between the two supports while the model has MUST-NOT-MARRY pointers in the same place. The combination produces a comparison description with a must-not-be-satellite-pair comparison note that positively prevents a match.

Identification with a particular model is also rejected if the difference description contains exits or supplementary-pointer comparison notes which involve must-be satellites. Such comparison notes occur when essential relations or properties are missing in the unknown. Two bricks lying on a table do not form a pedestal because the model for the pedestal has a MUST-BE-SUPPORTED-BY pointer. The result is a supplementary-pointer comparison note involving the must-be satellite MUST-BE-SUPPORTED-BY. Again there is no match.

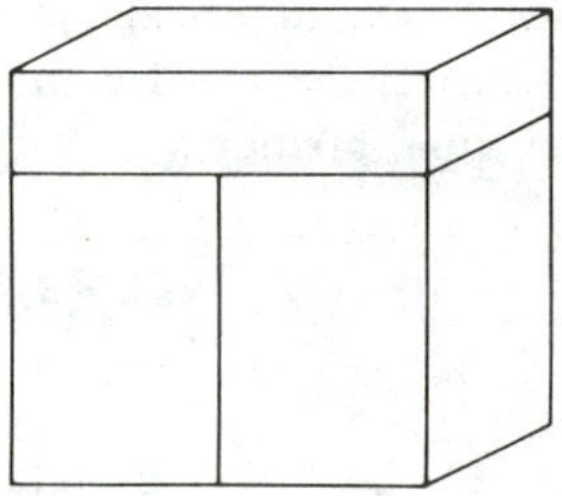

Suppose we have a HOUSE but its identity is as yet unknown. Match of a HOUSE against the PEDESTAL, the TENT, and the ARCH all lead to difference descriptions with comparison notes that forbid identification. The PEDESTAL fails because a merge indicates that the top object and BRICK is missing. The TENT similarly fails because both of its objects must be wedges. The ARCH fails because the model has a MUST-BE-SUPPORTED-BY pointer to an object missing in the HOUSE. This in turn causes a fatal exit comparison note in the difference description.

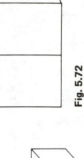

Fig. 5.72

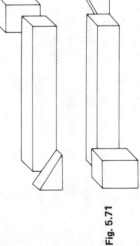

Fig. 5.71

The next problem emerges because some unknown may acceptably match more than one model in a trail list. Given several possible identifications, there should be some way of ordering them such that one could be reported to be best in some sense. To do this I associate each kind of difference with a number and combine the results by forming a weighted sum for each comparison. This seems to work well enough for the moment, but I do not think it would pay to put much effort into tuning such a formula. Instead more knowledge about the priorities of differences should lead to far better programs that do not use such a primitive scoring mechanism.

5.7.3 Best Match for Structures in a Context

Examine Fig. 5.73. Notice that object B seems to be a brick while object D seems to be a wedge. This is curious because B and D show exactly the same arrangement of lines and faces. The result also seems at odds with the models and identification process of the system as described so far, because so far anything identified as a wedge must have a triangular face.

But of course context is the explanation. Different rules must be used when programs try to identify objects or groups of objects that are only parts of scenes, rather than the whole scene. In the case where the question is whether or not the whole scene can be identified as a particular model, it is reasonable to insist that all relations deemed essential by the model be present, while all those forbidden be absent. But when the question is whether or not a few parts of a scene can be identified as a particular model, then there is the possibility that some important part may be obscured by other objects. In these situations, my identification program uses two special heuristics:

First, the coincidence of objects lying in a line seems to suggest that each object is the same type as the one obscuring it unless there is good reason to reject this hypothesis. This is what suggests object D is a wedge in Fig. 5.73.

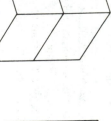
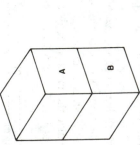

Fig. 5.73

Second, essential properties in the model may be absent in the unknown because the parts involved are hidden. This is why identification of object D with wedge works even though D lacks the otherwise essential triangular face. The requirement that forbidden properties do not occur remains in force, however.

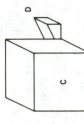
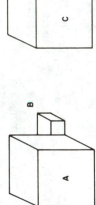

Fig. 5.74

Elaborate work can be done on the problem of deciding if the omission of a particular feature of some model is admissable in any particular situation. My program takes a singularly crude view and ignores all omissions. Rejection of the hypothesis that the obscured is like the obscuror happens only if the machine notices details specifically forbidden by relations in the model. Thus the effort is not to select the best matching model, but only to verify that a particular identification is not contradictory. This means that object B in Fig. 5.74 is confirmed to be brick-like while brick-ness is denied to D because of the ruinous apparent triangularity of the side face.

Of course if the propagation of a property like brick-ness or wedge-ness down a series of objects is interrupted, then the unknown must be compared with a battery of models with the program still forgiving omissions but now searching for the best of many possible identifications.

5.7.4 Learning from Mistakes

Suppose the program attempts to identify a house as a pedestal. Identification fails because the wedge will not match the top of the pedestal and the resulting type of a-kind-of-merge comparison note cannot be tolerated. Still it would be a pity to throw away the information about why the match failed. Instead the otherwise wasted matching effort can be used to suggest new identification candidates.

The way this works is quite simple. First the machine spends idle time comparing the various models in its armamentarium with each other. Whenever the number of differences observed are few, a simplified description of those differences is stored. Thus the machine knows that a house is similar to a pedestal, from which it differs only in the nature of the top object.

These descriptions link the known models together in a sort of similarity network.

This network and the difference descriptions noted in the course of identification failure help decide what model should be tried next. The

...of the differences between an unknown and a particular model is compared with the descriptions of the similarity net. If the difference between the unknown and a particular model matches the difference between that model and some other model, then identification with that other model is likely.

For example, an unknown which happened to be a house relates to the model of a pedestal in roughly the same way that the model of a house relates to the model of a pedestal. HOUSE is consequently elevated to the top of the list of trial models. Notice that the process requires the same steps as do analogy problems as described earlier. Figure 5.75 clarifies the procedure.

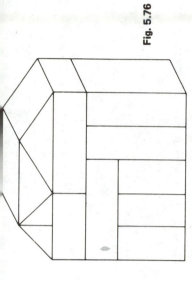

Fig. 5.76

5.7.5 Finding a Needle in a Haystack

The scene of Fig. 5.76 is curious in that one can find an arch, a pedestal, a house, and a tent in it if one is looking for them. But if they are not specifically searched for, mention of these particular models is unlikely to appear in a description of the scene. Although the configurations are present, they are hidden by extraneous objects so well that general grouping programs are unlikely to sort them out. Yet the question, "Does a certain model appear in the scene?" is certainly a reasonable one. One way to attack it divides nicely into three parts:

1. Find those objects in the scene that have the best chance of being identified with the model. If the model has unusual pointers or references unusual concepts, the program pays particular attention to them. Similarly, extra attention is paid to the emphasized parts of the model, for if mates cannot be established for them, solid identification cannot be affirmed. The result is a set of links between the objects of the model and their nearest analogues in the scene.

2. Once a good group of objects is picked, then the pointers relating these objects to the other objects in the scene are temporarily forgotten. In human terms, this is like painting the subgroup a special color.

3. Finally, with the best group of objects set into relief by the previous excision, the ordinary identification routines are applied with the expectation of reasonable performance.

The problem with direct application of the identification programs lies in the myriad irrelevant exit comparison notes that the extra objects in the scene would cause. Such clutter leaves the machine as bewildered as it does humans.

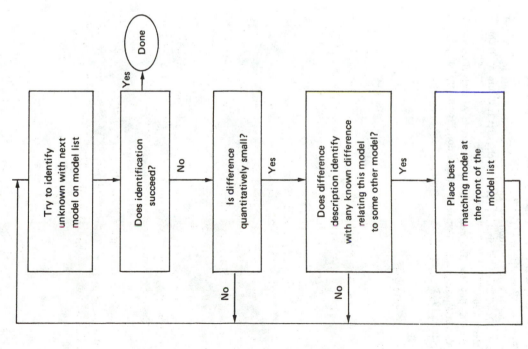

Try to identify unknown with next model on model list

Does identification succeed? — Yes → Done; No

Is difference quantitatively small? — Yes; No

Does difference description identify with any known difference relating this model to some other model? — Yes; No

Place best matching model at the front of the model list

Fig. 5.75

REFERENCES

1. Mahabala, H. N. V.: Preprocessor for Programs which Recognize Scenes, *M.I.T. Artificial Intelligence Laboratory Memo* 177, 1969.
2. Guzman, Adolfo: "Computer Recognition of Three-dimensional Objects in a Visual Scene," Ph.D. thesis, MAC-TR-59, Project MAC, Massachusetts Institute of Technology, Cambridge, Mass., 1968.
3. Evans, Thomas G.: "A Heuristic Program to Solve Geometric Analogy Problems," Ph.D. thesis, in Marvin Minsky (ed.), "Semantic Information Processing," The M.I.T. Press, Cambridge, Mass., 1963.

9 / Anthony S. Maida and Stuart C. Shapiro
Intensional Concepts in Propositional Semantic Networks

This paper proposes a particular semantic network formalism apparently capable of handling three important problems having to do primarily with natural language processing. One of these—the "telephone number problem"—is presented in McCarthy's "First Order Theories" paper [Chapter 31] in this volume. But more interestingly, the authors take and defend a very strong position with respect to the meanings of the nodes in their networks. Partially in response to [Woods, Chapter 11], but going substantially further, they interpret all information in the network *intensionally*—that is, as representing concepts and not items or sets in the world. The claimed value of this strict intensional stance is the ability of the formalism to handle tricky cases of sentences about beliefs. Since their nets are taken to model "the belief structure of a thinking, reasoning, language using being," Maida and Shapiro attempt to take opaque contexts (where, for example, equals cannot be substituted for equals) as the norm. While related in some ways to other formalisms discussed in this book, this creates an interesting contrast to KL-ONE [Brachman, Chapter 10], KRYPTON [Brachman *et al.*, Chapter 24], and KRL [Bobrow and Winograd, Chapter 13]. For example, the authors claim that their nets have no structural or definitional information, only assertions (which they claim is consistent with network models in the psychological literature). Further, the authors explain that in their model there can be no semantic primitives of the sort discussed in [Schank and Rieger, Chapter 7], and indeed draw upon the work of Quillian (see [Quillian, Chapter 6]) in defense of the non-compositional nature of their networks. There is, however, a bit of confusion in this paper, for example, when the authors get involved in discussions of "computational overhead" or in the direct representation of natural language questions, but the paper is valuable nevertheless. In particular, it is very well connected to the literature, and provides some good perspective on a number of other papers in this volume.

Appeared in *Cognitive Science* 6(4), 1982, 291–330.

Intensional Concepts in Propositional Semantic Networks*

ANTHONY S. MAIDA
Brown University

STUART C. SHAPIRO
State University of New York at Buffalo

An integrated statement is made concerning the semantic status of nodes in a propositional semantic network, claiming that such nodes represent only intensions. Within the network, the only reference to extensionality is via a mechanism to assert that two intensions have the same extension in some world. This framework is employed in three application problems to illustrate the nature of its solutions.

The formalism used here utilizes only assertional information and no structural, or definitional, information. This restriction corresponds to many of the psychologically motivated network models. Some of the psychological implications of network processes called node *merging* and node *splitting* are discussed. Additionally, it is pointed out that both our networks and the psychologically based networks are prone to memory confusions about knowing unless augmented by domain-specific inference processes, or by structural information.

INTRODUCTION

In this paper, we discuss a particular kind of semantic network. It is a representation of knowledge consisting of nodes and labeled, directed arcs in which the following conditions hold (cf. Shapiro, 1971): 1) each node represents a unique concept; 2) each concept represented in the network is represented by a node; 3) each concept represented in the network is represented by a node (the *Uniqueness Principle*); 4) arcs represent non-conceptual

*The work presented here was partly supported by the National Science Foundation under Grant No. MCS78–02274 and MCS80–06314. We appreciate the comments and suggestions of the members of the Graduate Group in Cognitive Science and of the SNePS Research Group, both of SUNY at Buffalo. We also thank one of the anonymous reviewers for very extensive comments.

tual binary relations between nodes; 5) the knowledge represented about each concept is represented by the structure of the entire network connected to the node representing the concept. The term *propositional* semantic network is sometimes used to distinguish those semantic networks in which *every* assertion that can be stored or accessed in the network is considered a concept, and therefore represented by a node, from those networks in which some such assertions are represented by arcs (most notably set membership and subset relationships, cf. Hendrix, 1979, p. 54; or statements without handle nodes, cf. Fahlman, 1979, p. 112). This paper is concerned with propositional semantic networks so understood. Conceivably, conceptual dependency networks (cf. Schank, 1975) could be classified as propositional semantic networks if their syntax were explicated. We are using the term proposition because propositions are the intensions of sentences. The definition also allows for the use of nodes corresponding to functional individuals.

We will more closely examine the Uniqueness Principle in order to help understand the semantics of semantic networks. In doing this, we follow the line of research exemplified by Woods (1975) and Brachman (1977, 1979). The major point will be that nodes represent only intensions and not extensions, e.g., individual concepts rather than referents, and propositions rather than truth values. Insisting that semantic networks be allowed to represent only intensions suggests promising approaches to several knowledge representation problems which often lead to confusion. One of our goals is to devise a representation which is rich enough to maintain the subtle distinctions related to referential opacity and extensional equivalence. The purpose of the representation is to provide a substrate by which processes (e.g., programs, production rules, and inference rules) can operate.

The first problem we treat concerns indirect reference, originally raised by Frege (1892) and recently discussed by McCarthy (1979). McCarthy has put the problem into the following form:

the meaning of the phrase *"Mike's telephone number"* in the sentence *"Pat knows Mike's telephone number"* is the concept of Mike's telephone number, whereas its meaning in the sentence *"Pat dialled Mike's telephone number"* is the number itself. Thus if we also have *"Mary's telephone number = Mike's telephone number,"* then *"Pat dialled Mary's telephone number"* follows, but *"Pat knows Mary's telephone number"* does not. (p. 129-130, italics in original)

Knowing is said to create an opaque context in its complement position and *dialling* is said to create a transparent context. The Uniqueness Principle suggests a solution strategy for this problem. We treat the concept of Mike's phone number and the concept of the number itself as distinct intensions, and thereby create a representational substrate with sufficient resolution to control inference processes which differentially apply in opaque and transparent contexts.

treatment would relate to the issues raised in this paper. His primary goal was to show how a speaker's beliefs about a hearer's beliefs influences the speaker's planning of speech acts. Anderson (1977, 1978) has sketched a semantic network based procedure for processing referring expressions. Anderson's approach involves creating two distinct nodes in the network for the two concepts (i.e., the concept of Mike's phone number and its referent), and perhaps was inspired by Woods' (1975) important paper. He does not work out the details of representing belief, as they are not his primary goal. He does some interesting reaction time experiments which partly test the psychological reality of the Anderson-Woods proposal and these will be discussed later in the paper.

The solution we propose is in the spirit of Anderson but is more thoroughly articulated in the following ways: 1) we specify exactly how the nodes are related and which features of the representation trigger which kinds of inference processes; 2) we provide the solution with well articulated philosophical underpinnings; 3) we point out that these same philosophical assumptions provide an identical solution to some, at first glance, unrelated problems; 4) Anderson's experiments used stimulus materials which involved only transparent contexts. We suggest that the experimental results will not generalize to opaque contexts; and, 5) We point out that Anderson's model, if it is straight-forwardly extended, predicts some counter intuitive memory confusions.

The second problem we treat is that of representing the concept of the truth value of a proposition. Since it is meaningful to talk about the truth value of a proposition independently of whether we know the proposition is true or false, we should have the ability to explicitly represent the truth value if we need to. For example, any semantic representation of the sentence "John knows whether he is taller than Bill" seems to explicitly reference the proposition underlying the sentence "John is taller than Bill." This seems clear after examining the paraphrase "John knows the truth value of the proposition John is taller than Bill."

Finally, we show how questions may be represented in propositional semantic networks. By this we mean how to represent the proposition that someone requested certain information of someone else. Such a proposition is contained in the sentence "I got mad because John asked me whether I was a boy or a girl."

HISTORY OF THE PROBLEMS

In this section, we briefly review the histories of three problems in knowledge representation for which we propose new solutions later in the paper. The main thrust of this paper is an investigation of the semantics of one kind of semantic network. That the theory leads to nice solution strategies for the three problems should be taken as a further explication of and support for the theory.

We can trace the emergence in artificial intelligence (AI) of the first problem to a paper by McCarthy and Hayes (1969) and it surfaced in its present form in later papers by McCarthy (1977, 1979). A well known philosophical solution to this problem, offered by Quine (1956) is to treat *knows* as an operator which creates an opaque context and to disallow substitution of equals by equals in an opaque context. Another approach has been adopted by Moore (1977, 1980). He encodes Hintikka's (1971) modal logic of knowledge within first-order logic and then builds an inference engine for that logic. An approach also using first-order logic is taken by McCarthy (1979) and Creary (1979). These researchers propose to view a concept as an object of discourse within the logic. They have one term which denotes Mike's phone number and another which denotes the concept of that phone number. This enables them to bypass the problem of replacement of equals by equals because the concept of Mike's phone number and the number itself are different entities. We differ from McCarthy in that we use one node to denote the concept of Mike's phone number and another node to denote the *concept* of the number itself.

One attempt to represent information about knowledge and belief in a semantic network was offered by Cohen (1978), but it is unclear how his

The second problem, of representing the notion of truth value, has not received much attention in the AI literature, probably because the problem domains which have been attacked by AI researchers have allowed domain specific solutions. We feel the problem deserves more attention for two reasons. First, the notion of truth value in general and the notion of the truth value of a specific proposition in particular can be objects of thought themselves. Since propositional semantic networks are supposed to be knowledge representations in which every concept (object of thought) is represented by a node, the notion of truth value should also be so represented. Second, having decided that truth values of propositions might be represented by nodes in a semantic network, we quickly find where such nodes can be useful. For example, utterance (1)

(1) John knows whether he is taller than Bill.

can be taken as an assertion that mentions the truth value of the proposition that John is taller than Bill without taking a position on whether it is true or false. Thus, in order to represent (1) as a proposition about a truth value, we need to be able to represent a truth value independently of the specific value (true or false) it happens to be. An alternative solution used by Allen (1979) and Cohen and Perrault (1979) involves specifying the meaning of "knowing whether" as a disjunction of correct beliefs. For instance, the disjunction (2) could serve as the representation for "John knows whether P."

THE THEORETICAL FRAMEWORK

What Does a Semantic Network Model?

The first issue we must be clear about is what we intend a semantic network to model. We first exclude two possibilities.

One possibility is the real world. This would require nodes to represent objects in the world (as opposed to individual concepts) and facts about such objects (as opposed to propositions). Although some people might be interested in semantic networks as models of the world, we are not.

A second possibility is that a semantic network models a corpus of natural language text, or perhaps that a semantic network is a data structure in which a text is stored and from which pieces of the text can be retrieved easily. In this case, nodes of the network would represent words, lexemes, morphemes, strings, phrases, clauses, sentences, and so forth. In Woods (1975), for example, it is argued that the semantic network representation of "The dog that had rabies bit the man" must distinguish between the proposition of the main clause, "The dog bit the man," and the proposition of the subordinate clause, "The dog had rabies." Woods proposed this for semantic reasons (p. 62). Had he made the proposal for purely syntactic reasons, then he would have been representing sentences as opposed to meanings. Although we feel that semantic networks can be used to model natural language text (cf. Shapiro & Neal, 1982), this is not the use with which we are concerned in this paper.

A third possibility, and the one that we are concerned with, is that a semantic network models the belief structure of a thinking, reasoning, language using being (e.g., a human). In this case, nodes represent the concepts and beliefs such a being would have. The point is that these concepts are intensions rather than extensions.

This is not, perhaps, the majority view of researchers in "knowledge representation." In their survey of knowledge representation research, Brachman and Smith (1980) asked researchers, "between what two things do you envisage the 'representation' relationship?" (p. 68). They report, "The one interesting thing to be said in summary, it seems, is that the phrase which we use as a commonplace label of our endeavor—'the representation of knowledge'—is perhaps surprisingly not taken in a particularly literal sense . . . what was considered to be 'represented', typically, were various kind of object [sic] in the world" (p. 71). Nevertheless, in answer to the question, "Would you characterize your inquiry as primarily an investigation into the structure of *language*, or more as an investigation into the structure of thought? . . . The great majority gave their prime allegiance to the study of thought" (p. 71).

(2) (*P* & John believes *P*) or
   (not *P* & John believes not *P*)

We claim that this representation uses the intensions *P*, John believes *P*, not *P*, and John believes not *P*, but it does not use the intension of the truth value of *P*, which is, we believe, the intension of "whether *P*."

A simpler example which we shall use throughout this paper is shown in (3) with its disjunctive reading in (4).

(3) John holds an opinion about whether he is taller than Bill.
(4) John believes he is taller than Bill or John believes he is not taller than Bill.

This disjunctive solution does not generalize to some embedding verbs such as "wonder," which is shown as sentence (5)

(5) John wondered whether *P*.

Perhaps (5) could be paraphrased as (6a) and thence, via the disjunctive reading of "knows whether," as (6b). We feel, however, that a better paraphrase is (6c), which mentions the concept of a truth value explicitly.

(6a) John wanted to know whether *P*.
(6b) John wanted to know *P* or to know not *P*.
(6c) John was curious about the truth value of *P*.

Our only claims are that a node for the concept of a truth value should explicitly exist in the network and is useful for certain representation tasks. We agree that (3) and (4) are logically equivalent and this can be captured by inference rules of some kind. However, logical equivalence is not the same as intensional identity.

The last of the three problems we discuss, that of representing questions, acquires salience because of our position that propositional semantic networks represent only intensions and the combined facts that: 1) intensions are meant to correspond to individual concepts or propositions, and 2) questions are neither individual concepts nor propositions. Other representational schemes can trivially represent questions by tagging the symbol structure which describes the content of the question as being a question and not an assertion. For instance, Schank (1975) represents yes-no questions in conceptual dependency diagrams by indicating that the mode of the diagram is a question, rather than an assertion. Wh-questions are indicated by placing the symbol "*?*" in the question slot. That is, the question "Where is the salt?" would be represented as something like (LOC SALT *?*). A propositional network would interpret the notation (LOC SALT *?*) as a proposition stating that the salt is at the question mark, or a proposition involving a free variable.

It happily turns out that by viewing yes-no questions as enquiries about truth values we can immediately represent them. Later in the paper, we attempt to generalize this solution to wh-questions as well.

Intensions

The term "intension" derives from Frege's (1892) term "sense". He was concerned with the relationship between *equality* and the meanings of designating expressions in a language. The fact that (7a) is true and (7b) is false illustrates the problem which concerned Frege.

(7a) Necessarily, the Morning Star is the Morning Star.
(7b) Necessarily, the Morning Star is the Evening Star.

Frege took this as evidence that the designating phrases "the Morning Star" and "the Evening Star" do not have the same meaning, even though they denote the same object. If the expressions were equal then (7a) and (7b) should have identical meaning. Frege used the term "sense" of an expression to intuitively correspond to the meaning of that expression, and he used the term "reference" to correspond to the denotation of the expression.

Carnap (1947) attempted to formalize Frege's notion of the sense of an expression as a function from possible states of affairs to denotations. The function was called an "intension" and the denotation was called an "extension" (cf. Dowty, Wall, & Peters, 1981, p. 145). The approach was refined through Kripke's (1963) semantics of necessity and Montague's intensional logic (p. 145).

When we say that nodes of a semantic network represent intensions as opposed to extensions, we mean sense as opposed to reference. Additionally for the purposes of this paper, we will not view intensions as functions, although it might be helpful to do so in the future. When we say that nodes of a semantic network represent intensions we mean intension as Frege (1892), McCarthy (1979), and Creary (1979) view intension, as opposed to Carnap (1947), Kripke (1963), Montague (cf. Dowty, et al.), or Moore (1980). We take intensions to correspond to concepts, ideas, objects of thought, or things which can be conceived of.

The Need for Intensional Representations

Woods (1975) appears to have been the first to emphasize that some nodes of a semantic network should represent intensions. One reason for this is to enable the cognitive agent being modeled to conceive of things which do not exist in the actual world such as unicorns and Santa Claus. Although unicorns do not exist, they can be reasoned about. Indeed, the reader can say, as McCawley (1980) points out, how many horns a two-headed unicorn would have. Thus, we should be able to describe within a semantic network any conceivable concept, independently of whether it is realized in the actual world, and we should also be able to describe whether in fact it is realized.

Returning to the Morning Star—Evening Star example, Woods (1975) concluded that, "there must be two mental entities (concepts, nodes, or whatever) corresponding to the two different intensions, morning star and evening star. There is then an assertion about these two intensional entities that they denote one and the same external object (extension)" (p. 50). Woods continues with the observation that "there must be some nodes in the network which correspond to descriptions of entities rather than entities themselves. . . . We have to decide how to tell the two kinds of nodes apart" (p. 68). Semantic network theorists have not universally agreed with this position. Schubert, Goebel, and Cercone (1979), for instance say, "We take the position that terms (nodes, subnets) *already have both extensions and intensions*" (p. 128, italics in original). Brachman (1977) takes a position on the other side of Woods, stating, "*Semantic networks are representations of the intensions of natural language designators*" (p. 139, italics in original). Yet Brachman still allows some extensional information in his networks: "some of the operations in the network scheme are purely intensional, while others are not" (p. 150).

We want to go even further than Brachman and say that all information in the network is intensional. The only reference to extensions will be propositions stating that two intensions pick out the same extension in some world, such as the proposition that the Morning Star is the Evening Star in the actual world.

The Absence of a Need for Extensional Representation

If, as Woods pointed out, at least some nodes represent intensions, do any represent extensions? Indeed, should every node be seen as having both an intension and an extension as Schubert et al. claim and as most philosophers usually treat designating expressions? Our answer derives from what we take our networks to model (see above). If a network modeled the real world, then a node would represent (or denote) an extension, but we take our networks to model conceptual belief structures.

A node that represents only an intension carries no commitment that an object realizing the intension exists in the real world. The standard translation of "The present king of France is bald" into a logical notation seems to require asserting the existence of the present king of France.

(EXISTS x) (x is-the-present-king-of-France & x is bald).

However, this is because of the normal extensional interpretation of statements in standard logic. A constant node in a semantic network is like a Skolem constant derived from a extensionally quantified variable that asserts only the existence of the intension.

STRUCTURAL IMPLICATIONS OF INTENSIONAL REPRESENTATION

The Need for Co-referential Propositions

If a semantic network has a node for the intension of the Morning Star and a different node for the intension of the Evening Star, what should be done when the assertion is made that the Morning Star is the Evening Star? If the nodes were merged by transferring all of the arcs from one node to the other and eliminating the first, then this would eliminate the distinction between the two concepts and make it impossible to represent the sentence ''John did not know that the Morning Star is the Evening Star'' differently from the sentence ''John did not know that the Morning Star is the Morning Star.'' The solution Woods (1975) proposed is to add a node to the network representing the proposition underlying the sentence ''The Morning Star is co-referential with the Evening Star in the actual world.'' The co-referential proposition can be used by the system's reasoning processes to infer that certain beliefs about the intension of the Morning Star can be transferred to (and from) the intension of the Evening Star. This will be discussed further below.

Order Dependency

The set of nodes existing in a network will depend not only on what information is presented to the network but also on the order of presentation. We shall call this property *order dependency*. Consider Russell's (1906) example, ''George IV wished to know whether Scott was the author of *Waverly*'' (p. 108). This apparently came about because, even though Scott was well known at the time, *Waverly* was published anonymously. George the IV had an intension for Scott and an intension for the author of *Waverly* but did not know whether they were extensionally equivalent. A semantic network simulating George IV, or just recording this fact, would need a different node for each of these intensions. But what does this imply for how we should represent the information that Scott wrote *Waverly* (assuming that the sentence ''Scott wrote *Ivanhoe*'' is our first introduction to the novel)? Must we represent this as two propositions, one for asserting the co-referentiality of the intension for Scott and the intension for the author of *Waverly*, and another for asserting that the author of *Ivanhoe* wrote *Ivanhoe*. Our answer is that the cognitive system creates intensions only as needed for storing information about them. A separate concept was needed for the intension of the author of *Waverly* only because there was thought of that author before an identification was made with any previous intension. Psychological evidence for this analysis has been provided by the work of Anderson and Hastie (1974), Anderson (1977, 1978), and McNabb (1977). This will be discussed in a later section.

This theory would predict that a sentence such as ''George IV thought that the author of *Waverly* was older than Scott,'' which requires two intensions having the same extension, would be harder to understand by someone whose first introduction to the intension of the author of *Waverly* was via the statement, ''Scott wrote *Waverly*,'' than by someone who had already thought about Scott and the author of *Waverly* independently. The second person would at first access the same intension for both Scott and the author of *Waverly*, but would then create at least one new concept for the intension of the author of *Waverly*. We call this process *splitting* and will return to a more detailed description of it later. This phenomenon would explain part of the cuteness of the example ''Shakespeare's plays weren't written by him, but by someone else of the same name'' (Hofstadter, Clossman, & Meredith, 1980).

Opacity as the Norm

A system that conforms to the Uniqueness Principle does not need the substitutivity of equals for equals as a basic reasoning rule, because no two distinct nodes are equal. Co-referentiality between two nodes must be asserted by a proposition. It requires inference rules to propagate assertions from one node to another node which is co-referential with it. Thus, intensional representation implies that referential opacity is the norm and transparency must be explicitly sanctioned by an inference process, unless nodes are ''merged.'' Merging will be discussed in a later section.

Connections with Reality

The main objection to exclusive intensional representation seems to be that if nodes represent only intensions, how could any alleged understanding system so based have any connections with the outside world? To consider this question, we must endow our modeled cognitive agent with sense and effector organs. We will look at a robot system with sight and manipulators.

The robot needs a perceptual system in which some node, set of features, and so forth is triggered consistently when a given object is seen. If it is to communicate reasonably with people about perceptual topics, it must be able to make approximately the same perceptual distinctions that we make. These perceptual nodes need not extensionally represent the objects that trigger them. The perceptual nodes can be connected to the semantic-conceptual nodes. This allows the robot to ''recognize'' objects, although it could be fooled.

The robot also needs effector organs that operate the manipulators consistently, and connections between some semantic-conceptual nodes and the effector organs so that it can operate its manipulators in a manner dictated by its reasoning (decide what to do).

Sensors and effectors, by supplying a connection between some node in the semantic network and some object(s) in the actual world, finally provide referents for the node in one particular world. However, these referents are only exemplars of the concept represented by the node. The significance of the node remains its intension.

The Meaning of the Nodes

There are a number of formalisms compatible with the definition of propositional semantic network presented at the beginning of this paper. The formalism used here contains only propositions and individual concepts. We will not specify a formal semantics for the network structures because the meaning units of the network, the nodes, violate Frege's Principle of Compositionality (cf. Dowty, Wall, & Peters, 1981; p. 42). If a formal language obeys the principle of compositionality, then for any non-atomic expression in the language, there is a set of rules which enable one to determine the expression's meaning from the meaning of the expression's subexpressions. In turn, the meaning of the subexpressions can be determined on the basis of the meaning of the sub-subexpressions, and so on, recursively.

There are two properties of a formal semantic system that must hold before one can even think of writing the above mentioned rules. The networks which appear in this paper have neither of those properties. First, in order for the above mentioned recursion to terminate, the language must have atomic expressions, or semantic primitives. However, the only primitives used in the networks are arc labels, which are non-conceptual, serve a syntactic function, and have no meaning. Second, in order for the principle of compositionality to apply at all, the meaning of an expression must not change when it is embedded in another expression. The meaningful expressions in our network, the nodes, get their meaning from the expressions they are embedded in (in addition to getting meaning from their subexpressions) and thereby change their meaning whenever they are embedded in a new expression.

Although our formalism does not obey Frege's principle, its characteristics which violate the principle can be found in Quillian's (1968) writings. Quillian, as Brachman (1979) has pointed out, is most known for suggesting that semantic information be stored in a subclass-superclass hierarchy so that properties could be inherited from superclass to subclass. There is, however, a less well known aspect of his writing that is relevant to

our discussion. The next two quotations, taken from Quillian (1968), seem to argue for a data structure that violates the principle of compositionality for the two reasons stated above. In the quotations, we will interpret the term "word concept" to mean node. First, Quillian argued that there are no primitives:

> there are no word concepts as such that are "primitive." Everything is simply defined in terms of some ordered configuration of other things in memory. (p. 239)

Second, Quillian argues that the meaning of a node is determined by a search process which begins with that node:

> a word's full concept is defined in the memory model to be all the nodes that can be reached by an exhaustive tracing process, originating at its initial, patriarchal type node . . . (p. 238, italics in original)

This implies that, as additional structure is added to the network, it changes the modeled cognitive agent's understanding of the concepts represented by every node connected to the added structure. Martin (1981) has applied the term *decompositional* to nodes whose meaning is dependent upon what they are constituents of. Because of this extreme form of decompositionality, the network described here will be inclined to memory confusions precisely because of these decompositional meanings. The mechanics of these confusions will be described in a later section. Anderson (1978, p. 51, Figure 1) appears to use decompositional meanings. It is an empirical question as to whether humans are inclined to make the above mentioned confusions. It may be the case that we will have to augment the network notation so that the meanings are more stable and conform to the second prerequisite for compositionality. Woods' (1975) arguments for the need to distinguish between the definitional information associated with a node and the assertional information associated with a node are relevant here.

THE REPRESENTATION CONSTRUCTS

Here we introduce the network notation used in this paper. It is not the only network notation compatible with semantic networks but uses perhaps the fewest constructs. The network will have two kinds of nodes which we will call base nodes and proposition nodes. The proposition nodes represent propositions and the base nodes represent individual concepts. All arcs are directional and are either ascending or descending, and come in pairs such that one arc of a pair is descending and the other is ascending. In the diagrams of this paper, only the descending arc of a pair is shown but there is always an ascending arc (corresponding to the inverse of the descending arc) which is not shown. A node is a base node if it has no descending arcs emanating from it other than a LEX arc. Otherwise, a node is a proposition node.

The LEX Arc

The purpose of the LEX arc is to form an access route from an individual concept to a word in a lexical memory. The LEX arc is a device used in this paper only to simplify the presentation. One drawback of the LEX arc is that its function is different than the function of the other arcs. This is because the object which it points to is not an intension, but rather an entity in lexical memory. Using the LEX arc to associate a name, say "John", with a concept, say the intension of John, does not give the network knowledge (in a conceptual sense) that John's name is "John," and we cannot tell the network that it has the wrong name for the person it thinks is named "John." A more consistent way to do this would be to have an intension for the word "John" as well as for the person John, and then use a proposition to assert that the intension for "John" is the word for the intension John. Any links to lexical memory would then emanate from the intension for "John" and not the intension for John. For the purposes of exposition we are representing an approximate distinction between a concept and a word denoting the concept but we would not be able to describe the process of acquiring word meanings with this scheme. So the current scheme is being used only to make the diagrams and presentation simpler.

The important things to know about the LEX arc are that: 1) it points from a concept to a word, and 2) the node it emanates from is an individual concept and not a proposition.

Other Descending Arcs

Other than the LEX arc, descending arcs always point to arguments of propositions and the nodes from which they descend represent propositions. A proposition node which has no descending arcs coming into it is said to be a non-dominated node and represents a proposition that is believed by the system. It is also necessary to be able to attach erasable, nonconceptual, assertion tags to proposition nodes which are dominated. The purpose of these tags is to indicate that the system believes those propositions. If a dominated proposition does not have a belief tag then the system has no opinion about its truth. The belief set of the semantic network consists exactly of the nodes which are non-dominated or which are tagged as true by an assertion tag.

Extensional Equivalence

There is a case frame, called the equivalence case frame, which is used to represent extensional equivalence. This case frame is used to assert that two distinct intensions have the same extension in the real world. It does not say what the extension is but rather only that they have the same extension. Thus "The Morning Star is the Evening Star," is represented in the simplified network structure of Figure 1 and can be paraphrased as "The conceptual object denoted by 'Morning Star' is extensionally equivalent to the conceptual object denoted by 'Evening Star'." The reason the case frame has a special status is that it will interact with propositions involving knowing and believing in ways that other propositions will not interact.

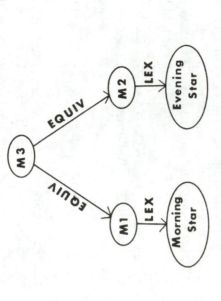

Figure 1. A representation (node M3) for the propositional information in the sentence "The Morning Star is the Evening Star."

Knowing and Believing

We will also use two different *know* relations. One will be used for knowing a fact as in the sentence "John knows that he is taller than Bill." The other will indicate familiarity with a concrete or abstract object as in knowing a person or game, or as in the sentence "Pat knows Mike's phone number.". We will call the sense of knowing a fact "know 1" and the sense of being acquainted with a thing "know 2". We justify these relations on the basis of the introspection that knowing an object is different than knowing a fact. Similarly, we will use two different *believe* relations, called "believe 1" and "believe 2," to correspond to the two different *know* relations.

As stated earlier a propositional semantic network models the belief system of a cognitive agent, which we will call "the system." Whenever any of the relations involving knowing or believing appear in the network, they will represent beliefs about beliefs.

We shall treat know1 only as correct belief rather than justified, correct belief for the following reason. If a cognitive agent believes that someone *knows* a facts, then the agent believes: 1) that the someone believes the fact; 2) the fact is true; and 3) that the someone believes the fact for the

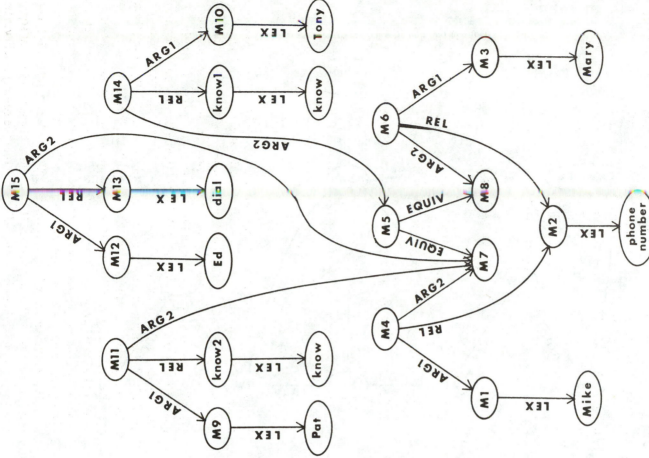

Figure 2. A representation for the information in the sentence sequence: "Pat knows Mike's phone number; Ed dials Mike's phone number; and Tony correctly believes that Mike's phone number is the same as Mary's phone number."

right reasons (as far as the cognitive agent can tell). The third stipulation about "right reasons" is necessary to rule out belief for the wrong reasons such as superstition or guessing. For example, there is at least one person who believes that white can force a win in chess, and there is at least one person who believes that white cannot. Therefore we know there is a person who has a correct opinion about whether white can force a win. Nonetheless, no one currently knows whether white can force a win. Since we are not able to specify what "believing for the right reasons" means, we will discuss knowing only in the sense of correct belief.

McCARTHY'S TELEPHONE NUMBER PROBLEM

The Main Example

We now address ourselves to McCarthy's telephone number problem. What follows is our representation, and its rationale, for sentence sequence (8).

(8) Pat knows Mike's phone number; Ed dials Mike's phone number; and, Tony correctly believes that Mike's phone number is the same as Mary's phone number.

This sentence sequence illustrates the distinctions upon which McCarthy's example focuses. On the basis of (8) the system should conclude that Ed dials Mary's phone number, yet it should not conclude that Pat knows Mary's phone number. Furthermore, it should not conclude that Tony knows either Mike's or Mary's phone number; however, if the system is subsequently told that Tony knows one of the numbers in particular, it should conclude that Tony also knows the other number. Figure 2 shows the network representation of the information contained in (8). (Note: Although it does not appear in the figure, assume M5 has been tagged as true by an assertion tag.)

Critical to our discussion is an explication of the system's understanding the concept of node M7 of that figure. Node M7 is:

Something which Pat knows, and
something which Ed dials, and
something which is Mike's phone number, and
something that is co-referential with Mary's phone number, and
something that Tony knows is co-referential with Mary's phone number.

In order to explicate the node's full concept, it was necessary to traverse the entire network, and the network is the sum total of the system's beliefs.

The assertion that node M7 is co-referent with Mary's phone number is just as much a part its meaning as the assertion that it is Mike's phone number. However, we do not want the system to decide that Pat knows Mary's phone number, so how do we avoid this? This is where extensional equivalence links acquire their special status. If the system believes that

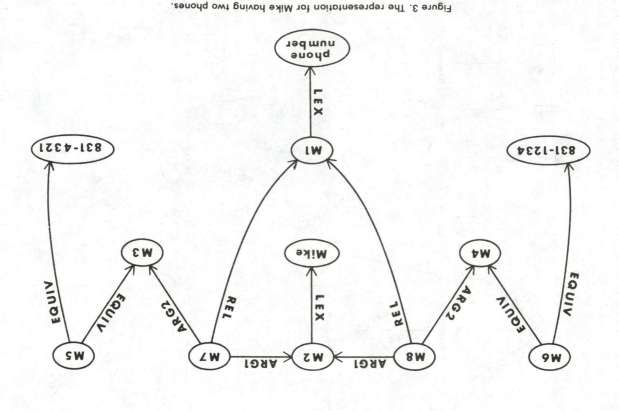

Figure 3. The representation for Mike having two phones.

some agent knows some intensional concept, then it will assume that the agent knows all of the propositions asserted about the intensional concept except those propositions which consist of the extensional equivalence case frame (e.g., M5) or which contain the extensional equivalence case frame (e.g., M14). So the system will assume that Pat knows M4, M11, and M15. Now the system could be mistaken; Pat need not necessarily know M15. This performance characteristic would predict corresponding kinds of memory confusions in humans. Further discussion of this appears later in the paper in the section titled "Merging and Splitting Nodes."

Further Examples

To further illustrate how we would use the representation, we will look at two more sentences, and then return to the question of transparency verses opacity. Consider (9) below.

    (9) Mike has two phones. One is 831-1234. The other is 831-4321.

Figure 3 shows how we represent it. The next example illustrates how we handle designators which fail to refer, as seen in (10) below.

    (10) Mike doesn't have a phone.

There are two ways to represent this utterance. The first involves the intension of nothing (for a discussion of this intensional object see, Heath, 1967). It is the notion of non-existence. The representation is depicted in Figure 4, and if one of the non-dominated nodes were submitted to a language generator (node M4 or M5), it might produce the sentence "Mike's phone number is non-existent." The other way employs universal quantification and, as shown in Figure 5, asserts that for all x, x is not Mike's phone number. The quantification arc is taken from the SNePS semantic network formalism (Shapiro, 1979a).

Transparent Relations Propogate by Inference

We now return to describing how the representation for McCarthy's telephone number problem can support processes which simulate referential transparency and opacity. Opacity is the norm because for instance, in the situation of sentence sequence (8), Mike's phone number and Mary's phone number are distinct intensions which are extensionally equivalent; but extensional equivalence is not equality, so we do not encounter the problem of substitution of equals for equals. Transparency, however, requires some sort of inference process. What is needed is an inference or production rule which propogates assertions across equivalence arcs, but which has an antecedent trigger pattern that matches only assertions involving transparent operators. This entails that the system have the conceptual knowledge that the relation *dial* is transparent but *know* is not. Such an inference rule would then enable the system to add to its data base that Ed dials Mary's phone number from the information given in (8); yet the system would not add that Pat knows Mary's phone number, because *know* is not transparent and would not satisfy the trigger pattern of the inference rule.

There are situations in which assertions involving opaque operators can also propagate across equivalence paths. Tony in (8) knows that Mike's phone number and Mary's phone number are extensionally equivalent, so any assertion with Tony as the agent and Mike's phone number (node M7) as the object, regardless of whether it involves an opaque operator, should be able to propagate across that equivalence path. In short then, if a cognitive agent knows that two concepts are extensionally equivalent, then for that agent all operators are transparent with respect to that path. The appendix contains examples of inference rules which propagate assertions across an equivalence path. No claim is made that they are complete.

REPRESENTING TRUTH VALUE

This section makes several points. First, the concept of the truth value of some proposition is intensionally distinct from its particular truth value (true or false) and at times it is necessary to make this distinction explicit in the representation. Second, the same information can be represented by two different configurations of concepts. This illustrates what we mean by order dependency. And third, we contrast the behavior of the system's beliefs about believing with its beliefs about knowing (correct belief).

Figure 6 shows the representation for sentence (11), with the proviso that the system has already wondered about the truth value of the proposition underlying the sentence "John is taller than Bill." An implication of our discussion of order dependency is that a distinct intension for the truth value of a proposition will be created only if the system wonders about the truth value of that proposition before actually learning its truth value.

(11) It is true that John is taller than Bill.

This treatment embodies the claim that the extension of a proposition is its truth value. Node M8 is the intension for the truth value of the proposition underlying the sentence "John is taller than Bill." Node M6 represents the individual concept of truth. When John wonders whether he is taller than Bill as in sentence (5), he is trying to determine the co-reference of node M8.

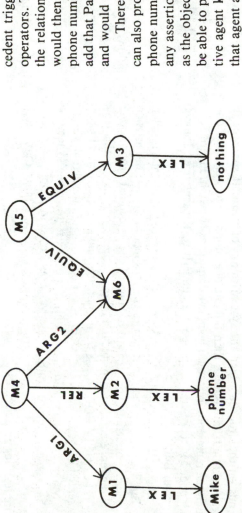

Figure 4. The representation for *Mike* not having a phone.

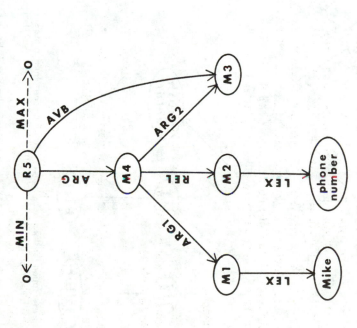

Figure 5. Another representation for *Mike* not having a phone.

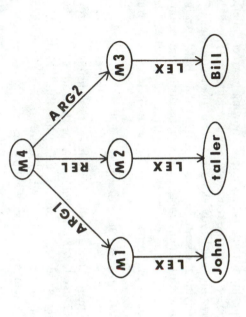

Figure 7. The representation (node M4) for the propositional information contained in the sentence "John is taller than Bill."

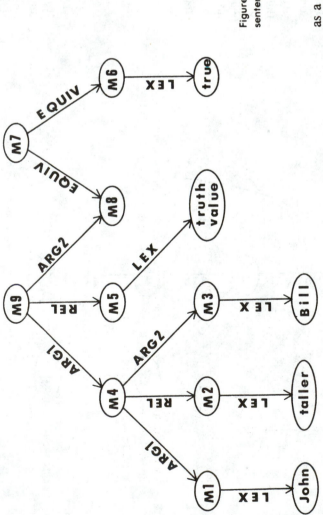

Figure 6. The representation for the propositional information contained in the sentence "It is true that John is taller than Bill."

If Tony believes, as in sentence (1), John knows whether John is taller than Bill, then Tony believes John's description of node M8 is complete even though Tony's is not necessarily complete.

We emphasize that the configuration of nodes used to represent (11) depends on the order in which the system thinks of them. If someone is directly told that John is taller than Bill and does not have to wonder about it, then the representation would be much simpler, as shown in Figure 7, in which node M4 represents the proposition underlying the sentence "John is taller than Bill."

Since (11) is an extraposed version of the sentence "That John is taller than Bill is true," we suspect it carries the presupposition that the listener has in fact wondered about the truth value of the embedded proposition, and so the representation depicted in Figure 6 is the correct one for this sentence. The EQUIV-EQUIV case frame indicates that two intensions already represented in the network are extensionally equivalent in the actual world. Node M6 of Figure 6 would presumably already exist in anyone's memory who has some notion of truth. Mode M8 would exist in people's memory who have wondered about the truth value of "John is taller than Bill" before learning its actual truth value.

The reader might entertain the possibility of using the above technique as a general method of asserting propositions in the network. This is not possible because it would lead to an infinite regress of assertion embeddings. If the EQUIV-EQUIV case frame were necessary to assert a proposition then Figure 6 would not assert utterance (11) because node M7 has not been asserted by the EQUIV-EQUIV case frame. The convention of taking top-level nodes as being asserted alleviates this problem.

In order to represent sentence (3), duplicated below, we use "believe 2." As already mentioned, it means to be familiar

(3) John holds an opinion about whether he is taller than Bill.
(4) John believes he is taller than Bill or John believes he is not taller than Bill.

with, or apprehend, some intension. Figures 8 and 9 contrast our representations of sentences (3) and (4). In Figure 9, sentence (4) is represented by node M8 which is a proposition involving exclusive-or. A feature inherent in the use of "know 2" is that the task of appraising in exactly what manner the agent of the "know 2" relation is familiar with, or apprehends, an individual concept requires the use of inference rules. "Know 2" says nothing in itself except that the agent is familiar in some domain specific way with the individual concept that is the object of the relation. There must also be a

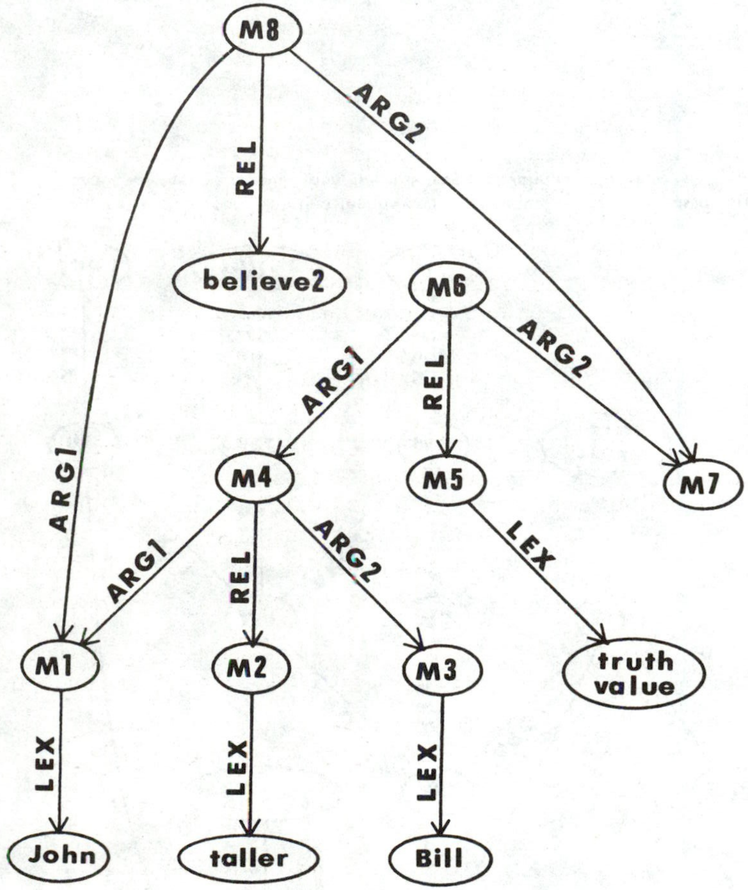

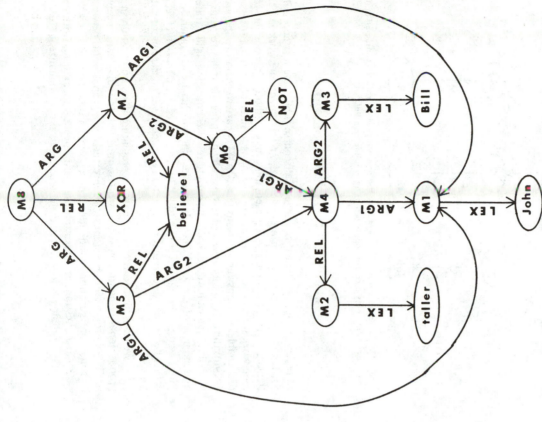

Figure 8. The representation (node M8) for the propositional information contained in the sentence "John holds an opinion about whether he is taller than Bill."

way for the specific facts that an agent knows about the concept to be independently asserted. An illustration of this point is depicted in Figures 10 and 11. Node M8 in Figure 10 does not directly represent

(12) John knows that he is taller than Bill.

sentence (12), but rather entails sentence (12). Node M5 in Figure 11 does directly represent (12). Believing that P and having a correct opinion about

Figure 9. The representation (node M8) for the propositional information contained in the sentence "John believes he is taller than Bill or John believes he is not taller than Bill."

whether P are two different intensions and therefore should be represented by two distinct nodes. The network structure of Figure 10 does not explicitly assert what John's opinion actually is. Using the inference rule (13) below, the information in Figure 11 could be deduced from the information in Figure 10.

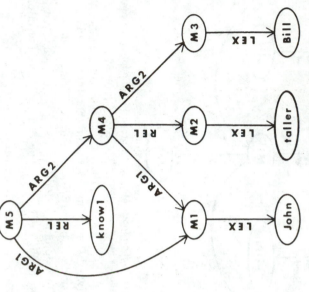

Figure 11. The representation (node M5) for the propositional information contained in the sentence "John holds a correct opinion that he is taller than Bill."

(13) If the system believes1 that some cognitive agent knows2 whether some proposition P and the system believes1 that P, then the system can conclude that the agent believes1 that P.

The following example illustrates the behavior of this kind of system. Suppose you were a college freshman majoring in computer science, and suppose you believed (incorrectly) that pi was a rational number. Naturally, you would also believe that your computer science professor also knew whether pi was rational. By applying the above inference rule, you would erroneously, but properly, conclude that your professor believed that pi was rational.

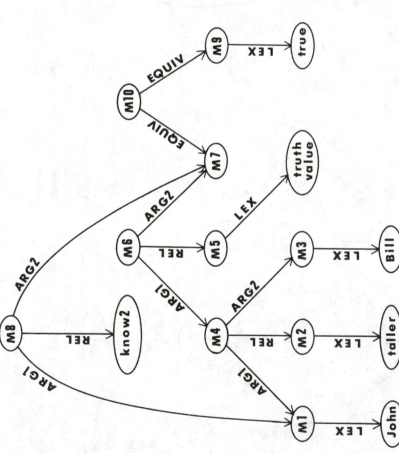

Figure 10. The representation for the sentence sequence: "John holds a correct opinion about whether he is taller than Bill; it is true that John is taller than Bill."

REPRESENTING YES-NO QUESTIONS

In order to support the entire range of discourse processing it is necessary for a knowledge representation in general, and a semantic network in particular, to have the ability to represent questions. Although it is possible for a network which does not represent questions to interface with a processor that enables it to answer questions (e.g., an ATN parser-generator; Shapiro, 1979b), the network itself would intrinsically not have the ability to remember which question were asked. The need to represent questions is illustrated by sentences of the sort "Since John asked me whether he was taller than Bill, I assumed he had never met Bill." In order to represent this sentence, it is first necessary to represent the question embedded within the subordinate clause.

We now turn to the problem of representing a yes-no question in a propositional semantic network. A question is not an individual concept, nor is it a proposition, but it must be represented in a propositional network by some configuration of individual concepts and propositions. It is not the case that a question can be paraphrased into a propositional form. Consider the line of dialog below (14) and the attempt to propositionalize it (15).

(14) Mary said, "John are you taller than Bill?"

(15) Mary asked John whether he was taller than Bill.

The paraphrased form superficially resembles a proposition except for a constituent centered around "whether," which cannot be propositionalized. There is a way to circumvent the obstacle by noticing that the sentence resembles sentence (5). We can generate (16) from (15) by replacing "ask" with "wonder" as shown below.

(16) Mary wondered whether John was taller than Bill.

Our treatment of "wonder" described earlier applies here and can be extended to "ask." Sentence (15) is an enquiry about the truth value of the proposition underlying the sentence "John is taller than Bill." The literal interpretation of all yes-no questions can be handled in this manner. Our representation of (15) is shown in Figure 12. The important thing to note is that the representation captures the fact that the question is an enquiry about the reference of the truth value of a proposition. The ability to represent this concept supplies the groundwork to build processes (e.g., programs, production rules, inference rules) in the system which uses this concept. The representation can trigger inference rules which will ensure that the system appropriately understands word senses like "ask." "Ask" means something like "enquire into the identity of."

The indirect speech act literature contains many examples of questions such as, "Can you pass the salt?" which are not interpreted in natural discourse as questions. Rather they effect the listener as if he had heard some other illocutionary act; in this case it is a request. However, humans are able to understand that, literally, this sentence is a yes-no question and it follows that they must be able to represent this literal interpretation. Furthermore, most accounts of indirect speech acts build on the assumption that the propositional content of the speech act has been extracted. Hence, we would like to represent this literalness in our network.

We will discuss wh-questions in the section after next section, after we discuss the process of node splitting.

MERGING AND SPLITTING NODES

Merging Nodes

Many writers point out the need for merging nodes which refer to the same physical object (e.g., Anderson, 1977, 1978; Hofstadter, Clossman, & Meredith, 1980). This kind of process seems attractive because it would serve to reduce "clutter" and simplify the crossreferencing problems between multiple nodes that are known to be co-referential is inefficient. This view is expressed by Hofstadter et al.:

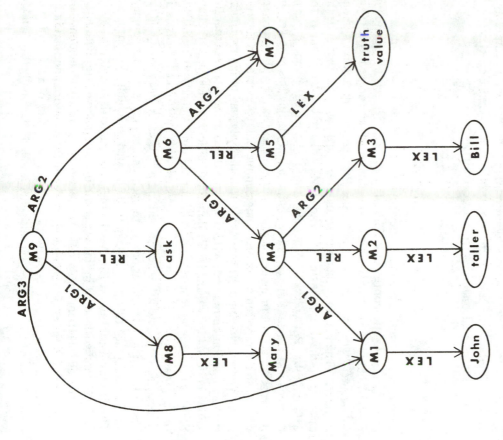

Figure 12. The representation (node M9) for the propositional information contained in the sentence "Mary asks John whether he is taller than Bill."

It is inevitable in any representational formalism that distinct nodes will sometimes be manufactured that, it turns out later, stand for the same thing.... What happens when one finally finds out that the two nodes represent the same thing? Clearly, they have to be fused somehow into one new node. (p. 4)

It is true that this kind of heuristic leads to increased ability to perform inferences in transparent contexts, however it has the disadvantage of not being able to inhibit spurious inference processes in domains involving opaque contexts. For instance, as already pointed out, if a system has two separate nodes for Mary's phone number and Mike's phone number, along with an assertion that they are extensionally equivalent, then it is not difficult to inhibit the system from concluding that John knows Mike's phone number if it is told that John knows Mary's phone number. But if a merge or copy process were to operate on the two nodes known to be extensionally equivalent, as Hofstadter et al., and Anderson propose, so that all of the information separately associated with each of the nodes is merged onto one node, then the spurious inference in the above example would be difficult to inhibit if the system were still going to make transparent inferences. Thus the process of merging nodes must not always take place.

Constraints on Merging Nodes

One possibility for policing this process is to set the constraint that a maximum of one predicate (assertions about co-reference are exempt) can be asserted per node. This amounts to a total suppression of any process which merges nodes; and, although it guarantees a representation with sufficient resolution to appropriately trigger both opaque and transparent inference processes, it creates a maximally inefficient system for cross referencing properties among extensionally equivalent concepts in transparent contexts. This option seems drastic and cumbersome, and we concur with Anderson and Hofstadter et al., in that it does not agree with our intuition either. Furthermore, there is experimental evidence that some merging of nodes does take place in humans. Anderson (1977), in addition to demonstrating that a subject can have two distinct nodes which are extensionally equivalent, has obtained evidence that subjects are strongly biased against maintaining two such distinct nodes if they know that the nodes are extensionally equivalent. Usually in such situations one of the two nodes is less strongly memorized than the other node. What subjects are inclined to do during the course of use is to place duplicate copies of the information which reside at the less established node to the more established node and then gradually abandon use of the less established node.

However, back in McCarthy's telephone number problem, the nodes for Mary's phone number and Mike's phone number cannot be merged. The nodes exist in an opaque context. In all of Anderson's experiments, his stimulus materials were instances of transparent reference. As we said earlier, in transparent contexts, merging of nodes leads to optimal performance. Subjects were asked to memorize the following kinds of sentences:

(17) The smart Russian is the tall lawyer.
(18) The smart Russian cursed the salesgirl.
(19) The smart Russian rescued the kitten.
(20) The tall lawyer adopted the child.
(21) The tall lawyer caused the accident.

These materials contain no opaque operators. However, we can prefix each of these study sentences with the phrase "John believes that"; then if a subject memorizes these modified study sentences, he or she will generate the same subconfiguration of nodes in memory as before but this time within an opaque context. If a subject fully processes the semantics of the word "believe" (unfortunately, tuning the task demands to force the subject to fully process "believe" might not be so easy) then during the experiment, he or she must process the nodes in a way that maintains the separate intensions. Specifically, the trend in the reaction time data which was observed that indicated subjects were copying information from one coreferent node to another should be absent.

We suggest that the process of merging nodes is inhibited when an opaque context is created but not otherwise. This creates a compromise system which will process instances of transparent reference efficiently yet process instances of opaque reference accurately.

Confusions

We as yet have not succeeded in devising a representation which does not make any semantic confusions. The problem can be seen by examining Figure 2. After the system is told the information in sentence sequence (8), it will answer "yes" to the question "Does Pat know Ed dials Mike's phone number?" The reason is that any straight-forward algorithm that adds the assertion to the data base that Pat knows M4 will also cause it to add to the data base that Pat knows M15 because both nodes have the same status in the network. Humans are certainly able to avoid making this mistake, but the representation can be patched up, either by augmenting the processes which use the representation or by augmenting the representation itself.

Without changing the representation, the only way to inhibit adding the fact that Pat knows node M15 while still allowing the inference that Pat knows node M4 is by using highly domain specific inference rules. Perhaps humans can generate these hypothesized rules quite quickly. It seems that this approach however would lead to a system whose performance was likely to degrade very time it learned something new because there would be the possibility of a new confusion. With each new confusion, a new domain specific inference rule would have to be created to inhibit the confusion. This is reminiscent of an EPAM-like theory of forgetting.

The networks used in this paper use only assertional information. Instead of adding domain specific inference rules, we could augment the representation to include structural, or definitional, information, and then change the semantics of the network so that the meaning of a node was only what the structural information said what it was. Notationally this could be done by adding functional individuals to the present representation constructs (cf. Maida, 1982). The purpose of definitional information would be to define intensions. Although Woods (1975, p. 58) argued for the need to distinguish between structural and assertional information, psychologists have not as yet been inclined to make such a distinction and tend to accept Quillian's formulation (cf. Collins & Loftus, 1975) of a node's full concept as adequate. Anderson (1976, p. 243) does use structural information to represent transparent versus opaque reference but he does not refer to the distinction in his experimental work (e.g., Anderson, 1978).

Splitting

Consider the following situation. What if a memory node created in a transparent context and with several descriptions fused or merged onto it, gets puts into an opaque context? Returning to the phone number problem, what if a cognitive agent learns that Mike and Mary have the same phone number as a consequence of learning that they live together? Then the two descriptions would be attached to the same node as shown in Figure 13. Now suppose this cognitive agent hears sentence (22).

(22) Pete doesn't know that Mike's phone number is the same as Mary's phone number.

The network structure depicted in Figure 13 could not become part of the representation structure for sentence (22) because that structure treats the concepts of Mike's and Mary's phone numbers as being the same, rather than being extensionally equivalent. Our cognitive agent must make a new

distinction before he can comprehend (22). It seems necessary that two nodes be constructed to separately represent Mike's phone number and Mary's phone number, and they must be made extensionally equivalent to the original node. We call this process *splitting* and it was mentioned earlier in our discussion of Scott writing *Waverly*. The final representaiton is shown in Figure 14 in which node M16 represents the proposition of (22). This analysis predicts that a person who learns about Mike's and Mary's phone number in a transparent context will have more difficulty subsequently comprehending (22) than a person who learns this same information in an opaque context because a split must take place.

Because of the probable computational overhead involved in splitting nodes, perhaps this kind of strategy might only be utilized when the system is operating in "careful node," as in social situations where misunderstandings could be embarrassing or costly. Also from a cognitive developmental perspective, this operation should occur late in the developmental sequence. And perhaps the usual mode of human functioning leads to treating opaque operators as transparent. Witness the difficulty a teacher has in trying to understand why a student does not understand. If the teacher was facile at processing opaque contexts, he or she would be able to accurately assess the student's knowledge state.

In light of the optional nature of processing associated with opacity, some unanswered experimental questions are raised? What are the factors which trigger opaque processing in humans? Developmentally, when does the ability for opaque processing appear in children? For instance, suppose that a person knows that Jim's wife is Sally's mother and is then told that Mike wants to meet Jim's wife (adapted from Creary, 1979). Under what circumstances might the person *assume that* Mike realizes he would like to meet Sally's mother and under what circumstances might that person feel the need to *determine whether* Mike knows Jim's wife is Sally's mother.

Consider the following two sentences taken from Anderson (1978). Anderson points out that the former sentence is an instance of

(23) I am looking for the best lawyer in town.
(24) I am looking for my little old mother.

opaque reference and the latter is an instance of transparent reference. Given that the difference in interpretation is probably not attributable to their very slight differing syntactic structure, what is determining whether the interpretation is transparent or opaque? The type of interpretation seems to depend on inference processes taking place in the listener which actively assess the knowledge state of the speaker. To illustrate, consider the interpretation of sentence (25) below, depending on whether a foster child, or an earthquake survivor is speaking.

(25) I am looking for my lost mother.

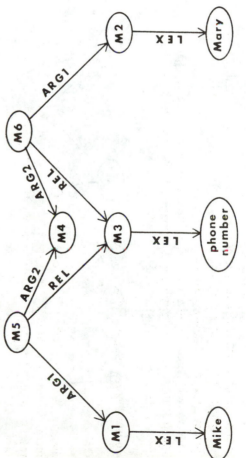

Figure 13. The representation for Mike's and Mary's phone number being the same if there is no immedicte need to treat them as separate intensions.

In the case of the foster child, the listener realizes that the child has probably never known its mother. Whereas in the case of the earthquake survivor, the listener knows that the survivor has someone specific in mind.

REPRESENTING WH-QUESTIONS

The treatment of wh-questions becomes clearer when one recognizes the opacity of the complement position of *ask*. The meaning of sentence (26) is changed if we substitute the phase "Mary's phone number" in place of "Mike's phone number" even if Mike and Mary have the same phone number.

(26) Pat asks Joe for Mike's phone number.

Therefore, in order to represent (26), we must create a new node which represents the intension of the Mike's phone number which Pat asks Joe for. We then equivalence it to the existing node. The resulting interpretation is depicted in Figure 15.

There are additional constraints to consider. We do not want to create a split to answer a simple question if we have already postulated splitting to be computationally expensive; and we want to use as much shared network structure as possible. The representation is constructed and integrated into the rest of memory as follows. The relation *ask* has three arguments: 1) the person doing the asking; 2) the person asked; and, 3) the thing being asked about. Only the thing being asked about is treated opaquely, so it is the only node that does not get matched to the network as the question is being parsed. Rather, it must be asserted to be extensionally equivalent to some other node in memory. Referring to Figure 15, node M8 gets matched to memory via the network pattern determined by nodes M9, M2, and M1. The node which is found as a result of this pattern match (M7 in this case) will be asserted to be extensionally equivalent to node M8. The system should be able to use information which is asserted about M7 to answer the question. In summary then, the listener constructs a representation of the question, matches it to the rest of the network, and finds a node which plays two roles: 1) it is treated as being extensionally equivalent to the concept being asked about; and, 2) it should serve as the access route to information suitable for answering the question. Note also that the system remembers who asked whom what question.

The question is, in fact, an enquiry about a particular intension, and that is the feature the representation unambiguously captures. But it is not so clear for the system as to how to determine what constitutes a good answer to the enquiry about the intension. This sort of task requires domain specific knowledge. It seems necessary to include discourse rules in the

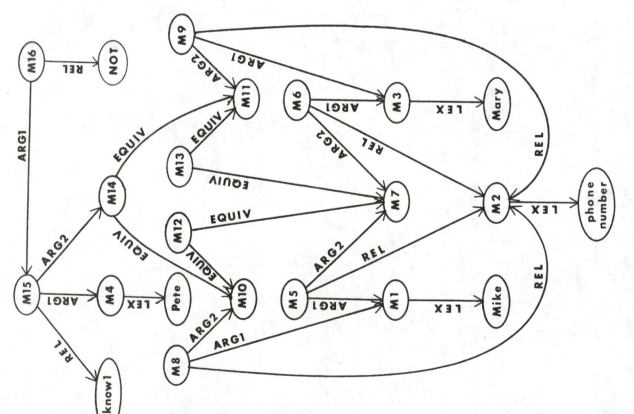

Figure 14. An illustration of the result of a splitting operation.

system to decide exactly what information the questioner is looking for. It is a mysterious phenomenon that humans perceive wh-questions as asking for specific information; on a literal level, they are vague, (e.g., Where is the salt? In the salt shaker). One possible rule for answering questions about phone numbers is given below in (27).

(27) If a person asks you for a description of a phone number that you believe2 or know2, then he wants you to generate a linguistic description of a digit sequence that is extensionally equivalent to the phone number.

Lehnert (1978), Allen (1979), and Allen and Perrault (1980) have extensively treated the problem of deciding what is so specific about specific questions in natural language discourse.

A more general rule for answering wh-questions, probably reserved for use when the system cannot find relevant domain specific knowledge, is given below in (28).

(28) When answering a wh-question, use any identifying description of the entity that the questioner asked about, but which the questioner himself did not use in formulating the question.

Thus if Joe answered (26) by saying, "Oh, Mike's phone number" then rule (28) would be violated. Alternatively, if he said "Oh, that's Mary's phone number," then rule (28) would be satisfied but not rule (27).

CONCLUSION

This paper makes an integrated statement concerning the semantic status of nodes in a propositional semantic network, claiming that nodes in such a network represent only intensions. Within the network, the only reference to extensionality should be via some mechanism to assert that two intensions have the same extension (e.g., The Morning Star is the Evening Star). We have also shown how processes which simulate referential transparency or referential opacity can operate on the network. Our analyses have been influenced by analytic philosophy, artificial intelligence, and cognitive psychology.

We have employed this framework in three application areas to illustrate the nature of its solutions. First, we map out a solution to McCarthy's telephone number problem, which he devised to succinctly capture the difference between referential transparency and opacity. Second, we directly represent the notion of the truth value of a proposition as is needed to represent a sentence like "John knows whether he is taller than Bill." Finally, we represent sentences like "Since John asked me whether I was taller than Bill, I assumed he never met Bill."

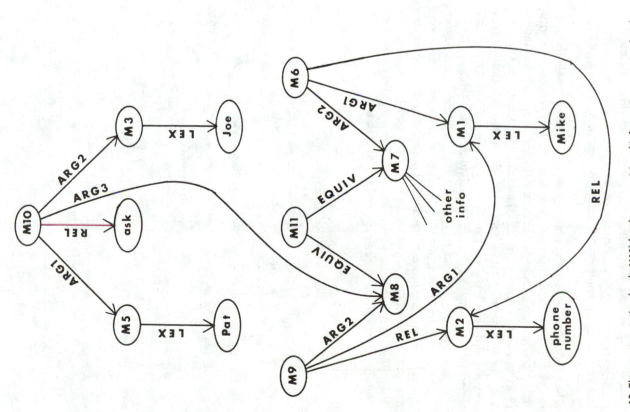

Figure 15. The representation (node M10) for the propositional information contained in the sentence "Pat asks Joe for Mike's phone number."

We also discuss some of the psychological implications of network processes which we call node *merging* and node *splitting*. It has been well recognized that a merge process should occur for co-referential nodes but little attention has been given to restrictions on this merge process and to the need for a splitting process. We theorize that merging should be inhibited in opaque contexts and suggest that Anderson's results on node merging will not generalize to opaque contexts. We also point out the need for a splitting process.

The formalism we use in this paper employs only assertional information and no structural, or definitional, information. This is consistent with network models in the psychological literature. In particular, neither Anderson (1978), nor Collins and Loftus (1975) mention the distinction. Our networks our prone to memory confusions to which the psychologically based networks will also be vulnerable. The notation employed in this paper can be augmented, by the use of functional individuals (cf. Maida, 1982) to eliminate the tendency for memory confusions. Whether psychologists should employ the use of functional individuals is an empirical question. This change in formalism, however, results in a drastic change in the semantic interpretation of network structure, as Quillian proposed it.

Propositional semantic networks continue to be a fruitful data structure by which to model the organization of the human mind.

REFERENCES

Allen, J. F. *A plan-based approach to speech act recognition* (Tech. Rep. 131). Toronto: University of Toronto, Department of Computer Science, 1979.

Allen, J. F., & Perrault, C. R. Analyzing intention in utterances. *Artificial Intelligence*, 1980, *15*, 143–178.

Anderson, J. R. *Language, memory, and thought*. Hillsdale, NJ: Lawrence Erlbaum Associates, 1976.

Anderson, J. R. Memory for information about individuals. *Memory and Cognition*, 1977, *5*, 430–442.

Anderson, J. R. The processing of referring expressions within a semantic network. *Theoretical issues in natural language processing-2*. New York: Association for Computing Machinery, 1978.

Anderson, J. R., & Hastie, R. Individuation and reference in memory: Proper names and definite descriptions. *Cognitive Psychology*, 1974, *6*, 495–541.

Brachman, R. J. What's in a concept: structural foundations for semantic networks. *International Journal for Man-Machine Studies*, 1977, *9*, 127–152.

Brachman, R. J. On the epistemological status of semantic networks. In N. V. Findler (Ed.), *Associative Networks: Representation and use of knowledge by computers*. New York: Academic Press, 1979.

Brachman, R. J., & Smith, B. R. Special issue on knowledge representation. *SIGART Newsletter*, February 1980, (70).

Carnap, R. *Meaning and necessity*. Chicago, IL: University of Chicago Press, 1947.

Cohen, P. R. *On knowing what to say: planning speech acts* (Tech. Rep. 118). Toronto: University of Toronto, Department of Computer Science, 1978.

Cohen, P. R., & Perrault, C. R. Elements of a plan-based theory of speech acts. *Cognitive Science*, 1979, *3*, 177–212.

Collins, A. M., & Loftus, E. F. A spreading activation theory of semantic processing. *Psychological Review*, 1975, *82*, 407–428.

Creary, L. G. Propositional attitudes: Fregean representation and simulative reasoning. *IJCAI Proceedings*, 1979, *6*, 176–181.

Dowty, D. R., Wall, R. E., & Peters, S. *Introduction to Montague Semantics*. Boston, MA: D. Reidel Publishing Company, 1981.

Fahlman, S. *NETL: A system for representing and using real-world knowledge*. Cambridge, MA: MIT Press, 1979.

Frege, G. Über Sinn und Bedeutung. *Zeitschrift für Philosophie und philosophiche Kritik*, 1892, *100*, (all). (Translation available in P. Geach & M. Black (Eds.), *Translations from the philosophical writings of Gottlob Frege*. Oxford: Basil Blackwell, 1960.

Heath, P. L. Nothing. In P. Edwards (Ed.), *The Encyclopedia of Philosophy* (Vol. 5). New York: Macmillan, 1967.

Hendrix, G. Encoding knowledge in partitioned networks. In N. Findler (Ed.), *Associative Networks: Representation and use of knowledge by computers*. New York: Academic Press, 1979.

Hintikka, J. Semantics for propositional attitudes. In L. Linsky (Ed.), *Reference and modality*. London: Oxford University Press, 1971.

Hofstadter, D. R., Clossman, G. A., & Meredith, M. J. *Shakespeare's plays weren't written by him, but by someone else of the same name* (Tech. Rep. 96). Bloomington, IN: Indiana University, Computer Science Department, 1980.

Kripke, S. Semantical considerations on modal logic. *Acta Philosophica Fennica*, 1963, *16*, 83–89.

Maida, A. S. Using lambda abtraction to encode structural information in semantic networks, 1982, available from the Center for Cognitive Science, Box 1911, Brown University, Providence, RI 02912.

Martin, W. A. Roles, co-descriptors, and the formal representation of quantified English expressions. *American Journal of Computational Linguistics*, 1981, *7*, 137–147.

McCarthy, J. Epistemological problems of artificial intelligence. *IJCAI Proceedings*, 1977, *5*, 1038–1044.

McCarthy, J. First-order theories of individual concepts and propositions. In J. Hayes, D. Michie, & L. Mikulich (Eds.), *Machine Intelligence 9*. New York: Halsted Press, 1979.

McCarthy, J., & Hayes, P. J. Some philosophical problems from the standpoint of artificial intelligence. In B. Meltzer & D. Michie (Eds.), *Machine Intelligence 4*. Edinburgh: Edinburgh University Press, 1969.

McCawley, J. Paper given at the Symposium in Cognitive Science, Vassar College, Poughkeepsie, NY, April 25-26, 1980.

McNabb, S. D. *The effects of encoding strategies and age on the memory representation for sentences containing proper names and definite descriptions* (Rep. No. 77-3). Bloomington, IN: Indiana University, Indiana Mathematical Psychology Program, 1977.

Moore, R. C. Reasoning about knowledge and action. *IJCAI Proceedings*, 1977, *5*, 223–227.

Moore, R. C. *Reasoning about knowledge and action* (Tech. Note 191). SRI International, 1980.

Quillian, M. R. Semantic memory. In M. Minsky, (Ed.), *Semantic information processing*. Cambridge, MA: MIT Press, 1968.

Quine, W. V. O. Quantifiers and propositional attitudes. *Journal of Philosophy*, 1956, *53*, 177–187.

Russell, B. On denoting. *Mind*, 1906, *14*. (Reprinted in H. Feigl & W. Sellars (Eds.), *Readings in philosophical analysis*. New York: Appleton-Century-Crofts, 1949.

Schank, R. C. *Conceptual information processing*. New York: American Elsevier, 1975.

Schubert, L. K., Goebel, R. G., & Cercone, N. J. The structure and organization of a semantic net for comprehension and inference. In N. Findler (Ed.), *Associative Networks: Representation and use of knowledge by computers*. New York: Academic Press, 1979.

Shapiro, S. C. A net structure for semantic information storage, deduction and retrieval. *IJCAI Proceedings*, 1971, *2*, 512–523.

Shapiro, S. C. Generation as parsing from a network into a linear string. *American Journal of Computational Linguistics*, 1975, Microfiche 33, 45–62.

Shapiro, S. C. Path-based and node-based inference in semantic networks. In D. Waltz (Ed.), *Theoretical issues in natural language processing-2*. New York: Association for Computing Machinery, 1978.

Shapiro, S. C. The SNePS semantic network processing system. In N. Findler (Ed.), *Associative Networks: Representation and use of knowledge by computers*. New York: Academic Press, 1979. (a)

Shapiro, S. C. Generalized augmented transition network grammars for generation from semantic networks. *Proceedings of the 17th Annual Meeting of the Association for Computational Linguistics*, 1979. (b)

Shapiro, S. C., & Neal, J. A knowledge engineering approach to natural language understanding. *Proceedings of the 20th Annual Meeting of the Association for Computational Linguistics*, 1982.

Woods, W. A. What's in a link: the semantics of semantic networks. In D. G. Bobrow & A. M. Collins (Eds.), *Representation and Understanding*. New York: Academic Press, 1975.

APPENDIX

This appendix contains a list of inference rules whose purpose is to propagate assertions across extensional equivalence paths. This is not a complete list to enable all valid inferences, and the specific format of these rules would depend on the specific notation one used. The rules consist of condition-action pairs in which the condition specifies a pattern that must match the network in order for the rule to apply and the action builds more network structure. The condition of a rule consists of a sequence of clauses which all must match the network. Clauses specify network structure as follows:

> (1st-arg-slot relation-slot 2nd-arg slot)
> or,
> (property-slot arg-slot)
> or,
> (arg-slot equivalent arg-slot)

Variables are prefixed with a question mark and while unbound will match any node in the network provided the rest of the clause matches that part of the network. Once a variable matches a node, it is bound to that node for the rest of the application of that rule.

Rule 1:

(is-transparent ?rel) &
(?agent ?rel ?obj1) &
(?obj1 equivalent ?obj2) = = >   (?agent ?rel ?obj2)

Note: For example,

If likes is a transparent relation and
John likes Mary and
Mary is Sally's mother then
    John likes Sally's mother.

However, he may not believe he likes Sally's mother.

Rule 2:

(?agent believe (?agent ?rel ?obj1)) &
(?agent believe (?obj1 equivalent ?obj2))
    = = > (?agent believe (?agent ?rel ?obj2))

If a person believes Jim's wife is Sally's mother and he believes he wants to meet Jim's wife, then he believes he wants to meet Sally's mother regardless of whether Jim's wife in fact is Sally's mother.

Rule 3:

(?agent know (?agent ?rel ?obj1)) &
(?agent believe (?obj1 equivalent ?obj2))
    = = > (?agent believe (?agent ?rel ?obj2))

Note: For example,

If John knows he likes Mary and
John believes that Mary is Sally's mother
then he believes he likes Sally's mother.

Although the premises of this rule are stronger than those of rule 2, the conclusion is the same as rule 2.

Rule 4:

(?agent know (?agent ?rel ?obj1)) &
(?agent know (?obj1 equivalent ?obj2))
    = = > (?agent know (?agent ?rel ?obj2))

The conclusion of this rule is stronger than that of rule 3 because the system believes the agent is correct in his belief about the coreferentiality of objects 1 and 2.

10 / Ronald J. Brachman
On the Epistemological Status of Semantic Networks

This paper presents a comprehensive survey and analysis of semantic network representation schemes (*circa* 1979). The survey pinpoints a large number of the seminal contributions to the history of semantic networks. It also helps remove some of the confusion about such schemes by illustrating how modern semantic networks evolved first from strict psychological models, and then from linguistic structures, neither of which methodologies intended to produce representation *languages*. Brachman's subsequent analysis involves the level of primitives used in the various networks. He proposes that the similarity among network notations is illusory, and that there are really at least five different types of links used. The levels range from *implementational*, simple pointers in the memory of a computer, all the way to *linguistic*, links whose meaning is tied to natural language. Brachman also distinguishes between *logical* primitives and *epistemological* ones. The latter form the basis for KLONE (subsequently KL-ONE), a representation language that Brachman sketches in the third part of the paper (see [Brachman and Schmolze 85] for a much more extensive introduction to that system and [Brachman *et al.*, Chapter 24] for some recent KL-ONE-based developments). While KL-ONE has received much attention and has been a significant contribution to the field, this paper is worth reading for the survey alone.

Appeared in *Associative Networks: Representation and Use of Knowledge by Computers*, 3–50, edited by N. V. Findler, New York: Academic Press, 1979.

ON THE EPISTEMOLOGICAL STATUS OF SEMANTIC NETWORKS*

Ronald J. Brachman

ABSTRACT

This chapter examines in detail the history of a set of network-structured formalisms for knowledge representation—the so-called "semantic networks." Semantic nets were introduced around 1966 as a representation for the concepts underlying English words, and since then have become an increasingly popular type of language for representing concepts of a widely varying sort. While these nets have for the most part retained their basic associative nature, their primitive representational elements have differed significantly from one project to the next. These differences in underlying primitives are symptomatic of deeper philosophical disparities, and I discuss a set of five significantly different "levels" at which networks can be understood. One of these levels, the "epistemological," or "knowledge-structuring," level, has played an important implicit part in all previous notations, and is here made explicit in a way that allows a new type of network formalism to be specified. This new type of formalism accounts precisely for operations like individuation of description, internal concept structure in terms of roles and interrelations between them, and structured inheritance. In the final section, I present a brief sketch of an example of a particular type of formalism ("Structured Inheritance Networks") that was designed expressly to treat concepts as formal representational objects. This language, currently under development, is called KLONE, and it allows the explicit expression of epistemological level relationships as network links.

INTRODUCTION

The idea of a memory based on the notion of *associations* is apparently a very old one—Anderson and Bower [1973] trace the idea back as far as Aristotle. However, only in the last ten years has the associative memory idea taken a firm hold with those interested in modeling human memory or providing working memories for intelligent computer programs. Yet in

* Prepared in part at Bolt Beranek and Newman Inc. under contracts sponsored by the Defense Advance Research Projects Agency and the Office of Naval Research. The views and conclusions stated are those of the author and should not be interpreted as necessarily representing the official policies, either express or implied, of the Defense Advanced Research Projects Agency or the U.S. Government.

the short time since Ross Quillian first introduced the idea of a "semantic network" in his Ph.D. thesis [1966], network models of information and their computer implementations have become rampant.

While Quillian's original intent was to represent the semantics of English words in his nets, representations that looked very similar were soon being used to model all sorts of nonsemantic things (e.g., propositions, physical object structure, "gated one-shot state coupling"). Yet, virtually every networklike formalism that has appeared in the literature since 1966 has at one time or another been branded by someone a semantic net. The possibility of confusion over the real nature of the network slipped by virtually unnoticed, since everyone working in the area already "knew" with what they were working. But as interest has developed over the last two years in the semantics of the semantic net itself, the epistemological status of the representation has become increasingly suspect. This chapter is an attempt to clear up what we mean when we call our representations semantic nets, and to examine what claims about the structure of knowledge these so-called representations actually make.

To this end, I shall first examine the history of semantic networks, covering as broadly as possible in a limited space the major developments in associative memory models from 1966 through the present. I shall then attempt to explain why so many of the earlier formalisms are inadequate in several ways, and why the more recent ones approaching complete logical adequacy are perhaps not as useful for knowledge representation as it was hoped they might be. The substance of this analysis will be a close look at the kinds of entities chosen by designers to be primitive in their network schemes. By elucidating the different kinds of primitives employed in these nets, I hope to illustrate how there are at least five different kinds of knowledge that have become confusingly called "semantic" by their association with semantic networks. For the purposes of the analysis, I shall postulate and discuss five levels of semantic net primitive corresponding to these kinds of knowledge—the "implementational," "logical," "epistemological," "conceptual," and "linguistic" levels.

One of these levels has been less used and understood than the others, but may have significantly more utility in the near future for general knowledge representation tasks than the others. This is the *epistemological* level of knowledge representation—the one on which several new nonnetwork formalisms like KRL [Bobrow and Winograd, 1977] and FRL [Goldstein and Roberts, 1977; Roberts and Goldstein, 1977] are built, and the one dealing with things like "inheritance," "abstraction," and concept structuring. In Section 3, I examine some of the implications of this level of thinking, and show how it has influenced my own work on what I used to think of as semantic networks. I shall present some of the prominent aspects of a new netlike formalism—the "Structured Inheritance Network." A structured inheritance network (SI-Net) has a fixed set of node and link

"word concepts," and links from a concept node pointed to other word concepts, which together made up a definition, just as dictionary definitions are constructed from sequences of words defined elsewhere in the same volume. The structure thus ultimately became an interwoven network of nodes and links.

In Quillian's structure, each word concept node was considered to be the head of a "plane," which held its definition. Figure 1 [Quillian, 1968, p. 236] illustrates a set of three planes (indicated by solid boxes) for three senses of the word "plant." Pointers *within* the plane (the solid links in the figure) are those which form the structure of the definition. Quillian postulated a small set of these, which included *subclass* (e.g., the relationship of PLANT 2 to APPARATUS in the figure), *modification* (e.g., APPA-RATUS is modified by the USE structure), *disjunction* (labeled by OR), *conjunction* (labeled by AND), and *subject/object* (e.g., the parallel links from USE to PEOPLE (the subject) and to = A (the object)). Pointers leading *outside* the plane (the broken links in the figure) indicate other planes in which the referenced words are themselves defined. The fact that in Quillian's structure words used in definitions of other words had their own planes, which were *pointed to* by place-holder nodes within those definitions, corresponded to the important "type/token" distinction. Each word was defined in only one plane in the structure (the head of the plane being the "type" node), and all references to a word went through intermediate "token" nodes. Thus definitions were not repeated each time a word concept was referenced.

Quillian's desire of his semantic memory model was that it might serve as a general *inferential* representation for knowledge. He presented in his thesis several examples of an inference technique based on the notion of a spreading activation *intersection search*—given two words, possible relations between them might be inferred by an unguided, breadth-first search of the area surrounding the planes for the words; this search was carried out by a propagation of some kind of activation signal through the network. A search would fan out through links from the original two planes to all planes pointed to by the originals, until a point of intersection was found. The paths from the source nodes to the point of contact of the two "spheres of activation" formed by the search would indicate a potential relationship between the two word concepts.* Quillian hoped that in this way information input in one frame of reference might be used to answer questions asked in another. The use of information implicit in the memory, but not stated explicitly, was one of the important features of the memory model.

---

* The belief that properties of a node could be found by an expanding search led Quillian to the idea that a word concept's "full meaning" comprised *everything* that could be reached from the patriarchal type node (the head of its defining plane) by an exhaustive tracing process.

types (the number of which is small), thereby providing the basis for a fixed and well-defined interpreter. The links in this kind of net are used to explicitly express "epistemological" relationships between Concepts and their parts ("Roles" and "Structural Descriptions"), that is, structuring relationships between formal objects used to represent knowledge. SI-Nets can be used to illustrate the level of concern of epistemological formalisms in general, and I shall use a particular SI-Net language, called KLONE, to help elucidate some of the representational responsibilities of such formalisms.

1. A LOOK AT THE EVOLUTION OF SEMANTIC NETWORKS

The last ten years have seen a tremendous explosion in the number of efforts directed toward developing memory models that might be considered networks, and the literature has expanded to the point where only with extreme effort can one maintain familiarity with the entire field. To treat fairly all of the work that has led to our current state of knowledge about network knowledge representation would be a Herculean task, and one requiring far more space and time than is convenient here. Therefore, my analysis will begin with Quillian's [1966] work and will not discuss the many earlier efforts of Gestalt psychology, perception-by-reconstruction theories (especially Bartlett [1967] and Neisser [1967]), and artificial intelligence that have had significant effects on the current shape of semantic nets. I shall only briefly outline the various major contributions to the semantic network literature, and hope that the bibliography at the end of this chapter will provide sufficient direction for the reader more interested in historical trends and details on the representations sketched here. I shall not proceed strictly chronologically (many of these projects developed simultaneously), but shall instead broadly outline three major groups of work: the early nets that provided the basic structure, those which attempted to incorporate linguistic case structure, and several more recent important foundational studies.

1.1. The Early Nets

The idea of a semantic network representation for human knowledge is generally acknowledged to have originated in the work of Quillian [1966, 1967, 1968, 1969; Bell and Quillian, 1971]; Quillian proposed an associational network model of "semantic memory" in his Ph.D. thesis in 1966. His intent was to capture in a formal representation the "objective" part of the meanings of words so that "humanlike use of those meanings" would be possible [1966, p. 1]. The representation was composed of *nodes*, interconnected by various kinds of *associative links*, and closely reflected the organization of an ordinary dictionary. The nodes were to be considered

Part of the reason that certain properties could be inferred from such a memory was its use of a link indicating a "subclass" relationship and a link specifying a "modifies" relation. A concept could be defined in terms of a more general concept (of which it was a subclass) and a modifying property, which was a combination of an attribute and a particular value for that attribute.* In this characterization, properties true of a class were assumed true of all of its subclasses, except for the modifications. As a result, the superclass chain extending upward from a concept embodied all of the properties true of that concept. Thus the semantic net represented the combination of two important types of memory feature—a superclass–subclass taxonomic hierarchy, and the description of properties (attribute/value pairs) for each class. Earlier work done by Lindsay (see Lindsay [1973] for a later discussion of Lindsay's original work) and Raphael [1968] can be seen to be the precursors of this important marriage.

Quillian later cleaned up his memory model a bit. He eliminated the type/token distinction by making everything in the net a pointer, and, in a project called the "Teachable Language Comprehender" (TLC) [1969], he investigated its utility as a knowledge base for the reading of text. In TLC, a property was formally defined to be an attribute (some relational concept), a value, and possibly some further "subproperties." Properties were used in the definitions of "units," which represented the concepts of objects, events, ideas, assertions, etc.: a unit was defined by its superset and a set of refining properties. For reading, an intersection technique was used to find relations between words encountered in a text (this was augmented by the application of certain "form tests" as syntax checks). Figure 2 [Quillian, 1969, p. 462] illustrates a simple unit. The unit being defined in this figure is the one for "client." The unit indicates that a CLIENT is a PERSON (i.e., PERSON is its superset), with a further qualification indicated by the second pointer from the unit to a restricting property. That property combines the attribute EMPLOY with a value PRO-FESSIONAL and the subproperty BY THE CLIENT.

While TLC was an interesting model for finding connections between word meanings, its success in reading was limited. TLC's failure to achieve understanding was at least in part due to its insufficient set of link types and the fact that the search did not take into account the meanings of the various links. Despite the many shortcomings of his model, however, Quillian's early papers contain the seeds of most of the important ideas that are today the mainstays of semantic nets.

Quillian's revised TLC format gave rise to two other important studies. With Collins, Quillian undertook a series of experiments to test the psychological plausibility of his network scheme [Collins and Quillian, 1969,

* Quillian claimed that his nodes corresponded "to what we ordinarily call 'properties'" [1966, p. 26].

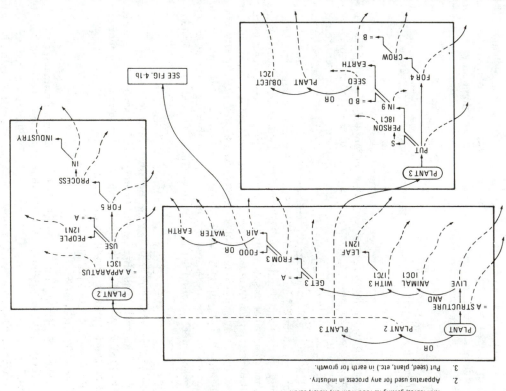

Fig. 1. Quillian's planes. Reprinted from Quillian [1968], by permission of the MIT Press, Cambridge, Massachusetts. Copyright 1968 by the Massachusetts Institute of Technology.

SEE FIG. 4-1b

PLANT 1. Living structure which is not an animal, frequently with leaves, getting its food from air, water, earth.
2. Apparatus used for any process in industry.
3. Put (seed, plant, etc.) in earth for growth.

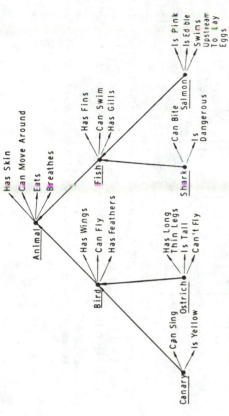

Fig. 3. A simple hierarchy. From Collins and Quillian [1970a].

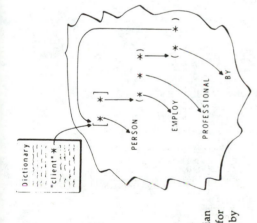

Fig. 2. A TLC unit. From Quillian [1969]. Copyright 1969, Association for Computing Machinery, Inc., reprinted by permission.

1970a,b, 1972a],* and the networks they used to check reaction time are easily recognized as the direct forerunners of recent networks (see Fig. 3 [Collins and Quillian, 1970a, p. 305]). The nets were simple superset hierarchies of concepts like *Animal*, *Bird*, and *Canary*, with each node having attached a set of properties defining its corresponding concept (e.g., "has skin," "has wings," "is yellow"). Since more general properties were supposedly stored higher up the generalization hierarchy, one would expect it to take more time to affirm a statement like "A canary has skin" than one like "A canary is yellow." The reaction time studies seemed to confirm the plausibility of a hierarchical model for human memory, although not conclusively. In any case, the experiments crystallized the notion of *inheritance of properties* in a semantic net (the passing of values like "has skin" from the general concept of *Animal* to the more specific one of *Canary*) and gave rise to a concrete notion of *semantic distance* between concepts (i.e., the number of links to be traversed between two nodes). More recently, Collins and Loftus [1975] have discussed in much detail the psychological implications of an extended version of this model, and have examined some experimental results in regard to their "spreading-activation" theory of processing (a sophistication of Quillian's semantic intersection technique). The reader is referred to that paper for some clarification of Quillian's original theory and a defense of the original experiments.

The other significant project arising directly from Quillian's TLC work was established by Carbonell [1970a,b] and attempted to use Quillian's

*The reader is also referred to an interesting article by Collins and Quillian called "How to make a language user" [1972b], in which they summarize many of the things that they learned from their experiments about language and memory.

networks as a data structure in an implemented computer-aided instruction program. The SCHOLAR program had a knowledge base that described in network terms the geography of South America. A student could participate in a "mixed-initiative" dialogue with the system, asking and being asked questions about the data base.

SCHOLAR's data base made some important new contributions to Quillian's nets. Carbonell began to distinguish "concept units" (like LATITUDE) from "example units" (like ARGENTINA), setting the stage for the later notion of *instantiation*.* In addition, a notion of Quillian's called *tags* was expanded and used extensively. Figure 4 [Carbonell, 1970b, p. 194] illustrates the SCHOLAR units for latitude and Argentina; in the text part of the figure, the name of a unit follows RPAQQ (a LISP value-setting function), and anything within the unit that follows a left parenthesis is an attribute. Tags on relations are indicated by parenthesized pairs following the attribute names [e.g., the SUPERP of LATITUDE is LOCATION, and has the tag (I 2)]. The most important of the tags in SCHOLAR was the *irrelevancy tag* (I-tag), which could explicitly increase the semantic distance between two nodes. I-tags were used to determine the relevance of certain facts in a given context, and allowed the system to start with the

*Instantiation has become one of the most well-known aspects of semantic net formalisms. The general idea is the association of a particular individual with the class of which it is a member, and in most notations, this is reflected by the construction of an individual description based on a generic description that the individual satisfies. Thus, while we primarily think of instances as things *in the world* that are manifestations of our abstract concepts, the term "instantiation" is very often used to refer to the production of a *description* of an individual based on a more general description. I shall later (Section 3) use the term, "individuation" (of description) for this latter intent, avoiding the potential confusion over what the term "instance" really means.

STATE

COUNTRY
(SUPERC (STATE INDEPENDENT))
(SUPERP CONTINENT)
(EXAMPLES ARGENTINA
BOLIVIA BRAZIL ·······
URUGUAY U.S. VENEZUELA)

LATITUDE

CONTINENT

URUGUAY
(SUPERC COUNTRY)

ARGENTINA
(SUPERC COUNTRY)
(LOCATION SOUTH/AMERICA)
(LATITUDE (RANGE -22-55))
(BORDERING COUNTRIES
(EASTERN BRAZIL URUGUAY)

SOUTH/AMERICA
(SUPERC CONTINENT)
(COUNTRIES ARGENTINA
URUGUAY VENEZUELA)

```
(RPAQQ LATITUDE (((CN LATITUDE)
        (DET THE DEF 2))
    NIL
    (SUPERC  NIL (DISTANCE NIL ANGULAR (FROM NIL
            EQUATOR)))
    (SUPERP (I 2)
        LOCATION)
    (VALUE (I 2)
        (RANGE NIL -90 90))
    (UNIT (I 2)
        DEGREES)))
```

```
(RPAQQ ARGENTINA (((XN ARGENTINA)
        (DET NIL DEF 2))
    NIL
    (SUPERC NIL COUNTRY)
    (SUPERP (I 6)
        SOUTH\AMERICA)
    (AREA (I 2)
        (APPROX NIL \ 1200000))
    (LOCATION NIL SOUTH\AMERICA (LATITUDE (I 2)
            (RANGE NIL -22` -55))
        (LONGITUDE (I 4)
            (RANGE NIL -57 -71))
        (BORDERING\COUNTRIES (I 1)
            (NORTHERN (I 1)
                BOLIVIA PARAGUAY)
            (EASTERN (I 1)
                (($L BRAZIL URUGUAY
                NIL
                (BOUNDARY NIL URUGUAY\RIVER)))
    (CAPITAL (I 1)
    BUENOS\AIRES)
    (CITIES (I 3)
        (PRINCIPAL NIL ($L BUENOS\AIRES CORDOBA ROSARIO
            MENDOZA LA\PLATA TUCUMAN)))
    (TOPOGRAPHY (I 1)
    VARIED
    (MOUNTAIN\CHAINS NIL (PRINCIPAL NIL ANDES
        (LOCATION NIL (BOUNDARY NIL (WITH NIL
                CHILE)))
            (ALTITUDE NIL (HIGHEST NIL ACONCAGUA
                (APPROX NIL 22000))))
        (SIERRAS NIL (LOCATION NIL ($L CORDOBA
            BUENOS\AIRES))))
    (PLAINS NIL (FERTILE NIL USUALLY)
        (($L EASTERN CENTRAL)
        NIL PAMPA)
        (NORTHERN NIL CHACO)))
```

Fig. 4. SCHOLAR units. From Carbonell [1970b]

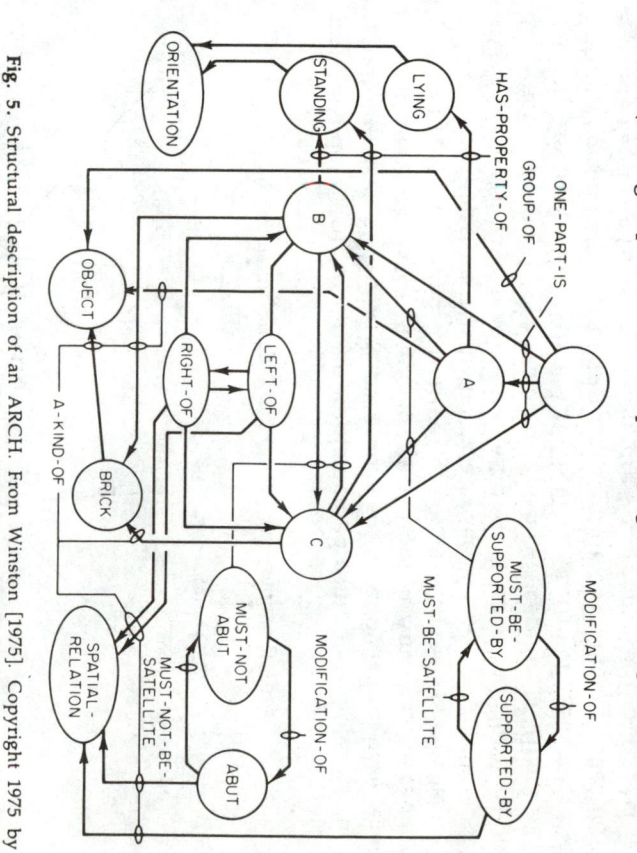

Fig. 5. Structural description of an ARCH. From Winston [1975]. Copyright 1975 by McGraw–Hill, Inc., New York. Used with permission of McGraw–Hill Book Company.

* While Carbonell claimed that no links were privileged [1970a, p. 112], that those like "SUPERC" are very special indeed is illustrated in Brachman [1978b].

most relevant aspects of a unit when describing a concept to the student. In addition, SCHOLAR introduced temporary, time-dependent tags. Also, while SCHOLAR's units looked much like Quillian's TLC units, the properties associated with a unit had as their first elements the *names* of attributes, rather than pointers (resurrecting the type/token distinction). Thus the precedent was set for *naming links*—associating arbitrary labels with the associations between units. In addition to several special attributes (SUPERC for superconcept, SUPERP for superpart, and SUPERA for superattribute), things like LOCATION, TOPOGRAPHY, CITIES, and UNIT were now being encoded directly into the network.* Another important precedent set in the SCHOLAR net was the intermixing of *procedures* with the declarative structure. LISP functions associated with units were used to actively infer properties that were not stated as declarative facts.

Another early effort, which proceeded independently of the Quillian/SCHOLAR work but made use of similar structures, was Winston's "structural descriptions" work at MIT [1970, 1975]. Winston created a program that could infer the "concept" of a physical structure such as an ARCH (see Fig. 5 [Winston, 1975, p. 198]), given encodings of a set of ex-

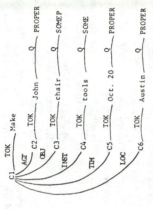

Fig. 6. A Simmons case structure. From Simmons and Bruce [1971]. Used with permission of International Joint Conferences on Artificial Intelligence, Inc.

amples of the structure in a network description language. The descriptions included nodes for concepts of physical objects (like BRICKs) in a scene, and labeled links representing physical relationships between the objects (e.g., LEFT-OF, SUPPORTED-BY). The interesting thing about Winston's networks (aside from the fact that he had actually written a program to induce generalizations from them) is that the relationships between concepts could themselves be modified or talked about as concepts. For example, in the very same notation, B could be described as LEFT-OF C, and LEFT-OF described as OPPOSITE RIGHT-OF. Winston also used the same language as his comparison language for determining differences between examples.

One problem with Winston's notation, as with each of the others mentioned so far, was its complete uniformity. While the notions of superconcept and instance were included in these nets, there was no acknowledgement of their difference from domain-specific notions like location and support. One could not "see" a hierarchy by looking at the structure, and important notions like inheritance were obscured by an overly uniform mixture of domain-specific and general "properties." However, with the groundwork laid by Quillian, Collins, Carbonell, and Winston, almost all of the semantic net apparatus used in the 1970s is already accounted for, and very little has really changed since then (at least until very recently, as Section 3 will attempt to show).

1.2. Case Structures

The work of Fillmore on linguistic case structure [1968] helped focus network attention onto *verbs*. Those interested in processing natural language with semantic nets began to think of a sentence as a *modality* coupled with a *proposition*, where a modality captured information such as tense, mood, manner, and aspect, and a proposition was a verb and a set of filled-in *cases*. There were believed to be a reasonably small number of cases (i.e., relationships in which nominals could participate relative to the verb of a sentence), and several people set out to incorporate this belief in network formalisms. The fact that properties in semantic nets were clustered around nodes made the nodes ideal places to anchor cases—if a node were thought of as a verbal concept, its associated attribute/value pairs could easily be case/filler pairs.

Simmons et al. [1968], Simmons and Bruce [1971], Simmons and Slocum [1972], Simmons [1973], Hendrix et al. [1973] used this notion very early in work that developed from the older Protosynthex system. Simmons' networks became centered around verbal nodes, with pointers labeled with case names to the participants in the action represented by the node (see Fig. 6 [Simmons and Bruce, 1971, p. 525]—the verbal node here is C1, a TOKen of the verb *Make*). The verbs themselves were grouped into "para-

digms," according to the sets of case relations in which they participated. Simmons' networks focused on the understanding and generation of particular sentences—not much attention seems to have been given in the original work to the place of general "world knowledge" in the overall scheme. Thus no classification of verbs, or nouns, for that matter, existed outside the similar case-frame grouping (the paradigms), and no definitions of general concepts seemed to exist at all. Recently, however, some sophistication has been added to these networks, including substantial use of superconcept and instance links. In addition, quantification and deductive mechanisms are discussed in Simmons and Chester [1977].

A similar incorporation of case structures into a network framework was achieved by Rumelhart et al. [1972], Norman [1972, 1973], Norman et al. [1975], and Rumelhart and Norman [1973]. Their attempt, spanning several years, included many of the features that Simmons had left out, although their orientation was more psychological and thus dealt with more aspects of memory. The Rumelhart et al. networks included nodes for concepts, nodes for *events*, and nodes for *episodes*—sequences of events clustered together. General definitions of concepts in the network were encoded in a straightforward manner, with caselike pointers indicating parts of nominal concepts and agents and objects of verbs, as illustrated in Fig. 7 [Rumelhart et al., 1972, p. 224]. Unfortunately, their notation was also very uniform, so that all links looked the same. In addition, the infamous IS-A link (see Woods [1975] and Cercone [1975]) was used to indicate type–token relations as well as subset relations, and many other relations were not motivated or explained—the English mnemonics are all that we have to indicate their semantics. Relatively little attention was given to the structure at the foundational, logical adequacy level, so that the inheritance relations between concepts were not always clear.

On the other hand, the Rumelhart and Norman group made an effort to account for procedural-type information directly in their notation (using a link called IS-WHEN), and integrated case-type information with other

should be built (this is in contrast to what we shall later refer to as *epistemological primitives*, operations for structuring pieces of the representation). Schank's contribution to the study of knowledge representation, while controversial, is an important one. His cases are "deeper" than those of Simmons, and begin to attack knowledge structure at the primitive level. Conceptual dependency was incorporated as the memory structure of the MARGIE system, which was a natural language understanding system that could parse an input sentence into the deep conceptual structure and rephrase it in a number of different ways. Schank and Rieger [1974] developed some important inferential properties for their memory structures, and their work has had a great influence on much of the later work in the field. The reader should consult Wilks [1974] and Cercone [1975] for two excellent expositions of Schank's work.

In more recent work, Rieger has attempted to deal in greater depth with the relations between actions and states [1975, 1976, 1977; Rieger and Grinberg, 1977]. Commonsense Algorithms (CSAs) capture information of a much more dynamic sort than that handled by the traditional, static concept networks. Rieger has nodes that represent not only primitive actions, but states, statechanges, wants, and "tendencies" (a tendency in CSA representation is a kind of action that takes place without the effort of an intentional force; one such tendency, for example, is gravity). There is a small repertoire of primitive link types, which are used to represent the underlying dynamic relationships between the actions, states, etc. ("ten theoretical forms of inter-event causal interaction" [Rieger and Grinberg, 1977, p. 250]). CSA links stand for relations like causality, enablement, concurrency, and the like, with the primary emphasis on expressing the cause and effect relationships that make physical systems work. While the notion that causality can be captured in a single link is debatable, CSAs may provide a useful way to express dynamic information that in other systems is supposedly captured by unstructured relational links, and may do so in a complete enough way to allow the simulation of certain physical mechanisms, like the reverse-trap flush toilet [Rieger, 1975] and the reasonably complex home gas forced-air furnace [Rieger and Grinberg, 1977].

Two other important treatments of memory with verb-centered caselike systems surfaced in the early 1970s. Heidorn's thesis [1972] parlayed a simple hierarchical network and instantiation mechanism into a system (called NLPQ) which could "understand" a queuing problem described to it in English. From this description, NLPQ could produce both an English restatement of the problem and a complete program (written in GPSS) for simulating the situation described. By including in advance some simple case frame definitions of actions relevant to queuing situations (for example, "unload" takes an agent, a goal, a location, and a duration), Heidorn provided his system with a built-in definitional context for the description of a particular situation. During an initial conversation with

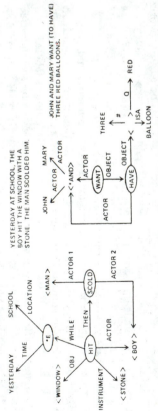

Fig. 7. Some Rumelhart *et al.* concepts. From Rumelhart *et al.* [1972].

"world knowledge." They included definitional as well as instantiated (propositional) constructs, and, all in all, they captured many good ideas in their nets.

Another important piece of work that deserves at least brief mention here is Schank's "conceptual dependency" representation [1972, 1973a,b; Schank *et al.*, 1973]. While Schank himself does not seem to believe in semantic memory [1974, 1975], his *conceptualizations* very much resemble concepts in systems like Simmons' and Rumelhart and Norman's, as evidenced in Fig. 8 [Schank, 1973b, p. 201]. A conceptualization consists of a *primitive act* and some associated cases, like "instrument" and "direction." In conceptual dependency diagrams, arrows with different shapes and labels indicate the case relations. For example, in Fig. 8 the R relation (a three-pronged arrow) indicates the recipient case, while the I relation indicates the instrument of the conceptualization (one interesting idea that is illustrated here is that the instrument of an action is itself a conceptualization). Each primitive act (e.g., TRANS, INGEST) has a particular case structure associated with it, and the higher-level verbs that one sees in the other notations must be broken down into canonical structures of primitives here. Thus, not only does Schank specify a set of *knowledge primitives* out of which concepts

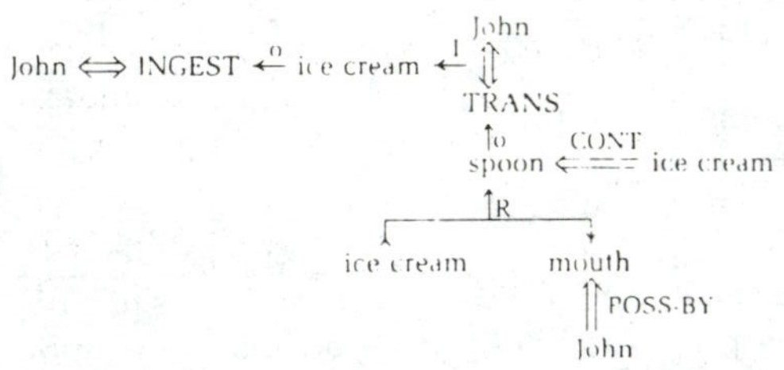

Fig. 8. A Conceptual Dependency conceptualization. From Schank [1973b]. Copyright 1973 by W. H. Freeman and Company.

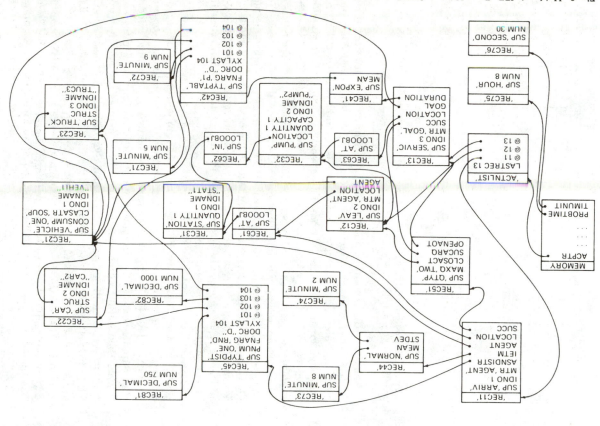

Fig. 9. Heidorn's IPD. From Heidorn [1974]. Copyright 1974, Association for Computing Machinery, Inc., reprinted by permission.

the user, the NLPQ system would build an "internal problem description (IPD)." This IPD comprised a set of instances connected appropriately to the general definitions (see Fig. 9 [Heidorn, 1974, p. 95]). NLPQ could consult those definitions and tell when the problem description was incomplete; it could thus intelligently ask the user for missing information. Although Heidorn's network was very simple and uniform (it was not very deep, concepts had very simple structure, and the SUP link was used for both subconcepts and instances), he achieved a rather dazzling effect by incorporating it in a general grammar-rule language and by starting with a set of concepts well-matched to the simulation language in which the output was produced.

The other "case" study produced a strongly psychologically oriented memory structure called HAM (for Human Associative Memory) [Anderson and Bower, 1973, 1974]. The elements of HAM were *propositions*, binary trees that represented the underlying structure of sentences. A simple proposition of this sort is depicted in Fig. 10 [Anderson and Bower, 1973, p. 165]. Relations allowed between nodes in the trees included set membership (the E links in Fig. 10) and subset, some cases like subject (S in Fig. 10), object (O), location (L), and time (T), and some logical indicators like predicate (P), context (C), and fact (F)—all represented uniformly. Propositions in HAM had truth values, and were supposed to convey assertions about the world; Anderson and Bower's notation failed to account for the internal structure of nominal entities. There were many problems with this simple notation, some of which are discussed in Schubert [1976], a work whose detail on the logical structure of semantic networks in terms of predicates and propositions makes it clear that HAM's propositional notation is insufficient. However, Anderson and Bower produced an extensive investigation into the state of the relevant philosophical and scientific work at the time of their own work, and their detailed psychological discussions should be consulted. Although their model is admitted to be inadequate and the semantics of their representation is not thoroughly worked out, their book is a milestone of start-to-finish research in a field often plagued by less than thorough work.

1.3. Concern for the Foundations

Unfortunately, most of the early work covered above suffers from a lack of explicit acknowledgement of some fundamental principles of knowledge representation design. Authors are most often intuitive when describing the semantics of their representations,* and as the network no-

* For example, "Intuitively, the nodes in the tree represent *ideas* and the links *relations or associations* between the ideas" [Anderson and Bower, 1973, p. 139]; "In this system a large part of the information is about the words and concepts of the relevant domain of discourse . . ." [Heidorn, 1972, p. 35].

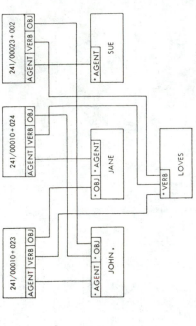

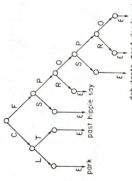

Fig. 10. A HAM proposition. From Anderson and Bower [1974]. Copyright 1974 by V. H. Winston and Sons, Inc., Washington, D. C. Used with permission of Hemisphere Publ. Co., and J. R. Anderson.

Fig. 11. Separating system relations from item relations. From Shapiro [1971a]. Used with permission of the author.

tations get more complex, more and more of the assumptions are left to the reader's imagination. Most of the early representations were not extensible in a general way (i.e., the system designer must intervene to add new case relations), and in general, the combination of set operations and descriptive concept operations that the semantic net is based upon has been poorly understood (see Brachman [1978b], especially Chapter 4, for details). All of the notations mentioned so far are seductively uniform—conceptual relations (e.g., agent, color, left-of) and underlying knowledge mechanisms (e.g., superset, "iswhen," member) are expressed in indistinguishable terms. In Section 2, I shall contend that this homogeneity is misguided and confusing.

However, in addition to that described in Section 3, some recent efforts have set out to remedy this inadequacy. Among the more important of the earlier and concurrent projects that attempted to deal with the expressive inadequacy of semantic nets are the work of Cercone and Schubert at the University of Alberta, and the work of Levesque and Mylopoulos at the University of Toronto, to which we turn in a moment. Several years earlier, however, Shapiro [1971a,b] introduced the important distinction between the "item," or conceptual level of network, and the "system" level—the structural level of interconnection that ties structured assertions of facts to items participating in those facts (i.e., indicates bindings). System relations are the labeled links in the network, and their semantics is determined by the set of processing routines that operate on them. Item relations are concepts that happen to be relational in nature, and are represented by nodes (items) just as are other, nonrelational concepts. Thus, a relationship like LOVES would appear not as a link in the net, but as a node. Particular assertions of the relationship would also be nodes, with AGENT and OBJECT system links to nodes for the participants, and a VERB link back to the node for LOVES (see Fig. 11 [Shapiro, 1971a, p. 43]. In Fig. 11, the top three nodes are assertions of particular LOVES relationships). Shapiro makes no suggestion as to how the general verb itself should be defined in network terms (that is, what makes a concept LOVES as opposed to any other verb with a similar case frame).

Shapiro's distinction explicitly separates underlying primitive cases from all other (conceptual) relations. He also explains how rules for deduction can be encoded directly in his formalism, and discusses at length a language for doing retrieval from his network structure. His early work gives us no guidelines for what the set of system relations should be (his examples suggest linguistic cases), nor does he talk about the semantics of items, except to imply through his search mechanism that sets are important. Shapiro's claim is only that what he has given us is an epistemologically neutral structure, a general language on top of which many models of knowledge might be constructed. This in itself, however, represents a significant advance over previous networks in the distillation of two very different levels of representation.

Between the time of Shapiro's thesis [1971a] and the more recent work to which I have alluded, others have tried to resolve some of the inadequacies of the homogeneous standard evolved from Quillian's Semantic Memory. Hays [1973a,b], in his "cognitive networks," has attempted to differentiate some of the semantics of network notations, and to be more formal than earlier authors about network structures (he specifies four node types, including "modalities," and five major link types). Among other things, his work has contributed the distinction between a "manifestation" of an object and an "instance."*

Hendrix [1975a,b, 1976], in attempting to provide an adequate quantification mechanism for semantic network concepts, introduced what has become a very broadly utilized facility—*partitions*,† or formal

---

* Objects in Hays' epistemology are permanent. However, they do change over time (e.g., a person is at various times an infant, a child, an adolescent, an adult, etc.). Manifestations are different concepts of the same object at different places or stages of its existence.

† Scragg [1975] has, apparently independently, introduced a very similar mechanism, which he calls "planes."

and subset), then they are open to the kind of complaint we shall lodge in that section. That is, each partition (space) type used in a system is open to its own epistemological constraints, just as is each use of the simple, general notion of a node.

In 1975, a very important paper by Woods appeared; this study of "what's in a link" for the first time seriously challenged the logical adequacy of previous semantic network notations [Woods, 1975]. Woods pointed out the *intensional* nature of many of the things we call upon nets to represent (see also Chapter 5 of Brachman [1978b]), and discussed in detail several important challenges for network notations that had not been previously acknowledged, let alone successfully met. We were asked to begin to consider the *semantics of the representation itself*, and to be held accountable for things previously brushed aside under the auspices of "intuition." The work to be described in Section 3 is, to some extent, a broader and deeper investigation in the same spirit as the Woods paper, a continuation of the semantic investigative work only begun there. It is hoped that many of Woods' challenges have been overcome by the structures illustrated in that section and in [Brachman, 1978b].

Some of the issues raised by Woods—the more logically oriented ones—have been recently treated in a series of papers by Cercone and Schubert [1978], Cercone [1975], and Schubert [1976]. In their attempts to extend the expressive power of network notation, Schubert and Cercone have expended considerable effort in the investigation of the underlying logical content of the node-plus-link formalism. Many of the issues of knowledge representation that were emphasized in my thesis [Brachman, 1978b] were raised in various papers from Alberta; in particular, an excellent criticism of the naive notion of the existence of a small number of "conceptually primitive relations" (i.e., cases) reflects a similar intuition about roles (see Section 5.1.3.1 of Brachman [1978b], Schubert [1976, pp. 168–170], and Cercone [1975, pp. 79–80]).

The notation developed by Schubert and Cercone is *propositional*—an important basic node type in the network is the predicative concept node, which is instantiated by conjoining at a *proposition node* a pointer to the predicate and a pointer to each argument of the predicate (see Fig. 13 [Cercone, 1975, p. 36]). The links used are all predefined system links, used only to point out the particular predicate invoked and to order the arguments. All of the conceptual work is done by the particular predicates pointed to with PRED links from the proposition nodes. Schubert and Cercone claim also to have concept nodes for *individuals* and *sets*, although it is not clear from the notation where these interpretations are expected. Given the propositional nature of the notation, a series of logical connectives and quantification conventions can be unambiguously (and explicitly) represented. In addition, Schubert and Cercone provide facilities for lambda-abstraction and various other intensional operations, and include time primitives for certain types of predicates. Schubert [1976] discusses

groupings of concept nodes. Figure 12 [Hendrix, 1975a, p. 239] illustrates the use of partitions (indicated by rectangular dashed boxes) to represent "Every city has a dogcatcher who has been bitten by every dog in town." In this figure, the two larger "spaces" hold the scopes of the universal quantifiers: the "form" link points to a space representing the scope of the universally quantified variable, which is encoded by a node pointed to by a "for all v" link. The node labeled "p" is an implicitly existentially quantified node, representing the particular dogcatcher for any given town.

Partitioning has many potential uses; for example, it can be used to provide a context mechanism, whereby entire areas of memory may be opened up or sealed off at relevant times (this allows reasonable groupings of beliefs). It should be pointed out that the nodes in many of Hendrix's nets represent sets as well as "prototypes", and the introduction of case-like properties for concept nodes makes them susceptible to the same confusions as all of the older, uniform nets (this is evidenced by relations like "creature" and "assailant" being directly encoded as links in his nets). Apparently, however, different space-types are used to distinguish different uses of the same link, and the nonlogical links are not really primitive in the system—they are introduced by "delineations" associated with general verbal concepts like OWNINGS. This is not obvious in some of the earlier papers, but see Hendrix (this volume) for the supporting details.

Partitions have become a mainstay of many recent semantic nets and are an indisputably helpful mechanism for representing higher level phenomena like quantification, context, and structural "plots" [Grosz, 1977]. When viewed as a *mechanism*, with no epistemological claims about their expressive adequacy (which depend on each individual's use of them), partitions do not come under the jurisdiction of our criticisms in Section 2. When partitions implement mixed sets of relationships (like "creature"

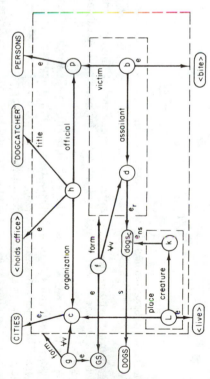

Fig. 12. A partitioned set of nodes. From Hendrix [1975a]. Used with permission of the author.

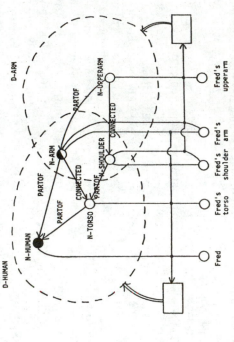

Fig. 14. Hayes' depictions and binders. From Philip Hayes [1977a]. Used with permission of the author.

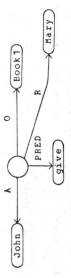

Fig. 13. A proposition node. From Cercone [1975]. Used with permission of the author.

the clear correspondence of his notation to predicate calculus, providing for the first time a clear standard of reference for network (logical) adequacy.*

While the work of Cercone and Schubert begins to answer some of the questions raised in Woods' paper, theirs is still only a neutral logical language. This notation, as all others discussed so far, offers no guidelines to its users on how to structure concepts in terms of the primitives of the notation. The language is as general, uniform, and low-level as predicate calculus and it is up to the designer of the particular network how to structure his world in terms of predicates and propositions. While Schubert's notation unambiguously accounts for many of the underlying logical operations of the semantic network, something more seems to be needed for it to be a truly useful representation of knowledge. This seems to involve looking at network structures at a slightly "higher" level.

Some hints on higher level primitives have been afforded us by some more recent efforts in network formalisms. Fahlman [1977] has designed a network system comprising two major parts: a parallel memory scheme, which allows propagation of markers through a network composed of special-purpose hardware, and a language (called NETL) for representing knowledge on top of the parallel memory. There are several important things to note about Fahlman's work. His is perhaps the first attempt to account for network-implementing hardware in its own right. The marker propagation and detection mechanism eliminates much of the costly search intrinsic to previous, nonparallel systems. Further, he introduces the idea of a "virtual copy" as a dominant organizing concept. This is a convenient way to think about inheritance in semantic nets, since it lets us assume that all properties at a parent node are (virtually) available at its subnodes. When a real copy is needed, as, for instance, when a property is to be explicitly modified, Fahlman has us create a MAP-node. The parallel-processing scheme makes virtual copy and map links act as short circuits in the appropriate circumstances, thereby allowing any inherited definitions to be immediately available.

Further, Fahlman introduces the "role" as a type of individual, whose universe of existence is another concept. While he at times, I believe, confuses the notion of a functional role (like AGENT) with that of a role *filler* (like PERSON), he seems to be on the right track in terms of the structure

* See also Simmons and Bruce [1971] for an earlier discussion of the correspondence between semantic nets and predicate calculus.

of concepts. In my own work (see Section 3 here), I have found this role notion to be critical, and have what amount to MAP-nodes also. A good deal of Fahlman's foundations could be used to support other network schemes.

Role-nodes as parts of structured descriptions also constitute a critical element in the work of Philip Hayes [1977a,b]. Hayes' networks have two levels of structure, just as those to be presented in Section 3 have: the internal structure of "depictions" (concepts), and relationships between depictions as wholes. Briefly, a depiction expresses the structure of an entity through a set of PART-OF and CONNECTED relationships between other entities that make up its parts. For example, in Fig. 14 [Philip Hayes, 1977a, p. 93], the depiction D-HUMAN (indicated by dashed lines) partially expresses the structure of a human (represented by the node N-HUMAN) in terms of an ARM and a TORSO. In the depiction D-HUMAN, N-ARM acts as a depic*ter*; at the same time, in D-ARM, N-ARM is the depic*tee*—the subject of the depiction.* Thus, while it is a thing unto itself in one structure, it acts as the specifier of a role to be filled in another. In some cases, Hayes contends (and I concur), the role can only exist within the larger context. For example, an arm cannot exist without implying the existence of some human; in that case, N-ARM would be an SQNODE for D-HUMAN, and the dependency would be expressed in an SQN structure (for *sine qua non*) involving D-ARM and D-HUMAN.

* While N-ARM is the same node in both depictions, links to it are only "visible" from the depiction from which it is viewed. That way various uses of ARM from more than one context can be kept distinct.

While Hayes does not distinguish the role itself from the role filler (see Section 3), and CONNECTED is much too simplistic to capture relations between roles, the very fact that Hayes has roles at all is significant. Concept structure involving roles is strictly enforced in instantiation, using a structure called a "binder." In Fig. 14, there are two binders (indicated by the rectangular boxes, the arrows coming in to them, and the dots at intersections), representing Fred and Fred's arm. The binder captures the fact that roles are inherited *as part of a structure*. There are explicit connections between role definitions (in the depictions) and role filler/instance pairs (in the binders), just as I propose in Section 3 (although the exact nature of the relationships is not spelled out in Hayes' structure). The explicit acknowledgement of these relationships is a very important development in the history of semantic networks.

Finally, a joint concern for higher-level (nonlogical) structures and their semantics in a semantic network formalism has surfaced in the work of Levesque and Mylopoulos at Toronto [in this volume; Levesque, 1977]. Their efforts attempt to provide a procedural semantics for the relations in a network by associating with a class (concept) a set of four operations: *add* an instance, *remove* an instance, *fetch* all instances of the class, and *test* for being an instance of the class. Classes are given internal structure with slots; parts fill these slots, generating a "PART-OF hierarchy." The classes themselves are organized in an "IS-A hierarchy," which expresses generalization relationships between classes and subclasses.

In addition to these two hierarchies, the system of Levesque and Mylopoulos also has an "instance hierarchy." Every class is itself an instance of the class CLASS, which is termed a "metaclass." Adding this distinction allows a precise account of inheritance and of relations often mistaken in more uniform schemes—including the descriptions of the programs themselves. Levesque and Mylopoulos also provide (in this volume) nice accounts of the distinctions between *structural* and *assertional* properties and between property *attributes* and property *values*, and account with their procedures for the interdependencies between pieces of a structure. As such, their account would provide a good set of tools for exploring the semantics of the representation to be presented in Section 3. The only major shortcoming is the lack of an explicit representation of the relationships between the parts of a class, since their dependencies are only implicitly accounted for in the four programs associated with a class definition.

discussed formalisms is their connectivity—the fact that they all claim to be made of links and nodes. But these two kinds of entity are really just descriptive of implementations—they have nothing to say about the epistemological import of these networks. While Hendrix states, "Broadly speaking, any representation interlinking nodes with arcs could be called a semantic network . . ." [Hendrix, 1977, p. 984], I believe that there is something amiss in this interpretation. Hendrix's definition is indistinguishable from that of a *graph*—and there is nothing inherently "semantic" about a graph.

The "semanticness" of semantic nets lies in their being used in attempts to represent the semantics of English words. Besides nodes and links, the common thread that has held together the many efforts described in Section 1 is the fact that most of the networks were to be used in understanding natural language. Semantic nets have become a popular meaning representation for use in natural language understanding systems.

Despite the fact that virtually all semantic networks have been used to represent the "concepts" corresponding to words and sentences, there has been very little agreement on how to factor such knowledge. The most important disagreement—as evidenced by the fact that we find no two sets of links the same in the literature—has to do with the structural decomposition of a concept. While only the most recent work [Brachman, 1978a,b; Levesque and Mylopoulos, in this volume; Smith, 1978] has dealt with concept-structuring *per se*, every network implicitly embodies a theory of the primitive elements that make up a concept. Structural links holding together the arguments of a logical predicate, "deep semantic cases," and even conceptual relations that are supposed to exist between objects in the world have all been proposed as semantic network links.

The distinction between these alternatives *appears* to be a significant one since logical forms are clearly formal *languages* within which meanings of surface strings are represented, whereas the latter are *labelled graphs* which somehow represent these same meanings. This distinction quickly evaporates, however, the moment one observes that a network is basically a particular choice of representation (at the *implementation* level) for some (*conceptual* level) logical form. [Nash-Webber and Reiter, 1977, p. 121]

(1) The distinction between these alternatives *appears* to be a significant one since logical forms are clearly formal *languages* within which meanings of surface strings are represented, whereas the latter are *labelled graphs* which somehow represent these same meanings. This distinction quickly evaporates, however, the moment one observes that a network is basically a particular choice of representation (at the *implementation* level) for some (*conceptual* level) logical form. [Nash-Webber and Reiter, 1977, p. 121]

(2) If someone argues for the superiority of semantic networks over logic, he must be referring to some other property of the former than their meaning. . . [Pat Hayes, 1977, p. 561]

(3) A semantic network purports to represent concepts expressed by natural-language words and phrases as nodes connected to other such concepts by a particular set of arcs called semantic relations. Primitive concepts in this system of semantic networks are word-sense meanings. Primitive semantic relations are those that the verb

2. "ONE MAN'S CEILING IS ANOTHER MAN'S FLOOR"*

Given this rich and interesting history, what, can we conclude, is a "semantic net"? About the only thing in common among all of the above-

* Copyright 1973, Paul Simon. Used by Permission. "One Man's Ceiling Is Another Man's Floor" provided courtesy of CBS Records.

of a sentence has with its subject, object, and prepositional phrase arguments in addition to those that underlie common lexical, classificational and modification relations. [Simmons, 1973, p. 63]

How are we to rationalize such disparate views of what has always seemed to be a single formalism?

2.1. Will the Real Semantic Network Please Stand Up?

The key issue here is the isolation of the *primitives* for semantic network languages. The primitives of a network language are those things that the interpreter is programmed in advance to understand, and that are not usually represented in the network language itself. While there is, of course, no one set of primitives that is *the* set, for any single language there should be one fixed group of primitive elements. Only with a fixed set of primitives can a fixed interpreter be constructed.* It would be difficult to justify an interpreter in which the set of primitives changed meaning, or for which it was expected that new primitives were to be added in the course of interpretation.

The view I shall take here is that the history of semantic nets and their utility as a representational device can best be understood by carefully examining the nature of the primitives that have been proposed. Since the semantics of any given language is dependent on the interpretation of the primitive elements and a set of rules for combining them into nonprimitive elements, the "well-definedness" of a network language rests heavily on the set of node and link types that it provides. While it is difficult to make simple, clear-cut comparisons of primitives from one language to the next, it is possible to distill a small number of distinctive types of nodes and links from the formalisms discussed in Section 1. Each of these types can be considered to form a consistent conceptual "level"; I shall therefore propose a set of levels, or viewpoints, with which to understand the range of semantic network primitives that have been used in the past. Each of the levels will have a set of link types whose import is clearly distinct from those of other levels.

Any network notation could be analyzed in terms of any of the levels, since they do not really have any absolute, independent "existence." For example, a particular concept might be structured with semantic cases. These cases can be understood as sets of logical predicates, which in turn are implemented with some set of atoms and pointers. However, each network scheme does propose an *explicit* set of primitives as part of the language's in-

terpreter. The particular sets of primitives that are proposed in particular languages are the ones of interest to us here. Understanding past problems with semantic nets and what one is getting when one uses a particular semantic net scheme are both facilitated by looking closely at these explicit primitive sets.* As we shall see, one set of difficulties has arisen because most network notations freely intermix primitives of different types.

The diverse opinions on the primitives of semantic networks expressed both explicitly in the literature and implicitly in the style of existing networks indicate that there are at least four main levels of primitive to be considered. The first view, expressed by the quote from Nash-Webber and Reiter above, considers a semantic network to be an implementational mechanism for a higher-level logical language. This view we might call the *implementational* form of semantic nets. In implementation level networks, links are merely pointers, and nodes are simply destinations for links. These primitives make no important substantive claims about the structure of knowledge, since this level takes a network to be only a data structure out of which to build logical forms. While a useful data-organizing technique, this kind of network gives us no more hint about how to represent (factor) knowledge than do list structures.

A second view sees a semantic network as a set of logical primitives with a structured index over those primitives. In this type of *logical* level net, nodes represent predicates and propositions. Links represent logical relationships, like AND, SUBSET, and THERE-EXISTS. The above quote from Pat Hayes expresses a viewpoint that is essentially the same as those implicitly expressed in networks by Schubert and Hendrix, to some extent Shapiro, and to a lesser extent Woods. In this point of view, logical adequacy, including quantificational apparatus, is taken to be the responsibility of semantic network representations of knowledge. The aforementioned efforts express a tacit dependence on predicate calculus for knowledge factoring and espouse network schemes as useful organizing principles over normally nonindexed predicate calculus statements. In doing so, they make at least some claim about how knowledge can be meaningfully factored. It is interesting to note that almost all of the "foundational" work on semantic networks has been done at this logical level of interpretation.

The most prevalent view of networks is reflected in Simmons' above statement and almost all of the work discussed in Section 1. This is, in some sense, the "real" semantic net—a network structure whose primi-

---

* It is probably also desirable to have this set as small as possible. However, at the current stage, we shall settle for any set that is adequate. One of the purposes of this chapter (see Section 3) is to begin to circumscribe what would be an adequate set of primitives, and therefore, an adequate interpreter.

* The assignment of a notation to a particular level should not be taken as a value judgment (very few formalisms can, in fact, be assigned to a single level). Different level notations are useful for different tasks. Here it is asked only that one become aware of the level at which one stops decomposing concepts, and understands the meaning of one's primitives as potentially decomposed into "lower" level ones.

tives are word-senses and case relations. As Simmons notes, in these *conceptual* level nets, links represent semantic or conceptual relationships. Networks at this level can be characterized as having small sets of language-independent conceptual elements (namely, primitive object- and action-types) and conceptually primitive relationships (i.e., "deep cases") out of which all expressible concepts can be constructed. The strongest view at this level is that of Schank and followers, which picks a small set of act types (e.g., GRASP, INGEST, PTRANS) and cases (e.g., INSTRUMENT, RECIPIENT) and claims that this set is adequate to represent the knowledge expressed in any natural language.* Weaker views are embodied in the Norman and Simmons nets, where it is difficult to tell if there are any truly primitive knowledge pieces. In these nets, the belief in cases, and the particular sets settled upon, seem to be the unchanging elemental units.

Finally, going one step higher, we might consider networks whose primitive elements are language-specific. The only formalism that I know of at the current time that embodies this view is OWL, whose elements are expressions based on English.† In such a formalism, one would presumably "take seriously the Whorfian hypothesis that a person's language plays a key role in determining his model of the world and thus in structuring his thought" [Martin, 1977, p. 985]. In OWL there is a basic concept-structuring scheme (see Hawkinson [1975]) that is used to build expressions, and strictly speaking, the principles of "specialization," "attachment," and "reference" are the primitives of the language. However, these primitives are neutral enough to be considered implementational, and thus the knowledge itself can be considered to form the structure of the data base. This seems operationally reasonable when OWL is looked at in detail—the two expressions (HYDRANT FIRE) and (MAN FIRE), while both specialized by FIRE, can have the specializations "mean" different things based on the rest of the network structure. This *linguistic* level represents perhaps the most radical view of semantic nets, in that the "primitives" are language-dependent, and are expected to change in meaning as the network grows. Links in linguistic level networks stand for arbitrary relationships that exist in the world being represented.

It should be obvious that each of the above viewpoints implies a set of primitive relationships substantially different from the others. Relationships between predicates and propositions (e.g., AND, ARGUMENT1, PRED) are distinctly different than those between verbs and associated "cases" (e.g., AGENT, INSTRUMENT, RECIPIENT). Both of these are not

* In general, a characteristic of this level is that it should be language-independent.
† "We have taken English as the basis for our knowledge representation formalism" [Szolovits et al., 1977, p. 2]. Not surprisingly, the view of the OWL group is that their "Linguistic Memory System" is a semantic network: "The most novel aspects of OWL are the structure of the semantic net (Hawkinson, 1975) . . ." [Martin, 1977, p. 985]

the same as arbitrary relationships between things in the world (i.e., relations between the entities that the concepts are supposed to denote, e.g., COLOR, HIT). And further, none of these is the same as the relations between the parts of an intensional description, to which we now turn.

2.2. The Missing Level

While this characterization of the levels of semantic network representations covers virtually all of the work that has been done, there appears to be at least one level missing from the analysis. That this is the case is suggested by some of the more recent phenomena appearing in network languages, including "partitions," "delineations" [Hendrix, 1975a,b, 1976], and "binders" [Philip Hayes, 1977a,b].* These features suggest the possibility of organizations of conceptual knowledge into units more structured than simple nodes and links or predicates and propositions, and the possibility of processing over larger units than single network links. The predominant use of concepts as intensional descriptions of objects in a world also hints that there is a class of relationship that is not accounted for by the four levels already discussed. This kind of relationship relates the parts of an intension [Carnap, 1947] to the intension as a whole, and one intension to another. Intensional descriptions can be related directly by virtue of their internal structures, or indirectly by virtue of their corresponding extensions.† In addition, even the single most common trait of semantic networks—"inheritance"—suggests a level of knowledge structure between the logical and conceptual ones described above. Inheritance of properties is not a logical primitive; on the other hand, it is a mechanism assumed by almost all conceptual level nets, but not accounted for as a "semantic" (deep case) relation.

There must be some intermediate level at which a precise formal account of such notions can be constructed. The very attempt to give conceptual units more structure than that of uniform configurations of links hints that at least some network designers have been thinking about "concepts" as formal objects, with predetermined internal organization that is more sophisticated than sets of cases. The formal structure of conceptual units and their interrelationships *as conceptual units* (independent of any knowledge expressed therein) forms what could be called an *epistemology*. I shall propose, then, an intermediate level of network primitive that embodies this formal structuring. This will be called the *epistemological* level, and it lies between the logical and conceptual levels.

The epistemological level of semantic network permits the formal def-

* Nonnetwork languages, like KRL [Bobrow and Winograd, 1977], have similar types of mechanisms playing a more and more prominent part.
† KRL has also focused intensively on the issue of description—most notably, what constitutes a description, and how descriptions in the above sense are inherently partial.

inition of knowledge-*structuring* primitives, rather than particular knowledge primitives (as in the Schank networks). Note that networks at the next higher level (conceptual) take as their primitives pieces of semantic knowledge and cases, but with no explicit accounting for their internal structure. While there is no universal agreement on what cases there are, everyone agrees that there are probably at least *some* cases, and they all seem to have a feel for what a case is. The basis for this agreement on the concept of case (or "slot") and the inheritance of cases in a network is provided by the epistemological level, which explains the meaning of cases in general and provides a defining mechanism for particular ones.

In Section 3, I shall touch on some of the other operations that nets built out of explicit epistemological primitives should account for. In that section, I shall also introduce a formalism expressly based on those notions. Briefly, relations at the epistemological level include those used to structure intensional descriptions and those used to interrelate them. The former involves piecing together aspects of a description, including descriptions of the conceptual subpieces of an object and how they intertwine. One such type of conceptual subpiece is a case, the meaning of which is taken to be something built out of epistemological primitives. The latter type of relation specifies inheritance of subdescriptions between descriptions.

Table I summarizes our discussion of the five levels. The examples listed with the levels are suggestive of the philosophy of those levels; none is really a "pure" example of a single primitive type. Although a desirable goal (as we shall see below), it is not clear that a pure network at any level is attainable. Our task here, then, is to understand as well as possible each

type of primitive so that the semantics of any formalism can be clearly and completely specified, even if it mixes elements of more than one level.

2.3. Neutrality, Adequacy, and Semantics

Despite the fact that we have isolated five distinct types of semantic net, there are some universal notions that can be applied equally well to each type of network. These are *neutrality, adequacy,* and *semantics*. Each of these can be used as a criterion for judging the utility and formality of a given network language. It is desirable that a formalism be as pure as possible, adequate to handle its appointed representation task, and have a clean, explicitly specified semantics.

A network implemented at some level should be *neutral* toward the level above it. For example, logical nets are "epistemologically neutral," in that they do not force any choice of epistemological primitives on the language user. Making "concepts" in logical nets, then, is a mixing of levels. Conceptual level nets must support many different linguistic systems and should be linguistically neutral (as Schank puts it, "the principal problem that we shall address here is the representation of meaning in an unambiguous language-free manner" [1973b, p. 187]). By the same token, of course, epistemological formalisms must be neutral in regard to particular semantic relationships. It is the job of the epistemological formalism to provide case-defining facilities—not particular cases.

A formalism at any of the four lower levels that is neutral toward the one above is a useful tool for designers of those at higher levels. Epistemological neutrality, for example, ensures flexibility in the design and definition of particular cases or nonstandard types of inheritance. It should be clear, then, that one of the main problems with many of the older formalisms was their lack of a clear notion of what level they were designed for. Almost universally, semantic networks have mixed primitives from more than one level (for example, particular cases were links in the same systems in which set membership was a link). In terms of neutrality, these formalisms were all less flexible than they could have been in serving knowledge base designers who were building structures on top of them. Decisions were forced at more than one level at a time; the simultaneous freedom on some issues and lack of flexibility on others (at the same level) has been a constant source of confusion for network language users throughout the history of semantic nets.

Any level network can also be judged on its *adequacy* for supporting the level above it. If a semantic net can somehow support all possible linguistic systems of knowledge, then it has achieved conceptual adequacy. While the particular features of conceptual adequacy are open to debate, the notion of adequacy for the logical level is well understood (see Shubert [1976], for example). At the current time, it is less clear

TABLE I
Levels of "Semantic" Networks

Level	Primitives	Examples (nonexclusive)
Implementational	Atoms, pointers	Data structures [Schubert, 1976]
Logical	Propositions, predicates, logical operators	[Cercone, 1975] [Hendrix, 1975a,b]
Epistemological	Concept types, conceptual subpieces, inheritance and structuring relations	[Brachman, 1978a,b]
Conceptual	Semantic or conceptual relations (cases), primitive objects and actions	[Schank, 1972] [Simmons, 1973] [Norman et al., 1975]
Linguistic	Arbitrary concepts, words, expressions	[Szolovits et al., 1977]

what it would take for a network representation language to be epistemologically adequate. This is a subject (as, for example, treated in Brachman [1978b]) that is ripe for study, and to which I would like to draw the reader's attention. Treatments of criteria for epistemological adequacy have heretofore been missing from network studies. Yet it seems that the understanding of knowledge representation languages in general will depend intimately on an understanding of what the elements of epistemological adequacy are, and how well given languages handle them. We shall look at some aspects of this in the next section.

Thinking in terms of adequacy gives us another reason why previous semantic networks have been difficult to assess. Given networks that mixed levels of primitives, it was impossible to tell what exactly the networks were adequate for. The recent push toward completely logical networks was in part motivated by the desire to achieve for the first time a network that was demonstrably adequate in a well-understood way.

Finally, each type of network language must be held accountable for its *semantics*—what, formally, do each of its elements mean, and what are the legal operations on them?* In this respect, the attempts to define logically adequate nets (Schubert, Cercone, Hendrix, etc.) have a clear advantage over all of the others: once a mapping to predicate calculus is established, a formal semantics (i.e., Tarskian truth-theoretic) is available, essentially for free. This requirement, on the other hand, makes a formal semantics for linguistic level nets almost impossible to achieve, since it would require a formal semantics to be defined for the particular natural language involved. For conceptual level nets, only Schank and Rieger [1974] have provided a well-defined semantics, in that they have, in advance, specified sets of ''inferences'' for each of their predetermined primitive acts. Thus an act is defined in terms of its inferences, and there are rules for combining inferences into interpretations of larger, nonprimitive structures, based only on the primitives out of which they are built. Other conceptual level nets do not have fixed primitives, thereby making it difficult to provide an acceptable semantics.

Formal semantics for epistemological level languages are currently under study; studies of such semantics must however be done in parallel

with those attacking epistemological adequacy, since the nature of the epistemological primitives is not yet understood, which therefore makes it hard to define a semantics. Three particular studies are of note here:

(1) In Brachman [1978b], I attempt to ferret out the meaning of a network language by making each basic relationship available as a link, and then explaining in detail the epistemological significance of each link.

(2) The work of Levesque and Mylopoulos at Toronto [in this volume; Levesque, 1977] investigates a procedural semantics in a similar manner—except that the nature of the procedures themselves is being dealt with in a general, network-expressible way.

(3) Smith [1978] is working on a comprehensive paradigm for knowledge representation languages in general, which includes a noncircular explanation for the interpreter of the procedures,* as well as accounts of ''meta-description,'' structured inheritance, believing as an active process that denotes, etc.

3. AN EPISTEMOLOGICALLY EXPLICIT REPRESENTATION

In this final section, I hope to illustrate what a network formalism at the epistemological level of knowledge representation should be concerned with. Such a formalism should have a clean, well-understood semantics, should not depend in any way upon the domain to which it is applied, and should adequately handle the significant epistemological relationships of concept structuring, attribute/value inheritance, multiple description, etc.

In order to make the ideas more concrete, I shall discuss epistemological primitives in terms of a particular type of formalism called *Structured Inheritance Networks* (SI-Nets) [Brachman, 1978a,b]. SI-Nets were developed expressly to address the above cited epistemological issues and to provide a useful explanatory tool for semantic level languages. SI-Nets constitute a class of network languages whose links represent epistemologically primitive relations. For the purposes of this discussion, we shall use a paradigmatic example of this class, called KLONE. While KLONE will be discussed only briefly here, details are available in Brachman [1978a,b].

The basic elements of KLONE (as they are in most semantic net schemes) are *Concepts*. Concepts are formal objects used to represent objects, attributes, and relationships of the domain being modeled. A Concept is thought of as representing an intensional object, and no Concepts

* The reader should be warned here that I am using the term ''semantics'' in its currently popular AI sense, wherein the meaning of a primitive is provided by the programs that operate on it. While the notion of links being meaningful by virtue of the programs that use them seems intuitively clear and reasonably precise, there is a lot more to be said on the issue. Semantics deals with the relationship between a symbol and what it denotes. Therefore not only should we take careful account of what here is a symbol (e.g., some marks on a piece of paper, an arrow with a word next to it, a set of bits in a computer), but we must also be precise about what these symbols denote (i.e., what are ''epistemological relations'' anyway?). Smith treats these problems in insightful depth in his Master's thesis [1978]. See also Fodor [1978] for a recent critique of ''procedural semantics.''

* The account of the procedures of Levesque and Mylopoulos is, of necessity, circular since the procedures are being defined in the same network for which they attempt to provide the semantics.

are used to represent directly extensional (world) objects. There are two main Concept types—generic and individual. Generic Concepts represent classes of individuals by describing the characteristics of a prototypical member of the class. Individual Concepts represent individual objects, relationships, etc. by *individuating* more general Concepts. Individuation is a relationship between Concepts. The term "instance" has been used in many network models to refer to an individuating description, as well as to the thing in the world that the individual description describes. Here, however, we shall use "instantiation" *only* as a relationship between a thing in the world and a Generic Concept, and not as a relationship between Concepts. Thus, the Arc de Triomphe (i.e., the one in Paris) is an "instance" of the Concept ARCH; the Individual Concept (call it ARC-DE-TRIOMPHE) that denotes the Arc de Triomphe "individuates" the Concept ARCH. The relationship between ARC-DE-TRIOMPHE and the real Arc is "denotation." See Fig. 15 for a schematic picture of this three-way relationship.

3.1. Internal Concept Structure

The key observation of SI-Nets is that objects in the world have complex relational structure—they cannot, in general, be usefully taken as atomic entities or mere lists of properties (see Brachman [1977, 1978b] for detailed justification). A Concept must therefore account for this internal structure as well as for the object as a wholistic entity. The KLONE formal entities that support this view of structured objects are *Role/Filler Descriptions* (Roles) and *Structural Descriptions* (SDs). Roles represent the conceptual subpieces of an entity, while SDs account for the structuring relationships between them.

The Roles represent the various kinds of attributes, parts, etc. that things in the world are considered to "have." These include, for example,

such things as parts (e.g., fingers of a hand), inherent attributes of objects and substances (e.g., color), arguments of functions (e.g., multiplier and multiplicand of a multiplication), and "cases" of verbs in sentences (e.g., "agent").* Any generalized attribute of this sort has two important pieces: (1) the particular entity that becomes the value for the attribute in an instance of the Concept, and (2) the functional role which that entity fills in the conceptual complex. A Role is a formal entity that captures both of these aspects in a structured way, by packaging up information about both the role filler and the functional role itself.

In KLONE, the substructure of a Role indicates the following: the type of entity that can fill the functional role, how many fillers of that role are to be expected, whether it is important in some way to have the role filled in an instance, and the name of the functional role itself. Notice, then, that the formal entity, Role, is somewhat more than a description of either the potential filler or the functional role alone. It is a very special type of epistemological entity that ties together the functional role, the context in which that role is played, and the (set of) filler(s) of the role. Figure 16 schematically illustrates the internal structure of a Role and its place in a Concept (Roles will henceforth be pictured as small squares, while Concepts will be depicted as ovals).

As just mentioned, while the "internal" Role structure indicates information about the particular fillers in themselves, the Role itself is the meeting place for information about how those fillers fit into the entire conceptual complex. It is the Concept's set of Structural Descriptions (SDs) that is the source of information about how role fillers interact with each other. Each SD is a set of relationships between two or more of the Roles. Just as a Role indicates that for any instance of the Concept there will be the appropriate number of fillers (with the corresponding characteristics) for the given functional role, an SD indicates that any instance of the Concept will exhibit the relationships specified in that SD. So, for example,

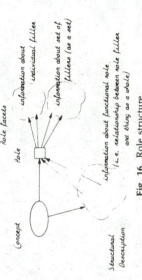

Role facets

Role

information about
'individual filler

Concept

information about set of
fillers (as a set)

Structural
Description

information about functional role
(i.e. relationship between role filler
and thing as a whole)

Fig. 16. Role structure.

* I have in the past [Brachman, 1978a,b] referred to the generalization of this kind of conceptual subpart as a "dattr." Here I shall use the term, "generalized attribute."

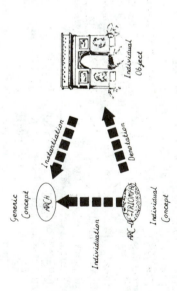

Generic
Concept

ARCH

Instantiation

Individual
Object

Denotation

Individual
Concept

ARC-DE-TRIOMPHE

Individuation

Fig. 15. A sketch of the individuates/instantiates dichotomy.

To determine the exact nature of this Concept, let us look at the way that we have expressed the relationship in English: first, the definite determiner for "ground" indicates that we mean a unique individual.* To reflect this, our network would have an Individual Concept, GROUND, which corresponded to that "constant." Further, there should be some individuator of the DISTANCE Concept with one of its Roles satisfied by GROUND. In Fig. 18, we illustrate this partial state of affairs—D1 is an individuator of DISTANCE (indicated by the *Individuates* link), and the fact that its TO Role (R1) is satisfied is captured by R2, whose *Satisfies* link indicates the appropriate Role, and whose *Value* link points to the filler. Now—back to our English description—we have still to account for "its lintel" and "the distance." By "its," we mean that for each arch, there is one lintel, and that is precisely what we meant by the Role R1 in Fig. 17. The "the" with "distance" then follows as saying that for each instance of ARCH, there is one unique distance involving the lintel of that arch. Thus, what we thought was an individuator of DISTANCE, is not quite—it has Role fillers tied down to lintels, but not to a single constant one.

The fact that the FROM Role of D1 is to be "filled" not by a constant, but by a type of existential, makes it a different sort of entity than R2. It is not quite a general Role, since it can only be filled by the lintel of a particular arch; nor is it a filled Role. Instead, it is an argument of a Concept that is parameterized by another Concept—D1, parameterized by ARCH. Once a particular arch is selected, the filler of the corresponding DISTANCE's FROM Role is fixed. We call this type of Concept a "Parametric Individ-

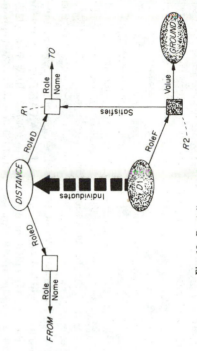

Fig. 18. Partially specified DISTANCE.

* To be precise, this use of "the" probably means "the ground under the arch." Let us assume that in this world all ground is at the same level and is, in fact, all one large individual entity, and therefore allow "the ground" to refer to that individual. Otherwise, the treatment of GROUND would be analogous to that of LINTEL.

the Concept for a simple arch, which has three bricks as its parts, might be factored as in Fig. 17 (SDs are indicated by diamonds).

In this figure, Role R1 expresses the fact that this kind of arch has one LINTEL, which must be a WEDGE-BRICK. The *RoleD* link expresses the relationship between the Concept ARCH and one of its Role descriptions; the *V/R* (Value Restriction) link points to the type predicate that must be true of the eventual role filler; the *Number* link indicates the restriction on the number of fillers of the role; the *Modality* link indicates the importance of the attribute to the Concept; and finally, the *RoleName* link names the relationship (conceptual, not epistemological) between the filler and the whole. R2 similarly indicates that any example of this type of object has two UPRIGHTs, which are BRICKs. R3 defines the generalized attribute of VERTICAL-CLEARANCE. The *Modality* INHERENT means that, while every arch has one of these, knowing its value is not critical to the recognition of some object as an ARCH.* In addition, DERIVABLE means that the value can be computed from the values of the other Roles, once they are found. As for the SDs, S1 is a set of relationships that expresses how every UPRIGHT supports the LINTEL, S2 specifies that no two UPRIGHTs touch each other, and S3 embodies the definition of the VERTICAL-CLEARANCE in terms of the LINTEL and an Individual Concept, GROUND. We now turn briefly to the internal structure of these relational parts of the Concept.

Let us say that we want to define the VERTICAL-CLEARANCE of an ARCH to be the distance between its lintel and the ground. There will thus be some Concept related to DISTANCE in one of the SDs of ARCH.

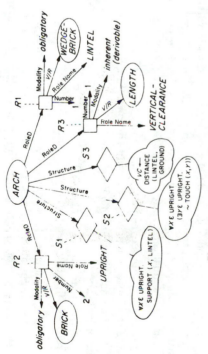

Fig. 17. A simple KLONE concept.

* There is a general problem here, of mixing recognition information with more neutral descriptive information. This aspect of the representation is currently under scrutiny.

formal representational objects. It should be clear at this point that there is no sense to having links like COLOR and ASSAILANT in the same formalism with links for epistemological operations (nor links like AND and PRED, for that matter). The relationship between a Concept and a Role/Filler structure is *not* the same as that between the object that the Concept represents and the thing that fills the functional role for that object.

The semantics of each of these links is, of course, built into the interpreting functions that operate over the network structure. While I shall not detail that interpreter here (except briefly; see Section 3.4), it should be noted that with a small, predetermined set of link types, a fixed interpreter can, at least in principle, be designed. In languages that claim to have no primitives at all, the status of an interpreter is in question.*

3.2. Epistemological Primitives for Inheritance

One type of epistemological relation that we have so far glossed over is that which connects formal objects of the same type—Concept to Concept, Role to Role, and SD to SD. This type of link is a critical one in the SI-Net scheme, since it accounts for *inheritance*. For example, as mentioned, individuation is a relationship between Concepts, such that there is always some description (Concept) that is being individuated. That Concept is composed of various subdescriptions, all of which must be satisfied by the individuating Concept. Not only is there a relation between the two Concepts involved (i.e., *Individuates*), there is a set of subrelations between the generalized attribute descriptions (Roles) of the parent Concept and the values of those attributes in the individuator (i.e., the relation *Satisfies* expresses this in the above examples).

* See Smith [1978] for a philosophical account of the place and nature of interpreters in knowledge representation schemes.

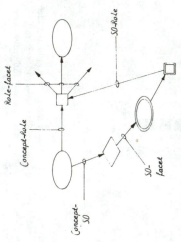

Fig. 20. Schematic Concept structure.

ual" (ParaIndividual), and express it as in Fig. 19. In this figure, the double oval represents the ParaIndividual, which is linked to DISTANCE by a *ParaIndividuates* link. The double square is a "Coref Role," which equates (as coreferential) the filler of the FROM role of the particular distance in some instance of ARCH with the filler of the LINTEL role for that same arch. *CorefValue* links the equated Roles, and *CorefSatisfies* performs an analogous task to that of *Satisfies* in an ordinary filled Role.

3.1.1. Epistemological Relations for Structuring Concepts

Our notions of Concept, Role, and SD give us the picture of structured conceptual objects schematically illustrated in Fig. 20. This structure implies that a knowledge representation language that is based on structured conceptual objects must account for at least the following relationships:

(1) the relationship between a Concept and one of its Roles,
(2) the relationship between a Concept and one of its SDs,
(3) the "internal" structure of a Role—the relationship between a Role and one of its facets,
(4) the "internal" structure of an SD,
(5) relationships between parts of SDs and Roles.

In SI-Nets, we account for these explicitly as link types, most of which were illustrated in the above figures. Thus, the primitives in this notation are epistemological (knowledge-structuring) relationships that compose

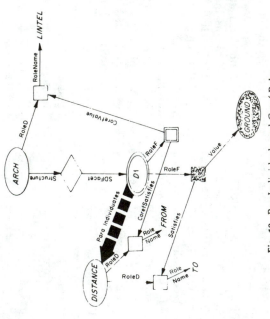

Fig. 19. ParaIndividuals and Coref Roles.

The notion of inheritance is broader, however, than just the defining of an Individual Concept by a more general Generic Concept. "Subconcepts," themselves also Generic, can be formed from Generic Concepts by restricting some of the subparts of the description embodied by the Generic Concept. As we have seen in the history of semantic nets, the formation of more and more specific descriptions is an important common feature, and taxonomic hierarchies depend on this for the backbone of their structure. There has generally been a single link (e.g., IS-A) to specify inheritance along sub/superconcept chains, and the assumption has been that everything relevant to a general class (e.g., MAMMAL) is relevant to its more specific subclasses (e.g., DOG, CAT). Looking at this with our epistemological eye, however, we find this to be an oversimplification of a multifaceted relationship.

The Roles and SDs of a parent Concept each contribute to the inheritance of a subConcept. Thus the inheritance link is effectively a "cable" carrying down each of these to the inheritor; the Roles and SDs must be transmitted as a group, since they do not have an existence independent of the Concept of which they are parts. Just as Fahlman's "virtual copy" link implies that all parts of the structure are immediately available at a subconcept, we think of inheritance as a *structured* epistemological relationship between Concepts.

Further, properties are usually not all inherited intact, but instead are often modified so as to give the subConcept a more restricted definition than the parent Concept.* In that case, each of the modifications must be represented in an explicit and precise way. Figure 21 sketches the set of epistemological relations between a parent Concept and one of its descendants. For each Role and SD that is to be modified in some way, we must say precisely what type of modification applies, and what Role or SD the modification applies to. The latter is indicated by an inter-Role or inter-SD link stating the relationship between the original Role or SD and

* In addition, further properties can be added to form more specialized Concepts, e.g., PRIME-NUMBER from NUMBER.

the new, modified one. The modification itself is then indicated just as if the modifying Role were a new Role description. KLONE currently allows three types of Role modification (satisfaction, or filling; differentiation, or the creation of subRoles; and restriction of the Role constraint). At the moment, only one type of SD modification (preempting) is provided. These relationships are explicitly indicated by appropriate links with unambiguous interpretations.

The reader should consult Brachman [1978a] for further details on KLONE. Here I have attempted only to illustrate the flavor of relationship for which it is necessary to account. More specifically, it is the job of an epistemological level formalism to provide internal Concept-, Role-, and SD-structuring relationships, and inheritance-specifying inter-Concept, inter-Role, and inter-SD relationships.

3.3. The "Conceptual Coat Rack"

In many of today's representation languages, there is a way for the knowledge base designer to go directly to the language in which the system is implemented (e.g., LISP) in order to express certain facts or associate certain procedures with network structures. Such "escape" mechanisms are used either when the knowledge to be expressed is too complex to be represented in the network itself, when knowledge about the network itself is to be encoded, or when certain procedures are to be triggered by operations on the data base. With the work of Smith [1978], the epistemological import of "procedural attachment' is now clear. There are, according to Smith, *two* different types of attachment that are most often confused under the guise of "procedural attachment": (1) "metadescription," wherein knowledge about knowledge is expressed in the same network language as the primary knowledge; and (2) interpretive intervention, in which direct instructions to the interpreter are expressed in the language that implements the interpreter itself.

In the case of metadescription, the interpreter is being asked to make a type or level jump when processing a Concept.* Metainformation is information about a Concept (or Role or SD) as a formal entity, and is not information about the thing(s) that the Concept describes. To support this kind of information, KLONE provides an explicit link to a node representing a separate sense of the Concept as a formal entity. This link is called a '*metahook*,' and it can attach to a Concept, a Role, or an SD. Metahooks always point to Individual Concepts, and those Individual Concepts express knowledge in the normal KLONE way—except that their "referents" are formal entities in the net, and not objects in the world.

KLONE provides another kind of hook, the "interpretive hook" (*ihook*), for attaching interpreter code directly to a Concept, Role, or SD. The code

* This is the case in the Levesque and Mylopoulos "instance hierarchy," for example

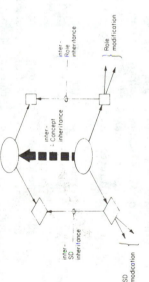

Fig. 21. Inter-Concept structured inheritance.

pointed to by an ihook must be constructed from interpreter primitives (e.g., functions like "CreateConcept," "SatisfyRole"), and the ihook must specify the place in the interpreter from which the code is to be invoked. These hooks are not intended as escapes in which arbitrary information can be encoded when the formalism makes it hard to express a fact about the world, but as a means of direct advice to the interpreter with clear import.*

The two kinds of hooks express important relationships between the KLONE interpreter and data base. These relationships are different in nature from those expressed by the intensional, structure-building links discussed above. They allow us to look at the part of the network built out of those links as a structure on which to hang knowledge about knowledge or advice to the interpreter—as kind of a "conceptual coat rack." The knowledge-structuring relationships can be thought of as forming a representation "plane" out of which hooks emerge orthogonally.

3.4. Interpreting KLONE Structures

While I have given the impression that there is a single KLONE interpreter that deals with the node- and link-types described, that is a bit misleading. KLONE is implemented (in INTERLISP) as a set of interpreter primitives, all of which together, in some sense, form an "interpreter." However, these primitive functions for building, accessing, and removing structure are not organized into a single cohesive program. Instead, they may be used in combination by higher-level functions (matching, reasoning by analogy, deduction, etc.) to construct and maintain a KLONE data base. Each function guarantees structural integrity, and the set of functions together constitute the only possible access to the KLONE structures. In this way, Concepts, Roles, and SDs are like abstract data types in CLU [Liskov and Zilles, 1974]. The functional interface provides a clean, implementation-independent definition for the types of entities that KLONE supports.

The principal motivation for providing a set of primitive functional pieces out of which "higher-level" procedures can be built, and not a particular set of matching, deduction, etc. procedures, is that it is felt that we do not have a clear enough understanding of these issues to allow us to provide powerful procedures at this higher level. Experience with matchers in the field in general has been equivocal, and we have chosen instead to provide a basic set of tools for building different variants on an experimental basis. Since there is no general understanding of things like matching and reasoning by analogy, it seems wise not to commit the basic package to some ad hoc set of processing routines. This does not mean to

say, however, that there do not exist such higher-level routines for KLONE—we have, in fact, been experimenting with a variety of approaches to structure-matching, paraphrasing, question-answering, and situation recognition. KLONE is well-suited to some of these tasks, and where possible, we have provided the obvious functions. With some of these, we are investigating the use of "parallel" marker-passing algorithms (see Woods and Brachman [1978], for example).

The KLONE functions depend on the fact that the set of connections between Concepts, Roles, and SDs is fixed in advance. In order to implement, say, a function that finds a (possibly inherited) facet of a Role, we need to be able to anticipate all possible forms of inheritance that will be encountered. The function can then look for immediately accessible values, and if not found, can call a variant of itself recursively, depending on the type of Role inheritance connector it encounters. A complete set of Role inheritance functions, including the provision for multiple super-Concepts and multiple super-Roles, has been implemented, based on the small set of possible inter-Role relationships.

Since the user of KLONE "sees" only abstract structures for Concepts, etc., it is not necessary to think of the network as a set of nodes interconnected by links, but instead to view Concepts as sets of Roles and SDs, etc. The functions deal only with those entities (and their "epistemological" relations), and never attempt to make or break simple local linklike connections. This is important, considering that structured inheritance is a central feature of KLONE; a "cable" contains many connections that are not independent. One problem with the traditional semantic network metaphor in general is the apparent independence of each link from all other links.

There are currently two significant uses being made of the KLONE interpreter package. One involves a natural language understanding system that combines general English ATN-based parsing with the benefits of "semantic grammar" [Brown and Burton, 1975; Burton, 1976]. A KLONE taxonomy has been built that encodes semantic categories for certain types of phrases, and the parser, guided by a very general grammar of English, interacts with this taxonomy to build up the representation of a sentence. The Concept-Role paradigm is ideal for expressing the relationships between categories like "person-NP" and its possible modifiers, since it provides a completely general case-definition facility. Further, the interpretations of sentences are built incrementally from their syntactic representations using the ihook and metadescription facilities to map syntactic structures into those of a conceptual network. The conceptual net expresses the relationships between the entities discussed in the sentences, which at the moment, include people, places, and research topics. Structural Descriptions play a large part in handling paraphrase utterances and determining answers to queries.

* See Smith [1978] for details on the interaction of interpretive "planes" and meta-descriptive "layers."

The other domain to which the package has been applied is the description of general graphics knowledge and how to use the display facilities of a bit-map terminal. This knowledge includes coordinate system transformations, projections of entities onto display surfaces, and interrelations between actual domain objects (like ships and land masses) and their corresponding display forms. For example, one might incorporate into the general knowledge base the desire to see ships displayed as circles with centers at their projected positions, and augment that with the instruction to display ships with radar with a special symbol. Once particular ships were described to the system (and incorporated into the portion of the network dealing with domain objects), their displays would be handled automatically. The knowledge is encoded in KLONE so that it will not only be useful in producing the displays, but will also be available for discussion and easy manipulation by the system's user.

CONCLUSIONS

In this chapter, I have examined the history of the "semantic" network, looking for the major conceptual breakthroughs that have made it such a popular representation technique. It was found that through that ten-year history, at least five different interpretations of nodes and links have crept together to create confusing languages with limited expressive power. In the last two years, efforts have been mounted to crack that expressive deadlock; these efforts have concentrated on the logical status of network primitives, and have begun to take a hard look at the foundations of network representations. At the same time, the field has begun to see higher-level structures (e.g., partitions, frames) imposed on nodes and links. These structures appear to be useful and significant, but no comprehensive effort has been made to understand exactly what their status is.

In Section 2, I postulated a set of conceptual levels for interpreting primitives in semantic networks. The four that were immediately apparent from the history of the semantic net were the *implementational, logical, conceptual,* and *linguistic* levels. Each of these has had at least one (perhaps implicit) proponent in the literature. In addition, to account for some more recent aspects of knowledge representation, and the standard descriptional use of network concepts, I proposed an intermediate level to account for the internal structures of Concepts, and the relations of inheritance that exist between them. I called this the *epistemological* level of knowledge representation.

Section 3 attempted to make more apparent the kinds of relationships that an epistemological level representation should express. It was noted that descriptions of functional roles in complex objects and descriptions of the fillers of those roles were a critical part of knowledge about the world,

and that, in addition, the meaning of a functional role was bound up in a set of relationships between its fillers and the fillers of other roles in the object. Given this interpretation of structured objects, the set of epistemological relations that a formalism must account for becomes clear. Finally, I tried to illustrate how a network language might account for all of these relations with explicit epistemological links, and how the structure thus formed could be used to hang information for the network interpreter.

In conclusion, it is in general useful to try to produce a knowledge representation language that is built on a small, fixed set of primitive node and link types. Settling on a fixed set of primitives, with well-understood import in terms of the operations of a particular level, enables the network designer to construct a well-defined and fixed interpreter. In addition, consistency at a single level affords the best position from which to achieve adequacy toward the level above.

ACKNOWLEDGMENTS

I would like to thank Norton Greenfeld, Austin Henderson, Rusty Bobrow, Bill Woods, and especially Martin Yonke, for their great help in understanding and implementing KLONE.

REFERENCES

[Anderson, J. R., and Bower, G. H., 1973]. *Human Associative Memory*. Holt, New York.

[Anderson, J. R., and Bower, G. H., 1974]. A propositional theory of recognition memory. *Memory and Cognition* **2**, No. 3, 406–412.

[Bartlett, F. C., 1967]. *Remembering: A Study in Experimental and Social Psychology*. Cambridge Univ. Press, London and New York (first published, 1932).

[Bell, A., and Quillian, M. R., 1971]. Capturing concepts in a semantic net. In *Associative Information Techniques*. E. L. Jacks (ed.). Am. Elsevier, New York, pp. 3–25.

[Bobrow, D. G., and Winograd, T., 1977]. An overview of KRL, a knowledge representation language. *Cognitive Science* **1**, No. 1, 3–46.

[Brachman, R. J., 1977]. What's in a concept: Structural foundations for semantic networks. *International Journal of Man-Machine Studies* **9**, 127–152.

[Brachman, R. J., 1978a]. Structured inheritance networks. In "Research in Natural Language Understanding." W. A. Woods and R. J. Brachman, Quarterly Progress Report No. 1, BBN Report No. 3742. Bolt Beranek & Newman, Cambridge, Massachusetts, 36–78.

[Brachman, R. J., 1978b]. "A Structural Paradigm for Representing Knowledge." BBN Report No. 3605. Bolt Beranek & Newman, Cambridge, Massachusetts.

[Brown, J. S., and Burton, R. R., 1975]. Multiple representations of knowledge for tutorial reasoning. In *Representation and Understanding*. D. G. Bobrow and A. M. Collins (eds.). Academic Press, New York, pp. 311–349.

[Burton, R. R., 1976]. "Semantic Grammar: An Engineering Technique for Constructing Natural Language Understanding Systems," BBN Report No. 3453 (ICAI Report No. 3). Bolt Beranek & Newman, Cambridge, Massachusetts.

[Carbonell, J. R., 1970a]. "Mixed-Initiative Man-Computer Instructional Dialogues," BBN Report No. 1971. Bolt Beranek & Newman, Cambridge, Massachusetts.

[Carbonell, J. R., 1970b]. AI in CAI: An artificial intelligence approach to computer-aided instruction. *IEEE Transactions on Man-Machine Systems* **MMS-11**, No. **4**, 190–202.

[Carnap, R., 1947]. *Meaning and Necessity*. University of Chicago Press, Chicago, Illinois.

[Cercone, N., 1975]. "Representing Natural Language in Extended Semantic Networks," Technical Report TR75-11. Department of Computing Science, University of Alberta. Edmonton, Alberta, Canada.

[Cercone, N., and Schubert, L., 1975]. Toward a state based conceptual representation. *Proceedings of the 4th International Joint Conference on Artificial Intelligence*, 1975 pp. 83–90.

[Collins, A. M., and Loftus, E. F., 1975]. A spreading-activation theory of semantic processing. *Psychological Review* **82**, No. 6, 407–428.

[Collins, A. M., and Quillian, M. R., 1969]. Retrieval time from semantic memory. *Journal of Verbal Learning and Verbal Behavior* **8**, 240–247.

[Collins, A. M., and Quillian, M. R., 1970a]. Facilitating retrieval from semantic memory: The effect of repeating part of an inference. In *Acta Psychologica 33 Attention and Performance III.* A. F. Sanders (ed.). North-Holland Publ., Amsterdam, pp. 304–314.

[Collins, A. M., and Quillian, M. R., 1970b]. Does category size affect categorization time? *Journal of Verbal Learning and Verbal Behavior* **9**, 432–438.

[Collins, A. M., and Quillian, M. R., 1972a]. Experiments on semantic memory and language comprehension. In *Cognition in Learning and Memory.* L. W. Gregg (ed.). Wiley, New York, pp. 117–137.

[Collins, A. M., and Quillian, M. R., 1972b]. How to make a language user. In *Organization of Memory.* E. Tulving and W. Donaldson (eds.). Academic Press, New York, pp. 309–351.

[Fahlman, S. E., 1977]. A system for representing and using real-world knowledge. Ph.D. thesis draft, Artificial Intelligence Laboratory, MIT, Cambridge, Massachusetts.

[Fillmore, C., 1968]. The case for case. In *Universals in Linguistic Theory.* E. Bach and R. Harms (eds.). Holt, New York, pp. 1–88.

[Fodor, J. A., 1978]. Tom Swift and his procedural grandmother (unpublished ms.), MIT, Cambridge, Massachusetts.

[Goldstein. I. P., and Roberts, R. B., 1977]. Nudge, a knowledge-based scheduling program. *Proceedings of the 5th International Joint Conference on Artificial Intelligence*, 1977 pp. 257–263.

[Grosz, B. J., 1977]. The representation and use of focus in a system for understanding dialogue. *Proceedings of the 5th International Joint Conference on Artificial Intelligence*, 1977 pp. 67–76.

[Hawkinson, L., 1975]. The representation of concepts in OWL. *Proceedings of the 4th International Joint Conference on Artificial Intelligence*, 1975 pp. 107–114.

[Hayes, Pat J., 1977]. In defence of logic. *Proceedings of the 5th International Joint Conference on Artificial Intelligence*, 1977 pp. 559–565.

[Hayes, Philip J., 1977a]. "Some Association-Based Techniques for Lexical Disambiguation by Machine," TR25. Department of Computer Science, University of Rochester, Rochester, New York.

[Hayes, Philip J., 1977b]. On semantic nets, frames and associations. *Proceedings of the 5th International Joint Conference on Artificial Intelligence*, 1977 pp. 99–107.

[Hays, D. G., 1973a]. "A Theory of Conceptual Organization and Processing." State University of New York at Buffalo (unpublished draft).

[Hays, D. G., 1973b]. Types of processes on cognitive networks. *Paper presented at the 1973 International Conference on Computational Linguistics.*

[Heidorn, G. E., 1972]. "Natural Language Inputs to a Simulation Programming System," NPS-55HD72101a. Naval Postgraduate School, Monterey, California.

[Heidorn, G. E., 1974]. English as a very high level language for simulation programming. *ACM SIGPLAN Notices* **9**, No. 4, 91–100.

[Hendrix, G. G., 1975a]. "Partitioned Networks for the Mathematical Modeling of Natural Language Semantics," Technical Report NL-28. Department of Computer Science, University of Texas at Austin.

[Hendrix, G. G., 1975b]. Expanding the utility of semantic networks through partitioning. *Proceedings of the 4th International Conference on Artificial Intelligence*, 1975 pp. 115–121.

[Hendrix, G. G., 1976]. The representation of semantic knowledge. In *Speech Understanding Research: Final Technical Report.* D. E. Walker (Ed.). Stanford Research Institute, Menlo Park, California.

[Hendrix, G. G., 1977]. Some general comments on semantic networks. *Proceedings of the 5th International Joint Conference on Artificial Intelligence*, 1977 pp. 984–985.

[Hendrix, G. G., Thompson, C. W., and Slocum, J., 1973]. Language processing via canonical verbs and semantic models. *Proceedings of the 3rd International Joint Conference on Artificial Intelligence*, 1973 pp. 262–269.

[Levesque, H. J., 1977]. "A Procedural Approach to Semantic Networks," Technical Report No. 105. Department of Computer Science, University of Toronto, Toronto, Canada.

[Lindsay, R., 1973]. In defense of ad hoc systems. In *Computer Models of Thought and Language.* R. C. Schank and K. M. Colby (eds.). Freeman, San Francisco, California, pp. 372–395.

[Liskov, B., and Zilles, S., 1974]. Programming with abstract data types. *ACM SIGPLAN Notices* **9**, No. 4, 50–59.

[Martin, W. A., 1977]. OWL. *Proceedings of the 5th International Joint Conference on Artificial Intelligence*, 1977 pp. 985–987.

[Nash-Webber, B., and Reiter, R., 1977]. Anaphora and logical form: On formal meaning representations for natural language. *Proceedings of the 5th International Joint Conference on Artificial Intelligence* 1977 pp. 121–131.

[Neisser, U., 1967]. *Cognitive Psychology*. Appleton. New York.

[Norman, D. A., 1972]. "Memory, Knowledge, and the Answering of Questions," CHIP Technical Report 25. Center for Human Information Processing, University of California at San Diego. La Jolla, California.

[Norman, D. A., 1973]. Learning and remembering: A tutorial preview. In *Attention and Performance IV.* S. Kornblum (ed.). Academic Press, New York, pp. 345–362.

[Norman, D. A., Rumelhart, D. E., and the LNR Research Group, 1975]. *Explorations in Cognition.* Freeman, San Francisco, California.

[Quillian, M. R., 1966]. "Semantic Memory," Report AFCRL-66-189. Bolt Beranek & Newman, Cambridge, Massachusetts.

[Quillian, M. R., 1967]. Word concepts: A theory and simulation of some basic semantic capabilities. *Behavioral Science* **12**, No. 5, 410–430.

[Quillian, M. R., 1968]. Semantic memory. In *Semantic Information Processing.* M. Minsky (ed.). MIT Press, Cambridge, Massachusetts, pp. 227–270.

[Quillian, M. R., 1969]. The Teachable Language Comprehender: A simulation program and theory of language. *Communications of the ACM* **12**, No. 8, 459–476.

[Raphael, B., 1968]. SIR: Semantic Information Retrieval. In *Semantic Information Processing.* M. Minsky (ed.). MIT Press, Cambridge, Massachusetts, pp. 33–145.

[Rieger, C., 1975]. The Commonsense Algorithm as a basis for computer models of human memory, inference, belief and contextual language comprehension. In *Proceedings of the Workshop on Theoretical Issues in Natural Language Processing.* B. L. Nash-Webber and R. Schank (eds.). Bolt Beranek & Newman, Cambridge, Massachusetts, pp. 180–195.

[Rieger, C., 1976]. An organization of knowledge for problem solving and language comprehension. *Artificial Intelligence* **7**, No. 2, 89–127.

[Rieger, C., 1977]. Spontaneous computation in cognitive models. *Cognitive Science* **1**, No. 3, 315–354.

[Rieger, C., and Grinberg, M., 1977]. The declarative representation and procedural simulation of causality in physical mechanisms. *Proceedings of the 5th International Joint Conference on Artificial Intelligence*, 1977 pp. 250–256.

[Roberts, R. B., and Goldstein, I. P., 1977]. "FRL Users' Manual," A.I. Memo No. 408. Artificial Intelligence Laboratory, MIT, Cambridge, Massachusetts.

[Rumelhart, D. E., and Norman, D. A., 1973]. Active semantic networks as a model of human

[Woods, W. A., 1975]. What's in a link? Foundations for semantic networks. In *Representation and Understanding*. D. G. Bobrow and A. M. Collins (eds.). Academic Press, New York, pp. 35–82.

[Woods, W. A., and Brachman, R. J., 1978]. "Research in Natural Language Understanding." Quarterly Progress Report No. 1, BBN Report No. 3742. Bolt Beranek & Newman, Cambridge, Massachusetts.

memory. *Proceedings of the 3rd International Joint Conference on Artificial Intelligence, 1973* pp. 450–457.

[Rumelhart, D. E., Lindsay, P. H., and Norman, D. A., 1972]. A process model for long-term memory. In *Organization of Memory*. E. Tulving and W. Donaldson (eds.). Academic Press, New York, pp. 197–246.

[Schank, R. C., 1972]. Conceptual dependency: A theory of natural language understanding. *Cognitive Psychology 3*, 552–631.

[Schank, R. C. 1973a]. The conceptual analysis of natural language. In *Natural Language Processing*. R. Rustin (ed.). Algorithmics Press, New York, pp. 291–309.

[Schank, R. C., 1973b]. Identification of conceptualizations underlying natural language. In *Computer Models of Thought and Language*. R. C. Schank and K. M. Colby (eds.), Freeman, San Francisco, California, pp. 187–247.

[Schank, R. C., 1974]. "Is There a Semantic Memory?" Technical Report 3. Istituto per gli Studi Semantici e Cognitivi, Castagnola. Switzerland.

[Schank, R. C., 1975]. The structure of episodes in memory. In *Representation and Understanding*. D. G. Bobrow and A. M. Collins (eds.). Academic Press, New York, pp. 237–272.

[Schank, R. C., and Rieger, C. J., III, 1974]. Inference and the computer understanding of natural language. *Artificial Intelligence 5*, No. 4, 373–412.

[Schank, R. C., Goldman, N., Rieger, C. J., III, and Riesbeck, C., 1973]. MARGIE: Memory, analysis, response generation, and inference on english. *Proceedings of the 3rd International Joint Conference on Artificial Intelligence, 1973* 255–261.

[Schubert, L. K., 1976]. Extending the expressive power of semantic networks. *Artificial Intelligence 7*, No. 2, 163–198.

[Scragg, G. W., 1975]. "Frames, Planes, and Nets: A Synthesis," Working Paper 19. Istituto per gli Studi Semantici e Cognitivi, Castagnola, Switzerland.

[Shapiro, S. C., 1971a]. "The MIND System: A Data Structure for Semantic Information Processing," Technical Report R-837-PR. Rand Corporation.

[Shapiro, S. C., 1971b]. A net structure for semantic information storage, deduction, and retrieval. *Proceedings of the 2nd International Joint Conference on Artificial Intelligence, 1971* pp. 512–523.

[Simmons, R. F., 1973]. Semantic networks: Their computation and use for understanding English sentences. In *Computer Models of Thought and Language*. R. C. Schank and K. M. Colby (eds.). Freeman, San Francisco, California, pp. 63–113.

[Simmons, R. F., and Bruce, B. C., 1971]. Some relations between predicate calculus and semantic net representations of discourse. *Proceedings of the 2nd International Joint Conference on Artificial Intelligence, 1971* pp. 524–529.

[Simmons, R. F., and Chester, D., 1977]. Inferences in quantified semantic networks. *Proceedings of the 5th International Joint Conference on Artificial Intelligence, 1977* pp. 267–273.

[Simmons, R. F., and Slocum, J., 1972]. Generating English discourse from semantic networks. *Communications of the ACM 15*, No. 10, 891–905.

[Simmons, R. F., Burger, J. F., and Schwarcz, R. M., 1968]. A computational model of verbal understanding. *AFIPS Conference Proceedings 33*, 441–456.

[Smith, B., 1978]. Levels, layers, and planes: The framework of a system of knowledge representation semantics. Master's thesis, Artificial Intelligence Laboratory, MIT, Cambridge, Massachusetts.

[Szolovits, P., Hawkinson, L. B., and Martin, W. A., 1977]. "An Overview of OWL, a Language for Knowledge Representation," MIT/LCS/TM-86. Laboratory for Computer Science, MIT, Cambridge, Massachusetts.

[Wilks, Y., 1974]. "Natural Language Understanding Systems Within the AI Paradigm," Memo. AIM-237. Stanford Artificial Intelligence Laboratory, Stanford, California.

[Winston, P. H., 1970]. "Learning Structural Descriptions from Examples," Project MAC TR-76. MIT, Cambridge, Massachusetts.

[Winston, P. H., ed., 1975]. *The Psychology of Computer Vision*. McGraw-Hill, New York.

11 / William A. Woods
What's in a Link: Foundations for Semantic Networks

Woods' "What's in a Link" was a milestone in the history of semantic networks. Until this time, the semantics of semantic network languages were mostly a mystery, with the meanings of various constructs relying strictly on the intuitions of the reader and based normally only on suggestive naming conventions (see [Brachman, Chapter 10] for more on how this state of affairs came about). Woods addresses the question directly, by focusing on the kinds of meanings links can take on. First he asks, "What is semantics?", and then applies the answer to that question to semantic network representations. Woods points out several problems with typical network representations, and introduces the key distinction between *structural* links (those for merely setting up parts of a proposition or description) and *assertional* links (those that make an assertion about the world by their presence). The KRYPTON system [Brachman *et al.*, Chapter 24] is a hybrid representation scheme built around this distinction. It is also interesting to reflect on the different ways in which Woods' emphasis on intensionality was picked up in other work like [Maida and Shapiro, Chapter 9] and [Bobrow and Winograd, Chapter 13]. Woods concludes with two difficult representation problems for semantic nets—how to handle relative clause-type constructs, and how to represent quantified information—and suggests why the obvious approaches are inadequate. In sum, this paper gets at the very heart of what semantic networks are all about, and sets a standard for all subsequent representation work.

Appeared in *Representation and Understanding: Studies in Cognitive Science*, 35–82, edited by D. G. Bobrow and A. M. Collins, New York: Academic Press, 1975.

WHAT'S IN A LINK:

Foundations for Semantic Networks

William A. Woods

Bolt Beranek and Newman
Cambridge, Massachusetts

I. INTRODUCTION

This chapter is concerned with the theoretical underpinnings for semantic network representations of the sort dealt with by Quillian (1968,1969), Rumelhart, Lindsay, & Norman (1972), Carbonell & Collins (1973), Schank (1975), Simmons (1973), etc. (I include Schank's conceptual dependency representations in this class although he himself may deny the kinship.) I am concerned specifically with understanding the semantics of the semantic network structures themselves, i.e., with what the notations and structures used in a semantic network can mean, and with interpretations of what these links mean that will be logically adequate to the job of representing knowledge. I want to focus on several issues: the meaning of "semantics", the need for explicit understanding of the intended meanings for various types of arcs and links, the need for careful thought in choosing conventions for representing facts as assemblages of arcs and nodes, and several specific difficult problems in knowledge representation—especially problems of relative clauses and quantification.

I think we must begin with the realization that there is currently no "theory" of semantic networks. The notion of semantic networks is for the most part an attractive notion which has yet to be proven. Even the question of what networks have to do with semantics is one which takes some answering. I am convinced that there is real value to the work that is being done in semantic network representations and that there is much to be learned from it. I feel, however, that the major discoveries are yet to be made and what is currently being done is not really understood. In this chapter I would like to make a start at such an understanding.

I will attempt to show that when the semantics of the notations are made clear, many of the techniques used in existing semantic networks are inadequate for representing knowledge in general. By means of examples, I will argue that if semantic networks are to be used as a representation for storing human verbal knowledge, then they must include mechanisms for representing propositions without commitment to asserting their truth or belief. Also they must be able to represent various types of intensional objects without commitment to their existence in the external world, their external distinctness, or their completeness in covering all of the objects which are presumed to exist. I will discuss the problems of representing restrictive relative clauses and argue that a commonly used "solution" is inadequate. I will also demonstrate the inadequacy of certain commonly used techniques which purport to handle quantificational information in semantic networks. Three adequate mechanisms will be presented, one of which to my knowledge has not previously been used in semantic nets. I will discuss several different possible uses of links and will discuss some of the different types of nodes and links which are required in a semantic network if it is to serve as a medium for representing knowledge.

The emphasis of this chapter will be on problems, possible solution techniques, and necessary characteristics of solutions, with particular emphasis on pointing out nonsolutions. No attempt will be made to formulate a complete specification of an adequate semantic network notation. Rather, the discussion will be oriented toward requirements for an adequate notation and the kind of explicit understanding of what one intends his notations to mean that are required to investigate such questions.

II. WHAT IS SEMANTICS?

First we must come to grips with the term "semantics". What do semantic networks have to do with semantics? What is semantics anyway? There is a great deal of misunderstanding on this point among computational linguists and psychologists. There are people who maintain that there is no distinction between syntax and semantics, and there are others who lump the entire inference and "thought" component of an AI system under the label "semantics". Moreover, the philosophers, linguists, and programming language theorists have notions of semantics which are distinct from each other and from many of the notions of computational linguists and psychologists. What I will present first is my view of the way that the term "semantics" has come to be associated with so many different kinds of things, and the basic unity that I think it is all about. I will attempt to show that the source of many confusing claims such as "there is no difference between syntax and semantics" arise from a limited view of the total role of semantics in language.

A. The Philosopher and the Linguist

In my account of semantics, I will use some caricatured stereotypes to represent different points of view which have been expressed in the literature or seem to be implied. I will not attempt to tie specific persons to particular points of view since I may thereby make the error of misinterpreting some author. Instead, I will simply set up the stereotype as a possible point of view which someone might take, and proceed from there.

First, let me set up two caricatures which I will call the Linguist and the Philosopher, without thereby asserting that all linguists fall into the first category or philosophers in the second. Both, however, represent strong traditions in their respective fields. The Linguist has the following view of semantics in linguistics: he is interested in characterizing the fact that the same sentence can sometimes mean different things, and some sentences mean nothing at all. He would like to find some notation in which to express the different things which a sentence can mean and some procedure for determining whether a sentence is "anomalous" (i.e., has no meanings). The Philosopher on the other hand is concerned with specifying the meaning of a formal notation rather than a natural language. (Again, this is not true of all philosophers--just our caricature.) His notation is already unambiguous. What he is concerned with is determining when an expression in the notation is a "true" proposition (in some appropriate formal sense of truth) and when it is false. (Related questions are when it can be said to be necessarily true or necessarily false or logically true or logically false, etc.) Meaning for the Philosopher is not defined in terms of some other notation in which to represent different possible interpretations of a sentence, but he is interested in the conditions for truth of an already formal representation.

Clearly, these caricatured points of view are both parts of a larger view of the semantic interpretation of natural language. The Linguist is concerned with the translation of natural languages into formal representations of their meanings, while the Philosopher is interested in the meanings of such representations. One cannot really have a complete semantic specification of a natural language unless both of these tasks have been accomplished. I will, however, go further and point out that there is a consideration which the philosophers have not yet covered and which must be included in order to provide a complete semantic specification.

B. Procedural Semantics

While the types of semantic theories that have been formulated by logicians and philosophers do a reasonable job of specifying the semantics of complex constructions involving quantification and combination of predicates with operators of conjunction and negation, they fall down on the specification of the semantics of the basic "atomic" propositions consisting of a predicate and specifications of its arguments--for example, the specification of the meanings of elementary statements such as "snow is white" or "Socrates is mortal". In most accounts, these are presumed to have "truth conditions" which determine those possible worlds in which they are true and those in which they are false, but how does one specify those truth conditions? In order for an intelligent entity to know the meaning of such sentences it must be the case that it has stored somehow an effective set of criteria for deciding in a given possible world whether such a sentence is true or false. Thus it is not sufficient merely to say that the meaning of a sentence is a set of truth conditions--one must be able to specify the truth conditions for particular sentences. Most philosophers have not faced this issue for atomic sentences such as "snow is white."

Elsewhere I have argued (Woods, 1967, 1973a) that a specification of truth conditions can be made by means of a procedure or function which assigns truth values to propositions in particular possible worlds. Such procedures

for determining truth or falsity are the basis for what I have called "procedural semantics" (although this interpretation of the term may differ slightly from that which is intended by other people who have since used it). This notion has served as the basis of several computer question-answering systems (Woods, Kaplan, & Nash-Webber, 1972; Woods, 1973b; Winograd, 1972).

The case presented above is a gross oversimplification of what is actually required for an adequate procedural specification of the semantics of natural language. There are strong reasons which dictate that the best one can expect to have is a partial function which assigns true in some cases, false in some cases, and fails to assign either true or false in others. There are also cases where the procedures require historical data which is not normally available and therefore cannot be directly executed. In these cases their behavior must be predicted on the basis of more complex inference techniques. Some of these issues are discussed more fully by Woods (1973a).

C. Semantic Specification of Natural Language

You now have the basics of my case for a broader view of the role of semantics in natural language. The outline of the picture goes like this:

There must be a notation for representing the meanings of sentences inside the brain (of humans or other intellects) that is not merely a direct encoding of the English word sequence. This must be so, since (among other reasons) what we understand by sentences usually includes the disambiguation of certain syntactic and semantic ambiguities present in the sentence itself.

The linguist is largely concerned with the process for getting from the external sentence to this internal representation (a process referred to as "semantic interpretation"). The philosopher is concerned with the rules of correspondence between expressions in such notations and truth and falsity (or correctness of assertion) in the real or in hypothetical worlds. Philosophers, however, have generally stopped short of trying to actually specify the truth conditions of the basic atomic propositions in their systems, dealing mainly with the specification of the meanings of complex expressions in terms of the meanings of elementary ones. Researchers in artificial intelligence are faced with the need to specify the semantics of elementary propositions as well as complex ones and are moreover required to put to the test the assembly of the entire system into a working total --including the interface to syntax and the subsequent inference and "thought" processes. Thus the researcher in artificial intelligence must take a more global view of the semantics of language than either the linguist or the philosopher has taken in the past. The same, I think, is true of psychologists.

D. Misconceptions about Semantics

There are two misconceptions of what semantics is about (or at least misuses of the term) which are rather widely circulated among computational linguists and which arise I think from a limited view of the role of semantics in language. They arise from traditional uses of the term which, through specialized application, eventually lose sight of what semantics is really about. According to my dictionary, semantics is "the scientific study of the relations between signs or symbols and what they denote or mean". This is the traditional use of the term and represents the common thread which links the different concerns discussed previously. Notice that the term does not refer to the things denoted or the meanings, but to the *relations* between these things and the linguistic expressions which denote them.

One common misuse of the term "semantics" in the fields of computational linguistics and artificial intelligence is to extend the coverage of the term not only to this relation between linguistic form and meaning, but to all of the retrieval and inference capabilities of the system. This misuse arises since for many tasks in language processing, the use of semantic information necessarily involves not only the determination of the object denoted, but also some inference about that object. In absence of a good name for this further inference process, terms such as "semantic"

inferences" have come to be used for the entire process. It is easy then to start incorrectly referring to the entire thought process as "semantics". One may properly use the term "semantic inferences" to refer to inferences that cross the boundary between symbol and referent, but one should keep in mind that this does not imply that all steps of the process are "semantic".

At the opposite extreme, there are those who deny any difference in principle between syntax and semantics and claim that the distinction is arbitrary. Again, the misconception arises from a limited view of the role of semantics. When semantics is used to select among different possible parsings of a sentence by using selectional restrictions on so-called semantic features of words, there is little difference between the techniques usually used and those used for checking syntactic features. In another paper (Woods, 1973a) I make the case that such techniques are merely approximations of the types of inferences that are really required, and that, in general, semantic selectional restrictions need to determine the referent of a phrase and then make inferences about that referent (i.e., they involve semantic inferences as I defined the term above). The approximate technique usually used, however, requires no special mechanism beyond what already exists in the syntax specification, and when taken as the paradigm for "semantic inferences" can lead to the false conclusion that semantics is no different from syntax. Likewise, if the representation constructed by a parser purports to be a semantic representation, with no intervening purely syntactic representation, then one might argue that the techniques used to produce it are syntactic techniques and therefore there is nothing left to be semantics.

As we have pointed out, however, a semantic specification requires more than the transformation of the input sentence into a "semantic" representation. The meanings of these representations must be specified also. Recall that semantics refers to the correspondence between linguistic expressions and the things that they denote or mean. Thus although it may be difficult to isolate exactly what part of a system is semantics, any system which understands sentences and carries out appropriate actions in response to them is somehow completing this connection. For systems which do not extend beyond the production of a so-called semantic representation, there may or may not be a semantic component included, and the justification for calling something semantic may be lost. Again, if one takes the production of such "semantic" representations as the paradigm case for what semantics is, one is misunderstanding the meaning of the term.

E. Semantics of Programming Languages

Before proceeding it is probably worth pointing out that the use of the term "semantics" by programming language theorists has been much closer to the tradition of the philosophers and less confused than in computational linguistics. Programming language theory is frequently used as a paradigm for natural language semantics. Programming languages, however, do not have many of the features that natural languages do and the mechanisms developed there are not sufficient for modeling the semantics of natural language without considerable stretching.

The programming language theorists do have one advantage over the philosophers and linguists in that their semantic specifications stand on firmer ground since they are defined in terms of the procedures that the machine is to carry out. It is this same advantage which the notion of procedural semantics and artificial intelligence brings to the specification of the semantics of natural language. Although in ordinary natural language not every sentence is overtly dealing with procedures to be executed, it is possible nevertheless to use the notion of procedures as a means of specifying the truth conditions of declarative statements as well as the intended meaning of questions and commands. One thus picks up the semantic chain from the philosophers at the level of truth conditions and completes it to the level of formal specifications of procedures. These can in turn be characterized by their operations on real machines and can be thereby anchored to physics. (Notice that the notion of procedure shares with the notion of meaning that elusive quality of being impossible to

present except by means of alternative representations. The procedure itself is something abstract which is instantiated whenever someone carries out the procedure, but otherwise, all one has when it is not being executed is some representation of it.)

III. SEMANTICS AND SEMANTIC NETWORKS

Having established a framework for understanding what we mean by semantics, let us now proceed to see how semantic networks fit into the picture. Semantic networks presumably are candidates for the role of internal semantic representation—i.e., the notation used to store knowledge inside the head. Their competitors for this role are formal logics such as the predicate calculus, and various representations such as Lakoff-type deep structures, and Fillmore-type case representations. (The case representations shade off almost imperceptibly into certain possible semantic network representations and hence it is probably not fruitful to draw any clear distinction.) The major characteristic of the semantic networks that distinguishes them from other candidates is the characteristic notion of a link or pointer which connects individual facts into a total structure.

A semantic network attempts to combine in a single mechanism the ability not only to store factual knowledge but also to model the associative connections exhibited by humans which make certain items of information accessible from certain others. It is possible presumably to model these two aspects with two separate mechanisms such as for example, a list of the facts expressed in the predicate calculus or some such representation, together with an index of associative connections which link facts together. Semantic network representations attempt instead to produce a single representation which by virtue of the way in which it represents facts (i.e., by assemblies of pointers to other facts) automatically provides the appropriate associative connections. One should keep in mind that the assumption that such a representation is possible is merely an item of faith, an unproven hypothesis used as the basis of the methodology. It is entirely conceivable that no such single representation is possible.

A. Requirements for a Semantic Representation

When one tries to devise a notation or a language for semantic representation, one is seeking a representation which will precisely, formally, and unambiguously represent any particular interpretation that a human listener may place on a sentence. We will refer to this as "logical adequacy" of a semantic representation. There are two other requirements of a good semantic representation. One is that beyond the requirement of logical adequacy, there must be an algorithm or procedure for translating the original sentence into this representation and the other is that there must be algorithms which can make use of this representation for the subsequent inferences and deductions that the human or machine must perform on them. Thus one is seeking a representation which facilitates translation and subsequent intelligent processing, in addition to providing a notation for expressing any particular interpretation of a sentence.

B. The Canonical Form Myth

Before continuing, let me mention one thing which semantic networks should not be expected to do: that is to provide a "canonical form" in which all paraphrases of a given proposition are reduced to a single standard (or canonical) form. It is true that humans seem to reduce input sentences into some different internal form that does not preserve all of the information about the form in which the sentence was received (e.g., whether it was in the active or the passive). A canonical form, however, requires a great deal more than this. A canonical form requires that *every* expression equivalent to a given one can be reduced to a single form by means of an effective procedure, so that tests of equivalence between descriptions can be reduced to the testing of identity of canonical form. I will make two points. The first is that it is unlikely that there could be a canonical form for English, and the second is that for independent reasons, in order to duplicate human behavior in paraphrasing, one would still need all of the inferential machinery that canonical forms attempt to avoid.

Consider first the motivation for wanting a canonical form. Given a system of expressions in some notation (in this case English, or more specifically an internal semantic representation of English) and given a set of equivalence-preserving transformations (such as paraphrasing or logical equivalence transformations) which map one expression into an equivalent expression, two expressions are said to be equivalent if one can be transformed into the other by some sequence of these equivalence transformations. If one wanted to determine if two expressions $e1$ and $e2$ were equivalent, one would expect to have to search for a sequence of transformations that would produce one from the other—a search which could be nondeterministic and expensive to carry out. A canonical form for the system is a computable function c which transforms any expression e into a unique equivalent expression $c(e)$ such that for any two expressions $e1$ and $e2$, $e1$ is equivalent to $e2$, if and only if $c(e1)$ is equal to $c(e2)$. With such a function, one can avoid the combinatoric search for an equivalence chain connecting the two expressions and merely compute the corresponding canonical forms and compare them for identity. Thus a canonical form provides an improvement in efficiency over having to search for an equivalence chain for each individual case (assuming that the function c is efficiently computable).

A canonical form function is, however, a very special function, and it is not necessarily the case for a given system of expressions and equivalence transformations that there is such a function. It can be shown for certain formal systems [such as the word problem for semigroups (Davis, 1958)] that there can be no computable canonical form function with the above properties. That is, in order to determine the equivalence of a particular pair of expressions $e1$ and $e2$ it may be necessary to actually search for a chain of equivalence transformations that connects these two particular expressions, rather than performing separate transformations $c(e1)$ and $c(e2)$ (both of which know exactly where to stop) and then compare these resulting expressions for identity. If this can be the case for formal systems as simple as semigroups, it would be foolhardy to assume lightly that there is a canonical form for something as complex as English paraphrasing.

Now, for the second point. Quite aside from the possibility of having a canonical form function for English, I will attempt to argue that one still needs to be able to search for individual chains of inference between pairs of expressions $e1$ and $e2$ and thus the principal motivation for wanting a canonical form is superfluous. The point is that in most cases where one is interested in some paraphrase behavior, the paraphrase desired is not one of full logical equivalence, but only of implication in one direction. For example, one is interested in whether the truth of some expression $e1$ is implied by some stored expression $e2$. If one had a canonical form function, then one could store only canonical forms in the data base and ask simply whether $c(e1)$ is stored in the data base without having to apply any equivalence transformations in the process. This is, however, just a special case. It is rather unlikely that what we have in the data base is an expression exactly logically equivalent to $e1$ (i.e., some $e2$ such that $e2$ implies $e1$ and $e1$ implies $e2$). Rather, what we expect in the typical case is that we will find some $e2$ that implies $e1$ but not vice versa. For this case, we must be able to find an inference chain as part of our retrieval process. Given that we must devise an appropriate inferential retrieval process for dealing with this case (which is the more common), the special case of full equivalence will fall out as a consequence; thus the canonical form mechanism for handling the full equivalence case gives no improvement in performance and is unnecessary.

There is still benefit from "partially canonicalizing" the stored knowledge (the term is reminiscent of the concept of being just a little bit pregnant). This is useful to avoid storing multiple equivalent representations of the same fact. There is, however, little motivation for making sure that this form does in fact reduce all equivalent expressions to the same form (and as I said before, there is every reason to believe that this may be impossible).

Another argument against the expectation of a canonical form solution to the equivalence problem comes from the following situation. Consider the kinship relations program of Lindsay (1963). The basic domain of discourse of the system is family relationships such as mother, father, brother, sister, etc. The data structure chosen is a logically minimal representation of a family unit consisting of a male and female parent and some number of offspring. Concepts such as aunt, uncle, and brother-in-law are not represented explicitly in the structure but are rather implicit in the structure and questions about unclehood are answered by checking brothers of the father and brothers of the mother. What does such a system do, however, when it encounters the input "Harry is John's uncle"? It does not know whether to assign Harry as a sibling of John's father or his mother. Lindsay had no good solution for this problem other than the suggestion to somehow make both entries and connect them together with some kind of a connection which indicates that one of them is wrong. It seems that for handling "vague" predicates such as uncle, i.e., predicates which are not specific with respect to some of the details of an underlying representation, we must make provision for storing such predicates directly (i.e., in terms of a concept of uncle in this case), even though this concept may be defined in terms of more "basic" relationships (ignoring here the issue that there may be no objective criterion for selecting any particular set of relationships as basic).

If we hope to be able to store information at the level of detail that it may be presented to us in English, then we are compelled to surrender the assumptions of logical minimality in our internal representation and provide for storing such redundant concepts as "uncle" directly. We would not, however, like to have to store all such facts redundantly. That is, given a Lindsay-type data base of family units, we would not want to be compelled to store explicitly all of the instances of unclehood that could be inferred from the basic family units. If we were to carry such a program to its logical conclusion, we would have to store explicitly all of the possible inferable relations, a practical impossibility since in many cases the number of such inferables is effectively infinite. Hence the internal structure which we desire must have some instances of unclehood stored directly and others left to be deduced from more basic family relationships, thus demolishing any hope of a canonical form representation.

C. Semantics of Semantic Network Notations

When I create a node in a network or when I establish a link of some type between two nodes, I am building up a representation of something in a notation. The question that I will be concerned with in the remainder of this chapter is what do I mean by this representation. For example, if I create a node and establish two links from it, one labeled SUPERC and pointing to the "concept" TELEPHONE and another labeled MOD and pointing to the "concept" BLACK, what do I mean this node to represent? Do I intend it to stand for the "concept" of a black telephone, or perhaps I mean it to assert a relationship between the concepts of telephone and blackness--i.e., that telephones are black (all telephones?, some telephones?). When one devises a semantic network notation, it is necessary not only to specify the types of nodes and links that can be used and the rules for their possible combinations (the syntax of the network notation) but also to specify the import of the various types of links and structures--what is meant by them (the semantics of the network notation).

D. Intensions and Extensions

To begin, I would like to raise the distinction between intension and extension, a distinction that has been variously referred to as the difference between sense and reference, meaning and denotation, and various other pairs of terms. Basically a predicate such as the English word "red" has associated with it two possible conceptual things which could be related to its meaning in the intuitive sense. One of these is the set of all red things--this is called the *extension* of the predicate. The other concept is an abstract entity which in some sense characterizes what it *means* to be red, it is the notion of *redness* which may or may not be true of a given object; this is called the *intension* of the predicate. In many philosophical theories the intension of a predicate is identified with an abstract function which applies to possible worlds and assigns to any such world a set of extensional objects (e.g., the intension of "red" would assign to each possible world a set of red things). In such a theory, when one wants to refer to the concept of redness, what is denoted is this abstract function.

E. The Need for Intensional Representation

The following quotation from Quine (1961) relating an example of Frege should illustrate the kind of thing that I am trying to distinguish as an internal intensional entity:

The phrase "Evening Star" names a certain large physical object of spherical form, which is hurtling through space some scores of millions of miles from here. The phrase "Morning Star" names the same thing, as was probably first established by some observant Babylonian. But the two phrases cannot be regarded as having the same meaning; otherwise that Babylonian could have dispensed with his observations and contented himself with reflecting on the meanings of his words. The meanings, then, being different from one another, must be other than the named object, which is one and the same in both cases. (Quine, 1961, p. 9).

In the appropriate internal representation, there must be two mental entities (concepts, nodes, or whatever) corresponding to the two different intensions, morning star and evening star. There is then an assertion about these two intensional entities that they denote one and the same external object (extension).

In artificial intelligence applications and psychology, it is not sufficient for these intensions to be abstract entities such as possibly infinite sets, but rather they must have some finite representation inside the head as it were, or in our case in the internal semantic representation.

F. Attributes and Values

Much of the structure of semantic networks is based on,

or at least similar to, the notion of attribute and value which has become a standard concept in a variety of computer science applications and which was the basis of Raphael's SIR program (Raphael, 1964)--perhaps the earliest forerunner of today's semantic networks. Facts about an object can frequently be stored on a "property list" of the object by specifying such attribute-value pairs as HEIGHT : 6 FEET, HAIRCOLOR : BROWN, OCCUPATION : SCIENTIST, etc. (Such lists are provided, for example, for all atoms in the LISP programming language.) One way of thinking of these pairs is that the attribute name (i.e., the first element of the pair) is the name of a "link" or "pointer" which points to the "value" of the attribute (i.e., the second element of the pair). Such a description of a person named John might be laid out graphically as:

```
JOHN
    HEIGHT        6 FEET
    HAIRCOLOR     BROWN
    OCCUPATION    SCIENTIST
```

Now it may seem the case that the intuitive examples which I just gave are all that it takes to explain what is meant by the notion of attribute-value pair, and that the use of such notations can now be used as part of a semantic network notation without further explanation. I will try to make the case that this is not so and thereby give a simple introduction to the kinds of things I mean when I say that the semantics of the network notation need to be specified.

The above examples seem to imply that the thing which occurs as the second element of an attribute-value pair is the *name* or at least some unique handle on the value of that attribute. What will I do, however, with an input sentence "John's height is greater than 6 feet?" Most people would not hesitate to construct a representation such as:

```
JOHN
    HEIGHT (GREATERTHAN 6 FEET)
```

Notice, however, that our interpretation of what our

network notations mean has just taken a great leap. No longer is the second element of the attribute-value pair a name or a pointer to a value, but rather it is a predicate which is asserted to be true of the value. One can think of the names such as 6 FEET and BROWN in the previous examples as special cases of identity predicates which are abbreviated for the sake of conciseness, and thereby consider the thing at the end of the pointer to be always a predicate rather than a name. Thus there are at least two possible interpretations of the meaning of the thing at the end of the link--either as the name of the value or as a predicate which must be true of the value. The former will not handle the (GREATERTHAN 6 FEET) example, while the latter will.

Let us consider now another example--John's height is greater than Sue's." We now have a new set of problems. We can still think of a link named HEIGHT pointing from JOHN to a predicate whose interpretation is "greater than Sue's height", but what does the reference to Sue's height inside this predicate have to do with the way that we represented John's height? In a functional form we would simply represent this as HEIGHT(JOHN) > HEIGHT(SUE). or in LISP type "Cambridge Polish" notation,

```
(GREATER (HEIGHT JOHN)(HEIGHT SUE))
```

but that is departing completely from the notion of attribute-value links. There is another possible interpretation of the thing at the end of the HEIGHT link which would be capable of dealing with this type of situation. That is, the HEIGHT link can point from JOHN to a node which represents the intensional object "John's height". In a similar way, we can have a link named HEIGHT from SUE to a node which represents "Sue's height" and then we can establish a relation GREATER between these two intensional nodes. (Notice that even if the heights were the same, the two intensional objects would be different, just as in the morning star/evening star example.) This requires a major reinterpretation of the semantics of our notation and a new set of conventions for how we set up networks. We must now introduce a new intensional node at the end of each attribute link and then establish predicates as facts that are true about such intensional objects. It also raises for us a need to somewhere indicate about this new node that it was created to represent the concept of John's height, and that the additional information that it is greater than Sue's height is not one of its defining properties but rather a separate assertion about the node. Thus a distinction between defining and asserted properties of the node become important here. In my conception of semantic networks I have used the concept of an EGO link to indicate for the benefit of the human researcher and eventually for the benefit of the system itself what a given node is created to stand for. Thus the EGOs of these two nodes are John's height and Sue's height respectively. The EGO link represents the intensional identity of the node.

G. Links and Predication

In addition to considering what is at the end of a link, we must also consider what the link itself means. The examples above suggest that an attribute link named Z from node X to Y is equivalent to the English sentence "the Z of X is Y" or functionally $Z(X)=Y$ or (in the case where Y is a predicate) $Y(Z(X))$, (read Y of Z of X). Many people, however, have used the same mechanism and notation (and even called it attribute-value pairs) to represent arbitrary English verbs by storing a sentence such as "John hit Mary" as a link named HIT from the node for John to the node for Mary, as in the structure:

```
JOHN    HIT    MARY
```

and perhaps placing an inverse link under Mary:

```
MARY    HIT*    JOHN
```

If we do this, then suddenly the semantics of our notation has changed again. No longer do the link names stand for attributes of the node, but rather arbitrary relations between the node and other nodes. If we are to mix the two notations together as in:

```
JOHN    HEIGHT    6 FEET
        HIT
        MARY
```

then we need either to provide somewhere an indication that these two links are of different types and therefore must be treated differently by the procedures which make inferences in the net, or else we need to find a unifying interpretation such as considering that the "attribute" HEIGHT is now really an abbreviation of the relation "height of equals" which holds between JOHN and (the node?) 6 FEET. It is not sufficient to leave it to the intuition of the reader, we must know how the machine will know to treat the two arcs correctly.

If we use Church's lambda notation, which provides a convenient notation for naming predicates and functions constructed out of combinations or variations of other functions (this is used, for example, as the basic function specification notation in the LISP programming language), we could define the meaning of the height link as the relation (LAMBDA (X Y) (EQUAL (HEIGHT X) Y)). By this we mean the predicate of two arguments X and Y which is true when and only when the height of X is equal to Y. Thus a possible unifying interpretation of the notation is that the link is always the name of a relation between the node being described and the node pointed to, (providing that we reinterpret what we meant by the original link named HEIGHT). Whatever we do, we clearly need some mechanism for establishing relations between nodes as facts (e.g., to establish the above GREATER relation between the nodes for John's height and Sue's height).

H. Relations of More Than Two Arguments

In the example just presented, we have used a link to assert a relation between two objects in the network corresponding to the proposition that John hit Mary. Such a method of handling assertions has a number of disadvantages, perhaps the simplest of which is that it is constrained to handling binary relations. If we have a predicate such as the English preposition "between" (i.e., (LAMBDA (X Y Z) (Y is between X and Z))), then we must invent some new kind of structure for expressing such facts. A typical, but not very satisfying, notation which one might find in a semantic network which uses links for relations is something like:

$$Y \xrightarrow{\text{LOCATION}} (\text{BETWEEN } X\ Z)$$

usually without further specification of the semantics of the notation or what kind of thing the structure (BETWEEN X Z) is. For example, is it the name of a place? In some implementations it would be exactly that, in spite of the fact that an underlying model in which there is only one place between any given pair of places is an inadequate model of the world we live in. Another possible interpretation is that it denotes the range of places between the two endpoints (this interpretation requires another interpretation of what the LOCATION link means-- the thing at the end is no longer a name of a place but rather a set of places, and the LOCATION link must be considered to be implicitly existentially quantified in order to be interpreted as asserting that the location is actually one of those places and not all).

Given the notion which we introduced previously that interprets the thing at the end of the location, we have perhaps the best interpretation—we can interpret the expression (BETWEEN X Z) at the end of the link as being an abbreviation for the predicate (LAMBDA (U) (BETWEEN X U Z)), i.e., a one place predicate whose variable is U and whose values of X and Z are fixed to whatever X and Z are.

Although this representation of the three-place predicate "between" (when supplied with an appropriate interpretation of what it means) seems plausible, and I see no major objections to it on the grounds of logical inadequacy, one is left with the suspicion that there may be some predicates

of more than two places which do not have such an intuitively satisfying decomposition into links connecting only two objects at a time. For example, I had to introduce the concept of location as the name of the link from Y to the special object (BETWEEN X Z). In this case, I was able to find a preexisting English concept which made the creation of this link plausible, but is this always the case? The account would have been much less satisfying if all I could have produced was something like:

$$X \xrightarrow{\text{BETWEEN1}} (\text{BETWEEN2 } Y\ Z)$$

with an explication of its semantics that (BETWEEN2 Y Z) was merely some special kind of entity which when linked to X by a BETWEEN1 link represented the proposition (BETWEEN X Y Z). It may be the case that all predicates in English with more than two arguments have a natural binary decomposition. The basic subject-predicate distinction which seems to be made by our language gives some slight evidence for this. It seems to me, however, that finding a natural binary decomposition for sentences such as "John sold Mary a book" (or any of Schank's various TRANS operations) is unlikely.

I. Case Representations in Semantic Networks

Another type of representation is becoming popular in semantic networks and handles the problem of relations of more than one argument very nicely. This representation is based on the notion of case introduced by Fillmore (1968). Fillmore advocates a unifying treatment of the inflected cases of nominals in Latin and other highly inflected languages and the prepositions and positional clues to role that occur in English and other largely noninflected languages. A case as Fillmore uses the term is the name of a particular role that a noun phrase or other participant takes in the state or activity expressed by the verb of a sentence. In the case of the sentence "John sold Mary a book" we can say that John is the agent of the action, and Mary is the recipient or beneficiary of the action, and the book is the *object* or *patient* of the action (where I have taken arbitrary but typical names for the case roles involved for the sake of illustration). When such a notation is applied to semantic network representations, a major restructuring of the network and what it means to be a link takes place. Instead of the assertion of a fact being carried by a link between two nodes, the asserted fact is itself a node. Our structure might look something like:

```
SELL
     AGT     JOHN
     RECIP   MARY
     PAT     BOOK
```

(ignoring for the moment what has happened to turn "a book" into BOOK or for that matter what we mean by JOHN and MARY--we will get into that later). The notation as I have written it requires a great deal of explanation, which is unfortunately not usually spelled out in the presentation of a semantic network notation. In our previous examples, the first item (holding the position where we have placed SELL above) has been the unique name or "handle" on a node, and the remaining link-value pairs have been predicates that are true of this node. In the case above, which I have written that way because one is likely to find equivalent representations in the literature, we are clearly not defining characteristics of the general verb "sell", but rather setting up a description of a particular instance of selling. Thus to be consistent with our earlier format for representing a node we should more properly represent it as something like:

```
S13472
     VERB    SELL
     AGT     JOHN
     RECIP   MARY
     PAT     BOOK
```

where S13472 is some unique internal handle on the node representing this instance of selling, and SELL is now the internal handle on the concept of selling. (I have gone through this two-stage presentation in order to emphasize that the relationship between the node S13472 and the concept of selling is not essentially different at this level from the relationship it has to the other nodes which fill the cases.)

J. Assertional and Structural Links

Clearly the case structure representation in a semantic network places a new interpretation on the nodes and arcs in the net. We still seem to have the same types of nodes that we had before for JOHN, MARY, etc., but we have a new type of node for nodes such as S13472 which represent assertions or facts. Moreover, the import of the links from this new type of node is different from that of our other links. Whereas the links which we discussed before are assertional, i.e., their mere presence in the network represents an assertion about the two nodes that they connect, these new link names, VERB, AGT, RECIP, PAT, are merely setting up parts of the proposition represented by node S13472, and no single link has any assertional import by itself; rather these links are definitional or structural in the sense that they constitute the definition of what node S13472 means.

Now you may argue that these links are really the same as the others, i.e., they correspond to the assertion that the agent of S13472 is JOHN and that S13472 is an instance of selling, etc. just like the "hit" link between John and Mary in our previous example. In our previous example, however, the nodes for John and for Mary had some a priori meanings independent of the assertion of hitting that we were trying to establish between them. In this case, S13472 has no meaning other than that which we establish by virtue of the structural links which it has to other nodes. That is, if we were to ask for the ego of the node S13472, we would get back something like "I am an instance of John selling a book to Mary" or "I am an instance of selling whose agent is John, whose recipient is Mary and whose patient is a book." If we were to ask for the ego of JOHN, we would get something like "I am the guy who works in the third office down the hall, whose name is John Smith, etc." The fact which I am trying to assert with the "hit" link is not part of the ego of JOHN or else I would not be making a new assertion.

This difference between assertional and structural links is rather difficult for some people to understand, and is often confused in various semantic network representations. It is part of the problem that we cited earlier in trying to determine whether a structure such as:

```
N12368              TELEPHONE
    SUPERC          BLACK
    MOD
```

is to be interpreted as an intensional representation of a black telephone or an assertion that telephones are black. If it is to be interpreted as an intensional representation of the concept of a black telephone, then both of these links are structural or definitional. If on the other hand, it is to be interpreted as asserting that telephones are black, then the first link is structural while the second is assertional. (The distinction between structural and assertional links does not take care of this example entirely since we still have to worry about how the assertional link gets its quantificational import for this interpretation, but we will discuss this problem later.)

The above discussion barely suffices to introduce the distinction between structural and assertional links, and certainly does not make the distinction totally clear. Moreover, before we are through, we may have cause to repudiate the assumption that the links involved in our non-case representation should be considered to have assertional import. Perhaps the best way to get deeper into the problems of different types of links with different imports and the representation of intensional entities is to consider further some specific problems in knowledge representation.

IV. PROBLEMS IN KNOWLEDGE REPRESENTATION

In previous sections I hope that I have made the point that the same semantic network notations could be used by different people (or even by the same person at different times for different examples) to mean different things, and therefore one must be specific in presenting a semantic network notation to make clear what one means by the notations which one uses (i.e., the semantics of the notation). In the remainder of this chapter, I would like to discuss two difficult problems of knowledge representation and use the discussion to illustrate several additional possible uses of links and some of the different types of nodes and links which are required in a semantic network if it is to serve as a medium for representing human verbal knowledge. The specific problems which I will consider are the representation of restrictive relative clauses and the representation of quantified information.

A. Relative Clauses

In attaching modifiers to nodes in a network to provide an intensional description for a restricted class, one often requires restrictions which do not happen to exist in the language as single-word modifiers but have to be constructed out of more primitive elements. The relative clause mechanism permits this. Anything that can be said as a proposition can be used as a relative clause by leaving some one of its argument slots unfilled and using it as a modifier. (We will be concerned here only with restrictive relative clauses and not those which are just parenthetical comments about an already determined object.) Let me begin my discussion of relative clauses by dispensing with one inadequate treatment.

The Shared Subpart Fallacy: A mechanism which occasionally surfaces as a claimed technique for dealing with relative clauses is to take simply the two propositions involved, the main clause and the relative clause, and represent the two separately as if they were independent propositions. In such a representation, the sentence "The dog that bit the man had rabies" would look something like that in Fig. 1. The point of interest here is not the names of the links (for which I make no claims) nor the type of representation (case oriented, deep conceptual, or whatever), but simply the fact that the only relationship between the two propositions is that they share the same node for dog. There are a number of problems with this representation: First, since there is no other relationship between the two sentences except sharing of a node (which is a symmetric relationship) there is no indication of which is the main clause and which is the relative clause. That is, we would get the same internal representation for the sentence "The dog that had rabies bit the man."

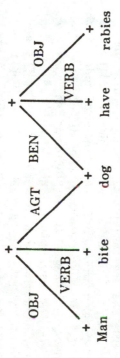

Fig. 1. A shared subpart representation.

Another difficulty is that there is nothing to indicate that the two sentences go together at all in a relative clause relationship. It is possible that on two different occasions we were told about this dog. On one occasion that he had rabies and on another that he bit a man. Then the presence of the two propositions in our data base both sharing the same node for dog would give us a structure identical to that for the example sentence. Now there is a subtle confusion which can happen at this point which I would like to try to clarify. You may say to me, "So what is the problem? Suppose I have told you the two facts at different times, suppose I have told you this dog and then it is still true that the dog that bit the man has rabies." How do I answer such an argument? On the face of it it seems true. Yet I maintain that the argument is fallacious and that it results from too shallow a treatment of the issues. The crux of the matter I think rests in the notion of which dog we are talking about. Unfortunately, this issue is one that gets omitted from almost all such discussions of semantic networks. If the two facts were told to me at different times, how did I know that they were about the same dog? (Without further explication of the semantics of the network notation, it is not even clear that we are talking about a particular dog and not about dogs in general.) It is exactly in order to relate the second fact to the first that we need the relative clause mechanism. In the next section we will consider the problem in more detail.

The Transient-Process Account. Quillian[1] once made the observation that a portion of what was in an input sentence was essentially stage directions used to enable the understanding process to identify an appropriate internal concept or node and the rest of the utterance was to be interpreted as new information to be added somehow to the network (and similar observations have been made by others). This gives an attractive account of the relative clause problem above. We interpret the relative clause not as something to be added to the network at all, but rather as a description to be used by the understander to determine which dog is in question. After this, we can forget about the relative clause (it has served its usefulness) and simply add the new information to the network. We might call this the "transient-process account". Under this account, if I was told about a dog that bit a man and later told that the dog that bit the man had rabies, then I would simply use the relative clause to find the internal concept for the dog that bit the man, and then add the new information that the dog had rabies. What's wrong with that account? Doesn't that explain everything?

Well, no. First, it simply evades the issue of representing the meaning of the sentence, focusing instead on the resulting change in memory contents. It says essentially that the role of the relative clause is a temporary and transient one that exists only during the processing of the utterance and then goes away. But you say, "well, isn't that a plausible account, does not that take care of the problem nicely, who says you have to have a representation of the original sentence anyway?"

[1]Personal communication.

Let's start from the first question--yes, it is a plausible account of the interpretation of *many* sentences, including this one in the context I just set up, and it may also be a correct description of what happens when humans process such sentences. It does not, however, take care of all occurrences of relative clauses. What about a situation when I read this sentence out of context and I haven't heard about the dog before? Then my processing must be different. I must infer that there must be a dog that I do not know about, perhaps create a new node for it, and then assert about this new node that it has rabies. Clearly also I must associate with this new node that it is a dog and that it bit a man. How then do I keep these two different types of information separate--the information which designates what I set the node up to stand for and that which the sentence asserted about it. We're back to the same problem. We need to distinguish the information that is in the relative clause from that in the main clause.

One possible way would be the use of an EGO link which points to a specification of what the node represents. Using such a link, when one creates the new node for the dog which bit the man, one would give the new node an EGO link which in essence says "I am the node which represents the dog that bit the man." When one then adds information to this node asserting additional facts about it, the original motivation for creating the node in the first place is not forgotten and the difference between the sentences "The dog that bit the man had rabies" and "The dog that had rabies bit the man" would lie in whether the facts about biting or about rabies were at the end of the EGO link. (There are a number of other questions which would require answers in order to complete the specification of the use of EGO links for this purpose--such as whether the propositions at the end of the EGO link are thereby made indirectly available as properties of this node or whether they are redundantly also included in the same status as the additional asserted properties which come later. We will not, however, go into these issues here.)

The above argument should have convinced you that the simple explanation of using relative clauses always only to identify preexisting nodes does not cover all of the cases. For certain sentences such as the above example, the object determined by the relative clause does not previously exist and something must be created to exist in the semantic network which will continue to exist after the process is finished. This thing must have an internal representation which preserves the information that it is an object determined by a relative clause.

A second argument against the transient process account is that even for sentences where nothing needs to remain in memory after the process has completed (because the relative clause has been used to locate a preexisting node), something needs to be extracted from the input sentence which describes the node to be searched for. In our previous example something like the proposition "the dog bit the man" needs to be constructed in order to search for its instances, and the process must know when it finds such an instance that it is the dog that is of interest and not the man. This specification of the node to be searched for is exactly the kind of thing which a semantic interpretation for the noun phrase "the dog that bit the man" should be. Thus even when no permanent representation of the relative clause needs to remain after the understanding process has completed, something equivalent to it still needs to be constructed as part of the input to the search process. The transient process account does not eliminate the need for such a representation, and the issue of whether a complete representation of the entire sentence (including the relative clause) gets constructed and sent off to the understanding process as a unit or whether small pieces get created and sent off independently without ever being assembled into a complete representation is at this point a red herring. The necessary operations which are required for the search specification are sufficient to construct such a representation, and whether it is actually constructed or whether parts of it are merely executed for effect and then cast away is a totally separate question.

A third argument against the transient process account, which should have become apparent in the above discussion, is that it is not an account at all, but merely a way of avoiding the problem. By claiming that the relative clause is handled during the transient process we have merely pushed the problem of accounting for relative clauses off onto the person who attempts to characterize the understanding process. We have not accounted for it or solved it.

B. Representation of Complex Sentences

Let us return to the question of whether one needs a representation of the entire sentence as a whole or not. More specifically, does one need a representation of a proposition expressed about a node which itself has a propositional restriction, or can one effectively break this process up in such a way that propositions are always expressed about definite nodes? This is going to be a difficult question to answer because there is a sense in which even if the answer is the former, one can model it with a process which first constructs the relative clause restricted node and then calls it definite and represents the higher proposition with a pointer to this new node. The real question, then, is in what sense is this new node definite? Does it always refer to a single specific node like the dog in our above example, or is it more complicated than that? I will argue the latter.

C. Definite and Indefinite Entities

Consider the case which we hypothesized in which we had to infer the existence of a heretofore unknown dog because we found no referent for "the dog that bit the man". This new node still has a certain definiteness to it. We can later refer to it again and add additional information, eventually fleshing it out to include its name, who owns it, etc. As such it is no different from any other node in the data base standing for a person, place, thing, etc. It got created when we first encountered the object denoted (or at least when we first recognized it and added it to our memory) and has subsequently gained additional information and may in the future gain additional information still. We know that it is a particular dog and not a class of dogs and many other things about it.

Consider, however, the question "Was the man bitten by a dog that had rabies?" Now we have a description of an indefinite dog and moreover we have not asserted that it exists but merely questioned its existence. Now you may first try to weasel out of the problem by saying something like, "Well, what happens is that we look in our data base for dogs that have rabies in the same way that we would in the earlier examples, and finding no such dog, we answer the question in the negative." This is another example of pushing the problem off onto the understanding process; it does not solve it or account for it, it just avoids it (not to mention the asumption that the absence of information from the network implies its falsity).

Let us consider the process more closely. Unless our process were appropriately constructed (how?) it would not know the difference (at the time it was searching for the referent of the phrase) between this case and the case of an assertion about an unknown dog. Hence the process we described above would create a new node for a dog that has rabies unless we block it somehow. Merely asking whether the main clause is a question would not do it, since the sentence "Did the dog that bit the man have rabies?" still must have the effect of creating a new definite node. (This is due to the effect of the presupposition of the definite singular determiner "the" that the object described must exist.) Nor is it really quite the effect of the indefinite article "a", since the sentence "a dog that had rabies bit the man" should still create a definite node for the dog. We could try conditions on questioned indefinites. Maybe that would work, but let me suggest that perhaps you do not want to block the creation of the new node at all but rather simply allow it to be a different type of entity, one whose existence in the real world is not presupposed by an intensional existence in the internal semantic network.

If we are to take this account of the hypothetical dog in our question, then we have made a major extension in our notion of structures in a semantic network and what they mean. Whereas previously we construed our nodes to correspond to real existing objects, now we have introduced a new type of node which does not have this assumption. Either we now have two very different types of nodes (in which case we must have some explicit indicator or other mechanism in the notation to indicate the type of every node) or else we must impose a unifying interpretation. If we have two different types of nodes, then we still have the problem of telling the process which constructs the nodes which type of node to construct in our two examples.

One possible unifying interpretation is to interpret every node as an intensional description and assert an explicit predicate of existence for those nodes which are intended to correspond to real objects. In this case, we could either rely on an implicit assumption that intensional objects used as subjects of definite asserted sentences (such as "the dog that bit the man had rabies") must actually exist, or we could postulate an inferential process which draws such inferences and explicitly asserts existence for such entities.

Since the above account of the indefinite relative clause in our example requires such a major reinterpretation of the fundamental semantics of our network notations, one might be inclined to look for some other account that was less drastic. I will argue, however, that such internal intensional entities are required in any case to deal with other problems in semantic representation. For example, whenever a new definite node gets created, it may in fact stand for the same object as some other node which already exists, but the necessary information to establish the identity may only come later or not at all. This is a fundamental characteristic of the information that we must store in our nets. Consider again Frege's morning star / evening star example. Even such definite descriptions, then, are essentially intensional objects. (Notice as a consequence that one cannot make negative identity assertions simply on the basis of distinctness of internal semantic representations.)

Perhaps the strongest case for intensional nodes in semantic networks comes from verbs such as "need" and "want". When one asserts a sentence such as "I need a wrench", one does not thereby assert the existence of the object desired. One must, however, include in the representation of this sentence some representation of the thing needed. For this interpretation, the object of the verb "need" should be an intensional description of the needed item. (It is also possible for the slot filler to be a node designating a particular entity rather than just a description, thus giving rise to an ambiguity of interpretation of the sentence. That is, is it a particular wrench that is needed, or will any wrench do?)

D. Consequences of Intensional Nodes

We conclude that there must be some nodes in the semantic network which correspond to descriptions of entities rather than entities themselves. Does that fix up the problem? Well, we have to do more than just make the assumption. We have to decide how to tell the two kinds of nodes apart, how we decide for particular sentences which type to create, and how to perform inferences on these nodes. If we have nodes which are intensional descriptions of entities, what does it mean to associate descriptions of entities with the nodes or to assert facts about the nodes. We cannot just rely on the arguments that we made when we were assuming that all of the nodes corresponded to definite external entities. We must see whether earlier interpretations of the meanings of links between nodes still hold true for this new expanded notion of node or whether they need modification or reinterpretation. In short we must start all over again from the beginning but this time with attention to the ability to deal with intensional descriptions.

Let me clarify further some of the kinds of things which we must be able to represent. Consider the sentence "Every boy loves his dog". Here we have an indefinite node for the dog involved which will not hold still. Linguistically it is marked definite (i.e., the dog that belongs to the boy), but it is a variable definite object whose reference changes with the boy. There are also variable entities which are indefinite as in "Every boy needs a dog." Here we plunge into the really difficult and crucial problems in representing quantification. It is easy to create simple network structures that model the logical syllogisms by creating links from subsets to supersets, but the critical cases are those like the above. We need the notion of an intensional description for a variable entity.

To summarize, then, in designing a network to handle intensional entities, we need to provide for definite entities that are intended to correspond to particular entities in the real world, indefinite entities which do not necessarily have corresponding entities in the real world, and definite and indefinite variable entities which stand in some relation to other entities and whose instantiations will depend on the instantiations of those other entities.

E. Functions and Predicates

Another question about the interpretation of links and what we mean by them comes in the representation of information about functions and predicates. Functions and predicates have a characteristic that clearly sets them apart from the other types of entities which we have mentioned (with the possible exception of the variable entity which depends on others)--namely, they take arguments. Somewhere in the internal representation of an entity which is a function or a predicate there must be information about the arguments which the function or predicate takes, what kinds of entities can fill those arguments, and how the value of the function or the truth of the predicate is determined or constrained by the values of the arguments. There is a difference between representing the possible entities that can serve as arguments for a predicate and expressing the assertion of the predicate for particular values or classes of values of those arguments. Unfortunately this distinction is often confused in talking about semantic networks. That is, it is all too easy to use the notation:

```
LOVE
   AGT      HUMAN
   RECIP    HUMAN
```

to express constraints on the possible fillers for the arguments of the predicate and to use the same link names in a notation such as:

```
S76543
   VERB     LOVE
   AGT      JOHN
   RECIP    SALLY
```

to represent the assertion that John loves Sally. Here we have a situation of the same link names meaning different things depending on the nodes which they are connected to.

Without some explicit indication in the network notation that the two nodes are of different types, no mechanical procedure operating on such a network would be able to handle these links correctly in both cases. With an explicit indication of node type and an explicit definition that the meaning of an arc depends on the type of the node to which it is connected (and how), such a procedure could be defined, but a network notation of this sort would probably be confusing as an explanatory device for human consumption. This is functionally equivalent, however, to an alternative mechanism using a dual set of links with different names (such as R-AGT and AGT, for example) which would make the difference explicit to a human reader and would save the mechanical procedure from having to consult the type of the node to determine the import of the link. Notice that in either case we are required to make another extension of the semantics of our network notation since we have two different kinds of links with different kinds of import. The ones which make statements about possible slot fillers have assertional import (asserting facts about the predicate LOVE in this case) while the ones that make up the arguments of S76543 have structural import (building up the parts of the proposition, which incidentally may itself not be asserted but only part of some intensional representation).

We conclude that the difference between the specification of possible slot fillers for a predicate as part of the information about the predicate and the specification of particular slot fillers for particular instances of the predicate requires some basic distinction in our semantic network notation. One is left with several questions as to just how this distinction is best realized (for example does one want a dual set of link names--or is there a preferable notation?). For the moment, however, let us leave those questions unexplored along with many issues that we have not begun to face and proceed with another problem of knowledge representation that imposes new demands on the interpretations of links and the conventions for representing facts in semantic networks.

F. Representing Quantified Expressions

The problem of representing quantified information in semantic networks is one that few people have faced and even fewer handled adequately. Let me begin by laying to rest a logically inadequate way of representing quantified expressions which unfortunately is the one most used in implemented semantic networks. It consists of simply tagging the quantifier onto the noun phrase it modifies just as if it were an adjective. In such a notation, the representation for "every integer is greater than some integer" would look something like:

```
S11113
    VERB    GREATER
    ARG1    D12345
    ARG2    D67890

D12345
    NOUN    INTEGER
    MOD     EVERY

D67890
    NOUN    INTEGER
    MOD     SOME
```

Now there are two possible interpretations of this sentence depending on whether or not the second existential quantifier is considered to be in the scope of the universal quantifier. In the normal interpretation, the second integer depends on the first and the sentence is true, while a pathological interpretation of the sentence is that there is some integer which every integer is greater than. (Lest you divert the issue with some claim that there is only one possible interpretation taking the quantifiers in the order in which they occur in the sentence consider a sentence such as "Everybody jumped in some old car that had the keys in it", in which the normal interpretation is the opposite.) Since our semantic network notation must provide a representation for whichever interpretation we decide was meant, there must be some way to distinguish the difference. If anything, the representation we have

given seems to suggest the interpretation in which there is some integer that every integer is greater than. If we take this as the interpretation of the above notation, then we need another representation for the other (and in this case correct) interpretation--the one in which the second integer is a variable entity dependent on the first.

To complicate matters even further, consider the case of numerical quantifiers and a sentence such as "three lookouts saw two boats". There are three possible interpretations of the quantifiers in this case. In the one that seems to correspond to treating the quantifier as a modifier of the noun phrase, we would have one group of three lookouts that jointly participated in an activity of seeing one group of two boats. There is, however, another interpretation in which each of three lookouts saw two boats (for an unknown total number of boats between 2 and 6 since we are not told whether any of them saw the same boats as the others) and still another interpretation in which each of two boats was seen by three men. We must have a way in our network notation to represent unambiguously all three of these possible interpretations. Quillian's (1968) suggestion of using "criterialities" on the arcs to indicate quantification will fail for the same reasons unless some mechanism for indicating which arguments depend on which others is inserted.

Before proceeding to discuss logically adequate ways of dealing with quantification, let me also lay to rest a borderline case. One might decide to represent the interpretation of the sentence in which each of three men saw two boats, for example, by creating three separate nodes for the men and asserting about each of them that he saw two boats. This could become logically adequate if the appropriate information were indicated that the three men were all different (it is not adequate to assume that internal nodes are different just because they are different nodes--recall the morning star/evening star example) and if the three separate facts are tied together into a single fact somewhere (e.g., by a conjunction) since otherwise this would not be an expression of a single fact (which could not a denied, for example). This is, however, clearly not a reasonable representation for a sentence such as "250 million people live in the United States", and would be a logical impossibility for representing universally quantified by expressions over sets whose cardinality was not known.

A variant of this is related to the transient process account. One might argue that it is not necessary to represent a sentence such as "Every boy has a dog" as a unit, but one can simply add an assertion to each internal node representing a boy. To be correct, however, such an account would require a network to have perfect knowledge (i.e., an internal node for every boy that exists in the world), a practical impossibility. We cannot assume that the entities in our network exhaust those that exist in the world. Hence we must represent this assertion in a way that will apply to future boys that we may learn about and not just to those we know about at this moment. To do this we must be able to store an intensional representation of the universally quantified proposition.

Quantifiers as Higher Operators: The traditional representation of quantifiers in the predicate calculus is that they are attached to the proposition which they govern in a string whose order determines the dependency of the individual variables on other variables. Thus the two interpretations of our first sentence are:

$$(\forall X/integer) \quad (\exists Y/integer) \quad (GREATER\ X\ Y)$$

and

$$(\exists Y/integer) \quad (\forall X/integer) \quad (GREATER\ X\ Y)$$

where I have chosen to indicate explicitly in the quantifier prefix the range of quantification of the variable (see Woods, 1967) for a discussion of the advantages of doing this--namely the uniform behavior for both universal and existential quantifiers). In the question-answering systems that I have constructed, including the LUNAR system, I have used a slightly expanded form of such quantifiers which uniformly handles numerical quantifiers and definite determiners as well as the classical universal and existential quantifiers. This formulation treats the quantifiers as higher predicates which take as arguments a variable name, a specification of the range of quantification, a possible restriction on the range, and the proposition to be quantified (which includes a free occurrence of the variable of quantification and which may be already quantified by other quantifiers). In this notation, the above two interpretations would be represented as:

(FOR EVERY X / INTEGER : T
  ; (FOR SOME Y / INTEGER : T ; (GREATER X Y)))

and

(FOR SOME Y / INTEGER : T
  ; (FOR EVERY X / INTEGER : T ; (GREATER X Y)))

where the component of the notation following the ":" in these expressions is a proposition which restricts the range of quantification (in this case the vacuously true proposition T) and the component following the ";" is the proposition being quantified. This type of higher-operator representation of quantification can be represented in a network structure by creating a special type of node for the quantifier and some special links for its components. Thus we could have something like:

```
S39732
    TYPE            QUANT
    QUANT-TYPE      EVERY
    VARIABLE        X
    CLASS           INTEGER
    RESTRICTION     T
    PROP            S39733

S39733
    TYPE            QUANT
    QUANT-TYPE      SOME
    VARIABLE        Y
    RESTRICTION     T
    PROP            S39734

S39734
    TYPE            PROPOSITION
    VERB            GREATER
    ARG1            X
    ARG2            Y
```

This is essentially the technique used by Shapiro (1971), who is one of the two people I know of to suggest a logically adequate treatment of quantifiers in his nets. (The other one is Martin Kay, whose proposal we will discuss shortly.) This technique has an unpleasant effect, however, in that it breaks up the chains of connections from node to node that one finds attractive in the more customary semantic network notations. That is, if we consider our sentence about lookouts and boats, we have gone successively from a simple-minded representation in which we might have a link labeled "see" which points from a node for "lookout" to one for "boats", to a case representation notation in which the chain becomes an inverse agent link from "lookout" to a special node which has a verb link to "see" and a patient link to "boats", and finally to a quantified representation in which the chain stretches from "lookout" via an inverse CLASS link to a quantifier node which has a PROP link to another quantifier node which has a CLASS link to "boats" and a PROP link to a proposition which has a VERB link to "see". Thus our successive changes in the network conventions designed to provide them with a logically adequate interpretation are carrying with them a cost in the directness of the associative paths. This may be an inevitable consequence of making the networks adequate for storing knowledge in general, and it may be that it is not too disruptive of the associative processing that one would like to apply to the memory representation. On the other hand it may lead to the conclusion that one cannot accomplish an appropriate associative linking of information as a direct consequence of the notation in which it is stored and that some separate indexing mechanism is required.

Other Possible Representations: There are two other possible candidates for representing quantified information, one of which to my knowledge has not been tried before in semantic networks. I will call them the "Skolem function method" and the "lambda abstraction method", after well-known techniques in formal logic.

Skolem Functions: The use of Skolem functions to represent quantified expressions is little known outside the field of mechanical theorem proving and certain branches of formal logic, but it is a pivotal technique in resolution theorem proving and is rather drastically different from the customary way of dealing with quantifiers in logic. The technique begins with a quantified expression containing no negative operators in the quantifier prefix (any such can be removed by means of the transformations exchanging "not every" for "some not" and "not some" for "every not"). It then replaces each instance of an existentially quantified variable with a functional designator whose function is a unique function name chosen for that existential variable and whose arguments are the universally quantified variables in whose scopes the existential quantifier for that variable lies. After this the existential quantifiers are deleted and, since the only remaining variables are universally quantified, the universal quantifiers can be deleted and free variables treated as implicitly universally quantified. The expression $(\forall x)(\exists y)(\forall z)(\exists w)P(x,y,z,w)$, for example, becomes $P(x,f(x),z,g(x,z))$, where f and g are new function names created to replace the variables y and w.

Notice that the arguments of the functions f and g in the result preserve the information about the universally quantified variables on which they depend. This is all the information necessary to reconstruct the original expression and is intuitively exactly that information which we are interested in to characterize the difference between alternative interpretations of a sentence corresponding to different quantifier orderings--i.e, does the choice of a given object depend on the choice of a universally quantified object or not? Thus the Skolem function serves as a device for recording the dependencies of an existentially quantified variable. An additional motivating factor for using Skolem functions to represent natural language quantification is that the quantification operation implicitly determines a real function of exactly this sort, and there are places in natural language dialogs where this implicit function appears to be referenced by anaphoric pronouns outside the scope of the original quantifier (e.g., in "Is there someone here from Virginia? If so, I have a prize for him", the "him" seems to refer to the value of such a function). We can obtain a semantic network notation based on this Skolem function analogy by simply including with every existentially quantified object a link which points to all of the universally quantified objects on which this one depends. This is essentially the technique proposed by Kay (1973).

It must be pointed out that one difficulty with the Skolem function notation which accounts for its little use as a logical representation outside the theorem proving circles is that it is not possible to obtain the negation of a Skolem form expression by simply attaching a negation operator to the "top". Rather, negation involves a complex operation which changes all of the universal variables to existential ones and vice versa and can hardly be accomplished short of converting the expression back to a quantifier prefix form, rippling the negation through the quantifier prefix to the embedded predicate and then reconverting to Skolem form. This makes it difficult, for example, to store the denial of an existing proposition. It seems likely that the same technique of explicitly linking the quantified object to those other objects on which it depends might also handle the case of numerically quantified expressions although I am not quite sure how it would all work out--especially with negations.

Lambda Abstraction: We have already introduced Church's lambda notation as a convenient device for expressing a predicate defined by a combination or a modification of other predicates. In general, for any completely instantiated complex assemblage of predicates and propositions, one can make a predicate of it by replacing some of its specific arguments with variable names and embedding it in a lambda expression with those variables indicated as arguments. For example, from a sentence "John told Mary to get something and hit Sam" we can construct a predicate (LAMBDA (X) John told Mary to get something and hit X) which is true of Sam if the original sentence is true and may be true of other individuals as well. This process is called "lambda abstraction".

Now one way to view a universally quantified sentence such as "all men are mortal" is simply as a statement of a relation between a set (all men) and a predicate (mortal) --

namely that the predicate is true of each member of the set (call this relation FORALL). By means of lambda abstraction we can create a predicate of exactly the type we need to view every instance of universal quantification as exactly this kind of assertion about a set and a predicate. For example, we can represent our assertion that every integer is greater than some integer as an assertion of the FORALL relation between the set of integers and the predicate

(LAMBDA (X) (X is greater than some integer))

and in a similar way we can define a relation FORSOME which holds between a set and a predicate if the predicate is true for some member of the set, thus giving us a representation:

(FORALL INTEGER (LAMBDA (X)
    (FORSOME INTEGER (LAMBDA (Y)
        (GREATER X Y)))))

which can be seen as almost a notational variant of the higher-operator quantifier representation. Notice that the expression (LAMBDA (Y) (GREATER X Y)) is a predicate whose argument is Y and which has a free variable X. This means that the predicate itself is a variable entity which depends on X--ie, for each value of X we get a different predicate to be applied to the Ys.

The use of this technique in a semantic network notation would require a special type of node for a predicate defined by the lambda operator, but such a type of node is probably required anyway for independent reasons (since the operation of lambda abstraction is an intellectual operation which one can perform and since our semantic network should be able to store the results of such mental gymnastics). The structure of the above expression might look like:

```
S12233    PROPOSITION
TYPE      FORALL
VERB      INTEGER
CLASS     P12234
PRED
```

distinctness, or their completeness in covering all of the objects which are presumed to exist in the world. I have also pointed out the logical inadequacies of almost all current network notations for representing quantified information and some of the disadvantages of some logically adequate techniques.

I have not begun to address all of the problems that need to be addressed, and I have only begun to discuss the problems of relative clauses and quantificational information. I have not even mentioned other problems such as the representation of mass terms, adverbial modification, probabilistic information, degrees of certainty, time, and tense, and a host of other difficult problems. All of these issues need to be addressed and solutions integrated into a consistent whole in order to produce a logically adequate semantic network formalism. No existing semantic network comes close to this goal.

I hope that by focusing on the logical inadequacies of many of the current (naive) assumptions about what semantic networks do and can do, I will have stimulated the search for better solutions and flagged some of the false assumptions about adequacies of techniques that might otherwise have gone unchallenged. As I said earlier, I believe that work in the area of knowledge representation in general, and semantic networks in particular, is important to the further development of our understanding of human and artificial intelligence and that many essentially correct facts about human performance and useful techniques for artificial systems are emerging from this study. My hope for this chapter is that it will stimulate this area of study to develop in a productive direction.

```
P12234
TYPE        PREDICATE
ARGUMENTS   (X)
BODY        S12235

S12235
TYPE        PROPOSITION
VERB        FORSOME
CLASS       INTEGER
PRED        P12236

P12236
TYPE        PREDICATE
ARGUMENTS   (Y)
BODY        S12237

S12237
TYPE        PROPOSITION
VERB        GREATER
ARG1        X
ARG2        Y
```

V. CONCLUSION

In the preceding sections, I hope that I have illustrated by example the kinds of explicit understanding of what one intends various network notations to mean that must be made in order to even begin to ask the questions whether a notation is an adequate one for representing knowledge in general (although for reasons of space I have been more brief in such explanations in this chapter than I feel one should be in presenting a proposed complete semantic network notation). Moreover, I hope that I have made the point that when one does extract a clear understanding of the semantics of the notation, most of the existing semantic network notations are found wanting in some major respects--notably the representation of propositions without commitment to asserting their truth and in representing various types of intensional descriptions of objects without commitment to their external existence, their external

REFERENCES

Carbonell, J. R., & Collins, A. M. Natural semantics in artificial intelligence. *Proceedings of Third International Joint Conference on Artificial Intelligence*, 1973, 344-351. (Reprinted in the American Journal of Computational Linguistics, 1974, *1*, Mfc. 3.)

Davis, M. *Computability and unsolvability.* New York: McGraw-Hill, 1958.

Fillmore, C. The case for case. In Bach and Harms (Eds.), *Universals in linguistic theory,* Chicago, Ill.: Holt, 1968.

Kay, M. The MIND system. In R. Rustin (Ed.) *Natural language processing.* New York: Algorithmics Press, 1973.

Lindsay, R. K. Inferential memory as the basis of machines which understand natural language. In E. A. Feigenbaum & J. Feldman (Eds.), *Computers and thought.* New York: McGraw-Hill, 1963.

Quillian, M. R. Semantic memory. In M. Minsky (Ed.), *Semantic information processing.* Cambridge, Mass.: MIT Press, 1968.

Quillian, M. R. The teachable language comprehender. *Communications of the Association for Computing Machinery,* 1969, *12,* 459-475.

Quine, W. V. *From a logical point of view.* (2nd Ed., rev.) New York: Harper, 1961.

Raphael, B. A computer program which 'understands'. *AFIPS Conference Proceedings,* 1964, *26,* 577-589.

Rumelhart, D. E., Lindsay, P. H., & Norman, D. A. A process model for long-term memory. In E. Tulving & W. Donaldson (Eds.), *Organization of memory.* New York: Academic Press, 1972.

Schank, R. C. *Conceptual information processing.* Amsterdam: North-Holland, 1975.

Shapiro, S. C. A net structure for semantic information storage, deduction, and retrieval. *Proceedings of the Second International Joint Conference on Artificial Intelligence,* 1971, 512-523.

Simmons, R. F. Semantic networks: Their computation and use for understanding English sentences. In R. C. Schank & K. M. Colby (Eds.), *Computer models of thought and language.* San Francisco, Ca.: Freeman, 1973.

Winograd, T. *Understanding natural language.* New York: Academic Press, 1972.

Woods, W.A. Semantics for a Question-Answering System. Ph.D. Thesis, Division of Engineering and Applied Physics, Harvard University, 1967. (Also in Report NSF-19, Harvard Computation Laboratory, September 1967. Available from NTIS as PB-176-548.)

Woods, W.A. Meaning and machines. *Proceedings of the International Conference on Computational Linguistics,* Pisa, Italy, August 1973(a).

Woods, W.A. Progress in natural language understanding: An application to lunar geology. *AFIPS Conference Proceedings,* 1973(b), *42,* 441-450.

Woods, W.A. Syntax, semantics, and speech, presented at IEEE Symposium on Speech recognition, Carnegie-Mellon University, April 1974.

Woods, W. A., Kaplan, R. M., & Nash-Webber, B. The lunar sciences natural language information system: final report. BBN Report No. 2378, June 1972.

III / Structured Object Representations

12 / Marvin Minsky
A Framework for Representing Knowledge

This paper by Minsky was one of the more influential contributions to Knowledge Representation and is certainly one of the most referenced in the entire history of the field. (The paper has appeared in at least three different versions, the one here being the most recent. A revised and greatly extended version of this theory is to be published in *The Society of Mind* (New York: Simon and Schuster, 1986).) In it, Minsky presents the idea of *frames* and frame systems, the basis of a generation of KR formalisms (especially KRL [Bobrow and Winograd, Chapter 13]). Drawing from a number of ideas in the air at the time, Minsky sketches in broad strokes a representation architecture based on prototypes, defaults, multiple perspectives, analogies, and partial matching. In contrast to some of the other approaches represented in this collection (*e.g.*, those described in [Moore, Chapter 18] and [Hayes, Chapter 28]), this results in a representational framework that seems to have much more to do with cognitive memory models than with mathematical logic and logical inference. (Hayes, of course, denies this completely in [Hayes, Chapter 14].) In fact, in an appendix to the paper, Minsky argues that the pursuit of formal logic in AI has been very misleading and that some of the demands of logic such as consistency and completeness are probably not even *desirable* in a representation language. On the other hand, he can only sketch somewhat impressionistically what a possible alternative would be like. This problem of vagueness and general lack of rigor has unfortunately followed many of those who pursued the frame ideas, as if the topic itself demanded a certain informal style of research.

Appeared in *Mind Design*, 95–128, edited by J. Haugeland, Cambridge, MA: The MIT Press, 1981.

A Framework for Representing Knowledge

MARVIN MINSKY

1. Frames

IT SEEMS TO ME that the ingredients of most theories both in Artificial Intelligence and in Psychology have been on the whole too minute, local, and unstructured to account—either practically or phenomenologically—for the effectiveness of common-sense thought. The "chunks" of reasoning, language, memory, and perception ought to be larger and more structured; their factual and procedural contents must be more intimately connected in order to explain the apparent power and speed of mental activities.

Similar feelings seem to be emerging in several centers working on theories of intelligence. They take one form in the proposal of Papert and myself (1972) to divide knowledge into substructures, "micro-worlds." Another form is in the "problem-spaces" of Newell and Simon (1972), and yet another is in the new, large structures that theorists like Schank (1973), Abelson (1973), and Norman (1973) assign to linguistic objects. I see all these as moving away from the traditional attempts both by behavioristic psychologists and by logic-oriented students of Artificial Intelligence in trying to represent knowledge as collections of separate, simple fragments.

I try here to bring together several of these issues by pretending to have a unified, coherent theory. The paper raises more questions than it answers, and I have tried to note the theory's deficiencies.

Here is the essence of the theory: When one encounters a new situation (or makes a substantial change in one's view of the present problem), one selects from memory a structure called a *frame*. This is a remembered framework to be adapted to fit reality by changing details as necessary.

A *frame* is a data-structure for representing a stereotyped situation, like being in a certain kind of living room, or going to a child's birthday party. Attached to each frame are several kinds of information. Some of this information is about how to use the frame. Some is about what one can expect to happen next. Some is about what to do if these expectations are not confirmed.

We can think of a frame as a network of nodes and relations. The top levels of a frame are fixed, and represent things that are always true about the supposed situation. The lower levels have many *terminals*—slots that must be filled by specific instances or data. Each terminal can specify conditions its assignments must meet. (The assignments themselves are usually smaller subframes.) Simple conditions are specified by *markers* that might require a terminal assignment to be a person, an object of sufficient value, or a pointer to a subframe of a certain type. More complex conditions can specify relations among the things assigned to several terminals.

Collections of related frames are linked together into *frame-systems*. The effects of important actions are mirrored by *transformations* between the frames of a system. These are used to make certain kinds of calculations economical, to represent changes of emphasis and attention, and to account for the effectiveness of imagery.

For visual scene analysis, the different frames of a system describe the scene from different viewpoints, and the transformations between one frame and another represent the effects of moving from place to place. For nonvisual kinds of frames, the differences between the frames of a system can represent actions, cause-effect relations, or changes in conceptual viewpoint. *Different frames of a system share the same terminals*; this is the critical point that makes it possible to coordinate information gathered from different viewpoints.

Much of the phenomenological power of the theory hinges on the inclusion of expectations and other kinds of presumptions. *A frame's terminals are normally already filled with "default" assignments.* Thus a frame may contain a great many details whose supposition is not specifically warranted by the situation. These have many uses in representing general information, most likely cases, techniques for bypassing "logic," and ways to make useful generalizations.

The default assignments are attached loosely to their terminals, so that they can be easily displaced by new items that fit better the current situation. They thus can serve also as variables or as special cases for reasoning by example, or as textbook cases, and often make the use of logical quantifiers unnecessary.

The frame-systems are linked, in turn, by an *information retrieval network*. When a proposed frame cannot be made to fit reality—when we cannot find terminal assignments that suitably match its terminal marker conditions—this network provides a replacement frame. These interframe structures make possible other ways to represent knowledge about facts, analogies, and other information useful in understanding.

Once a frame is proposed to represent a situation, a *matching* process tries to assign values to each frame's terminals, consistent with the markers at each place. The matching process is partly controlled by information associated with the frame (which includes information about how to deal with surprises) and partly by knowledge about the system's current goals. There are important uses for the information, obtained when a matching process fails. I will discuss how it can be used to select an alternative frame that better suits the situation.

An apology: The schemes proposed herein are incomplete in many respects. First, I often propose representations without specifying the processes that will use them. Sometimes I only describe properties the structures should exhibit. I talk about markers and assignments as though it were obvious how they are attached and linked; it is not.

Besides the technical gaps, I will talk as though unaware of many problems related to "understanding" that really need much deeper analysis. I do not claim that the ideas proposed here are enough for a complete theory, only that the frame-system scheme may help explain a number of phenomena of human intelligence. The basic frame idea itself is not particularly original—it is in the tradition of the "schemata" of Bartlett and the "paradigms" of Kuhn; the idea of a frame-system is probably more novel. Winograd (1974)

discusses the recent trend, in theories of AI, toward frame-like ideas.

In the body of the paper I discuss different kinds of reasoning by analogy, and ways to impose stereotypes on reality and jump to conclusions based on partial-similarity matching. These are basically uncertain methods. Why not use methods that are more logical and certain? Section 6 is a sort of Appendix which argues that traditional logic cannot deal very well with realistic, complicated problems because it is poorly suited to represent *approximations* to solutions—and these are absolutely vital.

Thinking always begins with suggestive but imperfect plans and images; these are progressively replaced by better—but usually still imperfect—ideas.

1.3[1] ARTIFICIAL INTELLIGENCE AND HUMAN PROBLEM SOLVING

In this essay I draw no boundary between a theory of human thinking and a scheme for making an intelligent machine; no purpose would be served by separating them today, since neither domain has theories good enough to explain, or produce, enough mental capacity. There is, however, a difference in professional attitudes. Workers from psychology inherit stronger desires to minimize the variety of assumed mechanisms. I believe this leads to attempts to extract more performance from fewer "basic mechanisms," than is reasonable. Such theories especially neglect mechanisms of procedure control and explicit representations of processes. On the other side, workers in AI have perhaps focused too sharply on just such questions. Neither has given enough attention to the structure of knowledge, especially procedural knowledge.

It is understandable that psychologists are uncomfortable with complex proposals not based on well-established mechanisms, but I believe that parsimony is still inappropriate at this stage, valuable as it may be in later phases of every science. There is room in the anatomy and genetics of the brain for much more mechanism than anyone today is prepared to propose, and we should concentrate for a while longer on *sufficiency* and *efficiency* rather than on *necessity*.

1. *Editor's note*: Section numbers have been retained from the original, and hence are not always sequential in this abridged edition.

1.11 DEFAULT ASSIGNMENT

Although both seeing and imagining result in assignments to frame terminals, imagination leaves us wider choices of detail and variety of such assignments. I conjecture that frames are never stored in long-term memory with unassigned terminal values. Instead, what really happens is that frames are stored with weakly bound default assignments at every terminal! These manifest themselves as often-useful but sometimes counterproductive stereotypes.

Thus if I say, "John kicked the ball," you probably cannot think of a purely abstract ball, but must imagine characteristics of a vaguely particular ball; it probably has a certain default size, default color, default weight. Perhaps it is a descendant of one you first owned or were injured by. Perhaps it resembles your latest one. In any case your image lacks the sharpness of presence because the processes that inspect and operate upon the weakly bound default features are very likely to change, adapt, or detach them.

Such default assignments would have subtle, idiosyncratic influences on the paths an individual would tend to follow in making analogies, generalizations, and judgements, especially when the exterior influences on such choices are weak. Properly chosen, such stereotypes could serve as a storehouse of valuable heuristic plan-skeletons; badly selected, they could form paralyzing collections of irrational biases. Because of them one might expect, as reported by Freud, to detect evidences of early cognitive structures in free-association thinking.

2. Language, Understanding, and Scenarios

2.1 WORDS, SENTENCES AND MEANINGS

The device of images has several defects that are the price of its peculiar excellences. Two of these are perhaps the most important: the image, and particularly the visual image, is apt to go farther in the direction of the individualisation of situations than is biologically useful; and the principles of the combination of images have their own peculiarities and result in constructions which are relatively wild, jerky and irregular, compared with the straightforward unwinding of a habit, or with the somewhat orderly march of thought.

The concepts of frame and default assignment seem helpful in discussing the phenomenology of "meaning." Chomsky (1957) points out that such a sentence as

(A) colorless green ideas sleep furiously

is treated very differently from the nonsentence

(B) furiously sleep ideas green colorless

and suggests that because both are "equally nonsensical," what is involved in the recognition of sentences must be quite different from what is involved in the appreciation of meanings.

There is no doubt that there are processes especially concerned with grammar. Since the meaning of an utterance is encoded as much in the positional and structural relations between the words as in the word choices themselves, there must be processes concerned with analyzing those relations in the course of building the structures that will more directly represent the meaning. What makes the words of (A) more effective and predictable than (B) in producing such a structure—putting aside the question of whether that structure should be called semantic or syntactic—is that the word-order relations in (A) exploit the (grammatical) conventions and rules people usually use to induce others to make assignments to terminals of structures. This is entirely consistent with theories of grammar. A generative grammar would be a summary description of the exterior appearance of those frame rules—or their associated processes—while the operators of transformational grammars seem similar enough to some of our frame transformations.

But one must also ask: to what degree does grammar have a separate identity in the actual working of a human mind? Perhaps the rejection of an utterance (either as nongrammatical, as nonsensical, or, most important, as *not understood*) indicates a more complex failure of the semantic process to arrive at any usable representation; I will argue now that the grammar-meaning distinction may illuminate two extremes of a continuum but obscures its all-important interior.

We certainly cannot assume that logical meaninglessness has a precise psychological counterpart. Sentence (A) can certainly generate an image! The dominant frame (in my case) is that of

—F. C. Bartlett (1932)

someone sleeping; the default system assigns a particular bed, and in it lies a mummy-like shape-frame with a translucent green color property. In this frame there is a terminal for the character of the property. In this frame there is a terminal for the character of the sleep—restless, perhaps—and "furiously" seems somewhat inappropriate at that terminal, perhaps because the terminal does not like to accept anything so "intentional" for a sleeper. "Idea" is even more disturbing, because a person is expected, or at least something animate. I sense frustrated procedures trying to resolve these tensions and conflicts more properly, here or there, into the sleeping framework that has been evoked.

Utterance (B) does not get nearly so far because no subframe accepts any substantial fragment. As a result no larger frame finds anything to match its terminals, hence, finally, no top level "meaning" or "sentence" frame can organize the utterance as either meaningful or grammatical. By combining this "soft" theory with gradations of assignment tolerances, I imagine one could develop systems that degrade properly for sentences with poor grammar rather than none; if the smaller fragments—phrases and subclauses—satisfy subframes well enough, an image adequate for certain kinds of comprehension could be constructed anyway, even though some parts of the top level structure are not entirely satisfied. Thus we arrive at a qualitative theory of "grammatical": *if the top levels are satisfied but some lower terminals are not, we have a meaningless sentence; if the top is weak but the bottom solid, we can have an ungrammatical but meaningful utterance.*

I do not mean to suggest that sentences must evoke visual images. Some people do not admit to assigning a color to the ball in "he kicked the ball." But everyone admits (eventually) to having assumed, if not a size or color, at least some purpose, attitude, or other elements of an assumed scenario. When we go beyond vision, terminals and their default assignments can represent purposes and functions, not just colors, sizes and shapes.

2.6 SCENARIOS

Thinking . . . is biologically subsequent to the image-forming process. It is possible only when a way has been found of breaking up the 'massed' influence of past stimuli and situations, only when a device has already been discovered for conquering the sequential tyranny of past reactions. But though it is a later and a higher development, it does not supersede the method of images. It has its own drawbacks. Contrasted with imaging it loses something of vivacity, of vividness, of variety. Its prevailing instruments are words, and, not only because these are social, but also because in use they are necessarily strung out in sequence, they drop into habit reactions even more readily than images do. [With thinking] we run greater and greater risk of being caught up in generalities that may have little to do with actual concrete experience. If we fail to maintain the methods of thinking, we run the risks of becoming tied to individual instances and of being made sport of by the accidental circumstances belonging to these.

—F. C. Bartlett (1932)

We condense and conventionalize, in language and thought, complex situations and sequences into compact words and symbols. Some words can perhaps be "defined" in elegant, simple structures, but only a small part of the meaning of "trade" is captured by:

first frame   *second frame*

A has X   B has Y   ———>   *B has X   A has Y*

Trading normally occurs in a social context of law, trust, and convention. Unless we also represent these other facts, most trade transactions will be almost meaningless. It is usually essential to know that each party usually wants both things but has to compromise. It is a happy but unusual circumstance in which each trader is glad to get rid of what he has. To represent trading strategies, one could insert the basic maneuvers right into the above frame-pair scenario: in order for A to make B want X more (or want Y less) we expect him to select one of the familiar tactics:

Offer more for Y.
Explain why X is so good.
Create favorable side-effect of B having X.
Disparage the competition.
Make B think C wants X.

These only scratch the surface. Trades usually occur within a scenario tied together by more than a simple chain of events each linked to the next. No single such scenario will do; when a clue about trading appears, it is essential to guess which of the different available scenarios is most likely to be useful.

Charniak's thesis (1972) studies questions about transactions that seem easy for people to comprehend yet obviously need rich default structures. We find in elementary school reading books such stories as:

Jane was invited to Jack's Birthday Party.
She wondered if he would like a kite.
She went to her room and shook her piggy bank.
It made no sound.

Most young readers understand that Jane wants money to buy Jack a kite for a present but that there is no money to pay for it in her piggy bank. Charniak proposes a variety of ways to facilitate such inferences—a "demon" for *present* that looks for things concerned with *money*, a demon for "piggy bank" which knows that shaking without sound means the bank is empty, etc. But although *present* now activates *money*, the reader may be surprised to find that neither of those words (nor any of their synonyms) occurs in the story. "Present" is certainly associated with "party," and "money" with "bank," but how are the longer chains built up? Here is another problem raised by Charniak. A friend tells Jane:

He already has a Kite.
He will make you take it back.

Take *which* kite back? We do not want Jane to return Jack's old kite. To determine the referent of the pronoun "it" requires understanding a lot about an assumed scenario. Clearly, "it" refers to the proposed *new* kite. How does one know this? (Note that we need not agree on any single explanation.) Generally, pronouns refer to recently mentioned things, but as this example shows, the referent depends on more than the local syntax.

Suppose for the moment we are already trying to instantiate a "buying a present" default subframe. Now, the word "it" alone is too small a fragment to deal with, but "take it back" could be a plausible unit to match a terminal of an appropriately elaborate *buying* scenario. Since that terminal would be constrained to agree with the assignment of "present" itself, we are assured of the correct meaning of *it* in "take X back." Automatically, the correct kite is selected. Of course, that terminal will have its own

constraints as well; a subframe for the "take it back" idiom should know that "take X back" requires that:

X was recently purchased.
The return is to the place of purchase.
You must have your sales slip.
Etc.

If the current scenario does not contain a "take it back" terminal, then we have to find one that does and substitute it, maintaining as many prior assignments as possible. Notice that if things go well, the question of *it* being the old kite never even arises. *The sense of ambiguity arises only when a "near miss" mismatch is tried and rejected.*

Charniak's proposed solution to this problem is in the same spirit but emphasizes understanding that because Jack already has a kite, he may not want another one. He proposes a mechanism associated with "present":

(A) If we see that a person P might not like a present X, then look for X being returned to the store where it was bought.

(B) If we see this happening, or even being suggested, assert that the reason why is that P does not like X.

This statement of "advice" is intended by Charniak to be realized as a production-like entity to be added to the currently active data-base whenever a certain kind of context is encountered. Later, if its antecedent condition is satisfied, its action adds enough information about Jack and about the new kite to lead to a correct decision about the pronoun.

Charniak in effect proposes that the system should watch for certain kinds of events or situations and inject proposed reasons, motives, and explanations for them. The additional interconnections between the story elements are expected to help bridge the gaps that logic might find it hard to cross, because the additions are only "plausible" default explanations, assumed without corroborative assertions. By assuming (tentatively) "does not like X" when X is taken back, Charniak hopes to simulate much of ordinary "comprehension" of what is happening. We do not yet know how complex and various such plausible inferences must be to get a given level of performance, and the thesis does not answer this because it did not include a large simulation. Usually he proposes terminating the process by asserting the allegedly plausible motive without further analysis unless necessary. To understand why Jack might return the additional kite, it should usually be enough to assert that he does not like it. A deeper analysis might reveal that Jack would not really mind having two kites but he probably realizes that he will get only one present; his utility for two different presents is probably higher.

2.7 SCENARIOS AND "QUESTIONS"

The meaning of a child's birthday party is very poorly approximated by any dictionary definition like "a party assembled to celebrate a birthday," where a party would be defined, in turn, as "people assembled for a celebration." This lacks all the flavor of the culturally required activities. Children know that the "definition" should include more specifications, the particulars of which can normally be assumed by way of default assignments:

DRESS ———— *SUNDAY BEST.*
PRESENT ———— *MUST PLEASE HOST.*
MUST BE BOUGHT AND GIFT-WRAPPED.

GAMES ———— *HIDE AND SEEK. PIN TAIL ON DONKEY.*
DECOR ———— *BALLOONS. FAVORS. CREPE-PAPER.*
PARTY-MEAL ———— *CAKE. ICE-CREAM. SODA. HOT DOGS.*
CAKE ———— *CANDLES. BLOW-OUT. WISH. SING BIRTHDAY SONG.*

ICE-CREAM ———— *STANDARD THREE-FLAVOR.*

These ingredients for a typical American birthday party must be set into a larger structure. Extended events take place in one or more days. A Party takes place in a Day, of course, and occupies a substantial part of it, so we locate it in an appropriate day frame. A typical day has main events, such as

Get-up Dress Eat-1 Go-to-Work Eat-2

but a School-Day has more fixed detail:

Get-up Dress
Eat-1 Go-to-School Be-in-School
Home-Room Assembly English Math (arrgh)

Eat-2 Science Recess Sport
Go-Home Play
Eat-3 Homework Go-To-Bed

Birthday parties obviously do not fit well into school-day frames. Any parent knows that the Party-Meal is bound to Eat-2 of its Day. I remember a child who did not seem to realize this. Absolutely stuffed after the Party-Meal, he asked when he would get Lunch.

Returning to Jane's problem with the kite, we first hear that she is invited to Jack's Birthday Party. Without this party scenario, or at least an invitation scenario, the second line seems rather mysterious:

She wondered if he would like a kite.

To explain one's rapid comprehension of this, I will make a somewhat radical proposal: *to represent explicitly, in the frame for a scenario structure, pointers to a collection of the most serious problems and questions commonly associated with it.* In fact we shall consider the idea that the frame terminals are exactly those questions. Thus, for the birthday party:

Y must get P for X ———— Choose P!
X must like P ———— Will X like P?
Buy P ———— Where to buy P?
Get money to buy P ———— Where to get money?
(Sub-question of the "present" frame?)
Y must dress up ———— What should Y wear?

Certainly these are one's first concerns, when one is invited to a party.

The reader is free to wonder, with the author, whether this solution is acceptable. The question, "Will X like P?" certainly matches "She wondered if he would like a kite?" and correctly assigns the kite to P. But is our world regular enough that such question sets could be precompiled to make this mechanism often work smoothly? I think the answer is mixed. We do indeed expect many such questions; we surely do not expect all of them. But surely "expertise" consists partly in not having to realize *ab initio* what are the outstanding problems and interactions in situations. Notice, for example, that there is *no* default assignment for the Present in our party-scenario frame. This mandates attention to that assignment problem and prepares us for a possible thematic concern. In any case, we probably need a more active mechanism for understanding "wondered" which can apply the information currently in the frame to produce an expectation of what Jane will think about.

The third line of our story, about shaking the bank, should also eventually match one of the present-frame questions, but the unstated connection between Money and Piggy-Bank is presumably represented in the piggy-bank frame, *not* the party frame, although once it is found, it will match our Get-Money question terminal. The primary functions and actions associated with piggy banks are Saving and Getting-Money-Out, and the latter has three principal methods:

1. Using a key. Most piggy banks don't offer this option.
2. Breaking it. Children hate this.
3. Shaking the money out, or using a thin slider.

In the fourth line does one know specifically that a *silent* Piggy Bank is empty, and hence out of money (I think, yes), or does one use general knowledge that a hard container which makes no noise when shaken is empty? I have found quite a number of people who prefer the latter. Logically the "general principle" would indeed suffice, but I feel that this misses the important point that a specific scenario of this character is engraved in every child's memory. The story is instantly intelligible to most readers. If more complex reasoning from general principles were required, this would not be so, and more readers would surely go astray. It is easy to find more complex problems:

A goat wandered into the yard where Jack was painting. The goat got the paint all over himself. When Mother saw the goat, she asked, "Jack, did you do *that?*"

There is no one word or line, which is the referent of "that." It seems to refer, as Charniak notes, to "cause the goat to be covered with paint." Charniak does not permit himself to make a specific proposal to handle this kind of problem, remarking only that his "demon" model would need a substantial extension to deal with such a poorly localized "thematic subject." Consider how much

one has to know about our culture, to realize that *that* is not the *goat-in-the-yard* but the *goat-covered-with-paint.* Charniak's thesis —basically a study rather than a debugged system—discusses issues about the activation, operation, and dismissal of expectation and default-knowledge demons. Many of his ideas have been absorbed into this essay.

In spite of its tentative character, I will try to summarize this image of language understanding as somewhat parallel to seeing. The key words and ideas of a discourse evoke substantial thematic or scenario structures, drawn from memory with rich default assumptions. The individual statements of a discourse lead to temporary representations—which seem to correspond to what contemporary linguists call "deep structures"—which are then quickly rearranged or consumed in elaborating the growing scenario representation. In order of "scale," among the ingredients of such a structure there might be these kinds of levels:

Surface Syntactic Frames. Mainly verb and noun structures. Prepositional and word-order indicator conventions.

Surface Semantic Frames. Action-centered meanings of words. Qualifiers and relations concerning participants, instruments, trajectories and strategies, goals, consequences and side-effects.

Thematic Frames. Scenarios concerned with topics, activities, portraits, setting. Outstanding problems and strategies commonly connected with topic.

Narrative Frames. Skeleton forms for typical stories, explanations, and arguments. Conventions about foci, protagonists, plot forms, development, etc., designed to help a listener construct a new, instantiated Thematic Frame in his own mind.

A single sentence can assign terminals, attach subframes, apply a transformation, or cause a gross replacement of a high level frame when a proposed assignment no longer fits well enough. A pronoun is comprehensible only when general linguistic conventions, interacting with defaults and specific indicators, determine a terminal or subframe of the current scenario.

In *vision* the transformations usually have a simple grouplike structure, in *language* we expect more complex, less regular systems of frames. Nevertheless, because *time*, *cause*, and *action* are so important to us, we often use sequential transformation pairs that replace situations by their temporal or causal successors.

Because syntactic structural rules direct the selection and assembly of the transient sentence frames, research on linguistic structures should help us understand how our frame systems are constructed. One might look for such structures specifically associated with assigning terminals, selecting emphasis or attention viewpoints (transformations), inserting sentential structures into thematic structures, and changing gross thematic representations.

Finally, just as there are familiar "basic plots" for stories, there must be basic superframes for discourses, arguments, narratives, and so forth. As with sentences, we should expect to find special linguistic indicators for operations concerning these larger structures; we should move beyond the grammar of sentences to try to find and systematize the linguistic conventions that, operating across wider spans, must be involved with assembling and transforming scenarios and plans.

2.8 QUESTIONS, SYSTEMS, AND CASES

Questions arise from a point of view—from something that helps to structure what is problematical, what is worth asking, and what constitutes an answer (or progress). It is not that the view determines reality, only what we accept from reality and how we structure it. I am realist enough to believe that in the long run reality gets its own chance to accept or reject our various views.

—A. Newell (1973a)

Examination of linguistic discourse leads thus to a view of the frame concept in which the "terminals" serve to represent the questions most likely to arise in a situation. To make this important viewpoint more explicit, we will spell out this reinterpretation.

A Frame is a collection of questions to be asked about a hypothetical situation: it specifies issues to be raised and methods to be used in dealing with them.

The terminals of a frame correspond perhaps to what Schank (1973) calls "conceptual cases," although I do not think we should restrict them to as few types as Schank suggests. To understand a

narrated or perceived action, one often feels compelled to ask such questions as

What caused it (agent)?
What was the purpose (intention)?
What are the consequences (side-effects)?
Whom does it affect (recipient)?
How is it done (instrument)?

The number of such "cases" or questions is problematical. While we would like to reduce meaning to a very few "primitive" concepts, perhaps in analogy to the situation in traditional linguistic analysis, I know of no reason to suppose that that goal can be achieved. My own inclination is to side with such workers as W. Martin (1974), who look toward very large collections of "primitives," annotated with comments about how they are related. Only time will tell which is better.

For entities other than actions one asks different questions; for thematic topics the questions may be much less localized, *e.g.*,

Why are they telling this to me?
How can I find out more about it?
How will it help with the "real problem"?

and so forth. In a "story" one asks what is the topic, what is the author's attitude, what is the main event, who are the protagonists, and so on. As each question is given a tentative answer, the corresponding subframes are attached and the questions they ask become active in turn.

The "markers" we proposed for vision-frames become more complex in this view. If we adopt for the moment Newell's larger sense of "view", it is not enough simply to ask a question; one must indicate how it is to be answered. Thus a terminal should also contain (or point to) suggestions and recommendations about how to find an assignment. Our "default" assignments then become the simplest special cases of such recommendations, and one certainly could have a hierarchy in which such proposals depend on features of the situation, perhaps along the lines of Wilks's (1973) "preference" structures.

For syntactic frames, the drive toward ritualistic completion of assignments is strong, but we are more flexible at the conceptual level. As Schank (1973a) says,

People do not usually state all the parts of a given thought that they are trying to communicate because the speaker tries to be brief and leaves out assumed or unessential information [. . .]. The conceptual processor makes use of the unfilled slots to search for a given type of information in a sentence or a larger unit of discourse that will fill the needed slot.

Even in physical perception we have the same situation. A box will not present all of its sides at once to an observer, and although this is certainly not because it wants to be brief, the effect is the same; the processor is prepared to find out what the missing sides look like and (if the matter is urgent enough) to move around to find answers to such questions.

Frame-Systems, in this view, become choice-points corresponding (on the conceptual level) to the mutually exclusive choice "Systems" exploited by Winograd (1970). The different frames of a system represent different ways of using the same information, located at the common terminals. As in the grammatical situation, one has to choose one of them at a time. On the conceptual level this choice becomes: *what questions shall I ask about this situation?*

View-changing, as we shall argue, is a problem-solving technique important in representing, explaining, and predicting. In the rearrangements inherent in the frame-system representation (for example, of an action), we have a first approximation to Simmons' (1973) idea of "procedures which in some cases will change the contextual definitional structure to reflect the action of a verb."

Where do the "questions" come from? That is not in the scope of this paper, really, but we can be sure that the frame-makers (however they operate) must use some principles. The methods used to generate the questions ultimately shape each person's general intellectual style. People surely differ in details of preferences for asking "Why?", "How can I find out more?", "What's in it for me?", "How will this help with the current higher goals?", and so forth.

Similar issues about the style of *answering* must arise. In its simplest form the drive toward instantiating empty terminals would appear as a variety of hunger or discomfort, satisfied by any default or other assignment that does not conflict with a prohibition. In more complex cases we should perceive less animalistic strategies for acquiring deeper understandings.

It is tempting, then, to imagine varieties of frame-systems that span from simple template-filling structures to implementations of the "views" of Newell—with all their implications about coherent generators of issues with which to be concerned, ways to investigate them, and procedures for evaluating proposed solutions. But I feel uncomfortable about any superficially coherent synthesis in which one expects the same kind of theoretical framework to function well on many different levels of scale or concept. We should expect very different question-processing mechanisms to operate our low-level stereotypes and our most comprehensive strategic overviews.

3. Learning, Memory, and Paradigms

To the child, Nature gives various means of rectifying any mistakes he may commit respecting the salutary or hurtful qualities of the objects which surround him. On every occasion his judgements are corrected by experience; want and pain are the necessary consequences arising from false judgement; gratification and pleasure are produced by judging aright. Under such masters, we cannot fail but to become well informed; and we soon learn to reason justly, when want and pain are the necessary consequences of a contrary conduct.

In the study and practice of the sciences it is quite different: the false judgements we form neither affect our existence nor our welfare; and we are not forced by any physical necessity to correct them. Imagination, on the contrary, which is ever wandering beyond the bounds of truth, joined to self-love and that self-confidence we are so apt to indulge, prompt us to draw conclusions that are not immediately derived from facts.

—A. Lavoisier (1949)

How does one locate a frame to represent a new situation? Obviously, we cannot begin any complete theory outside the context of some proposed global scheme for the organization of knowledge in general. But if we imagine working within some bounded domain, we can discuss some important issues:

EXPECTATION: How to select an initial frame to meet some given conditions.
ELABORATION: How to select and assign subframes to represent additional details.

ALTERATION: How to find a frame to replace one that does not fit well enough.

NOVELTY: What to do if no acceptable frame can be found. Can we modify an old frame or must we build a new one?

LEARNING: What frames should be stored, or modified, as a result of the experience?

In popular culture, memory is seen as separate from the rest of thinking: but finding the right memory—it would be better to say: finding a *useful* memory—needs the same sorts of strategies used in other kinds of thinking!

We say someone is "clever" who is unusually good at quickly locating highly appropriate frames. His information-retrieval systems are better at making good hypotheses, formulating the conditions the new frame should meet, and exploiting knowledge gained in the "unsuccessful" part of the search. Finding the right memory is no less a problem than solving any other kind of puzzle! Because of this, a good retrieval mechanism can be based only in part upon basic "innate" mechanisms. It must also depend largely on (learned) knowledge about the structure of one's own knowledge! Our proposal will combine several elements—a Pattern Matching Process, a Clustering Theory, and a Similarity Network.

In seeing a room or understanding a story, one assembles a network of frames and subframes. Everything noticed or guessed, rightly or wrongly, is represented in this network. We have already suggested that an active frame cannot be maintained unless its terminal conditions are satisfied.

We now add the postulate that *all satisfied frames must be assigned to terminals of superior frames.* This applies, as a special case, to any substantial fragments of "data" that have been observed and represented.

Of course, there must be an exception! We must allow a certain number of items to be attached to something like a set of "short term memory" registers. But the intention is that very little can be remembered unless embedded in a suitable frame. This, at any rate, is the conceptual scheme; in certain domains we would, of course, admit other kinds of memory "hooks" and special sensory buffers.

3.1 REQUESTS TO MEMORY

We can now imagine the memory system as driven by two complementary needs. *On one side are items demanding to be properly represented by being embedded into larger frames; on the other side are incompletely filled frames demanding terminal assignments.* The rest of the system will try to placate these lobbyists, but not so much in accord with general principles as in accord with special knowledge and conditions imposed by the currently active goals.

When a frame encounters trouble—when an important condition cannot be satisfied—something must be done. We envision the following major kinds of accommodation to trouble:

MATCHING: When nothing more specific is found, we can attempt to use some "basic" associative memory mechanism. This will succeed by itself only in relatively simple situations, but should play a supporting role in the other tactics.

EXCUSE: An apparent misfit can often be excused or explained. A "chair" that meets all other conditions but is much too small could be a "toy."

ADVICE: The frame contains explicit knowledge about what to do about the trouble. Below, we describe an extensive, learned, "Similarity Network," in which to embed such knowledge.

SUMMARY: If a frame cannot be completed or replaced, one must give it up. But first one must construct a well-formulated complaint or summary to help whatever process next becomes responsible for reassigning the subframes left in limbo.

In my view, all four of these are vitally important. I discuss them in the following sections.

3.3 EXCUSES

We can think of a frame as describing an "ideal." If an ideal does not match reality because it is "basically" wrong, it must be replaced. *But it is in the nature of ideals that they are really elegant simplifications; their attractiveness derives from their simplicity, but their real power depends upon additional knowledge about interactions between them!* Accordingly we need not abandon an ideal because of a failure to instantiate it, provided one can explain the discrepancy in terms of such an interaction. Here are some examples in which such an "excuse" can save a failing match:

OCCLUSION: A table, in a certain view, should have four legs, but a chair might occlude one of them. One can look for things like T-joints and shadows to support such an excuse.

FUNCTIONAL VARIANT: A chair-leg is usually a stick, geometrically; but more important, it is *functionally* a support. Therefore, a strong center post, with an adequate base plate, should be an acceptable replacement for all the legs. Many objects are multiple purpose and need functional rather than physical descriptions.

BROKEN: A visually missing component could be explained as in fact physically missing, or it could be broken. Reality has a variety of ways to frustrate ideals.

PARASITIC CONTEXTS: An object that is just like a chair, except in size, could be (and probably is) a toy chair. The complaint "too small" could often be so interpreted in contexts with other things too small, children playing, peculiarly large "grain," and so forth.

In most of those examples, the kinds of knowledge to make the repair—and thus salvage the current frame—are "general" enough usually to be attached to the thematic context of a superior frame. In the remainder of this essay, I will concentrate on types of more sharply localized knowledge that would naturally be attached to a frame itself, for recommending its own replacement.

3.5 CLUSTERS, CLASSES, AND A GEOGRAPHIC ANALOGY

Though a discussion of *some* of the attributes shared by a *number* of games or chairs or leaves often helps us to learn how to employ the corresponding term, there is no set of characteristics that is simultaneously applicable to all members of the class and to them alone. Instead, confronted with a previously unobserved activity, we apply the term 'game' because what we are seeing bears a close 'family resemblance' to a number of the activities we have previously learned to call by that name. For Wittgenstein, in short, games, chairs, and leaves are natural families, each constituted by a network of overlapping and crisscross resemblances. The existence of such a network sufficiently accounts for our success in identifying the corresponding object or activity.

To make the Similarity Network act more "complete," consider the following analogy. In a city, any person should be able to visit any other; but we do not build a special road between each pair of houses; we place a group of houses on a "block." We do not connect roads between each pair of blocks, but have them share streets. We do not connect each town to every other, but construct main routes, connecting the centers of larger groups. Within such an organization, each member has direct links to some other individuals at his own "level," mainly to nearby, highly similar ones; but each individual has also at least a few links to "distinguished" members of higher level groups. The result is that there is usually a rather short sequence between any two individuals, if one can but find it.

To locate something in such a structure, one uses a hierarchy like the one implicit in a mail address. Everyone knows something about the largest categories, in that he knows where the major cities are. An inhabitant of a city knows the nearby towns, and people in the towns know the nearby villages. No person knows all the individual routes between pairs of houses; but, for a particular friend, one may know a special route to his home in a nearby town that is better than going to the city and back. *Directories* factor the problem, basing paths on standard routes between major nodes in the network. Personal shortcuts can bypass major nodes and go straight between familiar locations. Although the standard routes are usually not quite the very best possible, our stratified transport and communication services connect everything together reasonably well, with comparatively few connections.

At each level, the aggregates usually have distinguished foci or *capitals*. These serve as elements for clustering at the next level of aggregation. There is no nonstop airplane service between New Haven and San Jose because it is more efficient overall to share the trunk route between New York and San Francisco, which are the capitals at that level of aggregation.

As our memory networks grow, we can expect similar aggregations of the destinations of our similarity pointers. Our decisions about what we consider to be primary or trunk difference features and which are considered subsidiary will have large effects on our abilities. Such decisions eventually accumulate to become episte-

—T. Kuhn (1970)

mological commitments about the conceptual cities of our mental universe.

The nonrandom convergences and divergences of the similarity pointers, for each difference d, thus tend to structure our conceptual world around

(1) the aggregation into d-clusters
(2) the selection of d-capitals

Note that it is perfectly all right to have *several capitals in a cluster*, so that there need be no one attribute common to them all. The "crisscross resemblances" of Wittgenstein are then consequences of the local connections in our similarity network, which are surely adequate to explain how we can feel as though we know what a chair or a game is—yet cannot always define it in a logical way as an element in some class-hierarchy or by any other kind of compact, formal, declarative rule. The apparent coherence of the conceptual aggregates need not reflect explicit definitions, but can emerge from the success-directed sharpening of the difference-describing processes.

The selection of capitals corresponds to selecting stereotypes or typical elements whose default assignments are unusually useful. There are many forms of chairs, for example, and one should choose carefully the chair-description frames that are to be the major capitals of chair-land. These are used for rapid matching and assigning priorities to the various differences. The lower priority features of the cluster center then serve either as default properties of the chair types or, if more realism is required, as dispatch pointers to the local chair villages and towns. Difference pointers could be "functional" as well as geometric. Thus after rejecting a first try at "chair," one might try the functional idea of "something one can sit on" to explain an unconventional form. This requires a deeper analysis in terms of forces and strengths. Of course, that analysis would fail to capture toy chairs, or chairs of such ornamental delicacy that their actual use would be unthinkable. These would be better handled by the method of excuses, in which one would bypass the usual geometrical or functional explanations in favor of responding to contexts involving art or play.

It is important to re-emphasize that there is no reason to restrict the memory structure to a single hierarchy; the notions of "level" of aggregation need not coincide for different kinds of differences. The d-capitals can exist, not only by explicit declarations, but also implicitly by their focal locations in the structure defined by convergent d-pointers. (In the Newell-Simon GPS framework, the "differences" are ordered into a fixed hierarchy. By making the priorities depend on the goal, the same memories could be made to serve more purposes; the resulting problem-solver would lose the elegance of a single, simple-ordered measure of "progress," but that is the price of moving from a first-order theory.)

Finally, we should point out that we do not need to invoke any mysterious additional mechanism for *creating* the clustering structure. Developmentally, one would assume, the earliest frames would tend to become the capitals of their later relatives, unless this is firmly prevented by experience, because each time the use of one stereotype is reasonably successful, its centrality is reinforced by another pointer from somewhere else. Otherwise, *the acquisition of new centers is in large measure forced upon us from the outside: by the words available in one's language; by the behavior of objects in one's environment; by what one is told by one's teachers, family, and general culture.* Of course, at each step the structure of the previous structure dominates the acquisition of the later. But in any case such forms and clusters should emerge from the interactions between the world and almost any memory-using mechanism; it would require more explanation were they *not found!*

3.6 ANALOGIES AND ALTERNATIVE DESCRIPTIONS

We have discussed the use of different frames of the same system to describe the same situation in different ways: for change of position in vision and for change of emphasis in language. Sometimes, in "problem-solving," we use two or more descriptions in a more complex way to construct an analogy or to apply two radically *different* kinds of analysis to the same situation. For *hard problems, one "problem space" is usually not enough!*

Suppose your car battery runs down. You believe that there is an electricity shortage and blame the generator.

The generator can be represented as a mechanical system: the rotor has a pulley wheel driven by a belt from the engine. Is the belt tight enough? Is it even there? The output, seen mechanically, is a cable to the battery or whatever. Is it intact? Are the bolts tight? Are the brushes pressing on the commutator?

Seen electrically, the generator is described differently. The rotor is seen as a flux-linking coil, rather than as a rotating device. The brushes and commutator are seen as electrical switches. The output is current along a pair of conductors leading from the brushes through control circuits to the battery.

We thus represent the situation in two quite different frame-systems. In one, the armature is a mechanical rotor with pulley; in the other, it is a conductor in a changing magnetic field. The same or analogous-elements share terminals of different frames, and the frame-transformations apply only to some of them.

The differences between the two frames are substantial. The entire mechanical chassis of the car plays the simple role, in the electrical frame, of one of the battery connections. The diagnostician has to use both representations. A failure of current to flow often means that an intended conductor is not acting like one. For this case, the basic transformation between the frames depends on the fact that electrical continuity is in general equivalent to firm mechanical attachment. Therefore, any conduction disparity revealed by electrical measurements should make us look for a corresponding disparity in the mechanical frame. In fact, since "repair" in this universe is synonymous with "mechanical repair," the diagnosis *must* end in the mechanical frame. Eventually, we might locate a defective mechanical junction and discover a loose connection, corrosion, wear, or whatever.

Why have two separate frames, rather than one integrated structure to represent the generator? I believe that in such a complex problem, one can never cope with many details at once. At each moment one must work within a reasonably simple frame-work. I contend that any problem that a person can solve at all is worked out at each moment in a small context and that the key operations in problem-solving are concerned with finding or constructing these working environments.

Indeed, finding an electrical fault requires moving between at least three frames: a visual one along with the electrical and

mechanical frames. If electrical evidence suggests a loose mechanical connection, one needs a visual frame to guide one's self to the mechanical fault.

Are there general methods for constructing adequate frames? The answer is both yes and no! There are some often-useful strategies for adapting old frames to new purposes; but I should emphasize that humans certainly have no magical way to solve *all* hard problems! One must not fall into what Papert calls the Superhuman-Human Fallacy and require a theory of human behavior to explain even things that people cannot really do!

One cannot expect to have a frame exactly right for any problem or expect always to be able to invent one. But we do have a good deal to work with, and it is important to remember the contribution of one's culture in assessing the complexity of problems people seem to solve. *The experienced mechanic need not routinely invent;* he already has engine representations in terms of ignition, lubrication, cooling, timing, fuel mixing, transmission, compression, and so forth. Cooling, for example, is already subdivided into fluid circulation, air flow, thermostasis, etc. Most "ordinary" problems are presumably solved by systematic use of the analogies provided by the transformations between pairs of these structures. The huge network of knowledge, acquired from school, books, apprenticeship, or whatever is interlinked by difference and relevancy pointers. No doubt the culture imparts a good deal of this structure by its conventional *use of the same words* in explanations of different views of a subject.

3.8 FRAMES AND PARADIGMS

Until that scholastic paradigm [the medieval 'impetus' theory] was invented, there were no pendulums, but only swinging stones, for scientists to see. Pendulums were brought into the world by something very like a paradigm-induced gestalt switch.

Do we, however, really need to describe what separates Galileo from Aristotle, or Lavoisier from Priestly, as a transformation of vision? Did these men really *see* different things when *looking at* the same sorts of objects? Is there any legitimate sense in which we can say they pursued their research in different worlds?

[I am] acutely aware of the difficulties created by saying that when Aristotle and Galileo looked at swinging stones, the first saw constrained fall, the second a pendulum. Nevertheless, I am convinced that we must learn to make sense of sentences that at least resemble these.

According to Kuhn's model of scientific evolution, normal science proceeds by using established descriptive schemes. Major changes result from new paradigms, new ways of describing things that lead to new methods and techniques. Eventually there is a redefining of "normal."

Now while Kuhn prefers to apply his own very effective redescription paradigm at the level of major scientific revolutions, it seems to me that the same idea applies as well to the microcosm of everyday thinking. Indeed, in that last sentence quoted, we see that Kuhn is seriously considering that the paradigms play a substantive rather than metaphorical role in visual perception, just as we have proposed for frames.

Whenever our customary viewpoints do not work well, whenever we fail to find effective frame systems in memory, we must construct new ones that bring out the right features. Presumably, the most usual way to do this is to build some sort of pair-system from two or more old ones and then edit or debug it to suit the circumstances. How might this be done? It is tempting to formulate the requirements, and then solve the construction problem.

But that is certainly not the usual course of ordinary thinking! Neither are requirements formulated all at once, nor is the new system constructed entirely by deliberate preplanning. Instead we recognize unsatisfied requirements, one by one, as deficiencies or "bugs," in the course of a sequence of modifications made to an unsatisfactory representation.

I think Papert (1972; see also Minsky, 1970) is correct in believing that the ability to diagnose and modify one's own procedures is a collection of specific and important "skills." *Debugging*, a fundamentally important component of intelligence, has its own special techniques and procedures. Every normal person is pretty good at them; or otherwise he would not have learned to see and talk! Although this essay is already speculative, I would like to point here to the theses of Goldstein (1974) and Sussman (1973) about the explicit use of *knowledge about debugging* in learning symbolic representations. They build new procedures to satisfy multiple requirements by such elementary but powerful techniques as:

1. Make a crude first attempt by the first order method of simply putting together procedures that *separately* achieve the individual goals.

2. If something goes wrong, try to characterize one of the defects as a *specific* (and undesirable) kind of interaction between two procedures.

3. Apply a debugging technique that, according to a record in memory, is good at repairing that *specific kind* of interaction.

4. Summarize the experience, to add to the "debugging techniques library," in memory.

These might seem simple-minded, but if the new problem is not too radically different from the old ones, they have a good chance to work, especially if one picks out the right first-order approximations. If the new problem *is* radically different, one should not expect *any* learning theory to work well. Without a structured cognitive map—without the "near misses," of Winston or a cultural supply of good training sequences of problems, we should not expect radically new paradigms to appear magically whenever we need them.

What are "kinds of interactions," and what are "debugging techniques?" The simplest, perhaps, are those in which the result of achieving a first goal interferes with some condition prerequisite for achieving a second goal. The simplest repair is to reinsert that prerequisite as a new condition. There are examples in which this technique alone cannot succeed because a prerequisite for the second goal is incompatible with the first. Sussman presents a more sophisticated diagnosis and repair method that recognizes this and exchanges the order of the goals. Goldstein considers related problems in a multiple description context.

If asked about important future lines of research on Artificial or Natural Intelligence, I would point to the interactions between these ideas and the problems of using multiple representations to deal with the same situation from several viewpoints. To carry out such a study, we need better ideas about interactions among the transformed relationships. Here the frame-system idea by itself begins to show limitations. Fitting together new representations from parts of old ones is clearly a complex process itself, and one that could be solved within the framework of our theory (if at all) only by an intricate bootstrapping. This, too, is surely a special skill with its own techniques. I consider it a crucial component of a theory of intelligence.

We must not expect complete success in the above enterprise; there is a difficulty, as Newell (1973) notes in a larger context:

'Elsewhere' is another view—possibly from philosophy—or other 'elsewheres' as well, since the views of man are multiple. Each view has its own questions. Separate views speak mostly past each other. Occasionally, of course, they speak to the same issue and then comparison is possible, but not often and not on demand.

6. Appendix: Criticism of the Logistic Approach

If one tries to describe processes of genuine thinking in terms of formal traditional logic, the result is often unsatisfactory; one has, then, a series of correct operations, but the sense of the process and what was vital, forceful, creative in it seems somehow to have evaporated in the formulations.
—M. Wertheimer (1959)

I here explain why I think more "logical" approaches will not work. There have been serious attempts, from as far back as Aristotle, to represent common sense reasoning by a "logistic" system—that is, one that makes a complete separation between

(1) "propositions" that embody specific information, and
(2) "syllogisms" or general laws of proper inference.

No one has been able successfully to confront such a system with a realistically large set of propositions. I think such attempts will continue to fail, because of the character of logistic in general rather than from defects of particular formalisms. (Most recent attempts have used variants of "first order predicate logic," but I do not think *that* is the problem.)

A typical attempt to simulate common-sense thinking by logistic systems begins in a microworld of limited complication. At one end are high-level goals such as "I want to get from my house to the Airport." At the other end we start with many small items— the *axioms*—like "The car is in the garage," "One does not go outside undressed," "To get to a place one should (on the whole) ... in its direction," etc. To make the system work, one designs

heuristic search procedures to "prove" the desired goal, or to produce a list of actions that will achieve it.

I will not recount the history of attempts to make both ends meet—but merely summarize my impression: in simple cases one can get such systems to "perform," but as we approach reality, the obstacles become overwhelming. The problem of finding suitable axioms—the problem of "stating the facts" in terms of always-correct, logical assumptions—is very much harder than is generally believed.

FORMALIZING THE REQUIRED KNOWLEDGE: Just constructing a knowledge base is a major intellectual research problem. Whether one's goal is logistic or not, we still know far too little about the contents and structure of common-sense knowledge. A "minimal" common-sense system must "know" something about cause-and-effect, time, purpose, locality, process, and types of knowledge. It also needs ways to acquire, represent, and use such knowledge. We need a serious epistemological research effort in this area. The essays of McCarthy (1969) and Sandewall (1970) are steps in that direction. I have no easy plan for this large enterprise; but the magnitude of the task will certainly depend strongly on the representations chosen, and I think that "Logistic" is already making trouble.

RELEVANCY: The problem of selecting relevance from excessive variety is a key issue! A modern epistemology will not resemble the old ones! Computational concepts are necessary and novel. Perhaps the better part of knowledge is not propositional in character, but interpropositional. For each "fact" one needs meta-facts about how it is to be used and when it should not be used. In McCarthy's "Airport" paradigm we see ways to deal with some interactions between "situations, actions, and causal laws" within a restricted microworld of things and actions. But though the system can make deductions implied by its axioms, it cannot be told when it should or should not make such deductions.

For example, one might want to tell the system to "not cross the road if a car is coming." But one cannot demand that the system "prove" no car is coming, for there will not usually be any such proof. In PLANNER, one can direct an *attempt* to prove that a car IS coming, and if the (limited) deduction attempt ends with

system. "Look right, look left" is a first approximation. But if one tells the system the real truth about speeds, blind driveways, probabilities of racing cars whipping around the corner, proof becomes impractical. If it reads in a physics book that intense fields perturb light rays, should it fear that a mad scientist has built an invisible car? We need to represent "usually"! Eventually it must understand the trade-off between mortality and accomplishment, for one can do nothing if paralyzed by fear.

MONOTONICITY: Even if we formulate relevancy restrictions, logistic systems have a problem in using them. In any logistic system, all the axioms are necessarily "permissive"—they all help to permit new inferences to be drawn. Each added axiom means more theorems; none can disappear. There simply is no direct way to add information to tell such a system about kinds of conclusions that should *not* be drawn! To put it simply: if we adopt enough axioms to deduce what we need, we deduce far too simply: if we adapt enough axioms to deduce what we need, we deduce far too many other things. But if we try to change this by adding axioms about relevancy, we still produce all the unwanted theorems, plus annoying statements about their irrelevancy.

Because Logicians are not concerned with systems that will later be enlarged, they can design axioms that permit only the conclusions they want. In the development of Intelligence the situation is different. One has to learn which features of situations are important and which kinds of deductions are not to be regarded seriously. The usual reaction to the "liar's paradox" is, after a while, to laugh. The conclusion is not to reject an axiom, but to reject the deduction itself! This raises another issue:

PROCEDURE-CONTROLLING KNOWLEDGE: The separation between axioms and deduction makes it impractical to include classificational knowledge about propositions. Nor can we include knowledge about management of deduction. A paradigm problem is that of axiomatizing everyday concepts of approximation or nearness. One would like nearness to be transitive:

(A near B) and (B near C) ==> (A near C)

but unrestricted application of this rule would make everything near everything else. One can try technical tricks like

(A near *1 B) AND (B near *1 C) ==> (A near *2 C)

and admit only (say) five grades of near *1, near *2, near *3, etc. One might invent analog quantities or parameters. But one cannot (in a Logistic system) decide to make a new kind of "axiom" to prevent applying transitivity after (say) three chained uses, conditionally, unless there is a "good excuse." I do not mean to propose a particular solution to the transitivity of nearness. (To my knowledge, no one has made a creditable proposal about it.) My complaint is that because of acceptance of Logistic, no one has freely explored this kind of procedural restriction.

COMBINATORIAL PROBLEMS: I see no reason to expect these systems to escape combinatorial explosions when given richer knowledge-bases. Although we see encouraging demonstrations in microworlds, from time to time, it is common in AI research to encounter high-grade performance on hard puzzles—given just enough information to solve the problem—but this does not often lead to good performance in larger domains.

CONSISTENCY and COMPLETENESS: A human thinker reviews plans and goal-lists as he works, revising his knowledge and policies about using it. One can program some of this into the theorem-proving program itself—but one really wants also to represent it directly, in a natural way, in the declarative corpus—for use in further introspection. Why then do workers try to make Logistic systems do the job? A valid reason is that the systems have an attractive simple elegance; if they worked, this would be fine. An invalid reason is more often offered: that such systems have a mathematical virtue because they are

(1) Complete—"All true statements can be proven"; and
(2) Consistent—"No false statements can be proven."

It seems not often realized that Completeness is no rare prize. It is a trivial consequence of any exhaustive search procedure, and any system can be "completed" by adjoining to it any other complete system and interlacing the computational steps. Consistency is more refined; it requires one's axioms to imply no contradictions. But I do not believe that consistency is necessary or even desirable in a developing intelligent system. No one is ever completely consistent. What is important is how one handles paradox or conflict, how one learns from mistakes, how one turns aside from suspected inconsistencies.

Because of this kind of misconception, Godel's Incompleteness Theorem has stimulated much foolishness about alleged differences between machines and men. No one seems to have noted its more "logical" interpretation: that enforcing consistency produces limitations. Of course there will be differences between humans (who are demonstrably inconsistent) and machines whose designers have imposed consistency. But it is not inherent in machines that they be programmed only with consistent logical systems. Those "philosophical" discussions all make these quite unnecessary assumptions! (I regard the recent demonstration of the consistency of modern set-theory, thus, as indicating that set-theory is probably inadequate for our purposes—not as reassuring evidence that set-theory is safe to use!)

A famous mathematician, warned that his proof would lead to a paradox if he took one more logical step, replied "Ah, but I shall not take that step." He was completely serious. A large part of ordinary (or even mathematical) knowledge resembles that in dangerous professions: When are certain actions unwise? When are certain approximations safe to use? When do various measures yield sensible estimates? Which self-referent statements are permissible if not carried too far? Concepts like "nearness" are too valuable to give up just because no one can exhibit satisfactory axioms for them. To summarize:

1. "Logical" reasoning is not flexible enough to serve as a basis for thinking: I prefer to think of it as a collection of heuristic methods, effective only when applied to starkly simplified schematic plans. The Consistency that Logic absolutely demands is not otherwise usually available—*and probably not even desirable!*—because consistent systems are likely to be too weak.

2. I doubt the feasibility of representing ordinary knowledge effectively in the form of many small, independently true propositions.

3. The strategy of complete separation of specific knowledge from general rules of inference is much too radical. We need more direct ways for linking fragments of knowledge to advice about *how* they are to be used.

accessible to deduction in the form of declarative statements; but this seems less urgent as we learn ways to manipulate structural and procedural descriptions.

I do not mean to suggest that "thinking" can proceed very far without something like "reasoning." We certainly need (and use) something like syllogistic deduction; but I expect mechanisms for doing such things to emerge in any case from processes for "matching" and "instantiation" required for other functions. Traditional formal logic is a technical tool for discussing either *everything that can be deduced from some data* or *whether a certain consequence can be so deduced*; it cannot discuss at all what *ought* to be deduced under ordinary circumstances. Like the abstract theory of Syntax, formal Logic without a powerful procedural semantics cannot deal with meaningful situations.

I cannot state strongly enough my conviction that the preoccupation with Consistency, so valuable for Mathematical Logic, has been incredibly destructive to those working on models of mind. At the popular level it has produced a weird conception of the potential capabilities of machines in general. At the "logical" level it has blocked efforts to represent ordinary knowledge, by presenting an unreachable image of a corpus of context-free "truths" that can stand almost by themselves. And at the intellect-modeling level it has blocked the fundamental realization that *thinking begins first with suggestive but defective plans and images that are slowly (if ever) refined and replaced by better ones.*

13 / Daniel G. Bobrow and Terry Winograd
An Overview of KRL, a Knowledge Representation Language

KRL represents one of the more ambitious efforts in the history of AI representation frameworks. Its scope ranged from representation of objects from multiple points of view to an elaborate description-matching framework to a complex process/control mechanism. As the authors put it, KRL is "a knowledge representation language that will integrate procedural knowledge with a richly structured declarative representation designed to combine logical adequacy with a concern for issues of memory structure and recognition-based reasoning processes." As such, it is among the more psychologically-inspired of the modern representation frameworks (but see [Maida and Shapiro, Chapter 9] for a different slant). KRL was also among the first to take head-on the idea of frame-like units as *descriptions* (see [Winograd, Chapter 20] for the immediate roots of this point of view, and [Maida and Shapiro, Chapter 9] and [Brachman, Chapter 10] for more on this). In addition, the work fits in well with the tradition initiated by Minsky in [Minsky, Chapter 12], advocating a complex form of resource-limited matching based on comparison to prototypes as the fundamental basis for reasoning. Bobrow and Winograd further stress that *associative* links are not derivable from the logical structure of descriptions, and therefore worry about access and indexing over and above expressive adequacy. KRL is also noted for having concretely specified how and why to do procedural attachment (see [Minsky, Chapter 12] and [Winograd, Chapter 20] for some suggestive comments on this issue), and meta-description (see [Davis and Buchanan, Chapter 22] for a related account). Ultimately, the KRL language was a failure, collapsing perhaps under the weight of its own features, but the attempt nonetheless stands out as the high point of a certain style of Knowledge Representation.

Appeared in *Cognitive Science* 1(1), 1977, 3–46.

An Overview of KRL, a Knowledge Representation Language*

DANIEL G. BOBROW

Xerox Palo Alto Research Center

TERRY WINOGRAD

Stanford University

This paper describes KRL, a **Knowledge Representation Language** designed for use in understander systems. It outlines both the general concepts which underlie our research and the details of KRL-0, an experimental implementation of some of these concepts. KRL is an attempt to integrate procedural knowledge with a broad base of declarative forms. These forms provide a variety of ways to express the logical structure of the knowledge, in order to give flexibility in associating procedures (for memory and reasoning) with specific pieces of knowledge, and to control the relative accessibility of different facts and descriptions. The formalism for declarative knowledge is based on *structured conceptual objects* with associated *descriptions*. These objects form a network of *memory units* with several different sorts of linkages, each having well-specified implications for the retrieval process. Procedures can be associated directly with the internal structure of a conceptual object. This *procedural attachment* allows the steps for a particular operation to be determined by characteristics of the specific entities involved.

The control structure of KRL is based on the belief that the next generation of intelligent programs will integrate data-directed and goal-directed processing by using multiprocessing. It provides for a priority-ordered multiprocess agenda with explicit (user-provided) strategies for scheduling and resource allocation. It provides *procedure directories* which operate along with *process frameworks* to allow procedural parameterization of the fundamental system processes for building, comparing, and retrieving memory structures. Future development of KRL will include integrating procedure definition with the descriptive formalism.

AN OVERVIEW OF KRL

This paper is an introduction to KRL, a **Knowledge Representation Language**, whose construction is part of a long-term program to build systems for language understanding, and through these to develop theories of human language use. What we describe is a formal computer language for representing knowledge. It has been shaped by our understanding of what is needed to build natural language understanders, and by analogies with human information processing, particularly in the areas of memory and attention.

Our ideas are in the course of active expansion and modification, and there

*Requests for reprints should be sent to Dr. Daniel G. Bobrow, Computer Science Laboratory, Xerox Palo Alto Research Center, 3333 Coyote Hill Road, Palo Alto, CA. 94304.

will be many changes before KRL comes close to our goals. We have implemented a subset of our ideas in a system which we call KRL-0, and the facilities we describe here are those that existed on May 1, 1976. We have conducted some experiments in system building in KRL-0 to test its utility and habitability. Although we have planned a number of features that will be incorporated in its successors, we feel it useful to present our current ideas for discussion and evaluation.

1. WHY WE ARE DOING IT

There is currently no suitable base on which to build sophisticated systems and theories of language understanding. A complete understander system demands the integration of a number of complex components, each resting on those below, as illustrated in Fig. 1. Current systems, even the best ones, often resemble a house of cards. The researchers are interested in the higher levels, and try to build up the minimum of supporting props at the lower levels. The standard available bases, such as LISP, QLISP, CONNIVER, production systems, etc., are at a low enough level that many middle layers must be built up in an ad hoc way for each project. The result is an extremely fragile structure, which may reach impressive heights, but collapses immediately if swayed in the slightest from the specific domain (often even the specific examples) for which it was built.

Much of the work in AI has involved fleshing in bits and pieces of human knowledge structures, and we would like to provide a systematic framework in which they can be assembled. Someone who wishes to build a system for a particular task, or who wishes to develop theories of specific linguistic

TASK DOMAINS:
    Travel Arrangements, Medical Diagnosis, Story Analysis, etc.

LINGUISTIC DOMAINS:
    Syntax and Parsing Strategies; Morphological and Lexical Analysis;
    Discourse Structures; Semantic Structures, etc.

COMMON SENSE DOMAINS:
    Time, Events and States;   Plans and Motivations;   Actions and
    Causes;
    Knowledge and Belief Structures; Hypothetical Worlds

BASIC STRATEGIES:
    Reasoning; Knowledge Representation; Search Strategies

UNDERLYING COMPUTER PROGRAMMING LANGUAGE AND ENVIRONMENT
    Representation Language; Debugging Tools; Monitoring Tools

FIG. 1   A layered view of a language understanding system.

phenomena should be able to build on a base that includes well thought out structures at all levels. In providing a framework, we impose a kind of uniformity (at least in style) which is based on our own intuitions about how knowledge is organized. We state our major intuitions here as a set of aphorisms, and provide justification and explanation in the body of the paper.

Knowledge should be organized around conceptual entities with associated descriptions and procedures.

A description must be able to represent partial knowledge about an entity and accommodate multiple descriptors which can describe the associated entity from different viewpoints.

An important method of description is comparison with a known entity, with further specification of the described instance with respect to the prototype.

Reasoning is dominated by a process of recognition in which new objects and events are compared to stored sets of expected prototypes, and in which specialized reasoning strategies are keyed to these prototypes.

Intelligent programs will require multiple active processes with explicit user-provided scheduling and resource allocation heuristics.

Information should be clustered to reflect use in processes whose results are affected by resource limitation and differences in information accessibility.

A knowledge representation language must provide a flexible set of underlying tools, rather than embody specific commitments about either processing strategies or the representation of specific areas of knowledge.

2. DESCRIPTION AS THE BASIS FOR A DECLARATIVE LANGUAGE

A natural organization for declarative knowledge is to center it around a set of *conceptual entities* with associated *descriptions*. Much of the detailed syntax and data structuring in KRL flows from a desire to explore the consequences of an object-centered factorization of knowledge, rather than the more common factorization in which knowledge is structured as a set of facts, each referring to one or more objects.

Objects, relations, scenes, and events are all examples of conceptual entities that can be associated with appropriate descriptions in KRL. A description is fundamentally *intensional*—the structure of the description can be used in recognizing a conceptual entity and comparing it with others. The three underlying operations in the system are *augmenting* a description to incorporate new knowledge, *matching* two given descriptions to see if they are compatible

for the current purposes, and *seeking* referents for entities that match a specified description. In this section we will describe the forms of description available in the system, the dimensions of matching as we see them, and the basic facilities for context dependent search and retrieval.

2.1 Multiple Descriptions of Conceptual Entities

A *description* is made up of one or more *descriptors*. For example, the description associated with a particular object in a scene might include descriptors corresponding to "the thing next to a table," "something made of wood," "something colored green," "something for sitting on," and "a chair." Some of these descriptors express facts that might be thought of as additional propositions about the objects, while others reflect different viewpoints for description by comparison.

The description of a complex event such as *kissing* involves one viewpoint from which it is a physical event, and should be described in terms of body parts, physical motion, contact, etc. The descriptors used from this viewpoint would have much in common with those used to describe other acts such as eating and testing someone's temperature with your lips. In the same description, we want to be able to describe kissing from a second viewpoint, as a social act involving relationships between the participants with particular combinations of motivations and emotions. Viewing *kissing* in this way, it would be described analogously to other social acts including hugging, caressing, and appropriate verbal communications. In general we believe that the description of a complex object or event cannot be broken down into a single set of primitives, but must be expressed through multiple views.[1]

In addition to containing descriptors corresponding to different viewpoints, a description can combine different modes of description. These include:

Assigning an object to membership in a *category* (such as "is a city"); stating its role in a complex object or event (the "destination" of a particular trip);

providing a unique identifier (this includes using a proper name like "Boston");

stating a relationship in which the object is a participant (being "to the north of Providence");

asserting a complex logical formula which is true of the object ("Either this person must be over 65, or a widow or widower with dependent children.");

describing an object in terms of membership in a set, or a set in terms of the objects it contains ("One of the 50 Model Cities");

[1]MERLIN (Moore & Newell, 1973) was an early attempt to use multiple viewpoints of this sort.

combining these other descriptors into time-dependent or contingent descriptions ("The place you are today").

In creating a set of descriptor forms, we have been guided by our intuitions about how they will be used in reasoning processes. They represent an alternative to the standard, more uniform notations (such as predicate calculus) that were developed for the purposes of formal logic and mathematics. We believe that it is more useful and perspicuous to preserve in the notation many of the conceptual differences which are reflected in natural language, even though they could be reduced to a smaller basis set. We expect this to ease the task of designing the strategies which guide the application of declarative knowledge.

We believe that multiple descriptions containing redundant information are used in the human representation system to trade off memory space for computation depth, and that computer systems can take advantage of the same techniques. The choice of where to put redundancy provides further structure for memory, and can be used to limit search and deduction. As a simple example, an understander system might know that every plumber is a person, and that Mary is a plumber. The memory unit for Mary would contain a descriptor stating that she is a plumber, and would very likely also contain an explicit descriptor stating that she is a person. This is redundant, but without it the system would be continually re-deducing simple facts, since personhood is a basic property often used in reasoning about entities. Memory structure in KRL is organized in a way that makes it possible to include redundant information for immediacy while keeping the ability to derive information not explicitly stated.

2.2 Descriptions Based on Comparison to Other Individuals and Prototypes

In designing KRL we have emphasized the importance of describing an entity by comparing it to another entity described in the memory. The object being used as a basis for comparison (which we call the prototype) provides a perspective from which to view the object being described. The details of the comparison can be thought of as a further specification of the prototype. Viewed very abstractly, this is a commitment to a wholistic as opposed to reductionistic view of representation. It is quite possible (and we believe natural) for an object to be represented in a knowledge system only through a set of such comparisons. There would be no simple sense in which the system contained a "definition" of the object, or a complete description in terms of its structure. However if the set of comparisons is large and varied enough, the system can have a functionally complete representation, since it could find the answer to any question about the object. This represents a fundamental difference in spirit between the KRL notion of representation, and standard logical representations based on formulas built out of primitive predicates.

In describing an object by comparison, the standard for reference is often not a specific individual, but a stereotypical individual which represents the typical member of a class. Such a prototype has a description which may be true of no one member of the class, but combines the default knowledge applied to members of the class in the absence of specific information. This default knowledge can itself be in the form of intensional description (for example, the prototypical family has "two or three" children) and can be stated in terms of other prototypes.

A single object or event can be described with respect to several prototypes, with further specifications from the perspective of each. The fact that last week Rusty flew to San Francisco would be expressed by describing the event as a typical instance of Travel with the mode specified as Airplane, destination San Francisco, etc. It might also be described as a Visit with the actor being Rusty, the friends a particular group of people, the interaction warm, etc.

The further specifications in a description by comparison can provide more detail to go along with less specific properties associated with the prototype, or can contradict the default assumptions which are assumed true in the absence of more specific information. The default for the destination of a trip simply specifies that it is some city, and in a particular event is further specified to be Boston. The default for a trip also includes the fact that the traveler starts from and ends at home, which might be violated in a specific instance. A comparison can be based on an individual rather than an abstract prototype ("He's like Brian, but shorter and with red hair."), again with the assumption that the properties of the prototype individual are assumed true of the individual being described unless explicitly counterindicated. It has been pointed out in many places how important it is to make heavy use of typical and expected properties in contexts in which the reasoner has incomplete information about the world, and cannot prove logically that a particular individual has a desired property.[2] It is important to see this analysis as an intuition about how people structure descriptions, rather than as a specific technical device. Many of the mechanisms proposed in the literature on memory representation (e.g., semantic networks, frames, etc.) can be used in a style compatible with this kind of inheritance of properties.[3] We emphasize perspectives as a fundamental part of the notation. Other systems for simulation of human cognitive processing have used similar ideas[4] with further specifications which must follow constraints specified in the prototype.

---

[2] The use of prototypes is the subject of much current research, in computer science (e.g., Minsky, 1975), psychology (e.g., Rosch & Mervis, 1975), and linguistics (e.g., Fillmore, 1975).

[3] See Winograd (1975a) for a discussion of property inheritance, and Woods (1975) for a discussion of the issues involved in building networks with sufficient intensional information.

[4] Schank (1975a) uses conceptual dependency primitives as prototypes, with constraints on objects which can fill various roles; Norman, Rumelhart, and the LNR Research Group (1975) allow constraints on arguments of processes whose prototypes are word definitions.

2.3 The Detailed Structure of Units and Perspectives

In Sections 2.1 and 2.2 we presented our overall notion of the structure of descriptions. In order to better discuss the ways in which descriptions are used, we will introduce in this section some specific notations of KRL. Through the remainder of the paper, terms such as "unit," "perspective," and "description" will be used in the narrower technical sense defined here.

The data structures of KRL are built of descriptions, clustered together into structures called *units*, that serve as unique mental referents for entities and categories. Each unit has a unique *name*, is assigned to a *category type* (see below), and has one or more named *slots* containing descriptions of entities associated with the conceptual entity referred to by the unit as a whole. Slots are used among other things to describe those substructures of a unit that are significant for comparison. Each slot has a *slot name* which is unique within the unit, and significant only with respect to that unit. One distinguished slot in each unit (named SELF) is used to describe the entity represented by the unit.

Associated with each slot is a set of procedures which can be activated under certain conditions of use of the unit. The use of this *procedural attachment* is described further in Section 3.1. Our convention is to capitalize the initial letter of unit names, but not of slot names. Each description is a list of *descriptors*, each with a set of associated *features* (discussed at the end of Section 2.4). There is a limited set of distinct descriptor types (twelve types in the May 1 version), each with a distinct syntactic form. The descriptor type used for description by comparison is called a *perspective*. An entity is further specified in a perspective by further describing its slots. A perspective is expressed in KRL-0 notation:

(a *prototype* with *identifier*$_1$ = *fillerdescription*$_1$ · · ·
identifier$_n$ = *fillerdescription*$_n$

where *prototype* names a unit being used as the basis for the comparison, there are indefinitely many pairs of the form *identifier* = *fillerdescription*, and each *identifier* is either a slot name naming a slot in the prototype unit, or a description which matches only one of the slot descriptions in the prototype unit. Thus the descriptor (a Person) when used to describe an object represents the fact that the object is one instance of the general class *Person*. A descriptor (a Person with name = "Joe") implies that *name* is a slot associated with the unit for *Person*, and would be used to describe a particular individual. The descriptor:

(a Person with
name = "Joe"
(an Address) = "1004 Main Street")

includes both the name and address information, and assumes that there is only one slot in the unit for *Person* whose description could be matched by the descriptor (an Address). Thus a perspective combines classification with a set of

bindings called *fillers*, which establishes the correspondence between specific descriptions (often indicating individuals and roles associated with the prototype unit in general, as indicated by the pairing of the identifiers and additional descriptions.

In Fig. 2 we show some simple units which describe Rusty's trip to San Francisco. These illustrate some KRL-0 notation using a simplified example. The overall syntax is like that of LISP, using paired delimiters as an explicit representation of the tree structure. Brackets [···] enclose each unit, and angles <···> enclose each slot in a unit. Each complex descriptor form is delimited by parentheses (···), and braces {···} are used to combine multiple descriptors into a single description. As in LISP, division of text into separate lines and indentation are used to clarify the structure for human readers; they are not used to convey syntax information to the system.

2.3.1 Categories of Units

The *unit* is a formal data structure in the KRL language for descriptions. It is used for entities at a number of different levels of abstraction—individuals, prototypes, relations, etc. It can be thought of as a mechanism for providing a larger structure which encompasses a set of descriptions, relating them to a set of

```
[Travel UNIT Abstract                    ...Travel is the unit name.
  <SELF  (an Event) >                        Its category type is Abstract.
                                          ...description of the Travel unit itself.
  <mode (OR Plane Auto Bus)>             ...Event, Plane, Auto etc. are known units
                                          ...either Plane or Auto or Bus
  <destination (a City)>]                ...can fill the slot named mode.


[Visit UNIT Specialization               ... a specific category of SocialInteraction
  <SELF (a SocialInteraction)>
  <visitor (a Person)>
  <visitees (SetOf (a Person))>]


[Event137 UNIT Individual                ...an event described by comparison
                                             with two different prototypes
  <SELF  {(a Visit with                  ...The actor is the known unit Rusty
           visitor =  Rusty
           visitees = (Items Danny Terry)]    ...Items indicates a set containing at least
                                                 Danny and Terry

          (a Travel with                 ...SanFrancisco is a unit described
           destination = SanFrancisco         as a City
           mode = Plane)}>]
```

FIG. 2 KRL representation of Rusty's trip to San Francisco.

procedures. Each unit has a category type, selected from: *Basic, Abstract, Specialization, Individual, Manifestation, Relation,* and *Proposition*. The category types determine certain modes of operation for the basic system procedures which manipulate descriptions.

Abstract, basic, and specialization. Units of these three types are used for categories such as *Person, Integer, MakeReservation*, etc. These units are used principally as prototypes for perspectives; the distinction between them is used primarily by the matcher.

Basic categories represent a simple nonoverlapping partition of the world into different kind of objects (such as *dog, bacteria,* ...). The matcher assumes that no individual is in two distinct basic categories. Therefore, quick tests of basic category match or conflict can be used in a many cases to decide whether a specific object fits a description. This use of simple disjoint categories corresponds to the use of selection restrictions as proposed in some linguistic and semantic theories[5] and data types in programming.

Specializations represent further distinctions within a basic category (such as *Poodle,* or *E. Coli*). A specialized prototype will have descriptions and procedures associated with it which are more specific than those for a basic category. In general, they are more useful for their procedural attachment and described properties than for any uniform treatment by the matcher. The description of a specialized prototype can indicate a *primary* perspective which describes it as a subclass of some basic category or other specialization. The partial tree formed by these primary links[6] is used by the matcher in comparing individuals from two categories which are not explicitly comparable.

An *abstract category* (such as *action* or *living thing*) primarily serves as a way of chunking a set of descriptions and procedures to be inherited by any entity described by a perspective for which the abstract unit is a prototype. Very general problem-solving information will often be attached at this level of abstraction. There is no commitment at what level of concepts in the domain should be represented at what level of categorization. The specific three types are based on psychological studies (Rosch, 1975; Rosch & Mervis, 1975) that human reasoning makes extensive use of a layered system of categories. The choice of whether a particular prototype (such as *Person* or *Visit*) should be basic, abstract, or a specialization depends on the way in which descriptions are built up and used in matching. What is provided is a mechanism by which the careful use of levels can result in achieving many of the efficiency benefits of semantic marker mechanisms and classification trees.

Individuals. The KRL matcher and other primitive mechanisms for building

descriptions assumes that different individuals are different unique entities in the world being modeled. For example, no individual can match (in a simple sense) a different individual. An inconsistency is signaled whenever there is an attempt to use pointers to two different individuals as descriptors in a single description. However, there are no built-in assumptions about how individuality should be assigned. The definition of what should constitute an individual within a domain is relative to a particular set of reasoning purposes. As a simple example, in the air travel domain, a particular flight (including date) could be an individual, with the flight number as a property (filling a slot), or, alternatively, each flight in the schedule (by number) could be treated as an individual, with a particular flight instance represented as a manifestation (see below).

Manifestations. Often it is useful to group together a set of descriptions which belong to some individual. There are three main cases in which we anticipate this need, and units with category type *manifestation* can be used for all of them:

1. *Further specified individuals:* A manifestation can be used to provide a single memory unit (for purposes of retrieval and content-dependent description) containing a set of descriptions belonging to an individual within one context. For example, we might separate out the physical properties of an object for which we also have functional or historical descriptions, or the description of some person as a scientist from the description of that person as a friend.

2. *Contingent properties:* An individual can be described using time-dependent descriptions without creating a separate manifestation. However, it is often useful to collect a set of descriptions which are true at some time (or in some hypothesized world) and treat them as *time-independent descriptions* of a manifestation which represents the individual at that particular time.

3. *Ghosts:* A representation must enable us to describe entities whose unique identity is not known. There are many cases in which we may know many properties of some object without knowing which of the known objects in our world it is. Such objects have at times been called "formal objects" (Sussman, 1975) and "ghosts" (Minsky, 1975). A standard detective story plot involves knowing that one of the people in a house is a murderer, knowing many properties of the murderer, and not knowing which individual it is. The unit used to represent the murderer is a manifestation that has no associated individual.

Relations and propositions. An abstract relationship, such as the relative magnitude of two numbers, can be described using the ideas of slots and description we have used so far. There is a unit, with category class *relation*, which represents the relationship (or predicate) as an abstract mapping; a *proposition* unit represents each instantiation of the relationship. The truth value of a proposition is specified explicitly rather than being determined as an implicit consequence of its existence in the data base.

[5] This includes much of the work on semantics associated with transformational grammar (e.g., Katz & Fodor, 1964), AI formalisms such as conceptual dependency (Schank, 1975a), and most forms of case grammar (see Bruce, 1975, for a summary).

[6] This tree corresponds to a simple generalization hierarchy, as discussed in Winograd (1975a).

2.4 The Family of Descriptors

Each descriptor in a description is an independent characterization of the object associated with the description. The variety of descriptor types corresponds to the notion of natural description discussed above. Each descriptor type is intended to express a different mode of describing conceptual objects. The syntax of descriptors depends on key words (such as *a, the, from, which*) based on analogy with simple English phrases. They are mnemonic indicators for a set of precisely defined structures within the formalism.

This set of descriptors was not designed with the goal of boiling everything down to the smallest possible set of mechanisms. On the contrary, it is based on an attempt to provide a simple and natural way of stating information conceptualized in different ways. There is a great deal of overlap. For example, the notion of "bachelor" might be represented in any of the following ways:

There could be a prototype unit for *Bachelor*, with an individual described as

(a Bachelor with. . .)

Bachelorhood could be represented indirectly by having a prototype for *MalePerson* and *Adult*, and a predicate for *IsMarried*, and using the description:

{(a MalePerson) (an Adult) (NOT (which IsMarried))}

There could be a unit representing a *Marriage* with slots for the *malePartner* and *femalePartner*, and a description:

{(a MalePerson) (an Adult)
(NOT (the malePartner from (a Marriage)))}

There could be a one-place predicate, *IsBachelor*. The predicate definition might (but need not) include a special procedural test for bachelorhood. An individual would then be described using the *predication*

(which IsBachelor)

These KRL forms are described in general in Fig. 3. No one of these forms is automatically primary. All of them could coexist, and be defined in terms of each other. The system provides the necessary reasoning mechanisms to interrelate the different forms in which essentially equivalent information could appear, and the hope is that additional knowledge (especially procedural knowledge) which is best stated with respect to any one form can be represented directly. Our intuition leads us to believe that prototypes and perspectives will most often serve as the fundamental organizing representation, with the others serving to provide secondary information.

In order to demonstrate the different uses of these descriptors, we present here a more extended example. It is based on a hypothetical system that acts as a travel assistant, making reservations and computing costs of trips. As with the example above, this is greatly oversimplified and is not intended as a careful

---

Descriptor name: direct pointer

Format: a unit name, number, string, or quoted LISP object

Use: A pointer to units, or to data directly in the description. Provides a unique identifier (this includes using a proper name like "Boston")

Examples: Block17, PaloAlto, 356, "a string", (QUOTE (A PIECE (OF LIST STRUCTURE)))

****

Descriptor name: perspective

Format: (a *prototype* with $identifier_1 = filler_1$ ... $identifier_n = filler_n$)

Use: Assigns an object to membership in a category (such as "city"). A comparison of the current object with the "prototype", with slots further specifying this object

Examples: (a Trip with destination = Boston airline = TWA)

****

Descriptor name: specification

Format: (the *slotSpecifier* from view *targetDescription*)

Use: Specifies the current object in terms of its role in a perspective of prototype: "view". States a role in a complex object or event (e.g., the "destination" of a particular trip)

Examples: (the actor from Act (a Chase with quarry = {Car22 (a Dodge)})

****

Descriptor name: predication

Format: (which *predicateName* . *predicateArgs*)

Use: Describes a relationship in which the object is a participant (being "to the North of Providence"). Defined in terms of a specification. A way of specifying an object in terms of a relation and arguments; allows special procedural attachment.

Examples: (which Owns (a Dog)) (which IsBetween Block17 (a Pyramid))

****

Descriptor name: logical boolean

Format: (OR . *booleanArgs*) or (XOR . *booleanArgs*) or (NOT *booleanArg*)

Use: Simple logical connectives. A description is an implicit AND of descriptors, thus AND is not needed

Examples: (OR (a Dog) {(a Cat)(which hasColor Brown)})
(NOT (a Pet with owner = (a Student)))

****

FIG. 3 Different descriptor types in KRL-0 (a partial list).

Descriptor name: restriction

Format: (theOne restrictionDesc)

Use: Marks the enclosed description as being sufficient to refer to a unique object in context

Examples: (theOne {(a Mouse)(which Owns (a Dog))})

****

Descriptor name: selection

Format: (using selectionDesc

selectFrom selectionPattern₁ ~ selection₁ ...

selectionPatternₙ ~ selectionₙ

otherwise defaultSelection)

Use: This is a declarative form corresponding to CASE or SELECT statements in programming languages.

Examples: (using (the age from Person ThisOne)

selectFrom (which isLessThan 2) ~ Infant

(which isAtLeast 12) ~ Adult

otherwise Child)

****

Descriptor name: set specification

Format: one of: (SetOf setElementDescription), (In . setDescription),

(Items . elements), (NotItems . elements), (AllItems . elements),

(ListOf . elements), (Sequence . elements),

Use: These descriptors allow specification of partial information about sets, sequences and lists. Describes an object in terms of membership in a set, or a set in terms of the objects it contains

Examples: (SetOf {(an Integer)(which hasFactor 2)})

... all elements are even numbers

(Items 2 4)

... at least 2 and 4 are in this set

(AllItems 2 4 64 {(an Integer)(which hasFactor 3)})

... a four element set

(NotItems 51)

... 51 is not in this set

(In {(SetOf (an Integer) (Items 2 5 8) (NotItems 4)})

... describes an object in a set of integers which

contains at least 2 5 8, and not 4

****

Fig. 3 Continued.

Descriptor name: contingency

Format: (during timeSpecification then contingentDescription)

Use: Specifies a time (or hypothetical world) dependent description.

Examples: (during State24 then (the top from (a Stack with height = 3)))

... part of the description of an individual block

(during (a Dream with dreamer = Jacob) then (an Angel))

... part of the description of an individual person

****

Fig. 3 Continued.

analysis of the travel domain. Figures 4 and 5 show a number of units with which we construct our examples. There is a basic unit for *Person*, and the different things we might know about a person are further grouped according to the ways they are used in this system. A person viewed as a *Customer* has a set of properties different from a person viewed as a *Traveller*. These specialized units can share information which is generally true of people. The decision of how to group the slots which make up units is up to the programmer and the purpose of the representation. In this example, *age* as associated with a traveller is that of *Infant*, *Child*, or *Adult*, the necessary distinctions for fare determination, while age for a *Person* is an integer.

Figure 6 shows a description of an individual traveller, G0043, described from two perspectives using these basic units. These three figures use a number of different types of descriptors, including specifications, set descriptors, predications, and units representing individuals. Individuals are either LISP objects (such as the string "*Juan*", and the integer 3) or units, such as *UniversalCharge*. Specifications provide a way to refer to fillers in perspectives associated with either the unit in which they appear or other units. The descriptor (*the age from Person G0043*) would refer to the age of the individual referred to by the unit named *G0043* when viewed as a *Person* (and thus is an integer), while (*the age from Traveller G0043*) refers to his age as a *Traveller*, and thus is one of *Infant*, *Child*, or *Adult*. Specifications can be nested. The special unit *ThisOne* is interpreted to refer to the entity being described when the description is used as a prototype. Thus, for example, the descriptor:

(the preferredAirports from City (the homeTown from Person ThisOne))

which appears in the unit for *Traveller* includes a nesting of one implicit and one explicit **target**. The descriptor (*the hometown from Person ThisOne*) is interpreted as referring to whatever fills the *hometown* slot in a perspective whose prototype is *Person*. The descriptor (*the localAirports from City* {···}) is based on the unit for *City*, which has a slot *localAirports*. This descriptor assumes that

```
[Person UNIT Basic
  <SELF>      ... There is no description for Person since it is not further
                 analyzed in the travel planning task

  <firstName (a String)>
  <lastName (a String)>
  <age (an Integer)>  ...A person's age in years; distinct from the age slot
                 in the unit for Traveller.

  <hometown {(a City) PaloAlto ; DEFAULT}>>
  ...semicolons are used to attach features to individual
     descriptors. Unless otherwise specified, the hometown of a
     Person will be assumed to be PaloAlto (which is in turn a unit
     described as a City).

  <streetAddress (an Address)>]


[Traveller UNIT Specialization
  <SELF (a Person)>   ...a specialization of the unit Person
  <age {(XOR Infant Child Adult)
     ...the age for any specific Traveller will be one of these units
     (using (the age from Person ThisOne) selectFrom
       (which isLessThan 2)  ~ Infant
       (which isGreaterThan 11)  ~ Adult
       otherwise Child)}>
     ...the selection descriptor provides a way of determining which
        case this is from the age field in the view of this Traveller
        viewed as a Person

  <preferredAirport {(In (the localAirports from City
                          (the hometown from Person ThisOne)))
                      ; DEFAULT
                      (an Airport)}>>
     ...the airport is found in the set of preferred airports found
        from the City in the hometown slot from a view of this
        Traveller viewed as a Person


[Customer UNIT Specialization
  <SELF (a Person)>
  <billingAddress {(an Address)
                   (the streetAddress from Person ThisOne)
                   ; DEFAULT}>
  <credit (a CreditCard)>]
```

Fig. 4   Some units for an airline travel system.

```
[Airport UNIT Basic
  <SELF>
  <location (a City)>]

[City UNIT Basic
  <SELF>
  <localAirports
     (SetOf (an Airport with location = ThisOne)) ; DEFAULT}>>]

[PaloAlto UNIT Individual
  <SELF (a City with localAirports = (Items SJO SFO OAK))>]
  ...these airports are units too

[SJO UNIT Individual
  <SELF (an Airport with location = SanJose )>]

[UniversalCharge UNIT Individual
  <SELF (a CreditCompany)>]

[Magnitude UNIT Relation
  <SELF (an ArithmeticRelation)
     (TRIGGERS (ToTest ...some LISP code appears here...))>
  <greater (a Quantity)>
  <lesser (a Quantity)>]

[IsGreaterThan PREDICATE Magnitude greater lesser]
  ... defines the Predicate IsGreaterThan with focus being the slot
      greater in Magnitude.  The argument which follows the predicate is
      to fill the lesser slot.  This predicate is used in predications having
      a form like (which IsGreater Than 2) as an equivalent for
      (the greater from Magnitude (a Magnitude with lesser = 2))

[IsLessThan PREDICATE Magnitude lesser greater]
  ... a second predication based on Magnitude, with its focus on lesser
```

Fig. 5   Some units and predicates used in travel information.

In the case in which a town had only one airport, this could be used directly to find the departure airport.

The predication (*which IsLessThan 2*) is a descriptor using the predicate *IsLessThan* which relates pairs of numbers, and in turn is based on a unit *Magnitude*. Predicates are defined with respect to a unit in which the arguments to the predicate are among the slots. Two different predicates are defined in terms of the *Magnitude* relation, as shown in Fig. 5. This unit includes in its SELF slot a procedure to test for the truth of the relation.

A predication is always used in describing one specific argument, as opposed to a proposition relating several variables in formal logic, which states the relationship without focusing on any one argument. Figure 7 shows another example of multiple predicates based on a single unit. In some cases, the

the object which is the *hometown* specified by the embedded specification can be viewed as a *City*.

There is a group of descriptors based on sets which have the obvious intuitive interpretations. In the example, the *localAirports* for a *City* are described as a set each of whose members is an *Airport*. The default for *preferredAirports* is described as an unspecified member of the set of local airports for the hometown.

2.4.1 Features and Meta-Descriptions

Often it is important to represent knowledge about knowledge. KRL allows any descriptor to have associated with it a *feature* (a lisp atom) or a *meta-description* (a full-fledged unit characterizing the descriptor viewed as a piece of knowledge). In the example of Fig. 4, there are descriptors marked with the feature *Default*, indicating that they can be assumed valid in the absence of other information, but should be superseded by any other information, and should not be used in looking for contradictions. Two other features are used in standard ways by the matching, searching, and data-adding routines: *Criterial*, indicating the set of descriptors whose satisfaction can be counted as proving a match, even if there are other descriptors around; and *Primary*, indicating the primary perspective for inheritance of properties in a hierarchy.

The ability to associate a complete unit at this meta-level makes it possible to have representations which include facts about facts (e.g., justifications, histories of when things were learned or inferred, interdependencies between assumptions, etc.). We have not yet worked out a standard notation for use at this level. As we build different domain programs, we will develop a set of standard units for talking about descriptors and propositions, and a set of facilities for modifying and using them when appropriate.

2.5 Description Matching as a Framework for Reasoning

We believe that reasoning is dominated by a process of *recognition* in which new objects and events are compared to a stored set of expected prototypes.[7] The key part of a recognition process is a *description matcher* which serves as a *framework* for comparing descriptions. We have intentionally used the term *matching* for a range of functions which is broader than its standard use in AI languages.

First, we have separated the issue of indexed data base retrieval from that of matching two descriptions. In Section 2.7 we deal separately with the processes of indexing, context searching, and retrieval. Our matcher takes two inputs: a pattern, and a specific object to be tested. Second, we use the abstract concept of matching in a very general sense, to include all sorts of reasoning processes that are used to decide whether a given entity fits a given description. Much of what is usually thought of as "deduction" comes under this heading, as do the notions which Moore and Newell (1973) have called "mapping."

We think of the matching process as a *framework* because the user has choices along several dimensions which determine how the matcher operates. In its simplest form, the matcher compares the exact forms of two given representa-

---

different predicates focus on different parts of the total relationship, as in the case of *IsHusbandOf* and *IsMotherOf* which relate different slots in the *Family* unit. In other cases, they simply provide different points of view by choosing a different argument as the implicit primary argument, as in the difference between *IsHusbandOf* and *IsWifeOf*. Each predicate can have associated procedures for proving and matching both for the relationship as a whole, and the particular focus of its use. Except for this procedural attachment, and for economy of writing, predicates and predictions can be replaced in a uniform way by specifications. For example, the following two descriptors are equivalent based on the definitions in Fig. 7:

(which IsHusbandOf Mary)
(the maleParent from (a Family with femaleParent = Mary))

```
[G0043 UNIT Individual
  <SELF {(a Person with
      firstName = "Juan"
      lastName = {(a ForeignName)
                  (a String with firstCharacter = "M")}
      ... These descriptors give partial information.  A unique
          string need not be specified in describing a name
      age = (which IsGreaterThan 21))
    (a Traveller with
      preferredAirport = SJO
      age = Adult)
    (a Customer with
      credit = (a CreditCard with
                  company = UniversalCharge
                  number = "G45-7923-220")}>]
```

FIG. 6   A unit describing a specific traveller.

```
[Family UNIT Abstract
  <SELF>
  <femaleParent {(a Person)(a Female)}>
  <maleParent {(a Person)(a Male)}>
  <children (SetOf (a Person))>]

[IsWifeOf PREDICATE Family femaleParent maleParent
  (TRIGGERS (ToTest ...some LISP code appears here...))]
    ...only this predicate has a special trigger

[IsHusbandOf PREDICATE Family maleParent femaleParent]

[IsMotherOf PREDICATE Family femaleParent (In children)]
```

FIG. 7   Multiple predicates defined on the basis of one relation.

---

[7]This basic approach has been advocated as "frame theory" by Minsky (1975) and Winograd (1974—Lecture 1), as "scripts" by Schank (1975b), and as "Beta-structures" by Moore and Newell (1973). There are many related notions in the current AI literature.

by the syntactic structure of the pattern. The process continues until all subtasks have succeeded, at which point it returns the variable assignments, or until any subtask fails, at which point the entire match fails.

In a multiprocess system, there are additional strategy decisions in choosing when to carry out subtasks in serial or parallel. Further, since the match process as a whole may be only one of several competing processes (for example, several patterns being compared for "best match") there are choices of when the match process should be suspended or resumed, and how it should compete for processing resources. At a still more sophisticated level, there can be sharing of overlapping subtasks between two match processes.

2.5.1 The Match Framework in KRL

We provide a framework for carrying out a match process, and an appropriate set of building blocks from which a matching strategy can be constructed within this framework for a specific user or domain or process. In Section 3.3 we describe in more detail how such "procedural parameterization" is done. We do not believe that any one combination of features will provide a universally applicable matcher. In the course of working with KRL, we plan to experiment with and develop a set of generally applicable strategies that can be used in building a user-tailored match process. The following list of extensions is intended to give some feeling for the scope and variety of issues we believe must be dealt with. At the moment, what exists in KRL-0 is the framework into which they will be integrated, and a set of simple strategies which handle straightforward cases. Figure 8 contains some simple data that will be used in illustrating some problems in matching.

Matching multiple descriptions. The pattern and datum in a KRL match are both descriptions which may contain any number of individual descriptors. In order for a match to be completed, all of the descriptors in the pattern should be satisfied in some way by the datum. But there is no simple sense in which the sequence of descriptors in one can be set into correspondence with the sequence of descriptors in the other. The matcher includes a set of strategies for *alignment* of descriptors. If, for example, both pattern and datum contain a descriptor which is a pointer to an individual, these two individuals will be compared and the match will succeed or fail depending on whether they are identical. If both pattern and datum contain perspectives with the same prototype, the two perspectives (including all of the filler pairs) will be compared in detail. If pattern and datum each contain a perspective whose prototype is a basic unit, those two prototypes will be compared. If the pattern contains a logical descriptor (such as a NOT) and its argument corresponds in one of these simple ways to a descriptor in the datum, the two will be compared.

The algorithm for alignment makes decisions both about what subtasks will be attempted, and in what order the attempts will be made. In the default algorithm built into the matcher, only those subtasks which can be set up simply (like those

---

tional structures; at the other extreme it guides the overall processing of the system. The matcher may use the semantics of descriptors as well as their syntactic form to decide whether two descriptions match. The matcher may search for a referent of a description (in order to use its properties), invoke special match procedures associated with a descriptor type or a specific pattern, and invoke a general reasoning process to search for chains of implications.

In extending the notion of matching, we have adopted and extended ideas that have been implemented in a variety of systems. Our attempt has been to integrate them into a coherent framework which gives the user of KRL a choice of the strategies best suited to the specific task. The choices can be viewed as representing four interacting dimensions. We will first list these dimensions and give examples of the choices made in well known match systems, then describe the range of possibilities provided for each in KRL.

Subtasks. In all but the most trivial matching operations, the pattern and the *datum* to which it is compared are complex objects with an internal structure. The match is carried out by setting up a series of subtasks, each of which matches one piece of the structure of the pattern against a corresponding piece of the datum. In the case of simple syntactic matchers (as in the AI languages) the division into subtasks is a direct reflection of the syntax of the structures—if the pattern and datum are represented as lists, each subtask involves matching one element of the pattern list against the corresponding structural element of the datum list, using a recursive application of the same matching algorithm.

Terminals. In applying a match process recursively to a complex structure, there is a choice of where the recursion "bottoms out." In matchers operating on individual data structures (such as *assertions* in the AI languages, or *well-formed formulas* in the unification algorithm of a logic-based system) there is a natural set of terminals provided by the underlying language. In a LISP-based system, pattern variables and atoms form the terminals—the task of matching them is not done by recursively setting up match subtasks, but by calling the appropriate procedure for deciding the match for that kind of object directly. Even though atoms have an internal structure, they conventionally serve as terminals. In logic, the predicate, variable, constant, and function symbols form a set of terminals. In simple network matchers, the individual links (and their labels) usually serve as terminals.

Results. The simplest kind of result from a matching process is a binary answer—MATCH or FAIL. Most matchers add to this some kind of mechanism for returning a set of associations between variables in the pattern and constants (or other variables) in the datum, either as an explicit output or implicitly through side effects.

Process. There are a number of control questions which decide how the match process should proceed. These include deciding what subtasks to carry out in what sequence, and when the match as a whole should be stopped. In the simplest case, the subtasks are taken serially, usually in the sequence provided

match should succeed. It can do so only by further reference to the information about Pluto. *The KRL matcher can vary the level of what it considers to be terminals.* Faced with comparing a descriptor to an individual (which corresponds loosely to an atom or constant in other matchers) it can set up a subtask of matching the pattern descriptor against the description stored in the unit for that individual. This is done only when the alignment strategies cannot find an appropriate descriptor in the datum, but can find a pointer to an individual.

This extension is naturally recursive. In matching the descriptor (*which Owns (a Dog)*) against the unit *Mickey* we first need to use the description within the *Mickey* unit to find (*which Owns Pluto*), then to use this we need to further look within the *Pluto* unit. The problem of finding the correct information in a general way has been called the "symbol mapping problem" (Fahlman, 1975), and has been handled to some degree by matchers based on networks rather than propositions (e.g., Hendrix, 1975; Nash-Webber, 1975). These matchers do not have a rigid notion of scope and terminals, since matching follows open-endedly along links, rather than operating within a specified formula.

Using deduced properties. The example above assumes that the desired properties are explicit in the data base, but are not local to the datum being matched. The matcher sets up a subtask which is a recursive call to the same matching process, with an expanded datum to work on. A further generalization of recursive subtasks in the matcher allows it to set up subtasks which are not primitive match operations or recursive calls to the match functions, but which require that a needed property be derived from known facts about the elements. This is the province of a theorem prover.

As a simple example, we might want to match (*which Owns (a Dog)*) against *Minnie*, having as our description of Minnie (*which Owns (a DogLicense)*), and having other information asserting that only dog owners own dog licenses. The appropriate subtask to set up is not one that can be done as a simple match operation, but one corresponding to the goal of proving that a dog license owner is a dog owner. This kind of subtask requires general capacities for reasoning and deduction. There is a search problem in deciding what alignments should be tried (which of the conclusions the system should try to prove on the basis of which parts of the available description). The KRL matching framework does not include any automatic mechanisms for making these decisions, but it does provide a natural superstructure in which specific deductive goals arise and, in the overall flow of control, it is typical that deduction tasks arise as subtasks called by the matcher.

In our example of Fig. 8 we have associated a specialized procedure with the general unit for *Ownership*. In a realistic system, it would be associated with the combination of the concepts *Ownership* and *Dog*, using the index mechanism described in Section 2.7.

```
[Cat UNIT Basic
 <SELF {(an Animal)(a Pet)}>]

[Dog UNIT Basic
 <SELF {(an Animal)(a Pet)}>]

.[Pluto UNIT Individual
 <SELF (a Dog)>]

[Mickey UNIT Individual
 <SELF (which Owns Pluto)>]

[Minnie UNIT Individual
 <SELF (which Owns (a DogLicense))>]

[Ownership UNIT Specialization
 <SELF (a State)
   TRIGGERS (ToEstablish
     (AND (Match \(the possession) \(a Dog))
          (Match \(the owner)
                 \(which Owns (a DogLicense with
                              licensed = (the possession)))))))>

 <owner (a Person)>
 <possession (a Thing)>]

[Owns PREDICATE Ownership owner possession]

[DogLicense UNIT Specialization
 <SELF>
 <licensed (a Dog)>]
```

FIG. 8 Sample knowledge base used in matching.

listed above) will be tried. The order in which these simple strategies will be tried can be determined by the user, and they can be intermixed with user defined strategies. The simple matching strategies handle a large number of the typically occurring cases, but do not account for all possible ways in which two descriptions might be matched. Whenever there is a descriptor in the pattern for which no simple alignment can be found, the system looks for a strategy program provided by the user for this specific match (either written for the special case, or chosen from the set of building blocks). The following examples illustrate possibilities for setting up an appropriate subtask for testing whether a pattern descriptor is matched.

Using properties of the datum elements. Consider matching the pattern descriptor (*which Owns (a Dog)*) against a datum which explicitly includes a descriptor (*which Owns Pluto*). The SELF description in the memory unit for Pluto contains a perspective indicating that he is a dog. In a semantic sense, the processes (such as asking a question of a user in a natural language system, or doing a visual scan in a vision system) in addition to the demons, so that the attempt to match the pattern serves as a driving force for deriving new possibly relevant information.[9]

Admission of ignorance and partial results. The KRL matcher is designed to distinguish among four possible results, both in reporting the result of the match as a whole and using the results of subtasks. In addition to a result of success, it separates two kinds of failures: those in which the pattern demonstrably does not match the datum; and those in which there is insufficient evidence. The case of insufficient evidence is further distinguished according to whether the matcher has been limited by resources it has used in the match, or the matcher failed to decide after trying every strategy it knew.

The general multiprocess capabilities of KRL can be used to suspend a match process and return a partial result. Thus, a match can be started, and after some amount of processing (using the resource limitation mechanisms described in Section 3.2) if no definite success or failure has occurred, it can return a result of "don't know yet." The process using the match can decide whether to accept this as sufficient for an assumed "yes," or to consider it a "no," or to abandon whatever it was doing for lack of sufficient information, or to resume the match process, giving it more resources.

Resource limitation and pinpointing of further problems. In a case in which the processing so far has not produced a definite answer, the matcher should be able to return specific details in addition to the result of "don't know yet." Given the problem of matching (which Owns (a Pet)) against Mickey, with sufficient resources (and the data of Fig. 8), it could answer "Yes." With fewer resources, it could answer "Yes, if (a Dog) matches (a Pet)," and with still fewer, "Yes, if Pluto matches (a Pet)." In general we want to limit the depth of the reasoning, and have the matcher return a list of yet unresolved problems if no definite answer has been found within the limitation.[10] We hope to integrate this mechanism with the means of returning bindings relating specific elements in the pattern and those which matched them in the datum. As of the current version, only the "hooks" for calling these mechanisms exist, and no details have been filled in.

Evaluation of the quality of a match. Many uses of the matching paradigm are not simple cases of matching a single pattern against a single datum, but involve finding the *best match* among a set of patterns. An example of the matching of a set of disease patterns against a specific symptom set in doing medical diagnosis. The matcher should have some way of assigning values on

Specialized procedures for subtasks. The previous example involves setting up subtasks that are not simple recursive applications of the matcher. The match framework provides for a general capability for calling arbitrary procedures as subtasks of a match. This can including setting up nonserial control regimes for running subtasks in parallel.

We believe that the most important weapon for attacking the combinatorial problems that arise in matching and deduction is the ability to attach specialized matching procedures to descriptions and units. When the matcher is faced with a pattern and datum that cannot be simply matched, it looks in several places for specific procedural information telling it what to do to decide what the result of the match should be:

There can be procedures associated with general types of alignment—for example, the user can provide a special procedure to be used when a perspective with its prototype in some specified set can be matched against another perspective with a prototype in that set.

Procedures can be associated with a unit, to be used whenever a perspective having that unit as its prototype appears as a pattern descriptor. These procedures can either be general (to match the perspective as a whole) or associated with specific slots.[8] The *ToEstablish* procedure associated with *Ownership* in Fig. 8 is an example of such a procedure.

Interleaving a match with ongoing processes. In the standard notions of matching, a match is a unitary process with respect to the rest of the system. The matcher is called as a subroutine, and other processing continues when it is done. In using a matcher as the basis for a general process of reasoning by recognition, this is not an acceptable strategy. The attempted match of a "frame" or "script" or "schema" begins when its presence is first conjectured, but may continue through a series of further inputs and other processing by the system. This is a natural extension of the ability for specific match situations to set up arbitrary subtasks as described above. Rather than calling a specific subtask and waiting for its answer, the specialized procedures can start up tasks (in a coroutine fashion) that will direct the processing of the system, while the match process remains in the background, waiting for the appropriate information to be found.

There are a number of ways the processing can be organized. In a simple case, the matcher can set up a demon waiting for each piece of information it needs (for example, a demon for each slot to be filled in a perspective) and simply resume the normal processing, waiting for the information to come in. In other cases, the specialized match procedures might start up information-seeking

[9]Some of the possible methods are discussed in Minsky (1975), Kuipers (1975), and Bobrow et al. (1976).

[10]This is similar to the idea of residues proposed by Srinivasin (1976) in MDS, a language with many similarities to KRL in both goals and mechanisms.

[8]This is a generalization of the notion of active elements in patterns, as in the elements originally called *actors* by Hewitt (1972).

some scale to the individual parts of a match, and combining these to return a "goodness measure" chosen along a scale of values, rather than just "yes," "no," or "I don't know."

Along with a value for how good the match seems to be, there should be a separate value for how reliable the information is, depending on how much work has been done, and perhaps on reliability measures stored with the information used. This can be combined with progressive deepening, such that each time a match process is resumed, it can further evaluate the match, updating its factor for the goodness of fit, and increasing the factor for reliability of the knowledge.[11] As with the binding of specific elements, we have so far only provided a place in the framework where such measures could be used.

Interaction of multiple matching processes. In looking for a best match, it is useful not to think of the separate matching operations as independent, but to allow interactions between them. A simple level of interaction occurs in operating them in a progressively deepening mode, and using some sort of heuristic strategy (e.g., best first generation) to decide which alternative to pursue at each step. At a deeper level, there can be additional information associated with specific ways in which a pattern fails to match (an *error pointer*), which indicates a specific alternative or provides direct information on the goodness of other matches being simultaneously attempted.[12] This capability should include the potential of triggering new patterns as candidates for a match, on the basis of new data turned up in the match process.[13]

Forced match. A matcher can be operated in a mode in which the question instead of "Does this match?" is "What would you have to believe in order to make this match?"[14] If asked to match (*which Owns (a Cat)*) against *Mickey*, instead of responding with failure, it should return "You have to view a *Dog* as a *Cat.*" This is a natural extension for the KRL matcher, since there is a general facility by which the user can provide procedures for alignment and the treatment of types of match (i.e., what to do when you try to match two different individuals).

Using individuals as patterns. Given the ability to do forced match and to return an indication of the differences, the matcher can be used in a mode in which the pattern is an actual individual, rather than a general prototype. The result of matching two individuals would be a specification of the ways in which they differ. This needs to be combined with a further mechanism (associated with resource limitation) which heuristically guides the choice of which properties to follow up and which to ignore. We hope that this style of matching,

---

[11]Simple versions of goodness evaluation are implemented in MYCIN (Shortliffe, 1976) and Rubin (1975).

[12]See Minsky (1975) and Kuipers (1975) for an extended discussion of the ways in which systems of patterns can be linked into a network.

[13]See Rubin (1975) for a discussion of this kind of triggering in medical diagnosis.

[14]The general issue of forced matching (or *mapping*) is developed in Moore and Newell (1973).

---

together with a basic commitment to description by comparison, will provide us with a strong base for doing more interesting sorts of reasoning by analogy.

2.6 *Chunking of Knowledge, Accessibility, and Redundancy*

One of the fundamental problems in artificial intelligence is the "combinatorial explosion." A large knowledge base provides an exponentially expanding set of possible reasoning chains for finding desired information. We believe that the solution to this problem must be found by dealing with it directly through explicit concern with the *accessibility* of information. The representation language must provide the user with a set of facilities for controlling the way in which memory structures are stored, so that there will be a correspondence between "salience" or "relevance" and the information accessed by procedures for search and reasoning operating under processing resource limitations.

Much of the current research on memory structures in artificial intelligence deals with ways of organizing knowledge into *chunks* or *clusters* which are larger than single nodes or links in a semantic net or formulas in a logic-based system. This is particularly important in reasoning based on prototypes, using description by comparison, in which typical properties are assumed true of an object unless more specific information is *immediately available.* It is also necessary in recognition, in which identification of an object is based on recognizing some set of *salient* properties, and in analogies in which only the *relevant* properties of one object are inherited by the other.[15]

The KRL data structures were designed to be used in processes that are subject to resource limitation and differences in accessibility. Two forms which are equivalent in a strict logical sense are not at all equivalent if used by a processor which takes different numbers of steps to come to the conclusion, and which may well be stopped or suspended before reaching completion. In KRL the unit is treated as a basic memory chunk, and processes such as the matcher operate differently when using information within a unit, and when retrieving information from a unit being pointed to or referenced by it. By making explicit decisions about how to divide information up between units, the user has structural dimension of control over the matching and reasoning processes.

Figures 9 and 10 illustrate the use of redundant information in building up descriptions to be used in matching. Figure 9 gives an example of a set of facts representing a particular event, presenting several different forms that are equivalent in abstract logical content, but different in their behavior with respect to memory chunking and accessibility. Figure 10 gives the units which are referred to by these alternatives.

The unit named *Event234* represents a specific event that is being remembered by a KRL program. In all of the versions, the recipient is represented by a pointer

---

[15]For a general discussion of these issues, see Bobrow and Norman (1975). A system which tries to distinguish the salience of different descriptors is described in Carbonell and Collins (1974).

to the unit for the individual *Person1*, corresponding to a situation in which the identity of that individual was the salient fact. Also, in every version the object is represented only by a description (*a Pen*), indicating that the specific identity of the pen is not remembered. Of course, these are arbitrary choices representing the way one particular program (or person) would remember the event. Someone else remembering the same event might store a description containing the identity of the pen (for example, if it were a special memento) and only a description of the person who received it.

The four versions differ in how much detail about the other person is considered salient to the specific event. In Version 1, the giver's identity is all that is included. In Version 2, the identity of his wife is included as well, and in Version 3, so is her occupation. Version 4 differs from the others in omitting the specific identities altogether. It corresponds to the kind of incomplete memory that might be expressed as ''Let's see, David got the pen from some guy who was married to a lawyer.''

If we try to match *Event234* with the pattern (*a Give with giver = (which Is HusbandOf (a Lawyer))*), the amount of processing needed to determine the

answer differs for the different versions. The matcher must look into the contents of the units for Person2 and Person3 in the cases in which there is less redundant information. The results for the various versions could differ as well. Matching (*a Give with giver = Person2*) against version 4, all we could say is that it is potentially compatible, while the other versions all provide a definite ''Yes.'' In a system with competing parallel processes, these differences can have a significant effect on the results of reasoning.

It should be apparent that the kind of knowledge structuring involved in chunking facts into units is very different from the structuring of facts into truth *contexts*, as provided by the AI languages such as CONNIVER and QLISP. In those systems, each context contains a set of objects and assertions whose connection derives from being present and true within a particular state representing a hypothetical world, or time. This grouping is orthogonal to KRL's object-oriented chunking based on grouping a set of facts (or properties) about a particular conceptual object. In KRL there are descriptors (the *contingency* form) that are applicable only in some worlds, and facts that are true in some worlds, but this mechanism is separate from the clustering of relevant facts into a memory structure.

```
[Give UNIT  Specialization
   <SELF (an Event)>
   <object (a Thing)>
   <giver (a Person)>
   <recipient (a Person)>]

[Lawyer UNIT  Specialization
   <SELF (a Person)>]

[Pen UNIT  Basic
   <SELF (a PhysicalObject)>]

[Person1 UNIT  Individual
   <SELF (a Person with firstName = ''David'')>]

[Person2 UNIT  Individual
   <SELF {(a Person with firstName = ''Jonathan'')
          (which IsHusbandOf Person3)}>]

[Person3 UNIT  Individual
   <SELF {(a Person with firstName = ''Ellen'')
          (a Lawyer)}>]
```

FIG. 10   Units used in the alternative forms in Fig. 9.

```
[Event234 UNIT  Individual
   <SELF (a Give with
       object = (a Pen)
       giver = Person2
       recipient = Person1)>]                 Version 1

[Event234 UNIT  Individual
   <SELF (a Give with
       object = (a Pen)
       giver = {Person2  (which IsHusbandOf Person3)}
       recipient = Person1)>]                 Version 2

[Event234 UNIT  Individual
   <SELF (a Give with
       object = (a Pen)
       giver = {Person2
           (which IsHusbandOf {Person3 (a Lawyer)})}
       recipient = Person1)>]                 Version 3

[Event234 UNIT  Individual
   <SELF (a Give with
       object = (a Pen)
       giver = (which IsHusbandOf (a Lawyer))
       recipient = Person1)>]                 Version 4
```

FIG. 9   Alternative memory structures with different redundancy.

In addition to the internal structure of units, and the associations represented by the index, there is a third type of structuring in which a set of units is collected in a context or *focus list*.[16] These focus lists are primitive building blocks for use in experimenting with notions of attention and differential access to data at different "levels of consciousness." There are primitives for adding and deleting items, and for finding all (or the most recent) units in a given focus list matching a given description. A focus list provides one mechanism by which to implement and test models of short-term memory.

One aspect of memory structure that we plan to explore in KRL is the use of context-dependent description.[17] The results of human reasoning are *context dependent*; the structure of memory includes not only the long-term storage organization (what do I know?) but also a current context (what is in focus at the moment?). We believe that this is an important feature of human thought, not an inconvenient limitation. It allows great simplifications in the form of descriptions by allowing them to be context dependent. A descriptor which is going to be interpreted in a context with other descriptions and objects around can implicitly describe its connections to them, rather than needing to make all of the links explicit. The descriptor form (*theOne...*) is used to specify a unit by giving a description which will pick it out uniquely in a context. This context might be a stored focus list, or one dynamically created as part of a current process.

3. EXTENDED CONTROL STRUCTURES

In designing KRL-0 we chose to concentrate our efforts on the declarative side of the language. The control mechanisms and procedure specification formalism make use of LISP as much as possible, extending what was already there, rather than building from the ground up. There is no such thing in KRL-0 as a "KRL-procedure." When a procedure is to be specified, it is done as a LISP function that makes use of a set of primitives (LISP functions) provided for manipulating the KRL-0 data structures. Arguments and values are passed in the normal LISP way, and subroutine calling obeys the usual stack discipline rules, as provided by INTERLISP. This includes the use of generators and other coroutines made possible by the spaghetti stack.

The underlying control structure has been extended in several directions: object-oriented process specification (*procedural attachment*); a general *signal* mechanism for error handling, notification, and dynamic procedural parameterization; organization of the basic system functions around *process frameworks*; and a multiprocess executive, based on a *multilevel scheduling agenda* with resource and priority management facilities.

[16] Focus lists have been used by Deutsch (1975) to establish a context for utterances in natural language dialogue.

[17] For an extended discussion of this idea, see Bobrow and Norman (1975).

2.7 Indexing and Retrieval

One of the fundamental problems in the use of memory is the *retrieval* of appropriate knowledge from a large data base. As mentioned in Section 2.5, KRL makes a distinction between the process of retrieval and the process of matching. In finding a desired object in memory, there are two steps. The first is a rough retrieval step, designed to produce a small set of units which potentially fit the specification for what is being sought. This is followed by a more thorough matching process in which each candidate is matched against the retrieval pattern, using the mechanisms discussed above.

This separation between retrieval and matching is carried over in the form of the memory. In most existing AI systems (and models of human memory) there is an underlying assumption that there is a single set of data linkages, used both for retrieval and for matching or deduction. The data structures must contain all of the logical form of what is being stored, and be usable in some uniform way for memory search. Many researchers have explored the problems that arise in trying to create structures which have desirable properties for retrieval processes while also being an adequate representation of the logical structure; for example, see Anderson and Bower (1973), Woods (1975), and Hendrix (1975). Many human memory experiments (beginning with Collins and Quillian, 1969) have been based on the same assumption that a single set of links must handle both tasks. The uniformity of logical and retrieval structure is also basic in systems that use complete indexing (as in CONNIVER, QLISP, etc.), and those which retrieve through a complex search process (as in the derivatives of Quillian's original network representation; see Quillian, 1968).

We believe that the presence of *associative links* for retrieval is an additional dimension of memory structure that is not derivable from the logical structure of the knowledge being associated. KRL has a separate independent mechanism for creating associative links between arbitrary combinations of units, and for retrieving those units on the basis of the associations. These associations would be closely related to the rest of the knowledge structure, but in a way determined by specific memory strategies. One of the major topics for research is the development of strategies for deciding when to put in associative links and when to look for them in retrieval.

KRL-0 has a simple indexing mechanism which allows the user to catalog any unit under a list-structured pattern of *keys*. There is a primitive to retrieve all units matching a key combination and another for matching all units indexed under any subset of a given key pattern. For most of what has been typically stored in AI language data bases, no indexing at all is needed in KRL-0, since the way in which descriptions are combined into units explicitly gathers together the information that would be retrieved by a data base mechanism. In the future, we hope to explore other retrieval mechanisms, perhaps involving spreading activation models, and parallel computation structures.

3.1 Procedural Attachment

One of the major current directions in programming language research involves factoring procedural knowledge orthogonally to the traditional programming formalisms. Each primitive program step can be viewed as applying some *operation* to one or more data objects each of which belongs to some *class*. The traditional way of organizing programs is to have a procedure keyed to each operation. The internal structure of this procedure takes into account the alternatives for the data objects on which it will operate. Languages such as SMALLTALK (Learning Research Group, 1976) and SIMULA (Dahl & Nygaard, 1966) and the various ACTOR formalisms (Hewitt, Bishop, & Steiger, 1973; Hewitt & Smith, 1975) group together the different procedures to be carried out on objects of a single class. The programmer defines classes of objects, and associates with each class a procedure whose internal structure takes into account the different operations which will be carried out. The *to-fill* and *when-filled* triggers discussed in the context of frame representations (Winograd, 1975a; Bobrow et al., 1976) are further examples of this *procedural attachment*. AI languages such as QLISP and the PLANNER family represent a different method of factoring the procedures, according to *configurations* defined in terms of patterns which are to be matched against goals and assertions. These configurations represent potentially arbitrarily overlapping classes, which is quite different from the use of classes in SMALLTALK and SIMULA.

We have extended the notion of object-oriented procedure definition in two important directions. The first is an integration of the ideas of object-associated procedures with those of frame structure and multiple description. In associating procedures with a class represented by a unit in KRL, procedures can be linked to the slots of a unit, and specifically associated with several different descriptor types. This makes the clustering of the procedures correspond better to the conceptual structuring of the domain. In addition, KRL provides through its use of perspectives a notion of *subclass* that allows objects to inherit procedural as well as declarative properties. Since each unit can contain multiple perspectives it can be a member of a number of subclasses.

KRL-0 provides facilities for procedural attachment that can be divided along two dimensions. The first is based on when the procedure is intended to be used—whether it is a *servant* or a *demon* which causes a secondary effect of some event. The second dimension corresponds to whether the procedure is associated with an individual data element or with a class (prototype).

A servant is invoked when the system has the goal of applying some specific operation to a data object (or set of objects), and needs a procedure for accomplishing the specified task. The interpreter looks for servant procedures associated with the data object or its class, and if it finds one, executes it to carry out the operation. If there is more than one, a strategy procedure is called (using the signal mechanism described below) to choose. A typical use of servants is to attach a procedure describing how to match a descriptor involving a particular relation or prototype. In Fig. 8, there is a *ToEstablish* servant, associated with the unit for *Ownership*, which uses the LISP function *And* and the KRL function *Match*. It provides a specific procedure for determining ownership in a special case.

A demon is invoked as a side effect of actions taken by the system. All of the primitive data-manipulating operations check for demons, whenever they use or add information. A demon can be associated with a description of the operation to be done, and the object to which it is done. A unique object can be specified, or a demon can be invoked for any object of a specified class. The antecedent theorems or if-added methods of the AI languages are examples of demon-like mechanisms, in which the invoking events are asserting and erasing, and the classes of data objects are specified by patterns. Demons can be awakened when something is about to be done or has just been done (there are both types). A demon typically might be invoked when a unit representing an individual is filled in as part of the description in an instance. This could trigger further processing which requires knowing the individual.

The second dimension of procedural attachment is the distinction between procedures associated with individual data objects (*traps*) and those associated with classes (*triggers*). Triggers are class-based—they apply to operations and events that take place on objects whose description includes a perspective whose prototype is the unit to which the trigger is attached. Traps are instance-based—they apply to operations and events directly involving the unit to which they are attached. A list of triggers and a list of traps can be associated with each slot within a unit. Both triggers and traps can be either servants or demons.

In addition to the servants explicitly sought by the system (in the frameworks for the matching and searching processes described below) and the demons explicitly triggered (by the data manipulating functions), the user can also provide arbitrary demons and servants and check them explicitly. The user can independently define a set of trap and trigger names, and use them for organizing a computation. There is a primitive used to *probe* for attached procedures, and if multiple traps or triggers are applicable, they can set up multiple processes (see below).

3.2 Multiprocessing and Variable Depth of Processing

The overall control structure of KRL is based on our belief that the next generation of intelligent programs will be built using multiprocessing with explicit (user-provided) scheduling heuristics and resource allocation. This view is based partly on looking at current multiprocess oriented systems,[18] and partly

[18] Such as in syntactic analysis (Kaplan, 1973b) and in speech understanding systems, as described in Reddy and Erman (1975).

on looking at properties of human processing, such as *partial output* based on *variable processing depth*.[19] We want to provide ways to build a system whose components can run on varying amounts of effort, producing some initial results with a small effort, and improving the quality of their results (either in amount of data, or certainty) as the effort is increased. We also want to explore issues of *attention* or *focus* in choosing which of competing procedures to run.[20] By beginning with a multiprocess system whose control structure is explicit and visible, we hope to have a base from which to experiment with a variety of control and resource allocation strategies.

We expect one of the major research areas to be the integration of data-directed and goal-directed processing. In the course of running, there will be an explicit goal structure for the program as a whole, while new processes will continually be triggered through procedural attachment and data from external sources. Resource manipulation and priorities will be used to provide a global direction to the processing, yet maintaining flexibility to deal with unanticipated combinations.

Many of the specific facilities in KRL, such as procedural attachment and the extended notion of matching discussed earlier, presuppose some sort of multiple process system, in which a set of procedures can be set up and control can be passed between them in a systematic way. The central executive of KRL is based on an *agenda*[21] of "runnable" processes, and a scheduler for running them in a systematic order. The agenda is a priority ordered list of queues, with all processes on a higher priority queue run before any on lower priority queues.

All scheduling is done by cooperation, not preemption. A process runs until it explicitly returns control to the scheduler. It can add any number of other calls to the agenda before it gives up control, including a call to continue itself. Whenever the scheduler runs, it scans down a series of *priority levels* on the agenda, and runs the first process in the highest priority nonempty queue. It removes that process from the agenda and starts it (if it is new) or resumes it (if it has been suspended).

The agenda levels can be used to achieve a variety of standard control disciplines. As one example, new inputs can be checked for periodically, and can put actions on the agenda at a high priority level, which will then be done before ongoing processing at lower levels, and may even remove such processes from the agenda. This makes it possible to write procedures (e.g., story understanders) whose depth of processing varies with the rate of the inputs. As another example, a part of the computation can be made *relatively continuous* (Fisher, 1970) with respect to another by causing all of its processes to be

scheduled at a higher priority level. A higher priority process is relatively continuous with respect to a lower priority process in that it is guaranteed to run to completion between any successive actions in the lower priority process. Use of relatively continuous processes is especially useful for coordinating processes with intermediate steps which leave data in states that would be inconsistent for use in other parts of the computation.

Part of the information associated with each process includes a pointer to a *resource pool*, which can be shared between any number of processes. There is no automatic assignment or checking of resources, but any process can check and increment or decrement its resource pool, and invoke a user-provided procedure if resources have run out. The agenda itself is an accessible data structure, and the scheduler looks for specialized strategy procedures (using the signal mechanism described below) in all of the places in which resource and scheduling decisions are made. The user can design combinations of strategy procedures (called a *control idiom*) suited to the particular program or component. This will be described further below in discussing process frameworks.

3.3 *Procedure Directories, Modules, and Process Frameworks*

For dealing with complex descriptions and matching processes, it is critical that the user be able to build up different mechanisms and strategies at a high conceptual level which do not demand detailed concern with all the ways in which different descriptor types may appear. There need to be processes built into the system which do the necessary bookkeeping and basic alignment for carrying out matching, description building, and searching operations. At the same time, there is no one way that things should be done. The strategy for carrying out a particular matching task can be selected along many dimensions, and detailed decisions at each step depend on the particular design choices.

Our solution to the desire for both generality and automatic handling of detail is to provide *process frameworks* for all of the basic operations, and a *procedure directory* which provides a mapping from a set of names (designating the procedure to be done) to procedures. For example, rather than having a semantically complete definition of what happens in a match, the system provides a matching framework which contains processes for setting up the structures to compare two descriptions, doing the alignment of comparable descriptors, looking for procedures attached to specific patterns, and handling all of those cases in which a simple syntactic match will work.

Whenever there is a "hard case," of any sort (i.e., something which cannot be resolved by simple syntactic properties), the system looks in the procedure directory for an entry corresponding to the unique name associated with that case. The directory is dynamically maintained—entries can be added and removed either singly or in groups called *directory modules*. *The user can specify with each call to the matcher a directory module that has entries to take the appropriate actions for all of the hard cases he wants to handle.* There is a set of initial default entries in the directory which take some action (the best that

---

[19]See Norman and Bobrow (1975) for a discussion of human processes which are limited by resources.

[20]See Hayes-Roth and Lesser (1976) and Paxton and Robinson (1975).

[21]See Kaplan (1975) for the use of an agenda in a system for parsing natural language.

heuristically guided search according to different strategies. We expect to build up a vocabulary of generally useful control idioms, including complex ones involving resource allocation.

The mechanism used in KRL-0 to implement procedure directories is based on a notion of signals.[22] The system maintains a *signal path* associated with each independent process, which is a linked list of *signal tables*, each of which is an association list pairing *signal names* with actions. There is a primitive which, given a signal name, looks on the signal path for the first place where that signal name is found, then executes the action associated with it. In addition, there is a range of primitives for putting actions into a signal table, pushing one onto or popping one off the signal path, resetting the current signal path, etc.

The signal mechanism is used for two other purposes in addition to providing procedure directories for process frameworks.

Errors. Whenever an error condition arises, a signal is generated whose name specifies the error condition. The default action is to stop and interact with the user on line, but the user can specify in the current signal path any action whatsoever to be taken to handle the error. This could include patching things up so the computation can go on, or could involve aborting the process in which it occurred, or any complex computation that might be built in as part of a debugging system.

Notification. Whenever any one of a specified set of system operations occurs (e.g., adding a new process to the agenda) a signal is generated. The default is to do nothing, but the user can specify any action, which typically would include printing out monitoring or debugging information, taking special actions, or keeping statistics. This makes it easier to provide debugging and monitoring tools for use in a multiprocess environment, which by its essential nature makes it difficult to keep track of just what is going on and when. These notification signals can also be used directly to trigger event-driven processes. For example, a data base indexing mechanism might operate by catching the signal generated by the primitive that augments a description with a new descriptor and taking the appropriate indexing actions.

Communication between the procedure assigned to the signal (according to the current signal path) and the context in which it is invoked is handled through the use of free variables.

4. WHERE WE ARE HEADED

4.1 Experimental Implementation and Recycling

Our approach in building KRL has been guided by a philosophy of working from actual domains and problems toward a habitable representation system, rather than starting with an abstractly designed representation and trying to force

[22]The concept of signals has been adapted from MESA (Lampson, Mitchell, & Satterthwaite, 1974).

can be done without further information) in the absence of a user-supplied entry. Typically, a program will include a set of alternative modules, with one of them being "plugged in" to the directory for each call to the matcher.

In some sense, this can be thought of as defining the system's basic functions (such as Match) using calls to subprocedures which are to be provided by the user. The additional directory mechanisms make it possible for the user to provide alternative definitions in a much more flexible way than with the static lexical procedure-naming conventions used by most programming languages. The use of directory modules makes it easy for the user to bind and unbind clusters of "functional arguments" in a single operation.

As an example within the matcher, the user could provide a module with an entry telling what to do when matching two perspectives whose prototypes represent abstract categories such as (a PhysicalObject) and (an Animal). One possible entry would indicate that the match should be abandoned without further work, while a different one might call on a complex procedure that uses a classification hierarchy. We expect to build up a vocabulary of standard modules (that we call *match idioms*) which represent different combinations of the features described above. One module (used for quick checking to see if there is an easy match) returns "don't know" if the built-in syntactic checks do not give an immediate yes or no answer. A module for quick disconfirmation checks only for those kinds of descriptors that give definite negative evidence easily (e.g., conflicting individuals or conflicting basic categories). One for forced match would perform a complete mapping process when faced with two conflicting individuals, returning the places in which their descriptions differ. The standard modules can be augmented with specialized individual entries for specific situations. The user can also control the way in which new entries take precedence over preexisting ones.

Briefly summarizing, a process framework provides a basic structure which sets up an environment and divides the process up into a set of cases (subtasks) to be handled. Each case is given a unique name (as part of defining the framework). For each such name, there are three different places to look for a detailed procedure: in the built-in mechanisms of the framework (e.g., the simple syntactic cases of matching); in procedures attached to the data on which it is working (e.g., To Match triggers associated with a pattern); and in the current procedure directory (e.g., an entry stating that when two conflicting individuals are to be matched, a given mapping process should be called).

There are several occurrences other than matching in which process frameworks are used in KRL-0. The primitive process for adding a new description to an already existing unit is a framework that allows for event-triggered side effects of each of its actions. The scheduler described in the previous section is a framework that allows for modules specifying different control strategies. As an example, a simple program has been written to search an AND-OR tree, along with two different modules that cause the search to be breadth-first or depth-first, respectively. Other modules could specify a

the world into it. To some degree we have drawn on our collective experience with designing language understanders. However, we believe that complex systems are "Whorfian" in that the underlying structure and style of a representation language can have a strong effect on what people attempt to do with it. Therefore, we see a need for a feedback loop in which systems are built, used, and then redesigned on the basis of experience.

Our current research strategy includes a cycle of three steps, with a step time on the order of six months to a year:

1. Design a system based on our current understanding and experience.
2. Build an experimental implementation that captures as much of this as feasible.
3. Use the system in a number of test domains to understand its capabilities and push its limits.

In the summer of 1976, we entered the third step on our first major round of design of KRL as embodied in KRL-0. For our experiments with KRL-0, we have chosen the strategy of implementing a set of already existing AI programs, each of which we hope will exercise different subsets of its facilities, and raise additional representation issues. Our current plan is for the Xerox Understander group and several Stanford students to work on 5 to 10 programs.[23] Each of these benchmark programs makes use of well-understood AI techniques, which push the current facilities of AI languages and systems, but which are clearly formulated in the already existing programs (or extended program descriptions). In some cases (such as MYCIN) much of the actual program deals with issues of smooth user interface, and the accumulation of large bodies of knowledge. We will not try to imitate these aspects, but only try to duplicate the basic modes of operation and reasoning. For most of the systems, however, it seems quite feasible to duplicate the complete published performance.

By beginning with systems whose behavior and general outline are well defined, we can concentrate on the ways in which the KRL representation can be used to full advantage, and the places in which it does not meet the needs. We expect each of these systems to take on the order of 1–2 person-months of work, and to provide part of the feedback cycle for the design of KRL.

4.2 Goals for Future Versions of KRL

Although we cannot predict all the changes which our experience will force on us, we are aware of several major issues which we consciously avoided in designing KRL-0. Major areas of expansion in our future designs will include: a LISP-independent specification of the primitive data objects; a descriptive formalism for specifying procedures; integration of the different procedure-calling facilities and indexes; development of an integrated system for programming and debugging; and development of a more convenient syntax.

Procedure specification. We need a way to specify procedures other than by giving a LISP function or expression. We believe that a representation system should make it possible to describe processes with the same generality and flexibility as any other objects. We want to take the ideas of multiple perspective, process frameworks, signals, and multiprocessing and integrate them directly into the ways procedures and arguments are specified, data are passed back and forth, etc. In particular we will be developing a notion of *factored description* in which a procedure is defined through a description based on multiple perspectives. This description may combine high level statements about the structure of the process, its results, conditions on various parts, etc., along with detailed statements about the individual steps. The system should be able to look at and understand descriptions of its procedures as well as run them.

In most current formalisms there are completely different representations for the declarative statements (networks, or assertions, or clause sets) and the procedures. In those systems in which there is a uniform base,[24] the declarative form is used primarily as a notation for writing programs as a sequence of steps to be executed. We want to greatly expand the conceptual tools for describing and talking about procedures from multiple perspectives.[25] We believe that this is necessary for two complementary reasons.

First, the ability to describe and reason about procedures is useful for making programs easier to write, and necessary for the kinds of self-conscious strategy choosing, debugging, explanation, and self-modification that are increasingly becoming a part of complex computer systems. One of the major beauties of LISP is the fact that programs are themselves built from the language's data structures (atoms and lists), making it easy to write editors, debuggers, program analyzers, and programming assistants. We would like to apply this kind of self-analytic power at a higher level, using the reasoning, matching, and problem solving

---

[23] Candidates being considered (some in progress) are: a simple cryptarithmetic problem solver (see Newell & Simon, 1972, for a description of the task); SAM, the Yale story understander (Lehnert, 1976; Schank and the Yale AI Project, 1975); a learning program for recognizing a simple kind of ARCH (Winston, 1975); the Blocks world planning programs HACKER (Sussman, 1975) and NOAH (Sacerdoti, 1975); the Rutgers action understander, BELIEVER (Schmidt, 1975); MYCIN (Shortliffe, 1976), a simple medical advice system; a more complex medical reasoner, perhaps CASNET (Kulikowski, 1974) or a diagnosis program sketched at MIT (Rubin, 1975); a legal reasoner based on a recent MIT dissertation (Meldman, 1975); GSP, a general syntactic processor (Kaplan, 1973a); and travel assistant programs that are part of the series of GUS programs at Xerox PARC (Bobrow et al., 1976). We will not do all of the programs on the list, but include them as examples of the kinds of programs we would like to do.

[24] As in MEMOD (Norman, et al., 1975), or for that matter, simple LISP structures.

[25] Systems like HACKER (Sussman, 1975) and MYCROFT (Goldstein, 1974) are first steps in this direction.

names in a program context) can be put into the same mold. In future versions, we hope to provide a better structured, more uniform mechanism for all of these.

Integrated system. All of the interfaces between programs and the world (user interactions, file systems, etc.) are currently done using INTERLISP (Teitelman, 1975) and will have to be defined independently. This includes the obvious sorts of input–output, and also the user-interaction facilities for writing, filing, editing, compiling, running, and debugging programs. It also includes multiprocessing facilities such as the spaghetti stack of Bobrow and Wegbreit (1975). We believe that the expanded reasoning powers of KRL programs will make it possible to write systems that are more flexible and useful than those existing in LISP. One of our research goals will be to develop intelligent programming apprentices[27] within an integrated KRL system. In the area of input–output, we want to deal explicitly with different types of output device (random access stream, formatted page) and input device (streams, pointing devices, asynchronous event devices, such as keysets) in a style which makes it easy to apply the general tools of KRL to programs demanding sophisticated user interaction.

Syntax. The current syntax for KRL-0 is quite clumsy, since it was designed to operate in a LISP based system with a minimum of intermediate parsing. Except for the use of multiple bracket types, it is essentially LISP syntax. This results in an inordinately large number of bracketing characters in complex descriptions, and sequences such as ''})})}>]'' are not uncommon. We need to work out a more natural syntax. This will become even more important when we design the forms for describing programs and integrate them with the existing description forms.

4.3 Building a Layered System

Throughout this paper we have described ways in which KRL provides a flexible set of underlying tools, rather than embodying specific commitments about processing strategies, or the representation of specific areas of knowledge. In terms of Fig. 1, all we have described is the bottom layer. One of our major goals will be to build a set of strategy and knowledge modules on top of it. This will be done in the context of designing one or more specific systems for language understanding in a limited domain, with an emphasis on clean, well-defined interfaces.

The construction of an integrated system will demand building many components. As we construct each one, we want to do it in a style that does not limit its usefulness to the specific context for which it was written. There is no one solution to the problems at a given level that will be satisfactory for all systems. But we believe that it is possible to develop a set of alternative modules at each

[27]See Hewitt and Smith (1975) and Winograd (1975b) for some ideas in this direction.

powers of KRL as a fundamental element in our tools for designing, building, and working with KRL programs.

Second, as we explore the kinds of asynchronous, factored multiprocess styles of program organization that are coming into existence, we will move away from the notion of a program as a sequence of steps (or simple control structures), and will explore alternative views of a process description in the language itself. In addition to being able to describe procedure definitions statically, we also need ways of describing and manipulating descriptions of dynamic states of processes. Even in systems such as LISP in which programs can be represented in the data structures of the language, the state of a process is represented in a totally separate set of data structures (stacks, registers, etc.). One advantage of production systems[26] is that all control information is explicitly represented in the data structures. We hope to retain this property of uniformity and visibility, while providing a more structured set of mechanisms for building and manipulating control structures. These include primitives for building a priority ordered agenda of things to be done, assigning descriptions (in the declarative forms of the language) to processes on the agenda or currently being run, and assigning and consuming shared resource measures. This extension of the way in which programs can be written is the largest part of what needs to be done. We hope it will be one of the major advances achieved by KRL as a programming language. It will involve a good deal of further research into how programs for a multiprocess environment are naturally conceptualized, and how people can best use the power of signals, procedural attachment, and other mechanisms that extend normal definition and control structures. We also need to find ways of implementing interpreters and compilers who operate from complex descriptions of a desired procedure rather than a step-by-step program.

Data objects. We need to formally specify the semantics of those data objects we are currently borrowing from LISP (atoms, strings, numbers, lists, arrays) and provide the necessary primitives. We will add some new data types oriented more toward a multiprocessing approach, such as *streams, partially specified lists* and *sets*. There are currently some mechanisms for working with specified lists and sets within KRL-0, but they need to be better integrated with the procedures and the primitive use of lists. Along with the primitive data objects, there will be a corresponding set of descriptions (in the KRL formalism) for use in programs that explicitly manipulate data and do reasoning about its form.

A more uniform approach to indexing. KRL-0 contains a number of different mechanisms that can be viewed as carrying out a common task of using some kind of indexing mechanism to associate data objects (units or procedures) with names. Signal tables, the attachment of procedures to slots of units, and the associative index are very similar in structure. Other mechanisms (such as the use of variable

[26]See Davis and King (1975) for a discussion of control structures used in production systems.

level which are sufficiently broad and flexible that someone interested in working at the next higher level could choose between them, rather than building all the way down.

Over the course of several years and the design of several different systems, we hope to develop a large inventory of modules, each containing a substantial body of knowledge, and all expressed in a compatible formalism. If we are successful at finding the appropriate lines along which to decompose the knowledge which goes into language understanding (and thought processes in general), it will be possible to construct from them programs of much greater size and complexity than those now feasible.

4.4 Summary

We are in the process of developing a knowledge representation language that will integrate procedural knowledge with a richly structured declarative representation designed to combine logical adequacy with a concern for issues of memory structure and recognition-based reasoning processes. The representation provides for several independent dimensions of structuring which deal with the logical content, the relative accessibility of different pieces of knowledge, and the association of specialized processes with data at various levels of specificity.

The system provides a basic orientation toward a recognition process based on a procedural framework for matching. The control structure is based on multiprocessing with explicit (user-provided) scheduling and resource control. Process frameworks and procedure directories are used to give the user detailed control over the semantics of the fundamental system operations. These include: adding new descriptions to memory; searching for a memory unit matching a given description; matching a given pattern against a specific description; and scheduling processes, based on resource allocation.

The system is complex, and will continue to get more so in the near future. We are intentionally trying to be eclectic rather than reductive, what we can learn from our experiments with early implementations. As continuing experience indicates to us which of the facilities are most important, and points out ways in which they can be simplified, we will refine the language. However, we do not expect that it will ever be reduced to a very small set of mechanisms. Human thought, we believe, is the product of the interaction of a fairly large set of interdependent processes. Any representation language that is to be used in modeling thought or achieving "intelligent" performance will have to have an extensive and varied repertoire of mechanisms.

ACKNOWLEDGMENTS

This paper describes work being done jointly by the Understander Group at Xerox Palo Alto Research Center, and by a research group at the Artificial Intelligence Laboratory at Stanford. Ronald Kaplan, Martin Kay, David Levy, Paul Martin, Donald A. Norman, and Henry Thompson have played significant roles in its development. We have profited from extensive and insightful comments on earlier versions of this paper by Drew McDermott, Donald A. Norman, Aaron Sloman, and Ben Wegbreit.

REFERENCES

ANDERSON, J., & BOWER, G. *Human associative memory.* Washington. D.C.: Winston, 1973.

BOBROW, D. G., KAPLAN, R. M., KAY, M., NORMAN, D. A., THOMPSON, H. & WINOGRAD, T. GUS, a frame driven dialog system. *Artificial Intelligence.* 1977. **8**, No.1.

BOBROW, D. G. & NORMAN, D. A. Some principles of memory schemata. In D. G. Bobrow & A. M. Collins (Eds.), *Representation and understanding.* New York: Academic Press, 1975. pp. 131–150.

BOBROW, D. G., & WEGBREIT, E. B. A model and stack implementation of multiple environments. *Communication of the Association for Computing Machinery;* 1973. **16**. 591–603.

BRUCE, B. Case systems for natural language. *Artificial Intelligence.* 1975. **6**.

CARBONELL, J. R., & COLLINS, A. M. Natural semantics in artificial intelligence. *American Journal of Computational Linguistics,* 1974, **1**. Mfc. 3.

COLLINS, A., & QUILLIAN, M. R. Retrieval time from semantic memory. *Journal of Learning and Verbal Behaviour,* 1969, **9**, 432–438.

DAHL, O. J., & NYGAARD, K. SIMULA—an ALGOL-based simulation language. *Communication of the Association for Computing Machinery,* 1966, **9**, 671–678.

DAVIS, R., & KING, J. An overview of production systems. Memo AM-271. Stanford University Artificial Intelligence Laboratory, October 1975.

DEUTSCH, B. Establishing context in a task oriented dialog. *Journal of the Association for Computational Linguistics,* **4**, Microfiche 35, 1975.

FAHLMAN, S. A system for representing and using real-world knowledge. MIT AI-Memo-331. 1975.

FILLMORE, C. Against a checklist theory of meaning. *Proceedings of the First Annual Meeting of the Berkeley Linguistics Society.* Berkeley: Institute of Human Learning. 1975.

FISHER, D. A. Control structures for programming languages. Department of Computer Science, Carnegie University, May 1970.

GOLDSTEIN, I. P. Understanding simple picture programs. AI-TR-294. MIT AI Laboratory. September 1974.

HAYES-ROTH, F., & LESSER, V. Focus of attention in a distributed-logic speech understanding system. Department of Computer Science, Carnegie-Mellon University, January 1976.

HENDRIX, G. G. Expanding the utility of semantic networks through partitioning. *Advance Papers of the Fourth International Joint Conference on Artificial Intelligence, Tbilisi,* 1975, pp. 115–121.

HEWITT, C. Description and theoretical analysis (using schemata) of PLANNER: A language for proving theorems and manipulating models in a robot. AI-TR-258, MIT-AI Laboratory, April 1972.

HEWITT, C., BISHOP, P., STEIGER, R. A universal modular ACTOR formalism for artificial intelligence. *Proceedings of the Third International Joint Conference on Artificial Intelligence.* 1973, 235–245.

HEWITT, C., & SMITH, B. Towards a programming apprentice. *IEEE Transactions on Software Engineering,* 1975, **SE-1**, 26–45.

KAPLAN, R. M. A general syntactic processor. In R. Rustin (Ed.), *Natural language processing.* New York: Algorithmic Press, 1973. (a)

KAPLAN, R. M. A multi-processing approach to natural language. *Proceedings of the 1973 National Computer Conference.* Montvale, N.J.: AFIPS Press, 1973. Pp. 435–440. (b)

KAPLAN, R. M. On process models for sentence analysis. In Norman, D. A., Rumelhart, D. E., & the LNR Research Group, *Explorations in cognition*. San Francisco: Freeman, 1975.

KATZ, J. J., & FODOR, J. A. The structure of a semantic theory. In J. Fodor & J. Katz (Eds.), *The structure of language*. Englewood Cliffs, N.J.: Prentice Hall, 1964.

KUIPERS, B. A frame for frames: Representing knowledge for recognition. In D. G. Bobrow & A. M. Collins (Eds.), *Representation and understanding*. New York: Academic Press, 1975. Pp. 151–184.

KULIKOWSKI, C. A. A system for computer-based medical consultation. *Proceedings of National Computer Conference*, 1974.

LAMPSON, B., MITCHELL, J., & SATTERTHWAITE, E. On the transfer of control between contexts. In B. Robnet (Ed.), *Programming symposium, Paris 1974*. Heidelberg: Springer-Verlag, 1974.

LEARNING RESEARCH GROUP. *Personal dynamic media*. Xerox Palo Alto Research Center, SSL76-1, 1976.

LEHNERT, W. Human and computational question answering. *Cognitive Science*, 1977, **1**, 47–73.

MELDMAN, J. A. A preliminary study in computer-aided legal analysis. MIT project MAC TR 157, 1975.

MINSKY, M. A framework for representing knowledge. In P. Winston (Ed.), *The psychology of computer vision*. New York: McGraw-Hill, 1975.

MOORE, J., & NEWELL, A. How can MERLIN understand? In L. Gregg (Ed.), *Knowledge and cognition*. Hillsdale, N.J.: Lawrence Erlbaum Assoc., 1973.

NASH-WEBBER, B. The role of semantics. In automatic speech understanding, in D. G. Bobrow & A. M. Collins, *Representation and understanding*. New York: Academic Press, 1975. Pp. 351–383.

NEWELL, A., & SIMON, H. A. *Human problem solving*. Englewood Cliffs, N.J.: Prentice Hall, 1972.

NORMAN, D. A., & BOBROW, D. G. On data-limited and resource-limited processes. *Cognitive Psychology*, 1975, **7**, 44–64.

NORMAN, D. A., RUMELHART, D. E., & the LNR RESEARCH GROUP. *Explorations in cognition*. San Francisco: Freeman, 1975.

PAXTON, W., & ROBINSON, A. System integration and control in a speech understanding system. AI Center Technical Note 111, Menlo Park: SRI, 1975.

QUILLIAN, M. R. Semantic memory. In M. Minsky (Ed.), *Semantic information processing*. Cambridge: MIT Press, 1968.

REDDY, D. R., & Erman, L. Tutorial on system organization for speech understanding. In D. R. Reddy (Ed.), *Speech recognition*. New York: Academic Press, 1975.

ROSCH, E. Cognitive representations of semantic categories. *Journal of Experimental Psychology: General*, 1975, **104**, 192–233.

ROSCH, E., & MERVIS, C. Family Resemblances: Studies in the internal structure of categories. *Cognitive Psychology*, 1975, **7**, 573–605.

RUBIN, A. D. Hypothesis formation and evaluation in medical diagnosis (MIT-AI Technical Report 316). Cambridge: MIT, 1975.

SACERDOTI, E. The non-linear nature of plans. In *Advance papers of the fourth international conference on artificial intelligence, Tbilisi, 1975*. Pp. 206–214.

SCHANK, R. C. (Ed.) *Conceptual information processing*. Amsterdam: North-Holland, 1975. (a)

SCHANK, R. C. The structure of episodes in memory. In D. G. Bobrow & A. Collins (Eds.), *Representation and understanding*. New York: Academic Press, 1975. (b)

SCHANK, R. C., & the YALE AI PROJECT. SAM—A story understander. Yale University Computer Science Research Report #43, August 1975.

SCHMIDT, E. Understanding human actions. In B. L. Nash-Webber & R. C. Schank (Eds.), *Theoretical issues in natural language processing*. Cambridge, Mass., 1975.

SHORTLIFFE, E. *MYCIN: Computer-based medical consultations*. New York: American Elsevier, 1976.

SRINIVASAN, C. The architecture of coherent information systems. *IEEE Transactions on Computers*, **C-25**, 1976.

SUSSMAN, G. J. *A computational model of skill acquisition*. Amsterdam: North Holland, 1975.

TEITELMAN, W. *INTERLISP reference manual*. Xerox Palo Alto Research Center, December, 1975.

WINOGRAD, T. Five lectures on artificial intelligence (Stanford AI-Memo-246). Stanford. California: Stanford University, September 1974.

WINOGRAD, T. Frames and the declarative-procedural controversy. In D. G. Bobrow & A. Collins (Eds.), *Representation and understanding*. New York: Academic Press, 1975. (a)

WINOGRAD, T. Breaking the complexity barrier (again). *ACM SIGPLAN Notices*, 1975, **10**, 13–30. (b)

WINSTON, P. Learning structural descriptions from examples. In P. Winston (Ed.), *The psychology of computer vision*. New York: McGraw-Hill, 1975.

WOODS, W. A. What's in a link? In D. B. Bobrow & A. Collins (Eds.). *Representation and understanding*. New York: Academic Press, 1975.

14 / Patrick J. Hayes
The Logic of Frames

The extraordinary influence of frame representations led Pat Hayes in 1979 to take a closer look at what this movement had produced since Minsky's original work in 1975 (see [Minsky, Chapter 12]). According to Hayes—and his arguments are convincing—there are few positive suggestions to come out of this movement. In fact, outside of some new directions in "reflexive reasoning," there are virtually no new insights to be had at all from this line of work. One may argue with Hayes' pronouncement that "most of 'frames' is just a new syntax for first-order logic," but this was nonetheless the first serious attempt to cast work on frames in a formal light, that is, to carefully analyze in some standard logical way the meaning of frame structures. Hayes directs his analysis mainly at KRL [Bobrow and Winograd, Chapter 13], but his comments apply to other frame systems and beyond to other representation schemes. In particular, Hayes comments on what it is exactly that makes something a representation language (reminiscent of similar comments made in his earlier paper [Hayes, Chapter 1]). He also points the way to subsequent work on understanding default reasoning in frame systems (see [Etherington and Reiter, Chapter 17]), as well as further work that deals more carefully with the epistemological/heuristic distinction (see [McCarthy, Chapter 2]).

Appeared in *Frame Conceptions and Text Understanding*, 46–61, edited by D. Metzing, Berlin: Walter de Gruyter and Co., 1979.

The Logic of Frames

Introduction: Representation and Meaning

Minsky introduced the terminology of 'frames' to unify and denote a loose collection of related ideas on knowledge representation: a collection which, since the publication of his paper (Minsky, 1975) has become even looser. It is not at all clear now what frames are, or were ever intended to be.

I will assume, below, that frames were put forward as a (set of ideas for the design of a) formal language for expressing knowledge, to be considered as an alternative to, for example, semantic networks or predicate calculus. At least one group have explicitly designed such a language, KRL (Bobrow/Winograd, 1977a, 1977b), based on the frames idea. But it is important to distinguish this from two other possible interpretations of what Minsky was urging, which one might call the metaphysical and the heuristic (following the terminology of (McCarthy/Hayes, 1968)).

The "metaphysical" interpretation is, that to use frames is to make a certain kind of assumption about what entities shall be assumed to exist in the world being described. That is, to use frames is to assume that a certain *kind* of knowledge is to be represented by them. Minsky seems to be making a point like this when he urges the idea that visual perception may be facilitated by the storage of explicit 2-dimensional view prototypes and explicit rotational transformations between them. Again, the now considerable literature on the use of 'scripts' or similar frame-like structures in text understanding systems (Charniak, 1977; Lehnert, 1977; Schank, 1975) seems to be based on the view that what might be called "programmatic" knowledge of stereotypical situations like shopping-in-a-supermarket or going-somewhere-on-a-bus is 'necessary in order to understand English texts about these situations. Whatever the merits of this view (its proponents seem to regard it as simply *obvious*, but see (Feldman, 1975) and (Wilks, 1976) for some contrary arguments), it is clearly a thesis about what sort of things a program needs to know, rather than about *how* those things should or can be *represented*. One could describe the sequence of events in a typical supermarket visit as well in almost any reasonable expressive formal language.

The "heuristic", or as I would prefer now to say, "implementation", interpretation is, that frames are a computational device for organising stored representations in computer memory, and perhaps also, for organising the processes of retrieval and inference which manipulate these stored representations. Minsky seems to be making a point like this when he refers to the computational ease with which one can switch from one frame to another in a frame-system by following pointers. And many other authors have referred with evident approval to the way in which frames, so considered, facilitate certain retrieval operations. (There has been less emphasis on undesirable computational features of frame-like hierarchical organisations of memory.) Again, however, none of this discussion engages representational issues.

A given representational language can be implemented in all manner of ways: predicate calculus assertions may be implemented as lists, as character sequences, as trees, as networks, as patterns in an associative memory, etc: all giving different computational properties but all encoding the same representational language. Indeed, one might almost characterise the art of programming as being able to deploy this variety of computational techniques to achieve implementations with various computational properties. Similarly, any one of these computational techniques can be used to implement many essentially different representational languages. Thus, circuit diagrams, perspective line drawings, and predicate calculus assertions, three entirely distinct formal languages (c.f. Hayes, 1975), can be all implemented in terms of list structures. Were it not so, every application of computers would require the development of a new specialised programming language.

Much discussion in the literature seems to ignore or confuse these distinctions. They are vital if we are to have any useful taxonomy, let alone theory, of representational languages. For example, if we confuse representation with implementation then LISP would seem a universal representational language, which stops all discussion before we can even begin.

One can characterise a representational language as one which has (or can be given) a semantic theory, by which I mean an account (more or less formal, more or less precise — this is not the place to argue for a formal model theory, but see Hayes, 1977) of how expressions of the language relate to the individuals or relationships or actions or configurations, etc., comprising the world, or worlds about which the language claims to express knowledge. (Such an account may — in fact must — entail making some metaphysical assumptions, but these will usually be of a very general and minimal kind (for example, that the world consists of individual entities and relationships of one kind or another which hold between them: this is the ontological commitment needed to understand predicate logic)). Such a semantic theory defines the *meanings* of expressions of the language. That's what makes a formal language into a representational language: its expressions carry meaning. The semantic theory should explain the way in which they do this carrying. To sum up, then, although frames are sometimes understood at the metaphysical level, and sometimes at the computational level, I will discuss them as a representational proposal: a proposal for a language for the representation of knowledge, to be compared with other such representational languages: a language with a meaning.

What Do Frames Mean?

A frame is a data structure — we had better say *expression* — intended to represent a 'stereotypical situation'. It contains named '*slots*', which can be filled with other expressions — *fillers* — which may themselves be frames, or presumably simple names or identifiers (which may themselves be somehow associated with other frames, but not by a slot-filler relationship: otherwise the trees formed by filling slots with frames recursively, would always be infinitely deep). For example, we might have a frame representing a typical house, with slots called *kitchen, bathroom, bedrooms, lavatory, room-with-TV-in-it, owner, address,* etc.. A particular house is then to be represented by an *instance* of this *house* frame, obtained by filling in the slots with specifications of the corresponding parts of the particular house, so that, for example, the *kitchen* slot may be filled by an instance of the frame *contemporary-kitchen* which has slots *cooker, floorcovering, sink, cleanliness,* etc., which may contain in turn respectively an instance of the *split-level* frame, the identifier *vinyl*, an instance of the *double-drainer* frame, and the identifier '13' (for "very clean"), say. Not all slots in an instance need be filled, so that we can express doubt (e.g. "I don't know where the lavatory is"), and in real 'frame' languages other refinements are included, e.g. descriptors such as "which-is-red" as slot fillers, etc. We will come to these later. From examples such as these (c.f. also Minsky's birthday-party example in Minsky, 1975), it seems fairly clear what frames mean. A frame instance denotes an individual, and each slot denotes a relationship which may hold between that individual and some other. Thus, if an instance (call it G00097) of the *house* frame has its slot called *kitchen* filled with a frame instance called, say G00082, then this means that the relationship *kitchen* (or, better, *is kitchen of*) holds between G00097 and G00082. We could express this same assertion (for it is an assertion) in predicate calculus by writing: is kitchen of (G00097, G00082).

Looked at this way, frames are essentially bundles of properties. *House* could be paraphrased as something like $\lambda x. (\text{kitchen}(x,y_1)$ & bathroom (x,y_2) & ...) where the free variables y_i correspond to the slots. Instantiating *House* to yield a particular house called *Dunroamin* (say), corresponds to applying the λ-expression to the identifier *Dunroamin* to get kitchen (dunroamin, y_1) & bathroom (dunroamin, y_2) & ... which, once the "slots" are filled, is an assertion about Dunroamin.

Thus far, then, working only at a very intuitive level, it seems that frames are simply an alternative syntax for expressing relationships between individuals, i.e. for predicate logic. But we should be careful, since although the meanings may appear to be the same, the inferences sanctioned by frames may differ in some crucial way from those sanctioned by logic. In order to get more insight into what frames are supposed to mean we should examine the ways in which it is suggested that they be *used*.

One inference rule we have already met is *instantiation*: given a frame representing a concept, we can generate an instance of the concept by filling in its slots. But there is another, more subtle, form of inference suggested by Minsky and realised explicitly in some applications of frames. This is the "criteriality" inference. If we find fillers for all the slots of a frame, then this rule enables us to infer that an appropriate instance of the concept does indeed exist. For example, if an entity has a kitchen and a bathroom and an address and ..., etc.; then it must be a house. Possession of these attributes is a sufficient as well as necessary condition for an entity to qualify as a house, criteriality tells us.

An example of the use of this rule is in perceptual reasoning. Suppose for example the concept of a letter is represented as a frame, with slots corresponding to the parts of the letter (strokes and junctions, perhaps), in a program to read handwriting (as was done in the Essex Fortran project (Brady/Wielinga, 1977)). Then the discovery of fillers for all the slots of the 'F' frame means that one has indeed found an 'F' (the picture is considerably more complicated than this, in fact, as all inferences are potentially subject to disconfirmation: but this does not affect the present point).

Now one can map this understanding of a frame straightforwardly into first-order logic also. A frame representing the concept C, with slot-relationships $R_1, ..., R_n$, becomes the assertion

$$\forall x\ (C(x) \equiv \exists y_1,...,y_n.\ R_1(x,y_1)\ \&\ ...\ \&\ R_n(x,y_n))$$

or, expressed in clausal form:

$$\forall x\ C(x) \supset R_1(x,f_1(x))$$
$$\&\ \forall x\ C(x) \supset R_2(x,f_2(x))$$
$$\&\ \vdots$$

$$\&\ \forall x \forall y_i\ R_1(x,y_1)\ \&\ R_2(x,y_2)\ \&\ ...\ \&\ R_n(x,y_n).\ \supset C(x)$$

The last long clause captures the criteriality assumption exactly. Notice the Skolem functions in the other clauses: they have a direct intuitive reading, e.g. for *kitchen*, the corresponding function is *kitchenof*, which is a function from houses to their kitchens. These functions correspond exactly to the *selectors* which would apply to a frame, considered now as a data structure, to give the values of its fields (the fillers of its slots). All the variables here are universally quantified. If we assume that our logic contains equality, then we could dispense altogether with the slot-relations R_i and express the frame as an assertion using equality. In many ways this is more natural. The above then becomes:

$$C(x) \supset \exists y.\ y = f_1(x)$$
$$\&\ \text{etc.}$$
$$f_1(x) = y_1\ \&\ ...\ \&\ f_n(x) = y_n.\ \supset C(x)$$

ever. So far as one can tell, the processes of reasoning involved may be expressible only in higher-order logic. For example, it may be necessary to construct new relations by abstraction during the "matching" process. It is known (Huet, 1972; Pietrzykowski/Jensen, 1973) that the search spaces which this gives rise to are of great complexity, and it is not entirely clear that it will be possible to automate this process in a reasonable way.)

This reading of a frame as an assertion has the merit of putting frames, frame-instances and 'matching' assumptions into a common language with a clear extensional semantics which makes it quite clear what all these structures *mean*. The (usual) inference rules are clearly correct, and are sufficient to account for most of the deductive properties of frames which are required. Notice, for example, that no special mechanism is required in order to see that J.S. is a Dogowner: it follows by ordinary first-order reasoning.

One technicality is worth mentioning. In KRL, the same slot-name can be used in different frames to mean different relations. For example, the *age* of a person is a number, but his *age* as an airline passenger (i.e. in the traveller frame) is one of {infant, child, adult}. We could not allow this conflation, and would have to use different names for the different relations. It is an interesting exercise to extend the usual first-order syntax with a notion of name-scope in order to allow such pleasantries. But this is really nothing more than syntactic sugar.

Seeing As

One apparently central intuition behind frames, which seems perhaps to be missing from the above account, is the idea of *seeing* one thing *as though* it were another: or of specifying an object by comparison with a known prototype, noting the similarities and points of difference (Bobrow/Winograd, 1977a). This is the basic analogical reasoning behind MERLIN (Moore/Newell, 1973), which Minsky cites as a major influence.

Now this idea can be taken to mean several rather different things. Some of them can be easily expressed in deductive-assertional terms, others less easily.

The first and simplest interpretation is that the 'comparison' is filling-in the details. Thus, to say JS is a man tells us something about him, but to say he is a bus conductor tells us more. The bus conductor frame would presumably have slots which did not appear in the Man frame (*since-when* for example, and *bus-company*), but it would also have a slot to be filled by the Man instance for JS (or refer to him in some other way), so have access to all his slots. Now there is nothing remarkable here. All this involves is asserting more and more restrictive properties of an entity. This can all be done within the logical framework of the last section.

The second interpretation is that a frame represents a 'way of looking' at an entity, and this is a *correct* way of looking at it. For example a Man may also

(Where the existential quantifiers are supposed to assert that the functions are applicable to the individual in question. This assumes that the function symbols f_i denote partial functions, so that it makes sense to write $\neg \exists y. \ y = f_i(x)$. Other notations are possible.)

We see then that criterial reasoning can easily be expressed in logic. Such expression makes clear, moreover (what is sometimes not clear in frames literature) whether or not criteriality is being assumed. A third form of frames reasoning has been proposed, often called *matching* (Bobrow/Winograd, 1977a). Suppose we have an instance of a concept, and we wish to know whether it can plausibly be regarded as also being an instance of another concept. Can we view John Smith as a dog-owner?, for example, where J.S. is an instance of the Man frame, let us suppose, and Dogowner is another frame. We can rephrase this question: can we find an instance of the dog-owner frame which *matches* J.S.? The sense of *match* here is what concerns us. Notice that this cannot mean a simple syntactic unification, but must rest — if it is possible at all — on some assumptions about the domain about which the frames in question express information.

For example, perhaps Man has a slot called *pet*, so we could say that a sufficient condition for J.S.'s being matchable to Dog-owner is that his *pet* slot is filled with as object known to be canine. Perhaps Dog-owner has slots *dog* and *name*: then we could specify how to build an instance of dog-owner corresponding to J.S.: fill the *name* slot with J.S.'s name (or perhaps with J.S. himself, or some other reference to him) and the *dog* slot with J.S.'s pet. KRL has facilities for just this sort of transference of fillers from slots in one frame to another, so that one can write routines to actually perform the matchings.

Given our expressions of frames as assertions, the sort of reasoning exemplified by this example falls out with very little effort. All we need to do is express the slot-to-slot transference by simple implications, thus: $Isdog(x)$ & $petof(x,y). \supset dogof(x,y)$ (using the first formulation in which slots are relations). Then, given:

name (J.S., "John Smith")   (1)
& pet (J.S., Fido)   (2)
& Isdog (Fido)   (3)

(the first two from the J.S. instance of the 'man' frame, the third from general world-knowledge: or perhaps from Fido's being in fact an instance of the Dog frame) it follows directly that

dogof (J.S., Fido)   (4)

whence, by the criteriality of Dogowner, from (1) and (4), we have:

Dogowner (J.S.).

The translation of this piece of reasoning into the functional notation is left as an exercise for the reader.

All the examples of 'matching' I have seen have this rather simple character. More profound examples are hinted at in (Bobrow/Winograd, 1977b), how-be a Dog-owner, and neither of these is a *further* specification of the other: each has slots not possessed by the other frame. Thus far, there is nothing here more remarkable than the fact that several properties may be true of a single entity. Something may be both a Man *and* a Dog-owner, of course: or both a friend *and* an employee, or both a day *and* a birthday. And each of these pairs can have its own independent criteriality.

However, there is an apparent difficulty. A single thing may have apparently contradictory properties, seen from different points of view. Thus, a man viewed as a working colleague may be suspicious and short tempered; but viewed as a family man, may have a sweet and kindly disposition. One's views of oneself often seem to change depending on how one perceives one's social role, for another example. And in neither case, one feels, is there an outright contradiction: the different viewpoints 'insulate' the parts of the potential contradiction from one another.

I think there are three possible interpretations of this, all expressible in assertional terms. The first is that one is really asserting different properties in the two frames: that 'friendly' *at work* and 'friendly' *at home* are just different notions. This is analogous to the case discussed above where 'age' means different relations in two different contexts. The second is that the two frames somehow encode an extra parameter: the time or place, for example: so that Bill really is unfriendly *at work* and friendly *at home*. In expressing the relevant properties as assertions one would be obliged then to explicitly represent these parameters as extra arguments in the relevant relations, and provide an appropriate theory of the times, places, etc. which distinguish the various frames. These may be subtle distinctions, as in the self seen-as-spouse or the self seen-as-hospital-patient or seen-as-father, etc., where the relevant parameter is something like interpersonal role. I am not suggesting that I have any idea what a theory of these would be like, only that to introduce such distinctions, in frames or any other formalism, is to assume that there *is* such a theory- perhaps a very simple one. The third interpretation is that, after all, the two frames contradict one another. Then of course a faithful translation into assertions will also contain an explicit contradiction.

The assertional language makes these alternatives explicit, and forces one who uses it to choose which interpretation he means. And one can always express that interpretation in logic. At worst, *every* slot-relation can have the name of its frame as an extra parameter, if really necessary.

There is however a third, more radical, way to understand seeing-as. This is to view a seeing-as as a metaphor or analogy, without actually asserting that it is *true*. This is the MERLIN idea. Example: a man may be looked at as a pig, if you think of his home as a sty, his nose as a snout, and his feet as trotters. Now such a caricature may be useful in reasoning, without its being taken to be veridically true. One may *think of* a man as a pig, knowing perfectly well that as a matter of fact he isn't one.

MERLIN's notation and inference machinery for handling such analogies are very similar respectively to frames and "matching", and we have seen that this is merely first-order reasoning. The snag is that we have no way to distinguish a 'frame' representing a mere caricature from one representing a real assertion. Neither the old MERLIN (in which *all* reasoning is this analogical reasoning) nor KRL provide any means of making this rather important distinction.

What does it *mean* to say that you can look at a man as a pig? I think the only reasonable answer is something like: certain of the properties of (some) men are preserved under the mapping defined by the analogy. Thus, perhaps, pigs are greedy, illmannered and dirty, their snouts are short, upturned and blunt, and they are rotund and short-legged. Hence, a man with these qualities (under the mapping which defines the analogy: hence, the man's *nose will be* upturned, his *house* will be dirty) may be plausibly be regarded as pig-like. But of course there are many other properties of pigs which we would *not* intend to transfer to a men under the analogy: quadrupedal gait, being a source of bacon, etc. (Although one of the joys of using such analogies is finding ways of extending them: "Look at all the little piggies ... sitting down to eat their bacon" [G. Harrison]). So, the intention of such a caricature is, that some -not all- of the properties of the caricature shall be transferred to the caricaturee. And the analogy is correct, or plausible, when these transferred properties do, in fact, hold of the thing caricatured: when the man *is* in fact greedy, slovenly, etc.....

This is almost exactly what the second sense of seeing-as seemed to mean: that the man 'matches' the pig frame. The difference (apart from the systematic rewriting) is that here we simply cannot assume criteriality of this pig frame. To say that a man *is* a pig is false: yet we have assumed that this fellow does fit this pig frame. Hence the properties expressed in this pig frame cannot be criterial for pig. To say that a man *is* a pig is to use criteriality incorrectly.

This then helps to distinguish this third *sense* of seeing-as from the earlier senses: the failure of criteriality. And this clearly indicates why MERLIN and KRL cannot distinguish caricatures from factual assertions; for criteriality is not made explicit in these languages. We can however easily express a non-criterial frame as a simple assertion.

One might wonder what use the 'frame' idea is when criteriality is abandoned, since a frame is now merely a conjunction. Its boundaries appear arbitrary: why conjoin just these properties together? The answer lies in the fact that not *all* properties of the caricature are asserted of the caricaturee, just those bundled together in the seeing-as frame. The bundling here is used to delimit the scope of the transfer. We could say that these properties were criterial for *pig-likeness* (rather than *pig-hood*).

In order to express caricatures in logic, then, we need only to define the systematic translations of vocabulary: nose — snout, etc., this seems to require some syntactic machinery which logic does not provide: the ability to substitute one relation symbol for another in an assertion. This kind of "analogy map-

"ping" was first developed some years ago by R. Kling and used by him to express analogies in mathematics. Let ϕ be the syntactic mapping 'our' of the analogy (e.g. 'snout¹ → 'nose¹, 'sty¹ → 'house¹), and suppose $\lambda x. \psi(x)$ is the defining conjunction of the frame of Pig-likeness:

Pig-like $(x) \equiv \psi(x)$

(Where ψ may contain several existentially bound variables, and generally may be a complicated assertion). Then we can say that Pig-like (Fred) is true just when $\phi(\psi)$ holds for Fred, i.e. the asserted properties are *actually* true of Fred, when the relation names are altered according to the syntactic mapping ϕ. So, a caricature frame needs to contain, or be somehow associated with, a specification of how its vocabulary should be altered to fit reality. With this modification, all the rest of the reasoning involved is first-order and conventional.

Defaults

One aspect of frame reasoning which is often considered to lie outside of logic is the idea of a default value: a value which is taken to be the slot filler in the absence of explicit information to the contrary. Thus, the default for the *home-port* slot in a traveller frame may be the city where the travel agency is located (Bobrow et al. 1977).

Now, defaults certainly seem to take us outside first-order reasoning, in the sense that we cannot express the assumption of the default value as a simple first-order consequence of there being no contrary information. For if we could, the resulting inference would have the property that $p \vdash q$ but $(p \& r) \vdash \neg q$ for suitable p, q and r (p does not deny the default: q represents the default assumption: r overrides the default), and no logical system behaves this way (Curry [1956] for example, takes $p \vdash q \Rightarrow p \& r \vdash q$ to be the fundamental property of all 'logistic' systems).

This shows however only that a *naive* mapping of default reasoning into assertional reasoning fails. The moral is to distrust naivety. Let us take an example. Suppose we have a Car frame and an instance of it for my car, and suppose it has a slot called *status*, with possible values {OK, *struggling, needs-attention, broken*}, and the default is OK. That is, in the absence of contrary information, I assume the car is OK. Now I go to the car, and I see that the tyre is flat: I am surprised, and I conclude that (contrary to what I expected), the correct filler for the *status* slot is *broken*. But, it is important to note, my state of knowledge has changed. I was previously making an assumption — that the car was OK — which was reasonable *given my state of knowledge at the time*. We might say that if ψ represented my state of knowledge, then status (car) = OK was a reasonable inference from ψ: $\psi \vdash$ status (car) = OK. But once I know the tyre is flat, we have a new state of knowledge ψ_1, and of course

$\psi_1 \vdash$ status (car) = broken. In order for this to be deductively possible, it must be that ψ_1 is got from ψ not merely by adding new beliefs, but also by removing some old ones. That is, when I see the flat tyre I am *surprised*: I had expected that it was OK. (This is not to say that I had explicitly considered the possibility that the tyre might be flat, and rejected it. It only means that my state of belief was such that the tyres being OK was a consequence of it). And of course this makes sense: indeed, I was surprised. Moreover, there is no contradiction between my earlier belief that the car was OK and my present belief that it is broken. If challenged, I would not say that I had previously been irrational or mad, only misinformed (or perhaps just *wrong*, in the sense that I was entertaining a false belief).

As this example illustrates, default assumptions involve an implicit reference to the whole state of knowledge at the time the assumption was generated. Any event which alters the state of knowledge is liable therefore to upset these assumptions. If we represent these references to knowledge states explicitly, then 'default' reasoning can be easily and naturally expressed in logic. To say that the default for *home-port* is Palo Alto is to say that unless the current knowledge-state says otherwise, then we will assume that it is Palo Alto, *until the knowledge-state changes*. Let us suppose we can somehow refer to the current knowledge-state (denoted by NOW), and to a notion of derivability (denoted by the turnstile $\vdash$). Then we can express the default assumption by:

$\exists y.$ NOW $\vdash$ ⌜homeport (traveller)⌝ $= y^1 \vee$ homeport (traveller) $=$ Palo Alto. The conclusion of which allows us to infer that *homeport* (traveller) = Palo-Alto *until the state of knowledge changes*. When it does, we would have to establish this conclusion for the new knowledge state.

I believe this is intuitively plausible. Experience with manipulating collections of beliefs should dispel the feeling that one can predict all the ways new knowledge can affect previously held beliefs. We do not have a theory of this process, nor am I claiming that this notation provides one.* But *any* mechanism — whether expressed in frames or otherwise — which makes strong assumptions on weak evidence needs to have some method for unpicking these assumptions when things go wrong, or equivalently of controlling the propagation of inferences from the assumptions. This inclusion of a reference to the knowledge-state which produced the assumption is in the latter category. An example of the kind of axiom which might form part of such a theory is this. Suppose $\phi \vdash p$, and hence p, is in the knowledge-state ϕ, and suppose we wish to generate a new knowledge-state ϕ' by adding the observation q. Let ψ be $\phi - $ ⌜$\phi \vdash p^1$ and all inferred consequences of ⌜$\phi \vdash p^1$. Then if $\psi \cup \{q^1\} \nvdash \neg p$, define ϕ' to be $\psi \cup$ ⌜$\psi \vdash p^1; q^1$. This can all be written, albeit rather rebarbitively, in logic augmented with notations for

---

* Recent work of Doyle, McDermott and Reiter is providing such a theory: see (Doyle, 1978) (McDermott/Doyle, 1978) (Reiter, 1978)

describing constructive operations upon knowledge-states. It would justify for example the transfer of *status* (car) = OK past an observation of the form, say, that the car was parked in an unusual position, provided that the belief state did not contain anything which allowed one to conclude that an unusual parking position entailed anything wrong with the car. (It would also justify transferring it past an observation like *it is raining*, or *my mother is feeling ill*, but these transfers can be justified by a much simpler rule: if p and q have no possible inferential connections in φ — this can be detected very rapidly from the 'connection graph' (Kowalski 1973) — then addition of q cannot affect p.)

To sum up, a close analysis of what defaults mean shows that they are intimately connected with the idea of *observations*: additions of fresh knowledge into a data-base. Their role in *inference* — the drawing of consequences of assumptions — is readily expressible in logic, but their interaction with observation requires that the role of the state of the system's own knowledge is made explicit. This requires not a new *logic*, but an unusual *ontology*, and some new primitive relations. We need to be able to talk *about the system itself*, in its own language, and to involve assumptions about itself in its own processes of reasoning.

Reflexive Reasoning

We have seen that most of 'frames' is just a new syntax for parts of first-order logic. There are one or two apparently minor details which give a lot of trouble, however, especially defaults. There are two points worth making about this. The first is, that I believe that this complexity, revealed by the attempt to formulate these ideas in logic, is not an artefact of the translation but is intrinsic to the ideas involved. Defaults just *are* a complicated notion, with far-reaching consequences for the whole process of inference-making. The second point is a deeper one.

In both cases — caricatures and defaults — the necessary enrichment of logic involved adding the ability to talk about the system itself, rather than about the worlds of men, pigs and travel agents. I believe these are merely two relatively minor aspects of this most important fact: much common-sense reasoning involves the reasoner in thinking about himself and his own abilities as well as about the world. In trying to formalise intuitive common-sense reasoning I find again and again that this awareness of one's own internal processes of deduction and memory is crucial to even quite mundane arguments. There is only space for one example.

I was once talking to a Texan about television. This person, it was clear, knew far more about electronics than I did. We were discussing the number of lines per screen in different countries. One part of the conversation went like this.

Texan: You have 900 lines in England, don't you?
Me: No, 625.
Texan (confidently): I *thought* it was 900.
Me (somewhat doubtfully): No, I think it's 625.
(pause)
  Say, they couldn't change it without altering the sets, could they? I mean by sending some kind of signal from the transmitter or.....
Texan: No, they'd sure have to alter the receivers.
Me (now confident): Oh, well, it's definitely 625 lines then.

I made a note of my own thought processes immediately afterwards, and they went like this. I *remembered* that we had 625 lines in England. (This remembering cannot be introspectively examined: it *seems* like a primitive ability, analogous to FETCH in CONNIVER. I will take it to be such a primitive in what follows. Although this seems a ludicrously naive assumption, the internal structure of remembering will not concern us here, so we might as well take it to be primitive.) However, the Texan's confidence shook me, and I examined the belief in a little more detail. Many facts emerged: I remembered in particular that we had changed from 405 lines to 625 lines, and that this change was a long, expensive and complicated process. For several years one could buy dual-standard sets which worked on either system. My parents, indeed, had owned such a set, and it was prone to unreliability, having a huge multigang sliding-contact switch: I had examined its insides once. There had been newspaper articles about it, technical debates in the popular science press, etc... It was not the kind of event which could have passed unnoticed. (It was this *richness of detail*, I think, which gave the memory its subjective confidence: I couldn't have imagined all *that*, surely?) So if there had been another, subsequent, alteration to 900 lines, there would have been another huge fuss. But I had no memory at all of any such fuss: so it couldn't have happened. (I had a definite subjective impression of *searching* for such a memory. For example, I briefly considered the possibility that it had happened while my family and I were in California for 4 months, being somehow managed with great alacrity that time: but rejected this when I realised that our own set still worked, unchanged, on our return). Notice how this conclusion was obtained. It was the kind of event I would remember; but I don't remember it; so it didn't happen. This argument crucially involves an explicit assertion about my own memory. It is not enough that I didn't remember the event: I had to *realise* that I didn't remember it, and *use* that realisation in an argument.

The Texan's confidence still shook me somewhat, and I found a possible flaw in my argument. *Maybe* the new TV sets were constructed in a new sophisticated way which made it possible to alter the number of lines by remote control, say, by a signal from the transmitter. (This seems quite implausible to me now; but my knowledge of electronics is not rapidly accessible, and it did seem a viable possibility at the moment). How to check whether this was possible? Why, ask the expert: which I did, and his answer sealed the only hole I could find in the argument.

This process involves taking a previously constructed argument — a proof, or derivation — as an object, and inferring properties of it: that a certain step in it is weak (can be denied on moderately plausible assumption), for example. Again, this is an example of *reflexive reasoning*: reasoning involving descriptions of the self.

Conclusion

I believe that an emphasis on the analysis of such processes of reflexive reasoning is one of the few positive suggestions which the 'frames' movement has produced. Apart from this, there are no new insights to be had there: no new processes of reasoning, no advance in expressive power.

Nevertheless, as an historical fact, 'frames' have been extraordinarily influential. Perhaps this is in part because the original idea was interesting, but vague enough to leave scope for creative imagination. But a more serious suggestion is that the *real force* of the frames idea was not at the representational level at all, but rather at the implementation level: a suggestion about how to organise large memories. Looked at in this light, we could sum up 'frames' as the suggestion that we should *store* assertions in nameable 'bundles' which can be retrieved via some kind of indexing mechanism on their names. In fact, the suggestion that we should store assertions in non-clausal form.

Acknowledgements

I would like to thank Frank Brown and Terry Winograd for helpful comments on an earlier draft of this paper.

Appendix: Translation of KRL-φ into Predicate Logic

KRL	many-sorted predicate logic
Units	
(i) Basic	Unary predicate (sort predicate: assuming a disjoint sort structure.)
(ii) Specialisation	Unary predicate
(iii) Abstract	Unary predicate
(iv) Individual	name (individual constant)
(v) Manifestation	sometimes a λ-expression $\lambda x.\, P(x)\, \&\, \ldots\, \&\, Q(x)$ sometimes an $\in$-expression $\in x.\, P(x)\, \&\, \ldots\, \&\, Q(x)$ (i.e. a variable over the set $\{x: P(x)\, \&\, \ldots\, \&\, Q(x)\}$
(vi) Relation	relation

Slot	binary relation or unary function
Descriptors	
(i) direct pointer	name
(ii) Perspective e.g. (a trip with destination = Boston airline = TWA)	λ-expression e.g. $\lambda x.\, trip(x)\, \&\, destination(x) = Boston\, \&\, airline(x) = TWA$ (in this case both fillers are unique. If not we would use a relation, e.g. $airline(x, TWA)$) ι-expression
(iii) Specification e.g. (the actor from Act E17(a chase...))	e.g. $\iota x.\, actor(E17) = x$ or $\iota x.\, actor(E17) = x\, \&\, Act(E17)$ λ-expression
(iv) predication	non-atomic expression
(v) logical boolean	ι-expression
(vi) restriction e.g. (the one (a mouse) (which owns (a dog)))	e.g. $\iota x.\, mouse(x)\, \&\, \exists y.dog(y)\, \&\, owns(x,y)$ ι-expression with conditional body
(vii) selection e.g. (using (the age from Person this one) select from (which is less than 2) ~ Infant (which is at least 12) ~ Adult otherwise child	e.g. $\iota x.\, (age(this\ one) < 2\, \&\, x = infant\, \vee\, (age)(this\ one) \geq 12\, \&\, x = adult)\, \vee\, (age(this\ one) < 2\, \&\, age(this\ one) \geq 12\, \&\, x = child)$
(viii) set specification	λ-expression (sets coded as predicates) or set specification (if we use set theory. Only very simple set theory is necessary)
(ix) contingency e.g. (during state 24 then (the topblock from (a stack with height = 3)))	ι-expression or $\in$-expression whose body mentions a state or has a bound state variable. e.g. $\iota x.\exists y.\, is\ stack(y, state\ 24)\, \&\, height(y) = 3\, \&\, topblock(y, x)$ where I have taken stack to be a contingent property: other choices are possible (e.g. stacks always "exist" but have zero height in some states).

Examples

$Traveller(x) \supset Person(x)\, \&$
$\qquad (category(x) = infant$
$\qquad \vee\, category(x) = child$
$\qquad \vee\, category(x) = adult)$
$\qquad \&\, \exists y.\, airport(y)\, \&\, preferredairport(x,y)$

$Person(x) \supset string(first\ name(x))\, \&\, string(last\ name(x))$
$\qquad \&\, integer(age(x))$
$\qquad \&\, city(nametown(x))$
$\qquad \&\, address(streetaddress(x))$

Person (G0043)
& firstname (G0043) = "Juan"
& foreignname (lastname (G0043))
& firstcharacter (lastname (G0043)) = "M"
& age (G0043) > 21

Traveller (G0043)
& category (G0043) = Adult
& preferredairport (G0043, SJO)

References

Bobrow, D.G., Kaplan, R.M., Norman, D.A., Thompson, H. and Winograd, T.
1977
"GUS, a Frame-Driven Dialog System", *Artificial Intelligence* 8, 155–173.

Bobrow, D.G. and Winograd, T.
1977a
"An Overview of KRL", *Cognitive Science* 1, 3–46.
1977b
"Experience with KRL-O: One Cycle of a Knowledge Representation Language", Proc. 5th Int. Joint Conf. on AI, MIT, (vol 1), 213–222.

Brady, J.M. and Wielinga, B.J.
1977
"Reading the Writing on the Wall", Proc. Workshop on Computer Vision, Amherst Mass.

Charniak, E.
1977
"Ms. Malaprop, a Language Comprehension Program", Proc. 5th Int. Joint Conf. on AI, MIT, (vol 1), 1–8.

Curry, H.B.
1956
Introduction to Mathematical Logic (Amsterdam: Van Nostrand)

Doyle, J.
1978
Truth Maintenance System for Problem Solving, Memo TR-419, A.I. Laboratory, MIT

Feldman, J.
1975
"Bad-Mouthing Frames", Proc. Conf. on Theor. Issues in Natural Language Processing", Cambridge Mass, 102–103.

Hayes, P.J.
1975
"Some Problems and Non-problems in Representation Theory", Proc. 1st AISB Conf, Brighton Sussex.
1977
"In Defence of Logic", 5 Int. Joint Conf. on AI, MIT, (vol 2), 559–565.

Huet, G.P.
1972
Constrained Resolution: a Complete Method for Type Theory, Jenning's Computer Science, Report 1117, Cace Western University.

Kowalski, R.
1973
An Improved Theorem-Proving System for First Order Logic, DCL Memo 65, Edinburgh.

Lehnert, W.
1977
"Human and Computational Question Answering", *Cognitive Science* 1, 47–73.

McCarthy, J. and Hayes, J.P.
1969
"Some Philosophical Problems from the Standpoint of Artificial Intelligence", *Machine Intelligence* 4, 463–502.

McDermott, D. and Doyle, J.
1978
Non-monotonic logic I, Memo AI-486, A.I. Laboratory, MIT

Minsky, M.
1975
"A Framework for Representing Knowledge", in P. Winston (Ed.) *The Psychology of Computer Vision*, (New York: McGraw-Hill), 211–277.

Moore, J. and Newell, A.
1973
"How Can MERLIN Understand?", in L. Gregg (Ed.) *Knowledge and Cognition* (Hilsdale New York: Lawrence Erlbaum Assoc), 201–310.

Pietrzykowski, T. and Jensen, D.
1973
Mechanising W-Order Type Theory through Unification, Dept. of Applied Analysis and Comp. Science, Report CS-73-16, University of Waterloo.

Reiter, R.
1978
"On Reasoning by Default", Proc. 2nd Symp. on Theor. Issues in Natural Language Processing, Urbana, Illinois.

Schank, R.
1975
"The Structure of Episodes in Memory", in D. G. Bobrow and A. Collins (Eds) *Representation and Understanding*, (New York: Academic Press), 237–272.

Wilks, Y.
1976
"Natural Language Understanding Systems within the AI Paradigm: a Survey", in M. Penny (Ed) *Artificial Intelligence and Language Comprehension*, (National Institute of Education, Washington, Oc).

IV / Formal Logic-Based Representations

15 / John McCarthy
Programs with Common Sense

This is the paper that started it all. It is not only the first paper that can clearly be seen to be about Knowledge Representation, it is one of the very first papers in all of Artificial Intelligence. Its central theme is that of a hypothetical system (called the "Advice Taker") whose performance could improve over time as a result of receiving advice, rather than by being reprogrammed. Essentially, the proposal is to construct a program that reasons deductively from a body of knowledge until it concludes that it should do certain actions, which it then performs, and the cycle repeats. The actual technical content of the paper, however, is more narrowly focused on representational issues. The most important, perhaps, is the use of a calculus of *situations*, based on first-order logic, to make statements about causality, the ability of agents, and the effect of actions. This was a very influential proposal for dealing with change in a representation system, although it is being questioned by recent work like [Hayes, Chapter 28] and [Allen, Chapter 30]. On the other hand, perhaps the main contribution of the paper is the methodology it suggests, with formal logic playing a key role in the larger enterprise. Indeed, with slogans like

> We believe that human intelligence depends essentially on the fact that we can represent in language facts about our situation, our goals, and the effects of the various actions we can perform.

and

> We base ourselves on the idea that in order for a program to be capable of learning something, it must be capable of being told it.

the paper reads somewhat like a manifesto, anticipating much of what was to follow in the field and most of the papers included in this volume.

Appeared in *Semantic Information Processing*, 403–418, edited by M. Minsky, Cambridge, MA: The MIT Press, 1968.

Programs with Common Sense

John McCarthy

7.1 The Advice Taker

The "Advice Taker" is a proposed program for solving problems by manipulating sentences in formal languages.* The main difference between it and other programs or proposed programs for manipulating formal languages, such as the Logic Theory Machine (6) and the Geometry Program of Gelernter (2), is that in the previous programs the formal system was the subject matter but the heuristics were all embodied in the program. In this program the procedures will be described as much as possible in the language itself and, in particular, the heuristics are all so described.

The main advantages we expect the advice taker to have is that its behavior will be improvable merely by making statements to it, telling it about its symbolic environment and what is wanted from it. To make these statements will require little if any knowledge of the program or the previous knowledge of the advice taker. One will be able to assume that the advice taker will have available to it a fairly wide class of immediate logical consequences of anything it is told and its previous knowledge. This property is expected to have much in common with what makes us describe certain humans as having common sense. We shall therefore say that a program has common sense if it automatically deduces for itself a sufficiently wide class of immediate consequences of anything it is told and what it already knows.

*Section 7.1 is a reprint of a paper taken from "Mechanisation of Thought Processes," Vol. 1, pp. 77-84, Proc. Symposium, National Physical Laboratory, London, November 24-27, 1958.

Before describing the advice taker in any detail, I would like to describe more fully our motivation for proceeding in this direction. Our ultimate objective is to make programs that learn from their experience as effectively as humans do. It may not be realized how far we are presently from this objective. It is not hard to make machines learn from experience how to make simple changes in their behavior of a kind which has been anticipated by the programmer. For example, Samuel has included in his checker program (8) facilities for improving the weights the machine assigns to various factors in evaluating positions. He has also included a scheme whereby the machine remembers games it has played previously and deviates from its previous play when it finds a position which it previously lost. Suppose, however, that we wanted an improvement in behavior corresponding, say, to the discovery by the machine of the principle of the opposition in checkers. No present or presently proposed schemes are capable of discovering phenomena as abstract as this.

If one wants a machine to be able to discover an abstraction, it seems most likely that the machine must be able to represent this abstraction in some relatively simple way.

There is one known way of making a machine capable of learning arbitrary behavior, and thus to anticipate every kind of behavior: This is to make it possible for the machine to simulate arbitrary behaviors and try them out. These behaviors may be represented either by nerve nets (5), by Turing machines (3), or by calculator programs (1). The difficulty is twofold. First, in any of these representations the density of interesting behaviors is incredibly low. Second, and even more important, small interesting changes in behavior expressed at a high level of abstraction do not have simple representations. It is as though the human genetic structure were represented by a set of blueprints: then a mutation would usually result in a wart, a failure of parts to meet, or even an ungrammatical blueprint which could not be translated into an animal at all. It is very difficult to see how the genetic representation scheme manages to be general enough to represent the great variety of animals observed and yet be such that so many interesting changes in the organism are represented by small genetic changes. The problem of how such a representation controls the development of a fertilized egg into a mature animal is even more difficult.

In our opinion, a system which is to evolve intelligence of human order should have at least the following features:

1. All behaviors must be representable in the system. Therefore, the system should either be able to construct arbitrary automata or to program in some general-purpose programming language.

2. Interesting changes in behavior must be expressible in a simple way.

3. All aspects of behavior except the most routine must be improvable. In particular, the improving mechanism should be improvable.

4. The machine must have or evolve concepts of partial success because on difficult problems decisive successes or failures come too infrequently.

5. The system must be able to create subroutines which can be included in procedures as units. The learning of subroutines is complicated by the fact that the effect of a subroutine is not usually good or bad in itself. Therefore, the mechanism that selects subroutines should have concepts of an interesting or powerful subroutine whose application may be good under suitable conditions.

Of the five points mentioned, our work concentrates mainly on the second. We base ourselves on the idea that in order for a program to be capable of learning something it must first be capable of being told it. In fact, in the early versions we shall concentrate entirely on this point and attempt to achieve a system which can be told to make a specific improvement in its behavior with no more knowledge of its internal structure or previous knowledge than is required in order to instruct a human. Once this is achieved, we may be able to tell the advice taker how to learn from experience.

The main distinction between the way one programs a computer and modifies the program and the way one instructs a human or will instruct the advice taker is this: A machine is instructed mainly in the form of a sequence of imperative sentences, while a human is instructed mainly in declarative sentences describing the situation in which action is required together with a few imperatives that say what is wanted. The advantages of imperative sentences are as follows:

1. A procedure described in imperatives is already laid out and is carried out faster.

2. One starts with a machine in a basic state and does not assume previous knowledge on the part of the machine.

The advantages of declarative sentences are as follows:

1. Advantage can be taken of previous knowledge.

2. Declarative sentences have logical consequences and it can be arranged that the machine will have available sufficiently simple logical consequences of what it is told and what it previously knew.

3. The meaning of declaratives is much less dependent on their order than is the case with imperatives. This makes it easier to have afterthoughts.

4. The effect of a declarative is less dependent on the previous state of the system so that less knowledge of this state is required on the part of the instructor.

The only way we know of expressing abstractions (such as the previous example of the opposition in checkers) is in language. That is why we have decided to program a system which reasons verbally.

7.1.1 The Construction of the Advice Taker

The advice taker system has the following main features:

1. There is a method of representing expressions in the computer. These expressions are defined recursively as follows: A class of entities called terms is defined and a term is an expression. A sequence of expressions is an expression. These expressions are represented in the machine by list structures (5).

2. Certain of these expressions may be regarded as declarative sentences in a certain logical system which will be analogous to a universal Post canonical system. The particular system chosen will depend on programming considerations but will probably have a single rule of inference which will combine substitution for variables with *modus ponens*. The purpose of the combination is to avoid choking the machine with special cases of general propositions already deduced.

3. There is an immediate deduction routine which when given a set of premises will deduce a set of immediate conclusions. Initially, the immediate deduction routine will simply write down all one-step consequences of the premises. Later this may be elaborated so that the routine will produce some other conclusions which may be of interest. However, this routine will not use semantic heuristics; i.e. heuristics which depend on the subject matter under discussion. The intelligence, if any, of the advice taker will not be embodied in the immediate deduction routine. This intelligence will be embodied in the procedures which choose the lists of premises to which the immediate deduction routine is to be applied. Of course, the program should never attempt to apply the immediate deduction routine simultaneously to the list of everything it knows. This would make the deduction routine take too long.

4. Not all expressions are interpreted by the system as declarative sentences. Some are the names of entities of various kinds. Certain formulas represent objects. For our purposes, an entity is an object if we have something to say about it other than the things which may be deduced from the form of its name. For example, to most people, the number 3812 is not an object: they have nothing to say about it except what can be deduced from its structure. On the other hand, to most Americans the number 1776 is an object because they have filed somewhere the fact that it represents the year when the American Revolution started. In the advice taker each object has a property list in which are listed the specific things we have to say about it. Some things which can be deduced from the name of the object may be included in the property list anyhow if the deduction was actually carried out and was difficult enough so that the system does not want to carry it out again.

5. Entities other than declarative sentences which can be represented by formulas in the system are individuals, functions, and programs.

6. The program is intended to operate cyclically as follows: The immediate deduction routine is applied to a list of premises and a list of individuals. Some of the conclusions have the form of imperative sentences. These are obeyed. Included in the set of imperatives which may be obeyed is the routine which deduces and obeys.

We shall illustrate the way the advice taker is supposed to act by means of an example. Assume that I am seated at my desk at home and I wish to go to the airport. My car is at my home also. The solution of the problem is to walk to the car and drive the car to the airport. First, we shall give a formal statement of the premises the advice taker uses to draw the conclusions. Then we shall discuss the heuristics which cause the advice taker to assemble these premises from the totality of facts it has available. The premises come in groups, and we shall explain the interpretation of each group.

1. First, we have a predicate "at." "at(x,y)" is a formalization of "x is at y." Under this heading we have the premises

1. at(I, desk)
2. at(desk, home)
3. at(car, home)
4. at(home, county)
5. at(airport, county)

We shall need the fact that the relation "at" is transitive, which might be written directly as

6. at(x,y), at(y,z) → at(x,z)

or alternatively we might instead use the more abstract premises

6'. transitive (at)

and

7'. transitive (u) → $(u(x,y), u(y,z) \to (u(x,z))$

from which 6. can be deduced.

2. There are two rules concerning the feasibility of walking and driving.
8. walkable(x), at(y,x), at(z,x), at(I,y)→can(go$(y,z$, walking))
9. drivable(x), at(y,x), at(z,x), at(car,y), at(I,car)→can(go$(y,z$,driving))
There are also two specific facts.
10. walkable(home)
11. drivable(county)

3. Next we have a rule concerned with the properties of going.
12. did(go(x,y,z)) → at(I,y)

4. The problem itself is posed by the premise:
13. want(at(I,airport))

5. The above are all the premises concerned with the particular problem. The last group of premises are common to almost all problems of this sort. They

14. $(x→\text{can}(y))$, (did$(y)→z$)→canachult(x,y,z)
The predicate "canachult(x,y,z)" i.e., "can achieve ultimately," means that in a situation to which x applies, the action y can be performed and brings about a situation to which z applies. A sort of transitivity is described by

15. canachult(x,y,z), canachult(z,u,v) → canachult$(x,\text{prog}(y,u),v)$.
Here prog(u,v) is the program of first carrying out u and then v. (Some kind of identification of a single action u with the one step program prog(u) is obviously required, but the details of how this will fit into the formalism have not yet been worked out).
The final premise is the one which causes action to be taken.

16. x, canachult$(x,\text{prog}(y,z), w)$, want$(w)→\text{do}(y)$
The argument the advice taker must produce in order to solve the problem deduces the following propositions in more or less the following order:

1. at(I,desk) → can (go (desk,car,walking))
2. at(I,car) → can (go (home,airport,driving))
3. did (go (desk,car,walking)) → at (I,car)
4. did (go (home,airport,driving)) → at (I,airport)
5. canachult (at (I,desk), go (desk,car,walking), at (I,car))
6. canachult (at (I,car), go (home,airport,driving), at (I,airport))
7. canachult (at (I,desk), program (go (desk,car,walking), go (home,airport, driving)), → at (I,airport))
8. do (go (desk,car,walking))

The deduction of the last proposition initiates action.

This reasoning raises two major questions of heuristics: The first is that of how the 16 premises are collected, and the second is that of how the deduction proceeds once they are found. We cannot give complete answers to either question in the present paper; they are obviously not completely separate since some of the deductions might be made before some of the premises are collected. Let us first consider the question of where the 16 premises come from.

First of all, we assert that except for the 13th premise (want (at (I,airport)) which sets the goal) add the 1st premise (at (I,desk) which we shall get from a routine which answers the question "where am I"), all the premises can reasonably be expected to be specifically present in the memory of a machine which has competence of human order in finding its way around. That is, none of them is so specific to the problem at hand that assuming its presence in memory constitutes an anticipation of this particular problem or of a class of problems narrower than those which any human can expect to have previously solved. We must impose this requirement if we are to be able to say that the advice taker exhibits common sense.

On the other hand, while we may reasonably assume that the premises are in memory, we still have to describe how they are assembled into a list by themselves to which the deduction routine may be applied. Tentatively, we expect the advice taker to proceed as follows: initially, the sentence "want (at (I,airport))" is on a certain list L, called the main list, all by itself. The program begins with an observation routine which looks at the main list and puts certain statements about the contents of this list on a list called "observations of the main list." We shall not specify at present what all the possible outputs of this observation routine are but merely say that in this case it will observe that "the only statement on L has the form "want(u(x))"." (We write this out in English because we have not yet settled on a formalism for representing statements of this kind.) The "deduce and obey" routine is then applied to the combination of the "observations of the main list" list, and a list called the "standing orders list." This list is rather small and is never changed, or at least is only changed in major changes of the advice taker. The contents of the "standing orders" list has not been worked out, but what must be deduced is the extraction of certain statements from property lists. Namely, the program first looks at "want (at (I,airport))" and attempts to copy the statements on its property list. Let us assume that it fails in this attempt because "want (at (I,airport))" does not have the status of an object and hence has no property list. (One might expect that if the problem of going to the airport had arisen before, "want (at (I, airport))" would be an object, but this might depend on whether there were routines for generalizing previous experience that would allow something of general use to be filed under that heading.) Next in order of increasing generality the machine would see if anything were filed under "want(at (I,x))" which would deal with the general problem of getting somewhere. One would expect that premises 6 (or 6' and 7'), 8, 9, 12 would be so filed. There would also be the formula

$$\text{want (at (I,x))} \rightarrow \text{do (observe (where am I))}$$

which would give us premise 1. There would also be a reference to the next higher level of abstraction in the goal statement which would cause a look at the property list of "want(x)". This would give us 14, 15, and 16.

We shall not try to follow the solution further except to remark that for "want(at(I,x))" there would be a rule that starts with the premises "at(I, y)" and "want (I,x)" and has as conclusion a search for the property list of "go(y,x,z)". This would presumably fail, and then there would have to be heuristics that would initiate a search for a y such that "at(I,y)" and "at (airport,y)". This would be done by looking on the property lists of the origin and the destination and working up. Then premise 9 would be found which has as one of its premises "at (I,car)". A repetition of the above would find premise 8, which would complete the set of premises since the other "at" premises would have been found as by-products of previous searches.

We hope that the presence of the heuristic rules mentioned on the property lists where we have put them will seem plausible to the reader. It should be noticed that on the higher level of abstraction many of the statements are of the stimulus-response form. One might conjecture that division in man between conscious and unconscious thought occurs at the boundary between stimulus-response heuristics which do not have to be reasoned about but only obeyed, and the others which have to serve as premises in deductions.

7.2 Situations, Actions, and Causal Laws*

Although formalized theories have been devised to express the most important fields of mathematics and some progress has been made in formalizing certain empirical sciences, there is at present no formal theory in which one can express the kind of means-ends analysis used in ordinary life. The closest approach to such a theory of which I am aware is made by Freudenthal (2).

Our approach to the artificial-intelligence problem requires a formal theory. We believe that human intelligence depends essentially on the fact that we can represent in language facts about our situation, our goals, and the effects of the various actions we can perform. Moreover, we can draw conclusions from the facts to the effect that certain sequences of actions are likely to achieve our goals.

In Section 7.1 I discussed the advantages of having a computer program, the Advice Taker, that will reason from collections of facts about its problem and derive statements about what it can do. The name "advice taker" came from the hope that its behavior could be improved by giving it advice in the form of new facts rather than by rewriting the program. The reader is referred to Minsky (4) for a general introduction to the subject of artificial intelligence.

The first requirement for the advice taker is a formal system in which facts about situations, goals, and actions can be expressed and which contains general facts about means and ends as axioms. A start is made here on providing a system meeting the following specifications:

1. General properties of causality, and certain obvious but until now unformalized facts about the possibility and results of actions, are given as axioms.

2. It is a logical consequence of the facts of a situation and the general axioms that certain persons can achieve certain goals by taking certain actions.

3. The formal descriptions of situations should correspond as closely as possible to what people may reasonably be presumed to know about them when deciding what to do.

*Section 7.2 copies a memorandum originally distributed in 1963.

7.2.1 Situations and Fluents

One of the basic entities in our theory is the *situation*. Intuitively, a situation is the complete state of affairs at some instant of time. The laws of motion of a system determine all future situations from a given situation. Thus a situation corresponds to the notion of a point in phase space. In physics, laws are expressed in the form of differential equations which give the complete motion of the points of that space.

Our system is not intended to supply a complete description of situations nor the description of complete laws of motion. Instead, we deal with partial descriptions of situations and partial laws of motion. Moreover, the emphasis is on the simple qualitative laws of everyday life rather than on the quantitative laws of physics. As an example, take the fact that if it is raining and I go outside I will get wet.

Since a situation is defined as a complete state of affairs, we can never describe a situation fully; and we therefore provide no notation for doing so in our theory. Instead, we state facts about situations in the language of an extended predicate calculus. Examples of such facts are:

1. raining (s)
   meaning that it is raining in situation s
2. time $(s) = 1963.7205$
   giving the value of the time in situation s. It will usually prove convenient to regard the time as a function of the situation rather than vice versa, because the numerical value of the time is known and important only where the laws of physics are involved.
3. (at(I,home,s) or at(I,home)(s)
   meaning that I am at home in situation s. We shall use the second of the given notations that isolates the situation variable since in most, if not all, cases we will be able to suppress it completely.

We shall not describe here the logical system we intend to use. Basically, it is a predicate calculus, but we shall use the λ-notation and if necessary conditional expressions, as in LISP or ALGOL. We shall extend the meaning of the Boolean operators to operate on predicates. Thus by

   at(I,home) ∧ raining

we mean the same as

   $\lambda s.$ at(I,home)(s) ∧ raining(s)

A predicate or function whose argument is a situation will be called a *fluent*. Thus, *raining*, *time*, and *at(I,home)* are all fluents, the first and last being propositional fluents. The predicate being called a *propositional fluent*. The term was used by Newton for a physical quantity that depends on time, and we therefore feel that the present use of the term is justified.

In our formulas we can usually use the fluents without explicitly writing variables that represent situations. This corresponds to the use of random variables in probability theory without using variables representing points in the sample space, even though random variables are supposed to be regarded as functions defined on a sample space. In fact, we shall go further and give an interpretation of our theory as a type of modal logic in which the fluents are not regarded as functions at all.

7.2.2 Causality

In order to express causal laws, we introduce the second-order predicate *cause*. The statement

   cause$(\pi)(s)$,

where π is a propositional fluent, is intended to mean that the situation s will lead in the future to a situation that satisfies the fluent π. Thus, cause (π) is itself a propositional fluent. As an example of its use we write

   $\forall s.\ \forall p.$ [person(p) ∧ raining ∧ outside(p) ⊃ cause (wet(p))] (s),

which asserts that a person who is outside when it is raining will get wet. We shall make the convention that, if π is a fluent, then $\forall \pi$ means the same as $\forall s.\ \pi (s)$.

With this convention we can write the previous statement as

   $\forall s.\forall p.$ person(p) ∧ raining ∧ outside (p) ⊃ cause (wet(p)),

thereby suppressing explicit mention of situations.

As a second example we discuss a special case of the law of falling bodies in the form:

$$\forall\forall t.\ \forall b.\ \forall t^1.\ \forall h\ \text{real}(t) \wedge \text{real}(t^1) \wedge \text{real}(h) \wedge \text{body}(b)$$
$$\wedge\ \text{unsupported}(b) \wedge [\text{height}(b) = h] \wedge [\tfrac{1}{2}gt^2 < h] \wedge$$
$$[\text{time} = t'] \supset \text{cause}\,(\text{height}(b) = h - \tfrac{1}{2}gt^2 \wedge \text{time} = t' = t).$$

The concept of causality is intended to satisfy the three following general laws, which may be considered as axioms:

C1. $\forall.$ cause $(\pi) \vee [\forall.\pi \supset p] \supset$ cause (p)
C2. $\forall.$ cause (cause $(\pi)) \supset$ cause (π)
C3. $\forall.$ cause $(\pi_1) \vee$ cause $(\pi_2) \supset$ cause $(\pi_1 \vee \pi_2)$.

The fact that we can suppress explicit mention of situations has the following interesting consequence: Instead of regarding the π's as predicates we may regard them as propositions and regard *cause* as a new modal operator. The operator $\forall$ seems then to be equivalent to the N (necessary) operator of ordinary modal logic. Conversely, it would appear that modal logic of necessity might be regarded as a monadic predicate calculus where all quantifiers are over situations.

In the present case of causality, we have a choice of how to proceed. **Regarding** the system as a modal logic seems to have the following two advantages:

1. If we use the predicate calculus interpretation, we require second-order predicate calculus in order to handle cause (π) (s), whereas if we take the modal interpretation we can get by with first-order predicate calculus.

2. We shall want decision procedures or at least proof procedures for as much of our system as possible. If we use the modal approach, many problems will involve only substitution of constants for variables in universal statements and will therefore fall into a fairly readily decidable domain.

Another example of causality is given by a 2-bit binary counter that counts every second. In our formalism its behavior may be described by the statement:

$$\forall s \forall t \forall x_0 \forall x_1 . time = t \wedge bit0 = x_1 \supset cause ($$
$$time = t+1 \wedge (bit0 = x_0 \oplus 1) \wedge (bit1 = x_1 \oplus (x_0 \wedge 1)))$$

In this example time, bit0, and bit1 are fluents, while t, x_0, and x_1 are numerical variables. The distinction is made clearer if we use the more long-winded statement

$$\forall s \forall t \forall x_0 \forall x_1 . time (s) = t \wedge bit0 (s) = x_0 \wedge bit1(s) = x_1 \supset$$
$$cause (\lambda s' . time (s') = t+1 \wedge (bit0(s') = x_0 \oplus 1) \vee bit1 (s') = x_1 \oplus (x_0 \wedge 1)))(s)$$

In this case, however, we can rewrite the statement in the form

$$\forall s . cause (\lambda s' . [time (s') = time (s) + 1] \wedge [bit0 (s') = bit0(s) \oplus 1] \wedge$$
$$[bit1 (s') = bit1 (s) \oplus (bit0 (s) \wedge 1)]) (s)$$

Thus we see that the suppression of explicit mention of the situations forced us to introduce the auxiliary quantities t, x_0, and x_1 which are required because we can no longer use functions of two different situations in the same formula. Nevertheless, the s-suppressed form may still be worthwhile because it admits the modal interpretation.

The time as a fluent satisfies certain axioms. The fact that there is only one situation corresponding to a given value of the time may be expressed by the axiom

T1. $\forall s \forall \pi \forall \rho \forall t . cause (time = t \wedge \pi) \wedge cause (time = t \wedge \rho) \supset cause$
$(time = t \wedge \pi \wedge \rho)$

Another axiom is

T2. $\forall s \forall t . real (t) \wedge t > time \supset cause (time = t)$

7.2.3 Actions and the Operator can

We shall regard the fact that a person performs a certain action in a situation as a propositional fluent. Thus

$$moves(person, object, location)(s)$$

is regarded as asserting that person moves object to location in the situation s. The effect of moving something is described by

$$\forall \rho \forall o \forall l . moves (\rho, o, l) \supset cause (at (o,l))$$

or in the long form

$$\forall s \forall p \forall o \forall l . moves (p, o, l) (s) \supset cause (\lambda s' . at (o, l) (s')) (s)$$

In order to discuss the ability of persons to achieve goals and to perform actions we introduce the operator can.

$$can(p, \pi)(s)$$

asserts that the person p can make the situation s satisfy π. We see that can(p, π) is a propositional fluent and that like cause, can may be regarded either as a second-order predicate or a modal operator. Our most common use of can will be to assert that a person can perform a certain action. Thus we write

$$can(p, moves(p, o, l))(s)$$

to assert that in situation s, the person p can move the object o to location l.

The operator can satisfies the axioms

K1. $\forall s \forall \pi \forall \rho \forall p . [can(p, \pi) \wedge (\pi \supset \rho) \supset (can(p,\rho)]$

K2. $\forall s \forall p_1 \forall p_2 . [\sim can(p_1, \pi) \wedge can(p_1, \sim \pi)]$

K3. $\forall s \forall p \forall \pi \forall \rho [can(p, \pi) \wedge can(p,\rho) \quad can(p, \pi \wedge \rho)]$

Using K1 and

$$can(p, moves(p, o, l)$$

and

$$\forall s \forall \rho \forall o \forall l . moves(p, o, l) \supset cause(at(o,l)),$$

we can deduce

$$can(p, cause(at(o,l)),$$

which shows that the operators can and cause often show up in the same formula. The ability of people to perform joint actions can be expressed by formulas like

$$can(p_1, can(p_2, marry(p_1, p_2))),$$

which suggests the commutative axiom

K4. $\forall \forall p_1 \forall p_2 \forall \pi . can(p_1, can(p_2, \pi)) \supset can(p_2, can(p_1, \pi))$

A kind of transitivity is empressed by the following

Theorem: From

1. $can(p, cause(\pi))$;

and

2. $\forall . \pi \supset can(p, cause(\rho))$;

it follows that

3. $can(p, cause(can(p, cause(\rho))))$.

Proof: Substitute can$(p, cause(\rho))$ for ρ in axiom C1 and substitute cause (π) for π and cause$(can(p, cause(\rho)))$ for ρ in axiom K1. The conclusion then follows by propositional calculus.

In order to discuss the achievement of goals requiring several consecutive actions, we introduce canult(p, π) which is intended to mean that the person p can ultimately bring about a situation satisfying π. We connect it with can and cause by means of the axiom

KC1. $\forall.\forall p \forall \pi.\pi \lor$ can $(p,$cause $($canult $(p,\pi))) \supset$ canult (p,π)

This axiom partially corresponds to the LISP-type recursive definition:

canult $(p,\pi) = \pi \lor$ can $(p,$ cause $($canult $(p,\pi)))$

We also want the axiom

KC2. $\forall p \forall \pi.$ cause $($canult $(p,\pi)) \supset$ canult (p,π)

7.2.4 Examples

The first example we shall consider is a situation in which a monkey is in a room where a bunch of bananas is hanging from a ceiling too high to reach. In the corner of the room there is a box, and the solution to the monkey's problem is to move the box under the bananas and climb onto the box from which the bananas can be reached.

We shall describe the situation in such a way that it will follow from our axioms and the description that the monkey can get the bananas. We shall not discuss the heuristic problem of how monkeys might or even do solve the problem. Specifically, we shall prove that

canult(monkey, has(monkey, bananas)).

The situation is described in a very simplified way by the following statements:

H1. $\forall\forall u.$ place $(u) \supset$ can (monkey, move (monkey, box, u))
H2. $\forall\forall u \forall v \forall p$ move $(p,v,u) \supset$ cause (at (v,u))
H3. $\forall$ can (monkey,climbs (monkey,box))
H4. $\forall\forall u \forall v \forall p.$ at $(v,u) \land$ climbs $(p,v) \supset$ cause (at $(v,u) \land$ on (p,v))
H5. $\forall$ place (under (bananas))
H6. $\forall$ at (box, under (bananas)) $\land$ on (monkey, box) $\supset$ can (monkey,reach (monkey,bananas))
H7. $\forall$ $\forall p$ $\forall x$ reach $(p,x) \supset$ cause (has (p,x))

The reasoning proceeds as follows: From H1 and H5 by substitution of under (bananas) for u and by propositional calculus we get

1. can(monkey, move(box, under(bananas)))

Using 1, H2, and axiom C1, we get

2. can(monkey, cause(at(box, under(bananas))))

Similarly, H3, H4, and C1 give

3. at (box, under (bananas)) $\supset$ can (monkey,cause (at (box, under (bananas)) $\land$ on(monkey,box)))

Then H6 and H7 give

4. at (box, under (bananas)) $\land$ on (monkey,cause (has(monkey, bananas)))

Now, Theorem 1 is used to combine 2, 3, and 4, to result in

5. can(monkey,cause(can(monkey,cause(can(monkey,cause(has(monkey, bananas)))))))

Using KC1, we reduce this to

canult(monkey, has(monkey, bananas)))

Another example concerns a two-person game where player p_1 has two moves, but whichever one he chooses, player p_2 has a move that will beat him. This situation may be described as follows:

1. can $(p_1,m_1) \land$ can $(p_1,m_2) \land (m_1 \lor m_2)$
2. $[m_1 \supset$ cause $(\pi_1)] \land [m_2 \supset$ cause $(\pi_2)]$
3. $\forall.\pi_1 \lor \pi_2 \supset [$can $(p_2, n_1) \land$ can $(p_2,n_2) \land (n_1 \lor n_2)]$
4. $\forall.(\pi_1 \land n_1) \lor (\pi_2 \land n_2) \supset$ cause (win (p_2))

We would like to be able to draw the conclusion

3. canult$(p_2,$win$(p_2))$

We proceed as follows: From 1 and 2 we get

4. cause $(\pi_1) \lor$ cause (π_2)

and and we use Axiom C3 to get

5. cause $(\pi_1 \lor \pi_2)$

Next we weaken 3 to get

6. $\forall.$ $\pi_1 \supset$ can $(p_2, \pi_1 \land n_1)$ and
7. $\forall.$ $\pi_2 \supset$ can $(p_2, \pi_2 \land n_2)$

and then we use K1 to get

8. $\forall.$ $\pi_1 \supset$ can $(p_2, \pi_1 \land n_1)$ and
9. $\forall.$ $\pi_2 \supset$ can $(p_2, \pi_2 \land n_2)$

The propositional calculus gives

10. $\forall.$ $\pi_1 \lor \pi_2 \supset$ can $(p_2, \pi_1 \land n_1)$ can$(p_2, \pi_2 \land n_2)$

and using K3 we get

11. $\forall.$ $\pi_1 \lor \pi_2 \supset$ can $(p_2, (\pi_1 \land n_1)$ $(\pi_2 \land n_2))$

which together with 4 and K1 gives

12. $\forall.$ $\pi_1 \lor \pi_2 \supset$ can $(p_2,$ cause (win $(p_2)))$

which together with 5 and C1 gives

13. cause (can$(p_2,$ cause(win(p_2))))

Using the axioms for *canult* we now get

14. canult $(p_2,$ win $(p_2))$.

7.2.5 Note

After finishing the bulk of this investigation I came across the work of Prior (7). He defines modal operators P and F, where P (π) means 'it has been the case that π' and F (π) means 'it will be the case that π'

He subjects these operators to a number of axioms and rules of inference in close analogy to the well-known (9) modal logic of possibility, and also interprets this logic in a restricted predicate calculus where the variables range over times. This logic is then extended to include a somewhat undetermined future and he claims (unconvincingly) that it cannot be interpreted in predicate calculus.

I have not yet made a detailed comparison of our logic with Prior's, but here are some tentative conclusions:

1. The causality logic should be extended to allow inference about the past.

2. Causality logic should be extended to allow inference that certain propositional fluents will always hold.

3. cause (π) satisfies the axioms for his F(π), which means that his futurity theory possesses, from his point of view, nonstandard models. Specifically, a collection of functions $p_1(t)$, $p_2(t)$ may satisfy his futurity axioms and assign truth to $p(1) \wedge \sim (Fp)(0)$. In our system this is acceptable because something can happen without being caused to happen.

4. If we combine his past and futurity axioms, our system will no longer fit his axioms and

PF1. $p \sim F(\sim P(p))$
PF2. $p \sim P(\sim F(p))$

since we do not wish to say that whatever is was always inevitable.

Bibliography

1. Friedberg, R. A., "A Learning Machine,"*IBM J. of Research and Development*, Part I: Vol. 2, No. 3, 1958; Part II: Vol. 3, No. 3, 1959.

2. Freudenthal, H. A., *Lincos: Design of a Language for Cosmic Intercourse*, North-Holland Press, Amsterdam, 1960.

3. McCarthy, J., "Inversion of Functions Defined by Turing Machines," *Automatic Studies*, Princeton, 1956.

4. Minsky, M., "Steps Toward Artificial Intelligence," *Proc. IRE*, Vol. 49, No. 1, 1961.

5. Minsky, M., "Neural Models for Memory," *Proc. Internatl. Congr. Physiological Sciences*, Vol. III, Leiden, 1962 (*Excerpta Medica* Internatl. Congr. Series 49).

6. Newell, A., et al., "Empirical Explorations of the Logic Theory Machine: A Case Study in Heuristics," *Proc. WJCC, IRE*, 1957.

7. Prior, A. N., *The Syntax of Time Distinctions*, Franciscan Studies, 1958

8. Samuel, A. L., "Some Studies in Machine Learning Using the Game of Checkers," *IBM J. of Research and Development*, Vol. 3, No. 3, 1959.

16 / Richard W. Weyhrauch
Prolegomena to a Theory of Mechanized Formal Reasoning

While there have been many representation systems based on semantic networks, frames, production rules, and the like, there have not been very many based on full first-order logic that were not simply theorem-provers of some sort. The FOL system described here by Weyhrauch is a notable exception. The system is not even an automatic theorem-prover, in that it only does certain bounded kinds of inference automatically, although it can be *led* through proofs of arbitrary complexity. The main distinction of FOL is that the symbols of a logical language can be attached to procedures and data structures, so that certain kinds of deduction can be done by *evaluating* expressions. Moreover, this form of semantic attachment can also be applied at a meta-level, where symbols are attached to terms and expressions at the base level. This allows the system to use shortcuts in its reasoning (such as derived rules of inference) provided that these are established at the meta-level (see [Davis and Buchanan, Chapter 22] for more on this). Allowing a meta-theory to be attached to its own structures gives the system a (rudimentary, at least) reflective capability [Smith, Chapter 3], allowing deduction at one level to be viewed as evaluation one meta-level higher. This, claims Weyhrauch, provides a technical account of the declarative/procedural controversy [Winograd, Chapter 20] in that what appear to be declarative sentences at one level can be viewed as arguments to procedures (deduction, simplification, *etc.*) higher up. As is the case with [McCarthy, Chapter 31], what unfortunately seems to be lacking is a crisp statement of what can or cannot be done using theories whose terms refer to the propositions of other theories.

Appeared in *Artificial Intelligence* **13**(1,2), 1980, 133–170.

Prolegomena to a Theory of Mechanized Formal Reasoning

Richard W. Weyhrauch

Stanford University, Stanford, CA, U.S.A.

Recommended by Daniel G. Bobrow

ABSTRACT

This is an informal description of my ideas about using formal logic as a tool for reasoning systems using computers. The theoretical ideas are illustrated by the features of FOL. All of the examples presented have actually run using the FOL system.

1. Introduction

The title of this paper contains both the words 'mechanized' and 'theory'. I want to make the point that the ideas presented here are not only of interest to theoreticians. I believe that any theory of interest to artificial intelligence must be realizable on a computer.

I am going to describe a working computer program, FOL, that embodies the mechanization of the ideas of logicians *about* theories of reasoning. This system converses with users in some first order language. I will also explain how to build a new structure in which theory and metatheory interact in a particularly natural way. This structure has the additional property that it can be designed to reason about itself. This kind of self reflexive logical structure is new and a discussion of the full extent of its power will appear in another paper.

The purpose of this paper is to set down the main ideas underlying the system. Each example in this paper was chosen to illustrate an *idea* and each idea is developed by showing how the corresponding FOL feature works. I will not present difficult examples. More extensive examples and discussions of the limits of these features will be described in other places. The real power of this theory (and FOL) comes from an understanding of the interaction of these separate features. This means that after this paper is read it still requires some work to see how all of these features can be used. Complex examples will only confuse the issues at this point. Before these can be explained the logical system must be fully understood.

The FOL project can be thought of in several different ways:

(1) Most important, FOL is an environment for studying epistemological questions. I look on logic as an empirical, applied science. It is like physics. The data we have is the actual reasoning activity of people. We try to build a theory of what that's like. I try to look at the traditional work on logic from this point of view. The important question is: in what way does logic adequately represent the actual practice of reasoning? In addition, its usefulness to artificial intelligence requires a stronger form of adequacy. Such a theory must be *mechanizable*. My notion of mechanization is informal. I hope by the end of this note it will be clearer. Below, I outline the mechanizable analogues of the usual notions of model, interpretation, satisfaction, theory, and reflection principle.

(2) FOL is a conversational machine. We use it by having a conversation with it. The importance of this idea cannot be overestimated. One of the recurring themes of this paper is the question: what is the nature of the conversation we wish to have with an expert in reasoning? In AI we talk about *expert systems*. FOL can be thought of as a system whose expertise is reasoning. We have tried to explore the question: what properties does an expert conversational reasoning machine have to have, independent of its domain of expertise? I believe that we will begin to call machines intelligent when we can have the kinds of discussions with them that we have with our friends. Let me elaborate on this a little. Humans are not ever likely to come to depend on the advice of a computer which has a simplistic one bit output. Imagine that you are asking it to make decisions about what stocks you should buy. Suppose it says "I have reviewed all the data you gave me. Sell everything you own and buy stock in FOL Incorporated." Most reasonable people would like to ask some additional questions! Why did you make that choice? What theory of price behavior did you use? Why is that better than using a dartboard? And so forth. These questions require a system that knows about more things than the stock market. For example, it needs to know how to reason about its *theories* of price movement. In FOL we have begged the question of *natural* language. The only important thing is having a sufficiently rich language for carrying out the above kinds of conversations. This paper should be looked at from this point of view.

This work has direct application in several areas. The details are referenced below.

(1) *Artificial Intelligence*. I propose that the *language/simulation structure* pairs described below are important building blocks in a viable and mechanizable theory of knowledge representation for AI. The central idea is that FOL makes systematic use of the distinction between a language and the objects that this language describes. This distinction allows us to deal with the questions of how to manipulate theories of theory building, how to deal with modalities, how to reason about possibly inconsistent theories, how to treat 'non-monotonic' reasoning and how

to build a mechanizable theory of perception. By perception I mean the question of how it is possible for us to go from sense impressions to theories about what our exterior is like.

(2) *Mathematical Theory of Computation.* FOL is an environment that can deal effectively both with a theory and its metatheory. Many aspects of program semantics are nicely expressable when this is viewed as a reasoning *system*. For a long time I have wanted to have a system in which I could develop the theory of LISP, following the ideas of Kleene (1952) when he developed recursion theory. The recent work of Cartwright (1977) and McCarthy (1978) have made this even more practicable. One main feature of this system is that it can incorporate both computation induction and the inductive assertion method in the same system. We can do this because both of these methodologies can be expressed as theorems of the metatheory. This is an example of the expressive power of the FOL system. If as above we claim that we want to be able to have discussions with FOL about anything, then programs are an interesting subject. We are currently building an 'expert' system for discussing LISP programs.

(3) *Logic.* The FOL system is not a formal system in the popular sense of the word. Logicians have used formal systems mainly to describe the sentences that are used in mathematical reasoning. I have tried on the other hand to build a structure which embodies the logicians theories of these theories and thus have a system capable of reasoning about theory building. There are several novel things about the logic of FOL that may be of interest to logicians and workers in AI. First is the way in which many sorted logic is treated. Second is the notion that simulation structures (i.e. partial models) should be represented explicitly. Third is the idea of the general purpose evaluator described below. Fourth is the use of reflection principles to connect a theory with its metatheory. Fifth is to notice that reflection and evaluation with respect to the metatheory is the technical realization of the procedural declarative discussions which appear in the AI literature. Sixth is the discovery of META, a self reflective structure with a 'locally' Tarskian semantics. This theory META is new and it has already produced some insight into the nature of meta reasoning that I will write about elsewhere.

As I reread this introduction it seems to contain a lot of promises. If they seem exaggerated to you then imagine me as a hopeless romantic, but at least read the rest of this paper. The things I describe here already exist.

2. FOL as a Conversational Program

FOL has previously been advertised as a proof-checker. This sometimes brings to mind the idea that the way you use it is to type out a complicated formal proof, and is founded on then FOL reads it and says yes or no. This picture is all wrong, and is founded on the theorem proving idea that simply stating a problem is all that a reasoning system should need to know. What FOL actually does is to have a dialogue with a user about some subject. The first step in this conversation is to establish what

language we will speak to each other by establishing what words we will use for what parts of speech. In FOL the establishment of this agreement about language is done by making *declarations.* This will be described below.

We can then discuss (in the agreed upon language) what facts (axioms) are to be considered true, and then finally we can chat about the consequences of these facts.

Let me illustrate this by giving a simple FOL proof. We will begin where logic began, with Aristotle (−335). Even a person who has never had a course in formal logic understands the syllogism:

Socrates is a man
and
All men are mortal
thus
Socrates is mortal

Before we actually give a dialogue with FOL we need to think informally about how we express these assertions as well formed formulas, WFFs of first order logic. For this purpose we need an individual constant (INDCONST), Socrates, two predicate constants (PREDCONSTs), MAN and MORTAL, each of one argument, and an individual variable (INDVAR), x, to express the all men part of the second line. The usual rules for forming WFFs apply (see Kleene (1967), pp. 7, 78). The three statements above are represented as

MAN (Socrates)
$\forall x.(\text{MAN}(x) \supset \text{MORTAL}(x))$
MORTAL(Socrates)

Our goal is to prove

$(\text{MAN}(\text{Socrates}) \land \forall x.(\text{MAN}(x) \supset \text{MORTAL}(x)))$
$\supset \text{MORTAL}(\text{Socrates})$

As explained above the first thing we do when initiating a discussion with FOL is to make an agreement about language we will use. We do this by making declarations. These have the form

*****DECLARE INDCONST Socrates;
*****DECLARE PREDCONST MORTAL MAN 1;
*****DECLARE INDVAR x;

The FOL program types out five stars when it expects input. The above lines are exactly what you would type to the FOL system.

FOL knows all of the natural deduction rules of inference (Prawitz (1965)) and many more. In the usual natural deduction style proofs are trees and the leaves of these trees are called assumptions. The assume command looks like

*****ASSUME MAN(Socrates) $\land \forall x.(\text{MAN}(x) \supset \text{MORTAL}(x))$;
1 MAN(Socrates) $\land \forall x.(\text{MAN}(x) \supset \text{MORTAL}(x))$ (1)

The first line above is typed by the user the second is typed by FOL. For each node in the proof tree there is a set of open assumptions. These are printed in parentheses after the proofstep. Notice that assumptions depend on themselves. We want to instantiate the second half of line one to the particular MAN, Socrates. First we must get this WFF onto a line of its own. FOL can be used to decide tautologies. We type TAUT followed by the WFF we want, and then the line numbers of those lines from which it follows.

```
*****TAUT ∀x.(MAN(x) ⊃ MORTAL(x)) 1;
2 ∀x.(MAN(x) ⊃ MORTAL(x))   (1)
```

This line also has the open assumption of line 1. We then use the ∀-elimination rule to conclude

```
*****∀E 2 Socrates;
3 MAN(Socrates) ⊃ MORTAL(Socrates)   (1)
```

It now follows, tautologically, from lines one and three, that Socrates must be MORTAL. Using the TAUT command again gets this result. More than one line can be given in the reason part of the TAUT command.

```
*****TAUT MORTAL(Socrates) 1,3;
4 MORTAL(Socrates)   (1)
```

This is almost the desired result, but we are not finished yet; this line still depends upon the original assumption. We close this assumption by creating an implication of the first line implying the fourth. This is done using the deduction theorem. In the natural deduction terminology this is called *implication* (⊃) *introduction*.

```
*****⊃I 1 ⊃ 4;
5 (MAN(Socrates) ∧ ∀x.(MAN(x) ⊃ MORTAL(x)))
    ⊃ MORTAL(Socrates)
```

This is the WFF we wanted to prove. Since it has no dependencies, it is a theorem. It is roughly equivalent to the English sentence, If Socrates is a man, and for all x if x is a man, then x is mortal, then Socrates is mortal.

This example was also used in Filman and Weyhrauch (1976) and illustrates the sense in which FOL is an interactive proof constructor, not simply a proof checker.

3. The Logic Used by FOL

The logic used by FOL is an extension of the system of first order predicate calculus described in Prawitz (1965). The most important change is that FOL languages contain equality and allow for sorted variables where there is a partial order on the sorts. This latter facility is extremely important for making discussions with FOL more natural. The properties of this extension of ordinary logic together with detailed examples appear in Weyhrauch (1979). In addition there are several features which are primarily syntactic improvements. A somewhat old description of how to use FOL is found in Weyhrauch (1977).

Prawitz distinguishes between individual variables and individual parameters. In FOL individual variables may appear both free and bound in WFFs. As in Prawitz individual parameters must always appear free. Natural numbers are automatically declared individual constants of sort NATNUM. This is one of the few defaults in FOL. The only kind of numbers understood by FOL are natural numbers, i.e. non-negative integers. −3 should be thought of not as an individual constant, but rather as the prefix operator − applied to the individual constant 3.

A user may specify that binary predicate and operation symbols are to be used as infixes. The declaration of a unary application symbol to be prefix makes the parentheses around its argument optional. The number of arguments of an application term is called its *arity*.

FOL always considers two WFFs to be equal if they can both be changed into the same WFF by making allowable changes of bound variables. Thus, for example, the TAUT rule will accept $\forall x. P(x) \supset \forall y. P(y)$ as a tautology if x and y are of the same sort.

We have also introduced the use of conditional expressions for both WFFs and TERMs. These expressions are not used in standard descriptions of predicate calculus because they complicate the definition of satisfaction by making the value of a TERM and the truth value of a WFF mutually recursive. Hilbert and Bernays (1934) proved that these additions were a conservative extension of ordinary predicate calculus so, in some sense, they are not needed. McCarthy (1963) stressed, however, that the increased naturalness when using conditional expressions to describe functions, is more than adequate compensation for the additional complexity.

Simple derivations in FOL are generated by using the natural deduction rules described in Prawitz (1965) together with some well-known decision procedures. These include TAUT for deciding tautologies, TAUTEQ for deciding the propositional theory of equality and MONADIC which decides formulas of the monadic predicate calculus. In actual fact MONADIC decides the case of ∀∃ formulas. These features are not explained in this paper. This is probably is a good place to mention that the first two decision procedures were designed and coded by Ashok Chandra and the last by William Glassmire. The important additions to the deductive mechanisms of first order logic are the syntactic and semantic simplification routines, the convenient use of metatheory and a not yet completed goal structure (Juan Bulnes (1979)). It is these later features that are described below.

4. Simulation Structures and Semantic Attachment

Here I introduce one of the most important ideas in this paper, i.e. *simulation structures*. Simulation structures are intended to be the *mechanizable* analogue of the notion of model. We can intuitively understand them as the computable part of some model. It has been suggested that I call them *effective partial interpretations*, but I have reserved that slogan for a somewhat more general notion. A full mathematical description of these ideas is beyond the scope of this paper but appears in Weyhrauch [Note 15]. In this paper I will give an operational description, mostly by means of some examples.

Consider the first order language L, and a model M.

L = (P,F,C)

M = (D,P,F,C)

As usual, L is determined by a collection, P, of predicate symbols, a collection, F, of function symbols, and a collection, C, of constant symbols (Kleene (1952, pp. 83–93)). M is a structure which contains a domain D, and the predicates, functions and objects which correspond to the symbols in L.

S = (D,P,F,C)

Loosely speaking, a simulation structure, S, also has a domain, D, a set of 'predicates', P, a set of 'functions', F, and a distinguished subset, C, of its domain. However, they have strong restrictions. Since we are imagining simulation structures as the mechanizable analogues of models we want to be able to actually implement them on a computer. To facilitate this we imagine that we intend to use a computer language in which there is some reasonable collection of data structures. In FOL we use LISP. The domain of a simulation structure is presented as an algorithm that acts as the characteristic function of some subset of the data structures. For example, if we want to construct a simulation structure for Peano arithmetic the domain is specified by a LISP function which returns T (for true) on all natural numbers and NIL (for false) on all other s-expressions. Each 'predicate' is represented by an algorithm that decides for each collection of arguments if the predicate is true or false or if it doesn't know. This algorithm is also total. Notice that it can tell you what is false as well as what true. Each 'function' is an algorithm that computes for each set of arguments either a value or returns the fact that it doesn't know the answer. It too is total. The distinguished subset of the domain must also be given by its characteristic function. These restrictions are best illustrated by an example. A possible simulation structure for Peano arithmetic together with a relation symbol for 'less than' is

S = (natural numbers, $\langle\{2 < 3, \neg\, 5 < 2\}\rangle$, $\langle$plus$\rangle$, {2,3}}

I have not presented this simulation structure by actually giving algorithms but they can easily be supplied. This simulation structure contains only two facts about 'less than'—two is less than three, and it's false that five is less than two. As mentioned above, since this discussion is informal $\{2 < 3, \neg\, 5 < 2\}$ should be taken as the description of an algorithm that answers correctly the two questions it knows about and in all other cases returns the fact that it cannot decide 'plus'

is the name of an algorithm that computes the sum of two natural numbers. The only numerals that have interpretations are two and three. These have their usual meaning.

Intuitively, if we ask is '2 < 3' (where here '2' and '3' are numerals in L) we get the answer yes. If we ask is '5 < 2' it says, "I don't know"! This is because there is no interpretation in the simulation structure of the numeral '5'. Curiously, if you ask is '2+3 < 2' it will say false. The reason is that the simulation structure has an interpretation of '+' as the algorithm 'plus' and 5 is in the domain even though it is not known to be the interpretation of any numeral in L.

A more reasonable simulation structure for Peano arithmetic might be

S = $\langle$natural numbers, $\langle$lessthan$\rangle$, $\langle$suc,pred,plus,times$\rangle$, natural numbers$\rangle$

Simulation structures are not models. One difference is that there are no closure conditions required of the function fragments. Thus we could know that three times two is six without knowing about the multiplicative properties of two and six.

Just as in the case of a model, we get a natural interpretation of a language with respect to a simulation structure. This allows us to introduce the idea of a sentence of L being satisfiable with respect to a simulation structure. Because of the lack of closure conditions and the partialness of the 'predicates', etc. (unlike ordinary satisfaction) this routine will sometimes return 'I don't know'. There are several reasons for this. Our mechanized satisfaction cannot compute the truth or falsity of quantified formulas. This in general requires an infinite amount of computing. It should be remarked that this is exactly why we have logic at all. It facilitates our reasoning about the result of an infinite amount of computation with a single sentence.

It is also important to understand that we are not introducing a three valued logic or partial functions. We simply acknowledge that, with respect to some simulation structures, we don't have any information about certain expressions in our language.

Below is an example of the FOL commands that would define this language, assert some axioms and build this simulation structure. As mentioned above, in the FOL system one of the few defaults is that numerals automatically come declared as individual constants and are attached to the expected integers. Thus the following axiomatization includes the numerals and their attachments by default.

The first group of commands creates the language. The second group are Robinson's axioms Q without the equality axioms (Robinson (1950)). The next is the induction axiom. The fourth group makes the semantic attachments that build the simulation structure. The expressions containing the word 'LAMBDA' are LISP programs. I will not explain the REPRESENT command as it is unimportant here. The parts of the declarations in square brackets specify binding power information to the FOL parser.

For example, $\forall x\ y.car(cons(x,y)) = x$ will rewrite any expression of the form $car(cons(t_1, t_2))$ to t_1, where t_1 and t_2 are arbitrary terms.

When given an expression to simplify, REWRITE uses its entire collection of rewrite rules over and over again until it is no longer possible to apply any. Unfortunately, if you give it a rule like

$$\forall x\ y.x+y = y+x$$

it will simply go on switching the two arguments to '+' forever. This is because the rewritten term again matches the rule. This is actually a desired property of this system. First, it is impossible in general to decide if a given collection of rewrite rules will lead to a non-terminating sequence of replacements. Second any simple way of guaranteeing termination will exclude a lot of things that you really want to use. For example, suppose you had the restriction that no sub-expression of the right hand side should match the left hand side of a rewrite rule. Then you could not include the definition of a recursive function even if you know that it will not rewrite itself forever in the particular case you are considering. This case occurs quite frequently.

This simplifier is quite complicated and I will not describe its details here. There are three distinct subparts.

(1) *A matching part*. This determines when a left hand side matches a particular formula.

(2) *An action part*. This determines what action to take when a match is found. At present the only thing that the simplifier can do under the control of a user is the replacement of the matched expression by its right hand side.

(3) *The threading part*. That is, given an expression in what order should the sub-expressions be matched.

The details of these parts are found in Weyhrauch [Note 6]. This simplifier behaves much like a PROLOG interpreter (Warren (1977)), but treats a more extensive collection of sentences. I will say more about first order logic as a programming language (Kowalski (1974)) below.

In Appendix E here is a detailed example which illustrates the control structure of the simplifier.

6. A General First Order Logic Expression Evaluator

Unfortunately, neither of the above simplifiers will do enough for our purposes. This section describes an evaluator for arbitrary first order expressions which is adequate for our needs. I believe that the evaluator presented below is the only natural way of considering first order logic as a programming language.

Consider adding the definition of the factorial function to the axioms above.

```
DECLARE OPCONST fact(NATNUM) = NATNUM;
AXIOM FACT: ∀n.fact(n) = IF n = 0 THEN 1 ELSE n*fact(pred(n));;
```

```
DECLARE INDVAR n m p q ∈ NATNUM;
DECLARE OPCONST suc pred (NATNUM) = NATNUM;
DECLARE OPCONST+(NATNUM, NATNUM) = NATNUM;
DECLARE OPCONST * (NATNUM, NATNUM) = NATNUM [R ← 458, L ← 455];
DECLARE PREDCONST ↔ (NATNUM, NATNUM) = NATNUM [R ← 558, L ← 555];
DECLARE PREDPAR P (NATNUM);

AXIOM    Q:
AXIOM    ONEONE: ∀n m.(suc(n) = suc(m) ⊃ n = m);
         SUCC1:  ∀n.¬(0 = suc(n));
         SUCC2:  ∀n.(¬0 = n ⊃ ∃m.(n = suc(m));
         PLUS:   ∀n.n+0 = n
                 ∀n m.n+suc(m) = suc(n+m);
         TIMES:  ∀n.n*0 = 0
                 ∀n m.n*suc(m) = (n*m)+m;;;

AXIOM    INDUCT: P(0) ∧ ∀n.(P(n) ⊃ P(suc(n))) ⊃ ∀n.P(n);;

REPRESENT {NATNUM} AS NATNUMREP;
ATTACH suc  ↔ (LAMBDA (X)(ADD1 X));
ATTACH pred ↔ (LAMBDA (X) (COND ((GREATERP X 0) (SUB1 X)) (T 0)));
ATTACH+     ↔ (LAMBDA (X Y)(PLUS X Y));
ATTACH *    ↔ (LAMBDA (X Y)(TIMES X Y));
ATTACH <    ↔ (LAMBDA (X Y)(LESSP X Y));
```

Using these commands we can ask questions like

```
*****SIMPLIFY 2+3 < pred(7);
*****SIMPLIFY 4*suc(2)+pred(3) < pred(pred(8));
```

Of course semantic simplification only works on ground terms, i.e. only on those quantifier free expressions whose only individual symbols are individual constants. Furthermore, such an expression will not evaluate unless all the constants have attachments, and there is a constant in the language for value of the expression. Thus a command like

```
*****SIMPLIFY n*0 < 3;
```

where n is a variable, will not simplify.

This facility may seem weak as we usually don't have ground expressions to evaluate. Below I will show that when we use the metatheory and the metatheory we frequently do have ground terms to evaluate, thus making this a very useful tool.

5. Syntactic Simplifier

FOL also contains a syntactic simplifier, called REWRITE. This facility allows a user to specify a particular set of universally quantified equations or equivalences as rewriting rules. We call such a collection a *simplification set*. The simplifier uses them by replacing the left hand side of an equation by its right hand side after making the appropriate substitutions for the universal variables.

(1) It will compute any function whose definition is hereditarily built up, in a quantifier free way, out of functions that have attachments, on domains that have attachments.

(2) Every step is a logical consequence of the function definitions and the semantic attachments. This implies that as a programming system this evaluator cannot produce an incorrect result. Thus the correctness of the expression as a 'program' is free.

This evaluator will be used extensively below. I would like to remark that this evaluator is completely general in that it takes an arbitrary set of first order sentences and an arbitrary simulation structure and does both semantic evaluation and syntactic evaluation until it no longer knows what to do. You should observe that the expressions you give it are any first order sentences you like. In this sense it is a substantial extension of PROLOG (Warren (1977)) that is not tied down to clause form and skolemization. In the examples below those familiar with PROLOG can see the naturalness that this kind of evaluation of first order sentences allows. Just look at the above definition of factorial. The introduction of semantic simplifications also gives arbitrary interpretations to particular predicates and functions.

7. Systems of Languages and Simulation Structures

As mentioned in the introduction, one of the important things about the FOL system is its ability to deal with metatheory. In order to do this effectively we need to conceptualize on what *objects* FOL is manipulating. As I have described it above, FOL can be thought of as always having its attention directed at a object consisting of a language, L, a simulation structure, SS, attachments between the two, and a set of facts, F, i.e. the finite set of facts that have asserted or proved. We can view this as shown in Fig. 1.

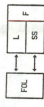

FIG. 1.

Below I will sometimes represent these 3-tuples schematically as

$$\langle L, SS, F \rangle$$

I will abuse language in two ways. Most of the time I will call these structures *LS pairs*, to emphasize the importance of having explicit representations as data structures for languages, the objects mentioned and the correspondence between the two. At other times I will call this kind of structure a *theory*.

The importance of LS pairs cannot be overestimated. I believe they fill a gap in the kinds of structures that have previously used to formalize reasoning.

Suppose we ask the semantic simplifier to

*****SIMPLIFY fact(3);

Quite justifiably it will say, "no simplifications". There is no semantic attachment to fact.

Now consider what the syntactic simplifier will do to fact(3) just given the definition of factorial.

fact (3) = IF 3 = 0 THEN 1 ELSE 3*fact(pred(3))
= IF 3 = 0 THEN 1
ELSE 3*(IF pred(3) = 0 THEN 1 ELSE pred(3)*fact(pred(pred(3))))

The rewriting will never terminate because the syntactic simplifier doesn't know anything about 3 = 0 or pred (3) = 0, etc. Thus it will blindly replace fact by its definition forever.

The above computation could be made to stop in several ways. For example, it would stop if

(3 = 0) ≡ FALSE
∀X Y. (IF FALSE THEN X ELSE Y) = Y
pred(3) = 2
fact(2) = 2
3*2 = 6

were all in the simplification set.

Or if we stopped after the first step and the semantic attachment mechanism knew about = on integers and pred then we would get

syn   fact(3) = IF 3 = 0 THEN 1 ELSE 3*fact(pred(3))
sem   = 3*fact(2)
syn   = 3*(IF 2 = 0 THEN 1 ELSE 2*fact(pred(2)))
sem   = 3*(2*fact(1))
syn   = 3*(2*(IF 1 = 0 THEN 1 ELSE 1*fact(pred(1))))
sem   = 3*(2*(1*fact(0)))
syn   = 3*(2*(1*(IF 0 = 0 THEN 1 ELSE 0*fact(pred(0)))))
sem   = 3*(2*(1*1))
            halt

This 'looks better'. The interesting thing to note is that if we had a semantic attachment to * this would have computed fully. On the other hand if we had added the definition of * in terms of + then it would have reduced to some expression in terms of addition. In this case if we didn't have a semantic attachment to * but only to + this expression would have also 'computed' 6.

Notice that this combination of semantic plus syntactic simplification acts very much like an ordinary interpreter. We have implemented such an interpreter and it has the following properties.

Informally their introduction corresponds to the recognition that we reason about objects, and that our reasoning makes use of our understanding of the things we reason about.

Let me give a mathematical example and a more traditional AI example.

Consider the following theorem of real analysis (Royden (1963)).

Theorem. *Let $\langle F_n \rangle$ be a sequence of nonempty closed intervals on the real line with $F_{n+1} \subseteq F_n$, then, if one of the F_n is bounded, the intersection of the F_n is nonempty.*

The goal I would like you to consider is: Give an example to show that this conclusion may be false if we do not require one of these sets to be bounded.

The usual counterexample expected is the set of closed intervals $[n,\infty]$ of real numbers. Clearly none of these are bounded and their intersection is empty. The idea of describing a counterexample simply cannot be made sense of if we do not have some knowledge of the models of our theories. That is, we need some idea of what objects we are reasoning about. The actualization of objects in the form of simulation structures is aimed in part at this kind of question.

As an AI example I will have to use the missionaries and cannibals puzzle. As the problem is usually posed we are asked to imagine three missionaries, three cannibals, a river, its two banks and a boat. We then build a theory about those objects. The point here is that we have explicitly distinguished between the objects mentioned and our theory of these objects. That is, we have (in our minds, so to speak) an explicit image of the objects we are reasoning about. This is a simulation structure as defined above.

One could argue that simulation structures are just linguistic objects anyway and we should think of them as part of the theory. I believe this is fundamentally wrong. In the examples below we make essential use of this distinction between an object and the words we use to mention it.

In addition to the practical usefulness that simulation structures have, they allow us, in a mechanized way, to make sense out of the traditional philosophic questions of sense and denotation. That is, they allow us to mention in a completely formal and natural way the relation between the objects we are reasoning about and the words we are using to mention them. This basic distinction is exactly what we have realized by making models of a language into explicit data structures.

One way of describing what we have done is that when we reason we have built a data structure that embodies the idea that when we reason we need a language to carry out our discussions, some information about the object this language talks about, and some facts about the objects expressed in the language. This structure can be thought of as a mechanizable analogue of a theory. Since it is a data structure like any other we can reason about this theory by considering it as an object described by some other theory. Thus we give up the idea of a 'universal' language about all objects to gain the ability to formally discuss our various theories of these objects.

Currently FOL has the facility to simultaneously handle as many LS pairs as you want. It also provides a facility for changing one's attention from one pair to another. We use this feature for changing attention from theory to metatheory as explained below.

8. Metatheory

I have already used the word 'metatheory' many times and since it is an important part of what follows I want to be a little more careful about what I mean by it. In this note I am not concerned with the philosophical questions logicians raise in discussions of consistency, etc. I am interested in how metatheory can be used to facilitate reasoning using computers. One of the main contributions of this paper is the way in which I use *reflection principles* (Feferman (1962)) to connect theories and metatheories. Reflection principles are described in the next section.

In this section I do not want to justify the use of metatheory. In ordinary reasoning it is used all the time. Some common examples of metatheory are presented in the next section. Here I will present examples taken from logic itself, as they require no additional explanation.

In its simplest form metatheory is used in the following way. Imagine that you want to prove some theorem of the theory, i.e. to extend the facts part, f, of some LS to F. One way of doing this is by using FOL in the ordinary theorem constructing way to generate a new fact about the objects mentioned by the theory. An alternative way of doing it may be to use some metatheorem which 'shortens' the proof by stating that the *result* of some complicated theorem generation scheme is valid. Such shortcuts are sometimes called *subsidiary deduction rules* (Kleene (1952), p. 86).

We represent this schematically by the following diagram.

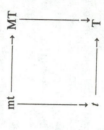

Consider the metatheorem: if you have a propositional WFF whose only sentential connective is the equivalence sign, then the WFF is a theorem if and each sentential symbol occurs an even number of times. In FOL this could be expressed by the metatheory sentence

$$\forall w. \, (\text{PROPWFF}\,(w) \land \text{CONTAINS\_ONLY\_EQUIVALENCES}\,(w)$$
$$\supset (\forall s.(\text{SENTSYM}(s) \land \text{OCCURS}(s,w) \supset \text{EVEN}(\text{count}(s,w)))$$
$$\supset \text{THEOREM}(w)))$$

The idea of this theorem is that since it is easier to count than to construct the proofs of complicated theorems, this metatheorem can save you the work of generating a proof. In FOLS metatheory this theorem can be either be proved or simply asserted as axiom.

We use this theorem by directing our attention to the metatheory and instantiating it to some WFF and proving that THEOREM(*w*). Since we are assuming that our axiomatization of the metatheory is sound, we are then justified in asserting *w* in the theory. The reflection principles stated below should be looked at as the *reason* that we are justified in asserting *w*. More detailed examples will be given in the next section.

In FOL we introduce a special LS pair META. It is intended that META is a general theory of LS pairs. When we start, it contains facts about only those things that are common to all LS pairs. Since META behaves like any other first order LS pair additional axioms, etc., can be added to it. This allows a user to assert many other things about a particular theory. Several examples will be given below.

An example of how we axiomatize the notion of well formed

$$\forall \text{Is expr}.(\text{WFF}(\text{expr,Is}) \equiv \text{PROPWFF}(\text{expr,Is}) \lor \\ \text{QUANTWFF}(\text{expr,Is})$$

An expression is a WFF (relative to a particular LS pair) if it is either a propositional WFF or a quantifier WFF.

$$\forall \text{Is expr}.(\text{PROPWFF}(\text{expr,Is}) \equiv \text{APPLPWFF}(\text{expr,Is}) \lor \\ \text{AWFF}(\text{expr,Is})$$

A propositional WFF is either an application propositional WFF or an atomic WFF.

$$\forall \text{Is expr}.(\text{APPLPWFF}(\text{expr,Is}) \equiv \text{PROPCONN}(\text{mainsym}(\text{expr})) \land \\ \forall n.(\emptyset < n \land n \leqslant \text{arity}(\text{mainsym}(\text{expr})) \\ \supset \text{WFF}(\text{arg}(n,\text{expr}),\text{Is})))$$

An application propositional WFF is an expression whose main symbol is a propositional connective, and if n is between 0 and the arity of the propositional connective then the n-th argument of the expression must be a WFF. Notice that this definition is mutually recursive with that of PROPWFF and WFF.

$$\forall \text{Is expr}.(\text{QUANTWFF}(\text{expr,Is}) \equiv \\ \text{QUANT}(\text{mainsym}(\text{expr})) \land \text{INDVAR}(\text{bvar}(\text{expr}),\text{Is}) \land \\ \text{WFF}(\text{matrix}(\text{expr}),\text{Is})$$

A quantifier WFF is an expression whose main symbol is a quantifier, whose bound variable is an individual variable and whose matrix is a WFF.

$$\forall \text{Is expr}.(\text{AWFF}(\text{expr,Is}) \equiv \text{SENTSYM}(\text{expr,Is}) \lor \\ \text{APPLAWFF}(\text{expr,Is}))$$

An atomic WFF is either a sentential symbol or an application atomic WFF.

$$\forall \text{Is expr}.(\text{APPLAWFF}(\text{expr,Is}) \equiv \text{PREDSYM}(\text{mainsym}(\text{expr}),\text{Is}) \land \\ \forall n.(\emptyset < n \land n \leqslant \text{arity}(\text{mainsym}(\text{expr}),\text{Is}) \\ \supset \text{TERM}(\text{arg}(n,e),\text{Is})))$$

An atomic application WFF is an expression whose main symbol is a predicate symbol and each argument of this expression in the appropraite range is a TERM.

$$\forall \text{Is expr}.(\text{TERM}(\text{expr,Is}) \equiv \text{INDSYM}(\text{expr,Is}) \lor \\ \text{APPLTERM}(\text{expr,Is}) \land$$

$$\forall \text{Is expr}.(\text{APPLTERM}(\text{expr,Is}) \equiv \text{OPSYM}(\text{mainsym}(\text{expr}),\text{Is}) \land \\ \forall n.(\emptyset < n \land n \leqslant \text{arity}(\text{mainsym}(\text{expr}),\text{Is}) \\ \supset \text{TERM}(\text{arg}(n,\text{expr}),\text{Is})))$$

A TERM is either an individual symbol or an application TERM, etc.

This is by no means a complete description of LS pairs but it does give some idea of what sentences in META look like. These axioms are collected together in appendix C. The extent of META isn't critical and this paper is not an appropriate place to discuss its details as implemented in FOL. Of course, in addition to the descriptions of the objects contained in the LS pair, it also has axioms about what it means to be a 'theorem', etc.

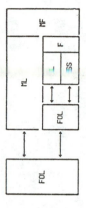

FIG. 2.

Thus META contains the proof theory and some of the model theory of an LS pair. As with any first order theory its language is built up of predicate constants, function symbols and individual constant symbols. What are these? There are constants for WFFs, TERMs, derivations, simulation structures, models, etc. It contains functions for doing 'and introductions', for substituting TERMs into WFFs, constructors and selectors on data structures. It has predicates 'is a well formed formula', 'is a term', 'equality of expressions except for change of bound variables', 'is a model', 'is a simulation structure', 'is a proof', etc.

Suppose that we are considering the metatheory of some particular LS pair, LSO = ⟨L,SS,F⟩. At this point we need to ask a critical question. What is the *natural* simulation structure for META?

The answer is: (1) we actually have in hand the object we are trying to axiomatize, LSO, and (2) the code of FOL itself contains algorithms for the predicates and functions mentioned above.

This leads to the picture of Fig. 2.It is this picture that leads to the first hint of how to construct a system of logic that can *look* at itself. The trick is that when we carry out the above construction on a computer, the two boxes labeled FOL are physically the same object. I will expand on this in the section on self reflection.

9. Reflection

A *reflection principle* is a statement of a relation between a theory and its metatheory. Although logicians use considerably stronger principles (see Feferman (1962)), we will only use some simple examples, i.e., statements of the soundness of the axiomatization in the metatheory of the theory. An example of a reflection principle is

(in T) $\backslash\!\!\|/$
             w
(in MT) Prf("$\backslash\!\!\|/$", "w")

In natural deduction formulations of logic proofs are represented as trees. In the above diagram let '$\backslash\!\!\|/$' be a proof and 'w' be the well formed formula which it proves. Let Prf be a predicate constant in the metatheory, with Prf(p,x) true if and only if p is a proof, x is a wff, and p is a proof of x. Also, let "$\backslash\!\!\|/$" and "w" be the individual constants in the metatheory that are the names of '$\backslash\!\!\|/$' and 'w', respectively. Then the above reflection principle can be read as: if '$\backslash\!\!\|/$' is a proof of 'w' in the theory we are allowed to assert Prf("$\backslash\!\!\|/$", "w") in the metatheory and vice versa.

A special case of this rule is 'w' has no dependencies, i.e. it is a theorem.

(in T)   w   with no dependencies
(in META) THEOREM("w")

A simpler example is

(in T)   an individual variable x
(in META) INDVAR("x")

Suppose we have the metatheorem

ANDI: ∀thm1 thm2. THEOREM(mkand(wffof(thm1),wffof(thm2)))

This (meta)theorem says that if we have any two theorems of the theory, then we get a theorem by taking the conjunction of the two wffs associated with these theorems. I need to remark about what I mean by the WFF associated with a theorem. Theorems should be thought of as particular kinds of facts. Facts are more complicated objects than only sentences. They also contain other information. For example, they include the reason we are willing to assert them and what other facts their assertion depends on. Facts also have names. Thus the above line is an incomplete representation of the metatheoretic fact whose name is ANDI. The WFF associated with this fact is just

∀thm1 thm2. THEOREM(mkand(wffof(thm1),wffof(thm2)))

Remember the reflection principle associated with THEOREM is

(in T)   w   with no dependencies
(in META) THEOREM("w")

Thus we can imagine the following scenario.

Suppose we have two theorems called T1 and T2 in the theory. These facts are represented as FOL data structures. Now suppose we want to assert the conjunction of these two in the theory. One way to do this is to use the *and introduction* rule of FOL. This example, however, is going to do it the hard way. First we switch to the metatheory carrying with us the data structures for T1 and T2. We then declare some individual constants t1 and t2 to be of sort theorem in the metatheory, and use the semantic attachment mechanism at the metatheory level to attach the data structures for T1 and T2 to the individual constants t_1 and t_2 respectively. We then instantiate the metatheorem ANDI to t1 and t2. Note that the resulting formula is a ground instance of a sentence without quantifiers. This means that if we have attachments to all the symbols in the formula we can evaluate this formula. In this theorem we have the predicate constant THEOREM. In META it is the only constant in this sentence that is not likely to have an attachment. This is because being a theorem is not in general decidable. Fortunately, we can still use the reflection principle, because we understand the intended interpretation of the metatheory. So if we use the evaluator on

mkand(wffof(t1),wffof(t2)),

we can pick up the data structure computed in the model, instead of one in the theory. Then since we know that it is a theorem we can make it into one in the theory.

This idea has been implemented in a very nice way. In FOL we have the following command.

*****REFLECT ANDI T1,T2;

The reflect command understands some fixed list of reflection principles, which includes those above. When FOL sees the word 'REFLECT' it expects the next thing in the input stream to be the name of a fact in the metatheory of the current theory. So it switches to the theory and scans for a fact. It then finds that this fact is universally quantified with two variables ranging over facts in the theory. It switches back to the theory and scans for two facts in the theory. It holds on to the data structures that it gets in that way and switches back to the metatheory. Once there it makes the attachments of these structures to two newly created individual constants, first checking whether or not it already has an attachment for either of these structures. We then instantiate the theorem to the relevant constants and evaluate the result. When we look at the result we notice that it will probably simply evaluate to

THEOREM(mkand(wffof(t1),wffof(t2)))

This is because we don't have an attachment to THEOREM and we also don't have an individual constant which names mkand(wffof(t1),wffof(t2)). But what we do notice is that we have reduced the theorem to the form THEOREM(−), and we know about reflection principles involving THEOREM. Thus we go back and evaluate its argument, mkand(wffof(t1),wffof(t2)), and see if it has a value in the model. In this case since it does we can reflect it back into the theory, by returning to the theory and constructing the appropriate theorem.

This example is a particularly simple one, but the feature described is very general. I will give some more examples below. One thing I want to emphasise here is that what we have done is *to change theorem proving in the theory into evaluation in the metatheory*. I claim that this idea of using reflection with evaluation is the most general case of this and that this feature is not only an extremely useful operation but a fundamental one as well. It is the correct technical realization of how we can *use* declarative information. That is, the only thing you expect a sentence to do is to take its intended interpretation seriously.

The metatheorem we use in reflection does not need to be of the form THEOREM(−). This is the reason for needing the evaluater rather than simply either the syntactic or the semantic simplification mechanisms alone. Consider the following general metatheorems *about* the theory of natural numbers. If you find it hard to read it is explained in detail in the next subsection.

$$\forall y1\, x .(\text{LINEAREQ}(\text{wffof}(v1),x) \supset \text{THEOREM}(\text{mkequal}(x,\text{solve}(\text{wffof}(v1),x))));$$
$$\forall w\, x .(\text{LINEAREQ}(w,x) \equiv$$
$$\quad \text{mainsym}(w) = \text{Equal} \;\wedge$$
$$\quad (\text{mainsym}(\text{lhs}(w)) = \text{Sum} \;\vee\; \text{mainsym}(\text{lhs}(w)) = \text{Diff}) \;\wedge$$
$$\quad \text{larg}(\text{lhs}(w)) = x \;\wedge$$
$$\quad \text{NUMERAL}(\text{rarg}(\text{lhs}(w))) \;\wedge$$
$$\quad \text{NUMERAL}(\text{rhs}(w)) \;\wedge$$
$$\quad (\text{mainsym}(\text{lhs}(w)) = \text{Sum} \supset \text{mknum}(\text{rhs}(w)) < \text{mknum}(\text{rarg}(\text{lhs}(w)))));$$

$$\forall w\, x .(\text{solve}(w,x) = \text{IF } \text{mainsym}(\text{lhs}(w)) = \text{Sum}$$
$$\quad \text{THEN } \text{mknumeral}(\text{mknum}(\text{rhs}(w)) - \text{mknum}(\text{rarg}(\text{lhs}(w)))+$$
$$\quad \text{ELSE } \text{mknumeral}(\text{mknum}(\text{rhs}(w))+$$
$$\qquad \text{mknum}(\text{rarg}(\text{lhs}(w))))) ;;$$

These axioms together with the reflection mechanism extend FOL, so that it can solve equations of the form $x+a = b$ or $x-a = b$, when there is a solution in natural numbers. We could have given a solution in integers or for n simultaneous equations in n unknowns. Each of these requires a different collection of theorems in the metatheory.

This axiomatization may look inefficient but let me point out that solve is exactly the same amount of writing that you would need to write code to solve the

same equation. The definition of LINEAREQ is divided into two parts. The first five conjunctions are to do type checking, the sixth conjunct checks for the existence of a solution before you try to use solve to find it. The above example actually does a lot. It type checks the argument, guarantees a solution and then finds it.

9.1. Can a program learn?

In this section I want to digress from the stated intent of the paper and speak a little more generally about AI. It is my feeling that it is the task of AI to explain how it might be possible to build a computer individual that we can interact with as a partner in some problem solving area. This leads to the question of what kinds of conversations we want to have with such an individual and what the nature of our interactions with him should be.

Below I describe a conversation with FOL about solving linear equations. As an example it has two purposes. First it is to illustrate the sense in which FOL is a conversational machine that can have rich discussions (even if not in natural language). And second to explore my ideas of what kinds of dialogues we can have with machines that might be construed as the computer individual learning. I believe that after the discussion presented below we could reasonably say that FOL had learned to solve linear equations. That is, by having this conversation with FOL we have taught FOL some elementary algebra.

Imagine that we have told FOL about Peano arithmetic. We could do this by reading in the axioms presented in Appendix B. We can then have a discussion about *numbers*. For example, we might say

*****ASSUME $n+2 = 7$;

1 $(n+2) = 7$ (1)

and we might want to know what is the value of n. Since we are talking about numbers in the language of Peano arithmetic the *only* way we have of discussing this problem is by using facts about numbers. Suppose that we already know the theorems

THM1: $\forall p\, q\, m. (p = q \supset p-m = q-m)$
THM2: $\forall p\, q\, m. (p+q)-r = p+(q-r)$
THM3: $\forall p. (p+0) = p$

Then we can prove that $n = 5$

*****AE THM1 $n+2,7,2$;
2 $(n+2) = 7 \supset ((n+2)-2) = (7-2)$
*****EVAL BY {THM2,THM3};
3 $(n+2) = 7 \supset n = 5$
***** $\supset$ E 1,3;
4 $n = 5$ (1)

In this case what we have done is proved that $n = 5$ by using facts about *arithmetic*. To put it in the perspective of *conversation*, we are having a discussion about numbers.

If we were expecting to discuss with FOL many such facts, rather than repeating the above conversation many times we might choose to have a single discussion about *algebra*. This would be carried out by introducing the notion of *equation* and a description of how to *solve* them. What is an equation? Well, it simply turns out to be a special kind of *atomic formula* of the theory of arithmetic. That is, we can discuss the solution to equations by using metatheory.

In FOL we switch to the metatheory. We make some declarations and then define what it means to be a linear equation with a solution by stating the axiom

$\forall w\, x. (\text{LINEAREQ}(w,x) \equiv$
$\quad \text{mainsym}(w) = \text{Equal} \wedge$
$\quad (\text{mainsym}(\text{lhs}(w)) = \text{Sum} \vee \text{mainsym}(\text{lhs}(w)) = \text{Diff}) \wedge$
$\quad \text{larg}(\text{lhs}(w)) = x \wedge$
$\quad \text{NUMERAL}(\text{rarg}(\text{lhs}(w))) \wedge$
$\quad \text{NUMERAL}(\text{rhs}(w)) \wedge$
$\quad (\text{mainsym}(\text{lhs}(w)) = \text{Sum} \supset \text{mknum}(\text{rhs}(w)) > \text{mknum}(\text{rarg}(\text{lhs}(w))))$

Here w is a (meta)variable ranging over WFFs, and x is a (meta)variable ranging over individual variables. Spelled out in English this sentence says that a well formed formula is a linear equation if and only if:

(i) it is an equality,

(ii) its left hand side is either a sum or a difference,

(iii) the left hand argument of the left hand side of the equality is x,

(iv) the right hand argument of the left hand side of the equality is a numeral,

(v) the right hand side of the equality is a numeral and

(vi) if the left hand side is a sum then the number denoted by the numeral on the right hand side is greater than the number denoted by the numeral appearing in the left hand side.

In more mathematical terminology it is: that the well formed formula must be either of the form $x+a = b$ or $x-a = b$ where a and b are numerals and x is an individual variable. Since here we are only interested in the natural numbers, the last restriction in the definition of LINEAREQ is needed to guarantee the existence of a solution.

We also describe how to find out what is the *solution* to an equation.

$\forall w\, x. (\text{solve}(w,x) = \text{IF } \text{mainsym}(\text{lhs}(w)) = \text{Sum}$
$\quad \text{THEN } \text{mknumeral}(\text{mknum}(\text{rhs}(w)) -$
$\qquad \text{mknum}(\text{rarg}(\text{lhs}(w))))$
$\quad \text{ELSE } \text{mknumeral}(\text{mknum}(\text{rhs}(w)) +$
$\qquad \text{mknum}(\text{rarg}(\text{lhs}(w))))) ;;$

This is a function definition in the meta theory. Finally we assert that if we have an equation in the theory then the numeral constructed by the solver can be asserted to be the answer.

$\forall vl\, x. (\text{LINEAREQ}(\text{wffof}(vl),x) \supset \text{THEOREM}(\text{mkequal}(x,\text{solve}(\text{wffof}(vl),x)))) ;$

We then tell FOL to remember these facts in a way that is convenient to be used by FOL's evaluator.

This then is the conversation we have with FOL about equations. Now we are ready to see how FOL can use that information, so we switch FOL's attention back to the theory. Now, whenever we want to solve a linear equation, we simply remark, using the reflect command, that he should remember our discussion about solving equations.

We can now get the effect of the small proof above by saying

*****REFLECT SOLVE 1 ;

$5\ n = 5$ (1)

In effect FOL has learned to solve simple linear equations.

We could go on to ask FOL to prove that the function solve actually provides a solution to the equation, rather than our just telling FOL that it does, but this is simply a matter of sophistication. It has to do with the question of what you are willing to accept as a justification.

One reasonable justification is that the teacher told me. This is exactly the state we are in above. On the other hand if that is not satisfactory then it is possible to discuss with FOL the justification of the solution. This could be accomplished by explaining to FOL (in the metatheory) not to assert the solution of the equations in the theory, but rather to construct a proof of the correctness of the solution as we did when we started. Clearly this can be done using same machinery that was used here. This is important because it means that our reasoning system does not need to be expanded. We only have to tell it more information.

A much more reasonable alternative is to tell FOL (again in the metatheory) two things. One is what we have above, i.e., to assert the solution of the equation. Second is that if asked to justify the solution, then to produce that proof. This combines the advantages each of the above possibilities. I want to point out that this is very close to the kinds of discussions that you want to be able to have with people about simple algebra.

Informally we always speak about solving *equations*. That is, we think of them as syntactic and learn how to manipulate them. This is not thinking about them as relations, which is their usual first order interpretation. In this sense going to the metatheory and treating them as syntactic objects is very close to our informal use of these notions.

I believe that this is exactly what we want in an AI system dealing with the question of *teaching*. Notice that we have the best of both worlds. On the one hand, at the theory level, we can 'execute' this learning, i.e. use it, and on the other hand, at the metatheory level, we can reason about what we have learned about manipulating equations. In addition the correct distinction between equations as facts and equations as syntactic objects has been maintained. The division between theory and metatheory has allowed us to view the same object in both these ways without contradiction or the possibility of confusion.

As is evident from the above description, one of the things we have here is a very general purpose programming system. In addition it is extendable. Above we have showed how to introduce any new subsidiary deduction rule that you chose, 'simply' by telling FOL what you would like it to do. This satisfies the desires of Davis and Schwartz (1977) but in a setting not restricted to the theory of hereditarily finite sets. As I said above: we are using first order logic in what I believe is its most general and natural setting.

There are hundreds of examples of this kind where their natural description is in the metatheory. In a later paper I will discuss just how much of the intent of natural language can only be understood if you realize that a lot of what we say is about our use of language, not about objects in the world. This kind of conversation is most naturally carried out in the metatheory with the use of the kind of self-reflective structures hinted about below.

9.2. Using metametatheory

We can take another leap by allowing ourselves to iterate the above procedure and using metametatheory. This section is quite sketchy but would require a full paper to write out the details.

We can use the metametatheory to describe declaratively what we generally call heuristics. Consider an idealized version of the Boyer and Moore (1979) theorem prover for recursive functions. This prover looks at a function definition and tries to decide whether or not to try to prove some property of the function using either CAR-induction or CDR-induction, depending on the form of the function definition.

CAR and CDR inductions are axiom schemas, which depend on the form of the function definition and the WFF being proved. Imagine that these had already told to FOL in the metatheory. Suppose we had called them CARIND and CDRIND. Then using the facilities described above we could use these facts by reflection. For example,

*****ASSUME $\forall u.\text{counta}(u) = $ if atom(u) then u else counta(car(u));

1 $\forall u.\text{counta}(u) = $ if atom(u) then u else counta(car(u))   (1)

*****REFLECT CARIND 1 $\forall u.\text{ATOM}(\text{counta}(u))$;

2 $\forall u.\text{ATOM}(\text{counta}(u))$ (1)

*****ASSUME $\forall u.\text{countd}(u) = $ if null(u) then 'NIL else countd(cdr(u));

3 $\forall u.\text{countd}(u) = $ if null(u) then 'NIL else countd(cdr(u))   (3)

*****REFLECT CDRIND 3 $\forall u.\text{countd}(u) = $ 'NIL;

4 $\forall u.\text{countd}(u) = $ 'NIL   (3)

The use of this kind of command can be discussed in the metametatheory. We introduce a function, T_reflect, in the metatheory, which we attach using semantic attachment to the FOL code that implements the above reflect command. Thus T_reflect takes a fact, $\vee$I and a list of arguments, and if it succeeds returns a new proof whose last step is the newly asserted fact and if it fails returns some error. Suppose also that Carind and Cdrind are the metametatheory's name for CARIND and CDRIND respectively. Then suppose in the metametatheory we let

$$\text{WFF1} = \text{mkforall}(\text{T\_}u,\text{mkapplw1}(\text{T\_ATOM},$$
$$(\text{mkapplt1}(\text{T\_counta},\text{T\_}u))))$$

$$\text{WFF2} = \text{mkforall}(\text{T\_}u,\text{mkequal}(\text{mkapplt1}(\text{T\_countd},\text{T\_}u),$$
$$\text{mksexp}(\text{'NIL})))$$

that is, $\lambda u.\ \text{ATOM}(\text{counta}(u))$ and $\forall u.\text{countd}(u) = $ 'NIL, respectively. We prefix things refering to the theory by "T_". The effect of the above commands (without actually asserting anything) is gotten by using the FOL evaluator on

$$\text{T\_reflect}(\text{Cdrind}, < \text{T\_fact}(1),\text{WFF1} >)$$
$$\text{T\_reflect}(\text{Cdrind}, < \text{T\_fact}(3),\text{WFF1} >).$$

Now suppose that $\vee$I ranges over facts in the theory, f ranges over function symbols, and w ranges over WFFs. The micro Boyer and Moore theorem prover can be expressed by

$$\forall \vee I f w.$$
$$(\text{IS\_T\_FUNDEF}(\vee I,f) \supset$$
$$(\text{CONTAINS\_ONLY\_CAR\_RECURSION}(\vee I,f) \wedge$$
$$\text{NOERROR}(\text{T\_REFLECT}(\text{Carind},\langle \vee I,w\rangle)) \supset$$
$$\text{T\_THEOREM}(\text{last\_T\_step}(\text{T\_REFLECT}(\text{Carind},\langle \vee I,w\rangle)))) \wedge$$
$$(\text{CONTAINS\_ONLY\_CDR\_RECURSION}(\vee I,f) \wedge$$
$$\text{NOERROR}(\text{T\_REFLECT}(\text{Cdrind},\langle \vee I,w\rangle)) \supset$$
$$\text{T\_THEOREM}(\text{last\_T\_step}(\text{T\_REFLECT}(\text{Cdrind},\langle \vee I,w\rangle)))))$$

In the metametatheory we call this fact BOYER_and_MOORE. It is read as follows: if in the theory, $\vee$I is a function definition of the function symbol f, then if this function definition only contains recursions on car, and if when you apply reflection from the theory level to the metatheorem called Carind you don't get an error, then the result of this reflection is a theorem at the theory level, similarly for cdr induction.

As explained in the previous sections, asserting this in the metametatheory allows it to be used at the theory level by using the same reflection device as before.

When our attention is directed to the theory we can say

*****MREFLECT BOYER_and_MOORE 1,counta,∀u.ATOM(counta(u));

5 ∀u.ATOM(counta(u))   (1)

*****MREFLECT BOYER_and_MOORE 3,countd,∀u.countd(u) = 'NIL;

6 ∀u.countd(v) = 'NIL   (3)

Here MREFLECT simply means reflect.into the metametatheory.

(1) If META has names for all of the LS pairs known to FOL then it has the entire FOL system as its simulation structure;

(2) Since META is a theory about any LS pair, we can use it to reason about itself.

We can illustrate this in FOL by switching to META and executing the following command.

*****REFLECT ANDI ANDI ANDI;

1 ∀thm1 thm2.THEOREM(mkand(wffof(thm1),wffof(thm2)) ∧
∨thm1 thm2.THEOREM(mkand(wffof(thm1),wffof(thm2)))

The effect we have achieved is that when FOL's attention is directed at itself, then when we reflect into its own metatheory we have a system that is capable of reasoning about itself.

When looking at human reasoning I am struck by two facts. First, we seem to be able to apply the Meta facts that we know to any problems that we are trying to solve, and second, even though it is possible to construct simple examples of use/mention conflicts, most people arrive at correct answers to questions without even knowing there is a problem. Namely, although natural language is filled with apparent puns that arise out of use/mention confusions, the people speaking do not confuse the names of things with the things. That is, the *meaning* is clear to them.

The above command suggests one possible technical way in which both of these problems can be addressed. The structure of FOL *knew* that the first occurrence of ANDI in the above command was a 'use' and that the second and third were 'mentions'. Furthermore, the same routines that dealt effectively with the ordinary non self reflective way of looking at theory/metatheory relations also dealt with this case of self reflection without difficulty.

Notice that I said, 'this case'. It is possible with the structure that I have described above to ask META embarrassing questions. For example, if you ask META twice in a row what the largest step number in its proof is you will get two different answers. This would seem to lead to a contradiction.

The source of this problem is in what I believe is in our traditional idea of what it means to be a *rule of inference*. Self reflective systems have properties that are different from ordinary systems. In particular, whenever you 'apply a rule of inference' to the facts of this system you change the structure of META itself and as a result you change the attachment to Meta. This process of having a rule of inference changes the models of a theory as well as the already proven facts simply does not happen in traditional logics. This change of point of view requires a new idea of what is a valid rule of inference for such systems.

The extent of the soundness of the structure that I propose here is well beyond the scope of this elementary paper. Also FOL was built largely before I understood anything about this more general idea of rule of inference, thus the current FOL

This example shows how the metametatheory, together with reflection, can be used to drive the proof checker itself. Thus we have the ability to declaratively state heuristics and have them effectively used. The ability to reason about heuristics and prove additional theorems about them provides us with an enormous extra power. Notice that we have once again changed theorem proving at the theory level into computation at the metametatheory level. This is part of the leverage that we get by having all of this machinery around simultaneously.

This example, as it is described above, has not yet been run in FOL. It is the only example in this paper which has not actually been done using the FOL system, but it is clear that it will work simply given the current features.

A good way of looking at all of this is that the same *kind* of language that we use to carry on ordinary conversations with FOL can be used to discuss the control structures of FOL itself. Thus it can be used to discuss its own actions.

10. Self Reflection

In the traditional view of metatheory we start with a theory and we axiomatize that theory. This gives us metatheory. Later we may axiomatize that theory. That gives us metametatheory. If you believe that most reasoning is at some level (as I do) then this view of towers of metatheories leads to many questions. For example, how is it that human memory space doesn't overflow. Each theory in the tower seems to contain a complete description of the theory below thus exponentiating the amount of space needed!

In the section on metatheory, I introduced the LS pair, META. Since it is a first order theory just like any other, FOL can deal with it just like any other. Since META is the general theory of LS pairs and META is an LS pair this might suggest that META is also a theory that contains facts about itself. That is, by introducing the individual constant Meta into the theory META and by using semantic attachment to attach the theory (i.e., the actual machine data structure) META to Meta we can give META its own name. The rest of this section is somewhat vague. We have just begun to work out the consequences of this observation.

FOL handles many LS pairs simultaneously. I have showed how given any LS pair we can direct FOL's attention to META using reflection. Once META has an individual constant which is a name for itself and we have attached META to this constant, then META is FOL's theory of itself. Notice several things:

code cannot adequately implement these ideas. One of many main current research interests is in working out the consequences of these self reflective structures. META has many strange properties which I have just begun to appreciate and is a large topic for further research.

11. Conclusion

11.1. Summary of important results

I want to review what I consider to be the important results of this paper.

One is the observation that, when we reason, we use representations of the objects we are reasoning about as well as a representation of the facts about these objects. This is technically realized by FOL's manipulation of LS pairs using semantic attachment. It is incorrect to view this as a procedural representation of facts. Instead we should look at it as an ability to explicitly represent procedures. That is, simulation structures give us an opportunity to have a machine representation of the objects we want to reason about as well as the sentences we use to mention them.

Second, the evaluator I described above is an important object. When used by itself it represents a mathematical way of describing algorithms together with the assurance that they are correctly implemented. This is a consequence of the fact that the evaluator only performs logically valid transformations on the function definitions. In this way we could use the evaluator to actually generate a proof that the computed answer is correct. In these cases evaluation and deduction become the same thing. This is similar in spirit to the work of Kowalski (1974), but does not rely on any normalization of formulas. It considers the usual logical function definitions and takes their intended interpretation seriously. This evaluator works on any expression with respect to any LS pair and its implementation has proved to be only two to three times slower than a lisp interpreter.

Third is the observation that the FOL proof checker is itself the natural simulation structure for the theory META of LS pairs. This gives us a clean way of saying what the intended interpretation of META is. This observation makes evaluation in META a very powerful tool. It is also the seed of a theory of self reflective logic structures that, like humans, can reason about themselves.

Fourth is the use of reflection principles to connect an LS pair with META. This, together with the REFLECT command, is a technical explanation of what has been called the declarative/procedural controversy. Consider the META theorem ANDI described above. When we use the REFLECT command to point at it from some LS pair, ANDI is viewed procedurally. We want it to do an *and introduction*. On the other hand when we are reasoning in META, it is a sentence like any other. Whether a sentence is looked at declaratively or procedurally depends on your point of view, that is, it depends where you are standing when you look at it.

I have presented here a general description of a working reasoning system that includes not only theories but also metatheories of arbitrarily high level. I have given several examples of how these features, together with reflection can be used to dynamically extend the reasoning power of the working FOL system. I have made some references to the way in which one can use the self reflective parts of this system. I have given examples of how heuristics for using subsidiary deduction rules can be described using these structures. In addition, since everything you type to FOL refers to some LS pair, all of the above things can be reasoned about using the same machinery.

11.2. Concluding remarks, history and thanks

I have tried in this paper to give a summary of the ideas which motivate the current FOL system. Unfortunately this leaves little room for complex examples so I should say a little about history, the kinds of things that have been done and what is being done now.

FOL was started in 1972 and the basic ideas for this system were already known in the summer of 1973. Many of the ideas of this system come directly out of taking seriously John McCarthy's idea that before we can ever expect the ideas involved in the problem solving we need a device that can represent the ideas involved in the problem. I started by attempting to use ordinary first order logic and set theory to represent the ideas of mathematics. My discovery of the explicit use of computable partial models (i.e. simulation structures) came out of thinking about a general form for what McCarthy (1973) called a 'computation rule' for logic, together with thinking about problems like the one about real numbers mentioned above. The first implementation of semantic evaluation was in 1974 by me. Since then it has been worked on by Arthur Thomas, Chris Goad, Juan Bulnes and most recently by Andrew Robinson. The first aggressive use of semantic attachment was by Bob Filman (1978) in his thesis.

This idea of attaching algorithms to function and predicate letters is not new to AI. It appears first in Green (1969) I believe, but since then in too many places to cite them all. What is new here is that we have done it uniformly, in such a way that the process can be reasoned about. We have also arranged it so that there can be no confusion between what parts of our data structure is code and what parts are sentences of logic.

The real push for metatheory came from several directions. One was the realization that most of mathematical reasoning in practice was metatheoretic. This conflicted with most current theorem proving ideas of carrying out the reasoning in the theory itself. Second was my desire to be able to do the proofs in Kleene (1952) about the correctness of programs. In the near future we are planning to carry out this dream. Carolyn Talcott and I plan to completely formalize LISP using all the power of the FOL system described above. In addition there will be people working on program transformations in the style of Burstall and Darlington

(1977). The third push for metatheory was a desire to address the question of common sense reasoning. This more than anything needs the ability to be able to reason about our theories of the world. One step in this direction has been taken by Carolyn Talcott and myself. We have worked out D. Michie's Keys and boxes problem using this way of thinking and are currently writing it up.

The desire to deal with metatheory led to the invention of the FOL reflection command. Metatheory is pretty useless without a way of connecting it to the theory. I believe that I am the first to use reflection in this way.

All of the above ideas were presented at the informal session at IJCAI 1973.

This panel was composed of Carl Hewitt, Allen Newell, Alan Kay and myself.

The idea of self reflection grew out of thinking about the picture in the section on metatheory.

It has taken several years to make these routines all work together. They first all worked in June 1977 when Dan Blom finished the coding of the evaluator. I gave some informal demos of the examples in this paper at IJCAI 1977.

I suppose that there is as good a place as any to thank all the people that helped this effort. Particularly John McCarthy for his vision and for supporting FOL all these years. I would not have had as much fun doing it alone. Thanks.

I hope to write detailed papers on each of these features with substantial examples. In the meantime I hope this gives a reasonable idea of how FOL works.

Appendices

A. An axiomatization of natural numbers

The commands below repeat those given in Section 4. They will be used in the examples below. One should keep in mind that this is an axiomatization of the natural numbers (including 0), not an axiomatization of the integers.

```
DECLARE INDVAR n m p q ∈ NATNUM:
DECLARE OPCONST suc pred(NATNUM) :: NATNUM:
DECLARE OPCONST +(NATNUM, NATNUM) = NATNUM [R ← 458.L ← 455]:
DECLARE OPCONST *(NATNUM, NATNUM) = NATNUM [R ← 558.L ← 5551:
DECLARE PREDCONST < (NATNUM, NATNUM) [INF]:
DECLARE PREDPAR P(NATNUM):

AXIOM Q:
  ONEONE: ∀n m. (suc(n) = suc(m) ⊃ n = m);
  SUCC1:  ∀n.¬ (0 = suc(n)):
  SUCC2:  ∀n.(¬ 0 = n ⊃ ∃m. (n = suc(m))):
  PLUS:   ∀n.n+0 = n
          ∀n m.n+suc(m) = suc(n+m):
  TIMES:  ∀n.n*0 = 0
          ∀n m.n*suc(m) = (n*m)+n: ::

AXIOM INDUCT: P(0) ∧ ∀n.(P(n) ⊃ P(suc(n))) ⊃ ∀n. P(n):::

REPRESENT {NATNUM} AS NATNUMREP:
ATTACH suc  ↔ (LAMBDA (X) (ADD1 X)):
ATTACH pred ↔ (LAMBDA (X) (COND ((GREATERP X 0) (SUB1 X)) (T 0))):
ATTACH+ ↔ (LAMBDA (X Y) (PLUS X Y)):
ATTACH* ↔ (LAMBDA (X Y) (TIMES X Y)):
ATTACH< ↔ (LAMBDA (X Y) (LESSP X Y)):
```

B. An axiomatization of s-expressions

These commands describe to FOL a simple theory of s-expressions. In addition it contains the definitions on the functions @, for appending two lists, and rev, for reversing a list.

```
DECLARE INDVAR x y z ∈ Sexp;
DECLARE INDVAR u v w ∈ List;
DECLARE INDCONST nil ∈ Null;

DECLARE OPCONST car cdr 1;
DECLARE OPCONST cons(Sexp,List) = List;
DECLARE OPCONST rev 1;
DECLARE OPCONST @ 2 [inf];

DECLARE SIMPSET Basic;
DECLARE SIMPSET Funs;

MOREGENERAL Sexp ≥ {List, Atom, Null};;
MOREGENERAL List ≥ {Null};

REPRESENT {Sexp} AS SEXPREP;

AXIOM CAR:  ∀x y. car(cons(x,y)) = x;;
AXIOM CDR:  ∀x y. cdr(cons(x,y)) = y;;
AXIOM CONS: ∀x y.¬ Null(cons(x,y));;

Basic← {CAR,COR,CONS};

AXIOM REV: ∀u.(rev(u) = IF Null (u) THEN (u) ELSE rev(cdr(u)) @. cons(car(u),nil));::
AXIOM APPEND: ∀u v.(u@v = IF Null(u) THEN v ELSE cons(car(u),cdr(u)@v);::

Funs← {REV.APPEND};
```

C. An axiomatization of well formed formulas

This is an example of how WFFs are axiomatized in META. It simply collects together the formulas of Section 8

$$\forall Is \ expr.(\text{WFF}(expr,Is) \equiv \text{PROPWFF}(expr,Is) \vee \text{QUANTWFF}(expr,Is) \vee$$

$$\forall Is \ expr.(\text{PROPWFF}(expr,Is) \equiv \text{APPLPWFF}(expr,Is) \vee \text{AWFF}(expr,Is) \vee$$

$$\forall Is \ expr.(\text{APPLPWFF}(expr,Is) \equiv \text{PROPCONN}(\text{mainsym}(expr)) \wedge$$
$$\forall n.(0 < n \wedge n \leqslant \text{arity}(\text{mainsym}(expr),Is) \supset \text{WFF}(\text{arg}(n,expr),Is))$$

$$\forall Is \ expr.(\text{QUANTWFF}(expr,Is) \equiv$$
$$\text{QUANT}(\text{mainsym}(expr)) \wedge \text{INDVAR}(\text{bvar}(expr),Is \wedge \text{WFF}(\text{matrix}(expr),Is)$$

$$\forall Is \ expr.(\text{AWFF}(expr,Is) \equiv \text{SENTSYM}(expr,Is) \vee \text{APPLAWFF}(expr,Is)$$

$$\forall Is \ expr.(\text{APPLAWFF}(expr,Is) \equiv \text{PREDSYM}(\text{mainsym}(expr),Is) \wedge$$
$$\forall n.(0 < n \wedge n \leqslant \text{arity}(\text{mainsym}(expr),Is) \supset \text{TERM}(\text{arg}(n,e),Is))$$

$$\forall Is \ expr.(\text{TERM}(expr,Is) \equiv \text{INDSYM}(expr,Is) \vee \text{APPLTERM}(expr,Is)$$
$$\forall Is \ expr.(\text{APPLTERM}(expr,Is) \equiv \text{OPSYM}(\text{mainsym}(expr),Is) \wedge$$
$$\forall n.(0 < n \wedge n \leqslant \text{arity}(\text{mainsym}(expr),Is) \supset \text{TERM}(\text{arg}(n.expr),Is))$$

D. Examples of semantic evaluations

We give two sets of examples of semantic evaluation.

In the theory of s-expressions

*****DECLARE OPCONST length(Sexp) = Sexp;

*****ATTACH length ↔ LENGTH;
length attached to LENGTH

*****SIMPLIFY length('(A B));

1 length ('(A B)) = '2

*****SIMPLIFY length ('(A B)) = 2;

2 length ('(A B)) = 2 ≡ '2 = 2

*****SIMPLIFY '2 = 2;

Can't simplify

*****SIMPLIFY '2 = '4;

3 ⌐ ('2 = '4)

In the theory of natural numbers

%6*****SIMPLIFY 2÷3 < pred(7);

1 2÷3 < pred(7)

*****SIMPLIFY 4*suc(2)+pred(3) < pred(pred(8));

2 ⌐ 4*suc(2)+pred(3) < pred(pred(8))

*****SIMPLIFY n*0 < 3;

no simplifications

E. An example of syntactic simplification

After

*****simplify Null(nil);

1 Null(nil)

the command

REWRITE rev cons(x,nil) BY Basic ∪ Funs ∪ {1} ∪ LOGICTREE;

produces the result

2 rev(cons(x,nil)) = cons(x,nil)

by a single syntactic simplification. The exact details of what the simplifier did are recorded below. The numbers on the left refer to notes below the example.

```
Trying to simplify
 |      rev(cons(x,nil))
 |
 succeeded using REV yielding
 |      IF Null(cons(x,nil))
 |        THEN cons(x,nil)
 |        ELSE (rev(cdr(cons(x,nil)))*cons(car(cons(x,nil)),nil))
```

```
Trying to simplify
 |      IF Null(cons(x,nil))
 |        THEN cons(x,nil)
 |        ELSE (rev(cdr(cons(x,nil)))*cons(car(cons(x,nil)),nil))
→→→Trying to simplify the condition
 |      Null(cons(x,nil))
 |
 succeeded using CONS yielding
 |      FALSE
failed
popping up
Trying to simplify
 |      IF FALSE
 |        THEN cons(x,nil)
 |        ELSE (rev(cdr(cons(x,nil)))*cons(car(cons(x,nil)),nil))
 succeeded using LOGICTREE yielding
 |      (rev(cdr(cons(x,nil)))*cons(car(cons(x,nil)),nil))
Trying to simplify
 |      (rev(cdr(cons(x,nil)))*cons(car(cons(x,nil)),nil))
1  |while trying to match *, SORT scruples do not permit me to bind u
   | to rev(cdr(cons(x,nil)))
→→→Trying to simplify argument 1
 |      rev(cdr(cons(x,nil)))
 |
   |while trying to match rev, SORT scruples do not permit me to bind u
   | to cdr(cons(x,nil))
   →→→Trying argument 1
 |      cdr(cons(x,nil))
 |
 |      nil
popping up
Trying to simplify
 |      rev(nil)
 |
 succeeded using REV yielding
 |      IF Null(nil) THEN nil ELSE (rev(cdr(nil))*cons(car(nil),nil))
2  |while trying to match *, SORT scruples do not permit me to bind u
   | to IF Null(nil) THEN nil ELSE rev(cdr(nil)*cons(car(nil),nil)
popping up
Trying to simplify
 |      (IF Null(nil) THEN nil ELSE (rev(cdr(nil))*cons(car(nil),nil))*
 |        cons(car(nil),nil)
3  |while trying to match *, SORT scruples do not permit me to bind u
   | to IF Null(nil) THEN nil ELSE rev(cdr(nil)*cons(car(nil),nil)
   →→→Trying to simplify argument 1
```

```
            IF Null(nil) THEN nil ELSE rev(cdr(nil)*cons(car(nil),nil)
        |_____
        failed
        →→→Trying to simplify condition
        |   Null(nil)
        |_____
            succeeded using line 1 yielding
            | TRUE
            |_____
        popping up
        Trying to simplify
            IF TRUE THEN nil ELSE rev(cdr(nil)*cons(car(nil),nil)
        |_____
            succeeded using LOGICTREE yielding
            nil
        |_____
    popping up
    Trying to simplify
        nil*cons(car(cons(x,nil)),nil)
    |_____
4   | while trying to match *, SORT scruples do not permit me to bind v
    |   to cons(car(cons(x,nil)),nil)
    →→→Trying to simplify argument 1
    |   nil
    |_____
5   failed but we are at a leaf: argument 1 completely simplified
    popping up
    →→→Trying to simplify argument 2
    |   cons(car(cons(x,nil)),nil)
    |_____
    failed
    →→→Trying to simplify argument 1
    |   car(cons(x,nil))
    |_____
        succeeded using CAR yielding
        |   x
        |_____
    popping up
    Trying to simplify
        cons(x,nil)
    |_____
    failed
    →→→Trying to simplify argument 1
    |   x
    |_____
    failed but we are at a leaf: argument 1 completely simplified
    popping up
    →→→Trying to simplify argument 2
    |   nil
    |_____
    failed but we are at a leaf: argument 2 completely simplified
```

```
    popping up
    argument 2 completely simplified
    popping up
    Trying to simplify
        nil*cons(x,nil)
    |_____

    succeeded using APPEND yielding
        IF Null(nil) THEN cons(x,nil) ELSE cons(car(nil),(cdr(nil)*cons(x,nil)))
    |_____
    Trying to simplify
        IF Null(nil) THEN cons(x,nil) ELSE cons(car(nil)*cons(x,nil)))
    |_____
    failed
    →→→Trying to simplify condition
    |   Null(nil)
    |_____
        succeeded using line 1 yielding
        |   TRUE
        |_____
    popping up
    Trying to simplify
        IF TRUE THEN cons(x,nil) ELSE cons(car(nil),(cdr(nil)*cons(x,nil)))
    |_____
        succeeded using LOGICTREE yielding
        |   cons(x,nil)
        |_____
    Trying to simplify
        cons(x,nil)
    |_____
6   this node already maximally simplified
    return cons(x,nil)
    11 substitutions were made
    26 calls were made to SIMPLIFY
```

Note 1. This is the FOL sort checking mechanism at work. FOL knows that x is an Sexp (by declaration) and that nil is a List because nil is of sort Null and Lists are more general than Nulls. This means that it knows by declaration that cons(x,nil) is a List. Unfortunately, it knows nothing about the cdr of a List. Thus since the definition of rev requires that u be instantiated to a Lists, this attempted replacement fails, and we try to simplify its arguments.

Note 2. Notice that the argument to rev actually simplifies to something that FOL can recognize as a List. This means that sort scruples do not prohibit the instantiation of the definition of rev.

Note 3. Unfortunately we have the same problem as in Note 1.

Note 4. This time the first argument to * is ok, but the second is not. Again we try to simplify the arguments.

Note 5. This time when we try to simplify nil nothing happens. In this case as a subterm it is completely simplified and gets marked in such a way that the simplifier never tries to do this again.

Note 6. It is very clever and remembers that it saw this before and since it is at the top level with a maximally simplified formula it stops.

F. An example of evaluation

This is an abbreviated trace of the evaluation of fact (2).

```
eval
|   fact (2)
interpreting
|   fact
fails
→→→Syntactic simplification succeeds, yielding
|   IF   2 = 0 THEN 1 ELSE 2*fact(pred(2))
|_
eval
|   IF   2 = 0 THEN 1 ELSE 2*fact(pred(2))
→→→eval
|   2 = 0
semantic evaluation succeeds, yielding
|   FALSE
popping up
semantic evaluation succeeds, yielding
|   2*fact(pred(2))
|_
interpreting
|   *
succeeds evaluating args
1   eval
|   2
semantic evaluation succeeds, yielding
|   2
|_
eval
|   fact(pred(2))
interpreting
|   fact
fails
Syntactic simplification succeeds, yielding
|   IF pred(2) = 0 THEN 1 ELSE pred(2)*fact(pred(pred(2)))
|_
→→→eval
```

```
|   pred(2) = 0
semantic evaluation succeeds, yielding
|   FALSE
popping up
semantic simplification succeeds, yielding
|   pred(2)*fact(pred(pred(2)))
|_
eval
|   pred(2)*fact(pred(pred(2)))
interpreting
|   *
succeeds evaluating args
1   eval
|   pred(2)
semantic simplification succeeds, yielding
|   1
2   eval
|   fact(pred(pred(2)))
interpreting
|   fact
fails
Syntactic simplification succeeds, yielding
|   IF pred(pred(2)) = 0
|       THEN 1 ELSE pred(pred(2))*fact(pred(pred(pred(2))))
|_
eval
|   IF pred(pred(2)) = 0
|       THEN 1 ELSE pred(pred(2))*fact(pred(pred(pred(2))))
|_
eval
|   pred(pred(2)) = 0
semantic evaluating succeeds, yielding
|   TRUE
semantic evaluation succeeds, yielding
|   1
|_

Evaluating 1 gives 1
Evaluating IF pred(pred(2)) = 0 THEN 1 ELSE pred(pred(2))*fact(pred(pred
                                                    (pred(2))) gives 1
Evaluating fact(pred(pred(2))) gives 1
Evaluating pred(2)*fact(pred(pred(2))) gives 1
Evaluating IF pred(2) = 0 THEN 1 ELSE pred(2)*fact(pred(pred(2))) gives 1
Evaluating fact(pred(2)) gives 1
Evaluating 2*fact(pred(2)) gives 2
Evaluating IF 2 = 0 THEN 1 ELSE 2*fact(pred(2)) gives 2
Evaluating fact(2) gives 2
1 fact(2) = 2
```

27. Weyhrauch, Richard W. (1978), Lecture notes on the use of logic in artificial intelligence and mathematical theory of computation, Summer school on the foundations of artificial intelligence and computer science (FAICS), Pisa.

The following series of notes refers to my working papers which are sometimes available from me. [Note 6]. Weyhrauch, Richard W., FOL: a reasoning system, Informal Note 6. Unpublished. [Note 15]. Weyhrauch, Richard W., The logic of FOL, Informal Note 15. Unpublished.

Received 22 January 1979

REFERENCES

1. Aristotle (–350) Organan.
2. Boyer, R. S. and Moore, J. S. (1979), *A Computational Logic*. To be published in the ACM Monograph Series (Academic Press).
3. Bulnes, J. (1978), GOAL: A goal oriented command language for interactive proof construction forthcoming Ph.D. thesis, Stanford University, Stanford.
4. Burstall, R. M. and Darlington, J. (1977), A transformation system for developing recursive programs, *JACM* **24** (1), 44–67.
5. Cartwright, R. (1977), Practical formal semantic definition and verification systems, Ph.D. thesis, Stanford University, Stanford.
6. Davis, M. and Schwartz, J. T. (1977), Correct-program technology/extensibility of verifiers– Two papers on program verification, Courant Computer Science Report #12, New York University.
7. Diffie, W. (1973), PCHECK: operation of the proof checker, unpublished.
8. Feferman, S. (1962), Transfinite recursive progressions of axiomatic theories, *J. Symbolic Logic* **27**, 259–316.
9. Filman, R. E. and Weyhrauch, R. W. (1976), A FOL Primer, Stanford Artificial Intelligence Laboratory Memo AIM–228, Stanford University, Stanford.
10. Filman, R. E. (1978), The interaction of observation and inference, forthcoming Ph.D. thesis, Stanford University, Stanford.
11. Green, C. (1969), The application of theorem proving to question-answering systems, Ph.D. thesis, Stanford University, Stanford.
12. Kelley, J. L. (1955), *General topology* (Van Nostrand, Princeton, NJ.) 298 pp.
13. Kleene, S. C. (1952), *Introduction to Metamathematics* (Van Nostrand, Princeton, NJ.) 60 pp.
14. Kleene, S. C. (1967), *Mathematical Logic* (Wiley, New York) 398 pp.
15. Kowalski, R. (1974), Predicate logic as a programming language, *Proc. IFIP Congress* **1974**.
16. Kreisel, G. (1971a), Five notes on the application of proof theory to computer science, Stanford University: IMSSS Technical Report 182, Stanford.
17. Kreisel, G. (1971b), A survey of proof theory, II in: Fenstad, J. E. (Ed.), *Proc. the Second Scandinavian Logic Symposium* (North-Holland, Amsterdam).
18. McCarthy, J. (1963), A basis for a mathematical theory of computation, in: Computer Programming and Formal Systems (North-Holland, Amsterdam).
19. McCarthy, J. and Hayes, P. J. (1969), Some philosophical problems from the viewpoint of Artificial Intelligence, in: Michie, D. (Ed.), *Machine Intelligence 7* (Edinburgh U.P., Edinburgh).
20. McCarthy, J. (1973), appendix to: Diffie, W., PCHECK: Operation of the proof checker. Unpublished.
21. McCarthy, J. (1978), Representation of recursive programs in first order logic, in: *Proc. International Conference on Mathematical Studies of Information Processing, Kyoto, Japan*.
22. Prawitz, D. (1965), *Natural Deduction—a proof-theoretical study* (Almqvist & Wiksell, Stockholm).
23. Robinson, R. M. (1950), An essentially undecidable axiom system, in: *Proc. Int. Cong. Math.* **1**, 729–730.
24. Royden, H. L. (1963), *Real Analysis* (Macmillan, New York).
25. Warren, D. (1977), Implementing PROLOG—compiling predicate logic programs, Vol. 1 and Vol. 2, DAI Research Reports Nos. 39 and 40, Edinburgh.
26. Weyhrauch, Richard W. (1977), FOL: A proof checker for first-order logic, Stanford Artificial Intelligence Laboratory Memo AIM–235.1, Stanford University, Stanford.

17 / David W. Etherington and Raymond Reiter

On Inheritance Hierarchies With Exceptions

In many ways, this paper is more about semantic networks than logic. Like the "Logic of Frames" paper by Hayes [Chapter 14], it attempts to put an existing representation framework on a more solid logical foundation. In this case, what is analyzed is inheritance hierarchies that allow exceptions. The utility of such hierarchies was covered in [Reiter, Chapter 23], and here the authors examine a specific network-based proposal. A crucial motivation for the kind of analysis they provide is the fact that the inheritance mechanism for an earlier version of this representation [Fahlman, Touretzky, and van Roggen 81] was discovered (after the fact) to have serious anomalies. This unexpected behavior raised a more general question, namely, how can one determine if a reasoning algorithm over inheritance structures is *correct?* Etherington and Reiter attempt to answer this question in terms of the Default Logic described by Reiter in [Reiter 80]. For each type of link in the network, they give a corresponding sentence or rule in their logic (which they misidentify as the semantics of the link). They then present an algorithm for inheritance that avoids the anomalies noted above and is, they claim, *provably* correct with respect to the specification provided by Default Logic. More importantly perhaps, they show why a certain style of parallel algorithm will *not* work properly. In particular, the kind of spreading activation behavior originally envisaged by Quillian (see [Chapter 6]) is based on finding shortest paths in networks, and Etherington and Reiter present convincing examples where this technique goes awry. If nothing else, the paper is a sobering lesson to those who would consider building (parallel) machines before critically analyzing the tasks to be performed by those machines.

Appeared in *Proc. AAAI-83*, Washington, D. C., 1983, 104–108.

On Inheritance Hierarchies With Exceptions

David W. Etherington[1]
University of British Columbia

Raymond Reiter[2]
University of British Columbia
Rutgers University

Abstract

Using default logic, we formalize NETL-like inheritance hierarchies with exceptions. This provides a number of benefits:

(1) A precise semantics for such hierarchies.

(2) A provably correct (with respect to the proof theory of default logic) inference algorithm for acyclic networks.

(3) A guarantee that acyclic networks have extensions.

(4) A provably correct quasi-parallel inference algorithm for such networks.

1. Introduction

Semantic network formalisms have been widely adopted as a representational notation by researchers in AI. Schubert [1976] and Hayes [1977] have argued that such structures correspond quite naturally to certain theories of first-order logic. Such a correspondence can be viewed as providing the semantics which "semantic" networks had previously lacked [Woods 1975].

More recent work has considered the effects of allowing exceptions to inheritance within networks [Brachman 1982, Fahlman 1979, Fahlman et al 1981, Touretzky 1982, Winograd 1980]. Such exceptions represent either implicit or explicit cancellation of the normal property inheritance which IS-A hierarchies enjoy.

In this paper, we establish a correspondence between such hierarchies and suitable theories in Default Logic [Reiter 1980]. This correspondence provides a formal semantics for networks with exceptions in the same spirit as the work of Schubert and Hayes for networks without exceptions. Having established this correspondence, we identify the notion of correct inference in such hierarchies with that of derivability in the corresponding default theory, and give a provably correct algorithm for drawing these inferences. As a corollary of the correctness of this algorithm, the default theories which formalize inheritance hierarchies with exceptions can be seen to be coherent, in a sense which we will define.

We conclude, unfortunately, on a pessimistic note. Our results suggest the unfeasibility of completely general massively parallel architectures for dealing with inheritance structures with cancellation (c.f. NETL [Fahlman 1979]). We do

[1] This research was supported in part by I.W. Killam Predoctoral and NSERC Postgraduate Scholarships.

[2] This research was supported in part by the Natural Science and Engineering Research Council of Canada grant A7642, and in part by the National Science Foundation grant MCS-8203954.

observe, however, that limited parallelism may have some applications, but that these appear to be severely restricted in general.

2. Motivation

In the absence of exceptions, an inheritance hierarchy is a taxonomy organized by the usual IS-A relation, as in Figure 1.

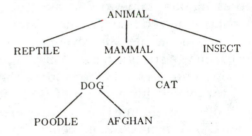

Figure 1 — Fragment of a Taxonomy

The *semantics* of such diagrams can be specified by a collection of first order formulae, such as:

$$(x).POODLE(x) \supset DOG(x)$$
$$(x).DOG(x) \supset MAMMAL(x)$$
$$(x).MAMMAL(x) \supset ANIMAL(x)$$
etc.

If, as is usually the case, the convention is that the immediate subclasses of a node are mutually disjoint, then this too can be specified by first order formulae:

$$(x).MAMMAL(x) \supset \neg REPTILE(x)$$
$$(x).MAMMAL(x) \supset \neg INSECT(x)$$
etc.

The significant features of such hierarchies are these:

(1) Inheritance is a logical property of the representation. Given that $POODLE(Fido)$, $MAMMAL(Fido)$ is provable from the given formulae. Inheritance is simply the repeated application of modus ponens.

(2) Formally, the node labels of such a hierarchy are unary predicates: e.g. $DOG(*)$, $ANIMAL(*)$.

(3) No exceptions to inheritance are possible. Given that Fido is a poodle, Fido must be an animal, regardless of what other properties he enjoys.

The logical properties of such hierarchies change dramatically when exceptions are permitted; non-monotonicity can arise. For example, consider the following facts about elephants:

(1)   Elephants are gray, except for albino elephants.

(2)   All albino elephants are elephants.

It is a feature of our common sense reasoning about prototypes like "elephant" that, when given an individual elephant, say Fred, not known to be an albino, we can infer that he is gray. If we subsequently discover — perhaps by observation — that Fred is an albino elephant, we must retract our conclusion about his grayness. Thus, common sense reasoning about exceptions is non-monotonic, in the sense that new information can invalidate previously derived facts. It is this feature which precludes first order representations, like those used for taxonomies, from formalizing exceptions.

In recent years, there have been several proposed formalisms for such non-monotonic reasoning (See e.g. [AI 1980]). For the purpose of formalizing inheritance hierarchies with exceptions, we shall focus on one such proposal — Default Logic [Reiter 1980]. A default theory consists of a set, W, of ordinary first order formulae, together with a set, D, of rules of inference called *defaults*. In general, defaults have the form:

$$\frac{\alpha(x_1,...,x_n) : \beta(x_1,...,x_n)}{\gamma(x_1,...,x_n)}$$

where α, β, and γ are first order formulae whose free variables are among $x_1,...,x_n$. Informally, such a default can be understood to say: For any individuals $x_1,...,x_n$, if $\alpha(x_1,...,x_n)$ is inferrable and $\beta(x_1,...,x_n)$ can be consistently assumed, then infer $\gamma(x_1,...,x_n)$. For our elephant example, the first statement would be represented by a default:

$$\frac{ELEPHANT(x) : GRAY(x) \,\&\, \neg ALBINO\text{-}ELEPHANT(x)}{GRAY(x)}$$

From the informal reading of this default, one can see that when given only ELEPHANT(Fred), GRAY(Fred) & ¬ALBINO-ELEPHANT(Fred) is consistent with this; hence GRAY(Fred) may be inferred. On the other hand, given ALBINO-ELEPHANT(Fred) one can conclude ELEPHANT(Fred) using the first order fact (x).ALBINO-ELEPHANT(x) ⊃ ELEPHANT(x), but ALBINO-ELEPHANT(Fred) "blocks" the default, thereby preventing the derivation of GRAY(Fred), as required.

The formal details of Default Logic are beyond the scope of this paper. Roughly speaking, however, for a default theory, (D,W), we think of the defaults of D as extending the first order theory given by W. Such an *extension* contains W and is closed under the defaults of D as well as first order theoremhood. It is then natural to think of an extension as defining the "theorems" of a default theory; these are the conclusions sanctioned by the theory. However, these extensions need not be unique [Reiter 1980]. For a default theory with more than one extension, any one of its extensions is interpreted as an acceptable set of beliefs that one may entertain about the world represented by that theory.

In the next section, we show how inheritance hierarchies with exceptions can be formalized as default theories. Default Logic will then be seen to provide a formal semantics for such hierarchies, just as first order logic does for IS-A hierarchies. As was the case for IS-A hierarchies, inheritance will emerge as a logical feature of the representation. Those properties, $P_1, . . . , P_n$, which an individual, b, inherits will be precisely those for which $P_1(b), ..., P_n(b)$ all belong to a common extension of the corresponding default theory. Should the theory

have multiple extensions — an undesirable feature, as we shall see — then b may inherit different sets of properties depending on which extension is chosen.

3. A Semantics for Inheritance Hierarchies With Exceptions

We now show that Default Logic can provide a formal semantics for inheritance structures with exceptions. We adopt a network representation with five link types. Although other approaches to inheritance may omit one or more of these, our formalism subsumes these as special cases. The five link types,[3] with their translations to default logic, are:

(1)   Strict IS-A: A.————▶.B: A's are always B's.
Since this is universally true, we identify it with the first order formula: (x).A(x) ⊃ B(x).

(2)   Strict ISN'T-A: A.⊬⊬⊬⊬▶.B: A's are never B's.
Again, this is a universal statement, identified with:
(x).A(x) ⊃ ¬B(x).

(3)   Default IS-A: A.————>.B: Normally A's are B's, but there may be exceptions.
To provide for exceptions, we identify this with a default:

$$\frac{A(x) : B(x)}{B(x)}$$

(4)   Default ISN'T-A: A.⊬⊬⊬⊬>.B: Normally A's are not B's, but exceptions are allowed.
Identified with:

$$\frac{A(x) : \neg B(x)}{\neg B(x)}$$

(5)   Exception: A.------>
The exception link has no independent semantics; rather, it serves only to make explicit the exceptions, if any, to the above default links. There must always be a default link at the head of an exception link; the exception then alters the semantics of that default link. There are two types of default links with exceptions; their graphical structures and translations are:

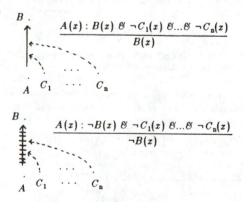

We illustrate with an example from [Fahlman et al 1981].

Molluscs are normally shell-bearers.
Cephalopods must be Molluscs but normally are *not* shell-bearers.
Nautili must be Cephalopods and must be shell-bearers.

---

[3] Note that strict and default links are distinguished by solid and open arrowheads, respectively.

Our network representation of these facts is given in Figure 2.

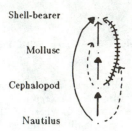

Figure 2 — Network representation of our knowledge about Molluscs.

The corresponding default theory is:

$$\{ \frac{M(x) : Sb(x) \ \& \ \neg C(x)}{Sb(x)}, \ (x).C(x) \supset M(x), \ (x).N(x) \supset C(x),$$

$$\frac{C(x) : \neg Sb(x) \ \& \ \neg N(x)}{\neg Sb(x)}, \ (x).N(x) \supset Sb(x)\}.$$

Given a particular Nautilus, this theory has a unique extension in which it is also a Cephalopod, a Mollusc, and a Shell-bearer. A Cephalopod not known to be a Nautilus will turn out to be a Mollusc with no shell.

It is instructive to compare our network representations with those of NETL [Fahlman et al 1981]. A basic difference is that in NETL there are no strict links; all IS-A and ISN'T-A links are potentially cancellable and hence are defaults. Moreover, NETL allows exception (*UNCANCEL) links only for ISN'T-A (*CANCEL) links. If we restrict the graph of Figure 2 to NETL-like links, we get Figure 3,

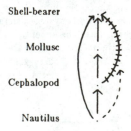

Figure 3 — NETL-like network representation of our knowledge about Molluscs.

which is essentially the graph given by Fahlman. This network corresponds to the theory:

$$\{ \frac{M(x) : Sb(x)}{Sb(x)}, \ \frac{C(x) : M(x)}{M(x)}, \ \frac{N(x) : C(x)}{C(x)},$$

$$\frac{C(x) : \neg Sb(x) \ \& \ \neg N(x)}{\neg Sb(x)}, \ \frac{N(x) : Sb(x)}{Sb(x)} \}.$$

As before, a given Nautilus will also be a Cephalopod, a Mollusc, and a Shell-bearer. A Cephalopod not known to be a Nautilus, however, gives rise to *two* extensions, corresponding to an ambivalence about whether or not it has a shell. While counter-intuitive, this merely indicates that an exception to shell-bearing, namely being a Cephalopod, has not been explicitly represented in the network. Default Logic resolves the ambiguity by making the exception explicit, as in Figure 2.

NETL, on the other hand, cannot make this exception explicit in the graphical representation, since it does not permit exception links to point to IS-A links.

How then does NETL conclude that a Cephalopod is not a Shell-bearer, without also concluding that it is a Shell-bearer? NETL resolves such ambiguities by means of an inference procedure which prefers shortest paths. Interpreted in terms of default logic, this "shortest path heuristic" is intended to favour one extension of the default theory. Thus, in the example above, the path from Cephalopod to ¬Shell-bearer is shorter than that to Shell-bearer so that, for NETL, the former wins. Unfortunately, this heuristic is not sufficient to replace the excluded exception type in all cases. Reiter and Criscuolo [1983] and Etherington [1982] show that it can lead to conclusions which are unintuitive or even invalid — i.e. not in any extension. Fahlman et al [1981] and Touretzky [1981, 1982] have also observed that such shortest path algorithms can lead to anomalous conclusions and they describe attempts to restrict the form of networks to exclude structures which admit such problems. From the perspective of default logic, these restrictions are intended to yield default theories with unique extensions.

An inference algorithm for network structures is correct only if it can be shown to derive conclusions all of which lie within a single extension of the underlying default theory. This criterion rules out shortest path inference for unrestricted networks. In the next section, we present a correct inference algorithm.

4. Correct Inference

The correspondence between networks and default theories requires defaults all of which have the form:

$$\frac{\alpha(x_1, \cdots, x_n) : \beta(x_1, \cdots, x_n) \ \& \ \gamma(x_1, \cdots, x_n)}{\beta(x_1, \cdots, x_n)}. \ [4]$$

Such defaults are called *semi-normal* , and can be contrasted with *normal* defaults, in which $\gamma(x_1, \ldots, x_n)$ is a tautology. Our criterion for the correctness of a network inference algorithm requires that it derive conclusions all of which lie within a single extension of the underlying default theory. Until recently, the only known methods for determining extensions were restricted to theories involving only normal defaults [Reiter 1980]. Etherington [1982] has developed a more general procedure, which involves a relaxation style constraint propagation technique. This procedure takes as input a default theory, (D,W), where D is a finite set of closed defaults,[5] and W is a finite set of first order formulae. In the presentation of this procedure, below, the following notation is used:

$S \vdash \omega$ means formula ω is first order provable from premises S.
$S \nvdash \omega$ means that ω is not first order provable from S.
$CONSEQUENT(\frac{\alpha : \beta}{\gamma})$ is defined to be γ.

---

[4] $\alpha(x_1, \cdots, x_n)$ and $(\beta(x_1, \cdots, x_n) \ \& \ \gamma(x_1, \cdots, x_n))$ are called the *prerequisite* and *justification* of the default, respectively.

[5] A default, $\frac{\alpha : \beta}{\gamma}$, is *closed* iff α, β, and γ contain no free variables.

$H_0 \leftarrow W; \quad j \leftarrow 0;$
repeat
$\quad j \leftarrow j + 1; \quad h_0 \leftarrow W; \quad GD_0 \leftarrow \{ \}; \quad i \leftarrow 0;$
$\quad$ **repeat**
$\quad\quad D_i \leftarrow \{ \frac{\alpha : \beta}{\gamma} \, \epsilon \, D \mid (h_i \vdash \alpha), (h_i \not\vdash \neg\beta), (H_{j-1} \not\vdash \neg\beta) \};$
$\quad\quad$ **if** $\neg null(D_i - GD_i)$ **then**
$\quad\quad\quad$ choose δ **from** $(D_i - GD_i);$
$\quad\quad\quad GD_{i+1} \leftarrow GD_i \bigcup \{\delta\};$
$\quad\quad\quad h_{i+1} \leftarrow h_i \bigcup \{CONSEQUENT(\delta)\};$ **endif**;
$\quad\quad i \leftarrow i + 1;$
$\quad$ **until** $null(D_{i-1} - GD_{i-1});$
$\quad H_j = h_{i-1}$
until $H_j = H_{j-1}$

Extensions are constructed by a series of successive approximations. Each approximation, H_j, is built up from any first-order components by applying defaults, one at a time. At each step, the default to be applied is chosen from those, not yet applied, whose prerequisites are "known" and whose justifications are consistent with both the previous approximation and the current approximation. When no more defaults are applicable, the procedure proceeds to the next approximation. If two successive approximations are the same, the procedure is said to *converge*.

The choice of which default to apply at each step of the inner loop may introduce a degree of non-determinism. Generality requires this non-determinism, however, since extensions are not necessarily unique. Deterministic procedures can be constructed for theories which have unique extensions, or if full generality is not required.

Notice that there are appeals to *non-provability* in this procedure. In general, such tests are not computable, since arbitrary first order formulae are involved. Fortunately, such difficulties disappear for default theories corresponding to inheritance hierarchies. For these theories, all predicates are unary. Moreover, for such theories, we are concerned with the following problem: Given an individual, b, which is an instance of a predicate, P, determine all other predicates which b inherits — i.e. given $P(b)$ determine all predicates, $P_1, \ldots, P_n$, such that $P(b), P_1(b), \ldots, P_n(b)$, belong to a common extension. For this problem it is clear that predicate arguments can be ignored; the appropriate default theory becomes purely propositional. For propositional logic, non-provability is computable.

Example

Consider the network of Figure 4. Given an instance of A, the corresponding default theory has a unique extension in which A's instance is also an instance of B, C, and D. When

the procedure is applied to this theory, it generates the approximations shown. (The formulae in each approximation are listed in the order in which they are derived.) $\neg D$ occurs in H_1 since it can be inferred *before* C.

The following result is proved in [Etherington 1983]:

> *For default theories corresponding to acyclic inheritance networks with exceptions, the procedure always converges on an extension.*

As a simple corollary we have:

> *The default theory corresponding to an acyclic inheritance network with exceptions has at least one extension.*

The latter result is comforting. It says that such networks are always coherent, in the sense that they define at least one acceptable set of beliefs about the world represented by the network.

5. Parallel Inference Algorithms

The computational complexity of inheritance problems, combined with some encouraging examples, has sparked interest in the possibility of performing inferences in parallel. Fahlman [1979] has proposed a massively parallel machine architecture, NETL. NETL assigns one processor to each predicate in the knowledge base. "Inferencing" is performed by nodes passing "markers" to adjacent nodes in response to both their own states and those of their immediate neighbours. Fahlman suggests that such architectures could achieve logarithmic speed improvements over traditional serial machines.

The formalization of such networks as default theories suggests, however, that there might be severe limitations to this approach. For example, correct inference requires that all conclusions share a common extension. For networks with more than one extension, inter-extension interference effects must be prevented. This seems impossible for a one pass parallel algorithm under purely local control, especially in view of the inadequacies of the shortest path heuristic.

Even in knowledge bases with unique extensions, structures requiring an arbitrarily large radius of communication can be created. For example, both the default theories corresponding to the networks in Figure 5 have unique extensions. A network inference algorithm must reach F before propagating through B in the first network and conversely in the second. The salient distinctions between the two networks are not local; hence they cannot be utilized to guide a purely local inference mechanism to the correct choices. Similar networks can be constructed which defeat marker passing algorithms with any fixed radius.

$H_0 = \{ A \}$

$H_1 = \{ A, B, \neg D, C \}$

$H_2 = \{ A, B, C \}$

$H_3 = H_4 = \{ A, B, D, C \}$

Figure 4 — Example of Procedure Behaviour

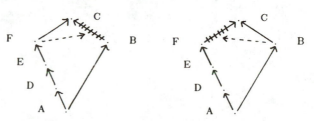

Figure 5a   *Figure 5b*

Touretzky [1981] has observed such behaviour and has developed restrictions on network structures which admit parrallel inferencing algorithms. In part, such restrictions appear to have the effect of limiting the corresponding default theory to one extension. Unfortunately, it is unclear how these restrictions affect the expressive power of the resulting networks. Moreover, Touretzky has observed that it is not possible to determine in parallel whether a network satisfies these restrictions.

A form of limited parallelism can be achieved by partitioning a network into a hierarchy of subnetworks, using an algorithm given in [Etherington 1983]. A parallel algorithm can then be applied to the individual subnets, in turn. The number of subnets which must be processed is bounded by the number of exception links in the network. Unfortunately, it can be shown that this technique may exclude some extensions of the theory. We have not yet characterized the biases which this induces in a reasoner.

6. Conclusions

By formalizing inheritance hierarchies with exceptions using default logic we have provided them with a precise semantics. This in turn allowed us to identify the notion of correct inference in such a hierarchy with that of derivability within a single extension of the corresponding default theory. We then provided an inference algorithm for acyclic inheritance hierarchies with exceptions which is provably correct with respect to this concept of derivability.

Our formalization suggests that *for unrestricted hierarchies*, it may not be possible to realize massively parallel marker passing hardware of the kind envisaged by NETL. Fortunately, this pessimistic observation does not preclude parallel architectures for suitably restricted hierarchies. This raises several open problems:

1a) Determine a natural class of inheritance hierarchies with exceptions which admits a parallel inference algorithm yet does not preclude the representation of our common-sense knowledge about taxonomies.

1b) Define such a parallel algorithm and prove its correctness with respect to the derivability relation of default logic.

2) In connection with (1a), notice that it is natural to restrict attention to those hierarchies whose corresponding default theories have unique extensions. Characterize such hierarchies.

7. Acknowledgments

We would like to thank Robert Mercer and David Touretzky for their valuable comments on earlier drafts of this paper.

8. References

AI (1980), Special issue on non-monotonic logic, *Artificial Intelligence 13 (1,2)*, April.

Brachman, R. (1982), "What 'IS-A' Is and Isn't", *Proc. Canadian Soc. for Computational Studies of Intelligence-82*, Saskatoon, Sask., May 17-19, pp 212-220.

Etherington, D.W. (1982), *Finite Default Theories*, M.Sc. Thesis, Dept. Computer Science, University of British Columbia.

Etherington, D.W. (1983), *Formalizing Non-monotonic Reasoning Systems*, TR-83-1, Dept. Computer Science, University of B.C. (To appear).

Fahlman, S.E. (1979), *NETL: A System For Representing and Using Real-World Knowledge*, MIT Press, Cambridge, Mass.

Fahlman, S.E., Touretzky, D.S., and van Roggen, W. (1981), "Cancellation in a Parallel Semantic Network", *Proc. IJCAI-81*, Vancouver, B.C., Aug. 24-28, pp 257-263.

Hayes, P.J. (1977), "In Defense of Logic", *Proc. IJCAI-77*, Cambridge, Mass., pp 559-565.

Reiter, R. (1980), "A Logic for Default Reasoning", *Artificial Intelligence 13*, (April) pp 81-132.

Reiter, R., and Criscuolo, G. (1983), "Some Representational Issues in Default Reasoning", *Int. J. Computers and Mathematics*, (Special Issue on Computational Linguistics), to appear.

Schubert, L.K. (1976), "Extending the Expressive Power of Semantic Networks", *Artificial Intelligence 7(2)*, pp 163-198.

Touretzky, D.S. (1981), Personal Communication.

Touretzky, D.S. (1982), "Exceptions in an Inheritance Hierarchy", Unpublished Manuscript.

Winograd, T. (1980), "Extended Inference Modes in Reasoning", *Artificial Intelligence 13*, (April), pp 5-26.

Woods, W.A. (1975), "What's In A Link?", *Representation and Understanding*, Academic Press, pp 35-82.

18 / Robert C. Moore
The Role of Logic in Knowledge Representation and Commonsense Reasoning

An often furious debate over the proper role of formal logic in Knowledge Representation has raged almost unabated since the very beginnings of the field. The issues involved in the debate are too intricate to go into here, but as noted in the Introduction, at least part of the problem has to do with the strange history of Knowledge Representation formalisms, the different ways they were used and understood. This paper by Moore is a very clear expression of one point of view in the debate. It was written partly in response to an AAAI presidential address given by Allan Newell in 1980 [Newell 82]. Newell claimed that logic is best viewed as a tool in the *analysis* of knowledge, that it allows us to assess the meaning of expressions in a Knowledge Representation language and to judge the soundness of the inferences made by a system. Moore argues that to actually capture real commonsense reasoning in a system, logic has to play a much more active role. In particular, he shows that to deal with *incomplete knowledge* of a problem domain, a system has to have the abilities possessed only by those systems based on formal logic. He also argues that the apparent failure of problem-solvers based on general purpose theorem-proving (which led, eventually, to the procedural school of representation, as discussed in [Winograd, Chapter 20]) was misunderstood as a failure of *logic*, when, in fact, it merely showed that better *control* of deduction and more attention to the computational properties of axioms were needed. The debate, of course, will not stop here, as there are many other factors to take into account (see the appendix to [Minsky, Chapter 12], for example). One hope for settling the debate once and for all, however, is the increasing popularity of hybrid representation schemes that combine logical and "non-logical" languages (see the discussion of KRYPTON in [Brachman *et al.*, Chapter 24], for example).

Appeared in *Proc. AAAI-82*, Pittsburgh, PA, 1982, 428–433.

THE ROLE OF LOGIC IN KNOWLEDGE REPRESENTATION AND COMMONSENSE REASONING*

Robert C. Moore
Artificial Intelligence Center
SRI International, Menlo Park, California 94025

ABSTRACT

This paper examines the role that formal logic ought to play in representing and reasoning with commonsense knowledge. We take issue with the commonly held view (as expressed by Newell [1980]) that the use of representations based on formal logic is inappropriate in most applications of artificial intelligence. We argue to the contrary that there is an important set of issues, involving incomplete knowledge of a problem situation, that so far have been addressed only by systems based on formal logic and deductive inference, and that, in some sense, probably can be dealt with only by systems based on logic and deduction. We further argue that the experiments of the late 1960s on problem-solving by theorem-proving did not show that the use of logic and deduction in AI systems was necessarily inefficient, but rather that what was needed was better control of the deduction process, combined with more attention to the computational properties of axioms.

I INTRODUCTION

In his AAAI presidential address, Allen Newell [1980] presented his view of the role that logic ought to play in representing and reasoning with commonsense knowledge. Probably the most concise summary of that view is his proposition that "the role of logic [is] as a tool for the analysis of knowledge, not for reasoning by intelligent agents" [p. 16]. What I understand Newell to be saying is that, while logic provides an appropriate framework for analyzing the meaning of expressions in representation formalisms and judging the validity of inferences, logical languages are themselves not particularly good formalisms for representing knowledge, nor is the application of rules of inference to logical formulas a particularly good method for commonsense reasoning.

As to the first part of this position, I could not agree more. Whatever else a formalism may be, at least some of its expressions must have referential semantics if the formalism is really to be a representation of knowledge. That is, there must be some sort of correspondence between an expression and the world, such that it makes sense to ask whether the world is the way the expression claims it to be. To have knowledge at all is to have knowledge** that the world is one way and not otherwise. If one's "knowledge" does not rule out any possibilities for how the world might be, then one really does not know anything at all. Moreover, whatever AI researchers may say, examination of their actual practice reveals that they do rely (at least informally) on being able to provide referential semantics for their formalisms. Whether we are dealing with conceptual dependencies, frames, semantic networks, or what have you, as soon as we say that a particular piece of structure represents the assertion (or belief, or knowledge) that John hit Mary, we have hold of something that is true if John did hit Mary and false if he didn't.

Now, mathematical logic (especially model theory) is simply the branch of mathematics that deals with this sort of relationship between expressions and the world. If one is going to provide an analysis of the referential semantics of a representation formalism, then, a fortiori, one is going to be engaged in logic. As Newell puts it [p. 17], "Just as talking of programmerless programming violates truth in packaging, so does talking of a non-logical analysis of knowledge." It may be objected that Newell and I are both overgeneralizing in defining logic so broadly as to include all possible methods for addressing this issue, but the fact remains that the only existing tools for this kind of semantic analysis have come from logic. I know this view is very controversial in AI, but I will

----
* Preparation of this paper was supported by the Defense Advanced Research Projects Agency under Contract N00039-80-C-0575 with the Naval Electronic Systems Command. The views and conclusions contained in this paper are those of the authors and should not be interpreted as necessarily representing the official policies, either expressed or implied, of the Defense Advanced Research Projects Agency of the United States Government.

** or at least a belief; most people in AI don't seem overly concerned about truth in the actual world.

not argue the point any further for two reasons. First, it has already been argued quite eloquently by Pat Hayes [1977], and second, I want to go on to those areas where I disagree with Newell.

The main point on which I take issue with Newell is his conclusion that logical languages and deductive inference are not very useful tools for implementing (as opposed to analyzing) systems capable of commonsense reasoning. Newell does not present any real argument in support of this position, but instead says [p. 17] "The lessons of the sixties taught us something about the limitations of using logics for this role." In my view, Newell has seriously misread the lessons of the sixties with regard to this issue.

It appears to me that a number of important features of commonsense reasoning can be implemented only within a logical framework. Consider the following problem, adapted from Moore [1975, p. 28]. Three blocks, A, B, and C, are arranged as shown:

A is green, C is blue, and the color of B is unstated. In this arrangement of blocks, is there a green block next to a block that is not green? It should be clear with no more than a moment's reflection that the answer is "yes." If B is green, it is a green block next to the nongreen block C; if B is not green then A is a green block next to the nongreen block B.

How is a person able to solve this problem? What sort of reasoning mechanisms are required? At least three distinctly "logical" factors seem to be involved: (1) the ability to see that an existentially quantified proposition is true, without knowing exactly which object makes it true, (2) the ability to recognize that, for a particular proposition, either it or its negation must be true, and (3) the ability to reason by cases. So far as I know, none of these abilities are possessed by any AI system not explicitly based on formal logic. Moreover, I would claim that, in a strong sense, these issues can be addressed only by systems that are based on formal logic.

To justify this claim we will need to examine what it means to say that a system uses a logical representation or that it reasons by deductive inference. Then we will try to re-evaluate what was actually shown by the disappointing results of the early experiments on problem-solving by theorem-proving, which we must do if the arguments presented here are correct and if there is to be any hope of creating systems with commonsense reasoning abilities comparable to those possessed by human beings.

II   WHAT IS A LOGICAL REPRESENTATION?

The question of what it means to use a logic for representing knowledge in a computer system is less straightforward than it might seem. In mathematics and philosophy, a logic is a language--i.e., a set of formulas--with either a formal inference system or a formal semantics (or both).* To use a logic in a computer system, we have to encode those formulas somehow as computer data structures. If the formulas are in "Cambridge Polish" notation, e.g.,

(EVERY X (IMPLIES (MAN X) (MORTAL X))),

we may be tempted to assume that the corresponding LISP S-expression must be the data structure that represents the formula in the computer. This is in fact the case in many systems, but using more sophisticated data structures certainly does not mean that we are not implementing a logical representation. For example, Sickel [1976] describes a theorem-proving system in which a collection of formulas is represented by a graph, where each node represents a formula, and each link represents a possible unification (i.e., pattern match) of two formulas, with the resulting substitution being stored on the link. Furthermore, Sickel notes that the topology of the graph, plus the substitutions associated with the links, carries all the information needed by the theorem-prover--so the actual structure of the formulas is not explicitly represented at all!

This example suggests that deficiencies attributed to logical representations may be artifacts of naive implementations and do not necessarily carry over when more sophisticated techniques are used. For instance, one of the most frequently claimed advantages of semantic nets over logic as a representation formalism is that the links in the semantic net make it easier to retrieve information relevant to a particular problem. Sickel's system (along with that of Kowalski [1975]) would seem to be at least as good as most semantic net formalisms in this respect. In fact, it may even be better, since following a link in a semantic net usually does not guarantee that the subsequently attempted pattern match will succeed, while in Sickel's or Kowalski's system, it does.

Given that the relationship between a logical formula and its computer implementation can be as abstract as it is in Sickel's system, it seems doubtful to me that we could give any clear criteria for deciding whether a particular system really implements a logical representation. I think that the best way out of this dilemma is to give up trying to draw a line between logical and

----
* For example, for several decades there were formal inference systems for modal logic [Hughes and Cresswell, 1968], but no semantics; Montague's [1974] intensional logic has a formal semantics, but no inference system.

nonlogical representations, and instead ask what logical features particular representation formalisms posses. If we adopt this point of view, the next question to ask is what logical features are needed in a general-purpose representation formalism. My answer is that, at a minimum, we need all the features of first-order classical logic with equality.

Perhaps the most basic feature of first-order logic is that it describes the world in terms of objects and their properties and relations. I doubt that anyone in AI could really complain about this, as virtually all AI representation formalisms make use of these concepts. It might be argued that one needs more than just objects, properties, and relations as primitive notions, but it should be kept in mind that first-order logic places no limits on what can be regarded as an object. Times, events, kinds, organizations, worlds, and sentences--not just concrete physical objects--can all be treated as logical individuals. Furthermore, even if we decide we need "nonstandard" features such as higher-order or intensional operators, we can still incorporate them within a logical framework.

For me, however, it is not the basic "metaphysical" notions of object, property, and relation that are the essential features of logic as a representation formalism, but rather the kinds of assertions that logic lets us make about them. Most of the features of logic can be seen as addressing the problem of how to describe an incompletely known situation. Specifically: existential quantification allows us to say that something has a certain property without having to know which thing has that property. Universal quantification allows us to say that everything in a certain class has a certain property without having to know what everything in that class is. Disjunction allows us to say that at least one of two statements is true without having to know which statement is true. Negation allows us to distinguish between knowing that a statement is not true and not knowing that it is true. Finally, logic lets us use different referring expressions without knowing whether they refer to the same object, but provides us with the equality predicate to assert explicitly whether or not they do.

One way that logic has been criticized is not to claim that the above features are unnecessary or harmful, but rather to argue that logic lacks some other essential feature--for instance, the ability to express control information. This was the basis of the early MIT-led criticism of theorem-proving research (e.g., [Winograd, 1972, Chapter 6]), which was, I believe, largely justified. This sort of problem, however, can be addressed and, in fact, has been [Hayes, 1973] [McDermott, 1978] [Kowalski, 1979] [Moore, 1975] by extending logic in various ways (see Section III), rather than by throwing it out and starting over. Moreover, the criticism quickly turned into a much more radical attack on any use of logic or deduction at all in AI [Hewitt, 1973] [Hewitt,

1975] [Minsky, 1974, Appendix]. That assault, in my view, was tremendously detrimental to serious research on knowledge representation and commonsense reasoning and represents the position I primarily want to argue against.

The major reason I regard the features of first-order logic as essential to any general-purpose representation formalism is that they are applicable to expressing knowledge about any domain. That is, it doesn´t really matter what part of the world we are talking about; it always may be the case that we have only partial knowledge of a situation and we need some of these logical features to express or reason with that knowledge. This can be seen in the example presented in Section I. Reasoning about the position and color of blocks is certainly no more inherently logical than reasoning about anything else. The logical complexity of the problem comes from the fact that we are asked whether any blocks satisfy a given condition, but not which ones, and that we don´t know the color of the middle block. If we had a complete description of the situation--if we were told the color of the middle block--we could just "read off" the answer to the question from the problem description without doing any reasoning at all.

Similar situations can easily arise in more practical domains as well. For instance, in determining a course of treatment, a physician may not need to decide between two possible diagnoses, either because the treatment is the same in either case or because only one of the two is treatable at all. Now, as far as I know, none of the inference methods currently being used in expert systems for medical diagnosis are capable of doing the sort of general reasoning by cases that ultimately justifies the physician´s actions in such situations. Some systems have ad hoc rules or procedures for these special cases, but the creators of the systems have themselves had to carry out the relevant instances of reasoning by cases, because the systems are unable to. But this means that, in any situation the system designers failed to anticipate, the systems will fail if reasoning by cases is needed. It seems, though, that the practical utility of systems capable of handling only special cases has created a false impression that expert systems have no need for this kind of logic.

To return to the main issue, I simply do not know what it would mean for a system to use a nonlogical representation of a disjunctive assertion or to use a nonlogical inference technique for reasoning by cases. It seems to me that, to the extent any representation formalism has the logical features discussed above, it is a logic, and that to the extent a reasoning procedure takes account of those features, it reasons deductively. It is conceivable that there might be a way of dealing with these issues that is radically different from current logics, but it would still be some sort of logic and, in any event, at the present time none of the systems that are even superficially different from standard logics have any way of dealing with them at all.

Furthermore, the idea that one can get by with only special-purpose deduction systems doesn't seem very plausible to me either. No one in the world is an expert at reasoning about a block whose color is unknown between two blocks whose color is known, yet anyone can see the answer to the problem in Section I. Intelligence entails being able to cope with novelty, and sometimes what is novel about a situation is the logical structure of what we know about it.

III   WHY DID EARLY EXPERIMENTS FAIL?

The bad reputation that logic has suffered from in AI circles for the past decade or so stems from attempts in the late 1960s to use general-purpose theorem-proving algorithms as universal problem-solvers. The idea was to axiomatize a problem situation in first-order logic and express the problem to be solved as a theorem to be proved from the axioms, usually by applying the resolution method developed by Robinson [1965]. The results of these experiments were disappointing. The difficulty was that, in the general case, the search space generated by the resolution method grows exponentially (or worse) with the number of formulas used to describe a problem, so that problems of even moderate complexity could not be solved in reasonable time. Several domain-independent heuristics were proposed to try to deal with this issue, but they proved too weak to produce satisfactory results.

The lesson that was generally drawn from this experience was that any attempt to use logic or deduction in AI systems would be hopelessly inefficient. But, if the arguments made here are correct, there are certain issues in commonsense reasoning that can be addressed only by using logic and deduction, so we would seem to be at an impasse. A more careful analysis, however, suggests that the failure of the early attempts to do commonsense reasoning and problem-solving by theorem-proving had more specific causes that can be attacked without discarding logic itself.

I believe that the earliest of the MIT criticisms was in fact the correct one, that there is nothing particularly wrong with using logic or deduction per se, but that a system must have some way of knowing which inferences it should make out of the many possible alternatives. A very simple, but nonetheless important, instance of this is deciding whether to use implicative assertions in a forward-chaining or backward-chaining manner. The deductive process can be thought of as a bidirectional search, partly working forward from premises to conclusions, partly working backward from goals to subgoals, and converging somewhere in the middle. Thus, if we have an assertion of the form (P -> Q), we can use it to generate either the assertion Q, given the assertion P, or the goal P, given the goal Q.

Some early theorem-proving systems utilized every implication both ways, leading to highly redundant searches. Further research produced more sophisticated methods that avoid some of these redundancies. Eliminating redundancies, however, creates choices as to which way assertions are to be used. In the systems that attempted to use only domain-independent control heuristics, a uniform strategy had to be imposed. Often the strategy was to use all assertions only in a backward-chaining manner, on the grounds that this would at least guarantee that all the inferences drawn would be relevant to the problem at hand.

The difficulty with this approach is that the question of whether it is more efficient to use an assertion for forward or backward chaining can depend on the specific form of that assertion. Consider, for instance, the schema

    (EVERY X (IMPLIES (P (F X)) (P X)))

Instances of this schema include such things as:

    (EVERY X (IMPLIES (JEWISH (MOTHER X))
                      (JEWISH X)))

    (EVERY X (IMPLIES (LESSP (SUCCESSOR X) Y)
                      (LESSP X Y)))

That is, a person is Jewish if his or her mother is Jewish,[*] and a number X is less than a number Y if the successor of X is less than Y.

Suppose we were to try to use an assertion of this form for backward chaining, as most "uniform" proof procedures would. It would apply to any goal of the form (P X) and produce the subgoal (P (F X)). This expression, however, is also of the form (P X), so the process would be repeated, resulting in an infinite descending chain of subgoals:

    GOAL: (P X)
    GOAL: (P (F X))
    GOAL: (P (F (F X)))
    GOAL: (P (F (F (F X)))), etc.

If, on the other hand, we use the rule for forward chaining, the number of applications is limited by the complexity of the assertion that originally triggers the inference:

    ASSERT: (P (F (F X)))
    ASSERT: (P (F X))
    ASSERT: (P X)

It turns out, then, that the efficent use of a particular assertion often depends on exactly what that assertion is, as well as on the context of other assertions in which it is embedded.

----
[*]   I am indebted to Richard Waldinger for suggesting this example.

Other examples illustrating this point are given by Kowalski [1979] and Moore [1975], involving not only the forward/backward-chaining distinction, but other control decisions as well.

Since specific control information needs to be associated with particular assertions, the question arises as to how to provide it. The simplest way is to embed it in the assertions themselves. For instance, the forward/backward-chaining distinction can be encoded by having two versions of implication--e.g., (P -> Q) to indicate forward chaining and (Q <- P) to indicate backward chaining. This approach originated in the distinction made in the programming language PLANNER between antecedent and consequent theorems. A more sophisticated approach is to make decisions such as whether to use an assertion in the forward or backward direction _themselves_ questions for the deduction system to reason about using "metalevel" knowledge. The first detailed proposal along these lines seems to have been made by Hayes [1973], while experimental systems have been built by McDermott [1978] and de Kleer et al. [1979], among others.

Another factor that can greatly influence the efficiency of deductive reasoning is the exact way in which a body of knowledge is formalized. That is, logically equivalent formalizations can have radically different behavior when used with standard deduction techniques. For example, we could define ABOVE as the transitive closure of ON in at least three ways:[*]

```
(EVERY (X Y)
       (IFF (ABOVE X Y)
            (OR (ON X Y)
                (SOME Z (AND (ON X Z)
                             (ABOVE Z Y))))))

(EVERY (X Y)
       (IFF (ABOVE X Y)
            (OR (ON X Y)
                (SOME Z (AND (ON Z Y)
                             (ABOVE X Z))))))

(EVERY (X Y)
       (IFF (ABOVE X Y)
            (OR (ON X Y)
                (SOME Z (AND (ABOVE X Z)
                             (ABOVE Z Y))))))
```

Each of these axioms will produce different behavior in a standard deduction system, no matter how we make such local control decisions as whether to use forward or backward chaining. The first axiom defines ABOVE in terms of ON, in effect, by iterating upward from the lower object, and would therefore be useful for enumerating all

----
[*] These formalizations are not quite equivalent, as they allow for different possible interpretations of ABOVE if infinitely many objects are involved. They are equivalent, however, if only a finite set of objects is being considered.

the objects that are above a given object. The second axiom iterates downward from the upper object, and could be used for enumerating all the objects that a given object is above. The third axiom, though, is essentially a "middle out" definition, and is hard to control for any specific use.

The early systems for problem-solving by theorem-proving were often inefficient because axioms were chosen for their simplicity and brevity, without regard to their computational properties--a problem that also arises in conventional programming. To take a well-known example, the simplest LISP program for computing the nth Fibonacci number is a doubly recursive procedure that takes $O(2^n)$ steps to execute, while a slightly more complicated and less intuitively defined singly recursive procedure can compute the same function in $O(n)$ steps.

Kowalski [1974] was perhaps the first to note that choosing among alternatives such as these involves very much the same sort of decisions as are made in conventional programming. In fact, he observed that there are ways to formalize many functions and relations so that the application fo standard deduction methods will have the effect of executing them as efficient computer programs. These observations have led to the development of the field of "logic programming" [Kowalski, 1979] and the creation of new computer languages such as PROLOG [Warren and Pereira, 1977].

IV   SUMMARY AND CONCLUSIONS

In this paper, I have tried to argue that there is an important class of problems in knowledge representation and commonsense reasoning, involving incomplete knowledge of a problem situation, that so far have been addressed only by systems based on formal logic and deductive inference, and that, in some sense, probably can be dealt with only by systems based on logic and deduction. I have further argued that, contrary to the conventional wisdom in AI, the experiments of the late 1960s did not show that the use of logic and deduction in AI systems was necessarily inefficient, but only that better control of the deduction process was needed, along with more attention to the computational properties of axioms.

I would certainly not claim that all the problems of deductive inference can be solved simply by following the prescriptions of this paper. Further research will undoubtedly uncover as yet undiagnosed difficulties and, one hopes, their solutions. My objective here is to encourage consideration of these problems, which have been ignored for a decade by most of the artificial-intelligence community, so that at future conferences we may hear about their solution rather than just their existence.

ACKNOWLEDGMENTS

I wish to thank Nils Nilsson and Bill Woods for helpful comments on previous versions of this paper.

REFERENCES

de Kleer, J. et al. [1979] "Explicit Control of Reasoning," in Artificial Intelligence: An MIT Perspective, Vol. 1, P. H. Winston and R. H. Brown, eds., pp. 93–116 (The MIT Press, Cambridge, Massachusetts, 1979).

Hayes, P. J. [1973] "Computation and Deduction," Proc. 2nd Symposium on Mathematical Foundations of Computer Science, Czechoslovak Academy of Sciences, pp. 105–116 (September 1973).

Hayes, P. J. [1977] "In Defence of Logic," Proc. Fifth International Joint Conference on Artificial Intelligence, Cambridge, Massachusetts, pp. 559–565 (August, 22–25 1977).

Hewitt, C. et al. [1973] "A Universal Modular ACTOR Formalism for Artificial Intelligence," Advance Papers of the Third International Conference on Artificial Intelligence, Stanford University, Stanford, California, pp. 235–245 (August, 20–23 1973).

Hewitt, C. [1975] "How to Use What You Know," Advance Papers of the Fourth International Joint Conference on Artificial Intelligence, Tbilisi, Georgia, USSR, pp. 189–198 (September, 3–8 1975).

Hughes, G. E. and Cresswell, M. J. [1968] An Introduction to Modal Logic (Methuen and Company Ltd, London, England, 1968).

Kowalski, R. [1974] "Predicate Logic as a Programming Language," in Information Processing 74, pp. 569–574 (North-Holland Publishing Company, Amsterdam, The Netherlands, 1974).

Kowalski, R. [1975] "A Proof Procedure Using Connection Graphs," Journal of the Association for Computing Machinery, Vol. 22, No. 4, pp. 573–595 (October 1975).

Kowalski, R. [1979] Logic for Problem Solving (Elsevier North Holland, Inc., New York, New York, 1979).

McDermott, D. [1978] "Planning and Acting," Cognitive Science, Vol. 2, No. 2, pp. 71–109 (April–June 1978).

Minsky, M. [1974] "A Framework for Representing Knowledge," MIT Artificial Intelligence Laboratory, AIM-306, Massachusetts Institute of Technology, Cambridge, Massachusetts (June 1974).

Montague, R. [1974] "The Proper Treatment of Quantification in Ordinary English," in Formal Philosophy, Selected Papers of Richard Montague, R. H. Thomason, ed., pp. 188–221 (Yale University Press, New Haven, Connecticut, and London, England, 1974).

Moore, R. C. [1975] Reasoning from Incomplete Knowledge in a Procedural Deduction System MIT Artificial Intelligence Laboratory, AI-TR-437, Massachusetts Institute of Technology, Cambridge, Massachusetts (December 1975). Also published by Garland Publishing, Inc. (New York, New York, 1980).

Newell, A. [1980] "The Knowledge Level," Presidential Address, American Association for Artificial Intelligence, AAAI80, Stanford University, Stanford, California (19 August 1980), printed in AI Magazine, Vol. 2, No. 2, pp. 1–20 (Summer 1981).

Robinson, J. A. [1965] "A Machine-Oriented Logic Based on the Resolution Principle," Journal of the Association for Computing Machinery, Vol. 12, No. 1, pp. 23–41 (January 1965).

Sickel, S. [1976] "A Search Technique for Clause Interconnectivity Graphs," IEEE Transactions on Computers, Vol. C-25, No. 8, pp. 823–835 (August 1976).

Warren, D. H. D. and Pereira, L. M. [1977] "PROLOG--The Language and its Implementation Compared with LISP," in Proceedings of the Symposium on Artificial Intelligence and Programming Languages (ACM); SIGPLAN Notices, Vol. 12, No. 8; and SIGART Newsletter, No. 64, pp. 109–115 (August 1977).

Winograd, T. [1972] Understanding Natural Language (Academic Press, New York, New York, 1972).

V / Procedural Representations and Production Systems

19 / Johan de Kleer, Jon Doyle, Guy L. Steele, Jr., and Gerald Jay Sussman
AMORD: Explicit Control of Reasoning

One of the original motivations for the PLANNER language developed by Carl Hewitt [Hewitt 71] (and for much of the procedural school of Knowledge Representation) was to provide a system with greater *control* over its reasoning than that supplied by standard logical theorem-provers. (The need for domain-specific control is discussed in [Hayes, Chapter 1] as well as in [Moore, Chapter 18].) In fact, a major criticism of PLANNER was that it did not go far enough and that, for example, automatic "chronological" backtracking was much too general and insensitive to the domain. One descendant of the language, CONNIVER, tried to remedy the situation by giving the user access to lower level implementation primitives that seemed to underly backtracking and other control regimes. However, as argued in [Hayes, Chapter 1], this was somewhat of a retrograde step. Another approach, exemplified in the AMORD language described in this paper, was to invent new primitives for the careful control of reasoning. Instead of the forward and backward chaining of PLANNER, AMORD does only forward reasoning, but over the state of the problem solver, which is explicitly represented over and above the facts about the domain, giving the system rudimentary reflective capabilities [Smith, Chapter 3]. Thus, based upon its currently asserted goals, and the antecedent rules in effect that state how facts should be used (that is, how goals can be achieved), it can reason and decide what new goals to pursue. By explicitly maintaining justifications among facts (and among goals), it can determine which assumptions have led to contradictions (and which subgoals have led to dead ends). A good part of the paper shows AMORD in operation on a small blocks-world problem-solving example. The emphasis throughout on the control of reasoning and the combinatorics of the problem domain is characteristic of the procedural school of Knowledge Representation (discussed more fully in [Winograd, Chapter 20]).

Appeared in *Proc. Symposium on Artificial Intelligence and Programming Languages,* *SIGPLAN Notices* **12**(8), and *SIGART Newsletter,* No. 64, August, 1977, 116–125.

AMORD
Explicit Control of Reasoning

by

Johan de Kleer, Jon Doyle[*],
Guy L. Steele Jr.[**], and Gerald Jay Sussman[***]

Artificial Intelligence Laboratory
Massachusetts Institute of Technology
545 Technology Square
Cambridge, Massachusetts 02139

Abstract

The construction of expert problem-solving systems requires the development of techniques for using modular representations of knowledge without encountering combinatorial explosions in the solution effort. This report describes an approach to dealing with this problem based on making some knowledge which is usually implicitly part of an expert problem solver explicit, thus allowing this knowledge about control to be manipulated and reasoned about. The basic components of this approach involve using explicit representations of the control structure of the problem solver, and linking this and other knowledge manipulated by the expert by means of explicit data dependencies.

[*] Fannie and John Hertz Foundation Fellow
[**] NSF Fellow
[***] Jolly Good Fellow

The Problem

A goal of Artificial Intelligence is to construct an "advice taker",[Advice Taker] a program which can be told new knowledge and advised about how that knowledge may be useful. One approach toward achieving this goal has been to use additive formalisms for the representation of knowledge. Those formalisms derived from mathematical logic have been the most popular. Unfortunately, the resulting systems are combinatorially explosive. It is difficult to provide incremental guidance for problem solvers because of the unsolved question of how to describe knowledge about how other knowledge may be profitably used in these additive formalisms.[Additive Knowledge]

Substantial progress has been made in constructing expert problem solvers for limited domains by abandoning the goal of incremental addition of knowledge. Experts have usually been constructed as procedures which embody in their control structure the knowledge of the problem domain and of how it is to be used. The "procedural embedding of knowledge"[Procedures] seems natural for capturing the knowledge of experts because of the apparent coherence we observe in the behavior of a human expert who is trying to solve a problem. For each specific problem he seems to be following a definite procedure with discrete steps and conditionals. In fact, an expert will often report that his behavior is controlled by a precompiled procedure. One difficulty with this theory is the flexibility of the expert's knowledge. If one poses a new problem, differing only slightly from one which we have previously observed an expert solve, he will explain his new solution as the result of executing a procedure differing in detail from the previous one. It really seems that the procedure is created on the fly from a more flexible base of knowledge.

We believe that the procedural explanation is an artifact of the explanation generator rather than a clue to the structure of the problem solving mechanism. The apparently coherent behavior of the problem solver may be a consequence of the individual behaviors of a set of relatively independent agents.[Coherence] As an example of coherent behavior on the part of a problem solver constructed from incoherent knowledge sources, we cite the operation of the EL electronics circuit analysis program.[EL] EL is constructed from a set of independent demons, each implementing some facet of electrical laws applied to particular device types. The nature of knowledge in the electrical domain is such that the analysis of a particular circuit is highly constrained, and so the traces of performance and explanations produced by EL are coherent. Like Simon's ant,[Simon's Ant] EL displays complex and directed behaviors which are largely determined by the nature of the terrain, that is, the circuit.

Our Approach

This paper presents a problem solving methodology by which the individual behaviors of a set of independent rules are coordinated so as to exhibit coherent behavior. This methodology establishes a set of conventions for writing rules, and a set of features which the rule interpreter must supply to support these conventions. Our rules operate on a data base of facts. Each fact is constructed with a justification which describes how that fact was deduced from antecedent facts.

The key to obtaining coherence is explicitly representing some of the knowledge which is usually implicit in an expert system:

We explicitly represent the control state of the problem solver. For example, each goal is asserted and justified in terms of other goals and facts. We distinguish various kinds of goals of deduction and action to which different subsets of rules apply. This information is used in reasoning about the problem solver's actions and its reasons for decisions.[Explicit Control]

We explicitly represent facts about how other facts are to be used. In traditional methods of representing knowledge the way a piece of knowledge is used is implicit rather than something that can be reasoned about. In PLANNER, for example, the use of a piece of knowledge is fixed at the time that the knowledge is built into the problem solver, and it is not possible to later qualify the use of this knowledge. One can specify a rule to be used as either a consequent or antecedent theorem, but one can not later say "But don't do that if ... is true." This shows that some facts are assertions about other facts.

We explicitly represent the reasons for belief in facts. Each fact has associated justifications which describe how the reasons for believing that fact depend on beliefs in other facts and rules. A fact is believed if it has well-founded support in terms of other facts and rules.[Well-Founded Support] The currently active data base context is defined by the set of primitive premises and assumptions in force.

The justifications can be used by both the user and the problem solver to gain insight into the operation of the set of rules on a particular problem. One can perturb the premises and examine the changed beliefs that result. This is precisely what is needed for reasoning about hypothetical situations. One can extract information from the justifications in the analysis of error conditions resulting from incorrect assumptions. This information can be used in dependency-directed backtracking[Backtracking] to pinpoint the faulty assumptions and to limit future search.

The explicit data dependencies allow us to control the connection between control decisions and the knowledge they are based on.[Separation] We can separate the reasons for belief in derived facts from the control decisions affecting their derivation when the facts are independent of the control decisions. Anomalous dependencies are produced when this separation is not made. In chronological backtracking[Micro-PLANNER] control decisions are confused with the logical grounds for belief in facts. This results in the loss of useful information when control decisions are changed.

This technique of using explicit control knowledge to guide a problem solver does not resolve all difficulties, since it is often unclear as to what knowledge is usefully made explicit. In the following we present examples of the use of explicit control knowledge in constructing coherent behaviors from incoherent knowledge sources.[Control Vocabulary]

Explicit Control Assertions

Suppose we know a few simple facts, which we can express in a bastard form of predicate calculus:

```
(-> (human :x) (fallible :x))     Every human is fallible!
(human Turing)                    Poor Turing.
```

If provided with a simple syntactic system with two derivation rules (which we may interpret to be the conjunction introduction and modus ponens rules of logic),

```
A             (-> A B)
B             A
----------    ---------
(AND A B)     B
```

then by application of these rules to the given facts we may derive the conclusion

```
(AND (fallible Turing) (human Turing)).
```

Since the rules are sound, we may believe this conclusion.

Several methods can be used to mechanically derive this conclusion. One scheme (the British Museum Algorithm) is to make all possible derivations from the given facts with the given rules of inference. These can be enumerated breadth-first. If the desired conclusion is derivable, it will eventually appear and we can turn off our machine.

The difficulty with this approach is the large number of deductions made which are either irrelevant to the desired

conclusion (they do not appear in its derivation) or useless, producing an incoherent performance. For instance, in addition to the above, conjunction introduction will produce such wonders as:[Suppression]

```
(AND (human Turing) (human Turing))
(AND (-> (human :y) (fallible :y)) (human Turing))
```

The literature of mechanical theorem-proving has concentrated on sophisticated deductive algorithms and powerful but general inference rules which limit the combinatorial explosion. These combinatorial strategies are not sufficient to limit the process enough to prevent computational catastrophe. Verily, as much knowledge is needed to effectively use a fact as there is in the fact.

Consider the problem of controlling what deductions to make in the previous example so that only relevant conjuncts are derived. The derivation rules can be modified to include in the antecedent a statement that the consequent is needed:

```
(SHOW (AND A B))      (SHOW B)
A                     (-> A B)
B                     A
----------------      -------
(AND A B)             B
```

Given these rules, only relevant conclusions are generated. The assertion (SHOW X) says nothing about the truth or falsity of X, but rather indicates that X is a fact which should be derived if possible. Since the "SHOW" rules only deduce new facts when interest in them has been asserted, explicit derivation rules are needed to ensure that if interest in some fact is asserted, interest is also asserted in appropriate antecedents of it. This is how subgoals are generated.[Implications]

```
(SHOW (AND A B))      (SHOW (AND A B))
----------------      A
(SHOW A)              ----------------
                      (SHOW B)

     (SHOW B)
     (-> A B)
     -------
     (SHOW A)
```

With these rules the derivation process is constrained. To derive

```
(AND (fallible Turing) (human Turing)),
```

interest must be first asserted:

```
(SHOW (AND (fallible Turing) (human Turing))).
```

Application of the derivation rules now results in the following sequence of facts:

```
(SHOW (fallible Turing))
(SHOW (human Turing))
(fallible Turing)
(AND (fallible Turing) (human Turing))
```

These are absolutely all the facts that can be derived, and no facts were derived which were not relevant to the goal.

Explicit Data Dependencies

This apparent coherence has been achieved by the manipulation of explicit control assertions. The use of explicit control necessitates the use of explicit dependencies. If the conclusions of a rule of inference uniformly depended on the antecedents of the rule then SHOW rules would cause belief in their consequents to depend on the statement of interest in them This is wrong. If the truth of a statement depends on the truth of the need for it, the statement loses support if interest in it is withdrawn. Even worse, if a conclusion derived is inconsistent, one might accidently blame the deducer for his curiosity instead of the faulty antecedent of the contradiction! The dependence of each new conclusion on other beliefs must be made explicit so that the dependencies of control assertions can be separated from the reasons for derived results. In the conjunction introduction rule, the truth of the conjunction depends only on the truth of the conjuncts but interest in the truth of the conjuncts propagates from interest in the truth of the conjunction.

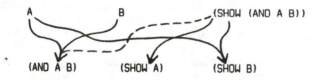

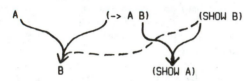

In this diagram, the target statement is derived if the source statements are known. Only the solid arrows construct dependency links.

The AMORD language

Primitives

To provide notation for expressing the explicit control and dependency structure of the problem solving process, we have developed an antecedent reasoning system called AMORD.[AMORD] AMORD is a language for expressing pattern-invoked procedures, which monitor a pattern-indexed data base, coupled with a system for automatic maintenance of dependency information. The basic AMORD constructs are RULEs and ASSERTions.

New facts can be inserted into the data base with

```
(ASSERT <pattern> <justification>),
```

where any variables in the arguments inherit their values from the lexically surrounding text, and <justification> is a specification of the reason for belief in the fact specified by <pattern>. The justification is constructed from {1} an arbitrary (possibly composite) name denoting the justification

type (often the name of a rule), and {2} the factnames of the assertions on which the belief depends. Variables are denoted by atoms with a ":" prefix. Each fact[Variants] has a unique factname.

A rule is a pattern-invoked procedure, whose syntax is:

```
(RULE (<factname> <pattern>) <body>),
```

where <factname> is a variable which will be bound to the factname of any fact which unifies[Unifies] with <pattern>, and <body> is a set of AMORD forms to be evaluated in the environment specified by adding the variable bindings derived from the unification and the binding of <factname> to those derived from the lexical environment of the rule. The primary use of <factname> is in specifying justifications for ASSERTs in the body. Rules are run on all matching facts.

Sometimes it is necessary to assume a truth "for the sake of argument". Such a hypothetical fact is used when we wish to investigate its consequences. Perhaps it is independently justifiable, but it is also possible that it is inconsistent with other beliefs and will be ruled out by a contradiction. We construct such a hypothetical assertion using ASSUME:

```
(ASSUME <pattern> <justification>)
```

Here <justification> provides support for the <u>need</u> for the assumption, not the assumed fact. If the assumed fact is contradicted and removed by backtracking, the negation of the assumed fact is asserted and supported by the reasons underlying the contradiction.[Nogood]

Examples

The forward version of conjunction introduction is implemented in AMORD as the following rule:

```
(Rule (:f :a)
      (Rule (:g :b)
            (Assert (AND :a :b) (&+ :f :g))))
```

To paraphrase this rule, the addition of a fact f with pattern a into the data-base results in the addition of a rule which checks every fact g in the data-base and asserts the conjunction of a and the pattern b of g. Thus if A is asserted, so will be (AND A A), (AND A (AND A A)), (AND (AND A A) A), etc. Note that the atom AND is not a distinguished symbol.

To control these deductions, the following rule can be defined to effect consequent reasoning about conjunctive goals.

```
(Rule (:g (SHOW (AND :p :q)))
      (Rule (:c1 :p)
            (Rule (:c2 :q)
                  (Assert (AND :p :q)
                          (&+ :c1 :c2)))
            (Assert (SHOW :q) ((BC &+) :g :c1)))
      (Assert (SHOW :p) ((BC &+) :g)))
```

In this rule the control statements (SHOWs) depend on belief in the relevant controlled facts so that the existence of a subgoal for the second conjunct of a conjunctive goal depends on the solution for the first conjunct. At the same time, no controlled facts depend on control facts, since the justification for a conjunction is entirely in terms of the conjuncts, and not on the need for deriving the conjunction. This means that the control over the derivation of facts cannot affect the truth of the derived facts. Moreover, the hierarchy of nested, lexically scoped rules allows the specification of sequencing and restriction information. For instance, the above rule could have been written as

```
(Rule (:g (SHOW (AND :p :q)))
    (Rule (:c1 :p)
        (Rule (:c2 :q)
            (Assert (AND :p :q)
                (&+ :c1 :c2)))))
    (Assert (SHOW :p) ((BC &+) :g))
    (Assert (SHOW :q) ((BC &+) :g)))
```

This form of the rule would also only derive correct statements, but would not be as tightly controlled as the previous rule. In this case, both subgoals are asserted immediately, although there is no reason to work on the second conjunct unless the first conjunct has been solved. This form of the rule allows more work to be done in that the possible mutual constraints of the conjuncts on each other due to shared variables is not accounted for. That is, in the first form of the rule, solutions to the first conjunct were used to specialize the subgoals for the second conjunct, so that the constraints of the solutions to the first are accounted for in the second subgoal. In the second form of the rule much work might be done on solving each subgoal independently, with the derivation of the conjunction performed by an explicit matching of these derived results. This allows solutions to the second subgoal to be derived which cannot match any solution to the first subgoal.

Other consequent rules for Modus Ponens, Negated Conjunction Introduction, and Double Negation Introduction are similar in spirit to the rule for Conjunction Introduction:

```
(Rule (:g (SHOW :q))
    (Rule (:i (-> :p :q))
        (Rule (:f :p)
            (Assert :q (MP :i :f)))
        (Assert (SHOW :p) ((BC MP) :g :i)))))

(Rule (:g (SHOW (NOT (AND :p :q))))
    (Rule (:t (NOT :p))
        (Assert (NOT (AND :p :q)) (-&+ :t)))
    (Rule (:t (NOT :q))
        (Assert (NOT (AND :p :q)) (-&+ :t)))
    (Assert (SHOW (NOT :p)) ((BC -&+) :g))
    (Assert (SHOW (NOT :q)) ((BC -&+) :g)))

(Rule (:g (SHOW (NOT (NOT :p))))
    (Rule (:f :p)
        (Assert (NOT (NOT :p)) (--+ :f)))
    (Assert (SHOW :p) ((BC --+) :g)))
```

The BLOCKS World

We will discuss problem solving in the blocks world as an example of our methodology. First, we formalize the domain with a set of logical axioms which express a McCarthy-Hayes situational calculus.Situations We use the syntax (TRUE

<statement> <situation>) to state that the indicated statement holds in the indicated situation. For example, the following axiom expresses the fact that in the situation arrived at after a PUTON operation the block which moved is on the block it was put on.

```
(Assert (-> (AND (TRUE (CLEARTOP :x) :s)
                (TRUE (SPACE-FOR :x :y) :s))
            (TRUE (ON :x :y) ((PUTON :x :y) . :s)))
    (Premise))
```

TRUE is a syntactic convenience. We could just as well add an extra argument to each of the predicates of the domain.

More axioms are needed for the blocks world. Blocks not moved by a PUTON remain on their former support:

```
(Assert (-> (AND (TRUE (ON :a :b) :s)
                (NOT (= :a :x)))
            (TRUE (ON :a :b)
                ((PUTON :x :y) . :s)))
    (Premise)).
```

A block is said to be CLEARTOP if no other block is ON it. We assume for simplicity that only one block can be ON another, and introduce statements of CLEARTOP for blocks made clear by PUTON:

```
(Assert (-> (AND (TRUE (ON :x :b) :s)
                (AND (NOT (= :b Table))
                    (NOT (= :y :b))))
            (TRUE (CLEARTOP :b)
                ((PUTON :x :y) . :s)))
    (Premise)).
```

If a block is CLEARTOP, it remains so after any action which does not place another block ON it.

```
(Assert (-> (AND (TRUE (CLEARTOP :b) :s)
                (NOT (= :y :b)))
            (TRUE (CLEARTOP :b)
                ((PUTON :x :y) . :s)))
    (Premise))
```

A block can be ON only one other block.

```
(Assert (-> (AND (TRUE (ON :x :z) :s)
                (NOT (= :z :y)))
            (NOT (TRUE (ON :x :y) :s)))
    (Premise))
```

The definition of CLEARTOP is:

```
(Assert (-> (TRUE (ON :x :y) :s)
            (NOT (TRUE (CLEARTOP :y) :s)))
    (Premise)).
```

If a block is CLEARTOP, it has SPACE-FOR any other block.

```
(Assert (-> (TRUE (CLEARTOP :x) :s)
            (TRUE (SPACE-FOR :y :x) :s))
    (Premise))
```

If a block is not CLEARTOP, it does not have SPACE-FOR

anything more. This assumes only one block can be ON another.

```
(Assert (-> (AND (NOT (TRUE (CLEARTOP :x) :s))
                 (NOT (= :x Table)))
            (NOT (TRUE (SPACE-FOR :y :x) :s)))
        (Premise))
```

The table always has SPACE-FOR everything.

```
(Assert (TRUE (SPACE-FOR :x Table) :s) (Premise))
```

We set up an initial state of the system by adding situation-specific axioms.

```
(Assert (TRUE (ON C A) INIT) (Premise))
(Assert (TRUE (ON A Table) INIT) (Premise))
(Assert (TRUE (ON B Table) INIT) (Premise))
(Assert (TRUE (CLEARTOP C) INIT) (Premise))
(Assert (TRUE (CLEARTOP B) INIT) (Premise))
```

Problem Solver Strategies

There are a number of strategies for using this description of this blocks world for problem solving. Consider the problem of finding a sequence of actions (PUTONs) which transforms the initial situation into a situation in which block A is ON block B. Such a sequence may be derived from a constructive proof of the statement (EXISTS (S) (TRUE (ON A B) S)) from the initial situation.[Construction]

One strategy is to derive all possible consequences of the axioms using the logical rules of inference without SHOW restrictions. If the goal state is a possible future of the initial state, then a solution sequence will eventually be generated. This forward chaining strategy generates piles of irrelevant states which, although accessible from the initial state, are not on any solution path to the goal state.

A dual strategy is backward chaining. This can be accomplished using the SHOW rules described previously to generate all possible pasts of the goal state. Although all the states so generated are relevant to the goal, most of these are inaccessible from the initial situation.[Subgoal Filters]

Refinement planning is the strategy of decomposing the problem into the sequential attainment of intermediate "islands" or subproblems.[Islands] Both forward and backward chaining are special cases of this strategy, in which the islands proposed are derived by finding states separated from the initial or goal states by the application of a single operator. The more general use is to propose subproblems which are not necessarily immediately accessible from the initial or goal states, but which, if solved, enormously restrict the size of the remaining subproblems. These intermediate subgoals are produced at the risk of being either irrelevant to the goal or impossible to achieve from the initial state, and so must be suggested by "methods" which "know" reasonable decompositions of a domain-specific nature.[HigherSpaceBC]

Several additional constraints influence the selection of problem solver strategies. Many operator sequences have no net effect (they are composite "no-ops"). A problem solver which fails to recognize that these sequences produce no change of state will loop unless its search is globally breadth-first. In addition, it will waste effort deriving solutions to problems isomorphic to ones it has already solved. To solve this problem, it is important to represent the properties of situations in such a way that two situations which are identical with respect to some purpose can be recognized as such.

Implementation of a Refinement-Planning Problem Solver

The principal difficulty of solving problems in worlds which can have arbitrarily many states is that any simple deduction mechanism will explore all of them. Our problem solver limits the potential combinatorial explosion by having domain specific rules which control the introduction of new states. The problem solver also contains rules which are domain independent, of which Modus Ponens and Conjunction Introduction are examples. These SHOW rules will only be invoked for questions which concern an existing state. They are not allowed to generate new or hypothetical states.

The statement (GOAL <condition> <situation>) is asserted when we want <condition> to be achieved in some situation which is a successor of <situation>. The following rule is triggered by this assertion and controls the solution process. When the goal is satisfied this rule will assert (SATISFIED (GOAL <condition> <situation>) <new-situation>) where <new-situation> is the name of the situation where <condition> now holds. The subrule first checks whether the goal is already true. It asserts (TRUE? <condition> <situation>) (asking the question, "Is <condition> true or false in <situation>?") and sets up two rules which wait for the answer. A convention of our rules is that an answer is guaranteed. Processing the goal will continue when the answer (YES or NO) is asserted. If the condition is not true in the current situation, planning proceeds by asserting (ACHIEVE <condition> <situation> <goal>), where <goal> is the fact name of the goal. The ACHIEVE facts trigger the relevant methods for achievement of the goal condition. These methods may introduce new situations and perform actions. If a method thinks that it has succeeded in producing a successor state of the given situation in which the goal condition is true it asserts (ACHIEVED? <goal> <new-situation>), where <new-situation> is the situation in which <goal> is thought to be satisfied. The goal rule then checks this suggestion with TRUE? and makes the SATISFIED assertion if successful. If the method is in error, the bug manifestation is noted in a BUG assertion.

This is marked as a contradiction and causes backtracking. A more sophisticated problem solver would at this point enter a debugging strategy. The justification of the contradiction can be traced. This information is helpful in diagnosing the fault and constructing a patch to the domain specific methods.

```
(Rule (:g (GOAL :c :s))
  (Assert (TRUE? :c :s) (Goal-true? :g))
  (Rule (:q (TRUE? :c :s))
    (Rule (:t (YES :q))
      (Assert (SATISFIED (GOAL :c :s) :s)
              (Goal-immed-satisfied :g :t)))
    (Rule (:t (NO :q))
      (Assert (ACHIEVE :c :s :g)
              (Goal-unsatisfied :g :t))
      (Rule (:w (ACHIEVED? :g :s1))
        (Assert (TRUE? :c :s1)
                (Did-it-succeed? :g :t :w))
        (Rule (:q2 (TRUE? :c :s1))
          (Rule (:f (YES :q2))
            (Assert (SATISFIED (GOAL :c :s) :s1)
                    (Win :g :f)))
          (Rule (:f (NO :q2))
            (Assert (BUG :g :w :f)
                    (Contradiction :w :f)))))))))))
```

To check whether a statement is true in a situation the SHOW mechanism is used. The assertion of (GOAL <condition> <situation>) requests <condition> to be true in some successor state of <situation>. The statement <condition> is relative to a situational variable. In order to test whether this statement is true or false this variable must be bound to the particular situation being considered. The condition of a GOAL assertion must be of the form (L <variable> <predicate>), ("L" abbreviates "LAMBDA") where <predicate> is a predicate form with an open situational variable <variable>. The unification of the trigger pattern of TRUE? with the assertion (TRUE? <condition> <situation>) has the effect of binding the particular situation <situation> being considered with the situational variable <variable> used in <predicate>. By lambda-abstracting the goal condition, we eliminate the explicit mention of any particular situation in the goal description. Equivalent goals are variants, and so will be identified by the AMORD interpreter.

```
(Rule (:g (TRUE? (L :s :p) :s))
    (Rule (:f :p)
          (Assert (YES :g) (Return :g :f)))
    (Rule (:f (NOT :p))
          (Assert (NO :g) (Return :g :f)))
    (Assert (SHOW :p) (Try-positive :g))
    (Assert (SHOW (NOT :p)) (Try-negative :g)))
```

If the goal is a conjunction of conditions, the following rule is triggered. Some conjunctive goals can be achieved by achieving each conjunct separately. This is called a LINEAR-PLAN. Sometimes the conjuncts can be achieved in one order but not in the other order.[PCBG] A conjunctive goal cannot always be decomposed in this way.[Anomalous] In the case of such a non-linear problem, our rule fails.

```
(Rule (:f (ACHIEVE (L :s (AND :c1 :c2))
                   :s1 :purpose))
      (Assume (LINEAR-PLAN :f) (First-order :f))
      (Rule (:p (LINEAR-PLAN :f))
            (Assume (STATED-ORDER :p)
                    (Conjunct-order :p))
            (Rule (:o (STATED-ORDER :p))
                  (Assert (ORDERED-PLAN
                            :s :c1 :c2 :s1 :purpose)
                          (Try :o)))
            (Rule (:o (NOT (STATED-ORDER :p)))
                  (Assert (ORDERED-PLAN
                            :s :c2 :c1 :s1 :purpose)
                          (Try :o))))
      (Rule (:p (NOT (LINEAR-PLAN :f)))
            ;This problem solver has no
            ;clever ideas about this case.
            (Assert (FAIL :p) (Contradiction :p))))
```

The next rule refines a conjunctive goal as an ordered linear plan. It produces the subgoal of finding an "island" in which the first conjunct is true. If the first subgoal can be satisfied, it then establishes the subgoal of satisfying the second conjunct in a successor of this island. If the second subgoal can be satisfied the resulting state is proposed as a solution to the conjunctive goal. The goal rule which triggered this method is resumed by the statement (ACHIEVED? <purpose> <new-situation>) which tests (using TRUE?) the original goal condition in <new-situation>. If this method is wrong, the GOAL rule will fail.

```
(Rule (:f (ORDERED-PLAN :s :c1 :c2 :s1 :purpose))
    (Assert (GOAL (L :s :c1) :s1)
            (Subgoal-1 :f))
    (Rule (:sat1 (SATISFIED
            (GOAL (L :s :c1) :s1) :s2))
          (Assert (GOAL (L :s :c2) :s2)
                  (Subgoal-2 :f :sat1))
          (Rule (:sat2 (SATISFIED
                  (GOAL (L :s :c2) :s2) :s3))
                (Assert (ACHIEVED? :purpose :s3)
                        (Win? :f :sat1 :sat2)))))
```

Methods redundantly incorporate knowledge included in the axioms. They embody the domain specific heuristics for constructing effective subgoals. The following rule suggests that to achieve (ON A B) one should first achieve a situation which A has a cleartop and B has space for A. From this situation, we can immediately (PUTON A B) producing a situation in which the goal is achieved. This method is the only rule which creates new situations.

```
(Rule (:f (ACHIEVE (L :s (TRUE (ON :a :b) :s))
                    :s1 :purpose))
  (Assert
   (GOAL (L :x
            (AND (TRUE (CLEARTOP :a) :x)
                 (TRUE (SPACE-FOR :a :b) :x)))
       :s1)
   (Prerequisite-for-PUTON :f))
  (Rule
   (:sat
    (SATISFIED
     (GOAL (L :x
              (AND (TRUE (CLEARTOP :a) :x)
                   (TRUE (SPACE-FOR :a :b) :x)))
         :s1)
     :s2))
    (Assert (ACHIEVED? :purpose
                       ((PUTON :a :b) . :s2))
            (Record-PUTON-purpose :f :sat))))
```

The following rules describe methods for achieving each predicate of the domain and its negation. To achieve NOT-ON, move the offending object to the table.

```
(Rule (:f (ACHIEVE
          (L :x (NOT (TRUE (ON :a :b) :x)))
            :s1 :purpose))
  (Assert (ACHIEVE
          (L :u (TRUE (ON :a Table) :u))
            :s1 :purpose)
          (Get-rid-of :f))))
```

To make space on something, achieve NOT-ON for all offending objects.

```
(Rule (:f (ACHIEVE
          (L :s (TRUE (SPACE-FOR :a :y) :s))
            :s1 :purpose))
  (Rule (:o (TRUE (ON :x :y) :s1))
    (Assert
     (ACHIEVE
      (L :u (NOT (TRUE (ON :x :y) :u)))
        :s1 :purpose)
      (Make-space-for :f :o))))
```

To clear a block, achieve NOT-ON for all other blocks on it.

```
(Rule (:f (ACHIEVE
          (L :s (TRUE (CLEARTOP :y) :s))
            :s1 :purpose))
  (Rule (:o (TRUE (ON :x :y) :s1))
    (Assert
     (ACHIEVE
      (L :u (NOT (TRUE (ON :x :y) :u)))
        :s1 :purpose)
      (Make-CLEARTOP :f :o))))
```

The methods introduce some incompleteness that was not present in the original axioms. In return the problem solver always halts by running out of further rules to run. The main reason the specific methods could be used successfully is that the deductions are explicitly controlled by control assertions (GOAL, ACHIEVE, ACHIEVED?, TRUE?).

Conclusions

Many kinds of combinatorial explosions can be avoided by a problem solver that thinks about what it is trying to do. In order to be able to meditate on its goals, actions and reasons for belief, these must be explicitly represented in a form manipulable by the deductive process. In fact, this "internal" control domain is a problem domain formalized using assertions and rules just like an "external" domain. How can we use assertions about control states to effectively control the deductive process?

The key to this problem is a set of conventions by which the explicit control assertions are used to restrict the application of sound but otherwise explosive rules. These conventions are supported by a vocabulary of control concepts and a set of systemic features. The applicability of a rule can be restricted by embedding it in a rule having a pattern which matches a control assertion as an entrance condition. The rule language allows the variables bound by matching the control assertions to further restrict the embedded rule. But we want the conclusions of sound rules to depend only on their correct antecedents and not on the control assertions used to restrict their derivation. This is necessary to enable fruitful deliberations about the reasons for belief in an assertion. The system must provide means for describing the reasons for belief in an assertion and means for referring to an object of belief.

Sometimes it is necessary to make assumptions -- to accept beliefs that may later be discovered false. Conclusions of rules which operate with incomplete knowledge must depend upon the control assumptions made. Accurate dependencies allow precise assignment of responsibility for incorrect beliefs. This is necessary for efficient search and perturbation analysis.

Acknowledgements:

We thank Charles Rich, Marvin Minsky, Drew McDermott, Richard Stallman, Marilyn McLennan, Richard Brown, and Gerald Roylance for suggestions, ideas and comments used in this paper. Jon Doyle is supported by a Fannie and John Hertz Foundation graduate fellowship. Guy Steele is supported by a National Science Foundation graduate fellowship. This research was conducted at the Artificial Intelligence Laboratory of the Massachusetts Institute of Technology. Support for the Laboratory's artificial intelligence research is provided in part by the Advanced Research Projects Agency of the Department of Defense under Office of Naval Research contract number N00014-75-C-0643.

Notes

Advice Taker

The term "Advice Taker" originates with McCarthy [1968].

Additive Knowledge

Is it possible to have an additive system in which knowledge about other knowledge can be expressed? Sometimes advice may be negative. For example, the process of sorting a list may be defined as finding a permutation of the list which is ordered. An obvious procedure derived from this definition is that of enumerating the permutations of the list and testing each for order. If better methods become known, we will want to give the advice that this method stinks. How can this be an additive piece of knowledge? Perhaps a way to make such knowledge additive is to formalize the "state of mind" of the problem solver, and let such advice change its state of mind.

Procedures

The "Procedural Embedding of Knowledge" is the philosophy popularized by Winograd [1972] and Hewitt [1972, 1975] that knowledge can be most profitably represented as computer programs.

Coherence

In *Human Problem Solving* [Newell and Simon 1972], the apparently coherent behavior of human subjects is also explained in terms of a set of relatively independent agents (formalized as productions). Minsky [1977] proposes a structure for human behavior in terms of a "society of agents".

EL

EL is a set of rules for electrical circuit analysis which embodies the method of propagation of constraints. [Sussman and Stallman 1975] EL is implemented in ARS. [Stallman and Sussman 1976]

Simon's Ant

Simon [1969] points out that apparently complex behavior can result from simple procedures operating in a complex but constraining domain.

Explicit Control

Production System devotees have tended to approach the problem of control through the architecture of the machine supporting the problem solver. Most of these studies are concerned with devices like production ordering, recency criteria for working memory elements, and priority measures on productions and memory elements. [Hayes-Roth and Lesser 1977, McDermott and Forgy 1976]

Drew McDermott's [1976] NASL interpreter explicitly records control assertions in guiding an electronic circuit design program. His system also records some dependency information, but does so in an automatic fashion rather than explicitly. Other uses of explicit representations of the problem solver control state are used in NOAH [Sacerdoti 1975] and MYCIN [Davis 1976]. Production System problem solvers (such as GPSR [Rychner 1976]) necessarily record goals explicitly in working memory, but only as an implementation of standard consequent reasoning, rather than as a mechanism for careful control.

Well-Founded Support

Means for effectively maintaining a well-founded justification for each believed fact have been investigated by Doyle [1977]. His system TMS (Truth Maintenance System) has been incorporated in our design of AMORD.

Backtracking

Dependency-Directed Backtracking is a technique for careful backtracking which was introduced by Stallman and Sussman [1976] in the context of electrical circuit analysis.

Separation

Hayes [1973], Kowalski [1974], and Pratt [1977] have advocated the separation of problem solving knowledge into "competence" and "performance" components. We feel that this is the wrong distinction to make, as the competence knowledge must necessarily be replicated in the performance knowledge. Our proposed methodology requires these forms of knowledge to be integrated for efficient control, but separated by explicitly recorded dependencies.

Micro-PLANNER

Micro-PLANNER [Sussman, Winograd, and Charniak 1970] was a language based on Hewitt's [1972] PLANNER which had a pervasive system of chronological backtracking.

Control Vocabulary

McDermott [1977] argues that it is the vocabulary used in explicit (production-like) control that is important, not the specific machine architecture. See also the detailed vocabularies he [McDermott 1976] and Sacerdoti [1975] develop for talking about tasks and actions.

Suppression

Of course, redundant conjuncts can be suppressed by building the semantics of conjunction into the problem solver. This just puts off the problem as non-primitive relations can also explode in this fashion. Resolution [Robinson 1965] and associated combinatorial strategies are domain independent techniques for suppressing some combinatorial explosions while maintaining completeness.

Implications

It is sometimes necessary to derive an implication as a subgoal, as in a conditional proof in natural deduction. In this example we have not provided for such subgoals. The details of conditional proof in the context of a truth maintenance system are described by Doyle [1977].

AMORD

A Miracle of Rare Device, a name taken from S. T. Coleridge's Kubla Khan.

Variants

In AMORD, facts are indexed so that variant statements of a fact are identified. If a fact is derived in different ways, it is justified by each of the various derivations. These multiple justifications are useful if a derivation is later withdrawn. [Stallman and Sussman 1976, Doyle 1977]

Unifies

Our matcher is based on the unification algorithm used in resolution, but ignores the restrictions of first order logic. In particular, there are no distinguished symbols or positions.

Nogood

A summary of the reasons for a contradiction which are independent of a particular set of assumptions is used in ARS [Stallman and Sussman 1976] to restrict future choices. Doyle [1977] extended and clarified this notion and its relationship to the logical notion of conditional proof.

Situations

The situational calculus formalizations of changing world was introduced by McCarthy [1968], and further developed by McCarthy and Hayes [1969]. This technique is closely related to the methods of modal logic. [Kripke 1963]

Construction

Green's [1969] method of constructive proof did not take into account the initial situation. For example, one should state the goal: (EXISTS (S) (AND (FUTURE INIT S) (TRUE (ON A B) S))) where FUTURE is defined according to the operators that are applicable.

Subgoal Filters

Some impossible subgoals can be pruned by using an external semantic filter. Gelernter's [1963] Geometry Machine uses an analytic geometry diagram for this purpose.

Islands

The concept of refinement planning with islands was introduced by Minsky [1963].

HigherSpaceBC

Refinement planning might be viewed from the GPS [Ernst and Newell 1969] and ABSTRIPS [Sacerdoti 1974] perspective as backward chaining in a higher level space which controls the activities in the action sequence space.

PCBG

One way in which a solution of a conjunction by a linear plan may be incorrect is the Prerequisite-Clobbers-Brother-Goal bug discussed by Sussman [1974, 1975]. This bug may be fixed by reordering the plan. Other related bugs in the world of fixed-instruction turtle programs are discussed by Goldstein [1974].

Anomalous

Allen Brown [Sussman 1975] discovered that it is impossible to use a linear plan to construct (AND (ON A B) (ON B C)) if the initial situation contains (ON C A). Tate [1974], Sacerdoti [1975], and Warren [1974] have proposed several solutions to this problem.

Bibliography

[Davis 1976]
Randall Davis, "Applications of Meta Level Knowledge to the Construction, Maintainance and Use of Large Knowledge Bases," Stanford AI Lab Memo AIM-283, July 1976.

[Doyle 1977]
Jon Doyle, "Truth Maintenance Systems for Problem Solving," MIT AI Lab TR-419, 1977.

[Ernst and Newell 1969]
George W. Ernst and Allen Newell, GPS: A Case Study in Generality and Problem-Solving, Academic Press, New York, 1969.

[Gelernter 1963]
H. Gelernter, "Realization of a Geometry-Theorem Proving Machine," in Feigenbaum and Feldman, Computers and Thought, pp. 134-152.

[Goldstein 1974]
Ira P. Goldstein, "Understanding Simple Picture Programs," MIT AI Lab, TR-294, September 1974.

[Green 1969]
C. Cordell Green, "Theorem-Proving by Resolution as a Basis for Question-Answering Systems," in Meltzer and Michie, Machine Intelligence 4, pp. 183-205.

[Hayes 1973]
P. J. Hayes, "Computation and Deduction," Proc. MFCS, 1973.

[Hayes-Roth and Lesser 1977]
F. Hayes-Roth and V.R. Lesser, "Focus of Attention in the Hearsay-II Speech Understanding System," CMU CS report, January 1977.

[Hewitt 1972]
Carl E. Hewitt, "Description and Theoretical Analysis (Using Schemata) of PLANNER: A Language for Proving Theorems and Manipulating Models in a Robot," MIT AI Lab, TR-258, April 1972.

[Hewitt 1975]
Carl Hewitt, "How to Use What You Know," IJCAI4, September 1975, pp. 189-198.

[Kowalski 1974]
Robert Kowalski, "Logic for Problem Solving," University of Edinburgh, Department of Computational Logic, DCL Memo 75, 1974.

[Kripke 1963]
S. Kripke, "Semantical Considerations on Modal Logic," Acta Philosophica Fennica, 83-94, 1963.

[McCarthy 1968]
John McCarthy, "Programs With Common Sense," in Minsky, Semantic Information Processing, pp. 403-418.

[McCarthy and Hayes 1969]
J. McCarthy and P. J. Hayes, "Some Philosophical Problems from the Standpoint of Artificial Intelligence," in Meltzer and Michie, Machine Intelligence 4, pp. 463-502.

[McDermott 1976]
Drew Vincent McDermott, "Flexibility and Efficiency in a Computer Program for Designing Circuits," MIT AI Lab TR-402, December 1976.

[McDermott 1977]
Drew McDermott, "Vocabularies for Problem Solver State Descriptions," IJCAI 5, August 1977.

[McDermott and Forgy 1976]
J. McDermott and C. Forgy, "Production System Conflict Resolution Strategies," CMU CS report, December 1976.

[Minsky 1963]
Marvin L. Minsky, "Steps Toward Artificial Intelligence," in Feigenbaum and Feldman, Computers and Thought, pp. 406-450.

[Minsky 1977]
Marvin L. Minsky, "Plain Talk about Neurodevelopmental Epistemology," IJCAI 5, August 1977.

[Newell and Simon 1972]
Allen Newell and Herbert Simon, *Human Problem Solving*, Prentice-Hall, Englewood Cliffs, NJ, 1972.

[Pratt 1977]
Vaughan R. Pratt, "The Competence/Performance Dichotomy in Programming," MIT AI Lab Memo 400, January 1977.

[Robinson 1965]
J. A. Robinson, "A Machine-Oriented Logic Based on the Resolution Principle," *JACM*, *12* (January 1965), pp. 23-41.

[Rychner 1976]
Michael D. Rychner, "Production Systems as a Programming Language for Artificial Intelligence Applications," CMU CS Report, December 1976.

[Sacerdoti 1974]
Earl D. Sacerdoti, "Planning in a Hierarchy of Abstraction Spaces," *Artificial Intelligence*, Vol. 5, No. 2, pp. 115-135.

[Sacerdoti 1975]
Earl D. Sacerdoti, "A Structure for Plans and Behavior," SRI AI Center, TN 109, August 1975.

[Simon 1969]
Herbert Simon, *The Sciences of the Artificial*, MIT Press, Cambridge, Massachusetts, 1969.

[Stallman and Sussman 1976]
Richard M. Stallman and Gerald Jay Sussman, "Forward Reasoning and Dependency-Directed Backtracking in a System for Computer-Aided Circuit Analysis," MIT AI Memo 380, September 1976.

[Sussman, Winograd and Charniak 1970]
Gerald Jay Sussman, Terry Winograd and Eugene Charniak, "MICRO-PLANNER Reference Manual," MIT AI Lab, AI Memo 203.

[Sussman 1974]
Gerald Jay Sussman, "The Virtuous Nature of Bugs," *Proc. AISB Summer Conference*, July 1974.

[Sussman 1975]
Gerald Jay Sussman, *A Computer Model of Skill Acquisition*, American Elsevier Publishing Company, New York, 1975.

[Sussman and Stallman 1975]
Gerald Jay Sussman and Richard Matthew Stallman, "Heuristic Techniques in Computer-Aided Circuit Analysis," *IEEE Transactions on Circuits and Systems*, Vol. CAS-22, No. 11, November 1975, pp. 857-865.

[Tate 1974]
Austin Tate, "INTERPLAN: A plan generation system which can deal with interactions between goals," University of Edinburgh, Machine Intelligence Research Unit, MIP-R-109, December 1974.

[Warren 1974]
David H. D. Warren, "WARPLAN: A System for Generating Plans," University of Edinburgh, Department of Computational Logic Memo No. 76, June 1974.

[Winograd 1972]
Terry Winograd, *Understanding Natural Language*, Academic Press, New York, 1972.

(Alice said),
"Would you tell me, please, which way I ought to go from here?" "That depends a good deal on where you want to get to," said the Cat. "I don't know where...," said Alice. "Then it doesn't matter which way you go," said the Cat.

From Lewis Carroll's *Alice's Adventures in Wonderland*

20 / Terry Winograd
Frame Representations and the Declarative/Procedural Controversy

This paper represents Winograd's attempt to synthesize what were, at the time of writing, two apparently competing positions on representing knowledge. On the one hand were the *proceduralists*, asserting that our knowledge is primarily a "knowing how." On the other were the *declarativists*, believing that the essence of knowledge did not reside in procedures for its use, but rather on a set of domain-specific facts and very general inference procedures (more like a "knowing that"). Winograd explores the advantages of each of the two approaches, and concludes that the debate is not a technical one, but rather it "is an expression of an underlying difference in attitude towards the problems of complexity. Declarativists and proceduralists differ in their approach to the duality between modularity and interaction. . ." He then goes on to explore a synthesis of procedures and declarative structures in a system based on the idea of frames (a notion generated in large part by [Minsky, Chapter 12]). Winograd introduces a "generalization hierarchy" of declarative frames (a fairly typical semantic network, actually), associates with them sets of important elements (or *IMPS*), and examines the way in which attached procedures give the user the flexibility to make the structure as modular or integrated as he sees fit. The formalism sketched in the second half of this paper is the precursor to the frame language KRL, a seminal contribution to the field (see [Bobrow and Winograd, Chapter 13]).

Appeared in *Representation and Understanding: Studies in Cognitive Science*, 185–210, edited by D. G. Bobrow and A. M. Collins, New York: Academic Press, 1975.

FRAME REPRESENTATIONS AND THE DECLARATIVE/PROCEDURAL CONTROVERSY

Terry Winograd
Computer Science Department
Stanford University
Stanford, California

I. INTRODUCTION

Any discussion today of "the representation problem" is likely to entail a debate between proponents of *declarative* and *procedural* representations of knowledge. Sides are taken (often on the basis of affinity to particular research institutions) and examples are produced to show why each view is "right". Recently a number of people have proposed theories which purport to solve many representational problems through the use of something called "frames". Minsky (1975) is the most widely known example, but very similar ideas are found in Moore & Newell's (1973) MERLIN system, the networks of Norman & Rumelhart (1975), and in the schemata of D. Bobrow & Norman (Chapter 5). Parts of the notion are present in many current representations for natural language [see Winograd (1974) for a summary].

This chapter is composed of two distinct parts. In the first half I want to examine the essential features of the opposing viewpoints, and to provide some criteria for evaluating ideas for representation. The second half contains a very rough sketch of a particular version of a frame representation, and suggests the ways in which it can deal with the issues raised.

II. THE SIMPLE ISSUES

First let us look at the superficial lineup of the argument. It is an artificial intelligence incarnation of the old philosophical distinction between "knowing that" and "knowing how". The proceduralists assert that our knowledge is primarily a "knowing how". The human information processor is a stored program device, with its knowledge of the world *embedded* in the programs. What a person (or robot) knows about the English language, the game of chess, or the physical properties of his world is coextensive with his set of programs for operating with it. This view is most often associated with MIT, and is emphasized by Minsky and Papert (1972), Hewitt (1973), and Winograd (1972).

The declarativists, on the other hand, do not believe that knowledge of a subject is intimately bound with the procedures for its use. They see intelligence as resting on two bases: a quite general set of procedures for manipulating facts of all sorts, and a set of specific facts describing particular knowledge domains. In thinking, the general procedures are applied to the domain-specific data to make deductions. Often this process has been based on the model of axiomatic mathematics. The facts are *axioms* and the thought process involves *proof procedures* for drawing conclusions from them. One of the earliest and clearest advocates of this approach was McCarthy (see

McCarthy & Hayes, 1969), and it has been extensively explored at Stanford, and Edinburgh.

From a strictly formal view there is no distinction between the positions. Anyone who has programmed in languages like LISP has been forced into believing that "programs are data". We can think of the interpreter (or the hardware device, for that matter) as the only program in the system, and everything else as data on which it works. Everything, then, is declarative.

From the other end, we can view everything as a program. Hewitt, Bishop, & Steiger (1973) actually propose this view. A fact is a simple program which accepts inputs equivalent to questions like "Are you true?" and commands like "Assume you are true!". It returns outputs like "true" and "false", while having lasting effects which will determine the way it responds in the future (equivalent to setting internal variables.) Everything is a procedure. Clearly there is no sharp debate on whether a piece of knowledge is a program or a statement. We must go below these labels to see what we stand to gain in *looking at* it as one or the other. We must examine the mechanisms which have been developed for dealing with these representations, and the kind of advantages they offer for epistemology. In this entire discussion, we could divide the question into two aspects: "What kind of representation do people use?" and "What kind of representation is best for machine intelligence?" I will not make this distinction, first of all since the issues raised are quite similar, and second, since I believe that at our current stage of knowledge these questions are most profitably attacked as if they were the same.

A. The Benefits of Declaratives

Flexibility - Economy. The primary argument against procedural representation is that it requires that a piece of knowledge be specified by saying how it is used. Often there is more than a single possible use, and it seems unsatisfactory to believe that each use must be specified in advance. The obvious example is a simple universal fact like "All Chicago lawyers are clever." This could be used to answer a question like "Is Dan clever?" by checking to see if he is a Chicago lawyer. It might be used to decide that Richard is not from Chicago if we know he is a stupid lawyer, or that he is not a lawyer if he is a dim-witted Chicagoan. Each of these might be done in response to a question which is asked, or as a response to a new piece of information which has just been added. In a strictly procedural representation, the fact would have to be represented differently for each of these deductions. Each would demand a specific form, like "If you find out that someone is a lawyer, check to see if he is from Chicago, and if so assert that he is clever." Traditional logic, however, provides a simple declarative representation in the predicate calculus:

$$\forall(x) [Chicagoan (x) \,\&\, Lawyer (x) \Rightarrow Clever (x)]$$

The different uses for this fact result from its access by a general deductive mechanism. In adding this formula to the system, we do not have to anticipate how it will be used, and the program is therefore more flexible in the sorts of deduction it will be able to make. Associated with this flexibility is an obvious economy in making multiple uses from a single statement.

Understandability - Learnability. The simplicity of the declarative statement above is more important than just an economy of storage. It also has important implications for the ease of understanding and modifying the body of knowledge in a system. If the knowledge base is a set of independent facts, it can be changed by adding new ones, and the implications of each statement lie directly in its logical content. For programs, on the other hand, the implications lie largely in questions of how a routine is to be used, under what conditions, with what arguments, etc. Minor changes can have far-reaching effects on other parts of the program. In addition, it is not easy to split programs into independent subprograms. Thus a single "piece" of knowledge may be embedded as a line in a larger integrated program. Changing or adding is much more difficult. This issue of modification applies both to programmers trying to build a system, and to any sort of self-modification or learning.

Accessibility - communicability. Much of what we know is most easily statable as a set of declaratives, and the usual way to give information to another person is to break it into statements. This has implications both for adding knowledge to programs, and communicating their content to other people. Quite aside from how the eventual program runs, there may be important advantages in stating things declaratively, from the standpoint of building it and working with it.

B. The Benefits of Procedures

Procedural - Modeling. It is an obvious fact that many things we know are best seen as procedures, and it is difficult to describe them in a purely declarative way. If we want a robot to manipulate a simple world (such as a table top of toy blocks), we do it most naturally by describing its manipulations as programs. The knowledge about building stacks is in the form of a program to do it. Since we specify in detail just what part will be called when, we are free to build in assumptions about how different facts interrelate. For example, we know that calling a program to lift a block will not cause any changes in the relative positions of other blocks (making the assumption that we will only call the lift program for unencumbered blocks). In a declarative formalism, this fact must be stated in the form of a *frame axiom* which states something equivalent to "If you lift a block X, and block Y is on block Z before you start, and if X is not Y and X is not Z and X is unencumbered, then Y is on Z when you are done." This fact must be used each time we ask about Y and Z in order to check that the relation still holds. Note that this knowledge is taken care of "automatically" in the procedural representation because we have control over when particular knowledge will be used, and deal explicitly with the interactions between the different operations.

In using procedures we trade some degree of flexibility for a tremendous gain in the ease of representing what we know about processes. This applies not only to obvious physical processes like moving blocks around, but equally well to deductive processes like playing games or proving geometry theorems.

Second Order Knowledge. One critical component of our knowledge is knowing about what we know and what we can know. We have explicit facts about how to use other facts in reasoning, and this must be expressed in our representation. These are not sophisticated logical tools, but straightforward heuristics. For example, if we want to generate a plan for getting to the airport, we know "If you do not see any obvious reason why the road should be impassable, assume you can drive." The catch is obviously the word "obvious". It is quite distinct from logical notions of truth and provability, referring to the complexity and difficulty of a particular reasoning process. Another such fact might be "The relation *NEAR* is transitive as long as you don't try to use it too many times in the same deduction."

It is theoretically possible to express second-order knowledge in a declarative form, but it is extremely difficult to do so outside the context of a particular reasoning process. In a procedural representation we can talk directly about things like the depth or duration of various computations, about the particular ways in which facts will be accessssed, etc.

The Need for Heuristic Knowledge. The strongest support for procedural representation comes from the fact that it works. Complex AI programs in all domains have a large amount of their knowledge built into their procedures. Those programs which attempt to keep domain-specific knowledge in a nonprocedural data base do so at the expense of limiting themselves to even more simplified worlds, and the simplest of goals. The obvious reason for this is that much of what we know about an area is neither "simple facts" nor general knowledge about reasoning, but is of the form "If you are trying to deduce this particular sort of thing under this particular set of conditions, then you should try the following strategies." In theory, this knowledge could be kept separate and integrated with the declarative knowledge of a domain. In practice, it is not at all clear how a real system could do this. Most systems which have been based on a declarative formalism have only the general heuristics built into the interpreter, and do not make it easy to add domain-specific strategies. By putting knowledge in a primarily procedural form, we gain the ability to integrate the heuristic knowledge easily. The deduction process is primarily under control of the specific heuristic knowledge.

III. SOME UNDERLYING ISSUES

At this point it is tempting to look for a synthesis -- to say "You need both. Some things are better represented procedurally, others as declarative facts, and all we need to do is work on how these can be integrated." This reaction misses what I believe is the fundamental ground for the dispute. It is not simply a technical issue of formalisms, but is an expression of an underlying difference in attitude towards the problems of complexity. Declarativists and proceduralists differ in their approach to the duality between modularity and interaction, and their formalisms are a reflection of this viewpoint.

In his essay, The Architecture of Complexity, Simon (1969, p. 100) describes what he calls *nearly decomposable systems*, in which "...the short-run behavior of each of the component subsystems is approximately independent of the short-run behavior of the other components.... In the long run, the behavior of any one of the components depends in only an aggregate way on the behavior of the other components." One of the most powerful ideas of modern science is that many complex systems can be viewed as nearly decomposable systems, and that the components can be studied separately without constant attention to the interactions. If this were not true, the complexity of real-world systems would be far too great for meaningful understanding, and it is is possible (as Simon argues) that it would be too great for them to have resulted from a process of evolution.

In viewing systems this way, we must keep an eye on both sides of the duality -- we must worry about finding the right decomposition, in order to reduce the apparent complexity, but we must also remember that "the interactions among subsystems are weak *but not negligible*". In representational terms, this forces us to have representations which facilitate the "weak interactions".

If we look at our debate between opposing epistemologies, we see two metaphors at opposite poles of the modularity/interaction spectrum. Modern symbolic mathematics makes strong use of modularity at both a global and a local level. Globally, one of the most powerful ideas of logic is the clear distinction between *axioms* and *rules of inference*. A mathematical object can be completely characterized by giving a set of axioms specific to it, without reference to procedures for using those axioms. Dually, a proof method can be described and understood completely in the absence of any specific set of axioms on which it is to operate. Locally, axioms represent the ultimate in decomposition of knowledge. Each axiom is taken as true, without regard to how it will interact with the others in the system. In fact, great care is taken to ensure the logical independence of the axioms. Thus a new axiom can be added with the guarantee that as long as it does not make the system inconsistent, anything which could be proved before is still valid. In some sense all changes are additive -- we can only "know different" by "knowing more".

Programming, on the other hand, is a metaphor in which interaction is primary. The programmer is in direct control of just what will be used when, and the internal functioning of any piece (subroutine) may have side effects which cause strong interactions with the functioning of other pieces. Globally there is no separation into "facts" and "process" -- they are interwoven in the sequence of operations. Locally, interactions are strong. It is often futile to try to understand the meaning of a particular subroutine without taking into account just when it will be called, in what environment, and how its results will be used. Knowledge in a program is not changed by adding new subroutines, but by a *debugging* process in which existing structures are modified, and the resulting changes in interaction must be explicitly accounted for.

Recent AI programming languages represent an attempt to achieve some *global modularity* within the programming context. [For a good overview, see Bobrow & Raphael (1974).] Through the use of pattern-directed call, and search strategies such as backup, they attempt to decouple the flow of control from the programmer. Procedures are specified whose meaning is in some sense free from the particular order in which they will be called, and the system has some sort of general mechanism for marshalling them in any particular case. So far, the general procedural knowledge is extremely primitive, and the potential modularity is rarely used. It is exploited much more fully in the *production systems* of Newell & Simon (1972). We can view production systems as a programming language in which all interaction is forced through a very narrow channel. Individual subroutines (productions) interact in only two ways, a static ordering and a limited communication area called the *short-term memory*. They can react to data left in the short-term memory and modify it as their means of communication. Their temporal interaction is completely determined by the data in this STM and a uniform ordering regime for deciding which productions will be activated in cases where more than one might apply. The orderings which have been most explored are a simple *linear* ordering of the productions, and a restricted system in which it is considered an error if there is not a unique production which matches the contents of short term memory at any time. Thus instead of the full ability to specify just what will happen when, the programmer can only determine the ordering, and the rest of the interaction is out of his hands. Of course, it is possible to use the STM to pass arbitrarily complex messages which embody any degree of interaction we want. The spirit of the venture, however, is very much opposed to this, and the formalism is interesting to the degree that complex processes can be described without resort to such tricks, maintaining the clear modularity between the pieces of knowledge and the global process which uses them.

If we look back to the advantages offered by the use of the two types of representation, we see that they are primarily advantages offered by different views toward modularity. The flexibility and economy of declarative knowledge come from the ability to decompose knowledge into "what" and "how". The learnability and understandability come from the strong independence of the individual axioms or facts. On the other hand, procedures give an immediate way of formulating the interactions between the static knowledge and the reasoning process, and allow a much richer and more powerful interaction between the "chunks" into which knowledge is divided. In trying to achieve a synthesis, we must ask not "how can we combine programs and facts?", but "How can our formalism take advantage of decomposability without sacrificing the possibilities for interaction?"

IV. STEPS TOWARD A MIDDLE

If the declarative and procedural formalisms represents endpoints on a spectrum of modularity/interaction, we should be able to see in each of them trends away from the extreme. Indeed, much current work in computing and AI can be seen in this light.

A. Modular Programming

One of the most prominent trends in computer programming today is toward some kind of *structured programming* as exemplified, say, by the work of Dahl, Dijkstra, & Hoare (1972). It represents a response to the tremendous complexities which arise when a programmer makes full use of his power to exploit interactions. Advocates maintain that understandability and modifiability of systems can only be maintained if they are forced to be "nearly decomposable". This is enforced by severely limiting the kinds of interaction which can be programmed, both in the flow of control and in the manipulation of data structures. This represents a move toward the kind of *local modularity* between the individual pieces of knowledge, and is carried to a logical extreme by Hewitt's actors.

an explanation of what frames "really are", or to represent anyone else's understanding of what they should be. Many different issues are still unsettled (many more perhaps unrecognized), and it will be a long time before any agreements on notation and operation can be reached. The notation also does not represent a worked-out design, but is intended to be suggestive of the necessary formalism. This example is specifically chosen to avoid many of the most interesting problems, in order to gain at least a small foothold for attacking them sensibly. Thus it oversimplifies and misrepresents my own views of frames as well. This version grew up in the same environment as Minsky's (1975) frames, but with a slightly different emphasis since they were initially applied with a view toward natural language rather than vision. Their development over the last year has been strongly influenced by discussions with Andee Rubin at MIT, and Daniel Bobrow at Xerox PARC. Further work is continuing in conjunction with Bobrow, leading toward the specification of the frame formalism and the development of reasoning programs which will use it.

With this caveat clearly in mind, let us look at the problem of understanding the connection between days, dates, and numbers. The context for this problem can be best understood by imagining some sort of program (or person) acting as an office assistant in matters such as scheduling. The assistant must be able to do things like writing schedules, accepting information about events to be scheduled, and accepting facts about dates in a natural input. This does not necessarily mean natural language, but in a form whose structure corresponds roughly to that which a person might use to another person.

A. The Generalization Hierarchy

We first note that the system would have a set of internal concepts appropriate to the subject matter. These might include things such as those in Fig. 1. These concepts are arranged in a *generalization hierarchy*, a structure of *isa* links connecting concepts to those of which they are *specializations*. This hierarchy contains both

B. Compiling Facts

Starting with a traditional logical-declarative system, Sandewall (1973) attempts to build in some of the specific control interactions which make programs effective. He compiles declarative information into *operators* in which specific decisions are embedded about what knowledge should be called into play when. These are then included as part of a system which in many ways is similar to GPS, the intellectual forerunner of the production systems. Another approach from this direction is Sussman's (1973) attempt to combine the effectiveness of procedures with the ease of modification which comes from modularity. His system contains both declarative and procedural knowledge, but combines them by being an *active programmer*. There is a body of declarative data about the specific subject domain, but it is not used directly in this form. As each piece is added, whether as a statement from a teacher, or from an experience in the model-world, it is perused by a programmer-debugger. General knowledge about procedures is brought into play to decide just how the new knowledge should be integrated into the domain-specific programs, and how the resulting interactions might be anticipated and tested. Thus what the system knows may be decomposed into "procedure" and "domain fact" modules, but these are internally combined into a procedural representation.

V. A FIRST ATTEMPT AT SYNTHESIS

Recently much excitement has been generated by the idea of a representational format called "frames" which could integrate many of the new directions described in the previous section. So far, this work is in a beginning state of development, and none of the available papers work out the actual implementation of such a scheme and its application to a significant set of problems. Therefore, most of what can be said is at the level of general system criteria, and ideas for organization.

In this section I give a simple example of a system which represents knowledge in a frame-like notation. I warn the reader strongly that this does not purport to be

specific objects (like *July 4, 1974*) and general objects (like *day, holiday,* and *Thursday*). I will avoid discussing the problems inherent in the combination of these in a single hierarchy, as that deserves at least another entire paper.

Associated with each node in this hierarchy is a *frame* tying together the knowledge we have of that concept. Often there will also be a particular English word or phrase associated with it, but that is not a necessary condition. Reference within the system can be made by using the internal concept names as shown in the hierarchy.

disagreements between them? For the purposes of this elementary discussion, we will ignore these (which of course does not make them go away for good).

B. Description and Classification

In the previous section we used the word "generalization" to describe the relationship between frames linked in the hierarchy. Another way to think of it would be as a system of *classification.* Each frame in fact represents a class of objects, and an *isa* link connects a class to some superclass which properly contains it. From an operational viewpoint it seems more useful to think of this as a hierarchy of *descriptions.* Of course there is a duality between the idea of descriptions and the idea of the classes of objects to which they apply. In making use of these frames, we will be specifying and modifying descriptions, not dealing with the sets of objects (mental or physical). Thus we will use the notion that a general description can be *further specified* to any one of a number of more specific ones. At the bottom we have descriptions which apply to unique objects in the system's model of the world. In attaching particular properties or facts to a node of this hierarchy, we are saying "Anything to which the description at this node applies also has these additional properties."

This operation of applying classifications is one of the basic modes of reasoning. We decide on the basis of partial evidence that some particular object with which we are concerned belongs to a known class (i.e., there is a particular frame for it in our hierarchy). On the basis of that decision, we can apply a whole set of additional knowledge associated with that frame. We can use the frame to guide our search for the specific facts associated with the object, or to make assumptions about things that must be true of it without checking specifically. [Minsky (1975) has an extended discussion of this vital aspect of frames as does Kuipers, Chapter 6.].

This type of reasoning can be extended to handle things more like analogy. In attempting to apply a full description to an object which would not normally be in

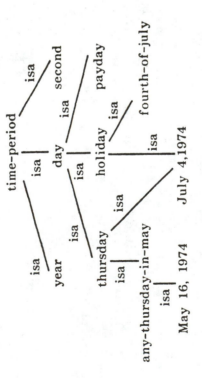

Fig. 1. A generalization hierarchy.

It is clear that this cannot be a simple tree, since often two different generalizations apply to the same specific concept. *July 4, 1974* is both a *fourth-of-july* and a *Thursday.* The use of this hierarchy is primarily through *inheritance of properties* Any property true of a concept in the hierarchy is implicitly true of anything linked below it, unless explicitly contradicted at the lower level. This is an old idea, to be seen, for example, in the work of Raphael and Quillian (in Minsky, 1968). At times it has been used to cover too much; however, as one of many deductive mechanisms, it is particularly efficient and intuitively reasonable. Again, many issues can be raised about the problem of "multiple isa links". If two generalizations apply, how do we choose the appropriate one to look for the properties we want, and how do we resolve

the corresponding class, the frame focuses our attention on those particular properties or facts which are applicable, and those which are contradictory.

C. Important Elements

What then are the elements attached to a description? In a simple predicate scheme, our classifications correspond to the set of predicates. All axioms (or clauses) containing a predicate are attached implicitly by the fact that they contain the symbol. Any statement which contains the predicate $day(x)$ says something about the concept *day*. In a semantic net system, the attachments are explicit, and essentially constitute all the links from the concept to anything else. The frame idea adds an important additional element to this -- the idea of *importance or centrality*. For each frame, there is a set of other frames marked as *important elements* having a specific relation to it. These are what Minsky (1975) calls "slots", Newell calls "components of the beta-structure", etc. The details of how these are determined and treated is probably the key area of frame theory, and the one on which there is the least agreement. Again with the warning that this oversimplification does not represent anyone's full views (including mine), I will pare away most of the interesting problems and go on a set of intuitive but unexplored assumptions for this particular case.

Associated with the frame for *day*, the important elements (or *IMPS*) might be, for example, *year, month, day-numbers, day-of-week, sequence-number* and *ASCII-form*. Immediately we note that the idea of important elements must be sensitive to what we are doing. The idea of *day* would have very different elements if we were thinking of it as a typical sequence of events for a person (getting up, going to work,....), as an astronomical phenomenon (period of rotation, orientation of axis,...), as a set of natural events (sunrise,...sunset, night), etc. We need separate frames for things like *day viewed as a calendar object, day viewed as an event sequence*, etc. Clearly more mechanism is needed to explain the connections between these (how do they relate in more ways than the fact they use the same

word), and the ability to choose the appropriate one for a given context. The idea of attaching IMPs to frames is not intended to avoid the more usual types of deduction and association, but to augment it by providing some kind of formalism for talking about the importance of certain ideas and relations with regard to a central concept (frame) within a context.

TABLE I.
Descriptions of the IMPs for "day"

IMP	DESCRIPTION
Year	Integer
Month	Month-name
Day-number	(Integer range (interval min 1 max 31))
Day-of-week	Weekday-name
Sequence-number	Integer
ASCII-form	(Integer
	length 6
	structure (concatenated-repetition
	element (integer length 2)
	number 3)))

When we further specify a frame (that is, move down the generalization hierarchy) we also further specify the IMPs that go with it. This makes sense only if we think of each IMP as being another frame (which in turn fits into the hierarchy, and so on recursively). Thus the IMPs associated with *day* might be initially filled by the descriptions of Table I. These of course imply a much more extended set of frames to cover things like "integer", "string", "6", the relation "length", etc. This knowledge will be common to many of the knowledge domains represented in a computer system, and one of the basic prejudices of this approach is that in looking at the knowledge of any part of the system we must do it in terms of its dependency on other parts. Our world knowledge is all tied together, and in any particular area we make use of our more general concepts. We have adopted a simple notation in which a frame is given by putting the name of its generalization (the thing to which it has an *isa* link) followed by a list of IMP names and their contents. If the appropriate frame is a simple named one, whose IMPS are not further specified, that name is used directly. This should definitely not be interpreted in the usual LISP sense of atoms and functions, and is also not isomorphic to a kind of straightforward atom-property list notation. Since the problems of all this do not arise at the level of detail used in the discussion below, they will be ignored for now [see Moore & Newell (1973) for a discussion of some of them].

At first glance these descriptions look like traditional computer language data types--integer, string, etc. Indeed, data types are one simple example of a shallow generalization hierarchy, but do not extend nearly far enough. We must be able to provide descriptions at any level of detail rather than choosing from a small finite set of categories. Newer computer-language formalisms are beginning to move in this direction. [See Dahl, Dijkstra, & Hoare, 1972; Cheatham & Wegbreit, 1973.] Also, it should be pointed out that the choice of descriptions is not strictly determined. The fact that the standard ASCII representation of a date is a six-digit integer is simple. But the fact that this integer is a sequence of three two-digit integers is less straightforward. Clearly any six-digit integer can be viewed in this way, but the fact that this description is used explicitly is a statement that this way of looking at it is in fact relevant and important for the purposes of this frame. One of the key points of the notation is that it allows (encourages) us to include facts which although in themselves "epistemological" (to use McCarthy's term) give us heuristic clues by their very presence in the representation. We want to represent not just the bare essence of what we know, but also the scheme of how we think about it. Here we are treading on that middle ground between declarative and procedural knowledge, by selecting our declarative statements with specific concern for how they will be used.

D. Relations between IMPs

We can now express a frame for a particular day as in Table II or a more specific but still general day as in Table III.

TABLE II.
Further Specification of IMPs for "July 4, 1974"

IMP	DESCRIPTION
Year	1974
Month	July
Day-number	4
Day-of-week	
Sequence-number	
ASCII-form	740704

TABLE III.
Further Specification IMPs for "Any Thursday in May"

IMP	DESCRIPTION
Year	
Month	May
Day-number	
Day-of-week	Thursday
Sequence-number	
ASCII-form	

TABLE IV.
Relations between IMPs

IMP	DESCRIPTION
Year	(Integer structure (concatenation first "19" second (! ASCII structure first)))
Month	(Month-name (position-in-list list "January, February,...,December" element (! month) number (! ASCII structure second)))
Day-number	(Integer range (interval min 1 max (! month length)))
Day-of-week	(Weekday-name (position-in-list list "Sunday, Monday,...,Saturday" element (! day-of-week) number (integer range (interval min 1 max 7))) (1-1 correspondence set1 (! day-of-week position-in-list number) set2 (quotient-mod-7 dividend (! sequence-number))))
Sequence-number ASCII-form	Integer (Integer length 6 structure (concatenated repetition element (integer length 2) number 3))

In each case, we have filled in those IMPs which correspond to the "natural" way of describing that day. The *filler* for each IMP is a further specification of the same IMP in the *day* frame. For example, *4* is a further specification of (*integer range (interval min 1 max 31)*) which in turn is a further specification of the general frame for *integer* in the part of the generalization hierarchy dealing with numbers. It is obvious that a more extended formalism is needed to express what we know about dates. The set of IMPs is not independent. Quite the opposite -- it is the interrelation between these important elements that provides most of the useful knowledge connected with the frame. Thus we need a notation which allows specific reference to IMPs associated with a frame. Newell seems to want to avoid this in his beta-structures, but it is not clear that this can be done at all, and certainly not without paying an untenable price in combinatorial explosion. We have chosen to represent an element of a frame as a path of IMP names implicitly beginning with the frame in which the path appears. Once again there are many issues buried here about variable binding, scoping, use of pointers versus names, etc., and the notation is far from settled. A list beginning with a "!" is used to indicate such a reference path. Thus in Table IV we include additional knowledge about our general concept of *day*, such as the fact that the year is actually the digits "19" concatenated with the first two digits of the ASCII form, or that we can expect each month name to have associated with it an IMP named *length*, and that the range of the *day-number* is determined by it. In adding this information, we have used material from still more of the fundamental set of frames used by a problem solver, such as *1-1 correspondence* and *position-in-list*.

E. Procedural Attachment

So far we have been building a declarative data structure. It contains somewhat more information than a simple set of facts, as it has grouped them in terms of importance, and made some of them implicit in the hierarchy. We can deduce that "The ASCII code for July 4 is a six-digit integer." using only the hierarchical link, while deciding "Its final four digits are 0704." would involve more complex computations, using the pointers and IMPs.

At this point we might try to describe a general deductive mechanism which made use of this elaborated structure, taking advantage of the additional information to help guide its computations. It seems possible to do so. The special use of the generalization hierarchy does not really provide any different power than that which could be expressed by a series of simple axioms like

$$\forall(x)\ Holiday(x) \Rightarrow Day(x).$$

There have been various schemes to use groupings of axioms to guide the theorem prover in selecting which to use (although it might be very difficult to prove things formally about its behavior). To the degree such a scheme succeeded, we would have been successful at embedding heuristic knowledge into the declarative structure. I believe, however, that to be useful, a representation must make much more specific contact with procedures.

In one sense, the idea of frame structure provides a framework on which to hang procedures for carrying out specific computations. Table V indicates some of the procedures which might be attached to our frame for *day*. The notations *TO-FILL* and *WHEN-FILLED* correspond loosely to the antecedent/consequent distinction of Planner-like formalisms, and indicate the two fundamental reasons for *triggering* a computation. The mechanism for doing this should, however be more general than the syntactic pattern match which controls the calling of procedures in these languages. Triggering should be based on a more general notion of mapping [see Moore & Newell (1973) and Minsky (1975) for different versions of this.] We will describe later one aspect of how this interacts with the abstraction hierarchy.

The procedures attached to a frame or IMP are not necessarily equivalent to the factual information in the same place. One obvious example is the procedure *use-calendar* associated with *day-of-week*. Our system would have a special algorithm which can take as inputs the day-number, month, and year, and produce as output a week-day. Its steps might be paraphrased as "Find a calendar. Find the page corresponding to *month-name*. Find the number corresponding to *day-number* on the page. Look at

TABLE V.
Possible Procedures to Attach to the "Day" Frame

IMP	PROCEDURE
Year	
Month	
Day-number	WHEN-FILLED
	(CHECK-RELATION day-number, month)
	TO-FILL
	(APPLY calendar-lookup
	TO year, month, day-number)
	(APPLY anchor-date-method
	TO year, month, day-number)
Day-of-week	
Sequence-number	WHEN-FILLED
ASCII-form	(FILL year, month, day-number)

the top of that column." This is the algorithm most of us use most of the time for this computation. It depends on a batch of additional knowledge about calendars and how they are printed, pages, columns, etc., but in using this procedure we do not worry about why calendars work -- only the direct steps needed. At a deep level it is based on the facts listed in Table IV, but that is far removed from the procedure itself. This is an important element of our frame notation -- there is a large degree of redundancy between the procedural and declarative knowledge. Many procedures are specific ways to deduce things which are implicit in the facts. Many facts are essentially statements about what the corresponding procedures do. Neither one is the "fundamental" representation--in any individual case one or the other may be learned first, one or the other may be used in more circumstances.

There may be a number of different procedures attached to any frame or IMP. In this example, we have another procedure for calculating dates, based on the use of an "anchor date". If asked "What day is June 28 this year?" I may perform a computation whose trace would be: "I know that May 12 is a Sunday, so the 19th is a Sunday, the 26th is a Sunday, the 33rd is a Sunday, but May has only 31 days, so June 2 is a Sunday, so the 23rd is, so the 28th is a Friday." This procedure involves a specific algorithm for beginning with some known date, stepping forward by 7 (or multiples of 7), accounting for the number of days in a month, and finally counting backward or forward from a known day of the week. (This last calculation often involves the use of peripheral digital devices (fingers) as well.) This procedure is much more closely tied to facts like the connection of the weekdays to the sequence of day numbers, but is not simply an application of them. The organization of these facts into a specific algorithm represents the addition of relevant knowledge, and its inclusion is not purely redundant. In operating it will also make fairly direct use of facts which are in the simple declarative form, such as that the *length* of May is 31. This new procedure is more generally applicable than the calendar one -- it works when we don't have a calendar at hand, and even works if we say "Imagine that May had 32 days this year. Then what day would June 28 be on?"

We can view the procedures as covering a whole spectrum, from very specific ones (attached to frames near the bottom of the hierarchy) to highly general ones nearer the top.

If we did not have a specific procedure for finding the name of the month from the ASCII representation, we could look at the facts and try applying whatever procedures were connected to the frame for *1-1 correspondence.* In fact we should have a number of different frames which are further specifications of *1-1 correspondence* for different cases. There may be only an abstract mathematical correspondence in which we know only of its existence, but not how to compute the actual correspondence between particular elements; a functional correspondence in which given a domain element we have a direct way of computing a range element, but not vice versa; a testable-pair correspondence in which we can test whether two elements correspond, but have no good way to search for one, etc. This enrichment of the set of terms used in the facts is crucial to integrating them properly with the procedures. The set of notations which

corresponds loosely to the quantifiers and connectives of logic would be much larger and richer, involving a correspondingly expanded set of inference rules. Again, this does not increase the abstract logical power, but allows us to include much more procedurally related information ("What can you do with this fact") into the declarative notation.

The procedural information attached to frames may be very specific, or may be simply a guide of what to do, like the statment (FILL month-name, year, day-number) in Table V. This does not indicate the specific procedures to be used for each of these, but is rather a piece of *control-structure* information. It tells the system that on filling the ASCII representation, it might be a good strategy to do these other computations. The system then must look for procedures attached to those particular IMPs (or generalizations of them) to do the work. One important area to be explored is the way in which this sort of explicit control structure can be included without paying a high price in loss of modularity.

F. Problems of Learning and Modularity

One important aspect of procedural attachment is that it should be dynamic -- the basic ways the system learns are by adding new facts (either from being told or by inducing a generalization), and by creating new procedures based on applying general procedures to specific facts. This is the type of learning described by Sussman (1973). We can think of this work as beginning with a very general set of procedures (near the top of our hierarchy) and a set of specific facts. The outcome is a set of more specific procedures associated with the particular tasks to be done at all levels of the hierarchy. The frame framework does not attack the details of this kind of debugging, but provides a way of representing what is going on and integrating the use of the results. Similarly we can think of the task of *automatic programming* as "pushing procedures down the hierarchy". Given very general procedural knowledge and declarative facts about further specified cases, the task is to write the procedures suited to those cases.

Returning to the issue of modularity, we find that it has been attacked directly by adding a whole new layer of structure. Instead of taking a modular view (each fact is independent) or a highly integrated view (everything knows enough about the others to know how to use them) we have created a set of mechanisms for allowing the writer (whether human or program) to impose a kind of modularity through the decision of what will be included in a frame, and how the procedures will be attached. Modularity then becomes not a fixed decision of system design, but a factor to be manipulated along with all the other issues of representation.

Most of what the system knows is included in *both a modular and an integrated form.* The procedures for learning and debugging continually use general knowledge of programming to take the individual facts and combine them into the specific integrated procedures which do most of the system's deductions. Faced with a problem for which no specific methods are available, or the ones available do not seem to work, the system uses the specific facts with more general methods. There is no sharp division between specific and general methods, since there is an entire hierarchy of methods attached at all levels of the generalization hierarchy for the concepts in the problem domain. The most critical problem for the representation is to make it possible for this shifting between levels of knowledge to occur smoothly, without demanding that the programmer anticipate the particular interactions.

VI. CONCLUSION

This formalism has clearly achieved one goal it set out to do: to blur many of the distinctions such as declarative/procedural, and heuristic/epistemological in the discussion of representations. It is yet to be seen whether this blurring will in the end clarify our vision, or whether it will only lead to badly directed groping. Many more issues are raised by it than are immediately solved, and for each solution there are many more problems. Hopefully this book will be one step on the way to sorting out what is useful and providing a new generation of representational tools for artificial intelligence.

REFERENCES

Bobrow, D. G., & Raphael, B. New programming languages for artificial intelligence research. *Computing Surveys*, 1974, *6(3)*, 153-174.

Dahl, O. J., Dijkstra, E., & Hoare, C. A. R. *Structured programming.* New York: Academic Press, 1972.

Hewitt, C., Bishop, P., & Steiger, R. A universal modular ACTOR formalism for artificial intelligence. *Proceedings of the Third International Joint Conference on Artificial Intelligence*, 1973, 235-245.

McCarthy, J., & Hayes, P. Some philosophical problems from the standpoint of artificial Intelligence. In B. Meltzer and D. Michie (Eds.), *Machine Intelligence 4.* Edinburgh, 1969, 463-502.

Marvin Minsky (Ed.), *Semantic Information Processing.* Cambridge: MIT Press, 1966.

Minsky, M. A framework for representing knowledge. In Winston, P. (Ed.), *The psychology of computer vision.* New York: McGraw-Hill, 1975.

Minsky, M., & Papert. S. Progress Report. Massachusetts Institute of Technology, Artificial Intelligence Laboratory, 1972.

Moore, J., & Newell, A. How can MERLIN understand?. In Gregg (Ed.). *Knowledge and cognition.* Baltimore, Md.: Lawrence Erlbaum Associates, 1973.

Newell, A., & Simon, H. A. *Human Problem Solving.* Prentice Hall, 1972.

Sandewall, E. Conversion of predicate-calculus axioms, viewed as non-deterministic programs, to corresponding deterministic programs. *Proceedings of the Third International Conference on Artificial Intelligence*, 1973, 230-234.

Simon, H. The architecture of complexity. In *The Sciences of the Artificial.* MIT Press, 1969.

Sussman, G., *A computational model of skill acquisition* (MIT-AI TR 297), 1973.

Winograd, T. *Understanding Natural Language*, New York: Academic Press, 1972.

Winograd, T., *Five lectures on artificial intelligence* (Stanford AI-Memo-246). September 1974.

21 / Randall Davis, Bruce Buchanan, and Edward Shortliffe
Production Rules as a Representation for a Knowledge-Based Consultation Program

The MYCIN system—one of the most well-known AI programs, and one of the first expert systems—was built in the mid-1970's to demonstrate the power of knowledge-based systems on "real-world" problems. The system provides consultative advice on diagnosis of (and therapy for) infectious diseases. The authors of this paper found that a production rule representation for the consultant's knowledge of symptoms, diseases, and therapies best met their three stated goals of producing a system that was useful, accommodating a large and changing body of expertise, and participating in an interactive dialog. The paper gives a comprehensive overview of the MYCIN system, including the key notions of confidence factors (although see [Garvey *et al.*, Chapter 27] for some comments on the inadequacy of simple confidence factors) and meta-rules (see [Davis and Buchanan, Chapter 22] for even more detail on this). But the most important contribution of this paper is its analysis of the effect and limitations of simple IF/THEN rules as a representation for knowledge. While not all of the claimed advantages of production rules touted here are as believable as they might originally have been (*e.g.*, the "explanations" taken from tracings are no longer very convincing as realistic explanations), this provides an important model for subsequent discussions of representations useful for expert reasoning. It would be nice to see more analyses of the exact positive and negative effects of representations as used in applications programs. It is important to determine the leverage—and limitations—imposed by different representations on different problems.

Appeared in *Artificial Intelligence* 8(1), 1977, 15–45.

Production Rules as a Representation for a Knowledge-Based Consultation Program [1]

Randall Davis and Bruce Buchanan

Computer Science Department, Stanford University, Stanford, CA 94305, U.S.A.

Edward Shortliffe

Department of Medicine, Stanford University School of Medicine

Recommended by Edward Feigenbaum

ABSTRACT

The MYCIN system has begun to exhibit a high level of performance as a consultant on the difficult task of selecting antibiotic therapy for bacteremia. This report discusses issues of representation and design for the system. We describe the basic task and document the constraints involved in the use of a program as a consultant. The control structure and knowledge representation of the system are examined in this light, and special attention is given to the impact of production rules as a representation. The extent of the domain independence of the approach is also examined.

1. Introduction

Two recent trends in artificial intelligence research have been applications of AI to "real-world" problems, and the incorporation in programs of large amounts of task-specific knowledge. The former is motivated in part by the belief that artificial problems may prove in the long run to be more a diversion than a base to build on, and in part by the belief that the field has developed sufficiently to provide techniques capable of tackling real problems.

The move toward what have been called "knowledge-based" systems represents a change from previous attempts at generalized problem solvers (as, for example, GPS). Earlier work on such systems demonstrated that while there was a large body of useful general purpose techniques (e.g., problem decomposition into subgoals, heuristic search in its many forms), these did not by themselves offer

[1] The work reported here was funded in part by grants from the Bureau of Health Sciences Research and Evaluation Grant HS01544 and NIH Grant GM 29662, by a grant from the Advanced Research Projects Agency under ARPA Contract DAHC15-73-C-8435, and the Medical Scientist Training Program under NIH Grant GM-81922.

sufficient power for high performance. Rather than non-specific problem solving power, knowledge-based systems have emphasized both the accumulation of large amounts of knowledge in a single domain, and the development of domain-specific techniques, in order to develop a high level of expertise.

There are numerous examples of systems embodying both trends, including efforts at symbolic manipulation of algebraic expressions [21], speech understanding [19], chemical inference [3], the creation of computer consultants as interactive advisors for various tasks [14, 29], as well as several others.

In this paper we discuss issues of representation and design for one such knowledge-based application program—the MYCIN system developed over the past three years as an interdisciplinary project at Stanford University, [1] and discussed elsewhere [27–30]. Here we examine in particular how the implementation of various system capabilities is facilitated or inhibited by the use of *production rules* as a knowledge representation. In addition, the limits of applicability of this approach are investigated.

We begin with a review of features which were seen to be essential to any knowledge-based consultation system, and suggest how these imply specific program design criteria. We note also the additional challenges offered by the use of such a system in a medical domain. This is followed by an explanation of the system structure, and its fundamental assumptions. The bulk of the paper is then devoted to a report of our experience with the benefits and drawbacks of production rules as a knowledge representation for a high performance AI program.

2. System Goals

The MYCIN system was developed originally to provide consultative advice on diagnosis of and therapy for infectious diseases—in particular, bacterial infections in the blood.[2] From the start, the project has been shaped by several important constraints. The decision to construct a high performance AI program in the consultant model brought with it several demands. First, the program had to be *useful* if we expected to attract the interest and assistance of experts in the field.

[1] The MYCIN system has been developed by the authors in collaboration with:

Drs Stanley Cohen, Stanton Axline, Frank Rhame, Robert Illa and Rudolpho Chavez-Pardo, all of whom provided medical expertise; William van Melle, who made extensive revisions to the system code for efficiency and to introduce new features; Carlisle Scott, who (with William Clancey) designed and implemented the expanded natural language question answering capabilities.

[2] We have recently begun investigating extending the system. The next medical domain will be the diagnosis and treatment of meningitis infections. This area is sufficiently different to be challenging, and yet similar enough to suggest that some of the automated procedures we have developed may be quite useful. The paper by van Melle [34] describes how an entirely different knowledge base—one concerned with a problem in automobile repair—was inserted into the system, producing a small but fully functional automobile consultant program.

To reflect this broadening of interests, the project has been renamed the Knowledge-Based Consultation Systems Project. MYCIN remains the name of the medical program.

The task area was thus chosen partly because of a demonstrated need: for example, in a recent year one of every four people in the U.S. was given penicillin, and almost 90% of those prescriptions were unnecessary [16]. Problems such as these indicate the need for more (or more accessible) consultants to physicians selecting antimicrobial drugs. Usefulness also implies competence, consistently high performance, and ease of use. If advice is not reliable, or is difficult to obtain, the utility of the program is severely impaired.

A second constraint was the need to design the program to accommodate a *large and changing body of technical knowledge.* It has become clear that large amounts of task-specific knowledge are required for high performance, and that this knowledge base is subject to significant changes over time [3, 13]. Our choice of a production rule representation was significantly influenced by such features of the knowledge base.

A third demand was for a system capable of handling an *interactive dialog,* and one which was not a "black box." This meant that it had to be capable of supplying coherent explanations of its results, rather than simply printing a collection of orders to the user. This was perhaps the major motivation for the selection of a symbolic reasoning paradigm, rather than one which, for example, relied totally on statistics. It meant also that the "flow" of dialog—the order of questions—should make sense to a physician and not be determined by programming considerations. Interactive dialog required, in addition, extensive human engineering features designed to make interaction simple for someone unaccustomed to computers.

The choice of a medical domain brought with it additional demands [28]. Speed, access and ease of use gained additional emphasis, since a physician's time is typically limited. The program also had to fill a need well-recognized by the clinicians who would actually use the system, since the lure of pure technology is usually insufficient. Finally, the program had to be designed with an emphasis on its supportive role as a tool for the physician, rather than as a replacement for his own reasoning process.

Any implementation selected had to meet all these demands. Predictably, some have been met more successfully than others, but all have been important factors in influencing the system's final design.

3. System Overview

3.1. The task

The fundamental task is the selection of therapy for a patient with a bacterial infection. Consultative advice is often required in the hospital because the attending physician may not be an expert in infectious diseases, as for example, when a cardiology patient develops an infection after heart surgery. Time considerations compound the problem. A specimen (of blood, urine, etc.) drawn from a patient may show some evidence of bacterial growth within 12 hours, but 24 to 48 hours (or more) are required for positive identification. The physician must therefore

often decide, in absence of complete information, whether or not to start treatment and what drugs to use if treatment is required. Both of these may be difficult questions.

```
------ PATIENT-1 ------
(1) Patient's name: (first-last)
**FRED SMITH                              {background data}
(2) Sex:
**MALE
(3) Age:
**55
(4) Have you been able to obtain positive cultures from a site at which Fred Smith
    has an infection?
**YES

------ INFECTION-1 ------
(5) What is the infection?
**PRIMARY-BACTEREMIA
(6) Please give the date and approximate time when signs or symptoms of the
    primary-bacteremia (INFECTION-1) first appeared. (mo/da/yr)
**MAY 5, 1975
The most recent positive culture associated with the primary-bacteremia
(INFECTION-1) will be referred to as:
------ CULTURE-1 ------
(7) From what site was the specimen for CULTURE-1 taken?
**BLOOD
(8) Please give the date and time when this blood culture (CULTURE-1)
    was obtained. (mo/da/yr)
**MAY 9, 1975
The first significant organism from this blood culture (CULTURE-1)
will be referred to as:
------ ORGANISM-1 ------
(9) Enter the identity of ORGANISM-1:
**UNKNOWN          {typically the identity is not known and must be inferred}
(10) Is ORGANISM-1 a rod or coccus (etc.):
**ROD
(11) The gram stain of ORGANISM-1:
**GRAMNEG
(12) Have there been POSITIVE cultures from sites which are NOT
     associated with infections about which you are seeking advice?
**NO
(13) Did ORGANISM-1 grow aerobically?
**YES (8)
(14) Did ORGANISM-1 grow anaerobically?
**YES
(15) What is the suspected portal of entry of ORGANISM-1
     into this sterile site?
**GI (6)
     ...
```

{more questions follow, to gather sufficient information to infer possible identities of the infecting organisms}

Fig. 1. Initial segment of a session with the consultation system. User responses are in **boldface** and follow the double asterisks. Italicized comments at the right are not part of the actual dialog.

The task will become clearer by reviewing the initial and final parts of a sample dialog with the MYCIN system, shown in Figs. 1 and 2 (italicized comments at the right are for explanatory purposes, and are not part of the actual dialog). A great deal of attention has been paid to making the interaction easy and natural. Questions have been carefully worded, for example, so as to set up expectations of responses without making them as uninteresting as multiple choice questions.

Currently the dialog is directed primarily by the system—patient information can be entered only by answering each question in turn.

There are several options available to make the interaction more informative. The user can, for instance, ask for a rephrasing of the question or a display of some (or all) of the acceptable responses. If a requested item of information is unavailable, he can respond with **UNKNOWN** (U, or **UNK** for short). The user can also modify any answer which he is unsure of by attaching a number indicating his degree of certainty (as, for example, in questions 13 and 15).

The main purpose of the system is to provide advice, and it does so via the *consultation program* (Fig. 3). In addition to this performance program, there are three adjunct programs that increase system utility and flexibility: (a) a *question answering program* which handles simple natural language inquiries about either the specific consultation, or about the general knowledge base of the program; (b) an *explanation program* for giving reasons why the performance program has requested an item of information or has drawn a particular conclusion; and (c) a *knowledge acquisition program* for extending the knowledge base through a dialog with an expert.

The system is written in INTERLISP, runs on a DEC KI-10 with approximately 130K of nonshared code, and is fast enough to permit convenient real-time

---

My therapy recommendation will be based on the following probable infection(s) and potential causative organism(s):

INFECTION-1 is PRIMARY-BACTEREMIA

⟨Item 1⟩ The identity of ORGANISM-1 may be PSEUDOMONAS-AERUGINOSA
⟨Item 2⟩ The identity of ORGANISM-1 may be KLEBSIELLA-PNEUMONIAE
⟨Item 3⟩ The identity of ORGANISM-1 may be E. COLI
⟨Item 4⟩ The identity of ORGANISM-1 may be BACTEROIDES-FRAGILIS
⟨Item 5⟩ The identity of ORGANISM-1 may be ENTEROBACTER
⟨Item 6⟩ The identity of ORGANISM-1 may be PROTEUS-NON-MIRABILIS

{*possible identities*}

(46) On a scale of 0 to 4, where higher numbers indicate increasing severity how would you rate Fred Smith's degree of sickness?

**3

(47) Does Fred Smith have a clinically significant allergic reaction to any antimicrobial agent?

**NO

(48) Fred Smith's weight in kilograms (or ⟨number⟩ POUNDS):

**70

{*note that 2 drugs cover for 6 potential organisms*}

[Rec 1] My preferred therapy recommendation is as follows:
In order to cover for Items ⟨1 2 3 5 6⟩:
  Give: GENTAMICIN
  Dose: 119 mg (1.7 mg/kg) q8h IV [or IM] for 10 days
  Comments: Modify dose in renal failure
In order to cover for Item ⟨4⟩:
  Give: CLINDAMYCIN
  Dose: 595 mg (8.5 mg/kg) q6h IV [or IM] for 14 days
  Comments: If diarrhea or other GI symptoms develop, patient should be evaluated for possible pseudomembranous colitis.

Do you wish to see the next choice therapy?

**Y

Which, if any, of the above drugs do you wish eliminated from consideration?

**CLINDAMYCIN

{*alternative choices are available*}

[Rec 2] Next best therapy recommendation:
In order to cover for Items ⟨2 3 4 5 6⟩:
  Give: CHLORAMPHENICOL
  Dose: 1 gm (15 mg/kg) q6h IV for 14 days
  Comments: Monitor patient's white count
In order to cover for Item ⟨1⟩:
  Give: GENTAMICIN
  Dose: 119 mg (1.7 mg/kg) q8h IV [or IM] for 10 days
  Comments: Modify dose in renal failure

FIG. 2. Final segment of a consultation. Alternative choices for therapies are generated if requested.

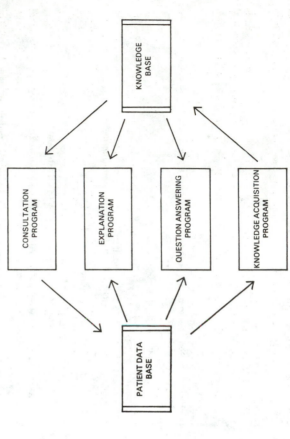

FIG. 3. The six components of the system: four programs, the knowledge base, and the patient data base. All of the system's knowledge of infectious disease is contained within the knowledge base. Data about a specific patient collected during a consultation is stored in the patient data base. Arrows indicate the direction of information flow.

interaction. The consultation program (with the required data structures) requires approximately 50K, the explanation program 10K, the question answering program 15K, the rule acquisition program 20K, and the rules themselves approximately 8K (the remainder includes a dictionary, information on drug properties, and various system utility features).

As described below, each of these four interrelated programs meets one or more of the goals outlined above.

3.2. The rules

The primary source of domain specific knowledge is a set of some 200 production rules, each with a premise and an action (Fig. 4).

```
PREMISE    $AND(SAME CNTXT INFECT PRIMARY-BACTEREMIA)
               (MEMBF CNTXT SITE STERILESITES)
               (SAME CNTXT PORTAL GI)
ACTION     (CONCLUDE CNTXT IDENT BACTEROIDES TALLY .7)
If   (1) the infection is primary-bacteremia, and
     (2) the site of the culture is one of the sterilesites, and
     (3) the suspected portal of entry of the organism is the gastro-
         intestinal tract,
then there is suggestive evidence (.7) that the identity of the organism is bacteroides.
```

Fig. 4. A rule from the knowledge base. $AND and $OR are the multivalued analogues of the standard Boolean AND and OR.

The premise is a Boolean combination of predicate functions on associative triples. Thus each clause of a premise has the following four components:

⟨predicate function⟩ ⟨object⟩ ⟨attribute⟩ ⟨value⟩

There is a standardized set of 24 predicate functions (e.g. SAME, KNOWN, DEFINITE), some 80 attributes (e.g. IDENTITY, SITE, SENSITIVITY), and 11 objects (e.g. ORGANISM, CULTURE, DRUG), currently available for use as primitives in constructing rules. The premise is always a conjunction of clauses, but may contain arbitrarily complex conjunctions or disjunctions nested within each clause. Instead of writing rules whose premise would be a disjunction of clauses, we write a separate rule for each clause. The action part indicates one or more conclusions which can be drawn if the premises are satisfied; hence the rules are (currently) purely inferential in character.

It is intended that each rule embody a single, modular chunk of knowledge, and state explicitly in the premise all necessary context. Since the rule uses a vocabulary of concepts common to the domain, it forms, by itself, a comprehensible statement of some piece of domain knowledge. As will become clear, this characteristic is useful in many ways.

Each rule is, as is evident, highly stylized, with the IF/THEN format and the specified set of available primitives. While the LISP form of each is executable code

(and, in fact, the premise is simply EVALuated by LISP to test its truth, and the action EVALuated to make its conclusions), this tightly structured form makes possible the examination of the rules by other parts of the system. This in turn leads to some important capabilities, to be described below. For example, the internal form can be automatically translated into readable English, as shown in Fig. 4.

Despite this strong stylization, we have not found the format restrictive. This is evidenced by the fact that of nearly 200 rules on a variety of topics, only 8 employ any significant variations. The limitations that do arise are discussed in Section 6.1.2.

3.3. Judgmental knowledge

Since we want to deal with real-world domains in which reasoning is often judgmental and inexact, we require some mechanism for being able to say that "A suggests B", or "C and D tend to rule out E." The numbers used to indicate the strength of a rule (e.g., the .7 in Fig. 4) have been termed Certainty Factors (CFs). The methods for combining CFs are embodied in a model of approximate implication. Note that while these are derived from and are related to probabilities, they are distinctly different (for a detailed review of the concept, see [30]). For the rule in Fig. 4, then, the evidence is strongly indicative (.7 out of 1), but not absolutely certain. Evidence confirming an hypothesis is collected separately from that which disconfirms it, and the truth of the hypothesis at any time is the algebraic sum of the current evidence for and against it. This is an important aspect of the truth model, since it makes plausible the simultaneous existence of evidence in favor and against the same hypothesis. We believe this is an important characteristic of any model of inexact reasoning.

Facts about the world are represented as 4-tuples, with an associative triple and its current CF (Fig. 5). Positive CF's indicate a predominance of evidence confirming an hypothesis, negative CFs indicate a predominance of disconfirming evidence.

```
(SITE CULTURE-1 BLOOD 1.0)
(IDENT ORGANISM-2 KLEBSIELLA .25)
(IDENT ORGANISM-2 E.COLI .73)
(SENSITIVS ORGANISM-1 PENICILLIN −1.0)
```

Fig. 5. Samples of information in the patient data base during a consultation.

Note that the truth model permits the coexistence of several plausible values for a single clinical parameter, if they are suggested by the evidence. Thus, for example, after attempting to deduce the identity of an organism, the system may have concluded (correctly) that there is evidence that the identity is E. coli and evidence that it is Klebsiella, despite the fact that they are mutually exclusive possibilities. As a result of the program's medical origins, we also refer to the attribute part of the triple as 'clinical parameter', and use the two terms interchangeably here. The object part (e.g., CULTURE-1, ORGANISM-2) is referred to as a context. This term was chosen to emphasize their dual role as both part of the associative triple and as a mechanism for establishing scope of variable bindings. As explained below, the contexts are organized during a consultation into a tree structure whose function is similar to those found in 'alternate world' mechanisms of languages like QA4.

3.4. Control structure

The rules are invoked in a backward unwinding scheme that produces a depth-first search of an AND/OR goal tree (and hence is similar in some respects to PLANNER's consequent theorems): given a goal to establish, we retrieve the (pre-computed) list of all rules whose conclusions bear on the goal. The premise of each is evaluated, with each predicate function returning a number between −1 and 1. $AND (the multivalued analogue of the Boolean AND) performs a minimization operation, and $OR (similar) does a maximization.[3] For rules whose premise evaluates successfully (i.e. greater than .2, an empirical threshold), the action part is evaluated, and the conclusion made with a certainty which is

$$\langle premise\text{-}value \rangle * \langle certainty\ factor \rangle$$

Those which evaluate unsuccessfully are bypassed, while a clause whose truth cannot be determined from current information causes a new subgoal to be set up, and the process recurs. Note that 'evaluating' here means simply invoking the LISP EVAL function—there is no additional rule interpreter necessary, since $AND, $OR, and the predicate functions are all implemented as LISP functions.

3.4.1. Variations from the standard depth-first search

Unlike PLANNER, however, the subgoal which is set up is a generalized form of the original goal. If, for example, the unknown clause is 'the identity of the organism is E. coli', the subgoal which is set up is 'determine the identity of the organism.' The new subgoal is therefore always of the form 'determine the value of ⟨attribute⟩' rather than 'determine whether the ⟨attribute⟩ is equal to ⟨value⟩'. By setting up the generalized goal of collecting all evidence about a clinical parameter, the program effectively exhausts each subject as it is encountered, and thus tends to group together all questions about a given topic. This results in a system which displays a much more focussed, methodical approach to the task, which is a distinct advantage where human engineering considerations are important. The cost is the effort of deducing or collecting information which is not strictly necessary. However, since this occurs rarely—only when the ⟨attribute⟩ can be deduced with certainty to be the ⟨value⟩ named in the original goal—we have not found this to be a problem in practice.

A second deviation from the standard rule unwinding approach is that every rule relevant to a goal is used. The premise of each rule is evaluated, and if successful, its conclusion is invoked. This continues until all relevant rules have all been used, or one of them has given the result with certainty. This use of all rules is in part an aspect of the model of judgmental reasoning and the approximate implication character of rules—unless a result is obtained with certainty, we should be careful to collect all positive and negative evidence. It is also appropriate to the system's current domain of application, clinical medicine, where a conservative strategy of considering all possibilities and weighing all the evidence is preferred.

If, after trying all relevant rules (referred to as 'tracing' the subgoal), the total weight of the evidence about a hypothesis falls between −.2 and .2 (again, empirically determined), the answer is regarded as still unknown. This may happen if no rule were applicable, the applicable rules were too weak, the effects of several rules offset each other, or if there were no rules for this subgoal at all. In any of these cases, when the system is unable to deduce the answer, it asks the user for the value (using a phrase which is stored along with the attribute itself). Since the legal values for each attribute are also stored with it, the validity (or spelling) of the user's response is easily checked. (This also makes possible a display of acceptable answers in response to a '?' answer from the user.)

The strategy of always attempting to deduce the value of a subgoal, and asking only when that fails, would insure the minimum number of questions. It would also mean, however, that work might be expended searching for a subgoal, arriving perhaps at a less than definite answer, when the user already knew the answer with certainty. In response to this, some of the attributes have been labelled as LABDATA, indicating that they represent quantities which are often available as quantitative results of laboratory tests. In this case the deduce-then-ask procedure is reversed, and the system will attempt to deduce the answer only if the user cannot supply it. Given a desire to minimize both tree search and the number of questions asked, there is no guaranteed optimal solution to the problem of deciding when to ask for information, and when to try to deduce it. But the LABDATA—clinical data distinction used here has performed quite well, and seems to embody a very appropriate criterion.

Three other recent additions to the tree search procedure have helped improve performance. First, before the entire list of rules for a subgoal is retrieved, the system attempts to find a sequence of rules which would establish the goal with certainty, based only on what is currently known. Since this is a search for a sequence of rules with CF = 1, we have termed the result a *unity path*. Besides efficiency considerations, this process offers the advantage of allowing the system

---

[3] Note that, unlike standard probability theory, $AND does not involve any multiplication over its arguments. Since CFs are not probabilities, there is no a priori reason why a product should be a reasonable number. There is, moreover, a long-standing convention in work with multi-valued logics which interprets AND as *min* and OR as *max* [20]. It is based primarily on intuitive grounds: if a conclusion requires all of its antecedents to be true, then it is a relatively conservative strategy to use the smallest of the antecedent values as the value of the premise. Similarly, if any one of the antecedent clauses justifies the conclusion, we are safe in taking the maximum value.

function call. The previewing mechanism uses the templates to extract the attribute from the clause in question, and can then determine whether or not it has been traced.

There are two points of interest here—first, part of the system is 'reading' the code (the rules) being executed by another part; and second, this reading is guided by the information carried in components of the rules themselves. The ability to 'read' the code could have been accomplished by requiring all predicate functions to use the same format, but this is obviously awkward. By allowing each function to describe the format of its own calls, we permit code which is stylized without being constrained to a single form, and hence is flexible and much easier to use. We require only that each form be expressible in a template built from the current set of template primitives (e.g., PARM, VALUE, etc.). This approach also insures that the capability will persist in the face of future additions to the system. The result is one example of the general idea of giving the system access to, and an "understanding" of its own representations. This idea has been used and discussed extensively in [7].

We have also implemented antecedent-style rules. These are rules which are invoked if a conclusion is made which matches their premise condition. They are currently limited to common-sense deductions (i.e. CF = 1), and exist primarily to improve system efficiency. Thus, for example, if the user responds to the question of organism identity with an answer of which he is certain, there is an antecedent rule which will deduce the organism gramstain and morphology. This saves the trouble of deducing these answers later via the subgoal mechanism described above.

3.5. Meta-rules

With the system's current collection of 200 rules, exhaustive invocation of rules would be quite feasible, since the maximum number of rules for a single subgoal is about 30. We are aware, however, of the problems that may occur if and when the collection grows substantially larger. It was partly in response to this that we developed an alternative to exhaustive invocation by implementing the concept of *meta-rules*. These are strategy rules which suggest the best approach to a given subgoal. They have the same format as the clinical rules (Fig. 7), but can indicate that certain clinical rules should be tried first, last, before others, or not at all.

PREMISE: ($AND (MEMBF SITE CNTXT NONSTERILESITES)
     (THEREARE OBJRULES(MENTIONS CNTXT PREMISE SAMEBUG))
     (CONCLIST CNTXT UTILITY YES TALLY –1.0)

ACTION:
If (1) the site of the culture is one of the nonsterilesites, and
  (2) there are rules which mention in their premise a previous
    organism which may be the same as the current organism
Then it is definite (1.0) that each of them is not going to be useful.

Fig. 7. A meta-rule. A previous infection which has been cured (temporarily) may reoccur. Thus one of the ways to deduce the identity of the current organism is by reference to previous infections. However, this method is not valid if the current infection was cultured from one of the non-sterile culture sites. Thus this meta-rule says, in effect, *if the current culture is from a non-sterile site, don't bother trying to deduce the current organisms identity from identities of previous organisms.*

---

to make 'common sense' deductions with a minimum of effort (rules with CF = 1 are largely definitional). Since it also helps minimize the number of questions, this check is performed even before asking about LABDATA type attributes as well. Because there are few such rules in the system, the search is typically very brief.

Second, a straightforward bookkeeping mechanism notes the rules that have failed previously, and avoids ever trying to reevaluate any of them. (Recall that a rule may have more than one conclusion, may conclude about more than a single attribute, and hence may get retrieved more than once).

Finally, we have implemented a partial evaluation of rule premises. Since many attributes are found in several rules, the value of one clause (perhaps the last) in a premise may already have been established, even while the rest are still unknown. If this clause alone would make the premise false, there is clearly no reason to do all the search necessary to try to establish the others. Each premise is thus 'previewed' by evaluating it on the basis of currently available information. This produces a Boolean combination of TRUEs, FALSEs, and UNKNOWNs, and straightforward simplification (e.g. $F \wedge U \equiv F$) indicates whether the rule is guaranteed to fail.

3.4.2. Templates

The partial evaluation is implemented in a way which suggests the utility of stylized coding in the rules. It also forms an example of what was alluded to earlier, where it was noted that the rules may be examined by various elements of the system, as well as executed. We require a way to tell if any clause in the premise is known to be false. We cannot simply EVAL each individually, since a subgoal which had never been traced before would send the system off on its recursive search.

However, if we can establish which attribute is referenced by the clause, it is possible to determine (by reference to internal flags) whether it has been traced previously. If so, the clause can be EVALed to obtain the value. A template (Fig. 6) associated with each predicate function makes this possible.

Function	Template	Sample function call
SAME	(SAME CNTXT PARM VALUE)	(SAME CNTXT SITE BLOOD)

Fig. 6. PARM is shorthand for clinical parameter (attribute); VALUE is the corresponding value; CNTXT is a free variable which references the context in which the rule is invoked.

The template indicates the generic type and order of arguments to the predicate function, much like a simplified procedure declaration. It is not itself a piece of code, but is simply a list structure of the sort shown above, and indicates the appearance of an interpreted call to the predicate function. Since rules are kept in interpreted form (as shown in Fig. 4), the template can be used as a guide to dissect a rule. This is done by retrieving the template for the predicate function found in each clause, and then using that as a guide to examining the clause. In the case of the function SAME, for instance, the template indicates that the clinical parameter (PARM) is the third element of the list structure which comprises the

Thus before processing the entire list of rules applicable to any subgoal, the meta-rules for that subgoal are evaluated. They may rearrange or shorten the list, effectively ordering the search or pruning the tree. By making them specific to a given subgoal, we can specify precise heuristics without imposing any extra overhead in the tracing of other subgoals.

Note, however, that there is no reason to stop at one level of meta-rules. We can generalize this process so that, before invoking any list of rules, we check for the existence of rules of the next higher order to use in pruning or rearranging the first list. Thus, while meta-rules are strategies for selecting clinical rules, second order meta-rules would contain information about which strategy to try, third order rules would suggest criteria for deciding how to choose a strategy, etc. These higher order rules represent a search by the system through "strategy space", and appear to be powerful constraints on the search process at lower levels. (We have not yet encountered higher order meta-rules in practice, but neither have we actively sought them).

Note also that since the system's rule unwinding may be viewed as tree search, we have the appearance of a search through a tree with the interesting property that each branch point contains information on the best path to take next. Since the meta-rules can be judgmental, there exists the capability of writing numerous, perhaps conflicting heuristics, and having their combined judgment suggest the best path. Finally, since meta-rules refer to the clinical rules by their content rather than by name, the method automatically adjusts to the addition or deletion of clinical rules, as well as modifications to any of them.

The capability of meta-rules to order or prune the search tree has proved to be useful in dealing with another variety of knowledge as well. For the sake of human engineering, for example, it makes good sense to ask the user first about the positive cultures (those showing bacterial growth), before asking about negative cultures. Formerly, this design choice was embedded in the ordering of a list buried in the system code. Yet it can be stated quite easily and explicitly in a meta-rule, yielding the significant advantages of making it both readily explainable and modifiable. Meta-rules have thus proved capable of expressing a limited subset of the knowledge formerly embedded in the control structure code of the system.

Meta-rules may also be used to control antecedent rule invocation. Thus we can write strategies which control the depth and breadth of conclusions drawn by the system in response to a new piece of information.

A detailed overview of all of these mechanisms is included in the Appendix, and indicates the way they function together to insure an efficient search for each subgoal.

The final aspect of the control structure is the tree of contexts (recall the dual meaning of the term, Section 3.3), constructed dynamically from a fixed hierarchy as the consultation proceeds (Fig. 8). This serves several purposes. First, bindings of free variables in a rule are established by the context in which the rule is invoked, with the standard access to contexts which are its ancestors. Second, since this

tree is intended to reflect the relationships of objects in the domain, it helps structure the consultation in ways familiar to the user. In the current domain, a patient has one or more infections, each of which may have one or more associated cultures, each of which in turn may have one or more organisms growing in it, and so on. Finally, we have found it useful to select one or more of the attributes of each context type and establish these as its MAINPROPS, or primary properties. Each time a new context of that type is sprouted, these MAINPROPS are automatically traced.[4] Since many of them are LABDATA-type attributes, the effect is to begin each new context with a set of standard questions appropriate to that context, which serve to 'set the stage' for subsequent questions. This has proved to be a very useful human engineering feature in a domain which has evolved a heavily stylized format for the presentation of information.

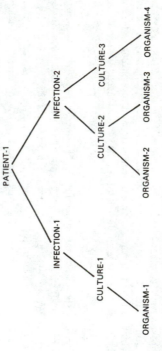

FIG. 8. A sample of the contexts which may be sprouted during a consultation.

4. Relation to Other Work

We outline briefly in this section a few programs that relate to various aspects of our work. Some of these have provided the intellectual basis from which the present system evolved, others have employed techniques which are similar, while still others have attempted to solve closely related problems. Space limitations preclude detailed comparisons, but we indicate some of the more important distinctions and similarities.

There have been a large number of attempts to aid medical decision making (see [27] for an extensive review). The basis for some programs has been simple algorithmic processes, often implemented as decision trees ([23, 37]), or more complex control structures in systems tailored to specific disorders [2]. Many have based their diagnostic capabilities on variations of Bayes' theorem [10, 36], or on techniques derived from utility theory of operations research [11]. Models of the patient or disease process have been used successfully in [32, 25 and 17]. A few

[4] As a result of this, the control flow is actually slightly more complicated than a pure AND/OR goal tree, and the flowchart in the appendix is correspondingly more complex.

recent efforts have been based on some form of symbolic reasoning. In particular, the glaucoma diagnosis system described in [17] and the diagnosis system of [26] can also be viewed as rule-based.

Carbonell's work [5] represents an early attempt to make uncertain inferences in a domain of concepts that are strongly linked, much as MYCIN's are. Although the purpose of Carbonell's system was computer-aided instruction rather than consultation, much of our initial design was influenced by his semantic net model.

The basic production rule methodology has been applied in many different contexts, in attempts to solve a wide range of problems (see, for example, [6] for an overview). The most directly relevant of these is the DENDRAL system [3], which has achieved a high level of performance on the task of mass spectrum analysis. Much of the initial design of MYCIN was influenced by the experience gained in building and using the DENDRAL system, which in turn was based in part on [38].

There have been numerous attempts to create models of inexact reasoning. Among the more recent is [18], which reports on the implementation of a language to facilitate fuzzy reasoning. It deals with many of the same issues of reasoning under uncertainty that are detailed in [30].

The approach to natural language used in our system has been thus far quite elementary, primarily keyword-based. Some of the work reported in [4] suggested to us initially that this might be a sufficiently powerful approach for our purposes. This has proven generally true because the technical language of this domain contains relatively few ambiguous words.

The chess playing program of [41] employs a knowledge representation which is functionally quite close to ours. The knowledge base of that system consists of small sequences of code which recognize patterns of pieces, and then conclude (with a variable weighting factor) the value of obtaining that configuration. They report quite favorably on the ease of augmenting a knowledge base organized along these lines.

The natural language understanding system of [39] had some basic explanation capabilities similar to those described here, and could discuss its actions and plans.

As we have noted above, and will explore further below, part of our work has been involved in making it possible for the system to understand its own operation. Many of the explanation capabilities were designed and implemented with this in mind, and it has significantly influenced design of the knowledge acquisition system as well. These efforts are related in a general way to the long sequence of attempts to build program-understanding systems. Such efforts have been motivated by, among other things, the desire to prove correctness of programs (as in [35] or [22]), and as a basis for automatic programming (as in [13]). Most of these systems attempt to assign meaning to the code of some standard programming language like LISP, or ALGOL. Our attempts have been oriented toward supplying meaning for the terms used in MYCIN's production rules (such as SAME). The task of program-understanding is made easier by approaching it at this higher conceptual level, and the result is correspondingly less powerful. We cannot for instance

prove that the implementation of SAME is correct. We can, however, employ the representation of meaning in other useful ways. It forms, for example, the basis for much of the knowledge acquisition program (see Section 6.3), and permits the explanation program to be precise in explaining the system's actions (see [7] for details). A similar sort of high level approach has been explored by Hewitt in his proposed INTENDER system [15].

Finally, similar efforts at computer-based consultants have recently been developed in different domains. The work detailed in [24] and [14] has explored the use of a consultation system similar to the one described here, as part of an integrated vision, manipulation, and problem solving system. Recent work on an intelligent terminal system [1] has been based in part on a formalism which grew out of early experience with the MYCIN system.

5. Fundamental Assumptions

We attempt here to examine some of the assumptions which are explicit and implicit in our use of production rules. This will help to suggest the range of application for these techniques, and indicate some of their strengths and limitations. Because such a listing is potentially open-ended, we include here the assumptions essential to the approach used in MYCIN, but which are not necessarily applicable to every interactive program.

There are several assumptions implicit in both the character of the rules and the ways in which they are used. First, it must be possible to write such judgmental rules. Not every domain will support this. It appears to require a field which has attained a certain level of formalization, which includes perhaps a generally recognized set of primitives and a minimal understanding of basic processes. It does not seem to extend to one which has achieved a thorough, highly formalized level, however. Assigning certainty factors to a rule should thus be a reasonable task whose results would be repeatable, but not a trivial one in which all CFs were 1.

Second, we require a domain in which there is a limited sort of interaction between conceptual primitives. Our experience has suggested that a rule with more than about six clauses in the premise becomes conceptually unwieldy. The number of factors interacting in a premise to trigger an action therefore has a practical (but no theoretical) upper limit. Also, the AND/OR goal tree mechanism requires that the clauses of a rule premise can be set up as non-conflicting subgoals for the purposes of establishing each of them (just as in robot problem solving; see [9] and the comment on side effects in [31]). Failure of this criterion causes results which depend on the order in which evidence is collected. We are thus making fundamental assumptions concerning two forms of interaction—we assume (a) that only a small number of factors (about 6) must be considered simultaneously to trigger an action; and (b) that the presence or absence of each of those factors can be established without adverse effect on the others.

Also, certain characteristics of the domain will influence the continued utility of this approach as the knowledge base of rules grows. Where there are a limited number of attributes for a given object, the growth in the number of rules in the knowledge base will not produce an exponential growth in search time for the consultation system. Thus as newly acquired rules begin to reference only established attributes, use of these rules in a consultation will not produce further branching, since the attributes mentioned in their premises will have already been traced. In addition, we assume that large numbers of antecedent rules will not be necessary, thus avoiding very long chains of 'forward' deductions.

There are essential assumptions as well in the use of this formalism as the basis for an interactive system. First, our explanation capabilities (reviewed below) rest on the assumption that display of either a rule or some segment of the control flow is a reasonable explanation of system behavior. Second, much of the approach to rule acquisition is predicated on the assumption that experts can be "debriefed", that is, they can recognize and then formalize chunks of their own knowledge and express them as rules. Third, the IF/THEN format of rules must be sufficiently simple, expressive, and intuitive that it can provide a useful language for expressing such formalizations. Finally, the system's mode of reasoning (a simple *modus ponens* chaining) must appear natural enough that a user can readily follow along. We offer below (Section 6) arguments that all these are plausible assumptions.

There is an important assumption, too, in the development of a system for use by two classes of users. Since the domain experts who educate the system so strongly influence its conceptual primitives, vocabulary, and knowledge base, we must be sure that the naive users who come for advice speak the same language.

The approach we describe does not, therefore, seem well suited to domains requiring a great deal of complex interaction between goals, or those for which it is difficult to compose sound judgmental rules. As a general indication of potentially useful applications, we have found that cognitive tasks are good candidates. In one such domain, antibiotic therapy selection, we have met with encouraging success.

6. Production Rules as a Knowledge Representation

In the introduction to this report we outlined three design goals for the system we are developing: usefulness (including competence), maintenance of an evolutionary knowledge base, and support of an interactive consultation. Our experience has suggested that production rules offer a knowledge representation that greatly facilitates the accomplishment of these goals. Such rules are straightforward enough to make feasible many interesting features beyond performance, yet powerful enough to supply significant problem solving capabilities. Among the features discussed below are the ability for explanation of system performance, and acquisition of new rules, as well as the general 'understanding' by the system

of its own knowledge base. In each case we indicate the current performance levels of the system, and evaluate the role of production rules in helping to achieve this performance.

6.1. Competence

The competence of the system has been evaluated in two studies in the past few years. In mid-1974, a semi-formal study was undertaken, employing five infectious disease experts not associated with the project. They were asked to evaluate the system's performance on fifteen cases of bacteremia selected from current inpatients. We evaluated such parameters as the presence of extraneous questions, the absence of important ones, the system's ability to infer the identity of organisms, and its ability to select appropriate therapy. The principal problem discovered was an insufficient number of rules concerned with evaluating the severity of a patient's illness. Nevertheless, the experts approved of MYCIN's therapy recommendation in 72% of the evaluations. (There were also considerable differences of opinion regarding the best therapy as selected by the experts themselves.)

A more formal study is currently under way. Building on our experience gained in 1974, we designed a more extensive questionnaire and prepared detailed background information on a new set of fifteen patients. These were sent to five experts associated with a local hospital, and to five others across the country. This will allow us to evaluate performance, and in addition measure the extent to which the system's knowledge base reflects regional trends in patient care.

6.1.1. *Advantages of production rules*

Recent problem solving efforts in AI have made it clear that high performance of a system is often strongly correlated with the depth and breadth of the knowledge base. Hence, the task of accumulation and management of a large and evolving knowledge base soon poses problems which dominate those encountered in the initial phases of knowledge base construction. Our experience suggests that giving the system itself the ability to examine and manipulate its knowledge base provides some capabilities for confronting these problems. These are discussed in subsequent sections.

The selection of production rules as a knowledge representation is in part a response to this fact. One view of a production rule is as a modular segment of code [40], which is heavily stylized [38, 3]. Each of MYCIN's rules is, as noted, a simple conditional statement: the premise is constrained to be a Boolean expression, the action contains one or more conclusions, and each is completely modular and independent of the others. Such *modular, stylized coding* is an important factor in building a system that is to achieve a high level of competence.

For example, any stylized code is easier to examine. This is used in several ways in the system. Initial integration of new rules into the knowledge base can be automated, since their premise and action parts can be systematically scanned, and the rules can then be added to the appropriate internal lists. In the question answering system, inquiries of the form 'Do you recommend clindamycin for bacteroides?' can be answered by retrieving rules whose premise and action contain the relevant items. Similarly, the detection of straightforward cases of contradiction and subsumption is made possible by the ability to examine rule contents. Stylized code also makes feasible the direct manipulation of individual rules, facilitating automatic correction of such undesirable interactions.

The benefits of modularized code are well understood. Especially significant in this case are the ease of adding new rules and the relatively uncomplicated control structure which the modular rules permit. Since rules are retrieved because they are relevant to a specific goal (i.e., they mention that goal in their action part), the addition of a new rule requires only that it be added to the appropriate internal list according to the clinical parameters found in its action. A straightforward depth first search (the result of the backward chaining of rules) is made possible by the lack of interactions among rules.

These benefits are common to stylized code of any form. Stylization in the form of production rules in particular has proved to be a useful formalism for several reasons. In the domain of deductive problems, especially, it has proven to be a natural way of expressing knowledge. It also supplies a clear and convenient way of expressing modular chunks of knowledge, since all necessary context is stated explicitly in the premise. This in turn makes it easier to insure proper retrieval and use of each rule. Finally, in common with similar formalisms, one rule never directly calls another. This is a significant advantage in integrating a new rule into the system—it can simply be 'added to the pot' and no other rule need be changed to insure that it is called (compare this with the addition of a new procedure to a typical ALGOL-type program).

6.1.2. Shortcomings of production rules

Stylization and modularity also result in certain shortcomings, however. It is, of course, somewhat harder to express a given piece of knowledge if it must be put into a predetermined format. The intent of a few of the rules in our system are thus less than obvious to the naive user even when translated into English. The requirement of modularity (along with the uniformity of the knowledge base), means all necessary contextual information must be stated explicitly in the premise, and this at times leads to rules which have awkwardly long and complicated premises.

Another shortcoming in the formalism arises in part from the backward chaining control structure. It is not always easy to map a sequence of desired actions or tests into a set of production rules whose goal-directed invocation will provide that sequence. Thus, while the system's performance is reassuringly similar to some human reasoning behavior, the creation of appropriate rules which result in such behavior is at times non-trivial. This may in fact be due more to programming experience oriented primarily toward ALGOL-like languages, rather than any essential characteristic of production rules. After some experience with the system we have improved our skill at 'thinking backward'.

A final shortcoming arises from constraining rule premises to contain "pure" predicates.[5] This forces a pure problem reduction mode in the use of rules: each clause of a premise is set up as an independent goal, and execution of the action should be dependent solely on the success or failure of premise evaluation, without referencing its precise value. It is at times, however, extremely convenient to write what amounts to a 'for each' rule, as in 'for each organism such that . . . conclude . . .'. A few rules of this form are present in the system (including, for example, the meta-rule in Fig. 7), and they are made to appear formally like the rest by allowing the premise to compute a value (the set of items that satisfy the premise), which is passed to the action clause via a global variable. While this has been relatively successful, the violation of the basic formalism results in other difficulties —in particular, in the explanation system, which produces somewhat murky explanations of such rules. We are working toward a cleaner solution of this problem.

6.2. Explanation

Augmentation or modification of any knowledge base is facilitated by the ability to discover what knowledge is currently in the system and how it is used. The system's acceptance (especially to a medical audience) will be strongly dependent upon the extent to which its performance is natural (i.e., human-like) and transparent. Lack of acceptance of some applications programs can be traced to their obscure reasoning mechanisms which leave the user forced to accept or reject advice without a chance to discover its basis. One of our original design criteria, then, was to give the system the ability to provide explanations of its behavior and knowledge. It soon became evident that an approach relying on some form of symbolic reasoning (rather than, for example, statistics) would make this feasible. This was one of the primary reasons behind the choice of the production rule representation, and has continued to influence the program's development.

Our initial efforts at explanation and question-answering were based on three capabilities: (i) display on demand during the consultation the rule currently being invoked, (ii) record rules which were invoked, and after the consultation, be able to associate specific rules with specific events (questions and conclusions) to explain why each of them happened, and (iii) search the knowledge base for a specific type of rule in answer to inquiries of the user. The first of these could be easily implemented via the single-word command format described below.

The latter two were intended for use after the consultation, and hence were provided with a simple natural language front end. Examples are shown in Fig. 9

[5] That is, a predicate that returns a value indicating only success or failure. Since we use a multi-valued logic, the predicate functions in rule premises return a number between 0 and 1. The alternative approach is to allow any non-NIL value to indicate success (e.g., the MEMBER function in LISP).

(additional examples can be found in [29]). Note that the capability for answering questions of type (ii) has been extended to include inquiries about actions the program *failed* to take (example [d], Fig. 9). This is based on the ability of the explanation system to simulate the control structure of the consultation system, and can be extremely useful in deciphering the program's behavior. For questions of type (iii), ([e] in Fig. 9) the search through the knowledge base is directed by a simple parsing of the question into a request for a set of rules, with constraints on premise and/or action contents. The retrieval of relevant rules is guided primarily by pre-established (but automatically generated) lists which indicate premise and action contents.

Some generalization of and extensions to the methodology of (i) and (ii) have been motivated by two shortcomings. Displaying the current rule is not particularly informative if the rule is essentially definitional and hence conceptually trivial. The problem here is the lack of a good gauge for the amount of information in a rule.

Recording individual rule invocations, questions and conclusions is useful, but as a record of individual events, it fails to capture the context and ongoing sequence. It is difficult therefore to explain any event with reference to anything but the specific information recorded with that event.

Two related techniques were developed to solve these problems. First, to provide a metric for the amount of information in a rule, we use (in a very rough analogy with information theory) $(-\log CF)$. Rules which are definitional ($CF = 1$) have by this measure no information, while those which express less obvious implications have progressively more information. The measure is clearly imperfect, since first, CFs are not probabilities, and there is thus no formal justification that $-(\log CF)$ is a meaningful measure. Second, any sophisticated information content measure should factor in the state of the observer's knowledge, since the best explanations are those which are based on an understanding of what the observer fails to comprehend. Despite these shortcomings, however, this heuristic has proven to be quite useful.

To solve the second problem (explaining events in context) the process of recording individual rule invocations has been generalized: all the basic control functions of the system have been augmented to leave behind a history of each of their executions. This internal trace is then read by various parts of the explanation system to provide a complete, in-context explanation of any part of the system's behavior.

Because the consultation process is essentially one of search through an AND/OR goal tree, inquiries during the course of a consultation fall quite naturally into two types: WHY a question was asked, and HOW a conclusion was (or will be) reached. The first of these looks "up" the goal tree, in examining rules which may help achieve a goal. This part of the system's explanation capability can thus be viewed in general as a process of tree traversal. By combining this concept with the information content metric, we make possible explanations in varying levels of detail: the tree may be traversed in steps whose information content size is specified by the user, rather than simply stepping from goal to goal. At the start of the traversal process, "information distance" from the current goal to the top of the tree is normalized to 10. The argument to the WHY command (an integer between one and ten, assumed to be one if absent) is then taken to indicate some part of that distance. Thus, **WHY 3** indicates an explanation which encompasses approximately one-third of the total "conceptual" distance. Repeated WHY questions have the effect of stepping up the goal tree. Examples are shown below; additional examples are found in [7] and [29].

(a) ** HOW DID YOU DECIDE THAT ORGANISM-1 MIGHT BE AN E.COLI ?

I used RULE021 to conclude that the identity of ORGANISM-1 is e.coli. This gave a cumulative CF of (.47).

Then I used RULE084 to conclude that the identity of ORGANISM-1 is e.coli. This gave a cumulative CF of (.55).

Finally, I used RULE003 to conclude that the identity of ORGANISM-1 is e.coli. This gave a cumulative CF of (.74).

(b) ** DID YOU USE RULE 163 TO FIND OUT ANYTHING ABOUT ORGANISM-1 ?

RULE163 was tried in the context of ORGANISM-1, but it failed because it is not true that the patient has had a genito-urinary tract manipulative procedure (clause 3).

(c) ** DID RULE 116 TELL YOU ANYTHING ABOUT INFECTION-1 ?

No. RULE116 would be relevant to the primary-bacteremia when applied to ORGANISM-1.

But clause 2 ("the gram stain of the organism is not known") was already known to be false for ORGANISM-1, so the rule was never tried.

(d) ** WHY DIDN'T YOU CONSIDER STREPTOCOCCUS AS A POSSIBILITY FOR ORGANISM-1 ?

The following rule could have been used to determine that the identity of ORGANISM-1 was streptococcus: RULE033

But clause 2 ("the morphology of the organism is coccus") was already known to be false for ORGANISM-1, so the rule was never tried.

(e) ** DO YOU RECOMMEND CLINDAMYCIN FOR BACTEROIDES ?

Yes.
RULE060
- - - - - - - - - -
If the identity of the organism is bacteroides
Then I recommend therapy be chosen from among the following:
CHLORAMPHENICOL, CLINDAMYCIN, RIFAMPIN, ERYTHROMYCIN, CARBENICILLIN, TETRACYCLINE, LINCOMYCIN

(f) ** IS BLOOD A STERILE SITE ?

Yes, blood is one of those sites that are normally sterile.

(g) ** WHAT ARE THE ORGANISMS ASSOCIATED WITH THE GASTRO-INTESTINAL TRACT ?

The likely pathogens associated with the gastro-intestinal tract are: ENTEROCOCCUS, CLOSTRIDIUM-GANGRENE, BACTEROIDES, KLEBISELLA, PSEUDOMONAS, E.COLI, ENTEROBACTER, PROTEUS.

FIG. 9. Examples of natural language question answering capabilities. Questions [a]-[d] reference a specific consultation, while [e]-[g] are general inquiries answered from the system knowledge base.

Similarly, HOW commands step "down" the tree. This can result in examining either branches which have already been traversed (as in the example below) or those which have yet to be tried (in which case the question becomes 'HOW will you determine . . .').

In this series, how many of the cultures were positive for the e.coli (ORGANISM-1) ?

*WHY   {typical system prompt}

[i.e. WHY is it important to determine the number of cultures which were positive for the organism?]   {request from user to determine motivation for question}

[1.0] This will help to determine whether there is significant disease associated with this occurrence of the organism.   {system's rephrasing of the WHY question, and answer}

It has already been established that
[1.1] the culture was taken from a sterile source
[1.2] the number of cultures in the series is greater than 2
Therefore, if
[1.3] the number of cultures which were positive for ORGANISM-1 is greater than 2
Then there is suggestive evidence (.5) that there is significant disease associated with this occurrence of the e.coli (ORGANISM-1).
[RULE 049]

**WHY   {repeated WHY to determine relevance of previous explanation}

[1.0]WHY is it important to determine if there is significant disease associated with this occurrence of the organism ?]

[2.0] This will help to determine a diagnosis for which the infection should be treated.
It has already been established that
[2.1] the infection is not one of: primary-bacteremia, meningitis
[2.2] for some current culture of the patient it is true that the site of the culture is blood
Therefore, if
[2.3] there is significant disease associated with this occurrence of the organism
Then
it is definite (1.0) that the diagnosis for which the infection should be treated is secondary-bacteremia
[RULE 103]

Fig. 10. Examples of explanation capabilities. User input is in **boldface** and follows the double asterisk. Expansion of each WHY or HOW question (enclosed in brackets) is produced by the system, to be sure the user is aware of the system's interpretation of them.

The system's fundamental approach to explanation is thus to display some recap of its internal actions, a trace of its reasoning. The success of this technique is predicated on the claim that the system's basic approach to the problem is sufficiently intuitive that a summary of those actions is at least a reasonable basis from which to start. While it would be difficult to prove the claim in any formal sense, there are several factors which suggest its plausibility.

First, we are dealing with a domain in which deduction, and deduction in the face of uncertainty, is a primary task. The use of production rules in an IF/THEN format seems therefore to be a natural way of expressing things about the domain, and the display of such rules should be comprehensible. Second, the use of such rules in a backward chaining mode is, we claim, a reasonably intuitive scheme.

**HOW 1.1   {the 1.1 refers to the information in the line labelled [1.1] in Fig. 10}

[i.e. HOW was it determined that the culture was taken from a sterile source?]

[3.1] RULE 001 was used to conclude that there is suggestive evidence (.7) that the culture was taken from a sterile source.
[3.3] RULE 022 was used to conclude that there is strongly suggestive evidence (.7) that the culture was taken from a sterile source.

**HOW 3.1   {another request from the user}

[i.e. HOW was RULE001 used?]

It has already been established that

[4.1] the site of the culture is one of: those sites from which the sterility of cultures depend upon the method of collection
[4.2] the method of collection of the culture is one of: the recognized methods of collection associated with the site of the culture, and
[4.3] it is not known whether care was taken in collecting the culture
Therefore
there is strongly suggestive evidence (.8) that the culture was taken from a sterile source
[RULE022]

FIG. 11. Examples of explanation capabilities—a HOW question.

Modus ponens is a well-understood and widely (if not explicitly) used mode of inference. Thus, the general form of the representation and the way it is employed should not be unfamiliar to the average user. More specifically, however, consider the source of the rules. They have been given to us by human experts who were attempting to formalize their own knowledge of the domain. As such, they embody accepted patterns of human reasoning, implying that they should be relatively easy to understand, especially for those familiar with the domain. As such, they will also attack the problem at what has been judged an appropriate level of detail. That is, they will embody the right size of "chunks" of the problem to be comprehensible.

We are not, therefore, recapping the binary bit level operations of the machine instructions for an obscure piece of code. We claim instead to be working with primitives and a methodology whose (a) substance, (b) level of detail, and (c) mechanism are all well suited to the domain, and to human comprehension, precisely because they were provided by human experts. This approach seems to provide what may plausibly be an understandable explanation of system behavior.

This use of symbolic reasoning is one factor which makes the generation of explanations an easier task. For example, it makes the display of a backtrace of performance comprehensible (as, for example, in Fig. 9). The basic control structure of the consultation system is a second factor. The simple depth-first-search of the AND/OR goal tree makes HOW, WHY, and the tree traversal approach natural (as in Fig. 10 and 11). We believe several concepts in the current system are, however, fairly general purpose, and would be useful even in systems which did not share these advantages. Whatever control structure is employed, the maintenance of an internal trace will clearly be useful in subsequent explanations of system behavior. The use of some information metric will help to insure that those explanations are at an appropriate level of detail. Finally, the explanation generating routines require some ability to decipher the actions of the main system.

By way of contrast, we might try to imagine how a program based on a statistical approach might attempt to explain itself. Such systems can, for instance, display a disease which has been deduced and a list of relevant symptoms, with prior and posterior probabilities. No more informative detail is available, however. When the symptom list is long, it may not be clear how each of them (or some combination of them) contributed to the conclusion. It is more difficult to imagine what sort of explanation could be provided if the program were interrupted with interim queries while in the process of computing probabilities. The problem, of course, is that statistical methods are not good models of the actual reasoning process (as shown in psychological experiments of [8] and [33]), nor were they designed to be. While they are operationally effective when extensive data concerning disease incidence are available, they are also for the most part, "shallow", one-step techniques which capture little of the ongoing process actually used by expert problem solvers in the domain.[6]

We have found the presence of even the current basic explanation capabilities to be extremely useful, as they have begun to pass the most fundamental test: it has become easier to ask the system what it did than to trace through the code by hand. The continued development and generalization of these capabilities is one focus of our present research.

6.3. Acquisition

Since the field of infectious disease therapy is both large and constantly changing, it was apparent from the outset that the program would have to deal with an evolving knowledge base. The domain size made writing a complete set of rules an impossible task, so the system was designed to facilitate an incremental approach to competence. New research in the domain produces new results and modifications of old principles, so that a broad scope of knowledge-base management capabilities was clearly necessary.

[6] However, the reasoning process of human experts may not be the ideal model for *all* knowledge-based problem solving systems. In the presence of reliable statistical data, programs using a decision theoretic approach are capable of performance surpassing those of their human counter-parts.

In domains like infectious disease therapy selection, however, which are characterized by "judgmental knowledge", statistical approaches may not be viable. This appears to be the case for many medical decision making areas. See [12] and [30] for further discussion of this point.

As suggested above, a fundamental assumption is that the expert teaching the system can be "debriefed", thus transferring his knowledge to the program. That is, presented with any conclusion he makes during a consultation, the expert must be able to state a rule indicating all relevant premises for that conclusion. The rule must, in and of itself, represent a valid chunk of clinical knowledge.

There are two reasons why this seems a plausible approach to knowledge acquisition. First, clinical medicine appears to be at the correct level of formalization. That is, while relatively little of the knowledge can be specified in precise algorithms (at a level comparable to, say, elementary physics) the judgmental knowledge that exists is often specifiable in reasonably firm heuristics. Second, on the model of a medical student's clinical training, we have emphasized the acquisition of new knowledge in the context of debugging (although the system is prepared to accept a new rule from the user at any time). We expect that some error on the system's part will become apparent during the consultation, perhaps through an incorrect organism identification or therapy selection. Tracking down this error by tracing back through the program's actions is a reasonably straightforward process which presents the expert with a methodical and complete review of the system's reasoning. He is obligated to either approve of each step or to correct it. This means that the expert is faced with a sharply focussed task of adding a chunk of knowledge to remedy a specific bug. This makes it far easier for him to formalize his knowledge than would be the case if he were asked, for example, "tell me about bacteremia."

This methodology has the interesting advantage that the context of the error (i.e., which conclusion was in error, what rules were used, what the facts of this case were, etc.) is of great help to the acquisition system in interpreting the expert's subsequent instructions for fixing the bug. The error type and context supply the system with a set of expectations about the form and content of the anticipated correction, and this greatly facilitates the acquisition process (details of this and much of the operation of the acquisition system are found in [7]).

The problem of educating the system can be usefully broken down into three phases: uncovering the bug, transferring to the system the knowledge necessary to correct the bug, and integrating the new (or revised) knowledge into the knowledge base. As suggested above, the explanation system is designed to facilitate the first task by making it easy to review all of the program's actions. Corrections are then specified by adding new rules (and perhaps new values, attributes, or contexts), or by modifying old ones. This process is carried out in a mixed initiative dialogue using a subset of standard English.

The system's understanding of the dialog is based on what may be viewed as a primitive form of 'model-directed' automatic programming. Given some natural language text describing one clause of a new rule's premise, the system scans the text to find keywords suggesting which predicate function(s) are the most appropriate translations of the predicate(s) used in the clause. The appropriate template for each such function is retrieved, and the 'parsing' of the remainder of the text is guided by the attempt to fill this in.

If one of the functions were SAME, the template would be as shown in Fig. 6. CNTXT is known to be a literal which should be left as is, PARM signifies a clinical parameter (attribute), and VALUE denotes a corresponding value. Thus the phrase "the stain of the organism is negative" would be analyzed as follows: the word "stain" in the system dictionary has as part of its semantic indicators the information that it may be used in talking about the attribute *gramstain* of an organism. The word "negative" is known to be a valid value of *gramstain* (although it has other associations as well). Thus one possible (and in fact the correct) parse is

(SAME CNTXT GRAM GRAMNEG)

or "the gramstain of the organism is gramnegative."

Note that this is another example of the use of higher level primitives to do a form of program understanding. It is the semantics of PARM and VALUE which guide the parse after the template is retrieved, and the semantics of the *gramstain* concept which allow us to insure the consistency of each parse. Thus by treating such concepts as conceptual primitives, and providing semantics at this level, we make possible the capabilities shown, using relatively modest amounts of machinery.

Other, incorrect parses are of course possible, and are generated too. There are three factors, however, which keep the total number of parses within reasonable bounds. First, and perhaps most important, we are dealing with a very small amount of text. The user is prompted for each clause of the premise individually, and while he may type an arbitrary amount at each prompt, the typical response is less than a dozen words. Second, there is a relatively small degree of ambiguity in the semi-formal language of medicine. Therefore a keyword-based approach produces only a small number of possible interpretations for each word. Finally, insuring the consistency of any given parse (e.g. that VALUE is indeed a valid value for PARM) further restricts the total number generated. Typically, between 1 and 15 candidate parses result.

Ranking of possible interpretations of a clause depends on expectation and internal consistency. As noted above, the context of the original error supplies expectations about the form of the new rule, and this is used to help sort the resulting parses to choose the most likely.

As the last step in educating the system, we have to integrate the new knowledge into the rest of the knowledge base. We have only recently begun work on this problem, but we recognize two important, general problems. First, the rule set should be free of internal contradictions, subsumptions, or redundancies. The issue is complicated significantly by the judgmental nature of the rules. While some inconsistencies are immediately obvious (two rules identical except for differing certainty factors), indirect contradictions (resulting from chaining rules, for example) are more difficult to detect. Inexactness in the rules means that we can specify only an interval of consistent values for a certainty factor.

The second problem is coping with the secondary effects that the addition of new

knowledge typically introduces. This arises primarily from the acquisition of a new value, clinical parameter or context. After requesting the information required to specify the new structure, it is often necessary to update several other information structures in the system, and these in turn may cause yet other updating to occur. For example, the creation of a new value for the site of a culture involves a long sequence of actions: the new site must be added to the internal list ALLSITES, it must then be classified as either sterile or non-sterile, and then added to the appropriate list; if non-sterile, the user has to supply the names of the organisms that are typically found there, and so forth. While some of this updating is apparent from the structures themselves, much of it is not. We are currently investigating methods for specifying such interactions, and a methodology of representation design that minimizes or simplifies the interactions to begin with.

The choice of a production rule representation does impose some limitations in the knowledge transfer task. Since rules are simple conditional statements, they can at times provide power insufficient to express some more complex concepts. In addition, while expressing a single fact is often convenient, expressing a larger concept via several rules is at times somewhat more difficult. As suggested above, mapping from a sequence of actions to a set of rules is not always easy. Goal-directed chaining is apparently not currently a common human approach to structuring larger chunks of knowledge.

Despite these drawbacks, we have found the production rule formalism a powerful one. It has helped to organize and build, in a relatively short period, a knowledge base which performs at an encouraging level of competence. The rules are, as noted, a reasonably intuitive way of expressing simple chunks of inferential knowledge, and one which requires no acquaintance with any programming language. While it may not be immediately obvious how to restate domain knowledge in production rule format, we have found that infectious disease experts soon acquired some proficiency in doing this with relatively little training. We have had experience working with five different experts over the past few years, and in all cases had little difficulty in introducing them to the use of rules. While this is a limited sample, it does suggest that the formalism is a convenient one for structuring knowledge for someone unfamiliar with programming.

The rules also appear capable of embodying appropriate-sized chunks of knowledge, and of expressing concepts that are significant statements. They remain, however, straightforward enough to be built of relatively simple compositions of conceptual primitives (the attributes, values, etc.). While any heavily stylized form of coding of course makes it easier to produce code, stylizing in the form of production rules in particular also provides a framework which is structurally simple enough to be translatable to simple English. This means that the experts can easily comprehend the program's explanation of what it knows, and equally easily specify knowledge to be added.

The control structure as it might be expressed in an ALGOL-like language. All predicates and functions refer to processes discussed in Sections 3.2–3.5. Examples of nonstandard 'data types' are shown below.

'data type'	example
item	IDENTITY
rule	RULE050
premise clause	(SAME CNTXT PORTAL GI)
action clause	(CONCLUDE CNTXT IDENTITY BACTEROIDES TALLY .8)

REFERENCES

1. Anderson, R. H. and Gillogly, J. J. RAND intelligent terminals agent: design philosophy, RAND R-1809-ARPA, The RAND Corporation, Santa Monica, CA. (January, 1977).

2. Bleich, H. L. The computer as a consultant, N. Engl. J. Med. 284 (1971) 141–147.

3. Buchanan, B. G. and Lederberg, J. The heuristic DENDRAL program for explaining empirical data, IFIP (1971), 179–188.

4. Colby, K. M., Parkinson, R. C. and Faught, B. L. Pattern matching rules for the recognition of natural language dialog expressions, A I Memo #234, (June 1974), Computer Science Department, Stanford University, Stanford, CA.

5. S. Carbonell, J. R. Mixed initiative man-computer instructional dialogues, BBN Report 1971, (31 May 1970), Bolt, Beranek and Newman, Cambridge, MA.

6. Davis, R. and King, J. An overview of production systems, in: Elcock and Michie (Eds.), Machine Intelligence 8: Machine Representations of Knowledge, Wiley, NY, 1977.

7. Davis, R. Use of Meta-level knowledge in the construction and maintenance of large knowledge bases, A I Memo #283 (July 1976) Computer Science Department, Stanford University.

8. Edwards, R. Conservatism in human information processing, in: Kleinmuntz (Ed.), Formal Representation of Human Judgment, Wiley, 1968, pp. 17–52.

9. Fahlman, S. E. A planning system for robot construction tasks, Artificial Intelligence 5 (1974) 1–50.

10. Gorry, G. A. and Barnett, G. O. Experience with a model of sequential diagnosis, Comput. Biomed. Res. 1 (1968) 490–507.

11. Gorry, G. A., Kassirer, J. P., Essig, A. and Schwartz, W. B., Decision analysis as the basis for computer-aided management of acute renal failure, Am. J. Med. 55 (1973) 473–484.

12. Gorry, G. A. Computer-assisted clinical decision making, Method. Inform. Med. 12 (1973) 42–51.

13. Green, C. C., Waldinger, R. J., Barstow, D. R., Elschlager, R., Lenat, D. B., McCune, B. P., Shaw, D. E. and Steinberg, L. I. Progress report on program-understanding systems, A I Memo #240, (August 1974), Computer Science Department, Stanford University, Stanford, CA.

14. Hart, P. E. Progress on a computer-based consultant, AI Group Technical Note 99, (January 1975), Stanford Research Institute, Menlo Park, CA.

15. Hewitt, C., Procedure semantics—models of procedures and the teaching of procedures, in: Rustin, R. (Ed.), Nat. Lang. Process., Courant Computer Science Symposium, 8 (1971) 331–350.

16. Kagan, B. M., Fannin, S. L. and Bardie, F. Spotlight on antimicrobial agents—1973, J. Am. Med. Assoc. 226 (1973) 306–310.

17. Kulikowski, C. A., Weiss, S. and Saifr, A., Glacoma Diagnosis and Therapy by Computer, Proc. Annu. Meet. Ass. Res. Vision Ophthamol. (May 1973).

18. Le Faivre, R. A. Fuzzy problem solving, Tech. Rept. 37, (September 1974), University of Wisconsin, Madison.

7. Conclusions

The MYCIN system has begun to approach its design goals of competence and high performance, flexibility in accommodating a large and changing knowledge base, and ability to explain its own reasoning. Successful applications of our control structure with rules applicable to other problem areas have been (a) fault diagnosis and repair recommendations for bugs in an automobile horn system [34], (b) a consultation system for industrial assembly problems [14], and (c) part of the basis for an intelligent terminal system [1].

A large factor in this work has been the production rule methodology. It has proved to be a powerful, yet flexible representation for encoding knowledge, and has contributed significantly to the capabilities of the system.

Appendix

```
Procedure FINDVALUEOF (item GOAL)
begin item X; list L; rule R; premise clause P;
if (X ← UNITYPATH(GOAL)) then return (X);
if LABDATA(GOAL) and DEFINITE_ANSWER(X ← ASKUSER(GOAL)) then return(X);
L ← RULES_ABOUT(GOAL);
L ← APPLY_METARULES(GOAL,L,0);
for R 0 L do
  unless PREVIEW(R) = false do
    begin "evaluate-rule"
    for P ∈ PREMISES_OF(R) do
      begin "test-each-premise-clause"
      if not TRACED(ATTRIBUTE_IN(P)) then FINDVALUEOF(ATTRIBUTE_IN(P));
      if EVALUATION_OF(P) < .2 then next(R);
      end "test-each-premise-clause";
    CONCLUDE(CONCLUSION_IN(R));
    if VALUE_KNOWN_WITH_CERTAINTY(GOAL) then
    begin MARK_AS_TRACED(GOAL); return(VALUEOF(GOAL)): end;
    end "evaluate-rule";
MARK_AS_TRACED(GOAL);
if VALUEOF(GOAL) = unknown and NOT_ALREADY_ASKED(GOAL)
                         then return(ASKUSER(GOAL))
                         else return(VALUEOF(GOAL));

end;

Procedure APPLY_METARULES(item GOAL; list L; integer LEVEL);
begin list M; rule Q;
if (M ← METARULES_ABOUT(GOAL,LEVEL+1))
                  then APPLY_METARULE_TO_ORDER_LIST(Q,L);
for Q ∈ M do USE_METARULE_TO_ORDER_LIST(Q,L);
return(L);
end;

Procedure CONCLUDE(action_clause CONCLUSION);
begin rule T; list I;
UPDATE_VALUE_OF(ATTRIBUTE_IN(CONCLUSION),VALUE_IN(CONCLUSION));
I ← ANTECEDENTRULES_ASSOCIATED_WITH(CONCLUSION);
I ← APPLY_METARULES(ATTRIBUTE_IN(CONCLUSION),I,0);
for T ∈ I do CONCLUDE(CONCLUSION_IN(T));
end;
```

19. Lesser, V. R., Fennell, R. D., Erman, L. D. and Reddy, D. R., Organization of the HEARSAY-II speech understanding system, *IEEE Trans. Acoust. Speech Signal Process.* ASSP-23, (February 1975), 11–23.

20. Lukasiewicz, J. A. Numerical interpretation of the theory of propositions, in: Borkowski (Ed.), *Jan Lukasiewicz: Selected Works*, North-Holland, Amsterdam, 1970.

21. The MACSYMA reference manual, The MATHLAB Group, (September 1974), Mass. Inst. Tech., Cambridge, MA.

22. Manna, Z., Correctness of programs, *J. Comput. Syst. Sci.* (1969).

23. Meyer, A. V. and Weissman, W. K. Computer analysis of the clinical neurological exam, *Comput. Biomed. Res.* **3** (1973) 111–117.

24. Nilsson, N. J. (Ed.), Artificial Intelligence—Research and Applications, A I Group Progress Report, (May 1975), Stanford Research Institute, Menlo Park, CA.

25. Pauker, S. G., Gorry, G. A., Kassirer, J. P. and Schwartz, W. B. Towards the simulation of clinical cognition: taking the present illness by computer, *Am. J. Med.* **60** (1976) 981–996.

26. Pople, H., Meyers, J. and Miller, R. DIALOG, a model of diagnostic logic for internal medicine, *Proc. Fourth Internl. Joint Conf. Artificial Intelligence* Tiblisi, U.S.S.R. (September 1975), 848–855.

27. Shortliffe, E. H., MYCIN: A rule-based computer progr⸍⸍ for advising physicians regarding antimicrobial therapy selection, A I Memo #251, (Octo⸍⸍ er Science Depart-ment, Stanford University. Also to appear as *Computer-I⸍ ⸍tations: MYCIN,* American Elsevier, New York, 1976.

28. Shortliffe, E. H., Axline, S. G., Buchanan, B. G. and Cc ⸍nsiderations for a program to provide consultations in clinical therapeutic.,. Diego Biomedical Symposium, (February 6–8, 1974).

29. Shortliffe, E. H., Davis, R., Buchanan, B. G., Axline, S. G., Green, C. C. and Cohen, S. N., Computer-based consultations in clinical therapeutics—explanation and rule acquisition capabilities of the MYCIN system, *Comput. Biomed. Res.* **8** (1975) 303–320.

30. Shortliffe, E. H. and Buchanan, B. G. A model of inexact reasoning in medicine, *Math. Biosci.* **23** (1975) 351–379.

31. Siklossy, L. and Roach, J. Proving the impossible is possible, *Proc. Third Internl. Joint Conf. Artificial Intelligence,* Stanford University, (1973) 383–387.

32. Silverman, H. A digitalis therapy advisor, MAC TR-143, (January 1975), Project MAC, Mass. Inst. Tech., Cambridge, MA.

33. Tversky, A. and Kahneman, D. Judgment under uncertainty: heuristics and biases, *Science,* **185** (1974) 1129–1131.

34. van Melle, W. Would you like advice on another horn, MYCIN project internal working paper, (December 1974) Stanford University, Stanford, California.

35. Waldinger, R. and Levitt, K. N. Reasoning about programs, *Artificial Intelligence* **5** (1974) 235–316.

36. Warner, H. R., Toronto, A. F. and Veasy, L. G. Experience with Bayes' theorem for computer diagnosis of congenital heart disease, *Am. N.Y. Acad. Sci.* **115** (1964) 558–567.

37. Warner, H. R., Olmstead, C. M. and Rutherford, B. D. HELP—a program for medical decision-making, *Comput. Biomed. Res.* **5** (1972) 65–74.

38. Waterman, D. A., Generalization learning techniques for automating the learning of heuristics, *Artificial Intelligence* **1** (1970) 121–170.

39. Winograd, T. Understanding natural language, *Cognitive Psychology* **3** (1972).

40. Winograd, T. Frame representation and the procedural/declarative controversy, in: Bobrow and Collins (Eds.), *Representation and Understanding,* Academic Press, 1975.

41. Zobrist, A. L., Carlson, F. R. An advice-taking chess computer, *Sci. Am.* **228** (1973) 92–105.

Received December 1975; revised version received March 1976

22 / Randall Davis and Bruce G. Buchanan
Meta-Level Knowledge: Overview and Applications

While the idea of meta-level knowledge (roughly, knowledge about knowledge) has been a recurrent theme in AI, very little convincing literature on it has been produced (although see [Smith, Chapter 3]). This lengthy conference paper presents nicely some specific proposals for a system's knowledge about what it knows. The paper looks at four types of meta-level knowledge in the context of TEIRESIAS, "a program designed to function as an assistant in the construction of high-performance [knowledge-based] systems." This work grew out of the MYCIN project, described in the immediately preceding paper [Davis *et al.*, Chapter 21]. Davis and Buchanan claim that the explicit representation of the data structures and rules of a basic knowledge-based system (at the object level) can contribute to knowledge acquisition, knowledge base management, and improved performance (*e.g.*, through strategies). They illustrate this kind of potential with examples of representations of complex data structures, typical rules (using empirically-derived rule models), function-invocation patterns, and perhaps most importantly, rules about rules. The last of these can be used to represent advice about the ordering of object-level rules and about the potential utility of rules given certain situations. Thus they can have an important impact on search, by ordering or even pruning entire branches of a search tree. They also appear to allow a kind of explanation of reasoning activity. Davis and Buchanan point out that their approach allows *content-directed invocation*, since meta-rules can refer to object rules by description (of a sort), rather than just by name.

Appeared in *Proc. IJCAI-77*, Cambridge, MA, August, 1977, 920–927.

META-LEVEL KNOWLEDGE: OVERVIEW AND APPLICATIONS

Randall Davis and Bruce G. Buchanan
Computer Science Department
Stanford University
Stanford, California 94305

Abstract

We define the concept of meta-level knowledge, and illustrate it by briefly reviewing four examples that have been described in detail elsewhere [2-5]. The examples include applications of the idea to tasks such as transfer of expertise from a domain expert to a program, and the maintenance and use of large knowledge bases. We explore common themes that arise from these examples, and examine broader implications of the idea, in particular its impact on the design and construction of large programs.

This work was supported in part by the Bureau of Health Sciences Research and Evaluation of HEW under Grant HS-01544 and by the Advanced Research Projects Agency under ARPA Order 2494. It was carried out on the SUMEX-AIM Computer System, supported by the NIH under Grant RR-00785. The views expressed are solely those of the author.

[1] Introduction

The representation and use of knowledge has been a central problem in AI research. A range of different encoding techniques have been developed, along with a number of approaches to applying knowledge. Most of the effort to date, however, has concentrated on representing and manipulating knowledge about a specific domain of application, like game-playing ([14]), natural language understanding ([15], [19]), speech understanding ([8], [11]), chemistry ([7]), etc.

This paper explores a number of issues involving representation and use of what we term *meta-level knowledge*, or knowledge about knowledge. It begins by defining the term, then exploring a few of its varieties and considering the range of capabilities it makes possible. Four specific examples of meta-level knowledge are described, and a demonstration given of their application to a number of problems, including interactive transfer of expertise and guiding the use of knowledge. Finally, we consider the long term implications of the concept and its likely impact on the design of large programs.

[2] Meta-level knowledge

In the most general terms, meta-level knowledge is knowledge about knowledge. Its primary use here is to enable a program to "know what it knows", and to make multiple uses of its knowledge. That is, the program is not only able to use its knowledge directly, but may also be able to examine it, abstract it, reason about it, or direct its application. To see in general terms how this can be accomplished, imagine taking some of the available representation techniques and turning them in on themselves, using them to describe their own encoding and use of knowledge. The result is a system with a store of both knowledge about the domain (the object level knowledge), and knowledge about its representations (the meta-level knowledge).

[3] Background

Some early efforts in AI involved the search for a single problem solving paradigm that would be both powerful and widely (or even universally) applicable. By the late 1960's it became clear that a single such paradigm was at best elusive, and that high (i.e., near human level) performance on non-trivial tasks required large stores of domain specific knowledge. A number of such knowledge-based systems have been developed and the methodology applied to a wide range of tasks, including speech understanding [11], algebraic symbol manipulation [12], and chemistry [7]. Because of the magnitude of the task of assembling the knowledge base for these systems, the accumulation, management and use of large stores of task specific knowledge has itself become a significant research problem.

It was this problem that provided the context for the development and exploration of meta-level knowledge reported here. The examples described below are all aimed toward the three aspects of the problem noted just above (knowledge accumulation, management, and use):

Schemata (Section 4.1) and rule models (Section 4.2) support accumulation of knowledge via interactive transfer of expertise from a human expert to the knowledge base of the system.

The schemata, along with the function templates (Section 4.3), provide a mechanism for handling some aspects of knowledge base maintenance.

Finally, meta-rules (Section 4.4) are applied to the problem of guiding the use of knowledge by offering a means of expressing strategies.

All of these are part of the TEIRESIAS system [2-5], an INTERLISP program designed to function as an assistant in the construction of high performance programs. A key element in this construction process is the transfer of expertise from a human expert to the program. Since the domain expert often knows nothing about programming, his interaction with the performance program usually requires a human programmer as intermediary. We have sought to create in TEIRESIAS a program to supply the same sort of assistance as that provided by the programmer, in order to remove the programmer from the loop.

We view the interaction between the domain expert and the performance program in terms of a teacher who continually challenges a student with new problems to solve, and carefully observes the student's performance. The teacher may interrupt to request a justification of some particular step the student has taken in solving the problem, or may challenge the final result. This may uncover a fault in the student's knowledge of the subject, and result in the transfer of information to correct it.

Figure 1 below shows the overall architecture of the sort of program TEIRESIAS is designed to help construct. The *knowledge base* is the program's store of task specific knowledge that makes possible high performance. The *inference engine* is an interpreter that uses the knowledge base to solve the problem at hand.

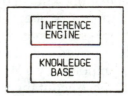

Figure 1 - architecture of the performance program

The main point of interest in this very simple design is the explicit division between these two parts of the program. This division allows us to assign the human expert the task of augmenting the knowledge base of a program whose control structure (inference engine) is assumed both appropriate and debugged. The question of *how* knowledge is to be encoded and used is settled by the selection of one or more of the available representations and control structures. The expert's task is to enlarge *what* it is the program knows. If all of the control structure information has been kept in the inference engine, then we can engage the domain expert in a discussion of the knowledge base and be assured that the discussion will have to deal only with issues of domain specific expertise (rather than with questions of programming and control structures).

In this discussion we will assume the knowledge base contains information about selecting an investment in the stock market; the performance program thus functions as an investment consultant.[1] Knowledge is in the form of a collection of associative triples (attribute, object, value) which characterize the domain, and approximately 400 inference rules built from them (Figure 2). Each rule is a single "chunk" of domain specific information indicating an action (in this case a conclusion) which is justified if the conditions specified in the premise are fulfilled.

```
RULE027
If   [1] the time-scale of the investment is long-term,
     [2] the desired return on the investment is
         greater than 10%,
     [3] the area of the investment is not known,
then there is evidence (.4) that the name of the stock
     to invest in is AT&T.

PREMISE   ($AND (SAME OBJCT TIMESCALE LONG-TERM)
                (GREATER OBJCT RETURNRATE 10)
                (NOTKNOWN OBJCT INVESTMENT-AREA))
ACTION    (CONCLUDE OBJCT STOCK-NAME AT&T .4)
```

Figure 2 - inference rule (English and LISP forms)

{4} Types of meta-level knowledge

We examine below four examples of meta-level knowledge, and review for each (i) the general idea; (ii) a specific instance, detailing the information it contains; (iii) an example of how that information is used to support knowledge base construction, maintenance, or use; and (iv) the other capabilities it makes possible. Figure 3 summarizes the type of information contained in each of the four examples.

KNOWLEDGE ABOUT	IS ENCODED IN
**************	************
representation of objects	schemata
representation of functions	function templates
inference rules	rule models
reasoning strategies	meta-rules

Figure 3 - four types of meta-level knowledge

{4.1} Example 1: Schemata
{4.1.1} Introduction: the need for knowledge about representations

As data structures go beyond the simple types available in most programming languages, to extended data types defined by the user, they typically become rather complex. Large programs may have numerous structures which are complex in both their internal organization and their interrelationships with other data types in the system. That is, the design and organization of data structures in any sizable system often involves a non-trivial store of detailed information. Yet such information is typically widely scattered, perhaps throughout comments in system code, in documents and manuals maintained separately, and in the mind of the system architect.

This presents a problem to someone who wants to make any sort of change to the system. Consider, for example, the difficulties typically encountered in such a seemingly simple problem as adding a new instance of an existing data type to a large program. Just finding all of the necessary information can be a major task, especially for someone unfamiliar with the system.

One particularly relevant set of examples comes from the numerous approaches to knowledge representations which have been tried over the years. While the emphasis in discussions of predicate calculus, semantic nets, production rules, frames, etc. has naturally concerned their respective conceptual power, at the level of implementation each of these has presented a non-trivial problem in data structure management.

The second example of meta-level knowledge involves describing to a system a range of information about the representations it employs. The main idea here is, first, to view every knowledge representation in the system as an extended data type, and write explicit descriptions of each of them. These descriptions should include all the information about structure and interrelations that was noted earlier as often widely scattered. Next, we devise a language in which all of this can be put in machine-comprehensible terms, and write the descriptions in those terms, making this store of information available to the system. Finally, we design an interpreter for the language, so that the system can use its new knowledge to keep track of the details of data structure construction and maintenance.

This is of course easily said and somewhat harder to do. It involves answering a number of difficult questions concerning the content of the required knowledge, and concerning how that information should be represented and used. This paper gives an overview of the answers, details can be found in [2] and [3]. The discussion here demonstrates briefly that the relevant knowledge includes information about the structure and interrelations of representations, and shows that it can be used as the basis for a form of knowledge acquisition.

The approach is based on the concept of a *data structure schema*, a device which provides a framework in which representations can be specified. This framework, like most, carries its own perspectives on its domain. One point it emphasizes strongly is the detailed specification of many kinds of information about representations. It attempts to make this specification task

easier by providing ways of organizing the information, and a relatively high level vocabulary for expressing it.

{4.1.2} Schema example

There are three levels of organization of the information about representations (Figure 4). At the highest level, a schema hierarchy links the schemata together, indicating what categories of data structures exist in the system and the relationships between them. At the next level of organization are the individual schemata, the basic unit around which the information about representations is organized. Each schema indicates the structure and interrelationships of a single type of data structure. At the lowest level are the slotnames (and associated structures) from which the schemata are built; these offer knowledge about specific conventions at the programming language level. Each of these three levels supplies a different sort of information; together they compose an extensive body of knowledge about the structure, organization, and implementation of the representations.

schema hierarchy	- indicates categories of representations and their organization
individual schema	- describes structure of a single representation
slotnames	- the schema building blocks, describe implementation conventions

Figure 4

The hierarchy is a generalization hierarchy that indicates the global organization of the representations. It makes extensive use of the concept of inheritance of properties, so that a particular schema need represent only the information not yet specified by schemata above it in the hierarchy. This distribution of information also aids in making the network extensible (see [2] for examples and further details).

Each individual schema contains several different types of information:

1) the structure of its instances
2) interrelationships with other data structures
3) a pointer to all current instances
4) inter-schema organizational information
5) bookkeeping information

Figure 5 shows the schema for a stock name; information corresponding to each of the categories listed above is grouped together.

```
STOCKNAME-SCHEMA
PLIST   [( INSTOF    STOCKNAME-SCHEMA          GIVENIT
           SYNONYM   (KLEENE (1 0) < ATOM >)   ASKIT
           TRADECON  (KLEENE (1 1 2)
                        <(MARKET-INST FIRSTYEAR-INST)>)
                                                ASKIT
           RISKCLASS CLASS-INST                 ASKIT
             CREATEIT]

RELATIONS ((AND* STOCKNAMELIST HILOTABLE)
           (XOR* COMMON PFD CUMPFD PARTICPFD)
           ((OR* PFD CUMPFD) PFDRATETABLE)
           ((AND* CUMPFD) OMITTEDDIVS) )

INSTANCES   (AMERICAN-MOTORS AT&T ... XEROX ZOECON)

FATHER      (VALUE-SCHEMA)
OFFSPRING   NIL

DESCR       "the STOCKNAME-SCHEMA describes the
            format for a stock name"
AUTHOR      DAVIS
DATE        1115
INSTOF      (SCHEMA-SCHEMA)
```

Figure 5 - schema for a stock name

The first five lines in Figure 5 contain structure information, and indicate some of the entries on the property list (PLIST) of the data structure which represents a stock name. The information is a triple of the form

       <slotname> <blank> <advice>

The *slotname* labels the "kind" of things which fills the *blank*, and serves as a point around which much of the "lower level" information in the system is organized. The *blank* specifies the format of the information required, while the *advice* suggests how to find it. Some of the information needed may be domain specific, and hence must be requested from the expert. But some may concern solely internal conventions of representation, and hence should be supplied by the system itself, to insulate the domain expert from such details. The *advice* provides a way of indicating which of these situations holds in each case.

The next five lines in the schema indicate its interrelations with other data structures in the system. The main point here is to provide the system architect with a way of making explicit all of the data structure interrelationships upon which his design depends. Expressing them in a machine-accessible form makes it possible for TEIRESIAS to take over the task of maintaining them, as explained below.

The schemata also keep a list of all current instantiations of themselves, primarily for use in maintaining the knowledge base. If the design of a data structure requires modification, it is convenient to have a pointer to all current instances to insure that they are similarly modified.

The next two lines contain organizational information indicating how the the stockname schema is connected to the schema hierarchy.

Finally, there is four lines of bookkeeping information that helps in keeping track of a large number of data structures: each structure is tagged with the date of creation and author, along with a free text description supplied by the author. In addition, each structure has a pointer to the schema of which it is an instance (note in this case that it is the schema itself which is the data structure being described by this information).

[4.1.3] Schemata: use in knowledge acquisition

Use of the schemata for knowledge acquisition relies on several ideas:
- information in the schema is viewed as a guide to creating a new instance of the representation it describes.
- that guidance is supplied by
  the structure description information, which is in the form of a prototype to be instantiated, and
  the *relations* information, which is interpreted as pointers to a number of structures which may require updating to insure that necessary data structure interrelations are maintained.
- it is this instantiation and interpretation process that drives the knowledge transfer dialog.
- the *advice* present in the schema adds a level of sophistication in the dialog.

For instance, suppose in the process of adding a new rule to the system the expert mentions a stock the system hasn't heard about yet. Learning about the new stock (i.e., creating a new instance of the concept *stock name*) becomes a subproblem in the task of acquiring the new rule. The stock name schema is retrieved, and used as the basis for a dialog that requests the necessary information from the expert. Detailed examples are found in [2] and [3]; an abbreviated version of the dialog is shown below. (In all traces, computer output is in mixed upper and lower case in this font, while user responses are in **BOLDFACE CAPITALS**, and commentary is {inside braces}.).

The new rule will be called RULE384
  If 1 - THE DESIRED RATE OF RETURN ON THE INVESTMENT IS
          GREATER THAN 10%
      2 - THE AMOUNT OF INVESTMENT EXPERIENCE OF THE CLIENT
          IS MODERATE
      3 - THE AREA OF THE INVESTMENT IS NATURAL RESOURCE
          DEVELOPMENT
  Then
      1 - THERE IS EVIDENCE (.5) THAT THE NAME OF THE STOCK
          TO INVEST IN IS GEORGIA PACIFIC

Sorry, but I don't understand
          THERE IS EVIDENCE (.5) THAT THE NAME OF THE STOCK TO
          INVEST IN IS GEORGIA PACIFIC
because these words are unknown: GEORGIA PACIFIC

{TEIRESIAS finds it cannot generate any interpretations of the text, so it reprints the original line, and specifies the trouble.}

Would you care to try rephrasing that?
++** Y
(Please use *'s to mark what you think might be a new attribute or a new value of an existing attribute)
      1 - THERE IS EVIDENCE (.5) THAT THE NAME OF THE STOCK
          TO INVEST IN IS * GEORGIA PACIFIC *

{While the language in this example is very simple, there are more complex cases where it would be quite hard to decide from the context what sort of new item the expert had in mind. To avoid the necessity for more sophisticated natural language handling, he is asked to mark off the new word or phrase with asterisks.}

It looks as though

GEORGIA PACIFIC
refers to a new value of an attribute, correct?
++** Y
...is it a name of a stock?
++** Y

{The system can then do some very simple pattern matching.}

Now please tell me a few things about it...

{TEIRESIAS retrieves the schema for a stock, and "reads" it to find out what it needs to know about any stock.}

On what markets is GEORGIA-PACIFIC traded?
The answer should be in the form of 1 or more of the following- <market name> <year first traded>
[Type 1 set to a line, then an empty line when done.]
++** NYSE 1945
++** PCE 1968

{Each of the questions from the system is prompted by the attempt to fill in some component of the data structure being built, according to the representation conventions indicated by the schema. A translated form of the "blank" is printed to guide the expert; it is then used to parse his answer and insure syntactic validity.}

What is the current risk classification of GEORGIA-PACIFIC? The answer should be in the form of a
          <risk classification>
++** AMEX
    Sorry, but the following are invalid -
    AMEX is not a recognized <risk classification>
    Please answer again.
++** BLUE-CHIP

{TEIRESIAS now beings working on updating other data structures in response to the addition of the new stock name.}

Should this new item be added to-
      1 - the list of common stocks, or
      2 - the list of preferred stocks, or
      3 - the list of cumulative prefered stocks, or
      4 - the list of participating prefered stocks
Select one of the above
++** 3
[Adding GEORGIA-PACIFIC to CUMULATIVEPFD]

{One of these tasks involves adding the new stock to one of four mutually exclusive lists. (Several other necessary updates are also performed; these have been edited out here for brevity, see [3] for details).}

Ok, done with GEORGIA-PACIFIC now... Back to the rule.

{Having finished acquiring the new stock, the system returns to parsing the new rule, and with some help from the expert gets the correct result (the parsing process is omitted here, see [4] for a detailed example).}

This may take a few moments.

This is my understanding of your rule:
  If 1 - the desired rate of return for the investment
          is greater than 10%
      2 - the amount of investment experience of the
          client is moderate
      3 - the area of the investment is natural-
          resource-development
  Then
      1 - there is evidence (.5) that the name of the
          stock to choose is georgia-pacific

[4.1.4] Schemata: other uses

The schemata also support a number of other capabilities. They are useful in maintaining the knowledge base, for instance, and offer a convenient mechanism for organizing and implementing data structure access and storage functions.

The data structure updating demonstrated in the previous section is one instance of their maintenance capabilities. This updating helps to insure that one change to the knowledge base (adding a new instance of representation) will not violate necessary relationships between data structures.

One of the ideas behind the design of the schemata is to use them as points around which to organize knowledge. The information about structure and interrelationships described above, for instance, is stored this way. In addition, access and storage information is also organized in this fashion. By generalizing the *advice* concept slightly, it is possible to effect all data structure access and storage requests via the appropriate schema. That is, code which wants to access a particular structure "sends" an access request, and the structure "answers" by providing the requested item[2]. This offers the well known advantages of insulating the implementation of a data structure from its logical design. Code which refers only to the latter is far easier to maintain in the face of modifications to data structure implementation.

While they have not yet been implemented, two other interesting uses of the schemata appear possible. First, straightforward extensions to the current system should support a more complex form of knowledge base maintenance. Suppose, for instance, it became necessary to modify the representation of a stock, i.e., we want to edit the stock name schema. It should be possible to have TEIRESIAS "watch" as the schema is modified and then carry out the same sequence of modifications on each of the current instances of the schema. Where new information was required (e.g., if new structure descriptors were added to the schema) the system could prompt for the appropriate entry for each instance. While major redesigns would be more difficult to carry out in this fashion, a number of common modifications could be accommodated, easing the task of making changes to structures in the knowledge base.

Second, the schema also appear to make possible a limited form of introspection. If the information in the *relations* slot were made accessible via simple retrieval routines, this would make it possible to answer questions like *What else in the system will be affected if I add a new instance of this data structure?* or *What are all the other structures that are related to this one?* This would be a useful form of on-line documentation.

{4.2} Example 2: Rule models
{4.2.1} Rule models as empirical abstractions of the knowledge base

In reviewing the rules in the knowledge base, a number of regularities become apparent. In particular, rules about a single topic tend to have characteristics in common -- there are "ways" of reasoning about a given topic. This idea of patterns of reasoning has been given a formal (statistical) definition, and provides the basis for the automated construction of a set of empirical generalities about the knowledge base: the rule models.

A rule model is an abstract description of a subset of rules, built from empirical generalizations about those rules. It is used to characterize a "typical" member of the subset (and in this sense is similar to the structures used in [20]), and is composed of four parts. First, a list of EXAMPLES indicates the subset of rules from which this model was constructed.

Next, a DESCRIPTION characterizes a typical member of the subset. Since we are dealing in this case with rules composed of premise-action pairs, the DESCRIPTION currently implemented contains individual characterizations of a typical premise and a typical action. Then, since the current representation scheme used in those rules is based on associative triples, we have chosen to implement those characterizations by indicating (a) which attributes "typically" appear in the premise (and in the action) of a rule in this subset, and (b) correlations of attributes appearing in the premise (action).[3]

Note that the central idea is the concept of *characterizing a typical member of the subset.* Naturally, that characterization would look different for subsets of rules, procedures, theorems, etc. But the main idea of characterization is widely applicable and not restricted to any particular representational formalism.

The two other parts of the rule model are pointers to models describing more general and more specific subsets of rules. The set of models is organized into a number of tree structures. These structures determine the subsets for which models will be constructed. At the root of each tree is the model made from all the rules which conclude about <attribute>, below this are two models dealing with all affirmative and all negative rules, and below this are models dealing with rules which affirm or deny specific values of the attribute.

There are several points to note here. First, these models are not hardwired into the system, but are instead formed by TEIRESIAS on the basis of the content of the knowledge base. Second, where the rules in the knowledge base contain object level information about a specific domain, the rule models contain information about those rules, in the form of empirical generalizations. As such they offer a global overview of the regularities in the rules, and may possibly reflect useful trends in the reasoning of the expert from whom those rules were acquired.

{4.2.2} Rule model example

Figure 6 shows an example of a rule model, one that describes the subset of rules concluding affirmatively about the area for an investment. (Since not all of the details of implementation are relevant here, this discussion will omit some. See [2] for a full explanation.) As indicated above, there is a list of the rules from which this model was constructed, descriptions characterizing the premise and the action, and pointers to more specific and more general models. Each characterization in the description is shown split into its two parts, one concerning the presence of individual attributes and the other describing correlations. The first item in the premise description, for instance, indicates that "most" rules about what the area of an investment should be mention the attribute *rate of return* in their premise; when they do mention it they "typically" use the predicate functions SAME and NOTSAME; and the "strength", or reliability, of this piece of advice is 3.83 (see [2] for precise definitions of the quoted terms).

The fourth item in the premise description indicates that when the attribute *rate of return* appears in the premise of a rule in this subset, the attribute *timescale of the investment* "typically" appears as well. As before the predicate functions are those typically associated with the attributes, and the number is a indication of reliability.

```
EXAMPLES   ((RULE116 .33)
            (RULE050 .70)
            (RULE037 .80)
            (RULE095 .90)
            (RULE152 1.0)
            (RULE140 1.0))
DESCRIPTION
PREMISE ((RETURNRATE SAME NOTSAME 3.83)
         (TIMESCALE SAME NOTSAME 3.83)
         (TREND SAME 2.83)
         ((RETURNRATE SAME) (TIMESCALE SAME) 3.83)
         ((TIMESCALE SAME) (RETURNRATE SAME) 3.83)
         ((BRACKET SAME)(FOLLOWS SAME)(EXPERIENCE SAME)
                                            1.50))
ACTION   ((INVESTMENT-AREA CONCLUDE 4.73)
          (RISK CONCLUDE 4.05)
          ((INVESTMENT-AREA CONCLUDE) (RISK CONCLUDE) 4.73))
MORE-GENL  (INVESTMENT-AREA)
MORE-SPEC  (INVESTMENT-AREA-IS-UTILITIES)
```

Figure 6 - example of a rule model

{4.2.3} Rule models: use in knowledge acquisition

Use of the rule models to support knowledge acquisition occurs in several steps. First, as noted above, our model of knowledge acquisition is one of interactive transfer of expertise in the context of a shortcoming in the knowledge base. The process starts with the expert challenging the system with a specific problem and observing its performance. If he believes its results are incorrect, there are available a number of tools that will allow him to track down the source of the error (see [2] for details). TEIRESIAS keeps track of this debugging process, and responds to the discovery of the source of the error by selecting the appropriate rule model. For instance, if the problem is a rule missing from the knowledge base that concludes about the appropriate area for an investment, then TEIRESIAS will select the model shown in Figure 6 as the appropriate one to describe the rule it is about to acquire. Note that the selection of a specific model is in effect an expression by TEIRESIAS of its *expectations* concerning the new rule, and the generalizations in the model become predictions about the likely content of the rule.

At this point the expert types in the new rule (Figure 7), using the vocabulary specific to the domain, and expressing it as much as possible in the associative triple format. TEIRESIAS's problem now is to try to understand what the expert has said. As is traditional, "understanding" is determined by converting the text into an internal representation (like that shown in Figure 2), then converting this back into English and requesting approval from the expert.

Since understanding natural language is known to be difficult, we have taken a simpler approach. The basic idea is to allow the text to "suggest" interpretations via a simple keyword-based approach, and to intersect those results with the expectations provided by the selection of a particular rule model. We thus have a data directed process (interpreting the text) combined with a goal directed process (the predictions made by the rule model). Each contributes to the end result, but it is the combination of them that is effective. Details of this process are described in [2] and [4].

The new rule will be called RULE383

```
If:    1 - THE CLIENT'S INCOME TAX BRACKET IS 50%
  and 2 - THE CLIENT IS FOLLOWING UP ON MARKET TRENDS
           CAREFULLY
  and 3 -
Then:  1 - THERE IS EVIDENCE (.8) THAT THE INVESTMENT AREA
           SHOULD BE HIGH TECHNOLOGY
  and 2 -
```

Figure 7

TEIRESIAS displays the results of this initial interpretation of the rule (Figure 8). If there are mistakes (as there are in this case), a rule editor is available to allow the expert to indicate required changes. This is easily accomplished, since TEIRESIAS can often make an effective second choice by determining the likely source of error in its initial guess.

```
This is my understanding of your rule:
RULE383
If   1) The client's income-tax bracket is 50%,
     2) The market has followed a upward trend recently
     3) The client manages his assets carefully
Then   there is evidence (.8) that the area of the
        investment should be high-technology
```

Figure 8

Once the expert is satisfied that TEIRESIAS has correctly understood what he said, it is the system's turn to see if *it* is satisfied with the content of the rule. The main idea is to use the rule model to see how well this new rule "fits in" to the system's model of its knowledge -- i.e., does it "look like" a typical rule of the sort expected?

In the current implementation, the presence of a partial match between the new rule and the generalizations in the rule model triggers a response from TEIRESIAS. Recall the last line of the premise description in the rule model of Figure 6:

((BRACKET SAME) (FOLLOWS SAME) (EXPERIENCE SAME) 1.50))

This indicates that when the tax BRACKET of the client appears in the premise of a rule of this sort, then how closely he FOLLOWS the market, and how much investment EXPERIENCE he has typically appear as well. Note that the new rule has the first two of these, but is missing the last, and TEIRESIAS points this out.

```
I hate to criticize, Randy, but did you know that most
rules about what the area of a investment might be,
that mention-
     the income-tax bracket of the client, and
     how closely the client follows the market
ALSO mention-
A] - the amount of investment experience of the client
Shall I try to write a clause to account for [A] ?
++** Y
How about-
A] The amount of investment experience of the client
   is moderate
Ok?
++** Y
```

Figure 9

If the expert agrees to the inclusion of a new clause, TEIRESIAS attempts to create it. The system relies on the context of the current dialog (which indicates that the clause should deal with the amount of the client's investment experience), and the fact that the rule must work for this case, or it won't fix the bug (earlier in the interaction [not shown] the expert indicated that the client had a *moderate* amount of experience). TEIRESIAS's guess is not necessarily correct, of course, since the desired clause may be more general, but it is at least a plausible attempt.

It should be noted that there is nothing in this concept of "second guessing" which is specific to the rule models as they are currently designed, or indeed to associative triples or rules as a knowledge representation. The most general and fundamental point was mentioned above -- testing to see how something "fits in" to the system's model of its knowledge. At this point the system might perform any kind of check, for violations of any established prejudices about what the new chunk of knowledge should look like. Additional kinds of checks for rules might concern the strength of the inference, number of clauses in the premise, etc. Different checks might be devised for other knowledge encoding schemes.

The automatic generation of the rule models by TEIRESIAS has several interesting implications, since it makes possible a synthesis of the ideas of model-based understanding and learning by experience. While both of these have been developed independently in previous AI research, their combination produces a novel sort of feedback loop: rule acquisition relies on the set of rule models to effect the model-based understanding process; this results in the addition of a new rule to the knowledge base, and this in turn prompts the recomputation of the relevant rule model(s).

Note first that performance on the acquisition of the next rule may be better, because the system's "picture" of its knowledge base has improved -- the rule models are now computed from a larger set of instances, and their generalizations are more likely to be valid.

Second, since the relevant rule models are recomputed each time a change is made to the knowledge base, the picture they supply is kept constantly up to date, and they will at all times be an accurate reflection of the shifting patterns in the knowledge base.

Finally, and perhaps most interesting, the models are not hand-tooled by the system architect, or specified by the expert. They are instead formed by the system itself, and formed as a result of its experience in acquiring rules from the expert. Thus despite its reliance on a set of models as a basis for understanding, TEIRESIAS's abilities are not restricted by the existing set of models. As its store of knowledge grows, old models can become more accurate, new models will be formed, and the system's stock of knowledge about its knowledge will continue to expand. This appears to be a novel capability for a model-based system.

{4.2.4} Rule models: other capabilities

As a form of meta-level knowledge, the rule models give the system a picture of its own knowledge. The system can, for instance, "read" a rule model to the user, supplying an overview of the information in part of the knowledge base. This may suggest global trends in the knowledge of the expert who assembled the knowledge base, and thus helps to make clear the overall approach of the system to a given topic (for examples see [2]).

{4.3} Example 3: Function templates

Associated with each predicate function in the system is a *template*, a list structure which resembles a simplified procedure declaration (Figure 10). It indicates the order and generic type of the arguments in a typical call of that function, and makes possible very simple versions of two interesting, parallel capabilities: code generation and code dissection.

```
FUNCTION        TEMPLATE
SAME            (OBJ ATTRIBUTE VALUE)
```

Figure 10 - template for the predicate function SAME

The template is used as the basis for the simple form of code generation alluded to in Section {4.2.3}. While details are beyond the scope of this paper (see [2]), code generation is essentially a process of "filling in the blanks": processing a line of text in a new rule involves checking for keywords that implicate a particular predicate function, and then filling in its template on the basis of connotations suggested by other words in the text.

Code dissection is accomplished by using the templates as a guide to extracting any desired part of a function call. For instance, as noted earlier, TEIRESIAS forms the rule models on the basis of the current contents of the knowledge base. To do this, it must be able to pick apart each rule to determine the attributes to which it refers. This could have been made possible by requiring that every predicate function use the same function call format (i.e., the same number, type, and order of arguments), but this would be too inflexible. Instead, we allow every function to describe its own calling format via its template. To dissect a function call, then, we need only retrieve the template for the relevant function (i.e., the template for the CAR of the form), and then use that as a guide to dissecting the remainder of the form. The template in Figure 10, for instance, indicates that the *attribute* would be the CADDR of the form. This same technique is also used by TEIRESIAS's explanation facility, where it permits the system to be quite precise in the explanations it provides (see [2] for details).

This approach also offers a useful degree of flexibility. The introduction of a new predicate function, for instance, can be totally transparent to the rest of the system, as long as its template can be written in terms of the available set of primitives like *attribute*, *value*, etc. The power of this approach is limited primarily by this factor, and will succeed to the extent that code can be described by a relatively small set of such primitive descriptors. While more complex syntax is easily accomodated (e.g., the template can indicate nested function calls), more complex semantics are more difficult (e.g., the appearance of multiple *attributes* in a function template can cause problems).

{4.4} Example 4: Meta-rules
{4.4.1} Strategies to guide the use of knowledge

Meta-rules embody strategies -- knowledge that indicates how to use other knowledge. This discussion considers strategies from the perspective of *deciding which knowledge to invoke next in a situation where more than one chunk of knowledge may be applicable.* For example, given a problem solvable by either heuristic search or problem decomposition, a strategy might indicate which technique to use, based on characteristics of the problem domain and nature of the desired solution. If the problem decomposition technique were chosen, other strategies might be employed to select the appropriate decomposition from among several plausible alternatives.

This view of strategies can be useful because many of the paradigms developed in AI admit (or even encourage) the possibility of having several alternative chunks of knowledge plausibly useful in a single situation (e.g., production rules, PLANNER-like languages, etc.). Faced with a set of alternatives large enough (or varied enough) that exhaustive invocation becomes infeasible, some decision must be made about which should be chosen. Since the performance of a program will be strongly influenced by the intelligence with which that decision is made, strategies offer an important site for the embedding of knowledge in a system.

This type of guidance can be especially useful in the sort of rule-based performance program that TEIRESIAS is designed to help build. The rules in this system are invoked in a simple backward-chaining fashion that produces an exhaustive depth-first search of an and/or goal tree. If the program is attempting, for example, to determine which stock would make a good investment, it retrieves all the rules which make a conclusion about that topic (i.e., they mention STOCK-NAME in their action). It then invokes each one in turn, evaluating each premise to see if the conditions specified have been met. The search is exhaustive because the rules are inexact: even if one succeeds, it was deemed to be a wisely conservative strategy to continue to collect all evidence about a subgoal.

The ability to use an exhaustive search is of course a luxury, and in time the base of rules may grow large enough to make this infeasible. As this point some choice would have to be made about which of the plausibly useful rules should be invoked. Meta-rules were created to address this problem.

{4.4.2} Meta-rules: examples

Figure 11 below shows two meta-rules. The first of them says, in effect, that in trying to determine the best investment for a non-profit organization, rules that base their recommendations on tax bracket are not likely to be successful. The second indicates that when dealing with clients nearing retirement age, more secure stocks should be considered before more speculative ones.

```
METARULE001
If  1) you are attempting to determine the best stock
       to invest in,
    2) the client's tax status is non-profit,
    3) there are rules which mention in their premise
       the income-tax bracket of the client,
then it is very likely (.9) that each of these rules
     is not going to be useful.

PREMISE
($AND(SAME OBJCT CURGOAL STOCK-NAME)
      (SAME OBJCT STATUS NON-PROFIT)
      (THEREARE OLRULES ($AND
          (MENTIONS FREEVAR PREMISE BRACKET)) SET1))
ACTION (CONCLUDE SET1 UTILITY NO .9)

METARULE002
If      1) the age of the client is greater than 60,
        2) there are rules which mention in their
           premise blue-chip risk,
        3) there are rules which mention in their
           premise speculative risk,
then    it is very likely (.8) that the former should
        be used before the latter.

PREMISE
($AND(GREATER OBJCT AGE 60)
     (THEREARE OLRULES ($AND
         (MENTIONS FREEVAR PREMISE BLUE-CHIP)) SET1)
     (THEREARE OLRULES ($AND
         (MENTIONS FREEVAR PREMISE SPECULATIVE)) SET2))
ACTION
     (CONCLUDE SET1 DOBEFORE SET2 .8)
```

Figure 11 - two meta-rules

It is important to note the character of the information conveyed by meta-rules. First, note that in both cases we have a rule which is making a conclusion about other rules. That is, where object level rules conclude about the stock market domain, meta-rules conclude about object level rules. These conclusions can (in the current implementation) be of two forms. As in the first meta-rule, they can make deductions about the likely utility of certain object level rules, or (as in the second) they can indicate a partial ordering between two subsets of object level rules.

Note also that (as in the first example) meta-rules make conclusions about the *utility* of object level rules, not their *validity*. That is, METARULE001 does not indicate circumstances under which some of the object level rules are invalid (or even "very likely (.9)" invalid). It merely says that they are likely not to be useful; i.e., they will probably fail, perhaps only after requiring extensive computation to evaluate their preconditions. This is important because it has an impact on the question of distribution of knowledge. If meta-rules did comment on validity, it might make more sense to distribute the knowledge in them, i.e., delete the meta-rule, and just add another premise clause to each of the relevant object level rules. But since their conclusions do concern utility, it does not make sense to distribute the knowledge.

Adding meta-rules to the system requires only a minor addition to the control structure described above. As before, the system retrieves the entire list of rules relevant to the current goal (call it L). But before attempting to invoke them, it first determines if there are any meta-rules relevant to that goal[4]. If so, these are invoked first. As a result of their action, we may obtain a number of conclusions about the likely utility, and relative ordering of the rules in L. These conclusions are used to reorder or shorten L, and the revised list of rules is then used. Viewed in tree-search terms, the current implementation of meta-rules can either prune the search space or reorder the branches of the tree.

{4.4.3} Meta-rules: guiding the use of the knowledge base

There are several points to note about this approach to encoding knowledge. First, the framework it presents for knowledge organization and use appears to offer a great deal of leverage, since much can be gained by adding to a system a store of (meta-level) knowledge about which chunk of object level knowledge to invoke next. Considered once again in tree search terms, we are talking about the difference between "blind" search of the tree, and one guided by heuristics. The advantage of even a few good heuristics in cutting down the combinatorial explosion of tree search is well known. Thus, where earlier sections were concerned about adding more object level knowledge to improve performance, here we are concerned with giving the system more information about how to use what it already knows.

Consider, too, that part of the definition of intelligence includes appropriate use of information. Even if a store of (object level) information is not large, it is important to be able to use it properly. Meta-rules provide a mechanism for encoding strategies that can make this possible.

Second, the description given in Section {4.4.2} has been simplified in several respects for the sake of clarity. It discusses the augmented control structure, for example, in terms of two levels -- the object and meta-levels. In fact, there can be an arbitrary number of levels, each serving to direct the use of knowledge at the next lower level. That is, the system retrieves the list (L) of object level rules relevant to the current goal. Before invoking this, it checks for a list (L') of first order meta-rules which can be used to reorder or prune L. But before invoking this, it checks for second order meta rules which can be used to reorder or prune L', etc. Recursion stops when there is no rule set of the next higher order, and the process unwinds, each level of strategies advising on the use of the next lower level.

Consider once again the issue of leverage, and recall the value of heuristics in guiding tree search. We can apply the same idea at this higher level, gaining considerable leverage by encoding heuristics that guide the use of heuristics. That is, rather than adding more heuristics to improve performance, we might add more information at the next higher level about effective use of existing heuristics.

The judgmental character of the rules offers several interesting capabilities. It makes it possible, for instance, to write rules which make different conclusions about the best strategy to use, and then rely on the underlying model of confirmation [16] to weigh the evidence. That is, the strategies can "argue" about the best rule to use next, and the strategy that presents the best case (as judged by the confirmation model) will win out.

Next, recall that the basic control structure of the performance program is a depth-first search of the and/or goal tree sprouted by the unwinding of rules. The presence of meta-rules of the sort shown in Figure 11 means that this tree has an interesting characteristic: at each node, when the system has to choose a path, there may be information stored advising about the best path to take. There may therefore be available an extensive body of knowledge to guide the search, but that knowledge is not embedded in the code of a clever search algorithm. It is instead organized around the specific objects which form the nodes in the tree; i.e., instead of a smart algorithm, we have a "smart tree".

Finally, there are several advantages associated with the use of strategies which are goal-specific, explicit, and embedded in a representation which is the same as that of the object level knowledge. That fact that strategies are *goal-specific*, for instance, makes it possible to specify quite precise heuristics for a given goal, without imposing any overhead in the search for any other goals. That is, there may be a number of complex heuristics describing the best rules to use for a particular goal, but these will cause no computational overhead except in the search for that goal.

The fact that they are *explicit* means a conceptually cleaner organization of knowledge and ease of modification of established strategies. Consider, for instance, alternative means of achieving the sort of partial ordering specified by the second meta-rule in Figure 11. There are several alternative schemes by which this could be accomplished, involving appropriate modifications to the relevant object level rules and slight changes to the control structure. Such schemes, however, share several faults that can be illustrated by considering one such approach: an agenda with multiple priority levels like the one proposed in [1]. That is, rather than dealing with a linear list L of relevant rules, those rules would be put on an agenda. Partial ordering could be accomplished simply by setting the priority for some rules higher than that of others: rules in subset A, for instance, might get priority 6 while those in subset B were given priority 5.

But this technique presents two problems: it is both opaque and likely to cause bugs. It will not be apparent from looking at the code, for instance, *why* the rules in A were given higher priority than the rules in B. Were they more likely to be useful, or is it desirable that those in A precede those in B no matter how useful they each may be? Consider also what happens if, before we get a chance to invoke any of the rules in A, an event occurs which makes it clear that their priority ought to be reduced (for reasons unrelated to the desired partial ordering). If the priority of only the rules in A are adjusted, a bug arises, since the desired relative ordering may be lost.

The problem is that this approach tries to reduce a number of different, incommensurate factors to a single number, *with no record of how that number was reached*. Meta-rules offer one mechanism for making these sorts of considerations explicit, and for leaving a record of why a set of processes has been queued in a particular order. They also make subsequent modifications easier, since all of the information is in one place -- changing a strategy can be accomplished by editing the relevant meta-rule, rather than searching through a program for all the places priorities have been set to effect that strategy.

Lastly, the use of a *uniform encoding of knowledge* makes the treatment of all levels the same. For example, second order meta-rules require no machinery in excess of that needed for first order meta-rules. It also means that all the explanation and knowledge acquisition capabilities developed for object level rules can be extended to meta-rules as well. The first of these (explanation) has been done, and works for all levels of meta-rules. Adding this to TEIRESIAS's explanation facility makes possible an interesting capability: in addition to being able to explain what it did, the system can also explain *how it decided to do what it did*. Knowledge in the strategies has become accessible to the rest of the system, and can be explained in just the same fashion. We noted above that adding meta-level knowledge to the system was quite distinct from adding more object level knowledge, since strategies contain information of a qualitatively different sort. Explanations based on this information are thus of a correspondingly different type as well.

{4.4.4}   Meta-rules: broader implications

There are a number of interesting generalizations of the basic scheme presented above, two of which we touch on briefly here. First, while we have been examining the idea of strategies in the context of the depth-first search used by the performance program, the concept is in fact more widely applicable and can be used with a range of control structures. Second, meta-rules effect their selection of the relevant object level rules by what we have termed *content-directed invocation*, an approach which offers advantages over previous knowledge source invocation techniques.

Applications to other control structures

The concept of strategies as a mechanism for deciding which chunk of knowledge to invoke next can be applied to a number of different control structures. We have seen how it works in goal-directed scheme, and it functions in much the same way with a data-directed process. In that case meta-rules offer a way of controlling the depth and breadth of the implications drawn from any new fact or conclusion. Pursing this further, we can imagine making the decision to use a data- or a goal-directed process itself an issue to be decided by a collection of appropriate meta-rules. At each point in its processing, the system might invoke one set of meta-rules to choose a control structure, then use another set to guide that control structure. This can be applied to many control structures, demonstrating the range of applicability of the basic concept of strategies as a device for choosing what to do next.

Content-directed invocation

If meta-rules are to be used to select from among plausibly useful object level rules, they must have some way of referring to the object level rules. The mechanism used to effect this reference has implications for the flexibility and extensibility of the resulting system.

To see this, note that the meta-rules in Figure 11 refer to the object level rules by *describing* them, and effect this description by direct examination of content. For instance, METARULE001 refers to *rules which mention in their premise the income tax bracket of the client*, a description, rather than an equivalent list of rule names. The set of object level rules which meet this description is determined at execution time by examining the source code of the rules. That is, the meta-rule "goes in and looks" for the relevant characteristic (in this case the presence of the attribute BRACKET), using the function templates as a guide to dissecting the rules. We have termed this *content-directed invocation*.

Part of the utility of this approach is illustrated by its advantages over using explicit lists of object level rules (e.g., if METARULE001 had been written to indicate "it is very likely (.9) that RULE124, RULE065, RULE210, and RULE113 are not going to be useful"). If such lists were used, then tasks like editing or adding an object-level rule to the system would require extensive amounts of bookkeeping. After an object level rule has been edited, for instance, we would have to check all the strategies that name it, to be sure that each such reference was still applicable to the revised rule. By using content-directed invocation, however, these tasks require no additional effort, since the meta-rules effect their own examination of the object level rules, and will make their own determination of relevance.

Additional advantages of this technique are discussed in more detail in [2] and [5].

{5} Implications

The examples reviewed above illustrate a number of general ideas about knowledge representation and use that may prove useful in building large programs.

We have, first, the notion that knowledge in programs should be made explicit and accessible. Use of production rules to encode the object level knowledge is one example of this, since knowledge in them may be more accessible than that embedded in the code of a procedure. The schemata, templates, and meta-rules illustrate the point also, since each of them encodes a form of information that is, typically, either omitted entirely or at best is left implicit. By making knowledge explicit and accessible, we make possible a number of useful abilities. The schemata and templates, for example, support the forms of system maintenance and knowledge acquisition described above. Meta-rules offer a means for explicit representation of the decision criteria used by the system to select its course of action. Subsequent "playback" of those criteria can then provide a form of explanation of the motivation for system behavior (see [2] for examples). That behavior is also more easily modified, since the information on which it is based is both clear (since it is explicit) and retrievable (since it is accessible). Finally, more of the system's knowledge and behavior becomes open to examination, especially by the system itself.

Second, there is the idea that programs should have access to their own representations. To put this another way, consider that over the years numerous representation schemes have been proposed and have generated a number of discussions of their respective strengths and weaknesses. Yet in all these discussions, one entity intimately concerned with the outcome has been left uninformed: the program itself. What this suggests is that we ought to describe to the program a range of information about the representations it employs, including such things as their structure, organization, and use.

As noted, this is easily suggested but more difficult to do. It requires a means of describing both representations and control structures, and the utility of those descriptions will be strongly dependent on the power of the language in which they are expressed. The schemata and templates are the two main examples of the partial solutions we have developed for describing representations, and both rely heavily on the idea of a task specific high level language -- a language whose conceptual primitives are task specific. The main reason for using this approach is to make possible what we might call "top down code understanding". Traditionally, efforts at code understanding (e.g., [18], [13]) have attempted to assign meaning to the code of some standard programming language. Rather than take on this sizable task, we have used the task specific languages to make the problem far easier. Instead of attempting to assign semantics to ordinary code, a "meaning" is assigned to each of the primitives in the high level language, and represented in one or more informal ways. Thus, for example, ATTRIBUTE is one of the primitives in the "language" in which templates are written; its meaning is embodied in procedures associated with it that are used during code generation and dissection (see [2] for details).

This convenient shortcut also implies a number of limitations. Most important, the approach depends on the existence of a finite number of "mostly independent" primitives. This means a set of primitives with only a few, well specified interactions between them. The number of interactions should be far less than the total possible, and interactions that do occur should be uncomplicated (as for example, the interaction between the concepts of *attribute* and *value*).

But suppose we could describe to a system its representations? What benefits would follow? The primary thing this can provide is a way of effecting multiple uses of the same knowledge. Consider for instance the multitude of ways in which the object level rules have been used. They are executed as code in order to drive the consultation (see [6] and [17] for examples); they are viewed as data structures, and dissected and abstracted to form the rule models; they are dissected and examined in order to produce explanations (see [2]); they are constructed during knowledge acquisition; and finally they are reasoned about by the meta rules.

It is important to note here that the feasibility of such multiplicity of uses is based less on the notion of production rules *per se*, than on the availability of a representation with a *small grain size* and a *simple syntax and semantics*. "Small", modular chunks of code written in a simple, heavily stylized form (though not necessarily a situation-action form), would have done as well, as would any representation with simple enough internal structure and of mangable size. The introduction of greater complexity in the representation, or the use of a representation that encoded significantly larger "chunks" of knowledge would require more sophisticated techniques for dissecting and manipulating representations than we have developed thus far. But the key limitations are size and complexity of structure, rather than a specific style of knowledge encoding.

Two other benefits may arise from the ability to describe representations. We noted earlier that much of the information necessary to maintain a system is often recorded in informal ways, if at all. If it were in fact convenient to record this information by describing it to the program itself, then we would have an effective and useful repository of information. We might see information that was previously folklore or informal documentation becoming more formalized, and migrating into the system itself. We have illustrated above a few of the advantages this offers in terms of maintaining a large system.

This may in turn produce a new perspective on programs. Early scarcity of hardware resources led to an emphasis on minimizing machine resources consumed, for example by reducing all numeric expressions to their simplest form by hand. More recently, this has meant a certain style of programming in which a programmer spends a great deal of time thinking about a problem first, trying to solve as much as possible by hand, and then abstracting out only the very end product of all of that to be embodied in the program. That is, the program becomes simply a way of manipulating symbols to provide "the answer", with little indication left of what the original problem was, or more important, what knowledge was required to solve it.

But what if we reversed this trend, and instead view a program as a place to store many forms of knowledge about both the problem and the proposed solution (i.e., the program itself). This would apply equally well to code and data structures, and could help make possible a wider range of useful capabilities of the sort illustrated above.

One final observation. As we noted at the outset, interest in knowledge-based systems was motivated by the belief that no single, domain independent paradigm could produce the desired level of performance. It was suggested instead that a large store of domain specific (object level) knowledge was required. We might similarly suggest that this too will eventually reach its limits, and that simply adding more object level knowledge will no longer, by itself, guarantee increased performance. Instead it may be necessary to focus on building stores of meta-level knowledge, especially in the form of strategies for effective use of knowledge.

Such "meta-level knowledge based" systems may represent a profitable future direction.

{6} Conclusions

We have reviewed four examples of meta-level knowledge, and demonstrated their application to the task of building and using large stores of domain specific knowledge. This has showed that supplying the system with a store of information about its representations makes possible a number of useful capabilities. For example, by describing the structure of its representations (schemata, templates), we make possible a form of transfer of expertise, as well as a number of facilities for knowledge base maintenance. By supplying strategic information (meta-rules), we make possible a finer degree of control over use of knowledge in the system. And by giving the system the ability to derive empirical generalizations about its knowledge (rule models), we make possible a number of useful abilities that aid in knowledge transfer.

Notes

(1)   TEIRESIAS was developed in the context of the MYCIN system [17,6], which deals with infectious disease diagnosis and therapy. The domain has been changed to keep the discussion phrased in terms familiar to a wide range of readers, and to emphasize that neither the problems attacked nor the solutions suggested are restricted to a particular domain of application. The dialogs shown are real examples of TEIRESIAS in action, with a few word substitutions: e.g, *primary bacteremia* became *Georgia Pacific*, *infection* became *investment*, etc.

(2)   Both of these are constructed via simple statistical thresholding operations.

(3)   This was suggested by the perspective taken in work on SMALLTALK [9] and actors [10].

(4)   That is, are there meta-rules directly associated with that goal. Meta-rules can also be associated with other objects in the system, but that is beyond the scope of this paper. The issues of organizing and indexing meta-rules are covered in more detail in [2] and [5].

References

[1]   Bobrow D, Winograd T, An Overview of KRL, *Cognitive Science*, vol 1, pp 3-47, Jan 1977.
[2]   Davis R, Applications of meta-level knowledge to the construction, maintenance, and use of large knowledge bases, Stanford HPP Memo 76-7, July 1976.
[3]   Davis R, Knowledge about representations as a basis for system construction and maintenance, to appear in *Pattern-Directed Inference Systems*, Academic Press, (in press).
[4]   Davis R, Interactive transfer of expertise, to appear in *Proc 5th IJCAI*, Aug 1977.
[5]   Davis R, Generalized procedure calling and content-directed invocation, to appear in *Proc AI/PL Conference*, Aug 1977.
[6]   Davis R, Buchanan B G, Shortliffe E H, Production rules as a representation for a knowledge-based consultation system, *Artificial Intelligence*, 8:15-45, Spring 1977.
[7]   Feigenbaum E A, et. al., On generality and problem solving, in *MI6*, pp 165-190, Edinburgh University Press, 1971.
[8]   Fennell R D, Multiprocess software architecture for AI problem solving, PhD Thesis, Computer Science Department, CMU, May 1975.
[9]   Goldberg A, Kay A, Smalltalk-72 User's Manual, Learning Research Group, Xerox PARC, 1976.
[10]   Hewitt C, A universal modular actor formalism for AI, *Proc 3rd IJCAI*, pp 235-245.
[11]   Lesser V R, Fennell R D, Erman L D, Reddy D R, Organization of the HEARSAY II speech understanding system, *IEEE Transactions*, ASSP-23, February 1975, pp 11-23.
[12]   Mathlab Group, MACSYMA reference manual, 1974, MIT.
[13]   Manna Z, Correctness of programs, *Journal of Computer Systems Sciences*, May 1969.
[14]   Samuel A L, Some studies in machine learning using the game of checkers II - recent progress, *IBM Jnl Res and Devel*, 11:601-617.
[15]   Schank R C, Abelson R P, Scripts, plans and knowledge, *Proc 4th IJCAI*, pp 151-157.
[16]   Shortliffe E H, Buchanan B G, A model of inexact reasoning in medicine, *Math Biosci* 23 (1975) pp 351-379.
[17]   Shortliffe E H, *MYCIN: Computer-based Medical Consultations*, American Elsevier, 1976.
[18]   Waldinger R, Levitt K N, Reasoning about programs, *Artificial Intelligence*, 5 (Fall 1974) pp 235-316.
[19]   Winograd T, *Understanding Natural Language*, Academic Press, 1972.
[20]   Winston P, Learning structural descriptions from examples, MIT TR-76, Sept 70.

VI / Other Approaches

23 / Raymond Reiter
On Reasoning by Default

Recently, a good deal of attention has gone into the study and formalization of reasoning by default, a special but very important form of *non-monotonic* reasoning (see [McCarthy, Chapter 2] for another form). The motivation for this research is the observation that in the presence of incomplete knowledge about the world, it is often necessary to make plausible inferences based on rules like "Unless there is knowledge to the contrary, assume that . . ." Not that the *use* of this form of reasoning in AI is a recent phenomenon; it can be traced back at least to the semantic net research described in [Quillian, Chapter 6]. The current work, however, aims at understanding in a general way the *logic* behind this form of reasoning. This paper by Reiter was one of the first in this area and is an excellent introduction to its problems and techniques. He shows how patterns of default reasoning are involved in a wide range of phenomena in AI including the "closed world assumption," the frame problem, exceptions, generalization hierarchies, and the negation-as-failure found in many procedural AI languages. He also sketches how a standard formal logic has to be modified to include default rules, and some of the serious problems that have to be faced in this formalization. Reiter's subsequent work articulates this formalization in detail and attempts to deal with some of the technical problems he predicted (see, for example, [Reiter 80], [Reiter 81], and [Reiter and Criscuolo 80]).

Appeared in *Proc. TINLAP-2, Theoretical Issues in Natural Language Processing-2,* University of Illinois at Urbana-Champaign, 1978, 210–218.

ON REASONING BY DEFAULT

Raymond Reiter

Department of Computer Science
University of British Columbia
Vancouver, B.C., Canada

ABSTRACT

This paper surveys a number of kinds of default reasoning in Artificial Intelligence, specifically, default assignments to variables, the closed world assumption, the frame default for causal worlds, exceptions as defaults, and negation in Artificial Intelligence programming languages. Some of these defaults provide clear representational and computational advantanges over their corresponding first order theories. Finally, the paper discusses various difficulties associated with default theories.

> If I don't know I don't know
> > > I think I know
> If I don't know I know
> > > I think I don't know
>
> > > R.D. Laing, Knots

1. INTRODUCTION

Default reasoning is commonly used in natural language understanding systems and in Artificial Intelligence in general. We use the term "default reasoning" to denote the process of arriving at conclusions based upon patterns of inference of the form "In the absence of any information to the contrary, assume..." In this paper, we take this pattern to have the more formal meaning "If certain information cannot be deduced from the given knowledge base, then conclude..." Such reasoning represents a form of plausible inference and is typically required whenever conclusions must be drawn despite the absence of total knowledge about a world.

In order to fix some of these ideas, we begin by surveying a number of instances of default reasoning as they are commonly invoked in A.I. Specifically, we discuss default assignments to variables, the closed world assumption, the frame default for causal worlds, exceptions as defaults,

and negation in A.I. programming languages. We shall see that these may all be formalized by introducing a single default operator $\not\vdash$ where $\not\vdash W$ is taken to mean "W is not deducible from the given knowledge base".

In addition, we shall discover that the closed world and frame defaults provide clear representational and computational advantages over their corresponding first order theories. The former eliminates the need for an explicit representation of negative knowledge about a world, while the latter eliminates the so-called frame axioms for dynamic worlds.

Finally, we discuss various problems which arise as a result of augmenting first order logic with a default operator.

2. SOME INSTANCES OF DEFAULT REASONING IN A.I.

The use of default reasoning in A.I. is far more widespread than is commonly realized. The purpose of this section is to point out a variety of seemingly different situations in which such reasoning arises, to accent common patterns which emerge when defaults are formalized, and to indicate certain representational and computational advantages of default reasoning.

2.1 Default Assignments to Variables

A number of knowledge representation schemes, e.g. FRL [Roberts and Goldstein 1977], KRL [Bobrow and Winograd 1977], explicitly provide for the assignment of default values to variables (slots, terminals). For example, in KRL the unit for a person in an airline travel system has the form:

```
[Person UNIT Basic
    .
    .
    .
<hometown{(a City) PaloAlto; DEFAULT}>
    .
    .
    .  ]
```

We can view this declaration as an instruction to the KRL interpreter to carry out the following: If x is a person, then in the absence of any information to the contrary, assume hometown(x)=PaloAlto, or phrased in a way which makes explicit the fact that a default assignment is being made to a variable:

If x is a person and no value can be determined for the variable y such that hometown(x)=y, then assume y=PaloAlto.

Notice that in assigning a default value to a variable, it is not sufficient to fail to find an explicit match for the variable in the data base. For example, the non existence in the data base of a fact of the form hometown(JohnDoe)=y for some city y does not necessarily permit the default assignment y=PaloAlto. It might be the case that the following information is available:

$$(x/EMPLOYER)(y/PERSON)(z/CITY)EMPLOYS(x,y) \wedge location(x)=z \supset hometown(y)=z$$ [1]

i.e. a person's hometown is the same as his or her employer. In this case the default assignment y=PaloAlto can be made only if we fail to deduce the existence of an employer x and city z such that

$$EMPLOYS(x,JohnDoe) \wedge location(x)=z$$

In general then, default assignments to variables are permitted only as a result of failure of some attempted deduction. We can formulate a general inference pattern for the default assignment of values to variables:

For all $x_1,\ldots,x_n$ in classes $\tau_1,\ldots,\tau_n$ respectively, if we fail to deduce $(Ey/\theta)P(x_1,\ldots,x_n,y)$ then infer the default statement

$$P(x_1,\ldots,x_n,\text{<default value for y>})$$

or more succinctly,

$$\frac{(x_1/\tau_1)\ldots(x_n/\tau_n) \quad \not\vdash (Ey/\theta)P(x_1,\ldots,x_n,y)}{P(x_1,\ldots,x_n,\text{<default value for y>})} \qquad (D1)$$

Here $\not\vdash$ is to be read "fail to deduce", θ and the τ's are types, and $P(x_1,\ldots,x_n,y)$ is any statement about the variables $x_1,\ldots,x_n,y$. There are some serious difficulties associated with just what exactly is meant by "$\not\vdash$" but we shall defer these issues for the moment and rely instead on the reader's intuition. The default rule for home towns can now be seen as an instance of the above pattern:

$$(x/PERSON) \ \frac{\not\vdash (Ey/CITY)hometown(x)=y}{hometown(x)=PaloAlto}$$

2.2 THE CLOSED WORLD ASSUMPTION

It seems not generally recognized that the reasoning components of many natural language understanding systems have default assumptions built into them. The representation of knowledge upon which the reasoner computes does not explicitly indicate certain default assumptions. Rather, these defaults are realized as part of the code of the reasoner, or, as we shall say, following [Hayes 1977], as part of the reasoner's process structure. The most common such default corresponds to what has elsewhere been referred to as the closed world assumption [Reiter 1978]. In this section we describe two commonly used closed world defaults.

2.2.1 Hierarchies

As an illustration of the class of closed world defaults, consider standard taxonomies (IS-A hierarchies) as they are usually represented in the A.I. literature, for example the following:

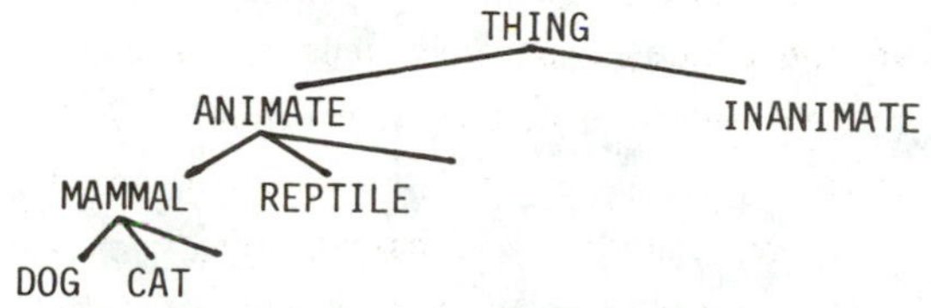

This has, as its first order logical representation, the following:

---

[1] Throughout this paper we shall use a typed logical representation language. Types, e.g. EMPLOYER, PERSON, CITY correspond to the usual categories of IS-A hierarchies. A typed universal quantifier like (x/EMPLOYER) is read "for all x which belong to the class EMPLOYER" or simply "for all employers x". A typed existential quantifier like (Ex/CITY) is read "there is a city x". The notation derives from that used by Woods in his "FOR function" [Woods 1968].

```
(x)DOG(x) ⊃ MAMMAL(x)
(x)CAT(x) ⊃ MAMMAL(x)                    (2.1)
(x)MAMMAL(x) ⊃ ANIMATE(x)
etc.
```

Now if Fido is known to be a dog we can conclude
that Fido is animate in either of two essentially
isomorphic ways:

1. If the hierarchy is implemented as some sort of
network, then we infer ANIMATE(fido) if the class
ANIMATE lies "above" DOG i.e. there is some pointer
chain leading from node DOG to node ANIMATE in the
network.

2. If the hierarchy is implemented as a set of first
order formulae, then we conclude ANIMATE(fido) if
we can forward chain (modus ponens) with DOG(fido)
to derive ANIMATE(fido). This forward chaining
from DOG(fido) to ANIMATE(fido) corresponds exactly
to following pointers from node DOG to node ANIMATE
in the network.

Thus far, there is no essential difference between a network representation of a hierarchy with
its pointer-chasing interpreter and a first order
representation with its forward chaining theorem
proving interpreter. A fundamental distinction
arises with respect to negation. As an example,
consider how one deduces that Fido is <u>not</u> a reptile.
A network interpreter will determine that the node
REPTILE does not lie "above" DOG and will thereby
conclude that DOGs are not REPTILEs so that
¬REPTILE(fido) is deduced. On the other hand, a
theorem prover will try to prove ¬REPTILE(fido).
Given the above first order representation, no such
proof exists. The reason is clear - nothing in
the representation (2.1) states that the categories
MAMMAL and REPTILE are disjoint. For the theorem
prover to deal with negative information, the
knowledge base (2.1) must be augmented by the
following facts stating that the categories of
the hierarchy are disjoint:

```
(x)ANIMATE(x) ⊃ ¬INANIMATE(x)
(x)MAMMAL(x) ⊃ ¬REPTILE(x)              (2.2)
(x)DOG(x) ⊃ ¬CAT(x)
```

It is now clear that a first order theorem proving
interpreter can establish ¬REPTILE(fido) by a pure
forward chaining proof procedure from DOG(fido)
using (2.1) and (2.2). However, unlike the earlier
proof of ANIMATE(fido), this proof of ¬REPTILE(fido)

is <u>not isomorphic to that generated by the network
interpreter</u>. (Recall that the network interpreter
deduces ¬REPTILE(fido) by <u>failing</u> to find a pointer
chain linking DOG and REPTILE). Moreover, while
the network interpreter must contend only with a
representation equivalent to that of (2.1), the
theorem prover must additionally utilize the negative information (2.2). Somehow, then, the process
structure of the network interpreter implicitly
represents the negative knowledge (2.2), while
computing only on declarative knowledge equivalent
to (2.1).

We can best distinguish the two approaches by
observing that two different logics are involved.
To see this, consider modifying the theorem prover
so as to simulate the network process structure.
Since the network interpreter tries, and fails, to
establish a pointer chain from DOG to REPTILE using
a declarative knowledge base equivalent to (2.1),
the theorem prover can likewise attempt to prove
REPTILE(fido) using only (2.1). As for the network interpreter, this attempt will fail. If we
now endow the theorem prover with the additional
inference rule:
"If you fail to deduce REPTILE(fido) then conclude
¬REPTILE(fido)"
the deduction of ¬REPTILE(fido) will be isomorphic
to that of the network interpreter. More generally,
we require an inference schema, applicable to any
of the monadic predicates MAMMAL, DOG, CAT, etc. of
the hierarchy:
"If x is an individual and P(x) cannot be deduced,
then infer ¬P(x)"
or in the notation of the previous section

$$(x) \quad \frac{\nvdash P(x)}{\neg P(x)} \qquad\qquad (D2)$$

What we have argued then is that the process
structure of a network interpreter is formally
equivalent to that of a first order theorem prover
augmented by the ability to use the inference
schema (D2). In a sense, a network interpreter is
the compiled form of such an augmented theorem
prover.

There are several points worth noting:

1. The schema (D2) is not a first order rule of
inference since the operator ⊬ is not a first
order notion. (It is a meta notion.) Thus a theorem

prover which evokes (D2) in order to establish negative conclusions by failure is not performing first order deductions.

2. The schema (D2) has a similar pattern to the default schema (D1).

3. In the presence of the default schema (D2), the negative knowledge (2.2), which would be necessary in the absence of (D2), is not required. As we shall see in the next section, this property is a general characteristic of the closed world default, and leads to a significant reduction in the complexity of both the representation and processing of knowledge.

2.2.2 The Closed World Default

The schema (D2) is actually a special case of the following more general default schema:

$$(x_1/\tau_1)\ldots(x_n/\tau_n) \ \frac{\not\vdash P(x_1,\ldots,x_n)}{\neg P(x_1,\ldots,x_n)} \qquad \text{(D3)}$$

If (D3) is in force for all predicates P of some domain, then reasoning is being done under the closed world assumption [Reiter 1978]. In most A.I. representation schemes, hierarchies are treated as closed world domains. The use of the closed world assumption in A.I. and in ordinary human reasoning extends beyond such hierarchies, however. As a simple example, consider an airline schedule for a direct Air Canada flight from Vancouver to New York. If none is found, one assumes that no such flight exists. Formally, we can view the schedule as a data base, and the query as an attempt to establish DIRECTLY-CONNECTS(AC, Van,NY). This fails, whence one concludes ¬DIRECTLY-CONNECTS(AC,Van,NY) by an application of schema (D3). Such schedules are designed to be used under the closed world assumption. They contain only positive information; negative information is inferred by default. There is one very good reason for making the closed world assumption in this setting. The number of negative facts vastly exceeds the number of positive ones. For example, Air Canada does not directly connect Vancouver and Moscow, or Toronto and Bombay, or Moscow and Bombay, etc. etc. It is totally unfeasible to explicitly represent all such negative information in the data base, as would be required under a first order theorem prover. It is

important to notice, however, that the closed world assumption presumes perfect knowledge about the domain being modeled. If it were not known, for example, whether Air Canada directly connects Vancouver and Chicago, we would no longer be justified in making the closed world assumption with respect to the flight schedule. For by the absence of this fact from the data base, we would conclude that Air Canada does not directly connect Vancouver and Chicago, violating our assumed state of ignorance about this fact.

The flight schedule illustrates a very common use of the closed world default rule for purely extensional data bases. In particular, it illustrates how this default factors out the need for any explicit representation of negative facts. This result holds for more general data bases. As an example, consider the ubiquitous blocks world, under the following decomposition hierarchy of objects in that world:

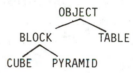

Let SUPPORTS(x,y) denote "x directly supports y" and FREE(x) denote "x is free" i.e. objects may be placed upon x. Then the following general facts hold:

$(x/OBJECT)(y/TABLE)\neg SUPPORTS(x,y)$ (1)

$(x/OBJECT)\neg SUPPORTS(x,x)$ (2)

$(x/PYRAMID)(y/BLOCK)\neg SUPPORTS(x,y)$ (3)

$(x\ y/BLOCK)SUPPORTS(x,y) \supset$
      $\neg SUPPORTS(y,x)$ (4)

$(x/PYRAMID)\neg FREE(x)$ (5)

$(x\ y/BLOCK)(z/TABLE)SUPPORTS(x,y) \supset$
      $\neg SUPPORTS(z,y)$ (6)

$(x/CUBE)FREE(x) \supset$
      $(y/BLOCK)\neg SUPPORTS(x,y)$ (7)

$(x/CUBE)(y/BLOCK)\neg SUPPORTS(x,y) \supset$
      $FREE(x)$ (8)

$(x/TABLE)FREE(x)$ (9)

Consider the following scene

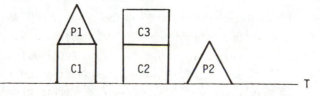

This is representable by

$$SUPPORTS(T,C1) \quad SUPPORTS(T,C2)$$
$$SUPPORTS(C1,P1) \quad SUPPORTS(C2,C3) \qquad (10)$$
$$SUPPORTS(T,P2)$$

together with the following negative facts

$$\neg SUPPORTS(C1,C2) \quad \neg SUPPORTS(C2,C1)$$
$$\neg SUPPORTS(C3,C1) \quad \neg SUPPORTS(C1,P2)$$
$$\neg SUPPORTS(C3,P1) \quad \neg SUPPORTS(C3,P2) \qquad (11)$$
$$\neg SUPPORTS(C1,C3) \quad \neg SUPPORTS(C2,P1)$$

Notice that virtually all of the knowledge about the blocks domain is negative, namely the negative specific facts (11), together with the negative facts (1)-(7)[1]. This is not an accidental feature. Most of what we know about any world is negative.

Now a first order theorem prover must have access to all of the facts (1)-(11). For example, in proving ¬SUPPORTS(C3,C2) it must use (4). Consider instead such a theorem prover endowed with the additional ability to interpret the closed world default schema (D3). Then, in attempting a proof of ¬SUPPORTS(C3,C2) it tries to show that SUPPORTS(C3,C2) is _not_ provable. Since SUPPORTS(C3,C2) cannot be proved, it concludes ¬SUPPORTS(C3,C2), as required.

It should be clear intuitively that in the presence of the closed world default schema (D3), none of the negative facts (1)-(7), (11) need be represented explicitly nor used in reasoning. This can be proved, under fairly general conditions [Reiter 1978]. One function, then, of the closed world default is to "factor out" of the representation all negative knowledge about the domain. It is of some interest to compare the blocks world representation (1)-(11) with those commonly used in blocks world problem-solvers (e.g.[Winograd 1972, Warren 1974]). These systems do not represent explicitly the negative knowledge (1)-(7), (11) but instead use the closed world default for reasoning about negation. (See Section 3 below for a discussion of negation in A.I. programming languages.)

Although the closed world default factors out negative knowledge for answering questions about a domain, this knowledge must nevertheless be available. To see why, consider an attempted update of the example blocks world scene with the new "fact" SUPPORTS(C3,C2). To detect the resulting inconsistency requires the negative fact (4). In general then, negative knowledge is necessary for maintaining the <u>integrity</u> of a data base. A consequence of the closed world assumption is a decomposition of knowledge into positive and negative facts. Only positive knowledge is required for querying the data base. Both positive and negative knowledge are required for maintaining the integrity of the data base.

2.3 DEFAULTS AND THE FRAME PROBLEM

The frame problem [Raphael 1971] arises in the representation of dynamic worlds. Roughly speaking, the problem stems from the need to represent those aspects of the world which remain invariant under certain state changes. For example, moving a particular object or switching on a light will not change the colours of any objects in the world. Painting an object will not affect the locations of the objects. In a first order representation of such worlds, it is necessary to represent explicitly all of the invariants under all state changes. These are referred to as the frame axioms for the world being modeled. For example, to represent the fact that painting an object does not alter the locations of objects would require, in the situational calculus of [McCarthy and Hayes 1969] a frame axiom something like

$$(x \ z/OBJECT)(y/POSITION)(s/STATE)(C/COLOUR)$$
$$LOCATION(x,y,s) \supset LOCATION(x,y,paint(z,C,s))$$

The problem is that in general we will require a vast number of such axioms e.g. object locations also remain invariant when lights are switched on, when it thunders, when someone speaks etc. so there is a major difficulty in even articulating a deductively adequate set of frame axioms for a given world.

A solution to the frame problem is a representation of the world coupled with appropriate rules of inference such that the frame axioms are neither represented explicitly nor used explicitly in reasoning about the world. We will focus on a

---

[1] The notion of a negative fact has a precise definition. A fact is negative iff all of the literals in its clausal form are negative.

proposed solution by [Sandewall 1972][1]. A related approach is described in [Hayes 1973]. Sandewall proposes a new operator, UNLESS, which takes formula W as argument. The intended interpretation of UNLESS(W) is "W can not be proved" i.e. it is identical to the operator $\nvdash$ of this paper. Sandewall proposes a single "frame inference rule" which, in the notation of this paper, can be paraphrased as follows:

For all predicates P which take a state variable as an argument

$$(x_1/\tau_1)\ldots(x_n/\tau_n)(s/\text{STATE})(f/\text{ACTION-FUNCTION})$$

$$\frac{\nvdash \neg P(x_1,\ldots,x_n,f(x_1,\ldots,x_n,s))}{P(x_1,\ldots,x_n,f(x_1,\ldots,x_n,s))} \qquad (\text{D4})$$

Intuitively, (D4) formalizes the so-called "STRIPS assumption" [Waldinger 1975]: Every action (state change) is assumed to leave every relation unaffected unless it is possible to deduce otherwise. This schema can be used in the following way, say in order to establish that cube33 is at location λ after box7 has been painted blue:

To establish LOCATION(cube33,λ,paint(box7,blue,s)) fail to prove $\neg$LOCATION(cube33,λ,paint(box7,blue,s))

There are several observations that can be made:

1. The frame inference schema (D4) has a pattern similar to the default schemata (D2) and (D3) of earlier sections of this paper. It too is a default schema.

2. The frame schema (D4) is in some sense a dual of the closed world schema (D3). The former permits the deduction of a positive fact from failure to establish its negation. The latter provides for the deduction of a negative fact from failure to derive its positive counterpart. This duality is preserved with respect to the knowledge "factored out" of the representation. Whereas the frame default eliminates the need for certain kinds of positive knowledge (the frame axioms), the closed world default factors out the explicit representation of negative knowledge.

2.4 DEFAULTS AND EXCEPTIONS

A good deal of what we know about the world is "almost always" true, with a few exceptions. For example, all birds fly except for penguins, ostriches, fledglings, etc. Given a particular bird, we will conclude that it flies unless we happen to know that is satisfies one of these exceptions. Nevertheless, we want it true of birds "in general" that they fly. How can we reconcile these apparently conflicting points of view? The natural first order representation is inconsistent:

(x/BIRD)FLY(x) "In general, birds fly"
(x)PENGUIN(x) $\supset$ BIRD(x) "Penguins are birds
(x/PENGUIN)$\neg$FLY(x) which don't fly."

An alternative first order representation explicitly lists the exceptions to flying

(x/BIRD)$\neg$PENGUIN(x) $\land$ $\neg$OSTRICH(x) $\land$ ... $\supset$
    FLY(x)

But with this representation, we cannot conclude of a "general" bird, that it can fly. To see why, consider an attempt to prove FLY(tweety) where all we know of tweety is that she is a bird. Then we must establish the subgoal

$\neg$PENGUIN(tweety) $\land$ $\neg$OSTRICH(tweety) $\land$ ...

which is impossible given that we have no further information about tweety. We are blocked from concluding that tweety can fly even though, intuitively we want to deduce just that. In effect, we need a default rule of the form

$$(x/\text{BIRD}) \quad \frac{\nvdash (\text{PENGUIN}(x) \lor \text{OSTRICH}(x) \lor \ldots)}{\text{FLY}(x)}$$

With this rule of inference we can deduce FLY(tweety), as required. Notice, however, that whenever there are exceptions to a "general" fact in some domain of knowledge we are no longer free to arbitrarily structure that knowledge. For example, the following hierarchy would be unacceptable, where the dotted link indicates the existence of an exception

Clearly there is no way in this hierarchy of establishing that penguins are animals. For hierarchies the constraint imposed by exceptions is easily

---

[1] [Kramosil 1975] claims to have proved that Sandewall's approach is either meaningless or equivalent to a first order approach. See Section 4 for a discussion of this issue.

articulated: If P and Q are nodes with P below Q, and if $(x)P(x) \supset Q(x)$ is true without exception, then there must be a sequence of solid links connecting P and Q. For more general kinds of knowledge the situation is more problematic. One must be careful to ensure that chains of implications do not unwittingly inherit unintended exceptions.

3. DEFAULTS AND "NEGATION" IN A.I. PROGRAMMING LANGUAGES

It has been observed by several authors [Hayes 1973, Sandewall 1972, Reiter 1978] that the basic default operator $\not\vdash$ has, as its "procedural equivalent" the negation operator in a number of A.I. programming languages e.g. THNOT in MICROPLANNER [Hewitt 1972, Sussman et al. 1970], NOT in PROLOG [Roussel 1975]. For example, in MICROPLANNER, the command (THGOAL <pattern>) can be viewed as an attempt to prove <pattern> given a data base of facts and theorems. (THNOT(THGOAL <pattern>)) then succeeds iff (THGOAL <pattern>) fails i.e. iff <pattern> is not provable, and this of course is precisely the interpretation of the default operator $\not\vdash$.

Given that "negation" in A.I. procedural languages corresponds to the default operator and not to logical negation, it would seem that some of the criticism often directed at theorem proving from within the A.I. community is misdirected. For the so-called procedural approach, often proposed as an alternative to theorem proving as a representation and reasoning component in A.I. systems, is a realization of a default logic, whereas theorem provers are usually realizations of a first order logic, and as we have seen, these are different logics.

In a sense, the so-called procedural vs. declarative issue in A.I. might better be phrased as the default vs. first order logic issue. Many of the advantages of the procedural approach can be interpreted as representational and computational advantages of the default operator. There is a fair amount of empirical evidence in support of this point of view, primarily based upon the successful use of PROLOG [Roussel 1975] - a pure theorem prover augmented with a "THNOT" operator - for such diverse A.I. tasks as problem solving [Warren 1974], symbolic mathematics [Kanoui 1976], and natural language question-answering [Colmeraurer 1973].

On the theoretical level, we are just beginning to understand the advantages of a first order logic augmented with the default operator:

1. Default logic provides a representation language which more faithfully reflects a good deal of common sense knowledge than do traditional logics. Similarly, for many situations, default reasoning corresponds to what is usually viewed as common sense reasoning.

2. For many settings, the appropriate default theories lead to a significant reduction in both representational and computational complexity with respect to the corresponding first order theory. Thus, under the closed world default, negative knowledge about a domain need not explicitly be represented nor reasoned with in querying a data base. Similarly under the frame default, the usual frame axioms are not required.

There are, of course, other advantages of the procedural approach - specifically, explicit control over reasoning - which are not accounted for by the above logical analysis. We have distinguished the purely logical structure of such representational languages from their process structure, and have argued that at least some of their success derives from the nature of the logic which they realize.

4. SOME PROBLEMS WITH DEFAULT THEORIES

Given that default reasoning has such widespread applications in A.I. it is natural to define a default theory as a first order theory augmented by one or more inference schemata like (D1), (D2) etc. and to investigate the properties of such theories. Unfortunately, some such theories display peculiar and intuitively unacceptable behaviours.

One difficulty is the ease with which inconsistent theories can be defined, for example $\frac{\not\vdash A}{B}$ coupled with a knowledge base with the single fact $\neg B$. Another, pointed out by [Sandewall 1972] is that the theorems of certain default theories will depend upon the order in which they are derived. As an example, consider the theory

$$\frac{\not\vdash A}{B} \qquad \frac{\not\vdash B}{A}$$

Since A is not provable, we can infer B. Since B

is now proved, we cannot infer A, so this theory has the single theorem B. If instead, we had started by observing that B is not provable, then the theory would have the single theorem A. Default theories exhibiting such behaviour are clearly unacceptable. At the very least, we must demand of a default theory that it satisfy a kind of Church-Rosser property: No matter what the order in which the theorems of the theory are derived, the resulting set of theorems will be unique.

Another difficulty arises in modeling dynamically changing worlds e.g. in causal worlds or in text understanding where the model of the text being built up changes as more of the text is assimilated. Under these circumstances, inferences which have been made as a result of a default assumption may subsequently be falsified by new information which now violates that default assumption. As a simple example, consider a travel consultant which has made the default assumption that the traveller's starting point is Palo Alto and has, on the basis of this, planned all of the details of a trip. If the consultant subsequently learns that the starting point is Los Angeles, it must undo at least part of the planned trip, specifically the first (and possibly last) leg of the plan. But how is the consultant to know to focus just on these changes? Somehow, whenever a new fact is deduced and stored in the data base, all of the facts which rely upon a default assumption and which supported this deduction must be associated with this new fact. These supporting facts must themselves have their default supports associated with them, and so on. Now, should the data base be updated with new information which renders an instance of some default rule inapplicable, delete all facts which had been previously deduced whose support sets relied upon this instance of the default rule. There are obviously some technical and implementation details that require articulation, but the basic idea should be clear. A related proposal for dealing with beliefs and real world observations is described in [Hayes 1973].

One way of viewing the role of a default theory is as a way of implicitly further completing an underlying incomplete first order theory. Recall that a first order theory is said to be <u>complete</u> iff for all closed formulae W, wither W or ¬W is provable. Most interesting mathematical theories turn out to be incomplete - a celebrated result due to Godel. Most of what we know about the world, when formalized, will yield an incomplete theory precisely because we cannot know everything - there are gaps in our knowledge. The effect of a default rule is to implicitly fill in some of those gaps by a form of plausible reasoning. In particular, the effect of the closed world default is to fully complete an underlying incomplete first order theory. However, it is well known that there are insurmountable problems associated with completing an incomplete theory like arithmetic. Although it is a trivial matter conceptually to augment the axioms of arithmetic with a default rule $\frac{\vdash W}{W}$ where W is any closed formula, we will be no further ahead because the non theorems of arithmetic are not recursively enumerable. What this means is that there is no way in general that, given a W, we can establish that W is not a theorem even if W happens not to be a theorem. This in turn means that we are not even guaranteed that an arbitrary default rule of inference is effective i.e. there may be no algorithm which will inform us whether or not a given default rule of inference is applicable. From this we can conclude that the theories of a default theory may not be recursively enumerable. This situation is in marked contrast to what normally passes for a logic where, at the very least, the rules of inference must be effective and the theorems recursively enumerable.

Finally, it is not hard to see that default theories fail to satisfy the <u>extension property</u> [Hayes 1973] which all "respectable" logics do satisfy. (A logical calculus has the extension property iff whenever a formula is provable from a set P of premises, it is also provable from any set P' such that $P \subseteq P'$.)

[Kramosil 1975] attempts to establish some general results on default theories. Kramosil "proves" that for any such theory, the default rules are irrelevant in the sense that either the theory will be meaningless or the theorems of the theory will be precisely the same as those obtainable by ignoring the default rules of inference. Kramosil's result, if correct, would invalidate the main point of this paper, namely that default theories play a prominent role in reasoning about the world. Fortunately, his "proof" relies on an incorrect definition of theoremhood so that the problem of characterizing the theorems of a default theory remain open.

5.   CONCLUSIONS

Default reasoning may well be the rule, rather than the exception, in reasoning about the world since normally we must act in the presence of incomplete knowledge. Moreover, aside from mathematics and the physical sciences, most of what we know about the world has associated exceptions and caveats. Conventional logics, such as first order logic, lack the expressive power to adequately represent the knowledge required for reasoning by default. We gain this expressive power by introducing the default operator.

In order to provide an adequate formal (as opposed to heuristic) foundation for default reasoning we need a well articulated theory of default logic. This requires, in part, a theory of the semantics of default logic, a suitable notion of theoremhood and deduction, and conditions under which the default inference rules are effective and the set of theorems unique. Since in any realistic domain, all of the default schemata of Section 2 will be in force (together, no doubt, with others we have not considered) we require a deeper understanding of how these different schemata interact. Finally, there is an intriguing relationship between certain defaults and the complexity of the underlying representation. Both the closed world and frame defaults implicitly represent whole classes of first order axioms. Is this an accidental phenomemon or is some general principal involved?

ACKNOWLEDGEMENTS

This paper was written with the financial support of NRC grant A 7642. I am indebted to Brian Funt, Randy Goebel and Richard Rosenberg for their criticisms of an earlier draft of this paper.

REFERENCES

Bobrow, D.G. and Winograd, T., (1977). "An Overview of KRL-0, a Knowledge Representation Language," Cognitive Science, Vol.1, No.1, Jan. 1977.

Colmeraurer, A., (1973). Un System de Communication Home-Machine en Français, Rapport interne, UER de Luminy, Université d'Aix-Marseille, 1973.

Hayes, P.J., (1973). "The Frame Problem and Related Problems in Artificial Intelligence," in Artificial and Human Thinking, A. Elithorn and D. Jones (Eds.), Jossey-Bass Inc., San Francisco, 1973, pp.45-49.

Hayes, P.J., (1977). "In Defence of Logic," Proc. IJCAI-5, M.I.T., Cambridge, Mass., August 22-25, 1977, pp. 559-565.

Hewitt, C., (1972). Description and Theoretical Analysis (Using Schemata) of PLANNER: A Language for Proving Theorems and Manipulating Models in a Robot, A.I.Memo No. 251, M.I.T. Project MAC, Cambridge, Mass., April 1972.

Kanoui, H., (1976). "Some Aspects of Symbolic Integration via Predicate Logic Programming," SIGSAM Bulletin, 10, Nov. 1976, pp. 29-42.

Kramosil, I., (1975). "A Note on Deduction Rules with Negative Premises," Proc. IJCAI-4, Tbilisi, USSR, Sept. 3-8, 1975, pp. 53-56.

McCarthy J. and Hayes, P.J., (1969). "Some Philosophic Problems from the Standpoint of Artificial Intelligence," in Machine Intelligence 4, B. Meltzer and D. Michie (Eds.), Edinburgh University Press, Edinburgh, 1969, pp. 463-502.

Raphael, B., (1971). "The Frame Problem in Problem-Solving Systems," in Artificial Intelligence and Heuristic Programming, N.V. Findler and B. Meltzer (Eds.), Edinburgh University Press, Edinburgh.

Reiter, R., (1978). "On Closed World Data Bases," in Logic and Data Bases, H. Gallaire and J. Minker (Eds.), Plenum Press, New York, to appear.

Roberts, R.B. and Goldstein, I., (1977). The FRL Manual, A.I. Memo No. 409, M.I.T., Sept. 1977.

Roussel, P., (1975). PROLOG, Manuel de Reference et d'Utilisation, Group d'Intelligence Artificielle, U.E.R. de Marseille, France, 1975.

Sandewall, E., (1972). "An Approach to the Frame Problem, and its Implementation," in Machine Intelligence 7, B. Meltzer and D. Michie (Eds.), Edinburgh University Press, Edinburgh, pp. 195-204.

Sussman, G., Winograd, T., and Charniak,E., (1970). MICRO-PLANNER Reference Manual, A.I. MEMO No. 203, M.I.T., Cambridge, Mass., 1970.

Waldinger, R., (1975). Achieving Several Goals Simultaneously, Artificial Intelligence Center Technical Note 107, Stanford Research Institute, Menlo Park, Calif., July 1975.

Warren, D., (1974). WARPLAN: A System for Generating Plans, Memo No. 76, Dept. of Computational Logic, University of Edinburgh, June 1974.

Winograd, T., (1972). Understanding Natural Language, Academic Press, New York, 1972.

Woods, W.A., (1968). "Procedural Semantics for a Question-Answering Machine," AFIPS Conference Proceedings, Vol. 3, Part I, 1968, pp. 457-471.

24 / Ronald J. Brachman, Richard E. Fikes, and Hector J. Levesque
KRYPTON: A Functional Approach to Knowledge Representation

In recent years, a number of efforts in Knowledge Representation have attempted various combinations of logic, networks, frames, and production rules. Here, Brachman, Fikes, and Levesque attempt a synthesis of frame-structures and logic to achieve a unique goal: a representation system that gives full status to the *definition* of complex terms, on top of a powerful *assertional* capability (see [Maida and Shapiro, Chapter 9] for a different approach to this distinction). Their approach is to use a network/frame-style language for forming terms (they discuss how a KL-ONE-style representation language [Brachman, Chapter 10] is particularly appropriate for the task) and a first-order predicate language for making statements (similarly, they briefly discuss how a first-order logical language is appropriate for the expression of beliefs; see also [Moore, Chapter 18]). They embed both languages within a functional framework, so that a user has no access to the structures that implement the terminological and assertional competences (after illustrating how this has been a bane of representation systems for some time). There is also substantial discussion of appropriate ways to implement the functions that define the system (called "KRYPTON"), including the key notion of how a theorem-prover in one component can make direct use of complex predicates defined in the other. The work was formally sound enough to allow the authors to explore the complexity of inference in the terminological component—see [Levesque and Brachman, Chapter 4] for details. The paper was written for a general computer science audience, and provides a good deal of motivation before it gets into the technical details.

Appeared as FLAIR Technical Report No. 16, Fairchild Laboratory for Artificial Intelligence Research, Palo Alto, CA, May, 1983 (revised version of an article published under the same name in *IEEE Computer* **16**(10), 1983, 67–73).

KRYPTON: A Functional Approach to Knowledge Representation

Ronald J. Brachman

Fairchild Laboratory for Artificial Intelligence Research

Richard E. Fikes

Xerox Palo Alto Research Center

Hector J. Levesque

Fairchild Laboratory for Artificial Intelligence Research

May, 1983

Abstract

Although knowledge representation systems based on frames and semantic networks have a certain computational and intuitive appeal, they tend to be severely restricted assertionally, and are often fraught with ambiguous and conflicting readings. Part of the problem is that users of frame systems have free access to the implementation data structures and use them in idiosyncratic ways to compensate for the assertional limitations of the language. We have attempted to overcome these difficulties in KRYPTON, a new knowledge representation system that is defined not in terms of the structures it can manipulate, but *functionally*, in terms of what it can be asked and told about the domain. KRYPTON integrates two representation languages, a frame-based one used only for forming descriptive terms, and a logic-based one for making assertions. We here describe the two languages, a functional interface to the system, and an implementation in terms of a taxonomy of frames and its interaction with a first-order theorem prover.

KRYPTON: A Functional Approach to Knowledge Representation

Ronald J. Brachman

Fairchild Laboratory for Artificial Intelligence Research

Richard E. Fikes

Xerox Palo Alto Research Center

Hector J. Levesque

Fairchild Laboratory for Artificial Intelligence Research

§1 Introduction

While much of current work in knowledge representation is fraught with disagreement, some trends seem to be emerging. In particular, a great deal of effort has focused on the development of 'frame'-based languages with the following features:

- the principal representational objects—known as "frames"—are taken to be non-atomic *descriptions* of some complexity;

- frames are defined as *specializations* of more general frames;

- individuals are represented by *instantiations* of generic frames; and

- the resulting connections between frames form *taxonomies.*

The widespread appeal of taxonomies of frames seems to arise from the fact that they match well with our intuitions about how to structure the world (as illustrated in folk taxonomies, for example). They also suggest enticing directions for processing (inheritance, defaults, *etc.*), and have found applications in other areas of computer science, such as database management and object-oriented programming.

While the basic ideas of frame systems are straightforward, complications arise in their design and use. These difficulties typically arise from the fact that

- structures are interpreted different ways at different times (the principal ambiguity being between definitional and factual interpretations);   and

- the meaning of the representation language is specified only in terms of the data structures used to implement it (typically inheritance networks).

We have developed a design strategy for avoiding these types of problems, and in this paper we outline our strategy and highlight some of the key features of a representation system we have defined using it. The representation system—called "KRYPTON"— clearly distinguishes between definitional and factual information. In particular, KRYPTON has two representation languages, one for forming descriptive terms and one for making statements about the world using these terms. Further, KRYPTON provides a *functional* view of a knowledge base, characterized in terms of what it can be asked or told, not in terms of the particular structures it uses to represent knowledge.

§2 The Trouble with Frames

As we have noted, a recurring theme in various knowledge representation languages is that of a *taxonomy of structured descriptions*. In such a language, we might have the following description of a family:

family:

> **isa** *social-structure*
>
> | |
> |---|
> | *male-parent: man* (**exactly** 1) |
> | *female-parent: woman* (**exactly** 1) |
> | *child: person* |

Even uninterpreted, this type of data structure is undeniably useful. For the purposes of knowledge representation, however, an interpretation must be imposed on the representational objects—that is, they have to *mean* something. As it turns out, there are an extraordinary number of possible interpretations of the links and nodes in a taxonomy of frames,[1] and typical frame systems leave much of the semantical work to the reader.

Yet despite the multitude of possible interpretations, there seem to be two basic approaches to the meaning of frames. The first takes them to be *assertions*, or statements about the way things are in the world. Under this interpretation, investigated in some depth in [Hayes 79], the presence of the *family* frame above in a frame system would be understood as asserting that every family is a social structure and that a family has a male parent, a female parent, and some number of children.

Unfortunately, the assertional point of view turns out to be quite restrictive, principally for two reasons:[2]

> ▸ 'instantiation' (filling in the slots of a frame), the basic form of assertion in frame systems, makes expressions of incomplete knowledge either difficult or impossible. For example, a statement such as "either Elsie or Bessie is the cow standing in Farmer Jones' field" cannot be made in a typical assertional frame system;

---

[1]See [Brachman 83] for a compendium of the ambiguous interpretations one finds for the ISA link.

[2]Since we cannot give adequate treatment to these issues here, we refer the reader to these more extensive discussions: first, see [Woods 75] for the distinction between *assertional* and *structural* links; further, see [Levesque 82] for a discussion of the inadequacy of instantiation as an assertional mechanism; finally, the failure of frame systems to handle structured descriptions is treated in section 3 of [Brachman 83].

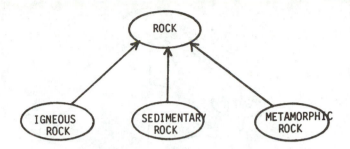

Figure 1. How many kinds of rocks are there?

▸ truly composite descriptions cannot be expressed. For example, instead of being able to form a description "a family with no children", we can only create a *childless-family* frame and assert that families of this type have no children (as if this were an incidental property, like having both parents working).

Frustration with limitations of an assertional stance might lead us to adopt the other predominant view of frames, as *descriptions*, with no direct assertional import. Representation languages such as KL-ONE [Schmolze and Brachman 82] and others take the view that frames and links between them are parts of the structure of descriptions; some other mechanism is needed to use the descriptions to state facts. Under this interpretation, the symbol "*family*" in the above example would be taken as an abbreviation for a description such as "a social structure with, among other things,[3] a male parent who is a man, a female parent who is a woman, and some number of children, all persons". This interpretation of frames is claimed to produce a cleaner language that does not suffer from the problems that plague strictly assertional frame systems.

Unfortunately, the cleanliness of the non-assertional approach does not quite allay *all* fears of misinterpretation of links and frames in these systems. What one gets when one gets a frame system—even a strictly interpreted structural one—is a package for manipulating symbolic *data structures*. This allows the user or the user program to draw unwarranted conclusions. Consider for example, Figure 1. It is all too easy to feel that one can answer the question, "How many kinds of rocks are there?" from this structure. It seems that all we would have to do is to count the nodes immediately below *rock*. But, as illustrated in Figure 2, counting 'kinds' in a structural network is meaningless. The intent of the language is exactly to allow the formation of descriptive terms such as *large grey igneous rock*, on a par with *igneous rock*.

A similarly seductive phenomenon arises from the user's access to links in a network. Figure 3 shows two different representations of *bachelor*; in the two cases,

---

[3]Whether or not the frame expresses sufficiency conditions is essentially independent of the choice to read it structurally or assertionally.

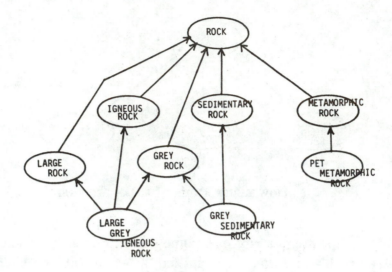

Figure 2. More rock-terms.

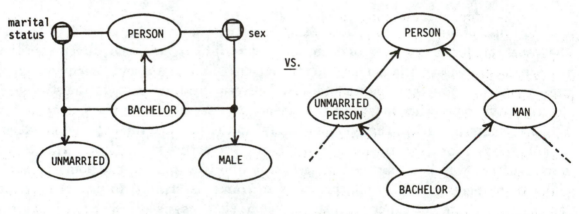

Figure 3. Conceptual distance.

the distance between *bachelor* and *person* is different. Spreading activation theories of processing in semantic nets might consider this distance to be significant.[4] But the links in a non-assertional frame system are simply for forming terms, and of themselves can have no contingent assertional consequence nor psychological import.

Another data-structure-generated mistake occurs when a link in a structurally-interpreted taxonomy is removed in response to new information. Figure 4 illustrates a case of this kind of error—it looks as if substituting link *y* for link *x* yields a new theory about whales, when in reality what has been achieved is a change in the structure of the Concept of a fish with properties *a*, *b*, and *c* to that of the Concept of a mammal with properties *a*, *b*, and *c*—not a terribly well-motivated move. Naming the node *"whale"*

---

[4]The distance between nodes is also considered significant in the inheritance of default properties, where a search is made for the 'closest' value.

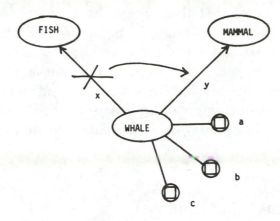

Figure 4. Whales mis-described.

does not change the fact that we have said nothing about whales at all.

The point of these imaginary (and somewhat extreme) examples is that even if the structures of a frame system are taken non-assertionally, their presence or absence can still be misread assertionally and used to encode facts about the world (geological or psychological, in the above). Moreover, real (but more subtle) occurrences of this phenomena can be found in KL-ONE-based applications.[5] For example, in the CONSUL system [Mark 81], Concepts are used as 'translation rules' (with 'antecedent' and 'consequent' Roles). The system determines whether or not a rule applies in a given situation (that is, whether or not something can be translated) based on the presence or absence of the Concept in the taxonomy. A similar kind of processing shows up in the PSI-KLONE system [Bobrow and Webber 80], where some Concepts are used as combinations of syntactic and (shallow) semantic categories. In PSI-KLONE, the presence or absence of a Concept for one of these categories determines the acceptability of a phrase structure (proposed by an independent parser). Finally, in the RABBIT system [Tou, *et al.* 82], there are Concepts standing for different kinds of restaurants (much as in the above geological example) and users attempt to locate an acceptable restaurant type looking only at the Concepts in the taxonomy. In all of these cases, the presence (or absence) of a Concept in a taxonomy *says* something about the problem domain.[6] This is particularly striking in the case of KL-ONE, where the taxonomy is explicitly advertised as an infinite virtual lattice of structurally composed terms.

---

[5]KL-ONE is perhaps the cleanest representation framework that advocates a strictly structural view of the taxonomy. In defense of its users, we might attribute the assertional uses described here to KL-ONE's impoverished assertional facilities, as compared to its richer description-formation capabilities.

[6]Giving an exact characterization of what the presence of a Concept means in these examples is somewhat difficult. The assertion appears to be that the domain includes a certain second-order entity (a 'kind'), represented by the Concept. However, our point here is merely that *something* is being asserted.

In sum, then, it seems that there are at least two serious problems that we are faced with in our frame representation systems. We must be careful to interpret structures unambiguously, so that we do not in one breath interpret a link as making an assertion and in the next interpret it as part of the meaning of a term. But, even when we are extremely careful about interpreting these structures, there is still the fundamental problem of having only *data structures* to manipulate. We are thus prey to unwarranted inferences, in counting data structures or assuming that their presence or absence means something.

§3 KRYPTON: A Functional Approach

Over the past year, we have been designing and implementing (in Interlisp-D) an experimental knowledge representation system, called "KRYPTON", attempting to avoid the kinds of problems engendered by the more traditional structure-oriented approaches. We focused on a *functional* specification of the knowledge base, replacing any question like "What structures should the system maintain for a user?" with one that asked "What exactly should the system *do* for a user?" In other words, we decided what kind of *operations* there should be for interacting with a knowledge base without assuming anything about its internal structure. By making only those operations available to a KRYPTON user we felt we could control precisely how the system would be used while having the freedom to implement the operations in any convenient way.

Of course, taking a functional view buys us nothing if the operations we provide are precisely the same ones as the standard ones. In such a case, our system would fall prey to the very same confusions between structural and assertional uses that we mentioned earlier. To avoid this problem, we have split the operations into two separate kinds, yielding two main components for our representation system: a terminological one (or 'TBox') and an assertional one (or 'ABox'). The TBox allows us to establish taxonomies of structured terms and answer questions about analytical relationships among these terms; the ABox allows us to build descriptive theories of domains of interest and to answer questions about those domains.

The separation between the two components arises naturally in the two kinds of expressions used to represent knowledge—(nominal) terms and sentences. The TBox deals with the formal equivalent of *noun phrases* such as "a person with at least 3 children", and understands that this expression is subsumed by (the formal version of) "a person with at least 1 child", and is disjoint from "a person with at most 1 child". The ABox, on the other hand, operates with the formal equivalent of *sentences* such as "Every person with at least 3 children owns a car" and understands the implications (in the logical sense) of assertions such as this one. Furthermore, just as there is no way for a user to specify, after the fact, what sentences are logical consequences of others in the ABox, there is no way for a user to specify, after the fact, where a term fits in a taxonomy in the TBox. The subsumption and disjointness relationships are based only on the structure of the TBox terms and not on any (domain-dependent) facts maintained by the ABox.

In what follows, we will describe the TBox and ABox languages, the operations that are available on these languages, and how these operations are being implemented in KRYPTON.

3.1 Two languages for representation

Given its division of representational labor, KRYPTON can afford to take a strict view of the constructs in its two languages. The expressions in the TBox language are used as structured descriptions, and have no direct assertional import. Moreover, the ABox language is used strictly for assertions and even universally quantified biconditionals have no special definitional import.

3.1.1 The language of the terminological component

Rather than simply use an existing frame language in our TBox, we have chosen to break out the primitives that seem to make up the essence of frames, carefully specify their meanings, and put them together in a compositional framework. In particular, the TBox supports two types of expressions: Concept expressions, which correspond roughly to frames (or, more closely, KL-ONE Concepts), and Role expressions, the counterparts of slots (or KL-ONE Roles).

In general, Concepts and Roles are formed by combining or restricting other Concepts and Roles. For example, the language includes an operator **ConjGeneric** ('conjoined generic'), which takes any number of Concepts, and forms the Concept corresponding to their conjunction. This operator could be used to define the symbol[7] *bachelor* by assigning it the expression

(**ConjGeneric** *unmarried-person man*)

(assuming that the symbols *unmarried-person* and *man* had appropriate definitions as Concepts).

Concepts can also be formed by restricting other Concepts using Roles. For example, KRYPTON has a **VRGeneric** ('value-restricted generic') operator that takes two Concepts c_1 and c_2 and a Role r and yields the term meaning "a c_1 any r of which

---

[7] As we will describe below, expressions can be assigned as definitions to atomic symbols. At this stage, however, this use of defined symbols is purely for the convenience of the user.

is a c_2", as in

(VRGeneric *person child bachelor*),

for "a person all of whose children are bachelors". The language also has an **NRGeneric** ('number-restricted generic') operator that restricts the cardinality of the set of fillers for a given Role; for example,

(NRGeneric *person child* 1 3),

for "a person with at least 1 and not more than 3 children".

Roles, like Concepts, can be defined as specializations of other Roles. One basic Role specialization operator **VRDiffRole** ('value-restricted differentiation'), takes a Role *r* and a Concept *c*, and defines the derivative Role corresponding to the phrase "an *r* that is a *c*". For example, *son* could be defined as

(VRDiffRole *child man*),

given the terms *child* (a Role) and *man* (a Concept).

All of the term-forming operators can be composed in the obvious way, as in, for example,

(VRGeneric (ConjGeneric *unmarried-person man*)
(VRDiffRole *sibling man*)
(NRGeneric *person child* 1 ∞)).

This expression can be read as "a bachelor whose brothers have children" or, more literally, "an unmarried person and a man all of whose siblings that are men have between 1 and ∞ children".

In many domains one wants to be able to give necessary but not sufficient conditions for a definition. To this end, KRYPTON includes facilities for specifying 'only-if' definitions. The **PrimGeneric** and **PrimRole** operators are used to form primitive specializations of a Concept or Role. A primitive Concept is one that is subsumed by its superConcept, but where no sufficient conditions exist for determining if something is described by it. To see how this relates to a language of frames, consider the *family* frame used as an example in Section 2. As a Concept, this might be expressed in KRYPTON as

(PrimGeneric (ConjGeneric
    (NRGeneric (VRGeneric *social-structure male-parent man*)
          male-parent 1 1)
    (NRGeneric (VRGeneric *social-structure female-parent woman*)
          female-parent 1 1)
    (VRGeneric *social-structure child person*))).

We have been experimenting with several different languages in the TBox; the principal operators that we are considering in the current version are summarized in Table 1.

Expression	Interpretation	Description
Concepts:		
(ConjGeneric $c_1 \ldots c_n$)	"a c_1 and ... and a c_n"	conjunction
(VRGeneric c_1 r c_2)	"a c_1 any r of which is a c_2"	value restriction
(NRGeneric c r n_1 n_2)	"a c with between n_1 and n_2 r's"	number restriction
(PrimGeneric c i)	"a c of the i-th kind"	primitive subConcept
(DecompGeneric c i j $disjoint?$)	"a c of the i-th type from the j-th [disjoint] decomposition"	decomposition
Roles:		
(VRDiffRole c r)	"an r that is a c"	role differentiation
(RoleChain $r_1 \ldots r_n$)	"an r_n of ... of an r_1"	role chain
(PrimRole r i)	"an r of the i-th kind"	primitive subRole
(DecompRole r i j $disjoint?$)	"an r of the i-th type from the j-th [disjoint] decomposition"	decomposition

Table 1. The TBox Language.

3.1.2 The language of the assertional component

As with the expressions of the TBox language, the sentences of the ABox language are constructed compositionally from simpler ones. The concerns behind the choice of sentence-forming operators, however, are quite different from those motivating the ones in the TBox language. As discussed in [Brachman and Levesque 82], the issue of expressive power in an assertional representation language is really the issue of the extent to which *incomplete knowledge* can be represented. Moreover, this issue can be seen to motivate the standard logical sentential constructs of disjunction, negation and existential quantification. So to provide the ability to deal systematically with incomplete knowledge and to compensate for the fact that the TBox had been purged of any assertional ability, our ABox language is structured compositionally like a first order predicate calculus language. In other words, the sentence-forming operators are the usual ones: **Not, Or, ThereExists**, and so on.

The major difference between our ABox language and a standard first order logical one lies in the primitive sentences. The non-logical symbols of a standard logical language—that is, the predicate symbols (and function symbols, if any)—are taken to be *independent, primitive, domain-dependent terms.* In our case, there is already a facility for specifying a collection of domain-dependent terms, namely the TBox. Our approach, therefore, is to make the non-logical symbols of the ABox language be the terms of the TBox language. As observed by Hayes [Hayes 79] among others, when the language of frames and slots is 'translated' into predicate calculus, the frames and slots become one- and two-place predicates, respectively. The main difference between what Hayes *et al.*, are suggesting and what we have done is that the resulting predicates are not primitive but can be definitionally related to each other (independently of any theory expressed in the ABox language).

Overall, the structure of a **KRYPTON** system can be visualized as in Figure 5: a

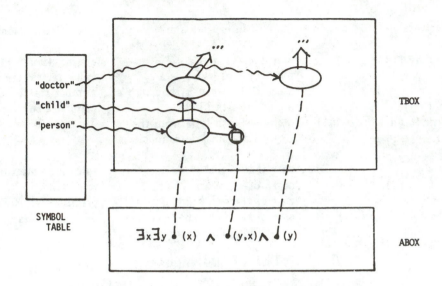

Figure 5. KRYPTON overview.

TBox of roughly KL-ONE-ish terms organized taxonomically, an ABox of roughly first-order sentences whose predicates come from the TBox, and a symbol table maintaining the names of the TBox terms so that a user can refer to them.

3.2 Operations on the components

So far, we have described the KRYPTON TBox and ABox in terms of two distinct but interconnected languages, without saying what a user actually *does* with expressions in these languages. Figure 5 is a somewhat misleading picture of KRYPTON since a user does not get access to either a network in the TBox or to a collection of sentences in the ABox. What a user does get is a certain fixed set of operations over the TBox and ABox languages. All interactions between a user and a KRYPTON knowledge base are mediated by these operations.

The operations on a KRYPTON knowledge base can be divided into two groups: the *TELL* operations are used to augment a knowledge base and the *ASK* operations are used to extract information. In either case, the operation can be definitional or assertional.

In terms of the ABox, the *TELL* operation takes an ABox sentence and asserts that it is true. The effect is to change the knowledge base into one whose theory of the world implies that sentence. The *ASK* operation takes a sentence and asks if it is true. The result is determined on the basis of the current theory held by the knowledge base *and* the vocabulary used in the sentence, as defined in the TBox. Schematically, we can describe these operations by

ABox: *TELL*: KB × SENTENCE → KB

Sentence *is true.*

ASK: KB × SENTENCE → {*yes, no, unknown*}

Is sentence *true?*

As for the TBox, the *TELL* operation takes a symbol and associates it with a TBox term (noun phrase). The effect is to change the knowledge base into one whose vocabulary includes the symbol, defined by the term. We have focused on two *ASK* operations: the first asks whether one TBox term subsumes another, and the second whether one TBox term is conceptually disjoint from another. Schematically, this gives us

TBox: *TELL*: KB × SYMBOL × TERM → KB

By symbol, *I mean* term.

ASK_1: KB × TERM × TERM → {*yes, no*}

Does term$_1$ *subsume* term$_2$?

ASK_2: KB × TERM × TERM → {*yes, no*}

Is term$_1$ *disjoint from* term$_2$?

Of course there have to be additional *ASK* operations on a knowledge base. So far, for instance, there is no way to get other than a yes/no answer. In the case of the ABox, we have to be able to find out what individuals have a given property; in the TBox, there has to be some way of getting information from the definitions that is not provided by the subsumption and disjointness questions (*e.g.*, the number of *angles* of a *triangle*).

It is important to stress that the service provided by KRYPTON as a knowledge representation system is completely specified by the above operations. In particular, the notions of a taxonomy or a set of first-order clauses in normal form are not part of the interface provided by the system. The actual symbolic structures used by KRYPTON to realize the *TELL* and *ASK* operations are not available to the user. While it might be useful to think of a knowledge base as structured in a certain way, this structure can only be inferred from the system's behavior. One might consider new operations that allow finer-grained distinctions to be made in the knowledge base, allowing even more of its structure to be deduced, but again it will be the operations that count, not the data structures used to implement them.

Essentially, this functional view of a knowledge base treats it like an abstract data type [Liskov and Zilles 74], characterized by a set of operations, rather than by a certain implementation structure. One can imagine a wide range of KRYPTON implementations realizing the behavior of these operations. Indeed, one of the advantages of our approach is that *what* the system does is defined independently from *how* it does it. This distinguishes KRYPTON from systems where the only account of what the primitives mean is in terms of the behavior of an implementation. In fact, since we have a non-algorithmic definition to begin with, we can actually talk about the *correctness* of an implementation.

One interesting property of this approach to knowledge representation is that there is a difference conceptuallly between what a system can be *told* (involving expressions in the interface language used as arguments to *TELL*) and what it has to actually *remember* (involving data structures in the implementation language). This allows us to consider an interface notation that is, in some sense, more expressive than the implementation one, provided that the difference can be accounted for in the translation. In [Levesque 82], a modal 'auto-epistemic' language is used to supply arguments to *TELL* and yet the resulting knowledge is always represented in first-order terms. For example, a sentence such as "The murderer is not among the known suspects" would be understood by calculating (at the time of the *TELL*) who the currently known suspects are and then remembering merely that the murderer is not one of them. The functional viewpoint allows us to use "the known suspects" *referentially* while "the murderer" is understood *attributively*.

From the point of view of a user, there are at least two major advantages to the functional approach. One is that a user of the system is isolated from implementation design decisions. This is in sharp contrast to typical knowledge representation systems where users have access to the implementation structures and are, therefore, very sensitive to changes in implementation methodology. But most importantly, a user cannot rely upon the symbolic structures to encode knowledge in a way contrary to the spirit of the language. In other words, incidental properties of an implementation that are not part of the defined interface (such as the current number of Concepts below another in a taxonomy or the current number of sentences in a theory) cannot be used as an alternate method of representing knowledge. This encourages a uniformity of usage that is in accordance with the intentions of the system designers.

3.3 Building KRYPTON

Having discussed the desired functionality of the KRYPTON knowledge representation system, we here sketch in general terms how we are building a system with these capabilitites.

3.3.1 Making an ABox

The first thing to notice about an implementation of the ABox is that because of the expressive power of the assertional language, very general reasoning strategies will be needed to answer questions. Specifically, we cannot limit ourselves to the special-purpose methods typical of frame-based representation systems.

For example, to find out if there is a cow in the field, it will not be sufficient to locate a representational object standing for it (*i.e.*, an instantiation of the *cow-in-the-field* Concept), since, among other things, we may not know all the cows or even how many there are. Yet, we may very well have been told that Jones owns nothing but cows and that at least one of his animals has escaped into the field.

The second point worth noticing about the ABox is that if the predicate symbols are indeed TBox terms, then the ABox reasoner needs to have access to the TBox definitions of those terms. For example, once told that Elsie is a cow, the ABox should know that Elsie is an animal and is not a bull. ABox predicates are not simply unconnected primitives (as in first-order logic), so if we want to use standard first-order reasoning techniques, we have to somehow make the connections implied by the TBox.

Conceptually, the simplest way to do this is to cause the definition of a term in the TBox to assert a sentence in the ABox and then to perform standard first-order reasoning over the resultant expanded theory. For example, after defining the Concept *cow* we could automatically assert sentences saying that every cow is an animal and that cows are not bulls, as if these were observed facts about the world. As far as the ABox is concerned, the definition of a term would be no more than the assertion of a 'meaning postulate'.[8]

In some sense, this would yield a 'hybrid' system like the kind discussed in [Rich 82] and elsewhere, since we would have two notations stating the same set of facts. Our goal, however, is to develop an ABox reasoner that avoids such redundancies, maintains the distinction between definitional and assertional information, and provides a significant gain in efficiency over simply asserting the meaning postulates as axioms. To this end, we are developing extensions to standard inference rules that take into account dependencies among predicates derivable from TBox definitions.

For example, the reasoning of a standard resolution theorem prover depends on noticing that an occurrence of $\phi(x)$ in one clause is inconsistent with $\neg\phi(x)$ in another. Given that realization, the two clauses can be used to infer a resolvent clause. The scope of this inference rule can be increased by using subsumption and disjointness information from the TBox as an additional means of recognizing the inconsistency of two literals.[9] That is, if ϕ and ψ are disjoint, then $\phi(x)$ and $\psi(x)$ are inconsistent, and if ϕ subsumes ψ, then $\neg\phi(x)$ and $\psi(x)$ are inconsistent. The situation is complicated by the fact that TBox definitions also imply 'conditional' inconsistencies. For example, assume that *rectangle* has been defined as "a *polygon* any *angle* of which is a *right-angle*". The literal $polygon(x)$ is inconsistent with $\neg rectangle(x)$ only when all the angles of x are right angles. In such cases, the clauses containing the conditionally

---

[8]Indeed, by far the most common rendering of definitions in systems based on first-order logic is as assertions of a certain form (universally quantified bi-conditionals), a treatment which simply fails to distinguish them from the more arbitrary facts that happen to have the same logical form.

[9]See [Stickel 83] for a similar approach to augmenting resolution by 'building-in' a theory.

inconsistent literals can still be resolved provided that we include the negation of the condition in the resolvent. Thus, if the TBox is asked whether *polygon* is disjoint from ¬*rectangle*, it should answer, in effect, "only when all the angles are right angles".

3.3.2 Making a TBox

If we take the point of view that an ABox reasoner has to be able to access TBox subsumption and disjointness information *between* steps in a deduction, we have to be very careful about how long it takes to compute that information. Absolutely nothing will be gained by our implementation strategy if the TBox operations are as hard as theorem proving; we could just as well have gone the standard 'meaning postulate' route. We are taking three steps to ensure that the TBox operations can be performed reasonably quickly with respect to the time needed by the ABox.

The first and perhaps most important limit on the TBox operations is provided by our TBox language itself. One can certainly imagine wanting a language that would allow arbitrary 'lambda-definable' predicates to be specified. The trouble is that no complete algorithm for subsumption would then be possible, much less an efficient one. By restricting our TBox language to what might be called the 'frame-definable' predicates (in terms of operators such as those we have already discussed), we stand at least a chance of getting a usable algorithm while providing a set of term-forming facilities that have been found useful in AI applications.

The situation is far from resolved, however. The computational complexity of term subsumption seems to be *very* sensitive to the choice of term-forming operators. For example, it appears that given a simple TBox language without the **VRDiffRole** operator, the term subsumption algorithm will be $O(n^2)$ at worst; with the **VRDiffRole** operator, however, the problem is not likely to have a non-exponential solution [Levesque 83].

As a second step towards fulfilling this efficiency requirement for the TBox, we have adopted a caching scheme in which we store subsumption relationships for symbols defined by the user in a tree-like data structure. We are, in effect, maintaining an explicit *taxonomy* of the defined symbols. We are also developing methods for extending this cache to include both absolute and conditional disjointness information about TBox terms. The key open question regarding these conditional relationships is how to determine a useful subset of the large number of possible ones that could be defined between the symbols.

As a final step towards an efficient TBox, we have adopted the notion of a *classifier* much like the one present in KL-ONE [Schmolze and Lipkis 83], wherein a background process sequentially determines the subsumption relationship between the new symbol and each symbol for which it is still unknown. Because the taxonomy reflects a partial-ordering, we can incrementally move the symbol down towards its correct position. In this way, the symbol taxonomy slowly becomes more and more informed about the relationship of a symbol to all the other defined symbols.

One very important thing to notice about this implementation strategy based on a taxonomy and classification is that it is precisely that—an implementation strategy. The meaning of the TBox language and the definition of the TBox operators do not depend at all on the taxonomy or on how well the classifier is doing at some point.

§4 Conclusion

As we have noted, there are some problems with the standard view of frames as a representation language: structural and assertional facilities are often confused, the expressive power is limited (particularly when instantiation is the principal operation), and frame systems are defined only in terms of the data structures used to implement them.

The KRYPTON system represents an attempt to deal directly with these problems in terms of a functional design strategy. It is an experiment in *strict* knowledge representation. By severely limiting the interface between a user and a knowledge base, certain misuses of the system can be minimized. A user is forced to concentrate on what his knowledge base is for, rather than on the implementation details supporting this functionality.

KRYPTON also advocates the division of the representation task into two distinct components: a terminological one and an assertional one. The terminological component supports the formation of structured descriptions organized taxonomically; the assertional component allows these descriptions to be used to characterize some domain of interest. In either case, we have a compositional language that is used to interact with a knowledge base.

An implementation of a KRYPTON system in Interlisp-D is underway. As of this writing, we have implemented the operations of the terminological component using the taxonomy/classification methodology discussed above, and are currently investigating its interaction with a version of the Stickel theorem-prover [Stickel 82].

Acknowledgement

Many people have made significant contributions to this work. Much of KRYPTON is derived from KL-ONE, whose development was strongly influenced by Rusty Bobrow, David Israel, Jim Schmolze, and Bill Woods. We would also like to thank Bill Mark, Tom Lipkis, Phil Cohen, and especially Danny Bobrow, Austin Henderson, and Mark Stefik for their participation in many discussions on KRYPTON and their help in the design of the incipient system. Thanks also to Mark Stickel for the use of his theorem-prover and the time spent in explaining it to us.

References

[Bobrow and Webber 80] Bobrow, R. and Webber, B. L., "PSI-KLONE: Parsing and Semantic Interpretation in the BBN Natural Language Understanding System," in *Proc. of the third CSCSI/SCEIO conference*, Victoria, B. C., 1980, 131–142.

[Brachman 83] Brachman, R. J., "What ISA Is and Isn't: An Analysis of Taxonomic Links in Semantic Networks," to appear in *IEEE Computer, Special Issue on Knowledge Representation*, September, 1983.

[Brachman and Levesque 82] Brachman, R. J., and Levesque, H. J., "Competence in Knowledge Representation," in *Proc. of the AAAI-82*, Pittsburgh, 1982, 189–192.

[Hayes 79] Hayes, P. J., "The Logic of Frames," in *Frame Conceptions and Text Understanding*, Metzing, D. (ed.), Walter de Gruyter and Co., Berlin, 1979, 46–61.

[Levesque 82] Levesque, H. J., "A Formal Treatment of Incomplete Knowledge Bases," FLAIR Technical Report No. 3, Fairchild Laboratory for Artificial Intelligence Research, Palo Alto, CA, February, 1982.

[Levesque 83] Levesque, H. J., "Some Results on the Complexity of Subsumption in a Frame-based Language," in preparation, 1983.

[Liskov and Zilles 74] Liskov, B., and Zilles, S., "Programming with abstract data types," *SIGPLAN Notices* **9**, 4 (1974).

[Mark 81] Mark, W., "Representation and Inference in the Consul System," in *Proc. of the IJCAI-81*, Vancouver, B. C., 1981, 375–381.

[Rich 82] Rich, C., "Knowledge Representation Languages and Predicate Calculus: How to Have Your Cake and Eat it Too," in *Proc. of the AAAI-82*, Pittsburgh, 1982, 193-196.

[Schmolze and Brachman 82] Schmolze, J. G., and Brachman, R. J., *eds.*, "Proceedings of the 1981 KL-ONE Workshop," FLAIR Technical Report No. 4, Fairchild Laboratory for Artificial Intelligence Research, Palo Alto, CA, May, 1982.

[Schmolze and Lipkis 83] Schmolze, J. G., and Lipkis, T. A., "Classification in the KL-ONE Knowledge Representation System," in *Proc. IJCAI-83*, Karlsruhe, West Germany, 1983.

[Stickel 82] Stickel, M. E., "A Nonclausal Connection-Graph Resolution Theorem-Proving Program," in *Proc. of the AAAI-82*, Pittsburgh, 1982, 229-233.

[Stickel 83] Stickel, M. E., "Theory Resolution: Building-In Nonequational Theories," in *Proc. of the AAAI-83*, Washington, D. C., 1983.

[Tou et al. 82] Tou, F., Williams, M. D., Fikes, R., Henderson, A., Malone, T., "RABBIT: An Intelligent Database Assistant," in *Proc. of the AAAI-82*, Pittsburgh, 1982, 314–318.

[Woods 75] Woods, W. A., "What's in a Link?: Foundations for Semantic Networks," in *Representation and Understanding*, Bobrow, D. G., and Collins, A. M. (ed.), Academic Press, New York, 1975, 35–82.

25 / Aaron Sloman
Afterthoughts on Analogical Representations

In somewhat of a rare occurrence in our field, Sloman here carefully looks back at a controversial paper he wrote some years earlier [Sloman 71]. That earlier paper attempted to distinguish representation by more or less direct analogy from the more propositionally-oriented representations—an important distinction, but apparently one that gave readers a lot of trouble. This paper is self-contained enough to introduce the reader to Sloman's idea, yet it gets at some deep and often subtle aspects of the representation problem, especially regarding the nature of analogical representations. Finally, in a bit of a twist, Sloman recants his earlier attempt to move some problem-solving work in the direction of using diagrams, maps, and the like. Ironically, the Funt paper in this volume [Chapter 26] shows in some detail how Sloman's original hopes were in fact more realistic than he came to think in 1975.

Appeared in *Proc. Theoretical Issues in Natural Language Processing*, Cambridge, MA, 1975, 164–168.

AFTERTHOUGHTS ON ANALOGICAL REPRESENTATIONS

Aaron Sloman
Cognitive Studies Programme
School of Social Sciences
University of Sussex
Brighton, England

In 1971 I wrote a paper attempting to relate some old philosophical issues about representation and reasoning to problems in Artificial Intelligence. A major theme of the paper was the importance of distinguishing "analogical" from "Fregean" representations. I still think the distinction is important, though perhaps not as important for current problems in A.I. as I used to think. In this paper I'll try to explain why.

Throughout I'll use the term "representation" to refer to a more or less complex structure which has addressable and significant parts, and which as a whole is used to denote or refer to something else. Thus maps, sentences, and phrases like "The paternal grandfather of the present mayor of Brighton" are representations. There is much that's puzzling and complex about the concept of using something to "denote" or "refer to" something else, but for the present I'll dodge that issue and rely on our intuitive understanding thereof.

The analogical/Fregean distinction is not new: people have been discovering and re-discovering it for a long time, though they rarely manage to say clearly and precisely what it is, despite agreement on (most) examples: e.g. maps, photographs and family trees are analogical representations whereas many sentences, referring phrases, and most logical and mathematical formulae are Fregean. I use the word "Fregean" because it was Gottleb Frege who first clearly saw that a great deal of natural-language syntax and semantics could be analysed in terms of the application of functions to arguments, and that this analysis was far superior to previous attempts to understand the structure of sentences. For instance, it enabled him to invent the logic of quantifiers and develop a notation which provided some of the essential ideas of Church's lambda-calculus, and thereby some of the goodies in programming languages like LISP, ALGOL and POP-2. I use the word "Fregean" not only to honour Frege but also because there is no unambiguous alternative. The most popular rivals - "symbolic" and "verbal" - are used in too many different ill-defined ways, and in addition the first seems too general, the second too narrow. People seem to have a lot of trouble seeing clearly what the distinction is, so I'll list and comment on some of the more common misrepresentations of what I wrote in the 1971 paper.

Misrepresentations
(1) "Analogical representations are continuous, Fregean representations discrete". Comment: I gave examples of discrete analogical representations, e.g. a list whose elements are ordered according to the order of what they represent.
(2) "Analogical representations are 2-dimensional, Fregean representations 1-dimensional." Comment: I gave examples of 1-d analogical representations (e.g. the list example). Much mathematical notation is 2-dimensional and Fregean (e.g. integral or summation symbols, the normal representation of fractions).

(3) "Analogical representations are isomorphic with what they represent." Comment: I discussed 2-d pictures which are _not_ isomorphic with the 3-d scenes they represent analogically.

(4) "Fregean representations are symbolic, analogical representations non-symbolic." Comment: I find this notion unintelligible. The only sense of "symbolic" which I can understand clearly includes both maps and sentences. People who arrive at this misinterpretation seem to be guilty of using "symbolic" in a sloppy, ill-defined sense, to contrast with some equally ill-defined alternative. Their excuse may be that this is frequently done (e.g. by Minsky and Papert in their Progress Report, and by Minsky in his more recent paper on frames - 1974.)

(5) "Sentences in a natural language are all Fregean." Comment: I pointed out that _some_ English sentences function in a partly analogical way, as is illustrated by the difference in meaning of "She shot him and kissed him" and "She kissed him and shot him". Compare "Tom, Dick and Harry stood in that order". Contrast "She shot him after she kissed him", where a relation is explicitly named, and the semantics is Fregean.

(6) "Analogical representations are complete: whatever is not represented in a picture or map is thereby represented as not existing. By contrast Fregean representations may abstract from as many or as few features of a situations as desired: if I say "Tom stood between Dick and Harry", then nothing is implied about whether anyone else was there or not." Comment: there may be an important distinction between descriptions or representations which are complete (relative to the resources of a language) and those which are incomplete, but this has nothing to do with the analogical/Fregean distinction. E.g. a map showing only some of the towns and roads of Britain is still an analogical representation. We are free to specify for some pictures of maps that they are to be interpreted as complete, and for others that they depict relations between some but not all parts of a situation or object. Similarly a LISP list might contain items representing events in the order in which the events occurred, yet be incomplete in that new items are added as new knowledge about the time-order of events is acquired.

(7) "Fregean representations have a grammar, analogical representations do not." Comment: it is easy to define a grammar for lists and trees, frequently used as analogical representations in computing. One can also define a grammar for a class of line-drawings which includes pictures of polyhedral scenes.

(8) "Although digital computers can use Fregean representations, only analog computers can handle analogical representations." Comment: see (1) and (2) above.

Explanation of the Distinction

What then is the distinction? Both Fregean and analogical representations are complex, i.e. they have parts and relations between parts, and therefore a syntax. They may both be used to represent, refer to, or denote, things which are complex, i.e. have parts and relations between parts. The difference is that in the case of analogical representations _both_ must be complex (i.e. representation and thing) and there _must_ be some correspondence between their structure, whereas in the case of Fregean representations there need be no correspondence. Roughly, in a complex

Fregean symbol the structure of the symbol corresponds not to the structure of the thing denoted, but to the structure of the procedure by which that thing is identified, or computed.

We can be a bit more precise about analogical representations. If R is an analogical representation of T, then (a) there must be parts of R representing parts of T, as dots and squiggles on a map represent towns and rivers in a country, or lines and regions in a picture represent edges and faces in a scene, and (b) it must be possible to specify some sort of correspondence, possibly context-dependent, between properties or relations of parts of R and properties or relations of parts of T, e.g. size, shape, direction and distance of marks on a map may represent size, shape, direction and distance of towns, and different 2-d relationships of lines meeting at a junction in a picture may represent (possibly ambiguously) 3-d configurations of edges and surfaces in a scene. The relationship between R and T need not be an isomorphism, for instance when a relation between parts of R (such as direction or distance) represents different relations between parts of T in different contexts. In a perspective drawing there is no simple, context independent, rule for translating angles between lines into angles between edges or surfaces in the scene depicted. In such cases the task of interpreting R, i.e. working out what T is, may involve solving quite complex problems in order to find a globally consistent interpretation. (See Clowes 1971.) From (a) and (b) it follows that in analogical representations, relationships within T do not need to be explicity named in R, i.e. there need not be a part of R corresponding to relations like "above", "behind", "intersects" in T. The conditions (a) and (b) do not hold for Fregean representations.

A Fregean formula may be very complex, with many parts and relationships, but none of the parts or relationships need correspond to parts or relations within the thing denoted. The phrase "the city 53 miles north of Brighton" contains the symbol "Brighton" as a part, but the thing denoted does not contain the town Brighton as a part. The thing denoted, London, has a complex structure of its own, which bears no relation whatsoever to the structure of the phrase. Similarly "the father of Fred", "63-24", "(CAR(CDR(CDR(CONS A (CONS B (CONS C NIL))))))" have structures which need bear no relationship to the structures of what they denote. In these, and the examples discussed by Frege, it is possible to analyse symbolic complexity as arising only from the application of functions to arguments. Predicate calculus, apparently invented independently by Frege and C.S. Peirce, is the consequence of this idea. A full explanation would require an exposition of Frege's distinctions between first-level and higher-level functions: e.g. he analysed "all", "exists", and the integral sign used by mathematicians, as names for second-level functions which take first-level functions as arguments.

Comments on the Distinction

The analysis proposed by Frege fails to account for the full richness and complexity of natural language, just as it fails to account for all the important features of programming languages. For instance, Frege apparently required every function to have a definite "level", determined by the levels of its arguments. In languages like POP2 and LISP, where variables need not have types, functions like MAPLIST and APPLY take functional arguments of any type, and therefore do not themselves have types. APPLY can even be applied to itself. In POP2, APPLY(4,SQRT,APPLY); has the same result as SQRT(4); for instance. Since one can use English to to explain how such functions work, English also cannot be restricted to Fregean semantics. There are many other ways in which a Fregean analysis of English breaks down: e.g. some adverbial phrases don't fit easily, and many linguists would quarrel with the analysis of "the capital of France" as an application of a function to France, according to the decomposition "the capital of (France)". (I am inclined to think the linguists are wrong, however.)

So I am not claiming that every symbolism, or representational system, must be analysed as being either analogical or Fregean. The distinction is not a dichotomy, though there may be some generalisation which is. Wittgenstein, in his Tractatus Logico Philosophicus outlined an all-embracing "picture" theory of meaning which attempted to subsume Fregean representations under analogical (e.g. by describing a structure such as R(a,b) as one in which the relation between the names "a" and "b" analogically represented the relation between their denotations corresponding to R. In his later writings he acknowledged that this attempt to eliminate the distinction was unsuccessful. Conversely, I once explored the possibility of interpreting all analogical representations as being composed of function-signs and argument-signs and decided that it could not be done, since an essential feature of Fregean symbolisms is that argument signs can be replaced by others without altering anything else, and in general this cannot be done with pictures: replace the representation of a man in a picture with the representation of an elephant, and there will often be some other syntactic change, since different outlines leave different things visible. Compare "My uncle is in the garden" and "My elephant is in the garden". Here any diffference in the implications depends not on structural differences between the sentences but on background premises about the differences between men and elephants. I conclude that attempts to obliterate the distinction cannot succeed, although, as remarked previously, a Fregean formula may analogically represent a procedure of evaluation or identification.

Linguists are not usually interested in the role of language in reasoning. Many philosophers, logicians, and mathematicians are under the mistaken impression that only proofs using a Fregean symbolism can be rigorous, or even valid. The suggestion is that the old proofs used in Euclidean geometry, which relied on diagrams, were not proofs at all. Real proofs were found only when axioms and inference rules were formulated which made the diagrams redundant. I believe that this denigration of analogical representations is connected with some of the worst features of mathematics teaching, especially at Universities. Excessive concern with too restricted a range of analogical representations is probably just as bad.

In the 1971 paper I tried to show that the concept of a rigorous valid inference could be applied to problem-solving using analogical representations just as it is normally applied to proofs in a Fregean language (e.g. predicate calculus). I tried to show that in some cases (some readers thought I meant all cases!) analogical representation combined rigour and validity with greater heuristic power than Fregean. I went on to suggest that program-writers and theoreticians in A.I. should pay more attention to analogical representations, and hinted that this would lead to programs which could solve problems much more easily and intelligently, since the possible manipulations of an analogical representation would be much more tightly restricted by its structure than the possible manipulations of Fregean representations. E.g. when relations are explicitly named, then any relation-name can be replaced by any other relation-name of the same syntactic category, whereas when relations are represented by relations (e.g. distance or order in a map) then the structure of the representing medium may constrain possible variations, thus usefully restricting search space.

The distinction between analogical and Fregean representations is real and important, though not exhaustive (as I pointed out in the paper). However, some of the things said or implied in my paper were erroneous, and sould be withdrawn, which is what I am now about to do.

Valid Criticisms of my 1971 paper

First of all I suggested that people in A.I. were not making use of analogical representation (except for the analogical relation between programs and processes). This was just wrong: any intelligent programmer will use ordering and other relationships within data-structures to correspond to the real relationships when this is useful. For example, Raphael's S.I.R. program did this. So did vision programs which used graph-like data-structures to represent the topology of pictures. Even PLANNER, with its apparently Fregean assertions, and procedure-invoking patterns, can be interpreted as a mechanism in which problems about actions or deductions are solved by simulating these actions or deductions: the simulation process then constitutes an analogical representation. However this was one of the major defects of PLANNER as a problem solver: often it is much more sensible to examine and describe possibilities for action than to execute them or simulate them, if one wishes to solve some problem about them. For a trivial case, consider the question "If I start in room A and then move back and forth between room A and room B, which room will I be in after exactly 377 moves?" The best way to solve this is not to simulate the moves but to form a generalisation about the effects of N moves where N is an odd number and where N is an even number. What we need are not my vague general exhortations to make more use of analogical representations, but detailed analysis of the differences between problems where it is and where it is not helpful to solve problems with the aid of some kind of partial simulation. The chess-board and domino problem is a good illustration of how an analogical representation can get in the way. Often one does better to manipulate descriptions of relationships than the relationships themselves.

Secondly I wrote as though anyone using a Fregean language, like predicate calculus, would not be interested in organizing the sets of assertions describing some world or problem. (Minsky and Papert make the same mistake.) However, intelligent programmers do not devise theorem-provers which blindly store all axioms in whatever order they are read in, and always have to search the whole lot in order to find assertions relevant to any particular sub-problem or sub-goal. If the set of stored assertions is large it will obviously pay to have some kind of indexing scheme, or to store assertions in a network such that each one is associated with pointers to others which might possibly be relevant. In fact, Bob Kowalski has shown that one can intimately combine the indexing system with a "resolution" inference system so that making inferences by resolution becomes a process of modifying the index to the data-base of axioms. However, no resolution theorem-prover, to my knowledge, gives the user sufficient access to the data-base handling mechanisms so that he can use a domain-specific indexing scheme. The same complaint can be made about PLANNER and CONNIVER. Once a set of Fregean formulae is stored in a structured network or graph the organisation of the network may itself have many properties of a non-Fregean, analogical representation. A trivial example would be the storage of a set of assertions of the form

$$R(a,b),R(b,c),R(c,d,),R(d,e,),R(a,d)$$

where R is a transitive asymmetric relation (e.g. "taller than" or "north of"). If each of the above assertions is stored in association with pointers to other assertions mentioning the same individuals, then the resulting structure can be used as an analogical representation of the order of the individuals, just as storing the names in a list like (A B C D E) can. The full equivalence could be obtained only if redundant assertions were pointed to in a different way, or perhaps removed, e.g. R(a,d). This might not be useful for all problem-domains (e.g. it could be less useful where R defines only a partial ordering).

Embedding one's analogical representation in a Fregean symbolism like this makes it easier to switch flexibly between different representation systems according to the needs of the problem. Of course, the mere presence in a computer of a data-structure which we can describe as an analogical representation is not enough: the program must embody procedures which make use of the analogical features of the representation. In the case of a predicate calculus theorem-prover, this means that there must be ways of controlling the order in which assertions or inference steps are tried, so as to correspond to the structure of the problem. E.g. if you wish to know whether c comes between a and e in the order defined by R, work through the set of assertions from a (or from e) in one direction at a time. A more complex illustration of all these points can be constructed by devising a scheme for storing predicate calculus assertions about family relationships with links which enable the data-base to be used like the usual kind of family tree, instead of an arbitrarily ordered list of facts. So questions like "Who were all X's cousins?" or "Was X the grandfather of Y?" can be answered with little or no searching, using the analogical properties of the data-base (i.e. relations represent relations).

More generally, it is possible (and maybe even fruitful) to think of all computation as being concerned with updating and accessing information explicit or implicity stored in a data base. The code for arithmetical functions implicitly represents, in a limited space, answers to a potentially infinite set of problems, for example. An important aspect of the intelligence of programmers, and programs, is the construction, manipulation, and use of indexes, so as to find relevant answers to questions quickly. However, an index is just as much a store of information as anything else, and problems of arbitrary complexity may be involved in finding a relevant index entry. (e.g. months of archeological research may be needed in order to decide which entry in a library or museum catalogue to follow up.) So the distinction between index and data-base disappears: any item or procedure may play a role in tracking down some other information. The data-base is its own index.

From this viewpoint one can assess the role of analogical representations as indexes, and note that relations of ordering and nearness, and distinctive substructures within analogical representations may define important access routes by which mutually relevant items of information may be linked. But, as Pat Hayes has pointed out, it doesn't matter how this is implemented so long as it works. Thus, storing visual input in a 2-d array enables the neighbourhood relationships between pairs of numbers (array subscripts) to be used as an analogical representation of neighbourhood relationships within the original input and to some extent within the scene represented. And one can make good use of this analogical representation even if the array is stored as a set of Fregean assertions about what value is located at co-ordinates n and m for all relevant integers n and m, provided there is a good index to these assertions.

So I should have acknowledged that all the benefits of analogical representations can be gotten from Fregean representations, suitably organised and interpreted. However, this does not imply that analogical representations are not needed, only that they can sometimes be implemented using Fregean ones. Similarly, it could be argued, at a still lower level, all Fregean formalisms used in a computer are ultimately represented analogically, even in a digital computer. But the matter is of little importance.

Finally I wrote as if it was going to be fairly straightforward to get programs to do things in the ways which people find easy. E.g. people often find it much easier to solve problems when they can see a picture of the problem-situation than when they are presented only with a set of assertions about it. However, doing this requires very complex visual abilities, which, although they feel easy to use, are probably the result of a very long and hard learning process extending back over millions of years of evolution (species-learning) and several years of individual learning. I do not believe anyone has very good ideas yet on how to give a computer the same kind of sophisticated grasp of two-dimensional structure as we use when we look at pictures, maps, mazes, diagrams, etc. It seems to be a mixture of a large store of general principles about topology and geometry, intricately combined with a large store of specific knowledge about particular shapes, shape-classes, and possibly patterns of change (translation, rotation, stretching, fitting together, going-through apertures, etc.).

And somehow all this knowledge is indexed for rapid access when relevant, though by no means infallibly indexed. I am sure that many of the problems in explaining how this is possible are common to both vision and natural language processing. (The links are especially clear in the case of reading poor handwriting.)

Thus my suggestion that A.I. workers interested in problem solving should design machines to solve problems by looking at diagrams, maps or other spatial structures may be many years premature. Even the best vision programs presently recognise and use only very few aspects of the 2-dimensional structure of the picture (or TV-inputs) which they attempt to interpret.

The upshot of all this is that I now realise that although it may be interesting and important from a philosophical or psychological standpoint to analyse the analogical/Fregean distinction, and to explore the relative merits of the two sorts of representations, such theoretical discussions don't necessarily help anyone engaged in tasks of designing intelligent programs. The really hard work is finding out what factual and procedural knowledge is required for intelligent performance in each domain. The most one can achieve by the philosophical analysis is the removal of prejudices. But was anyone in A.I. ever really prejudiced against analogical representations, properly defined?

Bibliography

Clowes, M. B. (1971) "On seeing things", in Artificial Intelligence, Vol. 2, 1971.

Frege, G. (1952) Philosophical Writings (translated by P. Geach M. Black), Blackwell, Oxford.

Hayes, P. J. (1974) "Some Problems and non-problems in representation theory", Proceedings AISB Summer Conference, Sussex University.

Kowalski, R. (1974) "A proof procedure using connections graphs". Memo No. 74, Department of Computational Logic, Edinburgh University.

Minsky, M. _ Papert, S. (1972) Progress Report on Artificial Intelligence, A.I. Memo 252, MIT Artificial Intelligence Laboratory.

Minsky, M. (1974) A Framework for Representing Knowledge, A.I. Memo 306, MIT Artificial Intelligence Laboratory.

Sloman, A. (1971) "Interactions between philosophy and A.I. - the role of intuition and non-logical reasoning in intelligence." Proceedings 2nd IJCAI, London, reprinted in Artificial Intelligence, Vol. 2, 1971.

26 / Brian V. Funt
Problem-Solving with Diagrammatic Representations

Brian Funt's thesis represents an extremely clear account of a kind of representation and inference mechanism that might better support a vision system than the more standard ones that dominate this volume. In the context of the WHISPER program, Funt here explores the role of reasoning more or less directly from *diagrams* of physical situations. The key to WHISPER's operation is its ability to imagine movements of physical objects by manipulating a direct analogue of a physical situation, and detecting potential instabilities and collisions by watching the objects' orientations and trajectories in its "mind's eye." WHISPER performs a kind of qualitative simulation using a parallel message-passing regime that implements a small set of perceptual primitives (*e.g.*, to find points of contact, to test for symmetry, etc.). Funt raises (although shallowly) the interesting issue of the potential integration of his analogical representation with more standard deductive mechanisms. This paper ties in very nicely with [Sloman, Chapter 25] in that it shows the details of an analogical reasoning system in action. See also [Levesque and Brachman, Chapter 4] for a discussion of the benefits and costs of reasoning with direct analogues.

Appeared in *Artificial Intelligence* **13**(3), 1980, 201–230.

Problem-Solving with Diagrammatic Representations*

Brian V. Funt

*Computer Science Department, State University of New York at Buffalo, Buffalo, NY 14226, U.S.A.***

Recommended by Daniel G. Bobrow and Aaron Sloman

ABSTRACT*

Diagrams are of substantial benefit to WHISPER, a computer problem-solving system, in testing the stability of a "blocks world" structure and predicting the event sequences which occur as that structure collapses. WHISPER's components include a high level reasoner which knows some qualitative aspects of Physics, a simulated parallel processing "retina" to "look at" its diagrams, and a set of re-drawing procedures for modifying these diagrams. Roughly modelled after the human eye, WHISPER's retina can fixate at any diagram location, and its resolution decreases away from its center. Diagrams enable WHISPER to work with objects of arbitrary shape, detect collisions and other motion discontinuities, discover coincidental alignments, and easily update its world model after a date change. A theoretical analysis is made of the role of diagrams interacting with a general deductive mechanism such as WHISPER's high level reasoner.

1. Introduction

Diagrams are very important tools which we use daily in communication, information storage, planning and problem-solving. Their utility is, however, dependent upon the existence of the human eye and its perceptual abilities. Since human perception involves a very sophisticated information processing system, it can be argued that a diagram's usefulness results from its suitability as an input to this powerful visual system. Alternatively, diagrams can be viewed as containing information similar to that contained in the real visual world, the canonical entity the human visual system was presumably designed through evolution to interpret. From this latter perspective, diagrams are a natural representation of certain types of primarily visual information, and the perceptual system simply provides an appropriate set of database accessing functions. Both these viewpoints underly the work described in this paper.

The role of diagrams is explored in a computer problem-solving program, named

WHISPER, which refers to diagrams during its processing. WHISPER's high-level reasoning component (HLR), built along the lines of traditional procedural AI problem-solving programs, has the additional option of requesting observations in a diagram. It does this by asking its "perceptual system" to "look at" the diagram with its parallel processing "retina". The questions that the perceptual system can answer are called *perceptual primitives*. If necessary, the HLR can also make changes to the current diagram. Fig. 1 shows WHISPER's overall structure.

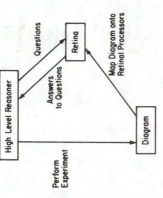

FIG. 1. The WHISPER proposal.

Upon receiving a diagram of a blocks world structure, WHISPER outputs a set of diagrams representing the sequence of events which occur as the structure collapses. The HLR contains knowledge about stability and the motion of falling objects. Using the retina to locate objects and their supports, it checks the stability of each object shown in the diagram. Unstable objects may either rotate or slide. In cases where one is rotationally unstable, the HLR asks the retina to "visualize" it rotating and thereby determine at what point it will hit some other object. Using this information WHISPER outputs an updated diagram showing the object rotated into its new position. Then with this new diagram, it restarts the problem-solving process from the beginning—rechecking the stability of each object, moving one of them, outputting another diagram, and restarting again. The process terminates when either all the objects are stable or the problem becomes too complex for the stability tester. A detailed discussion of the HLR will be postponed until Section 3.

1.1. Motivation

A strong case for computer use of diagrams as models for Geometry has been made by Gelernter (1963), and as general analogical representations by Sloman (1971). Networks with nodes representing "ideal integers" and arcs representing relationships between them were used as models for statements in arithmetic by Bundy (1973). Hayes (1974) and Bobrow (1975) comment on the theoretical nature of analogical representations; Hesse (1969) and Nagel (1961) discuss analogical reasoning.

* This paper is a substantially lengthened version of a similar paper appearing in IJCAI-5, [6].
** Now with: Dept. of Computing Science, Simon Fraser University, Vancouver, B.C., Canada V5A 1S6.

There is a variety of reasons for using diagrams in computer problem-solving. Diagrams such as maps, architectural plans, and circuit diagrams routinely facilitate human problem-solving. Perhaps diagrams function not merely to extend memory capacity, but rather present the important information in a particularly useable form. If they do, then the human visual system provides a paradigmatic example of a system for accessing these representations. Since it exploits a high degree of parallelism, it leads us into the realm of a different type of hardware. This is an exciting step, however, because we can see how much hardware characteristics influence our thinking about the difficulty of various problems and the feasibility of their solution. For example, we know we could compute with Turing Machines— but would we? Because WHISPER's retina harnesses parallelism, it in effect extends the available machine instruction set with special ones for diagram feature recognition. WHISPER is primarily an exploration of the question: to what extent can problem-solving be simplified through experiment and observation with diagrams? This is in contrast (but not in opposition) to the usual method of deduction within a formal theory as explained in the next section.

1.2. Theoretical framework

Any problem-solving system needs a representation of the problem situation. The standard approach in AI is to formalize the domain. We choose a language and write down a set of statements (axioms, productions, assertions, or a semantic network) describing the world. So that the problem-solver can generate new statements from this initial set, we provide a general deductive mechanism (theorem prover, programming language control structure, network algorithm). In terms of the predicate calculus the axioms define a theory, T, and so long as it is not self-contradictory there will be at least one model M (an assignment of predicates to the predicate symbols, functions to the function symbols, and individuals to the constant symbols) which satisfies it. Since our intention in axiomatizing the world was to accurately describe it, we expect it to be one of the models satisfying T.

We may find a second model M' satisfying T (in general there will be many such models). Now—and this is the main thrust of WHISPER—in some cases we can use M' to provide information about M without deriving it from T. What is required is that some of the predicates, functions and individuals of M' correspond to some of the predicates, functions and individuals of M in such a way that it is possible to translate the results obtained when these predicates and functions are applied to individuals in M' into the results that would be obtained if the corresponding predicates and functions were to be applied to the corresponding individuals in M. The similarity between M and M' means that experiments and observations made in M' yield results similar to those that would be obtained in M. As shown in Fig. 2, for WHISPER M' is the combination of its diagram and diagram re-drawing procedures. WHISPER obtains information about the blocks world by using its retina to observe the results of experimental changes made to its diagrams by the re-drawing procedures.

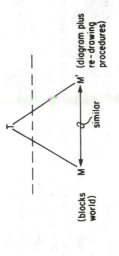

FIG. 2.

WHISPER is a prototype system designed to explore the extent to which problem-solving can be carried out below the dashed line of Fig. 2; however, it does do some reasoning above the line. WHISPER's success argues for working below the line, but not against working above the line. WHISPER's HLR is an above-the-line component.

A natural question is why use M' instead of M? If M is readily accessible then there is no reason not to use it; but, frequently it will not be. For example if we want to determine the stability of a pile of blocks on the surface of the moon, then we could construct a similar pile of blocks on earth and determine the result by experiment. In this case M, the pile of blocks on the moon is inaccessible. We can see that a lot can be learned from the blocks on earth, but some above-the-line inference must be done to handle the discrepancies arising as a result of the difference in gravity.[1]

2. Mechanisms for Diagram Interaction

The retina and perceptual primitives are designed to provide WHISPER with a new set of operations whose execution times are of the same order of magnitude as conventional machine instructions. To achieve this a high degree of parallelism has been incorporated into the system. The retina is a parallel processor, and the perceptual primitives are the algorithms it executes. (Do not be misled by the term "retina"; it refers to a general system of receptors and processors for the early stages of perceptual processing, rather than implying any close resemblance to the human retina.) Each perceptual primitive, when executed by the retina, determines whether some particular feature is present in the diagram. WHISPER's retina mixes parallel and sequential computation, so the features it can recognize are not subject to the same theoretical limitations as perceptrons (Minsky and Papert (1969)).

2.1. The retina

WHISPER's retina is a software simulation of hardware which, given the rapidly advancing state of LSI technology, should soon be possible to build. It consists of a collection of processors, each processor having its own input device called a *receptor*. There is a fixed number of processors, and they are all identical. As with the human eye, WHISPER's retina can be shifted to fixate at a new diagram location (also a feature

[1] I am grateful to Raymond Reiter for many of the ideas in Section 1.2.

of a program by Dunlavey (1975)), so that each processor's receptor receives a different input from the diagram. This fixation facility is important because the resolution of the retina decreases from its center to its periphery. Without being able to fixate, it would be impossible for WHISPER to examine the whole diagram in detail. Economy of receptors and processors dictates the use of decreasing resolution. (A declining resolution is also a characteristic of the human eye.) Each receptor covers a separate segment of the diagram and transmits a single value denoting the color of that region. The geometrical arrangement of the receptors and the area each covers is shown in Fig. 3.² The "circles" in the figure are called *bubbles*, and they are

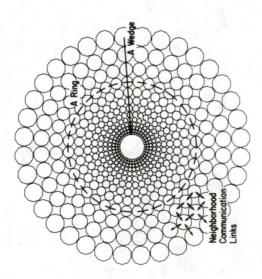

FIG. 3. WHISPER's retina.

arranged in *wedges* (rays emanating from the center) and *rings* (concentric circles of bubbles). The resolution varies across the retina because a larger portion of the underlying diagram is mapped onto a bubble depicted by a larger circle. Since the complete group of receptors is assumed to sense and transmit all signals in parallel, fixations are fast.

Each retinal processor has direct communication links to its nearest neighbors plus one additional link via a common databus connecting all the processors to a supervisory processor called the *retinal supervisor*. The communication topology has been restricted in this simple way to ensure a feasible future hardware implementation.

² There are more receptors filling the central blank area of Fig. 3; however, there is still one special case receptor in the very center which must be handled separately. In order to speed up the retinal simulation the bubbles lying in the blank central area can be fixated separately so they are mapped onto only when they are needed.

The bubble processors are each small computers with independent memory. They all simultaneously execute the same procedure; however, each bubble does not necessarily execute the same instruction at the same time. In the current implementation, a call to the LISP evaluator simulates a processor; and LISP MAPping functions simulate the parallel control structure.

Although the bulk of the processing of the perceptual primitives is done in parallel, there is also a small amount of sequential processing which is performed by the retinal supervisor. The retinal supervisor also directs the parallel processing by choosing which procedure the bubbles should execute next and broadcasting this common procedure to them.

2.2. The perceptual primitives

Each perceptual primitive detects a *problem domain independent* diagram feature. The HLR assigns these features interpretations pertinent to the problem it is solving. The current set of implemented perceptual primitives include ones to: find the center of area of a shape; find the points of contact between a shape of one color and a shape of another; examine curves for abrupt slope changes; test a shape for symmetry; test the similarity of shapes; and visualize the rotation of a shape while watching for a collision with another shape.

The CENTER-OF-AREA perceptual primitive is an illustrative example of the general operation of the perceptual primitives. It computes the center of area of a shape relative to the origin defined by the center of the retina. For each piece, ΔA, of the total area we need to compute the x and y components of its contribution to the total area. Dividing the vector sum of these contributions by the total area yields the coordinates of the center of area. Since each retinal bubble receives its input from a fixed sized area of the diagram and is at a fixed location relative to the retina's center, each bubble can independently compute the components of its contribution to the total area. The bubbles whose receptors do not lie over any part of the shape simply do not contribute. The retinal supervisor performs the summation and the division by the total area. A separate primitive computes the total area. It simply totals the area of all the contributing bubbles. If the computed center of area is far from the retina's center its accuracy can be improved by fixating the retina on the estimated center of area and then recomputing. The decision to iterate is made by the retinal supervisor. The accuracy improves because more of the central, high-resolution portion of the retina is used.

It is possible that systematic errors might lead to a discrepancy between the center of area as seen by the retina and the actual center of area of the object in the diagram. This is the case because the diagram-to-retina mapping does not take into account what fraction of a bubble's picture region is covered by an object. The bubble is simply marked whenever any portion of its region is covered. In practice, the accuracy of the center of area test was more than adequate for WHISPER; if necessary the accuracy could always be improved by adding more bubbles to the retina, increasing its resolution.

The center of area is used for more than simply providing the center of gravity of the objects in WHISPER's problem domain. Other primitives (symmetry, similarity, and contact finding) fixate on a shape's center of area before beginning their calculations. For example, if a shape is symmetrical its center of area will be on its axis of symmetry.

Another important primitive is RETINAL-VISUALIZATION. What is "visualized" is the rigid rotation of a shape about the retinal center. While the shape is rotating the collision detection primitive can be called as a demon to watch whether the rotation causes the shape to overlap with another stationary shape. This is useful both in "blocks world" environments involving moving objects and in testing whether two shapes are equivalent under rotation. The process is termed *visualization* because it does not involve modifying the diagram, but instead is totally internal to the retina itself. It simply entails an organized and uniform exchange of information amongst neighboring bubbles.

The geometrical arrangement of the bubble receptors facilitates the visualization of rotations. From Fig. 3 it can be seen that aligning the bubble centers along wedges results in a constant angular separation between bubbles of the same ring when they are from neighboring wedges, and that this constant is independent of the ring chosen. Thus, to rotate a shape clockwise each bubble marked by the shape simply sends a message to its clockwise ring neighbor asking it to mark itself. The sender then erases its own mark. A collision is detected if a bubble receives a message to mark when it is already marked by a shape other than the rotating one. Although the shape is rotated in sequential steps, the time required is still short because

(i) there are, as a maximum, only as many steps to be made as there are wedges on the retina (currently 36); and

(ii) all the message passing and collision checking occurs in parallel during each step.

The coarse retinal resolution means that the visualization process is much faster than the alternative of rotating the object by small increments directly in the diagram. However, the coarse resolution also means that the collision test may falsely predict a collision. Although the collision test will occasionally generate such "false alarms", it will never fail to correctly predict a true collision. The reason for this is that during the diagram-to-retina mapping a point in the diagram is blurred to fill a whole bubble on the retina with the result that the objects in the diagram appear slightly enlarged on the retina. To check out a possible false alarm the HLR

(i) calls the re-drawing procedures to rotate the object in the diagram to the point where the collision is expected,

(ii) fixates the retina at the predicted collision point,

(iii) asks the retina (now with its high resolution center) to see if the colliding objects are touching.

The CONTACT-FINDER primitive establishes the points at which an object touches other objects. The retina is first fixated on the center of area of the object and then the retinal supervisor directs each retinal bubble to execute the following steps:

Step 1. If the bubble value is not the color of the object then stop.

Step 2. For each of its neighboring bubbles do Step (3).

Step 3. If neighbor's value is the color of a different object send a "contact-found" message to the retinal supervisor.

Step 4. Stop.

The retinal supervisor may receive quite a number of messages from bubbles in the contact regions. It must sort these into groups—one for each distinct area of contact. To do this the retinal supervisor sequentially follows the chain of neighborhood links from one contact bubble to another. Each bubble in the chain is put in the same contact group. If no neighboring bubble is a contact bubble, then the chain is broken. Long chains indicate that the objects touch along a surface while short ones indicate that they touch only at a point. The bubble coordinates of the endpoints of the chain represent the extremities of a contact surface, and the average of the coordinates of all the bubbles in the group is a good place at which to fixate the retina for a more detailed analysis of the contact.

When two objects touch there is a good chance that one supports the other unless they are just sitting side by side. To determine which object is the supporter and which is the supportee, the coordinates of the touching bubbles are compared to find which is "above" the other in the diagram. The assignment of "up" is problem domain dependent and so is made by the HLR.

Another perceptual primitive, FIND-NEAREST, finds the bubble closest to the retinal center satisfying a given condition. For example, to find the object nearest to point P in the diagram the retina is fixated at P and then asked for the nearest marked bubble. The organization of the retina into rings, each an increasing distance from the center, facilitates the search for the required nearest bubble. To find the nearest bubble to the center of the retina satisfying condition C, the retinal supervisor executes the following algorithm:

Step 1. Direct each bubble to test C and save the result (either 'true' or 'false').

Step 2. For $n = 1$ to the number of rings on the retina do Steps 3 and 4.

Step 3. Direct each bubble to report its wedge and ring coordinates as a message to the retinal supervisor if the following hold: (a) it belongs to ring n, (b) its saved value is 'true'.

Step 4. If there is a message pending for the retinal supervisor from step (3), return the coordinates specified in that message (if there is more than one message pick any one of them—all bubbles in a ring are equidistant from the retinal center) to the calling procedure.

This algorithm is a good example of the difference between efficiency in sequential and parallel computation. Since testing C could be a lengthy computation, it is more efficient in terms of elapsed time to simultaneously test C on all bubbles as in Step 1, than to test it for only those bubbles in the scanned rings of Step 3. On a sequential processor it would be best to test C as few times as possible; whereas, on a parallel

Every ⊗ is two ● out from a ●

FIG. 4.

processor the total number of times C is tested is irrelevant (assuming the time to compute $C(x)$ is independent of x). It is the number of times C is tested sequentially which is important.

The SYMMETRY primitive tests for symmetry about a designated vertical axis by comparing the values of symmetrically positioned bubbles. An object is symmetrical (WHISPER tests for vertical and horizontal reflective symmetry), if each bubble having its "color" value has a symmetrically located bubble with the same value. If when testing the vertical reflective symmetry of a blue object, say, the bubble in the third wedge clockwise from the vertical axis and in the fourth ring from the center has the value 'blue', then the value of the bubble in the third wedge counter-clockwise from the vertical axis and in the fourth ring must be checked to see if it is also 'blue'. If it is not, then possibly the discrepancy can be ruled out as insignificant; otherwise, the object is asymmetrical. Neighborhood message passing is used to bring together the values from bubbles on opposite sides of the proposed axis. The technique is to cause whole wedges to shift in a manner perhaps best described as analogous to the closing of an Oriental hand fan. All the bubbles to the left of the axis send their values clockwise, while all those to the right send theirs counterclock-wise. Messages which meet at the axis are compared and will be equal if the object is symmetrical.

The symmetry test must be supplied a proposed axis of symmetry. The center of area offers partial information on determining this axis since it must lie on it if the object is symmetrical. This does not, however, provide the orientation of the axis. Although the simplest solution may be to test the object in all of the wedge orien-tations by using the rotational visualization, if one more point on the axis of sym-metry could be found the axis would be uniquely determined. Such a point is the center of the circumscribing circle of the object. The only problem is that thus far I have not managed to devise a quick parallel algorithm for finding this center. Although in some cases they may coincide, in general I expect the center of area and the center of the circumscribing circle to be distinct for objects with only a single axis of symmetry.

An unexpected and interesting property of WHISPER's retinal geometry leads to a simple method, employing neighborhood communication, for scaling the retinal 'image' of an object. The primitive is RETINAL-SCALING. An object is scaled correctly (i.e. without distorting its shape) if each bubble having its value, sends this value to a bubble in the same wedge, but a fixed number of rings away. As long as each value is moved the same number of rings either inwards or outwards from the bubble which originally holds it, the size of the 'image' of the object is changed but its shape is preserved (Fig. 4). This is the case because the constraint of aligning the bubbles into wedges such that each bubble touches all of its immediate neighbors is satisfied by increasing the bubble diameters by a constant factor from ring to ring. For a proof of this see Funt (1976). Scaling an object by neighborhood communi-cation is implemented by having each bubble simultaneously send its value as a message to its neighbor in the same wedge in either the appropriate inwards or

outwards direction, and repeating this message passing process sequentially as many times as necessary to bring about the required scaling.

The SIMILARITY PRIMITIVE determines whether two objects, A and B, are similar under some combination of translation, rotation and scaling, and if so returns the angle of rotation, direction and distance of translation, and the scale factor. It works by taking one object, say A, and translating, scaling and rotating it so it can be matched with the other. Since the center of area of an object is unique the centers of area of A and B must be aligned if they are to match. Thus the first step is to find the centers of area, and then to translate A. Rather than call the re-drawing transformations to move A in the diagram, its translation can be ac-complished entirely on the retina by:

   (i) fixating on the center of area of A,
   (ii) asking all bubbles not containing A to mark themselves as empty space,
   (iii) fixating on the center of area of B while superimposing this new image on the old one.

After translation A must be scaled. If A and B are to match, then their areas will need to be the same; therefore, we must scale A by a factor equal to the square root of the ratio of the areas of the two objects (i.e. scalefactor = squareroot(area(B)/ area(A)). The areas of A and B are available as a by-product of the center of area calculation. Now that the objects are aligned and the same size, A is rotated about its center of area using retinal visualization to see if there is any orientation at which it matches B.

CURVE-FEATURES analyses curves. In order to begin, it must first find the

testing whether any drastic slope change occurs over the length of the curve. To more accurately determine the slope at a particular point, the retina is fixated on it for higher resolution. The curve tangent is then the perpendicular to the bisector of the angle between wedges with the most bubbles on the curve. The angle between wedges can be used because they emanate directly from the center of the retina, just as the curve must when the retina is centered on it. This method is more accurate than measuring the angle between neighboring bubbles because there are more wedges than neighbors. The HLR mainly uses this test to decide whether or not an object will slide.

2.3. The underlying diagram

We began with the view that the retina is a special purpose parallel processor designed to detect diagrammatic features without saying anything about the precise nature of the diagrams themselves. With the retinal processor in hand, we can now see that the representation of the diagrams is unimportant as long as each bubble receives its correct input. This is analogous to a program which issues a READ command without caring whether the input is coming from a card reader, a file, or a terminal. The method of mapping from the diagram to the retinal bubbles' input must be fast, however, because the retina is re-filled everytime it is fixated at a new diagram location.

There are at least two different types of representing media for the underlying diagram. The first is the conventional medium of visible marks on a two-dimensional surface, usually paper. The map from diagram to human retina is accomplished by the lens of the eye focusing the incoming light. Since there is simultaneous stimulation of the receptors, it is a very fast process.

The second possible type of diagram representation is similar to that used in generating computer graphics. The diagram is specified as a list of primitive elements (in graphics applications, usually line segment equations). In a similar vein, Kosslyn (1975) proposes that human visual imagery is in some ways analogous to the storage and display of graphics images. The parallel processing capacity of WHISPER's retina can be used to quickly map each primitive element into the proper bubble inputs. To mark all bubbles lying on line segment, S, the retinal supervisor directs every bubble to determine independently if it is on S, and if so, to mark itself. Since this simple test—do a circle and a line segment intersect?—is performed by all bubbles simultaneously, the time required is independent of the length of S. The same method can mark all bubbles within any simple shape such as a circle, square or triangle in time independent of its area. Regardless of the type of primitive element, the time taken to "draw" the diagram on the retina is, however, proportional to the number of primitives in its description. They must be processed sequentially.

Due to the lack of true parallel processing, neither of the above two types of diagram representations is used in WHISPER. Instead, the diagram is implemented as a square array. Each array cell denotes a point on a real world, pencil and paper diagram.

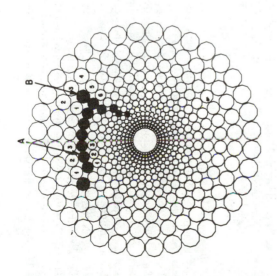

FIG. 5.

retinal bubbles on the curve. Given one bubble on the curve, the others can be found by following the chain of bubbles each having the same value. In WHISPER's diagrams the contours of objects are "colored" a different shade from their interiors, and this helps prevent the curve following process from getting lost tracing chains of bubbles which are part of an object's interior. It is not strictly necessary to color code the object contours, since a contour bubble can be determined by the type of neighbors surrounding it, but coding is cheaper and easier.

Once the set of bubbles on the curve is found, each bubble in the set can individually test for the occurrence of a particular feature; therefore, the whole curve is tested in parallel. A bubble detects a sharp bend in the curve if there is an imbalance in the number of its neighbors on opposite sides of the curve which are themselves not members of the curve. This is illustrated by Fig. 5 in which bubble A has three neighbors on each side of the curve, whereas bubble B has six neighbors on one side and none on the other. Thus, a bubble tests for bends by:

(i) asking its neighbors whether or not they are on the curve, and
(ii) comparing the number of responses originating from opposite sides of the curve.

For a simple closed curve, if the bubble knows which responding neighbors are interior and which are exterior, then it can additionally classify the bend as convex or concave.

The slope of a curve at any curve bubble is determined as the perpendicular to the bisector of the angle between the centers of its neighboring bubbles on the curve. This yields a rough approximation to the actual slope, but it is sufficient for quickly

2.4. The re-drawing transformations

The re-drawing transformations are the procedures the HLR can call to change the underlying diagram. In WHISPER there are transformations for adding and removing lines, and for rigidly translating and rotating shapes. Other non-linear transformations could be added if required. These re-drawing procedures are of course dependent upon the representation of the diagram they modify, and the ease and efficiency with which they can be implemented could affect the choice of diagram representation.

3. WHISPER in Operation

With the basic mechanisms for interaction with the diagram now understood, it is appropriate to see how they are used in the course of solving a problem. We will consider problems of the type: predict the sequence of events occurring during the collapse of a "blocks world" structure. The structure will be a piled group of *arbitrarily* shaped objects of uniform density and thickness. If the structure is stable, there are no events to describe; if it is unstable, then the events involve rotations, slides, falls, and collisions. WHISPER accepts a diagram of the initial problem state, and produces a sequence of diagrams, called *snapshots*, as its qualitative solution. A quantitative solution specifying precise locations, velocities, and times is not found; however, deriving one from a qualitative solution should not be too difficult (deKleer (1975)).

Fig. 6 is a typical example of WHISPER's input diagrams. They all depict a side view of the structure. Each object is shaded a different "color" (alphanumeric value) so it can be easily distinguished and identified. Objects' boundaries are also distinctly colored. The diagram depicts a problem, called the "chain-reaction problem," which is particularly interesting because the causal connection between objects B and D must be discovered.

3.1. The Qualitative HLR

The HLR is the top level of the WHISPER system. It is solely responsible for solving each problem; the diagram and retina are simply tools at its disposal. It consists of procedural specialists which know about stability, about the outcome of different varieties of instability, how to interpret each perceptual primitive, and how to call the transformation procedures to produce the solution snapshots. There are two types of instabilities—rotational and sliding. For clarity, sliding instabilities will not be discussed for the present. Operation of the system follows the steps:

Step 1. Determine all instabilities.
Step 2. Pick the dominant instability.
Step 3. Find pivot point for rotation of unstable object.
Step 4. Find termination condition of rotation using retinal visualization.
Step 5. Call transformation procedure to modify diagram as determined in Step 4.

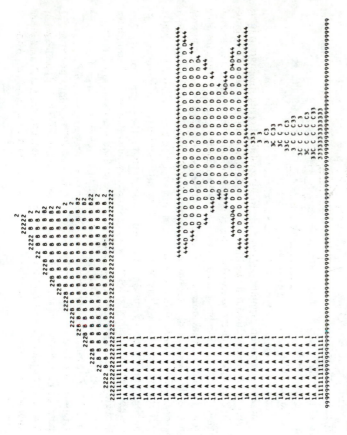

FIG. 6. Chain reaction problem.

Step 6. Output modified diagram as a solution snapshot.
Step 7. Use snapshot from Step 6 as input and restart from Step 1.
In what follows we elaborate on each of these steps.

The diagram and retina are an invaluable aid to the HLR in discovering what stops an object's motion, and in accomplishing the necessary state change. The chain reaction problem demonstrates this. The stability specialist directs the retina to fixate at numerous locations while perusing the diagram, and from an analysis (discussed below) of the visible support relationships determines that B is the only unstable object. B will pivot about the support point closest to its center of gravity. The retina is fixated there (the top right corner of A), so B's rotation can be visualized. As the object rotates, two events are possible. It may collide with another object, or it may begin to fall freely. The conditions under which either of these occur are monitored during the visualization. From this simulation of B's rotation, its collision with D is discovered, and its angle of rotation and location of first contact with D are found. Because of the coarseness of the retinal resolution, this angle of rotation is only approximate. This approximate value is used in conjunction with feedback from the diagram to refine the angle of rotation as follows. First the re-drawing transformations are called to produce a new diagram (Fig. 7) in which B is rotated by slightly less than the estimated value. The rotation is made on the short side so that B will not overshoot. The retina is then fixated on the anticipated point of collision so that the gap between the two objects can be examined. If there is none, then the update is complete; however, if there is, then B is rotated again until the gap is closed. The resulting diagram (Fig. 8) is output as WHISPER's first snapshot of the solution sequence.

3.2. Motion discontinuities and experimental feedback

There are several important observations to be made at this point. One is that discovering the reason for the interruption of an object's motion, accomplished so simply here for B through visualization, is generally found to be a very difficult problem. Physics provides equations for object motions, but these equations describe a condition which theoretically lasts indefinitely. They do not indicate when new boundary conditions should take effect. Certainly it is possible to design a set of special heuristics specifying when and where collisions are most likely to occur (e.g. below the rotating object). However, it is quite probable that the collision occurring in Fig. 9 would be overlooked, whereas WHISPER's visualization process would detect it as a matter of course.

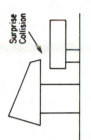

FIG. 9.

WHISPER relies on *experimental feedback* to successfully update its diagram in its method of visualization followed by gap closure. This method is basically a pragmatic equivalent to the unfeasible experiment of rotating the object in the diagram by very small increments until a collision occurs. Usually feedback is thought of in terms of a robot immersed in a real world environment. In WHISPER's case, however, the feedback is from a situation analogous to that in the real world—the diagram and diagram transformations—rather than from observation of actual falling objects. Alternatively, we can say that WHISPER is using M' to derive results about M. Using this feedback WHISPER is able to find when and where discontinuous changes in an object's motion occur without being forced to use sophisticated, "number-crunching" algorithms for touch tests (see Fahlman (1973)) for arbitrary shapes.

3.3. The frame problem

Once WHISPER has produced the first snapshot, it is ready to compute the next one. All the information the HLR needs for this is contained in the first snapshot diagram. Thus to produce the next snapshot, the HLR takes its last output snapshot as input, and begins processing exactly as if it were working on a fresh problem. Although

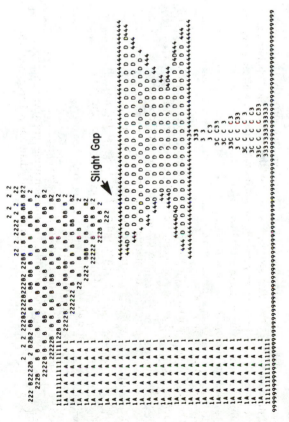

FIG. 7.

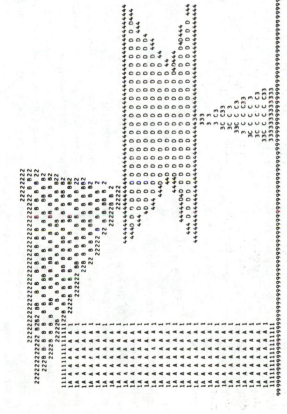

FIG. 8. First snapshot.

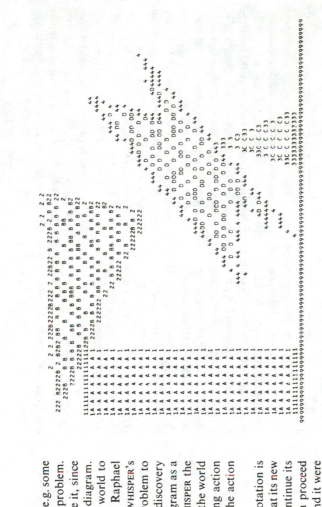

FIG. 10. Second snapshot.

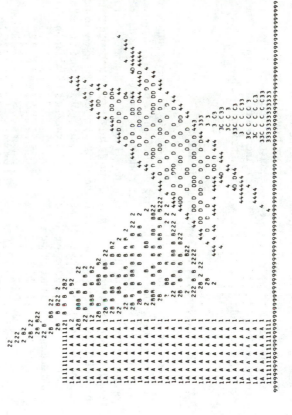

FIG. 11. Final snapshot.

some results derived while working on the previous snapshot remain valid (e.g. some contact relationships will still hold), many will be inapplicable to the new problem. It is easier to disregard this old information than to sort it out and update it, since the retina provides a fast and efficient method of fetching it from the new diagram.

The problem of updating a system's representation of the state of the world to reflect the effects of actions performed in the world is the *frame problem*. Raphael (1971) and Hayes (1971, 1976) discuss it in detail. The transition between WHISPER's snapshots is exactly the type of situation in which we expect the frame problem to arise. It involves the representation of action, the effects of action, and the discovery of chains of causal connection. However, because WHISPER relies on a diagram as a representation of the state of the world, it remains under control. For WHISPER the state of the world is represented by the state of the diagram, and action in the world is represented by corresponding action in the diagram. The corresponding action is the application of the appropriate transformation, and the effects of the action are correctly represented by the resulting state of the diagram.

In WHISPER's current problem, the HLR knows that the action of *B*'s rotation is represented by calling the rotation transformation procedure to re-draw *B* at its new location in the diagram. Almost all of the information that it needs to continue its problem solving is correctly represented by the updated diagram. It can proceed just as if the new snapshot (the updated diagram) were its original input and it were starting a brand new problem. The most important information which has changed in the transition between the states as a result of the rotation is: the position and orientation of object *B*; the position of its center of area; the contacts it makes with other objects; and the shape of the areas of empty space. There are also a multitude of things that will not have changed in the world and are correctly left unchanged by the rotational transformation, such as the position of all the other objects, the shape of all objects, the area of all objects, and the contact relationships of other objects not involving *B*. All of these things work out correctly without the need of any deduction or inference on WHISPER's part. All that it need do is to use its retina to look at the diagram and extract whatever information it needs from the updated diagram.

An expanded WHISPER system could not completely avoid the pitfalls of the frame problem because not all of the information about the current state of the world (e.g. velocities) can be represented by the state of the diagram.

3.4. Subsequent snapshots of the chain reaction problem

The analysis producing the second and third snapshots is very similar to that for the first. In Fig. 8, *B*'s weight on *D* causes *D* to be unstable. Its rotation is visualized with the retina fixated at the peak of *C* leading to the discovery of its collision with the table. The diagram is updated to produce the second snapshot, Fig. 10, which is again input for further analysis. *B* now lacks sufficient support, and topples to hit *D* again as shown in Fig. 11. The complexity of the problem rises sharply at this point, and WHISPER's analysis ends, as, I believe, would most peoples'.

B and *D* could be shown to fall simultaneously (WHISPER currently does not) by rotating *D* only part of the way to the table before allowing *B* to catch up, and then iterating this process a few times until *D* reaches the table.

3.5. Some limitations of WHISPER's qualitative knowledge

WHISPER's knowledge of Physics is far from comprehensive. As mentioned above, one obvious limitation is that a snapshot by its very nature portrays all objects as stationary, whereas some may be moving. To take velocities into account requires the addition of a quantitative reasoning component to the HLR's qualitative knowledge. Knowledge of velocity, acceleration, momentum and moments of inertia would have to be represented in terms of equations. The HLR's current qualitative predictions can be used to guide the application of these equations in the search for a quantitative solution.

Another limitation is that WHISPER approximates simultaneity by moving objects one after another. This process works for problems like the one discussed above; but this approximation is insufficient in some cases where two or more objects move at a time. In Fig. 12, for example, if *B* is moved after *A* is moved, then they will not

Fig. 12.

collide; however, if they are moved simultaneously they will collide. Again we can make use of the diagram by shading the areas each object will sweep through. If no two shaded areas overlap then there will not be a collision; wherever they do overlap a collision might occur and further quantitative analysis of the angular velocities of the objects is required.

3.6. Slide problems

Unstable objects may also slide. When Fig. 13 is given to WHISPER its reasoning up to the point where it generates the first snapshot, Fig. 14, is the same as for the chain reaction problem. At this point it is faced with a problem involving a sliding object. Although the basic outline of the solution process for slide problems—test stability, find termination point of motion, update diagram, output snapshot, restart with the output as input—is the same, there are some essential differences in handling sliding objects. The most important arises because it is not possible to visualize the slide of an object down an arbitrary curve. What WHISPER does instead is examine the curve itself with its retina.

A variety of conditions can terminate an object's slide. For example, there may be a sharp rise (a bump), a sharp fall (a cliff), or a hill which is higher than the starting point. Also the object may slide into another object resting on or near the surface.

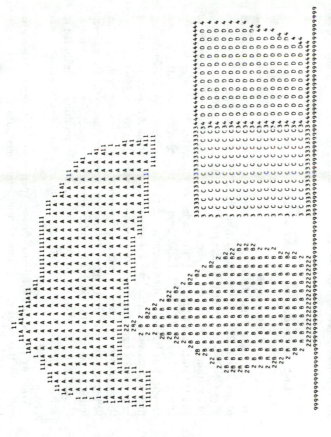

FIG. 13. A problem with a sliding object.

These conditions are illustrated in Fig. 15. In the current implementation WHISPER fixates only once (at the starting point of the slide) to test for these conditions. Multiple fixations at regular intervals along the curve would improve the accuracy of the tests.

The case shown in Fig. 15(e) of a "surprise collision" is one which requires multiple fixations. Although WHISPER does not yet handle this situation, it is clear how it easily could as illustrated in Fig. 16. In the figure an x indicates a fixation point, a semi-circle indicates the area of the diagram to be checked by the retina at each fixation (checking a circular region is easy because of the retina's ring structure), and the space between the dashed line and the surface indicates a clear "corridor" for the object. The radius of the semi-circle is a function of the object's size and the fixation interval. The same sized corridor can be examined with fewer fixations by using a larger radius. The only disadvantage is that the probability of false alarms is increased because the distance between the dashed line and the circumference of the semi-circles is greater. A false alarm can be investigated by making more fixations in the region where it occurs. This method of detecting collisions is good for two reasons:

(i) because the retina can check large segments of space in a single glance, the number of fixations required to examine the space near the surface is relatively small;
(ii) a collision will never be missed.

(i) those representing surfaces on the moving object (its underside) which will slide past a point on a stationary object, and

(ii) those representing surfaces of stationary objects (their topsides) which will have a point on the moving object ride over them.

Thus in the current example (Fig. 14) the HLR directs the retina to examine the surface of A from C1 to the left, and the surface of C, possibly continuing over to the surface of D, from C2 to the right. If there is more than one reason why the object's slide will end, then only the condition which occurs first (i.e. after the object has slid the shortest distance) is relevant. One more finepoint is that tests for some conditions, for example collisions, need only be made when the surface is a topside and not an underside.

3.7. Updating the diagram to reflect a slide

After the curve examination is complete and the spot where the object's slide will end is known, the next step is to update the diagram so that it will show the object at its new location. First the HLR calls the re-drawing procedures to translate the object. This is shown in the change from Fig. 14 to Fig. 17 in which point X is aligned with C1. This does not complete the diagram update however, since the object's orientation will most likely change during its slide. The contacts between the object and the surface it slides along should be the same when the slide ends as when it began. Knowing this the HLR can determine the object's correct orientation using retinal visualization. It directs the retina to fixate at the object's new location and then visualize its rotation while watching for the original contact relationships to be re-established. The angle of rotation is returned to the HLR which then calls the re-drawing procedures to rotate the object by that amount in the diagram. As before, the angle returned by the retina is only approximate so the HLR directs the retina to fixate on the expected point of contact and check for any remaining gap. If there is, a second corrective rotation is made. The resulting snapshot is Fig. 18. This two-step method—translation followed by a corrective rotation—works for curved as well as straight surfaces.

What we can see from all this is how experimental feedback combined with a first order theory of sliding motions results in a very natural form of qualitative reasoning.

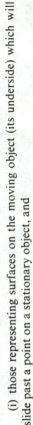

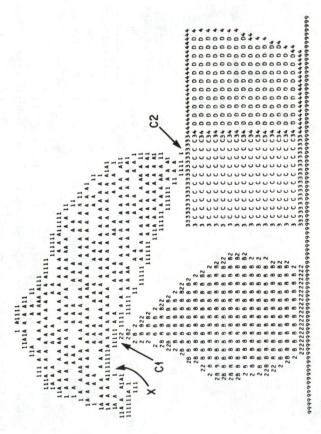

Fig. 14.

The HLR, in addition to specifying which conditions the retina should look for, must specify which curve segments it should look at. There are two kinds of curves to test:

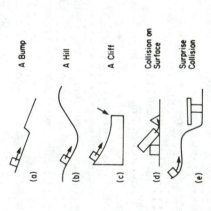

(a) A Bump

(b) A Hill

(c) A Cliff

(d) Collision on Surface

(e) Surprise Collision

Fig. 15.

Fig. 16.

3.8. Benefit of the diagram during slide analysis

In the curve examination and diagram update process, the diagram is very useful to the HLR in the course of curve following, and it also provides feedback as it did in the case of rotations. The main pitfall in curve following is the possibility that two objects will coincidentally align so that a smooth curve is formed across them both. An object could then begin its slide on one object and continue sliding along the other as A did when it slid across C and onto D. This *emergent* property of the curve must be noticed, and the two curve segments appended. In a system relying on an independent description of each object, this would pose a significant problem because one would require:

    (i) that it have a built in expectation that the situation might arise;
    (ii) that it continually check for the situation;
    (iii) that its check involve testing whether the first object touches any other object in the universe; and
    (iv) that it know how to amalgamate the two separate curve segment descriptions into a new curve description.

For WHISPER it does not create a problem because two aligned surfaces of neighboring objects form a continuous curve in the diagram; WHISPER only has to look at this curve, rather than, in a sense, discover or construct it.

4. The Stability Test

Rather than solve the stability problem with a sophisticated general method, as Fahlman (1973) did in his BUILD system, WHISPER seeks qualitative solutions using rules corresponding to those a person untrained in Physics might apply. The HLR has specialists which express rules like: "If an object hangs over too far, it will topple"; and "If an object and one of its supporters make contact along a surface (rather than at a single point) and if this surface is not horizontal, then the object will slide." A frictionless environment is assumed.

4.1. Sub-structuring

Overall organisation of the stability test is based on the observation that a complete structure is stable if each of its independent subparts is stable whenever their supporters are stable. Thus the initial structure is broken down into smaller substructures whose stability as individual units is easier to test than the stability of the structure as a whole. To perform the stability test the HLR first asks the retina for a list of the names of all objects in the scene. Each object, O, is then handled in turn. The retina is used to find whether or not O supports any other object(s). If it does not, then its stability is tested by SINGLE-STABLE, a specialist in individual object stability. At this point the assumption is that O's supporters are themselves stable. If O supports other objects then its stability is not tested, but rather it is amalgamated with its supportees as if it and they were all glued together to form a single conglomerate object, C. If C does not support anything, then its stability

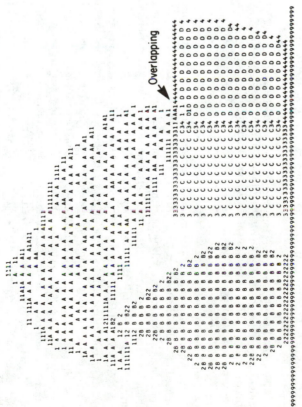

FIG. 17.

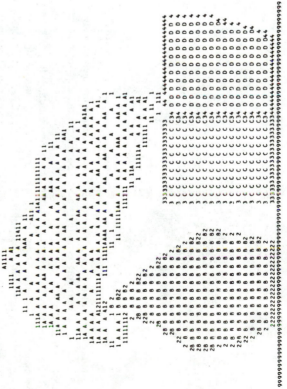

FIG. 18. Final snapshot of the sliding-object problem.

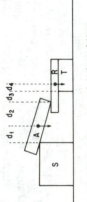

FIG. 19.

is tested by SINGLE-STABLE; if it does support something, then recursively it is combined with its supportees to form a new conglomerate, C', which is then also checked for supportees.

There is an important exception to the above description. When an object is a cosupporter, as one pillar in an arch for example, then it is not amalgamated with its supportee. In this case the object is sent to SINGLE-STABLE for testing with an addendum specifying the point of contact between it and the supportee.

The dotted curves in Fig. 19 encircle the sub-structures which are passed to SINGLE-STABLE. In (b), Q and RS are cosupporters of X, so they are not combined with it.

Incidentally, treating two objects such as A and B as a single object AB is another example of a situation in which two descriptions must be amalgamated. It is a trivial task for WHISPER to amalgamate two object descriptions, since all it need do is interpret their two color codings as the same color.

4.2. Single object stability

As we have seen, the problem of determining the stability of a complete structure is reduced at each stage to the determination of the stability of individual objects. For a single object there are only three basic types of instability. It can either rotate about some support point (rotational instability), slide along a surface (translational instability), or simply fall freely (free fall instability).

SINGLE-STABLE considers the relative positions of an object's center of gravity and its supporting contacts to decide on rotational stability. Consider first the case of an object with nothing on top of it. One with a single support must have its center of gravity positioned directly above the contact region. One with multiple supports must be positioned so that a vertical dropped from its center of gravity passes through either a contact region or the space between two contact regions. The restrictions of uniform density and thickness of objects mean that an object's center of area can be substituted for its center of gravity. SINGLE-STABLE thus sees that an object "hangs over too far" when its center of area falls outside its supports.

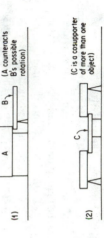

R is stable if $(d_4/d_3)w_R \geq (d_1/(d_1 + d_2))w_A$
where: w_A is the weight of A
$\quad\quad\quad w_R$ is the weight of R
$\quad\downarrow$ is an object's center of gravity

FIG. 20.

The stability of an object with something on top of it will be affected by the extra weight. Because of the way in which objects are formed into conglomerates before they are passed to SINGLE-STABLE, if one supports something then it must in fact be one of two or more cosupporters. Let us say SINGLE-STABLE is testing the stability of an object R which, along with cosupporter S, supports A. First it checks the easy cases:

(i) if ignoring A, R is already rotationally unstable and A's weight will only add to this instability, then R rotates;

(ii) if ignoring A, R is already rotationally unstable, but A's weight might counteract its rotation, then this is a counterbalancing type problem which is too difficult to handle without further quantitative investigation;

(iii) if A, no matter how heavy it is, will not topple R (i.e. test R's stability under the assumption that its center of gravity is located at the contact point between it and A) and R ignoring A is stable, then R remains stable.

The most difficult case is when ignoring A, R by itself is stable, but A may or may not be heavy enough to cause it to rotate. In this situation the location of A's center of gravity relative to its support must be considered. These distances are shown in Fig. 20. If $w_R(d_4/d_3) \geq w_A d_1/(d_1 + d_2)$ then R is stable; otherwise, it will rotate. SINGLE-STABLE cannot handle objects which participate in two or more cosupport relationships. Fig. 21 shows two problems the stability test does not handle. Objects, such as D in Fig. 6, which are balancing in an unstable equilibrium provide a special problem. Since the slightest deviation in the location of D's center

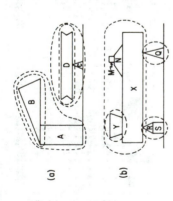

FIG. 21. Stability problems WHISPER cannot handle.

(1) Move to center of diagram; return names of all the objects in the scene.

(2–3) Find the center of gravity of A; find supportees of A.

(4–5) Find the center of gravity of B; find supportees and supporters of B.

(6) Move central section of retina; find exact contact point of A and B.

(7–8) Find center of gravity of AB; find supporters of AB.

(9) Move central section; find exact contact point of AB with table.

(10–11) Move central section; find extremities of contact surface.

(12) Find the slope of the contact surface.

(13) Move to center of gravity of B and look at contact between A and B.

(14–15) Move central section; find extremities of contact surface between A and B; (5, 72) and (19, 72) are returned.

(16) Determine the slope of the contact surface.

(17–20) Find center of gravity of D; look for supporters and supportees.

(21–22) Move both the central section and the periphery; find the exact point of contact with C. Discovers that support is a point not a surface indicating possible equilibrium situation.

(23) Move back to center of gravity of D to check for symmetry of D; equilibrium is found to be o.k.

(24) Finding center of gravity of C; look for supportees of C.

(25–26) Finding center of gravity of CD; find supporters of CD; finds the table.

(27) Move central section; find exact point of contact of CD with table.

(28–29) Move central section; find extremities of contact surface; returns (64, 22) and (76, 21).

(30) Determine the type of contact and its slope.

(31) Move to the pivot point of the rotation of B to visualize the rotation. The rotation is then carried out in the diagram, see Fig. 7.****
**** The rotation is carried out in the diagram, see Fig. 7.****

(32) Move central section to estimated point of collision between B and A to see if they touch; the gap is seen; the amount of the next rotation is estimated. **** Another rotation is carried out in the diagram, see Fig. 8.****

(33) Move central section to estimated point of collision between B and A (the same as (32)); now they are seen to touch.

---

of gravity would upset the balance, it must be known precisely. The CENTER-OF-AREA's estimation is not sufficiently accurate. We expect D to balance because it is symmetrical. Using the retina's symmetry test, WHISPER draws the same conclusion. For it to balance, D must be symmetrical about a vertical axis through its support point. Since D is, the stability test reports it as stable; if it were not, then the stability test would have to report that it was unable to decide.

4.3. The eye movement protocol for the chain reaction problem

During the problem-solving process the retina is constantly moving from place to place in the diagram. A trace of the eye movements is given by the circled numbers

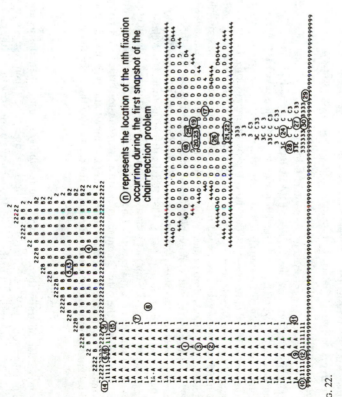

Ⓝ represents the location of the nth fixation occurring during the first snapshot of the chain-reaction problem

FIG. 22.

in Fig. 22 and Fig. 7. Each circle represents a fixation of the retina. The numbers give the order in which the fixations occurred. The retina was split so that its central and peripheral portions could be fixated separately. For some fixations in Fig. 22 only the center of the retina was used, while for others only the periphery. Although moving the two parts of the retina separately would be unnecessary if there actually were many processors operating in parallel, it saves a considerable amount of computation in the pseudo-parallel simulation. What follows is a list of the plotted fixations accompanied by the HLR's reasons for requesting them.

Although it would be rash to claim that WHISPER accurately models human problem-solving, the eye-movement protocol provides an unusual possibility for testing such a conjecture. An eye-tracking system could be used to record the eye movements of a human subject while he solves one of WHISPER's problems. This record could then be compared with WHISPER's protocol.

4.4 Translational stability

WHISPER decides translational stability by examining the object's contacts. There are three types of contact that are considered: surface-to-surface, surface-to-point, and point-to-surface. The stability criterion for a particular contact is whether or not the tangent to the surface involved in the contact is horizontal at the point of contact. (Tangents are found by the CURVE-FEATURES perceptual primitive.) If the tangent is not horizontal, then the direction of downward tilt is taken as the resultant direction of motion of the object. If a conflict in the direction arises—one contact indicating leftward motion and another indicating rightward motion—then WHISPER reports that it is unable to decide what the motion will be. In these situations a quantitative investigation is needed in order to resolve the qualitative ambiguity. (Resolving qualitative ambiguities by quantitative reasoning is discussed by deKleer (1975).) There is, of course, no conflict between a horizontal contact slope and a non-horizontal contact slope, the former simply does not contribute to the motion. After A rotates to hit C (Fig. 14), the HLR asks the retina to find and classify all the contacts. The A-to-B contact is classified as surface-to-point, with the rightward tilt of the surface of A at the contact noted as contributing to a rightward motion for A. Similarly, the A-to-C contact is classified as point-to-surface with no contribution to the motion of A because the slope of C is horizontal at the contact point. Thus WHISPER concludes that A will slide to the right along the surface of B.

5. Conclusion

WHISPER demonstrates the advantages and feasibility of using diagrams as an aid in problem-solving. We see from a theoretical standpoint that their role is one of a model M' which is similar to the model M—a blocks world structure in the problem domain. More simply stated, WHISPER's diagrams and diagram re-drawing procedures, M', are analogous to blocksworld situations, M. A fundamental component of the system is the retina which blends sequential and parallel processing while limiting the quantity of processors and processor interconnections to a fixed, not too large number. By asking questions of the retina, the HLR is able to obtain experimental feedback from M', and hence results about M—information it would otherwise have to deductively infer from general principles and assertions describing M.

ACKNOWLEDGMENT

I have benefited from the inspiration and assistance of Raymond Reiter, Alan K. Macworth, Richard S. Rosenberg, Gordon McCalla, Peter Rowat, Jim Davidson and Stuart C. Shapiro. I have also received valuable criticism from Zenon Pylyshyn and E. W. Elcock.

REFERENCES

1. Bobrow, D., Dimensions of Representation, in: D. G. Bobrow and A. Collins (Eds.), Representation and Understanding (Academic Press, New York, 1975), pp. 1–35.
2. deKleer, J., Qualitative and Quantitative Knowledge in Classical Mechanics, M.Sc. Thesis (1975), MIT, Cambridge, MA.
3. Dunlavey, M., An Hypothesis-Driven Vision System, Advance Papers of the Fourth International Conference on Artificial Intelligence, Tibilisi, Georgia, USSR, September 3–8, 1975, pp. 616–619.
4. Fahlman, S., A Planning System for Robot Construction Tasks, AI TR 283, MIT (May 1973).
5. Funt, B., WHISPER: A Computer Implementation Using Analogues in Reasoning, Tech. Report 76–9, Department of Computer Science, Univ. of British Columbia (1976).
6. Funt, B., WHISPER: A Problem-Solving System Utilizing Diagrams and a Parallel Processing Retina, Advance Papers of the Fifth International Joint Conference on Artificial Intelligence, MIT, August 1977.
7. Gelernter, H., Realization of a Geometry-Theorem Proving Machine, in: E. A. Feigenbaum and J. Feldman (Eds.), Computers and Thought (McGraw-Hill, New York, 1963), pp. 134–152.
8. Hayes, P., A Logic of Actions, in: B. Meltzer and D. Michie (Eds.), Machine Intelligence 6 (American Elsevier, New York, 1971), pp. 495–520.
9. Hayes, P., Some Problems and Non-Problems in Representation Theory. AISB Summer Conference Proceedings (July 1974), pp. 63–79.
10. Hesse, Mary, Models and Analogies in Science (University of Notre Dame Press, 1966).
11. Kosslyn, S. M., Information Representation in Visual Images, Cognitive Psychology 7 (1975). pp. 341–370.
12. Minsky, M. and Papert, S., Perceptrons: An Introduction to Computational Geometry (MIT Press, Cambridge, MA, 1969).
13. Nagel, E., The Structure of Science (Harcourt, Brace and World, 1961).
14. Sloman, A., Interactions Between Philosophy and Artificial Intelligence: The Role of Intuition and Non-Logical Reasoning in Intelligence, Artificial Intelligence 2 (1971), 209–225.
15. Raphael, B., The Frame Problem in Problem-Solving Systems, in: N. V. Findler and B. Meltzer (Eds.), Artificial Intelligence and Heuristic Programming (Edinburgh University Press, Edinburgh, 1971), pp. 159–169.

Received 23 January 1979; revised version received 9 July 1979

27 / Thomas D. Garvey, John D. Lowrance, and Martin A. Fischler
An Inference Technique for Integrating Knowledge from Disparate Sources

The representation systems highlighted in this book generally focus on all-or-nothing, deductive-type reasoning in non-perceptual domains. In this paper, Garvey, *et al.*, explain a popular new style of formalism based on graded evidential support for propositions, and explore the application of this work (due initially to Dempster and Shafer) to integrating evidence from multiple knowledge sources. This work on "probabilistic reasoning" ties into earlier work on expert systems (see [Davis *et al.*, Chapter 21]), which typically included simple confidence factors and Bayesian rules of combination. Instead, Dempster-Shafer representations use a *range* of probabilities to represent both the "support" for a proposition as well as its "plausibility." The paper is mathematical, but readable. It treats the statistical reasoning in a fairly pure form, but it is possible to imagine this kind of evidential combination in a more typical AI representation framework (for example, see [Rich 83] and [Ginsburg 84]).

Appeared in *Proc. IJCAI-81*, Vancouver, B. C., August, 1981, 319–325.

AN INFERENCE TECHNIQUE FOR INTEGRATING KNOWLEDGE FROM DISPARATE SOURCES

Thomas D. Garvey, John D. Lowrance, and Martin A. Fischler

SRI International, Menlo Park, California

ABSTRACT

This paper introduces a formal method for integrating knowledge derived from a variety of sources for use in "perceptual reasoning."[*] The formalism is based on the "evidential propositional calculus," a derivative of Shafer's mathematical theory of evidence [4]. It is more general than either a Boolean or Bayesian approach, providing for Boolean and Bayesian inferencing when the appropriate information is available. In this formalism, the likelihood of a proposition A is represented as a subinterval, $[s(A),p(A)]$, of the unit interval, $[0,1]$. The evidential support for proposition A is represented by $s(A)$, while $p(A)$ represents its degree of plausibility; $p(A)$ can also be interpreted as the degree to which one fails to doubt A, $p(A)$ being equal to one minus the evidential support for ~A. This paper describes how evidential information, furnished by a knowledge source in the form of a probability "mass" distribution, can be converted to this interval representation; how, through a set of inference rules for computing intervals of dependent propositions, this information can be extrapolated from those propositions it directly bears upon, to those it indirectly bears upon; and how multiple bodies of evidential information can be pooled. A sample application of this approach, modeling the operation of a collection of sensors (a particular type of knowledge source), illustrates these techniques.

I   INTRODUCTION AND OVERVIEW

We are pursuing a program of research aimed at developing a computer-based capability for "perceptual reasoning" [2] that will make it possible to interpret important aspects of a situation from information obtained by a collection of disparate sensors. Situational assessment implies the need to integrate sensory information with a body of relevant "expertise," or prior knowledge. This integration poses a number of difficult technical problems that must be examined.

Among the problems focused upon in our work are the following:

*   How to model sensors and other knowledge sources (KS), so as to know which situations they can provide information about and how to interpret their responses.

*   How to effectively combine (sometimes contradictory) information from multiple knowledge sources to compensate for their individual deficiencies.

*   How to automatically devise a data-acquisition/sensor-utilization strategy to maximize overall system effectiveness.

In this paper we shall concentrate on the approach to sensor modeling and knowledge integration that is currently under investigation. These form the core of the overall system.

A.   Previous Work

Earlier research [1, 2, 3] led to a number of important conclusions regarding the integration of perceptual information. First, because of the variety of knowledge types required and the particular uses of each, it became apparent that a proliferation of specialized representations was inevitable. This is a departure from standard approaches that attempt to develop a representation of sufficient scope to encompass all of the knowledge needed by a system. Use of nonmonolithic representations allows KSs to perform efficient operations on widely diverse, locally appropriate data formats. However, the problem then becomes one of somehow connecting these KSs in a flexible, effective manner.

We formulated several requirements of a reasoning paradigm for the combination and extrapolation of evidential information from disparate KSs. Whereas earlier work has focused upon a Bayesian-based probabilistic scheme, we feel that this is too restrictive. A likelihood represented by a point probability value is usually an overstatement of what is actually known, distorting the available precision.

----

[*] The work described here has been jointly supported by the Defense Advanced Research Projects Agency of the Department of Defense (monitored by the Air Force Avionics Laboratory under Contract No. F33615-80-C-1110) and the Office of Naval Research under Contract No. N00014-81-C-0115.

In particular, there is no adequate, non-ad hoc representation of ignorance within a Bayesian framework.*

Another problem with a Bayesian approach to the modeling of belief is the difficulty of ensuring and maintaining consistency in a collection of interrelated propositions. This difficulty also stems from the need to assign point probability values, even when the underlying models from which these values are derived are incapable of supplying such precise data.

There are many occasions when the inference technique of choice is probabilistic reasoning (e.g., particularly when reasoning is done with data close to the signal level), and other occasions when a (Boolean) logical formalism is preferred (e.g., when trying to combine "higher-level" knowledge). To avoid an ad hoc approach to "global" knowledge integration, the inference paradigm should flow smoothly from a probabilistic technique to a logical one, as the propositions in question become more nearly true or false. In addition, whenever the underlying model is complete and consistent enough for traditional methods to be effective, the technique should reduce to a Bayesian paradigm.

B. The Shafer Representation

The representation we have adopted to satisfy the preceding requirements for the integration of global knowledge is based on the work of Shafer [4]. It expresses the belief in a proposition A by a subinterval $[s(A), p(A)]$ of the unit interval, $[0,1]$. The lower value, $s(A)$, represents the "support" for that proposition and sets a minimum value for its likelihood. The upper value, $p(A)$, denotes the "plausibility" of that proposition and establishes a maximum likelihood. Support may be interpreted as the total positive effect a body of evidence has on a proposition, while plausibility represents the total extent to which a body of evidence fails to refute a proposition. The degree of uncertainty about the actual probability value for a proposition corresponds to the width of its interval. As will be shown, this representation with the appropriate inference rules satisfies the requirements established above.

In the remainder of this paper, we shall demonstrate Dempster's rule of combination [4] for pooling evidential information from independent knowledge sources, present an inference mechanism for updating proposition intervals based on other dependent proposition intervals, and demonstrate their use in sensor modeling and integration.

----

* For example, if no information is available concerning two initially exclusive and exhaustive possibilities, in a Bayesian framework they are usually assigned a probability of .5. This is quite different from specifying that nothing is known regarding such propositions.

II KNOWLEDGE REPRESENTATION AND INFERENCE

In what we call the "evidential propositional calculus," we represent a proposition using the following notation:

$$A_{[s(A), p(A)]},$$

where A is the proposition, $s(A)$ the support for the proposition, and $p(A)$ its plausibility. $p(A)$ is equivalent to $1-s(\sim A)$, the degree to which one fails to doubt A. The interval $[s(A), p(A)]$ is called the "evidential interval." The uncertainty of A, $u(A)$, corresponds to $p(A)-s(A)$. If $u(A)$ is zero for all propositions, the system is Bayesian.

The following examples illuminate some important points:

* $A_{[0,1]}$ => no knowledge at all about A.
* $A_{[0,0]}$ => A is false.
* $A_{[1,1]}$ => A is true.
* $A_{[.25,1]}$ => evidence provides partial support for A.
* $A_{[0,.85]}$ => evidence provides partial support for $\sim A$.
* $A_{[.25,.85]}$ => probability of A is between .25 and .85; i.e., the evidence simultaneously provides support for both A and $\sim A$.

A. Dempster's Rule of Combination

Dempster's rule is a method of integrating distinct bodies of evidence. This is most easily introduced through the familiar formalism whereby propositions are represented as subsets of a given set, here referred to as the "frame of discernment" (denoted θ). When a proposition corresponds to a subset of the frame of discernment, it is said to be "discerned." The primary advantage of this formalism is that it translates the logical notions of conjunction, disjunction, implication, and negation into the more graphic, set-theoretic notions of intersection, union, inclusion, and complementation. Dempster's rule combines evidential information expressed relative to those propositions discerned by θ.

1. Single Belief Functions

We assume that a knowledge source, KS_1, distributes a unit of belief across a set of propositions for which it has direct evidence,** in proportion to the weight of that evidence as it bears on each. This is represented by a function:

$$m_1: \{A_i \mid A_i \subseteq \theta\} \longrightarrow [0,1],$$
$$m_1(\phi) = 0,$$
$$\sum_{A_i \subseteq \theta} m_1(A_i) = 1.$$

** Those propositions are referred to as the KS's "focal elements."

$m_1(A_i)$ represents the portion of belief that KS_1 has committed exactly to proposition A_i, termed its "basic probability mass." m_1 can be depicted as a partitioned unit line segment, the length of each subsegment corresponding to the mass attributed to one of its focal elements (Figure 1). Any mass assigned to θ represents the residual "uncertainty" of the KS directly. That is, $m_1(\theta)$ is the mass that could not be ascribed to any smaller subset of θ on the basis of the evidence at hand, but must instead be assumed to be distributed in some (unknown) manner among the propositions discerned by θ. A similar interpretation is given to mass assigned any (nonunit) set.

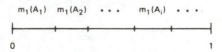

Figure 1 Probability Mass Assignment for KS_1

Once mass has been assigned to a set of propositions, the evidential interval can be determined directly. Support for a proposition A is the total mass ascribed to A and to its subsets; the plausibility of A is one minus the sum of the mass assigned to ~A and to subsets of ~A; the uncertainty of A is equal to the mass remaining, i.e., that attributed to supersets of A, including θ.

$$s_1(A) = \sum_{A_i \subseteq A} m_1(A_i).$$

$$p_1(A) = 1 - s_1(\tilde{A}).$$

$$u_1(A) = p_1(A) - s_1(A).$$

For example,

if A = {a},   A v B = {a,b},

~A = {b,c}, θ = {a,b,c},

and $m_1(\langle A, \tilde{A}, A \text{ v } B, \theta \rangle) = \langle .4, .2, .3, .1 \rangle$;

then $A_{[.4, .8]}$, $A \text{ v } B_{[.7, .1]}$,

~$A_{[.2, .6]}$, $\theta_{[1, 1]}$.

2. Composition of Mass Functions

If the belief function of a second KS, KS_2, is also provided, the information supplied by these KSs can be pooled by computing the "orthogonal sum;" this computation is illustrated by the unit square in Figure 2.

To combine the effects of KS_1, and KS_2, we consider the unit square as representing the combined probability mass of both KSs; KS_1 partitions the square into vertical strips corresponding to its focal elements, while KS_2 partitions it into horizontal strips that correspond to its focal elements. For example,

Figure 3 shows a vertical strip of measure $m_1(A_i)$ that is exactly committed to A_i by KS_1, and a horizontal strip of size $m_2(B_j)$ committed precisely to B_j by KS_2. The intersection of these strips commits exactly $m_1(A_i)m_2(B_j)$ to the combination of $A_i \cap B_j$:

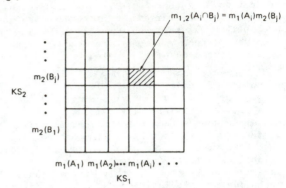

Figure 2 Composition of Mass from KS_1 and KS_2

Accordingly, we can compute the area commitment of each rectangle comprising the square A given subset of θ, C, may have more than one rectangle exactly committed to it; the total mass allocated to C is

$$\sum_{A_i \cap B_j = C} m_1(A_i)m_2(B_j).$$

This scheme is likely to commit a portion of mass to the empty set $\emptyset$. Every rectangle committed to $A_i \cap B_j$, where $A_i \cap B_j = \emptyset$, results in such a commitment. The "remedy" is to discard all such rectangles, proportionally increasing (i.e., normalizing) the size of the remaining rectangles by the following multiplicative factor:

$$N = (1 - k)^{-1},$$

where

$$k = \sum_{A_i \cap B_j = \emptyset} m_1(A_i)m_2(B),$$

thereby restoring the total probability mass to one.

There are several points of interest with respect to Dempster's rule of combination. The operation is commutative; therefore, the order of combination is immaterial. The operation is also associative, allowing the pairwise compositions of a sequence of KSs. When two Bayesian mass functions are combined, one associating its full unit of mass with a single proposition, the resulting support and plausibility values are the expected Bayesian conditionals. Yet when only less precise information is available, it too can be exploited.

The degree of conflict between two KSs can be measured intuitively by the size of the factor k. The greater the value of k, the greater the degree of conflict between the two KSs. When k is one, the KSs are irreconcilably different and the orthogonal sum does not exist.

B. Inference Rules

In addition to a technique for pooling distinct bodies of evidence, rules are needed that allow evidential information to be translated from those propositions it bears upon directly to those it bears upon indirectly. These rules are based on the following two principles of evidential support:

* The proposition corresponding to the frame of discernment always receives full support.

* Any support committed to a proposition is thereby committed to any other proposition it implies.

From the first principle we know that $s(\theta) = p(\theta) = 1$. The second principle dictates that any support committed to a subset of the frame of discernment is thereby committed to its supersets. This follows because one proposition implies another if it is a subset of that proposition in the frame of discernment. Of the total support committed to a given proposition A, some may be committed to one or more proper subsets of A, while the rest is committed exactly to A --and to no smaller subset, i.e., m(A). If it is assumed that a knowledge source expresses itself in terms of support and plausibility estimates for a selected set of propositions from the frame of discernment, a set of inference rules allows these estimates to be translated from proposition to proposition, thereby reducing uncertainty. A sampling of these rules follows. The statements above the line in each rule allow the statement below the line to be inferred.

$$\frac{}{\theta_{[1,1]}.}$$

$$\frac{A \subset \theta}{A_{[0,1]}.}$$

$$\frac{A_{[s1(A),p1(A)]}\quad A_{[s2(A),p2(A)]}}{A_{[s(A),p(A)]},\ \ s(A) = MAX[\ s1(A),\ s2(A)\ ],\ p(A) = MIN[\ p1(A),\ p2(A)\ ].}$$

$$\frac{A_{[s(A),p(A)]}}{\sim A_{[s(\sim A),p(\sim A)]},\ \ s(\sim A) = 1 - p(A),\ p(\sim A) = 1 - s(A).}$$

$$\frac{A_{[s(A),p(A)]}\quad B_{[s(B),p(B)]}}{A \vee B_{[s(A \vee B),p(A \vee B)]},\ \ s(A \vee B) = MAX[\ s(A),\ s(B)\ ],\ p(A \vee B) = MIN[\ 1,\ p(A) + p(B)\ ].}$$

$$\frac{A \vee B_{[s(A \vee B),p(A \vee B)]}\quad A_{[s(A),p(A)]}}{B_{[s(B),p(B)]},\ \ s(B) = MAX[\ 0,\ s(A \vee B) - p(A)\ ],\ p(B) = p(A \vee B).}$$

$$\frac{A_{[s(A),p(A)]}\quad B_{[s(B),p(B)]}}{A\ \&\ B_{[s(A\&B),p(A\&B)]},\ \ s(A\&B) = MAX[\ 0,\ s(A) + s(B) - 1\ ],\ p(A\&B) = MIN[\ p(A),\ p(B)\ ].}$$

$$\frac{A\ \&\ B_{[s(A\&B),p(A\&B)]}\quad A_{[s(A),p(A)]}}{B_{[s(B),p(B)]},\ \ s(B) = s(A\&B),\ p(B) = MIN[\ 1,\ 1 + p(A\&B) - s(A)\ ].}$$

As can be easily shown, when propositions are known to be true or false (that is, when their corresponding belief intervals become either [0,0] or [1,1]), these rules reduce to the corresponding rules of the propositional calculus. Thus, when appropriate knowledge exists, this method will enable easy transition from a probabilistic inference computation to the standard propositional calculus.

III   EXAMPLE: MODELING A KNOWLEDGE SOURCE

As our intention has been to treat sensors as specialized KSs, in this section we shall describe an approach to modeling such a KS. We shall begin by discussing the usual parameters measured by a (hypothetical) sensor, illustrating how, for this simple example, these measurements are converted to hypotheses by the inference mechanism.

A. Sensor Measurements

We assume that collections of electromagnetic signal "emitters" deployed in various configurations comprise the situation of interest. Measurements of characteristics of the signals emitted by these devices will be used to formulate hypotheses about their identities. In the complete system, these hypotheses will interact with those derived from other KSs to create a more comprehensive picture of the situation. Let us first concern ourselves with a single KS and then show how it may be composed with other KSs.

1. Emitter Characteristics

In this example, an emitter will radiate a pulsed radar signal whose pertinent characteristics will include the carrier frequency (rf) and the pulse width (pw), which are measured directly by the receiver. For the example we assume that the emitters of interest are of types E1, E2, E3, E4, or E5. The goal of the program is to identify a signal as having originated from one of those types.

The information about the parameter values likely to be exhibited by an emitter is presented in the form of parameter distribution graphs--for example, as shown in Figure 3. These curves indicate the probability that any given emitter (of the type indicated) will have a specific parameter value; the total area under each curve is one.

A typical approach to identifying an emitter is to look up the measured parameters in a table. In addition to difficulties traceable to the static nature of the table (e.g., emitter characteristics are not expected to remain stable and constant in actual operation), the technique gives little information regarding the relative likelihoods of ambiguous identifications.

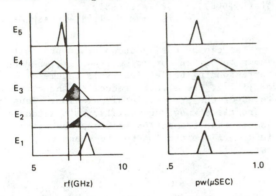

Figure 3 Examples of Typical Emitter
Parameter Distributions

2.   Sensor Characteristics

A sensor (receiver) will specify a range of possible values for the measured emitter parameter, as determined by the resolution of the sensor's measurements. For example, the receiver may specify an emitter's frequency value as lying within a band of frequencies, say from 5.5 to 5.6 GHz. Similarly, other emitter parameters will also be specified as falling within a range of values.

Our previous work [1] described how sensor models were modified in the event of changing environmental conditions. In the approach described here, such environmental factors will instead determine the total mass a sensor may allocate to propositions other than θ. In effect, the uncertainty U of a receiver in the prevailing conditions is its minimal commitment to θ (i.e., $m(\theta) \geq U$), leaving only $(1 - U)$ of the mass to be freely distributed.

B.   Modeling the Operation of a Sensor

The modeling process begins with the determination of a frame of discernment. If the task is to determine the true value of some variable, the frame of discernment is the set of all possible values for that variable. For the problem at hand, each element of the frame of discernment consists of an emitter type paired with a feature vector representing one possible electromagnetic signature that such an emitter might exhibit. Thus, θ is a subset of all of the combinations of emitter types (ET), radio frequencies (RF), and pulse widths (PW).

$$\theta \subseteq ET \times RF \times PW.$$

The key requirement of the frame of discernment is that all the propositions of interest be in correspondence with its subsets. In the current context the following propositions are some of those that might be of interest:

(The emitter is type E1)
    = {q| q $\in \theta$ and et(q) = E1};

(The radio frequency is between 5.5 and 5.6 GHz)
    = {q| q $\in \theta$ and $5.5 \leq$ rf(q) ≤ 5.6};

(The emitter is type E1 with pulse width between .68 and .7 μs)
    = {q| q $\in \theta$ and et(q) = E1
          and $.68 \leq$ pw(q) $\leq .7$}.

Once a frame of discernment has been determined, it can be represented as a dependency graph [5]. In this formalism propositions are represented by nodes, their interrelationships by arcs. These interrelationships can be interpreted either as set-theoretic notions relative to the frame of discernment (e.g., intersection, union, inclusion, and complementation), or as logical connectives (e.g., conjunction, disjunction, implication, and negation). The appropriate subset of propositions and relationships, so represented, depends on the preferred vocabulary of discourse among the KSs. Those propositions to which the KSs tend to assign mass need to be included, along with those relationships that best describe their interdependence. Once such a dependency graph has been established, it provides an integrated framework for both the combination and extrapolation of evidential information.

In the current context there is a subgraph for each emitter feature. At the lowest level of these subgraphs is a set of propositions representing the smallest bands into which that continuous feature has been partitioned--this partitioning being necessary within a propositional framework. These primitive bands form the basis of a hierarchy in each subgraph, relating larger bands to more primitive ones. The emitter types are similarly represented, the higher elements in the hierarchy corresponding to disjunctions of emitter types. All this is tied together by one last subgraph that relates the base elements of the hierarchies to elements of the frame of discernment, the frame of discernment consisting of the possible combinations of base elements. Figure 4 is a sketch of this dependency graph, with each node representing a proposition equal to the disjunction of those immediately below it, and the conjunction of those immediately above it.

This dependency graph contains all the information needed to determine the collective impact of several bodies of evidence on all the

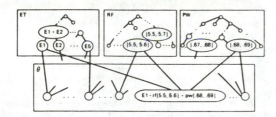

Figure 4 Dependency Graph for Sensor Model

propositions of interest. Given several distinct bodies of evidential information extracted from the environment by several knowledge sources, repeated applications of Dempster's rule followed by repeated applications of the inference rules for support and plausibility propagation--all based on the information embodied in the dependency graph-- results in a support and plausibility estimate for every proposition of interest [5]. There are no restrictions regarding which propositions serve as premises or conclusions. Information about radio frequency and pulse width can be used to determine the most likely types of emitters--or information about emitters and pulse width can be used to predict the expected radio frequency. Inferencing is unconstrained.

C. Simplification of the Sensor Model

In the preceding discussions, we showed how inferences could be drawn in a formal system that modeled all relevant elements of θ. It is frequently inconvenient to model these elements individually. For example, too many elements may be needed to represent the resolution of any particular sensor. An obvious simplification is to compute new propositions in θ as they are needed. For example, when a receiver reports a signal in a specific frequency band, propositions can then be created which assert that the signal originated from one element of a subset of possible emitter types. The exact hypotheses and their associated mass allocations are determined by comparing receiver measurements with tabulated information about the emitters.

1. Initial Mass Computations

The first step is to convert sensory measurements into a probability mass distribution over propositions. In essence, the parameter measurement range is overlaid on the curves representing distributions of emitter parameters, as shown in Figure 3. The area of the distribution curve is computed for each emitter (propositions are created only for those emitters whose parameter ranges overlap the sensor's report). A set of "basic mass numbers" is then computed by normalizing the resultant areas to bring their total area to one. This process is exactly equivalent to computing the probability of each emitter, conditioned upon the measured parameter's falling in the specified range (and assuming that only the tabulated emitter could radiate the received signal).

The uncertainty U of the receiver is accounted for through reducing each basic mass number by multiplying it by a factor equal to one minus U. This new set of mass numbers then represents the contribution of the receiver measurement to the support of the proposition.

2. Example

In this example we assume that there are five emitter types {E1, ..., E5}, whose rf and pw characteristics are shown graphically in Figure 3. The receiver has reported a frequency measurement of 7.6 to 7.7 GHz and a pulse width range of .68 to .7 μs. Assuming an uncertainty of .3 in the rf measurement and an uncertainty of .2 for pw, the resulting mass functions are

$$m_{rf}(\langle E1,E2,E3,E4,E5\rangle) = \langle .13,.22,.35,0,0\rangle$$

and

$$m_{pw}(\langle E1,E2,E3,E4,E5\rangle) = \langle .26,.085,.17,.034,.26\rangle.$$

Combining these with Dempster's rule gives the composite mass function,

$$m_{rf\&pw}(\langle E1,E2,E3,E4,E5\rangle)$$
$$= \langle .25,.16,.33,.018,.14\rangle,$$

with a resulting uncertainty of 0.11. This computation is illustrated in Figure 5, in which all rectangles attributed to ∅ are shaded and the remaining rectangles labeled with the proposition receiving that mass. These values convert directly to intervals on the propositions, as shown:

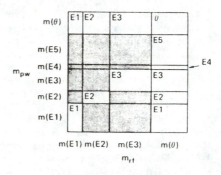

Figure 5 Composition of the Mass Assignments by Sensor Models

E1[.25, .36]
E2[.16, .27]
E3[.33, .43]
E4[.018, .13]
E5[.14, .25]

This information may be readily combined with information provided by other KSs. For example, a KS that indicated a high likelihood of encountering an E1 might produce the following mass function:

$$m_{prior}(\langle E1,E2,E3,E4,E5\rangle) = \langle .7,0,0,0,0\rangle,$$

which, when integrated with the receiver measurements, would result in a mass function

$$m_{composite}(\langle E1,E2,E3,E4,E5\rangle) = \langle .59,.089,.18,.01,.076\rangle,$$

with an uncertainty of .06. This leads to the following relevant hypotheses:

$$E1_{[.59,.65]} \text{ and } E3_{[.18,.24]}.$$

Based on sensor data alone, the method leads to two primary hypotheses, $E1_{[.25,.36]}$ and $E3_{[.33,.43]}$. E3 is slightly favored over E1. When external evidence is brought to bear, the support for E1 becomes significantly greater than for all others (and, in fact, all others except E3 drop to very low levels of support). Any other KS that provides a mass assignment over this set of propositions may also be combined.

This simplification of the formal method provides the ability to integrate information quickly from a variety of sources, even in those areas where the necessary propositions have not already been extracted from θ. The technique does not yet allow the propagation of evidence to arbitrarily selected propositions from the network. For example, it is not possible to take the structure defined for this problem and use it to determine what radio frequency values should be expected on the basis of pulse width data--a process easily carried out by the full representation. This is an area of current research. A related computational technique, restricted to evidence that either confirms or denies a single proposition, is also being investigated [6].

IV SUMMARY

We have briefly described an inference technique that appears to satisfy many of the requirements for reasoning in perceptual domains. In particular, the method provides the capability for (Bayesian) probabilistic reasoning when the appropriate underlying models are available (e.g., at the lowest levels of the system), (evidential) subjective reasoning when incomplete descriptions must be used (e.g., at the "middle" levels of the system), and (Boolean) logical reasoning when the truth values of propositions are true and false. This technique allows us to augment a static, incomplete model with current sensory information.

The approach provides a formal technique for updating the likelihoods of propositions in a consistent manner. In effect, by simultaneously performing computations over a collection of propositions, the method maintains global consistency without the problems frequently plaguing techniques that perform iterative updating by means of local rules. Most importantly, besides offering an inference technique that can be used

within a KS (as illustrated), the method provides a "language" for KSs to communicate with one another, as well as furnishing the means for linking disparate sources of information.

In our previous work on perceptual-reasoning systems, we evolved a number of effective generic (e.g., terrain, weather, etc.) and domain-specific (e.g., sensor) KSs. Our current research, focusing on the evidential propositional calculus as the integrating medium, aims at developing a general framework for linking these KSs together smoothly and flexibly.

REFERENCES

1. T. D. Garvey and M. A. Fischler, "Machine-Intelligence-Based Multisensor ESM System," Technical Report AFAL-TR-79-1162, Air Force Wright Avionics Laboratory, Wright-Patterson Air Force Base, Ohio (October 1979).

2. T. D. Garvey and M. A. Fischler, "Perceptual Reasoning in a Hostile Environment," Proceedings of the First Annual Conference on Artificial Intelligence, Stanford University, Stanford, California, pp. 253-255 (August 1980).

3. T. D. Garvey and M. A. Fischler, "The Integration of Multi-Sensor Data for Threat Assessment," Proceedings of the Fifth Joint Conference on Pattern Recognition, Miami Beach, Florida, pp. 343-347 (December 1980).

4. G. Shafer, A Mathematical Theory of Evidence (Princeton University Press, Princeton, New Jersey 1976).

5. J. D. Lowrance, "Dependency-Graph Models of Evidential Support," Ph.D. Dissertation, University of Massachusetts, Amherst, Massachusetts (in preparation).

6. B. A. Barnett, "Computational Methods for a Mathematical Theory of Evidence," Proceedings of the Seventh International Joint Conference on Artificial Intelligence, Vancouver, British Columbia, Canada (1981).

VII / Representations of Commonsense Knowledge

28 / Patrick J. Hayes
The Second Naive Physics Manifesto

While on the surface this update of Hayes' 1979 article looks simply like an ambitious research proposal, it is in actuality a broad and compelling methodological argument for the entire field of Knowledge Representation. In outlining what should be done and how it should be done, Hayes defends research that concentrates on the facts and that ignores implementation; he details some of the problems of premature implementation, and the inadequacy of dealing with "toy domains." He asks us to turn away from issues of *form,* and to concentrate instead on *content.* Rather than constructing new representation formalisms, the real task, he claims, is to construct a heuristically adequate (see [McCarthy, Chapter 2]) formalization of a very large and real domain: ordinary everyday knowledge of the physical world. There are basically two parts to the paper, the first covering characteristics of any formalism up to the task of representing commonsense physical knowledge, and the second discussing a number of concepts likely to play a part in the formalization. The discussion ranges through a number of issues, from the inadequacy of semantic primitives to a fascinating approach to representing space-time with four-dimensional "histories." The suggestive paragraphs on the various naive physics concept clusters are particularly thought-provoking, and the reader is engagingly drawn into the enterprise of thinking about how we think about the physical world.

Appeared in *Formal Theories of the Commonsense World,* 1–36, edited by J. R. Hobbs and R. C. Moore, Norwood, NJ: Ablex Publishing Corp., 1985.

The Second Naive Physics Manifesto

Patrick J. Hayes

Cognitive Science
University of Rochester
Rochester, New York

1 Preface

Five years ago I wrote a paper, ''The Naive Physics Manifesto'', complaining about AI's emphasis on toy worlds and urging the field to put away childish things by building large-scale formalizations, suggesting in particular that a suitable initial project would be a formalization of our knowledge of the everyday physical world: of naive physics (NP). At that time, I felt rather alone in making such a suggestion (which is why the paper had such a proselytizing tone) and quite optimistic that success in even this ambitious a project could be achieved in a reasonable time scale. As this volume testifies, both feelings are no longer appropriate. There is a lot of work going on, and there is more to be done than I had foreseen. A whole layer of professionalism has emerged, for example, in the business of finding out just what people's intuitive ideas are about such matters as falling rocks or evaporating liquids, a matter I had relegated to disciplined introspection. In 1978, I predicted that the overall task was an order of magnitude (but not ten orders of magnitude) more difficult than any that had been undertaken so far. I now think that two or three orders of magnitude is a better estimate. It's still not impossible, though.

My old paper now seems dated and, in places, inappropriately naive on some deep issues. The following is a revised version which attempts to correct some of these shortcomings, and repeats the points which need repeating because nobody seems to have taken any notice of them.

This is a revised version of the original, not a sequel to it. Since several years have passed, some of the passion may have gone, being replaced with (I hope) more careful discussion.

2 Introduction

Artificial intelligence is full of 'toy problems': small, artificial axiomatizations or puzzles designed to exercise the talents of various problem-solving programs or representational languages or systems. The subject badly needs some non-toy worlds to experiment with. In other areas of cognitive science, also, there is a need to consider the organization of knowledge on a larger scale than is currently done, if only because quantitatively different mental models may well be qualitatively different.

In this document I propose the construction of a formalization of a sizable portion of common-sense knowledge about the everyday physical world: about objects, shape, space, movement, substances (solids and liquids), time, etc. Such a formalization could, for example, be a collection of assertions in a first-order logical formalism, or a collection of KRL units, or a microplanner program, or one of a number of other things, or even a mixture of several. It should have the following characteristics.

2.1 Breadth

It should cover the whole range of everyday physical phenomena: not just the blocks world, for example. Since in some important sense the world (even the everyday world) is infinitely rich in possible phenomena, this will never be perfect. Nevertheless, we should *try* to fill in all the major holes, or at least identify them.

It should be reasonably detailed. For example, such aspects of a block in a block world as shape, material, weight, rigidity and surface texture should be available as concepts in a blocks-world description, as well as support relationships.

2.2 Density

The ratio of facts to concepts needs to be fairly high. Put another way: the units have to have *lots* of slots. Low-density formalizations are in some sense trivial: they fail to say enough about the concepts they mention to pin down the meaning of their symbols at all precisely. Sometimes, for special purposes, as for example in foundational studies, this can be an advantage: but not for us.

2.3 Uniformity

There should be a common formal framework (language, system, etc.) for the whole formalization, so that the inferential connections between the different parts (axioms, frames, . . .) can be clearly seen, and divisions into subformalisations are not prejudged by deciding to use one formalism for one area and a different one for a different area.

I (still) believe that a formalization of naive physics with these properties can be constructed within a reasonable time-scale. The reasons for such optimism are explained later. It is important however to clearly distinguish this proposal from some others with which it may be confused, because some of these seem to be far less tractable.

3 What the Proposal Isn't

3.1

It is *not* proposed to make a computer program which can 'use' the formalism in some sense. For example, a problem-solving program, or a natural language comprehension system with the representation as target. It is tempting to make such demonstrations from time to time. (They impress people; and it is satisfying to have actually *made* something which works, like building model railways; and one's students can get Ph.D.'s that way.) But they divert attention from the main goal. In fact, I believe they have several more dangerous effects. It is perilously easy to conclude that, because one has a program which *works* (in some sense), its representation of its knowledge must be more or less *correct* (in some sense). Now this is true, in some sense. But a representation may be adequate to support a limited kind of inference, and completely unable to support a slightly more general kind of behavior. It may be wholly limited by scale factors, and therefore tell us nothing about thinking about realistically complicated worlds. Images as internal pictures and the STRIPS representation of actions by add and delete lists are two good examples. I suspect that the use of state variables to represent time is another. Such representational devices are traps, tempting the unwary into dead ends where they struggle to overcome insurmountable difficulties, difficulties generated by the representation itself. I now believe, although I know this view is very controversial, that the famous frame problem is such a difficulty: an apparently deep problem which is largely artifact.

I emphasize this point because there is still a prevailing attitude in AI that research which does not result fairly quickly in a working program of some kind is somehow useless or, at least, highly suspicious. Of course implementability is the ultimate test of the validity of ideas in AI, and I do not mean to argue against this. But we must not be too hasty.

This is no more than a reiteration of John McCarthy's emphasis, since the inception of AI as a subject, on the importance of representational issues (McCarthy 1957, McCarthy & Hayes 1969). In 1969, McCarthy proposed the "Missouri Program", which would make no inferences of its own but would be willing to check proposed arguments submitted to it: a proof checker for common sense. Those who find it repugnant to be told to ignore programming considerations may find it more congenial to be urged to imagine the project of building a proof *checker* for naive physics.

3.2

It is *not* proposed to develop a new formalism or language to write down all this knowledge in. In fact, I propose (as my friends will have already guessed) that first-order logic is a suitable basic vehicle for representation. However, let me at once qualify this.

I have no particular brief for the usual syntax of first-order logic. Personally I find it agreeable: but if someone likes to write it all out in KRL, or semantic networks of one sort or another, or OMEGA, or KRYPTON, or what have you; well, that's fine. The important point is that one *knows what it means*: that the formalism has a clear *interpretation* (I avoid the word 's*m*nt*cs' deliberately). At the level of interpretation, there is little to choose between any of these, and most are strictly weaker than predicate calculus, which also has the advantage of a clear, explicit model theory, and a well-understood proof theory.

I have pointed out elsewhere (Hayes 1977, 1978) that virtually all known representational schemes are equivalent to first-order logic (with one or two notable exceptions, primarily to do with nonmonotonic reasoning). This is still true in 1983, but I should perhaps emphasize that care is needed in making comparisons. First, in claiming equivalence, one is speaking of representational (expressive) power, not computational efficiency. Given a simple "dumb" interpreter (i.e. a "uniform" theorem-prover), these may be at odds with one another. The moral is that simple, dumb interpreters are a bad idea, and interpreters should be sensitive to 'control' information, meta-information about the inferential process itself. This idea brings its own representational problems. I am not arguing that these should be ignored. On the contrary, they raise some of the most important questions in AI. But until we have some idea of the sorts of inferences we might want to control, speculation on the matter is premature. Second, in making comparisons between systems one must exercise care. Many "computational" systems have invisible, buried, assumptions about their domain, not explicitly documented in publications, which must be rendered explicit in a logical axiomatization.[1] Third, the use of logic imposes almost no restrictions on the kinds of thing about which we wish to speak: sequences of actions or views of a room or plans or goals, etc., are all perfectly fine candidates. One must not let lack of imagination in axiomatizing lead one to conclude that logical formalisms are weaker than some of the more superficially baroque systems which AI has devised. (In particular, first-order logic can be taken to quantify over some properties, functions and relations and still be essentially first-order. What makes it higher-order is when its quantifiers have to range over *all*[2] properties, functions and relations, a condition which cannot be enforced without something like a rule of λ-abstraction or a comprehension schema.)

Finally, let me emphasize that idiosyncratic notations may sometimes be useful for idiosyncratic subtheories. For example, in sketching an axiomatic theory of fluids (this volume) I found it useful to think of the possible physical states of fluids as being essentially states of a finite-state machine. This summarizes a whole lot of lengthy, and rather clumsy, first-order axioms into one neat diagram. Still, it *means* the same as the axioms: first-order logic is still, as it were, the reference language. It is essential that there be some standard reference language in this way, so that the different parts of the formalism can be related to one another.

---

[1] This touches on a basic terminological ambiguity. Shall we regard an axiom as a statement *in* a logic; or as a new *rule* to be *added* to the logic, so that the logic is somehow made stronger but the axiomatization is not enlarged? One always has the option: the second route tends to lead to less expressive but operationally more efficient systems, since a rule can often be neatly characterized as an axiom with a restriction imposed on its use, so that less can be inferred from it. I think we should take our axioms unrestricted for a while, until we can see more realistically what sorts of restriction we shall have to impose on their inferential behavior to achieve practical systems.

[2] There are two versions, in fact: "all nameable", which you get with the rule or schema, and "all", which can't be enforced by any schema or rule or computational device of *any* kind, since the set of theorems is then not recursively enumerable. If anyone claims to have implemented a reasoning system which can handle full higher order reasoning, he is wrong.

3.3

It is not proposed to find a philosophically exciting reduction of all ordinary concepts to some special collection of concepts (such as sets, or Goodmanesque "individuals", or space–time points, or qualia.) Maybe some such reduction will eventually turn out to be possible. I think it extremely unlikely and not especially desirable. but whether or not it is. is not the present issue. *First* we need to formalize the naive worldview. using whatever concepts seem best suited to that purpose—thousands or tens of thousands of them if necessary. Afterwards we can try to impose some a priori ontological scheme upon it. But until we have the basic theory articulated. we don't know what our subject matter is.

Now. this is not to say that we should not exercise some care in avoiding unnecessary proliferation of axioms. or some aesthetic sensibility in designing axioms to give clean proofs and to interact as elegantly as possible. But these are matters of general scientific style. not ends in themselves.

4 Theories, Tokens and Closure

Let us imagine that a NP formalization exists. It consists of a large number of assertions (*or*: frames, scripts, networks, etc.) involving a large number of relation, function and constant symbols (*or*: frame headers, slot names, node and arc labels, etc. From now on I will not bother to reemphasise these obvious parallels). For neutral words. let us call these formal symbols *tokens*, and the collection of axioms the *theory*. (in the sense of 'formal theory' in logic, not 'scientific theory' in history of science).

The success of a NP theory is measured by the extent to which it provides a vocabulary of tokens which allows a wide range of intuitive concepts to be expressed, and to which it then supports conclusions mirroring those which we find correct or reasonable. People know, for example, that if a stone is released, it falls with increasing speed until it hits something, and there is then an impact, which can cause damage if the velocity is high. The theory should provide tokens allowing one to express the concept of releasing a stone in space. And it should then be possible to infer from the theory that it will fall, etc.: **so** there must be tokens enabling one to express ideas of velocity, direction, impact, **and** so on. And then these same tokens must be usable in describing other kinds of circumstance, and the theory support the appropriate conclusions there, and so on. We want the overall pattern of consequences produced by the theory to correspond reasonably faithfully to our own intuition in both breadth and detail. Given the hypothesis that our own intuition is itself realized as a theory of this kind inside our heads, the NP theory we construct will then be equipotent with this inner theory.

More subtle tests than mere matching against intuition might be applied to an NP theory. Consequences which are *very* obvious should have shorter derivations then those which require some thought, perhaps. If, in proving *p* from *q*, the theory must make use of some concept token, perhaps psychologists can devise an experiment in which the "activation" of that concept can be tested for. while people are deciding whether or not *q*. given *p*. Pylyshyn (1979) discusses ways in which intermediate psychological states might be investigated: I will not discuss them further here, but focus instead on questions connected with getting a theory constructed in the first place.

The practical task of building such a theory begins with some 'target' concepts and desired inferences. Take the familiar example of formalising a world of cubical wooden blocks on a flat table. with the goal of being able to reason about processes of piling these into vertical stacks and rearranging such piles by moving blocks from place to place: the familiar blocks world. Notice that we have put quite a constraint on what inferences we are interested in. An actual tabletop of blocks admits of many more interesting and complicated activities: building walls and pyramids, pushing blocks around horizontally. juggling. etc.: but we deliberately exclude such matters from consideration for now.

I will go through this toy world in detail. in order to illustrate some general points. It is not intended as a serious exercise in naive physics. First, we obviously need the concept of block (a predicate $Block(b)$), and there will be several states of the little universe as things are moved, so we also need that concept ($State(s)$). A block will be on some other block or on the table in every state ($On(b,c,s)$, and the name $table$): four tokens so far, and now we can write some axioms, such as:

$$\forall s,b.\ State(s) \land Block(b) \supset$$
$$(\exists c.\ Block(c) \land On(b,c,s)) \lor On(b,table,s) \qquad (1)$$

(We could have done it differently: for example, a function $below(b,s)$ instead of the relation On, so that $On(b,c,s)$ translates into $below(b,s) = c$. Or a function $above$-(b,s), with the obvious meaning. and a constant, air, so that $above(b,s) = air$ corresponds to: $\forall c.\ \sim On(c,b,s)$, and being careful never to apply $above$ to the table. We could have decided not to use states at all, but to have thought of each block as having a temporal history. No doubt other variations are possible. (In the future, I will—to save paper and to improve readability—omit such antecedents as $Block(b)$ and $State(s)$ from formulae. It is straightforward to enrich the logic to a many-sorted logic in which this omission is syntactically normal. The concepts are there, though, and need inferential machinery of one kind or another, so they should be shown in the "reference language".)

Now, to describe change we need the idea of a state-transition. There are several ways to do this. We could have a relation $Next(s,t)$ between states, for example, or a function $next(s)$, corresponding to the intuitive feeling that one moment follows another, and there is always a unique next thing that will in fact happen (*que sera, sera*). Or we might say that, since we are talking about actions, and there are usually several things one *might* do in a given situation, so there are several different next-states. This leads to McCarthy's idea—now standard—of actions as state-to-state functions. We might have actions $pickup(b,s)$ and $putdown(b,s)$, for example. The result of picking up b is a state in which b is no longer on anything but rather is held in the hand:

$$Held(b, pickup(b)) \quad (2)$$

$$Held(b,s) \supset \forall x. \sim On(b,x,s) \quad (3)$$

We must now modify (1) by adding $Held(b,s)$ as a third possibility. The result of putdowning on b is that whatever is held gets to rest on b; provided of course there is nothing there already. To make this neater, let's define *Clear*:

$$Clear(x,s) \equiv \forall c.\ On(c,x,s) \lor x = table \quad (4)$$

Then we can say:

$$Held(b,s) \land Clear(c,s) \supset On(b,c,putdown(c,s)) \quad (5)$$

(This still doesn't explain what $putdown(c,s)$ is like if nothing is *Held* in s. We might decide there are two sorts of states, those in which the hand is holding something and those in which it is empty, and insist that $putdown$ applies only to the former. Or we might just say that:

$$\forall x \cdot \sim Held(x,s) \supset putdown(c,s) = s \quad (6)$$

We can now begin to see how the desired kinds of conclusion might follow. If we know that A is on C on the table and B is on the table and A and C are clear, then we can infer from (2) that after a suitable pickup, A is held. Unfortunately, we can't conclude that B is still clear: C may have jumped onto it, as far as our axioms are concerned. (Consider a world of jumping blocks, or stackable frogs, in which every time one is lifted, the one beneath hops onto a different block. This is a possible world, and all five of the axioms are true in it. So, nothing that they say rules this possibility out.) This is a tiny illustration of the notorious frame problem (McCarthy & Hayes 1969). We need to say that during a pickup of a block, no other *On* relations change.

Now, for the first time, we don't need to introduce any new tokens. We have a rich enough vocabulary at hand to state our axiom:

$$On(b,c,s) \land \sim On(b,c,pickup(d,s)) \lor b = d \quad (7)$$

Here, $\lor$ is exclusive-or, so that if b is not d, then $On(b,c)$ must still be true in $pickup(d,s)$; and we are sure that $\sim On(b,c,pickup(b,s))$ under any circumstances. Notice that the block picked up might itself carry others, and they go right along with it.

Given (7), we can quickly conclude that B is still clear and still on the table, so we can now putdown onto it and have a state in which A is on B—no longer clear, by (4)—and C is clear . . . well, not quite, since putting down might yet disturb things. But we can fix this with an even simpler frame axiom:

$$On(b,c,s) \supset On(b,c,putdown(d,s)) \quad (8)$$

and we can now discuss states reached by picking up and putting down things all over the place, as we desired. Given a sufficiently complete description of a layout of blocks, and a goal of some other configuration, then if there is a sequence of block movements which get us from the former to the latter, then this theory will show that there is.

For some time now we have not needed to introduce any other tokens. We can do the changes by adding or modifying axioms, working entirely in the given vocabulary. This collection of tokens (*block, table, state, on, held, pickup, putdown*) is enough to work with. Alternative worlds can be constructed within it. It is a large enough collection to support axioms describing general properties of the universe we have in mind, and descriptions of particular worlds in enough detail to allow the sorts of conclusion we wanted to be inferred. No subset will do the job, as we have seen:[3] but this is just enough to let us say what needs saying. We have reached what might be called a *conceptual closure*. This phenomenon is familiar to anyone who has tried to axiomatize or formalize some area. Having chosen one's concepts to start on, one quickly needs to introduce tokens for others one had not contemplated, and the axioms which pin down their meanings introduce others, and so on: until one finds suddenly there are enough tokens around that it is easy to say enough "about" them all: enough, that is, to enable the inferences one had had in mind all along to be made.

This sort of closure is by no means trivial. Suppose we had tried to use $next(s)$, following the idea that world-states are, after all, linearly ordered: then it becomes quite hard to achieve. We can say that a block may stay where it is, or become picked up:

$$On(b,c,s) \land \forall x. \sim Held(x,s) \supset On(b,c,next(s)) \lor Held(b,next(s)) \quad (9)$$

and we can insist that only one is held at once:

$$Held(b,s) \land Held(c,s) \supset b = c \quad (10)$$

---

[3] I omitted *clear* deliberately. It has an explicit definition and could be eliminated entirely at no real cost of expressive power. Having that token makes axioms more compact and deductions shorter, but it does not enable us to say anything new. since we could have replaced it everywhere else by its definition and gotten an equivalent set of axioms. Definitions don't add to the expressive power of a theory.

But putting down is more difficult. If we say

$$Held(b,s) \land Clear(c,s) \supset On(b,c,next(s)) \qquad (11)$$

then the held block has been put down into every clear space. We certainly want to say that the held block is put down in one of the potential putdown sites:

$$Held(b,s) \supset \exists c. \; Clear(c,s) \land On(b,c,next(s)) \qquad (12)$$

But we now have no way of inferring that the held block can actually be placed in any particular clear place. This axiom is consistent with a world in which blocks can be placed only on the table, for example, or in which blocks are always released from on high and falleth gently upon some random stack or other. There is no way within this vocabulary to describe one possible future state. We have no way of stating the properties we need: closure eludes us. It can be achieved, but only by bringing possible futures in by the back door.

Our theory, though closed, is by no means perfect. As stated, it can support all the inferences we had in mind. Unfortunately, it can also support some others which we didn't have in mind. For example, nothing in the axioms so far prevents two successive pickups, giving a handful of blocks (or, somewhat less plausibly, a handful of towers of blocks). This would be fine, except that (5) has it that anything held is deposited by a putdown, thus leaving several blocks on one; but they were supposed to be all the same size. The neatest way to fix this is to modify (2), say as follows:

$$\forall x. \sim Held(x,s) \supset Held(b,pickup(b,s)) \qquad (13)$$

We can also insist that only single blocks are picked up by adding $Clear(b,s)$ as another antecedent condition. Again: if a block is $Clear$, then we can pick it up—its still $Clear$—and put it down on *itself*: there's nothing in (5) to prevent this. (Consider a zero-gravity world in which blocks can be released in space, and they then just hang there: and say that in this case the block is On itself. Clearly all the axioms are satisfied in this world too.) So to rule this out we need another axiom, and to modify (5) slightly. Finding other such bugs is left as an exercise for the reader.

It is important to bear such negative properties of a formalization in mind even though they make the formalizer's life more complex. It is easy to overlook them.

5 Meanings, Theories and Model Theory

In developing this toy theory I have several times used an example world to show that something we wanted to follow didn't, or that something we didn't want to be

true might be. This ability to interpret our axioms in a possible world, see what they say and whether it is true or not, is so useful that I cannot imagine proceeding without it. But it is only possible if there is an idea of a *model* of the formal language in which the theory is written: a systematic notion of what a possible world is and how the tokens of the theory can be mapped into entities (or structures or values or whatever) in such worlds. We have to be able to *imagine* what our tokens *might* mean.

Now this semantic metatheory may be relatively informal, but the more useful it is defined, the more useful it will be as a tool for the theory-builder. The main attraction of formal logics as representational languages is that they have very precise model theories, and the main attraction of first-order logic is that its model theory is so simple, so widely applicable, and yet so powerful.

A first-order model is a set of entities and suitable mappings from tokens to functions and relations, of appropriate arity, over it.[4] Any collection of things will do: for example, for our blocks world, I could take the collection of papers on my desk, and interpret On to be the relation which holds between two pieces of paper when one partially or wholly overlaps the other, and *pickup* to be the action of picking up, and so on. (In fact, this isn't a model, because my desk is too crowded: axiom (5) is false. But it would be if I tidied my desk up.)

This is very satisfying, since we have found a model which is very close to the original intuition. But there are other models. Consider a table and a single block and the two states, one—call it A—with the block on the table, and the other—call it B—with the block held above the table. Let *pickup* and *putdown* denote the functions ($A \rightarrow B, B \rightarrow B$) and ($B \rightarrow A, A \rightarrow A$) respectively, let $Held$ be true just of

---

[4] This is usually presented, in textbooks of elementary logic, in a rather formal, mathematical way; and this fact may have given rise to the curious but widespread delusion that a first-order model is merely another formal description of the world, just like the axiomatization of which it is a model; and that the Tarskian truth-recursion is a kind of translation from one formal system to another (e.g. Wilks 1977). This is quite wrong. For a start, the relationship between an axiomatization and its models (or, dually, between a model and the set of axiomatizations which are true of it) is quite different from a translation. It is many-many rather than one-one, for example. Moreover, it has the algebraic character called a Galois connection, which is to say, roughly, that as the axiomatization is increased in size (as axioms are added), the collection of models—possible states of affairs—decreases in size. It is quite possible for a large, complex axiomizations to have small, simple models, and vice versa. In particular, a model can always be gratuitously complex. (e.g. contain entities which aren't mentioned at all in the axiomization). But the deeper mistake in this way of thinking is to confuse a formal description of a model—found in the textbooks which are developing a mathematical approach to the metatheory of logic—with the actual model. This is like confusing a mathematical description of Sydney Harbour Bridge in a textbook of structural engineering with the actual bridge. A Tarskian model can *be* a piece of reality. If I have a blocks-world axiomatization which has three block-tokens, 'A', 'B', and 'C' and if I have a (real, physical) table in front of me, with three (real, physical) wooden blocks on it, then the set of those three blocks can be the set of entities of a model of the axiomatization (provided, that is, that I can go on to interpret the relations and functions of the axiomatization as physical operations on the wooden blocks, or whatever, in such a way that the assertions made about the wooden blocks, when so interpreted, are in fact true). There is nothing in the model theory of first-order logic which a priori prevents the real world being a model of an axiom system.

the block in state B, and let On be true just of the block and the table in state A. All the axioms are true, so this is a possible world. This one is much simpler than my desk, and its existence shows that the axioms really say rather less than one might have thought they did: specifically, they say nothing about *how many* blocks or states there are, or about the direction of time's arrow.

One can find other very simple models, for example models made of dots being moved on a screen—so the theory says nothing about the three-dimensionality of the world.

This illustrates how the existence of a model theory for our formal language is not just a methodological convenience. It tells us what our formalizations could mean and hence, what they couldn't mean. We may think that we have captured some concept in a theory, but unless the theory is sufficiently rich to guarantee that *all* its models reveal the kind of structure we had in mind, then we are deluded: *a token of a theory means no more than it means in the simplest model of the theory*.

Returning to methodology for a moment, a crucial property of this way of characterizing meaning is that it transcends syntactic and operational variations. A given theory might be realized operationally in innumerable ways. Even ignoring heuristic 'control' issues, we have such variations as natural deduction rules, or semantic tableaux or Hilbert-style axiomatizations. We can make the theory look like a semantic network or a collection of frames or MOPS or any one of innumerable other variations. None of these variations will give the theory an ounce more expressive power. None of them *could* ever make good a representational inadequacy of the theory. It is easy to lose sight of this basic and uncomfortable truth. Thinking model-theoretically helps us to keep it in mind.

It also gives us a powerful theoretical tool. For example, I mentioned earlier that defined concept tokens, such as *Clear*, added no real expressiveness to a theory. This seems kind of intuitive once it is pointed out, but it has a quite conclusive model-theoretic statement (Beth's definability theorem) which completely settles the matter, and frees up time for more productive discussions.

An objection to the idea of models goes as follows. Any particular formalization or implementation consists entirely of the expressions and the inference rules or procedures which manipulate them. The idea of a model, and the mappings which relate expressions to denotations, etc., are just metatheorists' ideas, imposed from without. But we could have a different model theory for the same formal language, and declare that *this* semantic theory assigned meanings to the formal symbols. (e.g., see D. Israel, this volume.) And who is to say which of the many possible semantic theories is the right one?

But the relationship between a model theory and the (purely formal) inference rules or procedures attached to the formal language is not arbitrary in this way. Each model theory sanctions certain inferences (the ones that preserve truth in those models) and not others. And, sometimes, we also get the converse, viz., if some assertion is true in all those models, then the rules will indeed eventually declare it so. This is the content of the completeness theorem for a formal language. We should treasure completeness theorems: they are rare and beautiful things. Without

them, we have no good justification for our claims that we know how our theories say what we claim they say about the worlds we want them to describe. To emphasize this, consider enriching the formal language by introducing a new kind of symbol, say a quantifier M which I claim means 'most', so that $MxP(x)$ means P is true of *most* things. I can easily give a model theory: $MxP(x)$ is true in a model just when P is true of more than half the universe (with a little more subtlety for infinite domains, but let that pass). I can *claim* this, but the claim is premature until I can describe some mechanism of inference which captures that interpretation, generating all the inferences which it justifies and none which it refutes. And this might be difficult. For some model theories we know it is impossible.

A model theory can determine the actual meaning of the logical symbols of the formal language, but it does not determine the actual meaning of the tokens. The only way to do that is by restricting the set of possible models of the theory, for example by adding axioms. All we can say of a token is that in this model it means this, in that one it means that. There is no single 'meaning' of a formal token (unless there is only a single model): we cannot point to something and say, *that is the meaning*.

We might restate the goal of building a formal theory as being that of ensuring that all the models of the theory are recognizable as being the kind of possible world we were trying to describe, so that in each one, each token denotes what it should. But this notion of meaning raises a well-known philosophical specter, a second objection to a model-theoretic view of meaning. For no model theory can specify what *kinds* of entity constitute the universes of its models. It refers only to the presence of functions and relations defined over a set, not to what the set is a set *of*. And we could always make our universes out of entirely unsuitable things, in particular the tokens themselves.

Suppose we have a 'suitable' model of a theory. Make a ghost model as follows. Let each name denote itself. Every token which should denote an operation on things, interpret it rather as an operation on the *names* of things, whose result is the expression which would have referred to the thing got by performing the operation on the things named, so that for example a unary function symbol f denotes the function on expressions which takes the expression 'e' to the expression '$f(e)$', '$g(h(a))$' to '$f(g(h(a)))$', and so on. And interpret each relation symbol as that relation on expressions which is true when the relation is true of the thing named by the expressions in the 'suitable' model: so that 'P' denotes the predicate which is true of the symbol 'a' just if '$P(a)$' is true in the first model. In general, whenever you need to decide a question of fact, go and check in the ''suitable'' model to see what its facts are, and use those.

There is one of these ghostly (Herbrand) models for every model, and it makes exactly the same axioms true. So there could be no way of adding axioms (or frames or scripts or demons or MOPS or anything else, just to re-emphasize the point) which could ensure that all a theory is talking about might not be its own symbols.

This is an important point, considered as a criticism of a theory of meaning. Indeed, no formal operations, no matter how complex, can ever ensure that tokens denote any particular kinds of entity. There are, I think, three ways in which tokens can be attached to their denotations more rigidly (so to speak). One:: if the token is itself in a metatheory of some internal part of the theory, then the connection can simply be directly made by internal, formal, manipulations. Formally, these are "reflection principles", or rules of translation between a language and its metalanguage.

Two: if the theory is in a creature with a body—a robot, like us—then some of the tokens can be attached to sensory and motor systems so that the truth of some the propositions containing them is kept in correspondence to the way the real world actually is. These tokens—they might include the concept *vertical* connected to the inner ear, and those of a whole intricate theory of lighting and surfaces and geometry and texture and movement connected with visual perception, and a whole other collection associated with proprioceptive awareness of the body's position in space—have a special status. We might say that the body's sensorimotor apparatus *was* the model theory of this part of the internal formalization.

Three: tokens could be attached to the world through language. Again, let the theory be built into a physical computer, one without senses, but with a natural-language comprehension and production system. The tokens of the internal theory are now related to English words in the way we expect, so that the deep semantic meaning of a sentence is a collection of axiomatic statements in the formalism. Such a system could talk about things to other language users and could come to learn facts about an external world by communicating with them. Assuming that *their* beliefs and conversations really were about things—that they managed to actually refer to external entities—then I think we would have no reason to refuse the same honor to the conversing system.

These matters require and deserve fuller discussion elsewhere. But I suggest that for the purposes of developing a naive physics, this whole issue can be safely ignored. We can take out a promissory loan on *real* meanings. One way or another, parts of our growing formalization will have eventually to be attached to external worlds through senses or language or maybe some other way, and ghost models will be excluded. We must go ahead trying to formalize our intuitive world; paying attention indeed to the complexity and structural suitability of our models, but not worrying about what sort of stuff they are made from.

We have then to be ready to repay the loan, by looking out for areas of axiomatization where the tokens might be attachable to perceptual or motor or linguistic systems. For example, ideas connected with time must make some contact with our internal "clocks" of various sorts. Much of our intuitive knowledge of force and movement comes from *what it feels like* when we push, pull, lift and move. Much of our knowledge of three-dimensional space is connected with how things *look*; and so on.

6 Discovering Intuitions and Building Theories

We have been assuming all along that we are able to interpret tokens of the theory in intuitive terms. But this assumes that we can identify our own intuitive concepts sufficiently clearly to assign them to tokens. In practice, building axiomatic theories is in large part an exploration and clarification of our own intuitions. Just as professional grammarians tend to acquire an astonishingly acute sense of exactly which syntactic constructions are acceptable to a native speaker, so naive physicists will need to develop an acute sense of intuitive reasonableness of descriptions of the everyday physical world. It is not at all an easy thing to do.

Consider the earlier toy blocks-world example. It might be argued that here is a small theory with complete conceptual closure. But it is closed only with respect to the very limited range of inferences we required initially: this is exactly what makes it a toy theory. Try to expand it to deal with our own ideas of putting things on things. We have the token *On*: what exactly did that mean? It had a component of pure geometry, referring to the spatial arrangement of the blocks. It also seemed to have some idea of support contained within it: if *A* is on *B*, then *B* is holding *A* up; *B* is the reason why *A* isn't falling, it is bearing *A*'s weight. Now these are very different ideas. For example, the geometric *On* is asymmetrical (nothing is on anything which is on it—although it doesn't seem that this should be an axiom so much as a consequence of some more basic spatial theory), but the support *On* can be, e.g., two long blocks leaning on one another. They come together here in that the geometric *On* implies the support *On*, because blocks are rigid and strong, so they will bear weight without deforming or breaking. And this is because the stuff they are made of has these properties. To emphasize the separateness of these two ideas, imagine the alternative possible world with no gravity. The geometry is unchanged, but the 'support' idea is absent. So they must have distinct subtheories.

Both concepts are linked to clusters of others which we have not yet begun to formalize. The experience of doing so may well sharpen our sense of what the concept is, perhaps separating it out further into several slightly (or very) different ideas, each requiring its own axiomatic connections to the rest of the theory.

We have taken a proposed concept and seen it as a blend of two distinct components. As well as this analytic "division" of concepts there is what we might call a process of "broadening"; extending the range of a concept, trying it out in other areas where it seems natural. For example, imagine four blocks arranged in a compact square on the table, with adjacent faces in contact (the very fact that you can do that says a lot about the richness of the spatial-geometry part of our internal theories) and place a fifth block neatly on top, in the center. What is this block on? We might say it is on *each* of the other blocks, but this is a very different notion (e.g. pick up one of the lower blocks). Perhaps it is on the set of the four blocks . . . but a set hardly seems the kind of thing that can bear weight, and anyway only some sets will work. Perhaps we should abandon the notion of *on* altogether in this case in favor of some other, more subtle, relationship between the blocks. But it seems intuitively clear that the top block *is on something*, in much the same way that it could be on one block. The only reasonable conclusion, I believe, is that the fifth block is indeed on a (single) thing, which is made up of the four other blocks. By arranging them thus in a compact square, one has created a new object; we might call it a platform. (If someone points to it and asks; what is *that?*, the question is

from the rest of the theory: the meanings of its tokens would not be affected by the way in which the other axioms imposed interpretations on the rest of the tokens. It seems much more likely (it is in any case the most conservative assumption) that the whole theory is bound together, so that the meaning of any token depends on all of the rest of the theory.[6] But then how can we judge the correctness or suitability of part of such a theory? Since at any intermediate stage of theory construction there will be tokens not yet axiomatized, the process of formalizing those concepts may force changes in their correspondence to intuition and these changes might require our earlier partial theories to be rewritten. The toy blocks world's concepts came apart and its axioms became inappropriate to the new meanings, when we divided it into separate geometric and physical components, for example. Anyone who has tried to expand the scope of an existing representation will recognize the problem, but the methodology being urged here seems to preclude all the usual solutions.

One response is to proceed by enlarging the toy problems. On this approach we will work on progressively more ambitious subtheories, but always with a clear boundary on the kinds of inferences which the theory is expected to support. This approach is however very dangerous, since it can get caught in conceptual traps, as noted earlier. A technique might work well in a limited domain, and be applicable—with increasing difficulty—to a wider and wider range of phenomena, but be ultimately wrong. It is perilously easy to go on putting off consideration of the examples which clearly demonstrate its futility: one always plans to get to those later. Our toy blocks world embodies several such errors, notably the use of state-state functions to denote actions (completely unusable when several things are happening at once: see section 7).

Another response is to search for a small kernel theory of basic concepts, to which all others can be reduced by suitable definitions. Put another way: suppose we had a finished naive physics and eliminated all tokens which were explicitly defined in terms of others (as *clear* was in the blocks world), kept on doing this to the limit, and looked at what was left. This reduced theory must be conceptually closed, since the original one was: call it the kernel. Now, perhaps this is a smallish theory (less than a thousand tokens, say) so that to get it all done would be a feasible project. Filling in the rest can then be done piecemeal as needed, since adding definitions of new tokens does not affect the meanings of the old tokens; there can be no forced revision of the kernel axiomatization. This is the ''semantic primitives'' idea exemplified in the work of R. Schank and Y. Wilks.

It is worth pointing out that such a small kernel theory supporting a much larger

quite intelligible: there is some *thing* there. One might of course answer: nothing, its just four blocks.) So blocks can be on other things than blocks and tables. Its the same concept, but using it in a different situation forces a reevaluation of what can be said about it. We need to be able to state some criterion of put-on-ability, which seems to be having a firm horizontal surface. But now we have a new concept, that of a surface. This requires more axioms to relate it to existing concepts, and these in turn introduce other concepts (edge, side of a surface, direction, adjacency, contact, the object-surface relation, etc.: see Chapter 3, this volume, ''Naive physics I: Ontology for Liquids'', for a first attempt at such a list) and these require more axioms, each typically introducing other concepts, and so on. Conceptual closure becomes much harder to achieve: perhaps impossible to achieve completely.

This is what typically happens when one extends the scope of a concept. Closure is fragile, sensitive to the demands placed on them. In developing naive physics we expect far more of the theory, forcing it to be larger and making closure more remote. There is a constant tension between wanting a closed theory and wanting to pin down the meanings of tokens as precisely as we can: between closure and breadth.

This example illustrates an important and basic fact about the enterprise of knowledge representation. We want breadth and density: but you can't have the density without the breadth. If we want the theory to say a *lot* about a concept, the only way to do so is to relate that concept to many others. If there are many axioms in the theory which contain a certain token, there must ipso facto be many other tokens to which it is axiomatically related. It is exactly this, being tightly caught in a dense web of inferential connections to other parts of the theory, which gives a token meaning, by cutting out unwanted implausible models. And this is what we want, since the goal of the axiomatizing enterprise is to produce a theory from which we can rapidly draw the many conclusions corresponding to our intuitions, and this inferential richness goes along with model-theoretic constraint.

It is easy to find other things wrong with the toy blocks world: it was always just a toy, in any case, and we will now abandon it. But its limitations illustrate a serious general problem of how to get naive physics done.

A completed theory would be huge (a guess: between 10^4 and 10^5 tokens). It would be conceptually closed,[5] but it seems overwhelmingly likely that no reasonably sized subtheory of it will be. Such a subtheory would be completely isolated

---

[6] Some authors argue that cognitive structure consists of a large number of isolated units, with very weak connections between them. DiSessa (1983) for example refers to P-prims, which are ''simple . . . monolithic . . . knowledge structures whose meanings . . . are relatively independent of context''. But this is a very strong and optimistic assumption, and a dangerous one. If cognitive structure is really all fragmented and we don't assume that it is, then we will discover that it is. If however it is all bound together and we assume fragmentation, we will probably be unable to see (or express within our formalism) important aspects of its structure.

This issue is quite distinct, by the way, from the issue of ''modularity'' discussed by Fodor (1983). This entire discussion is concerned with the contents of Fodor's impenetrable non-modular central system.

---

[5] In fact, it wouldn't really. To *really* capture the notion of ''above'' it is probably not enough to stay even within naive physics. One would have to go into the various analogies to do with interpersonal status, for example. (Judge's seats are raised: Heaven is high. Hell is low: to express submission, lower yourself, etc.) Only a very broad theory can muster the power (*via* the Galois connection of model theory) to so constrain the meaning of the token 'above' that it fits to our concept *this* exactly. (Imagine a world in which the 'status' analogy was reversed, so that to be below someone was to be dominant and/or superior to them. That would be a possible model of naive physics, but not of the larger theory of common sense: and it would be a very different world from ours.)

theory by means of mere definitions does exist. It is axiomatic set theory, and it supports virtually the whole of pure mathematics. We have had 60 years to get used to the idea, but it is incredible that such an audacious program should have so nearly succeeded: a tiny theory (2 tokens and perhaps 8 axioms: details vary) enables one to define a large number of mathematical concepts, and then provides enough inferential power that the properties of these things follow from their definitions. The induction principle for the integers, for example, is not an axiom, but a *theorem* whose truth can be established within set theory.

Maybe such a small kernel can be found for our conceptual theory, but I very much doubt it. It seems a priori implausible that our knowledge of the rich variety of the everyday world could be merely a collection of lemmas to some small set of concepts. And there is a more technical objection, borne out by experience with schemes of scientific primitives. To pin down a concept exactly requires a rich theory and hence a large theory: exactness entails density which entails breadth, as noted earlier. It follows that a small theory which is conceptually closed and yet has a wide scope cannot be detailed. The concepts it discusses must be at a high level of generality not very tightly constrained by the theory. But then, if all else we have are definitions, we will never be able to get at the details. As Wilks (1977) says, no representation in terms of primitives can be expected to be able to distinguish between hammers, mallets and axes. But we must, somehow.

A third response, less idealistic but I think inevitable, is to accept the problem as real and find ways to live with it. We must build theories which are only partially closed. Some tokens will not yet have their meanings axiomatically specified: they will represent directions for future investigation. We will, indeed, always be in danger of having later theory construction come back and force an alteration in our present work, perhaps scrapping it entirely. The best we can hope for is to develop a good sense of style and scope in choosing groups of concepts and in formulating their subtheories.

Breadth seems to be crucial. If a concept makes intuitive sense in a wide variety of circumstances, but its candidate theory somehow presupposes a more limited framework, then something is wrong. Either the concept has several parts or cases, one of which is provisionally captured by the theory: or, more likely, the theory is limited by some inappropriate restriction (e.g. that blocks can be put only on other blocks) and needs to be recast in different terms. Applying this breadth criterion as a heuristic guide when building theories is what most clearly distinguishes this from the toy-worlds approach. Sometimes one has to accept a limitation for no better reason than that one can see no way to make progress without it, but this is to be resisted, rather than taken as a guiding principle.[7]

So far, I have assumed that concepts have been initially identified by no more than careful introspection. Other more objective and disciplined ways are also available. Detailed examination of the meanings of English spatial prepositions (Herskowitz 1982) provides many clues. Driving introspection deeper by sensitive interviews (Gentner & Stevens 1983) can uncover the outlines of whole inner theories. Showing subjects simplified physical situations (or tricking them with excruciatingly realistic ones: Howard 1978) and finding their intuitive predictions can clearly reveal centrally important concepts (such as "impetus", McCloskey 1983).

Many parts of the psychological and linguistic literature are ripe with clues. But one has to exercise great care. It is very difficult to make a *direct* connection between any aspect of overt behavior and any small part of the conceptual theory, if the present account is anything like correct. Single concepts may not emerge as English words, for example. Natural language is for communication, the internal language of thought is for thinking—in our model, inference-making in a highly parallel computer. These are vastly different requirements and so the languages can be expected to be very different. A communication language must be compact (since it has to be encoded as a time sequence, and time is short) but it can afford to be highly context sensitive in the way it encodes meaning (since the recipient is a powerful processor and shares a great deal of the context): neither applies to the internal language.

A word like "in" seems to expand into a whole complex of ideas when examined in detail: we must attempt to build a coherent formal theory of these before making judgements about the appropriateness or otherwise of the expansion, since tokens in isolation are meaningless (and they *seem* to be meaningful: see McDermott 1977).

7 Clusters

Concepts will not be evenly spread throughout a theory. Some groups of concept-tokens will have many tight axiomatic connections within the group, relatively few outside. Think of a graph with tokens as nodes, linked by an arc if there is an axiom containing both of them: call it the axiom-concept (a-c) graph. Then this graph, while connected, will have some areas more densely connected than others. Call such a collection a cluster. Our job as theory-builders is made easier if we can identify clusters: these are as close as one can get to isolated subtheories.

Identifying clusters is both one of the most important and one of the most difficult methodological tasks in developing a naive physics. I think that several serious mistakes have been made in the past here. For example, causality is, I now tend to think, not a useful, more-or-less self-contained theory of causality. "Causality" is a word for what happens when other things happen, and what happens, depends on circumstances. If there is liquid around, for example, things will often happen very differently from when everything is nice and dry. What happens with liquids, however, is part of the liquids cluster, not part of some

---

[7] Although perhaps one could not fight *too* hard. It is quite plausible that we might have several minitheories in our heads for some concepts. Perhaps we use one, oversimplified but useful, theory—a general utility version—and also special-purpose theories to handle idiosyncratic cases (such as porous solids in a theory of liquids). Or, more interestingly, a more sophisticated theory which can handle a very wide range of phenomena but is invoked only when needed (such as an atomic theory to explain porosity). c.f. Lucretius).

theory of "what-happens-when". This is not to say that the concept of causality is useless, but that it is an umbrella term for a large variety of particular relationships, each of which has its own detailed cluster of supporting theory, and its meaning is parasitic on theirs. If *all* you know is that A caused B, about all you can conclude is that A was before B.

Mistakes like this are hard to overcome, since a large conceptual structure can be entered anywhere. The symptom of having got it wrong is that it seems hard to say anything very useful about the concepts one has proposed (because one has entered the graph at a locally sparse place, rather than somewhere in a cluster). But this can also be because of having chosen one's concepts badly, lack of imagination, or any of several other reasons. It is easier, fortunately, to recognise when one is in a cluster: assertions suggest themselves faster than one can write them down.

A good strategy seems to be to work on clusters more or less independently at first: the meaning of the tokens in a cluster is more tightly constrained by the structure of a cluster than by the links to other clusters. It seems reasonable therefore to introduce concepts, which occur definitely in some other cluster, fairly freely, assuming that their meaning is, or will be, reasonably tightly specified by that other cluster. For example, in considering liquids, I needed to be able to talk about volumetric shape: assuming—and, I now claim, reasonably—that a shape cluster would specify these for me. Of course, their occurrence in the liquids cluster does alter their meaning: our concept of a horizontal surface would hardly be complete if we had never seen a large, still body of water—but the assumption of a *fairly* autonomous theory of shape still seems reasonable, at least as a working hypothesis.

The rest of this section discusses some likely clusters and some of the difficulties and issues which arise in formalizing them.

7.1 Places and Positions

Consider the following collection of words: inside, outside, door, portal, window, gate, way in, way out, wall, boundary, container, obstacle, barrier, way past, way through, at, in.

I think these words hint at a cluster of related concepts which are of fundamental importance to naive physics. This cluster concerns the dividing up of three-dimensional space in pieces which have physical boundaries, and the ways in which these pieces of space can be connected to one another, and how objects, people, events, and liquids can get from one such place to another.

There are several reasons why I think this cluster is important. One is merely that it seems so, introspectively. Another is that these ideas, especially the idea of a way through and the things that can go wrong with it, seem widespread themes in folklore and legend and support many common analogies. Another is that these ideas have cropped up fairly frequently in looking at other clusters, especially liquids and histories (see below). Another is that they are at the root of some important mathematics, viz. homotopy theory and homology theory. But the main reason is that *containment limits causality*. One of the main reasons for being in a

room is to isolate oneself from causal influences which are operating outside, or to prevent those inside the room from leaking out (respectively: to get out of the rain, to discuss a conspiracy). A good grasp of what kind of barriers are effective against what kinds of influence seem to be a centrally useful talent needed to be able to solve the frame problem.

There is another, closely related, idea which could be called a *position* (although the meanings of the English words "place" and "position" do not exactly coincide with the two concepts I am trying to distinguish). A position is a point within a space defined by some coordinate frame for that space. This need not necessarily be a Cartesian frame (in fact, it is rarely so), just some way of referring to parts of the space (such as the back, center and front of a stage, or a hotel room numbering system). A position is a place you can be *at*; a place is a place you can be *in*. Places always have boundaries, positions usually do not. (Although the boundary may not be marked by a physical barrier, it *is* there, and there is a clear notion of crossing it and getting into the place. Territorial animals have the same idea.) A position in a space is essentially pointlike in that space's coordinate system (i.e. it has no internal structure), but it may itself be a place, in which case its interior is a new space with its own coordinate system defining positions within it. The internal coordinate system need have no relation to the external one, even when there is no physical boundary. For example, one can be *in* a corner of a room, a place whose orientation is radially outwards, but the room's natural coordinate system might be in terms of a back and a front, left and right.

A room in an apartment building is a place which is a position in the interior of a place. To be *in* the interior of a place which is a position in the interior of a place. To be *in* the kitchen is to be *at* a position in the apartment (so answers the question: where are you?), and to be *in* the city is to be *at* a position in the state or country (so also answers the question, *if* the space being discussed is this larger one). This mutual nesting of places and positions can get very deep.[8] Notice that if one place is inside another then it must be a position within the latter. (After all, it must be *somewhere*, right?)

To get in or out of a place is to follow a path which must intersect the boundary. (This is the basic property of boundaries.) A path must consist of empty space, so if anything can get in or out, then there must be a part of the boundary of a place which is not solid: the door or portal, the *way* in or out. It follows that a way to prevent entry or exit is to ensure that there are no holes in the boundary of a place.

7.2 Spaces and Objects

Places and positions are concerned with space in the large, space to be in. But there is also a collection of concepts to do with local small-scale space, the space between and around solid objects. The two interact, if only in that suitable solid arrangements can define places, by being a boundary. But there seem to be some concepts and difficulties special to the small scale.

---

[8] Perhaps arbitrarily many or perhaps only seven plus or minus two.

For naive physics, vertical gravity is a constant fact of life, so vertical dimensions should be treated differently from horizontal dimensions: "tall" and "long" are different concepts. An object's shape is also often described differently (width and length; or depth—from the wall—and width or length along the wall: width if one thinks of the object as being put against the wall, length if one thinks of it as running along the wall). I suspect—the details have not been worked out—that these differing collections of concepts arise from the reconciliation of various coordinate systems. A wall, for example, defines a natural coordinate system with a semi-axis along its normal.

An important aspect is the relationship of surfaces to solids and edges to surfaces. The different names available for special cases indicates the richness of this cluster: top, bottom, side, rim, edge, lip, front, back, outline, end. Roget's Thesaurus (class two, section two) supplies hundreds more. Again, these are not invariant under change of orientation, especially with respect to the gravity vertical. Such boundary concepts are also crucial in describing the shape of space, and are the basis of homology theory and differential geometry. There is an obvious connection to the notion of place, in that places have boundaries. Let Δ be the function which defines the boundary of any piece of space: then $\Delta^2 p$ is the boundary of the boundary of p. If there is a gap in the boundary, then $\Delta^2 p$ is then outline of that gap (the door frame, for example). Homology theory takes it as axiomatic that $\Delta^2 = 0$, and studies the algebraic properties of triangulations which divide space into discrete pieces.

One concept which I currently find especially vexing is that of touching. Intuitively, it seems quite clear. Two bodies can touch, and when they do, there is *no space* between them: this could even be a definition of touching. It is also clear that they do not (usually) merge together or become attached or unified into one object: each retains the integrity of its bounding surface. And it also seems intuitively clear that the surface of a solid object is part of the object: the surface of a ballbearing is a *steel surface*, for example. And, finally, the local space we inhabit does seem to be a pseudo metric space (in the technical sense), i.e. there is a (fairly) clear notion of distance between two points. Unfortunately, taken together, these intuitions are incompatible with the basic assumptions of topology, and it is hard to imagine a more general theory of spatial relationships. Briefly, the argument goes: a pseudo-metric space is normal, which is to say that if two closed sets of points are disjoint, then there are disjoint open sets each containing one of them. (Intuitively, two closed sets cannot touch without having some points shared between them.) But if objects contain their surfaces, then they are closed sets: so they can never touch.[9]

My treatment of surfaces and contact in chapter 3 (this volume) escapes this problem by saying that when objects touch there is an infinitesimally thin layer of space (the "directed surface") between them. This works up to a point, but seems unintuitive and in any case does not address the basic issue, which is that our intuitive local space is, indeed, probably not a topological space.

It is certainly not three-dimensional Cartesian space, which contains such wildly implausible objects as space-filling curves and the Alexander Horned Sphere. Many mathematical intuitions at the basis of geometry and real analysis (from which topology is an abstraction) seem to be at odds with the way we think about everyday space. The idea of a point is itself one which people with no mathematical training seem to find difficult, or even incoherent.[10] As with many of the pathological constructions, the difficulty seems to arise from taking reasonable intuitions to unreasonable lengths by introducing infinite limits of one kind or another: infinitely small spots, or infinitely thin lines; surfaces which have no thickness *at all*, yet are actually there. etc. (see section 7.8). Intuitive space has a definite "grain" to it: when distances get *too* small, they cease to exist. It is a tolerance space (Zeeman 1962; Poston 1972) rather than a topological space.

All of this intricacy came from taking the idea of "touching" seriously, and illustrates again the way in which trying to capture one concept with some breadth of application can force major changes to large parts of the growing theory.

7.3 Qualities, Quantities and Measurements

Many everyday things have some properties which are more intrinsic than others, and might be called the possession of certain *qualities*. Objects have sizes, weights, colors; spaces have volumes: some objects have heights, others lengths. All of these qualities seem to exist independently of the entities which possess them. We can discuss heights, colors or smells as things in their own right: they form *quality spaces*. The set of possible heights is a quality space, as is the set of possible flavors.

There does seem to be a general theory of quality spaces. It always makes sense to consider the extent to which two qualities are alike: the degree of similarity between them. (Even when the answer is trivial, the question is never incoherent.) Thus there seems to always be a notion of "distance" defined on a quality space. Similarly, all quality spaces seem to have a tolerance. If two qualities are *very* similar, they become indistinguishable. (This may be the basic structure, as every tolerance defines a natural notion of distance between qualities to be the smallest number of steps by which one quality can be transformed into the other, each step being invisible under the tolerance. Poston (1972) develops this idea very thoroughly.) Many quality spaces are dense, in the sense that given any two distinct

---

[9] It may be felt that this concern with mathematical technicalities is out of place in judging the appropriateness of an axiomatization, since people don't think about mathematics in everyday affairs. This reaction is mistaken, however. We are judging the goodness of fit between a formal theory and intuitive reasoning. Intuition seems quite clear on all these matters of touching, which, when formalized, easily yield consequences which are the formal translates of very unintuitive ideas. That the formal derivation uses mathematical ideas is irrelevant to the failure of the match between theory and intuition.

[10] I think this consists in large part of becoming able to simply ignore the clash with raw intuition, rather than reconcile it. A point has position but no extent. How many are there in a 1-inch square, then? Such questions have no answer, and the training enables one to face this situation with equanimity. If points really were common-sense dots, there would have to be an answer.

them is at just before and just after each noteworthy event involving the other, for each world-state encompasses them both, being a state of the whole world. But this is clearly silly.

All we need to know about the other persons history is that at the time of their appointment it is contained in the same place as the first persons, and this can be established by its own train of reasoning. When their histories intersect, indeed, then the interactions between them need to be taken into account in an adequate description; but not until then.

There are other problems with the "situations" ontology (it is very hard to give a reasonable account of continuous processes, for example: see Allen, 1983 for some more), but this alone is enough to indicate that it is not a suitable foundation for a theory with any breadth.

Events happen in time, but also in space—they have a where as well as a when. They are four-dimensional spatiotemporal entities. So are objects, which have a position and shape and composition at a given time or period, which may differ at other times, and have temporal as well as spatial boundaries. All of which suggests that a basic ontological primitive should be a piece of spacetime with natural boundaries, both temporal and spatial. I will call these things *histories*. All the spatial concepts previously introduced can now be seen as instantaneous spatial cross-sections of histories. Thus, a place is a place-history at a time, and an object in a situation is that situations intersection with that objects history. Histories begin and end: the event of putting four blocks together in a square is the beginning of the history of a platform, and the end of that platform is when and where they are separated from one another. Situations themselves, perhaps now better referred to as time-instants, are themselves histories, although of a very special kind, being spatially unbounded and having temporal boundaries defined by the events between which they are fitted. [11] At the other extreme, spatial features which are permanent—notably, permanent places—are histories which are temporally unbounded but spatially restricted. Most objects in the common sense world fit between these extremes. Examples include the inside of a room during a meeting. Lyndon Johnson while he was president (this is an episode in the longer history of the man). Lac Leman (a permanent history) and the trajectory of USAir flight 130 from Washington to Rochester last Wednesday. This last is an example of a history which is more complicated in shape than just the direct algebraic product of a spatial object and a time-period. The projection of a trajectory onto the spatial reference frame is a path (e.g. an air traffic corridor), but the plane was only in a bit of it at each moment: its history slopes in spacetime.

The situations-actions language can be translated uniformly into a language which talks of histories, by replacing

[11] If time's passing is represented by a measuring scale, then we might say that time-instants form a quantity space with the measure function defined by a clock. On this account, the division of the conceptual time into discrete situations can be seen as the structuring of the past induced by the clock from the scale. This is how we make appointments to meet: they depend on there being a public clock and associated measuring scale.

qualities there is a third somewhere between them. (Colors and flavors aren't, I think.) Some spaces (colors, notably) seem to be structured in terms of a subset of prototype qualities, the others being defined by their distances from the prototypes. Some seem to be naturally n-dimensional, for some small n: others not.

Some quality spaces can be measured; i.e. there are functions (usually more than one) from them to a *measuring scale*, a linearly ordered set of some kind (e.g. the positive integers, the rational unit interval, the set {small, smallish, medium, tallish, tall}). Such measure functions (feet, meters) induce an order structure on the quality space (but it may not be a strict linear order). We can use this apparatus to talk about quantities: heights and distances are quantities, colors and smells aren't. We can write for example:

meters(height(Bill)) = 3.8

feet(height(Bill)) = 5.9

roughly(height(Bill)) = tallish

Notice that we can discuss heights directly, for example by writing

height(Bill) > height(Fred)

where the ordering relation > is that which is induced by the measuring functions *feet* and *meters*. (If we used the similar relation induced by the measuring function *roughly*, then this would say something like: Bill is *clearly* taller than Fred.) One remark which may be apposite here is this. It is often argued that "common sense" requires a different, fuzzy logic. The examples which are cited to support this view invariably involve fuzzy measuring scales or measure spaces. This, I believe, is where fuzziness may have a place: but that is *no* argument for fuzzy truth-values.

7.4 Change, Time and Histories

The now classical approach to describing time and change, invented first by J. McCarthy (1957), uses the idea of a state or situation (or: world-state, time instant, temporally possible world, . . .). This is a snapshot of the whole universe at a given moment. Actions and events are then functions from state to state. This framework of ideas is used even by many who deny that their formalism contains state variables, and has been deliberately incorporated into several AI programming languages and representational systems. We used it in the toy blocks world earlier. But a slightly broader view condemns it.

Consider the following example (which Rod Burstall showed me many years ago, but I decided to put off until later). Two people agree to meet again in a week. Then they part, and one goes to London, while the other flies to San Francisco. They both lead eventful weeks, each independently of the other, and duly meet as arranged. In order to describe this using world-states, we have to say what each of

$$R(o_1,\ldots,o_n,s)$$

by

$$R(o_1(\alpha s,\ldots,o_n(\alpha s)$$

where @ is the function which intersects a history and a time-instant, yielding a purely spatial object. But it is often more natural to describe histories and their relationships in other ways. The chapters "Liquids", in this volume, employs the histories ontology to describe an aspect of the world which I do not think could possibly be adequately approached using the situations ontology.

There are several kinds of history, and one does not expect that there will be a very rich theory of histories in general. Such as it is, it seems to be concerned with the relationships between histories and their boundaries, a sort of naive geometry of spacetime. Consider for example a stationary object being hit by a moving one and moving itself as a result. There are at least three histories involved in describing this: two successive episodes of the first object and one—that before the collision—of the second object. Call them A1, A2 and B. The temporal boundary between A1 and A2 is a purely spatial entity which itself has a spatial boundary (the surface of the object-at-that-moment: notice that this is the same as the surface-of-the-object at that moment, because space and time are orthogonal) which is in contact with the (isotemporal) surface of the last moment of B. Something evidently crossed that boundary ("impetus" (McCloskey 1983), probably) and put the first object into a different state: for if nothing had, then there would be no difference between A1 and A2. The event—itself a tiny history—which took place at the point of contact consisted of some kind of transfer between A and B, and so must have involved their boundaries, and this is the only place in spacetime where their boundaries intersect.

This vignette of analysis and the "liquids" axiomatization both illustrate a style of axiomatic description in which histories are classified into types and the kinds of relationship they can have with one another are defined by the nature of their boundary surfaces. Reasoning about the dynamics resembles a process of fitting together a jigsaw of historical pieces in an attempt to fill out spacetime, invoking interface properties of spatial and temporal boundaries at every stage. This appears to be a powerful and general technique, perhaps in part because it adapts so readily to constraint-propagation methods. Forbus (1981) uses a similar idea by partitioning space, as does Allen (1983) by classifying kinds of temporal interval. It depends on the use of taxonomies, i.e. listings of all the possible kinds of history of a certain type (all the kinds of falling history, or all the kinds of time interval, or all the ways in which a thing can be supported).[12]

---

[12] I think there are six. It can be resting on something which is bearing its weight; hanging from something; attached to something; floating on liquid; floating in the air—if it weighs nothing, and then only for a while—or flying, which takes continual effort.

7.5 Energy, Effort and Motion

There seems to be a significant distinction between events which can "just" happen, and those which require some effort or expenditure of energy to keep them going. The difference between falling and being thrown lies almost exactly in this, as far as I can tell. One importance of the distinction lies in the fact that if no effort is expended, then the second kind of history is ruled out, which eliminates a whole class of possibilities from consideration.

This notion of energy is not the physicists one: it is notoriously not conserved, for example (as in hitting ones head against a brick wall, or becoming exhausted by holding a heavy weight). Since real physics has taken the original term away from ordinary language, there are a number of informal terms in use: "oomph", and the German "schwung".

Typically, sources of schwung are of finite capacity and become exhausted in time, although may be self-replenishing. Also typically, schwung can exert force and thereby produce motion (or perhaps one should say rather that it can become motion, and pushing is giving the schwung = force = impetus to the object, c.f. the brief example given earlier).

McClosky (1983) and Clement (1982) have demonstrated convincingly what anyone who has talked to children knows informally, that naive physics is pre-Galilean. I can still remember the intellectual shock of being taught Newtonian laws of motion at the age of 11. How could something be moving if there were no forces acting on it: but yet, the argument was compelling: for if a surface was completely frictionless then nothing would stop a sliding object. My internal theory had a contradiction at its very center, the realization of which was acutely distressing. Another very convincing intuition is that heavy objects fall faster than light ones.[13]

I believe there are actually two ways of conceptualizing motion, which may be analogous to the distinction between large scale space and local metric space: as a displacement or as a trajectory. A displacement is a change of position, and requires constant effort to maintain: when the effort stops, the motion stops. They are changes of position, having no dynamic or geometric properties. In real-physics terms, they are dominated by friction. Trajectories are the motions of things with impetus. They are smooth motions along paths with a definite shape, and they keep going until they are stopped (when there may well be an impact, in which some or all of the schwung is transferred to other things). Displacement motion is Greek, trajectory motion is Galilean. Concepts such as going, coming, arriving, leaving, to, from, are connected with the former, concepts such as aiming, impact, speed (a

---

[13] Galileo's own argument why not is beautiful. Consider, he says, a stone cracked in half, falling alongside an identical one not split. Let the two halves separate just slightly. Will the split stone then suddenly decelerate? Surely not. If so, let the two halves just drift together and momentarily reunite: will it then accelerate? I tried this argument out on an intelligent ten year old, but he was unconvinced, arguing that the two halves would drift apart vertically, one falling faster than the other, even though they were identical. Why?—because two things never fell at exactly the same rate. Exasperated by this extraordinary obtuseness, my colleagues and I improvised a demonstration using two pennies. Within the limits of experimental error we could achieve at the dinner table, the child was right.

quantity space), towards, away from, are connected with the latter. Displacements are really mere transitions from their beginnings to their endings, whereas trajectories have a definite *shape*, and can be extrapolated in space and time. Speed is crucial. Walkings are displacements, but runnings have some of the quality of trajectories, and skiings are definitely trajectories. That position changes during the history is true of both kinds of movement, of course: if all we know is that Harry went to the store, it may have been either kind of motion.

7.6 Composites and Pieces of Stuff

Physical objects have many properties and relationships, many of them concerned with external attributes of the object such as shape or position. One category, however, concerns how objects are composed, what they are made of. As far as I can judge, all naive-physical objects are either a single piece of homogenous stuff. or are made up as a composite out of parts which are themselves objects. The essence of a composite is that its component parts *are* themselves objects, and that it can (conceptually if not in practice) be taken apart and reassembled, being then the same object. Examples of composites include a car, a cup of coffee, a house, four bricks making a platform. Examples of homogenous objects are a bronze statue, a plank of wood, the Mississippi, a brick. Homogenous objects have no parts, and can only be taken apart by being broken or divided in some way, resulting in *pieces*. Unlike parts, pieces have no independent status as objects in their own right, and the object has no natural internal boundaries which separate them: it comprises a *single* piece of stuff.

The physical characteristics of a composite depend on those of its parts, but also on the way in which they are arranged. There is a whole collection of concepts which have to do with putting parts together into assemblies: ways of attaching, strength and stability of connections, kinds of relative movement which are possible, how shapes can fit together, adhesive or frictional or lubricated relations between surfaces, etc.: one could put the whole of mechanical engineering in here. Central to the theory of composites is that this is *all* it depends on. so that if a composite is taken apart and reassembled so as to restore all the internal relations exactly, then it will behave in exactly the same way. And it will be the same object. Indeed, parts can be replaced with others—a new engine in a car—and the composite still be considered the same object.[14] A composite is more than the set of its parts. If we have a kit of parts for a model airplane, then after assembly all the parts are still there, but the aircraft exists *as well* as the parts. with its own unique properties. (Notice that the kit then no longer exists. It was also a composite, but of a different kind: not an assembly.)

A homogenous object comprises a single piece of stuff, but is not the same thing as the piece of stuff, since the criteria by which we individuate objects are different from those for pieces. If a statue is melted, the resulting pool is the same piece of (the same) stuff, but a very different object. In fact, the statue is gone forever. Even if the same metal is used in the same mold, the result is a new object. This contrasts sharply with the norm for composites, in which the set of parts is otherwise analogous to the piece of stuff. Pieces of some homogenous objects can be replaced by more of the same stuff and the object retain its identity. This is most obvious for liquid objects such as rivers, but applies also to solid objects, to a more limited extent. If a statue is broken and repaired, its the same statue (compare reassembling a car), although it has invisibly changed, and may now be a composite of the pieces of its former self (contrast reassembling a car).[15] But a piece of stuff is the piece it is, and cannot be added to or subtracted from without becoming a different piece.

Some of the properties of a homogenous object are properties of the object *qua* object (size, shape), others are properties of the piece of stuff it comprises (*amount* of stuff).[16] compare number of parts in a composite; color, surface hardness, rigidity). So long as the object remains the same piece, these both remain unchanged, but when they come apart, some properties can change. Many rivers change color with the seasons: topping up a cup of coffee increases the amount of coffee in the (same) cupful: freezing water produces an ice cube.

This last illustrates the distinction between stuffs and physical states (solid, liquid, paste, powder, jelly—a preliminary attempt a complete list produced over a hundred distinctions). Many stuffs can be put into a different physical state (by heating, cooking, grinding, squeezing, drying, etc.), and much of manufacturing depends on using such transitions to manipulate the object/piece distinction. An example is provided by casting. Take many small pieces of copper and heat them in a crucible. When the copper melts, each piece becomes liquid. Liquids can have no shape, so the copper objects which were the pieces cease to exist. Liquid objects in the same space merge together, so a new. larger, liquid copper object is produced. Now put this stuff into a mold—liquids take the shape of their containers. so the piece of copper now has this shape—and let it cool. Now it is a solid piece of copper and still an exact fit to the mold, so its shape is that of the mold. A new object has been created: an axehead, say. It may have seemed almost like a miracle four thousand years ago.

The parallel distinctions between an object and the piece of stuff which it is, and between a composite and the collection of parts which make it up. make it easy to see why a theory might fail to understand conservation of amount or number during manipulations which change the shape or physical layout of an object or group: for amount is a property of the *piece* (or collection), not the object. If that concept is not

---

[14] Borderline cases suggest themselves. If one simultaneously replaces everything but the body shell of a car, is it the same car? I think one can say yes, or could alternatively claim that this was a new car: but in that case, the body has been taken *from* the original car.

[15] Primitive atomic theory could be summarized as the idea that homogenous objects are really composites of atoms. and only atoms are truly homogenous (Lucretius). This explains why the recast statue is a new object: the interatomic relationships have changed. If one could get each atom back in the right place. it *would* be the same statue.

[16] *Amount* is a more basic idea than mass or volume. It takes considerable education to learn to distinguish these.

this similarly means *all* (describable) properties, such as being further north than the oldest plumber born in Philadelphia. Axiomatic theories must be very careful of comprehension axioms and schemes which guarantee the existence of entities: they should always state the relationship of the new thing to the other things on whose existence it was predicated. Thus we can speak of the space *between* two walls or *behind* a door, the falling history which is just *after* and *beneath* the moment and place where the object loses its support. and so on. In each case the relations which define the existence of the new entity also attach its boundaries to existing objects.

The use of public global metric coordinate frames restores unrestricted comprehension by the back door, for by using these we can describe the ``undescribable'' entities: *any* piece of three-dimensional space, such as an air traffic corridor. The resulting ontological freedom and uniformity may be why coordinate systems are so essential in (real) science.

7.8 A Sense of Scale

We seem to be remarkably good at imagining big and small things. One can imagine oneself inside a dolls house. or cupping the galaxy in ones hands. It is as though all our spatial intuitions have a free size parameter, which, while having a normal everyday default setting, can be adjusted so as to bring other things into their range. The incredible shrinking woman had the misfortune to have her actual size controlled by it. We sophisticated adults know this is impossible, but the idea certainly makes conceptual sense, which it would not if things and spaces had fixed sizes in our conceptual world.

This sliding size scale seems to be one of the sources of the intuition of continuity in the physical world, and of such geometric abstractions as points and lines. A dot, no matter how small, does have a size (or we wouldn't be able to see it, for example). Imagine it blown up, or equivalently oneself shrunk to match, and it would become an area, a place to be in. Then that space has tiny dots in it, being just like ordinary space. These are invisible in real space, or course, but they are certainly *there*, for how could it be otherwise? Just turn up the magnification and one would see them. And it must be like that all the way down, since one could always keep on turning the magnification up. That second-level dots are invisible in real life is shown from the observation that real dots are invisible from the next level *up*, achieved by looking at something from a long way away, so that it becomes small. Since—a basic assumption about scale change—it doesn't really matter which level one is at, the interlevel relationships must be transparent to shrinking and expansion as well. Mathematical points are now infinitely small dots, which are things that would appear dotlike at *all* levels. They aren't real physical things, because any real thing has a size and so would eventually stop looking like a dot, but points always resist magnification.

8 Getting It Done

One objection to the naive physics proposal is that it is impossibly ambitious: that we don't know enough about formalizations to embark on such a large representa-

available. there is no special reason why amount should be preserved, and many examples where it clearly isn't: rivers can get bigger and cause floods, for example. But when the concept is available and is used properly, conservation of amounts is very obvious. since amount of stuff in a piece is a property of the piece: and it is the very *same* piece after the transformation as before: *nothing* about it has changed. An ontological shift such as this may provide a convincing amount of the well known phenomenon. first noted by Piaget. of children's sudden acquisition of the ``concept'' of conservation. Notice however that conservation is not a concept, but a theorem.

7.7 Individuation

Establishing criteria for individuation must be done not only for objects but also for spaces. times. histories. quantities and any other kind of individual in our conceptual universe. When do we ascribe the status of being an individual thing to a piece of the world. since even the purely physical world can be carved up into pieces in arbitrarily many ways? I do not think there is a single neat answer, and there need not be: every kind of thing can have its own kind of reason for being a thing. But there do seem to be some general criteria.

We cut up spacetime into pieces so as to (a) keep important interactions as localized as possible: places are pieces of habitable space which are insulated from one another (by distance or by barriers); objects have a complete bounding surface which separates them from the rest of the world, and (b) to make the interactions as describable as possible. A square of blocks is a platform—a composite object—if we plan to stand something on it; for in that case we need its top surface to describe the *on* relation, so we need the object whose surface this is.

Solid objects have a shape (perhaps one that can change within some constraints, like that of an animal) and, while composites can have pieces replaced and retain their integrity. they tend to stay fairly stable. Liquid objects, on the other hand, are defined by their solid containers. and may be in a state of continual overhaul, like a river. The full story is more complex, however, since if the river dries up and refills it is the same river, while if I drink all my coffee, I go to get *another* cup.

This difference between an object and the piece of stuff which it comprises seems to run through many parts of naive physics, and perhaps all of common sense reasoning. The general phenomenon is that one history is an episode of two different histories, each corresponding to a different way of identifying an individual. ``Liquids'', this volume, describes a particularly intricate example: pouring one glass of water into another.

An important general point is that we do not want anything like universal individualhood. Common sense is prolix—many kinds of entity—but also very conservative—very few entities of each type. This contrasts with more ``universal'' schemes such as nominalism, in which *any* piece of spacetime can be an individual, allowing such things as the sphere of radius 20 meters centered on my left thumbnail *now*, during the month of August 1980 (say). Devotees of higher-order logic as a representational vehicle should realize that when one quantifies over all properties,

tional task; that it would take centuries, etc. Ultimately the only answer to such objections is make the attempt and succeed, so all I can do here is to convey my reasons for feeling optimistic. There are five.

The first is based on my experiences in tackling the ''liquids'' problem, which I had long believed was one of the most difficult problems in representation theory. The idea of quantifying over pieces of space (defined by physical boundaries) rather than pieces of liquid, enabled the major problems to be solved quite quickly, to my surprise. The key was finding the correct way of individuating a liquid object: the criterion by which one could refer to such a thing. I believe a similar concern for individuating criteria may well lead to progress in other clusters as well.

The second reason for optimism is the idea of histories outlined earlier. I believe that formalizations of the physical world have been hampered for years by an inadequate ontology for change and action and that histories begin to provide a way round this major obstacle.

The third reason is based on the no-programming methodology already discussed. To put it bluntly: hardly anybody has tried to build a large, epistemologically adequate formalization. We may find that, when we are freed from the necessity to implement performance programs, it is easier than we think.

The fourth reason is that, as the papers in this volume and (Gentner & Stevens, 1983) attest, physical intuitions seem to be relatively accessible by such techniques as in-depth interviewing. This was surprising (to me) and encouraging. A common view in AI is that, while expertise is ''surface'' knowledge and can be extracted by the expert system builders fairly easily, common sense knowledge is ''deeper'', more firmly buried in native machinery, and that to extract it would be much more difficult if not impossible. But it seems not: basic physical intuitions are near the ''surface''.[17]

The fifth reason is that there is an obvious methodology for getting it done, and this methodology has, in recent years, proved very successful in a number of areas.

Within AI, it has come to be called 'knowledge engineering', but essentially the same technique is used by linguists. It works as follows. In consultation with an 'expert' (i.e. a human being whose head contains knowledge: one knows it does because he is able to do the task one is interested in), one builds a preliminary formalization, based upon his introspective account of what the knowledge in his head is. This formalization then performs in a particular way, and its performance is compared with that of the expert. Typically it performs rather badly. The expert, observing this performance of the formalization in detail. is often able to pinpoint more exactly the inadequacies in his first introspective account and can offer a more detailed and corrected version. This is formalized, criticized and corrected: and so on. Typically, the expert, continually confronted with the formal consequences of his introspections, becomes better at detailed introspection as time goes by.

In ''knowledge engineering'', the expert is a specialist of some kind, and the formalization is, typically a collection of condition-action rules which can be run on a suitable interpreter: a very modular program, in a sense. In linguistics, the for-

malization is a grammar of some sort which assigns syntactic structures to sentences, and the expert is a native speaker. In both areas, the technique has proven extremely successful.

I believe this process of formalization, confrontation against intuition, and correction, can also be used to develop naive physics. Here is a domain in which we are all experts, in the required sense. The performance of a formalization is, here, the pattern of inferences which it supports. Performance is adequate when the ''experts'' agree that all and only the immediate, plausible consequences follow from the axioms of the formalization.[18] It seems to be sound to have several ''experts'' involved, as it is easy to miss some obvious distinctions when working alone.

The sheer size of a plausible formalization should give one pause, however. To even write down ten thousand axioms is not a light task. This can only be a group effort.

The ideal way to make progress is to have a committee. Each member is assigned what seems to be a cluster, and has to try to formalize it. They tell one another what they require from the other clusters: thus the ''histories'' cluster will need some ''shape'' concepts, and the ''assemblies'' cluster will need some ''histories'' concepts, and so on. Fairly frequently, the fragmentary formalizations are put together at a group meeting, criticized by other members (in their common-sense ''expert'' role), and tested for adequacy. I anticipate that some clusters will dissolve, and new ones will emerge, during these assembly meetings.

Initially, the formalizations need to be little more than carefully worded English sentences. One can make considerable progress on ontological issues, for example, without actually formalizing anything, just by being very careful what you say. The ''mental modelling'' field is at this stage now. But soon it will be necessary to formalize these insights and unify them into the common framework of a broad theory, and this is a new kind of task. It is here that the importance of a common reference language becomes clear, for it is only through this that the minitheories can be related to one another. It seems that this could be a real problem. because everybody has their own favorite notation. Many people find frame-like notations agreeable: others like semantic networks. etc. There is no reason why these. or even more exotic formalisms, should not be used: the only important requirement is that the inferential relationships between the various formalisms should be made explicit. In practice, this means that they should all be translatable into predicate calculus: but this is no problem. since they all are.

All of the suggestions and assumptions I have made are as conservative and minimal as possible. First-order logic is a very simple, basic, no-frills language. Other more structured ideas (procedural representations, frames, p-prims, concep-

---

[18] In fact, this is a weak notion of adequacy: the stronger notion would be that the derivations of the plausible consequences were also plausible. Attempting to use this stronger notion gives rise to severe methodological problems. since it requires one to have ''second-order'' introspections. Linguistics has an exactly analogous notion of strong adequacy for a grammatical theory. and suffers exactly similar methodological difficulties.

[17] Probably this whole depth metaphor is a mistake. like every other simple metaphor of the mind.

tual entities, scripts, . . .) make stronger assumptions about the representational language. It is *pessimistic* to assume that the a-c graph is connected, and that there is no small collection of primitive concepts. Maybe such special properties of the internal cognitive structure will emerge: but we should discover them, not assume them.

9 Why It Needs To Be Done

In the earlier version of this paper I argued at length that tackling a large-scale project such as this is essential for long-term progress in artificial intelligence. I will briefly review those arguments here, before turning to other reasons why large-scale formalization of ''mental models'' (Gentner & Stevens 1983) is of basic importance to other parts of cognitive science.

For AI there are three arguments: the importance of scale effects, the need to develop techniques of inference control, and the motivation of adequate representational languages.

AI has the aim of constructing working systems. This might be taken as the defining methodology of the field, in fact, in contrast to cognitive psychology. But there is a real danger in applying this criterion too early and too rigorously, so that a doctoral thesis must demonstrate a working program in order to be acceptable. Several areas of AI have outgrown this state, but work on knowledge representation is only just beginning to. As I have argued earlier, scale limitations mean that no matter how many short forays into small areas we make, we will never get an adequate formalization of commonsense knowledge. We have to take density seriously, and density requires breadth.

That weak, general techniques of controlling inference are inadequate to cope with the combinatorially explosive search spaces defined by large-scale assertional databases is now a matter for the textbooks. The moral is that the inference-makers need to be informed about what they are doing; they need a theory of control. I will not emphasize this point here, but note that the really large spaces which broad, dense formalizations yield may need qualitatively different metatheories of control, or other search processes entirely. I believe that the study of inferential control (which subsumes many questions of system architecture generally) is one of the most important facing AI at present. *But until we have some dense theories to experiment on, we won't know what the real problems are.* Many of the current ideas on controlling deductive search may be useful only on relatively sparse spaces; contrariwise, richly connected spaces may present new opportunities for effective strategies (the widespread use of relaxation, for example, may become newly effective). It would be interesting to find out, but something like naive physics has to be done first, otherwise our control theories will be little more than formalizations of the weak, general heuristics we already have.[19]

[19] The felt need for a nontrivially complex axiomatization to try out search heuristics on was my original motivation for embarking on this whole enterprise.

I will bet that there are more representational languages, systems and formalisms developed by AI workers in the last ten years than there are theories to express in them. This is partly because of the pressure to implement already mentioned, but is also due to a widespread feeling that the *real* scientific problems are concerned with how to represent knowledge rather than with what the knowledge is. When inadequacies arise in formalizations, the usual response is to attribute the cause less to the formalization than to a limitation of the language which was used to express it.[20] Many major recent efforts in the development of special knowledge representation languages are concerned with issues which have to do with the structure of the theories which are to be expressed in them. KLONE, for example appears to be a complex notation for describing interrelationships between concepts in a theory, including those between a concept and its constituent parts. The scientific questions of interest are to do with these relationships, not the idiosyncrasies of any particular notation for recording them. But all of this could be carried out in first order logic. The KLONE authors attribute considerable importance to the distinction between the structure of individual concepts on the one hand and the relationships between concepts on the other. In our terms this amounts to an extra layer of structural distinctions added on top of the simple axiomatic theory. Whether or not the distinction is worthwhile, it should not obscure the need to construct the underlying theory itself first.[21]

Progress in building nontrivially large axiomatizations of commonsense knowledge is also of importance to other fields than AI. Any theorizing about cognition has to take into account the structure of the internal theories which—if the whole computational view of mind is anything like correct—support it. If this is taken seriously, then large parts of cognitive and developmental psychology and psycholinguistics must refer to internal conceptual structures. This is a truism of cognitive science by now, but what is less widely appreciated is the need to be sensitive to the

[20] This may be connected with the fact that in computer science generally, development of programming languages is a respectable academic concern, while the development of particular programs isn't. After all, who knows what a language might be used for, especially a *general-purpose language*? And knowledge representation systems are almost invariably proud of their generality. This attitude is especially easy to comprehend when the Krep language is considered a species of programming language itself, which was a widespread confusion for several years.

[21] The deliberate eschewal of control (= computational) issues in the naive physics proposal represents a very *conservative* approach to questions of such structuring. First order logic makes very weak assumptions about the structure of theories couched in it, almost the weakest possible. They can be summarized as: the universe consists of individual entities, with relations between them. Nothing is said about the nature of the entities. (An attempt to find an area where this ''discreteness'' assumption breaks down was what led me to the liquids formalization, and an individualization assumption was, unexpectedly, crucial to its success.) It makes no assumptions whatever about control. Any insight into theory structure which is obtainable within naive physics must be readily transferable to more elaborate notations or systems of representation, therefore. It seems wisest, at this early stage in the development of large ''knowledge bases'', to be as conservative as possible. One might think that attempting to use first-order logic as a representational vehicle would be doomed to failure by its expressive inadequacy. In fact, however, the limitations seem to be on our ability to think of things to say in it.

details of these inner theories. Much work concerns itself with broad hypotheses about the functional architecture of cognitive structure, without paying attention to the detailed inferences which constitute the internal activities of the system. Some work assumes very simple internal theories, expressed in terms of "schemata", for example, or as an associative network of concept-nodes. But we know that internal theories, if they exist at all, must be extremely large and complex; and we know that we do not yet have any very reliable ideas about their structure, still less about their dynamics. Under these circumstances it seems risky at best to attempt to relate observable behavior to general hypotheses about cognitive structure. Word meanings in psycholinguistic theorizing, for example, often seem to be regarded as atomic entities related by some kind of association. But, as much AI work on language understanding even in restricted domains has shown, words must map into internal concepts in very complex and idiosyncratic ways, and the concepts themselves must be embedded in a network of internal theory, even to make possible such elementary operations as pronoun disambiguation or the interpretation of indirect speech acts.

The medieval alchemists had much empirical knowledge, and very grandiose but simple theories, and some success in relating the two together. Their view of the world attempted to make direct connections between philosophical and religious ideas and the colors and textures of the substances in their retorts. Modern chemistry began when the search for the Philosophers Stone was abandoned for the more modest goal of understanding the *details* of what was happening in the retorts. Cognitive Science is sometimes reminiscent of alchemy. We should, perhaps, give up the attempt to make grand, simple theories of the mind, and concentrate instead on the details of what must be in the heads of thinkers. Discovering them will be a long haul, no doubt, but when we know what it is that people know, we can begin to make realistic theories about how they work. Because they work largely by using this knowledge.

10 Is This Science?

The earlier manifesto ended on a note of exquisite methodological nicety: whether this activity could really be considered *scientific*. This second manifesto will end on a different note. Doing this job is necessary, important, difficult and fun. Is it really scientific? Who cares?

Acknowledgments

It is impossible to name all the people who have contributed to these ideas. I would, however, like to especially thank Maghi King, who let me get started; and Jerry Hobbs, who made me finish.

References

Allen, J. (1983). Towards a general theory of action and time, *AI Journal* (to appear).

Clement, J. (1982). Students preconceptions in introductory mechanics. *American Journal of Physics*, January.

DiSessa, A. (1983). Phenomenology and the evolution of intuition, in Gentner & Stevens, *Mental Models*. Hillsdale, NJ: Erlbaum.

Fodor, J. (1983). *The modularity of mind*. Bradford Books.

Forbus, K. (1981). *Qualitative reasoning about space and motion* (TR-615). Cambridge, MA: MIT AI Laboratory.

Gentner, D., & Stevens, A. (Eds.). (1983). *Mental models*. Hillsdale, NJ: Erlbaum.

Haak, S. (1973). Do we need fuzzy logic? Unpublished manuscript, University of Warwick, England.

Hayes, P. (1977). In defense of logic. *Proc. 5th IJCAI Conference*, MIT.

Hayes, P. (1978). The naive physics manifesto. In (Ed.), D. Michie *Expert systems in the micro-electronic age* Edinburgh, Scotland: Edinburgh University Press.

Herskowitz, A. (1982). *Space and the prepositions in English: regularities and irregularities in a complex domain*. unpublished doctoral dissertation. Stanford University, Stanford, CA.

Howard, I. P. (1978). Recognition and knowledge of the water-level principle. *Perception*. 7, 151–160.

McCarthy, J. (1957). Situations, actions and causal laws. (*AI-Memo* 1). Artificial Intelligence Project. Stanford University, Stanford, CA.

McCarthy, J., & Hayes, P. (1969). Some philosophical problems from the standpoint of artificial intelligence. In D. Michie & B. Meltzer, (Ed.), *Machine Intelligence 4*. Edinburgh. Scotland: Edinburgh University Press.

McCloskey, M. (1983). Naive theories of motion, in Gentner & Stevens. *Mental Models*. Hillsdale, NJ: Erlbaum.

McDermott, D. (1977). Artificial intelligence and natural stupidity. In J. Haugeland (Ed.). *Mind Design* Bradford Books.

Poston, T. (1972). *Fuzzy geometry*. unpublished doctoral dissertation. University of Warwick. England.

Pylyshyn, Z. (1979). Computational models and empirical constraints. *The Behavioral and Brain Sciences*, 3, 111–132.

Wilks, Y. (1977). *Good and bad arguments about semantic primitives*. (Memo 42). Edinburgh. Scotland: Department of Artificial Intelligence, University of Edinburgh.

Zeeman, C. (1962). The topology of the Brain and Visual Perception. In K. Fort (Ed.), *Topology of 3-manifolds* Englewood Cliffs, NJ: Prentice-Hall.

29 / Chuck Rieger
An Organization of Knowledge for Problem Solving and Language Comprehension

Historically at least, the form of this paper is as interesting as its content. It exhibits a type of Knowledge Representation research that has almost completely disappeared. Like the Minsky paper on frames [Minsky, Chapter 12], it is part of a more "Romantic" period in Knowledge Representation where the search was on for a few simple computational mechanisms that would account for a very large portion of intelligent behavior. As in the Minsky paper, the mechanism is presented quite informally using a wide variety of examples (in this case, from the areas of problem-solving and language comprehension) with little or no technical analysis. But with or without scientific rigor, the intuitive appeal of Rieger's approach is undeniable. The mechanism he proposes has two major components, a data structure for representing the causal changes and tendencies involved in the operation of algorithms or physical devices, and a discrimination network for determining which of a large number of such abstract algorithms might be relevant to a problem situation. This network, moreover, has the property that nodes can be bypassed as more is discovered about the situation, permitting a problem solver to quickly focus in on the methods that are relevant. Or so it is claimed. The validity of the mechanism is not argued in any detail and, unlike the Minsky proposal, it has never been followed up with a concrete implementation. It remains, however, a very clever and thought-provoking piece on the representation and use of causality information.

Appeared in *Artificial Intelligence* **7**(2), 1976, 89–127.

An Organization of Knowledge for Problem Solving and Language Comprehension[1]

Chuck Rieger

Department of Computer Science, University of Maryland, College Park, Md. 20742, U.S.A.

Recommended by D. Walker

ABSTRACT

Plan synthesis and language comprehension, or more generally, the act of discovering how one perception relates to others, are two sides of the same coin, because they both rely on a knowledge of cause and effect—algorithmic knowledge about how to do things and how things work. I will describe a new theory of representation for commonsense algorithmic world knowledge, then show how this knowledge can be organized into larger memory structures, as it has been in a LISP implementation of the theory. The large-scale organization of the memory is based on structures called bypassable causal selection networks. A system of such networks serves to embed thousands of small commonsense algorithm patterns into a larger fabric which is directly usable by both a plan synthesizer and a language comprehender. Because these bypassable networks can adapt to context, so will the plan synthesizer and language comprehender. I will propose that the model is an approximation to the way humans organize and use algorithmic knowledge, and as such, that it suggests approaches not only to problem solving and language comprehension, but also to learning. I'll describe the common-sense algorithm representation, show how the system synthesizes plans using this knowledge, and trace through the process of language comprehension, illustrating how it threads its way through these algorithmic structures.

1. Introduction

I want to talk today about human language comprehension and problem solving.

[1] This is the edited text of the "Computers and Thought Lecture" delivered to the 4th International Joint Conference on Artificial Intelligence, held in Tbilisi, Georgia, USSR, September 1975. Work reported herein was conducted partly at the University of Maryland, under support of a University Research Board grant, and partly at the Artificial Intelligence Laboratory, a Massachusetts Institute of Technology research program supported in part by the Advanced Research Projects Agency of the Department of Defense and monitored by the Office of Naval Research under Contract Number N00014-75-C-0643.

Investigations into how the human mind comprehends natural language have led model builders into progressively deeper cognitive issues. Until only very recently, most research had been directed toward the unit of the sentence, insofar as it represented an isolated thought. The primary areas of research were the sentence's syntactic analysis, its meaning representation, context-free inferences which could be drawn from it, its significance as a command or query within a microworld, and so forth. It is only recently that much attention has come to be directed toward the problem which, I feel, lies at the heart of language comprehension: the problem of understanding the interrelationships among the thoughts which underlie the sentences of a piece of text, of a story, or, more generally, of any sequence of perceptions.

Each step in the evolution of natural language model building over the past twenty years has required inclusion in the model of larger and larger memory structures for the model to consult in order to perform its job: from the lexical entries of the early translaters, to the syntactic rules of parsers, to the semantic and conceptual case frameworks of meaning-based parsers, to the context-sensitive data bases of micro-worlds. I *certainly* do not intend to reverse this evolutionary tendency today; instead, I want to show you stil larger structures which seem to be required by a model which is capable of relating one thought to the next.

Let us take as an informal definition of natural language comprehension "the art of making explicit the meaning relationships among sequences of thoughts which are presumed to be meaningfully relatable." My interest in language comprehension, as this defines it, has led me to the doorstep of another discipline which, historically at least, has developed quite independently of language comprehension. This is *problem solving*, or the art of influencing the world and self via planful actions. The independence of these two disciplines—language comprehension and human problem solving—sometimes was so acute that I can recall days when the language comprehenders and problem solvers would hiss at one-another when passing in the hallway! Perhaps those days will soon be over.

The thesis I wish to propose today is that these two core elements of human intelligence—language comprehension and problem solving—ought to be regarded as two sides of the same coin . . . that they are simply two ways of using one repertoire of memory processes and one memory organization. My belief, in other words, is that there ought to be a way of organizing world knowledge so that the very same memory structures can be used to solve problems and understand thought interrelationships. Watch any child as his level of problem solving expertise increases hand-in-hand with his ability to understand and connect his perceptions of the world as he must do, say, when listening to a story.

I come from the frenetic "build-a-model-then-rip-it-apart" persuasion within Artificial Intelligence, because it has been my experience that, no matter how clever one is, he never uncovers the real problems by gedankens-experiments. Rather, he thinks a while, builds a model, runs it, watches it fail, thinks some more, revises it, runs it again, and so on. So I will be describing some theoretical ideas today in the context of a computer model with which I have been preoccupied this past year. The resulting system is dual-purpose in that it serves as the core of a problem solver and language comprehender.

1. HOW TO REPRESENT CHUNKS OF COMMONSENSE ALGORITHMIC WORLD KNOWLEDGE

2. HOW TO ORGANIZE MANY SMALL CHUNKS OF THIS KNOWLEDGE INTO LARGER USEFUL PATTERNS

3. HOW TO USE THIS MEMORY WHILE COMPREHENDING LANGUAGE

FIG. 1.

Specifically, I want to talk about the three central questions which have served as motivation for my recent research (Fig. 1).

(1) First, how can we represent the kinds of knowledge about the world which underlie human problem solving and language comprehension abilities? That is, what kinds of primitive concepts do we need to express this kind of world knowledge? In particular, I want to focus on dynamic knowledge ... that which relates to actions, states and the notions of causality and enablement in the activities we all do day to day. Let's call this type of knowledge *commonsense algorithmic knowledge.* How are patterns of this knowledge built up from the set of primitive concepts?

(2) Second, how is this knowledge organized in a large system to provide a flexible and context-sensitive problem solver? This includes the question of how specific plans are actually synthesized by the problem solver which has access to this base of abstract commonsense algorithmic knowledge.

(3) Third, how can this commonsense memory organization be used as the basis of a language comprehension system?

My research shares many common goals with the research of others in the field. Bob Abelson, for instance, has long been interested in the nature of plans and themes from the point of view of a social psychologist interested in how humans incorporate notions of cause and effect in their representation of the world. In his Conceptual Dependency theory, Roger Schank has been interested for a number of years in developing a way to represent a conceptual knowledge of actions via a small set of primitives. More recently Schank and Abelson have been investigating techniques for representing the types of larger stereotyped patterns of "how-to-do-it" knowledge called "scripts" to

be used for understanding multi-sentence short stories. In the realm of understanding children's stories, Gene Charniak has also been developing a taxonomy of knowledge about actions in the context of applying that knowledge to understanding connected text. In fact, each of us is attacking the problems of representing a knowledge of how things work in the world, then using that knowledge to understand perceptions. This being the case, we are essentially generating language-related and problem solving-related instantiations of the much broader theory of intelligence proposed by Marvin Minsky: the "frames" theory. However, our methodologies for representing and using action-based world knowledge, and our focusses, differ consider-ably. Today, I want to show you mine.

2. Representing Algorithmic Knowledge

I suppose a good place to begin is to clarify what I mean by dynamic, or algorithmic world knowledge. Consider your knowledge of a bicycle (Fig. 2).

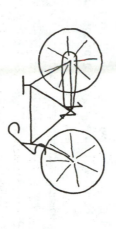

STATIC KNOWLEDGE

HEIGHT
SHAPE
RELATIVE POSITIONS OF COMPONENTS
CHARACTERISTICS OF COMPONENTS
PRICE
. . .

DYNAMIC KNOWLEDGE

FUNCTION OF THE WHOLE DEVICE:
TRANSLATE PUMPING INTO FORWARD MOTION
FUNCTIONS OF EACH COMPONENT

NOT INDEPENDENT, BUT DISTINGUISHABLE

FIG. 2.

You know for instance that it is roughly so tall, you know the shape of its handlebars, the relative positions of its seat, fenders and reflectors; you know that its pedals are free to pivot, that its chain is greasy, and you know its approximate price. These are *not* the kinds of things I mean by the term "commonsense algorithmic knowledge", but rather pieces of static knowledge about bicycles; they relate to the physical characteristics of a bicycle. Consider on the other hand your knowledge of the function of the bicycle and its various components . . . things like: the function of a bicycle is to translate an up-down pumping motion of the legs into a statechange in X–Y–Z location of the bicycle and rider; the kickstand is to provide support when the bicycle is not in use, thus interfering with gravity's desire to cause the bicycle to accelerate toward the earth; the horn, when air rushes through it as the result of squeezing the bulb, produces a sound which can cause others to become aware of the rider's presence, and so forth. These are examples of what I mean by the term "commonsense algorithmic knowledge", at least as it relates to mechanical objects and devices; it explains the "why's" and "how to's" of the various components, how the parts interface functionally with each other, and how and why a potential rider might want to interact with them. As you will soon see, I intend the term "commonsense algorithmic knowledge" to cover many other more diverse forms of cause and effect patterns outside the limited realm of mechanical devices.

Just for fun, let's see how we might represent part of our knowledge about the bicycle's horn (Fig. 3). What I am about to describe is a pattern built up from primitive event connectors which illustrate some of the commonsense algorithm representation I have been developing. I will describe this representation in more detail in a moment. Here is the description of how the bicycle horn works:

Actor P's performance of the action "grasp" will, provided the horn's bulb is not already flat, and provided P has situated his fingers around the bulb, cause a negative change in the volume of the bulb. This negative change will eventually threshold at the state in which the bulb is flat, contradicting a gate condition on the causality and shutting off the flow of causality. Meanwhile, provided there is air in the bulb and there are no leaks in the bulb itself, synonymous with the bulb's negative change in volume is a statechange of the location of the air from inside the bulb through the neck of the horn. This rush of air provides the requisite continuous enablement for the tendency "oscillation" to produce a "beep". The rush of air out of the bulb is synonymous with a negative change in amount of air in the bulb, this negative change eventually thresholding at the point at which there is no air left, contradicting a gate condition, and hence indirectly severing the continuous enablement needed by "oscillation". Meanwhile, provided there is a person nearby, the existence of the "beep" will amount to that person becoming aware of the horn honker!

And that, my friends, is the theory of a bicycle horn. Lest it be said that we model builders never verify our theories by psychological experimentation, I will now attempt to verify the correctness of this representation . . . (honk horn).

Now that I have everyone's renewed attention, and we have a sound

26 CONNECTIVE LINKS DEALING WITH CONCEPTS OF:

    CAUSALITY
    ENABLEMENT
    CONCURRENCY
    ITERATION
    INTENTION
    GATING
    THRESHOLDING

AMONG EVENTS OF 5 TYPES:

    ACTION
    STATE
    STATECHANGE
    TENDENCY
    WANT

FIG. 4. Commonsense algorithm representation.

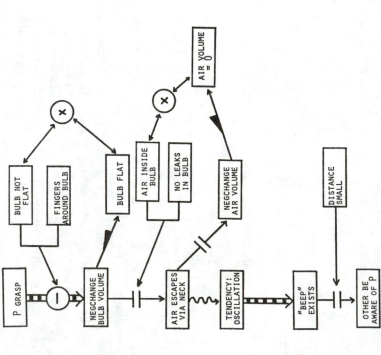

FIG. 3. Operation of a bicycle horn.

experimental basis upon which to proceed, let me briefly describe the common-sense algorithm approach to representing algorithmic world knowledge.

The essence of the representation (Fig. 4) is a set of 26 connecting links. The events which the links connect are assumed to be classifiable into five categories: actions, states, statechanges, tendencies and wants. Each of the 26 links has its own syntax of allowable event types. An *action* is something a potential actor can actually do: "grasp" is such a thing, while "honk a horn" is not, but is instead a reference to an entire commonsense algorithm pattern such as that I have just experimentally verified. *States* and *statechanges* are descriptions of actorless conditions in the world, such as STATE: (LOCATION IVAN HOME(IVAN)) and STATECHANGE: (LOCATION

tendency which causes an object to accelerate toward the earth, provided that the object is close to earth and unsupported; "metabolism" is another tendency which causes an organism to grow hungry, provided that the enabling condition "there is no food in its stomach" is satisfied. A *want* is a state or statechange which is desired by a potential actor.

The 26 connecting links are designed to express such concepts as causality, enablement, concurrency, iteration, gating, and intent among events of the five types I have described. There are eight links relating to forms of causality (Fig. 5): the four nominal causal forms (Fig. 5, top, one-shot/continuous, gated/non-gated), and the four counterpart byproduct forms (bottom).

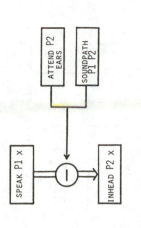

A PATTERN FOR VERBAL COMMUNICATION

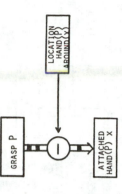

A PATTERN FOR PICKING UP A SMALL, HOLDABLE OBJECT

FIG. 6.

Suppose, for example, we wish to capture the essence of face-to-face verbal communication by a commonsense algorithm pattern. Then we write: Fig. 6, top. If, on the other hand, we wish to express one way of causing an object to be attached to one's hand, we write: Fig. 6, bottom.

The four causal byproduct forms allow the explicit representation of other

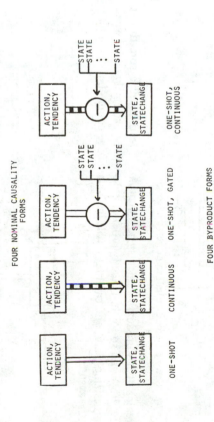

FOUR NOMINAL CAUSALITY FORMS

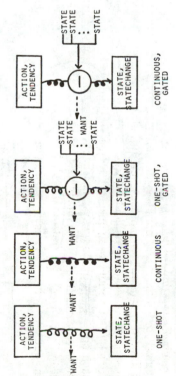

FOUR BYPRODUCT FORMS

FIG. 5. The eight causal link forms.

IVAN HOME(IVAN) OFFICE(IVAN)). States and statechanges can be caused by actions and their existence can enable other actions in turn. A *tendency* is an actorless action which, by definition, must occur whenever its set of enabling conditions is satisfied. For example, "earth gravity" is a

states and statechanges which are likely to result from an action, even though they are not related to the attainment of the intended goal of the action. For example, when we saw a board in half, we impart force to the board, causing it to move if unsupported; we cause small particles of wood fiber to begin existing in an unsupported state, and so on (Fig. 7(a)), or when a professor

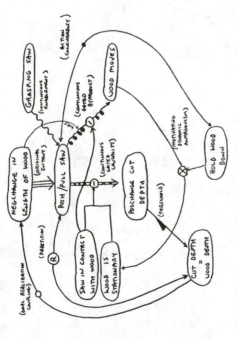

Fig. 7(a). Sawing a board in half to decrease its length.

screams at his graduate students, he sometimes gives himself a sore throat (Fig. 7(b)), and so forth. These byproduct links will be extremely useful when synthesizing plans, and can play a role in the language comprehension ability of the system.

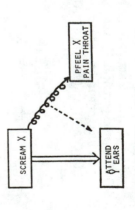

Fig. 7(b). Screaming at a graduate student.

There is another causal-like link, the *state coupling link* (Fig. 8, top), which gives us the ability to assert an implicit relationship of causality without having to explain the actual intervening actions. This link also gives us the ability to denote the equivalence of two different ways of viewing some state

or statechange. For example, to express a very common method of causing a statechange in location of a small object, we might write: Fig. 8, bottom left, or to express the synonymy of fluid entering a container with an increase in volume of fluid in the container, we would write: Fig. 8, bottom right.

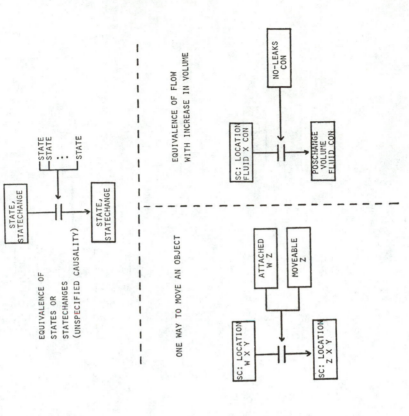

STATE COUPLING LINK

Fig. 8.

There is a link to capture the notion of good continuation of a statechange toward some desired level; this is the *threshold link*. For example, one way to cause oneself to be located at a place is to walk toward it, hoping eventually to reach it: Fig. 9.

There are links for representing the requisite preconditions of an action, or of an entire algorithm expressed as a commonsense pattern when we choose to regard the entire pattern as primitive for, say, problem solving purposes. For example, if for planning purposes, we choose to regard the "drive a car"

conditions which allow those actions to achieve the desired effects, and unleashing desirable tendencies while performing compensatory actions to suppress other undesirable ones.

THE ACT OF PROBLEM SOLVING IN THE COMMONSENSE ALGORITHM ENVIRONMENT WILL CONSIST OF THINGS SUCH AS:

-- EXECUTE A PRIMITIVE ACTION
-- SET UP ENABLING CONDITIONS OR GATE CONDITIONS
-- UNLEASH TENDENCIES
-- SUPPRESS UNDESIRED TENDENCIES
-- CONVERT GRAPH FORM COMMONSENSE ALGORITHMS TO LINEAR STEP SEQUENCES

FIG. 11(a).

3. Problem Solving

I will stop the description of the representation formalism even though there is a lot more to say, because I want to move to the second main topic (Fig. 11(b)): how to organize these small, isolated patterns of knowledge such as I have been showing you into larger complexes which will provide the basis for both problem solving and language comprehension. That is, imagine that we have the capability for representing, individually, the thousands upon thousands of small commonsense algorithmic patterns we all surely must possess. I want now to consider the structure of the larger fabric of the memory in which these patterns might be embedded.

1. HOW TO REPRESENT CHUNKS OF COMMONSENSE ALGORITHMIC WORLD KNOWLEDGE
2. HOW TO ORGANIZE MANY SMALL CHUNKS OF THIS KNOWLEDGE INTO LARGER USEFUL PATTERNS
3. HOW TO USE THIS MEMORY WHILE COMPREHENDING LANGUAGE

FIG. 11(b).

Let me introduce the approach to the organization I have been developing describing the theoretical considerations which led up to it (Fig. 12).

(1) First, if we assume, with regard to problem solving, that we have this ability to represent small, isolated patterns of algorithmic world knowledge, then the primary role of the larger structures must be to provide a matrix into which we can fit and interrelate the patterns. And this matrix should serve as a basis for making intelligent selections of alternative patterns when synthesizing a solution for a given problem. I mean by the phrase "intelligent

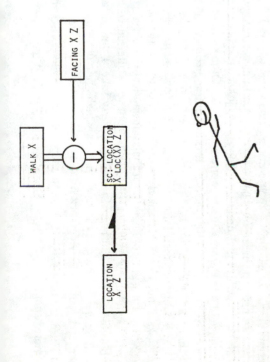

FIG. 9. Threshold link (good continuation).

commonsense algorithm as a primitive with a known solution, then all we need to know is the algorithm's cumulative set of preconditions: Fig. 10.

ENABLEMENT LINKS
(PRECONDITIONS FOR ACTIONS)

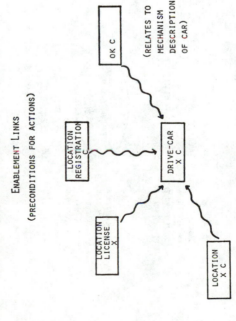

FIG. 10. Enablements for an entire algorithm, viewed as a black box.

I have described the most important aspects of the commonsense algorithm representation of dynamic world knowledge. Within this framework of event types and connective links, the act of problem solving (Fig. 11(a)) will be one of reacting to wants by constructing patterns which map out planful activities such as executing primitive actions, setting up preconditions and gate

problems. In particular, it would be desirable for knowledge discovered by one part of the system, during the solution of some *particular* problem, automatically to enhance the efficiency with which *other* parts of the system solve their problems. That is, as the system discovers things about its environment during the course of solving particular problems, its general level of problem solving expertise in that environment ought somehow to be heightened.

(4) Fourth, as regards use in language comprehension, the organization ought to be explicit, rather than embedded in procedures where the various causal and enablement relationships are only implicit in the structure of the procedure, and where the relations would normally be one-way subroutine calls or one-way pattern directed interfaces. The explicitness of the structures will be essential when the system needs to search through memory when seeking relationships among thoughts during language comprehension.

There is one other theoretical consideration which was perhaps an even more fundamental design criterion than these four. This is that the essence of both problem solving and language comprehension lies in knowing what are the relevant questions to ask during a selection or searching activity . . . that is, in knowing which aspects of the environment could possibly be relevant to the attainment of some goal. If a process which, say, selects one commonsense algorithm pattern over the rest does not know, in a context-free way, what is ultimately relevant to the functioning of the patterns among which it is selecting, how can that process ever be made to do different things in different environments? Perhaps this is a matter for the philosophers, but it has suggested to me that the heart of the problem of organizing world knowledge lies in encoding a knowledge of what *other* knowledge bears relevance to the solution of any given task, be it synthesizing a solution to a problem, or searching through algorithmic structures during language comprehension. *The system ought to behave in a way such that a knowledge of what is relevant can be used to seek out context, but one in which context, once discovered, can feed back, restricting that which is relevant.*

These four criteria—(1) the ability for intelligent algorithm selection, (2) the ability for higher level goals to influence the way in which subproblems are dealt with, (3) the ability for discoveries about the environment, the context, made during the solutions of particular problems to enhance the general ability to solve problems in that environment, and (4) explicitness— suggested an organization which I will call a *bypassable causal selection network* as the larger matrix into which to fit the thousands of small commonsense algorithm patterns (Fig. 13).

The purpose of such a network is, given a goal state or goal statechange, to select a most relevant algorithm pattern for achieving that goal state or statechange. Such a network consists of a set of nodes organized into a tree

---

"selections" that the organization ought to lend itself to interaction with both a static knowledge of the unchanging aspects of the world, and with the *context* in which the problem is being solved . . . that is, in which the commonsense algorithm pattern selection process is occurring. Where there are numerous alternative causal patterns for achieving some desired goal, the system ought to have good reasons for preferring one alternative over the rest in any given environment.

1. SHOULD PROVIDE THE ABILITY TO MAKE INTELLIGENT SELECTIONS FROM AMONG ALTERNATIVE CAUSAL PATTERNS
2. SOLUTIONS TO SUBPROBLEMS OUGHT TO BE SENSITIVE TO THE CONTEXT AND PURPOSES OF THE MAIN PROBLEM
3. ORGANIZATION OUGHT TO ADAPT DYNAMICALLY TO ENVIRONMENTAL CONTEXT
4. OUGHT TO BE EXPLICIT FOR USE BY PROCESSES OTHER THAN PROBLEM SOLVING

ALSO: MUST PROVIDE A WAY OF ENCODING A KNOWLEDGE OF WHAT IS RELEVANT TO SELECTING OR SEARCHING

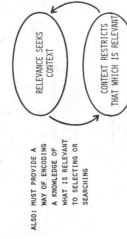

RELEVANCE SEEKS CONTEXT

CONTEXT RESTRICTS THAT WHICH IS RELEVANT

FIG. 12. Theoretical considerations for the large organization.

(2) Second, during the problem solving process, the solutions to subproblems ought somehow to be sensitive to the context and purposes of the larger problem. For example, suppose my goal is to insult Ivan. I decide the best way to proceed, based on what I know about him, is to make a dirty joke about his wife; but I don't know any dirty jokes, and hence have the subproblem of first learning an appropriate dirty joke. Of the many algorithm patterns organized under the "how to learn about something" part of my algorithmic knowledge, one is: "politely ask someone else." Certainly, in solving this subgoal, I would not want to go to Ivan and politely ask him for a dirty joke about wives! The structure of knowledge ought, therefore, to be such that certain aspects of higher level goals automatically diffuse throughout the system, guiding the problem solver *away* from some alternative solutions to subproblems, *toward* others. In seeking a dirty joke, I will either avoid Ivan altogether, or interact with him in ways which are compatible with my higher level goals as they concern him.

(3) Third, the organization ought to adapt dynamically as it discovers more and more about the environment—the context—in which it is solving

structure. Each node has associated with it a test and a set of one or more alternative branches, one of which will be followed on the basis of the test result. Tests are either memory queries about unchanging world knowledge, or queries about the environment in which the selection is being made, that is, in which the network is being traversed. There is one of these bypassable causal networks for each state concept and statechange concept in the system. For example, there is a causal selection network for deciding how to cause a statechange in the location of an object from one place to another (Fig. 13, left), there is a causal selection network for deciding on an appropriate approach to causing a piece of knowledge to begin existing in one's mind, or in the mind of another actor (Fig. 13, right), and so forth. This implies that there will be a relatively large number of networks, each being a specialist at solving problems relating to one particular state or statechange concept.

At the terminal nodes of these networks are what I will call *approaches*; these are the patterns, expressed in the commonsense algorithm representation I have shown you, which map out general, top-level plans for solving problems of the class for which the network is an expert. For example, among the hundreds of patterns at the terminal nodes of the AGENT W CAUSES STATECHANGE (LOCATION X Y Z) selection network will be linkers to commonsense algorithm patterns for driving cars, walking, taking elevators, grasping and carrying objects, hoisting things, throwing things, swallowing

things, and so on. The kinds of tests asked at the nodes of this network in order to select among the hundreds of alternatives a pattern for solving a particular instance of a STATECHANGE LOCATION goal will be things like class memberships of W, X, Y, Z, the distance between Y and Z, the nature of Y and Z (in a building, in the woods, under water, in the body), the weight and size of X, and so on. In other words, the causal selection network is the mother who asks all the right questions before choosing which son—which commonsense algorithm pattern—will be best for the job.

Each of the approaches at the bottom of a causal selection network is a commonsense algorithm pattern of one of three types (Fig. 14): (1) an *abstract*

THREE TYPES OF APPROACH:

-- ABSTRACT ALGORITHM
-- MECHANISM DESCRIPTION
-- SEQUENTIAL ABSTRACT ALGORITHM

ABSTRACT ALGORITHM FORMS:

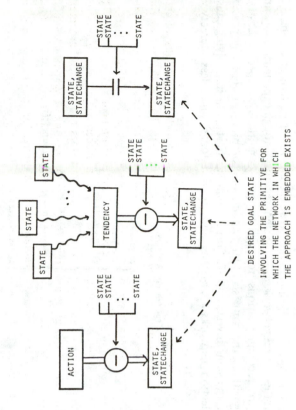

FIG. 14.

algorithm, (2) a *mechanism description,* or (3) a *sequential abstract algorithm.* An abstract algorithm is a pattern having one of the three forms: Fig. 14, left, center, right. For example, at the bottom of the AGENT W CAUSES STATECHANGE(LOCATION X Y Z) causal selection network, two of the

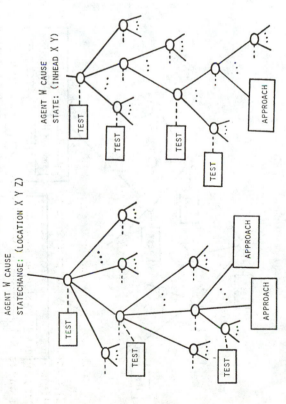

FIG. 13. Bypassable causal selection networks.

A recommendation represents a stereotyped way of solving the gate condition in the context peculiar to the abstract algorithm approach in which it occurs. Having the ability to store these recommendations allows the abstract algorithm patterns in effect to grow into larger and larger, more rigid forms. Without recommendations, the gate subgoals will be solved by applying other appropriate causal selection networks. But *with* recommendations, since a recommendation obviates the causal selection process for a subgoal by pointing directly to another abstract algorithm pattern at the base of another causal network, as the system records, through experience, more and more recommendations for specific gate conditions in specific abstract algorithms, the synthesis of larger and more complex plans becomes possible for the same investment of effort . . . that is, effort spent in applying causal selection networks . . . as was once needed for smaller, less stereotyped solutions.

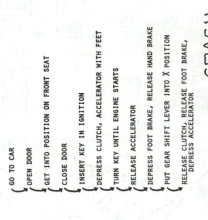

FIG. 16. Sequential abstract algorithms.

I will not get into the other two types of approach—mechanism descriptions and sequential abstract algorithms—except to show you an example of each. A sequential algorithm is essentially a commonsense algorithm pattern with explicit sequencing information . . . a linearized chunk of a plan which the system has successfully employed at one time and stored away with the simplifying sequencing information for future use. As such, it keys on action sequences rather than on unsequenced goal states. Fig. 16 illustrates a sequential algorithm for setting an automobile into motion.

A mechanism description captures the internal cause and effect relationships of the events which occur when the mechanism operates. From such a

---

hundreds of patterns we would find are: Fig. 15. One of these (Fig. 15, bottom left) would be in a part of the network which deals with changing the location of hand-graspable objects, the other (Fig. 15, bottom right) would be in a part of the network which deals with causing objects to come to be located inside the body. If we look at the "swallow" algorithm pattern, this says that, providing the object X is in the mouth, and it is small enough, the primitive action "gulp" will ordinarily cause X to change location to the stomach. In general, you can see that the gate conditions on the causal or state coupling link in an abstract algorithm will prescribe subgoals to be solved by other causal selection networks in the system.

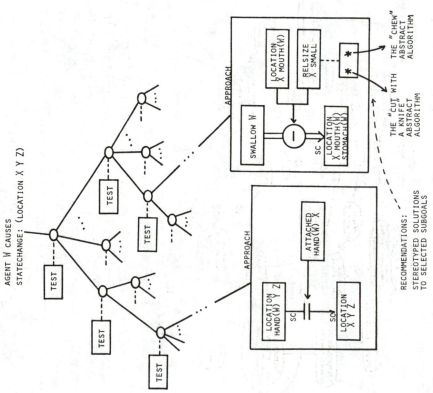

FIG. 15.

Notice in the swallow algorithm the existence of two *recommendations* attached to one of the gate conditions. Recommendations are direct pointers to other abstract algorithms which exist at the bottoms of other networks.

description, the system can figure out both how to use the mechanism and what using it can accomplish. Fig. 17 is the mechanism description of a reverse trap flush toilet. I have been carrying this particular mechanism description around with me for several months; you never know when you might need one!

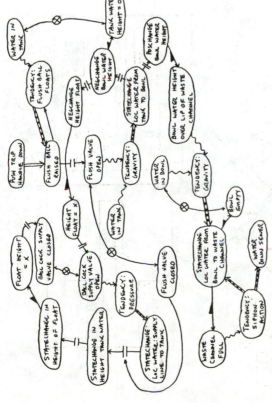

FIG. 17. Operation of the reverse trap flush toilet.

Let's return now to the causal selection network as a whole. The downward traversal of a network for any given state or statechange goal during problem solving results in the asking of many questions, and, finally, in the selection of an approach based on the answers to these questions. The network tests a context-layered data base, or, when simple lookups fail, a deduction mechanism which is itself organized as a system of discrimination networks. I will not describe these mechanisms today.

To illustrate how the causal selection networks function, and the kinds of tests they must make, let's confront the problem solver with a goal and observe what happens in response. Suppose I am at work and become thirsty. In other words, I have the goal: (LOCATION FLUID STOMACH(SELF)). This goal will cause the problem solver to apply the STATECHANGE LOCATION causal network for AGENT SELF CAUSES STATECHANGE (LOCATION FLUID? STOMACH(SELF)), this network being an expert at synthesizing plans for all sorts of statechanges in location of objects (Fig. 18). In this case, by asking questions about W, X, Y and Z, the network will lead the problem solver to a mechanism description at the bottom of the goal: "use the

water fountain out in the hall." In another environment, the network might have selected another quite different approach, such as drinking from a cup in the kitchen, drinking from a stream in the wilderness, going into a store and ordering a glass of water, and so forth. And of course, we have not even considered the rest of this extremely large causal selection network which would also be applied to the solution of vastly different varieties of STATE-CHANGE LOCATION goals involving people and various kinds of physical objects instead of fluids and bodyparts.

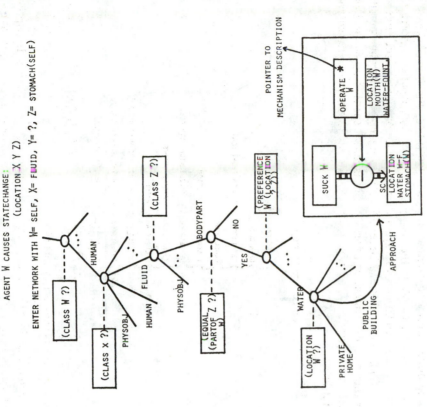

FIG. 18.

I imagine these causal selection networks as being extremely large, with perhaps thousands of nodes each. But their largeness, I believe, will be mostly a matter of extreme breadth rather than depth. I do not believe, for example, that they need ever exceed a depth of, say, 10 or 15. This characteristic will be important for the language comprehension search processes.

Note that, having selected the "drink from a water fountain" approach, specific subgoals are spelled out, the most significant one in this case being to achieve the statechange (LOCATION SELF OFFICE(SELF SELF) WATER-FOUNTAIN). (Since my mouth is attached, it will come along with me . . . the system knows about this through a statecoupling pattern!) Each subgoal will result in a planning process similar to this one. The end product of plan synthesis will be a large structure called a *synthesized algorithm* and will provide input to the linearization processes which will transform the synthesized algorithm, in graph form, into a linear, executable sequence of steps.

Before leaving this aspect of the system, let me reemphasize this notion of relevance. In the water fountain selection example, something in the system had to know that the current location of self bore extreme relevance to the

Now let me explain why I have called these causal selection networks "bypassable". Consider the system's character as a complete organism: if we look across all the networks in the system, we see that any particular test of the environment is apt to occur at numerous points throughout the system of networks. To take a very simple example, the test (CLASS X ?),

process of deciding how to go about quenching self's thirst. It is the purpose of the networks to carry out an orderly probe of the environment along relevant lines.

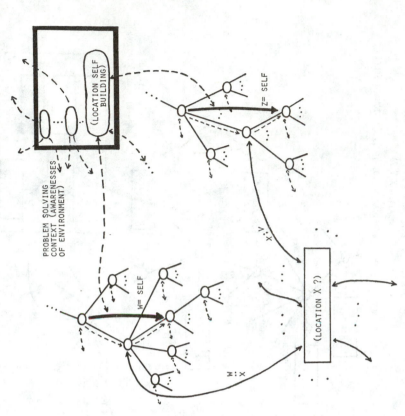

Fig. 20. Bypass implementation.

which inquires about the class membership of an object, except for different variable names, will occur at possibly hundreds of points throughout the system of networks. The presence of this test at different points within one network, or at points in different networks, will be for reasons peculiar to each network's requirements; the way one network uses this information may be quite a bit different from the way another network uses it. Nevertheless, if we disregard the reasons for the test's existence in the various

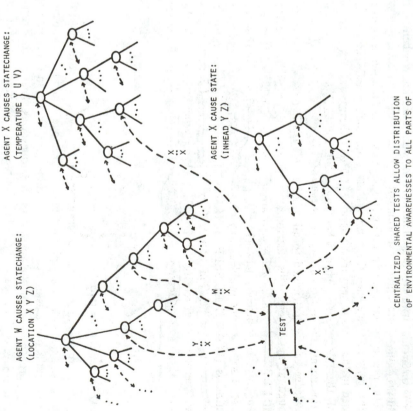

Fig. 19. Test sharing.

thus planted would be conditional upon X = SELF; the bypass will not be seen for other values of X.

In the implemented model, this is precisely what occurs. As each node in a network makes its test, the result is recorded as an active datum in the current environment, and then conditional bypasses are distributed to all parts of the system which could conceivably use the newly-acquired information.

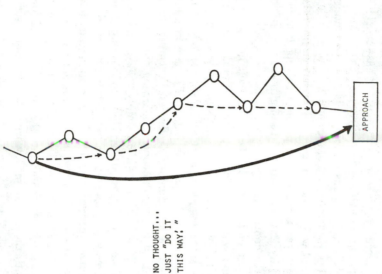

NO THOUGHT...
JUST "DO IT
THIS WAY!"

FIG. 22. Bypassing an entire causal selection network.

The significance of a bypass in a network is a key point of the model: a bypass will provide the problem solver with a *shortcut* in environments where the bypass remains valid. As more and more bypasses accumulate at scattered points throughout the system of networks via this distribution process, contiguous sequences of bypasses will begin to form (Fig. 21). If this bypass implantation process is overseen by a transitive closure seeker, then the system will automatically replace contiguous sequences of compatible bypasses by progressively longer, single-step bypasses. If the causal selection process is sensitive to these bypasses, preferring to follow them whenever it

networks, there will be quite a bit of overlap in the knowledge about the environment needed by the various networks.

This overlap can serve as the basis of a very interesting mechanism as follows (Fig. 19): First, we allow all network tests to be *shared*. What I mean by this is that suppose a given test occurs at 50 points throughout the system of networks. Then, instead of planting 50 instances of that test, we store one *central copy* and reference the central copy from each point that test is needed in the various networks. Suppose also that the central copy knows of all these occurrences. Then, when any network asks this question and obtains an answer in the current environment, the effects of that piece of knowledge can be distributed to all other points of that test's occurrence throughout the system. This distribution process is achieved by planting what I will call a *conditional bypass* around each occurrence of that test throughout the system of networks (Fig. 20). For example, if during the course of solving some problem, any network asks and discovers that self's location is (LOCATION SELF BUILDING), then every other network which might ask the question (LOCATION X ?), and which has BUILDING as an alternative, will receive a conditional bypass around the node in the network at which this question would be asked. In this case, the bypasses

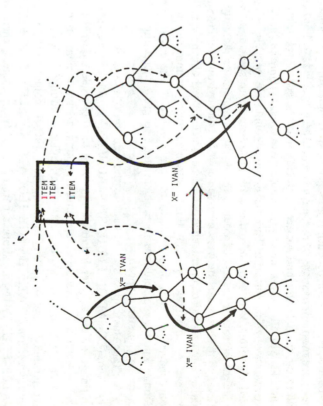

CLOSURE IS POSSIBLE ONLY
FOR COMPATIBLE SEQUENCES

FIG. 21. Closing bypass sequences.

can, then as more and more is discovered about the environment as the results of solving specific problems in that environment, the percentage of the total system which is bypassed increases. What this means is that the system automatically will tend increasingly to prefer the selection of approaches which are most appropriate in that environment, being guided, without any choice, through longer and longer stretches of bypassed causal selection networks. Some bypasses might grow to be quite long, even up to the point where some entire networks become effectively invisible because of the existence of one long bypass from the top node directly to some approach, A, at the bottom (Fig. 22). Of course, this bypass might never actually be needed; but, should that network ever be applied in an environment in which this total bypass exists, approach A would be selected "without thought" so to speak. As an overall organism, this bypassable network memory organization behaves in a way such that, as more and more of the environment becomes known, the solutions to problems tend to grow increasingly predetermined, or stereotyped.

If we take this bypass system back to the solution of the goal I posed a while ago, (LOCATION FLUID STOMACH(SELF)), you can see that by the time the "use a water fountain" approach has been selected at the top level, enough will have been determined about the environment—namely, that self is a human who is currently in an office building where there are predetermined ways of getting around—that when it comes time to solve the *subproblem* STATECHANGE (LOCATION SELF OFFICE(SELF) WATER-FOUNTAIN) in another part of the network system, there will already be bypasses pointing the problem solver *toward* approaches like "climb the stairs", or "take the elevator", and *away* from approaches such as "take an airplane", "swim", and so on.

No doubt the work "frame" is throbbing through your networks (Fig. 23), since we generally imagine a frame to be some sort of entity which imposes constraints on the way things are perceived, interpreted, or dealt with. But its bypass arrangement is indeed frame-like. But its frames aren't discernible as distinct packets of knowledge. Instead, they are distributed bundles of bypasses which can blend in essentially infinite variety. Notice that because of this, we get a continuity of context where, instead of "switching from one frame to another", the system can flow smoothly from context to context as individual aspects of the environment change. This is because "context" in the bypass system amounts to the set of questions posed and answered while solving problems so far in the environment, and of course, the cumulative set of bypasses introduced by this set of questions and answers. This serving as the definition of problem solving context, if we assume the existence of an overseer in the system who is responsible for monitoring the continued truth of items in this context, then as aspects of the context become no longer true, the bypasses associated with those aspects can be removed from the system of networks. This will cause the overall problem solving behavior of the system to grow slightly less automatic in the slightly altered environment. In other words, as the context changes, bypasses fade in and out. At any given moment, the set of bypasses in the system will guide the problem solver toward solutions which are most appropriate in that environment.

This model suggests a wealth of related mechanisms. I will mention two. The first is: suppose some item, such as (CLASS SELF HUMAN), to take the same very obvious example again, is found to remain in the problem solving context more or less continuously over time. Then perhaps it would be reasonable to discard it from the context, allowing only its bypasses to remain permanently. That is, after a while I simply *know* I am human, and, knowing this, am always one bypassed step closer to selecting an approach to problems whose networks care about my class membership. And this phenomenon of relatively permanent bypass implantation seems to occur in far subtler ways. One day I was repairing the plumbing under our kitchen sink. I had removed a section of the drain pipe, and as I did so, a considerable quantity of water rushed from the sink into the catch pail I had fortunately positioned underneath the operation. I worked several minutes more, but being annoyed by the bucket full of water, decided to dispose of it. Now, I won't swear to it, but I think I called up my causal selection network for how to dispose of objects, and it immediately told me that, since I was standing right next to a sink, and since the object to be disposed of was a fluid, that I should simply pour the water down the sink. I did so without a moment's hesitation, even as I held the section of disconnected drain pipe in my other hand! I spent the next few minutes mopping up under the cabinet and cursing my causal selection networks.

FRAME

FIG. 23.

system-wide increase in the degree of stereotypy in problem solving behavior. Perhaps that elusive packet of knowledge I envisioned when I first heard the term "frame" might simply be one of these distinguished configurations of bypasses which has occurred often enough, and with small enough variation, to have been frozen, and thus in effect named. To jumble metaphors a bit, perhaps this more continuous bypass system is the broth from which those more discrete animalcules, which I once imagined frames as being, emerge.

There is much, much more to be said about the organization of the causal selection networks and techniques of plan synthesis using them. There are also many interesting questions about learning in such an environment: how do the selection networks grow and evolve, how are abstract algorithm patterns initially composed from sequences of perceptions of the world, and so forth. These are current topics of research. But rather than continue along one of these lines, I will stop talking about the use of these commonsense algorithm memory structures in problem solving, and turn now to their use in *language comprehension* (Fig. 25).

---

1. How to represent chunks of commonsense algorithmic world knowledge

2. How to organize many small chunks of this knowledge into larger useful patterns

→ 3. How to use this memory while comprehending language

Fig. 25.

---

4. Language Comprehension

I view language comprehension as that process which elucidates the interrelationships among a collection or sequence of thoughts by consulting the kinds of world knowledge stored in an algorithmic memory of the sort I have been describing. And this process of elucidating the interrelationships should feed back, causing still other interrelationships to be perceived and awareness of context to expand. I feel the basic character of the language comprehension process is one of prediction/fulfillment, wherein every perception gives rise to general—and I want to emphasize the word "general"— expectations about what might follow, or it fits into some existing expectation, or both. While I will be talking in terms of language comprehension, where the source of incoming thoughts is linguistic, the approach I will be describing ought to apply to any collection of thoughts, regardless of their origin.

Let me first define language comprehension in a slightly more concise way (Fig. 26): Given a context $C(T_1, \ldots, T_i)$ which has been established by thoughts $T_1, \ldots, T_i$, make explicit the relationship between the next thought T_{i+1} and $C(T_1, \ldots, T_i)$. Call this explicit relationship the interpretation of T_{i+1} in this context: $I(T_{i+1}, C(T_1, \ldots, T_i))$.

The second mechanism one might envision in the bypass system is one which, as a particular overall bypass configuration—that is, set of awarenesses of the environment and their related bypass sets—was seen to recur frequently, could *freeze* that configuration, in effect naming it and forming a more packet-like snapshot of the environment (Fig. 24). Such frozen bypass configurations

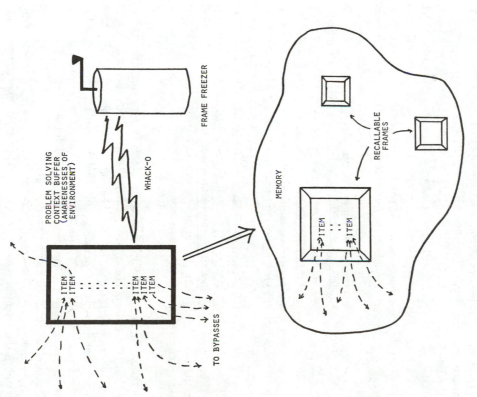

PROBLEM SOLVING
CONTEXT BUFFER
(AWARENESSES OF
ENVIRONMENT)

WHACK-O

FRAME FREEZER

ITEM
ITEM
ITEM
ITEM
ITEM

TO BYPASSES

MEMORY

ITEM
:
ITEM

RECALLABLE
FRAMES

Fig. 24.

could be stored away. Later, when evidence presented itself that the context represented by some frozen configuration was again likely to be present, the entire frozen chunk could be called in, its bypasses being implanted *en-masse* throughout the system of networks. This would cause a more sudden, discontinuous leap in the system's awareness of context, with a concomitant,

sense algorithm system, goals can be expressed as WANTs of states and statechanges. As such, an expected goal will be essentially a pointer, with suitable variable instantiations, to the top of what is implicitly an *extremely large structure in the memory* . . . that is, a pointer to the top of some causal selection network which explicitly ends in abstract algorithm approaches, but which *implicitly* extends deep into other causal selection networks via the various subgoals and recommendations mentioned in the various abstract algorithms at its bottom. If a prediction component can identify the *tops* of some networks as being actors' likely goals, then it has effectively identified an *entire realm* of things those actors might do to realize those goals, namely, those abstract algorithms at the bottom of the network, all the abstract algorithms at the *bottoms* of the networks involved as subgoals within each of the first level of approaches, and so forth. "Implicit" is a very important word here; rather than having to make thousands of *explicit* expectancies, we gain *implicit* access to them by pointing at the top of some network.

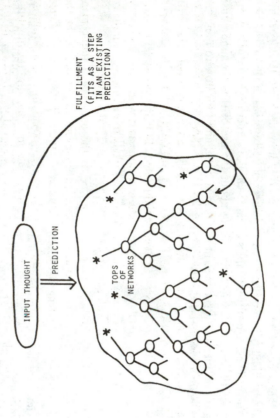

FIG. 28.

Now, suppose we have at each moment some collection of such predicted WANTs (Fig. 28). Then, the essence of the language comprehension reflex will be to identify how each subsequent thought fits into one of these implicitly large structures as a step towards achieving some expected goal. If the system

---

Now, the job will be to define $C(T_1, \ldots, T_i)$, which will represent the *predictive* component of the theory, and $I(T_{i+1}, C(T_1, \ldots, T_i))$, which will represent the *fulfillment* component. For the sake of simplicity, let's restrict the problem to the case $C(T_1)$, where we want to discover $I(T_2, C(T_1))$. Examples of this task are shown in Fig. 27.

> GIVEN A CONTEXT $C(T_1, \ldots, T_I)$ WHICH HAS BEEN ESTABLISHED BY THOUGHTS $T_1, \ldots, T_I$, ELUCIDATE THE RELATIONSHIP BETWEEN THE NEXT THOUGHT, T_{I+1}, AND $C(T_1, \ldots, T_I)$. CALL THIS RELATIONSHIP THE INTERPRETATION, $I(T_{I+1}, C(T_1, \ldots, T_I))$, OF T_{I+1} IN THIS CONTEXT.

FIG. 26. Language comprehension.

SIMPLEST CASE: $I(T_2, C(T_1))$

1. A1 IVAN FELT THE FIRST DROPS OF RAIN.
   B1 IVAN DIVED UNDER THE BUS.
   A2 IVAN HEARD A THUD AND SAW OIL LEAKING.
   B2 IVAN DIVED UNDER THE BUS.
   A3 IVAN HEARD HIS ANGRY WIFE COMING.
   B3 IVAN DIVED UNDER THE BUS.
2. A1 ANNA WANTED PETER TO NOTICE HER.
   B1 ANNA PICKED UP A ROCK.
   A2 WHEN PETER SAW HER, HE STUCK OUT HIS TONGUE.
   B2 ANNA PICKED UP A(NOTHER) ROCK.
3. A PETE STOLE JAKE'S CATTLE.
   B JAKE SADDLED HIS HORSE.

FIG. 27. Examples of $I(T_2, C(T_1))$.

How should we proceed? Suppose we can use T_1 to generate some expectancies about the kinds of commonsense activities we might expect the various potential actors to engage in in the situation we are perceiving. If these expectancies can be kept "defocussed" enough to provide a good target for the processes which will search for subsequent relations between T_1 and T_2, yet well enough organized to make searching through them practical, we will have the basis for computing $I(T_2, C(T_1))$.

The commonsense algorithm memory organization I have been describing provides both the essential breadth, or defocussedness, of expectancies, *and* enough internal organization to make searching practical. Suppose, by an inference process, we can predict each potential actor's probable reactions in a given situation; in other words, that we can infer a set of likely goals each potential actor might wish to accomplish in the situation. In the common

can do this, then the relationship between the thought which gave rise to the expectancies and the thought which has been identified as a step toward achieving one of these expectancies will be that *upward path* through layers of abstract algorithm approaches and causal selection networks which connects the fulfilling thought to the expectancy-generating thought. This path will be the desired interpretation, $I(T,K)$, of thought T in the context K, where K, the language comprehension context, is conveniently defined to be the composite set of various actors' expected WANTs which have been inferred from the sequence of preceding thoughts.

This being the general outline for language comprehension, let me first describe how the set of expectancies arises from the incoming thoughts. For this purpose, there are two other types of networks in the system: *inducement networks* and *prediction networks* (Fig. 29). Structurally, these two varieties

of network are similar to the causal selection networks, in that they participate in the same bypass and context mechanisms, and in that they are organized around state, statechange, and additionally, *action* concepts in the system. Their differences lie in their use and in the types of information at their terminal nodes.

An inducement network's purpose is to determine of a given event or state those internal, psychological states that event or state could induce in a potential actor. In other words, inducement networks are designed to relate what a potential actor *experiences* to what he might *feel internally* in reaction to those experiences. For example (Fig. 29, left), if we take KISS as an action concept expressible in the system—not primitive, since it references an abstract algorithm—then there will be an inducement network whose job it is to infer the internal states the event AGENT W CAUSES ACTOR X TO KISS OBJECT Y might induce in INDUCEE Z, who is assumed to be aware of the event. Suppose then, some thought tells us that agent IVAN caused actor IVAN to perform the action (KISS IVAN NATASHA) while BORIS was watching. Then, by entering the KISS inducement network with INDUCEE = BORIS, AGENT = IVAN, X = IVAN and Y = NATASHA to discover how this kissing event might affect BORIS, the system might discover, as the result of asking relevant questions as it worked its way down the KISS inducement network, that BORIS is likely to experience an induced state of extreme jealousy toward IVAN as a result: (MFEEL BORIS JEALOUSY IVAN). So that what we find at the bottoms of inducement networks are sets of internal states which an event might induce in the INDUCEE. Of course, exactly *which* induced states, if any, are predicted will be a function of the answers to questions posed by the inducement network . . . questions which selectively probe relevant aspects of the situation. If, for example, the network discovers no emotional ties between BORIS and NATASHA, no induced states may be predicted at all. On the other hand, if we run the KISS inducement network with INDUCEE = IVAN, we would perhaps arrive at the induced state "Ivan is self-satisfied". And who knows what we would get from applying the network with INDUCEE = NATASHA!

So, the inducement networks provide a method for inferring how various conditions in some situation might affect a potential actor. The system will put these networks to use during comprehension as follows. As each new thought enters, the comprehender applies the appropriate inducement network to it, varying the INDUCEE over all known potential actors in order to discover possible induced states for each. In this case, if IVAN causes (KISS IVAN NATASHA), we will run the KISS network once for INDUCEE = IVAN, once for NATASHA, and once for BORIS, if these are the three known potential actors.

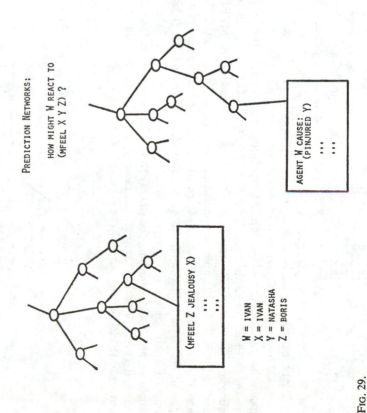

INDUCEMENT NETWORKS:

WHAT STATES MIGHT
AGENT W CAUSE (KISS X Y)
INDUCE IN Z ?

(MFEEL Z JEALOUSY X)
...
...

W = IVAN
X = IVAN
Y = NATASHA
Z = BORIS

PREDICTION NETWORKS:

HOW MIGHT W REACT TO
(MFEEL X Y Z) ?

AGENT W CAUSE:
(PINJURED Y)
...
...

FIG. 29.

If the inducement networks can thereby infer some induced states, these states will then serve as the input to the *prediction* networks (Fig. 29, right). It is the role of a prediction network to relate internal states of actors to goals they may be motivated to attempt as the result of being in those inferred states. Suppose, for example, the KISS inducement network decides that (MFEEL BORIS JEALOUSY IVAN) is likely. By applying the (MFEEL *X Y Z*) prediction network to this state, relevant questions will once again be posed to discover what, if any, *X*'s and *Z*'s responses might be, assuming again that each is aware of the MFEEL condition. For example, the section of the MFEEL prediction network dealing with JEALOUSY will ask questions about *X* and *Z*'s ages, social relationship, degree of the MFEEL, and so forth. If, for example, the prediction network discovers that BORIS and IVAN are school children, who are rivals and are off on some remote part of the playground away from teacher, then it might predict that BORIS might employ some sort of physical retaliation against IVAN . . . that he might set about accomplishing the state (PINJURED IVAN). On the other hand, if IVAN is BORIS' boss at the factory, some other reaction to the induced MFEEL would probably be expected.

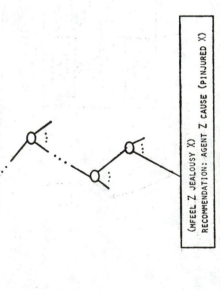

(MFEEL Z JEALOUSY X)
RECOMMENDATION: AGENT Z CAUSE (PINJURED X)

FIG. 30. Recommendations at bottoms of inducement and prediction networks.

As in the causal selection networks, we would like to have the mechanism for accumulating larger and larger stereotyped patterns at the bottoms of both the inducement and prediction networks. To illustrate, we may wish to obviate the application of the MFEEL prediction network by including as a *recommendation* in the KISS inducement set a direct reference to some sort of physical retaliation (Fig. 30). This would amount to saying that, in the *specific* context of an MFEEL JEALOUSY which has been caused by an

act of kissing where emotional relationships are involved, there may be a stereotyped reaction to the induced MFEEL JEALOUSY which is tightly attached to this inferred internal state. In other words, how one reacts to an induced state is often also dependent upon *how* that state arose. The recommendations allow the system to capture this dependency.

We have just been considering the manner in which the comprehender reacts to external thoughts as they arrive. In reality, all inducements and predictions generated internally are fed back into other appropriate networks in order to derive second-order and higher effects of the various inferences made by these networks. When, for example, the AGENT BORIS CAUSES (PINJURED IVAN) prediction arises, it can, being fed back into the PINJURED inducement net, give rise to expectancies about what IVAN might do in anticipation of this behavior on BORIS' part.

Now, let's return to the larger picture of the comprehender. As the sequence of thoughts arrives, each is processed via this inducement/prediction network sequence, which gives rise to a collection of likely goals all potential actors might possess. At this point, the prediction component has implicitly established contact with the tops of various causal selection networks (Fig. 31). As each new prediction is made, the comprehender will do one of two

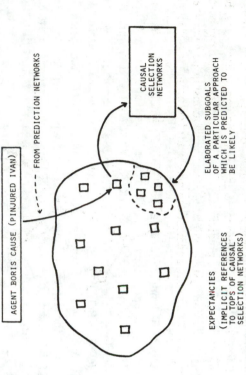

AGENT BORIS CAUSE (PINJURED IVAN)

FROM PREDICTION NETWORKS

CAUSAL
SELECTION
NETWORKS

EXPECTANCIES
(IMPLICIT REFERENCES
TO TOPS OF CAUSAL
SELECTION NETWORKS)

ELABORATED SUBGOALS
OF A PARTICULAR APPROACH
WHICH IS PREDICTED TO
BE LIKELY

FIG. 31. Continued forward elaboration of predictions via causal selection networks.

things: either stop the forward, predictive activity at that point, or go ahead and attempt to continue by predicting *how* the potential actor might actually attempt to realize his goal. That is, the prediction can be continued by applying the causal selection process to identify a likely approach. For example, if the system has reason to believe that BORIS will want to cause

IVAN to become PINJURED, it will attempt to continue the prediction by trying to guess how BORIS might go about the attack. Sometimes the environment will be constrained enough that such predictions are possible; other times, there will be no good basis for further prediction. In the latter case, the system will stop, finding that the majority of causal selection network questions being posed are not yet answerable.

Now let's look at the fulfillment side of the comprehender. In addition to being filtered through this prediction component, each input thought triggers a process of upward searching through layers of causal selection networks and abstract algorithm approaches at their bases (Fig. 32). Suppose, for

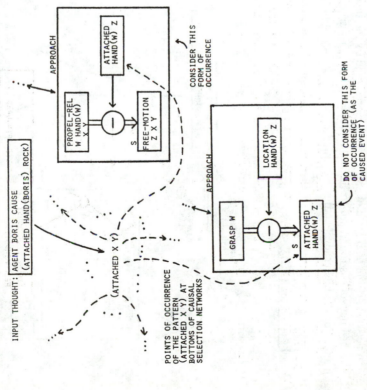

FIG. 32. Fulfillment: Locating points of occurrence of an activity throughout the causal selection networks.

example, we hear next, after this kissing incident, that BORIS grabbed a **rock**: BORIS CAUSE (ATTACHED HAND(BORIS) ROCK). First, the **system** locates all patterns in all abstract algorithms in the system which match this input pattern, preferring those matches which are most specific first. Locating all the occurrences of, say, an (ATTACHED X Y) pattern in the algorithmic base is possible in the system via a cross-indexing of each

concept's occurrence throughout the system. For the sake of illustration, suppose the searcher finds that the input thought matches (ATTACHED X Y) patterns at 25 points in various abstract algorithms at the bases of various causal selection networks. Then, each of these occurrences constitutes a place where the new thought could potentially fit as a step in some higher activity, hopefully one of the predicted activities from the prediction networks. Having identified these points of occurrence of the (ATTACHED X Y) pattern, the comprehender's goal becomes to search upward through the causal selection networks from these 25 points, hoping to encounter, before too long, some goal in the prediction set. If such an upward path can be found, the comprehension system will have found a relationship between the new thought and the context, and hence comprehended according to my definition.

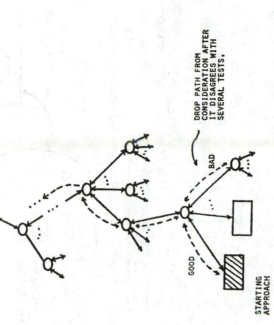

FIG. 33. Following an upward path from an approach to the top of a causal selection network.

This upward searching has the appearance of being a very time consuming operation. Indeed it would be without some means of deciding which of the 25 paths seem to be the most fruitful. But the structure of the causal selection networks offers a convenient means of doing just that. Let's consider what happens, starting from one of these 25 points of (ATTACHED X Y)'s occurrence in an abstract algorithm at the base of some causal selection network (Fig. 33). Abstract algorithms are backlinked to all points where they occur as the terminals of networks. Starting from each occurrence at the bottom of some network, the searcher works its way upward through the causal selection network one node at a time. At each node, the test stored at that node is posed. If the result of the test is such that, had the test been made by the problem solver during plan synthesis, it would have routed the system to the offspring node from which the searcher has just climbed in its upward search, then the search continues, retaining the path as still fruitful. If, on the other hand, the test would have routed the problem solver to some other alternative node at that point, then the path is considered less fruitful, and will eventually be dropped from consideration as an interpretation path after failing several causal network tests in this manner. Paths which survive this kind of reverse filtering eventually reach the top of the causal selection network. If the goal state or statechange represented by the successfully climbed network is found *not* to be in the prediction set, this process is begun anew for the higher level goal represented by the network just climbed

(Fig. 34); that is, occurrences of this newly-inferred higher level goal are located at the bottoms of yet other causal selection networks, and upward paths from each of those points sought. The process continues until a state or statechange in the set of predictions is reached, or until path length exceeds a cutoff value, indicating that, even if a path were to be discovered, it would be a rather remote interpretation. Path length is defined to be the number of causal selection networks passed through during the upward search.

Paths which survive this process will constitute possible interpretations of the new thought in the context of the preceding thoughts. In case there are several interpretations, the interpretation path finally preferred will be the shortest . . . that is, the one with the fewest subgoals intervening between the expectancy and the fulfillment. In case there are several shortest paths, the one which fared best during the application of the causal network tests on the upward search will be preferred.

Concerning the bypass mechanism's role during language comprehension, bypasses are not implanted until after the comprehender has obtained an interpretation path of which it is reasonably confident. Then, it reinforces that path by traversing it downward, distributing bypasses throughout the system from each test on the path. This amounts to *using* the interpretation path to infer pieces of the environmental context which were not known before; these can enhance the system's performance within that environment in the future. Also, as an interpretation path is found, the expectancy from which it has been derived is debunked from the set of expectancies and replaced by the more specific expectancies, if any, which represent those uncompleted steps in the abstract algorithm approach in which the fulfilling pattern occurred. Concerning recommendations throughout the causal selection network system, the upward searcher will prefer to follow a stereotyped recommendation rather than climb upward through a causal network.

5. Conclusion

I have described the essential character of the model. Let me now stimulate your various networks by reading a joke which I have been carrying around with me this last year. I promise to lay it to rest after this last reading:

A man was out shopping for groceries, pushing his three year old son around in the cart. As they passed by the oranges, the kid took a swipe and knocked over the whole pile. The father said "Cool it Oscar". As they walked passed the broom display, the kid yanked a handful of straws out of one of the brooms, in response to which the father again said levelheadedly "Cool it Oscar". On their way around the corner to the meat, the kid let loose an epithet he had wittingly absorbed from the family's conversation at the dinner table the evening before. To this, the father merely repeated calmly, "Cool it Oscar". Finally, as they were checking out, an elderly lady who had

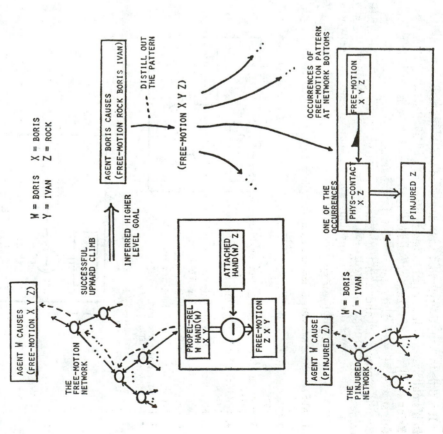

FIG. 34. Continuing upward path search through several networks.

been observing them remarked to the father that she greatly admired his restraint in dealing with his son. To that the father replied doggedly, "Lady, I'm Oscar".

It is time to stop. Everything I have described today has been implemented in a small system which can synthesize plans as well as discover $I(T_2,C(T_1))$. Being small, the system cannot handle complex plan synthesis or comprehend full stories yet. But I am happy with the model as a foundation for these cognitive processes, and with the underlying theory as an explanation of some aspects of human thought.

REFERENCES

1. Abelson, R. Frames for understanding social actions. Paper for Carbonell Conference 1974.

2. Charniak, E. A partial taxonomy of knowledge about actions. *Proc. 4IJCAI* (September 1975).

3. Fahlman, S. A planning system for robot construction tasks. M.I.T. AI–TR 283 (May 1973).

4. Goldstein, I. Understanding simple picture programs. M.I.T. AI–TR 294 (September 1974).

5. McDermott, D. Assimilation of new information by a natural language understanding system. M.I.T. AI–TR 291 (February 1974).

6. Minsky, M. A framework for representing knowledge. *The Psychology of Computer Vision*, Winston (ed.), McGraw-Hill, New York (1975).

7. Rieger, C. Conceptual overlays: A mechanism for the interpretation of sentence meaning in context. *Proc. 4IJCAI* (September 1975).

8. Rieger, C. The commonsense algorithm as a basis for computer models of human memory, inference, belief and contextual language comprehension. *Proc. Theoretical Issues in Natural Language Processing Workshop* (June 1975).

9. Schank, R. and Abelson, R. Scripts, plans and knowledge. *Proc. 4IJCAI* (September 1975).

10. Scragg, G. Answering process questions. *Proc. 4IJCAI* (September 1975).

11. Sussman, G. A computational model of skill acquisition. M.I.T. AI–TR 297 (August 1973).

12. Wilks, Y. Seven theses on Artificial Intelligence and natural languages. Working Paper 17, Fondazione Dalle Molle per gli Studi Linguistici e di Comunicazione Internazionale (1975).

Received October 1975; revised version received November 1975

30 / James F. Allen
Maintaining Knowledge about Temporal Intervals

The need to reason about time has turned out to be a recurring problem in many application domains, not only in Artificial Intelligence, but in many areas of Computer Science. Among the many possible ways of representing knowledge about time, Allen's scheme, described in this paper, has come to be accepted as a useful compromise between expressiveness and tractability [Levesque and Brachman, Chapter 4]. The approach Allen takes is to try to make the formalism reflect the way time is actually used in natural language. For example, to specify time knowledge that is vague or noncommittal, rather than using the usual logical operators over a set of atomic time assertions, the formalism expresses the uncertainty directly. In particular, events are labelled by time intervals of various sizes (rather than by time points), and, reflecting the fact that most of our temporal knowledge is relative, the time intervals can be related to each other by any of thirteen possible relationships. The main reasoning done by the system is to determine whether a new relationship between a pair of intervals is consistent with constraints existing among a set of intervals. While the given algorithm is efficient, it is incomplete, and what it actually *does* compute correctly is unfortunately left somewhat unclear. Time intervals can also be related to reference intervals which can be organized hierarchically and, on top of this, special mechanisms are provided for dealing with the present, as it moves inexorably forward. Of special interest here is the way *persistence* (that is, the fact that most of what is true remains true as time passes) is handled directly in terms of the interval mechanism.

Appeared in *Communications of the ACM* **26**(11), 1983, 832–843.

Artificial Intelligence and Language Processing

David Waltz Editor

Maintaining Knowledge about Temporal Intervals

JAMES F. ALLEN   The University of Rochester

James F. Allen's main interests are in artificial intelligence in particular natural language processing and the representation of knowledge.

Author's Present Address: James F. Allen, Computer Science Department, University of Rochester, Rochester, NY 14627.

The research described in this paper was supported in part by the National Science Foundation under Grants IST-80-12418 and IST-82-10564, and in part by the Office of Naval Research under Grant N00014-80-C-0197.

Permission to copy without fee all or part of this material is granted provided that the copies are not made or distributed for direct commercial advantage, the ACM copyright notice and the title of the publication and its date appear, and notice is given that copying is by permission of the Association for Computing Machinery. To copy otherwise, or to republish, requires a fee and/or specific permission. © 1983 ACM 0001-0782/83/1100-0832 75¢

1. INTRODUCTION

The problem of representing temporal knowledge and temporal reasoning arises in a wide range of disciplines, including computer science, philosophy, psychology, and linguistics. In computer science, it is a core problem of information systems, program verification, artificial intelligence, and other areas involving process modeling. (For a recent survey of work in temporal representation, see the special sections in the April 1982 issues of the ACM SIGART and SIGMOD Newsletters.)

Information systems, for example, must deal with the problem of outdated data. One approach to this is simply to delete outdated data; however, this eliminates the possibility of accessing any information except that which involves facts that are presently true. In order to consider queries such as, "Which employees worked for us last year and made over $15,000," we need to represent temporal information. In some applications, such as keeping medical records, the time course of events becomes a critical part of the data.

In artificial intelligence, models of problem solving require sophisticated world models that can capture change. In planning the activities of a robot, for instance, one must model the effects of the robot's actions on the world to ensure that a plan will be effective. In natural language processing, researchers are concerned with extracting and capturing temporal and tense information in sentences. This knowledge is necessary to be able to answer queries about the sentences later. Further progress in these areas requires more powerful representations of temporal knowledge than have previously been available.

This paper addresses the problem from the perspective of artificial intelligence. It describes a temporal representation that takes the notion of a *temporal interval* as primitive. It then describes a method of representing the relationships between temporal intervals in a hierarchical manner using constraint propagation techniques. By using *reference intervals*,

ABSTRACT: An interval-based temporal logic is introduced, together with a computationally effective reasoning algorithm based on constraint propagation. This system is notable in offering a delicate balance between expressive power and the efficiency of its deductive engine. A notion of reference intervals is introduced which captures the temporal hierarchy implicit in many domains, and which can be used to precisely control the amount of deduction performed automatically by the system. Examples are provided for a database containing historical data, a database used for modeling processes and process interaction, and a database for an interactive system where the present moment is continually being updated.

the amount of computation involved when adding a fact can be controlled in a predictable manner. This representation is designed explicitly to deal with the problem that much of our temporal knowledge is relative, and hence cannot be described by a date (or even a "fuzzy" date).

We start with a survey of current techniques for modeling time, and point out various problems that need to be addressed. After a discussion of the relative merits of interval-based systems versus point-based systems in Section 3, a simple interval-based deduction technique based on constraint propagation is introduced in Section 4. This scheme is then augmented in Section 5 with reference intervals, and examples in three different domains are presented. In the final sections of the paper, extensions to the basic system are proposed in some detail. These would extend the representation to include reasoning about the duration of intervals, reasoning about dates when they are available, and reasoning about the future given knowledge of what is true at the present.

The system as described in Section 5 has been implemented and is being used in a variety of research projects which are briefly described in Section 6. Of the extensions, the duration reasoner is fully implemented and incorporated into the system, whereas the date reasoner has been designed but not implemented.

2. BACKGROUND

Before we consider some previous approaches to temporal representation, let us summarize some important characteristics that are relevant to our work:

- The representation should allow significant imprecision. Much temporal knowledge is strictly relative (e.g., A is before B) and has little relation to absolute dates.
- The representation should allow uncertainty of information. Often, the exact relationship between two times is not known, but some contraints on how they could be related are known.
- The representation should allow one to vary the grain of reasoning. For example, when modeling knowledge of history, one may only need to consider time in terms of days, or even years. When modeling knowledge of computer design, one may need to consider times on the order of nanoseconds or less.
- The model should support *persistence*. It should facilitate default reasoning of the type, "If I parked my car in lot A this morning, it should still be there now," even though proof is not possible (the car may have been towed or stolen).

This does not exhaust all the issues, and others will come up as they become relevant. It provides us with a starting criteria, however, for examining previous approaches. Previous work can be divided roughly into four categories: state space approaches, date line systems, before/after chaining, and formal models.

State space approaches (e.g., [7, 17]) provide a crude sense of time that is useful in simple problem-solving tasks. A state is a description of the world (i.e., a database of facts) at an instantaneous point in time. Actions are modeled in such systems as functions mapping between states. For example, if an action occurs that causes P to become true and causes fact Q to be no longer true, its effect is simulated by simply adding fact P to the current state and deleting fact Q. If the previous states are retained, we have a representation of time as a series of databases describing the world in successive states. In general, however, it is too expensive to maintain all the pre-

vious states, so most systems only maintain the present state. While this technique is useful in some applications, it does not address many of the issues that concern us. Note that such systems do provide a notion of persistence, however. Once a fact is asserted, it remains true until it is explicitly deleted.

In datebase systems (e.g., [4, 5, 12, 13]), each fact is indexed by a *date*. A date is a representation of a time such that the temporal ordering between two dates can be computed by fairly simple operations. For example, we could use the integers as dates, and then temporal ordering could be computed using a simple numeric comparison. Of course, more complicated schemes based on calendar dates and times are typically more useful. Because of the nice computational properties, this is the approach of choice if one can assign dates for every event. Unfortunately, in the applications we are considering, this is not a valid assumption. Many events simply cannot be assigned a precise date. There are methods of generalizing this scheme to include ranges of dates in which the event must occur, but even this scheme cannot capture some relative temporal information. For instance, the fact that two events, A and B, did not happen at the same time cannot be represented using fuzzy dates for A and B. Either we must decide that A was before B, or B was before A, or we must assign date ranges that allow A and B to overlap. This problem becomes even more severe if we are dealing with time intervals rather than time points. We then need fuzzy date ranges for both ends of the interval plus a range for the minimum and maximum duration of the interval.

The next scheme is to represent temporal information using before/after chains. This approach allows us to capture relative temporal information quite directly. This technique has been used successfully in many systems (e.g., [4, 13]). As the amount of temporal information grows, however, it suffers from either difficult search problems (searching long chains) or space problems (if all possible relationships are precomputed). This problem can be alleviated somewhat by using a notion of reference intervals [13], which will be discussed in detail later. Note that a fact such as "events A and B are disjoint" cannot be captured in such systems unless disjunctions can be represented. The approach discussed in this paper can be viewed as an extension of this type of approach that overcomes many of its difficulties.

Finally, there is a wide range of work in formal models of time. The work in philosophy is excellently summarized in a textbook by Rescher and Urquhart [16]. Notable formal models in artificial intelligence include the situation calculus [14], which motivates much of the state space based work in problem solving, and the more recent work by McDermott [15]. In the situation calculus, knowledge is represented as a series of situations, each being a description of the world at an instantaneous point of time. Actions and events are functions from one situation to another. This theory is viable only in domains where only one event can occur at a time. Also, there is no concept of an event taking time; the transformation between the situations cannot be reasoned about or decomposed. The situation calculus has the reverse notion of persistence: a fact that is true at one instance needs to be explicitly reproven to be true at succeeding instants.

Most of the work in philosophy, and both the situation calculus and the work by McDermott, are essentially point-based theories. Time intervals can be constructed out of points, but points are the foundation of the reasoning system. This approach will be challenged in the upcoming section.

One other formal approach, currently under development, that is compatible with an interval-based temporal representation is found in the Naive Physics work of Hayes [10, 11]. He proposes the notion of a *history*, which is a contiguous block of space-time upon which reasoning can be organized. By viewing each temporal interval as one dimension of a history, this work can be seen as describing a reasoning mechanism for the temporal component of Naive Physics.

3. TIME POINTS VS. TIME INTERVALS

In English, we can refer to times as points or as intervals. Thus we can say the sentences:

> We found the letter at twelve noon.
> We found the letter yesterday.

In the first, "at twelve noon" appears to refer to a precise point in time at which the finding event occurred (or was occurring). In the second, "yesterday" refers to an interval in which the finding event occurred.

Of course, these two examples both refer to a date system where we are capable of some temporal precision. In general, though, the references to temporal relations in English are both implicit and vague. In particular, the majority of temporal references are implicitly introduced by tense and by the description of how events are related to other events. Thus we have

> We found the letter while John was away.
> We found the letter after we made the decision.

These sentences introduce temporal relations between the times (intervals) at which the events occurred. In the first sentence, the temporal connective "while" indicates that the time when the find event occurred is during the time when John was away. The tense indicates that John being away occurred in the past (i.e., before now).

Although some events appear to be instantaneous (e.g., one might argue that the event "finding the letter" is instantaneous), it also appears that such events could be decomposed if we examine them more closely. For example, the "finding the letter" might be composed of "looking at spot X where the letter was" and "realizing that it was the letter you were looking at." Similarly, we might further decompose the "realizing that it was the letter" into a series of inferences that the agent made. There seems to be a strong intuition that, given an event, we can always "turn up the magnification" and look at its structure. This has certainly been the experience so far in physics. Since the only times we consider will be times of events, it appears that we can always decompose times into subparts. Thus the formal notion of a time point, which would not be decomposable, is not useful. An informal notion of time points as very small intervals, however, can be useful and will be discussed later.

There are examples which provide counterintuitive results if we allow zero-width time points. For instance, consider the situation where a light is turned on. To describe the world changing we need to have an interval of time during which the light was off, followed by an interval during which it was on. The question arises as to whether these intervals are open or closed. If they are open, then there exists a time (point) between the two where the light is neither on nor off. Such a situation would provide serious semantic difficulties in a temporal logic. On the other hand, if intervals are closed, then there is a time point at which the light is both on and off. This presents even more semantic difficulties than the former case. One solution to this would be to adopt a convention that intervals are closed in their lower end and open on their upper end. The intervals could then meet as required, but each interval would have only one endpoint. The artificiality

of this solution merely emphasizes that a model of time based on points on the real line does not correspond to our intuitive notion of time. As a consequence, we shall develop a representation that takes temporal intervals as primitive.

If we allowed time points, intervals could be represented by modeling their endpoints (e.g., [4]) as follows: Assuming a model consisting of a fully ordered set of points of time, an interval is an ordered pair of points with the first point less than the second. We then can define the relations in Figure 1 between intervals, assuming for any interval t, the lesser endpoint is denoted by t− and the greater by t+.

We could implement intervals with this approach, even given the above argument about time points, as long as we assume for an interval t that t− < t+, and each assertion made is in a form corresponding to one of the interval relations. There are reasons why this is still inconvenient, however. In particular, the representation is too uniform and does not facilitate structuring the knowledge in a way which is convenient for typical temporal reasoning tasks. To see this, consider the importance of the *during* relation. Temporal knowledge is often of the form

> event E′ occurred during event E.

A key fact used in testing whether some condition P holds during an interval t is that if t is during an interval T, and P holds during T, then P holds during t. Thus *during* relationships can be used to define a hierarchy of intervals in which propositions can be "inherited."

Furthermore, such a *during* hierarchy allows reasoning processes to be localized so that irrelevant facts are never considered. For instance, if one is concerned with what is true "today," one need consider only those intervals that are during "today," or above "today" in the during hierarchy. If a fact is indexed by an interval wholly contained by an interval representing "yesterday," then it cannot affect what is true now. It is not clear how to take advantage of these properties using the point-based representation above.

4. MAINTAINING TEMPORAL RELATIONS

4.1. The Basic Algorithm

The inference technique described in this section is an attempt to characterize the inferences about time that appear to be made automatically or effortlessly during a dialogue, story comprehension, or simple problem-solving. Thus it should provide us with enough temporal reasoning to participate in these tasks. It does not, however, need to be able to account for arbitrarily complex chains of reasoning that could be done, say, when solving a puzzle involving time.

We saw above five relations that can hold between intervals. Further subdividing the *during* relation, however, pro-

Interval Relation	Equivalent Relations on Endpoints
t < s	t+ < s−
t = s	(t− = s−) & (t+ = s+)
t overlaps s	(t− < s−) & (t+ > s−) & (t+ < s+)
t meets s	t+ = s−
t during s	((t− > s−) & (t+ =< s+)) or ((t− >= s−) & (t+ < s+))

FIGURE 1. Interval Relation Defined by Endpoints.

vides a better computational model.[1] Considering the inverses of these relations, there are a total of thirteen ways in which an ordered pair of intervals can be related. These are shown in Figure 2.

Sometimes it is convenient to collapse the three *during* relations (d, s, f) into one relationship called *dur*, and the three *containment* relations (di, si, fi) into one relationship called *con*. After a quick inspection, it is easy to see that these thirteen relationships can be used to express any relationship that can hold between two intervals.

The relationships between intervals are maintained in a network where the nodes represent individual intervals. Each arc is labeled to indicate the possible relationship between the two intervals represented by its nodes. In cases where there is uncertainty about the relationship, all possible cases are entered on the arc. Note that since the thirteen possible relationships are mutually exclusive, there is no ambiguity in this notation. Figure 3 contains some examples of the notation. Throughout, let N_i be the node representing interval i. Notice that the third set of conditions describes disjoint intervals.

Throughout this paper, both the above notations will be used for the sake of readability. In general, if the arc asserts more than one possible relationship, the network form will be used, and in the case where only one relationship is possible, the relation form will be used.

For the present, we shall assume that the network always maintains complete information about how its intervals could be related. When a new interval relation is entered, all consequences are computed. This is done by computing the transitive closure of the temporal relations as follows: the new fact adds a constraint about how its two intervals could be related, which may in turn introduce new constraints between other intervals through the transitivity rules governing the temporal relationships. For instance, if the fact that i is *during* j is added, and j is *before* k, then it is inferred that i must be *before* k. This new fact is then added to the network in an identical fashion, possibly introducing further constraints on the relationship between other intervals. The transitivity relations are summarized in Figure 4.

The precise algorithm is as follows: assume for any temporal relation names r1 and r2 that T(r1, r2) is the entry in the transitivity table in Figure 4. Let R1 and R2 be arc labels, assume the usual set operations (∩ for intersection, ∪ for union, ⊂ for proper subset), and let ε be the empty set. Then *constraints* (R1, R2) is the transitivity function for lists of relation names (i.e., arc labels), and is defined by:

Constraints (R1, R2)
  $C \leftarrow \varepsilon$;
  For each r1 in R1
    For each r2 in R2
      $C \leftarrow C \cup T(r1, r2)$;
  Return C;

Assume we have a queue data structure named *ToDo* with the appropriate queue operations defined. For any two intervals i, j, let N(i, j) be the relations on the arc between i and j in the network, and let R(i, j) be the new relation between i and j to be added to the network. Then we have the following algorithm for updating the temporal network:

To **Add** R(i, j)
  Add ⟨i, j⟩ to queue *ToDo*;
  While *ToDo* is not empty **do**

---
[1] This fact was pointed out to me by Marc Vilain and was first utilized in his system [18].

Relation	Symbol	Symbol for Inverse	Pictoral Example
X *before* Y	<	>	XXX YYY
X *equal* Y	=	=	XXX YYY
X *meets* Y	m	mi	XXXYYY
X *overlaps* Y	o	oi	XXX YYY
X *during* Y	d	di	XXX YYYYYY
X *starts* Y	s	si	XXX YYYYY
X *finishes* Y	f	fi	XXX YYYYY

FIGURE 2. The Thirteen Possible Relationships.

Relation	Network Representation
1. i *during* j	N_i --(d)→ N_j

2. i *during* j or
    i *before* j or
    j *during* i
	N_i --(< d di)→ N_j

3. (i < j) or (i > j) or
    i *meets* j or
    j *meets* i
	N_i --(< > m mi)→ N_j

FIGURE 3. Representing Knowledge of Temporal Relations in a Network.

begin
  Get next ⟨i, j⟩ from queue *ToDo*;
  $N(i, j) \leftarrow R(i, j)$;
  For each node k such that Comparable(k, j) **do**
  begin
    $R(k, j) \leftarrow N(k, j) \cap$ Constraints$(N(k, i), R(i, j))$;
    If $R(k, i) \subset N(k, i)$
      then add ⟨k, i⟩ to *ToDo*;
  end
  For each node k such that Comparable(i, k) **do**
  begin
    $R(i, k) \leftarrow N(i, k) \cap$ Constraints$(R(i, j), N(j, k))$;
    If $R(i, k) \subset N(k, i)$
      then add ⟨i, k⟩ to *ToDo*;
  end
end;

We have used the predicate Comparable(i, j) above, which will be defined in Section 5. For the present, we can assume it always returns true for any pair of nodes.

4.2. An Example
Consider a simple example of this algorithm in operation. Assume we are given the facts:

  S *overlaps or meets* L

  S is *before, meets, is met by,* or *after* R.

B r2 C ／ A r1 B	<	>	d	di	o	oi	m	mi	s	si	f	fi
"before" <	<	no info	< o m d s	<	<	< o m d s	<	< o m d s	<	<	< o m d s	<
"after" >	no info	>	> oi mi d f	>	> oi mi d f	>	> oi mi d f	>	> oi mi d f	>	>	>
"during" d	<	>	d	no info	< o m d s	> oi mi d f	<	>	d	> oi mi d f	d	< o m d s
"contains" di	< o m di fi	> oi di mi si	o oi dur con =	di	o di fi	oi di si	o di fi	oi di si	di fi o	di	di si oi	di
"overlaps" o	<	> oi di mi si	o d s	< o m di fi	< o m	o oi dur con =	<	oi di si	o	di fi o	d s o	< o m
"overlapped-by" oi	< o m di fi	>	oi d f	> oi mi di si	o oi dur con =	>	o di fi	>	oi d f	oi > mi	oi	oi di si
"meets" m	<	> oi mi di si	o d s	<	<	o d s	<	f fi =	m	m	d s o	<
"met-by" mi	< o m di fi	>	oi d f	>	oi d f	>	s si =	>	d f oi	>	mi	mi
"starts" s	<	>	d	< o m di fi	< o m	oi d f	<	mi	s	s si =	d	< m o
"started by" si	< o m di fi	>	oi d f	di	o di fi	oi	o di fi	mi	s si =	si	oi	di
"finishes" f	<	>	d	> oi mi di si	o d s	> oi mi	m	>	d	> oi mi	f	f fi =
"finished-by" fi	<	> oi mi di si	o d s	di	o	oi di si	m	si oi di	o	di	f fi =	fi

FIGURE 4. The Transitivity Table for the Twelve Temporal Relations (omitting "=").

These facts might be derived from a story such as the following:

> John was not in the room when I touched the switch to turn on the light.

where we let S be the time of touching the switch, L be the time the light was on, and R be the time that John was in the room. The network storing this information is

$$R \leftarrow\text{-}(< \text{mmi} >)\text{-}\text{-} S \text{-}\text{-}(\text{om}) \rightarrow L.$$

When the second fact is added, the algorithm computes a constraint between L and R (via S) by calling the function *Constraints* with its two arguments, *R1* and *R2*, set to {oimi} and {(mmi)}, respectively. Note that we obtained the inverse of the arc from S to L simply by taking the inverse of each label. *Constraints* uses the transitivity table for each pair of labels and returns the union of all the answers. Since

$$T(\text{oi}, <) = (< \text{omdifi})$$
$$T(\text{oi}, m) = (\text{odifi})$$
$$T(\text{oi}, \text{mi}) = (>)$$
$$T(\text{oi}, >) = (>)$$
$$T(\text{mi}, <) = (< \text{omdifi})$$
$$T(\text{mi}, m) = (\text{ssi} =)$$
$$T(\text{mi}, \text{mi}) = (>)$$
$$T(\text{mi}, >) = (>)$$

we compute $(< > \text{omdi s sifi} =)$ as the constraint between L and R and thus obtain the network

$$R \leftarrow\text{-}(< \text{mmi} >)\text{-}\text{-} S \text{-}\text{-}(\text{om}) \rightarrow L$$
$$\uparrow \qquad\qquad\qquad |$$
$$\text{-}\text{-}\text{-}(< > \text{ooimdi s sifi} =)\text{-}\text{-}\text{-}\text{-}\text{-}$$

Let us consider what happens now when we add the fact

> L overlaps, starts, or is during R

This fact might arise from a continuation of the above story such as

> But John was in the room later while the light went out

Taking the intersection of this constraint with the previously known constraint between L and R to eliminate any impossible relationships gives

$$L \text{-}\text{-}(\text{os}) \rightarrow R$$

To add this constraint, we need to propagate its effects through the network. A new constraint between S and R can be calculated using the path:

$$S \text{-}\text{-}(\text{om}) \rightarrow L \text{-}\text{-}(\text{os}) \rightarrow R$$

From the transitivity tables, we find:

$$T(\text{o}, \text{o}) = (< \text{om})$$
$$T(\text{o}, \text{s}) = (\text{o})$$
$$T(\text{m}, \text{o}) = (<)$$
$$T(\text{m}, \text{s}) = (\text{m})$$

Thus the inferred constraint between S and R is

$$S \text{-}\text{-}(< \text{om}) \rightarrow R.$$

Intersecting this with our previous constraint between S and R yields

$$S \text{-}\text{-}(< m) \rightarrow R.$$

With respect to the example story, this is equivalent to inferring that John entered the room (i.e., R started) either after I touched the switch or at the same time that I finished touching the switch. Thus the new network is:

$$R \leftarrow\text{-}(< m)\text{-}\text{-} S \text{-}\text{-}(\text{om}) \rightarrow L$$
$$\uparrow \qquad\qquad\qquad |$$
$$\text{-}\text{-}\text{-}\text{-}\text{-}\text{-}\text{-}\text{-}\text{-}\text{-} (\text{o s}) \text{-}\text{-}\text{-}\text{-}\text{-}\text{-}\text{-}\text{-}$$

Of couse, if there were other nodes in the network, there would be other constraints derived from this new information. Thus, if we added a new interval D, say with the constraint D - -(d)→ S, we would infer the following new relationships as well:

$$D \text{-}\text{-}(<) \rightarrow R$$
$$D \text{-}\text{-}(< \text{o m d s}) \rightarrow L$$

4.3. Analysis

A nice property of this algorithm is that it only continues to operate as long as it is producing new further constrained relationships between intervals. Since there are at most thirteen possible relationships that could hold between two intervals, there are at most thirteen steps that could modify this relationship. Thus for a fixed number of nodes N, the upper limit on the number of modifications that can be made, irrespective of how many constraints are added to the network, is $13 \times$ the number of binary relations between N nodes, which is:

$$13 \times \frac{(N-1)(N-2)}{2}$$

Thus, in practice, if we add approximately the same number of constraints as we have nodes, the average amount of work for each addition is essentially linear (i.e., N additions take $O(N^2)$ time; one addition on average takes $O(N)$ time).

The major problem with this algorithm is the space requirement. It requires $O(N^2)$ space for N temporal intervals. Methods for controlling the propagation, saving time and space, will be discussed in the next section.

It should be noted that this algorithm, while it does not generate inconsistencies, does not detect all inconsistencies in its input. In fact, it only guarantees consistency between three node subnetworks. There are networks that can be added which appear consistent by viewing any three nodes, but for which there is no consistent overall labeling. The network shown in Figure 5 is consistent if we consider any three nodes; however, there is no overall labeling of the network.[2] To see this, if we assign the relationship between A and C, which could be f or fi according to this network, to either f alone, or fi alone, we would arrive at an inconsistency. In other words, there is no consistent labeling with A - -(f)→ C, or with A - -(fi)→ C, even though the algorithm accepts A - -(f fi)→ C.

To ensure total consistency, one would have to consider constraints between three arcs, between four arcs, etc. While this can be done using techniques outlined in Freuder [9], the computational complexity of the algorithm is exponential. In practice, we have not encountered problems from this deficiency in our applications of the model. We can verify the consistency of any subnetwork, if desired, by a simple backtracking search through the alternative arc labelings until we

---

[2] This network is due to Henry Kautz, personal communication.

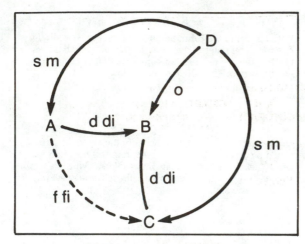

FIGURE 5. An Inconsistent Labeling.

arrive at a labeling for the whole subnetwork in which every arc has only one label.

5. CONTROLLING PROPAGATION: REFERENCE INTERVALS

In order to reduce the space requirements of the representation without greatly affecting the inferential power of the mechanism, we introduce *reference intervals*. Formally, a reference interval is simply another interval in the system, but it is endowed with a special property that affects the computation. Reference intervals are used to group together clusters of intervals for which the temporal constraints between each pair of intervals in the cluster is fully computed. Such a cluster is related to the rest of the intervals in the system only indirectly via the reference interval.

5.1. Using Reference Intervals

Every interval may designate one or more reference intervals (i.e., node clusters to which it belongs). These will be listed in parentheses after the interval name. Thus the node names

$$I1(R1)$$

$$I2(R1, R2)$$

describe an interval named I1 that has a reference interval R1, and an interval named I2 that has two reference intervals R1 and R2. Since I2 has two reference intervals, it will be fully connected to two clusters. An illustration of the connectedness of such a network is formed in Figure 6.

The algorithm to add relations using reference intervals is identical to the previous addition algorithm except that the comparability condition is no longer universally true. For any node N, let *Refs*(N) return the set of reference intervals for N. For any two nodes K and J, *Comparable*(K, J) is true if

1) *Refs*(K) ∩ *Refs*(J) is not null, that is, they share a reference interval; or
2) K ε *Refs*(J); or
3) J ε *Refs*(K).

Since reference intervals are simply intervals themselves, they may in turn have their own reference intervals, possibly defining a hierarchy of clusters. In most of the useful applications that we have seen, these hierarchies are typically tree-like, as depicted in Figure 7.

If two intervals are not explicitly related in the network, a relationship can be retrieved by finding a path between them through the reference intervals by searching up the reference hierarchy until a path (or all paths) between the two nodes are found. Then, by simply applying the transitivity relationships along the path, a relationship between the two nodes can be inferred. If one is careful about structuring the reference hierarchy, this can be done with little loss of information from the original complete propagation scheme.

To find a relationship between two nodes I and J, where N(i, j) represents the network relation between nodes i and j as in Section 4.1, we use the algorithm:

If N(I, J) exists
then return N(I, J)
else do
    Paths := Find-Paths(I, J)
    For each *path* **in** *Paths* do
      R := *R* ∩ *Constrain-along-path*(path)
    return *R*;
end;

The function *Find-Paths* does a straightforward graph search for a path between the two nodes with the restriction that each step of the path must be between a node and one of its reference intervals except for the one case where a direct connection is found. Thus, a path is of the general form

$$n_1, n_2, \ldots, n_k, n_{k+1}, \ldots, n_m$$

where all of the following hold:

-- for all i from 1 to $k - 1$, n_{i+1} is a reference interval for n_i;
-- n_k and n_{k+1} are connected explicitly;
-- for all i from $k + 1$ to $m - 1$, n_i is a reference interval for n_{i+1};

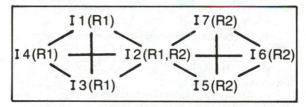

FIGURE 6. The Connectness of a Network with Two Reference Intervals.

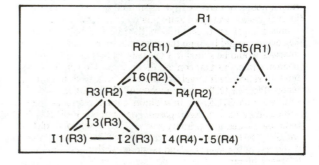

FIGURE 7. A Tree-Like Hierarchy Based on Reference Intervals.

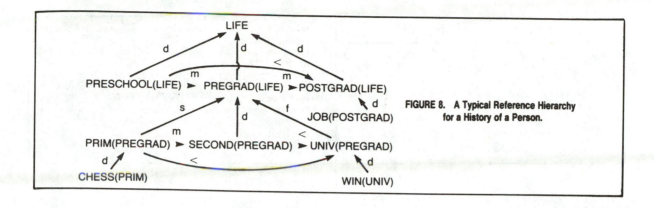

FIGURE 8. A Typical Reference Hierarchy for a History of a Person.

The function *Constrain-along-path* simply takes a path and computes the transitivity constraints along it. Thus if a path consisted of the nodes $n_1, n_2, n_3, \ldots, n_m$, we compute the relation between n_1 and n_m as follows:

$$R := N(n_1, n_2)$$

$$R := Constraints(R, N(n_2, n_3))$$

$$R := Constraints(R, N(n_3, n_4))$$

$$\ldots$$

$$R := Constraints(R, N(n_{m-1}, n_m))$$

where *Constraints* was defined in Section 4.1.

5.2. Examples

There are no restrictions imposed by the system on the use of reference intervals. Their organization is left up to the system designer. Certain principles of organization, however, are particularly useful in designing systems that remain efficient in retrieval, and yet capture the required knowledge. The most obvious of these is a consequence of the path search algorithm in the previous section: the more tree-like the reference hierarchy, the more efficient the retrieval process. The others considered in this section exploit characteristics of the temporal knowledge being stored.

With domains that capture historical information, it is best to choose the reference intervals to correspond to key events that naturally divide the facts in the domain. Thus, if modeling facts about the history of a particular person, key events might be their birth, their first going to school, their graduation from university, etc. Kahn and Gorry [13] introduced such a notion of reference events in their system. Other times in their system were explicitly related to these reference events (i.e., points). In our system, the intervals between such key events would become the reference intervals. Other time intervals would be stored in the cluster(s) identified by the reference intervals that contain them. Thus, we could have a series of reference intervals for the time from birth to starting school (PRESCHOOL), during school (PREGRAD), and after graduation (POSTGRAD). In addition, certain reference intervals could be further decomposed. For example, PREGRAD could be divided into primary and secondary school (PRIM and SECOND) and the time at university (UNIV). The times of the rest of the events would be stored with respect to this reference hierarchy. Figure 8 depicts this set of facts including its reference hierarchy, plus intervals such as the time spent

learning chess (CHESS), the time the person won the state lottery (WIN), and the time of the first job (JOB). If an event extended over two reference intervals, then it would be stored with respect to both. For example, if learning to play chess occurred during primary and secondary school, the interval CHESS would have two reference intervals, namely, PRIM and SECOND.

We can now trace the retrieval algorithm for this set of facts. Let us find the relationship between CHESS and WIN. There is no explicit relationship between the intervals, so we must search up the reference hierarchy. Only one path is found, namely:

CHESS(PRIM) - -(d)→ PRIM(PREGRAD) - -(<)→

UNIV(PREGRAD) - -(di)→ WIN(UNIV)

Applying the transitivity relations along the first path, we infer first that

CHESS *before* UNIV

and then

CHESS *before* WIN.

The fact that CHESS is *before* JOB can be inferred similarly from the path

CHESS - -(d)→ PRIM - -(s)→ PREGRAD - -(m)→

POSTGRAD - -(di)→ JOB.

Consider another domain, namely, that of representing information about processes or actions. Such knowledge is required for problem-solving systems that are used to guide the activity of a robot. Each process can be described as a partial sequence of subprocesses. Such a decomposition is not described in absolute temporal terms (i.e., using dates), but by the subprocess's relation to its containing process. Thus a natural reference hierarchy can be constructed mirroring the process hierarchy. For example, consider a process P consisting of a sequence of steps P1, P2, and P3 and another process Q consisting of subprocesses Q1 and Q2 occurring in any order, but not at the same time. Furthermore, let Q2 be decomposed into two subprocesses Q21 and Q22, each occurring simultaneously. To simulate a world in which process P begins before Q begins, we can construct the reference hierarchy in Figure 9. With this organization we can infer relationships between subprocesses of Q and subprocesses of P in the same manner as above. As long as the decomposition of

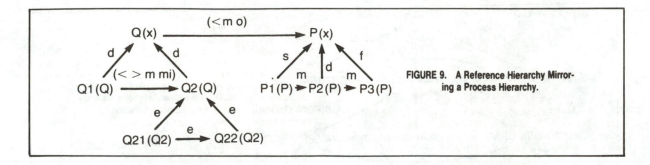

FIGURE 9. A Reference Hierarchy Mirroring a Process Hierarchy.

processes or actions can be done independently (such as in the NOAH system [17]), this organization will capture all the relevant temporal knowledge.

More interesting cases arise when there may be interactions among subprocesses. For instance, we might want to add that Q1 must occur before Q21. Note that, in adding Q1 *before* Q21, we can infer a new relationship between Q1 and Q2 from the path

$$Q1(Q) - -(<) \rightarrow Q21(Q2) - -(e) \rightarrow Q2(Q)$$

because Q1 and Q2 share the reference interval Q. It does not matter that Q21 does not share a reference interval with Q1. In more complicated cases, we will find relationships between subprocesses such that an important relationship between the processes containing the subprocesses will not be inferred because they do not share a reference interval. For instance, if we learn that Q2 overlaps P1, adding this will not cause the relationship between Q and P to be constrained to simply the *overlaps* relation even though that would be a consequence in the system without reference intervals. There is no path consisting of two arcs from Q to P that is affected by adding Q2 *overlaps* P1.

To allow this inference, we need to reorganize the reference hierarchy. For example, we could, when adding a relation between two noncompatible nodes, expand one of the node's reference intervals with the other node's reference intervals. In this scheme, to add Q2 *overlaps* P1, we would first add P to Q2's reference interval list. Then adding the relation will allow the appropriate changes. In particular, among others, we would infer that

$$Q2(Q, P) - -(o) \rightarrow P(X)$$

from the path

$$Q2(Q, P) - -(o) \rightarrow P1(P) - -(s) \rightarrow P(X),$$

and then infer

$$Q(X) - -(o) \rightarrow P(X)$$

from the path

$$Q(X) - -(di) \rightarrow Q2(Q, P) - -(o) \rightarrow P(X)$$

and the previous constraints between Q and P. The final state of the processes after these two additions is summarized in Figure 10.

Manipulating the reference hierarchies as in this example can be effective if used sparingly. With overuse, such tricks tend to "flatten out" the reference hierarchy as more intervals become explicitly related. In domains where such interactions are rare compared with the pure decompositional interactions, it can be very effective.

5.3. Representing the Present Moment

The technique of reference interval hierarchies provides a simple solution to the problem of representing the present moment. In many applications, such as natural language processing and process modeling, the present is constantly moving into the future. Thus a representation of *NOW* must allow for frequent updating without involving large-scale reorganization of the database each time.

Suppose we have a database in which all assertions are indexed by the temporal interval over which they hold. As time passes, we are interested in monitoring what is true at the present time, as well as in the past and future. The method suggested here is to represent *NOW* as a variable that, at any specific time, is bound to an interval in the database. To update *NOW*, we simply reassign the variable to a new interval that is *after* the previous interval representing the present moment. The key observation is that while the present is continually changing, most of the world description is remaining the same. We can exploit this fact by using refer-

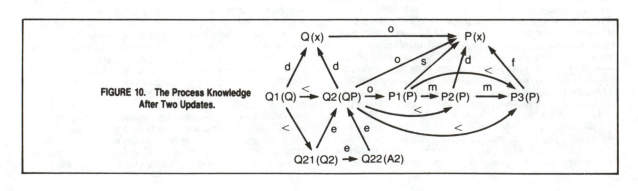

FIGURE 10. The Process Knowledge After Two Updates.

ence intervals to control the inferences resulting from updating *NOW*.

For example, let *NOW* be interval N1, which is *during* its reference interval R1. An example state of the database would be

N1(R1) *during* R1

R1 *before* I1, R1 *after* I2, R1 *during* I3

From this we can infer easily that the present (i.e., N1) is during I3, before I1, and after I2. If *NOW* then is updated (slightly), N2 can be defined as the new *NOW* using the same reference interval by adding the facts

N2(R1) *during* R1, N2(R1) *after* N1(R1)

Thus, *NOW* has been updated but most of the relations in the database have been unaffected, for the effects of N2 will only propagate to intervals referenced by R1. The reference interval R1 has "protected" the rest of the database from a minor change in the present moment.

Of course, eventually *NOW* will cease to be during R1 and a new reference interval will be needed. This will involve a more major update to the database, but the amount of work can be reduced if R1 itself has a reference interval that "protects" much of the database from it.

Thus we need a hierarchy of reference intervals, each containing the present moment. This hierarchy could be designed to mirror the set of English terms that can be used to refer to the present. For example, in English we can refer to the exact moment of an utterance (e.g., at a race, the starter may say "Go now!"), as well as to larger intervals such as "this morning," "today," and "this year." We can also refer to more event-oriented intervals such as "during this lecture" and "while at this bar." These are the types of intervals that should be maintained in the hierarchy representing the present. Furthermore, these intervals typically have well defined starting and termination points. Thus it is reasonable to assume that the temporal database will receive explicit notification when one of them ceases to contain the present. This allows the following important assumption:

When updating the *NOW* interval, unless otherwise stated, its relationship to its reference interval(s) remains constant.

When one of the reference intervals in the hierarchy ceases to contain the present moment, a new reference interval is selected. (This new interval should usually be provided by the user.) This update is done in the identical fashion as described above with *NOW*. In particular, the relationship with the higher-level reference interval remains constant. A new *NOW* interval, below the new reference interval in the hierarchy, must be introduced. For example, the beginning of a new day would make much of the old hierarchy part of the past (i.e., "yesterday").

While many intervals will be generated by this succession of intervals for *NOW*, many of them can be garbage collected when the reference intervals are updated. In particular, any interval that is not used to index any events or facts may be removed from the database. In a system modeling a natural language dialogue, a large number of these intervals would be used only to index the time of an utterance: These generally can be deleted without harm.

6. DISCUSSION

The temporal representation described is notable in that it is both expressive and computationally feasible. In particular, it does not insist that all events occur in a known fixed order, as

in the state space approach, and its allows disjunctive knowledge, such as that event A occurred either before or after event B, not expressible in date-based systems or simple systems based on before/after chaining. It is not as expressive as a full temporal logic (such as that of McDermott [15]), but these systems do not currently have viable implementations.

This balance between expressive power and computational efficiency is achieved by the restricted form of disjunctions allowed in the system. One can only assert disjunctive information about the relationship of two intervals. In other words, we can assert that A is *before* or *meets* B, but not that (A *meets* B) or (C *before* D). This limited form of disjunction is ideal for the constraint propagation algorithm.

The system has been implemented and is being used in a variety of applications. Both FRANZ LISP [8] and INTERLISP versions are running on a VAX 11/780 under UNIX. The system presently also includes the duration reasoner described below. It is currently being used in research in representing actions, events, and interactions that arise in natural language dialogues [1]. We are also using the representation as a world model for research in automatic problem-solving systems [3]. Such systems have long been constrained by their inadequate temporal models.

Vilain [18] has implemented a version of this system which, at the cost of greater space requirements, can perform consistency maintenance. In other words, in his system, when an inconsistency is found, the set of facts that caused the inconsistency can be identified. This system also explicitly allows time points in the representation and has a larger transitivity table, including all interval/point and point/point interactions. This violates the semantics of the interval representation, and so has not been adopted in our present system.

Let us consider why we would like time points, however. They seem to be referred to in English. We can, for instance, talk about the beginning and ending of events. There is no reason to assume, however, that these "endpoints" are truly zero-width points rather than intervals small enough so that they appear to be instantaneous. What this suggests is that there might be a minimum duration ε, such that all intervals of duration less than ε would be viewed as points. This would simplify our reasoning about such times for we would not have to worry about the possibility of two such intervals overlapping. It would be assumed either that these small intervals are equal or that one is before the other.

But this minimum size cannot be fixed in advance. A historian, for instance, may be happy to consider days as points, whereas the computer engineer, when reasoning about a logic circuit, would consider a day to be an eternity. Thus the interval size, where it is appropriate to simplify reasoning by assuming point-like times, varies with the reasoning task.

7. FUTURE RESEARCH AND EXTENSIONS

There are many areas in which this system is being extended. In particular, an interface to a *duration reasoner* has been incorporated into the system, and a system for reasoning about dates will be implemented in the near future. Finally, we are investigating reasoning systems that depend on the notion of persistence.

7.1. Duration Reasoning

We have designed a duration reasoning system based on the same principles as the interval relation reasoner described above. In particular, it is designed to allow relative information (e.g., interval A took longer than interval B) as well as representing uncertainty. The reasoner is again based on constraint propagation and a notion of reference durations can be defined.

Very briefly, the duration relationship between two intervals is expressed by outlining a range that includes the multiplicative factor which the duration of the first would be multiplied by to get the duration of the second. For example, the fact that the duration of A is less than the duration of B, expressed as $dur(A) < dur(B)$, is represented by the relation $A - -(0(1)) \rightarrow B$. In other words, $dur(A) >= 0*dur(B)$ and $dur(A) < 1*dur(B)$. The parentheses about the factor 1 indicate an open endpoint; thus the durations of A and B could not be equal. Both the upper and lower duration limits may be open or closed.

Duration information is encoded in a network orthogonal to the relationship network. Propagation across two duration restrictions is accomplished simply by multiplying the respective upper and lower duration limits. For example, if we have the facts

$$dur(A) <= dur(B)$$

$$dur(C) <= dur(B)$$

$$dur(B) < 2*dur(C)$$

which in network form would be

$$A - -(01) \rightarrow B - -(1(2)) \rightarrow C$$

we derive the relation

$$A - -(0(2)) \rightarrow C.$$

The duration reasoner and the interval reasoner are not independent of each other, however. They constrain each other by rules such as the following:

$$\text{If } I - -(dsf) \rightarrow J \quad \text{then} \quad dur(I) < dur(J).$$

Using this rule, constraints introduced in one network may introduce constraints in the other. In many examples, the networks may exchange information back and forth multiple times before the propagation terminates.

Reference durations correspond to the notion of scales, or common units. Constraints do not propagate through a reference duration. Thus, if the duration HOUR is a reference duration, and we add that $dur(A)$ is between 1 and 2 hours, and $dur(B)$ is less than one half an hour, no relation between $dur(A)$ and $dur(B)$ will be inferred. It will be derived at retrieval time via the reference duration HOUR. Further details on the duration reasoner can be found in [2].

7.2. Date Lines

Having considered the maintenance of relative temporal information in detail, we now consider how to exploit date information when available. Let a *date line* be any representation consisting of a fully ordered set of values taken to correspond to times. A date line corresponding to a simple calendar could be defined as follows:

values: ordered triples of integers, representing year, month (1–12), and day (1–31) (for example, (50 3 25) represents March 25, 1950)
comparison operation: orders triples in the obvious manner (for example, (50 3 25) < (75 1 1))

With date lines, the comparison operation between two times on the same date line is relatively inexpensive compared to searching the network of temporal relations.

Date line information could be incorporated into the present system by allowing any interval in the network to have date line information associated with it which identifies the dating system and dates associated with its start and end. The name of the date line is necessary to identify the operations for comparing values. A new interval, added with date line information specified, may affect the relationship to its reference interval and to the other intervals in its "reference class." For example, if two intervals are dated by the same date line, and have date values specified, those values can be used to calculate the exact relation between the intervals. If this relation is more specific than the information stored in the relational network, the network is updated and its effects propagated as usual.

When retrieving a relationship between two intervals dated by the same date line, the date information should be considered first before applying the usual network retrieval mechanism. Sometimes, however, the date line information will not be specific enough to pinpoint a specific relationship, and a network search will still be necessary. It may occur that one of the intervals being considered is dated but the other is not. In this case, the date information may be used only if a relationship can be found between the nondated interval and another interval dated by the same date line. In general, this may be too expensive to consider. A specific case that could be very useful, however, occurs when a reference interval involved in the search is dated by the appropriate date line. We can then compare the two dated intervals to obtain a relationship, which can be propagated back to the nondated interval.

A useful date line for dialogue systems is the time-of-day line. A reasonable implementation of this might have the basic duration of one minute, and have values consisting of an hour-minute pair. If the system were given access to a clock, this date line could be used extensively in the NOW hierarchy. Of course, the relative time database is still required to store the facts that are acquired during the dialogue as facts typically hold for much longer than the time that they are being talked about.

If the system does not have such easy access to an internal clock, it may still get time-of-day information occasionally during a dialogue. In this case, some of the NOW intervals will map onto the time-of-day line, while others will only be related to it by some relation (e.g., after 10 o'clock). In such a scheme, a new reference interval for the NOW interval would be created each time a precise time-of-day value was identified. For example, if the system learns that it is presently 10 o'clock, it can create an "after 10 o'clock" reference interval in which the NOW intervals will be contained until the next specific time is acquired. Whether such a technique is feasible requires further search.

7.3. Persistence of Intervals

The last requirement described in the introduction was that the representation should facilitate plausible inferences of the form "if fact P is true now, it will remain true until noticed otherwise." Most of the issues concerning this fall outside the range of this paper, as this system only knows about time intervals. However, a simple trick using this representation makes inferences of the above form easy to implement.

Typically, when a new fact is learned, its exact extent in time is not known. For instance, when I parked by car in the parking lot this morning I knew its location. Sitting at my desk now, I assume it is still there, though I have no proof of that fact. In general, I assume it will remain where it is until I pick it up. Thus, although I do not know the extent of the interval in which my car is parked, I want to be able to assume that this fact holds later in the day. The temporal representation is already based on the observation that most time intervals do not have precisely defined limits. If we allow the user to specify that some intervals should be assumed to extend as far as possible given the constraints, then we can use such intervals to index facts that are assumed to persist until discovered otherwise.

Thus, if we let a fact P be indexed by a *persistent interval* Tp, then testing P later during an interval t will succeed (by assumption) if it is possible that t is *during* Tp. Checking whether relationships between intervals are possible is easy, since the representation explicitly maintains this information.

For example, let Tp represent the interval in which my car is in the parking lot. I know that Tp is *met by* Tarrive, where Tarrive is the time that I arrived at school today. Then, if *NOW* is represented as interval Tnow, where Tnow *after* Tarrive, we can test if my car is on the parking lot. Since it is there during Tp, we are interested in whether it is possible that Tnow is *during* Tp. The known constraints allow us to infer the following:

Tp *met by* Tarrive, Tarrive *before* Tnow

$$\Rightarrow \text{Tp} \ \text{-} \ \text{-}(< \text{odi m}) \rightarrow \text{Tnow}$$

Thus it is possible that Tnow is *during* Tp, since it is possible that Tp contains ("di") Tnow. So the test succeeds.

Of course, if it is later learned that the car was found to be missing during time interval Tmiss, then Tp is constrained to be *before* Tmiss (even though it is still persistent). If Tnow is then after or during Tmiss, then it is not possible any longer that Tnow is during Tp.

Managing a system such as this is a difficult problem that requires some form of truth maintenance (e.g., see [6]). These issues, however, are independent of the temporal representation. All that is shown here is that the necessary temporal calculations are easily done within this framework.

An interesting technique suggested by the above may simplify much of the computation required for truth maintenance for this type of assumption. In particular, let us assume that P holds during interval Tp, where Tp is a persistent interval. Furthermore, assume that for any time, P implies Q. Then if we test P at time t, and find it is true by assumption, so we can infer Q during time t. However, if we index Q by Tp rather than by t, then we still can use the fact that Q is true during t (by assumption), but if we ever discover further constraints on Tp that then eliminate the possibility that t is during Tp, then both P *and* Q will cease to be true (by assumption) during t. Thus, by indexing all the consequences of P by the same interval, Tp, we can revise our beliefs about P and all its consequences simply by adding constraints about Tp. While this idea obviously requires further investigation, it appears that it may allow a large class of assumption-based belief revision to be performed easily.

8. SUMMARY

We have described a system for reasoning about temporal intervals that is both expressive and computationally effective. The representation captures the temporal hierarchy implicit in many domains by using a hierarchy of reference intervals, which precisely control the amount of deduction performed automatically by the system. This approach is par-

tially useful in domains where temporal information is imprecise and relative, and techniques such as dating are not possible.

Acknowledgments. Many people have provided significant help during the design and development of this work. In particular, I would like to thank Marc Vilain and Henry Kautz for work on developing and extending the system. I have also received many valuable criticisms from Alan Frisch, Pat Hayes, Hans Koomen, Drew McDermott, Candy Sidner, and the referees. Finally, I would like to thank Peggy Meeker for preparing the manuscript, and Irene Allen and Henry Kautz for the valuable editorial criticism on the final draft.

REFERENCES

1. Allen, J. F., Frisch, A. M., and Litman, D. J. ARGOT: The Rochester dialogue system, Proc. Nat. Conf. on Artificial Intelligence. AAAI 82, Pittsburgh, Pa., Aug. 1982.
2. Allen, J. F., and Kautz, H. A. "A model of naive temporal reasoning," to appear in J. R. Hobbs and R. Moore (Ed.), *Contributions in Artificial Intelligence, Vol. 1*, Ablex Pub. Co., Norwood, N.J., 1983.
3. Allen, J. F., and Koomen, J. A. Planning using a temporal world model. Submitted to 8th Int. Joint Conf. Artificial Intelligence, Aug. 1983.
4. Bruce, B. C. A model for temporal references and its application in a question answering program. *Artificial Intelligence 3* (1972), 1–25.
5. Bubenko, J. A., Jr. Information modeling in the context of system development. Proc. IFIP Congress 80, Oct. 1980, North-Holland, Amsterdam.
6. Doyle, J. A truth maintenance system. *Artificial Intelligence 12*, 3, (Nov. 1979), 231–272.
7. Fikes, R. E., and Nilsson, N. J. STRIPS: A new approach to the application of theorem proving to problem solving. *Artificial Intelligence 2*, (1971), 189–205.
8. Foderaro, J. K. *The FRANZ LISP Manual*. Dept. of Computer Science, U. of California, Berkeley, 1980.
9. Freuder, E. C. A sufficient condition for backtrack-free search. *J. ACM 29*, 1 (Jan. 1982), 24–32.
10. Hayes, P. J. The Naive Physics manifesto. In *Expert Systems*, D. Michie (Ed.), Edinburgh U. Press, 1979.
11. Hayes, P. J. Naive Physics I: Ontology for liquids. Working Paper 63, Institut pour les Etudes Semantiques et Cognitives, Geneva, 1978.
12. Hendrix, G. G. Modeling simultaneous actions and continuous processes. *Artificial Intelligence 4*, 3 (1973), 145–180.
13. Kahn, K. M., and Gorry, A. G. Mechanizing temporal knowledge. *Artificial Intelligence 9*, 2 (1977), 87–108.
14. McCarthy, J., and Hayes, P. Some philosophical problems from the standpoint of artificial intelligence. *Machine Intelligence 4*, Edinburgh U. Press, 1969.
15. McDermott, D. A temporal logic for reasoning about processes and plans. *Cognitive Science 6*, (1982), 101–155.
16. Rescher, N., and Urquhart, A. *Temporal Logic*. Springer-Verlag, New York, 1971.
17. Sacerdoti, E. D. *A Structure for Plans and Behavior*. Elsevier North-Holland, New York, 1977.
18. Vilain, M. A system for reasoning about time. Proc. AAAI 82, Pittsburgh, Pa., Aug. 1982.

CR Categories and Subject Descriptors: I.2.4 [Knowledge Representation Formalisms and Methods]: Representations—time, temporal representation; I.2.3 [Deduction and Theorem Proving]: Deduction—constraint propagation, temporal reasoning; H.3.3 [Information Search and Retrieval]: Clustering, Retrieval Methods
General Terms: Algorithms
Additional Key Words and Phrases: temporal interval, interval reasoning, interval representation.

Received 12/81; revised 3/83; accepted 5/83

31 / John McCarthy
First Order Theories of Individual Concepts and Propositions

This paper presents informally a theory of concepts and propositions in the language of a first-order logic and illustrates its use in representing modalities such as knowledge and necessity. It is thus an application of a representation language to a particular domain, and might be regarded as evidence for the expressive adequacy of first-order logic even for domains that seem to require more. This is certainly to be contrasted with the position of Maida and Shapiro [Chapter 9], who are interested in roughly the same subject matter, but build special features directly into a new representation scheme to deal with it. In presenting this subject matter, McCarthy touches on some of the puzzles in intensionality and opacity that have troubled philosophers of language for some time. An example is how it is possible for the telephone numbers of Mike and Mary to be one and the same, and yet have different properties, in that Pat may know one but not the other. Indeed, standard first-order logics with equality sanction the substitution of equals for equals in any sentence. McCarthy shows how this property can be preserved and yet still allow the phone number of Mike but not Mary to be known. On the other hand, the paper is at best a sketch of a solution. Very little is nailed down with any conviction, and examples substitute for analysis, a serious flaw given the work of Montague and others (acknowledged by McCarthy), apparently proving the inconsistency of this approach to modalities.

Appeared in *Machine Intelligence 9,* 129–147, edited by J. E. Hayes, D. Michie, and L. I. Mikulich, Chichester, England: Ellis Horwood, Ltd., 1979.

First Order Theories of Individual Concepts and Propositions

J. McCarthy
Computer Science Department
Stanford University, USA

Abstract

We discuss first order theories in which *individual concepts* are admitted as mathematical objects along with the things that *reify* them. This allows very straightforward formalizations of knowledge, belief, wanting, and necessity in ordinary first order logic without modal operators. Applications are given in philosophy and in artificial intelligence. We do not treat general concepts, and we do not present any full axiomatizations but rather show how various facts can be expressed.

INTRODUCTION

"... *it seems that hardly anybody proposes to use different variables for propositions and for truth-values, or different variables for individuals and individual concepts.*" – (Carnap 1956, p. 113).

Admitting individual concepts as objects – with concept-valued constants, variables, functions and expressions – allows ordinary first order theories of necessity, knowledge, belief and wanting without modal operators or quotation marks and without the restrictions on substituting equals for equals that either device makes necessary.

In this paper we will show how various individual concepts and propositions can be expressed. We are not yet ready to present a full collection of axioms. Moreover, our purpose is not to explicate what concepts are, in a philosophical sense, but rather to develop a language of concepts for representing facts about knowledge, belief, etc. in the memory of a computer.

Frege (1892) discussed the need to distinguish direct and indirect use of words. According to one interpretation of Frege's ideas, the meaning of the phrase "*Mike's telephone number*" in the sentence "*Pat knows Mike's telephone number*" is the concept of Mike's telephone number, whereas its meaning in the sentence "*Pat dialled Mike's telephone number*" is the number itself. Thus if

we also have "*Mary's telephone number = Mike's telephone number*", then "*Pat dialled Mary's telephone number*" follows, but "*Pat knows Mary's telephone number*" does not.

It was further proposed that a phrase has a *sense* which is a *concept* and is its *meaning* in *oblique contexts* like knowing and wanting, and a *denotation* which is its *meaning* in *direct contexts* like dialling. *Denotations* are the basis of the semantics of first order logic and model theory and are well understood, but *sense* has given more trouble, and the modal treatment of oblique contexts avoids the idea. On the other hand, logicians such as Carnap (1947 and 1956), Church (1951) and Montague (1974) see a need for *concepts* and have proposed formalizations. All these formalizations involve modifying the logic used; ours doesn't modify the logic and is more powerful, because it includes mappings from objects to concepts. Robert Moore's forthcoming dissertation also uses concepts in first order logic.

The problem identified by Frege – of suitably limiting the application of the substitutivity of equals for equals – arises in artificial intelligence as well as in philosophy and linguistics for any system that must represent information about beliefs, knowledge, desires, or logical necessity – regardless of whether the representation is declarative or procedural (as in PLANNER and other AI formalisms).

Our approach involves treating concepts as one kind of object in an ordinary first order theory. We shall have one term that denotes Mike's telephone number and a different term denoting the concept of Mike's telephone number instead of having a single term whose denotation is the number and whose sense is a concept of it. The relations among concepts and between concepts and other entities are expressed by formulas of first order logic. Ordinary model theory can then be used to study what spaces of concepts satisfy various sets of axioms.

We treat primarily what Carnap calls *individual concepts* like *Mike's telephone number* or *Pegasus* and not general concepts like *telephone* or *unicorn*. Extension to general concepts seems feasible, but individual concepts provide enough food for thought for the present.

This is a preliminary paper in that we don't give a comprehensive set of axioms for concepts. Instead we merely translate some English sentences into our formalism to give an idea of the possibilities.

KNOWING WHAT AND KNOWING THAT

To assert that Pat knows Mike's telephone number we write

$$true \; Know(Pat, Telephone \; Mike) \tag{1}$$

with the following conventions:

1. Parentheses are often omitted for one argument functions and predicates. This purely syntactic convention is not important. Another convention is to capitalize the first letter of a constant, variable, or function name

when its value is a concept. (We considered also capitalizing the last letter when the arguments are concepts, but it made the formulas ugly.)

2. *Mike* is the concept of Mike; that is, it is the *sense* of the expression "*Mike*". *mike* is Mike himself.

3. *Telephone* is a function that takes a concept of a person into a concept of his telephone number. We will also use *telephone* which takes the person himself into the telephone number itself. We do not propose to identify the function *Telephone* with the general concept of a person's telephone number.

4. If P is a person concept and X is another concept, then $Know(P, X)$ is an assertion concept or *proposition* meaning that P *knows* the value of X. Thus in (1) $Know(Pat, Telephone\ Mike)$ is a proposition and not a truth value. Note that we are formalizing *knowing what* rather than *knowing that* or *knowing how*. For AI and for other practical purposes, *knowing what* seems to be the most useful notion of the three. In English, *knowing what* is written *knowing whether* when the "knowand" is a proposition.

5. It is often convenient to write $know(pat, Telephone\ Mike)$ instead of $true\ Know(Pat, Telephone\ Mike)$ when we don't intend to iterate knowledge further. *know* is a predicate in the logic, so we cannot apply any knowledge operators to it. We will have

$$know(pat, Telephone\ Mike) \equiv true\ Know(Pat, Telephone\ Mike). \quad (2)$$

6. We expect that the proposition $Know(Pat, Telephone\ Mike)$ will be useful accompanied by axioms that allow inferring that Pat will use this knowledge under appropriate circumstances, that is, he will dial it or retell it when appropriate. There will also be axioms asserting that he will know it after being told it or looking it up in the telephone book.

7. While the sentence "*Pat knows Mike*" is in common use, it is harder to see how $Know(Pat, Mike)$ is to be used and axiomatized. I suspect that new methods will be required to treat knowing a person.

8. *true Q* is the truth value, t or f, of the proposition Q, and we must write *true Q* in order to assert Q. Later we will consider formalisms in which *true* has a another argument – a *situation*, a *story*, a *possible world*, or even a *partial possible world* (a notion we suspect will eventually be found necessary).

9. The formulas are in a sorted first order logic with functions and equality. Knowledge, necessity, etc. will be discussed without extending the logic in any way – solely by the introduction of predicate and function symbols subject to suitable axioms. In the present informal treatment, we will not be explicit about sorts, but we will use different letters for variables of different sorts.

The reader may be nervous about what is meant by *concept*. He will have to remain nervous; no final commitment will be made in this paper. The formalism is compatible with many possibilities, and these can be compared by using the models of their first order theories. Actually, this paper isn't much motivated by the philosophical question of what concepts really are. The goal is more to make a formal structure that can be used to represent facts about knowledge and belief so that a computer program can reason about who has what knowledge in order to solve problems. From either the philosophical or the AI point of view, however, if (1) is to be reasonable, it must not follow from (1) and the fact that Mary's telephone number is the same as Mike's, that Pat knows Mary's telephone number.

The proposition that Joe knows *whether* Pat knows Mike's telephone number, is written

$$Know(Joe, Know(Pat, Telephone\ Mike)), \quad (3)$$

and asserting it requires writing

$$true\ Know(Joe, Know(Pat, Telephone\ Mike)), \quad (4)$$

while the proposition that Joe knows *that* Pat knows Mike's telephone number is written

$$K(Joe, Know(Pat, Telephone\ Mike)), \quad (5)$$

where $K(P, Q)$ is the proposition that P knows *that* Q. English does not treat knowing a proposition and knowing an individual concept uniformly: knowing an individual concept means knowing its value, while knowing a proposition means knowing that it has a particular value, namely t. There is no reason to impose this infirmity on robots.

We first consider systems in which corresponding to each concept X, there is a thing x of which X is a concept. Then there is a function *denot* such that

$$x = denot\ X. \quad (6)$$

Functions like $Telephone$ are then related to *denot* by equations like

$$\forall P1\ P2.(denot\ P1 = denot\ P2 \supset denot\ Telephone\ P1 = denot\ Telephone\ P2). \quad (7)$$

We call *denot* X the *denotation* of the concept X, and (7) asserts that the denotation of the concept of P's telephone number depends only on the denotation of the concept P. The variables in (7) range over concepts of persons, and we regard (7) as asserting that $Telephone$ is *extensional* with respect to *denot*. Note that our *denot* operates on concepts rather than on expressions; a theory of expressions will also need a denotation function. From (7) and suitable logical axioms follows the existence of a function *telephone* satisfying

$$\forall P.(denot\ Telephone\ P = telephone\ denot\ P). \quad (8)$$

Know is extensional with respect to *denot* in its first argument, and this is expressed by

$$\forall P1\,P2\,X.(denot\,P1 = denot\,P2 \supset denot\,Know(P1,X) = denot\,Know(P2,X)),\tag{9}$$

but it is not extensional in its second argument. We can therefore define a predicate *know(p, X)* satisfying

$$\forall P\,X.(true\,Know(P,X) \equiv know(denot\,P,X)).\tag{10}$$

(Note that all these predicates and functions are entirely extensional in the underlying logic, and the notion of extensionality presented here is relative to *denot*.)

The predicate *true* and the function *denot* are related by

$$\forall Q.(true\,Q \equiv (denot\,Q = t))\tag{11}$$

provided that truth values are in the range of *denot*, and *denot* could also be provided with a (partial) *possible world* argument.

When we don't assume that all concepts have denotations, we use a predicate *denotes(X, x)* instead of a function. The extensionality of *Telephone* would then be written

$$\forall P1\,P2\,x\,u.(denotes(P1,x) \land denotes(P2,x) \land denotes(Telephone\,P1,u) \supset denotes(Telephone\,P2,u)).\tag{12}$$

We now introduce the function *Exists* satisfying

$$\forall X.(true\,Exists\,X \equiv \exists x.denotes(X,x)).\tag{13}$$

Suppose we want to assert that Pegasus is a horse without asserting that Pegasus exists. We can do this by introducing the predicate *Ishorse* and writing

$$true\,Ishorse\,Pegasus\tag{14}$$

which is related to the predicate *ishorse* by

$$\forall X\,x.(denotes(X,x) \supset (ishorse\,x \equiv true\,Ishorse\,X)).\tag{15}$$

In this way, we assert extensionality without assuming that all concepts have denotations. *Exists* is extensional in this sense, but the corresponding predicate *exists* is identically true and therefore dispensable.

To combine concepts propositionally, we need analogs of the propositional operators such as *And*, which we shall write as an infix and axiomatize by

$$\forall Q1\,Q2.(true(Q1\,And\,Q2) \equiv true\,Q1 \land true\,Q2).\tag{16}$$

The corresponding formulas for *Or, Not, Implies*, and *Equiv* are

$$\forall Q1\,Q2.(true(Q1\,Or\,Q2) \equiv true\,Q1 \lor true\,Q2),\tag{17}$$

$$\forall Q1\,Q2.(true(Q1\,Implies\,Q2) \equiv true\,Q1 \supset true\,Q2),\tag{19}$$

and

$$\forall Q1\,Q2.(true(Q1\,Equiv\,Q2) \equiv (true\,Q1 \equiv true\,Q2)).\tag{20}$$

The equality symbol "=" is part of the logic so that $X = Y$ asserts that X and Y are the same concept. To write propositions expressing equality, we introduce *Equal(X, Y)* which is a proposition that X and Y denote the same thing if anything. We shall want axioms

$$\forall X\,true\,Equal(X,X),\tag{21}$$

$$\forall X\,Y.(true\,Equal(X,Y) \equiv true\,Equal(Y,X)),\tag{22}$$

and

$$\forall X\,Y\,Z.(true\,Equal(X,Y) \land true\,Equal(Y,Z) \supset true\,Equal(X,Z))\tag{23}$$

making *true Equal(X, Y)* an equivalence relation, and

$$\forall X\,Y\,x.(true\,Equal(X,Y) \land denotes(X,x) \supset denotes(Y,x))\tag{24}$$

which relates it to equality in the logic. We can make the concept of equality *essentially* symmetric by replacing (22) by

$$\forall X\,Y.\,Equal(X,Y) = Equal(Y,X),\tag{25}$$

that is, making the two expressions denote the *same concept*.

The statement that Mary has the same telephone number as Mike is asserted by

$$true\,Equal(Telephone\,Mary,\,Telephone\,Mike),\tag{26}$$

and it obviously doesn't follow from this and (1) that

$$true\,Know(Pat,\,Telephone\,Mary).\tag{27}$$

To draw this conclusion we need something like

$$true\,K(Pat,\,Equal(Telephone\,Mary,\,Telephone\,Mike))\tag{28}$$

and suitable axioms about knowledge.

If we were to adopt the convention that a proposition appearing at the outer level of a sentence is asserted and were to regard the denotation-valued function as standing for the sense-valued function when it appears as the second argument of *Know*, we would have a notation that resembles ordinary language in handling obliquity entirely by context. There is no guarantee that general statements could be expressed unambiguously without circumlocution; the fact that the principles of intensional reasoning haven't yet been stated is evidence

FUNCTIONS FROM THINGS TO CONCEPTS OF THEM

While the relation $denotes(X, x)$ between concepts and things is many-one, functions going from things to certain concepts of them seem useful. Some things such as numbers can be regarded as having *standard* concepts. Suppose that $Concept1\ n$ gives a standard concept of the number n, so that

$$\forall n.(denot\ Concept1\ n = n). \tag{29}$$

We can then have simultaneously

$$true\ Not\ Knew(Kepler, Composite\ Number\ Planets) \tag{30}$$

and

$$true\ Knew(Kepler, Composite\ Concept1\ denot\ Number\ Planets). \tag{31}$$

(We have used *Knew* instead of *Know*, because we are not now concerned with formalizing tense.)

(31) can be condensed using $Composite1$ which takes a number into the proposition that it is composite, that is,

$$Composite1\ n = Composite\ Concept1\ n \tag{32}$$

getting

$$true\ Knew(Kepler, Composite1\ denot\ Number\ Planets). \tag{33}$$

A further condensation can be achieved by using $Composite2$ defined by

$$Composite2\ N = Composite\ Concept1\ denot\ N,$$

letting us write

$$true\ Knew(Kepler, Composite2\ Number\ Planets), \tag{34}$$

which is true even though

$$true\ Knew(Kepler, Composite2\ Number\ Planets) \tag{35}$$

$$true\ Knew(Kepler, Composite\ Number\ Planets) \tag{36}$$

is false. (36) is our formal expression of "*Kepler knew that the number of planets is composite*", while (31), (33), and (35) each expresses a proposition that can only be stated awkwardly in English, for example, as "*Kepler knew that a certain number is composite, where this number (perhaps unbeknownst to Kepler) is the number of planets*".

We may also want a map from things to concepts of them in order to formalize a sentence like, "*Lassie knows the location of all her puppies*". We write

$$\forall x.(ispuppy(x, lassie) \supset$$
$$true\ Knowd(Lassie, Locationd\ Conceptd\ x)). \tag{37}$$

Here *Conceptd* takes a puppy into a dog's concept of it, and *Locationd* takes a dog's concept of a puppy into a dog's concept of its location. The axioms

satisfied by $Knowd$, $Locationd$ and $Conceptd$ can be tailored to our ideas of what dogs know.

A suitable collection of functions from things to concepts might permit a language that omitted some individual concepts like *Mike* (replacing it with *Conceptx mike*) and wrote many sentences with quantifiers over things rather than over concepts. However, it is still premature to apply Occam's razor. It may be possible to avoid concepts as objects in expressing particular facts but impossible to avoid them in stating general principles.

RELATIONS BETWEEN KNOWING WHAT AND KNOWING THAT

As mentioned before, "*Pat knows Mike's telephone number*" is written

$$true\ Know(Pat, Telephone\ Mike). \tag{38}$$

We can write "*Pat knows Mike's telephone number is 333-3333*"

$$true\ K(Pat, Equal(Telephone\ Mike, Concept1\ "333-3333")) \tag{39}$$

where $K(P, Q)$ is the proposition that $denot(P)$ knows the proposition Q and $Concept1$ ("333-3333") is some standard concept of that telephone number.

The two ways of expressing knowledge are somewhat interdefinable, since we can write

$$K(P, Q) = (Q\ And\ Know(P, Q)), \tag{40}$$

and

$$true\ Know(P, X) \equiv \exists A.(constant\ A \wedge true\ K(P, Equal(X, A))). \tag{41}$$

Here *constant* A asserts that A is a constant, that is, a concept such that we are willing to say that P knows X if he knows it equals A. This is clear enough for some domains like integers, but it is not obvious how to treat knowing a person. Using the *standard concept* function $Concept1$, we might replace (41) by

$$true\ Know(P, X) \equiv \exists a.true\ K(P, Equal(X, Concept1\ a)) \tag{42}$$

with similar meaning.

(41) and (42) expresses a *denotational* definition of *Know* in terms of K. A *conceptual* definition seems to require something like

$$\forall P\ X.(Know(P, X) =$$
$$Exists\ X\ And\ K(P, Equal(X, Concept2\ denot\ X))), \tag{43}$$

where $Concept2$ is a suitable function from things to concepts and may not be available for all sorts of objects.

REPLACING MODAL OPERATORS BY MODAL FUNCTIONS

Using concepts we can translate the content of modal logic into ordinary logic. We need only replace the modal operators by *modal functions*. The axioms of modal logic then translate into ordinary first order axioms. In this section we will treat only *unquantified modal logic*. The arguments of the modal functions will not involve quantification, although quantification occurs in the outer logic.

Nec Q is the proposition that the proposition *Q* is necessary, and *Poss Q* is the proposition that it is possible. To assert necessity or possibility we must write *true Nec Q* or *true Poss Q*. This can be abbreviated by defining *nec Q* ≡ *true Nec Q* and *poss Q* correspondingly. However, since *nec* is a predicate in the logic with *t* and *f* as values, *nec* cannot be an argument of *nec* or *Nec*.

Before we even get to modal logic proper we have a decision to make — shall *Not Not Q* be considered the same proposition as *Q*, or is it merely extensionally equivalent? The first is written

$$\forall Q.\, Not\ Not\ Q = Q. \tag{44}$$

and the second

$$\forall Q.\, true\ Not\ Not\ Q \equiv true\ Q. \tag{45}$$

The second follows from the first by substitution of equals for equals.

In *Meaning and Necessity*, Carnap takes what amounts to the first alternative, regarding concepts as L-equivalence classes of expressions. This works nicely for discussing necessity, but when he wants to discuss knowledge without assuming that everyone knows Fermat's last theorem if it is true, he introduces the notion of *intensional isomorphism* and has knowledge operate on the equivalence classes of this relation.

If we choose the first alternative, then we may go on to identify any two propositions that can be transformed into each other by Boolean identities. This can be assured by a small collection of propositional identities like (44) including associative and distributive laws for conjunction and disjunction, De Morgan's law, and the laws governing the propositions *T* and *F*. In the second alternative we will want the extensional forms of the same laws. When we get to quantification a similar choice will arise, but if we choose the first alternative, it will be undecidable whether two expressions denote the same concept. I doubt that considerations of linguistic usage or usefulness in AI will unequivocally recommend one alternative, so both will have to be studied.

Actually there are more than two alternatives. Let *M* be the free algebra built up from the "atomic" concepts by the concept forming function symbols. If ≡≡ is an equivalence relation on *M* such that

$$\forall X1\ X2 \in M((X1 \equiv\equiv X2) \supset (true\ X1 \equiv true\ X2)), \tag{46}$$

then the set of equivalence classes under ≡≡ may be taken as the set of concepts. Similar possibilities arise in modal logic. We can choose between the *conceptual identity*

$$\forall Q.(Poss\ Q = Not\ Nec\ Not\ Q), \tag{47}$$

and the weaker extensional axiom

We will write the rest of our modal axioms in extensional form. We have

$$\forall Q.(true\ Nec\ Q \supset true\ Q), \tag{49}$$

and

$$\forall Q1\ Q2.$$
$$(true\ Nec\ Q1 \wedge true\ Nec(Q1\ Implies\ Q2) \supset true\ Nec\ Q2). \tag{50}$$

yielding a system equivalent to von Wright's T.

S4 is given by

$$\forall Q.(true\ Nec\ Q \equiv true\ Nec\ Nec\ Q), \tag{51}$$

and S5 by

$$\forall Q.(true\ Poss\ Q \equiv true\ Nec\ Poss\ Q). \tag{52}$$

Actually, there may be no need to commit ourselves to a particular modal system. We can simultaneously have the functions *NecT*, *Nec4* and *Nec5*, related by axioms such as

$$\forall Q.(true\ Nec4\ Q \supset true\ Nec5\ Q) \tag{53}$$

which would seem plausible if we regard S4 as corresponding to provability in some system and S5 as truth in the intended model of the system. Presumably we shall want to relate necessity and equality by the axiom

$$\forall X.\, true\ Nec\ Equal(X, X). \tag{54}$$

Certain of Carnap's proposals translate to the stronger relation

$$\forall X\ Y.(X=Y \equiv true\ Nec\ Equal(X, Y)) \tag{55}$$

which asserts that two concepts are the same if and only if the equality of what they may denote is necessary.

MORE PHILOSOPHICAL EXAMPLES – MOSTLY WELL KNOWN

Some sentences that recur as examples in the philosophical literature will be expressed in our notation, so the treatments can be compared.

First we have "*The number of planets = 9*" and "*Necessarily 9 = 9*" from which one doesn't want to deduce "*Necessarily the number of planets = 9*". This example is discussed by Quine (1961) and (Kaplan 1969). Consider the sentences

$$\neg nec\ Equal(Number\ Planets, Concept1\ 9) \tag{56}$$

and

$$nec\ Equal(Concept1\ number\ planets, Concept1\ 9). \tag{57}$$

Both are true. (56) asserts that it is not necessary that the number of planets be

that is necessarily equal to 9. It is a major virtue of our formalism that both meanings can be expressed and are readily distinguished. Substitutivity of equals holds in the logic but causes no trouble, because "*The number of planets = 9*" may be written

$$number(planets) = 9 \tag{58}$$

or, using concepts as

$$true\ Equal(Number\ Planets, Concept1\ 9), \tag{59}$$

and "*Necessarily 9=9*" is written

$$nec\ Equal(Concept1\ 9, Concept1\ 9), \tag{60}$$

and these don't yield the unwanted conclusion.

Ryle used the sentences "*Baldwin is a statesman*" and "*Pickwick is a fiction*" to illustrate that parallel sentence construction does not always give parallel sense. The first can be rendered in four ways, namely *true Statesman Baldwin* or *statesman denot Baldwin* or *statesman baldwin* or *statesman1 Baldwin* where the last asserts that the concept of Baldwin is one of a statesman. The second can be rendered only as *true Fiction Pickwick* or *fiction1 Pickwick*. Quine (1961) considers illegitimate the sentence

$$(\exists x)(Philip\ is\ unaware\ that\ x\ denounced\ Catiline) \tag{61}$$

obtained from "*Philip is unaware that Tully denounced Catiline*" by existential generalization. In the example, we are also supposing the truth of *Philip is aware that Cicero denounced Catiline*. These sentences are related to (perhaps even explicated by) several sentences in our system. *Tully* and *Cicero* are taken as distinct concepts. The person is called *tully* or *cicero* in our language, and we have

$$tully = cicero, \tag{62}$$

$$denot\ Tully = cicero \tag{63}$$

and

$$denot\ Cicero = cicero. \tag{64}$$

We can discuss Philip's concept of the person Tully by introducing a function $Concept2(p1, p2)$ giving for some persons $p1$ and $p2$, $p1$'s concept of $p2$. Such a function need not be unique or always defined, but in the present case, some of our information may be conveniently expressed by

$$Concept2(philip, tully) = Cicero, \tag{65}$$

asserting that Philip's concept of the person Cicero is *Cicero*. The basic assumptions of Quine's example also include

$$true\ K(Philip, Denounced(Cicero, Catiline)) \tag{66}$$

and

$$\neg true\ K(Philip, Denounced(Tully, Catiline)). \tag{67}$$

From (63), . . . (67) we can deduce

$$\exists P.true\ Denounced(P, Catiline)\ And\ Not\ K(Philip, Denounced(P, Catiline)), \tag{68}$$

from (67) and others, and

$$\neg\exists p.(denounced(p, catiline) \land \\ \neg true\ K(Philip, Denounced(Concept2(philip, p), Catiline))) \tag{69}$$

using the additional hypotheses

$$\forall p.(denounced(p, catiline) \supset p = cicero), \tag{70}$$

$$denot\ Catiline = catiline, \tag{71}$$

and

$$\forall P1\ P2.(denot\ Denounced(P1, P2) \equiv denounced(denot\ P1, denot\ P2)). \tag{72}$$

Presumably (68) is always true, because we can always construct a concept whose denotation is Cicero unbeknownst to Philip. The truth of (69) depends on Philip's knowing that someone denounced Catiline, and on the map $Concept2(p1, p2)$ that gives one person's concept of another. If we refrain from using a silly map that gives something like $Denouncer(Catiline)$ as its value, we can get results that correspond to intuition.

The following sentence attributed to Russell is discussed by Kaplan: "*I thought that your yacht was longer than it is*". We can write it

$$true\ Believed(I, Greater(Length\ Youryacht, \\ Concept1\ denot\ Length\ Youryacht)) \tag{73}$$

where we are not analysing the pronouns or the tense, but are using *denot* to get the actual length of the yacht and *Concept1* to get back a concept of this true length so as to end up with a proposition that the length of the yacht is greater than that number. This looks problematical, but if it is consistent, it is probably useful.

To express "*Your yacht is longer than Peter thinks it is*." we need the expression $Denot(Peter, X)$ giving a concept of what Peter thinks the value of X is. We now write

$$longer(youryacht, denot\ Denot(Peter, Length\ Youryacht)), \tag{74}$$

but I am not certain this is a correct translation.

Quine (1956) discusses an example in which Ralph sees Bernard J. Ortcutt skulking about and concludes that he is a spy, and also sees him on the beach, but doesn't recognize him as the same person. The facts can be expressed in our formalism by equations

$$true\ Believe(Ralph, Isspy\ P1) \tag{75}$$

and

$$true\ Believe(Ralph, Not\ Isspy\ P2) \tag{76}$$

where *P*1 and *P*2 are concepts satisfying *denot P1* = *orcutt* and *denot P2* = *orcutt*. *P*1 and *P*2 are further described by sentences relating them to the circumstances under which Ralph formed them.

We can still consider a simple sentence involving the persons as things — write it *believespy(ralph, orcutt)*, where we define

$$\forall p1\ p2.(believespy(p1,p2)) \equiv$$
$$true\ Believe(Concept1\ p1, Isspy\ Concept7\ p2) \tag{77}$$

using suitable mappings *Concept1* and *Concept7* from persons to concepts of persons. We might also choose to define *believespy* in such a way that it requires

true Believe(Concept1 p1, Isspy P) for several concepts *P* of *p*2, for example, the concepts arising from all of *p*1's encounters with *p*2 or his name. In this case *believespy(ralph, orcutt)* will be false and so would a corresponding *notbelievespy(ralph, orcutt)*. However, the simple-minded predicate *believespy*, suitably defined, may be quite useful for expressing the facts necessary to predict someone's behaviour in simpler circumstances.

Regarded as an attempt to explicate the sentence "*Ralph believes Orcutt is a spy*", the above may be considered rather tenuous. However, we are proposing it as a notation for expressing Ralph's beliefs about Orcutt so that correct conclusions may be drawn about Ralph's future actions. For this it seems to be adequate.

PROPOSITIONS EXPRESSING QUANTIFICATION

As the examples of the previous sections have shown, admitting concepts as objects and introducing standard concept functions makes "quantifying in" rather easy. However, forming propositions and individual concepts by quantification requires new ideas and additional formalism. We are not very confident of the approach presented here.

We want to continue describing concepts within first order logic with no logical extentions. Therefore, in order to form new concepts by quantification and description, we introduce functions *All*, *Exist*, and *The* such that *All(V,P)* is (approximately) the proposition that *for all values of VP is true*, *Exist(V,P)* is the corresponding existential proposition, and *The(V,P)* is the concept of *the V such that P*.

Since *All* is to be a function, *V* and *P* must be objects in the logic. However, *V* is semantically a variable in the formation of *All(V,P)*, *etc.*, and we will call such objects *inner variables* so as to distinguish them from variables in the logic. We will use *V*, sometimes with subscripts, for a logical variable ranging over inner variables. We also need some constant symbols for inner variables (got that?), and we will use doubled letters, sometimes with subscripts, for these. *XX* will be used for individual concepts, *PP* for persons, and *QQ* for propositions.

The second argument of *All* and friends is a "proposition with variables in it" but remember that these variables are inner variables which are constants

in the logic. Got that? We won't introduce a special term for them, but will generally allow concepts to include inner variables. Thus concepts now include inner variables like *XX* and *PP*, and concept-forming functions like *Telephone* and *Know* take the generalized concepts as arguments.

Thus

$$Child(Mike,PP)\ Implies\ Equal(Telephone\ PP, Telephone\ Mike) \tag{78}$$

is a proposition with the inner variable *PP* in it to the effect that if *PP* is a child of Mike, then his telephone number is the same as Mike's, and

$$All(PP, Child(Mike,PP)$$
$$Implies\ Equal(Telephone\ PP, Telephone\ Mike)) \tag{79}$$

is the proposition that all Mike's children have the same telephone number as Mike. Existential propositions are formed similarly to universal ones, but the function *Exist* introduced here should not be confused with the function *Exists* applied to individual concepts introduced earlier.

In forming individual concepts by the description function *The*, it doesn't matter whether the object described exists. Thus

$$The(PP,Child(Mike,PP)) \tag{80}$$

is the concept of Mike's only child. *Exists The(PP, Child(Mike, PP))* is the proposition that the described child exists. We have

$$true\ Exists\ The(PP,Child(Mike,PP)) \equiv$$
$$true(Exist(PP,Child(Mike,PP)$$
$$And\ All(PP1,Child(Mike,PP1)\ Implies\ Equal(PP,PP1)))), \tag{81}$$

but we may want the equality of the two propositions, that is,

$$Exists\ The(PP,Child(Mike,PP)) =$$
$$Exist(PP,Child(Mike,PP)$$
$$And\ All(PP1,Child(Mike,PP1)\ Implies\ Equal(PP,PP1))). \tag{82}$$

This is part of general problem of when two logically equivalent concepts are to be regarded as the same.

In order to discuss the truth of propositions and the denotation of descriptions, we introduce *possible worlds* reluctantly and with an important difference from the usual treatment. We need them to give values to the inner variables, and we can also use them for axiomatizing the modal operators, knowledge, belief and tense. However, for axiomatizing quantification, we also need a function α such that

$$\pi' = \alpha(V,x,\pi) \tag{83}$$

is the possible world that is the same as the world π except that the inner variable *V* has the value *x* instead of the value it has in π. In this respect our possible worlds resemble the *state vectors* or *environments* of computer science more than the possible worlds of the Kripke treatment of modal logic. This Cartesian product structure on the space of possible worlds can also be used to treat counterfactual conditional sentences.

Let $\pi 0$ be the actual world. Let $true(P, \pi)$ mean that the proposition P is true in the possible world π. Then

$$\forall P.(true\ P \equiv true(P, \pi 0)). \tag{84}$$

Let $denotes(X, x, \pi)$ mean that X denotes x in π, and let $denot(X, \pi)$ mean the denotation of X in π when that is defined.

The truth condition for $All(V, P)$ is then given by

$$\forall \pi \forall P.(true(All(V, P), \pi) \equiv \forall x.true(P, \alpha(V, x, \pi)). \tag{85}$$

Here V ranges over inner variables, P ranges over propositions, and x ranges over things. There seems to be no harm in making the domain of x depend on π. Similarly

$$\forall \pi \forall P.(true(Exist(V, P), \pi) \equiv \exists x.true(P, \alpha(V, x, \pi)). \tag{86}$$

The meaning of $The(V, P)$ is given by

$$\forall \pi \forall P\ x.(true(P, \alpha(V, x, \pi)) \wedge \forall y.(true(P, \alpha(V, y, \pi)) \supset y = x) \supset denotes(The(V, P), x, \pi)) \tag{87}$$

and

$$\forall \pi \forall P.(\neg \exists x.true(P, \alpha(V, x, \pi)) \supset \neg true\ Exists\ The(V, P)). \tag{88}$$

We also have the following "syntactic" rules governing propositions involving quantification:

$$\forall \pi\ Q1\ Q2\ V.(absent(V, Q1) \wedge true(All(V, Q1\ Implies\ Q2), \pi) \supset true(Q1\ Implies\ All(V, Q2), \pi)) \tag{89}$$

and

$$\forall \pi \forall Q\ X.(true(All(V, Q), \pi) \supset true(Subst(X, V, Q), \pi)). \tag{90}$$

where $absent(V, X)$ means that the variable V is not present in the concept X, and $Subst(X, V, Y)$ is the concept that results from substituting the concept X for the variable V in the concept Y. $absent$ and $Subst$ are characterized by the following axioms:

$$\forall V1\ V2.(absent(V1, V2) \equiv V1 \neq V2), \tag{91}$$

$$\forall V\ P\ X.(absent(V, Know(P, X)) \equiv absent(V, P) \wedge absent(V, X)), \tag{92}$$

axioms similar to (92) for other conceptual functions,

$$\forall V\ Q.absent(V, All(V, Q)), \tag{93}$$

$$\forall V\ Q.absent(V, Exist(V, Q)), \tag{94}$$

$$\forall V\ Q.absent(V, The(V, Q)), \tag{95}$$

$$\forall V\ X.Subst(V, V, X) = X, \tag{96}$$

$$\forall X\ V.Subst(X, V, V)| = X, \tag{97}$$

$$\forall X\ V\ P\ Y.(Subst(X, V, Know(P, Y)) = Know(Subst(X, V, P), Subst(X, V, Y))), \tag{98}$$

axioms similar to (98) for other functions,

$$\forall X\ V\ Q.(absent(V, Y) \supset Subst(X, V, Y) = Y), \tag{99}$$

$$\forall X\ V1\ V2\ Q.(V1 \neq V2 \wedge absent(V2, X) \supset Subst(X, V1, All(V2, Q)) = All(V2, Subst(X, V1, Q))), \tag{100}$$

and corresponding axioms to (100) for $Exist$ and The.

Along with these comes the axiom that binding kills variables, that is,

$$\forall V1\ V2\ Q.(All(V1, Q) = All(V2, Subst(V2, V1, Q))). \tag{101}$$

The functions $absent$ and $Subst$ play a "syntactic" role in describing the rules of reasoning and don't appear in the concepts themselves. It seems likely that this is harmless until we want to form concepts of the laws of reasoning.

We used the Greek letter π for possible worlds, because we did not want to consider a possible world as a thing and introduce concepts of possible worlds. Reasoning about reasoning may require such concepts or else a formulation that doesn't use possible worlds.

Martin Davis (in conversation) pointed out the advantages of an alternative treatment avoiding possible worlds in case there is a single domain of individuals each of which has a standard concept. Then we can write

$$\forall V\ Q.(true\ All(V, Q) \equiv \forall x.true\ Subst(Concept1\ x, V, Q)). \tag{102}$$

POSSIBLE APPLICATIONS TO ARTIFICIAL INTELLIGENCE

The foregoing discussion of concepts has been mainly concerned with how to translate into a suitable formal language certain sentences of ordinary language. The success of the formalization is measured by the extent to which the logical consequences of these sentences in the formal system agree with our intuitions of what these consequences should be. Another goal of the formalization is to develop an idea of what concepts really are, but the possible formalizations have not been explored enough to draw even tentative conclusions about that.

For artificial intelligence, the study of concepts has yet a different motivation. Our success in making computer programs with general intelligence has been extremely limited, and one source of the limitation is our inability to formalize what the world is like in general. We can try to separate the problem of describing the general aspects of the world from the problem of using such a description and the facts of a situation to discover a strategy for achieving a goal. This is called separating the epistemological and the heuristic parts of the artificial intelligence problem and is discussed in McCarthy and Hayes (1969).

We see the following potential uses for facts about knowledge:

1. A computer program that wants to telephone someone must reason

about who knows the number. More generally, it must reason about what actions will obtain needed knowledge. Knowledge in books and computer files must be treated in a parallel way to knowledge held by persons.

2. A program must often determine that it does not know something or that someone else doesn't. This has been neglected in the usual formalizations of knowledge, and methods of proving possibility have been neglected in modal logic. Christopher Goad (to be published) has shown how to prove ignorance by proving the existence of possible worlds in which the sentence to be proved unknown is false. Presumably proving one's own ignorance is a stimulus to looking outside for the information. In competitive situations, it may be important to show that a certain course of action will leave competitors ignorant.

3. Prediction of the behaviour of others depends on determining what they believe and what they want.

It seems to me that AI applications will especially benefit from first order formalisms of the kind described above. First, many of the present problem solvers are based on first order logic. Morgan (1976) in discussing theorem proving in modal logic also translates modal logic into first order logic. Second, our formalisms leaves the syntax and semantics of statements not involving concepts entirely unchanged, so that if knowledge or wanting is only a small part of a problem, its presence doesn't affect the formalization of the other parts.

ABSTRACT LANGUAGES

The way we have treated concepts in this paper, especially when we put variables in them, suggests trying to indentify them with terms in some language. It seems to me that this can be done provided that we use a suitable notion of *abstract language*.

Ordinarily a language is identified with a set of strings of symbols taken from some alphabet. McCarthy (1963) introduces the idea of *abstract syntax*, the idea being that it doesn't matter whether sums are represented $a+b$ or $+ab$ or $ab+$ or by the integer 2^a3^b or by the LISP S-expression (PLUS A B), so long as there are predicates for deciding whether an expression is a sum and functions for forming sums from summands and functions for extracting the summands from the sum. In particular, abstract syntax facilitates defining the semantics of programming languages, and proving the properties of interpreters and compilers. From that point of view, one can refrain from specifying any concrete representation of the "expressions" of the language and consider it merely a collection of abstract synthetic and analytic functions and predicates for forming, discriminating and taking apart *abstract expressions*. However, the languages considered at that time always admitted representations as strings of symbols.

If we consider concepts as a free algebra on basic concepts, then we can regard them as strings of symbols on some alphabet if we want to, assuming that we don't object to a non-denumerable alphabet or infinitely long expressions if we want standard concepts for all the real numbers. However, if we want to regard $Equal(X, Y)$ and $Equal(Y, X)$ as the same concept, and hence as the same "expression" in our language, and we want to regard expressions related by renaming bound variables as denoting the same concept, then the algebra is no longer free, and regarding concepts as strings of symbols becomes awkward even if possible.

It seems better to accept the notion of *abstract language* defined by the collection of functions and predicates that form, discriminate, and extract the parts of its "expressions". In that case it would seem that concepts can be identified with expressions in an abstract language.

ACKNOWLEDGEMENTS AND BIBLIOGRAPHY

The treatment given here should be compared with that in Church (1951b) and in Morgan (1976). Church introduces what might be called a two-dimensional type structure. One dimension permits higher order functions and predicates as in the usual higher order logics. The second dimension permits concepts of concepts, etc. No examples of applications are given. It seems to me that concepts of concepts will be eventually required, but this can still be done within first order logic.

Morgan's motivation is to use first order logic theorem-proving programs to treat modal logic. He gives two approaches. The syntactic approach – which he applies only to systems without quantifiers – uses operations like our *And* to form compound propositions from elementary ones. Provability is then axiomatized in the outer logic. His semantic approach uses axiomatizations of the Kripke accessibility relation between possible worlds. It seems to me that our treatment can be used to combine both of Morgan's methods, and has two further advantages. First, concepts and individuals can be separately quantified. Second, functions from things to concepts and concepts of them permit relations between concepts of things that could not otherwise be expressed.

Although the formalism leads in almost the opposite direction, the present paper is much in the spirit of Carnap (1956). We appeal to his ontological tolerance in introducing concepts as objects, and his section on intentions for robots expresses just the attitude required for artificial intelligence applications.

We have not yet investigated the matter, but plausible axioms for necessity or knowledge expressed in terms of concepts may lead to the paradoxes discussed in Kaplan and Montague (1960) and Montague (1963). Our intention is that the paradoxes can be avoided by restricting the axioms concerning knowledge, and necessity of statements about necessity. The restrictions will be somewhat unintuitive as are the restrictions necessary to avoid the paradoxes of naive set theory.

Chee K. Yap (1977) proposes *Virtual Semantics* for intensional logics as a generalization of Carnap's individual concepts. Apart from the fact that Yap does not stay within conventional first order logic, we don't know the relation between his work and that described here.

I am indebted to Lewis Creary, Patrick Hayes, Donald Michie, Barbara Partee and Peter Suzman for discussion of a draft of this paper. Creary in particular has shown the inadequacy of the formalism for expressing all readings of the ambiguous sentence *"Pat knows that Mike knows what Joan last asserted"*. There has not been time to modify the formalism to fix this inadequacy, but it seems likely that concepts of concepts are required for an adequate treatment.

REFERENCES

Carnap, R. (1956). *Meaning and Necessity*. Chicago: University of Chicago Press.

Church, A. (1951a). The need for abstract entities in semantic analysis, in "Contributions to the Analysis and Synthesis of Knowledge". *Proceedings of the American Academy of Arts and Sciences*, 80, No. 1, 100–112. Reprinted in *The Structure of Language* (eds. Fodor, A. and Katz, J.) Prentice-Hall, 1964.

Church, A. (1951b). A formulation of the logic of sense and denotation. In *Essays in honour of Henry Sheffer* (ed. Henle, P.), pp. 3–24. New York.

Frege, G. (1892). Uber Sinn und Bedeutung. *Zeitschrift fur Philosophie und Philosphische Kritik* 100:25–50. Translated by H. Feigl under the title "On Sense and Nominatum" in *Readings in Philosophical Analysis* (eds. Feigal, H. and Sellars, W). New York 1949. Translated by M. Black under the title "On Sense and Reference" in P. Geach and M. Black, *Translations from the Philosophical Writings of Gottlob Frege*. Oxford: 1952.

Kaplan, D. (1969). Quantifying in, from *Words and Objections: Essays on the Work of W. V. O. Quine* (eds. Davidson, D. and Hintikka, J.), pp. 178–214. Dordrecht-Holland: D. Reidel Publishing Co. Reprinted in (Linsky 1971).

Kaplan, D. and Montague, R. (1960). A paradox regained, *Notre Dame Journal of Formal Logic*, I, 79–90. Reprinted in (Montague 1974).

Linsky. L. (ed.) (1971) *Reference and Modality*, Oxford Readings in Philosophy. Oxford: Oxford University Press.

McCarthy, J. (1963). Towards a mathematical science of computation, in *Proceedings of IFIP Congress* 1962. Amsterdam: North-Holland Publishing Co.

McCarthy, J. and Hayes, P. J. (1969). Some philosophical problems from the standpoint of artificial intelligence. *Machine Intelligence* 4, pp. 463–502 (eds. Meltzer, B. Michie, D.). Edinburgh: Edinburgh University Press.

Montague, R. (1963). Syntactical treatments of modality, with corollaries on reflexion principles and finite axiomatizability, *Acta Philosophica Fennica* 16:153–167. Reprinted in (Montague 1974).

Montague, R. (1974). *Formal Philosophy*. New Haven: Yale University Press.

Morgan, C. G. (1976). Methods for automated theorem proving in nonclassical logics, *IEEE Transactions on Computers*, C-25, No. 8.

Quine, W. V. O. (1956). Quantifiers and propositional attitudes, *Journal of Philosophy*, 53. Reprinted in (Linsky 1971).

Quine, W. V. O. (1963). *From a Logical Point of View*. New York: Harper and Row. First published Harvard University Press (1953).

Yap, Chee K. (1977). A Semantical Analysis of Intensional Logics, Research Report *RC* 6893 (#29538). Yorktown Heights, New York: IBM, Thomas J. Watson Research Center.

VIII / A Knowledge Representation Bibliography

A Knowledge Representation Bibliography

We here present an extensive, partially annotated bibliography of research publications in Knowledge Representation. This is not, however, intended to be a complete bibliography of the field. For example, it contains almost nothing on visual knowledge, "analogical" representations, AI programming languages (and logic programming), and hardware implementations. We have, rather, selected a set of papers that we feel give a representative picture of work in Knowledge Representation (for individual authors, for example, we have included only the best papers by the author on a given topic). Any paper appearing in the bibliography is worth reading; however, those of special merit have a short annotation explaining their particular interest, or a comment indicating that they have been included in this volume.

In general, reports on research in Knowledge Representation are scattered throughout various journals, but have appeared mainly in *Artificial Intelligence* (North-Holland Publishing Company) and *Cognitive Science* (Ablex Publishing Corporation). Research results also appear in the proceedings of several conferences, notably the biennial International Joint Conference on Artificial Intelligence (IJCAI), the annual conference of the American Association for Artificial Intelligence (AAAI) and the biennial conference of the Canadian Society for the Computational Study of Intelligence (CSCSI). Finally, much information is disseminated more informally as technical reports from various AI research centers including those of BBN, CMU, Fairchild (FLAIR), MIT, SRI International, Stanford, and Xerox. A useful introduction to Knowledge Representation (and Artificial Intelligence in general) can be found in [Nilsson 80]; other surveys of the field appear in [Barr and Davidson 81], [Brachman and Smith 80], and [Mylopoulos and Levesque 83].

Like this volume, the bibliography below has entries from each of seven categories. These categories are indicated in the individual entries by the following symbols:

G: The Knowledge Representation Enterprise (G = <u>G</u>eneral)

N: Associational Representations (N = <u>N</u>etworks)

F: Structured Object Representations (F = <u>F</u>rames)

L: Formal Logic-Based Representations (L = <u>L</u>ogic)

P: Procedural Representations and Production Systems

O: Other Approaches

D: Representations of Common Sense Knowledge (D = <u>D</u>omain knowledge)

Abelson, R. P. "Concepts for Representing Mundane Reality in Plans." In *Representation and Understanding: Studies in Cognitive Science*. Edited by D. G. Bobrow and A. M. Collins. New York: Academic Press, 1975, 273–310. [**D**]

Aikins, J. S. "Prototypical Knowledge for Expert Systems." *Artificial Intelligence* **20** (2), 1983, 163–210. [**O**]
  - Aikins' system "represents its knowledge as a combination of frames and production rules and performs tasks in the domain of pulmonary (lung) physiology".

Allen, B. P., and Wright, J. M. "Integrating Logic Programs and Schemata." *Proc. IJCAI-83*. Karlsruhe, West Germany, 1983, 340–342. [**O**]

Allen, J. F. "Maintaining Knowledge about Temporal Intervals." *Communications of the ACM* **26** (11), 1983, 832–843. [**D**]
  - *This paper is included in this volume.*

Allen, J. F. "Towards a General theory of Action and Time." *Artificial Intelligence* **23** (2), 1984, 123–154. [**D**]

Allen, J. F., and Frisch, A. M. "What's in a Semantic Network?" *Proc. 20th Annual Meeting of the Association for Computational Linguistics*. Toronto, 1982, 19–27. [**O**]

Amarel, S. "On Representations of Problems of Reasoning About Actions." In *Machine Intelligence 3*. Edited by D. Michie. Edinburgh: Edinburgh University Press, 1968. [**G**]

Amarel, S. "Problems of Representation in Heuristic Problem-Solving: Related Issues in the Development of Expert Systems," Tech. Report CBM-TR-118, Lab. for Computer Science Research, Rutgers University, New Brunswick, NJ, 1981. [**G**]

Anderson, J. R., and Bower, G. H. *Human Associative Memory*. Washington, D.C.: V. H. Winston and Sons, 1973. [**N**]

Attardi, G., and Simi, M. "Consistency and Completeness of OMEGA, a Logic for Knowledge Representation." *Proc. IJCAI-81*. Vancouver, B. C., 1981, 504–510. [**O**]
  - This paper describes the logic of OMEGA, a Knowledge Representation system. OMEGA has a somewhat standard logic of sentences that is closely coupled to a unique logic of descriptions. For example, for each sentential operator, there is an analogous one for descriptions. The logical foundations of the system are emphasized in the paper.

Ballard, D. H., and Hayes, P. J. "Parallel Logical Inference." *Proc. of the Sixth Annual Conference of the Cognitive Science Society*. Boulder, CO, 1984, 114–120. [**L**]

Barnden, J. A. "Intensions as Such: An Outline." *Proc. IJCAI-83*. Karlsruhe, West Germany, 1983, 280–286. [**D**]
  - This paper presents a different formalization of concepts and propositions from the one by McCarthy [1979] (included in this volume). One interesting feature of Barnden's approach is that by using combinators, terms standing for variables can be avoided completely.

Barr, A. "Meta-Knowledge and Cognition." *Proc. IJCAI-79*. Tokyo, 1979, 31–33. [**G**]

Barr, A., and Davidson, J., eds. "Representation of Knowledge." In *The Handbook of Artificial Intelligence.* Edited by A. Barr and E. A. Feigenbaum. Los Altos, CA: William Kaufmann, Inc., 1981, 141–222. [**G**]

Bell, A., and Quillian, M. R. "Capturing Concepts in a Semantic Net." In *Associative Information Techniques.* Edited by E. L. Jacks. New York: American Elsevier Publishing Company, 1971. [**N**]

Besnard, P., Quiniou, R., and Quinton, P. "A Theorem-Prover for a Decidable Subset of Default Logic." *Proc. AAAI-83.* Washington, D.C., 1983, 27–30. [**L**]

Bledsoe, W. W. "Non-resolution Theorem Proving." *Artificial Intelligence* 9 (1), 1977, 1–35. [**L**]

Bobrow, D. G. "Dimensions of Representation." In *Representation and Understanding: Studies in Cognitive Science.* Edited by D. G. Bobrow and A. M. Collins. New York: Academic Press, 1975, 1–34. [**G**]

Bobrow, D. G., ed. "A Panel on Knowledge Representation." *Proc. IJCAI-77.* Cambridge, MA, 1977, 983–992. [**G**]

Bobrow, D. G., ed. *Special Volume on Qualitative Reasoning about Physical Systems. Artificial Intelligence* 24 (1–3), 1984. [**D**]
- This special issue of the *Artificial Intelligence* journal covers some of the current approaches to representing and reasoning about the structure and behavior of physical devices.

Bobrow, D. G., and Collins, A. M., eds. *Representation and Understanding: Studies in Cognitive Science.* New York: Academic Press, 1975. [**G**]

Bobrow, D. G., and Norman, D. A. "Some Principles of Memory Schemata." In *Representation and Understanding: Studies in Cognitive Science.* Edited by D. G. Bobrow and A. M. Collins. New York: Academic Press, 1975, 131–150. [**G**]

Bobrow, D. G., and Winograd, T. "An Overview of KRL, A Knowledge Representation Language." *Cognitive Science* 1 (1), 1977, 3–46. [**F**]
- *This paper is included in this volume.*

Bobrow, D. G., and Winograd, T. "KRL: Another Perspective." *Cognitive Science* (1), 1979, 29–42. [**F**]

Bobrow, D. G., Winograd, T., and the KRL Research Group. "Experience with KRL-0: One Cycle of a Knowledge Representation Language." *Proc. IJCAI-77.* Cambridge, MA, 1977, 213–222. [**F**]

Bobrow, R. J., and Webber, B. L. "Knowledge Representation for Syntactic/Semantic Processing." *Proc. AAAI-80.* Stanford, CA, 1980, 316–323. [**D**]

Boley, H. "Directed Recursive Labelnode Hypergraphs: A New Representation Language." *Artificial Intelligence* 9 (1), 1977, 49–85. [**N**]

Borgida, A. "On the Definition of Specialization Hierarchies for Procedures." *Proc. IJCAI-81.* Vancouver, B. C., 1981, 254–256. [**D**]

Brachman, R. J. "What's in a Concept: Structural Foundations for Semantic Networks." *International Journal of Man-Machine Studies* **9** (2), 1977, 127–152. [**N**]

Brachman, R. J. "A Structural Paradigm for Representing Knowledge," Ph.D. Thesis, Harvard University, May, 1977. Revised version available as BBN Report No. 3605, Bolt Beranek and Newman Inc., Cambridge, MA, May, 1978. Updated version to be published by Ablex Publishing Corp., Norwood, NJ, 1985. [**N**]
- The original thesis provides a detailed analysis of problems in semantic networks, and develops a new representation language with a "clean, epistemologically explicit" foundation. This language was the precursor to KL-ONE, and in the thesis it is used to represent information in two disparate domains— meanings of English nominal compounds and knowledge about an electronic mail system. The forthcoming book will provide retrospective addenda that trace various representational constructs through their history in KL-ONE and KRYPTON.

Brachman, R. J. "On the Epistemological Status of Semantic Networks." In *Associative Networks: Representation and Use of Knowledge by Computers*. Edited by N. V. Findler. New York: Academic Press, 1979, 3–50. [**N**]
- *This paper is included in this volume.*

Brachman, R. J. "What IS-A Is and Isn't: An Analysis of Taxonomic Links in Semantic Networks." *IEEE Computer* **16** (10), 1983, 30–36. [**N**]
- This paper examines in detail the taxonomic IS-A link found in most semantic networks, and concludes that a single representational link is being used to represent a wide variety of relations in confusing and ambiguous ways.

Brachman, R. J. "'I Lied About the Trees' (or, Defaults and Definitions in Knowledge Representation)." *The AI Magazine* **6** (3), 1985. [**F**]

Brachman, R. J., and Levesque, H. J. "Competence in Knowledge Representation." *Proc. AAAI-82.* Pittsburgh, PA, 1982, 189–192. [**O**]
- This paper argues that in a true "expert system" setting, a Knowledge Representation system has to provide facilities for incrementally capturing facts about a domain and for dealing with the technical vocabulary of that domain. It then suggests that these two orthogonal demands are best met by an amalgamation of two representation systems, a logical one and a frame-based one.

Brachman, R. J., and Levesque, H. J. "The Tractability of Subsumption in Frame-Based Description Languages." *Proc. AAAI-84.* Austin, TX, 1984, 34–37. [**F**]
- This paper demonstrates that the difficulty of determining whether one description is more general or specific than another is very sensitive to the constructs used in the descriptions. Part of this paper has been included in the Levesque and Brachman paper included in this volume.

Brachman, R. J., and Schmolze, J. "An Overview of the KL-ONE Knowledge Representation System." *Cognitive Science* **9** (2), 1985, 171–216. [**F**]
- KL-ONE was of the more influential semantic network/frame-based languages, and this paper is a clear explanation of what the language was, and what it was trying to accomplish.

Brachman, R. J., and Smith, B. C., eds. *Special Issue on Knowledge Representation. SIGART Newsletter*, No. 70, February, 1980. [**G**]
- This special issue of the *SIGART Newsletter* presents the results of an extensive questionnaire on Knowledge Representation answered by 83 groups who claimed to be working in the area. The questions asked cover a wide range of representation issues. Especially striking is the wide variety of answers to even the most basic foundational questions.

Brachman, R. J., Fikes, R. E., and Levesque, H. J. "KRYPTON: A Functional Approach to Knowledge Representation." *IEEE Computer* **16** (10), 1983, 67–73. [O]
- *This paper is included in this volume.*

Brachman, R. J., Gilbert, V. P., and Levesque, H. J. "An Essential Hybrid Reasoning System: Knowledge and Symbol Level Accounts of KRYPTON." *Proc. IJCAI-85.* Los Angeles, CA, 1985. [O]

Brooks, R. "A Comparison Among Four Packages for Knowledge-Based Systems." *Proc. Intl. Conference on Cybernetics and Society.* 1981, 279–283. [G]

Brown, J. S., and Burton, R. R. "Multiple Representations of Knowledge for Tutorial Reasoning." In *Representation and Understanding: Studies in Cognitive Science.* Edited by D. G. Bobrow and A. M. Collins. New York: Academic Press, 1975, 311–349. [O]

Bundy, A., Byrd, L., and Mellish, C. S. "Special-Purpose, but Domain-Independent, Inference Mechanisms." In *Progress in Artificial Intelligence.* Edited by L. Steels and J. A. Campbell. London: Ellis Horwood Ltd., 1985, 93–111. [O]
- This paper shows examples of various special-purpose reasoning techniques (such as reasoning with transitive closures) that need to be brought together in a single general-purpose system.

Bylander, T., Mittal, S., and Chandrasekaran, B. "CSRL: A Language for Expert Systems for Diagnosis." *Proc. IJCAI-83.* Karlsruhe, West Germany, 1983, 218–221. [D]

Carbonell, J. R. "AI in CAI: An Artificial Intelligence Approach to Computer-Aided Instruction." *IEEE Transactions on Man-Machine Systems* **11** (4), 1970, 190–202. [D]

Carbonell, J. R. "Mixed-Initiative Man-Computer Instructional Dialogues," BBN Report No. 1971. Bolt Beranek and Newman Inc., Cambridge, MA, 1970. [N]

Cercone, N., and Goebel, R. "Knowledge Representation and Databases: Science or Engineering." *Proc. CSCSI Fourth National Conference.* Saskatoon, Saskatchewan, 1982, 172–182. [G]

Cercone, N., and Schubert, L. "Toward a State Based Conceptual Representation." *Proc. IJCAI-75.* Tbilisi, Georgia, USSR, 1975, 83–90. [N]

Charniak, E. "A Framed PAINTING: The Representation of a Common Sense Knowledge Fragment." *Cognitive Science* **1** (4), 1977, 355–394. [F]

Charniak, E. "On the Use of Framed Knowledge in Language Comprehension." *Artificial Intelligence* **11** (3), 1978, 225–265. [F]
- Charniak describes a program that 'understands' simple stories about painting, using a frame-like representation. He particularly emphasizes inferences for understanding connected discourse.

Charniak, E. "A Common Representation for Problem-Solving and Language-Comprehension Information." *Artificial Intelligence* **16** (3), 1981, 225-255. [O]
- Charniak examines the role of representation in problem-solving and language-comprehension and concludes that a common representation is needed that meets the needs of both. His candidate combines frames and predicate calculus.

Charniak, E. "The Bayesian Basis of Common Sense Medical Diagnosis." *Proc. AAAI-83.* Washington, D.C., 1983, 70–73. [**P**]

- Most of the current theoretical work in evidential reasoning in Artificial Intelligence is based on the Dempster-Shafer theory. Charniak argues that the earlier and simpler Bayesian model is still appropriate in many circumstances.

Clancey, W. J. "The Epistemology of a Rule-Based Expert System–A Framework for Explanation." *Artificial Intelligence* **20** (3), 1983. [**P**]

Cohen, B., and Murphy, G. L. "Models of Concepts." *Cognitive Science* **8** (1), 1984, 27–59. [**F**]

- This paper reviews various models of concepts used in psychological studies of cognition, and concentrates in particular on "prototype theory." It looks at various accounts and criticisms of prototypes, and is interesting in its attempt to support prototype theory with a variation on a mainstream AI knowledge representation model.

Collins, A. M., and Loftus, E. F. "A Spreading-Activation Theory of Semantic Processing." *Psychological Review* **82** (6), 1975, 407–428. [**N**]

Cottrell, G. "Re: Inheritance Hierarchies with Exceptions." *Proc. of the Non-Monotonic Reasoning Workshop.* New Paltz, NY, 1984, 33–56. [**N**]

Creary, L. G. "Propositional Attitudes: Fregean Representation and Simulative Reasoning." *Proc. IJCAI-79.* Tokyo, 1979, 176–181. [**D**]

Dahl, V. "Logic Programming as a Representation of Knowledge." *IEEE Computer* **16** (10), 1983, 106–113. [**P**]

Davis, E. "The Mercator Representation of Spatial Knowledge." *Proc. IJCAI-83.* Karlsruhe, West Germany, 1983, 295–301. [**D**]

Davis, R. "Meta-Rules: Reasoning about Control." *Artificial Intelligence* **15** (3), 1980. [**P**]

- One concern with representations used for reasoning in AI systems is the effective application of knowledge, especially when the number of relevant facts is large. Davis here discusses a kind of 'meta-level knowledge' concerned with control of procedure invocation, and illustrates its utility in knowledge-based systems.

Davis, R., and Buchanan, B. G. "Meta-Level Knowledge: Overview and Applications." *Proc. IJCAI-77.* Cambridge, MA, 1977, 920–927. [**P**]

- *This paper is included in this volume.*

Davis, R., and King, J. "An Overview of Production Systems." In *Machine Intelligence 8.* Edited by E. Elcock and D. Michie. Chichester, England: Ellis Horwood, 1977, 300–332. [**P**]

- This is a clear statement of the basic principles of Production Systems, with some discussion of their advantages and limitations. It also presents a limited amount of cross-system comparison.

Davis, R., and Shrobe, H. "Representing Structure and Behavior of Digital Hardware." *IEEE Computer* **16** (10), 1983, 75–82. [**D**]

Davis, R., Buchanan, B. G., and Shortliffe, E. H. "Production Rules as a Representation for a Knowledge-Based Consultation System." *Artificial Intelligence* **8** (1), 1977. [**P**]
- *This paper is included in this volume.*

Davis, R., Shrobe, H., Hamscher, W., Wieckert, K., Shirley, M., and Polit, S. "Diagnosis Based on Description of Structure and Function." *Proc. AAAI-82.* Pittsburgh, PA, 1982, 137–142. [**D**]

Deering, M., Faletti, J., and Wilensky, R. "PEARL: A Package for Efficient Access to Representations in LISP." *Proc. IJCAI-81.* Vancouver, B. C., 1981, 930–932. [**P**]

de Kleer, J., and Brown, J. S. "Foundations of Envisioning." *Proc. AAAI-82.* Pittsburgh, PA, 1982, 434–437. [**D**]

de Kleer, J., Doyle, J., and Sussman, G. "AMORD: Explicit Control of Reasoning." *Proc. Symposium on Artificial Intelligence and Programming Languages. SIGPLAN Notices*, Vol. 12, No. 8, and *SIGART Newsletter*, No. 64, August, 1977, 116–125. [**P**]
- *This paper is included in this volume.*

Delgrande, J. P. "Theory Formation and Conjectural Knowledge in Knowledge Bases." *Proc. CSCSI-84.* London, Ontario, 1984. [**L**]
- Delgrande argues that there is a natural set of generalizations that can be induced from a body of data, and that these need not depend on any prior knowledge about prototypes, rules, or laws.

Deliyanni, A., and Kowalski, R. A. "Logic and Semantic Networks." *Communications of the ACM* **22** (3), 1979, 184–192. [**O**]

Doyle, J. "A Model for Deliberation, Action, and Introspection," AI-TR-581. M.I.T. AI Lab., Cambridge, MA, 1980. [**D**]

Doyle, J. "A Glimpse of Truth-maintenance." In *Artificial Intelligence: An MIT Perspective.* Edited by P. H. Winston and R. H. Brown. Cambridge, MA: The MIT Press, 1982, 119–135. [**P**]
- The paper describes the so-called Truth Maintenence System developed by the author. This is a system that performs deductions in a knowledge base, maintaining dependencies and justifications among sentences. These can then be examined when, for example, inconsistencies are discovered.

Doyle, J. "A Society of Mind: Multiple Perspectives, Reasoned Assumptions, and Virtual Copies." *Proc. IJCAI-83.* Karlsruhe, West Germany, 1983, 309–314. [**D**]

Doyle, J. "The Ins and Outs of Reason Maintenance." *Proc. IJCAI-83.* Karlsruhe, West Germany, 1983, 349–351. [**P**]
- Doyle attempts to put his earlier work on Truth Maintenance (which he now calls "Reason Maintenance") on a more sound mathematical footing so that, in particular, it might be possible to say what it is that the program was computing in an algorithm-independent way.

Doyle, J. "Admissible State Semantics for Representational Systems." *IEEE Computer* **16** (10), 1983, 119–123. [**G**]

Dreyfus, H. L. "From Micro-Worlds to Knowledge Representation: AI at an Impasse." In *Mind Design*. Edited by J. Haugeland. Cambridge, MA: The MIT Press, 1981, 161–204. [**G**]
- *This paper is included in this volume.*

Duda, R. O., Hart, P. E., Nilsson, N. J., and Sutherland, G. L. "Semantic Network Representations in Rule-Based Inference Systems." In *Pattern-Directed Inference Systems*. Edited by D. A. Waterman and F. Hayes-Roth. New York: Academic Press, 1978, 203-221. [**O**]

Elcock, E. W. "How Complete are Knowledge-Representation Systems?" *IEEE Computer* **16** (10), 1983, 114–118. [**G**]

Elschlager, B. "Consistency of Theories of Ideas." *Proc. IJCAI-79*. Tokyo, 1979, 241–243. [**D**]

Etherington, D. W., and Reiter R. "On Inheritance Hierarchies With Exceptions." *Proc. AAAI-83*. Washington, D. C., 1983, 104–108. [**L**]
- *This paper is included in this volume.*

Etherington, D., Mercer, R. E., and Reiter, R. "On the Adequacy of Predicate Circumscription for Closed-World Reasoning." *Proc. of the Non-Monotonic Reasoning Workshop*. New Paltz, NY, 1984, 70-81. [**L**]
- Etherington, Mercer, and Reiter analyze some of the properties and illustrates some of the shortcomings of McCarthy's notion of circumscription. In particular, circumscription is shown to be ineffectual when dealing with equality.

Fagan, L. M., Kunz, J. C., Feigenbaum, E. A., and Osborn, J. J. "Representation of Dynamic Clinical Knowledge: Measurement Interpretation in the Intensive Care Unit." *Proc. IJCAI-79*. Tokyo, 1979, 260–262. [**P**]

Fahlman, S. E. *NETL: A System for Representing and Using Real-World Knowledge*. Cambridge, MA: The MIT Press, 1979. [**N**]
- Fahlman's (MIT) thesis developed a semantic network-style representation in parallel with a hardware architecture for implementing it. This book duplicates that thesis, and provides an interesting view of the potential tight coupling between a network representation and inference routines implemented in parallel.

Fahlman, S. E., Touretzky, D. S., and van Roggen, W. "Cancellation in a Parallel Semantic Network." *Proc. IJCAI-81*. Vancouver, B.C., 1981, 257–263. [**N**]

Fain, J., Hayes-Roth, F., Sowizral, H., and Waterman, D. "Programming Examples in ROSIE," Tech. Report N-1646-ARPA. Rand Corporation, Santa Monica, CA, 1981. [**P**]

Feigenbaum, E. A. "The Art of Artificial Intelligence: Themes and Case Studies of Knowledge Engineering." *Proc. IJCAI-77*. Cambridge, MA, 1977, 1014–1029. [**D**]

Fikes, R. E. "Odyssey: A Knowledge-Based Assistant." *Artificial Intelligence* **16** (3), 1981, 331–361. [**D**]

Fikes, R., and Hendrix, G. "A Network-Based Knowledge Representation and its Natural Deduction System." *Proc. IJCAI-77*. Cambridge, MA, 1977, 235–246. [**N**]

Filman, R. E., Lamping, J., and Montalvo, F. S. "Meta-Knowledge and Meta-Reasoning." *Proc. IJCAI-83*. Karlsruhe, West Germany, 1983, 365–369. [**O**]

Findler, N. V., ed. *Associative Networks: Representation and Use of Knowledge by Computers*. New York: Academic Press, 1979. [**N**]

Finin, T. and Silverman, D. "Interactive Classification: A Technique for Building and Maintaining Knowledge Bases." *Proc. of the IEEE Workshop on Principles of Knowledge-Based Systems*. Denver, CO, 1984, 107–114. [**F**]

Fodor, J. *Representations*. Cambridge, MA: The MIT Press, 1981. [**G**]
- This book is a collection of articles by Fodor on various topics in cognitive science and the philosophy of mind, especially regarding the use of representations in thinking. Although dry at times, and occasionally only marginally relevant, the book does offer a stimulating perspective on issues related to Knowledge Representation from a leading figure in cognitive science.

Forbus, K. D. "Spatial and Qualitative Aspects of Reasoning about Motion." *Proc. AAAI-80*. Stanford, CA, 1980, 170–173. [**D**]

Forbus, K. D. "Modelling Motion with Qualitative Process Theory." *Proc. AAAI-82*. Pittsburgh, PA, 1982, 205–208. [**D**]
- A significant amount of work has been done in the area of representing the physical world in a qualitative, commonsense way. This paper describes Forbus' qualitative model of motion, which centers around the notion of *process* (rather than *state*).

Forgy, C., and McDermott, J. "OPS: A Domain-Independent Production System Language." *Proc. IJCAI-77*. Cambridge, MA, 1977, 933–939. [**P**]
- OPS was implemented to test certain claims about the superiority of production systems over other representational schemes. This paper discusses design issues for production systems in general, and describes OPS in particular.

Fox, M. S. "On Inheritance in Knowledge Representation." *Proc. IJCAI-79*. Tokyo, 1979, 282–284. [**N**]

Fox, M., Sathi, A., Greenberg, S. "Issues in Knowledge Representation for Project Management." *Proc. of the IEEE Workshop on Principles of Knowledge-Based Systems*. Denver, CO, 1984, 17–26. [**G**]

Fox, M., Wright, J. M., and Adam, D. "Experiences with SRL: An Analysis of a Frame-Based Knowledge Representation." *Proc. of the First International Workshop on Expert Database Systems*. Kiawah Island, SC, 1984, 224–237. [**F**]

Funt, B. V. "Problem-Solving with Diagrammatic Representations." *Artificial Intelligence* **13** (3), 1980, 201–230. [**O**]
- *This paper is included in this volume.*

Funt, B. V. "Analogical Modes of Reasoning and Process Modelling." *IEEE Computer* **16** (10), 1983, 99–105. [**O**]

Furukawa, K., Takeuchi, A., Kunifuji, S., Yasukawa, H., Ohki, M., and Ueda, K. "MANDALA: A Logic Based Knowledge Programming System." *Proc. of the International Conference on Fifth Generation Computer Systems*. Tokyo, 1984, 613–622. [L]

Gallaire, H., and Minker, J., eds. *Logic and Databases*. New York: Plenum Press, 1978. [L]

- This book is a collection of papers showing how database query evaluation can be understood in terms of (special cases of) first-order logic and logical deduction.

Garvey, T. D., Lowrance, J., and Fischler, M. A. "An Inference Technique for Integrating Knowledge from Disparate Sources." *Proc. IJCAI-81*. Vancouver, B. C., 1981, 319–325. [O]

- *This paper is included in this volume.*

Genesereth, M. R. "Metaphors and Models." *Proc. AAAI-80*. Stanford, CA, 1980. [G]

Genesereth, M. R. "An Overview of Meta-Level Architecture." *Proc. AAAI-83*. Washington, D. C., 1983. [O]

- This paper presents an interesting architecture intended to address the issue of explicit introspective reasoning and its practical use in AI systems. In particular, Genesereth presents a formal (predicate-calculus-based) language that allows one to describe system behavior as well as an interpreter that acts in accordance with behavioral descriptions expressed in the language.

Georgeff, M. P. "Procedural Control in Production Systems." *Artificial Intelligence* **18** (2), 1982, 175–201. [P]

Ginsberg, M. L. "Non-Monotonic Reasoning using Dempster's Rule." *Proc. AAAI-84*. Austin, TX, 1984, 126–129. [O]

Goebel, R. "Organizing Factual Knowledge in a Semantic Network," Technical Report TR77-8. Dept. of Computing Science, University of Alberta, Edmonton, Alberta, 1977. [N]

Goebel, R., and Cercone, N. "Representing and Organising Factual Knowledge in Proposition Networks." *Proc. CSCSI Second National Conference*. Toronto, 1978, 55–63. [N]

Goldstein, I. P., and Grimson, E. "Annotated Production Systems: A Model of Skill Acquisition." *Proc. IJCAI-77*. Cambridge, MA, 1977, 311-316. [P]

Goldstein, I. P., and Papert, S. "Artificial Intelligence, Language, and the Study of Knowledge." *Cognitive Science* **1** (1), 1977, 84–123. [G]

Goldstein, I. P., and Roberts, B. "Using Frames in Scheduling." In *Artificial Intelligence: An MIT Perspective*. Edited by P. H. Winston and R. H. Brown. Cambridge, MA: The MIT Press, 1979, 255–284. [D]

Green, C. "The Application of Theorem-Proving to Question Answering Systems," Ph.D. thesis. Department of Electrical Engineering, Stanford University, Stanford, CA, 1969. [**L**]

- Green was the first to show how mechanical theorem-proving could be used to answer other than yes-no questions. The idea (called "answer-extraction") involves adding an extra clause with free variables to the original question such that when the (Resolution) theorem-proving is complete, the variables in the clause are bound to a correct answer.

Greiner, R., and Lenat, D. "A Representation Language Language." *Proc. AAAI-80.* Stanford, CA, 1980, 105–169. [**F**]

Grosof, B. "Default Reasoning as Circumscription." *Proc. of the Non-Monotonic Reasoning Workshop.* New Paltz, NY, 1984, 115–124. [**L**]

Halpern, J. Y., and McAllester, D. A. "Likelihood, Probability, and Knowledge." *Proc. AAAI-84.* Austin, TX, 1984, 137–141. [**O**]

Halpern, J., and Moses, Y. "Towards a Theory of Knowledge and Ignorance: Preliminary Report." *Proc. of the Non-Monotonic Reasoning Workshop.* New Paltz, NY, 1984, 125–143. [**D**]

- The authors here attempt to formalize what it means for a certain sentence to be *all* that is known, something that arises repeatedly in non-monotonic reasoning. They present several versions of what this could mean, and then prove them equivalent.

Haugeland, J., ed. *Mind Design: Philosophy, Psychology, Artificial Intelligence.* Cambridge, MA: The MIT Press, 1981. [**G**]

- This book is an interesting compendium of articles on Artificial Intelligence by researchers in Philosophy, Psychology, and Artificial Intelligence. Although other areas of Artificial Intelligence are discussed, Knowledge Representation clearly is the central focus of the collection.

Havens, W., and Mackworth, A. "Representing Knowledge of the Visual World." *IEEE Computer* **16** (10), 1983, 90–98. [**D**]

- This paper shows how frame-like schemata can be useful for high-level vision in terms of both descriptive adequacy (that is, appropriately capturing the visual properties of objects) and procedural adequacy (that is, permitting efficient recognition and search).

Hayes, P. J. "The Frame Problem and Related Problems in Artificial Intelligence." In *Artificial and Human Thinking.* Edited by A. Elithorn and D. Jones. San Francisco: Jossey-Bass, 1973. [**G**]

Hayes, P. J. "Some Problems and Non-Problems in Representation Theory." *Proc. AISB Summer Conference.* University of Sussex, 1974, 63–79. [**G**]

- *This paper is included in this volume.*

Hayes, P. J. "In Defence of Logic." *Proc. IJCAI-77.* Cambridge, MA, 1977, 559–565. [**L**]

- Hayes argues eloquently that most of the criticism of logic as a representational language misses the point. He clearly explains the role of logic (for extensional analyses of meaning) and discusses some of the things it *isn't* (e.g., it is not a programming language).

Hayes, P. J. "The Naive Physics Manifesto." In *Expert Systems in the Electronic Age.* Edited by D. Michie. Edinburgh: Edinburgh University Press, 1979, 242–270. [**D**]

Hayes, P. J. "The Logic of Frames." In *Frame Conceptions and Text Understanding*. Edited by D. Metzing. Berlin: Walter de Gruyter and Co., 1979, 46–61. [**F**]
• *This paper is included in this volume.*

Hayes, P. J. "The Second Naive Physics Manifesto." In *Formal Theories of the Commonsense World*. Edited by J. R. Hobbs and R. C. Moore. Norwood, NJ: Ablex Publishing Corporation, 1985, 1–36. [**D**]
• *This paper is included in this volume.*

Hayes, P. J. "Naive Physics I: Ontology for Liquids." In *Formal Theories of the Commonsense World*. Edited by J. R. Hobbs and R. C. Moore. Norwood, NJ: Ablex Publishing Corporation, 1985, 71–107. [**D**]

Hayes, Philip J. "On Semantic Nets, Frames and Associations." *Proc. IJCAI-77*. Cambridge, MA, 1977, 99–107. [**N**]

Hays, D. G. "Types of Processes on Cognitive Networks." In *Computational and Mathematical Linguistics*, Vol. 1. Edited by A. Zampolli and N. Calzolari. Leo S. Olschki Publishers, 1973, 323–352. [**N**]

Hendrix, G. G. "Expanding the Utility of Semantic Networks through Partitioning." *Proc. IJCAI-75*. Tbilisi, Georgia, USSR, 1975, 115–121. [**N**]

Hendrix, G. G. "Encoding Knowledge in Partitioned Networks." In *Associative Networks: Representation and Use of Knowledge by Computers*. Edited by N. V. Findler. New York: Academic Press, 1979, 51–92. [**N**]
• This paper describes a semantic network formalism that includes facilities for encoding first order logical formulas as well as a unique way of grouping collections of nodes and links into partitions. These partitions play a number of roles in the representation including contexts, belief spaces and the scope of variable quantification.

Hewitt, C. "PLANNER: A Language for Proving Theorems in Robots." *Proc. IJCAI-71*. London, England, 1971, 295–301. [**P**]
• This paper is based on the author's doctoral dissertation and describes PLANNER, which was (more or less) the first procedural Knowledge Representation language and which established the direction for many of the developments in this area.

Hewitt, C. "How to Use What You Know." *Proc. IJCAI-75*. Tbilisi, Georgia, USSR, 1974, 189–198. [**P**]

Hewitt, C., and de Jong, P. "Analyzing the Roles of Descriptions and Actions in Open Systems." *Proc. AAAI-83*. Washington, D.C., 1983, 162–167. [**O**]

Hewitt, C., Attardi, G., and Simi, M. "Knowledge Embedding in the Description System Omega." *Proc. AAAI-80*. Stanford, CA, 1980, 157–163. [**O**]

Hewitt, C., Bishop, P., and Steiger, R. "A Universal Modular Actor Formalism for Artificial Intelligence." *Proc. IJCAI-73*. Stanford, CA, 1973. [**P**]

Hobbs, J. R., and Moore, R. C., eds. *Formal Theories of the Commonsense World*. Norwood, NJ: Ablex Publishing Corporation, 1985. [**D**]

Hurtubise, S. J., and Cumberbatch, R. "In Defense of Syllogism." *Proc. CSCSI Second National Conference.* Toronto, 1978, 311–314. [**L**]

Israel, D. J. "What's Wrong with Non-Monotonic Logic?" *Proc. AAAI-80.* Stanford, CA, 1980, 99–101. [**L**]

Israel, D. J. "On Interpreting Network Formalisms." *Computers and Mathematics with Applications* **9** (1), 1983. [**O**]

Israel, D. J. "The Role of Logic in Knowledge Representation." *IEEE Computer* **16** (10), 1983, 37–42. [**L**]

- This paper discusses the role of logic in reasoning in the context of a long standing disagreement between McCarthy and Minsky. Israel argues that even with its rules of inference, logic does not tell us how to reason, but only provides us with the consequences of reasoning one way or another, and so is at best a tool to be used in reasoning.

Israel, D. J., and Brachman, R. J. "Some Remarks on the Semantics of Representation Languages." In *On Conceptual Modelling: Perspectives from Artificial Intelligence, Databases, and Programming Languages.* Edited by M. L. Brodie, J. Mylopoulos, and J. W. Schmidt. New York: Springer-Verlag, 1984, 119–142. [**G**]

Joshi, A. K., and Kuhn, S. "Centered Logic: The Role of Entity Centered Sentence Representation in Natural Language Inferencing." *Proc. IJCAI-79.* Tokyo, 1979, 435–439. [**D**]

Kautz, H. A. "Planning Within First-Order Dynamic Logic." *Proc. CSCSI Fourth National Conference.* Saskatoon, Saskatchewan, 1982, 19–26. [**D**]

Kim, J. K., and Pearl, J. "A Computational Model for Causal and Diagnostic Reasoning in Inference Systems." *Proc. IJCAI-83.* Karlsruhe, West Germany, 1983, 190–193. [**D**]

Kogan, D. D., and Freiling M. J. "SIDUR — A Structuring Formalism for Knowledge Information Processing Systems." *Proc. of the International Conference on Fifth Generation Computer Systems.* Tokyo, 1984, 596–605. [**F**]

Kolata, G. "How Can Computers Get Common Sense." *Science* **217**, Sept. 24, 1982, 1237–1238. [**G**]

Konolige, K. "A Metalanguage Representation of Relational Databases for Deductive Question-Answering Systems." *Proc. IJCAI-81.* Vancouver, B. C., 1981, 496–503. [**D**]

Konolige, K. "A Deductive Model of Belief." *Proc. IJCAI-83.* Karlsruhe, West Germany, 1983, 377–381. [**D**]

- Konolige presents a model of belief composed of a base set of sentences and a deductive process over them. The model is very general, in that it allows the usual possible-world approaches to be simulated directly, as well as any number of restrictions to it (such as resource limitations) that one might want to model for specific agents.

Korf, R. E. "Toward a Model of Representation Changes." *Artificial Intelligence* **14** (1), 1980, 41–78. [**G**]

Kowalski, R. "Predicate Logic as a Programming Language." *Proc. IFIP Congress.* Toronto, 1974. [**O**]
- This is an early paper showing how a depth-first proof procedure for a restricted form of logic (namely Horn clauses) can be viewed as the execution of a programming language. The PROLOG programming language is, of course, based on this observation.

Kuipers, B. J. "A Frame for Frames: Representing Knowledge for Recognition." In *Representation and Understanding: Studies in Cognitive Science.* Edited by D. G. Bobrow and A. M. Collins. New York: Academic Press, 1975, 151–184. [**F**]
- Kuipers here attempts to build an intuitive model for frame representations as applied to (visual) recognition problems. Using this model, he is able to make much more precise statements about frames than had appeared previously.

Kuipers, B. "Modelling Spatial Knowledge." *Proc. IJCAI-77.* Cambridge, MA, 1977, 292–298. [**D**]

Kuipers, B. "On Representing Commonsense Knowledge." In *Associative Networks: The Representation and Use of Knowledge by Computers.* Edited by N. V. Findler. New York: Academic Press, 1979, 393–408. [**D**]
- Kuipers discusses the issue of what constitutes commonsense knowledge, and some practical limitations on representations of such knowledge. He also presents a particular model for commonsense knowledge of large-scale space.

Kuipers, B., and Kassirer, J. P. "How to Discover a Knowledge Representation for Causal Reasoning by Studying an Expert Physician." *Proc. IJCAI-83.* Karlsruhe, West Germany, 1983, 49–56. [**D**]

Langley, P. "Representational Issues in Learning Systems." *IEEE Computer* **16** (10), 1983, 47–52. [**D**]

Lehnert, W., and Wilks, Y. "A Critical Perspective on KRL." *Cognitive Science* **3** (1), 1979, 1–28. [**F**]

Levesque, H. J. "The Logic of Incomplete Knowledge Bases." In *Conceptual Modelling: Perspectives from Artificial Intelligence, Databases, and Programming Languages.* Edited by M. L. Brodie, J. Mylopoulos, and J. W. Schmidt. New York: Springer-Verlag, 1983, 165–186. [**L**]
- This paper argues that to properly query a knowledge base that has the kind of incomplete knowledge allowed by first-order logic, it is necessary to use a language that can talk about both the application domain and what the knowledge base knows about that domain. The paper motivates and presents a superset of first-order logic with this capability.

Levesque, H. J. "A Fundamental Tradeoff in Knowledge Representation and Reasoning." *Proc. CSCSI-84.* London, Ontario, 1984, 141–152. [**G**]
- *A revised version of this paper (by Levesque and Brachman) appears in this volume.*

Levesque, H. J. "Foundations of a Functional Approach to Knowledge Representation." *Artificial Intelligence* **23** (2), 1984, 155–212. [**G**]
- Levesque argues for a different view of Knowledge Representation based on what a system can be told and asked rather than on what structures and procedures it employs. In terms of this view, the paper rigorously demonstrates how a particularly expressive representation scheme that includes auto-epistemic facilities can be reduced to a less expressive one.

Levesque, H. J. "A Logic of Implicit and Explicit Belief." *Proc. AAAI-84*. Austin, TX, 1984, 198–202. [L]
- A standard problem with the concept of belief (or knowledge) based on logic is that logically equivalent beliefs are indistinguishable. This paper formalizes a more realistic and computationally tractable sense of belief where beliefs need not be closed under logical consequence.

Levesque, H., and Mylopoulos, J. "A Procedural Semantics for Semantic Networks." In *Associative Networks: Representation and Use of Knowledge by Computers*. Edited by N. V. Findler. New York: Academic Press, 1979, 93–120. [O]
- The authors describe a semantic network formalism called PSN that allows user-defined procedures to be attached to any component of a network and thereby extend or redefine every operation on the network. This allows the overall processor to be kept very simple, and dependencies among components to be captured succinctly.

Loveland, D. W. *Automated Theorem Proving: A Logical Basis*. New York: North-Holland Publishing Company, 1978. [L]
- This book is an excellent survey of Resolution-based theorem-proving (including many refinements) as of 1978. The emphasis is on the mathematical foundations (and especially the logical completeness) of these procedures.

McCarthy, J. "Programs with Common Sense." In *Semantic Information Processing*. Edited by M. Minsky. Cambridge, MA: The MIT Press, 1968, 403–418. [L]
- *This paper is included in this volume.*

McCarthy, J. "Epistemological Problems in Artificial Intelligence." *Proc. IJCAI-77*. Cambridge, MA, 1977, 1038–1044. [G]
- *This paper is included in this volume.*

McCarthy, J. "First Order Theories of Individual Concepts and Propositions." In *Machine Intelligence 9*. Edited by J. E. Hayes, D. Michie, and L. I. Mikulich. Chichester, England: Ellis Horwood, Ltd., 1979, 129–147. [L]
- *This paper is included in this volume.*

McCarthy, J. "Circumscription—A Form of Non-Monotonic Reasoning." *Artificial Intelligence* 13 (1,2), 1980, 27–39. [L]
- Circumscription, as presented in this paper, is one of the more successful and most analyzed formalizations of non-monotonic reasoning.

McCarthy, J. "Applications of Circumscription to Formalizing Common Sense Knowledge." *Proc. of the Non-Monotonic Reasoning Workshop*. New Paltz, NY, 1984, 295–324. [L]
- McCarthy presents ideas on a more general form of circumscription that appears to remedy some of the defects of his previous formulation.

McCarthy, J., and Hayes, P. J. "Some Philosophical Problems from the Standpoint of Artificial Intelligence." In *Machine Intelligence 4*. Edited by B. Meltzer and D. Michie. Edinburgh: Edinburgh University Press, 1969, 463–502. [G]
- This early but influential paper discusses general issues in Knowledge Representation that are still very relevant. Concrete progress has been made on some of the problems such as the formalization of belief, ability, and causality; but for others, such as the "frame" problem and the "qualification" problem, time has only increased our respect for their difficulty.

McCarty, L. T. "Permissions and Obligations." *Proc. IJCAI-83*. Karlsruhe, West Germany, 1983, 287–294. [**L**]

- The modalities of time, belief, and, to a certain extent, necessity and possibility have received most of the attention in Artificial Intelligence. This paper discusses a formalization of the modalities of permission and obligation within a context of reasoning about legalities.

McDermott, D. "The Last Survey of Representation of Knowledge." *Proc. AISB/GI Conference*. 1978, 206–221. [**G**]

McDermott, D. "A Theory of Metric Spatial Inference." *Proc. AAAI-80*. Stanford, CA, 1980, 246–248. [**D**]

McDermott, D. "Artificial Intelligence Meets Natural Stupidity." In *Mind Design*. Edited by J. Haugeland. Cambridge, MA: The MIT Press, 1981, 143–160. [**G**]

McDermott, D. "A Temporal Logic for Reasoning about Processes and Plans." *Cognitive Science* **6** (2), 1982, 101–155. [**D**]

- McDermott addresses the oft-ignored issue of time in AI programs. His "naive" theory of time is based on a temporal logic that can be used to reason about causality, continuous change, and plans. The logic uses "states" and "chronicles" arranged in a tree to represent complete possible histories of the universe.

McDermott, D. "Generalizing Problem Reduction: A Logical Analysis." *Proc. IJCAI-83*. Karlsruhe, West Germany, 1983, 302–308. [**D**]

McDermott, D., and Davis, E. "Planning Routes through Uncertain Territory." *Artificial Intelligence* **22** (2), 1984, 107–157. [**D**]

McDermott, D., and Doyle, J. "Non-Monotonic Logic I." *Artificial Intelligence* **13** (1,2), 1980, 41–72. [**L**]

McDermott, J., and Forgy, C. "Production System Conflict Resolution Strategies." In *Pattern-Directed Inference Systems*. Edited by D. A. Waterman and F. Hayes-Roth. New York: Academic Press, 1978, 177–199. [**P**]

McDermott, J., Newell, A., and Moore, J. "The Efficiency of Certain Production System Implementations." In *Pattern-Directed Inference Systems*. Edited by D. A. Waterman and F. Hayes-Roth. New York: Academic Press, 1978, 155–176. [**P**]

Mackinlay, J., and Genesereth, M. R. "Expressiveness of Languages." *Proc. AAAI-84*. Austin, TX, 1984, 226–232. [**G**]

- This paper discusses the use of specialized representation languages (such as diagrams) where some of the information represented is only stated implicitly, and shows how many such languages can co-exist by having axioms that describe exactly what is being represented.

McSkimin, J. R., and Minker, J. "A Predicate Calculus Based Semantic Network for Deductive Searching." In *Associative Networks: Representation and Use of Knowledge by Computers*. Edited by N. V. Findler. New York: Academic Press, 1979, 205–238. [**O**]

Maida, A. S. "Processing Entailments and Accessing Facts in a Uniform Frame System." *Proc. AAAI-84*. Austin, TX, 1984, 233–236. [**F**]

Maida, A. S., and Shapiro, S. C. "Intensional Concepts in Propositional Semantic Networks." *Cognitive Science* **6** (4), 1982, 291–330. [**N**]
- *This paper is included in this volume.*

Markusz, Z. "Knowledge Representation of Design in Many-Sorted Logic." *Proc. IJCAI-81.* Vancouver, B. C., 1981, 264–269. [**D**]

Martin, W. A. "Descriptions and the Specialization of Concepts." In *Artificial Intelligence: An MIT Perspective,* Vol. 1. Edited by P. H. Winston and R. H. Brown. Cambridge, MA: The MIT Press, 1979, 377–419. [**N**]
- This paper presents a view of OWL II, a language for representation based on the notion of descriptions. Martin presents a number of ways that a description can be specialized.

Martins, J. P., and Shapiro, S. C. "Reasoning in Multiple Belief Spaces." *Proc. IJCAI-83.* Karlsruhe, West Germany, 1983, 370–373. [**D**]

Mays, E. "A Modal Temporal Logic for Reasoning about Change." *Proc. of the 21st Annual Meeting of the ACL.* Cambridge, MA, 1983, 38–43. [**L**]

Mendelson, E. *Introduction to Mathematical Logic.* New York: Van Nostrand Reinhold Company, 1964. [**L**]
- This is an excellent reference on standard propositional and first-order logics and their applications in formal theories of numbers and sets. It also contains a very good chapter on computability.

Michener, E. R. "Representing Mathematical Knowledge." *Proc. CSCSI Second National Conference.* Toronto, 1978, 165–172. [**D**]

Minsky, M., ed. *Semantic Information Processing.* Cambridge, MA: The MIT Press, 1968. [**G**]

Minsky, M. "K-Lines: A Theory of Memory." *Cognitive Science* **4** (2), 1980. [**G**]

Minsky, M. "A Framework for Representing Knowledge." In *Mind Design.* Edited by J. Haugeland. Cambridge, MA: The MIT Press, 1981, 95–128. [**F**]
- *This paper is included in this volume.*

Mizoguchi, F., Ohwada, H., and Katayama, Y. "LOOKS: Knowledge Representation System for Designing Expert Systems in a Logic Programming Framework." *Proc. of the International Conference on Fifth Generation Computer Systems.* Tokyo, 1984, 606–612. [**D**]

Mizoguchi, R., and Kakusho, O. "Hierarchical Production Systems." *Proc. IJCAI-79.* Tokyo, 1979, 586–588. [**P**]

Moore, J., and Newell, A. "How Can Merlin Understand?" In *Knowledge and Cognition.* Edited by L. Gregg. Potomac, MD: Lawrence Erlbaum Associates, 1973. [**G**]

Moore, R. C. "Reasoning from Incomplete Knowledge in a Procedural Deduction System," Tech. Report AI-TR-347. M.I.T. AI Lab., Cambridge, MA, 1975. [**P**]

Moore, R. C. "Reasoning about Knowledge and Action." *Proc. IJCAI-77*. Cambridge, MA, 1977, 223–227. **[D]**

- This paper, based on the author's doctoral dissertation, discusses a system that can reason in a general way about both knowledge and action. For example, the system can deduce that after trying to open a safe with a certain number, no matter what the outcome of the attempt, it will know whether or not that number is the combination of the safe.

Moore, R. C. "Problems in Logical Form." *Proc. of the 19th Annual Meeting of the ACL*. Stanford, CA, 1981, 117–124. **[D]**

- Moore presents a clear overview of the some of the problems in representation having more to do with what is being represented than with the representational formalism itself. These problems, such as time and space and propositional attitudes, have yet to find a satisfactory solution in any formalism.

Moore, R. C. "The Role of Logic in Knowledge Representation and Commonsense Reasoning." *Proc. AAAI-82*. Pittsburgh, PA, 1982, 428–433. **[L]**

- *This paper is included in this volume.*

Moore, R. C. "Semantical Considerations on Nonmonotonic Logic." *Proc. IJCAI-83*. Karlsruhe, West Germany, 1983, 272–279. **[L]**

- Moore attempts to analyze semantically the non-monotonic logic of McDermott and Doyle and explain some of the anomalies they encounter in terms of an auto-epistemic interpretation.

Morgenstern, M. "Constraint Equations: A Concise Compilable Representation for Quantified Constraints in Semantic Networks." *Proc. AAAI-84*. Austin, TX, 1984, 255–259. **[N]**

Mylopoulos, J., and Levesque, H. J. "An Overview of Knowledge Representation." In *Conceptual Modelling: Perspectives from Artificial Intelligence, Databases, and Programming Languages*. Edited by M. L. Brodie, J. Mylopoulos, and J. W. Schmidt. New York: Springer-Verlag, 1983, 3–17. **[G]**

- Although the intended audience for this overview is the database and programming language communities, the issues addressed are of general interest.

Mylopoulos, J., Shibahara, T., and Tsotsos, J. "Building Knowledge-Based Systems: The PSN Experience." *IEEE Computer* **16** (10), 1983, 83–89. **[O]**

Mylopoulos, J., Wong, H. K. T., and Bernstein, P. A. "Semantic Networks and the Design of Interactive Information Systems." *Proc. CSCSI Second National Conference*. Toronto, 1978, 74–80. **[D]**

Mylopoulos, J., Cohen, P., Borgida, A., and Sugar, L. "Semantic Networks and the Generation of Context." *Proc. IJCAI-75*. Tbilisi, Georgia, USSR, 1975, 134–142. **[N]**

Nagao, M., and Tsujii, J. "S-Net: A Foundation for Knowledge Representation Languages." *Proc. IJCAI-79*. Tokyo, 1979, 617–624. **[N]**

Neches, R. "HPM: A Computational Formalism for Heuristic Procedure Modification." *Proc. IJCAI-81*. Vancouver, B. C., 1981, 283–288. **[D]**

Newell, A. "Production Systems: Models of Control Structure." In *Visual Information Processing*. Edited by W. Chase. New York: Academic Press, 1973. [**P**]
- This paper presents an introduction to production systems as models of control structures—what is left of an information processor when its particular tests and actions have been factored out. He shows how these models can be used to account for real psychological data.

Newell, A. "The Knowledge Level." *Artificial Intelligence* **18** (1), 1982, 87–127. [**G**]
- Newell argues that regardless of whether or not logic is a suitable representation language for knowledge-based systems (with reasoning understood in terms of theorem-proving), it is, at the very least, a useful tool in the analysis of the knowledge of an intelligent agent. The paper focuses on this sense of knowledge, that is, a potential for generating action, quite independent of the symbols used to represent it.

Nii, H. P., and Aiello, N. "AGE (Attempt to Generalize): A Knowledge-Based Program for Building Knowledge-Based Programs." *Proc. IJCAI-79.* Tokyo, 1979, 645–655. [**P**]

Nilsson, M. "A Logical Model of Knowledge." *Proc. IJCAI-83.* Karlsruhe, West Germany, 1983, 374–376. [**L**]

Nilsson, N. J. *Principles of Artificial Intelligence.* Palo Alto, CA: Tioga Publishing Co., 1980. [**G**]
- This book is an introduction to Artificial Intelligence that contains a good deal of useful material on Knowledge Representation. Of particular interest is the chapter on frame-structured representation languages that shows clearly both their logical basis and the special kinds of processing and organization that is their trademark. Also, the book contains a very good introduction to the area of mechanical theorem-proving using Resolution.

Norman, D. A., Rumelhart, D. E., and the LNR Research Group. *Explorations in Cognition.* San Francisco: W. H. Freeman and Co., 1975. [**N**]

Novak, G. S. "Representation of Knowledge in a Program for Solving Physics Problems." *Proc. IJCAI-77.* Cambridge, MA, 1977, 286–291. [**D**]

Nutter, J. T. "Default Reasoning using Monotonic Logic: A Modest Proposal." *Proc. AAAI-83.* Washington, D.C., 1983, 297–300. [**P**]

Palmer, S. E. "Fundamental Aspects of Cognitive Representation." In *Cognition and Categorization.* Edited by E. H. Rosch and B. B. Lloyd. Potomac, MD: Erlbaum Press, 1977. [**G**]

Papalaskaris, M. A., and Schubert, L. K. "Inference, Incompatible Predicates and Colours." *Proc. CSCSI Fourth National Conference.* Saskatoon, Saskatchewan, 1982, 97–102. [**D**]

Patel-Schneider, P. F. "Small can be Beautiful in Knowledge Representation." *Proc. of the IEEE Workshop on Principles of Knowledge-Based Systems.* Denver, CO, 1984, 11–16. [**F**]
- This paper argues that many representation schemes have suffered in their attempts at being too many things for too many applications, and that there is real value in attempting to design a facility that is limited along a variety of dimensions.

Patel-Schneider, P. F., Brachman, R. J., and Levesque, H. J. "ARGON: Knowledge Representation Meets Information Retrieval." *Proc. of the First Conference on AI Applications.* Denver, CO, 1984, 280–286. [**D**]

Patel-Schneider, P., Kramer, B., Gullen, A., Lesperance, Y., Myers, M., and Mylopoulos, J. "The Procedural Semantic Network: An Extensible Knowledge Representation Scheme." *Proc. CSCSI Fourth Biennial Conference.* Saskatoon, Saskatchewan, 1982, 108–115. [O]

Patil, R. S., Szolovits, P., and Schwartz, W. B. "Causal Understanding of Patient Illness in Medical Diagnosis." *Proc. IJCAI-81.* Vancouver, B. C., 1981, 893–899. [D]

Pentland, A. P., and Fischler, M. A. "A More Rational View of Logic." *The AI Magazine* **4** (4), 1983, 15–18. [G]
- This paper is another in what appears to be an endless series on the true role of logic in Artificial Intelligence. The point these authors try to make is that there appears to be a wide range of applications where objects themselves need to be represented directly (rather than theories of these objects), and that these direct representations permit reasoning algorithms that are inappropriate over sentences.

Pigman, V. "The Interaction Between Assertional and Definitional Knowledge in Krypton." *Proc. of the IEEE Workshop on Principles of Knowledge-Based Systems.* Denver, CO, 1984, 3–10. [O]
- In this paper, Pigman examines some of the issues arising in the implementation of the KRYPTON system (as described in this volume) in terms of modifications to an existing theorem-proving program.

Plaisted, D. A., and Greenbaum, S. "Problem Representations for Back Chaining and Equality in Resolution Theorem Proving." *Proc. of the First Conference on AI Applications.* Denver, CO, 1984, 417–423. [L]

Prawitz, D. *Natural Deduction, A Proof-Theoretical Study.* Stockholm: Almquist and Wiksell, 1965. [L]

Quillian, M. R. "Word Concepts: A Theory and Simulation of Some Basic Semantic Capabilities." *Behavioral Science* **12**, 1967, 410–430. [N]
- *This paper is included in this volume.*

Quillian, M. R. "Semantic Memory." In *Semantic Information Processing.* Edited by M. Minsky. Cambridge, MA: The MIT Press, 1968, 227–270. [N]

Quillian, M. R. "The Teachable Language Comprehender: A Simulation Program and Theory of Language." *Communications of the ACM* **12** (8), 1969, 459–476. [N]

Raphael. B. "SIR: A Computer Program for Semantic Information Retrieval." In *Semantic Information Processing.* Edited by M. Minsky. Cambridge, MA: The MIT Press, 1968, 33–145. [G]

Rapaport, W. J., and Shapiro, S. C. "Quasi-Indexical Reference in Propositional Semantic Networks." *Proc. COLING 84, Tenth Annual Conference on Computational Linguistics.* Stanford, CA, 1984, 65–71. [N]

Reimer, U. "A System-Controlled Multiple-Type Specialization Hierarchy." *Proc. of the First International Workshop on Expert Database Systems.* Kiawah Island, SC, 1984, 207–223. [N]

Reiter, R. "On Structuring a First Order Data Base." *Proc. CSCSI Second National Conference.* Toronto, 1978, 90–99. [L]

Reiter, R. "On Reasoning by Default." *Proc. TINLAP-2.* University of Illinois at Urbana-Champaign, 1978. [**O**]
- *This paper is included in this volume.*

Reiter, R. "A Logic for Default Reasoning." *Artificial Intelligence* **13** (1,2), 1980, 81–132. [**L**]

Reiter, R. "On Interacting Defaults." *Proc. IJCAI-81.* Vancouver, B. C., 1981, 270–276. [**L**]

Reiter, R., and Criscuolo, G. "Some Representational Issues in Default Reasoning," TR 80-7. Dept. of Computer Science, University of British Columbia, Vancouver, B. C., 1980. [**L**]

Rich, C. "Knowledge Representation Languages and Predicate Calculus: How to Have Your Cake and Eat It Too." *Proc. AAAI-82.* Pittsburgh, PA, 1980, 193–196. [**O**]
- Rich describes a hybrid system in which a specialized "planning" language (used in analyzing and designing computer programs) coexists with its translation in first-order predicate calculus. The utility of having both representations in a system became apparent only after the Programmer's Apprentice project was well underway, and this paper presents an interesting discussion of the unanticipated pragmatic merits of simultaneous representation.

Rich, C. "A Formal Representation for Plans in the Programmer's Apprentice." In *On Conceptual Modelling: Perspectives from Artificial Intelligence, Databases, and Programming Languages.* Edited by M. L. Brodie, J. Mylopoulos, and J. W. Schmidt. New York: Springer-Verlag, 1984, 239–269. [**D**]

Rich, E. "Default Reasoning as Likelihood Reasoning." *Proc. AAAI-83.* Washington, D.C., 1983, 348–351. [**O**]

Rieger, C. "An Organization of Knowledge for Problem Solving and Language Comprehension." *Artificial Intelligence* **7** (2), 1976, 89–127. [**D**]
- *This paper is included in this volume.*

Rieger, C. "Spontaneous Computation and its Roles in AI Modeling." In *Pattern-Directed Inference Systems.* Edited by D. A. Waterman and F. Hayes-Roth. New York: Academic Press, 1978, 69–97. [**O**]

Rieger, C., and Grinberg, M. "The Declarative Representation and Procedural Simulation of Causality in Physical Mechanisms." *Proc. IJCAI-77.* Cambridge, MA, 1977, 250–256. [**D**]

Rifkin, A. "A Model of Knowledge Representation Based on Deontic Modal Logic." *Proc. of the Sixth Annual Conference of the Cognitive Science Society.* Boulder, CO, 1984, 281–286. [**L**]

Roberts, R. B., and Goldstein, I. P. "The FRL Primer," AI Memo No. 408, Artificial Intelligence Laboratory, MIT, Cambridge, MA, 1977. [**F**]

Robinson, A. E., and Wilkins, D. E. "Representing Knowledge in an Interactive Planner." *Proc. AAAI-80.* Stanford, CA, 1980, 148–150. [**D**]

Rosenberg, S. "HPRL: A language for Building Expert Systems." *Proc. IJCAI-83*. Karlsruhe, West Germany, 1983, 215–217. [**F**]

Rosenschein, S. J. "The Production System: Architecture and Abstraction." In *Pattern-Directed Inference Systems*. Edited by D. A. Waterman and F. Hayes-Roth. New York: Academic Press, 1978, 525–538. [**P**]

Rosenschein, S. J. "Plan Synthesis: A Logical Perspective." *Proc. IJCAI-81*. Vancouver, B. C., 1981, 331–337. [**D**]
- Rosenschein presents a definition of planning that, unlike previous ones, very clearly shows its logical basis. The formalism used is a variant of Pratt's dynamic logic, restricted to keep the planning process computationally tractable.

Rulifson, J., Derkson, J. A., and Waldinger, R. J. "QA4: A Procedural Calculus for Intuitive Reasoning," Tech. Rep. TN-83. SRI International, AI Center, Menlo Park, CA, 1972. [**P**]

Rumelhart, D. E., and Norman, D. A. "Active Semantic Networks as a Model of Human Memory." *Proc. IJCAI-73*. Stanford, CA, 1973, 450–457. [**N**]

Rychener, M. D. "Production Systems as a Programming Language for Artificial Intelligence Applications," Technical Report, Computer Science Dept., Carnegie-Mellon University, Pittsburgh, PA, 1976. [**P**]

Rychener, M. D. "Control Requirements for the Design of Production System Architectures." *Proc. Symposium on Artificial Intelligence and Programming Languages. SIGPLAN Notices*, Vol. 12, No. 8, and *SIGART Newsletter*, No. 64, August, 1977, 37–44. [**P**]

Rychener, M. D. "A Semantic Network of Production Rules in a System for Designing Computer Structures." *Proc. IJCAI-79*. Tokyo, 1979, 738–743. [**O**]

Sandewall, E. "Representing Natural Language Information in Predicate Calculus." In *Machine Intelligence 5*. Edited by B. Meltzer and D. Michie. Edinburgh: Edinburgh University Press, 1970. [**L**]

Schank, R. C. "Conceptual Dependency: A Theory of Natural Language Understanding." *Cognitive Psychology* **3** 1972, 552–631. [**N**]

Schank, R. C. "Identification of Conceptualizations Underlying Natural Language." In *Computer Models of Thought and Language*. Edited by R. C. Schank and K. M. Colby. San Francisco: W. H. Freeman and Co., 1973, 187–247. [**N**]

Schank, R. C. *Conceptual Information Processing*. Amsterdam: North-Holland Publishing Company, 1975. [**N**]
- This book describes MARGIE, a natural language system developed at Stanford by the author and his students. The representation used is an early semantic network with nodes standing for primitive acts and objects, and links labelled with case relations. Of particular interest is the chapter by Rieger on the "reflex" inferences that are drawn from these conceptual structures.

Schank, R. C., and Abelson, R. *Scripts, Plans, Goals and Understanding*. Hillsdale, NJ: Lawrence Erlbaum Associates, 1977. [**N**]

Schank, R. C., and Colby, K. M., eds. *Computer Models of Thought and Language.* San Francisco: W. H. Freeman and Co., 1973. [**G**]

Schank, R. C., and Rieger, C. J. "Inference and the Computer Understanding of Natural Language." *Artificial Intelligence* **5** (4), 1974, 373–412. [**N**]
- *This paper is included in this volume.*

Schmolze, J. G., and Brachman, R. J., eds. "Proceedings of the 1981 KL-ONE Workshop," FLAIR Technical Report No. 4, Fairchild Laboratory for Artificial Intelligence Research, Palo Alto, CA. Also published as BBN Report No. 4842, Bolt Beranek and Newman Inc., Cambridge, MA, May, 1982. [**F**]
- This is a collection of position papers and technical discussions on the KL-ONE Knowledge Representation system. The topics range from practical applications of the system to current research topics and give a good indication of the issues faced by a representation system with a non-trivial user community.

Schmolze, J. G., and Lipkis, T. A. "Classification in the KL-ONE Knowledge Representation System." *Proc. IJCAI-83.* Karlsruhe, West Germany, 1983, 330–332. [**F**]

Schneider, P. "Organization of Knowledge in a Procedural Semantic Network Formalism," M.Sc. Thesis (and TR 115). Dept. of Computer Science, Univ. of Toronto, Toronto, Ontario, 1978. [**N**]

Schubert, L. K. "Extending the Expressive Power of Semantic Networks." *Artificial Intelligence* **7** (2), 1976, 163–198. [**N**]

Schubert, L. K. "On the Representation of Vague and Uncertain Knowledge." *Proc. COLING-78.* Bergen, Norway, August, 1978. [**N**]

Schubert, L. K. "Problems with Parts." *Proc. IJCAI-79.* Tokyo, 1979, 778–784. [**D**]
- While the IS-A relationship has received considerable attention, the complementary PART-OF one (between an object and its conceptual parts) has been more or less neglected. This paper is an interesting exception that shows, among other things, that simple questions such as "Is X a part of Y?" can be very difficult in the general case.

Schubert, L. K., Goebel, R. G., and Cercone, N. J. "The Structure and Organization of a Semantic Net for Comprehension and Inference." In *Associative Networks: Representation and Use of Knowledge by Computers.* Edited by N. V. Findler. New York: Academic Press, 1979, 121–175. [**N**]
- This paper describes a comprehensive semantic net formalism for encoding propositional knowledge. The formalism has a significantly logical flavor, including explicit structures for logical connectives, modal operators, etc. Its principal use is for inferences underlying natural language understanding.

Schubert, L. K., Papalaskaris, M., and Taugher, J. "Determining Type, Part, Color, and Time Relationships." *IEEE Computer* **16** (10), 1983, 53–60. [**D**]

Scragg, G. W. "Frames, Planes, and Nets: A Synthesis," Working paper 19. Istituto per gli Studi Semantici e Cognitivi, Castagnola, Switzerland, 1975. [**F**]

Shapiro, S. C. "Representing and Locating Deduction Rules in a Semantic Network." *SIGART Newsletter*, No. 63, June, 1977, 14–18. [**N**]

Shapiro, S. C. "Numerical Quantifiers and Their Use in Reasoning with Negative Information." *Proc. IJCAI-79.* Tokyo, 1979, 791–796. [**L**]

Shapiro, S. C. "The SNePS Semantic Network Processing System." In *Associative Networks: Representation and Use of Knowledge by Computers.* Edited by N. V. Findler. New York: Academic Press, 1979, 179–203. [**N**]
- The SNePS system described in this paper was one of the first semantic networks to have the expressive power of first-order logic. A special network representation of formulas and inference rules over them is discussed and an example of the system in operation is presented.

Siekmann J., and Wrightson G., eds. *Automation of Reasoning, Vols. I and II.* Berlin: Springer-Verlag, 1983. [**L**]

Simmons, R. F. "Semantic Networks: Their Computation and Use for Understanding English Sentences." In *Computer Models of Thought and Language.* Edited by R. C. Schank and K. M. Colby. San Francisco: W. H. Freeman and Co., 1973, 63–113. [**N**]
- This paper describes an early application of semantic networks to natural language understanding. Specifically, it examines a system that parses a sentence (using an ATN) and constructs a semantic network representation of the sentence, with a node standing for the verb, linked to its semantic cases (such as "agent" or "object").

Simmons, R. F., and Chester, D. "Inferences in Quantified Semantic Networks." *Proc. IJCAI-77.* Cambridge, MA, 1977, 267–273. [**N**]

Sloman, A. "Interactions Between Philosophy and Artificial Intelligence: The Role of Intuition and Non-Logical Reasoning in Intelligence." *Artificial Intelligence* **2**, 1971, 209–225. [**O**]

Sloman, A. "Afterthoughts on Analogical Representation." *Proc. Theoretical Issues in Natural Language Processing.* Cambridge, MA, 1975, 164–168. [**O**]
- *This paper is included in this volume.*

Smith, B. C. "Levels, Layers, and Planes: The Framework of a System of Knowledge Representation Semantics," Master's thesis, Artificial Intelligence Laboratory, M.I.T., Cambridge, MA, January, 1978. [**G**]

Smith, B. C. "Reflection and Semantics in a Procedural Language," Ph.D. thesis and Tech. Report MIT/LCS/TR-272, M.I.T., Cambridge, MA, 1982. [**G**]
- *The prologue of this dissertation is included in this volume.*

Smith, D. E. "Finding all of the Solutions to a Problem." *Proc. AAAI-83.* Washington, D.C., 1983, 373–377. [**O**]

Smith, D. E., and Clayton, J. E. "A Frame-Based Production System Architecture." *Proc. AAAI-80.* Stanford, CA, 1980, 154–156. [**O**]

Smith, E. E., and Oshershon, D. N. "Conceptual Combination with Prototype Concepts." *Cognitive Science* **8** (4), 1984, 337–363. [**N**]

Smith, R. G. "STROBE: Support for Structured Object Knowledge Representation." *Proc. IJCAI-83.* Karlsruhe, West Germany, 1983, 855–858. [**F**]

Sondheimer, N. K., Weischedel, R., and Bobrow, R. J. "Semantic Interpretation using KL-ONE." *Proc. COLING 84, Tenth Annual Conference on Computational Linguistics.* Stanford, CA, 1984, 101–108. [**F**]

Sowa, J. F. *Conceptual Structures: Information Processing in Minds and Machines.* Reading, MA: Addison-Wesley Publishing Co., 1984. [**G**]
- This impressive work is Sowa's attempt to provide a general, philosophically and psychologically sound foundation for most work in AI. It culminates many years of his work on Conceptual Graphs, and attempts a fairly ambitious synthesis.

Sridharan, N. S. "AIMDS User Manual—Version 2," Rutgers Univ. Computer Science Tech. Report CBM-TR-89, Rutgers Univ., New Brunswick, NJ, June, 1978. [**F**]

Srinivasan, C. V. "The Architecture of Coherent Information System: A General Problem Solving System." *IEEE Transactions on Computers* **C-25** (4), 1976, 390–402. [**F**]
- The "metadescription system" (MDS) has been developed at Rutgers over a number of years; this article presents an overview of the architecture of the system, emphasizing how it can be used for problemsolving in a general way.

Stefik, M. "An Examination of a Frame-Structured Representation System." *Proc. IJCAI-79.* Tokyo, 1979, 845–852. [**F**]

Stickel, M. E. "A Nonclausal Connection-Graph Resolution Theorem-Proving Program." *Proc. AAAI-82.* Pittsburgh, PA, 1982, 229–233. [**L**]

Stickel, M. E. "Theory Resolution: Building-in Nonequational Theories." *Proc. AAAI-83.* Washington, D. C., 1983. [**L**]

Sussman, G. J., and McDermott, D. "Why Conniving is Better than Planning," Memo 255A, M.I.T. AI Lab., Cambridge, MA, 1972. [**P**]

Sussman, G. J., and Steele, G. L. "CONSTRAINTS: A Language for Expressing Almost-Hierarchical Descriptions." *Artificial Intelligence* **14** (1), 1980, 1–40. [**P**]
- This paper presents an interactive system organized around hierarchical networks of constraints among several variables. Electrical circuits are used to illustrate an inference method called propagation which can detect inconsistencies among the constraints.

Szolovits, P., Hawkinson, L. B., and Martin, W. A. "An Overview of OWL, a Language for Knowledge Representation," MIT/LCS/TM-86. Laboratory for Computer Science, M.I.T., Cambridge, MA, June, 1977. [**N**]

Thompson, F. B. "Solution to Issues Depend on Knowledge Representation." *Proc. of the 20th Annual Meeting of the ACL.* Toronto, 1982, 169–171. [**G**]

Touretzky, D. S. "Implicit Ordering of Defaults in Inheritance Systems." *Proc. AAAI-84.* Austin, TX, 1984, 322–325. [**N**]

Tsotsos, J. K. "Knowledge and the Visual Process: Content, Form and Use." *Pattern Recognition* **17** (1), 1984, 13–29. [**D**]

van Melle, W. "A Domain-Independent Production-Rule System for Consultation Programs." *Proc. IJCAI-79.* Tokyo, 1979, 923–925. [**P**]

vanderBurg, G. J. "Problem Representations and the Formal Properties of Heuristic Search." *Information Sciences* II 1976. [**G**]

Vilain, M. B. "A System for Reasoning about Time." *Proc. AAAI-82*. Pittsburgh, PA, 1982, 197–201. [**D**]
- This paper shows a particular representation of time that seems well-suited for reasoning about contradictions. It is based on time intervals (with points as special cases), and a logic is described for reasoning about the relationships among intervals.

Waterman, D. A., and Hayes-Roth, F., eds. *Pattern-Directed Inference Systems*. New York: Academic Press, 1978. [**P**]

Webber, B. L. "Logic and Natural Language." *IEEE Computer* **16** (10), 1983, 43–46. [**L**]

Weiner, E. J. "A Knowledge Representation Approach to Understanding Metaphors." *The American Journal of Computational Linguistics* **10** (1), 1984, 1–14. [**D**]

Weiner, J. L., and Palmer, M. "The Design of a System for Designing Knowledge Representation Systems." *Proc. IJCAI-81*. Vancouver, B. C., 1981, 277-282. [**O**]

Weiss, S. M., Kulikowski, C. A., Amarel, S., and Safir, A. "A Model-Based Method for Computer-Aided Medical Decision-Making." *Artificial Intelligence* **11** (1 and 2), 1978. [**D**]

Westfold, S. J. "Very-High-Level Programming of Knowledge Representation Schemes." *Proc. AAAI-84*. Austin, TX, 1984, 344–349. [**G**]

Weyhrauch, R. W. "Prolegomena to a Theory of Mechanized Formal Reasoning." *Artificial Intelligence* **13** (1,2), 1980, 133–170. [**L**]
- *This paper is included in this volume.*

Wilensky, R. "KODIAK: A Knowledge Representation Language." *Proc. of the Sixth Annual Conference of the Cognitive Science Society*. Boulder, CO, 1984, 344–353. [**F**]

Wilkins, D. E. "Domain-Independent Planning: Representation and Plan Generation." *Artificial Intelligence* **22** (3), 1984, 269–302. [**D**]

Wilks, Y. "De Minimis: The Archaeology of Frames," Artificial Intelligence Dept., Univ. of Edinburgh, Edinburgh, 1976. [**F**]

Wilks, Y., and Bien, J. "Beliefs, Points of View, and Multiple Environments." *Cognitive Science* **7** (2), 1983, 95–121. [**D**]

Winograd, T. *Understanding Natural Language*. New York: Academic Press, 1972. [**P**]
- This book, a revised version of the author's doctoral dissertation, was somewhat of a milestone in Knowledge Representation. It demonstrated that, at least within the narrow confines of the blocks world, a system could be made to plan actions, reason effectively, and communicate in natural language using a procedural encoding (in a subset of PLANNER) of much of its knowledge.

Winograd, T. "Frame Representations and the Declarative/Procedural Controversy." In *Representation and Understanding: Studies in Cognitive Science*. Edited by D. G. Bobrow and A. M. Collins. New York: Academic Press, 1975, 185–210. [**P**]
- *This paper is included in this volume.*

Winograd, T. "On Primitives, Prototypes, and Other Semantic Anomalies." *Proc. TINLAP-2—Theoretical Issues in Natural Language Processing-2* Urbana, IL, 1978, 25–32. [**F**]

Winograd T., and Flores, F. *Understanding Computers and Cognition.* Norwood, NJ: Ablex Publishing Corporation, 1985. [**G**]

Winston, P. H., ed. *The Psychology of Computer Vision.* New York: McGraw-Hill Book Company, 1975. [**G**]
- This book contains a number of interesting applications of Knowledge Representation to topics related to computer vision. Of particular note are the chapters by Minsky and Winston (described elsewhere in this bibliography) as well as the work of Waltz and Shirai.

Winston, P. H. "Learning Structural Descriptions from Examples." In *The Psychology of Computer Vision.* Edited by P. H. Winston. New York: McGraw-Hill Book Company, 1975, 157–209. [**N**]
- *This paper is included in this volume.*

Woods, W. A. "What's in a Link: Foundations for Semantic Networks." In *Representation and Understanding: Studies in Cognitive Science.* Edited by D. G. Bobrow and A. M. Collins. New York: Academic Press, 1975, 35–82. [**N**]
- *This paper is included in this volume.*

Woods, W. A. "What's Important about Knowledge Representation." *IEEE Computer* **16** (10), 1983, 22–29. [**G**]

Wos, L., Pereira, F., Hong, R., Boyer, R., Moore, J., Bledsoe, W., Henschen, L., Buchanan, B., Wrightson, G., and Green, C. "An Overview of Automated Reasoning and Related Fields." *Journal of Automated Reasoning* 1 (1), 1985, 5–48. [**L**]
- This overview of automated reasoning is a good entry point into the area of theorem-proving, and features an extensive bibliography.

Zadeh, L. A. "PRUF—A Meaning Representation Language for Natural Languages," Memo No. ERL-M77/61, Electronics Res. Lab., College of Engineering, University of California at Berkeley, 1977. [**G**]

Zadeh, L. A. "Commonsense Knowledge Representation Based on Fuzzy Logic." *IEEE Computer* **16** (10), 1983, 61–66. [**O**]

Zdybel, F., Greenfeld, N. R., Yonke, M. D., and Gibbons, J. "An Information Presentation System." *Proc. IJCAI-81.* Vancouver, B. C., 1981, 978–984. [**D**]

INDEX

DATE DUE

31 '93